Malaysia, Singapore & Brunei

Simon Richmond, Marie Cambon, Damian Harper, Richard Watkins

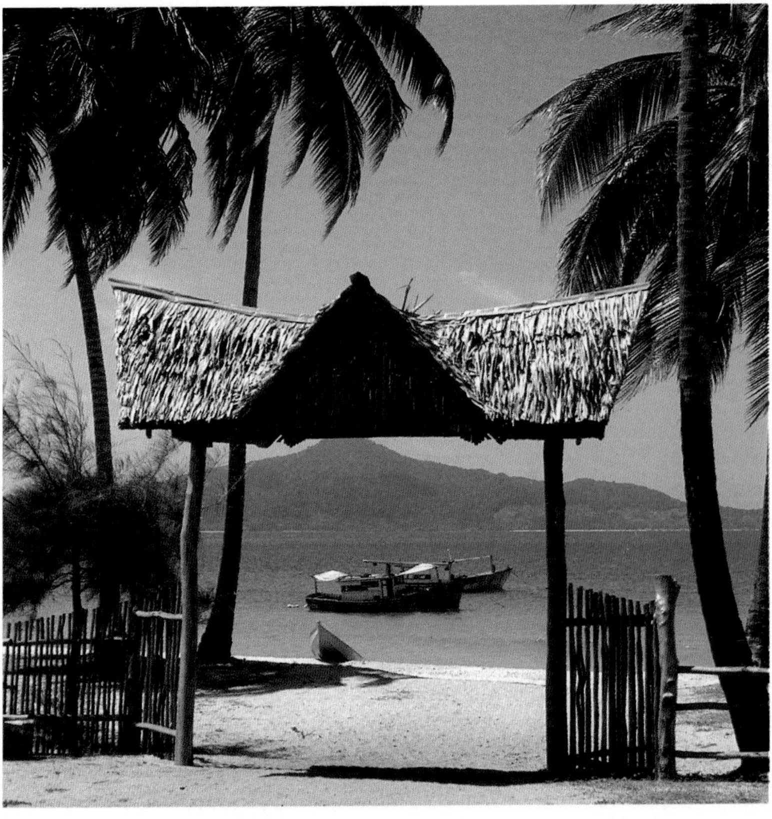

Contents

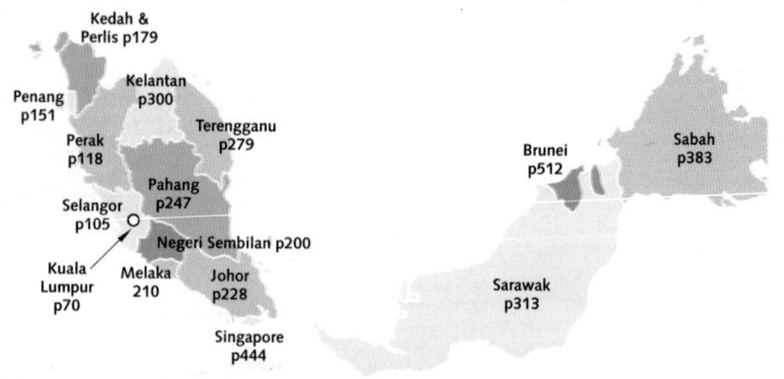

Lonely Planet books provide independent advice. Lonely Planet does not accept advertising in guidebooks, nor do we accept payment in exchange for listing or endorsing any place or business. Lonely Planet writers do not accept discounts or payments in exchange for positive coverage of any sort.

Buku-buku Lonely Planet memberikan nasihat bebas atau tersendiri. Lonely Planet tidak menerima iklan dalam buku-buku panduan dan juga tidak menerima pembayaran sebagai tukaran untuk menyenaraikan atau menyokong sebarang tempat atau perniagaan. Penulis-penulis Lonely Planet tidak menerima diskaun atau pembayaran sebagai tukaran untuk sebarang liputan positif.

Destination: Malaysia, Singapore & Brunei

As Southeast Asian countries go, Malaysia, Singapore and Brunei are models of how to get it right. Among the richest and safest nations in Asia, their transport facilities are good, accommodation standards are high, and the range and quality of food is fantastic.

The region offers amazing variety – one day you could be in Kuala Lumpur's gleaming Petronas Towers listening to a world-class orchestra, the next dancing with longhouse residents in the jungle heart of Malaysian Borneo. Lovers of beaches and tropical islands will be in heaven, particularly along the east coast of Peninsular Malaysia. If it's mountains, jungles and wildlife that fire you up, consider climbing Mt Kinabalu, exploring Brunei's Wasai Kandal forest and the rivers of Sarawak, or trekking in Taman Negara on the peninsula. Dive or snorkel your way around islands and encounter tropical fish, sea turtles and amazing coral reefs in clear warm waters. Then dip into city life, bargaining for kites in Kota Bharu, strolling around the historic old ports of Melaka and Penang's Georgetown, or the modern-as-tomorrow city of Singapore.

When it comes to people, you've got Malays, Chinese, Indians and a host of indigenous tribes, particularly in Sabah and Sarawak. In every town or city you will find markets with local produce, arts and crafts, and a gathering of folk utterly unique to the region. And although Malaysian Borneo may at times be a little pricey owing to its jungle-frontier situation, and Brunei can be expensive for what it offers, on the whole cost is another concern you can leave at home. These three countries are ideal for whatever type of travel you could desire.

ANDERS BLOMQVIST

PENINSULAR MALAYSIA & SINGAPORE

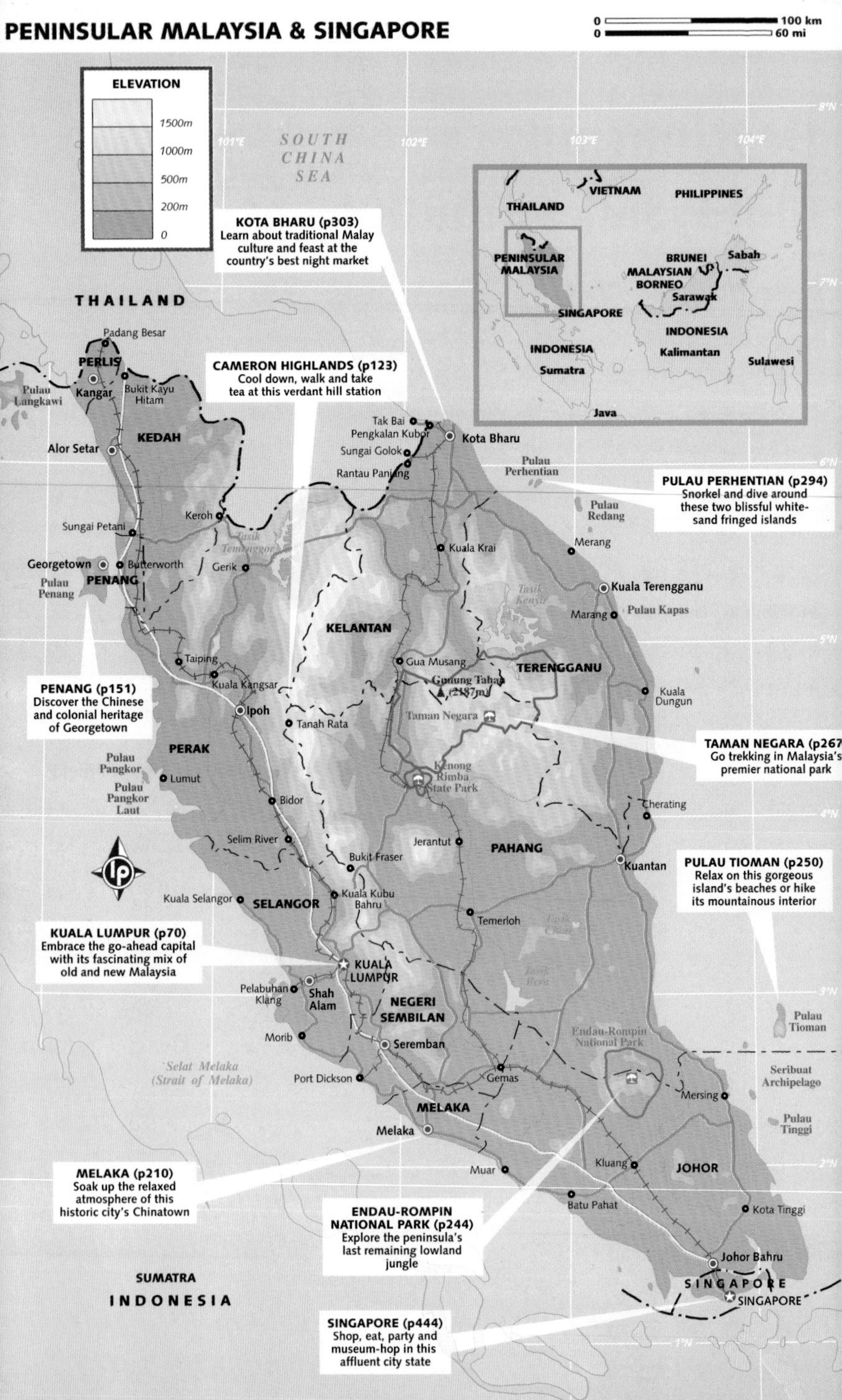
0 100 km
0 60 mi
ELEVATION
1500m
1000m
500m
200m
0
SOUTH CHINA SEA
101°E
102°E
103°E
104°E
8°N
7°N
6°N
5°N
4°N
3°N
2°N
1°N
VIETNAM
THAILAND
PHILIPPINES
PENINSULAR MALAYSIA
BRUNEI
Sabah
MALAYSIAN BORNEO
Sarawak
SINGAPORE
INDONESIA
Kalimantan
Sulawesi
Sumatra
Java
KOTA BHARU (p303)
Learn about traditional Malay culture and feast at the country's best night market
CAMERON HIGHLANDS (p123)
Cool down, walk and take tea at this verdant hill station
PULAU PERHENTIAN (p294)
Snorkel and dive around these two blissful white-sand fringed islands
PENANG (p151)
Discover the Chinese and colonial heritage of Georgetown
TAMAN NEGARA (p267
Go trekking in Malaysia's premier national park
PULAU TIOMAN (p250)
Relax on this gorgeous island's beaches or hike its mountainous interior
KUALA LUMPUR (p70)
Embrace the go-ahead capital with its fascinating mix of old and new Malaysia
MELAKA (p210)
Soak up the relaxed atmosphere of this historic city's Chinatown
ENDAU-ROMPIN NATIONAL PARK (p244)
Explore the peninsula's last remaining lowland jungle
SINGAPORE (p444)
Shop, eat, party and museum-hop in this affluent city state
THAILAND
Padang Besar
PERLIS
Pulau Langkawi
Kangar
Bukit Kayu Hitam
KEDAH
Alor Setar
Tak Bai
Pengkalan Kubor
Kota Bharu
Sungai Golok
Rantau Panjang
Pulau Perhentian
Pulau Redang
Keroh
Sungai Petani
Tasik Temenggor
Merang
Kuala Krai
Georgetown
Butterworth
Gerik
Pulau Penang
PENANG
Tasik Kenyir
Kuala Terengganu
Marang
Pulau Kapas
KELANTAN
Taiping
Gua Musang
TERENGGANU
Kuala Kangsar
Gunung Tahan (2187m)
Kuala Dungun
Ipoh
Tanah Rata
Taman Negara
PERAK
Pulau Pangkor
Kenong Rimba State Park
Lumut
Pulau Pangkor Laut
Bidor
Cherating
Selim River
Jerantut
PAHANG
Bukit Fraser
Kuantan
Kuala Selangor
SELANGOR
Kuala Kubu Bahru
Temerloh
Tasik Chini
KUALA LUMPUR
Pelabuhan Klang
Shah Alam
Tasik Bera
NEGERI SEMBILAN
Pulau Tioman
Morib
Seremban
Endau-Rompin National Park
Selat Melaka (Strait of Melaka)
Port Dickson
Gemas
Seribuat Archipelago
MELAKA
Mersing
Melaka
Pulau Tinggi
Muar
Kluang
JOHOR
Batu Pahat
Kota Tinggi
Johor Bahru
SUMATRA
INDONESIA
SINGAPORE
SINGAPORE

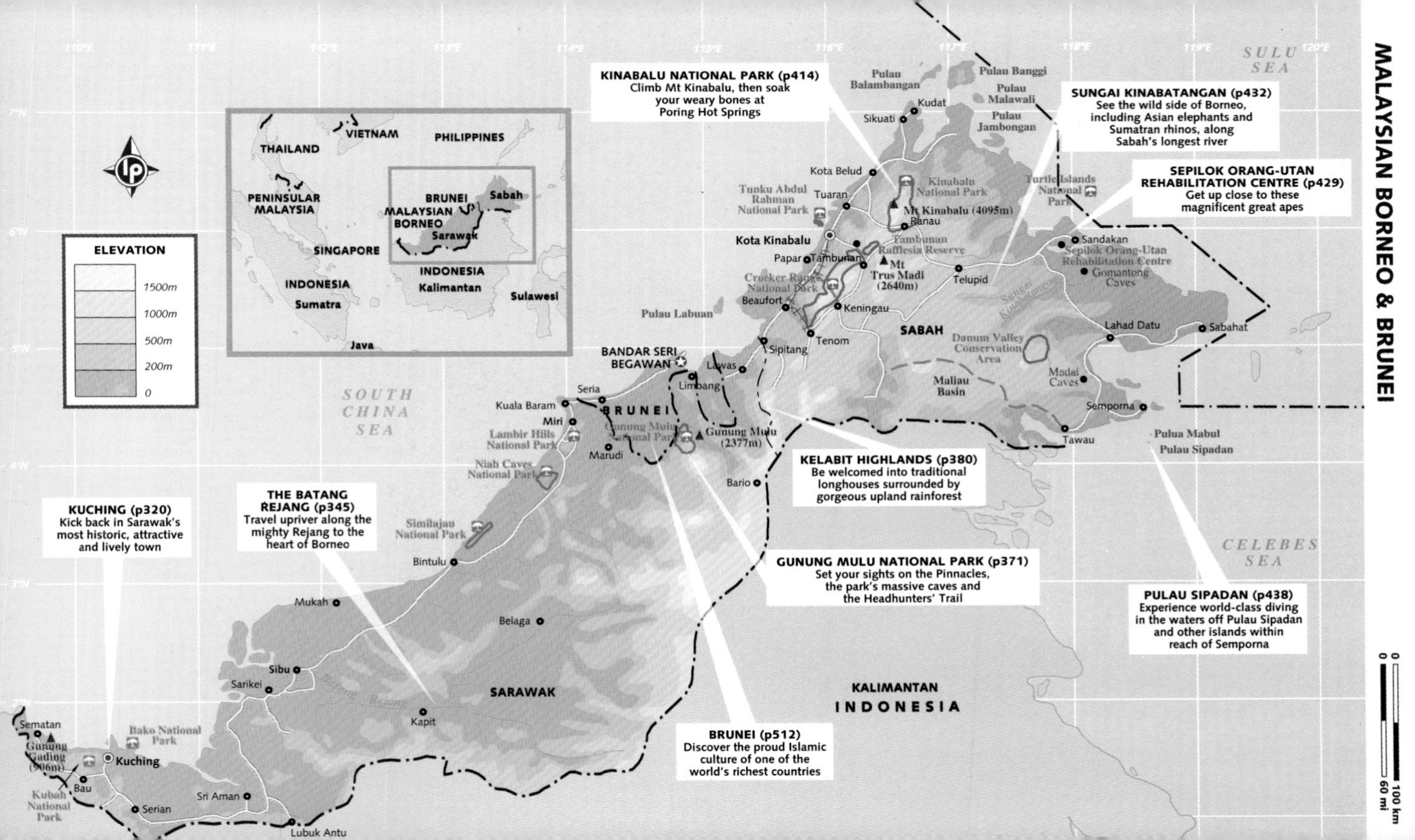

MALAYSIAN BORNEO & BRUNEI
0 100 km
0 60 mi
KINABALU NATIONAL PARK (p414)
Climb Mt Kinabalu, then soak your weary bones at Poring Hot Springs
SUNGAI KINABATANGAN (p432)
See the wild side of Borneo, including Asian elephants and Sumatran rhinos, along Sabah's longest river
SEPILOK ORANG-UTAN REHABILITATION CENTRE (p429)
Get up close to these magnificent great apes
KELABIT HIGHLANDS (p380)
Be welcomed into traditional longhouses surrounded by gorgeous upland rainforest
GUNUNG MULU NATIONAL PARK (p371)
Set your sights on the Pinnacles, the park's massive caves and the Headhunters' Trail
PULAU SIPADAN (p438)
Experience world-class diving in the waters off Pulau Sipadan and other islands within reach of Semporna
KUCHING (p320)
Kick back in Sarawak's most historic, attractive and lively town
THE BATANG REJANG (p345)
Travel upriver along the mighty Rejang to the heart of Borneo
BRUNEI (p512)
Discover the proud Islamic culture of one of the world's richest countries
ELEVATION
1500m
1000m
500m
200m
0
THAILAND
VIETNAM
PHILIPPINES
PENINSULAR MALAYSIA
BRUNEI
Sabah
MALAYSIAN BORNEO
Sarawak
SINGAPORE
INDONESIA
Sumatra
INDONESIA
Kalimantan
Sulawesi
Java
SULU SEA
SOUTH CHINA SEA
CELEBES SEA
SABAH
SARAWAK
BRUNEI
KALIMANTAN
INDONESIA
BANDAR SERI BEGAWAN
Pulau Balambangan
Pulau Banggi
Pulau Malawali
Pulau Jambongan
Kudat
Sikuati
Kota Belud
Tunku Abdul Rahman National Park
Tuaran
Kinabalu National Park
Mt Kinabalu (4095m)
Ranau
Turtle Islands National Park
Kota Kinabalu
Papar
Tambunan
Tambunan Rafflesia Reserve
Mt Trus Madi (2640m)
Telupid
Sandakan
Sepilok Orang-Utan Rehabilitation Centre
Gomantong Caves
Sungai Kinabatangan
Crocker Range National Park
Beaufort
Keningau
Pulau Labuan
Tenom
Sipitang
Danum Valley Conservation Area
Lahad Datu
Sabahat
Lawas
Limbang
Madai Caves
Maliau Basin
Seria
Kuala Baram
Miri
Semporna
Gunung Mulu National Park
Gunung Mulu (2377m)
Lambir Hills National Park
Marudi
Tawau
Pulua Mabul
Pulau Sipadan
Niah Caves National Park
Bario
Similajau National Park
Bintulu
Mukah
Belaga
Sibu
Sarikei
Batang Rejang
Kapit
Sematan
Gunung Gading (906m)
Bako National Park
Kuching
Bau
Kubah National Park
Serian
Sri Aman
Lubuk Antu

Islands & Beaches

Really, you're spoiled for choice, with great beaches and tropical islands where you can try a range of water sports or just lie back and soak up the sun and views. As well as the highlights on these pages, don't miss the beaches of **Pulau Pangkor** (p138) on Malaysia's west coast, and **Cherating** (p262) on the east. The **Similajau National Park** (p358) in Sarawak has decent beaches, but even better are the idyllic islands of Sabah's **Tunku Abdul Rahman National Park** (p398) and other islands within reach of Semporna.

CHRIS ROWTHORN

Discover the quiet rural beauty of the **Seribuat Archipelago** (p243)

Find paradise on **Pulau Tioman** (p250)

SIMON BRACKEN

Follow the sweep of white-sand beaches on **Pulau Perhentian** (p294)

CHRIS ROWT

SIMON BRACKEN

Island-hop from beautiful, legend-steeped **Pulau Langkawi** (p187)

MARK DAFFEY

Make tracks for stunning beach-views from the headlands of **Bako National Park** (p334)

Dive into deep waters off **Pulau Sipadan** (p438)

MICHAEL AW

Indulge every whim at the exclusive Pangkor Laut Resort on **Pulau Pangkor Laut** (p143)

SIMON RICHMOND

National Parks & Wildlife

Malaysia has an impressive network of national parks and other reserves, covering the wilderness gamut from jungles to caves, and offering opportunities to spot birds, apes, rhinos and more. Aside from the the highlights here, try the **Kenong Rimba State Park** (p277) or the **Endau-Rompin National Park** (p244) if you want your jungle experience without the crowds. In Sabah, there's the **Turtle Islands National Park** (p431).

CHRISTER FREDRIKSSON

Get up close with magnificent apes at the **Sepilok Orang-Utan Rehabilitation Centre** (p429)

Stumble upon a rock dinosaur in the **Bako National Park** (p334)

JANE SWEENEY

Tiptoe through the treetops on a canopy walkway in **Taman Negara** (p267)

JANE SW

MARK DAFFEY

Ascend to the Pinnacles, a stone forest in **Gunung Mulu National Park** (p371)

MARK DAFFEY

Face-off with monitor lizards and other wildlife at jungle camps along **Sungai Kinabatangan** (p432)

Go with the flow, take leisurely walks or go mountain climbing in **Kinabalu National Park** (p414)

MARK DAFFEY

Cities & Cultural Hotspots

This region isn't just for outdoor enthusiasts. There's plenty of urban action of the shopping and eating variety, and vibrant arts and festivals to discover. Not pictured here, but not to be missed, is handsome **Kuching** (p320), capital of Sarawak.

TOM COCKREM

Taste the delights of the markets at **Kota Kinabalu** (p388)

Discover traditional Malay culture in **Kota Bharu** (p303)

RICHARD I'ANSON

Stand small before the world's tallest building, the 88-storey Petronas Towers in **Kuala Lumpur** (p70)

SIMON BR

ALAIN EVRARD

Paint the town red during Chinese New Year in vibrant **Singapore** (p444)

LIZ BARRY

Listen as the call to prayer echoes from the Omar Ali Saifuddien Mosque in **Bandar Seri Begawan** (p516)

Tour the Cheong Fatt Tze Mansion in Georgetown, one of many displays of old-fashioned character in **Penang** (p152)

JOHN BORTHWICK

Open your eyes to the colourful culture and traditions of **Melaka** (p210)

CHRIS MELLOR

Adventurers' Agenda

Adventurous souls will be in their element, with many rivers to cross, mountains to climb and jungles trails to trek. Divers are well catered for, too. And there's no need to confine yourself to the highlights pictured here. Mountain climbers should head for **Gunung Tahan** (p272). There are treks aplenty in **Taman Negara** (p267), the **Endau-Rompin National Park** (p244), across the lush **Kelabit Highlands** (p380) and the **Cameron Highlands** (p123) hill station. Get into a tank with sharks at Underwater World in **Singapore** (p472), or swim or snorkel around the region's beautiful reefs and islands. For adventure of a different kind, there are boat trips into the heart of Borneo, up the mighty **Batang Rejang** (p345).

Swim with green turtles at dive sites off **Pulau Sipadan** (p438)

DAVE LEVITT

MARK DAFFEY

Go to ground at Gunung Mulu National Park's **Deer Cave** (p372)

Descend into clouds after conquering **Mt Kinabalu** (p414)

MARK

Getting Started

Between them Malaysia, Singapore and Brunei offer a wide range of travel possibilities with options to suit all budgets. Getting around much of the region is a breeze thanks to excellent transport infrastructure. The only part of the region you'll need to make more detailed advance preparations for is Malaysian Borneo, because of the remoteness of certain locations and the cost and time involved in getting to them.

WHEN TO GO

Rain occurs fairly evenly throughout the year in the region, and the differences between the main October-to-April rainy season and the rest of the year are not that marked, so travel is possible year round. The exception is the east coast of Peninsular Malaysia, which receives heavy rain from November to mid-February. During these months many east-coast resorts close and boat services dwindle or stop altogether. Travel along the west coast is not affected. The states of Sabah and Sarawak receive high rainfall throughout the year, but it is heaviest from October to March.

See Climate (p537) in the Directory chapter for more information.

With such a wide ethnic diversity, celebrations of one kind or another are held throughout the year. The locals like to get away during public holidays (see Directory, p531), so transport is crowded and hotel prices tend to increase in the resorts. The peak periods are Chinese New Year, Hari Raya and Christmas. If you're in the country during these times, it's best to wait until the holiday rush is over before travelling away from the major cities. The main beach- and hill-resorts also get crowded on Saturday and Sunday but are often deserted during the week.

The Muslim fasting month of Ramadan is generally not a problem for travel. Some services may be cut back, especially in the east-coast states of Kelantan and Terengganu, but transport, hotels, restaurants and many businesses function as normal.

COSTS & MONEY

Though one of the more expensive countries in Southeast Asia, Malaysia is still cheap by world standards and caters well to all budgets. Singapore and Brunei are a bit pricier, but there are still bargains to be had if you look carefully.

DON'T LEAVE HOME WITHOUT...

- Checking the visa situation (p551)... Those travelling on an Israeli passport cannot enter Malaysia.
- Checking travel advisory bureaus (see p539).
- Proof of vaccination for yellow fever (see p571) if coming from infected areas of Africa or South America.
- A copy of your travel insurance policy details (see p545).
- Packing a torch or headlamp, a pair of binoculars, mosquito net and leech-proof socks – all essential gear for a jungle trek.
- A sweater or light jacket – but only if you're planning a trip to the cooler highlands.
- Sharp elbows – for battling with Singaporeans over shopping bargains!

You can easily find a spartan double room in an old hotel for as little as US$5, but if you want to spend US$100 or more a night that's no problem either. Though still plentiful, the older cheap hotels are diminishing in number, but new travellers guesthouses are springing up in the tourist centres and offer dormitory beds for around US$2.50, as well as cheap rooms. The mid-range is well catered for and hotel rooms with air-con and attached bathroom start at around US$12.

Food is quite cheap. There's a good variety in the cities and you can usually get away with between US$1 and US$2 for a simple meal. A full meal at a food centre with a couple of drinks and dessert will come closer to US$3. At the other end of the scale, fancy hotels and restaurants in the main cities offer international cuisine at international prices.

Alcoholic drinks are usually quite expensive, particularly in Singapore, the conservative areas of the east coast or on islands. Beer costs about US$2 a can, almost double in isolated areas. Spirits are even more expensive – about 50% more than beer. With no alcohol available in Brunei at least you'll save money there.

Transportation is generally a real bargain. There are plenty of reasonably priced taxis for local travel. Drivers are fairly honest and prices are either fixed or there are meters. For long-distance journeys, Malaysia has excellent buses, trains and long-distance taxis, all at very reasonable prices, and even flying need not be too costly.

Besides the travel essentials of food, accommodation and transport you'll find nonessentials and luxuries are moderately priced, even downright cheap.

HOW MUCH?

Mid-range hotel double RM80/S$100/B$100

Cup of coffee RM2/S$4/B$4

Bowl of laksa RM5/S$4/B$4

Restaurant meal RM6/S$16/B$20

Newspaper RM1/S$1.20/B$0.80

LONELY PLANET INDEX

Litre of petrol RM1.10/S$1.20/B$0.53

Litre of bottled water RM1/S$1.50/B$1

Beer – large bottle of Tiger RM10/S$8

Souvenir T-shirt RM15/S$15/B$20

Street snack – satay stick RM0.50/S$0.40/B$1

TRAVEL LITERATURE

One of the most entertaining travel literature books written about this region is *Into the Heart of Borneo* (1987) by Redmond O'Hanlon. It's a hilarious account of O'Hanlon's and the poet James Fenton's journey by foot and boat into the Bornean interior in search of the fabled Sumatran rhinoceros. In a more serious vein is Eric Hansen's *Stranger in the Forest* (2000), in which the intrepid Hansen treks across Sarawak and Kalimantan, facing many perils along the way.

Rehman Rashad's *A Malaysian Journey* is an affectionate, insightful travelogue by a respected Malaysian journalist of his motorbike trip around the country. It's out of print so search for it in a library.

The Golden Chersonese and the Way Thither by Isabella Bird, first published in 1883, finds the doughty Victorian-era traveller wending her way through the Malaysian jungles of Selangor and Perak, and crossing the Bukit Genting pass on the back of an elephant.

Ian Buruma wrote *God's Dust* in the late 1980s. While the hard-line Islamic commune Buruma visits just outside of Kuala Lumpur (KL) was disbanded by the government in the late 1990s, many of his impressions of the cultural difficulties of the region remain pertinent today. Equally worth a look are VS Naipaul's *Among The Believers* (1982) and *Beyond Belief* (1999), both of which have chapters on Malaysia and its experience of Islam.

Among the travel literature on Singapore, the standout is Nigel Barley's entertaining *In the Footsteps of Stamford Raffles*, also titled *The Duke of Puddledock*. Julian Davison's *One For The Road* is a nostalgic collection of short stories drawn from the author's recollections of Singapore and Malaysia in the 1950s and 1960s, while Neil Humphreys brings the expat view up to date in *Notes From An Even Smaller Island* (2001) – he's not nearly as funny as he thinks he is but it still has a few pertinent points to make about contemporary Singaporean issues.

TOP TENS

MUST-SEE MOVIES

Neither Malaysia nor Singapore (let alone Brunei) is known for its cinematic output, and Hollywood tends to use the region mainly as an exotic backdrop. For some reviews of home-grown and international movies that give a flavour of the region see the Culture chapter, p40.

- *Penarik Becha (1955)*
  Director: P Ramlee
- *Entrapment (1999)*
  Director: Jon Amiel
- *Saint Jack (1979)*
  Director: Peter Bogdanovich
- *Rogue Trader (1999)*
  Director: James Dearden
- *King Rat (1965)*
  Director: Bryan Forbes
- *Bugis Street (Yao Jie Huang Hou; 1994)*
  Director: Yonfan
- *Mee Pok Man (1995)*
  Director: Eric Koo
- *Money No Enough (Qian Bu Gou Yong; 1998)*
  Director: TL Tay
- *Forever Fever (1998)*
  Director: Glen Goei
- *15 (2003)*
  Director: Royston Tan

TOP READS

Get a feel for the cultures of Malaysia and Singapore with the following acclaimed books by local and international writers. See the Culture chapter, p40, for reviews.

- *Foreign Bodies* and *Mammon Inc.*
  Hwee Hwee Tan
- *The Malayan Trilogy*
  Anthony Burgess
- *The Rice Mother*
  Rani Manicka
- *Lord Jim*
  Joseph Conrad
- *The Return*
  KS Maniam
- *The Consul's File* and *Saint Jack*
  Paul Theroux
- *Malaysian Stories*
  W Somerset Maugham
- *Love and Vertigo*
  Hsu-Ming Teo
- *Heartland*
  Daren VL Shia
- *Ceritalah* and *Journeys Through Southeast Asia: Ceritalah 2*
  Karim Raslan

OUR FAVOURITE FESTIVALS & EVENTS

It was a tough choice but the following is our Top Ten favourite festivals and events from the region.

- Thaipusam
  January (p109)
- Chinese New Year
  January (p542)
- Malaysian Grand Prix
  March (p542)
- Singapore Food Festival
  March to April (p479)
- Hari Raya Puasa
  March to April (p541)
- Singapore Arts Festival
  May to June (p479)
- Sultan of Brunei's Birthday Celebrations
  15 July (p522)
- Malaysian National Day (Hari Kebangsaan)
  31 August (p543)
- Thimithi
  October/November (p463)
- Deepavali
  October to November (p543)

INTERNET RESOURCES

For details of airline, bus and rail information websites for the region see the Transport chapter, p555.

Cari (www.cari.com.my) Cari means 'find' and, although it could be a lot more extensive, it is a great search engine for all things Malaysian.

Government of Brunei Darussalam (www.brunei.gov.bn) The official website with daily news updates, links to all the ministries and brief background info on the country.

Lonely Planet (www.lonelyplanet.com) Succinct summaries on travelling Malaysia, Singapore and Brunei, and the Thorn Tree bulletin board. Travel news and the subWWWay section with links to the most useful travel resources elsewhere on the Web.

Malaysiakini (www.malaysiakini.com) The best news site for Malaysia – great for finding out what's really going on in the country.

Singapore Tourism (www.visitsingapore.com) The official site for tourist information, with plenty of links to things to see and do.

Tourism Malaysia (www.tourismmalaysia.gov.my) The official government site for tourist information, with events calendars, regional links, background information and listings of domestic and international tourist offices.

Itineraries

CLASSIC ROUTES

THE GRAND TOUR Six weeks / Kuala Lumpur to Bandar Seri Begawan

In six weeks you could visit Malaysia, Singapore and Brunei, with time for some adventurous activities. Kick off in **Kuala Lumpur** (p70), where four days should be enough to acclimatise and see the sights. Next, cool off in **Cameron Highlands** (p123), then warm up again on the beaches of **Langkawi** (p187).

Take a rattling bus across the mountainous spine of the peninsula to **Kota Bharu** (p303), one of the best places in the country to encounter traditional Malay culture. Island- and beach-hop down the east coast, pausing at **Pulau Perhentian** (p294), **Cherating** (p262) and **Pulau Tioman** (p250), among many other options. Swing inland for a week to explore Malaysia's largest national park, **Taman Negara** (p267), then return to the west coast to historic **Melaka** (p210). From here you can head straight to **Singapore** (p444) for a week of shopping, museum viewing and world-class eating.

Fly across to **Kuching** (p320) and use it as your base for a longhouse excursion or for arranging a trek in the **Gunung Mulu National Park** (p371). Your next challenge, should you choose to accept it, is to climb **Mt Kinabalu** (p414). Finish up in **Bandar Seri Begawan** (p516), the capital of oil-rich Brunei.

The Grand Tour covers 5000km, taking in the key attractions of Malaysia with stopovers in Singapore and Brunei. A full two months would allow a more leisurely pace.

PENINSULAR MALAYSIA EXCLUSIVE

Three weeks / Kuala Lumpur to Melaka

Three weeks is enough to pack in a fair amount of Peninsular Malaysia. Use **Kuala Lumpur** (KL; p70) as a base for trips out to the atmospheric *kampung* (villages) of **Kuala Selangor** (p116), the **Batu Caves** (p108), even the hill station of **Bukit Fraser** (p111). Escape the crowds with a visit to **Bukit Larut** (p149), Malaysia's oldest hill station, then pitch yourself back into the fray amid the bustle of Penang's **Georgetown** (p158).

Return to KL at the start of your second week, then hit the jungle trails and waterways of **Taman Negara** (p267) or, if you're up for a more off-the-beaten-track jungle experience, head for either the **Endau-Rompin** (p244) or **Kenong Rimba** (p277) national parks. If that's not your scene, then consider a tour up the east coast, passing through **Cherating** (p262), **Marang** (p284), **Kuala Terengganu** (p286) and **Kota Bharu** (p303). Heading in this direction you could finish up with a leisurely week at **Pulau Perhentian** (p294).

Then again, if you've had your fill of beaches, spend your last few days taking the jungle railway from near Kota Bharu back south, perhaps pausing at **Kuala Lipis** (p311) en route. Finish up in **Melaka** (p210), where you can enjoy the mix of cultures, the colonial history, shopping for antiques and a fine range of cuisines.

On our Peninsular Malaysia Exclusive you'll cover around 2800km, making the most of both coasts, and trekking in the jungle interior. Add a few extra days to the three weeks if you take the jungle train and explore Melaka and the southern tip of the peninsula.

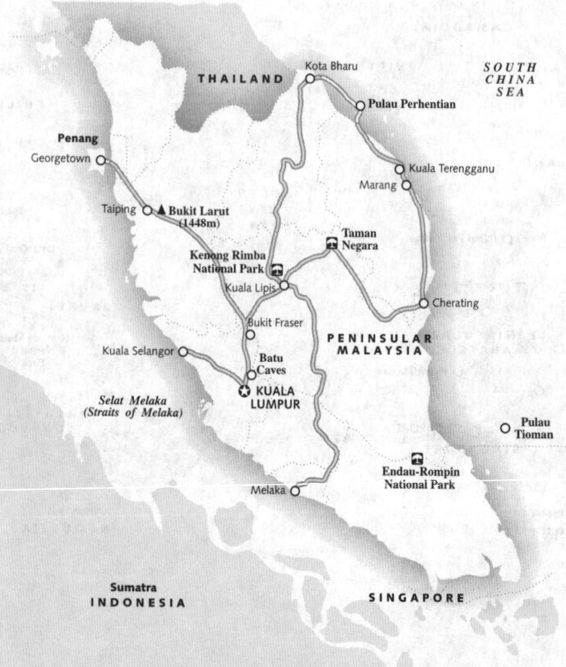

SINGAPORE & PENINSULAR MALAYSIA HIGHLIGHTS

Two weeks / Kuala Lumpur to Singapore

If you've only got a couple of weeks to spare then it's best to confine yourself to one side or other of the peninsula. Those interested in city life should stick to the west coast, spending around four days in **Kuala Lumpur** (p70), a couple of days each in **Penang** (p151) and **Melaka** (p210), and about four days in **Singapore** (p444). This will leave you a few days spare to add in a trip to the **Cameron Highlands** (p123).

If it's the great Malaysian jungle you've come to see, then top of your list should be **Taman Negara** (p267); four days will allow you to get the most out of the park, including spending a night or two in a jungle hide for wildlife spotting.

Confining yourself to the east coast, you could go straight from KL to **Kota Bharu** (p303) and then work your way down the coast taking in **Kuala Terengganu** (p286), and **Pulau Perhentian** (p294) for a few days, then the Royal Abu Bakar Museum and bustling night market of **Johor Bahru** (p231), before heading across the causeway to the relative sophistication of **Singapore** (p444).

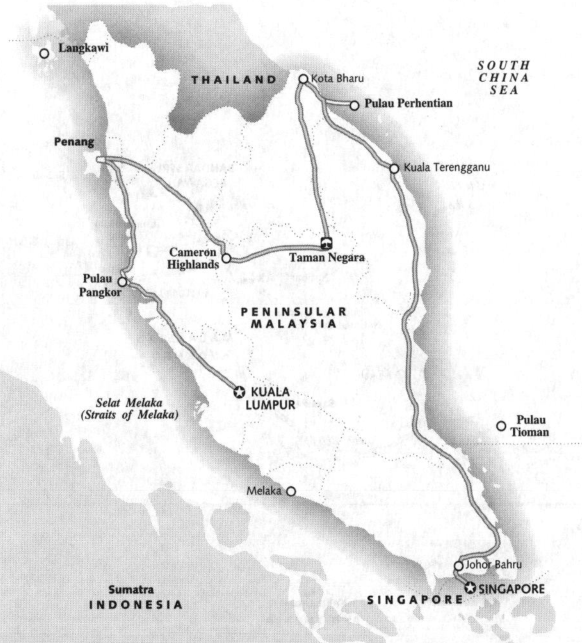

Covering the highlights of both the peninsula and Singapore in just a couple of weeks will involve some tough choices on what to leave out, but the excellent transport will allow you to travel 1100km up and down either the east or west coasts with a minimum of hassle.

ROADS LESS TRAVELLED

The following two itineraries could be combined for a grand tour of Malaysian Borneo.

SARAWAK & BRUNEI COMBINED

Three weeks / Kuching to Bandar Seri Begawan

Spend your first few days in Sarawak's handsome riverine capital **Kuching** (p320), using it as a base for trips to various longhouse communities and to **Bako National Park** (p334), which includes some of the state's best beaches.

Next head to **Sibu** (p346) to commence your journey up the mighty **Batang Rejang** (p345). Go beyond **Kapit** (p350) towards the atmospheric interior settlement of **Belaga** (p353), around which are the longhouses of the Kenyah and Kayan. A round trip takes about four days.

Return to Sibu and on to **Similajau National Park** (p358), a little-visited coastal park with good beaches, to chill out for a day or two. Press on to the **Gunung Mulu National Park** (p371) – reached by a flight from the city of **Miri** (p363) – where you'll find not only fine caves, but also challenging hikes to the Pinnacles and along the Headhunters' Trail.

Miri is also the jumping off point for **Bario** (p377), the lush valley settlement 1500m up in the Kelabit Highlands; the really adventurous could then tackle the four- to six-day trek to Long Lellang. Returning to Miri, head across the border into Brunei, spend a couple of days in the capital **Bandar Seri Begawan** (p516) then make a boat trip to the **Temburong district** (p528).

Travelling around both Sarawak and Brunei by road, river and sometimes air, you'll cover some 1900km, passing through a fascinating range of landscapes and encountering many of the different people of Borneo. To cover everything will easily take three weeks – a month would be better.

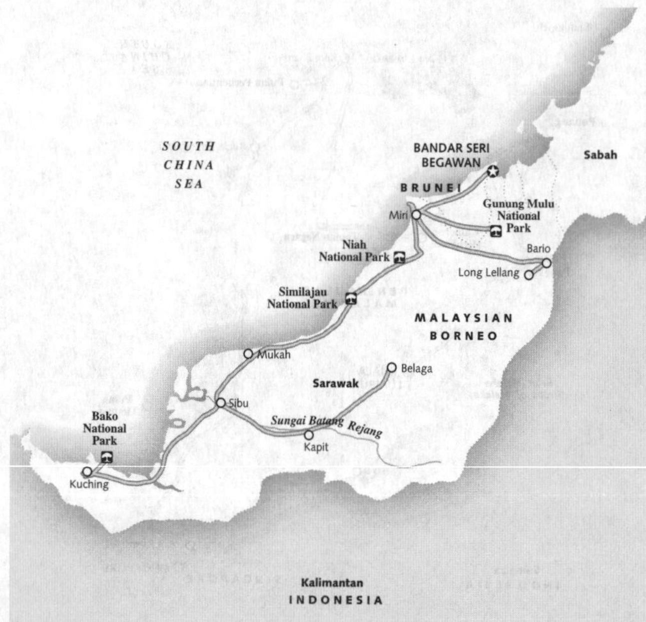

SABAH SOLO

Three weeks / Kota Kinabalu to Semporna

The main reason people come to Sabah is to climb **Mt Kinabalu** (p414); assaults on Malaysia's highest peak can be launched from the state capital, **Kota Kinabalu** (KK; p388). All up, a trip to the mountain and back, plus exploring the trails around the national park headquarters and a visit to **Poring Hot Springs** (p422), will take you five to six days. KK is also the jumping-off point for the **Tunku Abdul Rahman National Park** (p398), a cluster of five lovely islands offering beautiful beaches.

A six-hour bus ride will take you east to character-filled **Sandakan** (p425), the base for various wildlife-viewing activities, including a visit to the **Turtle Islands National Park** (p431), **Sepilok Orang-Utan Rehabilitation Centre** (p429) and **Sungai Kinabatangan** (p432), one of the best places in Southeast Asia to see fauna.

From Sandakan head south towards the **Danum Valley Conservation Area** (p434), where you can enjoy various ecotourism activities – including a not-to-be-missed night drive safari – from the luxurious Borneo Rainforest Lodge. Finish up your trip in **Semporna** (p437), from where you can organise diving and snorkelling trips to **Pulau Sipadan** (p438) and other nearby islands.

The 1300km you'll cover on this trip may seem like nothing once you've tramped the 18km up and down Mt Kinabalu, so sit back and enjoy the fantastic variety, from idyllic islands to wildlife-packed jungles, of this three-week itinerary.

TAILORED TRIPS

FOOD LOVER'S TOUR

Kuala Lumpur (KL; p70) has practically everything, from sizzling steaks to fantastic Chinese hawker fare. Heading north, pause at **Ipoh** (p132) for Ipoh *kway teow* (noodles) and *rendang tok* (beef cooked in coconut). Then make for **Cameron Highlands** (p123) and afternoon tea amid lush tea plantations.

Penang (p167) has a mouthwatering mix of specialities born of its past as a port for the spice trade. The classic dish is Penang laksa, a spicy, sour noodle dish. On the east coast, hit the night market in **Kota Bharu** (p307), with its staunchly Malay food; the dish not to miss is *nasi kerabu*, with its distinctive blue-coloured rice. In **Kuala Terengganu** (p289), fish dishes are popular; snack on *epok epok* – pastries filled with fried fish and coconut.

Melaka (p223) is justly famed for its Nonya cuisine, a hybrid of traditional Chinese and Malay culinary styles. You can also have fun trying *satay celup*, the local version of fondue.

Although you may be feeling quite full by this stage, don't miss the sumptuous culinary smorgasbord that is **Singapore** (p486). Chicken rice, chilli crab, satay and a whole host of other heavenly dishes are a must.

ISLANDS & BEACHES

From **Kuala Lumpur** (KL; p70) make a day trip to **Pulau Ketam** (p115) for tasty seafood served in an atmospheric fishing village. Moving north, **Pulau Pangkor** (p138) has good beaches but if possible, spend the night on the exclusive resort island of **Pulau Pangkor Laut** (p143) with access to Emerald Beach, one of the prettiest stretches of sand in the world.

Langkawi (p187) has several lovely beaches including Pantai Cenang and Pantai Kok. You can also make boat trips to the nearby island of Pulau Dayang Bunting. If you're heading for **Pulau Perhentian** (p294) – and who wouldn't want to? – choose Pulau Perhentian Besar if you want to escape the crowds. On gorgeous **Pulau Tioman** (p250) head over to Juara on the east coast for some quiet relaxation. There are numerous other equally attractive – and less touristed – islands off the east coast; try the islands of the **Seribuat Archipelago** (p243).

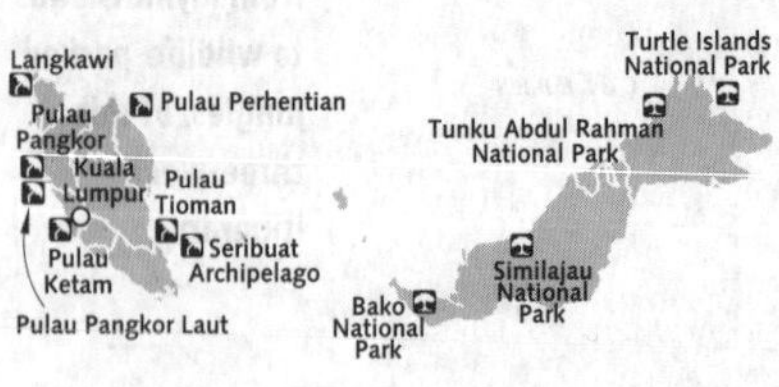

In Sarawak, good beaches can be found in both **Bako National Park** (p334) and **Similajau National Park** (p358). Sabah, though, is home to Malaysian Borneo's best collection of beaches and islands. Make time for swathes of white sand around the islands in **Tunku Abdul Rahman National Park** (p398). If you're interested in the conservation of turtles, then drop by **Turtle Islands National Park** (p431).

KIDS' MALAYSIA & SINGAPORE

Kuala Lumpur (KL; p86) has several attractions that will keep the kids happy. In the **Lake Gardens** (p77) there's Bird Park, Butterfly Park, Deer Park and Planetarium. The Skybridge at the **Petronas Towers** (p81) will be a hit, as will be the same complex's Petrosains interactive science discovery centre.

Within day-trip distance of KL are **Desa Waterpark** (p86) and **Sunway Lagoon Waterpark** (p86). There's also **Mines Wonderland** (p86), an amusement park packed with theme rides and musical fountains.

For an educational experience on the wonders of the jungle, take the family to **Taman Negara** (p267). Even if a long hike is out the question, the braver of your children will readily clamber across the canopy walkway or float down the river on an inner tube.

Out of the beaches and islands of the east coast, you might want to choose **Pulau Kapas** (p286) or **Cherating** (p262) which are slightly more geared towards family holidays.

Singapore (p477) is a great place to take the kids. You are just as likely as your little ones to enjoy the excellent **zoo and night safari** (p467). Monkeys can easily be spotted on walks around **Bukit Timah Nature Reserve** (p468) and the **MacRitchie Reservoir** (p469). It's fun pedalling around **Pulau Ubin** (p467) and you can hire bikes on **Sentosa Island** (p471) which also boasts a top-class aquarium, dolphin shows, an old fort and OK beaches.

PEAK & JUNGLE CHALLENGE

Malaysia's wealth of national parks provides many challenges for the adventurous traveller. Top of the list is **Taman Negara** (p267), the country's showcase national park; there are excellent trails and waterways to explore and good facilities. From inside the park you can climb Gunung Tahan, Peninsular Malaysia's highest peak; this would be a nine-day trip.

Also on the peninsula are the **Kenong Rimba** (p277) and **Endau-Rompin** (p244) national parks – both much less touristy than Taman Negara. Endau-Rompin has Malaysia's largest surviving population of Sumatran rhinos, although don't count on spotting these elusive beasts. To experience all three parks and do them justice, allow at least four days.

Malaysian Borneo has 16 national parks to choose from, including marine reserves and the rarefied heights of **Mt Kinabalu** (p413); you'll need to set aside three days to reach this summit. In **Gunung Mulu National Park** (p371) allow four days to tramp the Headhunters' Trail and climb to the jagged Pinnacles. A day is sufficient for **Niah National Park** (p359) with its interesting giant caves. Give yourself two days in **Bako National Park** (p334) to hunt out exotic flora and fauna, including the rare proboscis monkeys, and to enjoy walks along the rugged, sand- and mangrove-fringed coastline.

DIVER'S DELIGHT

Kick off at **Pulau Perhentian** (p294) where colourful reef fish, sea turtles, manta and blacktip reef sharks can be spotted. Move on to **Pulau Redang** (p292), one of Malaysia's most spectacular dive sites – nine islands surrounded by fine coral reefs and very clear water, or the much less visited gem of **Pulau Lang Tengah** (p293). The **Seribuat Archipelago** (p243) offers the same super dive conditions as nearby Pulau Tioman minus the crowds; the most accessible islands are Besar, Sibu and Rawa, but the best diving is around Pemanggil and Aur.

Over on Malaysian Borneo all the dive hot spots are in Sabah. **Pulau Labuan** (p408) offers wreck diving around sunken WWII boats. You'll certainly not want to miss spectacular **Pulau Sipadan** (p438), a world-class site with beautiful coral gardens, sea turtles, sharks and huge varieties of reef fish. The real pros will want to finish up at **Pulau Layang Layang** (p400), part of the famous Borneo Banks – here both shallow reefs and impressive drop-offs play host to shoals of tuna, barracuda and hammerhead sharks.

The Authors

SIMON RICHMOND

Coordinating Author & Singapore

Since the early 1990s Simon Richmond has made many trips to Malaysia and Singapore, travelling through the peninsula and to Sarawak. He spent two months in the country in 1996 and returned in 1998 to write about several adventure activities in Malaysia. In 2002, Simon spent a couple of more months digging into every corner of Singapore and making forays into Malaysia for Lonely Planet's *Singapore* city guide. In the face of SARS, he fearlessly returned in early 2003 to coordinate this book. Between trips to various far-flung corners of the globe for Lonely Planet and other publishers, Simon returns to his Sydney home.

The Coordinating Author's Favourite Trip

To get off the beaten track in Singapore, catch bus No 2 from the city centre to the Changi Village terminal. From there, hop on the ferry to Pulau Ubin (p467) and explore Singapore's most rural island by bicycle, grab a seafood lunch or hike to the tidal pools at Chek Jawa (p467). Return to the main island and reboard bus No 2 for the Changi Prison Museum & Chapel (p467), dedicated to those who suffered during WWII. Nip back on bus No 2, stop at the Payar Lebar MRT station and head for Joo Chiat Rd, 500m away. Walk south down Joo Chiat Rd into the heart of Katong (p466) to see pretty Peranakan terrace houses and colonial bungalows. There's a great local vibe and plenty of cheap restaurants offering delicious dishes.

MARIE CAMBON

Sarawak, Sabah & Brunei

Born and raised in Vancouver, Canada, Marie travelled to Asia after high school and eventually moved to Shanghai in the mid-80s to study Chinese. After some years in China, Marie visited Kalimantan and quickly became enamoured of Borneo's winding rivers and friendly people. Marie jumped at the chance offered by this book, her fifth for Lonely Planet, to become reacquainted with Borneo and its many faces. Her next trip there will have something to do with either tracking Sumatran rhinos or retracing the steps of Joseph Conrad. In the meantime, Marie lives in Vancouver with a dog named Marlowe.

DAMIAN HARPER

Kuala Lumpur, Negeri Sembilan, Melaka, Johor & Pahang

With degrees in modern and classical Chinese and the history of art, Damian worked in the book trade in the UK, before living and working in Singapore, Hong Kong and Beijing. A contributor to five guidebooks for Lonely Planet, Damian has also had a book published by *National Geographic Traveler*. He has an abiding interest in overseas Chinese communities in Malaysia, other Southeast Asian nations and Europe.

RICHARD WATKINS

Selangor, Perak, Penang, Kedah & Perlis, Terengganu and Kelantan

Born in Wales, Richard spent five years studying ancient history at university before a brief career teaching English as a foreign language eventually landed him in Singapore. Although he enjoyed his first taste of Asia, teaching grammar to bored businessmen held less appeal, and he travelled round Southeast Asia, Australia and New Zealand while deciding what to do next. Richard has written for Internet travel sites and other guidebooks. This is his first project for Lonely Planet.

CONTRIBUTING AUTHORS

Dr Trish Batchelor wrote the Health chapter (p571). Trish is a general practitioner and travel medicine specialist who works at the CIWEC Clinic in Kathmandu, Nepal, as well as being a medical advisor to the Travel Doctor New Zealand clinics. Trish teaches travel medicine through the University of Otago, and is interested in underwater and high-altitude medicine, and in the impact of tourism on host countries. She has travelled extensively through Southeast and East Asia, and loves high-altitude trekking in the Himalayas.

Alan D'Cruz wrote the History chapter (p28). Alan is a Malaysian writer and documentary film maker with a penchant for making films with a historical bias. He directed the acclaimed film, *Guardians of the Forest* (2001), which investigates the current predicament of Malaysia's indigenous people through an examination of their history. He is currently working on a documentary which explores the resilience of Malaysia's multiracial harmony.

Su-Lyn Tan wrote the Food & Drink chapter (p60). Su-Lyn is a freelance food writer based in Singapore and was the managing editor of *Wine & Dine* magazine, the most established food publication in the region. She is also the author of Lonely Planet's *World Food Malaysia & Singapore*. Su-Lyn is currently putting the final touches to a doctoral thesis examining the celebrity-chef phenomenon.

Snapshot

In early 2003 the region found itself at the centre of the SARS health scare with Singapore, in particular, and Malaysia, to a lesser extent, in the spotlight (for more information, see the Health chapter, p577). Both countries' economies were dealt an unexpected blow as locals stayed at home and overseas visitors stayed away. Having survived the regional economic crises of the late 1990s, this turn of events was a tough call for countries where tourism is a major income earner.

On the political front, Malaysia is steadying itself for its most momentous change in decades – the retirement of Dr Mahathir Mohamad as prime minister, a post he has commanded for the last 22 years. His successor, Deputy Prime Minister Abdullah Ahmad Badawi (also known, respectfully, as Pak Lah) was set to take over the top job in October 2003. But as the sorry experience of the former deputy, Anwar Ibrahim, shows, Malaysian politics can sometimes take unexpected turns. See the History chapter, p37, for more information.

Anwar was jailed in 2000 on charges of corruption and sodomy, despite much criticism of the legitimacy of his trial internationally and in Malaysia. He remains in jail, having lost his appeal in April 2003, but continues to battle on, taking his case to the country's highest judicial authority, the Federal Court; if he loses, he won't be freed until April 2009 at the earliest.

Some believe Badawi will grant Anwar's release as a magnanimous gesture prior to an election – which could happen during 2004; others that Anwar will stay locked up until after any election for fear that his release may detract from the ruling UMNO party's chances at the polls. Either way, the Anwar factor is something that UMNO cannot afford to ignore, especially as PAS, the main Islamic party, snaps at its heels. Anwar's wife, Wan Azizah, who heads the Keadilan party is respected for her loyalty to her beleaguered husband, but the party itself is no longer the force it promised to be a couple of years ago.

Such political battles – or indeed worries about any credible opposition – are unheard of in well-ordered Singapore, where Senior Minister Lee Kuan Yew keeps a beady eye on government despite having left the top job over a decade ago. Succession from the current Prime Minister Goh Chok Tong to Lee's son, Lee Hsien Loong, is assured. Meanwhile the nanny state continues to loosen up by cautiously fostering a more daring arts scene and allowing longer opening hours for bars.

Post-September 11, fears of Islamic fundamentalism permeate the region. A plot to blow up the US Embassy in Singapore was foiled in 2002. In Malaysia, PAS was virtually equated with the Taliban by the government, ignoring the fact that the party has drawn many Westernised Malays dissatisfied with UMNO. Nik Adli, the son of PAS leader Nik Aziz, was arrested in August 2001 under the country's notorious Internal Security Act (ISA) and continues to languish in jail, along with many others whose supposed crimes are unclear.

The most Islamic nation of the region, Brunei remains a haven of peace and prosperity, where the paternalistic sultan and his minions continue to work out how to prop up the economy once the oil runs out in around 20 years' time.

FAST FACTS: MALAYSIA

GDP per person: US$9000

Life expectancy: 71 years

Literacy rate: 83%

Inflation: 1.4%

Unemployment: 3.2%

Major exports: electronic components, petroleum and natural gas, chemicals and chemical products, textiles, timber

Number of sultans: nine

FAST FACTS: SINGAPORE

GDP per person: US$24,700

Life expectancy: 80 years

Literacy rate: 93%

Inflation: 1.5%

Unemployment: 4.7%

Major exports: electronics, consumer goods, chemicals, mineral fuels

Fine for littering: up to S$2000 for repeat offenders

FAST FACTS: BRUNEI

GDP per person: US$18,000

Life expectancy: 74 years

Literacy rate: 88%

Inflation: 2.7%

Unemployment: 5%

Major exports: crude oil, natural gas

Daily oil production: 163,000 barrels

History by Alan D'Cruz

Malaysia, Singapore and Brunei owe their tumultuous history to their geographical position. Situated between Asia's ancient civilisations of China and India, their destiny was shaped by the ebb and flow of the convergent sea trade of those two mighty nations.

ORIGINAL PEOPLE

The earliest evidence of human life in the region is a 40,000-year-old skull found in the Niah Caves of Sarawak. Little else is known about these early inhabitants, but they are believed to be related to the first people of Australia and New Guinea.

In Peninsular Malaysia, the oldest remains are the 13,000-year-old skeleton, 'Perak Man', which has been found to be genetically similar to the Negrito who now live in the mountainous rainforests of northern Malaysia. The Negritos were joined by Malaysia's first immigrants, the Senoi, who are thought to have slowly filtered down from central and southern Thailand around 2500 BC. These Neolithics had better stone tools, and archaeological findings in Gua Cha (Kelantan) include pottery and ornaments.

A third wave, the Proto-Malay, ancestors of today's Malays, came from the Indonesian islands between 1500 and 500 BC. They settled first on the coasts but later were forced upriver into deeper jungle. For more information see the boxed text The Indigenous People (p35).

EARLY TRADE

By the 2nd century Malaya was known as far away as Europe. Ptolemy, the Greek geographer, labelled it 'Golden Chersonese'. Indian traders were already making regular visits to Malaya in search of gold, tin and aromatic jungle woods.

The Indian traders had a significant impact on Malay social systems, beliefs and culture, introducing them to Hinduism, Buddhism and notions of kingship. Key Malay words like *bahasa* (language), *raja* (ruler) and *jaya* (success) are Sanskrit terms.

EARLY EMPIRES

The first kingdom to dominate the Malays is believed to have been the Funan empire, which was centred in what is now Cambodia. Although little is known about the Funans, Chinese travellers of the 3rd century record them as powerful overlords of the region.

Much more significant was the dominance of the mighty Srivijayan empire, which held sway from the 7th century to the 13th. Based in southern Sumatra, this Buddhist empire controlled the entire Malacca Straits, Java and southern Borneo. Under the protection of the Srivijayans, a significant Malay trading state grew in the Bujang Valley of Kedah. Relics of temple complexes that house both Buddhist and Hindu artefacts are still being excavated and provide a reminder of the Hindu Buddhist era in the Malay Peninsula.

Alan D'Cruz is a Malaysian writer and documentary film maker with a penchant for history. He directed the acclaimed *Guardians of the Forest* (2001) about Malaysia's indigenous people, and is currently working on a documentary exploring the resilience of multiracial harmony in Malaysia.

TIMELINE

700 The Buddhist Srivijayan empire dominates Malaya, Singapore, Indonesia and Borneo for 600 years

1400 Foundation of Melaka, the most successful Malay sultanate

New kingdoms in Thailand and the growth of the Hindu Majapahit empire of Java finally led to the demise of the Srivijayans in the 14th century.

THE MELAKA EMPIRE

Malaya's greatest empire was founded by a renegade prince.

Parameswara was from a little kingdom in southern Sumatra, which he declared independent of the Javanese Majapahit empire. This was a rash move, for an expedition was sent to crush the upstart. Parameswara escaped and landed on Temasek (today's Singapore) where he was welcomed by the local chief. Eight days later he killed his host and pronounced himself ruler – another foolish move. Temasek was a vassal state of the Thai empire. Over the next five years Parameswara and his fellow pirates wrought havoc on shipping and trade, until a huge Thai expedition saw them off. Parameswara fled up the Malay Peninsula, finally settling in Melaka, a tiny fishing village, where he foresaw its potential as a natural deep-water port.

Realising that Melaka could never grow without protection from the Thais, Parameswara sent envoys to China to offer tribute. The timing was fortuitous. The Ming emperor had just begun a series of maritime missions to find alternatives to the overland route to the West, and he agreed to offer protection. Melaka became a port of call for the massive Chinese junks that were to ply the oceans for several decades. The junks were also a magnet for the other key traders of the time, the Indians.

Melaka was ideally situated as a half-way point for trade between the two nations. The Indian ships sailed in on the southwest monsoon, berthed in Melaka and waited for the northeast monsoon, which blew in the Chinese junks. Their goods were traded, and the Indians sailed back to India on the same winds that brought in the Chinese. Business boomed as regional ships and *perahus* arrived to take advantage of trading opportunities.

DID YOU KNOW?

Malaysia has the world's only revolving monarchy. Malaysia has nine state sultans, each of whom takes a turn at being the *agong* (paramount ruler of Malaysia) for five years.

EARLY ISLAM

Islam first came to northern Sumatra through the Indian Muslim traders in the late 13th century. When the Melaka sultan and his subjects converted to Islam in the mid-15th century, the religion really took off. Melaka's population was a shifting melange of seafarers who spread the religion rapidly throughout the Indonesian islands. Melaka's role in the spread of Islam remains one of its greatest sources of pride.

Brunei received Islam through its trade with Melaka. In the 15th and 16th centuries the powerful Brunei sultanate controlled virtually the whole of Borneo and the Philippines.

THE PORTUGUESE ERA

By the 15th century, Europe had developed an insatiable appetite for spices, and the sole suppliers were Venetian merchants, who obtained them from Arab traders, who obtained them from Indian Muslim traders, who obtained them…from Melaka.

The Portuguese were determined to break this chain for 'God, glory and gold'. Their strategy was to build fortresses to control the sea trade

1445 Islam becomes Melaka's state religion and spreads throughout Southeast Asia

1511 Portuguese conquer Melaka

route between Lisbon and Melaka. In 1509 the Portuguese sailed into Melaka. Acting on the advice of his Indian Muslim councillors, the Melaka sultan captured 19 of the heathen sailors. Far from being discouraged, the Portuguese saw this as just the excuse they needed. In 1511, led by Viceroy Alfonso de Albuquerque, they returned with a fleet of 18 heavily armed ships. Within a month Melaka's army of 20,000 men and their war elephants had been defeated. The sultan and his court fled south to Johor, where they established a new base.

The Portuguese immediately built a fortress, the A Formosa, to protect their new acquisition. Expeditions were sent to the Moluccas, the source of the spices, where a monopoly agreement was signed with the local sultan. Within a few years Lisbon had replaced Venice as the greatest trading centre for Eastern goods.

The 130 years that the Portuguese held Melaka were fraught with wars and skirmishes. Their monopolistic attitude to trade and their determination to spread Christianity earned them few friends. The new Johor empire never gave up hope of recapturing Melaka and continually harassed Portuguese ships in the Melaka Straits.

THE DUTCH PERIOD

Unlike the Portuguese, the Dutch East India Company had no interest in God or national glory. It focused single-mindedly on wresting complete control of the spice trade. The Dutch set up a base in Batavia (now Jakarta) and negotiated directly for spices with the sultans of the spice islands. In 1641 they teamed up with the sultan of Johor, and together they laid a long and eventually successful siege on Melaka.

Over the 180 years that the Dutch controlled Melaka, its importance waned. Batavia was the main Dutch port, and the conquest of Melaka had been undertaken mainly to get rid of their Portuguese rivals.

THE BRITISH

British interest in the region began with the East India Company's (EIC) need for a halfway base for its ships plying the India-China maritime route. In 1786 Francis Light negotiated a deal with the sultan of Kedah to establish a settlement on largely uninhabited Penang Island. Light instituted a free trade policy at Penang, which was a clear contrast to the monopolistic methods of the Portuguese and Dutch. Penang thrived, and by 1800 it had a population of more than 10,000.

Unlike previous history books on Malaysia, which have invariably had a colonial bias, *A History of Malaya* by Barbara and Leonard Andaya brilliantly explores the evolution of 'Malayness' in Malaysia's history and the challenges of building a multiracial, post-independence nation.

Meanwhile, events in Europe were conspiring to consolidate British interests in the Malay Peninsula. When Napoleon overran the Netherlands in 1795, the British, fearing French influence in the region, took over Dutch Java and Melaka. When Napoleon was defeated, the British handed the Dutch colonies back – but not before they had destroyed the walls of A Formosa.

The British lieutenant-governor of Java, Stamford Raffles, had long felt that Britain, the most powerful nation in Europe, should expand its influence over Southeast Asia. He bitterly resented handing Java back to the Dutch and eventually managed to persuade the EIC that a settlement south of the Malay Peninsula was crucial to the India-China maritime route.

1641
Dutch wrest Melaka from Portuguese; end of Melaka's importance as a port

1786
The British open free trading port in Penang

BRITISH SINGAPORE

In 1819, Raffles landed on Singapore, which was a territory of the Johor empire and governed by a local chieftain. The Johor empire was engaged in a succession dispute. The former sultan had died while his elder son was away, and his younger son had been proclaimed sultan. The Dutch had a treaty with the young sultan, but Raffles threw his support behind the elder, recognising him as the rightful sultan. A treaty was signed between the new sultan, the local chief and Raffles for sole rights to build a trading settlement. In 1824 a second treaty was signed that ceded Singapore to Britain forever in exchange for cash and a life pension for the sultan and local chieftain.

Raffles Statue, next to the river at Raffles Landing, marks the spot where Stamford Raffles first set foot on the island.

GLENN BEANLAND

Raffles was delighted with the success of his skulduggery. Writing soon after, he waxed lyrical: 'It is impossible to conceive a place combining more advantages…it is the Navel of the Malay countries.'

Protests by the Dutch were silenced in 1824 when the two nations signed a treaty that divided the region into two distinct spheres of interest. The Dutch controlled what is now Indonesia, and the British had the Malay Peninsula and Singapore. Dutch Melaka and British Bencoolen, which were on the wrong side of the line, were exchanged.

SUCCESS OF RAFFLES' VISION

Raffles left instructions on the early development of Singapore with the new British Resident, Colonel William Farquhar. Singapore was to be a free port; a fort was to be built, and convenient watering places 'with firm shingle for rolling the casks' were to be installed.

Singapore's population of 150 fishermen and a small number of Chinese farmers swelled immediately. Chinese, Malays and Indonesians poured in, attracted by its free port status and the permanent British tenure. By 1821 the population had grown to 10,000; the harbour was filled with ships from all over the archipelago; and trade boomed.

Three years later Raffles returned to Singapore and governed it for one year. He initiated a town plan that included levelling a hill to form a new commercial district (now Raffles Place) and erecting government buildings around Forbidden Hill (now Fort Canning Hill). Wide streets of shop houses with covered walkways, shipyards, churches and a botanical garden were all built to achieve his vision of a Singapore that would one day be 'a place of considerable magnitude and importance'. The plan also embraced the colonial practice of administering the population according to neat racial categories, with the Europeans, Indians, Chinese and Malays living and working in their own distinct quarters.

AN ADVENTURER IN BORNEO

Travelling in Borneo takes on a whole different perspective when one looks at the adventures of James Brooke. In 1835 he inherited £30,000, bought a ship and sailed from London to Borneo, where he found the weak Brunei sultanate struggling to put down a rebellion by the native Dayaks and Sarawak Malays. He was offered a part of Sarawak if he would help quell the rebellion. With swashbuckling panache he succeeded, and in 1841 he was installed as raja of Sarawak, with the fishing village of Kuching as his capital. Through brutal naval force and skilful negotiation, James

1819
Stamford Raffles founds Singapore

1824
Dutch and British carve up region into what eventually becomes Malaya and Indonesia

Brooke extracted further territory from the Brunei Sultan and eventually brought peace to a land where piracy, headhunting and violent tribal rivalry had been the norm. The 'White Raja' dynasty was to rule Sarawak for more than a hundred years.

Unlike the British, the White Rajas included tribal leaders in their ruling council. They also discouraged large European companies from destroying native jungle to plant massive rubber plantations. They encouraged Chinese migration, and, without European competition, the Chinese came to dominate the economy.

British acquisition of Sabah was less romantic. In 1865 the American consul to Brunei persuaded the ailing sultan to grant him what is now Sabah in return for an annual payment. The rights eventually passed to an Englishman, Alfred Dent. In 1881, with the support of the British government, Dent formed the British North Borneo Company to administer the new settlement.

Brunei, the once mighty empire, was now a tiny and divided sultanate. To prevent a scramble for the remains, the British government decided to preserve the weakened sultanate and in 1888 declared it a British protectorate.

BRITISH MALAYA

In Peninsular Malaya, Britain's determined policy of 'trade, not territory' was challenged when trade was disrupted by fighting in the Malay sultanates. In 1874 the British intervened in a succession dispute in Perak, and a British Resident was installed, whom the sultan had to consult on all matters, 'other than those touching on religion and Malay customs'. The British Resident system was ingenious – it preserved the prestige of the sultans but effectively gave the British complete control.

The film *Kaki Bakar* (2001), directed by U-Wei Haji Saari and based on Faulkner's 'Barn Burning', was completed in 1995, but the censors considered it too controversial to be released at the time because of its suggestion about the origins of Malay roots. Despite winning an award for Best International Film at the Asian Film Festival '95, it was not until 2001 and after some minor re-editing that it found its way to the local theatres. It follows the struggle of a Javanese immigrant family as they resettle in Malaysia. It is also a coming-of-age tale of their son, who is faced with a difficult search for identity.

In 1896 Perak, Selangor, Negeri Sembilan and Pahang became known as the Federated Malay States, each governed by a British Resident. Kelantan, Terengganu, Perlis and Kedah were under Thai suzerainty. Fearing that they might fall into French or German hands, the British made a deal with the Thai king – they offered loans to build railways in exchange for his Malayan states. The sultan of Kedah, enraged by the Thai betrayal, is reported to have said his sultanate had been 'bought and sold like a buffalo'. Helpless against British power, the sultans of these 'Unfederated Malay States' accepted British advisers. Johor, though well ruled by its sultan, finally succumbed in 1913.

The British set about exploiting British Malaya's resources with gusto. Building ports, roads and railways, and selling huge swathes of virgin rainforest, they encouraged British entrepreneurs to invest in tin mines, rubber plantations and trading companies. Believing that the Malays were best suited to farming and fishing, they encouraged immigrants from China to work the mines, Indians to tap the rubber trees and build the railways, Ceylonese to be clerks in the civil service, and Sikhs to man the police force. The lesser Malay royals and 'the better-bred' Malays were encouraged to join a separate arm of the civil service. A 1931 census revealed that the Chinese numbered 1.7 million and the Malays 1.6 million. Malaya's economy had been revolutionised, but the problems of its liberal immigration policy would reverberate for decades to come.

1842 James Brook becomes first White Raja of Sarawak

1874 British intervention in Malay sultanate; first British Resident installed

WWII PERIOD

WWII came to Malaya a few hours before the Japanese bombed Pearl Harbor in December 1941. Landing at Kota Bharu in northeast Malaya, the Japanese made a lightning dash down the peninsula, and within a month they had taken Kuala Lumpur. A month later they were at Singapore's doorstep. With its guns pointing uselessly out to sea, Singapore capitulated in February 1942. The poorly defended Borneo states fell even more rapidly.

The Japanese ruled harshly from Singapore, which they had renamed Syonan – Light of the South. The governor, General Yamashita, slung the Europeans into the infamous Changi Prison, and Chinese communists and intellectuals, who had vociferously opposed the Japanese invasion of China, were targeted for Japanese brutality. Thousands were executed in a single week.

The Japanese achieved very little in Malaya. The British had destroyed most of the tin-mining equipment before their retreat, and the rubber plantations were neglected. The Malayan People's Anti-Japanese Army (MPAJA), comprising remnants of the British army and Chinese from the fledgling Malayan Communist Party, waged a weak, jungle-based guerrilla struggle throughout the war.

In Borneo, early resistance by the Chinese was brutally put down. In 1944 a primarily Australian force, Z Special Unit, parachuted into the Kelabit Highlands and won over the natives. Armed with blowpipes and led by Australian commandos, this unlikely army scored several victories over the Japanese.

The Japanese surrendered to the British in Singapore in 1945 after the devastating atom bombs had been dropped over Hiroshima and Nagasaki.

The Jungle is Neutral by F Spencer Chapman is a classic account of the hardships and adventures of a British guerrilla force based in the Malaysian jungles during the Japanese occupation of Malaysia and Singapore.

POSTWAR MALAYA & THE EMERGENCY

The British had already prepared a roadmap for Malaya's independence, starting with the Malayan Union. In 1946, through cajolery and coercion, the British persuaded the sultans to agree to the union, which amalgamated all the Peninsular Malayan states into a central authority; removed the sovereign rights of the sultans, who would remain as paid 'advisers'; offered citizenship to all residents regardless of race; abolished the special privileges of the Malays (which included favourable quotas in civil service employment and government scholarships); and vested ultimate sovereignty in the king of England. Singapore was to be administered separately. North Borneo and Sarawak became the Crown Colony of British Borneo (the third Raja Brooke realised he could not afford to rebuild after the war).

The War of the Running Dogs by Noel Barber, an account of the 12-year Emergency in Malaysia, is a classic.

The Malayan Union proposal caused an uproar among the normally acquiescent Malays. Rowdy protest meetings were held throughout the country, and the first Malay political party, the United Malays National Organisation (UMNO), was formed.

After intense meetings between the sultans, British officials and UMNO, the Malayan Union was revoked, and the Federation of Malaya was declared in 1948. The federation upheld the sovereignty of the sultans and the special privileges of the Malays. Citizenship for non-Malays was made more restrictive. Although the Malays were ecstatic about the British

1941-45
Japanese occupation of Malaya, Singapore and Brunei

1948-60
The Emergency in Malaya

climb-down, the Chinese felt they had been betrayed and that their role in resisting the Japanese was poorly appreciated. They were easy pickings for the Malayan Communist Party (MCP), which promised an equitable and just society.

The MCP took to the jungles and fought a guerrilla war against the colonial British. They received little support from the Malays, and their main Chinese supporters were subsistence farmers living along the jungle fringes. In 1948 an 'Emergency' was declared, and an all-out war was waged against the communists. The turning point came with the appointment of a military man, General Sir Gerald Templer, as high commissioner and the enforced resettlement of almost 500,000 rural Chinese into protected New Villages. Another key move was gaining the support of the jungle-dwelling Orang Asli. The communists were gradually forced further back into the jungles and towards the Thai border. In 1960 the Emergency was declared over – although sporadic fighting continued and the formal surrender was signed only in 1989.

Paloh (2002), directed by Adman Salleh, is a wartime drama based on real events that happened during the communist insurgency.

MERDEKA & MALAYSIA

UMNO led a less militant campaign towards independence. By forming the Alliance Party with the Malayan Chinese Association (MCA) and the Malayan Indian Congress (MIC), they presented a convincing argument for a racially harmonious, independent nation. In 1955 the British promised independence in two years and held an election to determine the government of the new nation. The Alliance Party, led by UMNO's Tunku Abdul Rahman, won a landslide victory, and on 31 August 1957 Merdeka (independence) was declared. A unique solution was found for the problem of having nine state sultans eligible for the position of paramount leader – they would take turns. Each sultan would be *agong* (federal ruler) for five years.

Singapore's politics were dominated by communists and left-leaning trade unions. In 1958 the People's Action Party (PAP) was voted into government. It was led by Lee Kuan Yew, a young Cambridge-trained lawyer, who garnered popular support through astute compromises with the trade union leaders. Britain remained responsible for defence and foreign relations.

Although Britain was keen to be rid of its remaining colonies, it was unlikely that Britain would grant Singapore independence while there was any possibility of a communist government. For Malaya, which was still fighting a rump communist guerrilla force, the thought of a communist-dominated, independent Singapore, 'a Cuba across the causeway', was highly unattractive.

In 1961 Tunku Abdul Rahman put forward a proposal suggesting a merger of Singapore and Malaya. To address the fear that the huge number of Singapore Chinese would tip the racial balance, his plan included the British Borneo territories in the new nation.

Malaysia was born in 1963 with the fusing of Malaya, Singapore, Sabah and Sarawak. Brunei, fearing loss of control of its oil wealth, decided not to join.

The day after Malaysia was created she faced a diplomatic crisis. The Philippines broke off relations claiming that Sabah was part of its territory. More seriously, Indonesia, under President Soekarno, laid claim to the whole of

Sayang Salmah (1995), directed by Mahadi J Murat, is a film set in the late 1950s and early 1960s in Johor and Singapore. Carefully entwined in this taut family drama is a sly observation of the complexities of post-independence Malay nationalism through the eyes of a nationalist campaigner and his extremist son.

1957
Merdeka (independence) in Malaya; Tunku Abdul Rahman becomes first prime minister.

1963
Singapore, Sabah and Sarawak join Malaya to form Malaysia

THE INDIGENOUS PEOPLE

Peninsular Malaysia has just under 100,000 Orang Asli (Original People), who are generally classified into three groups: the Negrito, the Senoi and the Proto-Malays. These can be further divided into 18 ethnic groups, which speak distinctly different languages. The majority remain animists, although there are ongoing attempts to convert them to Islam.

The Orang Asli played important roles in early trade, when products of the jungle were much sought after, but their significance waned as trade products became more sophisticated. During the Malayan Communist Emergency in the 1950s they became 'useful' again. The communists were fighting a jungle guerrilla war, and the Orang Asli were important providers of food, shelter and information. The British Malayan government realised that if they were to win the war, the support of the Orang Asli was crucial. They won them over by setting up jungle 'forts' close to their settlements, which supplied them with medical care and food.

After the communists were thwarted, 'guardianship' of the Orang Asli was undertaken by the Department of Orang Asli Affairs. Set up to represent Orang Asli concerns to the government, the department has now taken a 180° turn and become a conduit for government decisions. The main concerns of the Asli are land rights. Asli land rights are not recognised, and when logging, agricultural or infrastructure projects require their land, their claims are regarded as illegal.

In Sabah and Sarawak, despite indigenous people being in the majority and Native Customary Rights legislated, their lack of effective political representation has seriously compromised their land rights. Logging of their rainforests and, more recently, huge oil palm plantations have reduced their land areas considerably. Their enforced isolation from the land and the success of Christian missionaries over the last century has resulted in fragmented communities and the slow disappearance of traditional identity.

In Brunei the indigenous people comprise about 6% of the population. With Brunei's economic interests lying largely in off-shore oil and gas fields, encroachment on the indigenous people's land and rights has been minimal.

For an excellent introduction to the customs and culture of Malaysia's indigenous people, visit the Orang Asli Museum (p109), just north of Kuala Lumpur.

Borneo and decided the solution to this 'annexation' was 'Konfrontasi'. Indonesian armed forces crossed into Sabah and Sarawak from Kalimantan (Indonesian Borneo), and landings were made in Peninsular Malaysia and even Singapore. Although it was three years before Indonesia officially ended the confrontation, Malaysia was never seriously threatened.

Guardians of the Forest (2001), directed by Alan D'Cruz, is a sociological documentary that highlights the plight of the Orang Asli. It focuses on a tribe of Temuan whose way of life is changed forever because of a dam-building project.

BRUNEI'S SECOND CHANCE

The discovery of oil in 1929 revitalised a depressed Brunei. The most revered modern ruler of Brunei, Sultan Sri Muda Omar Ali Saifuddien III ascended the throne in 1950. During his reign he regained control over Brunei's internal affairs from the British and used Brunei's vast oil wealth to modernise and develop the infrastructure of the nation. In 1967 the sultan voluntarily abdicated in favour of his eldest son and the current ruler, the 29th in the unbroken royal Brunei line, Sultan Hassanal Bolkiah.

MALAYSIA SPLITS

The Malaysian marriage never really worked. Singapore refused to extend constitutional privileges to the Malays in Singapore and suggested working

1965

Singapore leaves Malaysia and Lee Kuan Yew becomes the first prime minister of Singapore

1969

Race riots in Malaysia result in national policy of positive discrimination for Malays

BAHASA MALAYSIA & MALAY

Malaysia has had a national language, Bahasa Malaysia, since Independence in 1957. This is often a cause of confusion for travellers, who logically give a literal translation to the two words and call it the 'Malaysian language'. In fact you cannot speak 'Malaysian'; the language is Malay.

The languages commonly spoken in Malaysia include Malay, Tamil, Hokkien, Cantonese, Mandarin and English, but there are also more Chinese dialects, various other Indian languages, and even a form of 16th-century Portuguese known as Christang. Although all Malaysians speak Malay, many are fluent in at least two other languages – a humbling thought for those of us who only speak English!

towards a 'Malaysian Malaysia'. Racial strife increased, and finally Malaysia decided that it would be best if Singapore left. A tearful Lee Kuan Yew took Singapore out in 1965.

RACIAL PROBLEMS

The Malaysian government's attempts to develop a Malaysian identity through the Malay language and national education were stymied by Chinese resistance. The Chinese were fiercely protective of their schools, which taught in Mandarin and were resistant to any moves that might threaten their continued existence.

DID YOU KNOW?

The Malay surname is the child's father's first name. This is why in Malaysia people use your Christian name after the Mr or Miss; to use your surname would be to address your father.

By the mid-1960s Malays were calling for measures to alleviate the stranglehold that foreign and Chinese companies had on the economy. Malays owned less than 2.5% of corporate wealth and, as they had little capital and know-how, things were not likely to change. Something had to give.

The 1969 general elections were contentious, and racial sentiments were strong. For the first time the Alliance Party lost its two-thirds majority in parliament. A celebration march by the opposition parties got out of hand, and the government's victory march the following day, 13 May, led to a full-scale riot. The government declared a state of emergency, but by the time things quietened down hundreds, mostly Chinese, had been killed. Stunned by the entire event the Malaysian government decided that racial harmony could be achieved only if there was economic parity between the races.

In 1970 a 'New Economic Policy' set a target whereby 30% of Malaysia's corporate wealth had to be in the hands of indigenous Malays, or *bumiputra* ('princes of the land'), within 20 years. Malay companies were heavily favoured for government contracts, low-interest *bumiputra* loans were made easily available, and thousands of Malays were sent abroad on government scholarships. To boost the *bumiputra* share in the corporate world, public listed companies were forced to relinquish 30% of their shares to *bumiputra* share-buyers – many of whom bought through *bumiputra* trust funds controlled by government institutions. By 1990 *bumiputra* corporate wealth had risen to 19%, poverty had fallen from 49% to 15%, and a new Malay middle class had emerged.

The Alliance Party invited opposition parties to join them and work from within. The expanded coalition was renamed the Barisan Nasional (National Front), which continues to rule to this day.

1981

Dr Mahathir becomes prime minister of Malaysia

1982

First edition of Lonely Planet's *Malaysia, Singapore & Brunei* published

RECENT HISTORY

Racial problems aside, the Malaysian economy has performed remarkably well since independence. Rubber, tin and timber are no longer the main export earners, and the manufacturing sector dominates. Seduced by tax incentives, hamstrung trade unions and a very pro-business government, multinationals have poured billions into the Malaysian economy. Much of Malaysia's exponential growth can be attributed to its charismatic and often controversial prime minister, Dr Mahathir Mohamad.

Since coming to power in 1981, his strong work ethic and ambition for Malaysia to be a fully developed nation by 2020 have been major driving forces for the country. A man of strong opinions, he has succeeded in establishing himself as the voice of the developing world, fulminating regularly on the subject of Western decadence and colonialist attitudes.

In 1997, after a decade of near 10% growth, a currency crisis that started in Thailand spread throughout Southeast Asia. Again Dr Mahathir railed at the West, blaming unscrupulous Western speculators for deliberately undermining the economies of the developing world for their personal gain. He famously ignored the economic recovery theories of the International Monetary Fund and prescribed his own remedies for the ailing economy. Pegging the Malaysian ringgit to the US dollar, bailing out what were seen as crony companies, forcing banks to merge and making it difficult for foreign investors to remove their money from Malaysia's stock exchange were measures that many predicted would spell disaster. However, Malaysia's recovery from the economic crisis, which was more rapid than that of many other Southeast Asian nations, has further bolstered Dr Mahathir's prestige.

In the wake of the economic crisis, Malaysia suffered a political crisis when Dr Mahathir sacked his deputy prime minister and heir apparent, Anwar Ibrahim. Analysts blamed their falling out on Anwar's disagreement with Mahathir's handling of the currency crisis, particularly the bailing out of crony companies. Two weeks after his sacking, Anwar was charged with corruption and sodomy. Many Malaysians, feeling that Anwar had been falsely arrested, took to the streets chanting Anwar's call for 'reformasi.' When he arrived in court with a black eye (the inspector general of police was eventually found guilty of his prison assault and sentenced to six months jail), the number of Anwar's supporters swelled and Kuala Lumpur saw weekly marches calling for his release. The demonstrations were harshly quelled. In trials that have been widely criticised, Anwar was sentenced to a total of 15 years imprisonment.

In the following general elections the Barisan Nasional suffered huge losses, particularly in the rural Malay areas. The gainers were Malaysia's Islamic party, PAS, who had vociferously supported Anwar, and a new political party, Keadilan (Justice Party), headed by Anwar's wife.

RISE OF ISLAMIC FUNDAMENTALISM

Islam has always played an important role in Malaysian politics, but the rapid rise of the fundamentalist Islamic party, PAS, which aims to install an Islamic government in Malaysia, is unlikely to have happened without the Anwar crisis. PAS now rules two state governments and is the leader of the opposition in the federal parliament.

The Other Malaysian by Farish A Noor is a collection of articles for the independent web-based daily, *Malaysiakini*. Farish Noor has a wonderful knack of using forgotten gems of Malaysia's history to comment on and critique contemporary Malaysian politics.

Khoo Boo Teik's book *Paradoxes of Mahathirism* is by far the best biography of Dr Mahathir and his political ideology. Khoo contends that Dr Mahathir's thoughts on nationalism, capitalism, Islam, populism and authoritarianism constitute a political ideology, which he terms 'Mahathirism'. He explores the evolution of these thoughts and, through them, attempts to resolve the apparent paradoxes in the politics of the enigmatic Dr Mahathir.

1984
Brunei becomes independent

1991
Lee Kuan Yew steps down as prime minister of Singapore; Goh Chok Tong takes over

DR MAHATHIR MOHAMAD – END OF AN ERA

Dr Mahathir first came to national attention in 1965 when, as a parliamentary backbencher, he locked horns with Singapore's Lee Kuan Yew (when Singapore was still part of Malaysia), accusing him of having 'the mad ambition of seeing himself as the first Chinese prime minister of Malaysia'. Lee Kuan Yew dismissed him as a 'Malay ultra'.

'Frankness' has continued to be a hallmark of Dr Mahathir. In 1969 he was expelled from UMNO for criticising the prime minister and causing disunity in the party. His first book, *The Malay Dilemma*, in which he postulated that Malay backwardness was due to hereditary and cultural factors, was banned in 1970.

He was reinstated a few years later and went on to become prime minister in 1981. One of the first things he did was to institute a 'Buy British Last' policy (after being criticised for the Malaysian government's successful corporate takeover of Britain's oldest plantation company, Guthrie Corporation) and the 'Look East' policy (favouring Japan, South Korea and Taiwan, which he admired for their strong work ethic and the close symbiotic relationship between government and business).

Over his 22 years as prime minister, Malaysia has grown from a commodity-based economy to an industrialised one. Government monopolies have been privatised, and heavy industries like steel manufacturing (a failure) and the Malaysian car (successful but heavily protected) have been encouraged. Multinationals have been successfully wooed to set up in Malaysia, and manufactured exports dominate the trade figures. Few would dispute the success of the good doctor's prescription for economic growth.

It has also been on his watch that some of Malaysia's most sacred institutions have been hamstrung. The judiciary (once proudly independent, now deemed subservient), the media (little more than government mouthpieces) and the sultans (their assent no longer needed to pass legislation) have all felt the wrath of Dr Mahathir. The worst blot on his copybook, however, must be the vicious treatment of his once heir-apparent, Anwar Ibrahim. Sacked, humiliated, beaten and languishing in jail, Anwar remains an unfortunate living memento of the Mahathir years, 1981–2003.

More worrying has been the unearthing of radical Islamic groups that the Malaysian government accuses of using deviant teachings to spread militant Islam. The revelation that many of the Bali bombers had spent years preaching in Malaysia and that some Malaysians were key members of Jemaah Islamiah, the Indonesian militant group connected to Al Qaeda, has shocked most Malaysians. Invoking the Internal Security Act, which allows detention without trial, the government acted swiftly to arrest and detain those whom it suspected of being associated with terrorist groups.

Magick River is the wonderfully eclectic website of Antares (formerly known as Kit Leee), writer, cartoonist, theatre critic and New-Age voyager. Besides the great rants, the site has excellent information and photographs of the Temuan Orang Asli with whom he now lives. www.xlibris.de /magickriver

Dr Mahathir announced his decision to step down in October 2003. Abdullah Badawi, his deputy and an Islamic scholar, is expected to provide able and moderate leadership in a period when sound Islamic credentials are proving to be crucial in Malaysian politics.

SINGAPORE TODAY

Lee Kuan Yew, who feared that Singapore would not survive on its own, can look back with pride at its economic achievement. Industrialisation, port facilities and financial services remain its mainstays of growth. First-rate infrastructure and a highly educated workforce that has accepted the maxim, 'No alternative but to work harder than everyone else', have kept the tiny nation well afloat.

1997
Economic crisis causes recession in all Southeast Asian nations

2003
Dr Mahathir steps down as prime minister; Abdullah Badawi takes over

In 1990 Lee Kuan Yew retired (though he still holds the position of 'senior minister'), and Goh Chok Tong, his successor, continues to run Singapore just as efficiently if a little less autocratically. Jailing political dissidents has been replaced with suing them for defamation.

Conspicuous too has been the relaxation of attempts to control every aspect of Singapore life. Sugarless chewing gum is now available at pharmacies; long-haired male travellers are no longer in danger of having SHIT (suspected hippy in transit) stamped in their passport; and the legalisation of bar-top dancing has made front-page news.

Singapore has struggled to recover from the economic downturn of 1997 and the competition from a growing China. But given Singapore's ability to overcome the greatest adversities, it is hard to imagine it not bouncing back.

Sisters in Islam, the website of Malaysia's Muslim women who refuse to be bullied by patriarchal interpretations of Islam, includes articles and legal advice about women's rights in Islam. sistersinislam.org.my

BRUNEI

In 1984 Sultan Hassanal Bolkiah somewhat reluctantly led his nation to independence. Since then Brunei has been drawn towards a stricter Islamic society. In 1991 the sale of alcohol was banned, and Islamic studies have been emphasised in schools. There have been a few signs of democratic reform, but the ruling monarchy is unlikely to let that go too far. The late 1990s were noted for the falling out of the sultan and his reckless younger brother, Prince Jefri, who was finance minister and head of Brunei's largest conglomerate, which spectacularly collapsed. The country's reserves have pulled it out of the crisis, but Brunei's economic arrogance has been dealt a blow.

The future of Brunei remains in the oil and gas industry as well as in its considerable overseas investments. Although its current reserves of oil and gas are expected to run out in 2018 and 2030, deeper sea exploration is expected to find significant new reserves. Recently moves have been made to develop Brunei into an offshore financial centre. Islamic banking, which offers financial facilities in keeping with Islamic principles (Islam strictly forbids usury), is expected to be an international growth industry in which Brunei hopes to take a leading role.

Director Erma Fatima weaves a tale of the search for cultural roots and the conflict with religious fundamentalism into the modern-day romance of *Perempuan Melayu Terakhir* (1999).

The Culture

THE NATIONAL PSYCHE

KS Maniam's *The Return* (1994) is one of the few works of contemporary fiction from Malaysia in English that can be wholeheartedly recommended. Maniam shines a light on the Indian Malaysian experience, through his character's search for a home on returning from being educated abroad.

Any discussion about the national psyche of Malaysians (that is, anyone born in Malaysia regardless of ethnic background) will immediately lead you into issues about the differences and similarities between the country's majority Malay population and the sizeable minorities of Chinese and Indians. The old images of Malays being a rural, traditional people and Chinese being an urban, capitalist class can still be applied, but the stereotypes are breaking down; in particular the number of urban Malays is growing, attracted by the new wealth and jobs of the cities.

The Indians, the next-largest group, are divided by religion and linguistic background. A small, English-educated Indian elite has always played a prominent role in Malaysian society, and a significant merchant class exists, but a large percentage of Indians – imported as indentured labourers by the British – remain a disadvantaged labouring class.

While there are undeniable tensions between the various groups, for the most part everyone gets along, partly because they have to, and also maybe because of the languid, generous spirit of the country – one fostered by a warm climate and a fruitful land. This friendliness and hospitality is what visitors see first and foremost.

Moving from the cities to the more rural, and thus Malay, parts of the country, the laid-back ethos becomes stronger and Islamic culture comes more to the fore, particularly on the east coast of the peninsula. Over in Malaysian Borneo you'll be fascinated by the communal lifestyle of the tribes who still live in jungle longhouses – again, here hospitality is a key ingredient of the social mix.

The movie *Money No Enough* (1998), directed by TL Tay, follows the fortunes of three Singaporean men unlucky in money and love. The dialogue is mainly in Hokkien and locals say it captures the Singaporean spirit of *kiasu*.

The cultural differences between easy-going Malaysia and fast-paced Singapore are striking, despite the island state having a similar ethnic mix, albeit one tilted firmly in favour of the Chinese. Commentators put this down to Singaporeans being *kiasu*. A Hokkien word literally meaning 'afraid to lose', the *kiasu* philosophy embraces a whole range of selfish and pushy behaviour, where the individual must win, get more and not lose out at all costs. And are Singaporeans *kiasu?* At the risk of generalising, it's true that they are competitive and a bargain will never pass a Singaporean by. But they are also admirably straightforward and have a no-nonsense approach that you're likely to find refreshing after travelling in other parts of Asia.

The citizens of Brunei, by contrast, coddled by the wealth of their oil-rich nation, would probably be the last people in the region to chase after a bargain.

LIFESTYLE

Hailed as the 'definitive Singaporean novel' *Heartland* (1999) by Daren VL Shiau is a contemporary work that focuses on the plight of an army conscript coming to terms with his place in society.

Although growing Westernisation and the pace of modern life is changing the cultures of Malaysia, Singapore and Brunei, traditional customs and religious values remain strong. Most Malays follow Islam devoutly, as well as adhering to older spiritual beliefs and systems of social law, known as *adat*. Many aspects of *adat* are still a part of everyday life in the *kampung* (village), and indeed in the suburbs of the cities.

The village-based social system of *adat*, with its roots in the Hindu period and earlier, is customary law that places great emphasis on collective rather than individual responsibility. The *kampung* and its obligations of kinship are at the heart of the Malay world. It is mutually supportive and places great emphasis on maintaining harmony. In principle, villagers are of equal status, though a headman is appointed on the basis of his wealth, greater experience or spiritual knowledge. Traditionally the founder of the village was appointed village leader *(penghulu* or *ketua kampung)* and often members of the same family would also become leaders. A *penghulu* is usually a haji, one who has made the pilgrimage to Mecca – a position of great importance.

As a religious leader, the imam holds a position of great importance in the community as the keeper of Islamic knowledge and the leader of prayer. The *pawang* and the *bomoh* are keepers of a spiritual knowledge that is part of an older tradition. A *pawang* possesses skills and esoteric knowledge about such things as the rice harvest, rain-making and fishing, and knows the rituals needed to ensure their success and appease the necessary spirits. The *bomoh* is a spiritual healer who has not only learned the knowledge of curative plants but can contact the spirit world and harness its power.

Hwee Hwee Tan's *Foreign Bodies* and *Mammon Inc.* are must-read books. Tan pinpoints precisely the peculiar dilemmas and contradictions facing Singaporean youth. Her ear for accurate dialogue is faultless and her morality-tale stories quite original.

Islamic fundamentalism and Western rationalism have helped to undermine the role of the *pawang* and the *bomoh*, but spirits, magic and such things as *keramat* (saint) worship still survive in the village – despite such ideas being at odds with Islamic teachings. Many traditional beliefs and *adat* customs have adapted to Islam, rather than having been destroyed by it.

The lure of the *kampung* lifestyle shouldn't be underestimated – many an urbanite from KL or Singapore hankers after it, despite the affluent Western-style living conditions they are privy to at home.

Religious customs and superstitions govern much of the Chinese community's home life, from the moment of birth (which is strictly recorded for astrological consultations later in life) to funerals (with many rites and rituals). Most Indians in the region originally come from South India, so the customs and festivals that are more important in the south, especially Tamil Nadu, are the most popular.

The cartoonist and artist Lat is a national institution in Malaysia. His witty sketches turn up in the *New Straits Times* newspaper, in advertisements and in four books, including *Kampung Boy*.

Both Malaysia and Singapore have dabbled to different degrees with social and economic policies to shape the lives of their citizens. In Malaysia, the New Economic Policy, or NEP (see History, p36) has promoted the position of Malays and to some extent has been successful.

Meanwhile, in Singapore the government notoriously encouraged birth control in the 1970s and 1980s (to stem a booming population), but that plan backfired and it now wants Singaporeans (in particular, educated Chinese Singaporeans) to have more children – see the boxed text on the next page.

POPULATION

Malaysia's population is currently around 22.7 million, with approximately 85% living in Peninsular Malaysia and the remaining 15% in Sabah and Sarawak. Malays, including indigenous groups, make up around 57% of the population, Chinese about 27%, Indians 8% and the remaining 8% others.

Singapore's resident population numbers 3.3 million, but if you include foreign residents it's 4.1 million. Chinese are the largest ethnic group (76.7%) followed by Malays (13.9%), Indian (7.9%) and 1.5% from other races.

Brunei's population is about 350,000, with Malays and some other indigenous people accounting for 67%. Chinese make up 15% of the total; Iban, Dayak and Kelabit people 6%; the rest are migrant workers and expats.

Rogue Trader (1999), directed by James Dearden, is based on the Nick Leeson biography. Ewan McGregor stars as the man who broke Barings Bank. A morality tale about the perils of expat life in Singapore.

THE GOVERNMENT PLAYS CUPID

To help alleviate Singapore's high population density, the government waged a birth control campaign in the 1970s and early 1980s. It was so successful that the birth rate dropped off alarmingly, especially in the Chinese community.

To reverse the trend and further the government's programme to breed intelligent children, tax incentives were introduced for university-educated women who produced children. At the same time financial rewards were offered to non-educated couples willing to undergo sterilisation. The government has since dropped such radical policies, although it still rewards couples for having more children through its Baby Bonus scheme.

The Social Development Unit (SDU) is another government scheme to get people together and, hopefully, procreating. What is in effect probably the world's only state-sponsored dating agency, the SDU runs programmes such as speed dating and blind dates at community centres around the island. There are dating cruises, too, in the SDU 'Love Boat'. Critics claim SDU really stands for Single, Desperate and Ugly.

MULTICULTURALISM

Malaysia is very much a multiracial society, something that has figured prominently and not always happily in its development. From the ashes of the interracial riots of 1969, when distrust between the Malays and Chinese peaked, the country has managed to forge a more tolerant, multicultural society. Though ethnic loyalties remain strong, the emergence of a single 'Malaysian' identity is now a much-discussed and lauded concept, even if not yet really embraced.

The government's *bumiputra* policy (see the History chapter, p36) has increased Malay involvement in the economy, albeit largely for an elite. This has helped defuse Malay fears and resentment of Chinese economic dominance, but has done little to quell Chinese or Indian fears, or the reality of their being discriminated against by government policy.

A widespread backlash from the Chinese community has not emerged, because the government has given the country a booming economy, benefiting Chinese entrepreneurs and delivering jobs to everyone. The government has also been careful to show even-handedness in cultural issues and keep the Chinese and Indian communities on side. It has also promised that the races will compete on an equal footing when the government's long-term economic growth plans, spelt out in Wawasan 2020, are achieved – a promise almost no-one in the country believes.

The once-bitter issue of the promotion of Bahasa Malaysia, the national language, has also ultimately helped unify the country as the proficiency and use of the language has spread among all races. The government has also allayed Chinese and Indian concerns at attempts to introduce it as the sole language of instruction in all levels of education and is again promoting English, for business and practical reasons.

Think *Saturday Night Fever* meets *Enter the Dragon* and you have *Forever Fever* (1998). This Singaporean romantic comedy, directed by Glen Goei, was well received in the USA and is quirky enough to retain interest.

Malaysia has made enormous strides in promoting racial harmony, but old divisions exist. Moves such as those by the Kelantan government to introduce Islamic law applying to all its citizens, including the Chinese, has the potential to open old wounds, but the federal government is keen to put a lid on any threats to the largely peaceful multicultural balance in today's Malaysia.

Singaporean government policy has always been to promote Singapore as a multicultural nation in which Chinese, Indians and Malays can live in equality and harmony while maintaining their distinct cultural identities. There are imbalances in the distribution of wealth and power among the racial groups, but on the whole multiculturalism seems to work much better in small-scale Singapore than it does in Malaysia.

MEDIA

No-one is under any illusions about the freedom of the press in either Malaysia or Singapore. In both countries, the governments tightly control the main media outlets in a variety of ways, often pursuing critics – even those with the mildest opposing views – through the courts. The main newspapers tend to parrot the official line, sometimes publishing articles that amount to little more than government propaganda. The less said about news on either Malaysian or Singaporean TV channels, the better.

It's on the Internet that anything of interest can be read. The courageous Web publication Malaysiakini at www.malaysiakini.com survived a police raid in January 2003 and has managed to remain in business – but only just. Its main protection has been former PM Mahathir's commitment of nongovernment interference in the Internet – a policy position adopted to encourage foreign businesses to invest in Malaysia's ambitious 'Multimedia Super Corridor' project, which aims to create an Asian Silicon Valley immediately south of KL.

Practically Malaysia's only independent daily news source with features and commentaries that are anything but the standard blather in the print media www.malaysiakini.com

Winner of Australia's Vogel literary award, Hsu-Ming Teo's *Love and Vertigo* (2001) is an evocatively written novel about a mother's suicide and its impact on her family. It takes a wry and insightful look at the experiences of the Straits Chinese in Singapore, Malaysia and Australia.

RELIGION

The variety of religions found in Malaysia is a direct reflection of the diversity of races living there. Although Islam is the state religion of Malaysia, freedom of religion is guaranteed. Hinduism has been practiced in Malaysia for at least 1500 years; Islam became dominant in the mid-14th century, but the arrival of Indian contract labourers in the 20th century brought an increase in the followers of Hinduism.

Although Christianity has made no great inroads into Peninsular Malaysia it has had a much greater impact upon Malaysian Borneo, where

THE PERANAKANS

Peranakan means 'half caste' in Malay, which is exactly what the Peranakans are: descendants of Chinese immigrants who from the 16th century onwards settled in Singapore, Melaka and Penang and married Malay women.

The culture and language of the Peranakans is a fascinating melange of Chinese and Malay traditions. The Peranakans took the name and religion of their Chinese fathers, but the customs, language and dress of their Malay mothers. They also used the terms Straits-born or Straits Chinese to distinguish themselves from later arrivals from China, whom they looked down upon.

Another name you may hear for these people is Baba-Nonyas, after the Peranakan words for males *(baba)* and females *(nonya)*. The Peranakans were often wealthy traders who could afford to indulge their passion for sumptuous furnishings, jewellery and brocades. Their terrace houses were gaily painted, with patterned tiles embedded in the walls for extra decoration. When it came to the interior, Peranakan tastes favoured heavily carved and inlaid furniture.

Peranakan dress was similarly ornate. Women wore fabulously embroidered *kasot manek* (beaded slippers) and *kebaya* (blouses worn over a sarong), tied with beautiful *kerasong* (brooches), usually of fine filigree gold or silver. Men, who assumed Western dress in the 19th century, reflecting their wealth and contacts with the British, saved their finery for important occasions such as the wedding ceremony, a highly stylised and intricate ritual dictated by *adat* (Malay customary law).

The Peranakan patois is a Malay dialect but one containing many Hokkien words – so much so that it is largely unintelligible to a Malay speaker. The Peranakans also included words and expressions of English and French, and occasionally practiced a form of backward Malay by reversing the syllables.

many of the indigenous people have converted to Christianity, although others still follow their animist traditions.

Ceritalah (1996) and *Journeys Through Southeast Asia: Ceritalah 2* (2002) are collections of newspaper and magazine features by the erudite Anglo-Malay lawyer Karim Raslan; widely available in bookshops in the region, but many of the pieces feel insubstantial. The first book in particular reads like history now that so much has changed politically in Malaysia. Still worth a look though.

Islam

Islam came to Malaysia with the South Indian traders and was not of the more-orthodox Islamic tradition of Arabia. It was adopted peacefully by the coastal trading ports of Malaysia and Indonesia, absorbing rather than conquering existing beliefs. Islamic sultanates replaced Hindu kingdoms, though the Hindu concept of kings remained. The traditions of *adat* continued, but Islamic law dominated.

Women had great influence in pre-Islamic Malay society; there were women leaders, and the descendants of the Sumatran Minangkabau in Negeri Sembilan still have a matriarchal society. The arrival of Islam weakened the position of women in Malaysia. Nonetheless, women were not cloistered or forced to wear full purdah as in the Middle East, and Malay women today still enjoy more freedom than their counterparts in many other Muslim societies.

Malay ceremonies and beliefs still exhibit pre-Islamic traditions, but most Malays are ardent Muslims and to suggest otherwise to a Malay would cause great offence. With the rise of Islamic fundamentalism, the calls to introduce Islamic law and purify the practices of Islam have increased, but while the federal government of Malaysia is keen to espouse Muslim ideals, it is wary of religious extremism. *Syariah* (Islamic law) is the preserve of state governments, as is the establishment of Muslim courts of law, which since 1988 cannot be overruled by secular courts.

DID YOU KNOW?

Brunei is proud of the fact that it was the first country in the region to introduce colour TV in 1975.

Only Muslims are tried in Islamic courts. Kelantan state is the country's hotbed of Islamic fervour, and the state government is keen to apply *syariah* to all of its citizens.

Chinese Religion

The Chinese religion is a mix of Taoism, Confucianism and Buddhism. Taoism contributes animistic beliefs to teach people to maintain harmony with the universe. Confucianism looks after the political and moral aspects of life, while Buddhism takes care of the afterlife. But to say that the Chinese have three religions is too simple a view of their traditional religious life. At the first level Chinese religion is animistic, with a belief in the innate vital energy in rocks, trees, rivers and springs. At the second level people from the distant past, both real and mythological, are worshipped as gods. Overlaid on this are popular Taoist, Mahayana Buddhist and Confucian beliefs.

On a day-to-day level the Chinese are much less concerned with the high-minded philosophies and asceticism of Buddha, Confucius or Lao Zi than they are with the pursuit of worldly success, the appeasement of the dead and the spirits, and the seeking of knowledge about the future. Chinese religion incorporates elements of what Westerners might call 'superstition' – if you want your fortune told, for instance, you go to a temple. The other thing to remember is that Chinese religion is polytheistic. Apart from Buddha, Lao Zi and Confucius there are many divinities, such as house gods, and gods and goddesses for particular professions.

Penang's Kek Lok Si Temple, the largest Buddhist shrine in Malaysia.

RICHARD I'ANSON

The most popular gods and local deities, or *shen*, are Kuan Yin, the goddess of mercy, and Toh Peh Kong, a local deity representing the spirit of the pioneers and found only outside China. Kuan Ti, the god of war, is also very popular and is regarded as the god of wealth.

Hinduism

Hinduism in Malaysia dates back at least 1500 years and there are Hindu influences in cultural traditions, such as *wayang kulit* (see below) and the wedding ceremony. However, it is only in the last 100 years or so, following the influx of Indian contract labourers and settlers, that it has again become widely practised.

Hinduism has three basic practices: *puja*, or worship; the cremation of the dead; and the rules and regulations of the caste system. Although still very strong in India, the caste system was never significant in Malaysia, mainly because the labourers brought here from India were mostly from the lower classes.

Westerners often have trouble understanding Hinduism, principally because of its vast pantheon of gods. You can look upon all these different gods simply as pictorial representations of the many attributes of one god. The one omnipresent god usually has three physical representations: Brahma, the creator; Vishnu, the preserver; and Shiva, the destroyer or reproducer. All three gods are usually shown with four arms, but Brahma has the added advantage of four heads to represent his all-seeing presence. The four *Veda*, the books of 'divine knowledge', which are the foundation of Hindu philosophy, are believed to have emanated from his mouths.

The debut novel *The Rice Mother* (2003), a potboiler by expat Malaysian Rani Manicka describes the epic story of Lakshmi who leaves pre-WWII Ceylon at 14 to move to rural Kuantan. Trials and tribulations over the following turbulent decades automatically follow.

Religions of Indigenous Peoples

The religions of indigenous peoples of Malaysia are as diverse as the peoples themselves. Despite their differences, they can generally be grouped together as animists. While animism does not have a rigid system of tenets or codified beliefs, it can be said of animist peoples that they perceive natural phenomena to be animated by various spirits or deities, and a complex system of practices are used to propitiate these spirits.

Ancestor worship is also a common feature of animist societies and departed souls are often considered to be intermediaries between this world and the next. Some examples of elaborate burial rituals can still be found in some parts of Sarawak in Malaysian Borneo, where the remains of monolithic burial markers and funerary objects still dot the jungle around Kelabit longhouses. However, most of these are no longer maintained and they're being rapidly swallowed up by the fast-growing jungle.

ARTS

Literature

Sejarah Melayu (Malay Annals) is the most famous of Malay literary works, dating from the 16th century. Modern Malay literature – both in the local language and English – is not prolific.

Singaporean writers are the ones to watch. Among the authors of note are Goh Sin Tub *(12 Best Singapore Stories)*; Philip Jeyaretnam *(Raffles Place Ragtime)*, Gopal Baratham *(A Candle or the Sun)*, Catherine Lim and Hwee Hwee Tan. See the individual book reviews in this chapter's margins for more on local and foreign writers who have taken inspiration from the region.

The Singaporean National Arts Council sponsors a huge range of arts and cultural events across the state www.nac.gov.sg

Wayang Kulit

Similar to the shadow-puppet performances of other Southeast Asian societies, in particular Java in Indonesia, the *wayang kulit* (shadow play) retells tales from the Hindu epic the *Ramayana*. You're most likely to see it performed in the east coast Malaysian states of Kelantan and Terengganu.

The best source of information on what's currently going on in the Malaysian arts scene www.kakiseni.com

The Malayan Trilogy by Anthony Burgess is the classic colonial expat experience: *Time For a Tiger*, *The Enemy in the Blanket*, and *Beds in the East*, all written in the 1950s, are recounted here. If you want to read of Burgess' own experiences in Kelantan, pick up the first volume of his memoirs, *Little Wilson and Big God* (1987).

The Tok Dalang, Father of the Mysteries, sits behind a semi-transparent screen and manipulates buffalo-hide puppets, whose images are thrown onto the screen. It's a feat of endurance both for performer and audience since the shadow plays can last for many hours. They often take place at weddings or after the harvest.

Dance

A variety of dances and dance-dramas are performed in Malaysia, usually for special occasions. If you're in KL you may be able to catch the Petronas Performing Arts Group when they put on one of their shows, drawing on a repertoire of over 100 dances and an ensemble of 30 musicians and 60 dancers.

Elsewhere, among the dances you may see are *menora*, a dance-drama of Thai origin performed by an all-male cast dressed in grotesque masks; and the similar *mak yong*, where the participants are female. These performances often take place at Puja Ketek, Buddhist festivals held at temples near the Thai border in Kelantan. The *rodat* is a dance from Terengganu. Often performed at Malay weddings by professional dancers, the *joget* is an upbeat dance with Portuguese origins; in Melaka it's better known as *chakunchak*.

Find out about traditional Malaysian performing arts – including shadow puppet theatre, dance and music – at Pusaka's website www.pusaka.com.my

Singapore's leading dance company Singapore Dance Theatre puts on performances ranging from classical ballet to contemporary dance. The Nrityalaya Aesthetics Society, which runs Singapore's only full-time troop of Indian dancers and musicians, puts on performances of South Indian dance and music and holds an annual drama festival.

Silat

Also known as *bersilat*, this is the Malay martial art that originated in Melaka in the 15th century. Today it is a highly refined and stylised activity. Demonstrations are often performed at ceremonies and weddings, accompanied by music from drums and gongs. Tourist shows are often put on in Kota Bharu (p305).

Music

Much Malay music has heavy Islamic and Chinese influences and takes different forms. The major types include the following:

Dondang sayang Chinese-influenced romantic songs accompanied by an orchestra, mainly in Melaka.

Hadrah Islamic chants, sometimes accompanied by dance and music.

Ghazal Female singers with orchestra, mainly in Johor.

Zikir A type of religious singing.

Traditional Malay music is based largely on the *gendang* (drum), of which there are more than a dozen types. Other percussion instruments include the gong, *cerucap* (made of shells), *raurau* (coconut shells), *kertuk* and *pertuang* (both made from bamboo), and the wooden *celampang*. The gamelan, a traditional Indonesian gong orchestra, is found in the state of Kelantan, where a typical ensemble will comprise four different gongs, two xylophones and a large drum. The region has a trio of top-class traditional orchestras. In Malaysia, the Malaysian Philharmonic Orchestra plays at the Dewan Filharmonik Petronas in the Petronas Towers.

DID YOU KNOW?

The *nobat* is an exclusive royal orchestra of four or five players performing on drums, flute, trumpet and gong. They play only on ceremonial occasions and are found these days only in the states of Kedah, Terengganu, Johor and Perak.

In Singapore, catch the Singapore Symphony Orchestra (SSO) at the Esplanade – Theatres on the Bay where it plays roughly 100 performances (usually sold-out) annually from January to December, with a break in June. Also in Singapore, the well-respected Singapore Chinese Orchestra has about 20 performances of traditional and symphonic Chinese music a year, as well as Indian, Malay and Western pieces.

Crafts

BATIK

Originally an Indonesian craft, batik – produced by drawing or printing a pattern on fabric with wax and then dyeing the material – has made itself equally at home in Malaysia. You'll find it in Penang on the west coast, but Kelantan and Terengganu are its true homes. Batik can be found as clothes, cushion covers, tablecloths, placemats or simply as works of art. Malay designs are usually less traditional than those found in neighbouring Indonesia.

KAIN SONGKET & MENGKUANG

A speciality of Kelantan and Terengganu, *kain songket* is a hand-woven fabric with gold and silver threads through the material. Clothes made from this beautiful fabric are usually reserved for the most important festivals and occasions. Mengkuang is a far more prosaic form of weaving using pandanus leaves and strips of bamboo to make baskets, bags and mats.

SILVER & OTHER METALWORK

Kelantan is famed for its silversmiths, who work in a variety of ways and specialise in filigree and repoussé work. In the latter, designs are hammered through the silver from the underside. Kampung Sireh at Kota Bharu is a centre for silverwork. Brasswork is an equally traditional skill in Kuala Terengganu.

ARTS & CRAFTS OF MALAYSIAN BORNEO

The indigenous peoples of Malaysian Borneo have a rich legacy of arts and crafts. *Pua kumbu* is a colourful weaving technique used to produce both everyday and ceremonial items decorated with a wide range of patterns. A special dyeing process known as ikat is used to produce the colours for *pua kumbu*. Ikat dyeing is performed while the threads of the pattern are already in place on the loom, giving rise to its English name, warp tie-dyeing.

The Malaysian equivalent of Frank Sinatra, celebrated crooner P Ramlee (1929–73) acted in some 70 movies. *Penarik Becha* (1955) was his first directorial effort; other movies he acted in include *Anakku Sazali*, *Ibu Mertua Ku* and the comedy *Madu Tiga*.

MALAYSIAN TOP OF THE POPS

While cruising the racks of KL's CD shops look out for these artists and titles:

- Siti Nurhaliza – Malaysia's answer to Kylie Minogue; she goes all acoustic on *Cindai*.
- Sheila Majid – Respected Malaysian jazz singer; listen to her on *Ratu*.
- Flop Poppy – This five-piece band from KL plays alternative rock on their eponymous album.
- Search – Heavy metal Malaysian style (not that much different from heavy metal elsewhere). Try their album *Terbaik*.
- Raihan – This group of singers presents religious-themed songs with a contemporary twist; albums include *On Gema Alam*.
- Krujaan – Boy band where the trio are all brothers; latest album is *Empayer*.
- Too Phat – Check out Malaysian hip hop on their album *360°*.
- Ning – This dreamy soul and R&B diva belts them out on *Selagi Adu*.
- Zainal Abidin – Blends *kampung* (village) beats with world music on *Refleksi*.

Woodcarving is a prized art among the peoples of Malaysian Borneo, and the most skilled carvers of all are held to be the Kenyah and Kayan peoples. In these societies, enormous burial columns carved from tree trunks were used to bury the remains of headmen. These columns, known as *kelirieng*, sometimes reached 2m in diameter and 10m in height and were covered with detailed carvings from top to bottom. Decaying remnants of *kelirieng* are still uncovered in the rainforest of Sarawak, and an example can be seen in Kuching Municipal Park. Less formidable, but equally beautiful, the Kenyah and Kayan also produced smaller wooden hunting-charms and ornate wooden knife-hilts known as *parang ilang*.

The woven baskets of the Iban, Kayan, Kenyah and Penan are among the most highly regarded in Borneo. The most common material for basket building is rattan, but bamboo, swamp nipah grass and pandanus palms are also used. In addition to baskets, related techniques produce sleeping mats, seats and materials for shelters. While each ethnic group has certain distinctive patterns, hundreds, or even thousands of years of trade and interaction has led to an intermixing of patterns. Some ethnic groups still produce baskets and other goods in the traditional way and these can be found in some of the markets of Malaysian Borneo. Others may be offered for sale upon a visit to a longhouse.

Royston Tan's *15* (2003) is an uncompromising look at the juvenile delinquents and teenage gangsters of Singapore – violence, drugs and all. Real teen gangsters star; one was arrested for a stabbing mid-way through the film's shoot.

Cinema

Although the Malaysian film industry dates back to the 1930s it has not yet managed to achieve world recognition in the way that some Thai or Vietnamese celluloid efforts have. Many of the Malay-language films made in this period were adaptations of the popular Chinese films of the time. After the WWII-imposed hiatus, the most popular Malaysian films were directed by Indian-born directors, who continued to adapt foreign plots for Malayan audiences.

In the1994 movie *Bugis Street* a Malaysian country girl Lian gets an eye-opening sexual education in a Singapore brothel on Bugis St where she rubs shoulders with transvestites and US-military clients.

The 1950s marked the golden age of Malay films and the first acting and directorial efforts of the king of Malaysian cinema, P Ramlee. His directorial debut was *Penarik Becha*, a commercial success released in 1955. Ramlee also acted in some 70 films in his lifetime and remains a national icon in Malaysia today. Today, though, Michelle Yeo is Malaysia's best known actress. The agile star of *Tomorrow Never Dies* and *Crouching Tiger, Hidden Dragon* hails from Ipoh, but gained her fame in Hong Kong.

Singapore has never been a leading light in film production either, but during the 1990s some local movies began to gain international attention, in particular *Bugis Street* and *Mee Pok Man*, both released in 1995, and *Army Daze* the following year. In 1998 the Singapore Film Commission was established. Its role is to 'nurture, support and promote' Singaporean talent in the film industry, which it does by dispensing grants, loans and scholarships, conducting training (including workshops in script writing and cinematography, and a master lecture series with international film makers) and supporting film-related events. The main chance to catch interesting local films is during the **Singapore International Film Festival** (www.filmfest.org.sg) held every April.

Eric Khoo directed the 1995 movie *Mee Pok Man* where a mentally disabled noodle-seller – the Mee Pok Man – falls for a prostitute who visits his stall. The all-amateur cast give standout performances.

Architecture

Of late, Malaysia and Singapore have both made their mark in the world of modern architecture with two ground-breaking buildings: the Petronas Towers in KL – the world's tallest building (p81); and the striking Esplanade – Theatres on the Bay complex in Singapore (p460). Both have been justly hyped as iconic structures and have drawn renewed attention to other interesting skyscrapers and civic buildings in the cities that take inspiration from both local culture (such as the Islamic motif of KL's Kompleks Dayabumi) or the environment – the space-age design of Sir Norman Foster's Expo MRT station, for example, which helps tackle Singapore's tropical heat.

Gaily coloured and handsomely proportioned, traditional wooden Malay houses are also perfectly adapted to the hot, humid conditions of the region. Built on stilts, with high, peaked roofs, they take advantage of even the slightest breeze to cool the interior. Further ventilation is achieved by full-length windows, a lack of internal partitions, and lattice-like grilles in the walls. The layout of a traditional Malay house reflects Muslim sensibilities. Notably, there are separate areas for men and women, as well as distinct areas where guests of either sex may be entertained.

DID YOU KNOW?

In the Hollywood jewel-heist caper *Entrapment* (1999), starring Sean Connery and Catherine Zeta Jones, Kuala Lumpur's Petronas Towers were superimposed to rise out of a squatter village in Melaka – which seriously annoyed the Malaysian government.

Although their numbers are dwindling, this type of house has not disappeared altogether. The best place to see examples are in the *kampung* (villages) of Peninsular Malaysia, particularly along the east coast in the states of Kelantan and Terengganu. Here you'll see that roofs are often tiled, showing a Thai and Cambodian influence (see the boxed text The East Coast House, p310).

In Melaka, the Malay house has a distinctive tiled front stairway leading up to the front veranda – to see examples take a wander around Kampung Morten (p217). The Minangkabau-style houses found in Negeri Sembilan are the most distinctive of the *kampung* houses, with curved roofs resembling buffalo horns – the design is imported from Sumatra.

Hardly any Malay-style houses have survived Singapore's rapid modernisation – the only place you'll see them is on Pulau Ubin (p467). The island state does have some magnificent examples of Chinese shophouse architecture, particularly in Chinatown, Emerald Hill – off Orchard Rd – and around Katong. Most noticeable of all, though, will be the rank upon rank of Housing Development Board (HDB) flats – over 900,000 units so far – that the vast majority of Singaporeans call home. If you want to find out more about Singapore's varied mix of architecture drop by the URA Gallery in Chinatown (p464).

Theatre

Singapore has the edge over Malaysia when it comes to theatre. Although there are the usual blockbuster plays and musicals from London and New York, local work gets a decent showing, too. The Esplanade – Theatres on the Bay's opening festival in October 2002 included the new musical *Forbidden City*, about the life of Empress Dowager Tzu Hsi, partly created by top Singaporean composer Dick Lee. It was a huge success. The city state runs several annual arts festivals, including the major **Singapore Arts Festival** (www.singaporeartsfest.com) every June, a good time to catch new productions by leading local theatre companies such as Action Theatre, Wild Rice, Toy Factory Ensemble and the Singapore Repertory Theatre.

Wallow in tales of life in Malaysia and Singapore during colonial times with *Malaysian Stories*, penned by one of the masters of the short story, W Somerset Maugham.

While the Singaporean government's support for the arts has been generous, in Malaysia such funding is pretty much nonexistent. In KL, your best chance of catching interesting local work is to check out what's playing at either the Actors Studio in the city centre or the Actors Studio in Bangsar. If it's anything by the Instant Cafe theatre group or local playwright Jit Murad, grab a ticket immediately. His recent play *Spilled Gravy on Rice* was a big hit both in Malaysia and Singapore; its subject matter included homosexuality, drug-taking, Zionism, not to mention child abuse, proving that English-language theatre can fly under the

The Catherine Cookson of Singapore, Catherine Lim is highly regarded. Her books, *Little Ironies – Stories of Singapore* (1978), *The Bondmaid* (1997) and *The Teardrop Story Woman* (1998), are mostly about relationships using the island as an exotic backdrop.

censorship radar. Aiming to boost the profile of the Malaysian theatre and arts scene are the Cameronean Arts Awards, funded by Boh Tea – the inaugural awards were in February 2003; check out the winners on the Kakiseni website (www.kakiseni.com).

CHINESE OPERA

In Malaysia and Singapore *wayang* or Chinese opera is derived from the Cantonese variety, which is seen as a more music hall mix of dialogue, music, song and dance. What the performances lack in literary nuance they make up for with garish costumes and the crashing music that follows the action. The scenery is virtually nonexistent, and props rarely consist of more than a table and chairs, but it is the action that is important.

Performances can go for an entire evening and it is usually easy for the uninitiated to follow the gist of the action. The acting is very stylised, and the music can be searing to Western ears, but seeing a performance is well worthwhile. Street performances are held during important festivals such as Chinese New Year (January/February), the Festival of the Hungry Ghosts (August/September) and the Festival of the Nine Emperor Gods (September/October) – head to the Chinatown areas of KL and Singapore, or to Melaka or Penang's Georgetown for the best chance of seeing performances.

Environment

THE LAND

Malaysia

Covering a total of 329,758 sq km, Malaysia consists of two distinct regions. Peninsular Malaysia is the long finger of land extending south from Asia as if pointing towards Indonesia and Australia. Much of the peninsula is covered by dense jungle, particularly its mountainous, thinly populated northern half. On the western side of the peninsula there is a long, fertile plain running down to the sea, while on the eastern side the mountains descend more steeply and the coast is fringed with sandy beaches.

The other part of the country, comprising more than 50% of its area, is Malaysian Borneo – the northern part of the island of Borneo (the larger, southern part is the Indonesian state of Kalimantan). Malaysian Borneo is divided into the states of Sarawak and Sabah, with Brunei a small enclave between them. Both states are covered by dense jungle, with many large river systems, particularly in Sarawak. Mt Kinabalu (4101m) in Sabah is the highest mountain between the Himalayas and New Guinea.

DID YOU KNOW?

The Malaysian jungle is believed to be 130 million years old. It supports over 145,000 species of flowering plant, 200 species of mammal, 600 species of bird and thousands of types of insect.

The Malaysian Nature Society, established in 1940, runs various nature-related projects across the country and has a range of publications. Visit its website at www.mns.org.my

Singapore

Singapore consists of the main, low-lying Singapore island and 63 much smaller islands within its territorial waters. It is situated just above 1° north in latitude, a mere 137km north of the equator. Singapore island is 42km long and 23km wide; with the other islands, the republic has a total landmass of 646 sq km (and growing through land reclamation).

Bukit Timah, in the central hills, is the highest point on Singapore island, at an altitude of 162m. The central area of the island is an igneous outcrop, containing most of Singapore's remaining forest and open areas. The western part of the island is a sedimentary area of low-lying hills and valleys, while the southeast is mostly flat and sandy. The undeveloped northern coast and the offshore islands are still home to some mangrove forest.

Visit Singapore's Ministry of the Environment website at www.env.gov.sg

Brunei

One of the smallest countries in the world, the sultanate covers just 5765 sq km. It has no mountain ranges or great rivers, and at its widest the larger, western part measures only 120km from side to side. White sandy beaches along the coast give way to low hills rising to around 300m in the interior. The capital Bandar Seri Begawan overlooks the estuary of the mangrove-fringed Sungai Brunei (Brunei River), which opens onto Brunei Bay and the eastern part of the country, Temburong.

Temburong consists of a coastal plain drained by Sungai Temburong, and rises to a height of 1850m at Bukit Pagon, the highest peak in the country. Two other main rivers drain the country – the Belait and Tutong.

Western Brunei is divided into the three administrative districts of Muara-Bandar Seri Begawan, Tutong and Belait. Apart from the capital city, the main settlements are Seria and Kuala Belait. Temburong makes up a fourth district, to the east, and is a sparsely populated area of largely unspoilt rainforest. Approximately 75% of Brunei retains its original forest cover.

WILDLIFE

An incredibly diverse and unusual array of mammals, birds, reptiles and insects make their home in the region. Although vast areas of forests have been cleared, some magnificent stands remain and the range of life

Visit the Worldwide Fund for Nature website at www.panda.org for information on a range of environmental-protection projects happening in Malaysia.

forms that can still be seen with a bit of patience is astonishing. Most of the best wildlife-viewing is to be had in the excellent system of reserves and national parks (p56).

Animals

ORANG-UTAN

Asia's only representative of the great apes, the orang-utan is increasingly rare and found only on the islands of Sumatra and Borneo. Unlike many primates, orang-utans are generally solitary animals; they are also unusual because they build a nest of sticks and branches in which to sleep each night. Adult males can weigh up to 100kg, stand up to 1.5m tall and can have an arm-span of nearly 3m. In contrast, females are of far more delicate build and seldom weigh more than 50kg. The best places to see them up close are the Sepilok Orang-Utan Rehabilitation Centre (p429) in Sabah and the Singapore Zoological Gardens (p467), where you can have breakfast or tea in their company.

A Field Guide to the Mammals of Borneo by Junaidi Payne, Charles M Francis and Karen Phillipps is a must for those travelling to Borneo. The illustrations are excellent.

GIBBONS

More closely related to apes than monkeys, gibbons dwell strictly in the trees, where they feed on fruits such as figs. Gibbons are superbly adapted to their lifestyle: they have small, slender bodies, and like apes have no tail. They have incredibly long arms for swinging effortlessly through the trees, their short legs dangling as they swing. Gibbons make an appalling racket in the predawn hour – a far-carrying, raucous hooting that is one of the most distinctive sounds of the Malaysian jungle. The calls help gibbons establish territories and find mates. Several species inhabit large stands of forest in Peninsular Malaysia and in Borneo, but they are generally shy of people.

MONKEYS

Malaysia has 10 species of monkey, divided by biologists into langurs and macaques. Langurs (or leaf monkeys) are mostly tree-dwelling, and generally have black palms and soles, and grey faces. Macaques have pale palms and soles, and brown- or red-coloured faces; they spend a great deal of time on the ground, although they are also agile climbers.

The greyish-brown long-tailed macaque is the most common and widespread of Malaysia's monkeys. The pig-tailed macaque is slightly bigger, with golden brown fur; its tail is reduced to a dangling stump. This species is sometimes trained to pick coconuts.

Malaysia's various species of langur are far more retiring than macaques and some are very attractively marked. The silvered leaf monkey's black fur is frosted with grey tips; this beautiful animal can be observed at Taman Alam Kuala Selangor (p116) in Peninsular Malaysia and at Bako National Park (p334) in Sarawak. The upper body of the banded langur is usually a black or dark grey colour; the spectacled langur has white rings around its eyes; and the maroon langur of Malaysian Borneo has reddish fur similar to that of the orang-utan.

Dusky langur (Presbytis obscura)

CHRISTER FREDRIKSSON

The fantastic proboscis monkey is a type of langur and is probably Malaysia's second-most famous animal, after the orang-utan. The male proboscis monkey is an improbable-looking creature with a pendulous nose and bulbous belly; females and youngsters are more daintily built, with quaint, upturned noses. Proboscis monkeys inhabit only the forests of Borneo, where they live almost entirely on leaves. The Sungai Kinabatangan (p432) in Sabah is the best place to look for these monkeys, although there are also colonies in Bako National Park (p334) in Sarawak, and in Brunei.

CATS

Malaysia has many species of wild cat, including the largest and some of the smallest. Several species – such as the tiger (see Endangered Species, p54) – are no longer common because of the pressures of hunting and, more recently, the trade in body parts for their supposed medicinal qualities. The leopard is still occasionally reported on the peninsula; it's a secretive animal and may actually be relatively common. The black form of the leopard – often called black panther – is more common in Malaysia than the spotted variety. Neither leopard nor tiger has been recorded in Borneo.

Several smaller species of cat hunt birds and small mammals in forests and adjoining plantations, although one – the bay cat – is a specialised fish-eater. The leopard cat is a widespread species a bit larger than a domestic cat; as its name suggests, it has spotted fur. The marbled cat is similar in size, with less-distinct markings.

Wild Malaysia: The Wildlife & Scenery of Peninsular Malaysia by Junaidi Payne and Gerald Cubitt is a lavishly illustrated, large-format coffee-table guide to Malaysian wildlife and habitats. Text is written by a leading environmentalist. Also includes information on the region's peoples and natural history.

CIVETS

Members of this diverse, sometimes attractive group of mainly carnivorous animals bear a superficial resemblance to cats. However, they differ in that they usually have long, pointed snouts. The common palm civet is found throughout Malaysia, even straying into the outskirts of urban areas (including Singapore). The Malay civet is slightly larger and attractively patterned, with a ringed tail and spotted or striped coat. The binturong is the largest of the civets; it has a shaggy black or dark-brown coat that helps keep it dry in its damp forest habitat.

The Encyclopaedia of Malaysia: The Environment by Prof. Dato' Dr Sham Sani is just one volume of an excellent illustrated series of encyclopaedias, covering much of what you may wish to know about Malaysia's environment – from its geology and climate to education and government policy.

TAPIR

An extraordinary animal that looks like a cross between a wild pig and a hippo, the Malaysian tapir's only living relatives inhabit the jungles of South and Central America. Tapirs can grow up to 2m in length and weigh some 300kg; they are vegetarian and are sometimes seen at the salt licks in the farther reaches of Taman Negara (p267). Adult tapirs have a two-tone colour scheme, almost black in the foreparts, changing to white hindquarters.

PANGOLINS

Also known as the scaly anteater, the pangolin feeds exclusively on ants and termites. It is a small, nonthreatening animal, measuring only 1m in length. It's covered in broad scales like a pine cone, and uses its powerful claws to dig open ant and termite mounds. Its method of self defence is to roll up into a ball. Pangolins are found throughout Peninsular Malaysia and Borneo, often straying into gardens and plantations.

BATS

Malaysia has more than 100 species of bat, most of which are tiny, insectivorous (insect-eating) species that live in caves, and under eaves and bark. Fruit bats, or flying foxes, are only distantly related to insectivorous bats; unlike them they have well-developed eyes and do not navigate by echolocation. There are fruit bats in Taman Negara (p267), and Deer Cave in Gunung Mulu National Park (p371) in Sarawak, where several million insectivorous bats stream out at dusk in wave after chittering wave.

Pocket Guide to the Birds of Borneo is published by the World Wide Fund for Nature (WWF) and the Sabah Foundation. They have condensed the weighty and definitive *Smythies' Birds of Borneo* into this handy book, which is brilliantly illustrated and ideal for the field.

BIRDS

The region is home to hundreds of unusual, colourful and unique bird species. Even in large cities there are usually a few species to see in parks and gardens, including bulbuls, starlings and house swifts. In Peninsular Malaysia there's excellent bird-watching within a day's reach of Kuala Lumpur (KL); prime locations include Taman Negara (p267), Bukit Fraser (p111) and Taman Alam Kuala Selangor (p116), where you may spot the secretive mangrove pitta, the stately crested serpent-eagle and various species of kingfisher.

Both Sabah and Sarawak have great bird-watching, including some 38 species found nowhere else. Good locations include Gunung Mulu National Park (p371); Mt Kinabalu (p415); Sungai Kinabatangan (p432) and the Danum Valley (p434). Species to keep an eye out for include brilliantly coloured pittas, trogons, jungle flycatchers, bulbuls, the bat hawk, hornbills and the Bornean bristlehead.

In Singapore, the place to head is the Sungei Buloh Wetland Reserve (p469), a nature reserve that is home to 140 species of bird.

REPTILES

There are far too many forms and species to name here, but a few groups stand out for their interest, beauty or – too often – for their rarity. Some 250 species of reptile have been recorded, including 100 of snake, 14 of tortoise and turtle, and three of crocodile.

Malaysia has a diverse range of wildlife, including the iguana.

JEAN-BERNARD CARILLET

Most snakes are inoffensive, but all should be treated with caution, because if you are bitten by a dangerous one you may find yourself far from help. Cobras and vipers are the most dangerous, although the chances of encountering them are low. Pythons are sometimes seen in national parks and one, the reticulated python, is reputed to grow to 10m in length. Several species of flying snake inhabit the rainforests; they don't literally fly, but glide from trees by extending a flap of loose skin along either side of their bodies. There are also 'flying' lizards and frogs.

The reptile you're most likely to see is the monitor lizard, which can be found in both Peninsular Malaysia and Borneo. These carrion-eaters are especially easy to spot on island beaches – Pulau Perhentian Besar is home to several monsters close to 2m in length. Although they look scary, they generally shy away from humans, unlike their close relative the Komodo dragon.

The Malay Archipelago by Alfred Russel Wallace is one of the definitive guides to this region's flora and fauna, despite being based on travels made in the mid-19th century.

ENDANGERED SPECIES

There are estimated to be less than 125 Sumatran rhinoceroses left in Malaysia, mainly in isolated areas of Sabah and Endau-Rompin National Park (p244) on the peninsula. Since they need at least 10 sq km of rainforest in which to roam, their chance of survival is very limited, given the rate at which such forest is disappearing. Habitat loss is also forcing down the numbers of Asian elephants, which number around 2000 spread over both sides of Malaysia; the extremely rare clouded leopard; and the Malaysian tiger – the country's national animal.

Among marine animals, turtles – especially the leatherback – and the dugong, found off the coast of Sabah, are seeing their numbers threatened. There are also reckoned to be fewer than 200 Storm's storks left in Malaysian Borneo.

DID YOU KNOW?

Found only in the rainforests of Malaysia and Sumatra (Indonesia), the parasitic rafflesia plant produces the world's largest flower, which can grow up to 1m across.

Plants

This region boasts a staggering range of trees, plants and flowers, including many that are unique to the area, such as the rafflesia, certain species of orchid and pitcher plants. The tropical climate and high rainfall promote the growth of dense rainforests and both the peninsula and Borneo once had extensive stands. Much of this forest cover has been

TURTLES UNDER THREAT

If you're fortunate you can see several species of turtle in Malaysia, including the hawksbill *(Eretmochelys imbricata)* and the green turtle *(Chelonia mydas)* – both of which have nesting areas within Sabah's Turtle Islands National Park (p431) – and the olive ridley *(Lepidochelys oliveacea)* and giant leatherback *(Dermochelys coriacea)* turtles, which, together with the first two, nest on Peninsular Malaysia's east coast.

However, leatherback numbers have declined by an incredible 98% since the 1950s, and sightings of these turtles at Rantau Abang (p283) have dropped from almost 1000 back in 1984 to just three in 2002. It's believed the drop is the result of decades of accidental capture in drift nets, turtle-egg harvesting and marine pollution. Biologists estimate that around one turtle hatchling in every thousand survives the 35 to 50 years it takes to reach maturity – turtle populations simply can't survive years of near-complete egg harvest.

While the collection and sale of leatherback eggs have been banned since 1988, in coastal markets it's common to see hundreds of eggs of the smaller green, hawksbill and olive ridley turtles, all of which have seen a marked decline in their populations. It may seem like an uphill battle, but there are some things you can do to help protect these magnificent creatures:

- Don't buy turtle eggs, turtle meat or anything made from turtle shell.
- Make sure your litter doesn't end up on beaches or in oceans.
- Make a donation to sea turtle conservation; check out the website of the Sea Turtle Outreach Program at www.kustem.edu.my/seatru and adopt a turtle or a turtle nest, or even volunteer for one of their research projects.

If you do get to see a turtle, the egg-laying process is amazing. After crawling well up the beach each female leatherback (who can weigh up to 750kg and reach up to 2m in length) digs a deep hole in the sand for her eggs. Into this cavity the turtle, with much huffing and puffing, lays between 50 and 140 eggs. Having covered them, she heads back towards the water. It all takes an enormous effort, and the turtle will pause to catch her breath several times. Back in the water, this heavy, ungainly creature glides off silently into the night.

You can take steps to ensure that the turtle is disturbed as little as possible. If no beach rangers are around:

- Stay at least 10m away from any turtle crawling up the beach.
- Don't use torches (flashlights) or camera flashes.
- If you see a turtle crawling ashore, sit and wait patiently for her to crawl to the top of the dunes – do not impede her emergence. It may be many hours before she is ready to lay eggs.
- Resist the temptation to take photos of hatchlings making their way to the ocean.

If beach rangers are around, they may allow you to get a little closer and take some flash photographs, but only once she has laid eggs (hopefully in time flash photography will be phased out).

cleared to make way for vast plantations of oil palms (see p56) and other cash crops, but near-pristine forests are preserved in national parks and other reserves.

Rainforest is often referred to as dipterocarp forest. Rainforest communities are extremely complex and a single hectare can support many species of tree, plus a vast diversity of other plants, including many thousands of species of orchid, fungi, fern and moss – some of them epiphytes (plants that grow on other plants). Other important vegetation types include mangroves, which fringe coasts and estuaries and provide nurseries for fish and crustaceans; the stunted rhododendron forests of Borneo's high peaks, which also support epiphytic communities of orchids and

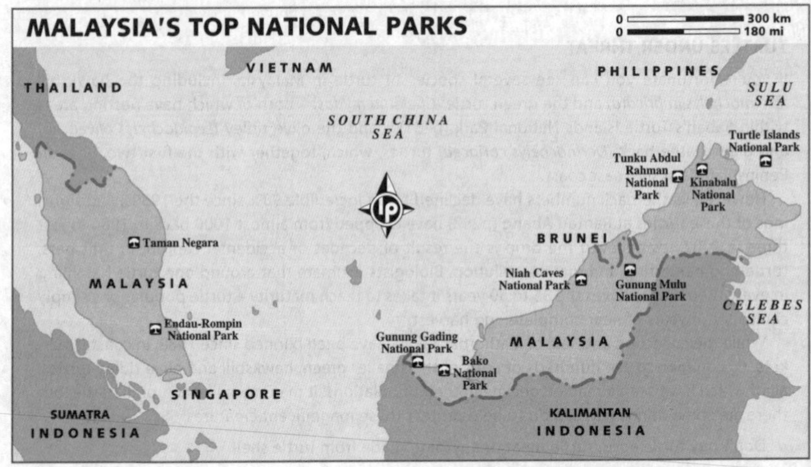

hanging lichens (beard moss); and the *kerangas* of Sarawak, which grows on dry, sandy soil and can support many types of pitcher plant.

Find out more about Singapore's parks and protected reserves at the National Parks Board's website at www.nparks.gov.sg. There's listings of events, news and conservation details.

PALM OIL

The oil palm *(Elaeis guineensis)* is probably the most common tree in Peninsular Malaysia today. When travelling along rural roads, particularly in Johor, Pahang and Sabah, you'll come across seas of oil-palm trees that stretch to the horizon.

The oil palm was first introduced in the 1860s; seeds were brought from Sri Lanka (although the tree itself is a native of West Africa), but it was not until 1917 that the first oil-palm plantation was established. Since WWII Malaysia has been the world's top producer of palm oil, and current annual output is around 7.2 million tonnes. The oil is extracted from the orange-coloured fruit, which grows in bunches just below the fronds. It is used primarily for cooking, although research is under way to find other uses, such as for engine fuel. Malaysia has invested heavily in palm oil, and it is one of the country's major primary industry exports.

NATIONAL PARKS & OTHER PROTECTED AREAS

The British established the first national park in Malaysia in 1938 and it is now included in Taman Negara (p267), Malaysia's major national park, which crosses the borders of Terengganu, Kelantan and Pahang on the peninsula. In addition to this and the 18 other national parks across the country (16 of them located in Malaysian Borneo), there are various government-protected reserves and sanctuaries for forests, birds, mammals and marine life. In all, though, it's estimated that only 5% of the country's natural habitat is protected.

Tropical Marine Life of Malaysia & Singapore, Tropical Birds of Malaysia & Singapore, Tropical Fruits of Malaysia & Singapore and *Tropical Plants of Malaysia & Singapore* are some of the titles in Periplus Editions' great series of field guides to the plants and animals of Malaysia.

Accommodation is not a problem when visiting most national parks. Various categories are available, from hostel to chalet. Transport and accommodation operations are increasingly being handled by private tour companies, and you have to book in advance and pay a deposit.

Marine Parks

Malaysia's marine parks range from inaccessible islands with no tourist facilities to tourist meccas like Pulau Tioman. In order to protect their fragile

MALAYSIA'S TOP NATIONAL PARKS

Park	Features	Activities	Best time to visit	Page reference
Taman Negara	canopy walkway, hides, jungle trails, rivers	trekking, wildlife spotting, river trips	Apr–Sep	p267
Endau-Rompin	lowland forest, unique plants, Sumatran rhinos, waterfalls and rivers,	trekking, wildlife spotting	Apr–Sep	p244
Niah Caves	caves	caving, trekking	May–Sep	p359
Gunung Mulu	caves, the Pinnacles, Gunung Mulu, Headhunters' Trail	caving, trekking, mountain climbing	May– Sep	p371
Tunku Abdul Rahman	gorgeous sand-fringed islands	snorkelling, diving	May–Sep	p398
Kinabalu	Mt Kinabalu	mountain climbing	May–Sep	p414
Bako	beaches, coastline walks, proboscis monkeys	trekking	May–Sep	p334
Gunung Gading	rafflesia plants	easy trekking, flower viewing	Nov–Feb	p343
Turtle Islands	turtle nesting sites, deserted beaches	turtle viewing, snorkelling, swimming	Jul–Oct	p431

underwater environments, no potentially destructive activities like fishing or motorised water sports are allowed. This makes these parks ideal for activities such as snorkelling, diving or just lazing around on the beach.

Some of the more-accessible marine parks are Pulau Payar (p192), Pulau Tioman (p250), the Seribuat Archipelago (p243), Pulau Kapas (p285), Pulau Redang (p292), and Pulau Perhentian (p294) in Peninsular Malaysia; and Tunku Abdul Rahman (p398) and Turtle Islands (p431) national parks in Sabah. There is a RM5 entry fee for all marine parks. However, collection of this fee is inconsistent at best.

ENVIRONMENTAL ISSUES

Malaysia attracts more than its fair share of criticism on the environmental front, and it remains a sensitive issue. The government has long maintained that Western concern about environmental issues in developing countries is a form of hypocrisy, and that it is doing its best to balance out the benefits of further development with conservation. This said, Malaysia does have some significant problems to deal with – see below.

In contrast, Singapore stands out as environmentally enlightened. Strict laws control littering and waste emissions and they are policed thoroughly. Though little of the island's original wilderness is left, growing interest in ecology has seen new bird sanctuaries and parkland areas created. In such a built-up urban environment, the government has always been aware of the need for sound planning, and ordinary Singaporeans, who perhaps crave wide-open spaces, are increasingly focusing on the environment.

The most significant contribution to a healthy environment has been the Singapore government's commitment to public transport and control of the motor car – the benefits of which are something that traffic-clogged KL has only recently woken up to.

Visit www.rainforestweb.org for global information on rainforests.

Pulau Ubin and *Chek Jawa* by Chua EE Kiam are coffee-table books beautifully illustrated by the photographs of Kiam, a dentist who has become one of Singapore's most high-profile environmental activists; his focus on the unique marine environment at Pulau Ubin's Chek Jawa helped save it from government development plans.

Forest Management & Logging

Logging is big business in Malaysia, reckoned to generate at least US$4.5 billion a year and provide hundreds of thousands of jobs. Yet it also wreaks untold ecological damage (see Banking on the Kinabatangan, p432) and has caused the displacement of many tribal people and the consequent erosion of their unique cultures.

There's a disparity between the figures of government and environmental groups, but it's probable that more than 60% of Peninsular Malaysia's rainforests have been logged, with similar figures applying to Malaysian Borneo. Government initiatives such as the National Forestry Policy have led to deforestation being reduced to 900 sq km a year, a third slower than previously. The aim is to reduce the timber harvest by 10% each year, but even this isn't sufficient to calm many critics who remain alarmed at the rate at which Malaysia's primary forests are disappearing.

Borneo Log: The Struggle for Sarawak's Forests by William W Bevis is an evocative narrative that starkly outlines the environmental and human impacts of the logging that goes on in Sarawak. A winner of the 1995 Western States Book Award.

Another government initiative is the Forestry Resource Institute of Malaysia (FRIM) – you can see its work on regenerating rainforests at its base outside KL (p110). For more details of what the government is doing in relation to forest management, see the websites of the forestry departments of Peninsular Malaysia (www.forestry.gov.my), Sarawak (www.forestry.sarawak.gov.my) and Sabah (www.sabah.gov.my/htan/).

One way forward perhaps lies in Sarawak, ironically the state where Malaysia's primary forests are most under threat. Here Kuching is the base for the Sarawak Biodiversity Centre (www.sbc.org.my), an organisation that aims to assist drug companies in their search for valuable medical compounds from the rainforest. If the multimillion dollar cure for cancer or AIDS can be found in these forests, it might just be their partial saviour.

Dam Construction & Displaced People

In addition to logging, Malaysia has been attacked for undertaking several large dam-construction projects, which critics claim are both economically and environmentally unsound. The most controversial of these is the Bakun Dam (p345) in Sarawak, which has been plagued by financing difficulties since its inception – it's currently scheduled to be commissioned in 2006. As well as drowning hundreds of square kilometres of virgin rainforest, construction of the dam will force up to 10,000 indigenous peoples from their homes.

For up-to-date stories and information about the various environmental struggles in Sarawak, visit www.rengah.c2o.org/, the website of Rengah Sarawak (Sarawak News).

Such projects are indicative of how the land rights of indigenous peoples are consistently ignored in Malaysia. Particularly affected have been the nomadic Penan of Sarawak, who to some extent have resisted government moves to have them resettle.

The local Friends of the Earth organisation SAM is now concerned about possible plans by the Sarawak government to set up an aluminium smelting plant in the state to take advantage of the excess power generated by the Bakun Dam.

Erosion & Landslides

Dam construction and logging are a couple of the causes of soil erosion. Overdevelopment of land for commercial and housing use has also taken its toll, particularly on hillsides in Peninsular Malaysia, where there have been several high profile landslides. Disasters such as the collapse of a 12-storey building in Selangor in December 1993, which killed 49 people, have caused the government to toughen up on construction codes, but development of such facilities continues apace in the cooler highland areas within easy reach of KL.

DID YOU KNOW?

Malaysia's largest lake, the 360-sq-km Tasik Kenyir in the state of Terengganu, was created in 1985 with the damming of Sungai Terengganu.

It's not just inland that Malaysia is facing erosion. The coastline is also under threat. Some 75% of Kelantan's coast is under attack from erosion; in the worst cases the shoreline is retreating by up to 10m a year.

Haze

More recently, the region's environment has been threatened by a force completely beyond its control – the so-called 'haze' from fires burning in the Indonesian states of Kalimantan and Sumatra. While some of these fires are of natural origin, most are set by Indonesian farmers to clear land for agricultural purposes. The haze is at its worst in Singapore and parts of Malaysia usually around September and October, just before the rainy season. Because this is a yearly problem in the region, it pays to check the Web for up-to-date reports before heading to Malaysia, Singapore and Brunei, particularly Malaysian Borneo.

Sahabat Alam Malaysia (SAM) is Sarawak's main environmental group. Its website is at surforever.com/sam

Food & Drink

by Su-Lyn Tan

Su-Lyn Tan is a freelance food writer based in Singapore and was the managing director of *Wine & Dine* magazine. She has written for the *Asian Wall Street Journal*, *Travel + Leisure* and the *Four Seasons Hotel Magazine*, among other publications. Su-Lyn is currently finishing a doctoral thesis examining the celebrity-chef phenomenon.

Variety is the spice of life. In Malaysia, Singapore and Brunei that claim certainly rings true. Here a simple staple like rice is transformed from *bubur* (rice porridge) to *nasi lemak* (coconut rice); from *ketupat* (compressed rice) to *tuak* (rice wine). Practically every dish offers fresh insight into the history and culture of this colourful region. A mouthful of the Nonya dish *babi pong teh* (stewed pork), for example, reveals how Malay cooking techniques and Chinese ingredients have been combined to create something new. The spices used in curries – turmeric, cumin, coriander – hint at the Arab and Indian merchants who tarried on the shores of Malaysia. The multicultural traditions of the region offer the food lover a gastronomic experience like no other – so dig in!

STAPLES & SPECIALITIES

Forget potatoes – rice *(nasi)* and noodles *(mee)* rule in this region. Rice is eaten steamed, fried with other ingredients, boiled into sweet or savoury porridge; or, with glutinous varieties, steamed and moulded into tubes or cubes. Noodles can be made from wheat, wheat and egg, rice, or mung beans, and are used in a bewildering number of dishes, either fried or boiled.

The variety of fresh fish *(ikan)* available is mind-boggling. Malays generally prefer their fish fried whole and stuffed with spices, or chopped into chunks or steaks and served in a spicy *asam* (tamarind) sauce. The Chinese prefer to cook larger fish either steamed (when the fish is extremely fresh), fried or braised. Fish also comes served in a variety of laksa (noodles in a spicy soup) and in the delicious *otak otak* (spiced rectangles of fish wrapped in banana leaf and grilled over charcoal).

Shellfish *(karang)* and crustaceans *(unam)* are also highly popular, with tiny oysters popping up in *or luah* (fried oyster omelette), cockles in *char kway teow* (broad, flat rice-flour noodles stir-fried with Chinese sausage and egg in a sweet, dark soy sauce), and whole crabs in pepper-crab and Singapore chilli-crab dishes.

Edited by Rosalind Mowe, *Southeast Asian Specialities*, a coffee-table book in Könemann's Culinaria series, is beautifully illustrated with many photographs. Focuses on Singapore, Malaysia and Indonesia, with everything from stinkbeans to shark's fin soup.

Apart from fish, chicken *(ayam)* is possibly the most consumed meat in the region, especially the ubiquitous Hainanese chicken-rice (chicken and rice with chilli-ginger sauce). Beef *(daging lembu)* and mutton (*daging kambing*, which also refers to lamb as well as kid and goat) are common in Malay dishes such as beef rendang (beef in a thick coconut-milk curry sauce), *daging masak kicap* (beef in soy sauce) and *gulai daging* (beef curry).

While pork *(babi)* is considered *haram* (forbidden) among Muslims, the Chinese, Peranakans and Eurasians (but not so much the Indians) revel in its flavour. The Chinese, especially, love the fatty layers of belly pork. Pork ribs are also used to make the peppery, herbal *bak kut teh* (pork-rib soup),

Protein-rich soya bean (*dao*, also called *tau*) is present in many dishes, whether in the form of bean curd, fermented beans or soy sauce. Pulses – dried beans, peas and lentils – form the basis of many an Indian vegetarian dish, including dhal (lentil, pea or bean, also called *daal*) curry and *dosa*, paper-thin rice-and-lentil crêpes served with coconut chutney and curry.

It is impossible to conceive of a Malaysian or Singaporean meal without chilli (*cili*). Blended and ground with other spices, it adds depth to a curry. Chillies blended on their own form the base for many a *sambal* (relish) and chilli sauce.

Considered the heart and soul of Malay curries and sauces, *rempah* is a mix of spices created by pounding a combination of wet (including shallots, lemongrass, garlic, chilli and ginger) and dry (items such as candlenuts, cinnamon, coriander seeds, cumin, cloves and peppercorns) ingredients together to form a paste.

Other flavourings you'll come across include oyster and fish sauces, ketchup, onion and garlic, ginger *(halia)*, turmeric *(kunyit)*, galangal (blue ginger), lemongrass *(serai)* and pandanus leaves *(daun pandan)*.

Among the region's many types of fruit and vegetable are some that you may not be so familiar with. The long, rigid and green bittergourd *(peria)* is usually sliced thinly and fried with shrimp, fried in an omelette, or stuffed with fish paste. With a hollow stem and large, arrowhead leaves, water convolvulus *(kangkong)* is a popular vegetable often served fried with *sambal belacan* (chilli and spicy shrimp-paste).

Butterfly or blue-pea flower *(bunga telang)* is a tiny, deep blue flower that provides the natural blue colouring for many Malay, Peranakan and Eurasian desserts and rice dishes (it gives the Kelantan speciality, *nasi kerabu* – cooked rice tossed with finely shredded herbs – its bluish hue). The white, mildly sweet, juicy flesh of the yam bean *(sengkuang)* – which is really a tuber – is often eaten raw in salads. When cooked, it is one of the major ingredients in the cooked vegetable stuffing that is served with *popiah* (Peranakan spring rolls that are not deep-fried).

Fruits are usually served raw, ripe and sliced, in a big, mixed fruit platter. They are sometimes used in salads such as *rojak* (salad with shrimp-paste-based dressing) or *kerabu tau geh* (bean-sprout salad).

It is almost impossible to stay neutral about the durian. The creamy, bittersweet flesh is eaten fresh or incorporated in a number of dishes (see the boxed text below). Almost always sold alongside durians, the dark-purple mangosteen (roughly the size of a tennis ball) has sweet, white flesh inside. Its tart sweetness is supposed to balance the rich creaminess of durian.

The red, leathery and hairy skin of rambutans conceals a sweet, succulent, semi-translucent white flesh. Also not so attractive on the outside is jackfruit, but its bright yellow flesh is sugary sweet and wonderfully fragrant. The brown-coloured flesh of the *chiku* is soft and sweet, but

Mangosteens are the perfect foil for durians.
SIMON BRACKEN

DID YOU KNOW?

Despite its stinky odour Malays believe that durian is a powerful aphrodisiac, hence the old adage, 'When the durians go down, the sarongs go up'.

VARIATIONS ON A STINKY THEME

When it comes to durians, Malaysians aren't happy to leave a great thing be. If this is indeed the king of fruit, then surely it has a long line of successors. Delicacies savoury and sweet: *durian pengat*, a porridge-like sweet made by cooking durian pulp, coconut cream and palm sugar until gooey-thick; the black saccharine chewiness of long-stewed *dodol durian*; and Nonya-style *yulian gao*, a cake sold in cylindrical 20cm sticks. Vendors add durian to their *ais kacang* (Malaysian iced-dessert), roti (bread) and Chinese mooncakes; batter and deep-fry it, tempura-style; and make it into chips. Restaurants serve durian gateau and tiramisu. Extremists may want to try *tempoyak* (fermented and near-alcoholic durian pulp) mixed with fish curry, *sambal* (chilli-based condiment) and rice. My vote, though, goes to durian pancakes at the Mandarin Oriental (p90) in Kuala Lumpur. They're really a veil of batter, like a crêpe, draped over layers of durian meat, and cream that has been folded through puréed durian. The whole thing is too big to eat in one mouthful – instead, biting through and pulling away the outer pancake layer mimics the act of eating the fruit itself. The reward is a stinky, lush and primordial durian ooze within that plays counterpoint to the floury dough without.

the texture is a little sandy. The *jambu* (rose apple) looks like a bell and, when ripe, is bright pink with a waxy skin. Its flesh is watery and sweet. Locals enjoy it sliced and dipped in a combination of dark soy sauce and sliced chillies.

Regional Variations

Although the food of the region is as varied as its people, the differences across the three countries can sometimes be very subtle, coming down to, for example, a choice of fish used in a laksa or whether the rice is served shaped into little balls rather than heaped onto a plate.

New Asia Cuisine gives you access to a range of food- and wine-related sites for the region; plus magazine features www.asiacuisine.com

In the west coast Malaysian states of Kedah and Perlis there's a strong Thai influence. Lemongrass, kaffir lime leaves, lime juice, and fish sauce are more common in dishes here. Ipoh, the state capital of Perak, is famed for its Chinese food.

The foods of Penang and Melaka both reflect the intermingling of cultures that has happened in these ports. Dishes such as *murtabak* (pan-fried rice dough with chicken, beef or mutton, or vegetables) and *jiu hoo char* (stir-fried shredded cuttlefish with yam bean) represent Penang's spice-trade-centric history, while Melaka is renowned for its Peranakan (or Nonya) dishes combining Malay, European and Chinese cooking styles and ingredients (for more information on Peranakan culture, see p43).

To experience true Malay cuisine dine along the Malaysian east coast in the states of Kelantan and Terengganu. Kelantan in particular boasts some unique specialities such as *nasi ayam percik* (barbecued chicken marinated with spicy coconut gravy) and *nasi kerabu* (blue-tinted rice served with fish crackers and fried salted-fish).

Learn all about the local version of fusion cuisine, blending Chinese and Malay ingredients and cooking methods, from *Ms Lee's Cookbook: Nonya Recipes and Other Favourite Recipes* by Chin Koon Lee.

Over in Malaysian Borneo, a variety of fish dishes are popular, including Sabah's *hinava* (raw fish marinated with lime juice and herbs). Sago palm is the main starch component of some tribal meals. Sago-based dishes include *linut*, a thick translucent paste eaten hot with *sambal*. Wild boar and deer are Sarawak favourites, and vegetable dishes made with jungle ferns and *paku* (fern shoots) are not to be missed.

In food-crazy Singapore you can eat just about anything; a couple of representative dishes are Hainanese chicken-rice and Singapore chilli crab.

DRINKS

Freshly-made fruit juices are readily available at most hawker centres and even in some shopping malls. As well as the familiar options, there's sugar cane juice, pressed straight from the cane and an amazing thirst-quencher when served with a wedge of lemon; soursop, a dark green, prickly fruit with a slightly acidic, tropical-flavoured pulp; and *kalamansi* – a tiny, mouth-watering type of lime.

Coconut water *(air kelapa)* is very popular, usually served in the actual coconut. The eye-catchingly pink *air bandung* combines rose syrup and condensed milk. There's also soya-bean milk *(air soya)*, and the black-coloured grass-jelly drink which is considered a great herbal tonic.

Tea *(teh)* and coffee *(kopi)* are both fantastically popular, with the per capita consumption of tea in Malaysia alone about half a kilogram a year. Tea is brewed for longer to give it stronger flavour and is often served with thick condensed milk; coffee is equally strong and again comes with condensed milk unless you specify otherwise.

Despite alcohol consumption being frowned upon in predominantly Muslim Malaysia, alcohol is available and there are some local tipples to try, including toddy (palm-sap wine) and *tuak* (rice wine), the latter a speciality of the tribal people of Borneo.

CELEBRATIONS

In this region every event, from Chinese New Year to the Muslim Hari Raya Puasa to the Indian Deepavali, is a banquet of delights.

Traditional weddings can include days of feasting. Much of the food bears symbolic significance. A Peranakan mother-in-law, for example, may present a special *nasi lemak* (coconut rice with fried fish) to the mother of her son's bride, to acknowledge that the bride is a virgin. At Malay weddings, guests are presented with ornate, beautifully packaged gifts of hard-boiled eggs when they leave – a wish for fertility and off-spring.

To celebrate births across most cultures in Malaysia, Singapore and Brunei, the baby's first month is marked with a banquet attended by friends and family. On the 100th day, some Chinese families cook a chicken and its tongue is rubbed on the baby's lips to ensure the child will be an eloquent speaker.

On progressive birthdays in Peranakan and Chinese families, for example, the birthday person is served *diam mee*, fine egg noodles and hard-boiled eggs (some use quail eggs) in a sweet, sugary soup. The noodles represent long life. One should take care never to break the noodles while lifting them up, as this represents a life cut short. *Shou tao* (longevity peach buns) shaped like peaches (believed to symbolise spring-time and beauty) and filled with red-bean or lotus-seed paste are another enduring favourite.

The 2003/4 editon of *Makansutra*, the popular guide to 1000 selected eating places around Singapore (mostly hawker stalls and mid-price restaurants), is organised by cuisine, also making it a great primer to all the popular foods of the region.

WHERE TO EAT & DRINK

The neighbourhood *kedai kopi* or *kopi tiam* (both the Malay and Hokkien terms are commonly used, the latter more so in Singapore) is a no-frills café where neighbours may stop for a *kopi* or *teh*, and a meal. They are usually open throughout the day and, much like the hawker centre (see Quick Eats, p64), you order from individual stalls that specialise in specific dishes.

Restaurants *(restoran)* can refer to a broad variety of eateries, ranging from humble joints with no air-conditioning, surly service and decidedly local items on the menu, to swish fine-dining establishments with designer interiors, foreign chefs and sommeliers, and cutting-edge cuisine.

Makansutra is also the best website for checking out the street-food scene in Singapore, with regularly updated features and reviews www.makansutra.com

TRAVEL YOUR TASTEBUDS

Here are a few of the region's more challenging dishes (to Western palates, at least):

- *Perut ikan* (fish stomach) – fish innards cooked in a coconut curry, lightly scented with mint, and presented on top of sliced beans and pineapple. A dish from Penang.
- *Tempoyak* (fermented salted durian) – locals in Perak mix durian flesh with salt and leave it in an airtight jar in the refrigerator for at least three days. Most commonly mixed with pounded chilli to make a *sambal* which is eaten with rice, it can also be incorporated in curry dishes.
- *Siat* (sago grubs) – stir-fried with shallots and ginger, these fat grubs are a protein-rich delicacy in Sarawak.
- Fish-head curry – Go on, this Singaporean specialty tastes fabulous, especially the soft muscle around the eyeballs.

Roving drink carts wheeled by vendors dishing up various drinks, usually juices, are commonly found on most busy street corners in Malaysia. In Singapore, search for them in hawker centres, food courts and shopping malls.

The handsomely revised 2003 edition of the 1994 *Raffles Hotel Cookbook* includes the history of Raffles Hotel as well as recipes, which have proved popular with guests, from the establishment's various restaurants.

Alcohol is freely available, but it's likely to be more expensive than you'd pay at home and recreational drinking is the preoccupation of a relatively younger set. Enclaves such as Jl Bukit Bintang in Kuala Lumpur and Boat Quay in Singapore have evolved into party strips, especially for tourists, but in more Malay (ie Muslim) parts of the country you'll be restricted to drinking at Chinese restaurants and cafés, and top-end hotels.

Quick Eats

The hawker meal is central to the experience of eating in Malaysia and Singapore. Great effort has been made to raise the hygiene standards of hawker food by moving hawker carts off the streets and into permanent stalls at hawker centres and food courts. But locals will argue that the best food is still found at the compact little kitchens-on-wheels that line alleyways and street corners, fill whole hawker enclaves and cluster around popular coffee shops.

Yvonne Tan's *Penang Food Odyssey* lists the favourite hawker food and meals of Penang, covering 35 locations around the island. It's nicely illustrated with colour pencil drawings and has 12 recipes, including *asam laksa* and curry Kapitan.

That said, it's difficult to define street food purely as food served at these roadside stalls. There is very little difference between the types of dish served from a street-side hawker cart and a stall in a hawker centre or food court (in Singapore these carts have almost disappeared, although they are still to be found throughout Malaysia).

VEGETARIANS & VEGANS

Although there's an abundance of fruit and vegetables available in these countries, purely vegetarian dishes are not common. Foods are often fried in pork lard and seafood products are used as flavouring for many dishes.

This said, the prevalence of Hindu and Buddhist cultures in the region also means that finding purely vegetarian restaurants in most of the big cities and towns shouldn't be too problematic. Head for the Little Indias of Kuala Lumpur or Singapore and you'll discover a wide range of restaurants serving great vegetarian food, from roti and dhal for breakfast to thali (meal platter of rice, curried veg. soup and breads) for lunch and dinner; see the Eating sections in KL (p91) and Singapore (p486) for reviews of Chinese and Western-style vegetarian restaurants and cafés.

WHINING & DINING

The good news for those travelling with children is that in the bigger towns and cities of the region you'll rarely be far from a fast food-joint of the variety that kids the world over crave. Having said this, the relatively high standards of food preparation and the good quality of ingredients and water mean that you shouldn't be afraid about having your kids (and you) eat what the locals do.

A meal at a hawker centre can be not only tasty but also an educational experience, an opportunity to get to know the various cultures of the region through their different foods. Dishes you should have no problems getting the little darlings to wolf down include satay beef or chicken, and the lurid shaved-ice mountains of *ais kacang*. If they don't mind a bit of spice and getting their fingers messy (and who doesn't?) then chilli crab is also fun for older kids.

For more information on travelling with children, see the Directory chapter (p536).

HABITS & CUSTOMS

Eating is pretty much an obsession with Malaysians and Singaporeans, and it may seem that they eat all the time! Breakfast is usually bought from a roadside or hawker stall on the way to work and may consist of anything from a filling *nasi lemak*, soupy Chinese noodles, delicate *dosa* or soft-boiled eggs and *roti kaya* (grilled bread with coconut egg jam), to an egg McMuffin. The mid-morning snack may be a curry puff filled with a dry chicken-and-potato curry, and a quarter of a hard-boiled egg, or *you char kway* (a deep-fried dough stick) – and a *kopi* (coffee with sweet condensed milk).

Lunch hour starts at around 12.30pm. At the numerous hawker areas and food centres you'll discover that diners first focus on scoring themselves a clean table and seat before ordering a one-course meal of local favourites such as noodles or clay-pot rice. Eating is a functional (and often hot and sweaty) affair at this time of day. It's common for diners to share the empty seats at their table with perfect strangers. In swankier, air-conditioned food courts expect, apart from the local specialities, renditions of Western, Japanese, Thai and other foods, all of which reveal the intrinsic openness the locals have towards different cuisines.

Celine Marbeck's *Cuzinhia Cristang: A Malacca-Portuguese Cookbook* offers an overview of the Portuguese-influenced food culture, still surviving after 600 years, of Melaka.

For busy couples and families, dinner is also often eaten at hawker stalls. Meals are more substantial, and diners tend to mix their cuisines, maybe opting for an Indian salad, a Malay rice dish and a Chinese dessert. Home-cooked dinners, on the other hand, tend to be centred around just one style of cuisine, usually that traditional to the family. Then, there's always supper. At 2am, it's back to the hawker stalls for barbecued chicken wings, peppery pork-rib soups and greasy *or luah* (oyster omelette).

COOKING COURSES

In Malaysia there are cooking courses in Kota Bharu (p306).

In Singapore you can gain hands-on experience of making the region's various dishes at the **at-sunrice cooking academy** (p477) as well as attending demonstration-only cookery courses at Raffles Hotel and the Coriander Leaf restaurant.

DINING DOS & DON'TS

If eating with your fingers:

- Wash your fingers first
- Remember to use serving spoons, not your fingers, to take food from the communal dish
- Use your right hand, and scoop up the food using just the tips of your fingers
- Mix your curries with your rice well, before raising a mouthful to your lips

And a few dining no-nos:

- Don't serve alcohol or pork to Muslims
- Avoid serving beef to Hindus or Buddhists
- Never stick your chopsticks into a bowl of rice – this symbolises death to the Chinese

EAT YOUR WORDS

Useful Phrases

These Malay phrases may help in off-the-beaten track eating adventures – at most places in the region English will be understood. For guidelines on pronunciation see p584.

Where's a...? — *...di mana?*
  restaurant — *kedai makan*
  hawker centre — *pusat penjaja*
Can I see the menu? — *Minta senarai makanan?*
I'd like... — *Saya mau...*
What's in this dish? — *Ini termasuk apa?*
Not too spicy, please. — *Kurang pedas.*
I like it hot and spicy! — *Saya suka pedas lagi!*
The bill/check, please. — *Minta bon.*
Thank you, that was delicious. — *Sedap sekali, terima kasih.*
I don't want any meat at all. — *Saya tak mau daging.*
I'm a vegetarian. — *Saya hanya makan sayuran.*

Menu Decoder

achar – vegetable pickle
ais kacang – dessert of ice shavings topped with syrups, coconut milk, red beans, seeds and jelly
aloo gobi – Indian potato-and-cauliflower dish
ayam goreng – fried chicken
bak chang – rice dumpling filled with savoury or sweet meat and wrapped in leaves
bak kut teh – pork-rib soup with hints of garlic and Chinese five-spice
belacan kangkong – water convolvulus stir-fried in prawn paste
biryani – steamed basmati rice oven-baked with spices and meat, seafood or vegetables
carrot cake – omelette-like dish made from radishes, egg, garlic and chilli; also known as *chye tow kway*
cendol – drink/dessert of coconut milk and palm-sugar syprup with fine short strings of green-bean flour dough
char kway teow – broad noodles, clams and eggs fried in chilli and black bean sauce
char siew – sweet roasted pork fillet
chicken-rice – steamed chicken, served with rice boiled or steamed in chicken stock, slices of cucumber and a chilli-ginger sauce
clay-pot rice – rice cooked in a clay pot with chicken, mushroom, Chinese sausage and soy sauce
congee – Chinese porridge
dhal – dish of pureed lentils
dim sum – sweet and savoury mini-dishes served at breakfast and lunch; also known as *dian xin* or *yum cha*
fish-head curry – red snapper in curry sauce
gado gado – cold dish of bean sprouts, potatoes, long beans, bean curd, rice cakes and prawn crackers, topped with a spicy peanut sauce
Hokkien mee – yellow noodles fried with sliced meat, boiled squid, prawns and strips of fried egg
idli – steamed rice cake
ikan asam – fried fish in sour tamarind curry
kari ayam – curried chicken
kofta – minced-meat or vegetable ball
korma – mild Indian curry with yoghurt sauce
kueh melayu – sweet pancakes filled with peanuts, raisins and sugar
laksa – noodles in a spicy coconut soup with bean sprouts, quail eggs, prawns, shredded chicken and dried bean curd; also called Nonya laksa to differentiate it from Penang laksa, a version that has a prawn-paste-based gravy instead of coconut milk

The Food of Malaysia, edited by Wendy Hutton, is a good collection of local recipes, all nicely photographed in colour.

SERVICE CHARGE AND TAXES

In the more expensive hotels and restaurants of Malaysia and Singapore you'll be charged a government tax of 5%, and most likely a service tax of 10%. This often expressed as ++ on the menu.

lontong – rice cakes in spicy coconut-milk gravy topped with grated coconut and, sometimes, bean curd and egg
lor mee – noodles with slices of meat, eggs and a dash of vinegar in a dark brown sauce
masala dosa – thin pancake rolled around spicy vegetables with *rasam* on the side
mee goreng – fried noodles
mee rebus – yellow noodles served in a thick sweetish sauce made from sweet potatoes and garnished with sliced hard-boiled eggs and green chillies
mee siam – white thin noodles in a sweet-and-sour gravy made with tamarind
mee soto – noodle soup with shredded chicken
murtabak – *roti canai* filled with pieces of mutton, chicken or vegetables
nasi biryani – saffron rice flavoured with spices and garnished with cashew nuts, almonds and raisins
nasi campur – buffet of curried meats, fish and vegetables, served with rice
nasi goreng – fried rice
nasi lemak – rice boiled in coconut milk, served with fried *ikan bilis*, peanuts and a curry dish
nasi padang – Malay rice and accompanying meat and vegetable dishes
pilau – rice fried in ghee and mixed with nuts, then cooked in stock
popiah – similar to a spring roll, but not fried
raita – side dish of cucumber, yoghurt and mint
rasam – spicy soup
rendang – spicy coconut curry with beef or chicken
rijstaffel – literally, rice table; a buffet of Indonesian dishes
rogan josh – stewed mutton in a rich sauce
rojak – salad doused in a peanut-sauce dressing that may contain shrimp paste
roti canai – unleavened flaky bread cooked with ghee on a hotplate; eaten dipped in dhal or curry; also known as *paratha or roti prata*
saag – spicy chopped-spinach dish
sambal udang – hot curried prawns
sambar – fiery mixture of vegetables, lentils and split peas
samosa – pastry filled with vegetables or meat
satay – pieces of chicken, beef or mutton that are skewered and grilled
soto ayam – spicy chicken soup with vegetables and potatoes
steamboat – meats, seafood and vegetables cooked at the table by being dipped into a pot of boiling clear stock
tauhu goreng – fried bean curd and bean sprouts in peanut sauce
teh kosong – tea without milk or sugar
teh tarek – tea made with evaporated milk, which is literally pulled or stretched *(tarek)* from one glass to another
teh-o – tea without milk
tikka – small pieces of meat or fish served off the bone and marinated in yoghurt before baking
tom yum kung – hot-and-sour spicy seafood soup
umai – raw fish marinated and served with onions
won ton mee – soup dish with shredded chicken or braised beef
yong tau foo – bean curd stuffed with minced meat
yu char kway – deep-fried Chinese bread sticks
yu yuan mian – fish-ball soup
yu tiao – deep-fried pastry eaten for breakfast or as a dessert

Lonely Planet's *World Food: Malaysia & Singapore by* Su-Lyn Tan gives an in-depth view of all that these countries offer in terms of food and drink, and includes tantalising photography, recipes, a culinary dictionary and glossary.

Street kitchen – Kuala Lumpur

RICHARD I'ANSON

Glossary

ayam – chicken
belacan – fermented prawn paste
bhindi – okra (lady's fingers)
brinjal – aubergine (eggplant)
chapati – griddle-fried wholewheat bread
chilli padi – extremely hot small chilli
choi sum – popular Chinese green vegetable, served steamed with oyster sauce
daun kunyit – turmeric leaf
daun pisang – banana leaf, often used as a plate in Malaysia
daun salam – leaves used much like bay leaves in cooking
dhal – pureed lentils
dosa – large, light, crispy pancake
dow see – fermented, salted black beans
fish sauce – liquid made from fermented anchovies and salt
galangal – ginger-like root used to flavour various dishes
garam masala – sweet, mild mixture of freshly ground spices
garoupa – white fish popular in Southeast Asia
ghee – clarified butter
gingko nut – meaty nut used in soups and desserts or roasted and chopped for sauces, salads and meat dishes
gula jawa – brown palm-sugar sold in thin blocks
halal – food prepared according to Muslim dietary laws
hoisin sauce – thick sweet-spicy sauce made from soya beans, red beans, sugar, flour, vinegar, salt, garlic, sesame, chillies and spices
ikan bilis – small deep-fried anchovies
kangkong – water convolvulus; thick-stemmed type of spinach
kecap – soy sauce
keema – spicy minced meat
kepala ikan – fish-head, usually in curry or grilled
kueh mueh – Malay cakes
kway teow – broad rice-noodles
lassi – yoghurt-based drink
lombok – type of hot chilli
mee pok – flat noodles made with egg and wheat
mee – noodles
naan – tear-shaped leavened bread baked in a clay oven
nasi – rice
pakora – vegetable fritter
pappadam – Indian cracker
phrik – chillies
pisang goreng – banana fritter
pudina – mint sauce
sambal – sauce of chilli, onions and prawn paste which has been fried
santan – coconut milk
Szechuan – region in south central China famous for its spicy cuisine; also spelt Sichuan
tamarind – large bean from the tamarind tree with a brittle shell and a dark brown, sticky pulp; used for its sweet-sour taste
tandoori – Indian style of cooking in which marinated meat is baked in a clay oven
taro – vegetable with leaves like spinach, stalks like asparagus, and a starchy root similar in size and taste to the potato

DID YOU KNOW?

'Ketchup' comes from the word *ke-tsiap* – a Chinese fish sauce encountered by European traders in the ports of Melaka and Penang.

Malaysia

MARK DAFFEY

Kuala Lumpur

CONTENTS

In its 120 years, Kuala Lumpur (KL) has grown from a Wild-West tin-mining town – harassed by civil war, fires and floods – into an affluent modern Asian capital. The city's 21st-century skyline of gleaming skyscrapers, crowned by the vertiginous and self-assured twin Petronas Towers, remains a triumphant legacy of the 1990's boom time.

Putrajaya, a US$8 billion centre for administration and government on Kuala Lumpur's southern periphery and Cyberjaya, an adjoining ultra-high-tech 'multimedia super corridor', further evince the slick ambitions of this erstwhile shantytown.

Mega projects and aspirations aside however, KL has no deficit of history or culture. Old colonial buildings and modern Islamic masterpieces stand proudly in the centre of town. With its street vendors and old shophouses, vibrant Chinatown is a cultural highlight; while bustling Little India and the Malay-dominated Chow Kit Market area north of the city centre add zest to the cultural potpourri. KL's multi-religious character is marked by an abundance of fascinating temples and religious customs. From the capital, many of Selangor's attractions such as the Batu Caves, Zoo Negara, Orang Asli Museum and Templer Park (see the Selangor chapter, p110) are an easy day trip away.

At first glance, KL may seem like just another noisy, Westernised Asian city. A further look reveals a city with a rich heritage full of colour and character, alongside all the trimmings of a modern metropolis.

HIGHLIGHTS

- Walking through the historic **colonial district** (p83) and vibrant **Chinatown** (p85)
- Taking in the jaw-dropping **Petronas Towers** (p81), the world's tallest building
- Shopping (and eating) 'til you drop at the showcase **Suria KLCC shopping complex** (p98)
- **Dining out** (p91) at the city's choice Malay, Chinese, Indian and international eateries followed by a beer in **Bangsar** (p96)
- Strolling or boating in the relaxing **Lake Gardens** (p77), visiting its showpiece Bird Park and admiring the colonial luxury of the Carcosa Seri Negara

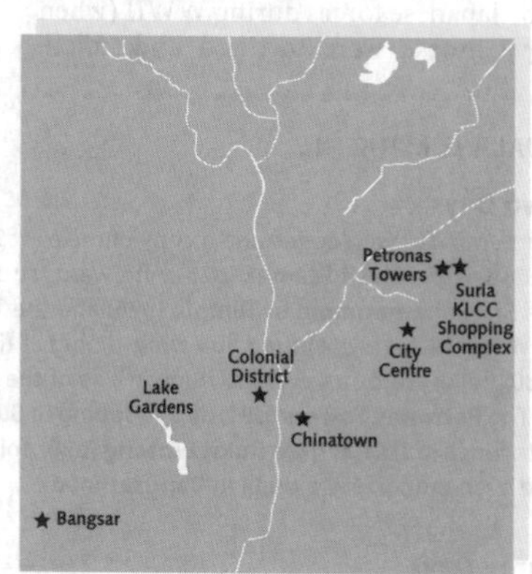

TELEPHONE CODE: 03 | POPULATION: 1.4 MILLION | AREA: 243 SQ KM

HISTORY

Kuala Lumpur came into being in 1857, when a band of prospectors in search of tin landed at the meeting point of the Klang and Gombak rivers and imaginatively named the place Kuala Lumpur – Muddy Confluence. More than half of those first arrivals died of malaria and other tropical diseases, but the tin they discovered in Ampang attracted more miners and KL quickly became a brawling, noisy, violent boomtown.

As in other parts of Malaysia, the local sultan appointed a Kapitan China to bring the unruly Chinese fortune-seekers and their secret societies into line – a problem that Yap Ah Loy (the Kapitan China from 1868–85) jumped at with such ruthless relish that he became known as the founder of KL.

In the 1880s successful miners and merchants began to build fine homes along Jl Ampang. British government representative Frank Swettenham pushed through a far-reaching new town plan, which transferred the central government here from Klang.

In 1881 the entire town was destroyed by fire and a subsequent flood, but it quickly got back on its feet. By 1886 a railway line linked KL to Klang; by 1887 several thousand brick buildings had been built; and in 1896 the city became the capital of the newly formed Federated Malay States.

KL has never looked back. After occupation by Japanese forces during WWII (when many Chinese were tortured and killed, and many Indians sent to work on Burma's 'Death Railway'), the British temporarily returned, only to be ousted when Malaysia finally declared its independence here in 1957 at Dataran Merdeka (Merdeka Square). The city officially became the Federal Territory of Kuala Lumpur when it was ceded by the sultan of Selangor state in 1974.

Today KL is not only Malaysia's political and commercial capital, but also its most populous and prosperous city.

CLIMATE

The temperature in Kuala Lumpur ranges from 21°C to 33°C and the average humidity exceeds 82%. Although there is rain through the year, March to April and September to November are the wettest months.

ORIENTATION

The traditional heart of KL is Merdeka Square, near the confluence of the two rivers from which KL takes its name. Its 100m-high flagpole – claimed to be the world's tallest – marks the square, in the heart of the old colonial district. Southeast across the river, the banking district merges into Chinatown – a bustling area with a range of accommodation and a lively night market.

The Masjid Negara (National Mosque) and the historic KL Train Station are south of Merdeka Square, west of which are the peaceful attractions of the Lake Gardens and Malaysian Parliament House.

KUALA LUMPUR IN...

Two Days

Start your day with coffee and a copy of the *New Straits Times* before walking to **Merdeka Square** (p83) and the **Masjid Jamek** (p76). Afterwards stroll through Chinatown to admire its shophouses, the **Sri Mahamariamman Temple** (p76) and the Taoist **Sze Yah Temple** (p85).

Watch KL revolve around you while dining at the **Seri Angkasa** (p92) high up in the **KL Tower** (p80), followed by an evening drink in one of the many bars in the **Golden Triangle** (p96).

The **Petronas Towers** (p81) and shopping in **Suria KLCC** (p98) are highlights of the second day, with lunch in **Jl Changkat Bukit Bintang** (p80), followed by a visit to the **Thean Hou Temple** (p80), and then dinner and a drink in **Bangsar** (p96).

Three Days

Follow the two-day itinerary, and on your third day hop onto the LRT to **KL Sentral** (p103) and walk to the **National Museum** (p79) and **Lake Gardens** (p77) with its vast **Bird Park** (p77) and other attractions. Sample a Nonya lunch in the Peranakan setting of the **Kapitan's Club** (p94) before returning to the heart of Chinatown to browse through **Jl Petaling Market** (p81). Dine at one of the area's many Chinese eateries.

East of Merdeka Square area is Masjid Jamek, at the intersection of the Star and Putra Light Rail Transit (LRT) lines. Jl Tun Perak, a major trunk road, leads east to the long-distance transport hub of the country, the Puduraya bus station.

To the east of Puduraya bus station, around Jl Sultan Ismail and Jl Bukit Bintang, the Golden Triangle is the modern heart of the new KL, crowded with mid-range and luxury hotels, shopping centres and office towers.

Running north of Merdeka Square is Jl Tunku Abdul Rahman (Jl TAR). It runs one way southbound through Chow Kit and Little India. Jl Raja Laut runs almost parallel to Jl TAR and takes the northbound traffic.

Jl Tun Sambanthan runs southwest from the KL Train Station through the Brickfields area where the transport hub KL Sentral station (and the KL City Air Terminal) are located. On the other side of the tracks (south), Bangsar is a nightlife nucleus of trendy bars and eateries.

KL is relatively easy to find your way around, although getting from place to place on foot can be frustrating. Distances are short, but footpaths are often missing. When in doubt, the slick LRT system is quicker and easier; taxis are another option.

INFORMATION

Bookshops

Kinokuniya (Map pp74-5; ☎ 2164 8133; Level 4, Suria KLCC) Huge and highly efficient bookstore with an excellent range of English-language titles.

MPH Bookstores BB Plaza (Map pp82-3; ☎ 2142 8231; Ground fl, Jl Bukit Bintang) Mid Valley Megamall (☎ 2983 3333; Bangsar) Good range of magazines and contemporary books.

Popular (Map pp82-3; ☎ 2145 8501; Sungei Wang Plaza)

Skoob (Map pp74-5; ☎ 2272 2731; 88 Jl Padang Belia, Brickfields) Excellent second-hand bookstore with a cultured collection; it's worth coming to Brickfields just to browse here.

Times (Map pp82-3; ☎ 2161 0217; the Weld)

Cultural Centres & Libraries

Alliance Française (☎ 2692 5929; www.alliancefrancaise.org.my; 15 Lg Gurney)

Australian Information Library (☎ 2146 5786; austh@po.jaring.my; 6 Jl Yap Kwan Seng)

British Council (☎ 2698 7555; arts@britishcouncil.org.my; Ground fl, West Block, Wisma Selangor Dredging, Jl Ampang)

Goethe Institut (☎ 2142 2011; 1 Jl Langgak Golf, off Jl Tun Razak)

Lincoln Resource Center (☎ 2168 4966; US Embassy, 376 Jl Tun Razak)

National Library of Malaysia (☎ 2687 1700; pnmweb@www1.pnm.my; 232 Jl Tun Razak)

New Zealand Education Centre (☎ 2078 4612; 21st fl, Menara IMC, 8 Jl Sultan Ismail)

Immigration Offices

The main **Immigration Office** (☎ 2095 5077; opsroom@imi.gov.my; Block I, Pusat Bandar Damansara) for visa extensions is about 1km west of the Lake Gardens. The more convenient **Kompleks Wilayah branch** (Map pp74-5; ☎ 2698 0377; fax 2698 0068; Jl Dang Wangi) is near Sogo department store.

Internet Access

Big-city rates for Internet access start at RM3 per hour. Several backpacker guesthouses also offer Internet access (not necessarily cheap or fast).

Adamz Cyber Café (Map pp78-9; Central Market Annexe; RM5 per hr; 🕒 10am-10pm) Offers Net-phone.

@Bintang Internet Centre (Map pp82-3; 1st fl, 146A Jl Bukit Bintang; RM4 per hr; 🕒 10am-1am)

Browse Internet Café (Map pp74-5; 118-m Jl Tun Sambanthan, Brickfields; RM3 per hr) pp78-9

HMI Multimedia Network (Map pp78-9; Jl Melayu; RM3 per hr; 🕒 10am-midnight, Fri from 2.30pm)

Internet Café (Map pp82-3; Jl Bukit Bintang; RM4 per hr; 🕒 8am-2am) Just north of Malaysia Hotel.

Master World Surfnet Café (Map pp78-9; Jl Cheng Lock; RM6 per hr; 🕒 9am-2am) Fast connections.

Media

Look out for the free magazine *Juice*, with the latest tips on entertainment, eating and leisure activities in KL and surrounding areas. *KLue* (www.klue.com.my) is a trendy bi-weekly entertainment magazine costing RM1.80 (available from Tower Records); *KL Vision* also has entertainment listings (available from top-end hotels).

Medical Services

Assunta Hospital (☎ 7782 3343; Petaling Jaya)

Kuala Lumpur General Hospital (Map pp74-5; ☎ 2692 1044; Jl Pahang)

Tung Shin Hospital (Map pp78-9; ☎ 2072 1655; 102 Jl Pudu)

Twin Towers Medical Centre KLCC (Map pp74-5; ☎ 2382 3500; fax 2382 9000; Lot 401 F&G, Level 4, Suria KLCC)

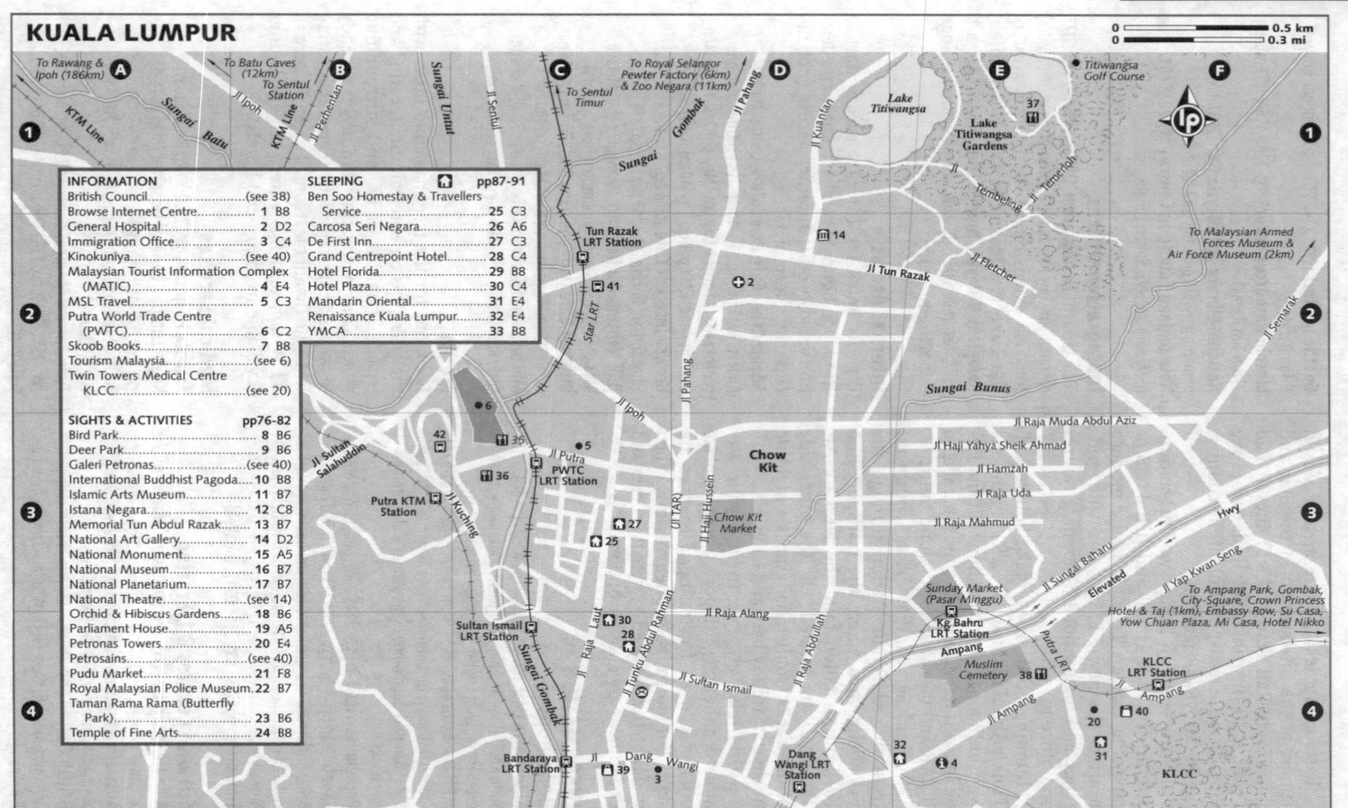
KUALA LUMPUR
0 0.5 km
0 0.3 mi
INFORMATION
British Council....(see 38)
Browse Internet Centre.... 1 B8
General Hospital.... 2 D2
Immigration Office.... 3 C4
Kinokuniya....(see 40)
Malaysian Tourist Information Complex (MATIC).... 4 E4
MSL Travel.... 5 C3
Putra World Trade Centre (PWTC).... 6 C2
Skoob Books.... 7 B8
Tourism Malaysia....(see 6)
Twin Towers Medical Centre KLCC....(see 20)
SIGHTS & ACTIVITIES pp76-82
Bird Park.... 8 B6
Deer Park.... 9 B6
Galeri Petronas....(see 40)
International Buddhist Pagoda.... 10 B8
Islamic Arts Museum.... 11 B7
Istana Negara.... 12 C8
Memorial Tun Abdul Razak.... 13 B7
National Art Gallery.... 14 D2
National Monument.... 15 A5
National Museum.... 16 B7
National Planetarium.... 17 B7
National Theatre....(see 14)
Orchid & Hibiscus Gardens.... 18 B6
Parliament House.... 19 A5
Petronas Towers.... 20 E4
Petrosains....(see 40)
Pudu Market.... 21 F8
Royal Malaysian Police Museum.... 22 B7
Taman Rama Rama (Butterfly Park).... 23 B6
Temple of Fine Arts.... 24 B8
SLEEPING pp87-91
Ben Soo Homestay & Travellers Service.... 25 C3
Carcosa Seri Negara.... 26 A6
De First Inn.... 27 C3
Grand Centrepoint Hotel.... 28 C4
Hotel Florida.... 29 B8
Hotel Plaza.... 30 C4
Mandarin Oriental.... 31 E4
Renaissance Kuala Lumpur.... 32 E4
YMCA.... 33 B8
To Rawang & Ipoh (186km)
To Batu Caves (12km)
To Sentul Station
KTM Line
Sungai Batu
Jl Ipoh
Jl Perhentian
Sungai Untut
Jl Sentul
To Sentul Timur
To Royal Selangor Pewter Factory (6km) & Zoo Negara (11km)
Sungai Gombak
Jl Pahang
Jl Kuantan
Lake Titiwangsa
Lake Titiwangsa Gardens
Titiwangsa Golf Course
Jl Tembeling
Jl Temerloh
To Malaysian Armed Forces Museum & Air Force Museum (2km)
Tun Razak LRT Station
Jl Tun Razak
Jl Fletcher
Jl Semarak
Star LRT
Sungai Bunus
Jl Raja Muda Abdul Aziz
Jl Haji Yahya Sheik Ahmad
Jl Hamzah
Jl Raja Uda
Jl Raja Mahmud
Chow Kit
Chow Kit Market
Jl Haji Hussein
(Jl TAR)
Jl Sultan Salahuddin
Jl Putra
PWTC LRT Station
Putra KTM Station
Jl Kuching
Jl Raja Laut
Jl Tunku Abdul Rahman
Jl Raja Alang
Jl Raja Abdullah
Jl Sultan Ismail
Sultan Ismail LRT Station
Sungai Gombak
Bandaraya LRT Station
Jl Dang Wangi
Dang Wangi LRT Station
Sunday Market (Pasar Minggu)
Kg Bahru LRT Station
Ampang
Muslim Cemetery
Putra LRT
Jl Sungai Baharu
Elevated Hwy
Jl Yap Kwan Seng
To Ampang Park, Gombak, City-Square, Crown Princess Hotel & Taj (1km), Embassy Row, Su Casa, Yow Chuan Plaza, Mi Casa, Hotel Nikko
KLCC LRT Station
Jl Ampang
KLCC

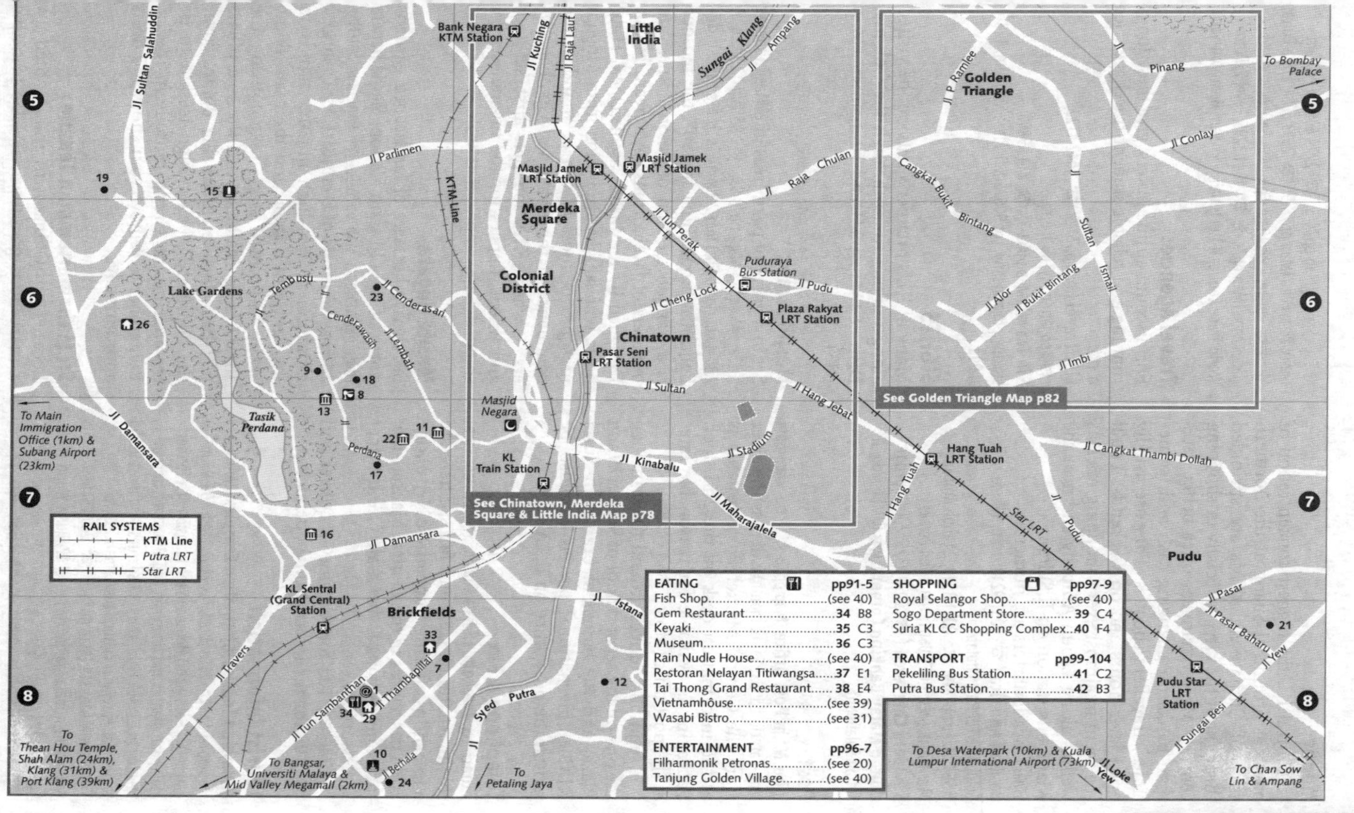
EATING pp91-5
Fish Shop (see 40)
Gem Restaurant 34 B8
Keyaki 35 C3
Museum 36 C3
Rain Nudle House (see 40)
Restoran Nelayan Titiwangsa 37 E1
Tai Thong Grand Restaurant 38 E4
Vietnamhôuse (see 39)
Wasabi Bistro (see 31)
ENTERTAINMENT pp96-7
Filharmonik Petronas (see 20)
Tanjung Golden Village (see 40)
SHOPPING pp97-9
Royal Selangor Shop (see 40)
Sogo Department Store 39 C4
Suria KLCC Shopping Complex 40 F4
TRANSPORT pp99-104
Pekeliling Bus Station 41 C2
Putra Bus Station 42 B3
RAIL SYSTEMS
KTM Line
Putra LRT
Star LRT
See Golden Triangle Map p82
See Chinatown, Merdeka Square & Little India Map p78
Golden Triangle
Little India
Merdeka Square
Colonial District
Chinatown
Pudu
Brickfields
Lake Gardens
Tasik Perdana
Masjid Negara
KL Train Station
KL Sentral (Grand Central) Station
Bank Negara KTM Station
Masjid Jamek LRT Station
Pasar Seni LRT Station
Plaza Rakyat LRT Station
Hang Tuah LRT Station
Pudu Star LRT Station
Puduraya Bus Station
Sungai Klang
KTM Line
Star LRT
Jl Sultan Salahuddin
Jl Parlimen
Jl Damansara
Jl Cenderasari
Cenderawasih
Tembusu
Perdana
Jl Lembah
Jl Travers
Jl Tun Sambanthan
Jl Thambapillai
Jl Berhala
Jl Kuching
Jl Raja Laut
Jl Tun Perak
Jl Cheng Lock
Jl Sultan
Jl Kinabalu
Jl Maharajalela
Jl Stadium
Jl Hang Jebat
Jl Pudu
Jl Raja Chulan
Jl Ampang
Jl Hang Tuah
Jl Imbi
Jl Alor
Jl Bukit Bintang
Cangkat Bukit Bintang
Jl Sultan Ismail
Jl P Ramlee
Jl Conlay
Jl Pinang
Jl Cangkat Thambi Dollah
Jl Pasar
Jl Pasar Baharu
Jl Yew
Jl Sungai Besi
Jl Loke Yew
Jl Istana
Jl Syed Putra
To Bombay Palace
To Chan Sow Lin & Ampang
To Desa Waterpark (10km) & Kuala Lumpur International Airport (73km)
To Petaling Jaya
To Bangsar, Universiti Malaya & Mid Valley Megamall (2km)
To Thean Hou Temple, Shah Alam (24km), Klang (31km) & Port Klang (39km)
To Main Immigration Office (1km) & Subang Airport (23km)

Money

In central KL the biggest concentration of banks is around Jl Silang at the northern edge of Chinatown. ATMs are sprinkled throughout the city, especially in shopping centres. Moneychangers offer better rates than banks for changing cash and (sometimes) travellers cheques. They are usually open later hours and on weekends. You'll see them in almost every shopping mall, as well as along Lebuh Ampang and near the Klang bus station on Jl Sultan.

Bank headquarters are numerous:

Bank of America (☎ 2031 9218; 1st fl, Wisma Goldhill, 67 Jl Raja Chulan)

HSBC (Map pp78-9; ☎ 2031 3510; 2 Lebuh Ampang)

Maybank (☎ 2053 8501; 100 Jl Tun Perak)

Standard Chartered (☎ 2070 2325; 2 Jl Ampang)

United Malay Banking Corporation (UMBC Bldg, Jl Sultan Sulaiman)

Post

The **Main Post Office** (Map pp78-9; 🕑 8.30am-6pm Mon-Sat, closed first Sat of month) is across the river from the Central Market. Poste restante is at the information desk on the 2nd floor. Packaging is available for reasonable rates at the post office store.

Useful post offices around town include the one on the second floor of Sungei Wang Plaza, and the basement branch in Suria KLCC. International parcels can also be sent at the post office on Jl TAR.

Telephone & Fax

Head to **Telekom** (Jl Raja Chulan; 🕑 8.30am-9pm) for international calls and faxes. There are a few shops offering competitive Net-phone and fax services in the Central Market area, including Adamz Cyber Café (see Internet Access, p73).

Call ☎ 103 for directory inquiries and ☎ 108 for the international operator.

Tourist Information

Malaysian Tourist Information Complex (MATIC; Map pp74-5; ☎ 2164 3929; fax 2162 1149; 109 Jl Ampang; 🕑 9am-6pm) Housed in the mansion of a former Malaysian planter and tin miner, and almost a tourist attraction in its own right, this is KL's largest and most useful tourist office; regular cultural performances.

Tourism Malaysia (Map pp74-5; ☎ 2693 5188; www.tourismmalaysia.gov.my; Level 17, Putra World Trade Centre, Jl Tun Ismail); Kuala Lumpur International Airport (KLIA; ☎ 8776 5647/51; International Arrival Hall, Sepang); KL Train Station (Map pp74-5; ☎ 2274 6063; 🕑 9am-6pm); Plaza Putra (Map pp78-9; ☎ 2693 6664; Plaza Putra; Merdeka Square; 🕑 10am-6pm Mon-Sat); Putra World Trade Centre (Map pp74-5; ☎ 4041 1295; Level 2; Putra World Trade Centre, Jl Tun Ismail; 🕑 9am-6pm Mon-Sat)

Travel Agencies

For discount airline tickets, give these long-running and reliable student-travel agencies a go:

MSL Travel (Map pp74-5; ☎ 4042 4722; msl@po.jaring.my; 66 Jl Putra)

STA Travel (Map pp82-3; ☎ 2143 9800; stakul@po.jaring.my; Lot 506, 5th fl, Plaza Magnum, 128 Jl Pudu)

SIGHTS

Many of KL's premier sights can be visited along walking tours through the Colonial District (Map p84) and Chinatown (Map p85).

Masjid Jamek

Set in a grove of palm trees, the **Masjid Jamek** (Friday Mosque; Map pp78-9; 🕑 8.30am-12.30pm & 2.30-4pm, closed Fri 11am-2.30pm) is KL's most delightful mosque. Built in 1907, the mosque is a tranquil creation of onion domes and minarets of layered pink and cream bricks. Designed by the British architect AB Hubbock, who sought inspiration from Moghul mosques in India, it can be found at the confluence of the Klang and Gombak rivers – where KL's founders first set foot and where supplies for the tin mines were shipped. Dress appropriately.

Masjid Negara

Set in five hectares of landscaped gardens north of the old train station, **Masjid Negara** (National Mosque; Map pp78-9; 🕑 9am-6pm Sat-Thu, 2.45-6pm Fri) is one of Southeast Asia's largest mosques. A 73m-high minaret stands in the centre of a pool, and the main dome is an 18-pointed star – symbolising the 13 states of Malaysia and the five pillars of Islam. Forty-eight smaller domes cover the courtyard; their design is said to be inspired by the Grand Mosque in Mecca. Remember to remove your shoes and dress appropriately.

Sri Mahamariamman Temple

Located in Chinatown and fronted by a marvellous gate-tower is KL's principal

PAUL BEINSSEN

Celebrating **Thaipusam** (p109), Kuala Lumpur

RUSSELL MOUNTFORD

Tasty tidbits, **Chinatown** (p85)

ALAIN EVRARD

Posters advertising **movies** (p96), Kuala Lumpur

Chinese **temples** (p86), Kuala Lumpur

PAUL BEINSSEN

RICHARD I'A

Some of Kuala Lumpur's numerous **hawker venues** (p95)

Street festival (p87), Kuala Lumpur

RICHARD I'ANSON

MANFRED GOTTSCHALK

Malaysia's Supreme Court, **Sultan Abdul Samad building** (p84)

MANFRED GOTTS

Cake display, **Chinatown** (p85)

Hindu temple, the **Sri Mahamariamman Temple** (Map pp78-9 ; Jl Tun HS Lee; admission free), a large and ornate South-Indian Hindu shrine dating to 1873. Fresh and vibrantly colourful, the temple houses a large silver chariot that is taken out and paraded to the Batu Caves (p108) during the Thaipusam festival in January or February each year. Leave your shoes at the entrance.

Lake Gardens

As in many planned, colonial cities in Malaysia, the **Lake Gardens** (Map pp74–5) district lies at the edge of the central city area, around landscaped hills. Here the British elite built their fine houses, away from the hurly burly of downtown commerce and people of other races. The official residence of British government representative Frank Swettenham is now the Carcosa Seri Negara, Malaysia's most expensive hotel (see Sleeping, p91).

At the centre of the 92-hectare gardens is **Tasik Perdana** (Premier Lake). You can rent boats on weekends and watch t'ai chi practitioners in the early morning.

The gardens contain a host of attractions and you can take a leisurely, if sweaty, stroll around them. Alternatively hop on the **shuttle bus** (adult/child 50/20 sen; 9am-7pm Mon-Thu, Sat & Sun, 9am-noon & 3-7pm Fri), which does a loop of the gardens.

Out on Jl Cendarasari, **Taman Rama Rama** (Butterfly Park; adult/child RM10/3, extra RM1 to take photos; 9am-6pm) is both enjoyable and educational. Exit through an insect gallery where you can see the size of the spiders awaiting you in the Cameron Highlands.

Other sights are all clustered together. One of the highlights is the 'world's largest covered' **Bird Park** (2273 5423; adult/child RM22/15; 9am-7.30pm), an enormous walk-in aviary with 160 (mostly Southeast Asian) species of birds. It's worth getting to the park for feeding times (eg, eagles 2.30pm daily). Opposite is **Taman Orkid** (Orchid Garden; admission free; 9am-6pm) and the adjacent **Taman Bunga Raya** (Hibiscus Garden; admission free; 9am-6pm).

The nearby **Memorial Tun Abdul Razak** has memorabilia of Malaysia's second prime minister. To the north, the **Deer Park** (admission free) has a number of tame species, including the tiny *kancil*.

The massive **National Monument** overlooks the Lake Gardens from the northern side. Sculpted in bronze in 1966 by Felix de Weldon, the creator of the Iwo Jima monument in Washington DC, this memorial commemorates the Communist defeat in 1950.

On the southern side, the **National Planetarium** (10am-4pm Tue-Sun) has a small space-exhibition (RM1). It also puts on audiovisual science demonstrations in English (RM3) and IMAX films on a 20m-domed screen (RM6).

Intrakota bus No 21C from the Sultan Mohammed bus stop, or bus Nos 21B, 22, 48C or F3 from in front of Kota Raya shopping complex in Chinatown will take you to the gardens.

Museums

Museums are scattered around the city, though most visitors only bother taking in the National Museum and maybe the Islamic Arts Museum or the National Art Gallery – the rest are for those with special interests.

ISLAMIC ARTS MUSEUM

Just outside the Lake Gardens is the impressive **Islamic Arts Museum** (Muzium Kesenian Islam Malaysia; Map pp74-5; 2274 2020; Jl Lembah Perdana; adult/under-6 RM8/free; 10am-6pm Tue-Sun). The spacious, dazzlingly white building incorporates a dome and other Islamic architectural features. On the third level are scale models of the world's most famous mosques and a full-scale interior reproduction of a typical Muslim room of the Ottoman Empire. Upstairs are exhibits of religious calligraphy, textiles, armour, metalwork and carpets. The museum shop sells beautiful Islamic crafts of higher quality (and at higher prices) than elsewhere in KL.

NATIONAL ART GALLERY & THEATRE

The **National Art Gallery** (Balai Seni Lukis Negara; Map pp74-5; 4025 4990; 2 Jl Temerloh, off Jl Tun Razak; admission free; 10am-6pm) has a permanent collection of work by contemporary Malaysian artists, and rotating exhibitions of Asian and international art, including photography. The gallery also conducts symposiums and art classes for kids.

The Malaysian kite-shaped **National Theatre** (Istana Budaya) next door, with its Langkawi marble and tropical-hardwood doors, is a work of art in and of itself. There's a **costume gallery** (10am-6pm Mon-Sat) on the 2nd floor.

CHINATOWN, MERDEKA SQUARE & LITTLE INDIA

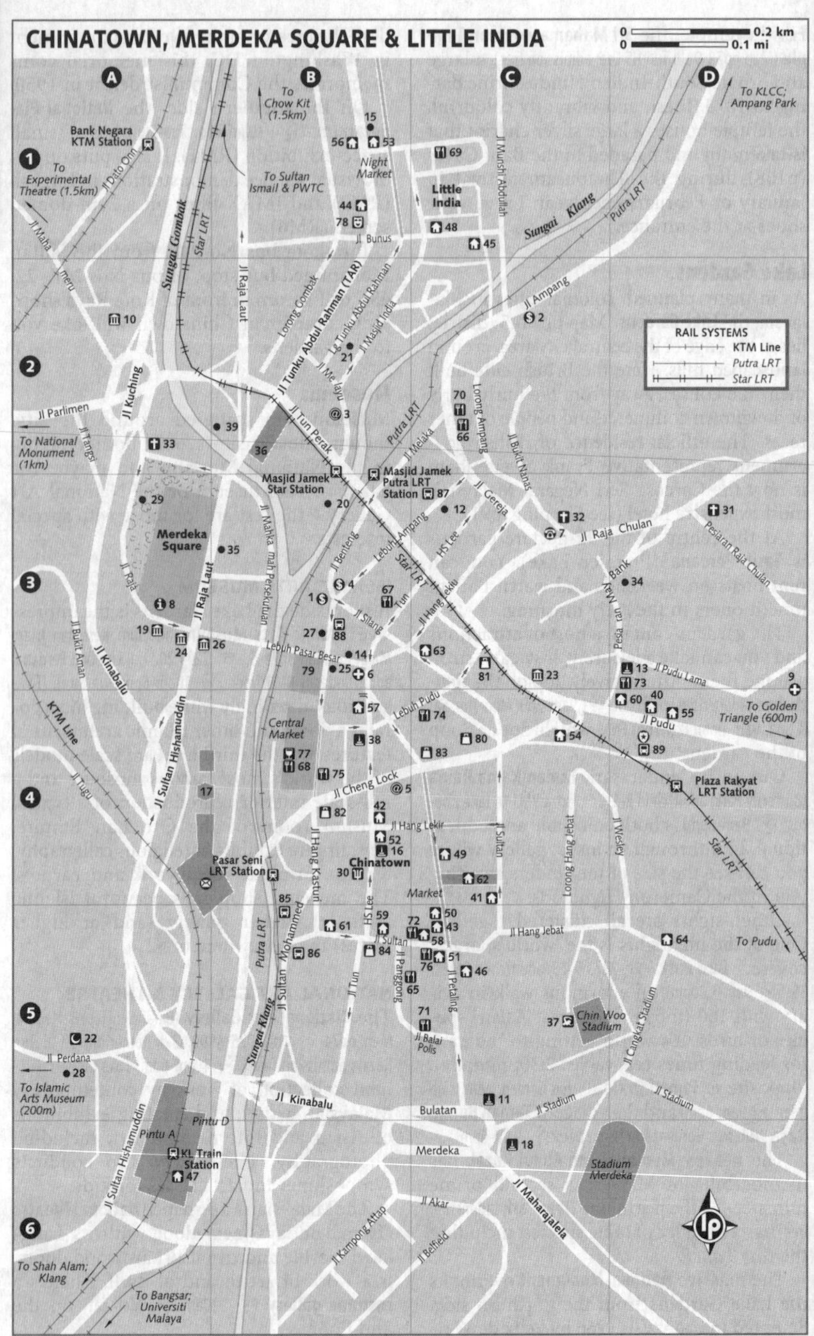

INFORMATION
Adamz Cyber Café.........................(see 79)
Bank Simpanan Building.................(see 57)
Citibank...1 B3
Citibank...2 C2
HMI Multimedia Network.....................3 B2
HSBC Bank.......................................4 B3
Master World Surfnet Café..................5 B4
Maybank..(see 23)
MS Ally Company...............................6 B3
Telekom Office..................................7 C3
Tourism Malaysia..............................8 A3
Tung Shin Hospital............................9 D4

SIGHTS & ACTIVITIES pp76-82
Bank Negara Money Museum..........10 A2
Chan See Shu Yuen Temple...........11 C5
Chettiar House................................12 C3
Court Hill Ganesh Temple...............13 D3
Federal Stores Building...................14 B3
Globe Silk Store..............................15 B1
Guandi Temple................................16 B4
Kompleks Dayabumi.........................17 A4
Koon Yam Temple............................18 C6
Kuala Lumpur Memorial Library......19 A3
Masjid Jamek..................................20 B3
Masjid Little India............................21 B2
Masjid Negara.................................22 A5
Maybank Numismatik Muzium........23 C3
National History Museum...............24 A3
OCBC Bldg......................................25 B3
Old City Hall....................................26 A3
Painted Shophouses........................27 B3
Pusat Islam Malaysia (Islamic Centre)...28 A5
Royal Selangor Club........................29 A3
Sri Mahamariamman Temple............30 B4
St Andrew's Presbyterian Church.....31 D3
St John's Cathedral..........................32 C3
St Mary's Cathedral..........................33 A2
Stock Exchange................................34 D3
Sultan Abdul Samad Bldg.................35 B3
Supreme Court..................................36 B2
Swimming Pool.................................37 C5
Sze Yah Temple................................38 B4
Telekom Muzium..............................(see 7)
Treehouse Fountain..........................39 B2

SLEEPING pp87-91
Anuja Backpackers Inn......................40 D4
Backpackers Travellers Inn...............41 C4
Backpackers Travellers Lodge...........42 B4
Chinatown Guest House...................43 C5
Coliseum Hotel..................................44 B1
Garden City Hotel.............................45 C1
Golden Plaza Hostel.........................46 C5
Heritage Station Hotel......................47 A6
Hotel Champagne.............................48 C1
Hotel China Town Inn.......................49 C4
Hotel Excel Inn.................................50 C5
Hotel Lok Ann...................................51 C5
Hotel Malaya.....................................52 B4
Hotel Noble.......................................53 B1
Impiana Hotel...................................54 C4
Katari Hotel......................................55 D4
Kowloon Hotel..................................56 B1
Le Village..57 B4
Lee Mun Guest House.......................58 C5
Mandarin Pacific Hotel......................59 B5
Pudu Hostel......................................60 D4
Starlight Hotel..................................61 B5
Swiss-Inn..62 C4
Travellers Moon Lodge......................63 C3
YWCA..64 D5

EATING pp91-5
Amata Vegetarian Restaurant............65 B5
Be My Friend Café...........................(see 79)
Bilal Restoran....................................66 C2
Charlies Restaurant.........................(see 47)
Coliseum Café.................................(see 44)
Fatt Yan Vegetarian Restaurant.........67 B3
Ginger..68 B4
Govinda's Vegetarian Restaurant.......69 C1
Kapitan's Club...................................70 C2
Old China Cafe...................................71 C5
Restoran Kam Lun Tai........................72 C5
Restoran Sri Ganesa...........................73 D3
Restoran Wilayah Baru.......................74 C4
Restoran Yusoof.................................75 B4
West Lake Restoran...........................76 C5

DRINKING p96
Bull's Head..77 B4
Liquid...(see 79)
Reggae Bar.......................................(see 42)

ENTERTAINMENT pp96-7
Actors Studio.....................................(see 8)
Coliseum Cinema...............................78 B1
Disco...(see 79)

SHOPPING pp97-9
Central Market Annexe......................79 B3
Kota Raya Shopping Complex.............80 C4
Metrojaya Department Store...............81 C3
Peter Hoe Evolution...........................82 B4
Plaza Putra...(see 8)
S&M Shopping Arcade........................83 C4
UDA Ocean Plaza...............................84 B5

TRANSPORT pp99-104
Jalan Sultan Mohammed Bus Stop......85 B5
Klang Bus Station...............................86 B5
Lebuh Ampang Bus Stop....................87 C3
Medan Pasar Bus Stop........................88 B3
Puduraya Bus Station.........................89 D4

Both the National Art Gallery and National Theatre are outside the Lake Titiwangsa Gardens, north of the city centre. Take any Len Seng-operated bus from Lebuh Ampang or from along Jl Raja Laut and get off at the hospital stop.

NATIONAL MUSEUM

South of Tasik Perdana, at the edge of the Lake Gardens, the **National Museum** (Muzium Negara; Map pp74-5; ☎ 2282 6255; Jl Damansara; adult/under-12 RM2/free; 🕑 9am-6pm) was built on the site of the old Selangor Museum, which was destroyed during WWII. There are colourful displays on Malaysia's history, economy, arts, crafts (kites, shadow play, weaving) and explanations of aspects of Malay culture, including circumcision. At the rear are old Malaysian motor vehicles including a fire engine and the Rolls Royce used by Malaysia's first prime minister.

OTHER MUSEUMS

Maybank Numismatic Museum (Map pp78-9; Maybank Bldg, 100 Jl Tun Perak; admission free; 🕑 10am-6pm) Under renovation at the time of writing, this museum displays a collection of Malay coinage and notes.

Bank Negara Money Museum (Map pp78-9; ☎ 2690 7461; Central Bank of Malaysia; Jl Dató Onn; admission free; 🕑 9am-4.30pm Mon-Fri, 9am-noon Sat) Has displays along the money theme.

Telekom Museum (Map pp78-9; ☎ 2031 9966; Jl Gereja; admission free; 🕑 9am-5pm Tue-Sun). This little place expounds the history of telecommunications in Malaysia from its earliest days to the IT era.

Royal Malaysian Police Museum (Map pp74-5; ☎ 2272 5689; 5 Jl Perdana; admission free; 🕑 10am-6pm Tue-Sun) In the Lake Gardens, this displays a mix of lethal weapons and anti-communist memorabilia.

The **Malaysian Armed Forces Museum** (☎ 2692 1333; Jl Padang Tembak; admission free; 🕑 10am-4pm Sat-Thu) a few kilometres northeast of the city, displays weapons, paintings, uniforms and other military paraphernalia; cannons and tanks rest outside. In the same area, the **Air Force Museum** (Jl Padang Tembak; admission free; 🕑 8am-4pm Mon-Thu, 8am-5pm Sat, 10am-5pm Sun) displays a few light planes.

Jl Tunku Abdul Rahman (Jl TAR)

Originally called Batu Road, Jl TAR was once a dusty track leading north out of the city to the caves and tin mines at Batu village (see

Batu Caves, p108, in the Selangor chapter). The modern Jl TAR leads through a historic section of the city, passing Little India.

Named for its South Indian-style mosque, the main street of **Little India** is Jl Masjid India, which is crammed with Indian sari shops and halal restaurants. Little India has all the feel of a Middle Eastern bazaar, especially during the Saturday *pasar malam* (night market).

Further north along Jl TAR many of the buildings are modern, but one surviving colonial relic is the **Coliseum Hotel** (see Sleeping, p88). Enter through the saloon doors to the bar, where you can relax and sip your drink in a planter's chair where Somerset Maugham once sat. The Coliseum's wealthy owner began his business empire here in 1921 and the hotel hasn't changed in decades – which is said to be good luck in the Chinese tradition. The Coliseum Cinema next door screens the latest Bollywood extravaganzas.

Jl TAR is good for shopping during the day, and you can browse in the long-running **Globe Silk Store** (185 Jl TAR) for cheap clothes and batik.

Further north is Chow Kit, once (and arguably still) KL's famed red-light district. Though attempts have been made to clean the area out, it's still fairly seedy, especially at night. The **Chow Kit Market** has a gaggle of roadside vendors, and all manner of goods are on sale (see Shopping, p98). The area around the City Villa Hotel is crammed with hawker stalls, good for satay and *nasi lemak* (rice boiled in coconut milk, served with accompaniments such as peanuts, fried anchovies and a curry dish).

Golden Triangle

A forest of high-rises, the Golden Triangle is central KL's business, shopping and entertainment district. Encompassing an area of several square kilometres, it extends north from its base along Jl Imbi to its apex at the landmark **Petronas Towers** (see 'The Petronas Towers' boxed text). These graceful twin skyscrapers surge up from the spacious landscaped gardens of the Kuala Lumpur City Centre (KLCC).

Most of KL's luxury hotels and several nightspots are spaced out along Jl Sultan Ismail, where it intersects with Jl Bukit Bintang, with the biggest concentration of shopping malls, mid-range hotels and eating establishments in Kuala Lumpur. The trendy Jl Changkat Bukit Bintang has emerged as a hotspot of cosmopolitan bars and restaurants.

At the western edge of the Golden Triangle soars the 421m **Menara Kuala Lumpur** (KL Tower) the fourth-highest telecommunications tower in the world. Visitors can pass through a rigorous security check and ride the lift to the **viewing deck** (☎ 2020 5448; Jl Punchak; adult/child incl audio tour & binoculars RM15/9; ⏰ 9am-10pm, last tickets 9.30pm), for a superb panorama of the city from a dizzy altitude of 276m (the Petronas Towers Skybridge is a mere 146m). You can't just scoot up a level to the Seri Angkasa revolving restaurant (see 'The Author's Choice' boxed text, p92) for a swift drink, as meals carry a minimum charge.

Off Jl Raja Chulan, the high-rise **Stock Exchange** (Map pp74–5) is a curious amalgam of postmodern and neoclassical styles. Downhill towards Jl Pudu is the tiny, busy **Court Hill Ganesh Temple** (Map pp74–5).

At the northern edge of the Golden Triangle, **Jl Ampang** was built up by early tin millionaires and is lined with impressive mansions. Many of these stately buildings have become embassies or consulates, so the street is nicknamed Embassy Row.

Thean Hou Temple

Dedicated to Thean Hou (Queen of Heaven), the modern and bustling **Thean Hou Temple** (☎ 2274 7088; Jl Klang Lama; admission free; ⏰ 9am-6pm) was completed in 1987. Thean Hou, variously spelt Tian Hou or Tin Hau and also called Mazu or Niangniang, is worshipped largely in coastal areas of China and is the protector of those who make their living from the sea. She is represented in the central statue in the main hall of this huge temple, with Guanyin (the Buddhist Goddess of Mercy) on her right and Shuiwei Shengniang (the Goddess of the Waterfront) to her left. Statues of Milefo (the laughing Buddha), Weituo and Guandi further contribute to this Taoist/Buddhist hodgepodge. The walls of the main hall are covered in thousands of tiles depicting representations of Guanyin and also rows of tiles with Chinese names – presumably those who dedicated money to the temple. As the temple is on a hill, there are long views from the upper decks and binoculars are available for use. Beneath

THE PETRONAS TOWERS

Rising some 451.9m above the flat plain of Kuala Lumpur, the **Petronas Towers** (Map pp74-5; www.petronas.com.my/petronas) – the world's tallest building – rapidly became a symbol of the new Malaysia. Completed in 1998 at a cost of $US1.9 billion, the 88-storey twin towers are an arresting sight. Unique in design, the twin towers' floor plan is based on an eight-sided star that echoes the arabesque patterns of Islamic art. Islamic influences are also evident in each tower's five tiers – representing the five pillars of Islam – and in the 63m masts that crown them, calling to mind the minarets of a mosque and the Star of Islam.

It is hardly surprising that other high-rise projects are on the drawing board to top the towers. New York's World Trade Center replacement may surge higher (depending on the final choice), the stop-start construction on the World Finance Building in Shanghai may one day make the record books, while in South Korea, the 110-storey International Business Centre is being earmarked for Seoul.

You can take the lift to the 41st-floor **Skybridge** (admission free; 10am-12.45pm & 3-4.45pm Tue-Sun) connecting the two towers, although you will only be a modest 146m above ground – less than a third of the building's total height. Arrive early, as queues are long at other times and tickets are issued for specific time slots (only 800 tickets are issued daily); leaving it late means less control over what time slot you get. Weekends and public holidays are packed.

the temple on the lower floors are rows of restaurants and shops. To reach the temple, 3km south of the centre of town, either take a taxi or bus No 27 or 52 from Klang bus station and then walk up the hill.

International Buddhist Pagoda

In the Brickfields area south of KL train station, the shrine at the modern **International Buddhist Pagoda** (Map p74–5) was built in the 1800s by Sinhalese Buddhists from Sri Lanka. There's a *bodhi* (enlightenment) tree on the grounds and daily services are held at 7.30pm.

The International Buddhist Pagoda is a centre for Buddhist teaching and meditation in KL (see Courses, p86). Bus No 12 from Klang bus station will take you there.

Markets

KL's streets are the scene of busy *pasar malam*, with hawker food stalls and vendors selling souvenirs and household goods.

In Kampung Bahru, northeast of the city centre, Jl Raja Muda comes alive on Saturday night for the **Pasar Minggu** (Sunday Market), so-called because it continues until Sunday morning. It's mainly a food and produce market.

Little India's **Saturday-night market**, along Lorong TAR, is another of the city's best.

Open day and night, **Jl Petaling** in Chinatown is a bustling street-market where you can have a Chinese alfresco meal or snack, bargain for clothes, or pick up a kilogram of lychees or mangoes.

North of the city centre, **Chow Kit Market** is incredibly busy from early morning until late at night. During the day vendors sell all manner of bits and pieces; after 6pm the food stalls take over.

The predominantly Chinese-run **Pudu Market**, 3km southeast of the city centre, is the largest wet (produce) market in KL. It's definitely a wet market – wear shoes rather than thongs or sandals. Here you can get every imaginable type of fruit, vegetable, fish and meat – everything from the foot of a chicken slaughtered and butchered on the spot, to a stingray fillet or a pig's penis. Pudu Market is five minutes' walk from Pudu Star LRT station; go north along Jl Pudu, right onto Jl Pasar, then right down Jl Pasar Baharu.

ACTIVITIES

Bowling

Federal Hotel (Map pp82-3; 35 Jl Bukit Bintang)
Mid Valley Megamall Bowling Alley (Mid Valley Megamall; off Jl Bangsar) State-of-the-art alley.
Pekeliling Bowl (Map pp74-5; Yow Chuan Plaza; on Jl Tun Razak)

Golf

There is no shortage of golf courses around Kuala Lumpur.

Kuala Lumpur Golf & Country Club (☎ 2093 1111; off Jl Bukit Kiara; green fees for non-members from RM120) A 32-hole course.

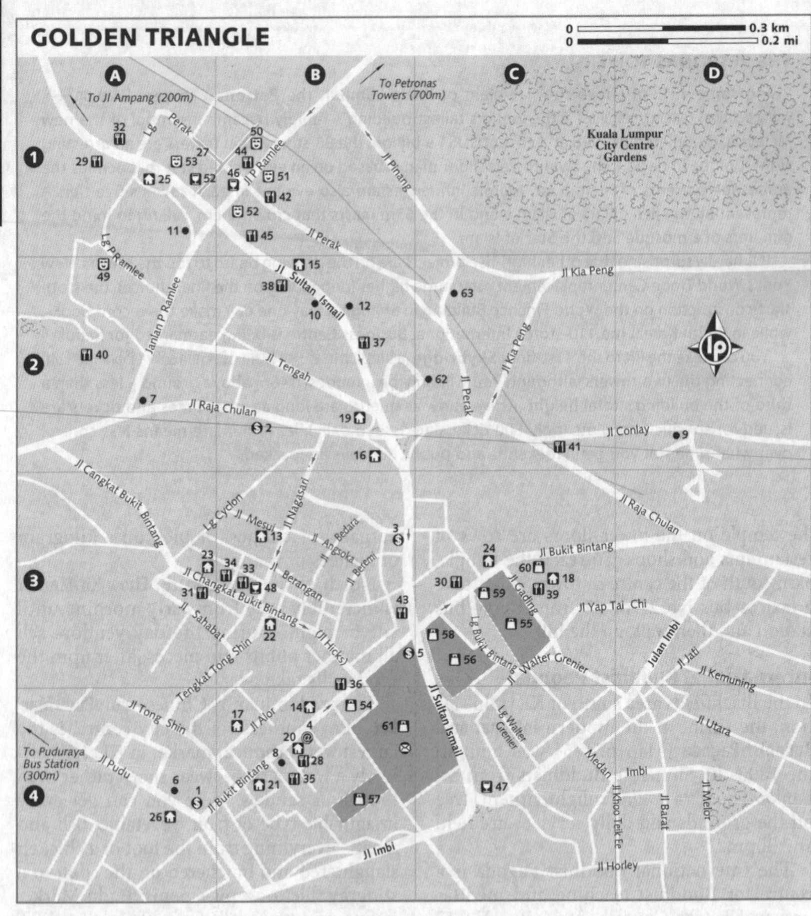

Royal Selangor Golf Club (☎ 9284 8433; off Jl Tun Razak; green fees RM250, incl caddy) Non-members can play at weekends.

Saujana Golf & Country Club (☎ 7846 1466; Shah Alam; green fees from RM170) Near the old Subang airport; a popular course.

Snooker

Snooker and Billiards room (2nd fl, Wisma Lai Choon, 10 Jl Pudu) Opposite Puduraya bus station, has seven snooker tables.

Swimming & Water Sports

Bangsar Sports Complex (☎ 2284 6065; 3 Jl Terasek Tiga; 🕑 8am-4.15pm Mon-Fri, 8am-1pm Sat) A swim costs RM1.50 per 2½ hours. Also has tennis courts, squash and badminton facilities.

Chin Woo Stadium (Map pp78-9; off Jl Hang Jebat)

National Sports Council Complex (☎ 9058 1390; Jl Duta)

For water sports, see Mines Wonderland, Desa Waterpark and Sunway Lagoon Waterpark (p86).

Tennis

Besides top-end hotels, you can play tennis at other courts:

Bangsar Sports Complex See Swimming & Water Sports earlier.

National Sports Council Complex (☎ 9058 1390; Jl Duta)

YMCA (Map pp74-5; ☎ 2274 1768; 95 Jl Padang Belia) Four courts.

INFORMATION	
@Bintang Internet Centre	(see 30)
Alliance Bank ATM	1 A4
Bank of America	2 B2
HSBC Bank	3 B3
Internet Café	4 B4
Maybank	5 B3
MPH Bookstores	(see 54)
Popular	(see 61)
STA Travel	6 A4
Times	7 A2
SIGHTS & ACTIVITIES	**pp76-82**
Federal Hotel	8 B4
Kompleks Budaya Kraf	9 D2
Malaysia Airlines	10 B2
Menara Kuala Lumpur (KL Tower)	(see 40)
Menara UBN	11 A1
Pernas International Building	12 B2
SLEEPING	**pp87-91**
AttapSana	13 B3
Bintang Warisan Hotel	14 B4
Hotel Equatorial	15 B2
Hotel Istana	16 B2
Hotel Nova	17 B4
JW Marriott	18 C3
Lodge Hotel	19 B2
Malaysia Hotel	20 B4
Novotel Century Kuala Lumpur	21 B4
Park Inn International	22 B3
Pondok Lodge	23 A3
Regent	24 C3
Shangri-La Hotel	25 A1
Swiss-Garden Hotel	26 A4
EATING	**pp91-5**
Afternoon Hawker-Food Stalls	27 A1
Bangkok Jam Thai Restaurant & Bar	28 B4
Beijing Wok	(see 57)
Bierkeller	29 A1
Dontaku Restoran Jepun	30 C3
Frangipani Restaurant Bar	31 A3
Hard Rock Cafe	32 A1
Lafite	(see 25)
Le Bernardin French Brasserie	33 B3
Moghul House	34 B3
Nyonya Wok	(see 54)
Outback Steakhouse	35 B4
Rasa Utara	(see 54)
Restoran Best Thai Cuisine	36 B3
Restoran Koryo Won	37 B2
Scalini's	38 B2
Sentidos Tapas	39 C3
Seri Angkasa	40 A2
Seri Melayu	41 C2
Shang Palace	(see 25)
Shook!	(see 18)
Sri Perak Hawker Centre	42 B1
Sushi King	43 B3
Talk	44 B1
TGI Friday's	45 B1
Toku Toku	(see 43)
DRINKING	**p96**
Beach Club Café	46 B1
Delaney's	47 C4
Flo	(see 15)
Green Man	48 B3
Havana Club	(see 18)
Sangria	(see 52)
ENTERTAINMENT	**pp96-7**
Atmosphere	(see 53)
Backroom	49 A2
Bar Ibiza	50 B1
Bliss	(see 53)
Modesto's	51 B1
No Black Tie	(see 13)
Nouvo	52 B1
TwelveSI	53 A1
SHOPPING	**pp97-9**
BB Plaza	54 B4
Galleriwan	(see 44)
Isetan Department Store	(see 56)
KL Plaza	55 C3
Lot 10 Shopping Complex	56 C3
Low Yat Plaza	57 B4
Manchester United Shop	58 C3
Planet Hollywood	59 C3
Star Hill Shopping Centre	60 C3
Sungei Wang Plaza	61 B4
Tower Records	(see 55)
TRANSPORT	**pp99-104**
Avis	62 C2
Hawk	63 C2
Hertz	(see 37)
Lufthansa	(see 12)
Orix	(see 8)
Royal Brunei Airlines	(see 11)

WALKING TOURS

With six-lane roads and fly-overs dividing KL up into sections unconnected by footpaths, it's no pedestrian's paradise.

However, the city is surprisingly compact and all the main areas of interest are close together. Walking from Little India and Jl TAR down through Merdeka Square to Chinatown takes only 20 to 30 minutes – if you know where to find the pedestrian crossings, that is. The walking tours in this section will take you to all the major sights (and a few off-beat places) in KL's old colonial district around Merdeka Square and Chinatown.

KL has some designated Heritage Trails covering Merdeka Square, Market Square, Chinatown and Jl TAR. These do-it-yourself walking tours focus on prewar architecture and early city history, pointing out odd buildings and temples you might otherwise overlook. Tourism Malaysia information centres stock the trail brochures, which are also available directly from **Badan Warisan Malaysia** (Heritage of Malaysia Trust; ☎ 2144 9273; www.badanwarisan.org.my; 2 Jl Stonor; ⌚ 10am-5pm Mon-Fri, 11am-4pm Sat).

Colonial District Walk

This walking tour begins at KL's magnificent **train station (1)**. Built in 1911, this delightful example of colonial whimsy designed by British architect AB Hubbock is a Moorish fantasy of spires, minarets, towers, cupolas and arches. It couldn't look any better if it had been built as a set for some Hollywood extravaganza. You will also find the grand **Heritage Station Hotel** (**2**; p90) here.

For the best views of the train station, take the pedestrian tunnel to the right of the station's west Pintu (Exit) A, underneath Jl Sultan Hishamuddin and stand in front of the superb **Malayan Railway Administration Building (3)**.

Walk north and turn the corner onto Jl Perdana. A short distance west you'll find the **Pusat Islam Malaysia (4)** (Islamic Centre) and, on the other side of the street, the **Masjid Negara** (**5**; p76).

Backtrack to the train station and take Pintu D on the eastern side. Then turn left and walk alongside the fenced-in train platforms underneath a covered footpath, until you arrive at the Pejabat Pos Besar (Main Post Office). Take the car ramp heading upward and skirt the eastern side of the post office until you find yourself at the small **Petronas Fountain (6)**, which features a globe highlighting all the world's petroleum-producing countries (which include Malaysia, of course).

Immediately to your right is the distinctive, multiple-sided **Kompleks Dayabumi (7)**. Note the Islamic arches and recurring motifs. Walk to the left of the tower and the building behind it (as you turn the corner, look northeast and you'll get a view of the KL Tower and the Petronas Towers framed by palm fronds), then north down the steps, alongside the **Old City Hall (8)** to your left. Go through the arched gate and turn left along Lebuh Pasar Besar.

Start/Finish: KL train station/Masjid Jamek
Distance: 2.2km
Duration: 1.5 hours

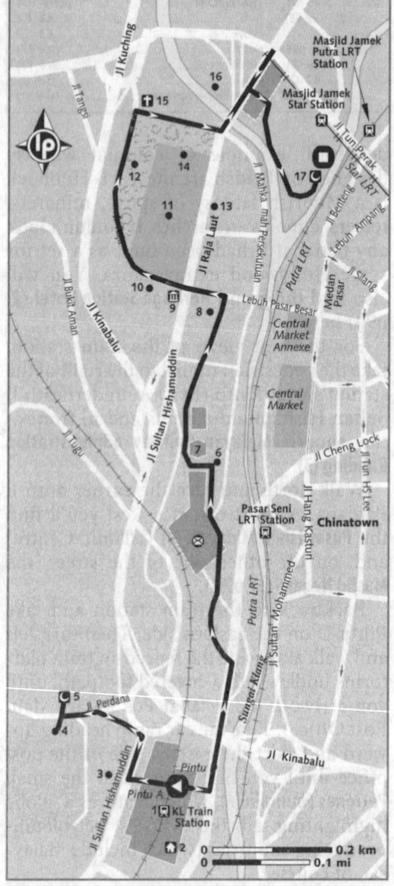

Walk west across Jl Sultan Hishamuddin to the **National History Museum (9**; ☎ 2694 4590; admission free; 9am-6pm), which originally housed KL's first bank, then a Japanese telecommunications base during WWII, and then one of the early administration offices after independence. The museum itself has rather scant exhibits. Adjacent is the **Kuala Lumpur Memorial Library (10)**.

Cross Jl Raja to the southern side of **Merdeka Square (11)**, once at the heart of colonial KL, and part of the open field formerly known as the Padang. It was here that Malaysia's British administrators engaged in that curious English rite known as cricket. It's no coincidence that in 1957 Malaysia's independence was proclaimed here, and dignitaries still gather on National Day to watch the parades (see Festivals & Events, p87).

From the flagpole, walk counter-clockwise around the perimeter of the square. The **Royal Selangor Club (12)**, a social centre for KL's high society in the tin-boom days of the 1890s, is across the field to your left. It's still a gathering place for the KL elite.

East of the square across Jl Raja Laut you can see the **Sultan Abdul Samad Building (13)**. Its blend of Victorian and Moorish architecture is typical of the colonial buildings that give the city much of its character. Designed by AC Norman (an associate of AB Hubbard, designer of the KL train station) and built between 1894 and 1897, it was once the Secretariat Building for the British administration and is now Malaysia's Supreme Court.

Continue walking north towards the **memorial arches (14)** inscribed with 'Dataran Merdeka' (Merdeka Square). Further north be careful crossing over Jl Raja from the square to another of AC Norman's creations, **St Mary's Cathedral (15)**, dating from 1894 and housing a fine pipe-organ.

As there are no crossings here, you'll have to head north up Jl Raja Laut past the spectacularly ugly **treehouse fountain (16)**. Make a U-turn via the lengthy pedestrian crossings and then head back south along the eastern side of Jl Raja Laut. You can cut through the Supreme Court grounds to get to the quiet riverside. Bear left and walk alongside the river until you arrive at the entrance to the landmark **Masjid Jamek** (**17**; p76).

Chinatown Walk

South of Masjid Jamek are the teeming streets of KL's Chinatown. This crowded, colourful area is the usual melange of Chinese signs and shops, activity and noise, and is bounded on two sides by Jl Hang Kasturi and Jl Sultan. The central section of **Jl Petaling** is closed to traffic and is a frantically busy market, at its most vivid at night when brightly lit.

All the activity may distract you from the area's historic Chinese shophouses. Local conservation groups are making efforts to protect these buildings from city development and to restore them to their former glory.

Starting from **Masjid Jamek** (1; p76), cross over to the northern side of Jl Tun Perak and walk one block east to Lebuh Ampang. A short detour up this narrow street reveals a South-Indian Chettiar community, full of moneychangers and street vendors selling Indian sweets and flower garlands. Note the striking **old shophouses (2)** at Nos 16 to 18 and Nos 24 to 30, and the ceramic peacock-tiles on the **Chettiar House (3)** at No 85.

Backtrack across Jl Tun Perak and follow the path along Jl Benteng until the street splits at the clock tower. This is **Medan Pasar** (Market Square), the site of the city's original market and gambling sheds set up for early tin miners. The row of **painted shophouses (4)** at Nos 2 to 8 on your right was all designed by the same Chinese architect in 1906.

Head south to where Medan Pasar meets Lebuh Pasar Besar. On the southeastern corner is the **OCBC Building (5)**, an imposing Art Deco structure built in 1938 for the Overseas Chinese Banking Company.

Turn east along this street, passing the whimsical, pink and green old **Federal Stores Building (6)**, dating from 1905 and taking up an entire side of the block on your left. Opposite is the rose-pink and white **MS Ally Company (7)**, one of KL's longest-running and most venerable pharmacies.

Turn south at the next block onto Jl Tun HS Lee. Twenty metres down on your right is the orange and green **Bank Simpanan Building (8)**, bearing the date 1914. It was originally a printing press and the upstairs is now home to the Backpackers Travellers Lodge (p87).

At the end of this block, cross Lebuh Pudu, turn right and, after 25m, duck left into an

Start/Finish: Masjid Jamek/Jl Petaling
Distance: 1.6km
Duration: 1.5 hours

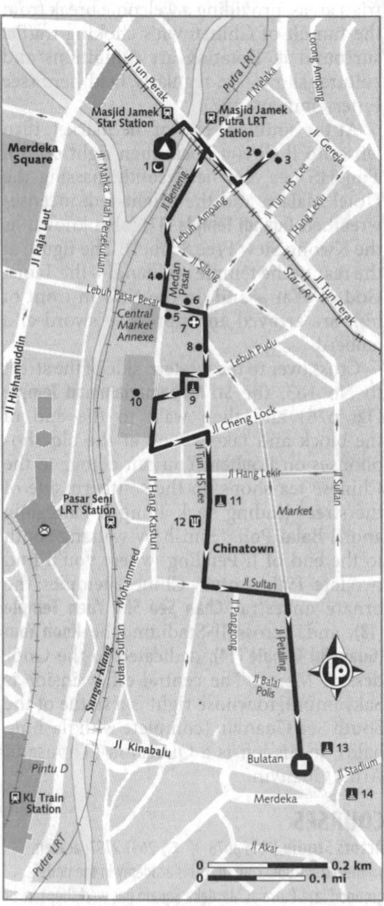

alleyway, which leads to the small Taoist **Sze Yah Temple (9)**. The construction of this fascinating Taoist temple was organised by 'Kapitan China' Yap Ah Loy himself in 1864 and to the left of the altar is a statue of his likeness. You may see worshippers crawling in homage and penitence under the altar in front of the main shrine. Outside the temple are two gilded sedan chairs.

Exit the way you came in, cross the street and walk through the alley opposite the enormous **Central Market (10)**. Previously the city's produce market, the Central Market is an Art Deco building that was saved by preservationists and refurbished as a centre for handicraft, antique and art sales. Pedestrian areas, providing a welcome break from the tumult of Chinatown's choking traffic, surround it. Rotating art exhibitions and cultural shows are regularly held here (see Entertainment, p97).

At the southern end of the market, turn left onto Jl Cheng Lock, then right onto Jl Tun HS Lee and head south, passing the Hotel Malaya and the bright-red, incense-wreathed **Guandi Temple (11)** (also known as the Kwong Siew Free School). The figure at the rear of the temple is Guandi – the Taoist God of War – and on the altar in front of him are arrayed an impressive sword and halberd.

Cross over to the western side of the street to No 163, the **Sri Mahamariamman Temple** (**12**; p76) and then walk to the end of the block and take a look at the old shophouses on **Jl Sultan**. You can detour to the Chinese tea shops on the southern side of the street leading back along Jl Panggong and Jl Balai Polis. Finish by walking south to the end of Jl Petaling, where you'll find two late-19th-century Chinese temples: the ornate ancestral **Chan See Shu Yuen Temple (13)**, and, across Jl Stadium, the **Koon Yam (Guanyin) Temple (14)**, dedicated to the Goddess of Mercy. The central effigy inside is Sakyamuni, to whose right is a statue of the South Sea Guanyin (complete with flashing halo); to his left is a Qianshou (Thousand Arm) Guanyin.

COURSES

Actors Studio (Map pp78-9; ☎ 2697 2797; academy@theactorsstudio.com.my) This academy in the underground Plaza Putra at Merdeka Square has workshops in everything from modern choreography and classical Indian dance to Chinese orchestral music.

International Buddhist Pagoda (Map pp74-5; ☎ 2274 1141; 123 Jl Berhala) This Brickfields landmark has a variety of courses and events at its Buddhist School, including Buddhism for Beginners (RM40). Meditation sessions are held at 8pm on Monday and Thursday, and chanting classes at 7.30pm on Tuesday and Friday. Dharma talks are given at 8pm on Friday.

Kompleks Budaya Kraf (Map pp82-3; ☎ 2162 7533; Jl Conlay) You can try your hand at batik or sign up for a basic batik course.

National Silat Federation (Pesaka; ☎ 4024 7240) Ask for a recommended class or course in the ancient Malaysian martial art of *silat*.

Temple of Fine Arts (Map pp74-5; ☎ 2274 3709; 114 Jl Berhala) Classes are offered in classical Indian dance and music.

YMCA (Map pp74-5; ☎ 2274 1439) This Brickfields hostel and community centre offers a variety of short- and long-term language classes in Bahasa Malaysia, Hindi, Thai, Mandarin/Cantonese, and Japanese, as well as courses in martial arts and even ballroom dancing.

KUALA LUMPUR FOR CHILDREN

Children will love the **Lake Gardens**, especially the Bird Park, Butterfly Park, Deer Park and Planetarium. The **Skybridge** at the Petronas Towers is an eye-opener or take them around **Petrosains** (Map pp74-5; ☎ 2331 8787; www.petrosains.com.my; Level 4, Suria KLCC, Petronas Towers; ⏰ 9.30am-4pm Tue-Thu, 1.30-4pm Fri, 9.30am-5pm Sat, Sun & holidays), an interactive science discovery centre for kiddies.

For toy shopping, take your mites to **Suria KLCC**: Twinkles on the second floor has a huge range of soft toys, cars and games; Toycity at Shop 329 has a colourful collection of models and cars. Stalls at the **Central Market** sell Malaysian kites – perhaps an ideal toy and souvenir.

South of KL (10km), **Desa Waterpark** (☎ 7118 8338; adult/child RM17/10; noon-8pm Mon-Fri, 10am-8pm Sat, Sun & holidays), has loads of fun rides and slides and a bubble pool. Also see the Selangor chapter for details on the **Sunway Lagoon Waterpark** (p114; ☎ 5635 6000).

Night-time family frolics can be had at **Mines Wonderland** (☎ 8942 5010; Jl Sungai Besi; adult/child RM25/17; 6-11pm Mon-Fri, 5pm-midnight Sat & Sun), a vast playground of theme rides, musical fountains and amusement facilities (take a KTM Komuter train to the Serdang station, from where you can walk).

TOURS

Ecstasy Travel (☎ 4042 5688; fax 4041 9864; 3rd fl, Jl 14/48A, Sentul Raya, off Jl Sentul), organises half-day city tours that briefly touch on the Lake Gardens, Merdeka Square, the National Museum and National Palace. Half-day stop-and-shop 'country tours' visit a pewter factory, insect farm, batik factory and a *kampung* (village) house, finishing at the Batu Caves (see the Selangor chapter, p108). Both tours run twice daily and cost RM25 (excluding minimal entry fees), but neither is very in-depth.

FESTIVALS & EVENTS

The capital is a good venue for Malaysia's major holidays and festivals, including Chinese New Year (January–February) and Deepavali (October–November). See p541 for more information.

City Day (1 February) KL commemorates becoming a federal territory. Celebrations take place at Tasik Perdana and Lake Titiwangsa gardens in the north of the city.

Flora Fest (July) KL goes flower-crazy with exhibitions and the international Floral Parade.

National Day (31 August) At midnight revellers crowd Merdeka Square to celebrate the anniversary of Malaysia's independence in 1957. There are parades and festivities the next morning, usually at Commonwealth Stadium, but check with the tourist information office.

Malaysia Fest (Colors of Malaysia; September) Two weeks of celebration, with exhibits of traditional arts and special cultural performances around town.

Shopping Carnival (October) A chance to find bargains at selected KL shopping centres during this annual sale.

SLEEPING

KL has a wide range of budget, mid-range and top-end accommodation options, offering good value for money. See under Accommodation (p531) in the Directory chapter for facilities you should expect in the various price ranges.

Budget Chinatown accommodation largely consists of crumbling hotels, cookie-cutter guesthouses and backpacker hostels, many simply functional, others with genuine charm. Competition generally keeps prices down and you can negotiate, but many establishments just offer a bed in a windowless box or (in the case of dorms) too many beds in a windowless box, partitioned from another box by way of thin plywood. Most guesthouses offer laundry facilities, have a noticeboard and, occasionally, Internet access. The better places in Chinatown tend to fill up quickly. If arriving late at night or early in the morning, call ahead to the smaller guesthouses before just turning up and expecting someone to let you in at 4am. North of Chinatown, colourful Little India and, further north along Jl TAR, the seedier Chow Kit area have some low-priced accommodation.

Mid-range hotels cluster in the Golden Triangle district. East of Puduraya bus station you'll also find much of KL's shopping and nightlife. Busy Jl Bukit Bintang, east of the city centre and in the Golden Triangle, is a good hunting ground for mid-range hotels; also try in Little India, along Jl TAR and the Chow Kit area.

Kuala Lumpur has a profusion of luxury hotels catering primarily to business travellers, and boasting some of the best restaurants and bars in town. Many offer promotional discounts (up to 50%) off regular room rates quoted here (which include the 5% tax and 10% service charge applied in the more expensive places). Top-end hotels are largely concentrated in the Golden Triangle and further north at KLCC.

Budget

CHINATOWN **Map pp78–9**

Le Village (☎ 2026 6737; hasnuljamil.@hotmail.com; 99A Jl Tun HS Lee; dm/s/d RM15/20/30) Set in a gorgeous old colonial building (built 1914) richly decorated with original features and ethnic chic (rattan furniture, woven rugs, coloured blinds), Le Village is a comfortable and easy-going establishment. Still finding its feet (check if smoke alarms have arrived), it's very friendly and ideal for the laid-back crowd. Clean toilet/shower area, cooking facilities and free coffee.

Backpackers Travellers Lodge (☎ 2031 0889; 1st fl, 158 Jl Tun HS Lee; dm/d with fan RM10/22, d with air-con & shower RM60; ❄ 💻) The cheapest rooms at this popular establishment are windowless doubles; doubles with shower are large, but pricey for what you get. There's a TV lounge and Internet access (not cheap).

Backpackers Travellers Inn (☎ 2078 2473; 60 Jl Sultan; dm RM10, d with fan/air-con RM25/50; ❄) This is a relatively clean, popular and well-run place, albeit cramped with windowless rooms. It has an excellent location, a great rooftop bar, nightly movies, TV and cooking facilities.

Lee Mun Guest House (☎ 2078 0639; 5th fl, 109 Jl Petaling; dm/s/d RM9/20/25, d with air-con RM35; ❄) Right in the heart of Chinatown, this no-frills hotel is a fun, cheap place although the cardboard partition walls compromise privacy. There's an energetic manager, busy and efficient staff, and a clean communal toilet and shower area. The entrance is on Jl Sultan.

Also recommended:

YWCA (☎ 2078 3225; 12 Jl Hang Jebat; s/d RM30/50) Very quiet establishment tucked away east of Chinatown, with plain but acceptable rooms (with fan and bathroom) for women or married couples.

THE AUTHOR'S CHOICE *Damian Harper*

Budget

Pudu Hostel (Map pp78-9; ☎ 2078 9600; puduhostel@hotmail.com; 3rd fl, Wisma Lai Choon, 10 Jl Pudu; 24hr; dm/s/d RM12/30/40;) The Pudu has it all – fine location opposite Puduraya bus station; well-equipped lobby/lounge area featuring cold Tiger beer (RM6), pool table (RM3 per game), ESPN-broadcast football, satellite TV, VCD library; clean dorm rooms with lockers and hygienic shower rooms. The noticeboard is full of travel tips and advice, and the whole enterprise is geared towards independent travellers (with daily shuttle buses to Taman Negara National Park). There's an Internet café on the first floor with fast connections (RM4 per hour; if you stay at the hostel, it's RM3 per hour); on the second floor there's a billiard hall, and breakfast is included.

Top End

Shangri-La Hotel (Map pp82-3; ☎ 2032 2388; www.shangri-la.com; 11 Jl Sultan Ismail; d RM565;) The distinctive foyer may be somewhat overblown, but there's the usual Shangri-La opulence and style – a winning formula that has made this chain one of the best in the Far East and this hotel one of KL's best. You get free laundry, free local calls and breakfast is complementary. Also at hand are Lafite restaurant, a popular English pub upstairs, live music in the lobby lounge and Shang Palace – a fine Chinese restaurant (see Eating, p91).

Chinatown Guest House (☎ 2072 0417; Wisma BWT, 103 Jl Petaling; dm RM12, s/d with fan RM25/30, s/d with air-con R32/40;) Rather simple but amiable establishment.

Anuja Backpackers Inn (☎ 2026 6479; anuja@sgsmc.com; 1st-3rd fl, 28 Jl Pudu; s/d with fan RM18/25, s/d with air-con RM30/40;) Convenient location opposite Puduraya bus station, fine rooftop beer garden and evening movies.

Golden Plaza Hostel (☎ 2026 8559; goldenplazakl@hotmail.com; 1st fl, 106 Jl Petaling; dm/s/d with fan RM10/25/35, s/d with air-con RM40/50;) Friendly, spacious with clean showers but many rooms without windows; mixed reviews.

Hotel Excel Inn (☎ 2031 8621; 89 Jl Petaling; r RM55;) Clean, neat, all rooms (windowless) with air-con, shower room, TV and phones, upper rooms away from noise outside.

Travellers Moon Lodge (☎ 2070 6601; 36B Jl Silang; dm/s/d/tr RM10/20/25/30) Many spacious windowless rooms, with top-floor terrace; mixed reviews.

GOLDEN TRIANGLE & KLCC Map pp82–3

AttapSana (☎ 2142 0710; attapsanakl@yahoo.com; 27 Jl Mesui; dm/tw/d RM20/25/50;) This welcoming and petite guesthouse to the west off Jl Nagasari is a truly homely and pretty place. Much effort has been invested in the Malay decoration and design (plus welcoming greenery outside), the rooms are clean and travellers enthuse about the management (complementary breakfast). Downstairs is the hip live-music club No Black Tie.

Pondok Lodge (☎ 2142 8449; pondok@tm.net.my; 3rd fl, 20 Jl Cangkat Bukit Bintang; dm/s/d RM15/40/55;) This is a spacious, beautifully decorated and popular retreat (one of KL's best) with airy common lounges and a rooftop sitting area. Bright Western- or Malay-style rooms provide for a pleasant stay and the four-/six-bed dorms come with either fan or air-con.

LITTLE INDIA, JL TAR AREA TO CHOW KIT

Coliseum Hotel (Map pp78-9; ☎ 2692 6270; 100 Jl TAR; s/d with fan RM28/33, s/d with air-con RM38/45;) With its famous old planters café and bar downstairs (see p93), the Coliseum has a potent sense of colonial history. Rooms are huge and quiet, albeit without bathrooms (some rooms have sinks), and come with ancient electric switches, tables and chairs, high ceilings and wardrobes. This atmospheric hotel is a KL institution; it's often full.

Ben Soo Homestay & Travellers Service (Map pp74-5; ☎ 2691 8096, 012-675 6110, bensoohome@yahoo.com; Front 2nd fl, 61B Jl Tiong Nam; s/d with fan RM30/36, s/d with air-con RM38/44;) Off Jl Raja Laut, this friendly, family-run homestay offers rare value with a variety of well-kept rooms, all with free tea and toast (8am to 10.30pm). The homestay is a 10-minute walk from both Sultan Ismail and PWTC Star LRT stations. For a small fee, the owner will pick you up from the train or bus stations, and can also help arrange tours and air tickets.

KL SENTRAL, BRICKFIELDS & TRAIN STATION

YMCA (Map pp74-5; ☎ 2274 1439; fax 2274 0559, 95 Jl Padang Belia; s/d with fan RM38/50, s/d with air-con RM68/78;) south of KL Sentral, is ideal for those arriving in KL, albeit out of the way for sightseeing. There's a good range of facilities, including a gym, shop and language courses (see Courses, p86). The rooms are comfortable; air-con rooms come with bathroom.

Mid-Range

CHINATOWN Map pp78–9

Impiana Hotel (☎ 2026 6060, www.impiana.net; Jl Cheng Lock; d RM120;) Just west of Puduraya bus station, this is a smarthotel that's of international standard. All rooms feature in-house movies, satellite TV, small fridge, coffee/tea-making facilities, and in-room safe; you also receive a complimentary newspaper.

Hotel Lok Ann (☎ 2078 9544; 113A Jl Petaling; d RM60;) Despite facing noisy Jl Sultan, this tidy and clean place has spacious rooms with windows, TV, phone and large shower rooms; better value than much of the competition.

Katari Hotel (☎ 2031 7777; katari@tm.net.my; 38 Jl Pudu; d/f RM138/265;) The Katari offers an economical level of mid-range comfort (coffee/tea-making facilities, TV with in-house movies, mini bar) in a central location opposite Puduraya bus station.

Mandarin Pacific Hotel (☎ 2070 3000; fax 2070 4363; 2-8 Jl Sultan; standard/deluxe d RM70/86;) This is a clean, presentable, quiet and friendly hotel. The standard rooms face inwards to a rather dismal shaft, but there are larger, better-positioned deluxe rooms and 24-hour room service. Good value for money (breakfast included).

Hotel China Town Inn (☎ 2070 4008; contact@chinatowninn.com; 52-54 Jl Petaling; s/d RM59/79;) This well-managed and good-value hotel has ample rooms and is well located in the bustling heart of Chinatown. Clean and attractive, all rooms (most with air-con) have attached shower room and TV (VCD players can be hired).

Starlight Hotel (☎ 2078 9811; 90 Jl Hang Kasturi; s/d RM50/60;) Well-managed and well located hotel with ample rooms that all come with shower room. The Klang bus station opposite can make things noisy.

Also recommended:

Swiss-Inn (☎ 2072 3333; resvns_sikl@swissgarden.com; 62 Jl Sultan; d RM100;) Comfortable, clean and centrally located; breakfast included.

Hotel Malaya (☎ 2072 7722; www.hotelmalaya.com.my; cnr Jl Hang Lekir & Jl Tun HS Lee; s/d RM140/165;)

GOLDEN TRIANGLE & KLCC

Novotel Century Kuala Lumpur (Map pp82-3; ☎ 2143 9898; cklhres@pd.jaring.my; Jl Bukit Bintang; d RM168;) Located at the southern end of Bukit Bintang, this stylish and very comfortable high-rise hotel offers spacious rooms (with high-speed Internet access, cable TV, complimentary newspaper), a bar, restaurant and health centre.

Hotel Nova (Map pp82-3; ☎ 2143 1818; novahtl@tm.net.my; 16-22 Jl Alor; r RM120;) The snazzy high-rise Nova offers great value for a hotel in an excellent position (overlooking the Jl Alor hawker stalls) and tucked away off the busy Bukit Bintang. All rooms have cable, ESPN and bathrooms. The complimentary breakfast is, however, rather unspectacular.

Crown Princess (☎ 2162 5522; crownprincess@fhikl.com.my; City Square Centre, Jl Tun Razak; s/d RM168/188;) With a great position next to the City Square shopping centre, this elegant hotel (home to the Taj restaurant – see Eating, p92) frequently has promotional rates, including breakfast, which make it a good deal indeed.

Park Inn International (Map pp82-3; ☎ 2715 3888; www.parkinn.com.my; 51A Jl Changkat Bukit Bintang; d RM330;) Excellently located for the bars and restaurants of Changkat Bukit Bintang, this recommended hotel offers some excellent promotions and high standards; breakfast included.

Lodge Hotel (Map pp82-3; ☎ 2142 0122; fax 2142 0122; 2 Jl Tengah; annexe room RM92, standard/deluxe d RM115/138;) This unassuming, conveniently located retro '60s-style motel is dwarfed by skyscrapers, and boasts a restaurant and small pool. The main advantage of staying here is the well-priced (for the area) spacious rooms.

Also recommended:

Malaysia Hotel (Map pp82-3; ☎ 2144 7733; fax 2142 8579; 67-69 Jl Bukit Bintang; d RM118;) Rather tatty but reasonable value.

Bintang Warisan Hotel (Map pp82-3; ☎ 2148 8111; www.bintangwarisan.com; 68 Jl Bukit Bintang; s/d RM150/170;) Attractive small hotel.

Swiss-Garden Hotel (Map pp82-3; ☎ 2141 3333; resvns_sghkl@swissgarden.com; 117 Jl Pudu; d RM350;) Decent mid-range hotel; the Bluechip lounge has live jazz Monday to Saturday.

LITTLE INDIA, JL TAR AREA TO CHOW KIT

Grand Centrepoint Hotel (Map pp74-5; ☎ 2693 3988; ubb@po.jaring.my; 316 Jl TAR; d/ste RM85/250;) This stylish 100-room hotel, mid-way between Little India and Chow Kit, is a smart and well presented business hotel, and offers good mid-range value for money (breakfast included). Rooms are clean and well insulated from traffic noise. It's a five-minute walk from Sultan Ismail LRT station.

Hotel Noble (Map pp78-9; ☎ 2711 7111; contact@hotelnoble.com; 4th fl, 165 Jl TAR; d RM150;) Good deals can be found at this modern and attractively laid-out hotel (ask for their promotional rate). Staff are polite; the ambience is smart, clean and comfortable. Rooms come with mini-bar, safe deposit box, coffee and tea making facilities, TV, shower and complimentary newspaper; breakfast included.

Garden City Hotel (Map pp78-9; ☎ 2711 7777; gardencityhotel@hotmail.com; 213-214 Jl Bunus; s/d RM120/140;) This pleasant hotel, off Jl Masjid India, is recommended for its cleanliness and friendly service (breakfast included). Ask for promotional rates.

Also recommended:

Kowloon Hotel (Map pp78-9; ☎ 2693 4246; kowloon@po.jaring.my; 142-146 Jl TAR; s/d RM90/115;) Friendly staff and value for money.

Hotel Plaza (Map pp74-5; ☎ 2698 2255; plazakl@po.jaring.my; Jl Raja Laut; s/d RM80/95;) Breakfast included.

De First Inn (Map pp74-5; ☎ 4045 2323; fax 4045 2939; 2 Lorong Haji Taib 5; d RM90;) Comfortable rooms with bathrooms.

Hotel Champagne (Map pp78-9; ☎ 2698 6333; 141 Jl Bunus; d RM74;)

KL SENTRAL, BRICKFIELDS & TRAIN STATION

Heritage Station Hotel (Map pp78-9; ☎ 2272 1688; thshkl@tm.net.my; Jl Sultan Hishamuddin; dm/d/superior RM35/110/130;) Housed in the magnificent neo-Moorish KL Train Station is this grand, cavernous colonial-era hotel. Despite the heavy historical patina, most rooms have modern decor but there are grander colonial-style suites available if you really want to get in the mood. Good-value long-term (more than one month) rates start from RM700 per month. Check out the original fixtures, including the lift (out of order at time of writing). Breakfast is included. Charlies Restaurant (see Eating, p93) on the ground floor adds to the yesteryear ambience.

There are a few mid-range options in this part of town (which has the added attraction of having a vibrant Indian community), but nothing outstanding. **Hotel Florida** (Map pp74-5; ☎ 2260 1111; 71-73 Jl Thambapillai; s/d RM60/75;) has decent rooms.

KUALA LUMPUR INTERNATIONAL AIRPORT

A useful pitstop for those in transit or arriving at odd hours, the **Airside Transit Hotel** (☎ 8787 4848; Satellite bldg, KLIA; d RM120;) has short-stay rates. There's a fitness centre, business centre, spa and sauna, and all rooms come with attached bathroom and TV.

Top End

GOLDEN TRIANGLE & KLCC

JW Marriott (Map pp82-3; ☎ 2715 9000; jwmh@po.jaring.my; 183 Jl Bukit Bintang; d RM345;) The sumptuous Marriott delivers some stupendous luxury; the additional lavishness of the attached Star Hill Shopping Centre is the icing on the cake. The foyer is astonishingly elegant, but just inspect the mind-blowing scale of the basement. The weekday promotional rate brings the price of a deluxe room to RM195. There is a restaurant and a celebrated international eatery, Shook! (see Eating, p93).

Mandarin Oriental (Map pp74-5; ☎ 2380 8888; mokul-reservations@mohg.com; next to Petronas Towers; r RM700;) One of KL's newest and finest hotels, with a magnificent location and excellent bars and restaurants. The five-star Mandarin has outstanding styling and design and is quite simply sumptuous.

Regent (Map pp82-3; ☎ 2141 8000; 160 Jl Bukit Bintang; d RM690;) This award-winning hotel is amazingly luxurious. The swimming pool is gorgeous; also at hand are air-con squash courts, gymnasium, the Lai Ching Yuen Chinese restaurant (also award-winning) and everything else you could need.

MiCasa Hotel Apartments (Map pp74-5; ☎ 2161 8833; micasa@po.jaring.my; 368B Jl Tun Razak; one-/two-/three-bedroom apt ste RM400/530/1000;) The homely hotel apartments of MiCasa, a few hundred metres south of Ampang Park LRT station, are fully equipped apartment suites ideal for long stays. Accommodation is made up of low-level, tiled houses and there's all the convenience of a small village with a full range of facilities. All suites come with kitchen plus utensils, satellite TV, fridge and room safe; long-stay rates are attractive.

Su Casa (☎ 4251 3833; sucasa@pd.jaring.my; 222 Jl Ampang; 1-/2-bed apt RM280/400;) These serviced apartments are ideal for those looking for long stays in KL; monthly rates start at RM5000. All apartments come with fully equipped kitchens; facilities include a pool, restaurants, gym and laundry. There's a relaxing and cooling café at the rear.

Also recommended:

Hotel Equatorial (Map pp82-3; ☎ 2161 7777, www.equatorial.com; Jl Sultan Ismail; s/d RM340/360;) This long-standing international hotel has an excellent coffee shop in the basement, a children's playroom and the funky Flo bar (see Drinking, p96).

Renaissance Kuala Lumpur (Map pp74-5; ☎ 2162 2233; ww.renaissance-kul.com; cnr Jl Sultan Ismail & Jl Ampang; d RM285;) Highly opulent five-star hotel with extravagant lobby.

Hotel Istana (Map pp74-5; ☎ 2141 9988, 1800-883 380; istana.hik@meritus-hotels.com; 73 Jl Raja Chulan; s/d RM525/550;)

Hotel Nikko (☎ 2161 1111; www.hotelnikko.com.my; 165 Jl Ampang; d RM600;) Prestigious Japanese business hotel in embassy district; ask for frequent, attractive promotional rates. Fine range of restaurants and an English pub.

KL SENTRAL, BRICKFIELDS & TRAIN STATION

At the time of writing, the unfinished twin towers ascending into the sky adjacent to KL Sentral in Brickfields were evolving into new five-star Hilton and four-star Le Meridien hotels. For those arriving at KL Sentral, the hotels should offer both convenience and comfort along with a host of other amenities, in 2004.

KUALA LUMPUR INTERNATIONAL AIRPORT

The first-rate **Pan Pacific KLIA** (☎ 8787 3333; KLIA; s/d RM560/590;) is linked by a skybridge to the main terminal and boasts undeniable luxury. There's a large range of restaurant and business-class facilities, including tennis court and gym. Ask for promotional discounts, which can shave 50% off the rack rate.

ELSEWHERE

The magnificent **Carcosa Seri Negara** (Map pp74-5; ☎ 2282 1888; fax 2282 6868; Taman Tasik Perdana; ste RM1100-RM3500;) comprises two colonial mansions in tranquil gardens at the western edge of the Lake Gardens. Carcosa was the residence of British government representative Sir Frank Swettenham, and Seri Negara was the official guesthouse. Visiting high-level dignitaries make this hotel, which has just 13 suites, their choice when in KL.

EATING

One of the main reasons to come to KL is to sample its eclectic cuisine. Dominated by Malay, Indian and Chinese cooking, city menus also feature an impressive spread of international dishes to suit all budgets.

Chinese

You'll find Chinese restaurants at every turn, but particularly in Chinatown and around Jl Bukit Bintang in the Golden Triangle.

Museum (Map pp74-5; ☎ 4042 9888 ext 8006; the Legend Hotel, 9th fl, the Mall, Putra Place, 100 Jl Putra; meals RM50) With fine Cantonese, Sichuan and Teochew cuisine served in a satisfying context of Chinese antiques and exhibits by very polite waiting staff, the Museum makes for a distinctive choice.

Old China Cafe (Map pp78-9; ☎ 2072 5915; 11 Jl Balai Polis) Push open the swinging wooden doors to the feel of a Shanghai teahouse, complete with quaint 1920s crooner music. Try the incredible coffee and generous servings of Nonya (Peranakan) fare.

Tai Thong Grand Restaurant (Map pp74-5; ☎ 2162 4433; 2nd fl, North Block, Wisma Selangor Dredging, Jl Ampang; meals RM25) This bright and spacious Cantonese restaurant is smart and well admired by KL diners. The abalone and/or suckling pig may rapidly empty your wallet, but there's also Peking duck (RM60), dim sum and a range of vegetable and *doufu* (bean curd) dishes.

Shang Palace (Map pp82-3; ☎ 2032 2388; Shangri-La Hotel, 11 Jl Sultan Ismail; meals RM40; noon-2.30pm & 7-10.30pm Mon-Sat, 11am-2.30pm & 7-10.30pm Sun) Relax in fine surroundings and enjoy a variety of Cantonese and Sichuan delicacies including Hong Kong–style roast duck (RM30) and hot-and-sour soup with assorted seafood (RM16), plus range of pricey abalone dishes; dim sum in mornings.

Fatt Yan Vegetarian Restaurant (Map pp78-9; ☎ 2070 6561; 57-59 Jl Tun HS Lee; meals RM14) Herbivores will approve of this Buddhist Chinese restaurant that eschews meat on religious principles. There's a large variety of *doufu* (beancurd) dishes including the spicy Sichuan *mapo doufu* (RM8), imitation-meat dishes like deep-fried spare ribs (RM10), or just the simple mixed vegetables (RM8). Eat with a clean conscience overlooked by statues of Guanyin, Milefo and Sakyamuni.

Amata Vegetarian Restaurant (Map pp78-9; ☎ 2026 9077; 2 Jl Panggong; meals RM15-20) Despite the name, the food here is actually vegan, dished up in a refined setting under a high ceiling in a historic building. On the Buddhist-influenced menu are *pandan* (screw pine leaf) mock chicken (RM12), chilli mock squid (RM8) and hot-and-sour soup (RM6) – all good.

Also recommended:

West Lake Restoran (Map pp78-9; 15 Jl Sultan; meals RM10-15) Long-running Chinatown eatery known for its *yong tau foo* (bean curd stuffed with minced meat) and *mee* (noodle) dishes.

Restoran Kam Lun Tai (Map pp78-9; ☎ 2078 0749; 1-14 Jl Sultan; meals RM10) Bustling Chinatown restaurant with Cantonese staples.

Beijing Wok (Map pp82-3; ☎ 2141 2998; 25 Low Yat Plaza, Jl Bukit Bintang; set meals RM10)

Indian

Indian food is naturally widespread in KL and Little India is obviously a good hunting ground. Plenty of coffee shops can be found in the Jl Masjid India/Jl TAR area, and food stalls in the area specialise in cheap tandoori chicken, and breads such as naan, *dosa* and chapati.

Bombay Palace (☎ 2145 4241; 215 Jl Tun Razak; meals RM25; noon-3pm & 6.30-11pm) You can 02dine in stylish surrounds here. High-quality North Indian dishes – including a decent spread of vegetarian cuisine – is on offer at this elegant restaurant.

Gem Restaurant (Map pp74-5; ☎ 2260 1373; 124 Jl Tun Sambanthan; meals RM18-20) This is an excellent restaurant for North and South Indian cuisine, in the Brickfields area. The chicken tikka (RM11) is chunky and plentiful; there's a range of vegetarian options, including creamy Indian-style veg (RM8), and service is good.

Govinda's Vegetarian Restaurant (Map pp78-9; ☎ 2698 6785; 1st fl, 16-1, Lorong Bunus 6, off Jl Masjid India; 7am-3pm Mon-Sat) Simple, spartan Govinda's offers a popular daily 'Karma Free Pure Vegetarian' buffet (breakfast 7am to 10am, lunch 11am to 3pm; RM5); look for the sign on the pavement and head upstairs. À la carte dinner mock-meat options made from soy include Indian, Malay and Chinese dishes, even *rendang* from Negeri Sembilan. Bhagavad-Gita (sacred Indian text) classes are held on Monday at 7.50pm.

Bilal Restoran (Map pp78-9; ☎ 2078 0804; 33 Jl Ampang; meals RM7) No points for ambience, but the Bilal, north of Chinatown, is highly popular for its South Indian Muslim dishes. There's a large range of roti (RM1.30): *chanai* (unleavened flaky flat bread), egg, *bawang* (onion), plus *ikan* (fish) and *kambing* (mutton) curries.

Restoran Sri Ganesa (Map pp78-9; 5 Jl Pudu Lama; meals RM5) This well-liked eatery has cheap and reliably filling vegetarian banana-leaf meals from around RM5. It's simple but popular.

Also worth considering:

Taj (☎ 2162 5522; Crown Princess Hotel, Jl Tun Razak; meals RM25) Three-time winner of the prestigious Malaysian Tourism Award for Best Indian Restaurant.

THE AUTHOR'S CHOICE

Damian Harper

Seri Angkasa (Map pp82-3; ☎ 2020 5055; www.serimelayu.com/angkasa.htm; KL Tower; meals RM50) Revolving high up in the KL Tower, this restaurant offers exhilarating views and fine dishes. Instead of paying to view KL from the observation deck below, enjoy a lunch buffet for RM64 and watch the city circle about you. Dining à la carte, there's a large range of local seafood (lobster RM21 per 100gm) and steaks, but book in advance for evening meals, especially sunset reservations.

Moghul House (Map pp82-3; ☎ 2142 1455; 34 Jl Changkat Bukit Bintang; meals RM25-30) Off Bukit Bintang, this smart diner has a fine menu and an unhurried air cultivated by pleasant staff and soft lighting. The prawn vindaloo is a searing dish, but milder dishes such as the *aloo palak* (potatoes and spinach in thick creamy sauce) make for soothing accompaniments and there's a large range of other vegetarian options.

Restoran Yusoof (Map pp78-9; ☎ 2072 6425; 40 Jl Hang Kasturi, opposite Central Market; meals RM10)

Sagar (Map p94; ☎ 2284 2532; 6 & 6A Jl Telawi; meals RM24) Decent North Indian cuisine.

International

Central KL has a surprising variety of Western restaurants and innovative places, which also concentrate in Bangsar, south of the city centre.

CENTRAL KL

Sentidos Tapas (Map pp82-3; ☎ 2145 3385; Lower ground fl, Star Hill Shopping Centre, 181 Jl Bukit Bintang; meals RM25) On the corner of the Marriott Hotel is this stylishly designed tapas bar. The dishes are scrumptious and measures are generous – try the eggplant and tomato stew, which is delectable. The menu boasts a large range of tortilla, seafood and vege dishes. This is a great place for a sociable meal with friends.

Frangipani Restaurant (Map pp82-3; ☎ 2144 3001; 25 Changkat Bukit Bintang; meals RM100) If you want elegance, modern styling and contemporary French and Fusion cuisine, this swish restaurant (with upstairs bar) is an attractive addition to this increasingly cosmopolitan street.

Le Bernardin French Brasserie (Map pp82-3; ☎ 2142 1755; 38 Changkat Bukit Bintang; meals from RM50) A smart and stylish gastronomical addition to Changkat Bukit Bintang, this fine French restaurant is owned by the affable Bernard, who also runs a restaurant in Singapore. The menu includes pan-fried duck liver (RM70), poached salmon, fillet of sole (RM55) and other treats.

Shook! (Map pp82-3; ☎ 2716 8535; Lower ground fl, Starhill Centre, 181 Jl Bukit Bintang; meals RM40) Sleek and smart restaurant offering three separate, but equally appetising menus: Japanese, Chinese and Western grill. Entrées hover around RM30 to RM40 and imaginative, tempting desserts are less than RM10. Reservations are advised.

Scalini's (Map pp82-3; ☎ 2145 3211; 19 Jl Sultan Ismail; meals RM40) Pleasant staff and fantastic Italian food in a stylish setting (with alfresco seating) make this a highly recommended restaurant.

Charlies Restaurant (Map pp78-9; ☎ 2272 1688; Jl Sultan Hishamuddin; meals RM30) Huge place with bar, in the colonial-era Heritage Station Hotel. Swirling ceiling fans contribute to the pervasive sense of history. Try the lamb chops (RM24.90), Irish stew (RM10.90) or pumpkin soup (RM7.90).

Coliseum Café (Map pp78-9; ☎ 2692 6270; 100 Jl TAR; meals RM30) Resisting the passage of time, the Coliseum still enjoys a great reputation for its sizzling steaks, but it's just worth coming for the colonial-era ambience. You can book a room at the hotel upstairs (see Sleeping, p88), or take in a drink at the bar (which closes at 10pm).

Fish Shop (Map pp74-5; Lower ground fl, Suria KLCC; meals RM14) Fast-food outlet dishing up some very scrumptious fish. There's excellent fried and battered fillets, and fish and chips (RM9.95).

Bierkeller (Map pp82-3; Jl Sultan Ismail; meals RM25-30) Hidden behind a petrol station, Bierkeller is full of expat Central Europeans savouring bratwurst and sauerkraut (RM15.50), gulping imported brews (from RM13) and perusing the selection of recent German newspapers and magazines. The bar is open until 1am, but the kitchen closes at 11pm.

Hard Rock Café (Map pp82-3; ☎ 2715 5555; Ground fl, Wisma Concorde, 2 Jl Sultan Ismail; meals RM25) On top of the fish and chips (RM22) and the Hard Rock veggie sandwich (RM19) you can get a fine coffee here (RM6.50) among the usual rock memorabilia.

Be My Friend Café (Map pp78-9; Lot 2.07, Central Market Annexe; coffees RM3.50) With a terrace overlooking the river, there's healthy home-cooked fare, sandwiches, some vegetarian options, as well as great coffee.

Also recommended:

Lafite (Map pp82-3; ☎ 2032 2388; Shangri-La Hotel; 11 Jl Sultan Ismail; meals RM50; 🕒 noon-2.30pm & 7-10.30pm Mon-Sat) Fantastic French restaurant.

Outback Steakhouse (Map pp82-3; ☎ 2144 9919; BB Park, Low Yat Plaza, 7 Jl 1/77, Bukit Bintang; meals RM30) Steaks and sports TV.

TGI Friday's (Map pp82-3; ☎ 2163 7761; Ground fl, Life Centre, Jl Sultan Ismail; meals RM25)

BANGSAR

This favourite haunt of expats and KL's trendy denizens has almost all of the city's stylish, innovative restaurants and a lot of foreigner-friendly pubs. To get there, take the Putra LRT to Bangsar station, then a feeder bus to the main strip around Jl Telawi or jump into a taxi.

La Bodega (Map p94; ☎ 2287 8318; 14 & 16 Jl Telawi 2; meals RM25-30; 🕒 noon-1am) Not the place for

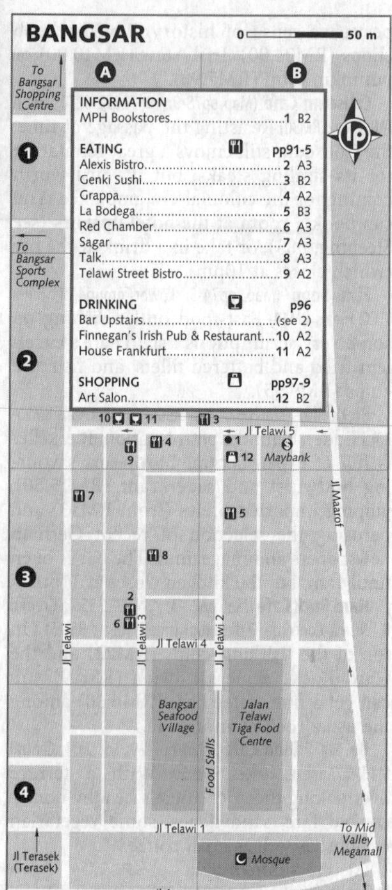

a romantic evening as there's loud music and a popular bar. The tapas are enjoyable, albeit modest in size; the *patatas bravas* (RM8) are spicy and tasty. There's an ample wine list (half-bottle RM58), and a choice of sherries and brandies.

Red Chamber (Map p94; ☎ 2283 1898; 33 Jl Telawi 3; meals RM18) You can dine from red-velvet couches on pan-Asian and fusion cuisine, including dumplings and noodle dishes, and take advantage of a full bar.

Alexis Bistro (Map p94; ☎ 2284 2880; 29 Jl Telawi 3; meals RM25-30) serves trendy international dishes and has the ultra-smooth Bar Upstairs (see Drinking, p96).

The popular **Grappa** (Map p94; ☎ 2287 0080; 1 Jl Telawi 5; meals RM45) cooks up Italian dishes, while **Telawi Street Bistro** (Map p94; ☎ 2284 3168; 1 Jl Telawi 3; meals RM 28) is a swish bistro with a bar upstairs.

Japanese

Wasabi Bistro (Map pp74-5; ☎ 2163 0968; Mandarin Oriental; meals from RM50) The finest in town, offering a modern interpretation of Japanese cuisine.

Keyaki (Map pp74-5; ☎ 4042 5555; Pan Pacific Hotel; Jl Putra; meals from RM50; open noon-3pm & 7-11pm) A highly recommended restaurant.

Talk Bangsar (Map p94; ☎ 2161 2643; 22 Jl Telawi 3) Golden Triangle (Map pp82-3; Jl P Ramlee; closed Sun) A stylish Japanese bistro with good-value lunch sets (RM15) and *ramen* noodles (RM10).

Also recommended:

Sushi King (Map pp82-3; Jl Sultan Ismail; meals RM18) Reasonably priced self-serve sushi at the conveyor-belt bar.

TokuToku (Map pp82-3; Jl Sultan Ismail; meals RM20) Atmospheric and affordable.

Dontaku Restoran Jepun (Map pp82-3; across from Lot 10; meals RM18) is an authentic-looking *izakaya*-style (Japanese pub) place.

Malay & Nonya

There are Malay *warung* (small eating stalls) and *kedai kopi* (coffee shops) throughout KL, but especially along and just off Jl TAR. Nonya (also known as Peranakan or Straits Chinese) food fuses Malay ingredients and spices with Chinese cooking methods, and includes elements of Portuguese Eurasian cuisines (for more information on Nonya culture see p43).

Kapitan's Club (Map pp78-9; ☎ 2031 0242; 35 Jl Ampang; meals RM15-20; 11am-3pm & 6-10.30pm) Relax in this marvellous, museum-like restaurant fashioned from an old Peranakan shophouse. The Kapitan chicken (RM11.50) is a speciality, as are 30 other Nonya creations. The beef rendang (Malay-style beef stewed in spices; RM13.50) is good, as is the wonton soup (RM5.50) and other staples.

Seri Melayu (Map pp82-3; ☎ 2145 1833; 1 Jl Conlay; meals from RM35; 11am-3pm & 7-11pm) This restaurant, set in a traditional Malay building, goes the whole hog with cultural performances and is embedded on the tour circuit, but the food is both varied and excellent, including a good-value lunch buffet (RM35).

Restoran Nelayan Titiwangsa (Map pp74-5; ☎ 4021 1284; Jl Kuantan, Taman Tasik Titiwangsa; meals RM25) In an enormous hut built over the water in the Lake Titiwangsa Gardens in northern KL, this restaurant (serving Malay seafood) is lively in the evenings when tour groups roll in for live performances (see Cultural Shows, p97).

Also recommended:

Restoran Wilayah Baru (Map pp78-9; 29 Lebuh Pudu; meals RM10) Excellent Chinatown eatery serving Malay food.

Rasa Utara (Map pp82-3; ☎ 2141 9246; Basement, BB Plaza, Jl Bukit Bintang; meals RM7) Inexpensive cuisine from Kedah state.

Nyonya Wok (Map pp82-3; ☎ 2141 4203; 2nd fl, BB Plaza, Jl Bukit Bintang; meals RM14)

Quick Eats

KL has plenty of indoor and outdoor hawker venues all around the city.

In Chinatown, Jl Petaling is closed to traffic between Jl Cheng Lock and Jl Sultan. Tables are set up in the evenings outside Chinese restaurants on Jl Hang Lekir between Jl Petaling and Jl Sultan. Puduraya bus station also has a variety of stalls and many open very late.

Night markets for Malay food include the **Sunday Market** (Kampung Bahru LRT station) and the **Chow Kit Market** (off Jl TAR). Night owls head to Chow Kit for the all-night *nasi lemak* stalls.

Little India's **Saturday night market** (Jl TAR) has many food vendors and a great atmosphere. Jl Masjid India is almost as good any evening of the week for Indian fare.

Jl Alor, one street northwest of Jl Bukit Bintang in the Golden Triangle district, has some of the best Chinese hawker stalls and coffee shops in KL, serving excellent *ikan bakar* (grilled fish). Stalls start after dark around 7pm and close late. Off Jl Sultan Ismail, the small Sri Perak, just back from Modesto's, and the lane of hawkers near the Beach Club are both busy places.

In Bangsar, the indoor Jl Telawi Tiga Food Centre is a popular alternative to the area's pricier competition; stalls also set up on the street outside in the evenings serving up Malay, East Asian and South Asian food.

Most shopping malls have food courts selling slightly more expensive hawker food in air-con surrounds. The top-floor **Medan Hang Tuah** (The Mall shopping complex) opposite the PWTC in the Chow Kit area is a re-creation of an old city street, complete with mock shophouses, and has an excellent selection of cheap Malay, Chinese and Indian favourites.

The **Lot 10 Shopping Complex** (Jl Sultan Ismail) has a wide range of Asian food. The **Asian Flavours food court** (Level 4, Suria KLCC) is a popular place. The **Ampang Park Shopping Complex** (Jl Tun Razak) has a popular spread of stalls.

Chinatown's **Central Market** (Jl Hang Kasturi) has an average selection of hawker food on the second level. KL Sentral has a large food court on the upper floors.

Look out for street-side soft drink stalls where you can pick up a variety of cheap drinks including soya milk (70 sen).

Self-Catering

You can find supermarkets in Chinatown at the **S&M Shopping Arcade** (Jl Cheng Lock) and at **UDA Ocean Plaza** (Cnr Jl Sultan & Jl Tun HS Lee). **Sogo department store** (Jl TAR) has a well-stocked basement supermarket.

Many of the shopping malls and department stores in the Golden Triangle also have supermarkets. There's one in the basement of the **Isetan department store** (Map pp82-3; Jl Sultan Ismail).

The **Mid Valley Megamall** (p98; Jl Bangsar) is partly anchored by a branch of the French hypermarket Carrefour.

Thai & Other Asian

Ginger (Map pp78-9; ☎ 2273 7371; Lot M12, Central Market; meals RM15), has good Thai, Malaysian and Indonesian fare. There's a tiny indoor waterfall, hardwood tables and soothing lighting.

Restoran Best Thai Cuisine (Map pp82-3; ☎ 2148 5255; 74 Jl Bukit Bintang; meals RM15) Favoured for its outstanding cooking and very reasonable prices.

Restoran Koryo Won (Map pp82-3; ☎ 2142 7655; 2nd fl, Kompleks Antarabangsa, Jl Sultan Ismail; meals RM20-25) A well-liked Korean barbecue restaurant, perfect for gregarious evenings with loads of beer and sizzling strips of meat.

Also recommended:

Rain Nudle House (Map pp74-5; ☎ 2382 0669; Lot 409, Level 4, Suria KLCC; meals RM25) Nifty noodle bar with RM34.50 set dinners.

Bangkok Jam Thai Restaurant & Bar (Map pp82-3; ☎ 2142 3449; BB Park, Low Yat Plaza, 7 Jl 1/77, Jl Bukit Bintang; meals RM15) Good-value set meals.

Vietnamhôuse (Map pp74-5; ☎ 294 1726; 6th fl, Sogo department store, Jl TAR; meals RM24; 🕑 noon-9pm) Wide menu of Vietnamese food.

DRINKING

Most of KL's nightlife was once found in the Golden Triangle, and Jl Sultan Ismail is still the centre of the universe for KL's middle class, as well as for some ravingly bored youth. However, many expats head to Bangsar, south of the city centre, to see and be seen.

Liquid (Map pp78-9; ☎ 2078 5909; liquid@tm.net.my; Central Market Annexe; beer RM14) This is one of KL's crispest and most sophisticated bars, all low lighting and low tables, situated beneath a gay disco of the same name. It's very smooth and the ultimate chill-out bar.

Reggae Bar (Map pp78-9; ☎ 2272 2158; 158 Jl Tun HS Lee; beer by the glass/jug RM10/26) Deep booming bass thumps endless Bob Marley while punters escape the interior gloom to tables on the pavement outside. The bar occasionally stages theme nights to give other music genres airplay and there's a DJ spinning house, jazz and blues after 10pm.

Sangria (Map pp82-3; ☎ 2164 6666; www.nouvoclub.com; 16 Jl Sultan Ismail) Spanish-themed bar with large, flat-screen TVs, mosaic bar and floor, velvet booths, alfresco seating, and relaxed and subdued lighting (it comes alive at night though). It's a nifty place with the club Nouvo upstairs (see Clubs, this page).

Delaney's (Map pp82-3; ☎ 2141 5195; Ground fl, Parkroyal Hotel, Jl Sultan Ismail; ⏰ noon-late; happy hour 4-8pm) This middle-of-the-road Irish pub has sports satellite TV, Irish food (meal for two RM60), live music (Tuesday to Sunday) and a clientele base of older expats and businessmen.

Havana Club (Map pp82-3; ☎ 2715 9000; Marriott Hotel; 183 Jl Bukit Bintang) This classy Cuban bar/cigar room is high on atmosphere and a great place to unwind when it all gets too much.

Bar Upstairs (Map p94; ☎ 2284 2881; 29A Jl Telawi 3; ⏰ 6pm-2am) Walk into this world of subdued red lighting and opaque furniture and take a seat – this bar above Alexis Bistro is a supreme chill-out venue.

Finnegan's Irish Pub & Restaurant (Map p94; ☎ 2284 9024; 6 Jl Telawi 5) This is a first-rate place for a knees-up, with live ESPN sports coverage, enthusiastic staff, stout and a decent menu (and kiddies' favourites like Marmite soldiers); packed at weekends but far quieter mid-week.

House Frankfurt (Map p94; ☎ 2284 1624; 12 Jl Telawi 5) This popular German bar has a range of imported German beers (Erdinger Dark, Weihenstephaner, etc) and doubles as a restaurant.

Also recommended:

Green Man (Map pp82-3; ☎ 2141 9924; 40 Changkat Bukit Bintang) Popular, unstuffy British expat hangout, with pool table and quieter reaches upstairs (RM3); there's simple food and outside seating.

Bull's Head (Map pp78-9; Central Market; beer RM13.50 per pint) English pub with jukebox and pool table.

Beach Club Café (Map pp82-3; ☎ 2166 9919; 97 Jl P Ramlee) Popular bar with live music every night apart from Saturday.

Flo (Map pp82-3; ☎ 2161 7777 ext 8224; Hotel Equatorial, Jl Sultan Ismail) The soothing, illuminated orange bar top makes this a novel setting for a drink.

ENTERTAINMENT

Cinemas

KL's most convenient multi-screen cinema is **Tanjung Golden Village** (Map pp74-5; ☎ 7492 2929; Level 3, Suria KLCC); the city's largest multiplex is the 18-screen multiplex **Golden Screen Cinemas** (☎ 2938 3366; Mid Valley Megamall) in Bangsar.

Classical Music

Dewan Filharmonik Petronas (Map pp74-5; ☎ 2051 7007; Level 2, Tower 2, Petronas Towers) Classical music performances are staged by the Malaysian Philharmonic Orchestra and international ensembles (Friday and Saturday evenings and Sunday matinees) in this state-of-the-art, dazzling auditorium.

National Theatre (Map pp74-5; ☎ 4025 2525; Lake Titiwangsa Gardens) Performances by the National Symphony and National Choir are staged here, as well as the occasional drama and dance performance.

Clubs

KL has a sparkling and varied club scene; for the latest information, check the pages of *Juice* or *KLue* (see Media, p73).

Atmosphere (Map pp82-3; ☎ 2145 9198; 12 Jl Sultan Ismail; RM25 incl drink; ⏰ 9pm-3am Thu-Sat) Centrepiece of the sleek two-storey and high-profile TwelveSI complex, this up-to-the-minute multi-tier club wills clubbers on with house and techno and a vast dance floor under the laser lights.

Nouvo (Map pp82-3; ☎ 2164 6666; 16 Jl Sultan Ismail; RM20 incl drink; ⏰ 10pm-3am Thu-Sat) On the corner of Jl P Ramlee and upstairs from Sangria (p96), this neat mezzanine-equipped club is besieged by the cream of KL's preening club dwellers at weekends.

Backroom (Map pp82-3; ☎ 2031 0688; Basement, Menara Pan Global, 8 Lg P Ramlee; RM35; 9pm-late Wed, Fri & Sat; ladies night Wed) A landmark on the KL dance circuit, the huge Backroom has regular international DJs spinning house, techno, R & B and hip hop.

Bliss (Map pp82-3; ☎ 2145 9198; 12 Jl Sultan Ismail; RM25 Fri-Sun; 7pm-2am Tue & Thu, 7pm-3am Wed, Fri, Sat & Sun) A component of the TwelveSI complex on Jl Sultan Ismail, this glitzy medium-sized bar and club (techno and funk) is decked out with velvet sofas and sees a stylish throng descending at weekends.

Disco (Map pp78-9; ☎ 2026 5039; 1st fl, 3.04, Central Market Annexe, Jl Hang Kasturi; 10pm-3am Wed, Fri & Sat) Operating from a former cinema, the Disco is a supreme venue for true enthusiasts of dance and music; a mezzanine area is at hand for recuperation.

Bar Ibiza (Map pp82-3; ☎ 2713 2333; 924 & 926 Jl P Ramlee; noon-3am Mon-Fri, 5pm-3am Sat & Sun) Just off Jl Sultan Ismail, this hip bar and dance club plays house most nights and R & B on Thursday. There are appearances by international DJs. Ladies night is Wednesday and Sunday; RM25 Saturday and Sunday.

Another popular nightclub and bar is **Modesto's** (Map pp82-3; ☎ 2713 2333; Lot 924 & 926 Jl P Ramlee; Wed, Fri & Sat) with R&B and house, and just off the happening Jl Changkat Bukit Bintang; cover charge RM25; **No Black Tie** (Map pp82-3; ☎ 2141 8110; 27 Jl Mesui) is a hip, live-music venue for jazz, rock and classical.

Cultural Shows

Malaysian Tourist Information Complex (MATIC; Map pp74-5; ☎ 2164 3929; 109 Jl Ampang; adult/under-12 RM5/free; 3-3.45pm Tue, Thu, Sat & Sun) Malaysian traditional dance and music performances are staged regularly in the mini auditorium.

Central Market (Map pp78-9; ☎ 22746542; admission free; 7.45pm Sat & Sun) You can catch a regular programme of open-air events, including Malay dance, Indian classical dance, Chinese dance and Ta'i chi performances, as well as musical presentations. Pick up a monthly calendar from the information desk

Hotels and restaurants have dinner-and-show, although some seem tacky. **Restoran Nelayan Titiwangsa** (Map pp74-5; ☎ 4021 1284; Lake Titiwangsa) has shows at 8.30pm daily except Monday. **Seri Melayu** (Map pp82-3; ☎ 2145 1833, 1 Jl Conlay; Malaysian buffet and show RM60.50) has traditional Malay music and dance performances between 6.30pm and 10.30pm.

GAY & LESBIAN KL

Liquid (Map pp78-9; ☎ 2078 5909; liquid@tm.net.my; Central Market Annexe; RM10; 10pm-3am Thu, Fri & Sat) KL's most famous and funkiest gay venue draws in an international and local crowd of young dancers to this hallmark club.

Bliss (Map pp82-3; ☎ 2145 9198; 12 Jl Sultan Ismail; Sun) Bliss Boys on Sunday night is gay night at this funky outfit at TwelveSI.

Frangipani Bar (Map pp82-3; ☎ 2144 3001; 25 Jl Changkat Bukit Bintang) Above the restaurant of the same name (see p93), Frangipani's seductive bar attracts a stylish gay and straight crowd.

Theatre

Actors Studio (Map pp78-9; ☎ 2694 5400; tickets@theactorsstudio.com.my; Lot 19, Plaza Putra; adult/student RM35/25) The studio puts on regular contemporary dance performances, as well as comedies. In addition, there are also new plays (often in English). The theatre also runs a small café and bookshop inside the mall.

Actors Studio Bangsar (☎ 2094 0400; tickets@theactorsstudio.com.my; Level 3, New Wing, Bangsar Shopping Centre, Jl Maarof; RM42-102) Theatre and comedy are staged at this studio located north of the Bangsar bar and restaurant quadrant.

See the National Theatre (p96) for information on classical music performances.

SHOPPING

KL promotes itself as a shopping haven. Clothes and shoes are inexpensive, though not as cheap as neighbouring Thailand and Indonesia – still, the range is better. Singapore has a much wider selection of electronics at lower prices, but KL is very competitively priced for camera gear, film, and computer software and hardware.

KL may be the best place to buy handicrafts in Malaysia, but higher wages mean that Malaysia produces fewer handicrafts these days. Traditional Malay batik cloth and kites can be found, but not cheaply, and almost everything else is imported from Indonesia, Thailand or elsewhere.

For books, see Bookshops (p73).

Art Galleries

Admission is free to all the following commercial galleries.

AP Art Gallery (Ground fl, Central Market)

Art Salon (Map p94; ☎ 2282 2601; 4 Jl Telawi 2, Bangsar Baru; 9am-6.30pm Mon-Sat) Displays contemporary Malaysian art.

ArtFolio Gallery (☎ 2162 3339; 3rd fl, City Square, Jl Tun Razak; 11am-8pm Mon-Sat) Sells contemporary Malaysian art.

Galeri Petronas (☎ 2051 7770; 3rd fl, Suria KLCC; 10am-8pm Tue-Sun) Fresh, thought-provoking exhibitions of contemporary photography and paintings, plus occasional historical exhibitions on Malaysia.

Galleriwan (Map pp82-3; ☎ 2161 4071; 1st fl; Crown Regency Service Apartments, 12 Jl P Ramlee; 10am-6pm Mon-Fri, 11am-5pm Sat) Deals in antique Peranakan slippers, majestic Malaysian kites, fine pottery and contemporary fine arts.

Shopping Malls

KL has plenty of shopping malls catering to affluent Malaysians. If it's clothes, shoes, electronics, cameras and everyday goods you're after, the Golden Triangle has the biggest selection. Shopping malls are generally open from 10am to 10pm, but smaller shops close earlier.

Sungei Wang Plaza (Map pp82-3; ☎ 2144 9988; Jl Sultan Ismail) and **BB Plaza** (Map pp82-3; Jl Bukit Bintang) adjoin to form one of KL's biggest and best complexes. Sungei Wang Plaza is especially good for camera gear and cheap (but possibly pirated) software and hardware components.

Lot 10 (Map pp82-3; ☎ 2141 0500; 50 Jl Bukit Bintang) and **Star Hill** (Map pp82-3; ☎ 2148 1000; 181 Bukit Bintang) both sell genuine designer-label clothes, shoes and perfume. Die-hard soccer fans can pay homage at the **Manchester United Shop** (Map pp82-3; ☎ 2145 2100; Lot G17, ground fl, Lot 10) – with another branch at Suria KLCC. **KL Plaza** (Map pp82-3; 2141 7288; 79 Jl Bukit Bintang), squeezed between Lot 10 and Star Hill, houses Tower Records and Planet Hollywood.

The **Mall** (Map pp74-5; ☎ 4042 7122; 100 Jl Putra) shopping centre opposite the Pan Pacific Hotel in Chow Kit, is a good place for brand-name goods.

Ampang Park (Jl Ampang) is on the northern outskirts of the Golden Triangle and has clothes and jewellery shops, and moneychangers offering very competitive rates. It's linked by a pedestrian bridge to the classier **City Square shopping complex** (Jl Tun Razak), which has interesting upmarket interior-design stores and art galleries.

Globe Silk Store (Map pp78-9; 185 Jl TAR), located in Little India, is a KL institution. This long-running, small department store has cosmetics, textiles and clothes at some of the cheapest prices in town.

The modern **Sogo department store** (Map p74–5) carries designer clothes, household goods and a few electronics.

Suria KLCC (Map pp74-5; ☎ 2382 2828; Petronas Twin Towers) is an excellent shopping complex at the foot of the Petronas Towers. The mall has several bookshops, designer clothes and shoe stores, and gourmet restaurants. Near Galeri Petronas on the third floor are some arts and crafts shops: Pucuk Rebung has antiques and fine Malay items.

Mid Valley Megamall (☎ 2983 3333; www.midvalley.com.my) is a colossal complex and Southeast Asia's largest shopping, dining and entertainment centre. There are 300 stores, an 18-screen cinema, a bowling alley, Carrefour, Tower Records and a huge food court.

Shops & Markets

For information on KL's most notable night markets, see p81.

The Central Market (Map pp78–9) is housed in a cavernous Art Deco building beside the river in Chinatown. It's easy to spend an hour or more wandering around the various craft outlets, which sell souvenirs, batik, kites, clothes and jewellery. Overpriced Asian artefacts and antiques are also available, so bargain hard. As a general rule, the higher the price, the more you should bargain. Some of the antique shops on the first floor are interesting for old bric-a-brac; **Oriental Style** (☎ 2273 2468; Lot M25) has a notable display of furniture and pots; **Oriental Spirit** (☎ 2273 2468) has a fascinating jumble of Asian antiques.

Peter Hoe Evolution (Map pp78-9; 2 Jl Hang Lekir) Just south of the Central Market, this small shop has tastefully arranged Malaysian and imported Asian goods, including true (not machine-printed) batik and silks, and contemporary pottery and jewellery; prices are saner than at the Central Market.

City Square shopping complex (Jl Tun Razak) Reasonably priced Asian art and crafts are available here (see also Shopping Malls, p96). You can also find great deals on carpets on the upper floors.

In the heart of Chinatown **Jl Petaling** (Map pp78–9) is one of the most colourful shopping streets in KL, particularly at night. This street-side market has cheap clothes, copy watches, pirated CDs and a smattering of crafts. Hard bargaining is definitely in order.

Kompleks Budaya Kraf (Map pp82-3; ☎ 2162 7459; Jl Conlay; 10am-6pm) This large handicrafts complex has a variety of locally produced batiks, carved wooden artefacts, pewter utensils, woven baskets, rattan furniture, glassware, glazed ceramics and more. The complex also offers batik-making courses.

Stalls at the Chow Kit Market (Map pp74–5) sell everything: clothes, basketware and leather goods are good buys if you bargain hard. Shops in the lanes around the market, particularly Jl Haji Hussein, specialise in made-to-order *songkok*, the traditional Malay male headdress.

In Little India, Jl Masjid India (Map pp74–5) is the place to shop for saris, Indian silks, carpets and other textiles.

Royal Selangor Pewter Factory (☎ 4022 1000; www.royalselangor.com; 4 Jl Usahawan Enam) Pewterware, made from 97% high-quality Malaysian tin, is an important local craft. Royal Selangor, located 8km northeast of central KL in the suburb of Setapak Jaya, is the main manufacturer and its pewter is available in department stores and shops around town. Free 15-minute tours of the factory (which has the world's largest pewter tankard at 1557kg) are conducted between 8am and 4.45pm daily. Take Len Seng bus W12 from Jl Ampang, or ride the Putra LRT to Wangsa Maju station and take a Putra feeder bus (50sen) to the factory. A metered taxi from central KL should cost RM7.

Alternatively, visit the **Royal Selangor shop** (Map pp74-5; ☎ 3182 0240; 118, 1st fl, Suria KLCC).

GETTING THERE & AWAY

Kuala Lumpur is Malaysia's principal international arrival gateway and the crossroads for domestic bus, train and taxi travel.

Air

Kuala Lumpur's International Airport, KLIA (www.klia.com.my) is 75km south of the city centre at Sepang. For transport options to get into town see Getting Around (p101).

KLIA takes all international flights to and from Kuala Lumpur and regular flights to domestic destinations including: Alor Setar, Ipoh, Johor Bahru, Kota Bharu, Kota Kinabalu, Kuala Terengganu, Kuantan, Kuching, Labuan, Langkawi, Miri and Penang. For a list of airlines with offices in KL see the Transport chapter (p555).

The **Tourism Malaysia office** (☎ 8776 5647/51; 9am-10pm) in the international arrival hall is useful, and there are several restaurants (on Level 4). TimeReach Phonecards bought at the terminal don't work anywhere else in Malaysia.

For short-stay accommodation, try the Airside Transit Hotel (p90) or the Pan Pacific KLIA (p91).

There are several car rental firms operating outside arrivals (Hertz, Mayflower, Pacific, Hawk and Orix).

Bus

From KL's main Puduraya bus station, just east of Chinatown, buses go all over Peninsular Malaysia, including the east coast, and to border countries Singapore and Thailand. The only long-distance destinations that Puduraya doesn't handle are Kuala Lipis and Jerantut, which leave from Pekeliling bus station.

The Pekeliling and Putra bus stations in the north of the city handle a greater number of services to the east coast. Buses at these stations often have seats available when Puduraya buses are fully booked.

For information on buses to Taman Negara, see p274.

KLANG BUS STATION

From the Klang bus station near the Pasar Seni LRT station in Chinatown, at the southern end of Jl Hang Kasturi, frequent buses include No 222 to Shah Alam, No 710 to Klang and Nos 58 and 793 for Pelabuhan (Port) Klang, as well as buses to Petaling Jaya.

PEKELILING BUS STATION

Buses to Jerantut – the jumping off point for Taman Negara National Park – and Kuala Lipis (Kenong Rimba State Park) operate only from Pekeliling bus station (☎ 4042 7256) in the north of the city, just off Jl Tun Razak (close to Tun Razak Star LRT station).

Transnasional Express (☎ 4256 8218) has departures to Kuala Lipis (RM9.50, 4 hours, 6 daily) and Raub (RM6.60, 2½ hours, 5 daily). Park May bus company has six buses a day to Kuantan (RM15, 4 hours). There are buses to/from KL's Pekeliling bus station (RM10.85, 3½ hours, last bus around 4pm) via Temerloh. There are also several buses to Jerantut via Temerloh (RM9.40, 3 hours) and hourly between 7.30am and 6.30pm to Temerloh (RM7), from where regular buses run to Jerantut. Buses also run to the Genting Highlands (RM3.60, every half-hour from 6.30am to 9pm). There are two buses a day to Terengganu (RM25, 9 hours) from Pekeliling.

The **left-luggage counter** (RM3 per bag per day) is open daily from 8am to 8pm.

PUDURAYA BUS STATION

This hot, confusing, clamorous bus-and-taxi station is centrally located on Jl Pudu. Whisperings suggest that Puduraya will close, with operations moving to a new bus station at KL Sentral. A few travellers have reported being robbed late at night, so stay alert.

The **Tourist Police** (main entrance) have an office just inside; opposite is an **information counter** (☎ 2070 0145). At the rear is a **left-luggage counter** (RM2 per day per bag; 🕒 8am-10pm), as well as a post office. A number of hawker stalls serve up food.

Inside are dozens of bus company ticket-windows. A large signboard in front lists which destinations are served by which ticket windows. As you walk down the row of ticket counters, staff will shout out destinations, but check to be sure the departure time suits you, as they sometimes try to sell tickets for buses that aren't leaving for many hours. Buses leave from numbered platforms in the basement, and note that you'll have to look for the name of the bus company rather than your destination.

On the main runs, services are so numerous that you can sometimes just turn up and get a seat on the next bus. However, tickets should preferably be booked at least the day before, and a few days before during peak holiday periods, especially to the Cameron Highlands and east-coast destinations.

With the largest office inside the terminal **Transnasional Express** (☎ 4256 1055) has buses to almost all major destinations. Your guesthouse or hotel may also be able to arrange ticketing, so ask. Transnasional buses are often slower than private companies', but that's because they're safer and more reliable. In a bid to pack in as many trips as possible, drivers from some other companies recklessly speed, resulting in frequent, often fatal, accidents. A bus that crashed at high speed in Negeri Sembilan in 2003, killing three and hospitalising 16, had previously been booked for 59 traffic offences.

Outside the terminal, on Jl Pudu, there are at least another dozen private companies handling tickets for buses to Thailand, Singapore and some Malaysian destinations. Also ask at the Pudu Hostel (see 'The Author's Choice' boxed text, p88) opposite, which can arrange ticketing.

There are only a few daily services to the Cameron Highlands and east-coast destinations, but frequent departures to most other places during the day, and at night to the main towns. For the latter, try to leave as late as possible; otherwise, shortened travel times on the Lebuhraya tollway mean you'll arrive at your destination too early in the morning.

Typical adult fares and journey times from KL are:

Destination	Fare	Duration
Alor Setar	RM 25	4/5 hr
Butterworth	RM 20	4 hr
Cameron Highlands	RM 16	5 hr
Ipoh	RM 11	2½ hr
Johor Bahru	RM 20	4 hr
Kota Bharu	RM 26	6½ hr
Kuala Kedah	RM 21	6 hr
Kuala Terengganu	RM 27	7 hr
Kuantan	RM 14	4½ hr
Lumut	RM 16	4 hr
Melaka	RM 9	2½ hr
Mersing	RM 19.50	5½ hr
Penang	RM 23	5 hr
Singapore	RM 25	5½ hr
Sungai Petani	RM 23	5 hr
Taiping	RM 16	3½ hr

You can get to Puduraya bus station by taking the Star LRT to Plaza Rakyat station.

PUTRA BUS STATION

Though Puduraya handles buses to the east coast, there are also a number of large-company coach services leaving from the quieter and less intimidating **Putra bus station** (☎ 4042 9530), opposite PWTC (easily reached by taking the Star LRT to PWTC station, or a KTM Komuter train to Putra station). Buses depart 8am to 10am and 8pm to 10pm daily.

There are services to Kota Bharu (RM26, 7 hours, 9am and 9.30pm), Kuantan (RM14.25, 4 hours, 10am) and Kuala Terengganu (RM25.70, 7 hours, 10am and 10pm).

Car

Navigating the city's complex (and mostly one-way) traffic system can be frustrating, but there are loads of car parks charging around RM7 per day. KL is the best place to hire a car for touring the peninsula. Rates start at around RM155 a day for a Malaysian-built Proton Wira 1.3L. The best deals are for longer rentals – RM900 per week or RM2000 per month, including insurance and unlimited kilometres.

All the major companies have offices at the airport as well as the following city offices, which are generally open from 9am to 6pm weekdays, and sometimes on weekends. The best deals are usually with Orix, Hawk or Mayflower.

Avis (Map pp82-3; ☎ 2141 7144; 40 Jl Sultan Ismail)
Hawk (Map pp82-3; ☎ 2164 6455; Ground fl, Wisma UOA, 19 Jl Pinang)
Hertz (Map pp82-3; ☎ 9025 6433; Kompleks Antarabangsa, Jl Sultan Ismail)
Mayflower (☎ 6252 1888; 13th fl, Wisma UOAII, 21 Jl Pinang)
National (☎ 2148 0522; 9th fl, Menara Boustead, 69 Jl Raja Chulan)
Orix (Map pp82-3; ☎ 2142 3009; www.orix.com.my; Ground fl, Federal Hotel, 35 Jl Bukit Bintang)

Taxi

Long-distance taxis – often not faster than taking a bus – depart from upstairs at Puduraya bus station. Early in the morning the chances are reasonable of finding other passengers waiting to share on the main west-coast runs to Johor Bahru, Melaka, Ipoh and Penang, but you may have to wait to get a full complement of four passengers. Otherwise, you'll have to charter a whole taxi.

Prices should include toll charges, but some taxi drivers, especially those on the Johor Bahru run, insist on charging extra.

FIXED TAXI FARES

Destination	Fare
Bukit Fraser (Fraser's Hill)	RM 120
Cameron Highlands	RM 140
Genting Highlands	RM 60
Ipoh	RM 160
Johor Bahru	RM 240
Lumut	RM 200
Melaka	RM 140
Penang	RM 240

Train

Kuala Lumpur is the hub of the **KTM** (☎ 2267 1200; www.ktmb.com.my) national railway system. Long-distance trains depart from KL Sentral in the Brickfields area. The KTM information office in the main hall can advise on schedules and check seat availability; it's open from 6.30am to 10.30pm daily. A **ticket delivery service** (☎ 2267 1200; 🕑 8.30am-4.30pm Mon-Sat) can get your ticket to you for a small fee. Children between four and 12 years of age are charged half the adult fare; children under four travel free.

There are daily departures for Butterworth, Wakaf Bharu (for Kota Bharu), Johor Bahru, Thailand and Singapore. Most express-train seats can be booked up to 60 days in advance. For fare and schedule information see Getting Around in the Transport chapter, p568. KTM Komuter trains also link KL with the Klang Valley and Seremban (see City Trains, p102 for information).

GETTING AROUND

Kuala Lumpur's public transport system is changing from slow, chaotic and crowded to speedy, comfortable and uncomplicated. Efforts to ease the city's chronic traffic congestion have seen massive investment in new infrastructure, including the construction of new expressways and public transport options.

KL Sentral station, situated in the Brickfields area 1km south of the historic old train station, is the hub of a new sophisticated rail-based urban network consisting of the KTM Komuter, KLIA Ekspres, KLIA Transit, Putra LRT and Monorail systems.

The systems unfortunately remain unintegrated, with no combined ticketing to facilitate passenger interchange between the various rail systems.

To/From the Airport

The new and efficient non-stop **KLIA Ekspres train** (☎ 2267 8000; first/last train 5am/1am, departures every 15 mins; adult/child one way RM35/15, adult/child return RM70/30) can whisk you between KL Sentral and KLIA in 28 minutes; it is the fastest way of reaching KL from the airport. From KL Sentral, you can continue to your destination by KMT Komuter, Putra LRT, Monorail or taxi.

The **KL Transit train** (adult/child one way RM35/15) also connects KLIA with KL Sentral, but stops at three other stations en route (Salak Tinggi, Putrajaya and Cyberjaya, and Bandar Tasik Selatan), taking about 35 minutes. If flying from KL on Malaysia Airlines, you can check your baggage in at KL Sentral before making your way to KLIA.

Express coaches connect KLIA with Hentian Duta terminal on the northern outskirts of KL. **Airport Coach** (☎ 6203 3154, 1800-880 495) buses leave for KLIA every 30 minutes from 5.30am to 10.15pm (adult/child one way RM20/9, adult/child return RM34/16, 1 to 1½ hrs). At KLIA, these buses depart from the lower terminal levels from 6.45am to 12.30am. As Hentian Duta is not connected to KL by public transport, Airport Coach minibuses do pick-ups and drop-offs at selected downtown hotels, (one way/return RM25/45). Coaches also run between KLIA and Chan Sow Lin Star LRT station (one way/return RM10/18; 45 minutes to 1 hour), about 20 minutes from Masjid Jamek Star LRT station north of Chinatown. From Chan Sow Lin, airport buses depart every half-hour from 6.30am to 9.30pm. In the reverse direction, buses depart from the airport between 7.30am and 9.30pm.

Taxis from KLIA operate on a fixed-fare coupon system. Purchase a coupon from a counter at the arrival hall and use it to pay the driver. Standard taxis cost RM67.10 to hire, and luxury taxis or family-sized minivans cost RM91; return tickets are significantly discounted. It's best to buy your taxi coupon before you exit the arrivals hall, to avoid the aggressive pirate taxis that hassle you to pay a few hundred ringgit for the same ride.

Going to the airport by taxi, make sure that the agreed fare includes tolls, typically RM65 from Chinatown.

Bus

The two main companies are **Intrakota** (☎ 7807 7771) and **Cityliner** (☎ 7982 6904).

Modern air-con buses run along key routes throughout the city, although the renumbering of some routes has further confused the already baffling bus system. Thankfully, both companies have helpful information booths, conveniently located on the northern side of Klang bus station (Cityliner) and at Jl Sultan Mohammed bus stand (Intrakota).

Local buses leave from many of the bus terminals around the city, including the huge Puduraya bus station on Jl Pudu, the Klang bus station, the Jl Sultan Mohammed bus stop south of the Central Market, and from along Medan Pasar and Lebuh Ampang near the Masjid Jamek LRT stations. The maximum fare is usually 90 sen or RM1 for destinations within the city limits; try to have correct change ready when you board, especially during rush hours or if you're boarding somewhere other than at a terminal.

Since KL's inexpensive taxis and reliable LRT systems are more efficient, not to mention air-conditioned, there's little point in trying to come to grips with the bus system unless you're going to be in KL for some time. You'll only really need the bus for trips to outlying areas, such as the Batu Caves.

City Train

The **KTM Komuter service** (☎ 2272 2828) runs along existing long-distance railway lines, stopping at KL Sentral. The service is primarily designed for those who commute from the vast, outlying urban sprawl. It is of limited use to visitors since it does not connect central KL with any of the city's attractions, but it may still be useful for day trips to Selangor and Negeri Sembilan.

The main north–south service runs from Sentul, just north of the city centre, to Pelabuhan Klang via Klang and Shah Alam in Selangor. The other line runs from Rawang, 20km northwest of the city centre, to Seremban in Negeri Sembilan, 66km southeast of KL.

Trains run every 15 to 20 minutes, beginning at approximately 6am and ending about 11pm. Tickets start from RM1 and a RM5 ticket allows unlimited travel on KTM Komuter trains after 9am.

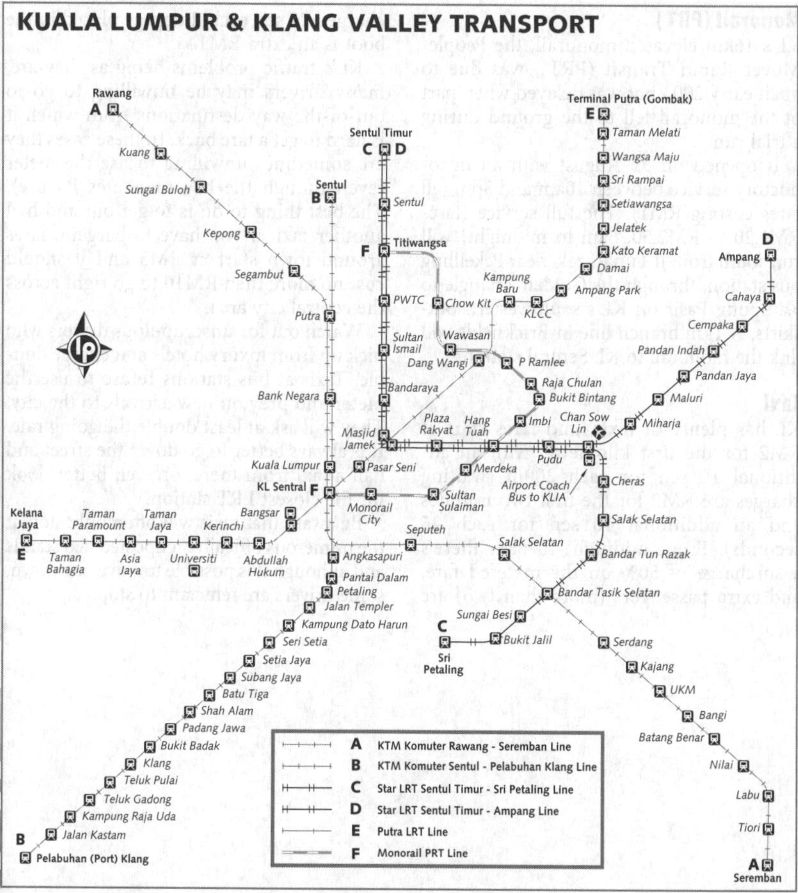

Light Rail (LRT)

KL's pride and joy is the **Light Rail Transit** (LRT; ☎ 1800-388 228), a fast, frequent and inexpensive 'metro'. The largely elevated LRT network is not integrated; however, transfers between the privately run Star and Putra LRT lines can be made at Masjid Jamek, by leaving one system and walking across the street to the other station. An electronic control system for each checks tickets as you enter and exit via turnstiles. Fares range from 70 sen to RM2.80 and stored-value tickets are also available, which can be used on the monorail (see following section). A monthly combined travel card for both lines costs RM125. Touch and Go is a bus and train card that can be used on Cityliner buses and Putra LRT lines; they're available from stations.

The Star LRT runs from Sentul Timur in northern KL via Masjid Jamek to Chan Sow Lin station, where it splits into two separate lines, heading east to Ampang and south to Sri Petaling. Star LRT trains run every six to 10 minutes from 6am to 11.50pm (11.30pm Sunday and holidays).

The Putra LRT runs from Terminal Putra (Gombak) in northeastern KL via Masjid Jamek, then south via KL Sentral station to Bangsar and Universiti Malaya, terminating at Kelana Jaya on KL's western outskirts. The Putra LRT runs about every 10 minutes from 6am to midnight (11pm Sunday and holidays).

Monorail (PRT)

KL's 16km elevated monorail, the People-Mover Rapid Transit (PRT), was due to open early 2003 but was delayed when part of the monorail fell to the ground during a trial run.

It opened on 31 August with an introductory service between 10am and 3pm (all fares costing RM1). The full service (fares RM1.20 to RM2.50, 6am to midnight) will run south from Jl Tun Razak, near Pekeliling bus station, through the Golden Triangle to Kampung Pasir on KL's southwestern outskirts. A 1km branch line in Brickfields will link the monorail to KL Sentral station.

Taxi

KL has plenty of taxis, and fares start at RM2 for the first kilometre, with an additional 10 sen for each 200m (waiting charges are RM2 for the first two minutes and an additional 10 sen for each 45 seconds). From midnight to 6am there's a surcharge of 50% on the metered fare, and extra passengers (more than two) are charged 20 sen each. Luggage placed in the boot is an extra RM1.

KL's traffic problems being as they are, many drivers may be unwilling to go to out-of-the-way destinations from which it is hard to get a fare back. In these cases they are sometimes unwilling to use the meter (even though the law mandates its use). The best thing to do is to get out and hail another taxi; if you have to bargain, fares around town start at RM5 and it should cost no more than RM10 to go right across the central city area.

Watch out for unscrupulous drivers who pick up from luxury hotels and charge double. Taxis at bus stations refuse to use the meter and prey on new arrivals to the city. They will ask at least double the going rate. It is always better to go down the street and hail a taxi from there, or even better, look for the closest LRT station.

Be aware that taxis will often only stop at the numerous offically signposted taxi stands and although it is possible to wave one down, some drivers are reluctant to stop.

Selangor

CONTENTS

Selangor state surrounds the federal territory of Kuala Lumpur (KL) city. Its major borders are aquatic: Selat Melaka (Strait of Melaka) to the west, Sungai Sepang (River Sepang) and Sungai Bernam (River Bernam) to the south and north respectively, and the Banjaran Titiwangsa mountain range watershed to the east.

Many of the state's attractions – such as the Batu Caves, Zoo Negara (National Zoo) and Templer Park on the northern outskirts of KL – are best visited on day trips from the capital. But for those with a little more time to spend, Selangor also has rewarding stopovers in Bukit Fraser (Fraser's Hill), a pleasantly cool hill-station which straddles the state's border with Pahang, and the old royal capital of Kuala Selangor with its wildlife watching and *kampung* (village) atmosphere.

Heading west from KL is the busy, industrial Klang Valley, which runs down to the coast at Pelabuhan Klang, once Malaysia's busiest port. Selangor's state capital, Shah Alam, has a few modern architectural glories and Klang has reminders of the old sultanate, but it is not until you reach Kuala Selangor on the coast that you finally leave the traffic and urban sprawl behind.

HIGHLIGHTS

- Hiking in **Bukit Fraser** (p111) and spotting rare and colourful birds and animals
- Watching the spectacular light shows put on by **fireflies** (p116) on **Sungai Selangor**
- Having a fun day out on the waterslides at **Sunway Lagoon** (p114)
- Visiting Shah Alam's magnificent **Blue Mosque** (p115) and relaxing by the lakeside
- Tucking into a feast of delicious chilli crabs at **Pelabuhan Klang** (p115)
- Spotting spoonbilled sandpipers and other exotic birds at **Taman Alam Kuala Selangor** (p116)
- Learning about Malaysia's aboriginal inhabitants at the **Orang Asli Museum** (p109)
- Climbing the 272 steps to the psychedelic Hindu galleries of **Batu Caves** (p108)

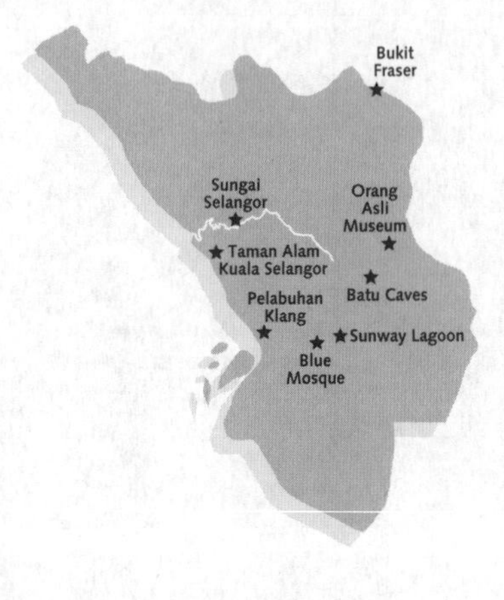

TEL CODES: 03, 09	POPULATION: 4.19 MILLION	AREA: 7960 SQ KM

History

In the 15th century, Selangor was under the control of Melaka's great *bendahara* (chief minister) Tun Perak. Once Melaka fell to the Portuguese, control of Selangor was hotly contested, partly because of its rich tin reserves. The Minangkabau settlers, who had migrated from Sumatra 100 years earlier, were displaced by Buginese immigrants from Celebes (present-day Sulawesi), who aided Dutch colonisation by hiring themselves out as mercenaries. By the middle of the 18th century, the Buginese had established the current sultanate, based at Kuala Selangor.

The 19th century was a boom time for the tin trade, attracting a large influx of Chinese merchants and miners. Many attained powerful positions – in 1857 two Chinese merchants went into partnership with two Selangor chiefs and opened tin mines at Ampang, out of which grew the city of Kuala Lumpur.

The success of the tin trade and the growing wealth of the Chinese communities led to conflicts among the Selangor chiefs and between the miners. The outcome was a prolonged civil war, which saw the destruction of KL before it was brought to an end in 1873.

By this time the British authorities were keen to impose some order on the chaos, especially as tin production had dropped to a fraction of its former volume. In 1874 the sultan was forced to accede to the installation of a British Resident at Klang, and for the next 25 years the state prospered, largely on the back of another boom in tin prices.

Perhaps the most famous of all of the British Residents was Frank Swettenham who, evincing more tolerance and cultural insight than his colleagues, smoothed relations between the sultan and the local chiefs. He cajoled the sultans of four states (Perak, Selangor, Negeri Sembilan and Pahang) into an alliance that eventually became the Federated Malay States in 1896.

The federation was centrally administered from a phoenix-like KL, which had become a well-ordered and prosperous city by the turn of the 20th century. The Federated Malay States led to the formation of the Federation of Malaya in 1948 and, finally, the Federation of Malaysia in 1963. In 1974 Kuala Lumpur city was ceded by the sultan of Selangor and became the federal territory, while Shah Alam took over the role of state capital. In recent years, Selangor has prospered and developed rapidly to become Malaysia's richest, most urbanised and most industrialised state.

Climate

Lowland Selangor has a tropical climate, with daily temperatures hovering between 21°C and 32°C year-round. There is occasional rain throughout the year. Temperatures in the highland areas of Bukit Fraser and the Genting Highlands are much cooler, ranging between 12°C and 22°C. Rainfall here is much heavier and more prolonged. Humidity averages around 85% to 90%.

National Parks

The Taman Alam Kuala Selangor (see p116) is an important wetland and forest reserve some 75km northwest of KL, home to a large number of rare bird species and best known for its fireflies (p116). Bukit Fraser (see p111), straddling the Selangor/Pahang state border, is an old colonial hill station, again rich in wildlife and a good place to go walking.

Getting There & Away

KL is the transport hub of Selangor – for more information on services originating from KL to Selangor and other parts of the region see Getting There & Away (p99) and Getting Around (p101) in the Kuala Lumpur chapter. Kuala Lumpur International Airport (KLIA) is located at Sepang, in the southeast corner of Selangor, with road and dedicated rail links to the capital. The North-South Highway, from Johor Bahru to the Thai border runs the length of the state. Ferries to Sumatra depart from Pelabuhan Klang (see p115).

Getting Around

Trains run to the north and south of KL, as well as westwards, along the Klang Valley through Shah Alam to Pelabuhan Klang. Bus services are more frequent and comprehensive, with links between KL and all major towns in Selangor. See Getting There & Away (p99) in the Kuala Lumpur chapter for information on the main bus and train stations and services.

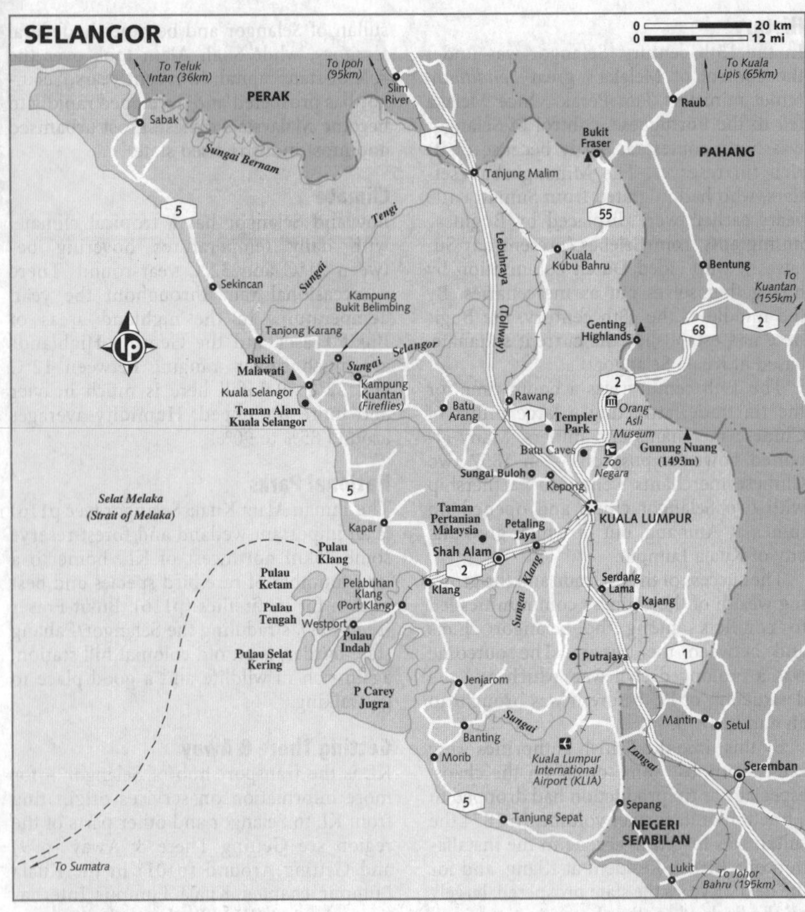

NORTH OF KUALA LUMPUR

Batu Caves

The huge **Batu Caves** (admission free, car park RM2; 8am-8pm) are the best-known attraction near KL. Just 15km north of the capital, a short distance off the Ipoh road, the caves are in a towering limestone formation and were little-known until about 100 years ago, when an American naturalist stumbled across them. Later a small Hindu shrine was built in the vast open space, later known as Temple Cave. Each year in late January or early February almost a million pilgrims come to the caves during the Thaipusam festival to watch the spectacular, masochistic-looking feats of devotees – see the boxed text 'Piercing Devotions' (opposite).

The main cave is reached by a straight flight of 272 steps. Delving into the cavern, it opens to an atrium-like cave at the rear. Many visitors are more spellbound by the monkeys that scale the vertical cliff faces than by the shrines on view (which are dwarfed by the scale of the cave). Several other caves exist in the same formation, including a small one at the base of the outcrop, reached by crossing over a turtle pond. This cave contains elaborately painted sculptures of various Hindu gods. Lord Subramaniam takes centre stage as the dancing Shiva, and other deities such as the fearsome Durga – Shiva's female half – are arranged to tell parables from the *Bhagavad Gita* and other Hindu scriptures.

PAUL BEINSSEN

Shrine to the elephant-god Ganesha, **Batu Caves** (p108)

MICHAEL AW

Blue Mosque (p115), Shah Alam

Sunway Lagoon (p114) theme park, Petaling Jaya

JOHN BORTHWICK

CLEM LINDEN

Istana Kenangan (p145), Perak

Boh's Sungai Palas Tea Estate (p126), Cameron Highlands

RICHARD I'ANSON

CLEM LINDENMAYER

Facade of an old Chinese house, **Taiping** (p146)

CLEM LINDENMAYER

Kellie's Castle (p137), near Ipoh

You can reach the caves on Intrakota bus No 11D (90 sen, 30 minutes) or Cityliner bus No 69 (RM1) from Medan Pasar, near the Central Market in KL. No 11D also stops along Jl Raja Laut in the Chow Kit area. During Thaipusam special trains and buses carry devotees and onlookers to the caves.

Zoo Negara

About 13km northeast of KL, **Zoo Negara** (National Zoo; ☎ 4108 3427; adult/child RM7/3, camera use RM2; ⏰ 9am-5pm) is laid out over 62 hectares around a central lake. The collection has a sampling of native Malaysian wildlife, as well as other animals from Asia and Africa. Though a good zoo by Asian standards, some of the animal enclosures are still sadly cramped. Elephant and pony rides (RM2) are available around lunchtime and there are elephant shows in the morning and afternoon. A shuttle takes visitors around the landscaped grounds.

Take bus No 170 from Lebuh Ampang in KL's Chinatown or from along Jl Raja Laut in Chow Kit, from where you could also catch bus No 17 to the zoo.

Orang Asli Museum

The excellent and highly educational **Orang Asli Museum** (☎ 6189 2122; Jl Pahang, Gombak; admission free; ⏰ 9.30am-5pm Sat-Thu), 25km north of KL, is a good introduction to the customs and culture of the Orang Asli – Malaysia's aboriginal people – who numbered over 92,000 in 1993 (see the boxed text 'The Indigenous People', p35). Within the Orang Asli there are 18 separate ethnic types, each with their own language (the principle language Mon-Khmer in origin). Groups include the Bateq, Jahai, Temiar, Semai and Semoq Beri (40% of Orang Asli are coastal, lowland dwellers). The exhibits are fascinating: you get to see some Orang Asli bark pants – trousers made from the bark of Terap and Ipoh trees. Also on view are

PIERCING DEVOTIONS

The most spectacular Hindu festival in Malaysia is Thaipusam, a wild orgy of seemingly hideous body piercings. The festival happens every year in the Hindu month of Thai (January/February), when the constellation of Pusam is in its ascendancy, and is celebrated with huge gusto at the Batu Caves where up to a million devotees and onlookers flock to honour Lord Muruga, also known as Lord Subramaniam. His chariot takes pride of place as it makes its way from the Sri Mahamariamman Temple in KL's Chinatown to the Batu Caves. If you want to see anything at all amid this heavy crowd get here by dawn at the latest and bring food and water with you.

The greatest spectacle is the *kavadi* carriers, the devotees who subject themselves to seemingly masochistic acts as fulfilment for answered prayers. Many of the devotees carry offerings of milk in *paal kudam*, or milk pots, often connected to the skin by hooks. Even more striking are the *vel kavadi*, great cages of spikes that pierce the skin of the carrier and are decorated with peacock feathers, pictures of deities and flowers. Some penitents go as far as to pierce their tongues and cheeks with hooks, skewers and tridents. Couples whose prayers for children have been answered carry their babies on their shoulders in saffron cradles made of sugar-cane stalks. To the beating of drums and chants of *'Vel, Vel'* the devotees form a constant procession through the caves and up the 272 steps to the main shrine.

The festival is the culmination of around a month of prayer, a vegetarian diet and other ritual preparations, such as abstinence from sex, or sleeping on a hard floor. While it looks excruciating, a trance-like state stops participants from feeling pain; later the wounds are treated with lemon juice and holy ash to prevent scarring. Like firewalking, only the truly faithful should attempt the ritual. It is said that insufficiently prepared devotees keep Indian doctors especially busy over the Thaipusam festival period with skin lacerations, or by collapsing after the strenuous activities.

Originating in Tamil Nadu and now banned in India, Thaipusam is also celebrated in Penang at the Nattukotai Chettiar Temple and the Waterfall Hilltop Temple, and in Johor Bahru at the Sri Thandayuthabani Temple. Ipoh attracts a large number of devotees, who follow the procession from the Sri Mariamar Temple in Buntong to the Sri Subramaniar Temple in Gunung Cheroh. In Singapore, Hindus march in a procession from the Sri Srinivasa Perumal Temple on Serangoon Rd to the Chettiar Hindu Temple.

personal adornments, musical instruments, hunting implements (blowpipes, poison spoons and bird lime sticks) and informative descriptions of Orang Asli wedding rites. Aboriginal dwellings, usually just temporary structures as the Orang Asli are nomadic, are also represented. The museum provides useful preparation for anyone visiting Orang Asli areas, such as Taman Negara National Park (p267). Also covered is their animistic religion and the role played by the *halaaq* (medicine man). Take bus No 174 from the Lebuh Ampang terminus in KL.

Forestry Research Institute of Malaysia (FRIM)

Surrounded by the Bukit Lagong Forest Reserve, the **Forestry Research Institute of Malaysia** (FRIM; ☎ 6279 7575; www.frim.gov.my; 🕓 8am-6.30pm) maintains a 600-hectare jungle park at Kepong, 16km northwest of KL. It is a centre for research into forest regeneration and, though not aimed at tourists, its displays roughly outline the work done by FRIM and explain the rainforest habitat and its renewal. Visitors can view close to 30 species of local and exotic bamboo, traditional medicinal-herb gardens and Malaysia's rainforest flora up close, but not much is labelled. On the grounds there is also a traditional Chengal wood house from the Terengganu region of east Peninsular Malaysia.

The main interest is the variety of short to strenuous jungle trails (night walks are also possible), where you can see a large variety of trees and plant life. There is also an arboretum, a museum and a wetland area. For a closer inspection of the rainforest canopy, you can book a canopy walk by calling the **Canopy Walkway Centre** (☎ 6279 7220; adult/child RM5/3; 🕓 Tue-Sat & 2nd Sun of each month); advance bookings are necessary. A round trip on the trail incorporating the walkway takes around two hours. Bring water with you. There is no public bus service from KL; a metered taxi to FRIM costs RM12 to RM15; alternatively take a KTM Komuter train to Kepong (RM1) and then a taxi (RM5).

Templer Park

Beside Hwy 1, 22km north of KL, **Templer Park** (☎ 6091 0022; 🕓 24hr) is a 1200-hectare tract of primary jungle named after the last British high commissioner of Malaysia. There are a number of marked jungle paths, swimming lagoons, an artificial lake and several waterfalls within the park boundaries.

On the outskirts of the northern boundary of Templer Park is a 350m-high limestone formation known as Bukit Takun, and nearby is the smaller Anak Takun, which has many caves for exploring.

Templer Park is a half-hour ride on the Tanjung Malim-bound bus No 66 from the Puduraya bus station.

Genting Highlands

☎ 03

Genting Highlands is a garishly modern hill station designed as a kind of Asian Disneyland for the affluent citizens of KL just 50km to the south. In contrast to the Old English style of other Malaysian hill stations, Genting's landscape is a forest of high-rise concrete blocks. With its huge theme parks and extensive entertainment and activity programmes, it's popular with young families, and can get extremely crowded, especially at weekends. You'll also find Malaysia's only casino here, along with a boating lake and golf course.

Genting has cooler weather like any other hill station; the main part of the resort is almost 2000m above sea level.

SLEEPING & EATING

There are five huge hotels on the Highlands proper, all run by **Genting Highlands Resort** (☎ 2718 1118; www.genting.com.my), which takes all reservations and inquiries. The KL office of **Genting Resort World** (☎ 2162 2666; Wisma Genting, Jl Sultan Ismail), also accepts reservations. Rates vary enormously over low, shoulder (school holidays and June), peak (Saturday night and November to January) and superpeak (Christmas and Chinese and Western New Year) seasons.

First World Hotel (s & d from RM65; ❄ 💻 🚭) The largest hotel in Malaysia, with a shopping arcade and indoor theme park complete with carousel. Rooms are fairly plain, but good value.

Theme Park Hotel (s & d from RM100; ❄ 💻) Has a vaguely medieval theme going on, though rooms are pretty ordinary.

Resort Hotel (s & d RM140; ❄ 💻 🚭) The rooms at this more upscale hotel are preferable to those at the Theme Park Hotel.

Genting Hotel (s & d from RM210, apt from RM1000;) A gigantic five-star place with every facility imaginable, try this for a bit of real luxury. Themed rooms furnished in English, Japanese or Indian styles are also available, as well as three-room apartments.

Highlands Hotel (s & d from RM230;) This grand hotel offers a luxury standard, with elegantly decorated rooms and a wide range of facilities.

Awana Golf & Country Resort (☎ 6101 3015; s & d from RM130;) A few kilometres below the bus and lower cable-car station, this is another top-class option, offering tennis, squash, golf and horse riding.

All the hotels have good restaurants.

Peak (☎ 6101 1118; dishes from RM39) on the 17th floor of the Genting Hotel, is the best. It serves first-class Asian and Western cuisine, and has great views.

Tropical Café (buffet RM29) in the First World Hotel, offers generous buffet lunches and dinners.

GETTING THERE & AWAY

Buses leave from KL's Puduraya bus station every 30 minutes for Genting Highlands (RM6.80, 1½ hours); the price includes the Skyway cable car. A taxi will cost RM55. There are also direct bus services from KLIA via Hentian Duta to the Highlands (RM22, including the Skyway).

From the Genting Highlands bus station, the precipitous 3.4km-long cable car **Genting Skyway** (one way/return RM4/7; 7.30am-11pm, until 2am Sat) hums up to the main resort – 700 vertical metres above – in 15 minutes. The **Awana Skyway** (one way/return RM4/7; 11.30pm-8am) runs up and down hourly at night.

Bukit Fraser

☎ 09

Bukit Fraser is named after Louis James Fraser, a reclusive ore-trader and mule-train operator who lived here at the turn of the 20th century. It's said he ran gambling-and-opium dens, but these had vanished (along with Fraser himself) by 1910, when Bishop Ferguson-Davie of Singapore came looking for Fraser and recognised the area's potential as a hill station.

Of all the hill stations, Fraser's retains the most colonial charm. The station, set at a cool 1524m altitude, is not the easiest place to get to without your own transport. It's a quiet and relatively undeveloped place, attracting only a fraction of the visitor numbers drawn to the overcrowded Genting Highlands or the backpacker-land of the Cameron Highlands. There is relatively little to do besides relax in the cool or enjoy a jungle stroll and indulge in a morning's bird-watching.

Bukit Fraser can be done as a (long) day trip from KL, if you have your own car, but it's best to take it easy and book into one of the charming state-run stone bungalows for an overnight stay.

Like the Genting Highlands, Bukit Fraser is on the Selangor/Pahang border, but almost all visitors come through Selangor, and the state border actually cuts right through the station. Note that the telephone area code for Bukit Fraser is the Pahang code (☎ 09), not the Selangor code (☎ 03).

INFORMATION

The tiny village at the western end of the golf course is the centre of Bukit Fraser.

Maybank (9.30am-4.30pm Mon-Fri, until 11am Sat) has a small branch at the Quest Resort. Back in Kuala Kubu Bharu (KKB), the turn-off to Bukit Fraser from Hwy 1, there is a Maybank with ATMs opposite the bus station.

Bukit Fraser Development Corporation (FHDC; ☎ 362 2248; fax 362 2273; Jl Genting; 8am-1pm & 2-10pm) Provides information, maps and brochures, and staff can book FHDC accommodation in Bukit Fraser.

WWF Nature Education Centre (☎ 362 2517; www.wwfmalaysia.org/fhnec; Sports Complex, Jl Genting; 9.30am-5.30pm Wed-Sun) Resource centre with a library and small museum on local flora and fauna. Up-to-date and detailed hiking trail guides and maps are available here. The knowledgeable staff can answer queries and organise guided jungle walks.

SIGHTS & ACTIVITIES

One of Fraser Hill's main attractions is its abundant flora and fauna, and in particular, its **birdlife**; some 265 species have been recorded here (see the boxed text 'Birds at Bukit Fraser', p113. There are many wild flowers, dense jungle and impressive towering trees, though walks are mostly limited to quick strolls off and on the quiet paved roads.

One of the only real trails of note is the **Maxwell Trail**, a two-hour walk (about 2km) from the children's playground (complete

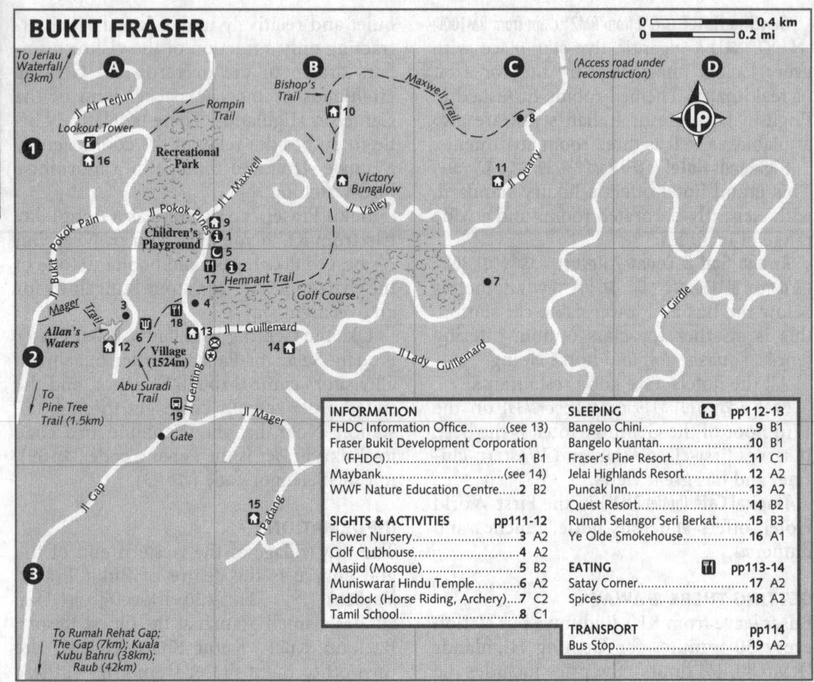

with go-karts and mini-golf) to the small Tamil school. The walk is strenuous and the trail is muddy in parts. For less-vigorous walkers, the **Hemmant Trail**, which takes only 30 minutes, is about 1km and leads from the side of the WWF office to Victory Bungalow. More rewarding, but also more difficult, the **Pine Tree Trail** starts a few kilometres west of town. The steep 6km trail takes about four hours to scramble to the peak of Pine Tree Hill; check in at the WWF office for a detailed trail guide before setting out.

At the picturesque nine-hole **golf course**, where you'll see dusky leaf monkeys wandering, a game costs RM30/40 on weekdays/weekends, plus RM15 for club rental. Table tennis, snooker, a gym and sauna are available at the clubhouse. At the paddock to the east of the golf course, you can go **horse riding** or practice **archery**. Aquatic enthusiasts can hire a paddle boat or do some fishing at **Allan's Waters**, a small lake next to the flower nursery and Muniswarar Hindu temple, both of which are open to the public.

About 5km northwest of the town centre is **Jeriau Waterfall**, with a swimming pool fed from the falls. It's easily reached via Jl Air Terjun, passing a **lookout tower** on the way.

SLEEPING

Most of the accommodation is run by the FHDC, a government-contracted *bumiputra* (indigenous Malaysian) organisation, and there are few budget options. Rates at FHDC lodgings are slightly lower Monday to Friday; peak times are Saturday, Sunday and public holidays when bookings are recommended (see Information, p111).

Rooms have bathrooms and showers, but are usually musty due to the cool, damp climate.

Budget

Puncak Inn (☎ 362 2201; s & d RM39-61) Above the little shopping centre close to where the bus stops is this convenient and reasonably priced place, though it has seen better days. Simple rooms, with TV and hot shower.

Rumah Selangor Seri Berkat (s & d RM40-60) This Selangor government resthouse on

Jl Padang is across the state line on the south side of Bukit Fraser. This two-storey colonial edifice built in 1926 has comfortable and spacious rooms with high ceilings. Book through the **District Office** (☎ 03-6064 1026) in KKB.

Rumah Rehat Gap (☎ 362 2227; s & d RM41) Situated at the Gap turn-off from the main road 8km south of Bukit Fraser, this place is also run by the Selangor government. Wonderfully old fashioned, its spacious rooms with bathrooms are big enough for three people, with room to spare.

Mid-Range

The FHDC has *bangelo* (bungalows); they are stone buildings with pleasant gardens, good views, large lounge areas and plenty of colonial grace. Many of the dozens of bungalows scattered around Bukit Fraser are privately leased out by the FHDC. Availability to the public changes, so ask in advance at the information office downstairs at the Puncak Inn.

At the time of writing, only the Kuantan and Chini bungalows were available.

Bangelo Kuantan has a pleasant hillside aspect but is almost 3km from the centre; **Bangelo Chini** sits up on a hillside above the FHDC headquarters, although the views are partly obscured. Most FHDC bungalows are a fair way from the bus stop, but once you get your gear there, it is a pleasant walk around the roads. The bungalows cost RM150, and sleep up to four. Food is provided by the caretakers if there is enough demand; negotiate the price beforehand, as the caretakers usually expect to be paid much more than the set price (RM28 per meal for four people).

Quest Resort (☎ 362 2300; fax 362 2284; Jl Lady Guillemard; s & d RM99-180; ❄ 💻) is a modern place that overlooks the golf course. It's in a very pleasant spot, and rooms are comfortable enough but a little overpriced.

Jelai Highlands Resort (☎ 362 2600; fax 362 2604; s & d RM80-120, f RM140) is situated on the south side of Allan's Waters, and has spacious, if slightly damp, doubles overlooking the lake.

Top End

Most of the top-end hotels charge around 20% to 30% more on weekends and public holidays.

BIRDS AT BUKIT FRASER

Bukit Fraser (Fraser's Hill) is a paradise for bird-watchers, with a large bird population in a quite small and limited area. There's a huge variety of birds to be seen – 265 different species at the last count – and many of these are brightly coloured and relatively tame; you'll have no trouble spotting the flashes of colour among the trees. With its lush, damp forest environment, the hill supports a distinct assortment of birdlife to the warmer and more humid lowlands. A high proportion of Malaysia's endemic birds can be seen here, including the Malaysian whistling thrush, the Kinabalu friendly warbler, the brilliantly coloured green magpie, and the long-tailed broadbill with its sky-blue chest.

For more information, check the website www.wwfmalaysia.org/fhnec.

Fraser's Pine Resort (☎ 362 2122; frasershill@hotmail.com; Jl Pecah Batu; s & d from RM288) Has roomy, well-kept apartments and a decent coffee house in the main lodge. Popular with young families.

Ye Olde Smokehouse (☎ 362 2226; fax 362 2035; Jl Air Terjun; s & d RM280-400) Fraser's classiest lodging has all the charm of a country manse, with its mock-Tudor building, with exposed beams, log fires, stained-wood armchairs and the lingering smell of roasts. English breakfasts and cream teas offer a taste of the old country.

Other privately owned bungalows and condominiums are sometimes available for rent, but advance bookings are necessary. The FHDC can help and the restaurants below the Puncak Inn sometimes advertise space on their bulletin boards.

EATING

The small shopping centre at the Puncak Inn has a range of simple restaurants, including the Chinese **Hill View** (☎ 362 2231; dishes from RM5) and **Restoran Puncak**, serving roti canai (flaky flat bread with dhal or curry) and other cheap Indian snacks.

Just uphill, **Spices** (☎ 362 2510; Jl Genting; dishes from RM11) serves Western food, including fish and chips. Further uphill, just south of the WWF office, **Satay Corner** (dishes RM2-3) has basic, delicious hawker fare.

GETTING THERE & AWAY

Bukit Fraser is 103km north of KL and 240km from Kuantan on the east coast. The usual access is via Kuala Kubu Bahru (KKB), 62km north of KL, just off Hwy 1 and the KL–Butterworth train line.

From KL's Puduraya bus station, take the half-hourly Tanjung Malim bus from platform 21 to KKB (RM4.50, 1½ hours). To ensure a connection, though, you must take one no later than 8.30am, as there's only one bus a day, at 10.30am, from KKB to Bukit Fraser (RM3.20, 1½ hours). The bus makes the return journey from Bukit Fraser to KKB at 2.45pm. A taxi from KKB to Bukit Fraser is RM50. A direct taxi all the way from KL's Puduraya bus station costs around RM120.

Buses to Bukit Fraser run via the Gap, a mountain pass on the KKB–Raub road. The 11km-long road up the back of Bukit Fraser via the Tamil school and Fraser's Pine Resort has been under reconstruction for years. For now, the old 8km-long road, which descends directly from Bukit Fraser village centre, has an alternating one-way traffic system, with fixed times for uphill and downhill traffic.

You can walk down the Gap in about 1½ hours (8km) and catch the KKB-bound bus from Raub that passes by the Gap around 3.30pm. If you're coming from Raub via that bus, wait at the Gap turn-off for the next bus up to Bukit Fraser. If you plan to head east after visiting Fraser's, the 4pm bus back to KKB can drop you off on the main road beneath the Gap to meet the Raub-bound bus that passes by at around 5pm. From Raub you can continue to Jerantut and Kuala Lipis, though maybe not the same day.

Bukit Fraser is open to private vehicles, but drivers are warned that there's no fuel station in Fraser's; the nearest places with fuel are Raub and KKB.

KLANG VALLEY

☎ 03

Heading southwest of KL along the Klang Hwy, the **Kota Darul Ehsan** ceremonial arch marks the boundary between KL and Selangor. It memorialises the sultan of Selangor's 'sacrifice' of Kuala Lumpur to the federal government. Apart from the archway, little else distinguishes this corridor of housing estates and industrial parks. Just over the boundary, Petaling Jaya (PJ) blends into Shah Alam, the state capital, which blends into Klang, the old royal capital. Efficient transport connections to and from KL make for easy day trips, but there's not a whole lot to see.

Petaling Jaya

☎ 03

Petaling Jaya (PJ) is a modern suburb of Kuala Lumpur, just 11km southwest of the city centre. Originally developed as a dormitory suburb, PJ has grown so successfully and rapidly that it is now a major industrial centre in its own right.

The Universiti Malaya is en route to PJ. On the university grounds is the **Muzium Seni Asia** (Museum of Asian Arts; ☎ 7959 3805; Jl Pantai Baru; admission free; 🕑 9am-5pm Mon-Thu, 9am-12.15pm & 2.45-5pm Fri, 9am-12.30pm Sat). It houses an overflowing collection of Asian ceramics, carvings and textiles, but there is little labelling in English. Take the Putra LRT from KL to the Universiti stop (RM1.60), then a shuttle bus (50 sen) or a metered taxi to the campus.

PJ is well supplied with shopping malls and amusement places popular with the residents of KL. Malaysia's first theme park, **Sunway Lagoon** (☎ 5635 8000; www.sunway.com.my/lagoon; 3 Jl PJS, Bandar Sunway; adult/child RM39/26; 🕑 11am-6pm Mon & Wed-Fri, 10am-6pm Sat & Sun) has waterslides, fairground rides and numerous shows, games and activities for children. Take the Putra LRT to Kelana Jaya terminus, from where shuttle bus No 900 runs every 30 minutes to Sunway Lagoon (50 sen). Cityliner bus No 51 and Metro bus Nos 10 and 11 go directly to Sunway Lagoon from KL's Klang bus station.

Shah Alam

☎ 03

The capital of Selangor state is an hour's drive west of KL. Two decades ago it was just a rubber-and-palm plantation, but in the late 1970s a massive building programme spawned a well-developed infrastructure, some enormous public buildings and a rapidly growing population.

The **Tourism Selangor** office (☎ 5513 2000; www.deselangortourism.com; P-7 Jl Indah; 🕑 9am-7pm) is in the centre of town, near the Quality Hotel. There's a range of brochures on hand, while helpful staff can answer Selangor-related queries.

Like many planned cities, Shah Alam has very wide streets and great distances between parts of the city, making it difficult to get around without your own transport. Most sights, however, are at or near the attractive central **Lake Gardens**. The showpiece is Masjid Sultan Salahuddin Abdul Aziz Shah, nicknamed the **Blue Mosque** for its blue aluminium dome covered in a rosette of verses from the Quran. This huge, gleaming mosque is Malaysia's largest and accommodates up to 24,000 worshippers; its four minarets are the tallest in the world at over 140m.

The **State Museum** (☎ 5519 0050; Persiaran Bandar Raya; admission free; 🕑 9.30am-5.30pm Sat-Thu, 9.30am-noon & 2.45-5.30pm Fri) is a short walk from the mosque through the Lake Gardens. Extensive displays cover the history and culture of Selangor from earliest times, while other galleries are devoted to natural history and the royal family.

SLEEPING & EATING

Shah Alam is an easy day trip from KL, and there's little call for an overnight stay. If you do decide to stay, there's only a limited choice of top-end hotels.

Grand Blue Wave Hotel (☎ 5031 3388; www.bluewavehotels.com; 14 Persiaran Perbandaran; s & d/ste RM239.20/322;) The best place in town, with a couple of top-class Chinese and Japanese restaurants.

Quality Hotel (☎ 5510 3696; www.quality.com.my; Plaza Perengsang; s & d/ste RM155/280;) A modern chain hotel, offering a high standard of comfort. It has a very good Szechuan restaurant, **Meisan** (dishes from RM25), open to nonguests.

Cheaper fast food is available from outlets in the central **Alam Sentar** mall, while just behind, overlooking the lake, **Restoran Tasik Indah** (☎ 5519 8388; 14 Jl Indah; dishes from RM28) serves excellent seafood.

GETTING THERE & AWAY

Bus Nos 222 and 338 go to Shah Alam from KL's Klang bus station (RM2) and will drop you in front of the PKNS Plaza mall, from where it's a short walk to all the sights. Alternatively, you could take a frequent Komuter train from KL to Shah Alam station, but from there it's another bus or taxi ride to the Lake Gardens.

Klang

☎ 03

Klang (sometimes spelt Kelang) is the old royal capital of Selangor, where the British installed their first Resident in 1874. Its few attractions are in the old city, south of the bus station and across the river, nearer to the train station.

Masjid Di Raja Sultan Suleiman, 1km south of the train station along Jl Raya Timur, is a blend of Art Deco and Middle Eastern influences. Behind the mosque, on Jl Istana, is **Istana Alam Shah**, the main palace of the sultan before the capital was moved to Shah Alam. There are other mosques and minor palaces scattered about, and all are signposted from the intersection in front of the train station.

GETTING THERE & AWAY

Klang's bus station is opposite the My Din shopping complex, on the northern side of the river. There are several buses every hour to KL's Klang bus station (RM2) or Kuala Selangor (RM2). Express buses between KL and Pelabuhan Klang also stop in Klang. Klang's taxi station is one block east, behind the bus station.

Coming from KL, KTM Komuter trains are more convenient as the train station, a 10-minute walk over the bridge from the bus station, is closer to the sights; there are trains every 30 minutes.

Pelabuhan Klang

☎ 03

Some 41km southwest of KL, 8km past Klang, is Pelabuhan Klang (formerly Port Swettenham). It's hard to believe, but Pelabuhan Klang was KL's main seaport until the establishment of a major new harbour at Westport on Pulau Indah.

Though not a particularly attractive place, Pelabuhan Klang is renowned for its excellent seafood, particularly chilli crabs (about RM35).

The 30-minute ferry trip to **Pulau Ketam** (Crab Island) is a popular weekend excursion for KL residents. The island has a stilt fishing village and Chinese seafood restaurants. Public ferries leave from the wharf roughly every hour between 9.40am and 5.10pm (until 7pm on Saturday); the last ferry back from Pulau Ketam is at 4.40pm (3.40pm on Sunday).

One of the few places to stay in Pelabuhan Klang is **Sealion Villa Lodge** (☎ 3110 4121; fax 3110 4072; s/d from RM25/35; ☒) next to the jetty, but there's little reason to linger.

GETTING THERE & AWAY

Buses from KL's Klang bus station run to Pelabuhan Klang via Klang, but they only stop in town about a kilometre from the port. KTM Komuter trains also run to/from the capital and Klang. Pelabuhan Klang is at the end of the KTM Komuter line and the station is just a stone's throw from the wharf.

Ferries to Tanjung Balai (Asahan) in Sumatra depart from Pelabuhan Klang every day except Sunday at 11am (one way/return RM95/190, 4 hours). **Doyan Shipping & Forwarding** (☎ 316 530731) has a ticket counter inside the passenger-ferry terminal, opposite the KTM station at the end of Persiaran Raja Muda Musa. You must have an Indonesian visa before boarding.

Kuala Selangor

☎ 03

Where Sungai Selangor meets the sea is the old royal capital of Kuala Selangor. This small town was conquered by the Dutch when they invaded Selangor in 1784, then became the scene of ongoing battles and civil disturbances.

Well off the beaten tourist track, Kuala Selangor has an enjoyable *kampung* atmosphere and a few notable points of interest. It's well worth a stopover for those venturing along this rewarding back route to Perak state.

SIGHTS & ACTIVITIES

Bukit Malawati

The flat coastal plain along this stretch of coast is broken by Bukit Malawati, the hill overlooking the town. It is a pleasant walk through landscaped parklands and forest to the top, with views across the mangrove coastline.

Bukit Malawati was an ideal site for monitoring shipping in the Selat Melaka, first for the sultans of Selangor, then for the British who intervened in 1874, and the Dutch. The Dutch destroyed the sultan's fort during their invasion in 1784, then rebuilt it, naming it Fort Atlingsburg after their governor general. The fort was recaptured quickly by the sultan in 1785, repeatedly changing hands and being fought over; all that remains today are some sections of wall and cannons.

The road up Bukit Malawati starts one block behind the shops facing the old bus station in the town centre. It does a clockwise loop of the hill; you can walk up and around in about an hour.

Taman Alam Kuala Selangor

This 240-hectare nature park is on the estuary of Sungai Selangor, 2km outside town towards the new station. The turn-off to the park is at Jl Klinik, set back a few hundred metres from the highway. This park of mangroves and secondary forest is noted

FLYING FIREWORKS

Of the 130-odd species of firefly (*kelip-kelip*), those of Southeast Asia are the most spectacular, noted for their displays of synchronised flashing. The folded-wing fireflies (*Pteroptyx tener*) are quite large at around 6cm long, and both males and females flash, though only the brighter males flash in unison. They gather in particular *berembang* trees along the banks of Sungai Selangor, sometimes in the thousands, when their flashing becomes synchronised, at intervals of roughly three seconds.

This natural light show can be seen at a few places, notably Kampung Kuantan, 9km east of Kuala Selangor. Malay-style wooden boats row out on the river to the 'show trees' and their dazzling displays. Boats take four people at RM10 each for the 45-minute trip, and leave on demand throughout the evening from around 7pm until midnight. The trips are not recommended on full-moon or rainy nights, when the fireflies are not at their luminous best. Take mosquito repellent.

To reach the village, take the turn-off to Batang Berjuntai, 2km south of Kuala Selangor. A taxi from Kuala Selangor costs RM40 for the return trip.

You can also see fireflies at Kampung Bukit Belimbing; see the entry for the Firefly Park Resort in Kuala Selangor (opposite).

for its **birdlife**, especially mangrove waders such as the rare spoonbilled sandpiper and Nordmann's greenshank, best seen at dusk. Around 150 species have been sighted. The park also operates a captive breeding programme, in conjunction with Zoo Negara, for the endangered milky stork; their aviary is next to the main lake. In the secondary forest, you may catch a glimpse of the noisy silver langurs, as well as otters, nocturnal leopard cats and civets.

To aid in better bird-watching, two watchtowers and several hides have been constructed, and two boardwalks lead through the mangroves to the sea. Tame nature trails, which take 25 minutes to 2½ hours to complete, radiate from the visitors centre. The main trails are dirt roads – the side trails are more interesting.

Entry to the park costs RM5 and the **visitors centre** (☎ 889 2294) is open daily, though opening hours may be erratic. Be warned, that the park is often deserted, and female travellers have been harassed by men here.

SLEEPING & EATING

Kuala Selangor is just one long block of shops next to the old bus station.

Hotel Kuala Selangor (☎ 3289 2709; 90B Jl Steysen; s & d RM40-90; ❄) Directly opposite the bus station, this hotel has simple rooms in a rather drab concrete block over some shops.

Melawati Ria Hotel (☎ 3289 1268; 15 Jl Raja Jalil; s & d RM40; ❄) One street back towards Bukit Malawati, this is a smaller place with a helpful, English-speaking owner who can suggest day trips and places to see the fireflies.

Firefly Park Resort (☎ 3289 1208; www.fireflypark.com; Kg Bukit Belimbing; chalets RM120-160; ❄) North of the river, this is a great option. This modern resort has comfortable four-person chalets perched on stilts over the river, and beautifully landscaped grounds. Boat trips to watch the fireflies cost RM10/6 for adults/children, and fishing trips cost RM30 per hour. Also on site, the **Firefly Park Seafood Restaurant** (dishes from RM10) serves very good fresh fish.

In town, there are a number of unexceptional Chinese restaurants on Jl Steysen, near the Hotel Kuala Selangor.

GETTING THERE & AWAY

Buses run roughly hourly between Kuala Selangor and KL's Puduraya bus and taxi station (RM6, 2 hours). Air-con buses run every 30 minutes between Kuala Selangor and Klang (RM2, 1¼ hours). Heading north from Kuala Selangor to Perak state, first take one of the old rattlers to Tanjong Karang for connections to Teluk Intan.

Many bus services originate from the bus station, 2km outside the town centre. If you're headed to KL or Teluk Intan, it's best to start there; take a local bus (60 sen) from the old bus station, or it's a 20-minute walk from town.

Approximate fares for a taxi from Kuala Selangor: KL (RM100), Klang (RM20) and Teluk Intan (RM60).

Perak

CONTENTS

For centuries Perak's fame rested on its rich tin deposits; in fact, it gained its name from the ore (*perak* means 'silver' in Malay). Perak (more specifically, Kuala Kangsar) was also the birthplace of the Malaysian rubber industry, a mainstay of the local and national economy to this day.

Perak is a relatively large state with a varied landscape. Much of the north of the state is dominated by jungle and sees very few foreign visitors, while the south contains a scattering of lazy towns, mostly of interest for their onward transport connections.

The capital, Ipoh, is a sprawling, ramshackle city with a certain rough-edged charm, but for most travellers the main attractions of Perak are the laid-back resort island of Pulau Pangkor, which lies just off the southern coast, the historic royal town of Kuala Kangsar, and Taiping, with its lush gardens, colonial remnants and zoo.

Perak is also the access point for the Cameron Highlands (in Pahang), Malaysia's premier hill station and one of the country's most justifiably popular tourist destinations. For a quieter retreat, Malaysia's oldest hill station is peaceful Bukit Larut, near Taiping.

HIGHLIGHTS

- Visiting one of the tea plantations and enjoying leisurely walks and lush scenery in the **Cameron Highlands** (p123)
- Sitting down to a traditional cream tea in **Tanah Rata** (p126) in the Cameron Highlands
- Exploring the caverns and grottoes of Perak Tong and other **cave temples** (p134) near Ipoh
- Taking a wander around the grand colonial ruin of **Kellie's Castle** (p137) and its pleasant grounds
- Hiking, snorkelling or lazing on one of the fine beaches of **Pulau Pangkor** (p138), a low-key resort island
- Admiring the palaces, mosque and other sights of **Kuala Kangsar's** (p144) impressive old royal district
- Luxuriating in one of the exclusive seaside villas on **Pulau Pangkor Laut** (p143)
- Relaxing in the lovely lush **Taman Tasik Taiping** (p146)

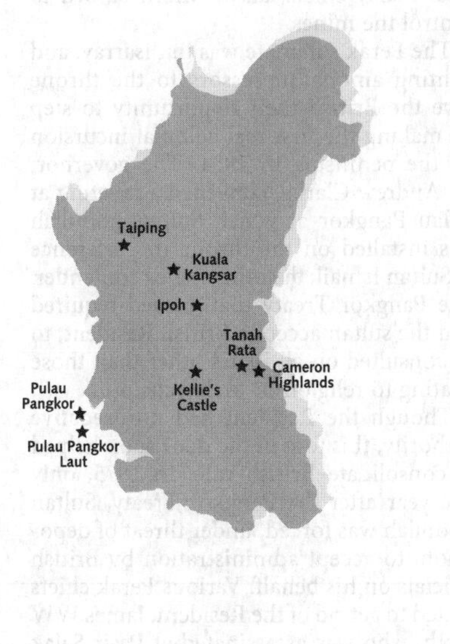

- TEL CODES: 05, 09
- POPULATION: 2.05 MILLION
- AREA: 21,005 SQ KM

History

The current sultanate of Perak dates back to the early 16th century, when the eldest son of the last sultan of Melaka, Sultan Muzaffar Shah, established his own dynasty on the banks of Sungai Perak (Perak River). Being so rich in tin, the state was regularly threatened.

Dutch efforts in the 17th century to monopolise the tin trade had little result, but remains of their forts can still be seen on Pulau Pangkor (Pangkor Island) and at the mouth of Sungai Perak. In the 18th century the Bugis from the south and the Siamese to the north made concerted attempts to dominate Perak; if it weren't for British assistance in the 1820s, the state would have come under Siam's domination.

The British had remained reluctant to intervene in the peninsula's affairs, but growing investment from the Strait settlements, along with the burgeoning rubber industry and rich tin mines of Perak, committed their interest. The mines also attracted a great influx of Chinese immigrants, who soon formed rival clan groups allied with local Malay chiefs, all of whom battled to control the mines.

The Perak sultanate was in disarray, and fighting among successors to the throne gave the British their opportunity to step in, making the first real colonial incursion on the peninsula in 1874. The governor, Sir Andrew Clarke, convened a meeting at Pulau Pangkor at which Sultan Abdullah was installed on the throne in preference to Sultan Ismail, the other major contender. The Pangkor Treaty that ensued required that the sultan accept a British Resident, to be consulted on all issues other than those relating to religion or Malay custom.

Though the Resident had no executive authority, this foot in the door soon helped to consolidate British rule. In 1875, only one year after the Pangkor Treaty, Sultan Abdullah was forced, under threat of deposition, to accept administration by British officials on his behalf. Various Perak chiefs united to get rid of the Resident, James WW Birch, who was assassinated at Pasir Salak in November 1875.

Colonial troops were called in to fight what proved to be a short-lived war, Sultan Abdullah was exiled to the Seychelles, and a new British-sanctioned sultan was installed. Sir Hugh Low, well-versed in Malay affairs and language, became the next British Resident in Kuala Kangsar and proved to be a much more able administrator. He assumed control of taxes from the tin mines and practised greater intervention in state affairs, and in 1877 he introduced the first rubber trees to Malaysia. The sultans, meanwhile, maintained their status but were increasingly effete figureheads, bought out with stipends.

The first railway in the state, from Taiping to Port Weld, was built in 1885, to transport the wealth of tin; the result was rapid development in Taiping and Ipoh. In 1896 Perak, along with Selangor, Pahang and Negeri Sembilan, became part of the Federated Malay States. The Resident system persisted, however, even after the Japanese invasion and WWII, ending only when Perak became part of the Federation of Malaya in 1948.

Climate

Perak has a tropical climate, and is hot and humid throughout the year; daily temperatures average between 21°C and 32°C, and humidity levels hover at a steady 90%. There are brief downpours and occasional lighter rain at all times of the year, with June and July usually being the driest. The Cameron Highlands are actually inside Pahang, and temperatures there are much cooler, rarely rising above 21°C. Rainfall is more frequent too.

Getting There & Away

Both the main rail line and the Lebuhraya (North-South Hwy) run the length of the state, from Johor Bahru in the south up to the Thai border in the north, giving easy access to the state capital, Ipoh, and other major towns. Ipoh is the transport hub of Perak, and there are bus connections to most major towns on the peninsula. Ipoh also has an airport, with regular flights to/from Kuala Lumpur (KL); see p136 for more information.

Getting Around

Almost everywhere in Perak is accessible by bus from Ipoh. Trains are infrequent, often leave at inconvenient times and are not particularly useful for travelling within the state. Lumut is the departure point for ferries to

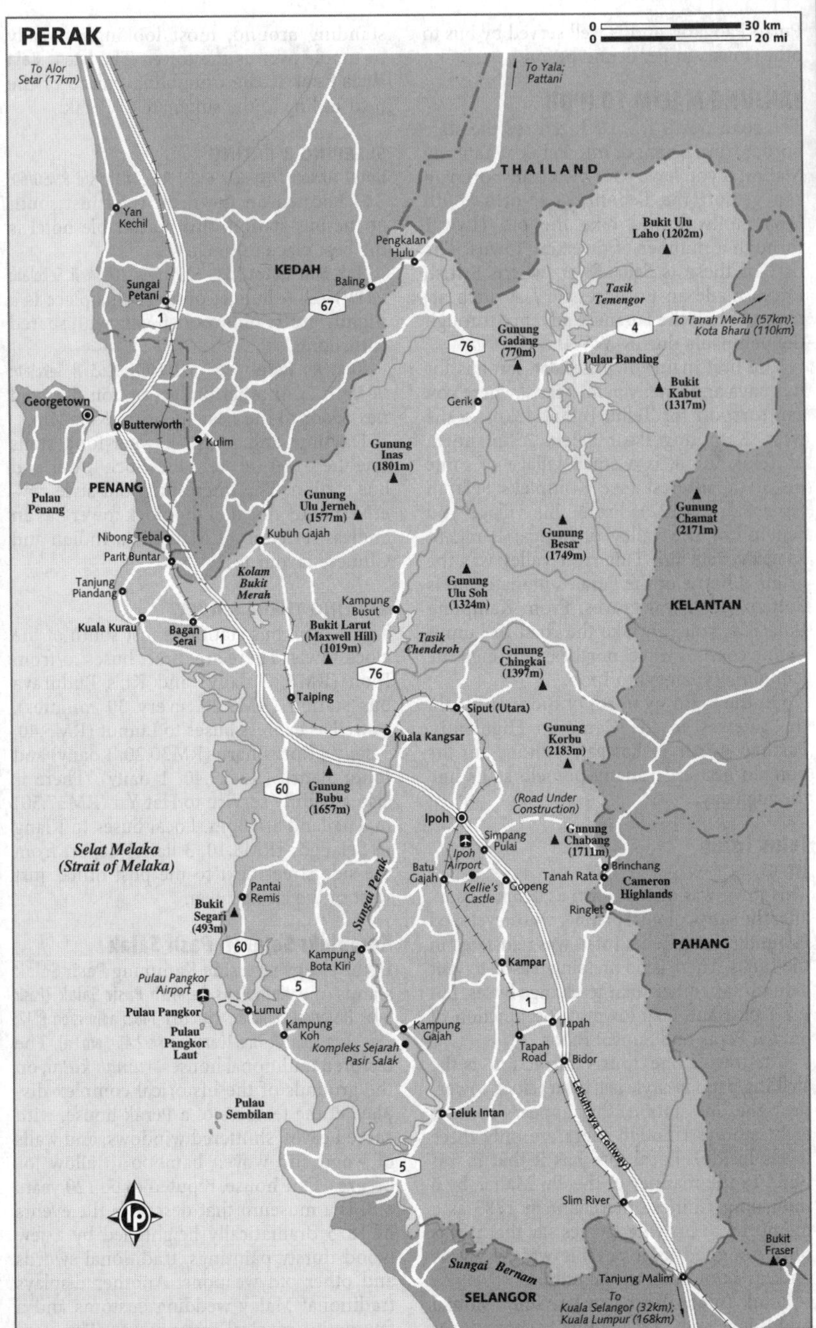
PERAK
0 30 km
0 20 mi
To Alor Setar (17km)
To Yala; Pattani
THAILAND
Yan Kechil
Sungai Petani
KEDAH
Pengkalan Hulu
Baling
Bukit Ulu Laho (1202m)
Tasik Temengor
To Tanah Merah (57km); Kota Bharu (110km)
Gunung Gadang (770m)
Pulau Banding
Bukit Kabut (1317m)
Gerik
Georgetown
Butterworth
Kulim
Gunung Inas (1801m)
PENANG
Pulau Penang
Gunung Ulu Jerneh (1577m)
Gunung Chamat (2171m)
Gunung Besar (1749m)
Nibong Tebal
Parit Buntar
Kubuh Gajah
Kolam Bukit Merah
Tanjung Piandang
Kuala Kurau
Bagan Serai
Kampung Busut
Gunung Ulu Soh (1324m)
Bukit Larut (Maxwell Hill) (1019m)
Tasik Chenderoh
KELANTAN
Gunung Chingkai (1397m)
Taiping
Siput (Utara)
Kuala Kangsar
Gunung Korbu (2183m)
Gunung Bubu (1657m)
(Road Under Construction)
Ipoh
Simpang Pulai
Gunung Chabang (1711m)
Ipoh Airport
Selat Melaka (Strait of Melaka)
Batu Gajah
Kellie's Castle
Gopeng
Brinchang
Tanah Rata
Cameron Highlands
Ringlet
Pantai Remis
Bukit Segari (493m)
Sungai Perak
PAHANG
Kampung Bota Kiri
Kampar
Pulau Pangkor Airport
Pulau Pangkor
Lumut
Pulau Pangkor Laut
Kampung Koh
Kampung Gajah
Kompleks Sejarah Pasir Salak
Tapah
Tapah Road
Bidor
Lebuhraya (Tollway)
Pulau Sembilan
Teluk Intan
Slim River
Sungai Bernam
Bukit Fraser
Tanjung Malim
SELANGOR
To Kuala Selangor (32km); Kuala Lumpur (168km)
1
4
5
60
67
76

Pulau Pangkor, and is well served by bus to other towns in Perak and beyond.

TANJUNG MALIM TO IPOH

The road north from KL crosses the state border from Selangor into Perak at Tanjung Malim. If you have your own transport, you can get off the Lebuhraya (North-South Hwy) tollway and take the old Hwy 1 through a number of diverting towns. The first of these is **Selim River**, where British forces made an unsuccessful last-ditch attempt to halt the Japanese advance through the peninsula during WWII.

The first main town is **Bidor**, famous for its guava and smelly *petai* beans, where you can turn off for Teluk Intan, 42km to the west. Kampung Pasir Salak, 25km north of Teluk Intan, is a small village of some historical interest (see Kompleks Sejarah Pasir Salak, p122). From this village you can follow the valley of Sungai Perak to **Kampung Bota Kiri**. This river valley was the original home of the Perak sultanate and is dotted with royal graves. From Kampung Bota Kiri you can take the road to Lumut on the coast or travel northeast through the *kampung* (villages) to Ipoh.

On the highway north of Bidor is Tapah, the gateway to the Cameron Highlands. Farther north is **Kampar**, famous for its pomelo orchards; many pomelo stalls line the highway.

Teluk Intan

☎ 05

This town was once known as Teluk Anson, after the early colonial planner who developed it, but the name Teluk Intan was reinstated in the 1980s. There is no pressing reason to visit Teluk Intan, other than to change buses, but it's a pleasant, lazy town at the junction of Sungai Perak and Sungai Bidor.

The town's one 'tourist attraction' is the striking pagoda-style **jam besar** (clock tower) near the bus station, that appears to have eight storeys (though there are only three levels inside). Local lore has it that it was built, in the manner of the Taj Mahal, by a mourning Chinese merchant in 1885 as a memorial to his wife; cynics say that it was only designed as a potable-water storage tank. It's not open to the public.

Teluk Intan also has a few fine colonial buildings and old Chinese shophouses standing around, most looking as ready to topple over as the tower. The **Istana Raja Muda Perak** is the crumbling palace of the next in line to the sultanate of Perak.

SLEEPING & EATING

Hotel Anson (☎ 622 6166; Jl Sekolah; s/d RM50/60; ❄) Located on the main road just south of the bus station, this reasonable hotel is the best place in town.

Kok Min Hotel (☎ 622 1529; 1065A Jl Sekolah; s/d RM18/22) A budget option. This place is a slightly grotty old wooden villa with shared bathrooms.

Kum Ah Hotel (☎ 622 1407; 1065 Jl Sekolah; s/d RM17/22) Another budget option. Located next door to the near-identical Kok Min.

Daytime and night, hawker-food stalls line the streets around the clock tower and bus station. The interesting, old-style covered market north of the clock tower has an endless selection of Malaysian, Indian and Chinese favourites.

GETTING THERE & AWAY

The central bus station is just south of the clock tower. There are direct buses to/from Ipoh (RM5, 3 daily) and KL's Puduraya bus station (RM9.20, every 30 minutes), as well as express buses to Lumut (RM5.40, 5 daily), Kota Bharu (RM30.20, 1 daily) and Johor Bahru (RM29.40, 1 daily). There is also a nightly service to Hat Yai (RM37.50) in Thailand at 10pm. Local buses to Klang in Selangor (RM8.10, 3 daily) depart from the side street next to the post office, just west of the clock tower.

Kompleks Sejarah Pasir Salak

In the sleepy riverside Kampung Pasir Salak stands the **Kompleks Sejarah Pasir Salak** (Pasir Salak Historical Complex; ☎ 631 1462; admission RM2; ⏲ 10am-5pm Sat-Thu, 10am-noon & 2.45-5pm Fri). The restored traditional houses, *rumah kutai*, on the grounds of the historical complex display all the features of a Perak house, with carved eaves, shuttered windows, and walls of wood and woven bamboo to allow for breezes. One house, reputed to be 120 years old, is a museum that describes the events of 1875 dramatically heightened by a few blood-thirsty paintings, traditional swords and other old weapons. Another displays traditional Malay wedding customs and a few native musical instruments. The largest house (admission RM5) has been transformed into a 'time tunnel' of historical dioramas depicting Perak from prehistoric times to independence, complete with a full-scale model of Birch's assassination and screaming soundtracks.

Pasir Salak became known for the 1875 murder of James WW Birch, the first British Resident of Perak. He was slain while bathing at a rafthouse on the river – a **memorial** marks the exact spot of the assassination. Birch is widely characterised as an intolerant man, insensitive to Malay customs and known to lecture Sultan Abdullah in public. However, his murder was as much a reaction to the colonial government's decision to assume direct control in Perak as it was to any shortcomings in Birch's personality. His killers, Maharaja Lela (a local chief), Dato Sagar and Pandak Indut, were arrested by British troops and later hanged. They have since been enshrined as national heroes, and the memorial dedicated to them here is in the shape of a traditional *sundang* (a knife widely used in rebellions against the British). Replicas of Maharaja Lela's **fort** and **house** are nearby.

GETTING THERE & AWAY

Pasir Salak is 4km across Sungai Perak bridge from the nearest town, Kampung Gajah. A chartered taxi from Teluk Intan to Pasir Salak costs about RM35 return.

Tapah

☎ 05

The small town of Tapah has no attractions, but is the main transit point for bus connections for the Cameron Highlands.

SLEEPING & EATING

If you get stuck overnight here, Tapah has a couple of budget hotels on Jl Stesyen; take the street directly opposite the bus station for two short blocks.

Hotel Utara (☎ 401 2299; 35 Jl Stesyen; s & d RM25/30; ❄) A small hotel with a few basic rooms; the slightly dearer air-con rooms are the best bet.

NH Hotel (☎ 401 7288; 24 Jl Stesyen; s & d RM50; ❄) Across the tiny lane from the Utara, this place offers a marginally higher standard of accommodation.

There's a good **Chinese coffee shop** (35 Jl Stesyen) at the Hotel Utara, though the whole town is just about bursting with them, along with simple Indian restaurants dishing up roti canai (flaky bread dipped in dhal or curry) and chicken biryani.

GETTING THERE & AWAY

The bus station on Jl Raja is only 200m from the main road. Local buses make the winding journey to Tanah Rata in the Cameron Highlands roughly every hour from 8am to 6pm (RM4.20, 2 hours). Taxis to Tanah Rata (RM50) leave from the taxi station 100m farther down Jl Raja away from the main road.

From the bus station there are a few departures to KL and Penang, but most express long-distance buses leave from the Restoran Caspian at 9 Main Rd. Turn right as you come out of the bus station, then left at Main Rd, and the Restoran Caspian is four shops down from KFC. The owner of the restaurant runs a sub-agent, the Kah Mee Agency, directly opposite the bus station.

From various whistlestops around the Restoran Caspian, passing air-con buses pick up passengers for Butterworth (RM16, 4 hours, 9.30am, 10.30am, 4.15pm and 5.30pm); Hat Yai, Thailand (RM36, 7 hours, 11pm); Ipoh (RM4.20, 1½ hours, hourly); Johor Bahru/Singapore (RM49, 7 hours, 10am and 9.30pm); KL (RM9 to RM10, 2 hours, hourly until 6.15pm); Kuala Terengganu (RM41, 8 hours, 9am); Kuantan (RM27, 7 hours, 9am and 9pm); Lumut (RM13.50, 3 hours, 11.30am); and Melaka (RM22, 4 hours, 10am). Some of these buses can also be booked for the same price or slightly more at **CS Travel & Tours** (☎ 491 1200; fax 491 2390; 47 Jl Besar) in Tanah Rata.

The nearest train station, known as **Tapah Road** (☎ 418 1345), is 9km west of town. The train for Butterworth leaves at 11.46pm and for KL at 4.34am. A taxi to Tapah Road station from Tapah is around RM7.

CAMERON HIGHLANDS

☎ 09

Malaysia's most extensive hill station, about 60km off the main KL–Ipoh–Butterworth road at Tapah, is at an altitude of 1300m to 1829m. The Cameron Highlands encompasses a large area stretching along the road from the town of Ringlet, then through the main towns of Tanah Rata, Brinchang and beyond. The Highlands are inside the state

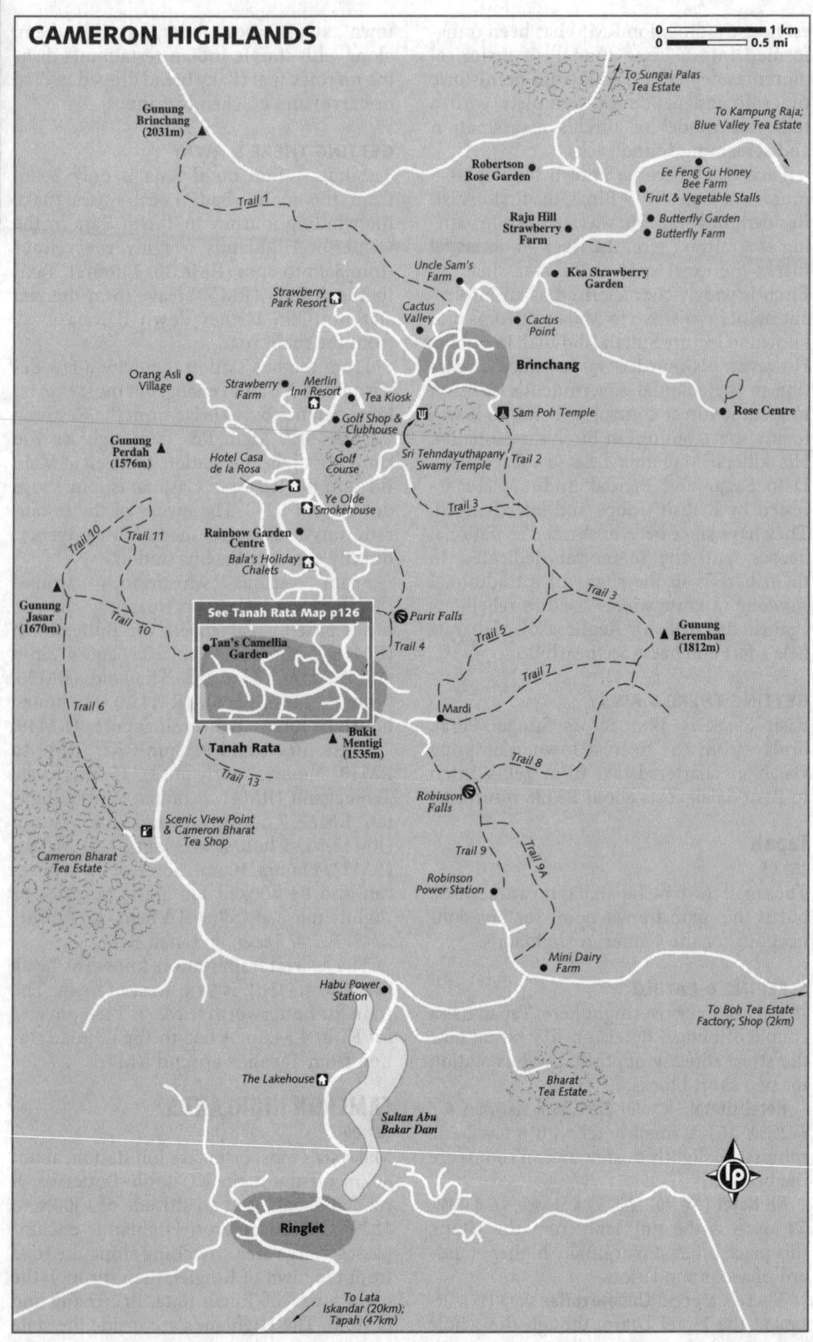
CAMERON HIGHLANDS
0 1 km
0 0.5 mi
To Sungai Palas Tea Estate
To Kampung Raja; Blue Valley Tea Estate
Gunung Brinchang (2031m)
Trail 1
Robertson Rose Garden
Ee Feng Gu Honey Bee Farm
Fruit & Vegetable Stalls
Raju Hill Strawberry Farm
Butterfly Garden
Butterfly Farm
Uncle Sam's Farm
Kea Strawberry Garden
Strawberry Park Resort
Cactus Valley
Cactus Point
Brinchang
Orang Asli Village
Strawberry Farm
Merlin Inn Resort
Tea Kiosk
Golf Shop & Clubhouse
Sam Poh Temple
Rose Centre
Gunung Perdah (1576m)
Golf Course
Sri Tehndayuthapany Swamy Temple
Trail 2
Hotel Casa de la Rosa
Ye Olde Smokehouse
Trail 3
Trail 10
Trail 11
Rainbow Garden Centre
Bala's Holiday Chalets
Trail 3
Gunung Jasar (1670m)
Trail 10
See Tanah Rata Map p126
Parit Falls
Tan's Camellia Garden
Trail 4
Trail 5
Gunung Beremban (1812m)
Trail 7
Trail 6
Mardi
Bukit Mentigi (1535m)
Tanah Rata
Trail 8
Trail 13
Robinson Falls
Scenic View Point & Cameron Bharat Tea Shop
Trail 9
Trail 9A
Cameron Bharat Tea Estate
Robinson Power Station
Mini Dairy Farm
Habu Power Station
To Boh Tea Estate Factory; Shop (2km)
The Lakehouse
Bharat Tea Estate
Sultan Abu Bakar Dam
Ringlet
To Lata Iskandar (20km); Tapah (47km)

borders of Pahang, but access is via Tapah in Perak.

The Cameron Highlands takes its name from William Cameron, the surveyor who mapped the area in 1885. He was soon followed by tea planters, Chinese vegetable farmers and wealthy colonialists seeking a cool escape from the heat of the lowlands.

The temperature rarely drops below 10°C or climbs above 21°C, and in this fertile area vegetables grow in profusion, flowers are cultivated for sale nationwide and wild flowers bloom everywhere. It's also the centre of Malaysian tea production.

The cool weather tempts visitors to exertions normally forgotten at sea level. There's a network of jungle trails, waterfalls and mountains, an excellent golf course and less-taxing points of interest such as colourful temples, rose gardens and tea plantations where visitors are welcome to try the local brew.

Until quite recently, development of the Cameron Highlands was fairly limited, but construction of hulking apartment blocks has somewhat changed the old-fashioned, English atmosphere. More seriously, massive, indiscriminate and often illegal land clearance has caused severe damage to the environment; hills have been levelled and streams filled in to make way for farmland, causing landslips and floods. So far, the Pahang state government has done little to halt this destruction, other than impose nominal fines on landowners. A new road is being pushed through Brinchang to link up with Simpang Pulai on the Lebuhraya tollway, which will make the Highlands much more accessible from Ipoh; this has been under construction for years, though it should finally be open by 2004.

Despite all the changes, the regular rain, dampness and visiting hordes, the Cameron Highlands is still a relaxing destination and one of Malaysia's most rewarding stopovers. If you bypass it, you'll really miss out.

Orientation

Though the Cameron Highlands lies just over the Perak state border in Pahang, it can be accessed only from Perak. From the turn-off at Tapah it's 47km up to Ringlet, the first village of the Highlands and a primarily Malay town. On the way you'll pass the eye-catching waterfall **Lata Iskandar** at the Km 20 marker (20km from Tapah).

Soon after Ringlet you skirt the lake created by Sultan Abu Bakar Dam. About 13km past Ringlet, Tanah Rata is the main town of the Highlands. As you enter, new apartment blocks towering above give way to the busy Jl Besar (Main Rd), lined with restaurants and old-fashioned shops. Tanah Rata has a large Indian population, descendants of the Indian workers originally brought here to pick tea. Most visitors stay in Tanah Rata for its lively atmosphere.

A few kilometres past Tanah Rata is the golf course, clustered around which you'll find many of the Highlands' more luxurious hotels. Beyond the golf course at around KM 65 you reach Brinchang, a more modern, Chinese town. Though Brinchang has a good range of facilities and is closer to many of the attractions, it has less character than Tanah Rata and is less served by public transport.

The road continues up beyond Brinchang to grungy Kampung Raja, a tea estate village, and the Blue Valley Tea Estate at Km 90. Flower gardens, strawberry stalls and butterfly farms are found along this stretch of road, as is the turn-off to Sungai Palas Tea Estate and Gunung Brinchang (Mt Brinchang; 2031m).

Information

The post office, banks, police and bus station are all on Jl Besar in Tanah Rata. Most guesthouses offer Internet access for around RM5 per hour.

CS Travel & Tours (☎ 491 1200; fax 491 2390; 47 Jl Besar) Organises coach tours of the Highlands and books bus and air tickets.

Dobi Highlands Laundry (62A Persiaran Camellia 3)

Pusat Computer CL (1st floor, 55c Persiaran Camellia 3; RM2.80 per hr) The cheapest Internet in Tanah Rata.

www.cameron.com.my Also worth a look, with similar information to the following website.

www.cameronhighlands.com An overview and brief history of the Highlands, as well as some information on accommodation and hiking, though it's not updated very often.

Yam Tourist Information (☎ 012-657 1084; Jl Besar) In the absence of an official tourist office, the friendly and knowledgeable Yam has added this tiny kiosk onto the front of his cobbler's stall, next to Restaurant Kumar. Operating hours are erratic, but he's happy to answer queries by phone.

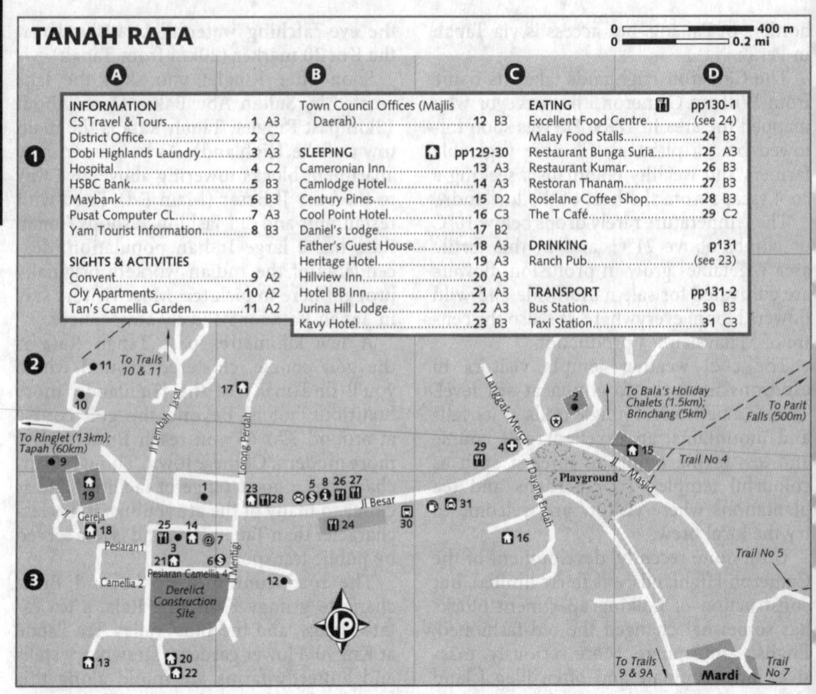

Sights

TEA PLANTATIONS

A visit to a tea plantation is a popular Highlands outing, and not to be missed. The first tea was planted here in 1929 by JA Russell, who founded the Boh Tea Estate. Boh brands still dominate the market for Cameron Highlands tea.

Boh's **Sungai Palas Tea Estate** is up in the hills north of Brinchang, off the road to Gunung Brinchang. The approach road leads past functional worker housing and a Hindu temple to the attractive visitors centre. You can buy tea and tea sets in the gift shop, or sample the brew of your choice along with scrumptious cakes in a tearoom offering grand vistas over the hills.

The tea is still cured with wood fires, which imparts flavour to the finished product. The process is almost all mechanised now, including the picking and sifting into grades from dust to choice leaf. Free 15-minute tours showing the process are conducted from 8.30am to 4.30pm (closed Monday). Wait for a staff member to collect you from the video presentation room.

Public buses running between Tanah Rata and Kampung Raja pass the turn-off to Gunung Brinchang. From there it's 4km along the winding road past **Robertson Rose Garden** (worth a detour for its hilltop views) to the plantation entrance, after which it's another 15 minutes downhill to the visitors centre.

You can also visit other tea estates, but guided tours are usually given only for organised groups. One exception is **Boh Tea Estate** (www.boh.com.my), southeast of Tanah Rata and 8km off the main road up to the Highlands. From the end of jungle trail 9A (see p128), it's only a 45-minute walk to the plantation and tours are given approximately hourly from 10am to 3.30pm.

Activities

The **Sam Poh Temple**, just below Brinchang about 1km off the main road, is a typically Chinese kaleidoscope of colours, with Buddha statues, countless Buddha wall plaques and stone guard-lions. It is signposted as the 'Tokong Temple' from the intersection at the main road in front of the Iris House Hotel. The nearby **Sri Tehndayuthapany Swamy**

Temple is an equally colourful Hindu place of worship – the bright sculptures were created by artists brought from India.

MARDI is an agricultural research station east of Tanah Rata – tours must be arranged in advance. CS Travel & Tours may be able to make arrangements for you (see p129).

There are a number of **apiaries**, **flower and cactus nurseries**, **vegetable farms** and **strawberry farms** in the Highlands. The main season for strawberries is January.

There is an Orang Asli (aboriginal Malaysian) settlement near Brinchang, but it's a real village and not a tourist site. If you want to visit, hire a local Malay guide to accompany you and to act as an interpreter.

About 10km beyond Brinchang is the **Butterfly Garden** (☎ 496 1364; admission RM3; 🕑 9am-6pm), where more than 300 varieties supposedly flutter around, including the majestic Raja Brooke butterfly. The collection also includes enormous rhinoceros beetles, scorpions and giant stick insects.

Gunung Brinchang (2031m) is the highest point accessible by surfaced road on the peninsula. The 7km road is narrow and incredibly steep in places, but the views from the summit are breathtaking.

HIKING

There are a variety of walks around the Highlands, many leading to waterfalls and mountain peaks. The start of the trails are marked with large yellow-and-black signboards that are sometimes obscured. Unfortunately there are no high-quality, up-to-date contour maps available.

The popular tracks are reasonably well maintained and periodically cleared with brush cutters, but it doesn't take long for tracks to become overgrown, especially the less popular ones. There is little or no signposting of side trails, and you occasionally come across false trails that go nowhere. Guesthouses in Tanah Rata often employ informal guides who lead daily hikes; they are a good source of information on the latest track conditions, which can change rapidly from one season to the next. Inexperienced hikers would be well advised to employ the services of a guide on the longer trails; in recent years, several people have become lost, in more than one case for a couple of days. Single women have also been attacked in remote areas.

TEA PROCESSING

Tea bushes are plucked every seven to eight days, and while once done by hand, the process is now almost entirely mechanised in Malaysia. It takes 5kg of leaves to make 1kg of tea. The collected leaves are weighed and 'withered' – a drying process in which fans blow air across troughs to reduce the moisture content by about 50%. The dried leaves are then rolled to twist and rupture the leaf cells and release the juices for fermentation. The finer leaves are separated out and the larger ones are rolled again.

Fermentation, which is the oxidisation of the leaf enzymes, has to be strictly controlled to develop the characteristic flavour and aroma of the tea. The fermented leaves are 'fired', a process in which excess moisture is driven off in a drying machine. At this time the leaves become black. Finally, the tea is sorted into grades, and stalks and fibres are removed before it is stored in bins to mature.

The trails generally pass through relatively unspoiled jungle, and the cool weather makes hiking a pleasure. You should take care to always carry water, some food, and rain gear for the unpredictable weather. Trails 4 and 9A (as far as Robinson Falls) are easy hikes taking an hour or less, while a combination of trails 10 and 11 is more challenging. The rest may be tough-going, depending on your level of fitness.

Note that Trail 14 has been taken over by an expanding farm, and closed. Trail 13 starts from behind the Cameronian Inn, but it stops at the concrete construction pylons.

Although hikes around the Highlands are all relatively short, there is obviously the potential for longer hikes. A glance at the Perak map (p121) will indicate what a short, steep distance it is from the Highlands down to Ipoh or the main road. For any hike outside the immediate area, however, the local authorities have to be notified and a guide is necessary.

Trail 1

This trail leads from around the side of the transmitter station on top of Gunung Brinchang down to the army camp just north of Brinchang. It is a steep, muddy, overgrown trail (often closed for repairs) and should only be tackled from the top down by experienced hikers. Take the 7km paved road to Gunung Brinchang through the tea plantations – a pleasant enough walk for a while, but dull eventually. The trail down takes about 1½ hours, unless you get lost and wander through the jungle for a couple of days, as a number of people have done in recent years.

Trail 2
Starting just before Sam Poh Temple outside Brinchang, this steep, strenuous hike follows a thin, slippery track for 1½ hours before it eventually joins Trail 3.

Trail 3
This starts at Arcadia Bungalow southeast of the golf course and climbs towards Gunung Beremban (1812m), getting steeper near the summit. It is a strenuous three-hour hike all the way to the mountain, or an easier hike if you only go as far as Trail 5 and take that back to MARDI; this too, though, is a steep path.

Trail 4
This trail starts next to the river just past the Century Pines resort in Tanah Rata. It leads to Parit Falls, but unfortunately garbage from the nearby village finds its way here, and it's not the most bucolic of spots. The falls can also be reached from the road around the southern end of the golf course. Both hikes are about half a kilometre.

JIM THOMPSON

The Cameron Highlands' most famous jungle trekker was a man who never came back from his walk. American Jim Thompson is credited with having founded the Thai silk industry after WWII. He subsequently made a fortune, and his beautiful, antique-packed house beside a canal in Bangkok is a major tourist attraction today. On 26 March 1967, while holidaying in the Highlands, Jim Thompson left his villa for a pre-dinner stroll – never to be seen again. Despite extensive searches, the mystery of his disappearance has never been explained. Kidnapped? Taken by a tiger? Or simply a planned disappearance or suicide? Nobody knows.

Trail 5
This starts at MARDI. Take the road inside the complex and follow the sign around to the left. It's a very steep 1½-hour hike though open country and forest, easier if done downhill from Trail 3.

Trail 6
Although recently cleared at the time of writing, Trail 6 is prone to neglect, and the path is unclear in places. It goes from the end of the road at the Cameron Bharat Tea Estate and merges with Trail 10 at the summit of Gunung Jasar (1670m). It's a 2½-hour uphill hike – take a guide.

Trail 7
This one also starts inside MARDI. The beginning can be tough to find and you should allow all day – it's at least a steady three-hour uphill hike, with a very steep final climb to the summit of Gunung Beremban.

Trail 8
This trail branches off Trail 9 just before Robinson Falls and is another steep three-hour approach to Gunung Beremban. Although a slightly easier hike, it's still a strenuous 2½ hours if done in reverse from the mountain.

Trails 9 & 9A
Popular Trail 9 starts 1.5km from the main road in Tanah Rata. Take the road past MARDI and follow it all the way around to the right, where it ends at a footbridge. From here the trail leads downhill past Robinson Falls to a metal gate, about 15 minutes away. Trail 9, which is not recommended, goes through the gate and follows the water pipeline down a very steep, slippery incline through the jungle to the power station. We recommend taking Trail 9A, which branches off to the left before the metal gate and in about an hour empties out onto Boh Rd. Follow this to the main road, where you can either head east to Boh Tea Estate or west to Habu Power Station for buses back to Tanah Rata.

Trails 10 & 11
Gunung Jasar is a fairly strenuous hike via Trail 10, starting behind the Oly Apartments in Tanah Rata. Go through Tan's

Camellia Garden and uphill to the left. After reaching the summit, you can continue on towards Gunung Perdah (1576m), but you must bypass it and return by Trail 11, which joins up with Trail 10 halfway back to Tanah Rata. Both these paths are unclear; take a guide.

OTHER ACTIVITIES

If you want a game of **golf**, you'll need to be suitably dressed (no T-shirts or shorts). The golf course is run by the **Strawberry Park Resort** (☎ 491 1166). Green fees are RM40 for a whole day (RM60 on Saturday and Sunday), or RM20 after 4pm. Club, shoe and ball hire costs around RM40.

You can also swim, play a few sets of tennis or squash, and steam in the sauna at Strawberry Park Resort, up in the hills west of the golf course. You should phone ahead to check available times and rates.

Tours

CS Travel & Tours (☎ 491 1200; fax 491 2390; 47 Jl Besar) sells tickets for popular half-day tours of the Highlands, leaving around 8.45am and 1.45pm (RM15). It will pick you up from your guesthouse. This can be a good way of seeing all the various attractions, which are spread out and are either difficult or impossible to reach by public transport. Places visited include a tea estate, a strawberry farm, the Sam Poh Temple, an apiary, a butterfly farm and a rose garden (entry fees not included). It also organises various longer tours of the area and can arrange guides for the hiking trails.

Sleeping

The Highlands are very popular with Malaysian families during the school holidays, in April, August and December. During these times especially, you should book accommodation in advance. Tanah Rata is a favourite stopover for backpackers, and most of the accommodation here is of the budget variety, of varying standards of cleanliness and comfort. Hostel touts will usually meet new arrivals at the bus station and you can inspect the rooms before deciding whether to stay. If you don't see the tout for the guesthouse you're headed to, ring them and most will pick you up for free. If you choose to walk, it's no more than 20 minutes to any place in town. Mid-range options are very limited, while the big luxury resorts are mostly located outside town.

The smaller town of Brinchang also has some hotels, but there's little atmosphere and it's an awkward place to stay if you're dependent on public transport.

TANAH RATA

Budget

Cameronian Inn (☎ 491 1327; 16 Jl Mentigi; dm/s/d RM6/18/30; 💻) Clean, friendly hostel with spacious rooms, TV and reading lounges, and a pleasant garden. At the time of writing, land clearance had begun right behind, so noise may become a problem. Rooms sleeping three or four are also available.

Father's Guest House (☎ 491 2484; fathersonline@hotmail.com; dm/d from RM8/20; 💻) Very sociable place on a hill at the western edge of town. The old, bunker-style Nissen huts from the British occupation are surprisingly clean and comfortable inside; there are also more attractive rooms available in the nearby house (RM35 to RM80). Access is via a long, steep flight of steps.

Camlodge Hotel (☎ 491 4975; 55C Persiaran Camelia 3; s/d RM35/45) Small guesthouse with neat, clean rooms but not much character, in the modern shopping complex at the western end of town. All rooms come with attached bathroom.

Hotel BB Inn (☎ 491 4551; 79A Persiaran Camelia 4; s & d RM35-45) Similar style place to the Camlodge; the more expensive rooms have balconies and are much more preferable.

Kavy Hotel (☎ 491 5652; fax 491 5423; 44 Jl Besar s & d RM29-39) Slightly dated hotel above a noisy bar in the town centre, though the price is very reasonable.

Daniel's Lodge (☎ 491 5823; 9 Lorong Perdah; dm/s/d from RM6/16/18; 💻) Scruffy hostel surrounded by tatty shanty-houses just off the main road. It's a very sociable place, but some travellers have reported bedbugs and complained of unhelpful staff.

Mid-Range

Hillview Inn (☎ 491 2915; fax 491 5212; 17 Jl Mentigi; s & d RM40-80; 💻) A bright, spotlessly clean hotel with large, airy rooms, most with balconies, in a quiet area south of the town centre.

Jurina Hill Lodge (☎ 491 5522; 819 Jl Mentigi; s & d from RM50; 💻) Cosy modern guesthouse in a quiet area directly behind the Hillview

Inn, with fully equipped hillside bungalows and apartments.

Bala's Holiday Chalet (☎ 491 1660; www.balaschalet.com; s & d RM88-120) Charming mock-Tudor style guesthouse, originally built as a boarding school in 1934, in well-tended grounds about 1.5km out of Tanah Rata, on the road to Brinchang. The colonial ambience has been preserved but rooms are rather small.

Cool Point Hotel (☎ 491 4914; hotelcph@tm.net.my; 891 Persiaran Dayang Endah; s & d RM75; 💻) Large, modern and somewhat characterless hotel in the town centre. Rooms for three and four people are also available, but note that prices virtually double at weekends (Saturday and Sunday).

Top End

Lakehouse (☎ 495 6152; www.lakehouse-cameron.com; s & d from RM407) Overlooking the lake 2km north of Ringlet, this 'Olde English'-style country house is one of the most delightful hotels in the Highlands. There are only 18 rooms, all with four-poster beds and antique furnishings. There's a restaurant serving traditional British cuisine and a cosy pub with a log fire. It's a little remote, though, and you'll need your own transport to stay here.

Ye Olde Smokehouse (☎ 491 1215; fax 491 1214; s & d from RM350) This atmospheric old country house near the golf course on the outskirts of town looks as if it's been lifted straight from deepest Surrey, complete with red British phone box outside. Indoors, the exposed beams, open fireplaces and chintzy décor complete the image. The restaurant serves traditional English food. Note that prices rise by a third on weekends.

Hotel Casa de la Rosa (☎ 491 1333; www.hotelcasadelarosa.com.my; 48 Jl Circular; s & d from RM320, ste from RM1000; 💻) Modern, quiet resort on the southern fringe of the golf course, with large, individually designed rooms and a couple of good restaurants.

Century Pines (☎ 491 5115; fax 491 1115; 42 Jl Masjid; s & d RM150-200; 💻 🏊) Modern, luxurious hotel in a quiet location at the eastern edge of town. Rooms are spacious and beautifully furnished and look out onto attractively landscaped grounds. Tennis courts and a gym were under construction at the time of writing.

Heritage Hotel (☎ 491 3888; www.heritage.com.my; Jl Gereja; s & d from RM350; 💻) This large, vaguely mock-Tudor concrete complex, set amid similarly designed holiday apartments, has a high standard of accommodation, but it's rather bland and very quiet. It's particularly popular with Japanese coach groups.

BRINCHANG

Budget

Hotel Sentosa (☎ 491 1907; 38 Jl Besar; s & d RM25) Basic, no-frills place that is just about the only real budget hotel in Brinchang. It's nothing special, but it's still a bargain.

Mid-Range

Iris House Hotel (☎ 491 1818; fax 491 2828; 56 Jl Kuari; s & d RM88-98) Big modern hotel on the edge of town. The rooms are rather plain but good value. It's at the turn-off to Sam Poh Temple.

Parkland Hotel (☎ 491 1299; fax 491 2366; 45 Jl Besar; s & d from RM99) Smart modern place with large rooms, though they're a little expensive; discounts are occasionally available.

Hill Garden Lodge (☎ 491 2988; 15 Jl Besar; s & d RM50) Neat enough little hotel in the town centre with small, comfortable rooms. It gets busy on Saturday and Sunday, but discounts are often available at other times.

Brinchang Hotel (☎ 491 1755; fax 491 3452; 36 Jl Besar; s & d RM55) Rather drab place in the middle of town. It also has larger rooms for three/four people (RM65/85). Some of the rooms don't have windows.

Top End

Strawberry Park Resort (☎ 491 1166; fax 491 1949; s & d from RM216) Huge, 'neo-Tudor' apartment-type setup in the hills west of town, popular with package tour groups. It has a nightclub and good facilities, which are also available for day-use (see p129). Three-bedroom penthouses go for RM950 and package deals are available.

Merlin Inn Resort (☎ 491 1211; www.merlinhotels.com.my; s & d from RM300) Overlooking the northern end of the golf course, this large resort has fairly plain-looking rooms, but it's popular with Asian tourists and, of course, golfers.

Eating

TANAH RATA

The cheapest food in Tanah Rata is found at the rows of mainly Malay food stalls stretching down Jl Besar towards the bus and taxi stations. One stall, the Excellent Food Centre, has an extensive menu of tasty cooking. Other places have Chinese fare and all the usual Malay dishes, including satay.

T-Café (☎ 019-572 2883; 4 Jl Besar; dishes from RM6) One of the most popular spots in town, this friendly café serves cheap and tasty Western food such as pasta, vegeburgers, steaks and sandwiches. The apple pie comes highly recommended, too, and it's a nice place just to sit out one of the frequent downpours with a coffee and meet up with other travellers.

Restaurant Bunga Suria (☎ 491 4666; 66A Persiaran Camellia 3; dishes from RM4) At the opposite end of town is this great place for delicious South Indian food. The banana-leaf set meals, either meat or vegetarian, are especially good value, and there's a wide range of samosas, curries, *dosa* (paper-thin rice-and-lentil crêpes) and roti as well.

Restaurant Kumar (☎ 491 2624; 26 Jl Besar; dishes from RM3) Offers inexpensive South Indian food, as well as *murtabak* (roti prata filled with mutton, chicken or vegetables) and roti canai – served for breakfast, too, if you feel up to it. It's a good spot to sit outside with a beer and watch the world go by.

Restoran Thanam (☎ 491 1645; 25 Jl Besar; dishes from RM3) Right next door to Restaurant Kumar, this place serves a similar range of simple Indian fare, including tandoori-chicken set meals.

Roselane Coffee Shop (☎ 491 1419; 44 Jl Besar; dishes from RM8) Offers Western food such as fish and chips, and it's also a good place to indulge in the local Highlands tradition of cream tea, with scones and jam.

All the hotels and hostels have their own restaurants. **Ye Olde Smokehouse** (☎ 491 1215) is ideal for homesick Brits, serving up traditional favourites like steak and kidney pie (RM48) and beef Wellington (RM65). You can even get a Devonshire cream tea (RM18).

BRINCHANG

Brinchang has a good night market, which sets up in the central square in the late afternoon. A permanent food-stall centre livens up the southern end of the square.

Palm Leaf Garden (☎ 491 4208; 3 Bandar Baru; dishes from RM10) A decent modern restaurant, serving good Thai and Malay cuisine.

Jew May Yen (☎ 491 4020; 6 Jl Besar; dishes from RM4) Farther along from Palm Leaf Garden, this typical Chinese cheapie offers a wide range of dishes including steamboat and vegetarian food.

Shal's Curry House (☎ 491 2408; 25 Jl Besar; dishes from RM7) A popular Indian restaurant specialising in roti and *dosa* served on banana leaves; try the intriguing clove and cardamom teas too.

Drinking

Bigger hotels in the Highlands have their own bars, sometimes done up as traditional British pubs, while beer is available at many restaurants. Hostels often have party nights and you can usually get a beer at any time. The only real bar in Tanah Rata is the **Ranch Pub** (44 Jl Besar), in the same building as the Kavy Hotel. It's a bit dark and dingy, with a curious 'Wild West' theme, but it's popular with backpackers. It also has a pool table.

Getting There & Away

BUS

It's a long, gradual and often scenic climb from Tapah in Perak state to the Highlands, with plenty of corners on the way. From the golf course down to the main road junction, one visitor reported counting 653 bends. The road passes a number of Orang Asli villages and roadside huts where their produce is sold.

Be warned that the Highlands is where old Malaysian buses come to die. The bus drivers on this route seem to be frustrated racing drivers, especially on the stretch up from Ringlet, and almost everyone overtakes on blind corners. There are seven daily buses from Tapah to Tanah Rata between 8am and 6pm (RM4.20, 2 hours). Many of these rattletraps stop to change vehicle and driver at Ringlet. From Tanah Rata, the first and last buses down to Tapah leave at 8am and 5.30pm.

A few direct long-distance services originate from the Tanah Rata bus station for KL (RM16, 5 hours, 5 daily) and Penang (RM22, 6 hours, 4 daily). See also Getting There and Away, p123 in the Tapah section earlier in this chapter.

TAXI

The taxi station in Tanah Rata is just east of the bus station on Jl Besar. Things are much busier in the morning, so it's best to go then if you are looking for someone to share your ride. Full-taxi fares are RM50 to Tapah, RM100 to Ipoh and RM180 to KL.

Getting Around

BUS

Regal Transport Company keeps a throttle-hold on all public transport in the Highlands. Posted timetables don't often match reality, as drivers leave when they feel like it and, if buses break down, routes go out of service.

Getting between Tanah Rata and Brinchang is not a problem between 6.30am and 6.30pm, as buses run every hour or so. There are scheduled buses every hour from Tanah Rata to Kampung Raja, 23km away across the Highlands, but it's more like two or three hours until the next one happens by. It's quite a scenic trip, and you can hop off at various fruit and vegetable farms along the way. These buses also pass the turn-off to Gunung Brinchang and the Sungai Palas Tea Estate.

TAXI

Taxi services from Tanah Rata include Ringlet (RM15), Brinchang (RM5), Sungai Palas Estate (RM15) and Boh Tea Estate (RM20). For touring around, a taxi costs RM18 per hour, or you can go up to Gunung Brinchang and back for RM60. When you head back downhill to Tanah Rata you may be able to bargain down to a few ringgit, as drivers are glad to pick up at least a few passengers on the return trip.

IPOH

☎ 05

The City of Millionaires made its fortune from the rich tin mines of the Kinta Valley. Some of the mines around Ipoh are still producing today, and the city's elegant mansions testify to the success of many Chinese miners. With a population of 390,000 (over half a million if the surrounding districts are included) Ipoh is Malaysia's third-largest city, but it's not as bustling as its size might indicate, and has retained many of its historic buildings.

For the visitor, Ipoh is mainly a transit town, a place where you change buses if you're heading for Pulau Pangkor or Tapah. It may be worth a longer visit to explore outlying sights like the Buddhist temples cut into the limestone outcrops, the royal town of Kuala Kangsar or the eccentric Kellie's Castle. Ipoh itself has some fine old colonial architecture, but it's a seedy city, with a notorious prostitution problem, and you're unlikely to want to linger longer than necessary.

'Old Town' Ipoh is west of Sungai Kinta, between Jl Sultan Idris Shah and Jl Sultan Iskandar, and is worth a wander for the old Chinese and British architecture. The grand civic buildings close to, and including, the train station give some idea of just how prosperous this city once was. At the end of the 19th century the city expanded east over the river into 'New Town', which is another repository of colonial shophouses. While the city centre remains largely preserved and free from development, it is rather lifeless in the evenings.

Orientation

Many of Ipoh's main streets have been renamed in recent years, and while the street signs give the new (and often overly lengthy) names, the streets may still be known by the old names. The main ones include Jl Chamberlain (now Jl CM Yussuf), Jl Leech (Jl Bandar Timah), Jl Station (Jl Dato' Maharajah Lela), Jl Clarke (Jl Sultan Idris Shah) and Jl Kelab (Jl Panglima Bukit Gantang Wahab!).

Information

HSBC Bank (Jl Dato' Maharajah Lela)
Magic Surfer Internet (88 Jl Mustapha Al-Bakri; RM2 per hr)
Maybank (Jl Bandar Timah)
Perak Tourist Information Centre (☎ 241 2957; Jl Tun Sambanthan; 🕓 9am-5pm Mon-Fri)
Standard Chartered Bank (Jl Dato' Maharajah Lela)
www.ipoh-online.com.my Has some useful information about the city.
www.perak.gov.my Information on Perak.

Sights

COLONIAL ARCHITECTURE

Ipoh's grand colonial architecture is found in the Old Town. Some structures look freshly whitewashed, but other buildings have fallen into disrepair. Known locally as the 'Taj Mahal', the **train station** is a blend of Moorish and Victorian architecture, similar to KL's train station. It houses the

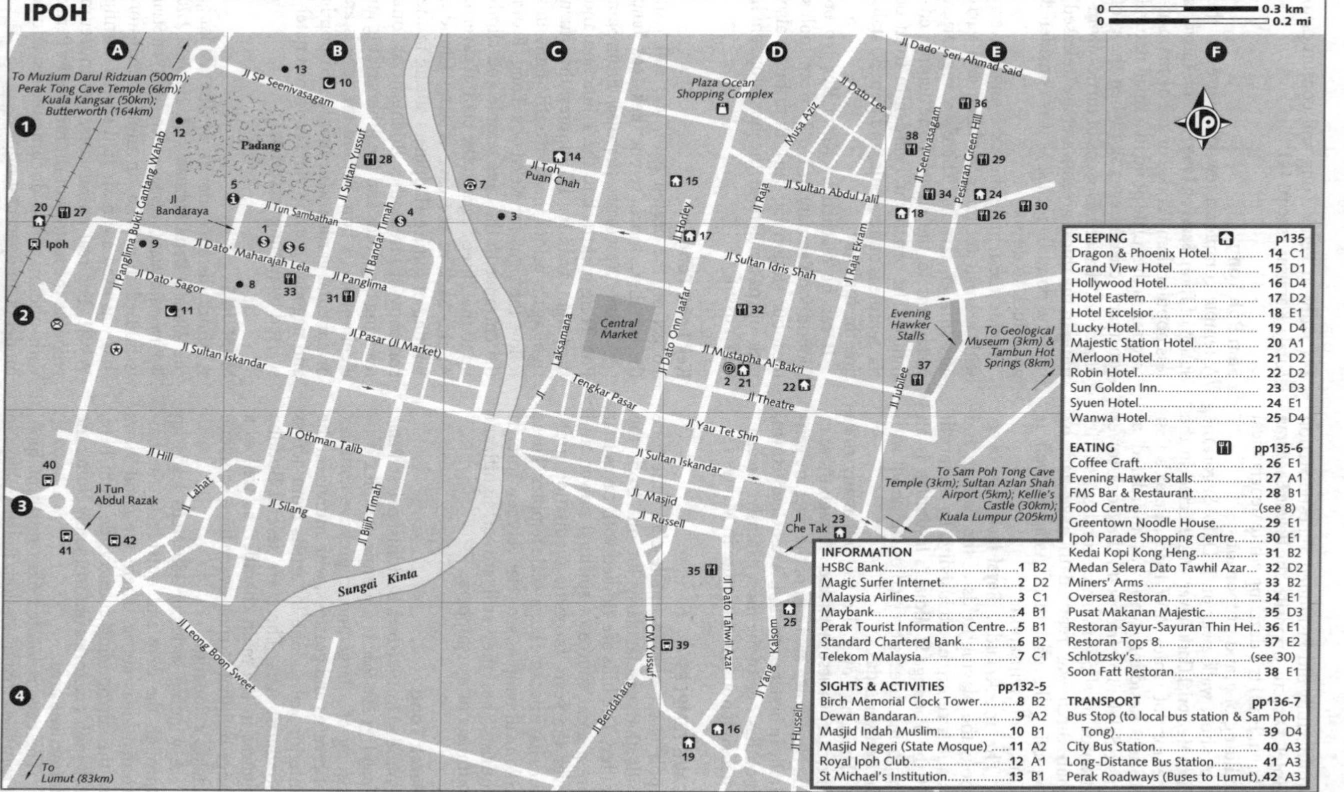
IPOH
0 0.3 km
0 0.2 mi
To Muzium Darul Ridzuan (500m); Perak Tong Cave Temple (6km); Kuala Kangsar (50km); Butterworth (164km)
To Geological Museum (3km) & Tambun Hot Springs (8km)
To Sam Poh Tong Cave Temple (3km); Sultan Azlan Shah Airport (5km); Kellie's Castle (30km); Kuala Lumpur (205km)
To Lumut (83km)
Padang
Plaza Ocean Shopping Complex
Central Market
Evening Hawker Stalls
Sungai Kinta
Ipoh
Jl SP Seenivasagam
Jl Panglima Bukit Gantang Wahab
Jl Bandaraya
Jl Tun Sambathan
Jl Dato' Maharajah Lela
Jl Dato' Sagor
Jl Sultan Yussuf
Jl Bandar Timah
Jl Panglima
Jl Pasar (Jl Market)
Jl Sultan Iskandar
Jl Othman Talib
Jl Hill
Jl Lahat
Jl Silang
Jl Bijih Timah
Jl Tun Abdul Razak
Jl Leong Boon Sweet
Jl Toh Puan Chah
Jl Laksamana
Tengkar Pasar
Jl Dato Onn Jaafar
Jl Horley
Jl Raja
Jl Sultan Abdul Jalil
Jl Sultan Idris Shah
Jl Mustapha Al-Bakri
Jl Theatre
Jl Yau Tet Shin
Jl Masjid
Jl Russell
Jl CM Yussuf
Jl Bendahara
Jl Dato Tahwil Azar
Jl Yang Kalsom
Jl Hussein
Jl Che Tak
Musa Aziz
Jl Dato Lee
Jl Raja Ekram
Jl Jubilee
Jl Dado' Seri Ahmad Said
Jl Seenivasagam
Pesiaran Green Hill
SLEEPING p135
Dragon & Phoenix Hotel 14 C1
Grand View Hotel 15 D1
Hollywood Hotel 16 D4
Hotel Eastern 17 D2
Hotel Excelsior 18 E1
Lucky Hotel 19 D4
Majestic Station Hotel 20 A1
Merloon Hotel 21 D2
Robin Hotel 22 D2
Sun Golden Inn 23 D3
Syuen Hotel 24 E1
Wanwa Hotel 25 D4
EATING pp135-6
Coffee Craft 26 E1
Evening Hawker Stalls 27 A1
FMS Bar & Restaurant 28 B1
Food Centre (see 8)
Greentown Noodle House 29 E1
Ipoh Parade Shopping Centre 30 E1
Kedai Kopi Kong Heng 31 B2
Medan Selera Dato Tawhil Azar 32 D2
Miners' Arms 33 B2
Oversea Restoran 34 E1
Pusat Makanan Majestic 35 D3
Restoran Sayur-Sayuran Thin Hei 36 E1
Restoran Tops 8 37 E2
Schlotzsky's (see 30)
Soon Fatt Restoran 38 E1
INFORMATION
HSBC Bank 1 B2
Magic Surfer Internet 2 D2
Malaysia Airlines 3 C1
Maybank 4 B1
Perak Tourist Information Centre 5 B1
Standard Chartered Bank 6 B2
Telekom Malaysia 7 C1
SIGHTS & ACTIVITIES pp132-5
Birch Memorial Clock Tower 8 B2
Dewan Bandaran 9 A2
Masjid Indah Muslim 10 B1
Masjid Negeri (State Mosque) 11 A2
Royal Ipoh Club 12 A1
St Michael's Institution 13 B1
TRANSPORT pp136-7
Bus Stop (to local bus station & Sam Poh Tong) 39 D4
City Bus Station 40 A3
Long-Distance Bus Station 41 A3
Perak Roadways (Buses to Lumut) 42 A3

wonderfully old-fashioned Majestic Station Hotel. Directly opposite, the **Dewan Bandaran** (Town Hall) is a dazzling white neoclassical building of grand proportions.

A short walk away on Jl Dato' Sagor, the **Birch Memorial Clock Tower** was erected in the memory of James WW Birch, Perak's first British Resident, who was murdered at Pasir Salak. The friezes on the clock tower attempt to show more cultural sensitivity than Birch was reputed to have had, by depicting the growth of Asian as well as European civilisation.

The mock-Tudor **Royal Ipoh Club** overlooks the playing fields of the Padang and is still a centre of exclusivity. To the north of the Padang, **St Michael's Institution** is an imposing three-storey colonial school with arched verandas.

The Old Town also features many rows of rickety **Chinese shophouses**, though those in the New Town area east of the river are generally in better condition. After Georgetown, Ipoh has one of the most extensive areas of later shophouse architecture in Malaysia.

CAVE TEMPLES

Ipoh is set among jungle-clad limestone hills that spectacularly jut out from the valley. The hills are riddled with caves that are a great source of spiritual power, and over the years favourite meditation grottoes have became large-scale temples. These colourful temples see relatively few foreign tourists, but they still attract significant numbers of worshippers.

Perak Tong

Founded in 1926 by a Buddhist priest, **Perak Tong** (⌚ 8am-6pm) is a temple complex consisting of a large and impressive complex of caverns and grottoes, with murals on the interior walls, done by artists from across Southeast Asia. There are several Buddha figures in the main chamber, as well as a huge bell that is rung every time someone makes a donation.

A winding series of 385 steps leads up through the cave and outside to the balconied areas above. There are good views of the surrounding countryside from here, but Ipoh's factories unfortunately clutter the immediate area.

The cave is located 6km north of Ipoh. From the city bus station, Reliance bus No 141 stops at Perak Tong and continues to Kuala Kangsar (see p144).

Sam Poh Tong

A temple complex a few kilometres to the south of Ipoh, **Sam Poh Tong** (⌚ 8am-4.30pm) is less popular than Perak Tong. The main attraction is the turtle pond in a small natural courtyard, created ages ago when the roof of a cave collapsed. Dozens of turtles swimming in the thick, green water are 'released' into the pond by locals, as it is considered good luck to do so.

Inside the temple there's a huge cavern with a small reclining Buddha, and various smaller caverns. There's a vegetarian restaurant to the right of the temple entrance. The ornamental garden in front of the temple is quite scenic, and pomelo stalls line the highway.

It can be reached by Kinta Bus No 66 (bound for Kampar) or No 73 from Ipoh's local bus station (50 sen). Both buses also pick up passengers at the bus stop on Jl CM Yussuf.

Kek Look Tong

To get off the beaten path, you can visit the smaller, more serene **Kek Look Tong** (⌚ 7.30am-7.30pm; donations requested). From Sam Poh Tong backtrack to the T-junction and turn right, walk for 15 minutes, then turn right again before the first traffic light and follow the signs for Kek Look Tong. From the entrance to the cave temple you climb up to the Three Sages in the central cavern. At the back of the cave is a fat Chinese Buddha of Future Happiness sitting in the company of three other Bodhisattvas, one teaching on a lotus and the others riding an elephant and a lion. Behind the cave is an ornamental garden with manicured ponds and pagodas, but the view is unfortunately scarred by fuming factories.

MUSEUMS

A short distance north of the Padang, the **Muzium Darul Ridzuan** (☎ 253 8906; 2020 Jl Panglima Gantang; admission free; ⌚ 9am-5pm) is housed in a 1926 tin miner's mansion that was used as an air-raid shelter during WWII. For real enthusiasts, the museum recounts the history of tin mining in Perak with photos, video documentaries and a model of an open-cast mine.

Rock buffs might enjoy a visit to the **Geological Museum** (☎ 557 644; Jl Sultan Azlan Shah; admission free; 🕑 8am-12.30pm & 2-4pm Mon-Thu, 8am-12pm & 2.45-4pm Fri, 8am-12.30pm Sat), 3km east of town. Hundreds of mineral samples and fossils are on display, including all the tin ore you could wish for. Take a Tanjung Rambutan bus from the city bus station, get off at the crossing of Jl Sultan Azlan Shah, then walk southeast for 10 minutes.

Sleeping

Ipoh's hotels are mostly scattered around the New Town on the eastern side of Sungai Kinta, and are generally a pretty uninspiring bunch. There are a few modern luxury hotels catering to business travellers, as well as some better-kept mid-range options, but there are also many old and downright shabby establishments around too. Decent budget places are in very short supply. Ipoh has an unsavoury reputation for prostitution, and there are lots of dingy little 'hotels' around that are actually brothels, even quite smart places offer hourly rates and 'spa treatments'; single travellers, especially women, may want to avoid these sleazy places.

BUDGET

Sun Golden Inn (☎ 243 6255; 17 Jl Che Tak; s & d RM35; ❄) Ipoh's best budget choice is a simple but very clean and friendly place, hidden down a side street away from the traffic noise. Larger rooms, for up to four people, are also available (RM50).

Wanwa Hotel (☎ 241 5177; 32 Jl Ali Pitchay; s/d from RM30/34.50; ❄) Basic budget option at the junction of two busy roads, which does get a little noisy. The slightly dearer air-con rooms are preferable.

Hollywood Hotel (☎ 241 5214; 72 Jl CM Yussuf; s/d RM36/46; ❄) Seedy city-centre place with rather scruffy rooms, which might just be OK for an overnight stay if everywhere else is full. Like other hotels in Ipoh, it sees its fair share of 'day use'.

Merloon Hotel (☎ 254 1363; www.pvghotels.com; 92 Jl Mustapha Al-Bakri; s & d RM50-60; ❄) Comfortable modern hotel offering a decent standard of accommodation for the price, but it does have 'spa' facilities.

MID-RANGE

Syuen Hotel (☎ 253 8889; syuenht@tm.net.my; 88 Jl Sultan Abdul Jalil; s & d from RM178; ❄ 💻 🏊) Ipoh's most luxurious hotel, with bright, spacious rooms and a good range of facilities including a gym, tennis court and beer garden.

Majestic Station Hotel (☎ 255 4242; www.majesticstationhotel.com; Jl Panglima Bukit Gantang Wahab; standard/deluxe RM78/150; ❄) This venerable colonial establishment in Ipoh's magnificent, Moorish-style train station has plenty of character, and taking high tea on its long, tiled veranda is an experience in itself. The 'standard' rooms, though, are drab and poor value; go instead for the much more comfortable 'deluxe' rooms, which face onto the veranda. Discounts of up to 45% may be available.

Hotel Excelsior (☎ 253 6666; fax 253 6908; 43 Jl Sultan Abdul Jalil; s/d RM128/138; ❄) Modern, city-centre high-rise, with a sauna and gym, as well as a couple of good restaurants.

Grand View Hotel (☎ 243 1488; fax 243 1811; 36 Jl Horley; s/d RM69/89; ❄) One of the smarter and better-value mid-range places, with clean, brightly furnished rooms in a quiet area near the city centre.

Dragon & Phoenix Hotel (☎ 253 4661; 23 Jl Toh Puan Chah; s & d RM59.80; ❄) Quiet Chinese hotel set back from the main road, with fairly ordinary but comfortable rooms.

Hotel Eastern (☎ 254 3936; fax 255 1468; 18 Jl Sultan Idris Shah; s & d from RM65; ❄) Somewhat dated, but adequate small hotel in the city centre. All rooms have refrigerators and there are free daily newspapers.

Robin Hotel (☎ 242 1888; 100 Jl Mustapha Al-Bakri; s & d RM59.80-71.30; ❄) Sister hotel of the nearby Merloon, but although perfectly clean and comfortable, it's a little seedy, with a 'massage parlour' and suchlike; staff at reception will even openly offer 'call-girl packages', so it's not exactly discreet.

Lucky Hotel (☎ 254 7777; luckyhot@tm.net.my; 79 Jl CM Yussuf; s & d from RM60; ❄) Pleasant, if rather characterless, modern hotel in the city centre. It can be a little noisy, though, especially with the adjoining karaoke lounge.

Eating

Ipoh is the home of the rice noodle dish known as *kway teow*, reputedly still the best in Malaysia. You'll find it at most of the numerous cheap Chinese eateries located all over the city. More upscale fare can be found on the parallel streets of Pesiaran Greenhill and Jl Seenivasagam to the north-east of the city centre, which are lined with a succession of good-quality restaurants serving up excellent Chinese, Thai, Malay and vegetarian food.

FMS Bar & Restaurant (☎ 253 7678; 2 Jl Sultan Idris Shah; dishes from RM7) Excellent Chinese restaurant in a beautifully restored old colonial building on the edge of the Padang. The main restaurant is upstairs, decorated with all manner of retro knick-knacks, antique prints and porcelain, and watched over by a large portrait of the young Queen Elizabeth. Seafood and beancurd dishes are particularly good. There's a small saloon-style bar downstairs.

Oversea Restoran (☎ 258 0885; 65 Jl Seenivasagam; dishes from RM13) Highly regarded Chinese seafood restaurant, which gets crowded in the evenings. The fish is about as fresh as it comes – you can choose your meal from the one of the many fish tanks on display.

Greentown Noodle House (☎ 241 5145; 58 Pesiaran Greenhill; dishes from RM4) Reasonably priced noodle and rice dishes are the order of the day here, and there's also a small bar.

Soon Fatt Restoran (32 Jl Seenivasagam; dishes from RM7) Appropriately named hole-in-the-wall style place specialising in claypot, noodles and other Chinese fare.

Restoran Sayur-Sayuran Thin Hei (25 Pesiaran Greenhill; dishes from RM7) Basic vegetarian option, serving good Thai and Chinese food. Meat dishes are also available.

Kedai Kopi Kong Heng (Jl Bandar Timah; dishes from RM4) Simple but venerable and very popular place specialising in *kway teow*. The seafood is also good.

Restoran Tops 8 (Jl Jubilee; dishes from RM3) More of a food court than a restaurant, with a range of cheap Chinese hawker fare.

Ipoh also has plenty of food-stall centres. There's a row of more low-key evening hawkers east of Jl Jubilee and in front of the train station, and a small daytime food centre next to the Birch Memorial Clock Tower.

Medan Selera Dato Tawhil Azar (Jl Raja Musa Aziz) Better-known as the Children's Playground, this large centre has food stalls arranged around a small square. It's a popular place for Malay food in the evening and is open late.

Pusat Makanan Majestic (Jl Dato Tahwil Azar) Gets rowdy when market stalls are set up on the streets in the late afternoon.

You'll find some smarter restaurants and a food court in the **Ipoh Parade Shopping Centre** (Jl Sultan Abdul Adil).

Drinking

All the restaurants listed earlier serve beer.

Miners' Arms (8 Jl Dato' Maharaja Lela) A popular British-style pub, which also serves grills and steak dinners.

Coffee Craft (81 Jl Sultan Abdul Jalil; noon-midnight) A great place to try a wide range of gourmet coffees, and it also serves light meals.

Schlotzsky's (Jl Sultan Abdul Adil), on the ground floor of the Ipoh Parade Shopping Centre, is a top-notch juice bar; try its giant 'Fresh Fruit Juggernauts'.

Getting There & Away

AIR

Malaysia Airlines (☎ 312 2460; Jl Sultan Idris Shah) has two daily departures to KL (RM111). Car rental is available at the airport from **Hertz** (☎ 312 7109).

BUS

Ipoh is on the main KL–Butterworth road; 205km north of the capital, 164km south of Butterworth. The long-distance bus station is south of the train station and the city centre, a taxi ride from the main hotel area. Numerous bus companies operate from this station, with services departing at varying times.

Destinations and standard fares include Alor Setar (RM17); Butterworth (RM9); Hat Yai in Thailand (RM33); Johor Bahru (RM38); Kota Bharu (RM19); Kuala Kangsar (RM3.95); KL (RM15); Lumut (RM4.50); Melaka (RM17); Taiping (RM5.45); Tapah (RM4.20) and Teluk Intan (RM5). Try to book your tickets in advance or turn up early, especially for the crowded, infrequent service to Tapah.

Perak Roadways has a separate terminus directly across Jl Tun Abdul Razak, with regular buses to Lumut (RM4.50, 1¾ hours).

The city bus station is northwest of the long-distance station on the other side of the roundabout. Local buses depart from here for outlying regions close to Ipoh, such as Batu Gajah and Gopeng (for Kellie's Castle), and Kuala Kangsar.

TAXI

Long-distance taxis depart from in front of the long-distance bus station, and there is another rank directly across the road. Whole-taxi fares include: Butterworth (RM150); Cameron Highlands (RM100); Ipoh airport (RM12); Kuala Kangsar (RM30); KL (RM160); Lumut (RM60); Taiping (RM60); and Tapah (RM50). Taxis from here cost RM5 to RM6 anywhere around town, but in the city centre should only cost RM2 to RM3.

TRAIN

Ipoh's **train station** (☎ 254 0481; Jl Panglima Bukit Gantang Wahab) is on the main Singapore–Butterworth line. The train to KL (RM18) leaves at 3.06am, arriving at 8.20am; in the opposite direction, a daily train heads to Butterworth (RM12) at 1.25am, arriving at 6.34am, before continuing to Hat Yai in Thailand.

AROUND IPOH

Kellie's Castle

A striking colonial remnant set by a small river about 30km south of Ipoh, **Kellie's Castle** (adult/child RM5/2; 🕒 8.30am-6pm) is, in fact, an old unfinished mansion, nicknamed Kellie's Folly. It was cast in the mould of great colonial houses, complete with Moorish-style windows and a lift (elevator). Wealthy British rubber-plantation owner William Kellie Smith, who already lived in another splendid mansion in this area, commissioned the building – which was to be the home of his son – in what was then a remote jungle area. Seventy Hindu artisans were brought from Madras to work on the mansion, but Smith died in Lisbon in 1926 on a trip home to England and the house was never completed. Today, the still imposing six-storey structure is a well-tended tourist site, set in a pleasant park that also includes a deer enclosure and a small aviary. The best-preserved rooms are the guest bedrooms, adorned with fine figurative plasterwork, and there are some splendid views of the surrounding countryside from the roof terrace.

About 500m from the castle is a **Hindu temple**, built for the artisans by Smith when a mysterious illness decimated the workforce and the remaining workers believed that the gods needed to be appeased. To show their gratitude to Smith, the workers placed a figure of him, complete with white suit and pith helmet, among the Hindu deities on the temple roof. The temple is now semi-derelict but still in use. The resident priest will point out the statue of Smith.

Kellie's Castle is inconvenient to reach without your own transport. From Ipoh's city bus station you can take either the frequent No 66 bus to Gopeng (RM1.30) or bus No 36 or 37 to Batu Gajah, which leaves every 20 minutes (RM1.50). The No 67 bus runs approximately every hour in either direction between Batu Gajah and Gopeng, passing in front of Kellie's Castle. You can also charter a taxi from Ipoh (RM35 return). A taxi from Batu Gajah costs RM5.

Tambun Hot Springs

A popular getaway for locals, the **Tambun Hot Springs** are 8km northeast of Ipoh, beside a lake, at the base of forested limestone cliffs. These natural thermal springs have various hot pools in which to 'take the waters' (RM5).

Regular buses from Ipoh's city bus station to Tanjung Rambutan pass the hot springs.

LUMUT

☎ 05

Lumut is the departure point for Pulau Pangkor and despite attempts to promote the town as a tourist destination in its own right, it has little to offer apart from souvenir shops, a few restaurants and some reasonable beaches outside town.

The Malaysian Navy has its principal base just outside town and some 25,000 sailors make up the overwhelming majority of the town's inhabitants. You'll see the huge apartment complexes of the naval quarters as you take the boat out to Pulau Pangkor.

The sailors frequent **Teluk Batik**, a good beach 7km from town. There's no bus service here, but a one-way taxi costs RM10.

Information

The **Tourism Malaysia Office** (☎ 683 4057; Jl Sultan Idris Shah; 🕒 9am-5pm Mon-Fri, 9am-1.45pm Sat) is midway between the jetty and the bus station. Next door you'll find a moneychanger offering better rates than on Pulau Pangkor, and **Maybank** (Jl Sultan Idris Shah) is farther down the street.

Motorists on their way to Pangkor can use the 24-hour, long-term car park behind the Shell petrol station, next to the bus station (RM10 per day).

Sleeping & Eating

If you get marooned on the way to Pangkor, Lumut has a few reasonable hotels and restaurants.

Phin Lum Hooi Hotel (☎ 683 5641, 93 Jl Titi Panjang; s & d from RM40; ❄) This clean and friendly hotel is about half a kilometre out of town; it also has a good, cheap restaurant downstairs.

Harbour View Hotel (☎ 683 7888; 13 Jl Titi Panjang; s & d from RM60; ❄) A few doors back from Phin Lum Hooi Hotel, offers comfortable rooms with attached bathroom.

Orient Star (☎ 683 4199; 203 Jl Iskandar Shah; s & d from RM300; ❄ 🏊) About 1km farther out towards the navy base, this international-class hotel is on the waterfront but has no beach. Discounts are often available.

Getting There & Away

BUS

Lumut is 170km south of Butterworth and 83km southwest of Ipoh, the main turn-off for Lumut on the KL–Butterworth road. The bus station is right by the ferry jetty. On Pulau Pangkor, the bus agent next to Pangkor town's Chuan Full Hotel handles bookings for the express buses.

Lumut is well connected to other destinations on the peninsula and several bus companies operate from here. The most-frequent buses take the highway to/from Ipoh (RM4.50, hourly). Direct buses run roughly hourly to/from KL (RM16). Other destinations include Butterworth (RM10.50, 5 daily); Johor Bahru/Singapore (RM37/40, 6 daily); Kuantan (RM25, 3 daily); Melaka (RM20, 2 daily); and Taiping (RM6, 5 daily). There are no direct buses from Lumut to the Cameron Highlands; take a bus to Ipoh, then transfer to a bus to Tapah, then yet another local bus to Tanah Rata. Allow at least half a day.

TAXI

Long-distance taxis from Lumut can be scarce late in the day. Typical fares are Butterworth (RM120); Ipoh (RM50); and KL (RM200).

PULAU PANGKOR

☎ 05

The island of Pangkor is just a short ferry ride from Lumut, and is easily accessible via Ipoh. It's a low-key resort island noted for its fine beaches. These can be visited via the road running around the island. The jungle-clad hills of the interior, though, are virtually untouched.

At 8 sq km, and with a population of 25,000, Pangkor is a relatively small island, but that hasn't stopped the state government from trying to promote it as one of Malaysia's main tourist destinations. Although development is relatively limited, Pangkor's laid-back, *kampung*-feel is slowly disappearing. Before tourism took off, Pangkor's economy relied on fishing. Fishing and dried fish products are still a major industry for the island, particularly on the east coast.

Pangkor was a bit-player in the battle to control trade in the Strait of Melaka. In earlier times, the island was a favourite refuge of fishermen, sailors, merchants and pirates. In the 17th century, the Dutch built a fort here in their bid to monopolise the Perak tin trade, but were less than keen to defend Perak against Acehnese and Siamese incursions. The Dutch were driven out by a local ruler before returning briefly some fifty years later. In 1874 a contender to the Perak throne sought British backing and the Pangkor Treaty was signed. As a result, British Resident James WW Birch was installed in Perak and the colonial era on the peninsula began.

Pangkor is a popular local resort and it can get very crowded on weekends and holidays, but during the week the beaches are almost empty.

Orientation

Finding things on Pangkor is very simple. The east coast of the island, facing the mainland, is a continuous village strip comprising Sungai Pinang Kecil (SPK), Sungai Pinang Besar (SPB) and Pangkor Town, the main centre of population.

The road that runs along the east coast turns west at Pangkor Town and runs directly across the island, which is only 2km wide at this point, to Pasir Bogak. From there it runs north to the village of Teluk Nipah, where you'll find most of the budget accommodation. It then goes to the northern end of the island, past the airport, to Pangkor's upmarket resorts. The road from there back to the eastern side of the island is winding and very steep in parts, but it's paved all the way.

nformation

Che Maybank in Pangkor Town, in the ame building as Min Lian Hotel, is open he usual hours and has an ATM. For travllers cheques and cash, the **moneychanger** Jl Sultan Idris Shah) back on the mainland in .umut (p137) offers better rates.

There are Internet cafes in Pangkor Town nd at some of the budget accommodation t Teluk Nipah. The cheapest is **Fisherman afé Internet** (☎ 685 1123; 62 Jl Besar; RM3 per hr) n Pangkor Town. Rates elsewhere remain igh (RM10 per hour), but the **Seagull Beach Resort** (☎ 685 2878) in Teluk Nipah charges RM7. Note that connection times can be gonisingly slow.

The **bus agent** (Jl Besar) next to the Chuan 'ull Hotel in Pangkor Town handles bookngs for express buses originating from .umut on the mainland.

Beaches

The beach at **Pasir Bogak** is fine for swimming, ut during holidays it's crowded – at least y Malaysia's 'empty beach' standards. It's lovely, if rather narrow, white-sand beach. **eluk Nipah**, a hilly 20-minute bicycle ride rther north, has a wider, better beach.

The best beach on this side is at **Coral Bay**, ıst north of Teluk Nipah. The water is a lear, emerald-green colour due to the presnce of limestone, and usually the beach is uite clean and pretty.

In May, June and July turtles used to come ı to lay their eggs at night on **Teluk Ketapang** each, north of Pasir Bogak. Increasing umbers of gawking tourists have seriously ffected the turtles and sightings are increasıgly rare. For more information on turtles ee the Environment chapter (p55).

At the northern end of the island at Teluk elanga, **Pantai Puteri Dewi** (Golden Sands each) is pleasant, but access is restricted) Pan Pacific Resort guests. Day-trippers ave to pay a ridiculous RM40 (including ınch). In between there are a number of irtually deserted beaches that you can each by boat, motorcycle or on foot.

On nearby Pulau Pangkor Laut, **Emerald ay** is a beautiful little horseshoe-shaped ay with clear water, fine coral and a gently oping beach. You'll have to be resident at ıe exclusive Pangkor Laut Resort, though, enjoy it (see the boxed text 'The Author's hoice', p143).

Exploring the Island

The island lends itself well to exploration by motorcycle, bicycle or on foot. Spend a day doing a loop of the island, following the paved road all the way around. By motorcycle it takes about two hours with stops, around three or four hours by bicycle, or you could even walk it in a very long day. Be warned, though, that local motorcycling youths seem oblivious to any kind of road rules and accidents are commonplace.

Along the western side are the main beaches of Pasir Bogak, Teluk Nipah and Coral Beach, and most of the tourist accommodation. On the northern edge of Coral Beach, look out for the small psychedelic **Lin Je Kong**, adorned with numerous outsize statues including a giant turtle, a mermaid and, of course, Donald Duck. From here, the road heads inland past the airport and, to the north, the Pan Pacific Resort at Teluk Belanga. Continuing eastwards, the road skirts Teluk Dalam, with its luxury resort, and crosses over the headland. This is a steep and twisting road through some superb **jungle**, though it's quite deserted and women travellers have been attacked here.

On the eastern side, from SPK it's a nearly continuous village strip on to grotty Pangkor Town. It's probably not somewhere you'd want to hang out for too long, though, unless you're absorbed by the sight of drying fish or want to stock up on cheap souvenir T-shirts. Nearby there's a colourful South Indian **Hindu temple**. In SPB, the **Foo Lin Kong**, on the side of the hill just west of the main road, is worth a quick look; there's a mini version of the Great Wall of China climbing up the hill behind.

Pangkor's one bit of history is 3km south of Pangkor Town at Teluk Gedong. The **Kota Belanda** (Dutch Fort) was built here in 1670, after the Dutch had been kicked out of Lower Perak by resentful local Malays. Despite frequent visits, the Dutch weren't able to reoccupy the site and rebuild the fort until 1743; only five years later they abandoned it for good after local warrior chiefs repeatedly attacked them. The old fort was totally swallowed by the jungle until 1973, when it was reconstructed as far as the remaining bricks would allow, which wasn't much.

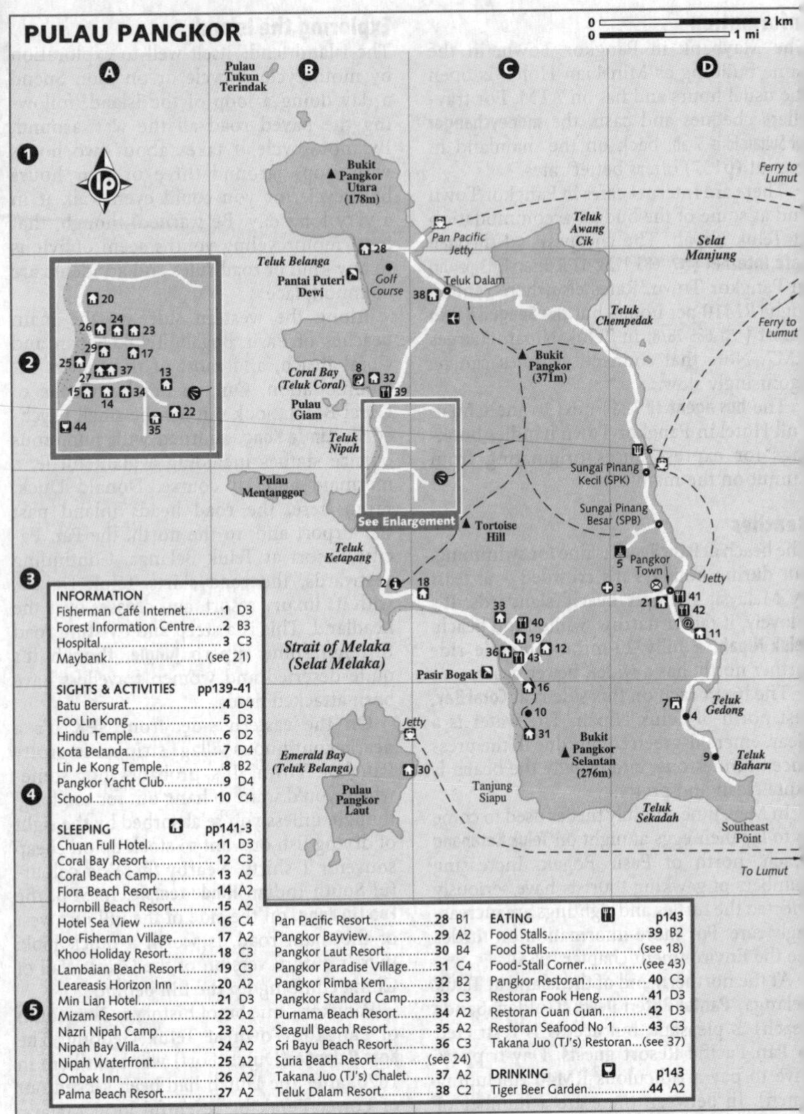

On the waterfront 100m beyond the fort is **Batu Bersurat**, a mammoth stone carved with the symbol of the Dutch East India Company (Vereenigde Oost-Indische Compagnie; VOC) and other ancient graffiti, including a faint depiction of a tiger stealing a child. This supposedly relates to an incident when the child of a local European dignitary disappeared whil[e] playing near the rock. The Dutch like[d] the idea of the tiger story; the more likel[y] explanation is that the girl was abducted b[y] disenchanted locals.

The road ends just past the fishing villag[e] of Teluk Gedong and the defunct Pangk[or] Yacht Club.

Activities

Snorkelling gear, boats and even jet skis can be hired at hotels or on the beach at Pasir Bogak and Teluk Nipah. A small boat to take you **snorkelling** at small nearby islands or less-accessible beaches costs RM30 for three people, after negotiation. Boats can also be hired to go to Pulau Sembilan, a group of nine islands with deserted white-sand beaches that are popular for **sports fishing**, about 1½ hours southwest of Pangkor.

The island offers some interesting **walking** opportunities. A four-hour jungle trail crosses the island from Teluk Nipah and comes out near the Foo Lin Kong; another trail goes from Pasir Bogak to Bukit Pangkor before joining the east-coast road. Walking trails are often overgrown. Take a guide and *parang* (bush knife), and protect yourself against leeches and ticks. The Forest Information Centre at the north end of Pasir Bogak, at the start of one of the trails, is rarely open. Most guesthouses have lots of information and can organise a guide.

Sleeping

Pasir Bogak is the most developed beach: it's a string of big, mid-range hotels, a few restaurants and not much else. It's very busy on weekends, but much quieter during the week. Teluk Nipah, the best beach on the island, is in transition from a *kampung* to another Pasir Bogak as mid-range hotels spring up around the backpacker hostels. The only other developments on Pangkor are luxury resorts on isolated beaches.

Rates at most places vary between peak (Saturday, Sunday and holidays) and off-peak seasons; the following prices quoted are 'off-peak', available from Monday to Friday and in the low season.

TELUK NIPAH

The most lively of Pangkor's beaches, Teluk Nipah is a popular backpacker haunt, with a variety of cheap hostel accommodation available. There are also a few mid-range places. Note that hotels on the main road do experience a fair bit of noise from local youths racing their motorbikes, which often continues well into the wee hours.

Budget

Seagull Beach Resort (☎ 685 2878; s & d RM20-50;) Very friendly guesthouse in a quiet spot back from the road. The small, basic huts are comfortable enough, but the pricier air-con doubles are preferable. There's a good restaurant on site, and the cheapest Internet access on Teluk Nipah (RM7 per hour).

Suria Beach Resort (☎ 685 3922; fax 685 3921; s & d RM50;) Sparkling modern hotel with spotless, comfortable rooms with balconies, which are a real bargain.

Mizam Resort (☎ 685 3359; s & d RM30-50;) A hidden gem set well back from the beach, at the very edge of the jungle. It's a quiet place, and the rooms all come with TV and attached bathroom.

Nazri Nipah Camp (☎ 685 2014; nipahcamp@yahoo.com; dm RM10, s & d RM15-40) Very friendly, sleepy place at the edge of the rainforest with a good range of accommodation including simple A-frames and more comfortable chalets with bathrooms.

Ombak Inn (☎ 685 5223; s & d RM20-70;) Low-key hotel with a variety of options, from basic A-frame huts to sparkling fan/air-con bungalows with attached bathrooms.

Takana Juo (TJ's) Chalet (☎ 685 4733; s & d RM25) Small place with a few basic, but often full, bungalows with bathrooms just behind its popular restaurant.

Coral Beach Camp (☎ 685 2711; s & d RM20-50) Long-running budget place with tiny A-frame huts and more comfortable doubles with bathrooms.

Pangkor Rimba Kem (☎ 685 5490; dm/d RM15/60) Basic place in a pleasant spot on Coral Beach. There's also space for tents (RM10).

Joe Fisherman Village (☎ 685 2389; s & d RM20-30) Rather scruffy place, verging on semi-derelict, opposite Nazri Nipah Camp. It has the usual, basic A-frame huts and travellers who stay here all seem to enjoy the boisterous, communal atmosphere. Bicycle rental is available (RM15 per day).

Mid-Range

Hornbill Beach Resort (☎ 685 2005; fax 685 2006; s & d RM120-150;) Spotless modern hotel facing the beach, with comfortable, well-equipped rooms, most with balconies, and friendly hosts. The rooms at the front have great views, but those at the back are quieter.

Purnama Beach Resort (☎ 685 3530; s & d RM45-75;) Spruce collection of chalets including fairly simple fan huts and neat, motel-style doubles. Larger family chalets are available, sleeping up to six (RM135).

There's a good restaurant and a very small pool. Prices include breakfast.

Palma Beach Resort (☎ 685 3693; s & d RM65-75; ❄) Reasonably priced mid-range option with quite nice wooden chalets with TV and bathroom. Prices are negotiable, especially for longer stays.

Nipah Bay Villa (☎ 685 2198; fax 685 2386; dm RM25, s & d RM85-95; ❄) Smart place with a range of accommodation including cosy chalets of various sizes, sleeping up to eight (RM180).

Flora Beach Resort (☎ 685 3878; s & d RM65-75; ❄) Comfortable collection of clean wooden chalets set back from the road, all with attached bathrooms. Motorbikes and bicycles (RM30 and RM10 respectively) are available for rent.

Nipah Waterfront (☎ 685 5485; s & d RM80-150; ❄) One of the newest places, with spacious and comfortably furnished rooms. Larger chalets sleep up to six people (RM200).

Horizon Inn (☎ 685 3398; s & d from RM70; ❄) Nice rooms facing the sea, with a good restaurant downstairs. It does get a fair bit of noise from the road though.

Pangkor Bayview (☎ 685 3540; s & d RM60; ❄) Smart place with decent size rooms, all with a TV and attached bathroom.

PASIR BOGAK

The rest of Pangkor's accommodation possibilities are grouped at each end of the beach at Pasir Bogak, where there is a mixture of top-end and cheaper places to stay. The atmosphere is lacking compared to Teluk Nipah, however, and fewer overseas travellers stay here. It's geared more to weekending Malaysian families.

Khoo Holiday Resort (☎ 685 2190; fax 685 1164; s & d from RM70; ❄) Located at the western end of the beach, the main building of this resort is a rather ugly concrete conglomeration, but the simple wooden chalets with bathrooms on the steep slope behind have great views across to Pulau Pangkor Laut.

Pangkor Standard Camp (☎ 685 1878; s & d from RM52; ❄) If you continue east on the main road you'll reach this similarly styled place that also has cramped three-person A-frame huts (RM31.50 to RM37.80). Bicycles are available for rent.

The other hotels are at the eastern end of the beach, where the road from Pangkor town crosses the island.

Lambaian Beach Resort (☎ 685 402; fax 685 4022; s & d from RM70; ❄) North of the intersection, this reasonable place has neat rooms and a Malaysian restaurant.

Sri Bayu Beach Resort (☎ 685 1929; fax 685 1050; s & d from RM250; ❄) Located opposite Lambaian, this luxurious complex has attractive, spacious rooms set in landscaped gardens. There's nightly live entertainment.

Hotel Sea View (☎ 685 1605; s & d from RM115; ❄) There is an inviting pool but rather plain doubles and brick chalets. Significant discounts may be available.

Pangkor Paradise Village (☎ 691 3241; s & d from RM50; ❄) A locals' retreat in a coconut grove at the southernmost end of Pasir Bogak, accessible only via a track leading around the side of a school. It has rather grubby chalets on an isolated little beach, which is the real attraction. There's a small restaurant right on the water.

Coral Bay Resort (☎ 685 5111; fax 685 5666; s & d from RM130; ❄) On the road to Pangkor Town is this huge gleaming-white complex with spotless rooms, but a little overpriced since it's not even on the beach. Discounts of more than 50% may be available.

PANGKOR TOWN

As the whole attraction of Pangkor is the beaches, there is little point in staying in Pangkor Town, but if you get stuck, there are a few cheap Chinese hotels.

Min Lian Hotel (☎ 685 1294; s & d RM40; ❄) Right above the Maybank is this tidy and welcoming hotel; staff don't speak English.

Chuan Full Hotel (☎ 685 1123; 60 Jl Besar; s/d RM15/20; ❄) This rickety, old, wooden hotel is immaculately kept and has a veranda at the back overlooking the waterfront. Aircon rooms cost RM35. The friendly owner also books coach tickets.

ELSEWHERE ON THE ISLAND

Pan Pacific Resort (☎ 685 1091/1399; fax 685 1852) You'll find the lush, secluded grounds of this resort at Teluk Belanga on the northern end of the island. Prices start at RM380 for standard rooms, RM580 for the 'house on the rocks' and RM780 for a bungalow. Recreational facilities include a golf course, and the resort is on a very pleasant stretch of beach. Access is restricted to hotel guests, although day-trippers are admitted for RM40 (including lunch).

THE AUTHOR'S CHOICE

Richard Watkins

Pangkor Laut Resort (☎ 699 1100; www.pangkorlautresort.com; s & d from RM920;) Malaysia's most exclusive tourist development occupies the tiny private island of Pangkor Laut, just opposite Pasir Bogak. The luxurious accommodation ranges from spacious hillside and seafront villas with king-size beds, balconies and huge bathrooms, to private 'estates' (uniquely designed houses, with two to four bedrooms, private pools and gardens, on a secluded bay away from the main resort). Minimum three-night packages start at a staggering RM30,400. Every conceivable amenity is at hand, and the resort boasts several fine restaurants, tennis courts and a Spa Village offering a wide choice of treatments, including Ayurvedic.

The island is a favourite getaway for the Italian tenor, Pavarotti, and you can even stay in the Pavarotti Suite (RM2415), an elegant hilltop retreat with a large, open-roofed bathroom and decorated with paintings from the opera star's private collection.

Teluk Dalam Resort (☎ 685 5000; www.pangkorresorts.com; s & d from RM172;) Farther to the east you'll find this four-star resort. Its collection of rustic wooden chalets and bungalows overlook the sea. Facilities include a tennis court, children's pool and a nursery.

Eating

TELUK NIPAH

Several of Teluk Nipah's guesthouses have restaurants, though outside high season, these often close down. There are some basic food stalls at the beach.

Takana Juo (TJ's) Restoran (dishes from RM6) A family-run Indonesian restaurant at the bungalows of the same name. TJ's cooks delicious, cheap food, though they certainly take their time serving it. It's open for breakfast, lunch and dinner, and is regularly full, so you'll need to get there early.

Restaurant Horizon (dishes from RM8) Downstairs from the Horizon Inn, this place has sunset views, alfresco dining and some good seafood, though it's a bit overpriced.

PASIR BOGAK

All the hotels have restaurants and there are a few other places to eat.

Khoo Holiday Resort (☎ 685 2190) has a good, inexpensive restaurant and there are food stalls nearby.

At the opposite end of the beach, near the Lambaian Beach Resort, is a permanent food-stall corner. Here you'll also find **Restoran Seafood No 1** (dishes from RM15) specialising in fresh prawns, fish and crab. The karaoke joint here constitutes Pangkor's only nightlife.

Tucked away along a small dirt road running alongside Pangkor Standard Camp, **Pangkor Restoran** (dishes from RM5) is cheap for Chinese seafood and popular with locals.

PANGKOR TOWN

Pangkor Town has a proliferation of cheap, Chinese *kedai kopi* (coffee shops), some of which serve excellent seafood. **Restoran Guan Guan** (Jl Besar; dishes from RM5) is an old favourite for seafood cooked any way you like; prices are posted on the wall-sized English menu. **Restoran Fook Heng** (Jl Besar; dishes from RM5) is also popular. Both serve beer.

Drinking

Most of the restaurants listed earlier serve alcohol. **Tiger Beer Garden** (Teluk Nipah), on the main road just down from the Hornbill Beach Resort, has a few outdoor tables where you can drink a beer and watch the sunset.

Getting There & Away

AIR

Berjaya Air (☎ 685 5828) has flights every day except Tuesday and Thursday between KL's Subang airport and Pangkor airport in the north (RM225).

BOAT

In the high season, **Pan Silver Ferry** (☎ 685 1046) runs between Lumut and Pangkor Town every 30 minutes from 6.45am to 7.30pm, while the **Duta Pangkor Ferry** (☎ 691 6753) does the same trip every hour between 7am and 7pm. Most ferries to Lumut stop at SPK before reaching Pangkor Town, so don't hop off too soon. Return tickets on both boats cost RM4 and can be bought from touts around the bus station and jetty; just check which service is leaving first.

The Pan Pacific and Teluk Dalam resorts on the northern end of the island are served by their own, expensive, ferry service from Lumut, running every 1½ to two hours in either direction (RM16).

Getting Around

There are no public buses available to tourists, so you will be forced to use Pangkor's candy-pink minibus taxis, which operate between 6.30am and 9pm. Set-fare services for up to three people from the jetty in Pangkor Town include: Pasir Bogak (RM4); Teluk Nipah (RM10); Pan Pacific Resort (RM18); the airport (RM18); and around the island (RM35 to RM40).

An ideal way to see the island is by motorcycle or bicycle (see Exploring the Island, p139). There are a number of places at Pangkor Town, Pasir Bogak and Teluk Nipah that rent motorcycles for around RM30 per day and bicycles for RM15. Cars must be left on the mainland.

KUALA KANGSAR

☎ 05

Beside the highway, northwest of Ipoh, Kuala Kangsar has been the royal town of Perak state since the sultan moved his capital here in the 18th century. It was also the first foothold for the British, who moved to control the peninsula by installing Residents at the royal courts in the 1870s. Kuala Kangsar was the birthplace of Malaysia's great rubber industry – see the boxed text this page. By the 1890s the rapid growth of the tin towns of Ipoh and Taiping overshadowed Kuala Kangsar, and the town remains a quiet backwater steeped in Malay tradition.

> **RUBBERY FACTS**
>
> In the late 1870s, a number of rubber trees were planted by British Resident Sir Hugh Low in his gardens in Kuala Kangsar, from seed stock allegedly either smuggled out of Brazil or taken from London's Kew Gardens. However, it was not until the invention of the pneumatic tyre in 1888, and then the popularity of the motorcar at the start of the 20th century, that rubber suddenly came into demand and rubber plantations sprang up across the country. Almost all of the trees in the new plantations were descended from Low's original rubber trees or from the Singapore Botanic Gardens. You can still see one of those first trees in Kuala Kangsar's District Office compound.

The small town centre is unremarkable, but to the southeast, overlooking Sungai Perak, the royal district is spacious and quiet – this is the most attractive of all Malaysia's royal cities. Kuala Kangsar's main sights are few, but they're quite impressive and can easily be explored in a morning or afternoon, or as a day trip from Ipoh, including a detour en route to Perak Tong (see p134).

Sights

Heading out on Jl Istana beside the wide Sungai Perak, the first striking example of the wealth of the sultanate is the small, but magnificent **Masjid Ubudiah** (Ubudiah Mosque). The mosque appears as if viewed through a distorting mirror, since its minarets are squeezed up tightly against the superb golden onion-dome. It was completed in 1917, after delays due to WWI and rampant elephants that destroyed the Italian marble tiles. The caretaker will show you around the outside of the building for a small donation, but non-Muslims are not allowed inside.

Overlooking the river, **Istana Iskandariah** is a suitably opulent palace built in 1933. It is best viewed from the river side to appreciate the original palace, which mixes Art Deco with Islamic motifs. The 1984 annexe, on the southern side, is less striking. Unfortunately, the palace is not open to visitors.

Farther east is a slightly earlier palace, **Istana Kenangan** (Palace of Memories), made entirely of wood and woven bamboo. It was built in 1931 and served as the temporary royal quarters until the Istana Iskandariah was completed. It now houses the **Muzium Di Raja** (Royal Museum; 🕒 9.30am-5.30pm, closed 12.15-2.45pm Friday), with displays on the state's history and the Perak royal family. Admission is by small donation.

Closer to town on Jl Istana near the Masjid Ubudiah, **Istana Hulu** is another substantial palace inspired by Victorian architecture. Built in 1903, it is now the Raja Perempuan Mazwin School.

The **Malay College** to the north of town is the most impressive colonial building in Kuala Kangsar. Established in 1905, it was the first and one of the only Malay schools to provide English education for the Malay elite destined for the civil service. It not only provided clerical workers for the British administration but also the nationalist leaders of the conservative 'Malaya for Malays' faction. In the 1950s Anthony Burgess wrote his first book while teaching here.

Opposite the Malay College, the **Pavilion Square Tower** is a delightful folly overlooking the surrounding parkland and playing fields. Built in 1930, this small, three-storey sports pavilion of Malay and colonial design allowed royalty and VIPs to view polo matches in comfort.

Sleeping & Eating

Kuala Kangsar has a couple of cheap hotels for an overnight stay.

Double Lion Hotel (☎ 776 1010; 74 Jl Kangsar; s/d from RM25/30; ❄) Conveniently close to the bus station. In addition to the rooms with fan, there are more comfortable air-con rooms available for RM70. There's a busy bar and bakery downstairs.

Rumah Rehat Kuala Kangsar (☎ 776 5872; Jl Istana; s & d RM80-100; ❄) The best place in town is this modernised resthouse situated in a quiet parkland area southeast of the centre. Many of the spacious rooms overlook the river, and it's worth paying the little bit extra for a room with a balcony. There's also a Malay restaurant with a river terrace.

Getting There & Away

Kuala Kangsar is 50km northwest of Ipoh, just off the main KL–Butterworth road. It's 123km south of Butterworth and 255km north of KL. Frequent bus connections include Butterworth (RM6.30); Ipoh (RM3.95); KL (RM14.10); Lumut (RM6.70); and Taiping (RM2.50). There are two daily services to Kota Bharu (RM18.80).

Taxis leave from next to the bus station for Butterworth (RM55); Ipoh (RM28); KL (RM100); and Taiping (RM25).

The **train station** (☎ 776 1095) is located less-conveniently to the northwest of town. All KL–Butterworth trains stop here.

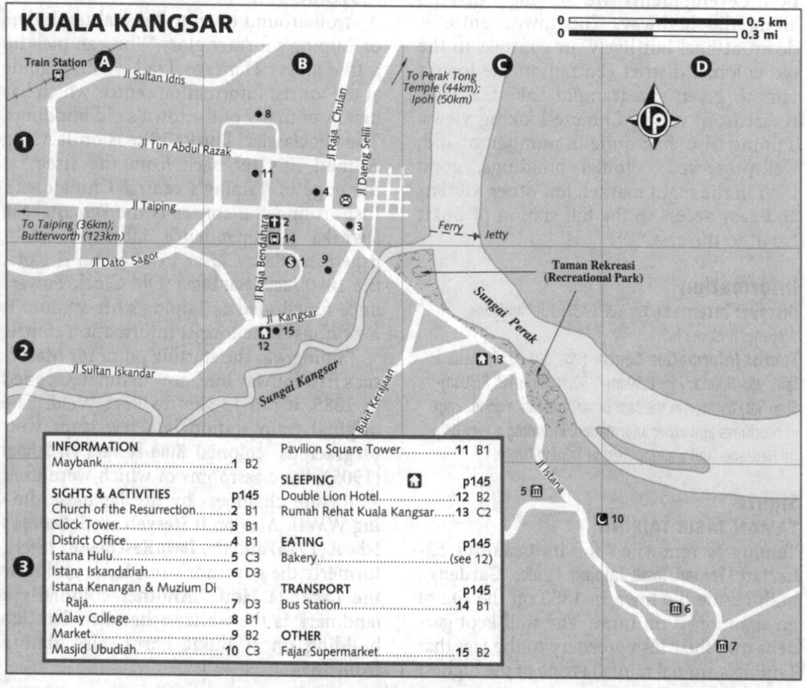

TAIPING

☎ 05

The Town of Everlasting Peace hardly started out that way. In the mid-nineteenth century, when it was known as Larut, the town was a raucous, rough-and-tumble tin-mining centre, the oldest one in Malaysia. Bitter feuds broke out three times between rival Chinese secret societies, with injury, torture and death taking place on all sides. When colonial administrators finally brought the bloody mayhem under control in 1874, they took the prudent step of renaming the town. Though it was then the largest and most important town in Perak, by 1890 Ipoh and the Kinta Valley had begun to overshadow Taiping as the centre of the tin industry, and the state capital was finally moved in 1935.

Though Taiping has lost its former status, the tourist brochures still boast of the town's '31 Firsts' for Malaysia including the first museum; the first railway; the first newspapers in English, Malay and Tamil; and the country's first zoo.

Taiping is now a low-key town and any new developments are on the outskirts along the highway. The town centre is down-at-heel but lively, in contrast to the old colonial district centred on the town's famous green and tranquil Lake Gardens. Apart from misty, Chinese-looking views, Taiping also has quite a number of old, well-preserved colonial buildings, good food in the night market, few other tourists and easy access to the hill station of Bukit Larut to the east.

Information

Discover Internet (☎ 806 9487; 3 Jl Panggong Wayang; RM2 per hr)

Tourist Information Centre (☎ 805 3245; Menara Jam, 355 Jl Kota; 🕑 8.30am-5.30pm Mon-Fri, 8.30am-3pm Sat) Located in the Jam Besar, and has a good range of brochures and other information, including a very helpful Heritage Trail walking map of Taiping (free).

Sights

TAMAN TASIK TAIPING

Taiping is renowned for its beautiful 62-hectare **Taman Tasik Taiping** (Lake Gardens), built beside the town in 1880 on the site of an abandoned tin mine. The well-kept gardens owe their lush greenery to the fact that Taiping's annual rainfall is one of the highest in Peninsular Malaysia. In the hills that rise above the gardens is Bukit Larut (Maxwell Hill), the oldest hill station in Malaysia.

The Lake Gardens also contain the **Zoo Taiping** (☎ 808 6577; www.zootaiping.gov.my; adult/child RM4/2; 🕑 8.30am-6.30pm), a pleasantly landscaped place where you can see all manner of creatures, if they're not snoozing in the midday heat. Watch out, though, for the wild monkeys, who drop from the trees to scavenge for food; they can be aggressive.

MUZIUM PERAK

Northwest of the gardens, the **Muzium Perak** (State Museum; ☎ 807 2057; Jl Taming Sari; admission free; 🕑 9am-5pm, closed 12.15-2.45pm Fri) is housed in an impressive colonial building. It's the oldest museum in Malaysia, opening in 1883, and doesn't seem to have changed that much since. Exhibits include an array of traditional kris (daggers), Orang Asli carvings, royal artefacts, costumes and stuffed animals. Outside, you can cast an eye over a few outsize exhibits such as an old British jet fighter.

HISTORIC BUILDINGS

A stroll around town will reveal reminders of Taiping's former glory. You can pick up a free glossy Heritage Trail walking guide at the tourist information centre, which has details of many of the town's old buildings. The neoclassical **District Office** is on Jl Alang Ahmad (it's set back from the street at the edge of Taiping's central Chinatown). Just around the corner is the **Perpustakaan Merdeka** (Independence Library), established in 1882. Closer to town on Jl Kota, the 1890 **Jam Besar Lama** (Old Clock Tower) once functioned as Taiping's fire station. It now houses the tourist information centre.

Taiping was the starting point for Malaysia's first railway line, now defunct. Opened in 1885, it ran 13.5km to Port Weld. The original train station is a few steps west of gracious, colonial **King Edward VII School** (1905), the classrooms of which were used as torture chambers by the Japanese during WWII. Also on Jl Stesyen are **St George's School** (1915) and the **Town Rest House** (1894), formerly the governor's residence and now the Lagenda Hotel. Another colonial-era landmark is the whitewashed **New Golf Club** building on Jl Bukit Larut, also dating from 1894.

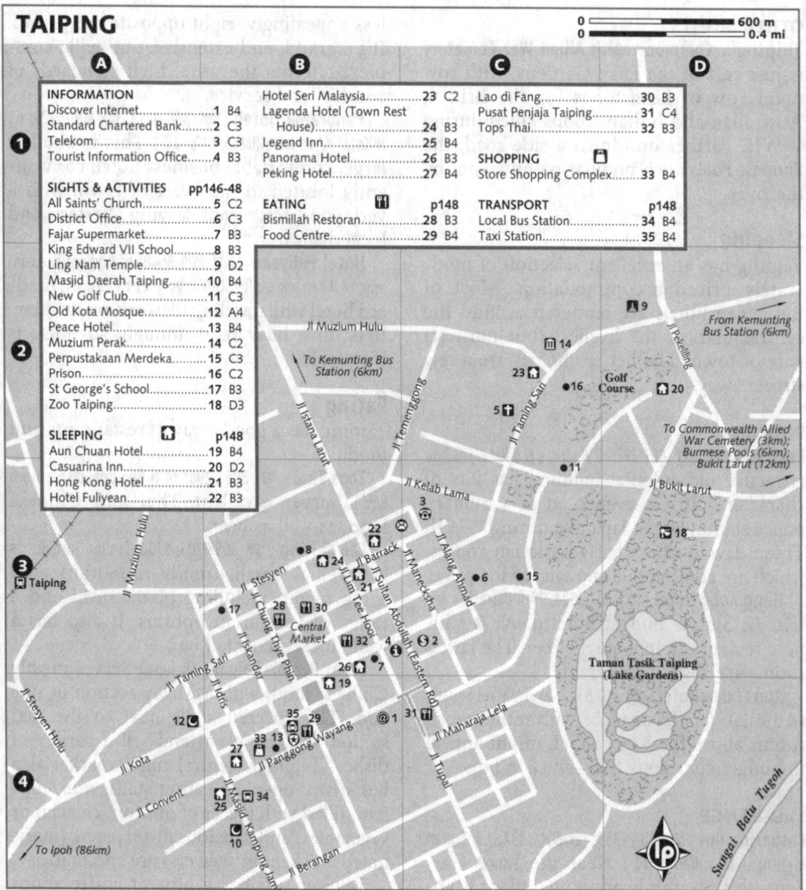

At the western end of town, the **Old Kota Mosque** (1897) is the oldest in Taiping. It's mainly of note for its hexagonal design.

Taiping has a number of fine old shophouses, such as the converted **Peace Hotel** on Jl Iskandar. The Peranakan architecture has stucco tiles, stained glass, and beautifully carved bird and flower designs on the upper wall dividers inside. A makeover would turn it into a real showpiece, but until then don't contemplate staying here – it's a seedy dive. Opposite the Muzium Perak, the **prison**, built in 1885 to house lawless miners, was used by the Japanese during WWII, later as a rehabilitation centre for captured Communists during the Emergency and then for housing political detainees under the Internal Security Act (ISA) ruling.

Just southwest of the museum and the prison, **All Saints' Church** (1886) is said to be the oldest Anglican church in Malaysia. It's looking its age. The cemetery contains the graves of early colonial settlers, most of whom died of tropical diseases or failed to achieve the colonial pension needed to return home to Britain or Australia.

To the north of the museum, the colourful, gaudy **Ling Nam Temple** is the oldest Chinese temple in Perak. The temple has been recently renovated and there's not much of the old temple left apart from a boat figure dedicated to the emperor who built China's first canal.

OTHER SIGHTS

Taiping's **Commonwealth Allied War Cemetery** is just east of the Lake Gardens, with row upon row of headstones for the British, Australian and Indian troops killed during WWII. Farther on, down a side road, the **Burmese Pools** are a popular bathing spot by the river.

Sleeping

Taiping has an excellent selection of moderately priced accommodation. Most of the cheap hotels are scattered around the central market, the liveliest (but noisiest) part of town. The better choices are a few streets away.

BUDGET

Peking Hotel (☎ 807 2975; 2 Jl Idris; s & d RM27) This attractive old colonial building has lots of character – it was even used as a military police station by the Japanese during WWII. These days it offers fairly basic fan rooms, which are comfortable enough for the price.

Hong Kong Hotel (☎ 807 3824; 79 Jl Barrack; s & d RM25-35) Simple budget hotel above a Chinese restaurant, in a quiet street. The larger rooms are slightly preferable.

Aun Chuan Hotel (☎ 807 5322; 25 Jl Market Square; s & d RM15) Very basic place with rather worn rooms above the KFC, which might appeal to budget conscious fried-chicken fans.

MID-RANGE

Casuarina Inn (☎ 804 1339; fax 804 1337; 1 Jl Sultan Mansur; s & d RM69; ❄) Near the Lake Gardens, this pleasantly appointed place is approached through the pillars of what was once the British Resident's house. Rooms are neat and spacious.

Legend Inn (☎ 806 0000; www.legendinn.com; 2 Jl Lorong Jafaar; d/ste from RM80/150; ❄) This smart modern hotel opposite the local bus station has spacious, well-equipped rooms, which are great value. There's also a good coffee bar downstairs.

Lagenda Hotel (☎ 805 3333; fax 805 3355; 101 Jl Stesyen; s & d RM70; ❄) This fine colonial building, once used as the governor's residence, has been tastefully restored, with all modern comforts. Rooms are on ground level, and there's a nice restaurant attached.

Hotel Seri Malaysia (☎ 806 9502; www.serimalaysia.com.my; s & d RM110; ❄ ♿) Spotless chain hotel near the Lake Gardens and, less appealingly, right opposite the prison. It's a grand, and extensive, pink villa complex, offering the usual high standards of comfort and service.

Panorama Hotel (☎ 808 4111; fax 808 4129; 61 Jl Kota; d/ste from RM75/140; ❄) This is another large, comfortable business hotel, conveniently located in the heart of town, with a very good restaurant serving Western and local dishes.

Hotel Fuliyean (☎ 806 8648; hf@cyberoffice.com.my; 14 Jl Barrack; s/d RM50/60; ❄) Very clean, modern hotel with dazzling tilework everywhere. It is on a busy road, though, so noise is inevitable.

Eating

Taiping has a good array of restaurants and food centres.

Tops Thai (☎ 808 6296; 14 Jl Boo Bee; dishes from RM5) Serves excellent Thai and Chinese food, as well as beer.

Lao di Fang (☎ 805 9705; 120 Jl Taming Sari; dishes from RM4) A small, trendy restaurant with a big menu, including pizza, sushi and a range of vegetarian options. It also has a well-stocked cocktail bar.

Pusat Penjaja Taiping (Jl Tupai) Serves mostly Chinese food, with a Malay section at one end. The covered stalls next to the taxi station are very clean and sell a variety of dishes. Taiping's central night market also has many open-air eating stalls; *murtabak* (roti filled with pieces of mutton, chicken or vegetables) and delicious *ayam percik* (marinated chicken on skewers) are specialities.

Taiping also has a host of coffee shops serving economical food.

Bismillah Restoran (138 Jl Taming Sari; dishes from RM3) One of the oldest coffee shops, Bismillah is a simple place noted for its roti and biryani.

Getting There & Away

Taiping is several kilometres off the main KL–Butterworth road. It's 99km south of Butterworth and 291km north of KL. The express-bus station is 7km north of the town centre, at Kemunting. Frequent buses go to Butterworth (RM6), Ipoh (RM5.45) and KL (RM16), with less-frequent connections to other destinations like Kota Bharu (RM20.75), Johor Bahru/Singapore (RM40), Lumut (RM6) and Kuala Terengganu (RM41.75).

There are no hotels nearby, nor any reason to stay in Kemunting – hop on the next bus (80 sen) or take a taxi (RM6) to the town centre. The local bus station is in the centre of Taiping, near the central market. Non-air-con buses depart for surrounding villages and Kuala Kangsar. You can get to Kemunting from the local bus station on the No 8 bus (80 sen).

Taiping's **train station** (☎ 807 5584) is 1km west of the town centre, on the KL–Butterworth line. The train to KL leaves at 12.36am, and towards Butterworth at 3.22am.

Regular long-distance taxis operate from the taxi station near the central market to Butterworth or Ipoh for RM560 and to Kuala Kangsar for RM28.

BUKIT LARUT

☎ 05

The oldest hill station in Malaysia, Bukit Larut (Maxwell Hill) is 12km from Taiping, at an altitude of 1019m. It was formerly a tea estate named for the first assistant British Resident in Perak, who 'opened' the hill, and this quiet little station is simply a cool and peaceful place to visit. There are no golf courses, fancy restaurants or other hill-station trappings, let alone casinos. Few people visit Bukit Larut – in fact, bungalows here only accommodate around 70 visitors. During the school holidays, all are full.

Even if you don't stay, Bukit Larut can be an excellent day trip. Getting up to the hill station is half the fun, and once there, you've got fine views over Taiping and the Lake Gardens far below. On a clear day, from the road near the top you can see the coast all the way from Penang to Pulau Pangkor.

Sights & Activities

Most visitors go up and back by Land Rover (RM2.50, one way) though the hill is also a favourite with locals who walk up in three to four hours. The walk along the road through the jungle is pleasant but taxing. You can also choose to take a Land Rover up and walk down.

The first stop is at the crumbling **Tea Gardens** checkpoint at the Batu 3.5 (Km 5.5) mark, where a ramshackle guesthouse and a few exotic trees are the only reminder of the former tea estate. Next up, at Batu 6 (Km 9.5), you'll find the Bukit Larut Guesthouse, Bungalow Beringin and a canteen for meals. The Land Rovers stop at the main administration office, where you book for the return journey if you haven't already – very advisable on weekends. There are some tame strolls through the nearby gardens from here.

The Land Rovers usually continue 2km up the hill to Gunung Hijau Rest House. Nearby are the Cendana, Tempinis and Sri Kanangan bungalows (see Sleeping & Eating this page). From here it's a 30-minute walk along the road, noted for its profusion of **butterflies**, to the Telekom transmitter station at the top of the hill.

The jungle on the hill is superb, but the only real trail for exploring leads off the main road from between the two transmission towers. (It's best to do all your walking in the mornings, as afternoon rains cause dangerous, gigantic sparks – large enough to hit your head – along the transmission lines.) The trail follows a practically abandoned path to **Gunung Hijau** (1448m). You can usually only follow the leech-ridden path for about 15 minutes to an old pumping station (now, curiously, functioning as a small Shiva shrine) but even on this short walk there's a good chance of seeing monkeys and numerous birds. Beyond the shrine the trail is periodically cleared but quickly becomes overgrown; it's advisable to take a guide with you.

Walking back down the road, it takes half an hour from Gunung Hijau Rest House to the main post at Bukit Larut Guesthouse, another hour to the Tea Gardens checkpoint, then another 1½ hours to get to the Land Rover station at the bottom of the hill, near the Taiping Lake Gardens.

Sleeping & Eating

You can book space in one of the bungalows by ringing ☎ 807 7241, or by writing to the Officer in Charge, Bukit Larut Hill Resort, Taiping. If you haven't booked earlier, you can ring from the Land Rover station at the bottom of the hill.

Bukit Larut Guesthouse (1036m) and **Gunung Hijau Rest House** (1113m) each has four doubles for RM15 per double. The bungalows **Beringin** (RM150) at 1036m, **Cendana** (RM100) at 1139m and **Tempinis** (RM100) at 1143m are equipped with kitchens, so you need to bring provisions. Beringin and Cendana both accommodate up to eight people; Tempinis can accommodate 10 people. You pay for the whole bungalow, regardless of how many people are in your party. Meals are available from the caretakers at the bungalows, but they need advance notice and they'll drive a hard bargain (as much as RM95 to start, just for dinner).

Rumah Angkasa and **Sri Kayangan** are more luxurious and not open to tourists, normally available only for VIPs. The Tea Gardens Guesthouse has long been closed, but there are vague plans to renovate and reopen it.

There is a basic **camping ground** (RM2 per person) below the main resthouse near the Tempinis bungalow.

Next to the upper Land Rover office, the Bukit Larut Guesthouse is usually open for meals and has impressive views. Simple rice and noodle dishes are the main menu items.

Getting There & Away

Prior to WWII, you had the choice of walking, riding a pony or being carried up in a sedan chair, as there was no road to the station. Japanese POWs were put to work building a road at the close of the war, and it was opened in 1948.

Private cars are not allowed on the road – it's only open to government Land Rovers, which run a regular service from the station at the foot of the hill, just above the Taiping Lake Gardens. They operate every hour on the hour from 9am to 5pm (until 4pm in the low season), and the trip takes about 40 minutes.

The winding road negotiates 72 hairpin bends on the steep ascent, and there are superb views through the trees on the way up. The Land Rovers going up and those going down pass each other midway at the Tea Gardens. Fares are paid at the bottom of the hill – it's RM2 to the administration office and RM2.50 to Gunung Hijau Rest House. Alternatively, you can walk to the top in three or four hours.

To book a seat on a Land Rover (which is advisable), ring the **station** (☎ 807 7243) at the bottom of the hill. A taxi from central Taiping to this station, about 2km east of the Lake Gardens, should cost RM5.

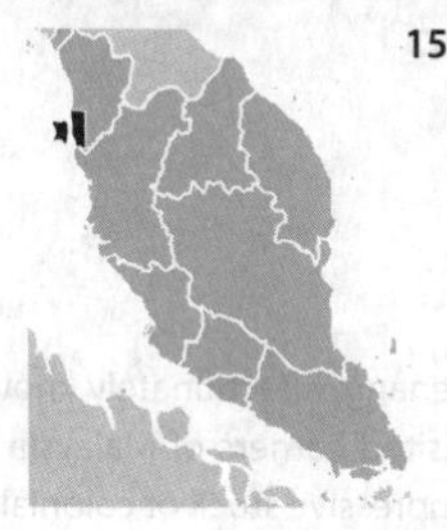

Penang

CONTENTS

Penang, affectionately known as the Pearl of the Orient, is one of the best-known and most-visited corners of Malaysia. Its main centre, Georgetown, attracts the most tourists with its impressive stock of colonial architecture, temples and museums, lively Chinese culture, great shopping and even better food. But there are many attractions elsewhere on the island, including the beaches on the northern coast, charming Penang Hill with its funicular and colonial hill station, and the amazing Kek Lok Si Temple – the largest Buddhist shrine in the country.

You can make a circuit of the island to discover a varied landscape of jungle and coast, farmland, plantations and fishing villages. Georgetown is also a transport hub with connections to other parts of Malaysia, Singapore and other Asian destinations.

Penang state also encompasses a narrow strip of mainland coast known as Seberang Perai (or Province Wellesley), although there's very little to see or do other than change buses or trains in the main town of Butterworth.

HIGHLIGHTS

- Riding a trishaw around the colonial heart of **Georgetown** (p159)
- Admiring the historical and cultural treasures of the **Penang Museum** (p162)
- Climbing up the pagoda at the **Kek Lok Si Temple** (p172) for some awe-inspiring views
- Jumping on the free **Heritage Trail shuttle** (p161) for a tour around Georgetown
- Taking in the sights, sounds and exotic scents of Georgetown's lively **Little India district** (p164)
- Taking tiffin in the opulent surroundings of the **Eastern & Oriental Hotel** (p166)
- **Shopping** (p171) for a piece of Penang pewter, art, crafts or antiques
- Stepping back in time at the dazzling **Cheong Fatt Tze Mansion** (p163)
- Water-ski or parasail off the beach at **Batu Ferringhi** (p176)

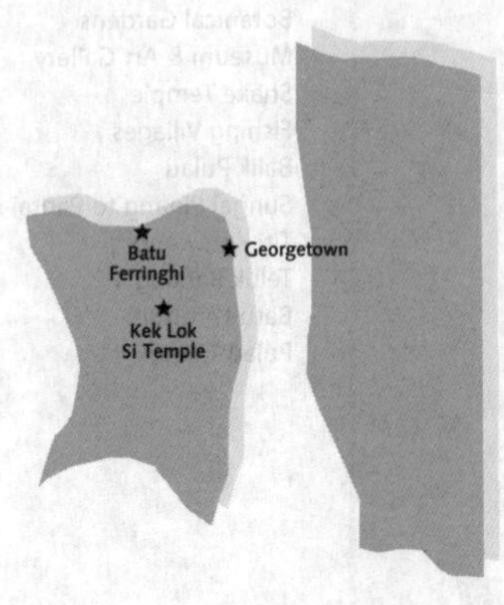

- TELEPHONE CODE: 04
- POPULATION: 1.31 MILLION
- AREA: 1031 SQ KM

History

Penang has always attracted adventurers, dreamers, artists, intellectuals, scoundrels and dissidents. In 1786 Captain Francis Light, on behalf of the East India Company, acquired possession of Pulau Penang from the local sultan in return for protection against various enemies. He renamed it Prince of Wales Island, as the acquisition date fell on the Prince's birthday. It's said that Light fired silver dollars from his ship's cannons into the jungle to encourage his labourers to hack back the undergrowth for settlement.

Whatever the truth of the tale, he soon established the small town of Georgetown, also named after the Prince of Wales who later became King George IV, with Lebuh Light, Lebuh Chulia, Lebuh Pitt and Lebuh Bishop as its boundaries. Founding towns must have been a tradition for the Light family – Francis Light's son is credited with the founding of Adelaide in Australia, which is today a sister city to Georgetown. By 1800 Light had negotiated with the sultan for a strip of the mainland adjacent to the island; this became known as Province Wellesley, after the governor of India.

Light permitted new arrivals to claim as much land as they could clear, and this, together with a duty-free port and an atmosphere of liberal tolerance, quickly attracted settlers from all over Asia. Virtually uninhabited in 1786, by the turn of the 18th century Penang was home to over 10,000 people.

The local economy was slow to develop, as mostly European planters set up spice plantations – slow-growing crops requiring a high initial outlay. Although the planters later turned to sugar and coconut, agriculture was hindered by a limited labour force.

In 1805 Penang became a presidency government, on a par with the cities of Madras and Bombay in India, and so gained a much more sophisticated administrative structure.

Penang briefly became the capital of the Straits Settlements in 1826 (including Melaka and Singapore) until it was superseded by the more thriving Singapore. By the middle of the 19th century, Penang had become a major player in the Chinese opium trade, which provided more than half of the colony's revenue. It was a dangerous, rough-edged place, notorious for its brothels and gambling dens, all run by the Chinese secret societies.

In 1867, the simmering violence came to a head when large-scale rioting broke out between two rival Chinese secret societies, who had each allied themselves with similar Malay groups. Once the fighting had been brought under control, the British authorities fined each group the then huge sum of $10,000, the proceeds going to establish a permanent police force in the colony.

Although Penang thrived as a centre of international trade, it never saw the rapid development experienced by Singapore, resulting in much of its early colonial architecture remaining intact to this day.

Climate

Penang has a tropical climate, with temperatures of between 21°C and 32°C year-round. There are brief, torrential downpours at all times of year, though the period between May and October sees more rain. Humidity is normally 85% to 90%.

Dangers & Annoyances

While generally a safe place to wander, Georgetown, like any big city, does have its seamy side. Foreign tourists have been attacked and mugged in Love Lane and other dimly lit side-streets, and it's unwise to linger in these areas alone after dark. Foreign motorists have also been targeted by motorcyclists who flag them down on the pretext that there has been an accident, and then attempt to attack and rob them.

Robberies have occurred in some backpacker hostels, so you should never leave valuables, especially your passport, unattended. Meanwhile, drug dealing still occurs in Georgetown, despite Malaysia's very stiff anti-drug laws; don't get involved.

Getting There & Away

The mainland strip of Seberang Perai is easily accessed by road and rail from other parts of the peninsula. Butterworth is the transport hub, and the departure point for ferries to Pulau Penang, which is also linked to the mainland by road-bridge; another bridge link is planned, but at the time of writing there was as yet no start date for construction. Buses to all major towns on the peninsula leave from both Georgetown

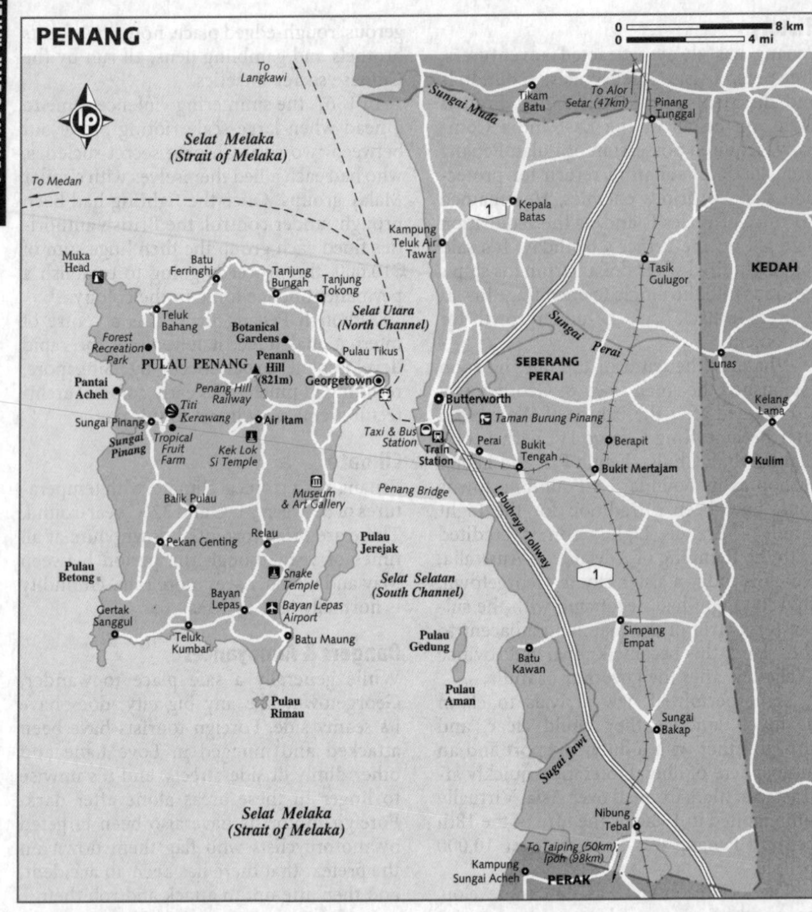

and Butterworth. Georgetown, the capital of Penang, also has ferry links to Langkawi and to Medan in Indonesia, and an airport with regular flights to KL, Singapore, Johor Bahru and Langkawi.

AIR

Airline Offices

Air Asia (☎ 644 8701; 463 Lebuh Chulia)
Cathay Pacific (☎ 226 0411; Menara PSCI, Jl Sultan Ahmad Shah)
Malaysia Airlines (Map p160; ☎ 262 0011; Komtar; 8.30am-5.30pm Mon-Sat)
Singapore Airlines (Map p160 ; ☎ 226 3201; Wisma Penang Gardens, Jl Sultan Ahmad Shah)
Thai Airways International (Map p160; ☎ 226 6000; Wisma Central, 41 Jl Macalister)

Domestic Flights

There are several daily connections between Penang and KL (RM281), Johor Bahru (RM481) and Langkawi (RM140).

International Flights

Penang is a major centre for cheap airline tickets, although international air fares are less competitive than they used to be. Long-running, reliable agents are listed under Travel Agencies, p159.

Malaysia Airlines has at least one flight daily to Medan in Sumatra (RM240) and with Singapore Airlines (SIA) to Singapore (RM255). Thai Airways International flies between Penang and Bangkok (RM590) with Malaysia Airlines.

Other international connections include Mumbai (SIA, RM1100); Los Angeles (Eva Air, RM1250); Hong Kong (Malaysia Airlines/SIA, RM650); and Sydney (Malaysia Airlines, RM1300). Return tickets on most routes offer substantial savings.

BOAT

Two companies currently operate boat services to Medan in Sumatra. These land in Belawan, and the journey to Medan is completed by bus (included in the price), usually taking about 4¼ hours (but sometimes as long as five or six).

Both **Langkawi Ferry Service** (LFS; Map p160; ☎ 264 3088; 8 Lebuh King) and **Ekspres Bahagia** (Map p160; ☎ 263 1943; PPC Bldg, Pesara King Edward) have offices near the Tourism Malaysia office in Georgetown. Their shared ferries leave Georgetown at 8.30am every day; departures from Belawan in Sumatra are at 10am daily (one way/return RM90/160).

If you're in a hurry, Langkawi Ferry Service offers slightly faster boats to Medan, though fares are the same.

The same two companies also run daily ferries from Georgetown to Kuah on Langkawi (RM35/65, 1¾ to 2½ hours). All boats leave at 8am, returning from Langkawi at 5.30pm.

BUS

Several long-distance bus services leave from Komtar in central Georgetown. Most depart from its basement, where the bus companies have ticket offices. While it may be more convenient to buy your tickets from travel agents on Lebuh Chulia or some guesthouses and hotels, it's a safer bet to buy your ticket in person.

From Komtar there are several daily buses to KL, as well as one bus each to Kota Bharu and Kuala Terengganu – book well in advance. There are four daily buses leaving Georgetown for the Cameron Highlands (RM20). Another option is to take a bus to Tapah, then change to a local bus up to Tanah Rata, the main Highlands town.

Many more buses leave from across the channel in Butterworth next to the mainland ferry terminal, and a few long-distance buses also leave from other parts of Georgetown. **Newsia Tours & Travel** (☎ 261 7933; fax 262 0243; 35-36 Pengkalan Weld) is a major agent. Buses for other operators in the immediate vicinity stop along the side street next to the Newsia office.

Many long-distance buses depart in the evening. Typical one-way fares:

Destination	Fare
Alor Setar	RM 5
Cameron Highlands	RM 20
Ipoh	RM 11.50
Johor Bahru	RM 45
Kota Bharu	RM 19.50
KL	RM 23
Kuala Perlis	RM 6.80
Kuala Terengganu	RM 24-28
Kuantan	RM 35
Lumut	RM 10.50
Melaka	RM 30.70
Singapore	RM 45
Taiping	RM 6
Tapah	RM 14

There are also bus and minibus services out of Malaysia to Thailand, including Hat Yai (RM30); Krabi (RM38); Phuket (RM60); Ko Pipi (RM65); Ko Samui (RM55) and even Bangkok (RM80), though it's a long haul. The minibuses usually don't go directly to some destinations; you'll probably be dumped for a change of vehicle in Hat Yai or Surat Thani, sometimes with significant waiting times. It's best to buy your ticket from a guesthouse that contracts directly with a minibus agency, instead of from bucket shops on Lebuh Chulia. Then, in the case of your minibus showing up two hours late, or not at all, you have someone to hold responsible.

CAR

Penang Bridge, completed in 1985, is one of the longest bridges in Asia at 13.5km. If you drive across to the island there's a RM7 toll payable at the toll plaza on the mainland, but no charge to return.

Rental

Penang's a good place to rent a car, but you'll probably have to reserve in advance, especially for weekends and holidays or if you need an automatic car. Rates start at around RM95 per day plus RM15 insurance but drop for longer rentals. Good deals can be found at smaller agents, though the main companies are also worth trying for special deals.

There are many car-hire companies in Georgetown:

Avis (☎ 643 9633; Bayan Lepas airport)
Budget (☎ 643 6025; Bayan Lepas airport)
Hertz (Map p160; ☎ 263 5914; 38 Lebuh Farquhar)
Mayflower Airport (☎ 262 8196); Georgetown (☎ 641 1191; 274 Lebuh Victoria)
National Airport (☎ 262 9404); Georgetown (☎ 643 4205; 1 Weld Quay)

In Batu Ferringhi, try **Smile Tours & Rent A Car** (Map p177; ☎ 881 3786; 208 Batu Ferringhi), which also rents motorbikes for RM20 per day.

TAXI

Long-distance taxis operate from a depot beside the Butterworth ferry terminal on the mainland. Typical whole-taxi fares are higher than anywhere else in Peninsular Malaysia, and include such rip-offs as Ipoh (RM150); KL (RM280); Kota Bharu (RM250); Lumut (RM180) and Taiping (RM150).

TRAIN

The **train station** (☎ 323 7962) is next to the ferry terminal and bus-and-taxi station in Butterworth.

The nightly train to KL leaves at 9.55pm, arriving at 8.20am the next morning. There is a daily train to Hat Yai in Thailand, leaving at 6.34am. Fares and timetables change rapidly, so check with the station before you travel.

Getting Around

Seberang Perai and Pulau Penang are linked by road-bridge and a 24-hour ferry service. Georgetown is well served by bus, and *trishaws* (see the Getting Around section, p157) are a popular way to get around the city centre.

Buses from Georgetown to other parts of the island are less frequent and getting around the island by road is easiest with your own transport, particularly since the road does not run along the coast except on the northern side, and you have to leave the main road to get to the small fishing villages and isolated beaches.

TO/FROM THE AIRPORT

Penang's Bayan Lepas International Airport is 18km south of Georgetown. There's a coupon system for taxis from the airport. The fare to Georgetown is RM23.

Taxis take about 45 minutes from the centre of town, while the bus takes at least an hour. Yellow Bus No 83 runs to and from the airport (RM1.50) hourly from 6am to 9pm, with stops along Pengkalan Weld, Komtar and Lebuh Chulia.

BOAT

There's a 24-hour ferry service between Georgetown and Butterworth. Ferries take passengers and cars every eight minutes from 6.20am to 9.30pm, every 20 minutes until 11.15pm, and hourly after that until 6.20 am. Fares are charged only for the journey from Butterworth to Penang; returning to the mainland is free. The adult fare is 60 sen; cars cost RM7 (depending on the size) and motorcycles RM1.40.

BUS

There are several main bus-departure points in Georgetown, and half a dozen bus companies. The main city bus terminal is in the Komtar basement and almost all buses (including minibuses) stop here. Another main stand is at Pengkalan Weld, next to the ferry terminal jetty. TransitLink city buses all run via Pengkalan Weld, originating from the company's own terminal nearby on Lebuh Victoria; and Yellow Bus, Hin Bus and Sri Negara buses all swing by the Pengkalan Weld stand. Most TransitLink buses also have stops along Lebuh Chulia.

Fares around town vary, but are typically under RM1. Some handy routes, as well as the operators, route numbers and pick-up points, are set out in the 'Penang Bus Routes' table on the next page. Minibuses all cost a standard 70 sen (exact change required) and you can only be sure of catching one at the Komtar centre, as wherever else they happen to stop along their route depends on the driver's whim.

For around RM5 you can circuit the island by public transport. Start with a Yellow Bus No 66 and hop off at the Snake Temple. This Yellow Bus No 66 will take you all the way to Balik Pulau, where you have to transfer to Yellow Bus No 76 for Teluk Bahang. There are only a few per day, roughly every 2¼ hours between 7.30am and 7.15pm, so it's wise to leave Georgetown early and check the departure times when you reach Balik Pulau. From Teluk Bahang, on the northern beach strip,

PENANG BUS ROUTES

Destination	Operator & route no	Pick-up
Air Itam	TL1, 101, 351, 361; YB 85	Pengkalan Weld, Lebuh Chulia, Komtar
Batu Ferringhi	HB93	Pengkalan Weld, Lebuh Chulia, Komtar
Bayan Lepas Airport	YB83	Pengkalan Weld, Lebuh Chulia, Komtar
Botanical Gardens	TL7	Lebuh Chulia, Komtar
Gurney Dr	HB93 TL202 Minibus 26, 31 or 88	Pengkalan Weld, Air Itam, Komtar
Penang Hill Railway	TL8	Air Itam
Pulau Tikus	HC93, TL202, Minibus 26, 32 or 88	Pengkalan Weld, Komtar
Snake Temple	YB66; Minibus 32	Pengkalan Weld, Lebuh Chulia, Komtar
Teluk Bahang	HB93	Pengkalan Weld, Komtar
Thai consulate	SN 136 or 137; TL7	Pengkalan Weld, Lebuh Chulia, Komtar

take a TransitLink bus No 202 or a blue Hin Bus No 93 back to Georgetown via Batu Ferringhi.

MOTORCYCLE & BICYCLE

You can hire bicycles from many places, including travellers guesthouses and shops along Lebuh Chulia or out at Batu Ferringhi. It costs RM10 to rent a bicycle, and motorcycles start at RM30 per day. Before heading off on a motorbike, just remember that if you don't have a motorcycle licence, your travel insurance in all likelihood won't cover you.

TAXI

Penang's taxis all have meters, which drivers flatly refuse to use, so negotiate the fare before you set off. Typical fares around town cost around RM3 to RM6. Outlying sights serviced by taxi from Georgetown include Pulau Tikus (RM8); Batu Ferringhi (RM20); Botanical Gardens (RM10); Penang Hill/Kek Lok Si Temple (RM10); Snake Temple (RM15); and Bayan Lepas airport (RM23).

TRISHAW

Bicycle rickshaws are an ideal way to negotiate Georgetown's backstreets and cost around RM1 per kilometre – but, as with taxis, it's important to make sure you agree on the fare before departure. You won't have any trouble finding a *trishaw* – more often than not, the drivers will hail you! From the ferry terminal, a *trishaw* to the hotel area around Lebuh Chulia should cost RM6 (or you can walk there in about 15 minutes). For touring around, the rate is about RM15 an hour.

SEBERANG PERAI

BUTTERWORTH

☎ 04

You probably won't spend much time in the industrial town of Butterworth, as the main reason most travellers come here is to cross the channel to visit Pulau Penang. The town has a large ferry port and an air-force base.

The sole point of interest is the **Taman Burung Pinang** (Penang Bird Park; ☎ 399 1899; Jl Todak; adult/child RM10/5; 9am-7pm), 7km east of the ferry terminal across the river. This landscaped park has more than 300 species of birds, mostly from Southeast Asia, including parrots, hornbills and hawks. To get there, take the frequent No 515 TransitLink bus from Butterworth bus station (80 sen).

Most of the land transport (buses, trains, taxis) between Penang and other places in peninsular Malaysia and Thailand leaves from Butterworth, not far from the train station and next to the terminal for ferries going to or from Georgetown.

Sleeping

Butterworth has a number of hotels, if for some reason you want to stop; the **Ambassadress Hotel** (☎ 332 7788; 4425 Jl Bagan Luar; s & d from RM63;) in the town centre is a reasonable choice.

Getting There & Away

See the Getting There & Away (p153) and Getting Around (p156) sections for information on transport services to/from Butterworth.

PULAU PENANG

Pulau Penang is the oldest of the British Straits settlements in Malaysia, predating both Singapore and Melaka. Penang's capital city, Georgetown, is often referred to as Penang.

Central Georgetown is a sprawling, largely Chinese city, steeped in history, with old-fashioned character that's fast disappearing. If you walk from the ferry to the main tourist area around Lebuh Chulia in Chinatown, it would seem Penang missed the development boom that swept the rest of Malaysia in recent years. High-rise apartments and industrial areas now crowd the outskirts of expanding Georgetown, especially south towards Penang Bridge and the airport, and west to the beaches.

The beaches along the north coast are the most visited and most accessible, but while the main resort of Batu Ferringhi has its appeal, the beaches are not nearly as spectacular as the tourist literature makes out. Beaches close to the city suffer from pollution, while those around the south of the island are undeveloped and rather inaccessible. Most aren't that good for swimming, but are kept alive by hordes of package-tour groups.

GEORGETOWN

☎ 04

Georgetown is a real Chinatown, with more traditional Chinese flavour than Singapore or Hong Kong. Those larger cities have had their Chinese characteristics partly submerged under a gleaming concrete, glass and chrome confusion. In the older parts of Georgetown, however, the clock seems to have stopped 50 years ago. Georgetown is an easy-going, colourful city full of crumbling old shophouses, *trishaws* and ancient trades such as carpentry, seal-making and prostitution.

The city has plenty of reminders of colonial rule, and its winding streets and old temples are always fascinating to wander around. Most visitors to the island stay in Georgetown, which has countless hotels, restaurants and all the facilities of a major city. Those looking for the beach (such as it is) head to Batu Ferringhi or the less developed Teluk Bahang, a little further west.

Orientation

Georgetown is on the northeastern corner of the island, where the channel between island and mainland is narrowest.

A 24-hour vehicle- and passenger-ferry service operates across the 3km-wide channel between Georgetown and Butterworth on the mainland. South of the ferry crossing is the Penang Bridge, reputedly the longest in Southeast Asia, which links the island with Malaysia's Lebuhraya (North-South Hwy).

Georgetown is a compact city and most places can easily be reached on foot or by *trishaw*. The old colonial district centres on Fort Cornwallis. Lebuh Pantai is the main street of the 'city', a financial district crammed with banks and stately buildings that once housed the colonial administration. After dark, exercise caution as this area becomes eerily deserted.

You'll find many of Georgetown's popular cheap hotels along Lebuh Chulia in Chinatown, packed amongst travel agencies, budget-priced restaurants and Internet cafés. At the northern end of Lebuh Chulia, Jl Penang is a main thoroughfare and a popular shopping street. In this area are a number of upmarket hotels, including the venerable Eastern & Oriental (E&O) Hotel at the waterfront end of the street. (See the boxed text on p168 for this hotel's amazing story.)

If you follow Jl Penang south, you'll pass the modern multipurpose Kompleks Tun Abdul Razak (Komtar) shopping mall, and eventually leave town and continue towards the Bayan Lepas International Airport. If you turn west at the waterfront end of Jl Penang you'll follow the coastline and eventually come to the northern beaches, including Batu Ferringhi. This road runs right around the island back into town, via the airport.

Finding your way around Georgetown can be slightly complicated. Jl Penang may also be referred to as Jl Pinang or as Penang Rd – but there's also a Penang St, which may also be called Lebuh Pinang! Similarly, Chulia St is Lebuh Chulia; Pitt St is sometimes Lebuh Pitt, but is shown on some maps and signposts as Jl Masjid Kapitan Keling. Some of the street signs still use the old spelling for Lebuh, which is Leboh. Maps are sold at bookshops (see opposite).

Trishaws are the ideal way of getting around Georgetown, particularly at night when travelling this way takes on an almost magical quality. For an excellent view over the whole sprawling scene of Georgetown, there's a viewing gallery on level 58 of Komtar. Buy your admission tickets (RM5) at the Penang Tourist Guides Association counter on the 3rd floor.

Information

BOOKSHOPS

The **Popular Bookshop** (☎ 263 6122; Komtar) stocks novels, travel books, maps and a reasonable selection of books on Penang and Malaysia.

For second-hand books, check out the small shops along Lebuh Chulia:

HS Sam Book Store (☎ 262 2705; 473 Lebuh Chulia) One of the best, the self-proclaimed 'most organised used book shop in town' has a fair range of popular paperbacks. The amicable, and versatile owner also sells reasonably priced souvenirs, organises car and bike rental, and provides luggage storage.

Kedai Buku Ali's Enterprise (☎ 261 6786; 40 Lebuh Chulia) Also buys and sells second-hand books.

IMMIGRATION OFFICES

Immigration Office (☎ 261 5122; 29A Lebuh Pantai)

INTERNET ACCESS

Eighteen Internet Café (☎ 264 4754; 18 Lebuh Cintra; RM3 per hr)

Harwich Backpackers' Internet (☎ 263 3335; 86 Love Lane; RM1 per hr)

Penang Online Café (☎ 264 3631; 69 Lebuh Pitt; RM2.50 per hr)

There are several more along Lebuh Chulia, and in and around Komtar.

LIBRARIES

Alliance Francaise Library (☎ 227 6008; 8 Jl Yeoh Guan Seok; 🕓 9am-5pm Tue-Sat, 9.30am-1pm Sun)

Malaysian German Society Library (☎ 229 6853; 250B Jl Air Itam; 🕓 9am-5pm Tue-Sat, 9.30am-1pm Sun)

The Penang Library was closed and in the process of relocating to a site on Scotland Rd at the time of writing; contact the Tourism Malaysia office for the new address.

MEDICAL SERVICES

General Hospital (☎ 229 3333; Jl Residensi)

Loh Guan Lye Specialist Centre (☎ 228 8501; 19 Jl Logan)

Penang Adventist Hospital (☎ 226 1133; 465 Jl Burma)

MONEY

Branches of major banks are on Lebuh Pantai and Lebuh Downing, near the main post office, and most have 24-hour ATMs.

At the northwestern end of Lebuh Chulia there are numerous moneychangers open longer hours than the banks and with more competitive rates. Moneychangers are also scattered around the banks on Lebuh Pantai and at the ferry terminal, although you'll probably get better rates on the mainland from the moneychangers at the Butterworth bus station.

TOURIST INFORMATION

Penang Heritage Trust (☎ 264 2631; 26A Lorong Stewart; 🕓 9.30am-12.30pm & 2.30-4.30pm Mon-Fri) Information on the history of Penang and conservation projects.

Penang Tourist Guides Association (☎ 261 4461; 3rd fl, Komtar, Jl Penang; 🕓 10am-6pm Mon-Sat) Information on everything going on in Penang.

Tourism Malaysia (☎ 262 0066; fax 262 3688; 10 Jl Tun Syed Sheh Barakbah; 🕓 8am-4.30pm Mon-Thu, 8am-12.15pm & 2.45-4.30pm Fri, 8am-1pm Sat) Georgetown's main tourist information office.

www.penang.net.my Has general-interest information, background on island cuisine, events calendars and English-language *Yellow Pages*.

Also extremely useful is the monthly **Penang Tourist Newspaper** (RM2), which has comprehensive listings of shops, tourist attractions and hotel promotions, as well as detailed pull-out maps. It's available from tourist offices and some shops.

TRAVEL AGENCIES

Most, but not all, of the agencies in Georgetown are trustworthy. Reliable operators that many travellers use to purchase discounted airline tickets:

Silver-Econ Travel (☎ 262 9882; 436 Lebuh Chulia)

Happy Holidays (☎ 262 9222; 432 Lebuh Chulia)

Sights

COLONIAL DISTRICT

As the oldest British settlement in Malaysia, many grand colonial buildings can still be found in Penang. Francis Light stepped ashore in 1786 on the site of Fort Cornwallis, which is the main attraction (see p162) and a good place to start a tour of the colonial district around the waterfront. Many of the buildings in the area are

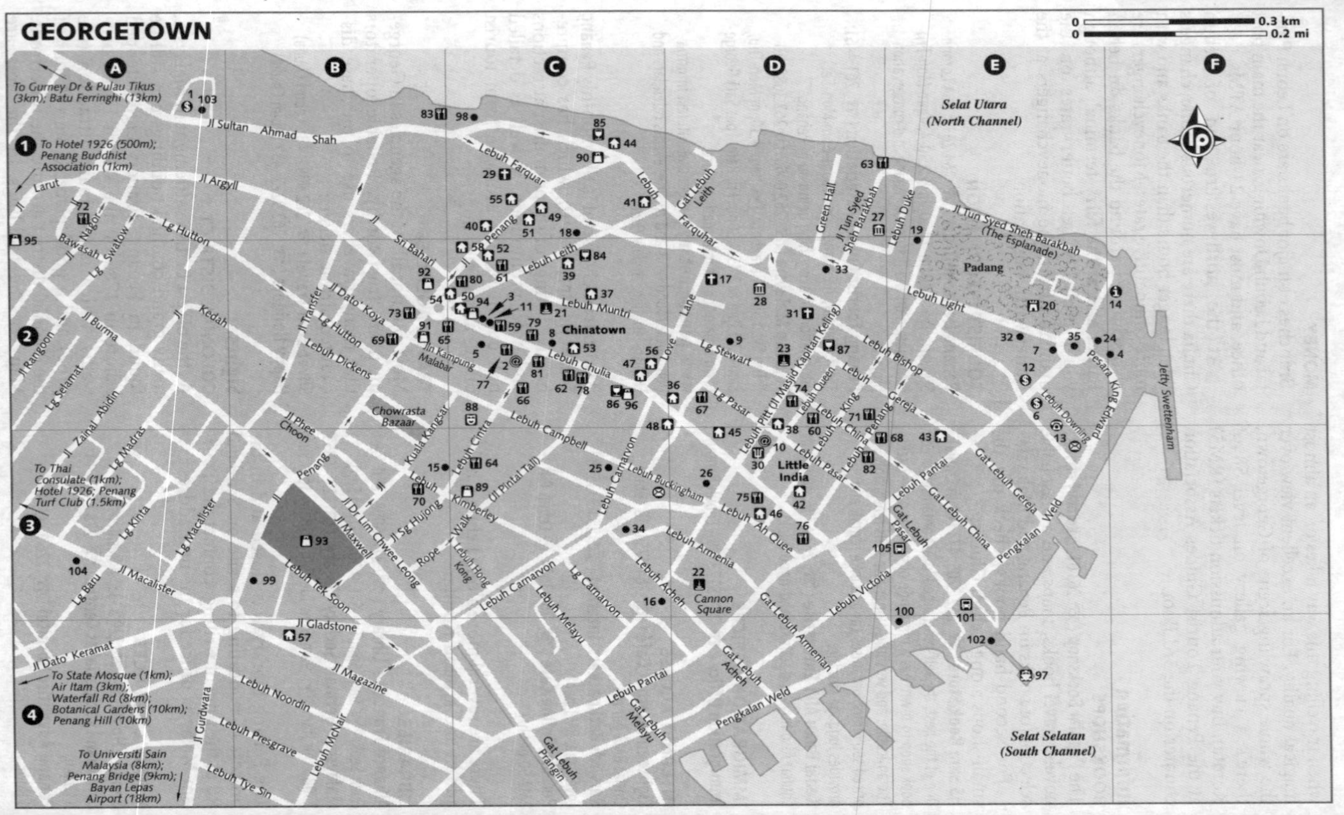
GEORGETOWN
0.3 km
0.2 mi
A
B
C
D
E
F
1
2
3
4
To Gurney Dr & Pulau Tikus (3km); Batu Ferringhi (13km)
To Hotel 1926 (500m); Penang Buddhist Association (1km)
To Thai Consulate (1km); Hotel 1926; Penang Turf Club (1.5km)
To State Mosque (1km); Air Itam (3km); Waterfall Rd (8km); Botanical Gardens (10km); Penang Hill (10km)
To Universiti Sain Malaysia (8km); Penang Bridge (9km); Bayan Lepas Airport (18km)
Selat Utara (North Channel)
Selat Selatan (South Channel)
Jetty Swettenham
Padang
Jl Tun Syed Sheh Barakbah (The Esplanade)
Pesara King Edward
Lebuh Downing
Pengkalan Weld
Gat Lebuh Gereja
Gat Lebuh China
Gat Lebuh Pasar
Gat Lebuh Armenian
Gat Lebuh Acheh
Gat Lebuh Melayu
Gat Lebuh Prangin
Gat Lebuh Leith
Lebuh Light
Lebuh Duke
Green Hall
Jl Tun Syed Sheh Barakbah
Lebuh Bishop
Lebuh Gereja
Lebuh King
Lebuh Pantai
Lebuh Victoria
Lebuh Penang
Lebuh China
Lebuh Queen
Lebuh Pasar
Little India
Lebuh Pitt (Jl Masjid Kapitan Keling)
Lg Stewart
Love Lane
Lg Pasar
Lebuh Leith
Lebuh Farquar
Lebuh Farquhar
Lebuh Muntri
Chinatown
Lebuh Chulia
Lebuh Ah Quee
Lebuh Armenia
Cannon Square
Lebuh Buckingham
Lebuh Acheh
Lebuh Carnarvon
Lg Carnarvon
Lebuh Melayu
Lebuh Campbell
(Jl Pintal Tali)
Lebuh Cintra
Lebuh Kimberley
Rope Walk
Lebuh Hong Kong
Jln Kampung Malabar
Chowrasta Bazaar
Lebuh Kuala Kangsar
Jl Sg Hujong
Jl Dr Lim Chwee Leong
Jl Maxwell
Lebuh Tek Soon
Jl Gladstone
Jl Magazine
Lebuh McNair
Lebuh Noordin
Lebuh Presgrave
Lebuh Tye Sin
Jl Gurdwara
Jl Sri Bahari
Jl Dato' Koya
Lg Hutton
Lebuh Dickens
Jl Transfer
Jl Phee Choon
Jl Penang
Jl Sultan Ahmad Shah
Jl Argyll
Jl Hutton
Jl Kedah
Jl Larut
Jl Nagor
Lg Swatow
Bawasah
Jl Burma
Jl Rangoon
Lg Selamat
Jl Zainal Abidin
Lg Madras
Lg Macalister
Jl Macalister
Lg Kinta
Lg Baru
Jl Dato' Keramat

INFORMATION
- Citibank 1 A1
- Eighteen Internet Café 2 C2
- Ekspres Bahagia (see 24)
- Happy Holidays 3 C2
- Harwich Backpackers' Internet (see 47)
- Hawaii Travel & Tours 4 F2
- HS Sam Book Store 5 C2
- HSBC Bank 6 E2
- Immigration Office 7 E2
- Kedai Buku Ali's Enterprise 8 C2
- Penang Heritage Trust 9 D2
- Penang Online Café 10 D3
- Penang Tourist Guides Association (see 93)
- Silver-Econ Travel 11 C2
- Standard Chartered Bank 12 E2
- Telekom Malaysia 13 E2
- Tourism Malaysia 14 F2

SIGHTS & ACTIVITIES pp159-65
- 100 Cintra Street 15 B3
- Acheen St Mosque 16 C3
- British Pool & Pub (see 93)
- Cathedral of the Assumption 17 D2
- Cheong Fatt Tze Mansion 18 C1
- City Hall 19 E2
- Fort Cornwallis 20 E2
- Hainan Temple 21 C2
- Khoo Kongsi 22 D3
- Kuan Yin Teng 23 D2
- Langkawi Ferry Services 24 E2
- Market 25 C3
- Masjid Kapitan Keling 26 D3
- Penang Library 27 D1
- Penang Museum 28 D2
- Protestant Cemetery 29 C1
- Sri Mariamman Temple 30 D3
- St George's Church 31 D2
- State Art Gallery (see 27)
- State Assembly Building 32 E2
- Supreme Court 33 D2
- Syed Alatas Mansion 34 C3
- Victoria Memorial Clocktower 35 E2

SLEEPING pp165-7
- 509 Café 36 D2
- 75 Travellers' Lodge 37 C2
- Broadway Hostel 38 D2
- Cathay Hotel 39 C2
- Cititel Hotel 40 C1
- City Bayview Hotel 41 C1
- Coral Hostel 42 D3
- D'Budget Hostel 43 E3
- Eastern & Oriental Hotel 44 C1
- Genesis 45 D3
- Golden Plaza Hostel 46 D3
- Harwich Backpackers' Lodge 47 C2
- Hong Ping Hotel 48 C2
- Hotel Continental 49 C1
- Island City Hotel 50 C2
- Malaysia Hotel 51 C1
- Merchant Hotel 52 C2
- New Eng Aun 53 C2
- Oriental Hotel 54 C2
- Peking Hotel 55 C1
- Pin Seng Hotel 56 C2
- Shangri-La 57 B4
- Towne House Hotel 58 C2
- Waldorf Hotel (see 39)

EATING pp167-70
- 1885 (see 44)
- Caribbean Rasta Café & Hostel 59 C2
- Ching Lotus Humanist Space 60 D2
- Cous-Cous (see 90)
- Eden Bakery 61 C2
- Eng Thai Cafe 62 C2
- Esplanade Food Centre 63 D1
- Gloria Jean's Coffees (see 90)
- Green Planet 64 C3
- Hang Chow Café 65 C2
- Hong Kong Restaurant 66 C2
- Hsiang Yang Fast Food 67 D2
- Kaliamans 68 D3
- Kayu Nasi Kandar 69 B2
- Kedai Kopi Kimberly 70 B3
- Madras New Woodlands Restaurant 71 D2
- Nyonya Baba Cuisine 72 A1
- Passage Thru' India 73 B2
- Peace & Joy 74 D2
- Restoran Kapitan 75 D3
- Restoran Tomyam 76 D3
- Rhak Café 77 C2
- SC Cuisine 78 C2
- Secret Garden 79 C2
- Shin Miyako 80 C2
- Sin Kuan Hwa Cafe 81 C2
- Sri Ananda Bahwan 82 D3
- Thirty Two 83 B1
- Winter Warmers (see 90)

DRINKING pp170-1
- 20 Leith Street 84 C2
- Baywatch Beach Club 85 C1
- Coco Island Travellers Corner (see 48)
- Farquhar's Bar (see 44)
- Hard Life Cafe 86 C2
- Pitt Street Corner 87 D2
- Slippery Senoritas (see 90)
- Soho Free House (see 55)

ENTERTAINMENT p171
- Lush (see 90)
- Rock World 88 C2

SHOPPING pp171-2
- Bee Chin Heong 89 C3
- Garage 90 C1
- Hong Giap Hang 91 B2
- Hong Seng Arts & Crafts 92 B2
- Komtar 93 B3
- Oriental Arts & Antiques 94 C2
- Penang Plaza 95 A1
- Tropical Art Corner 96 C2

TRANSPORT pp153-7
- Ferry Terminal 97 E4
- Hertz 98 C1
- Malaysia Airlines 99 B3
- Newsia Tours & Travel 100 E4
- Pengkalan Weld Bus Stop 101 E3
- Railway Booking Office 102 E4
- Singapore Airlines 103 A1
- Thai Airways International (THAI) 104 A3
- TransitLink City Bus Station 105 E3

marked with signs explaining their history and significance. You can follow the Heritage Trail walking tours, that also take in temples and mosques in Chinatown – pick up a pamphlet of the routes at the tourist offices or the Penang Heritage Trust (see Information, p159). There's also a free **bus shuttle** (⌚; 7am-7pm Mon-Fri, to 2pm Sat), which runs between the jetty and Komtar, winding its way through the colonial core of Georgetown. It's a good way to get a quick overview of the town, and you can get on and off again at various stops. A map of the route is in the *Penang Tourist Newspaper*.

Opposite the southeastern corner of Fort Cornwallis is the **Victoria Memorial Clocktower**, a gleaming white tower topped by a Moorish dome. Donated by a local Chinese millionaire to honour Queen Victoria's Diamond Jubilee in 1897, it stands 18m (60 feet) tall – one foot for each year of her reign.

A typical feature of Malaysian colonial cities is the *padang*, which is an open playing field surrounded by public buildings. Georgetown's *padang* stretches west from Fort Cornwallis to the **City Hall** (Dewan Bandaran), one of Penang's most imposing buildings, with fine porticos. The Penang Library behind it is not architecturally interesting. Although the library itself is relocating, a section of the **State Art Gallery** (admission free; ⌚ 9am-5pm Sat-Thu) remains on the ground floor with a rotating display of contemporary local art.

On the southern side of the *padang* is the neoclassical **State Assembly building** (Dewan Undangan Negeri), and northwest along Lebuh Light is the equally impressive **Supreme Court**.

Behind the Supreme Court, **St George's Church** on Lebuh Farquhar is the oldest Anglican church in Southeast Asia. This gracefully proportioned building, with its marble floor and towering spire, was built in 1818 with convict labour. In the grounds there is an elegant little pavilion, housing a memorial plaque to Francis Light. Also on Lebuh Farquhar is the double-spired **Cathedral of the Assumption**, named for the feast day on which its Catholic founders landed here from Kedah.

In the **Protestant Cemetery** on Jl Sultan Ahmad Shah, the mouldering tombs of colonial officials huddle together under a canopy of magnolia trees. Here you'll find the graves of Captain Francis Light (who was also Sir Thomas Stamford Raffles' brother-in-law) and Thomas Leonowens, the young officer who married Anna – the schoolmistress to the King of Siam who was made famous by Deborah Kerr in the *King and I*. The 1999 remake, *Anna and the King*, was filmed in Malaysia, some of it in Penang.

Fort Cornwallis

Among Penang's oldest sights are the timeworn walls of **Fort Cornwallis** (Lebuh Light; admission free; ⌚ 9am-7pm). It was here that Captain Light first set foot on the virtually uninhabited island in 1786 and established the free port where trade would, he hoped, be lured from Britain's Dutch rivals. At first a wooden fort was built, but between 1808 and 1810 convict labour replaced it with the present stone structure.

Today only the outer walls of the fort are standing, and the area within is now a park. There's not much to do except wander around the battlements, which are liberally studded with old cannons. Many of these were retrieved from local pirates, although they were originally cast by the Dutch.

Seri Rambai, the most-important and largest cannon, faces the north coast and dates back to 1603. It has a chequered history; the Dutch gave it to the sultan of Johor, after which it fell into the hands of the Acehnese. It was later given to the sultan of Selangor and then stolen by pirates before ending up at the fort. It is famed for its procreative powers, and childless women are advised to place flowers in the barrel of 'the big one' and offer special prayers.

Penang Museum

From the town's foundation site it's only a short stroll to the **Penang Museum** (☎ 261 3144; Lebuh Farquhar; admission RM1; ⌚ 9am-5pm Sat-Thu), one of the best-presented museums in Malaysia. In front is a bronze statue of Captain Light, which itself has an intriguing history. As no picture of Francis Light could be found at the time the statue was made, it was actually modelled on the features of his son, William, who founded Adelaide in South Australia. It was first put on show in 1939 but quickly spirited away when the Japanese invaded, and only saw light of day again in 1978, minus its impressive sword, according to some.

The excellent exhibits on the ground floor of the museum illustrate the customs and traditions of Penang's various ethnic groups, with photos, documents, costumes, furniture and other well-labelled displays. Look out for the beautifully carved opium beds, inlaid with mother-of-pearl.

Upstairs is the history gallery. An interesting section recounts the bloody ten days of rioting between Chinese secret societies in 1867, attributed by ill-prepared British authorities to a rambutan-throwing incident. Georgetown suffered a near civil war, with hundreds left dead, before the administrators took a firm hand. The societies were heavily fined and the proceeds used to build police stations that subsequently kept the peace.

There's also a collection of early-19th-century watercolours by Captain Robert Smith, an engineer with the East India Company, and prints showing landscape scenes of old Penang.

Outside, one of the original Penang Hill funicular railcars is now a kiosk selling an unusual array of souvenirs including antique costume jewellery and coins; all proceeds benefit the Penang Heritage Trust. Also on display is the battered Rolls Royce, in which the then British High Commissioner, Sir Henry Gurney, was travelling when he was gunned down by communist bandits in 1951.

CHINATOWN

Inland from the old colonial district lie the twisting streets of the old city, dotted with temples, mosques and traditional businesses. The large **Chinatown** stretches from Lebuh Pantai to Jl Penang. It's centred on Lebuh Chulia, which is still the lively heart of Georgetown, but pockets of Indian and Malay areas remain within and around it.

Chinatown is a delight to wander around any time of day. Set off in any direction and you're certain to find plenty of interest, whether it's the beautiful old Chinese shophouses, an early-morning vegetable market, a temple ceremony, the crowded antique shops or a late *pasar malam* (night market).

All the usual Chinese events are likely to be taking place: colourful parades at festival times or elderly women setting up their stalls for a day's business. All around you'll hear those distinctively Chinese noises – the clatter of mahjong tiles from inside houses, the trilling of caged songbirds, as well as the sound of loud arguments and conversations everywhere.

Kuan Yin Teng

On Lebuh Pitt (Jl Masjid Kapitan Keling) is the temple of **Kuan Yin** – the goddess of mercy, good fortune, peace and fertility. Built in the early 19th century by the first Hokkien and Cantonese settlers in Penang, the temple is not impressive, but it's very central and popular with the Chinese community. There's often something going on: worshippers burning paper money at the furnaces in front of the temple; devotees offering joss sticks (incense) inside; or night-time puppetry or Chinese theatre on the goddess' birthday, celebrated on the 19th day of the second, sixth and ninth lunar months.

Hainan Temple

This small gem demands a closer look. Dedicated to Mar Chor, the patron saint of seafarers, the **Hainan Temple** (Lebuh Muntri) was founded in 1866 but not completed until 1895. A thorough remodelling for its centenary in 1995 has refreshed its distinctive swirling dragon pillars and brightened up the ornate carvings. The small compound is usually buzzing with activity.

Khoo Kongsi

Near the end of Lebuh Pitt (Jl Masjid Kapitan Keling) is the **Khoo Kongsi** (Lebuh Cannon; admission RM5; ⏲ 9am-5pm). A *kongsi* is a clan house, a building that's partly a temple and partly a meeting hall for Chinese of the same clan or surname.

Penang has many *kongsi*, but the clan house of the Khoo is by far the finest and is not to be missed. Its construction was first considered around 1835, but the permanent structure wasn't built until 1894. The building was so magnificent and elaborate that nobody was surprised when the roof caught fire on the night it was completed in 1901! That misfortune was interpreted as a message from above that they had really overdone it and the ancestors were jealous, so the Khoo rebuilt it in a marginally less extravagant style.

The present *kongsi*, which dates from 1906 but was recently extensively renovated, is also known as the Dragon Mountain Hall. It's a colourful mix of dragons, statues, paintings, lamps, coloured tiles and carvings.

Acheen St Mosque

A short walk from the Khoo Kongsi, the Malay **Acheen St Mosque** (Lebuh Acheh) is unusual for its Egyptian-style minaret (most Malay mosques have Moorish minarets). Built in 1808 by a wealthy Arab trader, the mosque was the focal point for the Malay and Arab traders in this quarter – the oldest Malay *kampung* (village) in Georgetown.

Syed Alatas Mansion

Restored in 1994, the **Syed Alatas Mansion** (Lebuh Acheh; admission free; ⏲ 9am-5pm Mon-Fri, 9am-1pm Sat-Sun) was the residence of Syed Mohd Alatas, a powerful Acehnese merchant of Arab descent. Syed Alatas led the local Acehnese community during the Penang riots of 1867 and organised resistance to the Dutch siege of Aceh (Sumatra) in the 1870s.

Cheong Fatt Tze Mansion

Built in the 1880s, the magnificent 38-room, 220-window **Cheong Fatt Tze Mansion** (☎ 262 5289; 14 Lebuh Leith; admission RM10) was commissioned by Cheong Fatt Tze. He was a local Hakka merchant-trader who left China as a penniless teenager and eventually established a vast financial empire throughout East Asia, earning himself the sobriquet Rockerfeller of the East.

Eastern and Western influences blend and conform to precepts of feng shui by sitting on a 'dragon's throne' – a mountain (Penang Hill) behind and water (the Channel) in front. It's a rare surviving examples of the grandiose architectural style preferred by wealthy overseas Chinese who tried to imitate the opulence of the Ching dynasty. Its features include ingeniously crafted louvred windows, Art Nouveau stained-glass windows, elaborate wrought ironwork and a superb glazed-tile roof adorned with ceramic motifs.

The building was rescued from ruin in the 1990s and won the Unesco Heritage Conservation award in 2000. Although it's currently run as an exclusive homestay hotel (see p167), one-hour tours are given at 11am and 3pm Monday to Friday and at 11am on Saturday and Sunday.

100 Cintra Street

Dating from 1881, and restored a century later, the attractive old house at **100 Cintra Street** (☎ 264 3581; adult/child RM5/1; ⏰ 11am-6pm Tue-Sun) houses the tiny Pocket Cultural Exhibition celebrating Penang's rich Baba-Nonya heritage. Furniture, costumes, porcelain and household items are displayed in re-creations of late 19th-century interiors. Indian and Malay items are also laid out, and there's a small antiques bazaar and a tea shop downstairs.

LITTLE INDIA

Suffused with the scents of sandalwood and spices, **Little India** is alive with the sounds of Hindi music blaring from numerous shop-fronts and lined with Bollywood video stores, sari shops, temples and restaurants, is centred on Lebuh Pasar. Here, Tamils from the south of India cool boiled milk by nonchalantly hurling it through the air from one cup to another. Money changing is almost exclusively an Indian enterprise here, and stocky Sikhs holding antique-looking guns can be seen guarding many banks and jewellery shops.

Sri Mariamman Temple

About midway between Kuan Yin Teng and the Kapitan Keling Mosque you'll find this Hindu temple, another example of Penang's religious diversity. The **Sri Mariamman Temple** (Lebuh Pitt) is typically South Indian; an elaborately sculpted and painted superstructure representing Mt Meru (the cosmic mountain that supports the heavens) rises above its shrine. Built in 1883, it's Georgetown's oldest Hindu temple and a testimony to the strong Indian influence you'll find in this otherwise most Chinese of towns.

Penang's Thaipusam procession begins here (see Festivals & Events, p165), and in October a wooden chariot takes the temple's deity for a spin around the neighbourhood during Vijayadasami festivities.

Masjid Kapitan Keling

Penang's first Indian Muslim settlers (East India Company troops) built **Masjid Kapitan Keling** in 1801 at the junction of Lebuh Buckingham and Lebuh Pitt (Jl Masjid Kapitan Keling). The mosque's domes are yellow, in a typically Indian-influenced Islamic style, and it has a single minaret. It looks sublime at sunset.

OTHER SIGHTS

Wat Chayamangkalaram

At Lorong Burma just off Jl Burma, the main road to Batu Ferringhi, is the **Temple of the Reclining Buddha**. This brightly painted Thai temple houses a 33m-long reclining Buddha, draped in a gold-leafed saffron robe. The claim that it's the third-longest in the world is a dubious one but it's a colourful temple and worth a visit.

The **Dhammikarama Burmese Buddhist Temple** stands opposite, with two large stone elephants flanking the gates. Penang's first Buddhist temple, built in 1805, it has been significantly added to over the years.

You can get to both temples on Transit Link bus No 202; Minibus No 26, 31 or 88; or Hin Bus No 93 from Komtar or along Lebuh Chulia.

Penang Buddhist Association

Completed in 1931, this unusual Buddhist temple is on Jl Anson about 1km west of town. Instead of the typical colourful design of most Chinese temples, this one shows Art Deco influences and looks like a frosted cake, all white and pastel. Interior Buddha figures are carved from Italian marble, and glass chandeliers, made in Penang, hang from above. Penang's Buddhist community gathers here on Wesak Day (April/May) to celebrate the triple holy-day of the Buddha's birthday, attainment of enlightenment and death.

Other Mosques & Temples

The glossy, modern **Masjid Negeri** (State Mosque) at Air Itam, about 5km west of town, offers good views from its 50m-high minaret.

Nattukotai Chettiar Temple on Waterfall Rd, near the Botanical Gardens (see p173), is the largest Hindu temple in Penang and is dedicated to Bala Subramaniam. Further along on the left side is a gate leading up to the **Waterfall Hilltop Temple**, the destination of the Thaipusam procession from Little India's Sri Mariamman Temple.

Northwest of Georgetown, past Gurney Dr out at Tanjung Tokong, **Tua Pek Kong** is dedicated to the God of Prosperity and dates from 1837.

Activities

Malaysia is becoming a popular **golfing** destination and Penang has some exceptionally affordable international-standard golf courses – Japanese businessmen fly in for just a day or two to take advantage of them. The island's premier course is located at **Bukit Jambul Country Club** (☎ 644 2255; 2 Jl Bukit Jambul) near Bayan Lepas airport. Golf Malaysia rated it the second-most-beautiful course in Malaysia, and the stunning and very challenging 18 holes were carved straight out of the rocky jungle terrain.

At the **Penang Turf Club** (☎ 229 3233; www.penangturfclub.com; Batu Gantong) horse-racing events take place on two consecutive weekends every two months. Seats are cheap, but gambling is illegal. **Horse riding** is sometimes offered Monday to Friday.

For indoor pursuits, there's **Penang Bowl** (☎ 263 4702; 38B Lebuh Farquhar) in Georgetown. In the ritzy Pulau Tikus area west of Georgetown, Midlands 1-Stop has bowling alleys and a roller-skating rink.

There are several places to play a game of **pool** or **snooker** in Komtar; try **British Pool & Pub** (☎ 263 4881; 2nd fl), which also has a noisy karaoke lounge.

Tours

The big hotels and travel agents all book tours. **Hawaii Travel & Tours** (☎ 261 4325; 1 Jl Tun Syed Sheh Barakbah), a few doors from the Tourism Malaysia office, sells tickets for various tours including the half-day City Tour, full-day Round-Island Tour, Penang Hill & Kek Lok Si Temple Tour, Georgetown by Night Tour and the Mainland Tour, which takes in the Penang Bird Park. All cost RM28. On most of these tours, you're simply paying for transportation and not much else, though the Round-Island Tour is more convenient than relying on the public buses to reach remote sights.

Festivals & Events

All the usual festivals are celebrated in Penang, but with this island's extraordinary enthusiasm. Current events, including workshops, cultural talks and art exhibitions, are listed in the *Penang Tourist Newspaper*.

January–February

Thaipusam This masochistic-looking festival is celebrated as fervently as in Singapore and KL, but without quite the same crowds. The Sri Mariamman, Nattukotai Chettiar and Waterfall Hilltop temples (see those entries earlier) are the main centres of activity in Penang. (For more information on Thaipusam see the 'Piercing Devotions' boxed text, p109).

Chinese New Year Celebrated with particular gusto in Penang. The Khoo Kongsi is done up for the event, and dance troupes and Chinese opera groups perform all over the city. On the night before the 15th day of the new year, a fire ceremony takes place at Tua Pek Kong temple.

Chap Goh Meh The 15th day of the New Year celebrations, during which local girls throw oranges into the sea from the Esplanade. Traditionally, the girls would chant 'throw a good orange, get a good husband' while local boys watched and later contacted their dream girl through matchmakers. New Year is also one of the only times to see Baba-Nonya performances of *dondang sayang*, spontaneous and traditional love ballads bandied about between singers using Bahasa Malaysia and Hokkien dialects. Traditional *orang asli* (Malaysian aborigines) musical accompaniment consists of violins, accordions, tambourines and skin drums played slowly enough to give singers time to compose their replies.

June–August

Penang International Dragon Boat Festival (June) is a colourful and popular regatta featuring the traditional dragon boats.

Penang Food & Cultural Festivals (August) Highlights the best of Penang's multiethnic heritage.

September–December

Lantern Festival (mid-September) is celebrated by eating moon cakes, Chinese sweets once used to carry secret messages for underground rebellions in ancient China.

Pesta Pulau Penang (November–December) The annual Penang Islands Festival features various cultural events, parades and carnivals.

Sleeping

Penang has the wide variety of accommodation you would expect in a big, bustling tourist city, from the simplest hostels to the grandest hotels. Mid-range options are mostly found along Jl Penang, consisting of a number of ageing high-rises and a few more attractive modern places. Lebuh Chulia and Love Lane make up the heart of Penang's Backpacker-Land, crammed with cheap hostels and hotels, but the quality varies enormously and it certainly pays to check a few out before parting with your cash. Luxury hotels are spread out around the city and most offer discounts.

Be warned that during holidays, most notably Chinese New Year, hotels tend to fill up very quickly and prices can become ridiculously inflated; if you intend to stay at this time, book well in advance.

BUDGET

75 Travellers' Lodge (☎ 262 3378; 75 Lebuh Muntri; dm/d RM7/15;) Clean, comfortable and friendly place in a quiet street between Jl Penang and Love Lane. There's a TV room and a balcony for sunbathing. Air-con doubles (RM35) are also available.

Pin Seng Hotel (☎ 261 9004; 82 Love Lane; s/d RM20/25) Popular small hotel tucked down a little alley and well insulated from any street noise. Rooms, all with shared bathroom, vary in quality, so it pays to check a few.

Broadway Hostel (☎ 262 8550; 35-F Lebuh Pitt; dm/s/d RM7/20/30;) Friendly, well-placed hostel with clean rooms. Air-con doubles go for RM40.

Golden Plaza Hostel (☎ 263 0560, 32 Lebuh Ah Quee; dm/s/d RM8/16/25;) A popular place with a variety of rooms to choose from, including air-con rooms (from RM40). There are free newspapers available, and English-language movies play in its common lounge.

New Eng Aun (☎ 262 3889; 380 Lebuh Chulia; s/d from RM20/25) Quiet, rickety old house set back from the street, with large, simple rooms, all with shared bathrooms.

Genesis (☎ 283 5658; 208 Lebuh Chulia; dm/s/d RM7/15/18;) This is a very friendly, laid-back place with small but clean rooms. Downstairs there's a little café with a pool table and satellite TV.

Coral Hostel (☎ 264 4909; 99 Lebuh King; dm/s/d RM7/16/25;) Friendly hostel in the bustling, and noisy, Little India area of the city. The dorms are a little cramped, but the doubles are reasonably sized and comfortable.

D' Budget Hostel (☎ 263 4794; 9 Lebuh Gereja; dm/s/d RM7/16/22;) This is very basic hostel accommodation, with simple rooms (some windowless) and grotty shared bathrooms. The pricier air-con doubles (RM30) come with shower and are marginally preferable.

509 Café (☎ 016-487 0561; 298 Lebuh Chulia; dm/s/d from RM8/15/20;) Basic rooms above a popular café that serves good Western-style breakfasts. A bed in the air-con dorm is RM10.

THE AUTHOR'S CHOICE *Richard Watkins*

Budget

Harwich Backpackers' Lodge (☎ 263 3335; 86 Love Lane; s/d RM12/15;) One of the newest and most amenable of the backpacker hostels, with large, simple rooms and shared bathrooms over a busy pub. It also offers the cheapest Internet access in Georgetown (RM1 per hour).

Mid-range

Hotel 1926 (☎ 228 1926; hotel1926pq@penang-hotels.com; 227 Jl Burma; s & d from RM95;) An elegant modern hotel occupying a row of restored houses built in 1926 for British army officers, around 2km west of the city centre. The large, comfortable rooms are tastefully furnished in a vaguely Victorian style, and there's a good restaurant on site. Three-night packages are available from RM255.

Top end

Eastern & Oriental Hotel (☎ 222 2000; www.e-o-hotel.com; 10 Lebuh Farquhar; ste from RM345;) Undoubtedly Penang's grandest hotel, established in 1884 by the Sarkies brothers, who also ran Raffles Hotel in Singapore, it was completely refurbished in 2001. It's an all-suite hotel, and it's worth paying the extra for a sea view (RM440). The spacious suites are elegantly furnished, in a colonial style, and there are a number of very good restaurants too. The sea-facing lawn, where you'll find the biggest and oldest Java tree in Penang, is a nice place to relax. The pith-helmeted porters may be a touch over the top, though. (See the boxed text on p168.)

Island City Hotel (☎ 263 7107; 456 Lebuh Chulia; r RM45-50; ❄) Somewhat drab and character-less place with very simple, box-like rooms, though it's reasonably priced. Cheaper fan rooms are also available (RM30).

MID-RANGE

City Bayview Hotel (☎ 263 3161; 25A Lebuh Farquhar; r from RM150; ❄ 💻) Plush and sparkling high-rise, topped by a revolving restaurant with great views over Georgetown. There's a couple of other restaurants too, as well as a 'fun pub' with regular live music.

Cititel Hotel (☎ 370 1188; www.cititelhotel.com; 66 Jl Penang; s/d from RM145/160; ❄ 💻) Bright and airy modern hotel with a range of well-equipped rooms on offer, including suites (RM355). There's also a few good restaurants and a nightclub.

Malaysia Hotel (☎ 263 3311; 7 Jl Penang; r from RM156; ❄). Modern, centrally located high-rise with good-sized rooms and a high standard of service. Facilities include a health centre, restaurant and karaoke lounge.

Hotel Continental (☎ 263 6388; 5 Jl Penang; r from RM156; ❄ 💻 🏊) This is a modern high-rise with comfortable rooms, though they're nothing special.

Hong Ping Hotel (☎ 262 5243; 273-B Lebuh Chulia; s & d from RM60; ❄) Situated right in the heart of things on bustling Lebuh Chulia, offering plain but very clean rooms. Street-facing rooms may get a bit noisy; it's right above the Coco Island Travellers Corner pub (see p170).

Merchant Hotel (☎ 263 2828; 55 Jl Penang; s & d from RM78; ❄) A well-located but slightly age-ing hotel, with neat, comfortably furnished rooms, all with TV and fridge. It also has a good restaurant serving Malay and Western cuisine.

Oriental Hotel (☎ 263 4211; www.oriental.com.my; 105 Jl Penang; s & d from RM69; ❄) Modern high-rise hotel that offers fairly good value for money, though the rooms are pretty ordinary. Family rooms, sleeping four, are available (RM92) and there's a highly regarded Indian restaurant on site.

Cathay Hotel (☎ 262 6271; 15 Lebuh Leith; s/d RM69/92; ❄) Atmospheric old wooden colonial villa, with large, clean rooms.

Towne House Hotel (☎ 263 8621; 70 Jl Penang; s & d RM69; ❄) Old-fashioned city-centre hotel, with slightly shabby rooms; those facing the street can get noisy.

TOP END

Cheong Fatt Tze Mansion (☎ 262 5289; www.cheongfatttzemansion.com; 14 Lebuh Leith; r from RM232; ❄) Exclusive and unique owner-hosted home-stay, which is also one of the city's premier tourist attractions (see p163). The opulently furnished suites are individually styled, and each comes with a personal valet.

Shangri-La (☎ 262 2622; www.shangri-la.com; Jl Magazine; r from RM250; ❄ 💻 🏊) Huge luxury hotel beside the Komtar shopping centre. All the top-end facilities you could expect are here, including a gym and several restaurants and bars. Guests can also enjoy the facilities of the Shangri-La Resort in Batu Ferringhi at no extra charge, with a free shuttle-bus between the two.

Eating

The quality and variety of food in Penang is legendary, and deservedly so. You can try a vast array of Asian cuisine in a very small area, with numerous Indian, Chinese, Malay and Thai restaurants jostling for trade, and seemingly always full.

Laksa *assam*, or Penang laksa, is a fish soup with a sour taste from tamarind (*assam*) paste; it's served with special white laksa noodles. Originally a Thai dish, laksa lemak has been adopted by Penang. It's similar to the Thai dish, except tamarind is substituted for coconut milk.

Apart from Melaka, Penang is one of the best places to try Nonya (Straits Chinese) cuisine, although you will have to look hard to find the real thing. Seafood is also very popular in Penang and there are many restaurants that specialise in fresh fish, crabs and prawns – particularly along the northern beach.

Despite its Chinese character, Penang also has a strong Indian presence and there are some popular specialities to savour. Curry Kapitan is a chicken curry that is supposed to have been named when a Dutch sea captain asked his Indonesian mess boy what was to eat that night. The answer was 'curry, Kapitan' and it's been on the menu ever since.

BREAKFAST & SNACKS

Lebuh Chulia has some delightfully old-fashioned coffee shops, as well as numerous outlets serving Western breakfasts of bacon and eggs or cereals.

THE EASTERN & ORIENTAL HOTEL

The historic Eastern & Oriental Hotel stands at 10 Lebuh Farquhar, dominating the seafront end of Jl Penang. It was originally built in 1884, as the Eastern Hotel, which became so popular that the following year it was expanded and renamed the Eastern & Oriental Hotel. The stylish E&O was the archetypal 19th-century colonial grand hotel, established by two of the famous Armenian Sarkies brothers, Tigram and Martin, the most famous hoteliers in the East, who later founded Raffles Hotel in Singapore.

In the 1920s, the Sarkies promoted the E&O as 'The Premier Hotel East of Suez' (a catchy phrase the brothers later used to advertise *all* their hotels), which supposedly had the 'Longest Sea Front of any Hotel' in the world, at 842 feet. High-ranking colonial officials and wealthy planters and merchants filed through its grand lobby, and the E&O became firmly established as a centre for Penang's social elite. Rudyard Kipling, Noel Coward and Somerset Maugham were just some of the famous faces who passed through its doors.

The Sarkies almost closed the E&O when the rent was raised from £200 to £350 a month. Arshak Sarkies, a third brother (a gambler by nature), convinced the family to open the Raffles Hotel instead. Arshak's generosity was legendary; he often paid the £50 to £60 passage back to England for broken-hearted (and empty-pocketed) rubber planters and tin miners himself. Some observers said that Arshak ran the E&O not to make money, but to entertain: he seemed more keen to waltz around the ballroom with a whisky and soda balanced on his head than to add up a balance sheet. Shortly before his death, Arshak began lavish renovations to the E&O; this expense, coupled with loans to friends that were conveniently forgotten, finally bankrupted the family business in 1931. Still, Arshak's funeral was one of the grandest Penang has ever seen.

In the 1990s, the E&O closed and fell into disrepair, but a huge renovation programme was begun to rescue one of Georgetown's most prominent and glamorous landmarks, and in 2001 it once again opened for business, as a luxury, all-suite grand hotel, with elegant, spacious rooms decorated with the best of colonial style. Today, the E&O offers some fine dining, and a visit to Penang isn't complete until you've taken tiffin on its grand lawn (see 'The Author's Choice' boxed text, p166).

The E&O features in several stories by Somerset Maugham, who was a regular (and often difficult) guest. For more on dashing Arshak Sarkies, read George Bilainikin's entertaining *Hail Penang! Being the Narrative of Comedies and Tragedies in a Tropical Outpost Among Europeans, Chinese, Malays and Indians.*

Secret Garden (☎ 262 9996; 414 Lebuh Chulia; dishes from RM6) A very popular travellers hang-out. It's run by an Austrian expat who serves a range of wholesome breakfasts and better-than-average Western food including vegetarian options. There's also a free movie shown every evening, though you'll be lucky to get a seat if you don't turn up early. The owner can arrange tickets, rentals and so forth for travellers.

Green Planet (63 Lebuh Cintra; dishes from RM5) A popular travellers café offeringpizza, lasagne, felafel and nachos. Another favourite is **Rhak Café** (☎ 016-480 6780; 451 Lebuh Chulia; dishes from RM4) It serves economical and filling breakfasts and light meals throughout the day. Free movies are often shown.

Hang Chow Café (☎ 263 7609; 511 Lebuh Chulia; dishes from RM4) Basic little café serving a wide range of quick and cheap meals such as omelettes, ham and eggs, and pizza. Nearby, **Caribbean Rasta Café** (☎ 012-438 3962; dishes from RM4) is a small backpackers' café serving light meals and snacks. It also has a noisy bar.

Eden Bakery (☎ 263 8323; Lebuh Muntri; dishes from RM5) Small bakery with a sit-down café serving light snacks, rolls, sandwiches and cakes.

Gloria Jean's Coffees (the Garage, 2 Jl Penang) Popular place for pricey coffees and light meals with soft sofas and free newspapers at hand.

Komtar has a supermarket and numerous fast-food outlets. On the 5th floor there's a lively, crowded hawker centre serving all the usual Chinese and Malay dishes, plus some Indian food.

CHINESE

There are so many Chinese restaurants in Georgetown that it is difficult to give recommendations. A wander down any street in Chinatown is likely to turn up hidden gems.

Ching Lotus Humanist Space (☎ 261 8001; 83 Lebuh China; dishes from RM4.50) Oddly named place in a tastefully restored old wooden shophouse, with a small art and design bookshop, and reading area on the ground floor. The set meals of various forms of chicken with rice or noodles (RM8.80) are superb value, and come with soup, herbal tea and dessert.

SC Cuisine (☎ 262 3263; 397 Lebuh Chulia; dishes from RM2) Excellent-value place with a big menu of cheap and tasty Chinese fare. The set meals, such as honey lemon fish and rice (RM3.90) are a bargain, while claypot meals start at just RM5.

Hong Kong Restaurant (☎ 264 4375; 29 Lebuh Cintra; dishes from RM6) Very popular seafood and dim sum restaurant with an extensive menu.

Peace & Joy (87 Lebuh China; dishes from RM4) Basic and ever-busy Chinese coffee-shop, near Ching Lotus, serving up cheap roast pork and rice dishes.

INDIAN

Little India is replete with cheap eating places, especially along Lebuh Pasar and Lebuh Penang, serving up curries, roti, tandoori and biryani. Other places are scattered all around town. Several small restaurants and stalls in this area offer cheap North Indian and South Indian food.

Passage Thru' India (☎ 262 0263; 132 Jl Penang; dishes from RM11) Arguably the best Indian restaurant in Georgetown. It certainly has the most extensive menu, offering regional cuisine from all parts of the subcontinent. Set meals (vegetarian and non-vegetarian) are good value, and there's occasional live music. There's even a frock-coated doorman to show you in.

Restoran Kapitan (☎ 264 1191; 49 Lebuh Chulia; dishes from RM4) Very busy, 24-hour restaurant specialising in tandoori chicken and biryani. It also serves some excellent lassi.

Kaliammans (☎ 262 8953; 43 Lebuh Penang; dishes from RM4) Smart, air-con restaurant serving North and South Indian cuisine as well as Western food such as pizza. Best value are the tasty banana leaf set meals for RM4.

Madras New Woodlands Restaurant (☎ 263 9764; 60 Lebuh Penang; dishes from RM3) Very good vegetarian restaurant offering tasty banana leaf meals and North Indian specialities.

Sri Ananda Bahwan (☎ 264 4204; 55 Lebuh Penang; dishes from RM3) Basic Indian eatery, seemingly forever full of chatting locals, serving up tandoori chicken, roti canai (unleavened flaky flat bread) and *murtabak* (roti canai filled with pieces of chicken, beef, mutton or vegetables).

MALAY

Kayu Nasi Kandar (☎ 264 4767; 216 Jl Penang; dishes from RM4) Big 24-hour place serving up cheap and tasty Malay specialities, including lots of basic chicken and rice dishes, and vegetarian options.

NONYA

Penang, like Melaka and Singapore, was the home of the Straits-born Chinese, or Baba-Nonya, who combined Chinese and Malay traditions, especially in their kitchens. Penang's Nonya cuisine is a tad more fiery due to the island's proximity to Thailand. These days, though, true Nonya cuisine is becoming harder to find.

Nyonya Baba Cuisine (☎ 227 8035; 44 Nagore Road; dishes from RM6; closed Wed) The best place in Georgetown to sample traditional and authentic high-quality Nonya food – try the deep-fried fish or *hong bak* (pork in thick gravy). Set-lunch menus of three dishes plus dessert cost only RM6. The owners are considering moving, so you may need to ask around for its new location.

QUICK EATS

Georgetown has a big selection of street stalls, with nightly gatherings at places like the seafront Esplanade Food Centre. This is one of the best hawker centres, as much for the delightful sea breezes as the Malay stalls serving delicious Penang specialities. The more restaurant-like Chinese section features seafood and icy-cold beer.

Lorong Baru, just off Jl Macalister, is another lively location where food stalls set up in the evenings. Two other hawker areas can be found northwest of Komtar, just off Jl Burma on Lorong Selamat and Lorong Swatow. Lorong Swatow is good for laksa, *rojak* (green fruit salad in a spicy sauce) and *ais kacang*, a shaved-ice dessert.

In Chinatown a good Malay food market springs up every night along Lebuh

Kimberley on the corner of Lebuh Cintra. Lebuh Chulia is always a great place for noodles at night. After 9pm, small Chinese stalls set up tables on the footpath and the street is always a lively procession. Most stalls are found clustered around the Hong Ping Hotel at No 273.

Gurney Dr, 3km west along the coast on the way to Batu Ferringhi, is another popular seafront venue. Evening hawker-style restaurants here are noted for their seafood, including those in the lively New Golden Phoenix outdoor food court and at the northwestern end of the street.

Chinese fare of every imaginable type is sold from food carts and at small coffee shops around the old town. One of Georgetown's 'excellent Hainanese chicken-rice' purveyors is **Sin Kuan Hwa Cafe** (cnr Lebuh Chulia & Lebuh Cintra). Also very cheap is **Kedai Kopi Kimberly** (Lebuh Kimberly). Many other places serve classic dim sum in the mornings.

One of Chinatown's most popular outdoor fast-food places is **Hsiang Yang Fast Food** (off Lebuh Chulia). It's really a hawker centre, with an inexpensive Chinese buffet, noodles, satay and popiah (rice-paper roll) vendors.

THAI & JAPANESE

Shin Miyako (☎ 263 8702; 1st fl, 103-A Jl Penang; dishes from RM10; closed Wed) Good quality Japanese restaurant with seafood, sushi and other favourites on the menu.

Restoran Tomyam (☎ 263 2592; 21 Lebuh Chulia; dishes from RM4) Simple place serving interesting spicy combinations from Islamic southern Thailand, like steamed fish with garlic and sour plum.

WESTERN

1885 (☎ 261 8333; 10 Lebuh Farquahar; dishes from RM45) The elegant main restaurant of the E&O Hotel, serving excellent Western cuisine such as sea bass with truffle sauce and roast duck. Open for dinner only, with a smart casual dress code (no T-shirts, shorts or sandals).

Thirty Two (☎ 262 2232; 32 Jl Sultan Ahmed Shah; dishes from RM24) Genteel restaurant in an elegant seaside mansion. Pasta, steaks and roast lamb and duck are on the menu. There's also a cocktail bar and an outdoor seating area. There's live jazz on Friday and Saturday evenings. Dress code is smart casual.

Cous-Cous (☎ 263 6868; 2 Jl Penang; dishes from RM11) Mexican-style restaurant inside the Garage shopping mall, also serving a fusion of Cajun, Spanish and Malaysian cuisine. Grilled fish, fajitas, paella, steaks and curry are some of the eclectic offerings.

Winter Warmers (☎ 262 0848; Ground fl, 33-G Prangin Mall; dishes from RM8) Chintzy English tearoom serving light meals, such as pasta dishes, and lots of different teas, coffee and ice-cream.

Drinking

Pitt Street Corner (94 Lebuh Pitt) Friendly, atmospheric and authentic little Indian bar; a great place to sit down with a cold beer on a hot day.

Farquhar's Bar (10 Lebuh Farquhar) Upscale British pub inside the E&O Hotel, serving beer, traditional pub food and cocktails; try their signature drink, the Eastern & Oriental Sling (RM25).

Soho Free House (50 Jl Penang) Rather dimly-lit British-style pub serving a wide choice of draught beers.

20 Leith Street (20 Lebuh Leith) Lively bar situated right opposite the Cheong Fatt Tze Mansion, which promises 'the cheapest beer in town' at RM4.99 a glass. Happy hour is 4pm to 9pm.

Slippery Senoritas (the Garage, 2 Jl Penang) Vaguely Spanish-style bar attached to the Cous-Cous restaurant (see Western this page). The dress code is smart casual, and it's popular with Western expats.

Coco Island Travellers Corner (273 Lebuh Chulia) Big backpackers' pub with lots of outdoor tables. It's a good place to sit and watch the world go by with a beer or two.

THE AUTHOR'S CHOICE

Richard Watkins

No visit to Penang is complete without sitting down to a fine tiffin lunch at **Sarkies Corner** in the grand Eastern & Oriental Hotel. Served between noon and 2pm from Monday to Friday (RM14.90) in elegant surroundings, it's a filling and surprisingly inexpensive meal consisting of various items such as mussels, curried chicken and lamb, with a view out onto the lawn and the sea beyond. Try a pot of 'Prince of Wales' tea afterwards. The dress code is smart casual, so no shorts or sandals.

Hard Life Cafe (363 Lebuh Chulia) Busy place which grooves to a reggae beat and is usually full enough to spill out onto the footpath.

Entertainment

There are lots of place on Lebuh Chulia where you can catch some live music over a beer or two. **Coco Island Travellers Corner** at No 273 often has live bands until late.

Georgetown used to have more discos that stayed open till the wee hours, but **Rock World** (☎ 261 3168; off Lebuh Campbell) is the lone survivor. It still gets lively on weekends and features local Chinese bands. You can't miss the gargantuan neon spider web hanging over the front.

Baywatch Beach Club (☎ 262 6299; 10 Lebuh Farquhar) Right next to the E&O Hotel, this popular place features a resident DJ and live bands most nights. It's open till 2am during the week, and till 3am on weekends, though it doesn't have a dance floor.

Lush (the Garage; 2 JL Penang) Open till 3am every day except Sunday. It's basically an upmarket bar with occasional live music and a smart casual dress code.

Beans & Brews Café (☎ 263 6311; 33-G-59 Prangin Mall, Jl Dr Lim Chwee Leong) Serves a big range of coffees, teas and shakes, and there are live music performances every Friday, Saturday and Sunday from 9pm to midnight.

Shopping

Penang is a good place to shop, with plenty of outlets for cameras, electronics, CDs and clothes at competitive prices (though Kuala Lumpur has a wider range). Copies of brand-name goods are cheap and vary in quality. Bargaining is usually required, except in department stores. Jl Penang is the best shopping street in Georgetown.

Komtar (Jl Penang) This vast mall has hundreds of small and large shops selling everything from clothes, shoes and electronics to everyday goods.

Prangin Mall (Jl Penang) Adjoins Komtar and houses a huge number of shops and restaurants, including smarter chain stores such as the **Parkson Grand** (☎ 261 2133), with a wide range of clothes, cosmetics, household goods and suchlike.

Along Jl Penang you'll find shops selling locally made **Penang Pewter**, a rather more affordable version of the better-known Selangor Pewter, though of equal quality.

Hong Giap Hang (☎ 261 3288; 193 Jl Penang) If you're looking for pewter products, this place has a good range. There's also woodcarvings, jewellery, porcelain and batik.

Hong Seng Arts & Crafts (☎ 261 1210; 86 Jl Penang) This shop specialises in antique and modern Chinese porcelain.

A number of shops in Chinatown sell art, antiques and curios. Prices range from the reasonable to the ridiculous, so bargain hard.

Bee Chin Heong (☎ 261 9346; 58 Kimberley St) This interesting outlet sells a colourful, bewildering array of religious statues, furniture and temple supplies; if you're after a huge Chinese couch, a household shrine or a 2m-tall carved wood Buddha, this is the place to come. Even if you're not buying, it's still worth a look round.

Garage (Jl Penang) Located opposite the E&O Hotel, this artfully restored Art-Deco building, has been converted into an upscale mini-mall. It contains a few antique and craft shops such as **Little Heritage House** (☎ 262 6181), which sells a range of jewellery and porcelain, and **Tea Garden** (☎ 263 3686), where you can look over exquisitely decorated Chinese tea sets.

A wander along Lebuh Chulia will turn up a selection of interesting little shops.

Tropical Art Corner (☎ 262 6663; 369 Lebuh Chulia) Looking for silver jewellery or batik? How about stone seals, personally carved with your name in Chinese characters? Look no further.

Oriental Arts & Antiques (☎ 261 2748; 440 Lebuh Chulia) An array of antiques, including furniture, porcelain, silverware and general bric-a-brac are for sale here.

100 Cintra Street (see p164) A small collection of antique shops is housed here, as well as a tiny Baba-Nonya cultural exhibition on the top floor.

Lebuh Campbell is another good shopping street, and stalls at the intersection with Jl Penang have a broad range of leather and rattan goods.

Penang Plaza (Jl Burma) This mid-sized shopping mall has a large supermarket and a few bookshops.

Out at Pulau Tikus you'll find the typical suburban malls, including the Midlands 1-Stop shopping centre and Island Plaza shopping complex (with a cineplex and game centre).

The Thieves Market (a morning flea market, said to be liveliest on Sunday) has moved to a car park behind the City Stadium on Lorong Kulit. It has all sorts of unsorted bric-a-brac (much of which is useless junk) but there are also antique pieces for sale. Buses to Air Itam pass the flea market, but check the *Penang Tourist Newspaper* or at a tourist office to make sure it hasn't moved.

Getting There & Away

See the Getting There & Away (p153) and Getting Around (p156) sections for information on transport to and from Georgetown.

AROUND THE ISLAND

You can make a circuit of the island by car, motorcycle, bicycle (if you're very keen), public transport or on a tour. If travelling by motorcycle or car, plan to spend about five hours, with plenty of sightseeing and refreshment stops. If you're on a bicycle, allow all day.

It's 70km all the way round, but only the north-coast road runs beside the beaches. The route takes you from Georgetown around the island clockwise. The road to Bayan Lepas and the airport is congested and built up, but it gets much quieter further around on the island's western side.

Penang Hill

☎ 04

Rising 821m above Georgetown, the top of Penang Hill provides a cool retreat from the sticky heat below, being generally about 5°C cooler than at sea level. From the summit there's a spectacular view over the island and across to the mainland. There are pleasant gardens, an old-fashioned kiosk, a restaurant and a hotel, as well as a lavishly decorated **Hindu temple** and a mosque at the top. Penang Hill is particularly wonderful at dusk as Georgetown, far below, starts to light up.

Penang Hill was first cleared by Captain Light soon after British settlement in order to grow strawberries (it was originally known as Strawberry Hill). A trail to the top was opened from the Botanical Gardens waterfall and access was by foot or packhorse, or sedan chair for the wealthy. The official name of the hill was Flagstaff Hill (now translated as Bukit Bendera), but it is universally known as Penang Hill.

Efforts to make it a popular hill resort were thwarted by difficult access, and the first attempt at a mountain railway proved to be a dismal failure. In 1923 a Swiss-built **funicular** (one way/return RM3/4; ⌚ every 15-30 mins from 6.30am-9.30pm Sun-Thu, open to 11.15pm Fri & Sat) was completed. The tiny cable-pulled Penang Hill Railway cars have trundled up and down ever since. The trip takes a crawling 30 minutes, with a change of trains at the halfway point. On the way, you pass the bungalows originally built for British officials and other wealthy citizens. The original funicular cars were replaced by more-modern ones a few years back, but that hasn't deterred the punters. Queues on weekends and public holidays can be horrendously long (with waits of up to 30 minutes).

A number of roads and **walking trails** traverse the hill. You can walk the 5.5km to the Botanical Gardens (Moon Gate) in about three hours from the trail near the upper funicular station. The easier jeep track from the top also leads to the gardens, just beyond the Moon Gate. Take water and food on longer walks.

The **Bellevue Hotel** (☎ 829 9500; fax 829 2052; s/d RM120/160) is the only place to stay on top of the hill, but while it offers some great views over Georgetown, it's a little frayed at the edges and somewhat overpriced. Access is via the funicular railway and a five-minute walk. The hotel has a good map in the lobby that shows trails, as well as a small **aviary garden** (admission RM4; ⌚ 9am-6pm) featuring exotic birds.

GETTING THERE & AWAY

From Komtar, or along Lebuh Chulia, you can catch one of the frequent TransitLink buses (No 1, 101, 351 or 361) or Yellow Bus No 85 to Air Itam. From Air Itam, walk five minutes to the funicular railway station or take the half-hourly TransitLink shuttle bus No 8. A taxi from the ferry terminal in Georgetown to the funicular station is RM12.

The energetic can take one of the walking trails to/from the Botanical Gardens.

Kek Lok Si Temple

The largest Buddhist temple in Malaysia stands on a hilltop at Air Itam, near Penang

Hill. Founded by an immigrant Chinese Buddhist, construction started in 1890, took more than 20 years to complete and was largely funded by donations from Penang Straits Chinese elite.

To reach the entrance, walk through arcades of souvenir stalls, past a tightly packed turtle pond and murky fish ponds, until you reach **Ban Po Thar** (Ten Thousand Buddhas Pagoda; admission RM2) a seven-tier, 30m-high tower. The design is said to be Burmese at the top, Chinese at the bottom and Thai in between. In another three-storey shrine, there's a large Thai Buddha image that was donated by King Bhumibol of Thailand. Standing high above all the temple structures is a striking white figure of Kuan Yin, goddess of mercy.

It's an impressive temple, though crowded with tourists and shoppers as much as worshippers. The temple is about a 3km walk from Penang Hill station (see p172), or you can hop on the half-hourly TransitLink shuttle bus No 8 or Yellow Bus No 85.

Botanical Gardens

The 30-hectare **Botanical Gardens** (☎ 227 0328; Waterfall Rd; admission free; 🕒 5am-8pm) are also known as the Waterfall Gardens, after the stream that cascades through from Penang Hill. They've also been dubbed the Monkey Gardens for the many long-tailed macaques that appear on the lawn for a feed by the staff early each morning and late afternoon. (Monkeys do bite, so it's probably best to leave the feeding to the staff). Within the grounds are an orchid house, palm house, herbal garden, cactus garden and sun rookery. A path leads to the top of Penang Hill.

The half-hourly Sri Negara bus No 137 stops at a nearby hotel, from where it's a 1km walk to the gardens. TransitLink bus No 7 runs hourly from Komtar along Lebuh Chulia to the entrance.

Museum & Art Gallery

Six kilometres south of Georgetown, on the sprawling campus of Universiti Sains Malaysia, the **Museum and Art Gallery** (☎ 657 7888; admission free; 🕒 10am-5pm Sun-Thu, 10am-12.15pm & 2.45-5pm Fri, 10am-1pm Sat) has a fine collection of traditional Malaysian and Indonesian musical instruments (including several full gamelan orchestras), aboriginal and Baba-Nonya pieces, and fascinating contemporary Malaysian art and photography.

Take any Yellow Bus (except No 82 or 85) from Georgetown, but be sure to get off at the university stop before the bus turns onto the Penang Bridge and carries you away to the mainland.

Snake Temple

Three kilometres before the airport, you'll see Penang's **Snake Temple** (Temple of the Azure Cloud) on the western side of the road. The temple is dedicated to Chor Soo Kong, a Buddhist priest and healer, and was built in 1850 by a grateful patient. The several resident (venomous) Wagler's pit vipers and green tree snakes are said to be fixed and slightly doped by the incense smoke drifting around the temple during the day, but at night slither down to eat the offerings. Admission is technically free, although donations are demanded by the snake handlers.

Yellow Bus No 66 and Minibus No 32 run every 30 minutes from Komtar past the temple.

Fishing Villages

About 3km after the snake temple, you reach the turn-off to the Chinese fishing village of **Batu Maung**. The renovated seaside temple here has a shrine dedicated to the legendary Admiral Cheng Ho (see p216 for more information on this historic figure). The temple sanctifies a huge footprint on the rock that's reputed to belong to the famous eunuch. Yellow Bus No 69 and TransitLink No 303 from Komtar pass Batu Maung.

Back on the highway, the road climbs up, then drops down to Teluk Kumbar, from where you can detour to the fishing village of **Gertak Sanggul**, which has stalls on the seaside selling fresh fish. You'll pass some pint-sized scenic beaches on the way, although none are particularly good for swimming.

Balik Pulau

☎ 04

Balik Pulau is the main town on the island circuit. There are a number of restaurants and food stalls here, but no accommodation – circling the island has to be a one-day operation, unless you bring camping gear. Balik Pulau is a good place for lunch and the local speciality, *laksa balik pulau*, is a must. It's a tasty rice-noodle concoction with a thick fish-broth, mint leaves, pineapple slivers, onions and fresh chillies.

Balik's **Holy Name of Jesus Church** was built in 1854 and its twin spires stand impressively against the jungle behind.

Balik Pulau is the terminus of Yellow Bus No 66 from Georgetown. You can also take Yellow Bus No 85, which takes the inland route.

Sungai Pinang to Pantai Acheh

After Balik Pulau you pass through an area of Malay *kampung* and clove, nutmeg, rubber, even durian plantations. Sungai Pinang, a busy Chinese village built along a stagnant river, is worth a peek. Further on is the turn-off to Pantai Acheh, another small, isolated fishing village.

About 2km further north along the road to Teluk Bahang, the **Tropical Fruit Farm** (☎ 866 5168; 9am-5pm) raises over 140 types of tropical and sub-tropical fruit trees, native and hybrid. Visitors can stay, in return for helping on the farm (though you need to phone ahead to organise this). The two-hour tours (RM20) are very educational and include a fruit sampler tasting. Most visitors come on organised trips. The infrequent Yellow Bus No 76 runs between Balik Pulau and Teluk Bahang four times a day, passing Sungai Pinang and the fruit farm.

Titi Kerawang

☎ 04

After the turn-off to Pantai Acheh, the road starts to climb and twist, offering glimpses of the coast and the sea far below. During durian season, stalls are set up along the road selling the spiky orbs, and you can see nets strung below the trees themselves to protect the precious fruits when they fall.

The jungle becomes denser here and soon you reach Titi Kerawang. Until recently, a waterfall flowed into a natural swimming pool just off the road, but the nearby dam has left the stream a trickle.

As you descend towards the north coast you'll pass the new dam and come upon the **Forest Recreation Park**. Several kilometres south of Teluk Bahang, it has gentle trails through the jungle, a few small waterfall pools and a campsite. For more information, contact the Penang Tourist Guides Association (p159).

A little nearer the coast is the **Penang Butterfly Farm** (Map p175; ☎ 885 1253; 830 Jl Teluk Bahang; adult/child RM12.50/6.25; 9am-5pm Mon-Fri, 9am-6pm Sat & Sun) with several thousand live butterflies representing over 120 species. You can also see some fascinating beetles, lizards and spiders.

From here it's 1km north to the bus stop in Teluk Bahang, passing an **Orchid Garden** (Map p175) where the colourful display of blooms is sure to delight horticulturalists, and the **Craft Batik** (Map p175) factory and shop, a somewhat touristy and overpriced outlet for sarongs and the like, along the way.

Teluk Bahang

☎ 04

The village of Teluk Bahang marks the western end of the island's northern beach strip. It's a sleepy fishing village with not a great deal to see or do, other than take walks around the headland. The effluvia from the many fishing boats and the refuse washed down the river make this a dirty beach, but the stretch in front of the Mutiara Resort is good.

From Teluk Bahang you can trek down the beach to **Muka Head**, the isolated rocky promontory at the extreme northwestern corner of the island marked by a lighthouse, which is off-limits (note the barbed wire and the sign depicting a guard shooting a flailing civilian). The trail passes the University of Malaysia marine research station and the privately owned Teluk Duyong beach. South of Muka Head is **Pantai Keracut**, also called Monkey Beach, where there are shelters, pit toilets and lots of bird- and monkey-life; camping is permitted.

The **Pinang Cultural Centre** (☎ 885 1175), down the road from the Penang Mutiara Beach Resort, only opens for large, pre-arranged tour groups. Local handicraft exhibitions and cultural shows, including music and dancing are staged in the morning, at a cost of RM40 per person, while the nightly buffet and cultural show costs an extravagant RM110. A shuttle service from all beach hotels is included in the price.

SLEEPING

Penang Mutiara Beach Resort (☎ 885 2828; fax 885 2829; 1 Jl Teluk Bahang; s & d from RM650;) The biggest and most luxurious

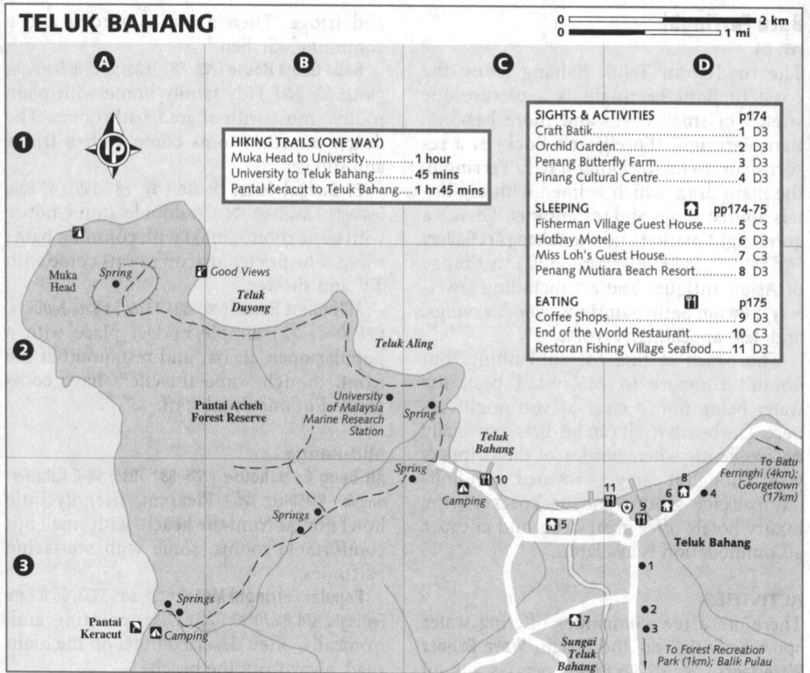

hotel development here, with an attractive and spotless beachfront location where the sand is raked and sifted with a net. Large comfortable rooms have balconies and big bathrooms. There's a water-sports centre, Chinese, Japanese and Italian restaurants, tennis and squash courts and a small putting green. Discounts are often available.

Miss Loh's Guest House (☎ 885 1227; 159 Jl Teluk Bahang; dm/s/d from RM8/15/20; ❄) This endearing place, set in a large garden, is so comfortable that some travellers end up staying a long, long time.

Fisherman Village Guest House (☎ 885 2936; Kampong Nelayan; s & d from RM20) This Malay fishing *kampung* offers simple, tidy rooms in a family home. Heading west from the roundabout, cross the water and take the first right after the T-intersection, then turn right again down a small lane and follow the signs.

Hotbay Motel (☎ 885 1323; s & d from RM50; ❄) In the main shopping area east of the roundabout, it offers good motel-style rooms; with air-con (RM65).

EATING

With all those fishing boats in the harbour, fresh and tasty seafood is guaranteed.

End of the World Restaurant (dishes from RM10) At the western end of the village by the jetty, this restaurant is famous; however, the seafood is overpriced and often just not very good.

Restoran Fishing Village Seafood (dishes from RM7) Expats in the know prefer this joint, hidden away just east of the End of the World.

The main shopping area along the road heading east to Batu Ferringhi also has a few coffee shops where you'll find cheaper Chinese dishes and seafood, as well as a couple of good South Indian places which sell *murtabak* and *dosa* (savoury Indian pancakes).

GETTING THERE & AWAY

Hin Bus No 93 runs from Georgetown every half-hour all the way along the north coast of the island as far as the roundabout in Teluk Bahang, as does the hourly Transit Link bus No 202.

Batu Ferringhi

☎ 04

The road from Teluk Bahang along the coast to Batu Ferringhi is a picturesque stretch of small coves and more beaches. Batu Ferringhi (Foreigner's Rock) is a resort strip stretching along Jl Batu Ferringhi, the main drag, which is lined with big hotels, tourist shops and restaurants. There's a good night market and the **Yahong Art Gallery** (☎ 881 1251; 58-D Batu Ferringhi) sells a vast range of Asian antiques and art including jewellery, pewter, batik paintings, woodcarvings, and, less appealingly, ivory.

The beach is fine for sunbathing, but doesn't compare to Malaysia's best, the water being not as clear as you might expect. The beach itself can be dirty, especially on weekends when hordes of day-trippers visit. Though it can get crowded with holiday package groups and backpackers, the luxury hotels offer great deals and cheaper accommodation is available.

ACTIVITIES

There are a few companies offering water sport activities on the beach. **Wave Runner Watersport** (☎ 012-405 0814) operates out of a small beach hut behind the Holiday Inn Resort. Among the activities on offer are jet skiing (RM70 for 30 minutes), water-skiing (RM50 for 15 minutes) and parasailing (RM40 for 15 minutes). You can also book a deep-sea fishing trip (RM500 for a full day).

SLEEPING

Batu Ferringhi, along with Teluk Bahang, was once a favourite stopover on the budget travellers' trail, and although there's still a clutch of backpacker hostels near the beach, these days the place is dominated by huge luxury developments. Outside high season (roughly December to February), big discounts are often available.

Budget

Shalini's Guest House (☎ 881 1859; 56 Batu Ferringhi; s/d from RM25/35; air-con) This old, two-storey wooden house has a friendly, family atmosphere. Rooms are basic but neat and some have balconies. Air-con doubles go for RM45.

Beng Keat Guest House (☎ 881 1987; 67-A Batu Ferringhi; r RM27-60; air-con) Comfortable ground-level chalet accommodation, all with TV and fridge. There's a nice garden and a communal kitchen.

Baba Guest House (☎ 881 1686; 52 Batu Ferringhi; r RM25-60; air-con) Tidy family home with plain rooms, most with shared bathrooms. The dearer air-con rooms come with a fridge and shower.

ET Budget Guest House (☎ 881 1553; 47 Batu Ferringhi; r RM20-60; air-con) A double-storey house with basic rooms, most with common bathroom. The pricier air-con rooms come with TV and shower.

Ali's Guest House (☎ 881 1316; 53 Batu Ferringhi; r RM30-65; air-con) Simple budget place with a popular open-air bar and restaurant at the front, though some travellers have complained of unhelpful staff.

Mid-Range

Ah Beng Guesthouse (☎ 881 1036; 54-C Batu Ferringhi; r RM50-60; air-con) Pleasant, friendly little hotel not far from the beach, with small but comfortable rooms, some with sea-facing balconies.

Popular Ferringhi Motel (☎ 881 3333; 66 Jl Batu Ferringhi; s/d RM70/90; air-con) Disappointing and, ironically, often deserted hotel on the main road, away from the beach.

Top End

Lone Pine Hotel (☎ 881 1511; www.lonepinehotel.com; 97 Jl Batu Ferringhi; r from RM385; air-con swimming pool) Batu Ferringhi's original hotel, established in 1948. In contrast to the nearby mega-resorts, it's a relatively small, low-rise hotel, with only 50 rooms, and it retains a charming old world, colonial ambience, though it has been completely renovated. Tastefully furnished rooms open out onto balconies or terraces with sea views, over a shady lawn just off the beach.

Shangri-La Rasa Sayang Resort (☎ 881 1966; www.shangri-la.com; Jl Batu Ferringhi; s/d from RM480/540; air-con internet swimming pool) Vast luxury resort on a fine stretch of beach. All rooms have balconies, many with sea views. There's a health club, tennis courts, putting green and several restaurants.

Shangri-La Golden Sands Resort (☎ 881 1911; fax 881 1880; Jl Batu Ferringhi; s & d from RM324; air-con internet swimming pool) A big luxury complex, under the same management as the neighbouring Rasa Sayang Resort, though not quite up to the same standard. Guests can use the facilities of both places.

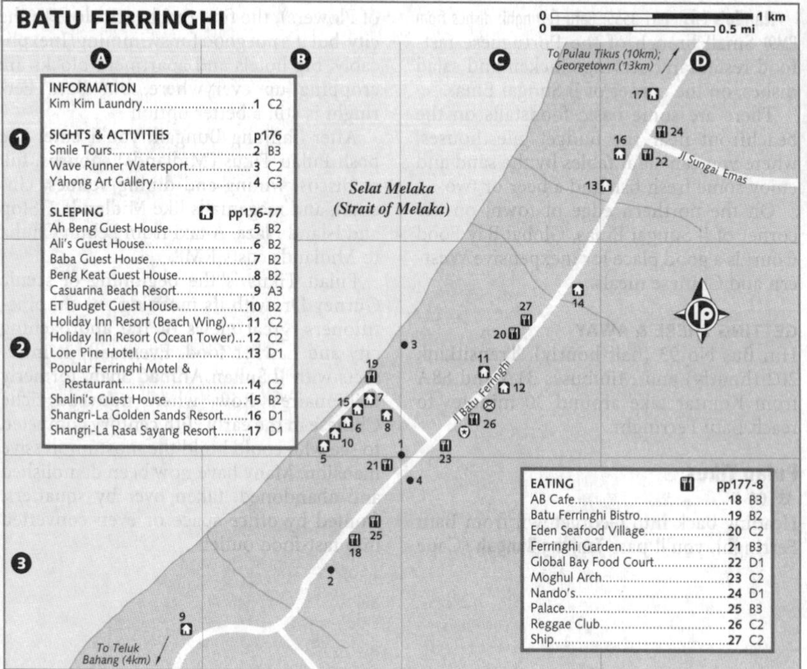

Holiday Inn Resort (☎ 881 1601; www.penang.holiday-inn.com; 72 Jl Batu Ferringhi; s & d from RM400;) Big, family-friendly resort with accommodation blocks either side of the main road; rooms in the sea-facing Beach Wing are dearer (from RM500). There's a wide range of rooms to choose from, including themed 'Kidsuites', which come with TV, video and playstation. There's also a well-equipped Kids Club, as well as a range of sporting activities for adults.

Casuarina Beach Resort (☎ 881 1711; www.casuarina.com; Jl Batu Ferringhi; r RM420;) Slightly ageing concrete resort at the western edge of the beach, with a good Italian restaurant and a British-style pub. A few pleasant beach bungalows are also available (RM865).

EATING & DRINKING

Ferringhi Garden (☎ 881 1193; 34C Jl Batu Ferringhi; dishes from RM16.80) Smart place serving up a varied menu of Western and Asian seafood, including lobster (RM45) and surf 'n' turf (RM48). Bottles of wine cost around RM79.

Eden Seafood Village (☎ 881 1236; 69A Jl Batu Ferringhi; dishes from RM24) Huge place serving seafood plucked from aquariums at the entrance. Prepared dishes include stir-fried cuttlefish and lobster. There are cultural shows and live music every evening.

Palace (☎ 881 1313; 78 Jl Batu Ferringhi; dishes from RM12) Very gaudily decorated Indian restaurant specialising in tandoori dishes, though it also serves Italian and Arabic cuisine.

Ship (☎ 881 2142; Jl Batu Ferringhi; dishes from RM28) You can't miss this one; it's a full-size replica of a wooden sailing ship, specialising in hefty steaks and seafood. It's quite smart inside, but rather dark.

Moghul Arch (☎ 881 1289; Jl Batu Ferringhi; dishes from RM7.50) A popular Indian restaurant serving a range of curries, tandoori and roti dishes.

AB Cafe (☎ 881 3220; Jl Batu Ferringhi; dishes from RM5) A good place for filling breakfasts of French toast, banana pancakes or oatmeal porridge.

Reggae Club (☎ 881 1743; Jl Batu Ferringhi, snacks RM3-4) Popular place to chat with other travellers over a cold beer.

Nando's (☎ 881 3555; Batu Ferringhi; dishes from RM9) Small branch of the Portuguese fast-food restaurant, serving chicken and salad dishes, on the corner of Jl Sungai Emas.

There are some basic foodstalls on the beachfront near the budget guesthouses, where you can sit at tables by the sand and enjoy some fresh fish and a beer or two.

On the northern edge of town, on the corner of Jl Sungai Emas, Global Bay Food Court is a good place for inexpensive Western and Chinese meals.

GETTING THERE & AWAY

Hin Bus No 93 (half-hourly), TransitLink 202 (hourly) and Minibuses 31A and 88A from Komtar take around 30 minutes to reach Batu Ferringhi.

Pulau Tikus

☎ 04

Heading back into Georgetown from Batu Ferringhi, you'll pass **Tanjung Bungah** (Cape of Flowers), the first real beach close to the city, but it's not good for swimming. Inexplicably, big hotels and apartment blocks are cropping up everywhere, but Batu Ferringhi is still a better option.

After Tanjung Bungah, you'll enter the posh Pulau Tikus (Midlands) suburbs, full of discos, wining-and-dining venues, cinemas, and megamalls like Midlands 1-Stop and Island Plaza. A taxi from Lebuh Chulia to Midlands costs RM8.

Pulau Tikus is the beginning of scenic Gurney Dr, with its morning t'ai chi practitioners, great views of the approaching city and hawker food. Eventually it intersects with Jl Sultan Ahmad Shah, formerly Millionaire's Row, where nouveau riche Chinese in the early 20th century competed to see who could build the most impressive mansion. Many have now been demolished and abandoned, taken over by squatters, fronted by office space or even converted into fast-food outlets.

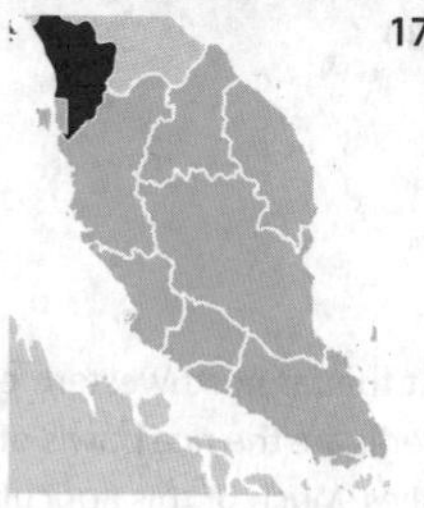

Kedah & Perlis

CONTENTS

At the far northwestern corner of Peninsular Malaysia, the picturesque states of Kedah and Perlis are the rice bowls of Malaysia, producing more than half of the country's domestic supplies. Much of this agricultural region is covered by a panoramic sea of rice paddies towered over by limestone outcrops that burst from the terrain.

Perlis, once part of Kedah, is also the smallest state in Malaysia (759 sq km), and both states are important gateways into Thailand. This northern area is also strongly Islamic. The state government of Perlis has recently enacted controversial legislation that effectively endorses polygamy (see Polygamy in Perlis p198) and has taken a hard-line, conservative stance on other social issues.

The top attraction here is the island resort of Pulau Langkawi, with its stunning beaches and jungle-clad hills. Although tourist development here is taking off, it's still possible to get away from it all on a quite beach.

Apart from Pulau Langkawi, this corner of Peninsular Malaysia sees very few tourists. Women travellers can expect more hassle here than elsewhere on the west coast, as social attitudes are more conservative.

HIGHLIGHTS

- Discovering Kedah's fascinating early history at the **Muzium Arkeologi** (p183) in Lembah Bujang
- Exploring the colonial town square and grand old buildings of **Alor Setar** (p185)
- Relaxing on one of the stunning beaches of **Pulau Langkawi** (p190)
- Driving the jungle road to the top of Langkawi's **Gunung Raya** (p191) to enjoy the spectacular views
- Swimming with the catfish in the clear lake waters of **Tasik Dayang Bunting** (p192)
- Hiking through the beautiful landscape of the **Taman Negara Perlis** (p199)

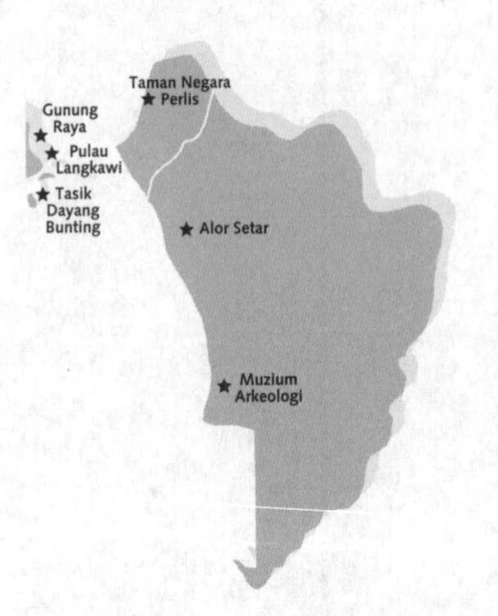

- TELEPHONE CODE: 04
- POPULATION: 1.85 MILLION
- AREA: 10,184 SQ KM

Climate

Kedah and Perlis both enjoy a typical tropical climate, with temperatures between 21° and 32°C throughout the year. The wettest time of year is between April and October, when the odd tropical storm can be expected, whereas there is intermittent rainfall and occasional downpours at other times. Pulau Langkawi tends to see less rain than the mainland. Humidity hovers at around 90%.

Dangers & Annoyances

Travellers crossing the land border into Malaysia from Thailand have reported a common scam practised by some travel operators. Foreigners are told that at the border crossing they need a certain amount of Malaysian ringgit (RM) to be allowed into the country (usually quite a high amount), and are then obliged to buy Malaysian currency at a highly disadvantageous rate. Don't be taken in by this con – it is not necessary to have a specified amount of Malaysian cash to cross the border.

Getting There & Away

The main train line and the Lebuhraya (North-South Hwy) run through Kedah and Perlis, heading southwards to Butterworth and beyond, and northwards to the Thai border. Alor Setar, the state capital of Kedah, is the main transport hub, with bus connections to most major cities on the peninsula.

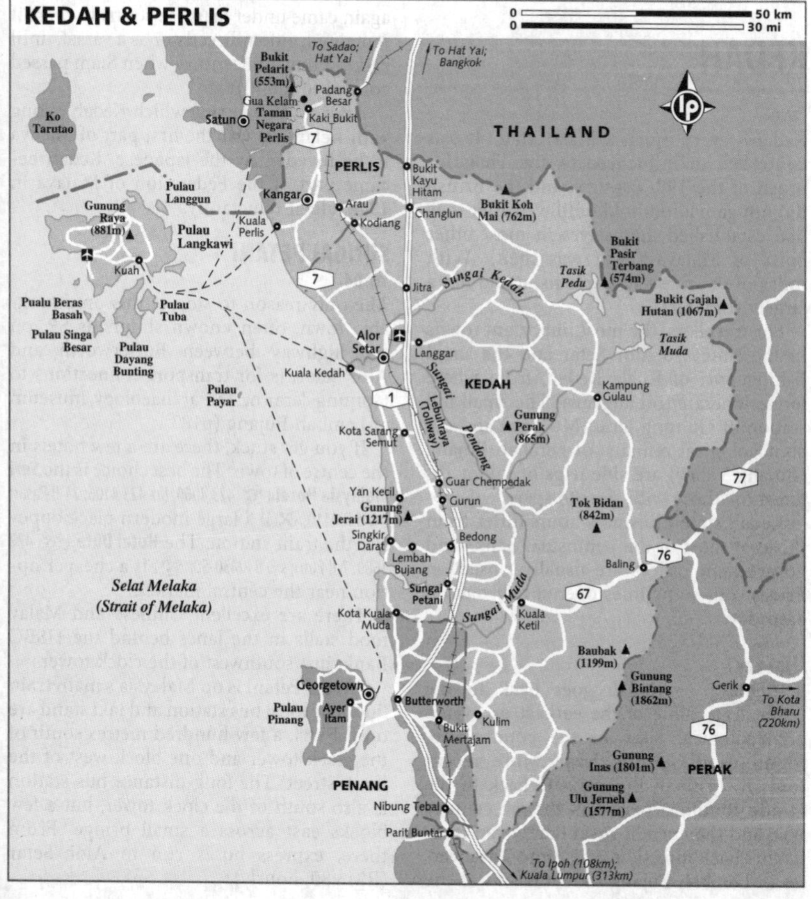

It also has an airport, with regular flights to KL. Bukit Kayu Hitam in Kedah and Padang Besar in Perlis are the border crossings into Thailand.

Langkawi can be reached by air from KL, Georgetown and Singapore and by ferry from Penang, Kuala Kedah and Kuala Perlis and from Satun in Thailand.

Getting Around

Most of the big towns in Kedah and Perlis are easily reached by bus. Trains are infrequent, often leave at inconvenient times and are not particularly useful for travelling within the two states. There is no public transport on Langkawi, and you will have to use taxis to get around, unless you rent a car or motorbike.

KEDAH

☎ 04

Kedah is very much a Malay state. It was controlled or influenced by the Thais for much of the 19th century, and the British did not gain a foothold until well after they had established themselves in most other parts of Malaya (as it was then). With miles of flat rice-paddy plains, it still has a largely rural feel.

For travellers, the most important towns in the state are Alor Setar and the small fishing port of Kuala Kedah, from where ferries operate to Langkawi. The small hill station of Gunung Jerai (Mt Jerai) and the archaeological remains of Lembah Bujang (Bujang Valley) are side trips of minor interest for those with time to spare.

Kedah state's business hours differ from those of most of the peninsula. Banks and government offices are usually closed on Friday, but sometimes open a half-day on Saturday.

History

Settlement in Kedah goes back to the Stone Age; some of the earliest excavated archaeological sites in the country are found near Gunung Jerai. More recent finds in Lembah Bujang date back to the Hindu-Buddhist period in the 4th century AD, and the current royal family can trace its line back directly to this time. Discoveries in Lembah Bujang show that it was the cradle of Hindu-Buddhist civilisation on the peninsula and one of the first places to come into contact with Indian traders.

During the 7th and 8th centuries, Kedah paid tribute to the Srivijaya Empire of Sumatra, but later fell under the influence of the Thais until the 15th century, when the rise of Melaka led to the Islamisation of the area. In the 17th century Kedah was attacked by the Portuguese, after their conquest of Melaka, and by the Acehnese, who saw Kedah as a threat to their own spice production.

In the hope that the British would help protect what remained of Kedah from Thailand, the sultan handed over Penang to the British in the late 18th century. Nevertheless in the early 19th century Kedah once again came under Siamese control, where it remained, either directly or as a vassal, until early in the 20th century when Siam passed control to the British.

After WWII, during which Kedah (along with Kelantan) was the first part of Malaya to be invaded by the Japanese, Kedah became part of the Federation of Malaya in 1948, albeit reluctantly.

SUNGAI PETANI

☎ 04

The only reason to stop at this unremarkable town, often known simply as SP, on the highway between Butterworth and Alor Setar, is for transport connections to Gunung Jerai or the archaeology museum at Lembah Bujang (p183).

If you get stuck, there are a few hotels in the centre of town. The best choice is the **Seri Malaysia Hotel** (☎ 423 4060; fax 423 4106; 21 Jl Pasar; s & d RM110; ❄), a large modern place opposite the train station. The **Hotel Duta** (☎ 422 1689; 7 Jl Putri; s & d RM30-50; ❄) is a cheaper option near the central market.

There are excellent Chinese and Malay food stalls in the lanes behind the HSBC Bank, just southwest of the clock tower.

Sungai Petani is on Malaysia's main train line. The local bus station and taxi stand are on Jl Putri, a few hundred metres south of the clock tower and one block west of the main street. The long-distance bus station is also south of the clock tower, but a few blocks east across a small bridge. From there, express buses run to Alor Setar (RM3.80, hourly).

LEMBAH BUJANG

☎ 04

The area west of Sungai Petani was home to the most important Hindu-Buddhist kingdom on the Malay peninsula, dating from the 4th century AD. By the 7th century AD it was part of the large Srivijaya Empire of Sumatra, and it reached its architectural peak in the 9th and 10th centuries. Hindu and Buddhist temples were scattered from Gunung Jerai south to Kuala Muda, and in Lembah Bujang alone 50 archaeological sites have been already excavated.

The kingdom traded with India and the Khmer and Srivijaya kingdoms, and was visited by the well-travelled Chinese monk I-Tsing in AD 671. In 1025 Srivijaya and Bujang were attacked by the Cholas of India, but the Lembah Bujang kingdom later forged an alliance with the Cholas against the waning Srivijaya Empire. The region continued to trade, but by the 14th century its significance had faded and the temples were deserted with the coming of Islam. They remained buried in the jungle until first excavated by British archaeologist HG Quaritch-Wales in 1936.

Along the banks of Sungai Bujang, the **Muzium Arkeologi** (Archaeological Museum; ☎ 457 2005; admission free; ⌚ 9am-5pm) chronicles the excavations, and displays stone carvings, pottery shards and other finds from the digs. Most of the carvings have been lost, though the temples were not noted for extravagant carvings like those of contemporaneous Borobudur in Java. Only a handful of items are on display, such as a fragment of a wall frieze and a statue of the elephant god Ganesh. Most numerous are the Shivaite yoni fertility stones.

Though of enormous archaeological significance, the exhibits are neither breathtaking nor well labelled. The most interesting exhibit is the partially restored *candi* (temples) behind the museum, but even these are unadorned and only the bases of most remain. The largest and most significant temple is 1000-year-old **Candi Bukit Batu Pahat**. The entire complex is scheduled to become a National Historic Park when excavations are complete, but this is a long way off.

The museum is off the Tanjung Dawai road, 2km north of the village of Merbok. From Sungai Petani, take a taxi (RM50) or one of the buses that run roughly every hour to Tanjung Dawai, get off at Merbok (RM1.40) and walk the 2km to the museum.

GUNUNG JERAI

At 1217m, forest-clad Gunung Jerai dominates the surrounding flat plains. It was a sacred mountain in the ancient Hindu period and a landmark for ships from India and Indonesia.

From the base of the mountain, a steep and narrow road snakes its way 13km through a forest recreation park to a sleepy hill resort. From here there are expansive views north across the rice paddies of Kedah and over to Langkawi. As hill resorts go, this is definitely a minor one, well off the tourist route. Bring a friend, or lots of books.

There are few opportunities for hiking or exploring away from the paved road. The road itself continues 3km past the resort to the peak and the remains of Candi Telaga Sembilan, a 6th-century Hindu bathing shrine, but the area is the property of the defence ministry and is off limits.

A few kilometres downhill from the resort is a tiny **forestry museum** with exhibits on native trees and their uses, but little on the mountain's flora and fauna. The highlight is an enormous fossilised elephant dropping. From the museum a paved trail leads through the forest to a waterfall and bathing pools.

Sleeping & Eating

Perangian Gunung Jerai (☎ 423 4345; s & d RM40-50; ⊠) The only place to stay, a low-key resort with accommodation in modern but worn chalets. Camping costs RM3 per site, plus RM2 per person (but tents cannot be hired). There's also a restaurant at the resort, serving Malaysian and Western dishes from around RM10.

Getting There & Away

Gunung Jerai is about 30km north of Sungai Petani, and the turn-off is 3km north of Gurun just before Guar Chempedak. From the car park at the bottom of the mountain, 10-seat minibuses run up to the resort approximately every 45 minutes from 8.30am to 5pm (RM4). Private vehicles can also use the road.

Although the local No 2 bus between Sungai Petani and Alor Setar passes right by the car park on Hwy 1, the express services use the Lebuhraya (North-South Hwy) instead. From Sungai Petani you could also take a taxi or a local Guar Chempedak bus to the car park.

ALOR SETAR

☎ 04

Also known as Alor Star, the capital of Kedah state is 93km north of Butterworth, on the main road to the Thai border. It's the turn-off point to Kuala Kedah, for ferries to Pulau Langkawi. Few travellers spend time here but it's worth a brief stopover before heading for Langkawi or off inland.

Alor Setar's long association with Thailand is evident in the Thai temples scattered around the city, but it's the area around the Padang, the old colonial town square, that draws most attention. Here you'll find some grand historic buildings, including the Masjid Zahir (Zahir Mosque) and the Balai Besar hall.

Since Alor Setar was under Thai suzerainty until the 1909 Anglo-Siamese Treaty transferred rights to the British, the city shows fewer signs of Western colonial influence, and it is very much a Malay town, with fewer Chinese and Indians than other west-coast cities. The Indian community, centred northwest of the Padang, stays lively with hawker stalls and epic Hindi

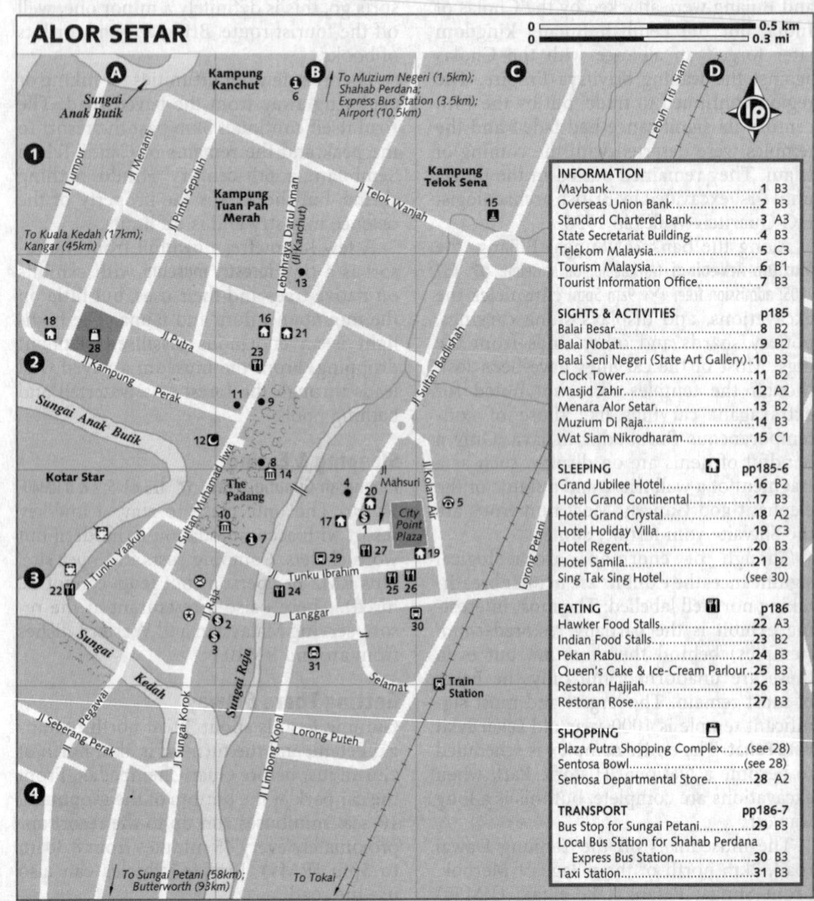

movies blaring from video shops, whereas the modest Chinatown, situated where Sungai Anak Butik flows into Sungai Kedah, is crammed with hawker stalls and crumbling shophouses.

Information

There are numerous Internet cafés in City Point Plaza; all charge around RM3 per hour. Banks, including branches of Maybank, are located around the town centre.

Tourist offices:

Tourism Malaysia Office (☎ 730 1322; 179B Kompleks Alor Setar, Lebuhraya Darul Aman; 🕒 9am-5pm, closed Fri) Small office out of town, which might relocate in 2004. Staff can answer queries by phone.

Tourist Information Office (☎ 731 2322; Jl Raya; 🕒 9am-5pm, closed Fri) Hands out a small range of useful brochures.

Sights

THE PADANG

The large, open town square has a number of distinctive buildings around its perimeter. The open-sided **Balai Besar** (Royal Audience Hall) was built in 1898 and is still used by the sultan of Kedah for royal and state ceremonies, though it is not open to the public. Supported on tall pillars topped with Victorian iron lacework, it also shows Thai influences in its decoration.

Around the side of the Balai Besar is the **Muzium Di Raja** (Royal Museum), which served as the royal palace for the sultan and other members of the family from 1856. It was closed for long-term repairs at the time of writing, though you can still see some of the royal carriages and boats in the courtyard.

At the southern edge of the square is the **Balai Seni Negeri**, the state art gallery, has been closed for major renovation; its small but fascinating collection of contemporary Malaysian art should be back in place by 2004.

On the western side of the square is the **Masjid Zahir**, the state mosque. It is one of the largest and grandest mosques in Malaysia, and with its Moorish domes and Mogul minarets, it looks like a vision from *The Arabian Nights*.

Further north, the **Balai Nobat** (Hall of Drums), an octagonal tower topped by an onion-shaped dome, houses the *nobat* (royal orchestra). The *nobat* is principally composed of percussion instruments, and the drums in this orchestra are said to have been a gift from the sultan of Melaka in the 15th century. It isn't open to the public, and the instruments are brought out only on special occasions.

On the opposite side of the road, the decorative **clock tower**, painted in the same yellow and white livery as the Balai Nobat, was erected in the early 1900s so that the muezzin at the neighbouring mosque would know when to call the faithful to prayer.

Further north stands the **Menara Alor Setar** (Telekom Tower) which, at 165.5m, is the tallest structure in town.

WAT SIAM NIKRODHARAM

This Thai Buddhist temple was built mostly by donations from the local Chinese community. There's an elaborate sculpture garden, and a golden Garuda hovers over the entry to the main hall, inside of which sits a recognisably Thai image of the Buddha in the 'subduing Mara' posture. Along the outer walls of the temple grounds are inscriptions of the Buddha's teaching in three languages.

MUZIUM NEGERI

The **Muzium Negeri** (State Museum; ☎ 733 1162; Lebuhraya Darul Aman; admission free; 🕒 10am-6pm) is 2km north of the Padang. The small collection includes early Chinese porcelain, artefacts from archaeological excavations at Lembah Bujang, and dioramas of royal and rural Malaysian life. A fabulous 'gold and silver tree', produced as a yearly tribute in the days when Siam ruled Kedah, stands near the entrance.

Most local buses from town to the express bus station pass by the museum. A taxi from the town centre costs RM5.

Sleeping

Alor Setar isn't overly blessed with good hotel accommodation. Most can be found within the compact city centre, though mid-range options are few and overpriced. Budget places, scattered around the city, are often pretty shabby affairs, more used to migrant workers than foreign tourists.

Sing Tak Sing Hotel (☎ 732 5482; 74 Jl Langgar; s & d RM27-38) Slightly seedy, grubby place over the local bus station, with basic fan rooms with or without bathroom.

Grand Jubilee Hotel (☎ 733 0055; 429 Lebuhraya Darul Aman; s & d RM38-49; ❄) White concrete box, set back from the road, opposite the Hotel Samila, offering plain but clean rooms with fan or air-con.

Hotel Regent (☎ 731 1900; 1536-G Jl Sultan Badlishah; s/d RM66/77; ❄) Small modern hotel in the centre of town with decent rooms, but it can be rather noisy.

Hotel Samila (☎ 731 8888; 27 Lebuhraya Darul Aman; s & d RM87; ❄) Somewhat dated, downbeat place north of the centre, which is overpriced for what's on offer, though there's a good café downstairs.

Hotel Grand Crystal (☎ 731 3333; fax 731 6368; 40 Jl Kg Perak; s & d RM100; ❄ 🖳) Smaller sister hotel of the Grand Continental, located down a quiet side street near the mosque. Rooms are pretty average, but staff are friendly and helpful.

Hotel Grand Continental (☎ 733 5917; 134 Jl Sultan Badlishah; s & d RM115-135; ❄) Modern and very central high-rise chain hotel, which offers a good standard of comfort, though it's rather lacking in character. Discounts are often available.

Holiday Villa (☎ 734 9999; 162 Jl Tunku Ibrahim; s & d from RM190; ❄ 🖳) Far and away the best hotel in town, with spacious, tastefully furnished rooms and a range of facilities including a gym, sauna and shopping arcade.

Eating

QUICK EATS

Queen's Cake & Ice Cream Parlour (☎ 731 9400; 33 Jl Tunku Ibrahim; dishes from RM3) A pleasant little café serving up a wide range of Western dishes such as fish and chips as well as the usual rice and noodle options. There's also a bakery at the front.

Pekan Rabu (Wednesday Market; Jl Langgar) This goes on all day, every day, until late at night. Ground floor food-stalls sell all manner of local fare; look for the *dodol durian*, a local sweet made from sticky rice, coconut and, yes, durian.

Food stalls along the riverbank serve typical Malaysian hawker fare until late. Indian food stalls about 1km south of the Telekom Tower sell takeaway snacks and mountains of Indian sweets.

RESTAURANTS

City One (☎ 732 2600; 3rd fl, City Point Plaza; dishes from RM10) Smart restaurant inside the City Point Plaza shopping mall, serving very good Asian and Western food, plus some more unusual options such as stir-fried ostrich.

Restoran Hajijah (☎ 731 3997; Jl Tunku Ibrahim; dishes from RM4) Ever-busy Thai Muslim place serving tasty curries and simple rice dishes, including good vegetarian options.

Restoran Rose (☎ 731 3471; Jl Sultan Baldishah; dishes from RM4) Popular Indian restaurant serving up a range of curries, roti and biryani dishes.

Getting There & Away

Alor Setar is 48km from the Bukit Kayu Hitam border to Thailand. Frequent buses go to the border, from where minibus taxis go to Hat Yai (see Bukit Kayu Hitam p196 for this border crossing). A direct train via the Padang Besar border may be quicker and is certainly more convenient.

AIR

Sultan Abdul Halim Airport is 11km north of town just off the Lebuhraya. **Malaysia Airlines** (☎ 731 1106) flies four times daily to Kuala Lumpur (RM123 to RM183). There are a few car-rental agencies at the airport, including **Hertz** (☎ 714 4959).

BUS

The small bus station on Jl Langgar handles only local buses, including the regular shuttle service to the Shahab Perdana express bus station on Jl Mergong, 4km north of the town centre (60 sen). A taxi costs RM6. All long-distance buses leave from here.

Frequent buses depart throughout the day for Bukit Kayu Hitam (RM3), Kangar (RM3) and Kuala Kedah (RM1). There are also regular coaches, operated by several different companies, to KL (RM26), Ipoh (RM17), Butterworth (RM6.30), Melaka (RM33) and Johor Bahru (RM45), as well as to east-coast destinations including Kuantan (RM35), Kuala Terengganu (RM33.60) and Kota Bharu (RM22.50).

Buses to Sungai Petani (RM3.70, 1 hour) stop on Jl Tunku Ibrahim opposite the Pekan Rabu market.

TAXI

Rates for a four-passenger taxi from the taxi station include RM25 to Bukit Kayu Hitam, RM48 to Butterworth, RM20 to Kangar, RM12 to Kuala Kedah and RM30 to Padang Besar.

TRAIN

The **train station** (☎ 731 4045; Jl Stesyen) is southeast of the town centre. The daily northbound train to Hat Yai in Thailand leaves at 8.40am, arriving at 10.15am, Thai time (RM8, 2½ hours). In the opposite direction, the train to KL departs at 7.11pm, reaching the capital at 8.20am the following morning (RM31).

KUALA KEDAH

☎ 04

This busy fishing village 11km from Alor Setar is the southern gateway to Langkawi. **Kota Kuala Kedah** is a fort, built around 1770, opposite the town on the far bank of Sungai Kedah. Constructed to protect this main port from Siam, it fell to the Thais in 1821. On show are the walls, cannons and gateway of the partially restored fort.

Ferries to Langkawi leave approximately every half-hour (1½ hours from April to October, the wet season) from 7am to 7pm (RM15).

PULAU LANGKAWI

☎ 04

The 104 islands of the Langkawi group are 30km off the coast from Kuala Perlis, at the northern end of Peninsular Malaysia bordering Thailand. They're accessible by boat from Penang, Kuala Perlis, Kuala Kedah and Satun, Thailand, or by air from Penang, KL and Singapore.

The only island with any real settlement is 478.5 sq km Pulau Langkawi, which has interior jungle-clad hills and some stunning beaches scattered around the coast. Since Langkawi was declared a duty-free zone in 1986, the island has been heavily promoted as one of the country's premier tourist destinations. Since then luxury hotels have sprung up around secluded bays and numerous shopping complexes have appeared in the main town, Kuah.

Recent efforts have been made to broaden Langkawi's appeal beyond simple beach holidays, with the construction of a host of artificial tourist attractions, along with major events including the Langkawi International Maritime and Aerospace (LIMA) exhibition around November and the biennial Langkawi International Festival of Arts (LIFA). Away from the built-up areas Langkawi is still a rural Malay island of small villages, rice paddies, water buffalo and natural beauty.

Orientation

Kuah, in the southeast corner of the island, is the main town and the arrival point for the ferries, but the beaches are elsewhere.

On Langkawi's west coast, the most developed beach is Pantai Cenang, crammed with mostly budget to mid-range hotels and restaurants. The water there can be murky and jellyfish are occasionally seen. Pantai Tengah is a southerly continuation of Pantai Cenang. The beach at Pantai Kok is reputedly one of the best on the island, and is lined with a string of luxury resorts.

The airport is on the island's central-west coast near Kuala Muda. There are a few isolated resorts here, but the beach is pretty poor.

LEGENDARY LANGKAWI

The name Langkawi combines the old Malay words *helang* (eagle) and *kawi* (strong). Classical Malay literature claims the island as one of the resting places of Garuda, the mythological bird that became Vishnu's vehicle. The whole island is steeped in legends, and the favourite story is of Mahsuri, a maiden who was wrongly accused of infidelity. Before finally allowing herself to be executed, she put a curse on the island for seven generations. As proof of her innocence, white blood flowed from her veins, turning the sands of Langkawi's beaches white. Her mausoleum can be seen near Kuah (p189).

Another legend concerns the naming of places around the island. Pulau Langkawi's two most powerful families became involved in a bitter argument over a marriage proposal. A fight broke out and all the kitchen utensils were used as missiles. The gravy *(kuah)* was spilt at Kuah and seeped into the ground at Kisap ('to seep'). A pot landed at Belanga Perak (Broken Pot) and finally the saucepan of hot water *(air panas)* came to land where Air Hangat village is today. The fathers of these two families got their comeuppance for causing all this mayhem – they are now the island's two major mountain peaks.

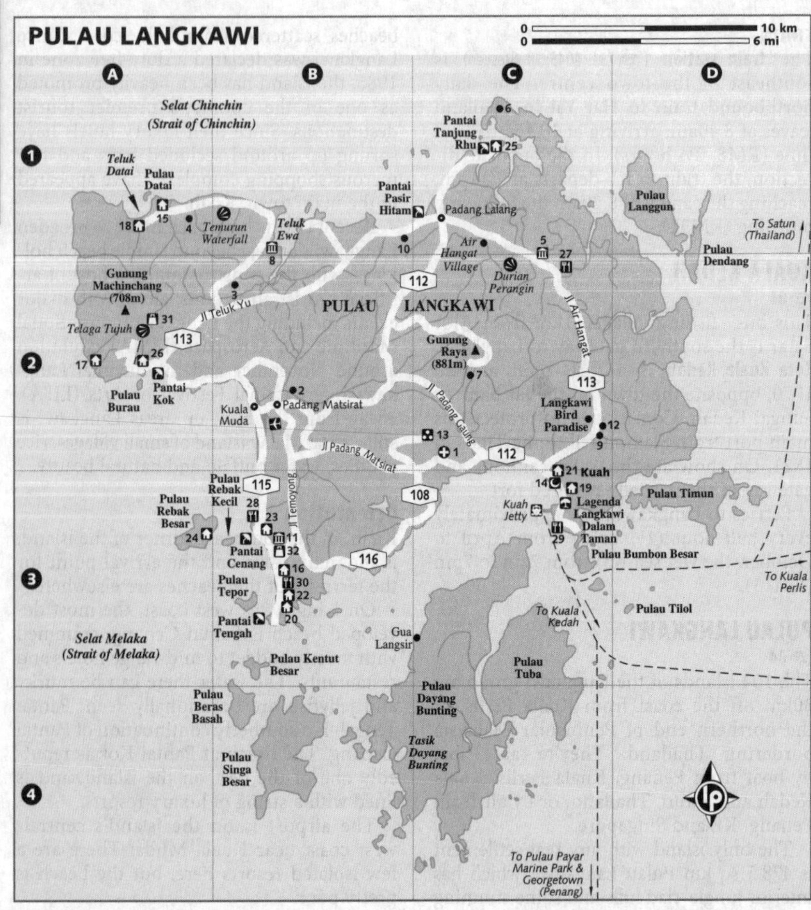

Along the north coast of the island are more upmarket resorts, two at Teluk Datai in the west and one at Tanjung Rhu in the east. Tanjung Rhu is a beautiful beach with white sand, turquoise waters and a panoramic view of rock islands off the coast, which you can practically walk to during low tide.

Information

For Internet access, try the **Langkawi Online Café** (☎ 966 6602; 79 Jl Kelibang, Kuah) at RM4 per hour.

The only banks on the island are at Kuah. Unlike elsewhere in Kedah, the banks here are usually open on Friday, but closed on Saturday and Sunday. You'll also find moneychangers tucked into and around the duty-free shops. There are a few moneychangers at Pantai Cenang but elsewhere you'll have to rely on the resort hotels, and they might not change money if you're not a guest at the hotel.

Tourism Malaysia (☎ 966 7789; fax 966 7889; Jl Persiaran Putra, Kuah; 🕑 9am-1pm & 2-6pm) hands out an excellent array of brochures and gives comprehensive information on the whole island.

INTERNET RESOURCES

www.langkawi-online.com One of the most comprehensive sources of information.

www.mylangkawi.com The official travel website, also worth a look.

INFORMATION	
Hospital	1 C2
Tourism Malaysia	(see 14)
SIGHTS & ACTIVITIES	**pp189-91**
Burnt Rice Area	2 B2
CHOGM Park	(see 14)
Crocodile Adventureland	3 B2
Datai Bay Golf Club	4 A1
Galeria Perdana	5 C1
Gua Cerita	6 C1
Gunung Raya Golf Resort	7 C2
Ibrahim Hussein Museum	8 B1
Kedah Marble	9 C2
Kompleks Budaya Kraf	10 B1
Laman Padi	11 B3
Langkawi Cable Car	(see 31)
Langkawi Crystaal	12 C2
Mahsuri's Tomb	13 C2
Masjid Al-Hana	14 C3
Underwater World	(see 32)
SLEEPING	**pp192-4**
Andaman Resort	15 A1
Aseania Resort	16 B3
Berjaya Langkawi Beach & Spa Resort	17 A2
Casa del Mar	(see 23)
Datai Langkawi	18 A1
Gates	19 C3
Holiday Villa	20 B3
Hotel Asia	21 C3
Hotel Central	(see 21)
Hotel Langkasuka	(see 21)
Langkawi Village Resort	22 B3
Oriental Village Inn	(see 31)
Pelangi Beach Resort	23 B3
Rebak Marina Resort	24 A3
Sheraton Langkawi Beach Resort	(see 26)
Tanjung Rhu Resort	25 C1
Tanjung Sanctuary Langkawi	26 A2
EATING	**pp194-5**
Barn Thai	27 C2
Bon Ton	28 B3
Charlie's Place	29 C3
Lighthouse	(see 30)
Prawn Village Restaurant	(see 21)
Sunvillage Restaurant	30 B3
SHOPPING	**pp195-6**
Oriental Village	31 A2
Zon Shopping Complex	32 B3

TRAVEL AGENCIES

Keng Chuan Travel (☎ 966 9688; 2 Jl Pandak Mayah 2, Kuah) Runs an array of tours around Langkawi.

Legend Admire Travel & Tours (☎ 966 9116; 13 Jl Pandak Mayah 4, Kuah) This leading tour operator runs a wide variety of trips around the island and to Pulau Payar.

Silver Miracle Travel (☎ 955 9341; silvermiracle@hotmail.com; 15 Jl Pantai Cenang) Organises various tours and books ferry tickets.

Sights & Activities

KUAH

The small fishing village of Kuah is the island's main town. Apart from the plethora of duty-free outlets and souvenir shops, there's little to stop you proceeding to the beaches. There are a number of newly built luxury hotels in Kuah, and the town centre, just over a kilometre from the jetty, is the only place on the island where you'll find banks.

Out of town, towards the jetty, is Kuah's picturesque **Masjid Al-Hana**. Its golden dome and Moorish arches rise above the palm trees of **CHOGM Park**, which, as a plaque proudly claims, was the site of the first ever international coconut-tree climbing championship in 1987 (won by Sri Lanka). Next to the jetty, the **Lagenda Langkawi Dalam Taman** (☎ 966 4223; Jl Persiaran Putra; adult/child RM5/2.50; 🕑 8am-7pm) is an uninspiring 'folklore' theme park stretching along the waterfront. The international- standard **Gunung Raya Golf Resort** (☎ 966 8148; www.golfgr.com.my; Jl Air Hangat; 🕑 7am-7pm) is around 8km north of town, in a spectacular location in the foothills of Langkawi's highest mountain. Green fees are RM150/200 for 9/18 holes.

Just south of the golf club is **Langkawi Crystaal** (☎ 966 1555; 1804 Jl Kisap; admission free; 🕑 9am-6pm), Malaysia's only glass-blowing works, and next door, the **Kedah Marble** quarry. Both are open to visitors, and are popular with stop-and-shop tour buses.

In the same area you'll find **Langkawi Bird Paradise** (☎ 966 5855; Jl Kisap; adult/child RM15/8; 🕑 9am-6pm), a very pleasant tropical garden where you can see 150 species of exotic birds, including toucans, hornbills and flamingoes.

A little further on is **Galeria Perdana** (☎ 959 1498; Mukim Kisap; admission RM3; 🕑 9am-6pm), established by Prime Minister Dr Mahathir to display hundreds of gifts bestowed on the state by foreign nations. While this may not sound enticing, the gallery is a showcase for the very best of Asian traditional crafts, as well as those of places as far flung as Africa and the South Pacific. Cambodian silver, Indonesian wayang kulit puppets and woodcarvings from Easter Island are just a sampling of the collection.

MAHSURI'S TOMB & PADANG MATSIRAT

These historic sites are west of Kuah, a few kilometres off the road leading to the west-coast beaches and to the airport. Mahsuri was a legendary Malay princess, unjustly accused of adultery and sentenced to death. Her magical powers were so great that all attempts to execute her failed until the indignant Mahsuri agreed to die, but not before issuing the curse that 'there shall be no peace or prosperity on this island for seven generations'. The disappointing **Mahsuri Mausoleum** (☎ 012-418 4033; Mukim Ula Melaka; admission RM2;

7.30am-6pm), however, is nothing more than a fenced-in slab of white stone.

A result of Mahsuri's curse can still sometimes be seen in the 'field of burnt rice' at nearby **Padang Matsirat**. There, villagers once burnt their rice fields rather than allow them to fall into the hands of Siamese invaders. It is said that heavy rain still sometimes brings traces of burnt grains to the surface.

PANTAI CENANG

This 2km-long beach strip lies at the southwestern corner of Langkawi, 25km from Kuah. Pantai Cenang is where almost all of Langkawi's beach chalets are concentrated. It has a good range of restaurants, bars and shops, though outside peak season it's still a fairly quiet and relaxed place.

A sandbar appears at low tide, allowing you to inspect the local sea life. Between November and January you can walk across this sandbar to the nearby island of **Pulau Rebak Kecil**, but only for two hours around low tide. Another nearby island is **Pulau Tepor**, which can be reached by hired boat from Pantai Cenang.

At the southern end of Pantai Cenang is the Zon duty-free shopping complex and **Underwater World** (955 6100; adult/child RM18/10; 10am-6pm), a large aquarium with a walk-through tunnel for peering at the many varieties of fish above you.

At the northern end right opposite the Casa del Mar hotel is the **Laman Padi** (Rice Garden; 955 4312; admission free; 10am-6pm), which has eye-catching rice fields and landscaped gardens in the grounds. The museum exhibits inside tell you (in English) everything you could possibly want to know about rice cultivation.

PANTAI TENGAH

Pantai Tengah is a smaller, quieter beach just south of Pantai Cenang after the road skirts around a small rocky point. There are a few big, all-inclusive resorts here, popular with young families, as well as some more basic chalets. There are also some excellent restaurants.

PANTAI KOK

On the western part of the island, 12km north of Pantai Cenang, Pantai Kok fronts a beautiful bay surrounded by limestone mountains and jungle. The water here isn't necessarily clearer than at any of the other beaches, however. The grandiose building stretching out into the water is the **Summer Palace** (959 2599; adult/child RM5/3.5; 9am-5pm), a set made for the 1999 movie *Anna & the King*; it now houses a collection of props, costumes and other memorabilia from the film.

Heading inland from Pantai Kok, you'll come across the Oriental Village shopping complex, where you'll find the station for the **Langkawi Cable Car** (959 3688; www.langkawicablecar.com; adult/child RM15/10; 10am-7pm). It will whisk you to the top of the majestic Gunung Machinchang (708m) for some magnificent views over Langkawi and the Andaman Sea. Note that temperatures on the top of the mountain will be 4° to 5° lower than at sea level.

TELAGA TUJUH

Telaga Tujuh is a 2.5km walk inland from Pantai Kok, just north of Oriental Village. Water cascades nearly 100m down a hillside through a series of seven *(tujuh)* wells *(telaga)*. You can slide down from one of these shallow pools to another near the top of the falls – the stone channels are very smooth.

You can also get there by rented car, motorbike or taxi; drive to the end of the road, about 1km past Pantai Kok, then turn along with the road to the right until you reach the car park. From here it's a steady 10-minute climb through the rainforest (stay to the right) to the wells at the top of the falls.

TELUK DATAI

The beaches and jungle around Teluk Datai are some distance off the main road around the island. Here you'll find Langkawi's most exclusive resorts and the upmarket **Datai Bay Golf Club** (959 2620). The resorts' beautiful beaches are only for guests, and day-trippers will unfailingly be driven away. The road continues past the resort to a headland where a short trail takes you through the jungle and down to the sea – a pleasant spot, but there is no beach to speak of.

On the way to Teluk Datai is **Crocodile Adventureland** (959 2559; adult/child RM15/10; 9am-6pm) where you can view saltwater crocodiles at various stages of their development, with twice-daily shows and hourly feedings. The 'stunt' shows and the shop selling a huge range of crocodile skin products won't be to everyone's taste, however.

Further along where the road turns west along the coast to Teluk Datai is the **Ibrahim Hussein Foundation Museum** (☎ 959 4669; www.gtitec.com.my/museums/kedibmus.htm; admission RM12; 10am-6pm). Completed in 1998, it is a quiet retreat in the forest. The museum displays the abstract and multi-media works of its founder, Ibrahim Hussein, some of whose work comments on Asian politics.

Temurun Waterfall is halfway between the museum and the resorts. The high falls are worth a look; the turn-off is just east of a huge concrete archway spanning the road.

PANTAI PASIR HITAM

Further eastwards along the north coast, this beach is noted for its black sand, although it's not a real black-sand beach – it only has streaks of black caused by a spring that deposits mineral oxides. It's really a contrived attraction, as the beach is only a couple of metres wide and is at the foot of a 5m drop, so you can't walk along it. The waters off Pasir Hitam are dotted with huge boulders, and the only other notable sight is the unique Y-shaped jetty.

Before reaching the beach, you'll pass the **Kompleks Budaya Kraf** (☎ 959 1913; admission free; 10am-6pm), an enormous handicrafts centre built in an extravagant neo-Islamic style. A wide range of regional and Malaysian-made goods are on sale, from batik and ikat to pottery and woodcarvings, though you can also find everything in KL and Penang.

TANJUNG RHU

Just beyond Pasir Hitam at the village of Padang Lalang there's a roundabout with a turn-off to the north to Tanjung Rhu, while the main road continues back to Kuah.

Tanjung Rhu has one of Langkawi's wider and better beaches. The water is shallow, and at low tide you can walk across the sandbank to the neighbouring islands, except during the monsoon season. The water swirls across the bank as the tide comes in. There are mangrove cruises, and kayaks can be hired.

Around the promontory, accessible by hired boat, is the **Gua Cerita** (Cave of Legends). Along the coast for a couple of kilometres before the beach, the tiny fish known as *ikan bilis* (anchovies) are spread out on mats to dry in the sun.

GUNUNG RAYA

The tallest mountain on the island (881m) can be reached by a snaking, paved road through the jungle. It is a spectacular drive to the top with views across the island and over to Thailand. At the top there's a lookout point and a small tea house with spectacular views, when it's not fogged over. Access to the mountain may occasionally be restricted by the government; the gate at the foot of the mountain will be lowered.

AIR HANGAT VILLAGE

This **hot-springs village** (☎ 959 1357; admission free; 9am-6pm) is towards the north of the island, not far from the turn-off to Tanjung Rhu. There's not much to see or do here, but as with so many places on Langkawi, the springs are associated with an intriguing legend (see boxed text Legendary Langkawi, p187).

DURIAN PERANGIN

Roughly 15km north of Kuah is the turn-off to these waterfalls, which are 3km off the main road. In the dry season they are not very spectacular, though the swimming pools, 10 minutes walk up through the forest, are always refreshingly cool. The falls are best seen at the end of the monsoon season: late September and early October.

Tours

There are travel agents in Kuah, along Pantai Cenang and at most upmarket resorts that organise tours (see Travel Agencies, p189). One of the most popular day trips is the **Island Hopping Tour**, offered by most companies and costing around RM35. The tour usually takes in Pulau Dayang Bunting and Pulau Singa Besar, which, at the time of writing, was home only to an abandoned zoo and a couple of emaciated horses, although there are plans to develop a wildlife sanctuary here. A stop at the undeveloped beach on Pulau Beras Basah is often included.

Eagle Feeding Tours (RM75-90) give an opportunity to see Langkawi's famous brahminy kite eagles and sea eagles up close, and usually include a trip to the mangroves and stopovers at a couple of islands. During the monsoon season from July to mid-September, the seas are usually too rough and unpredictable for boat trips.

There are also cheap sightseeing (read shopping) half-day tours that include Galeria Perdana, Langkawi Crystaal and Tanjung Rhu (RM35).

PULAU DAYANG BUNTING

Tasik Dayang Bunting (Lake of the Pregnant Maiden) is located on the island of the same name. It is a freshwater lake surrounded by craggy limestone cliffs and dense jungle, and is good for swimming. You can also rent a pedalo for a spin round the lake, or just sit on the edge of the jetty and have your toes nibbled by the resident catfish.

A legend states that a childless couple, after 19 years of unsuccessful effort, had a baby girl after drinking from this lake. Since then it has been a popular pilgrimage destination for those hoping for children. Legend also says that the lake is inhabited by a large white crocodile.

Also on Pulau Dayang Bunting north of the lake is **Gua Langsir** (Cave of the Banshee), which is inhabited by thousands of bats. Most of the island-hopping tours give it a miss.

PULAU PAYAR MARINE PARK

This marine park, 30km or 19 nautical miles south of Langkawi and around 32 nautical miles from Penang, incorporates a number of tiny islands, the largest of which is 2km-long Pulau Payar. A large floating platform is moored off the island and includes an underwater observation chamber for viewing the reef. From here you can go snorkelling and diving, or rent glass-bottom boats. Inquire about the water conditions before you go, as it can be murky and you might see more in eastern Malaysia or Thailand.

Langkawi Coral (☎ 966 7318; www.langkawicoral.com) at Kuah jetty is the main tour operator for Pulau Payar. Trips cost RM230 including snorkelling and RM299 for diving. Hotels and travel agents may be able to get you cheaper deals. You can also book tickets to the park from Penang.

Sleeping

Langkawi is marketed as Malaysia's top tourist draw, so there's no shortage of accommodation of all kinds, from budget beach chalets to the most sybaritic five-star resorts. Budget accommodation is available only on the island's southwest coast at Pantai Cenang and Pantai Tengah, though prices are rising, whereas mid-range options are expensive compared with elsewhere in Malaysia. Luxury resorts are situated on spectacular private bays on the west and north coasts of the island, and cheaper package deals can sometimes be arranged.

During school holidays and the peak tourist season from November to February, Pulau Langkawi can become crowded, though something can usually still be found. At other times of the year supply far outstrips demand.

KUAH

Kuah has seen the greatest tourist development, which is hard to understand given its lack of beaches. A short ride by taxi will take you from the pier to any of Kuah's cheaper accommodation, which is strung out along the waterfront, and will do for a late arrival or catching an early ferry.

Gates (☎ 966 8466; Jl Persiaran Putra; d/ste from RM192/429;) Not far from the jetty is this sprawling luxury resort with elegantly furnished wooden chalets as well as three-bedroom suites, complete with living room, dining room and kitchen (RM1320). There are tennis courts, restaurants and a nursery on site.

City Bayview Hotel (☎ 966 1818; fax 966 3888; 1 Jl Pandak Mayah; s & d RM140-200;) This high-rise hotel in the centre of town offers high standards of comfort, including a gym and sauna.

Right opposite CHOGM Park is the mid-range **Hotel Central** (☎ 966 8585; www.hotelcentral.com.my; 33 Persiaran Putera; s & d RM85;), which also has family rooms for RM145, while further along, roughly 1km from the pier, you'll come to the **Hotel Asia** (☎ 966 6216; 18 Jl Taman Sentosa; s & d RM50-120;), which has reasonably comfortable rooms, though they're a little overpriced. Further on again, **Hotel Langkasuka** (☎ 966 6751; A-14 Pokok Asam; s & d RM60-120;) is a comfortable, if rather bland modern hotel above a large duty-free store.

PANTAI CENANG

Pantai Cenang is the liveliest beach strip, and it has accommodation from budget to international standard, though most places are mid-range. They straggle along the 2km of beach between the turn-off to Kuah at the northern end and Pantai Tengah to the south. Unfortunately, because the blocks of land are long and narrow, the beach frontage is minimal so from some of the chalets the only view is of another chalet.

Budget

Lagenda Permai Chalet (☎ 955 2806; lagendapermai@hotmail.com; s & d RM40-70; ❄) A welcoming, vaguely budget place directly opposite the beach (but not on it), with simple fan and air-con chalets. Discounts are available for stays of three nights or more.

Beachview (☎ 955 8513; beachvu@hotmail.com; dm/d from RM18/35; ❄) Popular backpacker place, with helpful, friendly owners who organise various activities and excursions, but, again, it's across the road from the beach and rooms have no real view of the sea.

Cenang Beach Motel (☎ 955 1395; s & d RM55-75; ❄) Basic choice that offers fair value for your money, with clean fan and air-con doubles actually on the sand.

Mid-Range

Beach Garden Resort (☎ 955 1363; combeer@pd.jaring.my; s/d RM140/160; ❄ 🏊) Near the northern edge of the beach, this small, attractive place has a secluded and relaxed atmosphere. It also has a very nice beachfront bar.

Sandy Beach Resort (☎ 955 1308; s & d RM70-80; ❄ 💻) A very popular place that has a range of accommodation, including A-frame chalets and bungalows; the ones nearest the beach are best. The on-site spa offers Thai massage, shiatsu and other treatments, from RM50.

Langkapuri Beach Resort (☎ 955 1202; fax 955 1959; s & d RM95-160; ❄) Pleasant clutch of chalets at the southern end of the beach, near the Zon Shopping Complex. The chalets are small but clean and comfortable, and the pricier ones have a sea view.

Semarak Langkawi Beach Resort (☎ 955 1377; s & d RM75-125; ❄) Next door to the more welcoming Sandy Beach, the Semarak has roomy, if somewhat overpriced, fan/air-con chalets with bathrooms, set among coconut trees facing the beach. The chalets nearest the sea are preferable; those closer to the road can be noisy. Service, however, is oddly slack.

AB Motel (☎ 955 1300; s & d RM65-120; ❄) An older laid-back place facing the beach. The chalets, spaced among palms and casuarina trees, are big and quite neat, though they've seen better days.

Top End

Pelangi Beach Resort (☎ 952 8888; www.pelangibeachresort.com; d/ste from RM640/1150; ❄ 💻 🏊) The northernmost place on the beach, with tastefully furnished chalets in vast, landscaped grounds. A family-oriented place, it has sports facilities, restaurants and every imaginable luxury – even electric buggies to take you to your room. There's also a full programme of children's activities.

Casa del Mar (☎ 955 2388; www.casadelmar-langkawi.com; d/ste from RM510/780; ❄ 💻 🏊) Directly opposite the Laman Padi, this is a sumptuous, Spanish villa–style place on a lovely stretch of beach. Various package deals are available.

PANTAI TENGAH

Several new hotels have been built at Pantai Tengah, though it's still less built up than Pantai Cenang, and is popular with young families.

Green Hill Beach Resort (☎ 955 1935; s & d RM40-70; ❄) Just after the headland that separates the two beaches is this scruffy place, which has some basic wooden huts.

Tanjung Malie (☎ 955 1891; s & d RM35-60; ❄) Nearby is another basic, sleepy collection of huts, though the standard's a little better. Family rooms cost RM120.

Sunset Beach Resort (☎ 955 1751; sunvil@tm.net.my; s & d RM130-190; ❄) Next along is this more upmarket resort, with comfortably furnished chalets surrounded by lush tropical gardens, but they don't have sea views.

Charlie Motel (☎ 955 1200; fax 955 1316; s & d RM65-85; ❄) After a gap of undeveloped land you'll find Charlie Motel, which is the best value on this beach. There are simple chalets facing the beach and a good seafood restaurant.

Aseania Resort (☎ 955 2020; aseania@tm.net.my; d/ste from RM139-450; ❄ 💻 🏊) Just inland from Charlie Motel at the large intersection at the southern end of Pantai Cenang is this huge pink palace. Looking like a Californian vision of Ancient Rome, it has luxurious rooms, a very good restaurant and a spectacular outdoor pool with an artificial waterfall. Discounts might get you as much as 35% off.

Langkawi Village Resort (☎ 955 1511; www.langkawi-villageresort.com; s & d RM150-220; ❄ 🏊) Further along the beach is this large, quiet, family-friendly place with a range of spotless single and double-storey bungalows. There's a British-style pub and a couple of good restaurants, as well as a range of organised activities.

Holiday Villa (☎ 955 1701; fax 955 2211; s/d from RM320/335;) Another vast modern complex, with squash and tennis courts, a gym and an indoor pool, 'exclusively for ladies'. Rooms are airy and spacious, and look out over the lawns and the soft white-sand beach.

PANTAI KOK

Berjaya Langkawi Beach & Spa Resort (☎ 959 1888; www.berjayaresorts.com; d/ste from RM315/700;) Past the headland at the northwestern end of the beach, this is one of the largest on the island, with 400 rooms. Most attractive are the waterfront chalets; others look out on to the lush rainforest. It also has an excellent range of sports facilities and a spa.

Tanjung Sanctuary Langkawi (☎ 955 2977; sanctuar@tm.net.my; s & d RM245-350;) Several kilometres back towards Pantai Cenang, Tanjung Sanctuary offers stylish luxury in harmony with nature. It's built on a forested, rocky headland with its own small beach and a restaurant built on stilts over the water. The spacious chalets all have king-size beds and balconies overlooking the sea.

Sheraton Langkawi Beach Resort (☎ 955 1901; fax 955 1968; s & d RM500-580;) Further southeast, the Sheraton Langkawi has all the usual five-star amenities in an attractive setting on a shady headland between the rainforest and the sea. Discounts are often available.

Oriental Village Inn (☎ 959 1606; fax 959 1607; s & d RM140;) Inland from Pantai Kok, incorporated into the Oriental Village shopping development, is this modern boutique hotel with spacious, attractively furnished rooms. There's also a tennis court and a very good restaurant.

PULAU REBAK BESAR

Rebak Marina Resort (☎ 966 5566; www.rebakmarina.com; s & d RM245-595;) Lying just off Pantai Cenang, this small island is occupied by this exclusive resort, which has a variety of spacious and elegantly furnished chalets in beautifully landscaped grounds. It has all the facilities you would expect, including a gym, tennis courts, spa and restaurants. There are several different package deals available. The island also has the only fully equipped, international-standard yachting marina in Malaysia.

TELUK DATAI

The **Andaman** (☎ 959 1088; www.ghmhotels.com/theandaman; d/ste from RM900/1950;) Just past the Datai Bay Golf Club in a grand wooden Malay-style building within the rainforest is this luxurious retreat with a gym, spa, gourmet restaurants and its own private beach. There's also a children's playground in the forest and a babysitting service.

The **Datai Langkawi** (☎ 959 2500; www.ghmhotels.com/thedatai; d/ste from RM1325/2135;) The island's most exclusive beach resort. Attractive, spacious chalets, many built on stilts over the water, are rustically set in the large grounds. There's a spa, tennis courts and three top-notch restaurants, and the resort also has a knowledgeable jungle trekking guide on its staff.

TANJUNG RHU

Tanjung Rhu Resort (☎ 959 1033; www.tanjungrhu.com.my; s & d from RM1100;) The best place to escape to on the island, this resort is tucked into a secluded cove opposite several tiny islands and has a glorious golden beach. Its tasteful buildings are arranged around a central courtyard, and there are four excellent restaurants. A variety of packages is available, including a seven night Wedding Package (RM12,385). This serene, eco-conscious resort is within walking distance of the public beach, with its food stalls and boat hire for day trips.

Eating

KUAH

Kuah is hardly a gastronomic goldmine, but it does have a few good seafood restaurants. For Chinese seafood, try **Prawn Village** (☎ 966 6111; Jl Persiaran Putra; dishes from RM8) near the Hotel Asia. Deliciously cooked dishes are generously portioned and not too expensive. A little further back towards the town centre, **Saribina Bay Café** (Jl Persiaran Putra; dishes from RM3) is a cheap place serving tasty Malay and Indian snacks such as nasi goreng and roti naan. It's set on one of Kuah's rare bits of beach, and you can sit outside on the sand for some great views.

Nearer to the jetty, the Langkawi Fair shopping complex has fast food outlets and a large **supermarket**. About 500m uphill from the jetty at the yacht club is the breezy **Charlie's Place** (☎ 966 4078; Jl Pantai Dato Syed Omar; dishes from RM20), which has a great harbour view to complement its Western and Asian menu.

Nine kilometres north of Kuah on the island's east coast is **Barn Thai** (☎ 966 6699; Mukim Kisap; dishes from RM20), an upmarket Thai restaurant with live jazz on some nights (reservations advisable). It's accessible via an interesting 450m-long raised walkway through a mangrove forest reserve, which is worth experiencing even if you don't eat there.

You'll find food stalls in front of the City Bayview Hotel and on the nearby laneways of Lencongan Putra 1, 2 and 3, serving steaming hot hawker fare day and night. Inexpensive Chinese coffee shops are scattered all around town.

PANTAI CENANG

Many of the hotels at Pantai Cenang have restaurants, though the quality is variable. The best are at the **Casa del Mar** (tapas RM18) which serves excellent Western meals and the **Pelangi Beach Resort** (set dinner RM61).

About 1km north of the Laman Padi museum is **Bon Ton** (☎ 955 6787; dishes from RM32), a restaurant, art gallery and resort set in the middle of rice fields and serving a fusion of Asian and Western cuisine. The tempting deserts (RM15) include such novelties as Japanese green tea ice-cream and macadamia pudding.

Opposite the Semarak Beach Resort, the **Hot Wok** (☎ 955 3193; dishes from RM15) is a busy place serving good Thai and Chinese seafood. Nearby is **Champor-Champor** (☎ 955 1449; dishes from RM20), a tranquil garden restaurant offering imaginative Western-Asian-African fusion cuisine, including tasty vegetarian options.

In the same complex as the Zon shopping mall, **Restoran Kampung Siam** (☎ 955 7830; dishes from RM16) is a smart place serving excellent Thai cuisine, though it's frequently empty.

A little further on, the tiny **Little India Cuisine** (☎ 955 7308; dishes from RM14; 🕑 7-11pm), in a converted garage, is a great place for authentic North Indian food, including vegetarian set meals.

PANTAI TENGAH

Pantai Tengah also has some very good places to eat. **Lighthouse** (☎ 955 2586; dishes from RM18) overlooks the beach and serves excellent Malaysian and Mediterranean food; it also runs Malaysian cookery classes. Next to the Langkawi Village Resort, **Sunvillage** and **Matahari** (☎ 955 6200; www.sunvillage.com.my; dishes from RM8) are two adjoining, traditional Malay restaurants, under the same management. There's an extensive menu of Malay curries, including vegetarian options, as well as Western dishes such as Surf 'n' Turf (RM35).

Drinking

Nearly all hotels have bars, and most restaurants serve alcohol; as Langkawi is a duty-free island, prices are normally cheaper than elsewhere in Malaysia. You can get a beer in any of the Chinese coffee shops in Kuah, though as few foreign tourists stay here for long, there are no real bars. Roughly midway along Pantai Cenang, the **Irish Bar** is the place to go for a pint of Guinness and a game of darts. Further along, **Oasis Beach Pub** is a pleasant place to watch the sunset with a beer or two, and there are regular party nights with live music.

If you'd prefer to sip a cocktail in smarter surrounds, try the **Sunvillage** restaurant on Pantai Tengah, which also serves wine.

Shopping

Langkawi is promoted as a duty-free shopping paradise, but prices are much the same as elsewhere in Malaysia. Apart from cheap cigarettes and alcohol, shopping is geared to domestic visitors or to the Japanese market for imported designer labels at inflated prices. Electronics are no bargain and the variety is poor. You'll find a greater range of goods in KL and Penang.

Kuah is the main place to shop on Langkawi. Duty-free shops can also be found at the ferry terminal, the airport and the **Zon Shopping Complex** at Pantai Cenang. Some resorts also have small shopping plazas. The **Langkawi Fair** shopping mall near the jetty is largely taken up with shops selling batik shirts and souvenirs.

Oriental Village is a new upmarket shopping complex just north of Pantai Kok. There are thirty separate outlets selling designer clothes and other top-end goods.

Langkawi Crystaal (p189) glassware and marble souvenirs are significant locally made goods, and are best bought at the production sites on the road north from Kuah.

Legally, visitors must stay on the island for 48 hours before they are entitled to purchase duty-free items.

Getting There & Away

AIR

Malaysia Airlines (☎ 966 6622), at the Langkawi Fair shopping mall, and **Air Asia** (☎ 955 7752) have two flights daily between Langkawi and KL (RM216/200). Silk Air flies daily to Singapore (RM345), and Malaysia Airlines also flies to Penang (once daily, RM90).

BOAT

All passenger ferries to/from Langkawi operate out of Kuah.

From about 8am to 6.30pm, regular ferries operate roughly every 1½ hours in either direction between Kuah and the mainland ports of Kuala Perlis (45 minutes, RM12) and Kuala Kedah (one hour, RM15).

Two companies, **Langkawi Ferry Services** (LFS; ☎ 966 9439) and **Ekspres Bahagia** (☎ 966 5784), operate daily ferries between Kuah and Georgetown on Penang (RM35/65 one way/return, 2½ hours). Boats depart from Georgetown at 8.30am and leave Kuah at 2.30pm and 5.30pm.

Ferry to Thailand

From the Kuah jetty, Langkawi Ferry Services makes four daily runs between 9.30am and 4pm to Satun on the Thai coast (approximately 1 hour, RM18). From the port you could take either a *songthaew* (small pick-up truck used as buses or taxis) which costs about RM20, or a taxi to Satun town, for connections to Hat Yai or Phuket.

Getting Around

TO/FROM THE AIRPORT

Taxi destinations from the airport include Kuah jetty or Pantai Cenang (RM16), Pantai Kok (RM15), Tanjung Rhu (RM26) and Teluk Datai (RM40). Buy a coupon at the desk before leaving the airport terminal and use it to pay the driver.

CAR

Cars can be rented cheaply, and touts from the travel agencies at the Kuah jetty will assail you upon arrival. The going rate starts at RM80 per day, but drops with bargaining. Cars and jeeps can also be rented more expensively at the upmarket beach resorts.

MOTORCYCLE & BICYCLE

The easiest way to get around is to hire a motorbike for around RM35 per day. You can do a leisurely circuit of the island (70km) in a day. The roads are excellent, and outside Kuah it's very pleasant and easy riding. Motorbikes can be hired at stands all over the island. A few places also rent mountain bikes for RM15 per day.

TAXI

As there is no public transport available, taxis are the main way of getting around, but fares are relatively high. There is a taxi station at the Langkawi Fair mall and at the jetty (☎ 966 5249). From the Kuah jetty, sample fares include: RM5 to Kuah town, RM20 to Pantai Cenang/Pantai Tengah and RM26 to Pantai Kok.

BUKIT KAYU HITAM

This is the main border crossing between Malaysia and Thailand, 48km north of Alor Setar. The Lebuhraya handles the vast majority of road traffic between the two countries, and all the buses to Hat Yai, Thailand, come this way so immigration processing on both sides of the border can become jammed. Taking the train via Padang Besar is almost always a quicker and more convenient alternative.

At the border post there are a few restaurants, private car-parking facilities and a **Tourism Malaysia Office** (☎ 922 2078; 🕑 9am-5pm). The easiest way to cross the border is to take a through bus all the way to Hat Yai (though when the border opens in the morning, the lines can be horrendous). Buses and taxis from Alor Setar run right up to the Malaysian customs post. From here you can walk the roughly 2km to the border crossing or hop on one of the passing motrobikes which ply the route for around RM3. Taxis on the other side run to Sadao, from where there are buses on to Hat Yai.

If arriving from Thailand, ensure that your passport is stamped by the Malaysian border police – otherwise you may be fined for 'illegal entry' when you leave Malaysia.

JOHN BORTHWICK

Musician, **Fort Cornwallis** (p162)

Wat Chayamangkalaram (p164), Georgetown

SALLY DILLON

ERIC L WHEATER

Drink vendor (p169), Georgetown

JAMES BRAUND

Trishaw (p157) driver

CLEM LINDEN

Masjid Zahir (p185), Alor Setar

Mangrove swamp, **Pulau Singa Besar** (p191)

SIMON BRACKEN

SIMON BRACKEN

Tasik Dayang Bunting (p191), Pulau Dayang Bunting

WAYNE W

Moored fishing boats, **Pulau Langkawi** (p187)

There is no accommodation on the Malaysian side, and the few questionable hotels on the Thai side are extremely overpriced. Even with the expense of shelling out for a taxi, you'll end up saving money (and headaches) by proceeding immediately to your next destination.

Once in Malaysia, you'll find taxis (RM30) and regular buses (RM3) to Alor Setar, from where frequent buses go to Kuala Kedah (for Langkawi), Butterworth, KL and destinations across the peninsula. Kuala Perlis, the other departure point for Langkawi, is more difficult to reach – first take a bus to Changlun, another to Kangar and then another to Kuala Perlis.

PERLIS

☎ 04

The tiny state of Perlis, tucked away in far northwest Malaysia on the Thai border, tends to be the forgotten state of Malaysia. Apart from a sugar refinery and cement factory, its economy is still dominated by agriculture, and Perlis is primarily a state to transit through. Kuala Perlis is one of the access ports for Langkawi, and Padang Besar is the main border town if arriving by train from Thailand. If you have time, the small but beautiful **Taman Negara Perlis** state park is worth exploring.

In recent years, the state government's hard-line Islamic policies have caused controversy throughout Malaysia, not least the relaxing of rules governing polygamy (see box Polygamy in Perlis p198). Other proposed measures have included a nightly curfew for the under-18s and the establishment of single-sex karaoke lounges.

Being a predominantly Muslim state, Perlis observes the same business hours as neighbouring Kedah.

History

Perlis was originally part of Kedah, though it variously fell under Thai and Acehnese sovereignty. After the Siamese conquered Kedah in 1821, the sultan of Kedah made unsuccessful attempts to regain his territory by force until, in 1842, he agreed to accept Siamese terms. The Siamese reinstalled the sultan, but made Perlis into a separate vassal principality with its own raja.

As was the case in Kedah, power was transferred from the Thais to the British under the 1909 Anglo-Siamese Treaty, and the British installed a Resident at Arau. During the Japanese occupation in WWII, Perlis was 'returned' to Thailand, and then after the war it again returned to British rule until it became part of the Malayan Union, and then the Federation of Malaya in 1957.

KANGAR

☎ 04

Kangar, 45km northwest of Alor Setar, is the state capital of Perlis. It's a sleepy modern town surrounded by rice paddies and has little of interest for travellers. There are a few banks and countless restaurants and shops in the vicinity of the bus station. If you have a long wait between bus connections, you can do as the locals do and relax with a coffee at one of the many *kedai kopi* around town.

Sleeping & Eating

Putra Palace (☎ 976 7755; fax 976 1049; 135 Persiaran Jubli Emas; s & d RM120-270;) The best place in town, with luxurious and smart, comfortable rooms, an excellent restaurant, a gym and a children's pool. It's about 1km from the centre.

Federal Hotel (☎ 976 6288; 104 Persiaran Jubli Emas; s & d RM50-100;) Back towards town is this drab and sombre place with basic and overpriced rooms.

Hotel Ban Cheong (☎ 976 1184; 79 Jl Kangar; s & d RM20-40;) More amenable and much cheaper is this typical old Chinese hotel with basic fan and air-con rooms.

Malaysia Hotel (☎ 976 1366; 65 Jl Jubli Perak; s & d RM33-63;) Opposite the express bus station is this simple though convenient option, above a Chinese restaurant.

There are numerous restaurants and cafés sprinkled around the bus station, including the **Embassy** (Jl Jubli Perak) a food court a few doors from the Malaysia Hotel, which serves cheap Chinese food.

Much better though, is the **Bendang Coffee House** (Putra Palace hotel; dishes from RM8) which offers Western and Asian cuisine.

Getting There & Away

The express bus station is on the southern edge of town, off Jl Jubli Perak. There are a few daily departures to KL (RM27.90), Butterworth (RM7.60), Alor Setar (RM3.20)

POLYGAMY IN PERLIS

'If you want to practise polygamy, come to Perlis.' So said the chief mufti of Perlis when questioned about the ultra-conservative state's decision to abolish the legal requirement for men to seek their first wife's written permission before taking a second or even third wife. The move was intended to deter the increasing number of Muslim men – more than 500 in 2002 – who were crossing the border into southern Thailand in order to marry again secretly. The state government also did away with the usual obligation to attend marital instruction courses and made polygamy registration rates more affordable, at RM500 for Perlis residents and RM1000 for other Malaysians.

Although polygamy is allowed under Islamic law, it remains very rare in mainstream Malaysian society, and there has been a national outcry from women's groups and the press, who dubbed Perlis a 'Polygamists' Paradise', and expressed concerns about the possible harmful effects to family life. The national government wants the laws governing marriage to be standardised throughout Malaysia, but in the meantime, Perlis' hard-line lawmakers are unrepentant, declaring that the relaxation of the law will reduce illegal marriages and stop men taking mistresses.

and Kota Bharu (RM24.90) and regular buses to Kuala Perlis (RM1). Infrequent buses to Kaki Bukit (RM2.70) and Padang Besar (RM2.15) leave from the more central station on Jl Tun Abdul Razak.

If you're impatient to get to Langkawi, a taxi to Kuala Perlis from the bus station costs RM10.

KUALA PERLIS

☎ 04

This small port town in the extreme northwest of the peninsula is visited mainly as a departure point for Langkawi. It is also the closest access port to the island from Thailand. The landing jetty for ferries is only 700m from the town centre. The main part of Kuala Perlis consists of a couple of streets with a bank, several restaurants and shops, and a couple of hotels. The older part of town has interesting houses and mosques built on stilts over the mangrove swamps.

Sleeping & Eating

Pens Hotel (☎ 985 4122; Jl Kuala Perlis; s & d RM63-75; ❄) The only decent place in town, with neat, comfortable rooms. Along the same street are a few grotty, dirt-cheap hostels.

Near the jetty are several Malay food stalls serving Kuala Perlis' famous special laksa, as well as a few Chinese restaurants.

Getting There & Away

The bus and taxi station is a short walk from the jetty towards town. The frequent No 56 bus to Kangar (RM1) swings by the jetty before terminating at the station. Less frequent direct buses depart for Butterworth, Alor Setar, KL and Padang Besar. From the bus station or the jetty, taxis go to Kangar (RM10) and Padang Besar (RM20).

Ferries to Kuah, on Pulau Langkawi, leave at least hourly between 8am and 6pm (RM15). Private car parks between the jetty and the bus station will look after your vehicle for RM6 per day.

PADANG BESAR

☎ 04

This town on the Thai border is 35km northeast of Kangar. The town itself is nothing special, but it's a popular destination for Malaysians because of the duty-free markets in the neutral territory between the two countries. Near the large roundabout are a few banks that will change travellers cheques. Moneychangers will give you even better rates for bank notes (foreign or Thai baht) and have the added advantage of being open longer hours than banks every day.

If arriving from Thailand ensure that your passport is stamped by the Malaysian border police – otherwise you may be fined for 'illegal entry' when you leave Malaysia.

There's some accommodation on the Malaysian and Thai sides of the border, but you're better off avoiding these mostly disreputable budget hotels and hiring a taxi or catching a bus to your next destination.

Malaysian buses stop near the large roundabout around a kilometre from the large border-crossing complex on the Malaysian side. There are regular buses to/from Kangar (RM2.15) and infrequently to Kaki Bukit. The taxi stand is on the left before you reach the bus stop, and fares are posted for all destinations, including Kaki Bukit (RM10) and Kangar (RM12), as well as Kuala Perlis and Penang.

Very few people, if any, walk the more than 2km of no-man's land between the Thai and Malaysian sides of the border. Motorcyclists shuttle pedestrian travellers back and forth for about RM3 each way, though bargaining is possible.

On the Thai side you can flag down buses to Sadao and Hat Yai from the main road. If you're coming from Hat Yai, travel agencies on Thanon Niphat Uthit 2, a five-minute walk from Hat Yai's train station, run share taxis to the Thai side of the border, as well as through-bus tickets to popular Malaysian destinations and Singapore.

All in all, the train is a better bet, with a connection from Padang Besar to Hat Yai at 10.25am. Southbound trains leave Hat Yai at 2.50pm (Thai time). All passengers must disembark to clear customs and immigration (both Thai and Malaysian) before reboarding.

TAMAN NEGARA PERLIS

The small state park of Taman Negara Perlis in the northwest of the state runs along the Thai border, covering about 5000 hectares. It comprises the Nakawan Range – the longest continuous range of limestone hills in Malaysia – and the Mata Ayer and Wang Mu Forest Reserves. It has heavily forested slopes and numerous cave systems, such as **Gua Wang Burma**, with its intriguing limestone formations. It's also rich in wildlife; this is the only habitat in Malaysia for the stump-tailed macaque. White-handed gibbons and a rich array of birds can also be found here.

Just outside the park, **Gua Kelam** (Cave of Darkness; admission RM1; 9am-6pm), is a 370m-long cavern gouged out in tin-mining days; today it's the state's top tourist attraction. A river runs through the cave and emerges in a cascade at a popular swimming spot and a landscaped park. The old tin mine is a short walk from the far end of the cavern. Listen for motorcycles that may be rushing through, and watch out for exploding guano (the build-up of phosphates is highly flammable). The cave is a 1km walk from Kaki Bukit.

Other attractions include the **Wang Kelian Sunday Market**, which straddles the Malaysia-Thailand border. Fruit, vegetables and clothes from both countries are for sale, and no passport is needed, provided you stay in the market area. The Malaysian side of the market is open every day.

Information

The **Park Visitor Centre** (945 7898; wwfps@pd.jaring.my; Jl Kaki Bukit; Mon-Fri 9am-noon & 2-4pm) is signposted 3km from the small town of Kaki Bukit. All visitors must register here, and entry to the park is RM2 per day. Guides (RM30-50) can also be hired at the centre, and are obligatory for many areas.

The website http://ecoperlis.mediasite.de is a good source of information on the park.

Sleeping

The modern wooden chalets in the **Park Visitor Centre** (tents from RM6; dm/chalets RM10/RM30-80;) are very comfortable. Contact the **Visitor Centre** (945 7898; wwfps@pd.jaring.my).

Getting There & Away

There is no public transport to the park. The nearest town is Kaki Bukit, from where a winding mountain road leads to the tiny village of Kampung Wang Kelian. The Park Visitor Centre is signposted 3km further on.

Negeri Sembilan

CONTENTS

The small state of Negeri Sembilan (Nine States) is one of Malaysia's most unique, being a centre for the Minangkabau people, who originally came here from Sumatra in the 15th century. To some extent, the Minangkabau people still follow *adat perpatih*, a traditional matrilineal system of inheritance and communal village administration that is unique to Negeri Sembilan, though these customs are now weakening. Fortunately, the Minangkabau's fiery cooking style has survived.

Few visitors squeeze Negeri Sembilan into their itineraries. The lacklustre capital, Seremban, has few sights of note beyond the Taman Seni Budaya (Arts & Cultural Park). The area around the capital is worth exploring for those interested in the Minangkabau people (p202) and the distinctive architecture of their traditional houses. Within striking distance of Seremban is the lazy old royal town of Sri Menanti, notable for its impressive Istana Lama (Old Palace), a beautiful traditional building.

Most travellers to Negeri Sembilan make their way to the beach at Port Dickson and Tanjung Tuan (Cape Rachado), a long and pleasant stretch of sand and hotels. Popular with Kuala Lumpur city dwellers, it's a welcome respite from urban KL, but the beaches are not among the peninsula's best.

HIGHLIGHTS

- Discovering the traditional culture and **architecture** (p203) of the Minangkabau people around Seremban
- Marvelling at the grand **Istana Lama (Old Palace)** (p207) at Sri Menanti
- Admiring the old shophouses and ornate temples at **Kuala Pilah** (p207)
- Exploring Port Dickson's seaside resorts and the romantic old **Tanjung Tuan lighthouse** (p208)

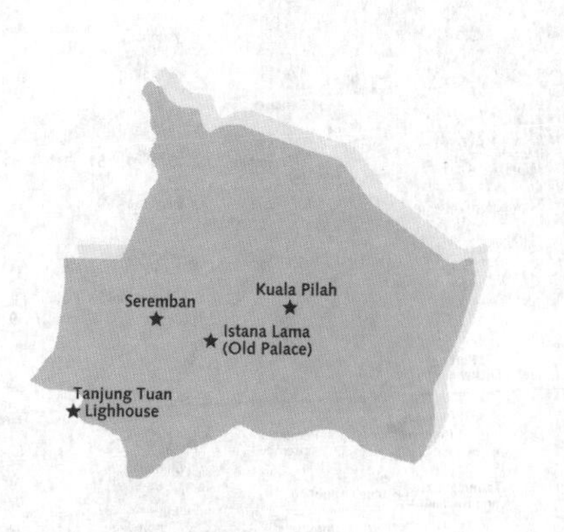

- TELEPHONE CODE: 06
- POPULATION: 859,924
- AREA: 6645 SQ KM

History

During the Melaka sultanate of the 15th century, many Minangkabau people from Sumatra settled here. They initially lived under the protection of the rulers of Melaka, but with the fall of Melaka to the Portuguese, the Minangkabau sought protection from the sultans of neighbouring Johor.

With the rising power of the Bugis (a seafaring group of warrior-like Malay settlers from Macassar – Ujung Padang – in Celebes) in Selangor, the Minangkabau felt increasingly insecure, so they turned back to the royal house of Sumatra for protection. Raja Melewar, a Minangkabau prince from Sumatra, was appointed the first *yang dipertuan besar* (head of state) of Negeri Sembilan in 1773 by the *undang* (territorial chiefs). Out of this initial union emerged a loose confederation of nine *luak* (fiefdoms), although there is some debate about its exact make-up. The royal capital of Negeri Sembilan was established at Sri Menanti, and Raja Melewar, though essentially powerless, indulged himself here.

Like Selangor to the north, Negeri Sembilan was rich in tin, and so suffered the unrest and political instability motivated by greed for much of the 19th century. After Raja Melewar's death, the title of *yang dipertuan* was taken on by a succession of Sumatran chiefs, until a series of protracted tin-related wars from 1824 to 1832 led to the severance of political ties with Sumatra.

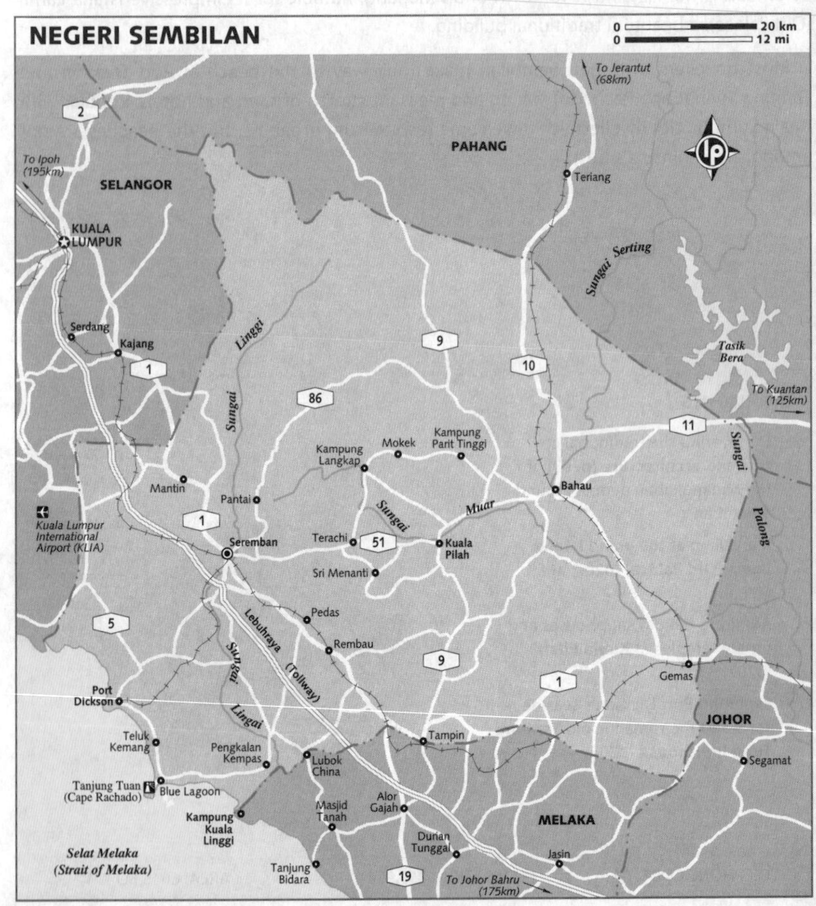

In the second half of the 19th century the civil disturbances and interstate rivalry continued, particularly in the northern state of Sungai Ujong. In the 1880s the British gradually intervened by increasing their influence in the area, and the territories of Sri Menanti, Tampin, Rembau and Jelebu were consolidated into a new confederacy controlled by a British Resident. In 1895 Sungai Ujong was added to the union, and these five districts now make up the bulk of the modern state of Negeri Sembilan, with an area of 6643 sq km.

Climate

The temperature in Negeri Sembilan ranges from 21°C to 33°C and average humidity exceeds 82%. Although there is rain through the year, September to November are the wettest months.

Getting There & Away

The North-South Hwy, connecting Johor Bahru and Kuala Lumpur, is the major road through the state. For details of trains to/from KL and buses to/from KL and Melaka see the Seremban section, p206. Details on buses to KL, Melaka and other peninsular destinations are in the Port Dickson section, p209.

SEREMBAN

☎ 06

Seremban, 64km southeast of KL, is the rather down-at-heel capital of Negeri Sembilan. The noisy central area is a shabby grid of traffic. Crumbling colonial-era shophouses, eroding from damp and neglect, and green with moss and opportunistic vegetation, lend the town a certain nobility (despite the myriad betting shops and the skulking presence of prostitution).

Not totally devoid of sights, Seremban is a centre for Minangkabau culture. Buffalo-horn roofs adorn many of the new buildings, such as the city hall, but the only real access to Minangkabau culture is at the Muzium Negeri, part of the Taman Seni Budaya (Arts & Cultural Park) on the outskirts of town.

Heading east to the hills bordering the city centre, Seremban takes on a different personality. The Lake Gardens are a low-key respite from the traffic, and further into the hills is the old colonial district, with scattered bungalows, colonial buildings and parks favoured by t'ai chi practitioners.

Information

An ATM (Visa/Plus) can be found in the **OCBC** (Cnr Jl Dato Lee Fong Yee & Jl Dato Bandar Tunggal) and also in the Terminal 1 and Seremban Parade shopping centres. A moneychanger is near the Catholic church on Jl Tam Yuan.

There are several Internet cafés in town.

Carryon Computer Center (Jl Dato Sheik Ahmad; RM2.50 per hr)

NS Internet Library (13 Jl Dato Lee Fong Yee; RM3 per hr)

Sights

ARCHITECTURE

No new building in Seremban is complete without a Minangkabau curved roof, but the only really fine melding of modern and traditional architecture is the **Dewan Undangan Negeri** (State Secretariat bldg; between Jl Dato Abdul Kadir & Jl Dato Abdul Malek), whose wonderful multiple roof points are a striking landmark for central Seremban. Opposite is the **Istana Besar** (Jl Bukit), home of the sultan of Negeri Sembilan (closed to the public). Directly south is the neoclassical (1912) **State Library** (off Jl Dato Hamzah, west of Lake Gardens), Seremban's most imposing colonial building and once the offices of the colonial administration.

Further south towards the city centre is the **Masjid Negeri** (State Mosque; Jl Dato Hamzah), with its nine pillars symbolising the nine original states of Negeri Sembilan. This monochrome, futuristic mosque is relatively restrained compared with some other mosques erected to the glory of Islam in Malaysia.

In the central area, colonial architecture includes the Catholic **Church of the Visitation** (JL Yam Tuang), with its gothic spires, and the more sober **Methodist Church** (Jl Dato Sheikh Ahmad) built in 1920. The **King George V School** (Jl Za'aba) was the premier colonial school for Seremban's elite and still functions as a high school.

The old Taoist **Liesheng Temple** (Jl Dr Samuel) has three Taoist idols positioned on the main altar; the central image is Guandi (the God of War). The Chinese characters above the altar mean 'Your needs will be answered' (often associated with Buddhism). Guanyin (Goddess of Compassion)

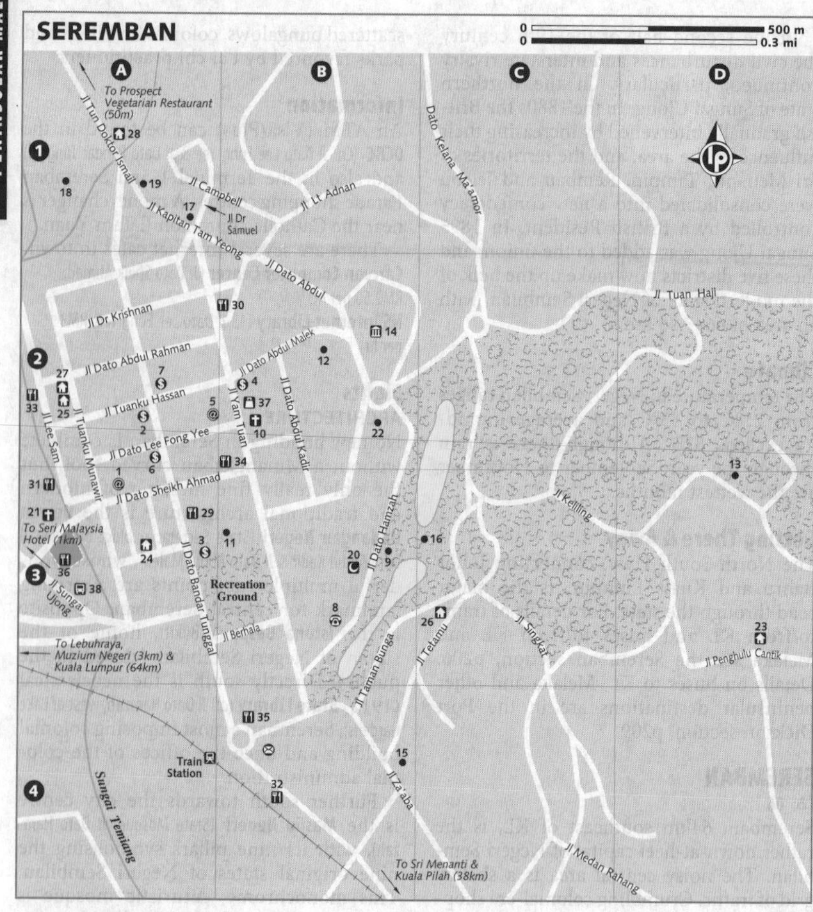

is also here, as are old drums, and the roof is decorated with dragons. On the pavement outside the shophouses to the north of the temple are two marvellous old-fashioned advertisements for Milkmaid Milk, dating perhaps from the 1940s.

LAKE GARDENS

The quaint Lake Gardens are a tame recreation reserve and the place where courting couples go in the evenings. There's a small **aviary** on the western side and an open pavilion where cultural events are sometimes staged. The gardens are at the edge of the green and tranquil colonial district that now mostly houses government quarters. There are many other parkland areas to the east of the Lake Gardens, including the **Hutan Rekreasi**, a small jungle park.

MUZIUM NEGERI

The **Muzium Negeri** (State Museum), built in the style of a Minangkabau palace, has some worn craft and historical exhibits. Displays cover the Emergency (see p33), complete with gruesome post-capture portraits of the Communist leaders – reminiscent of those of the bullet-ridden Che Guevara.

The museum is inside the **Taman Seni Budaya** (Arts & Cultural Park; admission free; 10am-6pm Tue, Wed, Sat & Sun, 8.15am-1pm Thu, 10am-12.15pm & 2.45-6pm Fri), which also includes a *gasing* (top spinning) pavilion and a small tourist information office.

INFORMATION		
Carryon Computer Center	1	A3
HSBC Bank	2	A2
Maybank	3	A3
Moneychager	4	B2
NS Internet Library	5	A2
OCBC Bank	6	A2
Standard Chartered Bank	7	A2
Telekom Malaysia	8	B3
SIGHTS & ACTIVITIES	**pp203-5**	
Aviary	9	B3
Church of the Visitation	10	B2
City Hall	11	B3
Dewan Undangan Negeri	12	B2
Hutan Rekreasi Entrance	13	D3
Istana Besar	14	B2
King George V School	15	B4
Lake Gardens	16	C3
Liesheng Temple	17	A1
Market	18	A1
Masjid Jamek	19	A1
Masjid Negeri	20	B3
Methodist Church	21	A3
State Library	22	B2
SLEEPING	**pp205-6**	
Allson Klana Resort	23	D3
Carlton Star Hotel	24	A3
Chiew Kee Hotel	25	A2
Hilton	26	C3
Seremban Inn	27	A2
Sun Lun Yik Hotel	28	A1
EATING	**p206**	
Bilal	29	A3
Blossom Court	(see 23)	
Chinese Hawker Centre	30	B2
Han Pi Yuen	(see 26)	
Hawker Centre	31	A3
Hawker Stalls	32	B4
Pasar Malam	33	A2
Restoran Negeri	34	B2
Seremban Parade Shopping Centre	35	B4
Terminal 1 Shopping Centre	36	A3
Yuri	(see 23)	
ENTERTAINMENT		
Golden Screen Cinemas	(see 36)	
SHOPPING		
Martial Arts Shop	37	B2
TRANSPORT	**p206**	
Bus & Taxi Station	38	A3

Outside are two traditional Minangkabau houses on the museum grounds. The **Istana Ampang Tinggi** (Ampang Tinggi Palace) was originally constructed in the 1860s near Sri Menanti, a gift from the sultan to his daughter. Though small, it shows the intricate carving of palace architecture and traditional thatch roof. Minangkabau houses were built entirely without nails, though apparently this is now a lost art, as nails were used when the palace was reconstructed here. Next to the palace, the **Rumah Negeri Sembilan** is a less ornate traditional house with a shingle roof, but it shows the hallmark curved-roof style based on the buffalo horn.

It's 3km west of the bus station on the road to KL. From the town centre, several local buses will drop you here (40 sen) or you can take a taxi (RM6).

Sleeping

There is no real need to overnight in Seremban as KL, the beach at Port Dickson and even Melaka are only about an hour away by bus or train. There is a good choice of mid-range and top-end hotels; most budget options in the town centre are filthy, dingy and badly run, several are also boarding houses or bordellos.

Sun Lun Yik Hotel (☎ 763 5735, 19 Jl Tun Dr Ismail; s/d RM50/60; ❄) This is a clean, well-run and homely Chinese hotel opposite the Central Market on the fringes of the town centre. It may be slightly removed from the action, but it does get you away from Seremban's worst reaches and there are some good restaurants nearby. Rooms come with TV and shower room; the cheaper doubles are windowless.

Carlton Star Hotel (☎ 762 5336; 47 Jl Dato Sheikh Ahmad; s/d RM58/68; ❄) Enjoying a useful position not far from the bus and train station, this six-storey hotel is otherwise unremarkable, although you can avail yourself of the steam bath, sauna, massage and karaoke facilities. There's also a Chinese restaurant here.

Seri Malaysia (☎ 764 4181; fax 764 4179; Jl Sungai Ujong; r RM110; ❄) Standard mid-range comfort and well furnished rooms can be found here at this hotel from the nationwide chain, although the location is an inconvenient 1km west of the bus station, on the road to Muzium Negeri.

Allson Klana Resort (☎ 762 9600; fax 763 9218; Jl Penghulu Cantik; s/d RM360/380; ❄ 🏊) This prestigious four-star hotel is set on a hill to the east of the Lake Gardens. Ensconced in large grounds and featuring all the luxuries of an international-class hotel, the resort has reputable Chinese and Japanese restaurants. One of the Allson's highlights is its colossal pool (poolside rooms cost marginally extra). Also at hand is a pub-style bar with a pool table. Visitors arriving at KLIA can consider staying here as the airport is only 20 minutes away.

Hilton (☎ 766 6666; info_seremban@hilton.com; Jl Dato AS Dawood; d RM400, superior d RM450; ❄ 🏊) Seremban's sole five-star hotel, located by the Lake Gardens, the new Hilton boasts an abundance of amenities. There's an excellent

Chinese restaurant, Han Pi Yuen (see Eating this page), a Fun Pub, a very relaxing bar and lounge, fitness centre, air-conditioned squash court and all rooms come with five-star facilities. Specially fitted rooms are available for guests with physical disabilities.

Chiew Kee Hotel (☎ 762 2095; 1st fl, 41 Jl Tuanku Munawir; d without/with air-con RM35/RM45; ❄) This cheap and simple hotel is better than many other central budget options, but a sign reads 'We regret that prostitutions are strictly prohibited here'.

The mid-range **Seremban Inn** (☎ 761 7777; fax 763 7777; 39 Jl Tuanku Munawir; d RM80; ❄) has hotel-quality rooms.

Eating

Minangkabau-style cooking is red-hot, due in part to generous additions of *chili padi*, a tiny firebomb of a thing. You should certainly dare to taste either *masak lemak* (fish, meat or vegetables cooked in coconut milk) or rendang (thick, dry meat curry usually served with rice cooked in coconut milk), all in a bamboo stem.

Food stalls, serving mostly Malay dishes and some spicy Minangkabau fare, can be found south of the train station and at the upstairs **hawker centre** (Jl Lee Sam). The lively Saturday **pasar malam** (night market; Jl Lee Sam) has plenty of food stalls. **Chinese hawker stalls** (Cnr Jl Yam Tuan & Jl Dr Krishnan) serve up favourites from alfresco tables in the car park on fine evenings. The ground floor of the Terminal 1 Shopping Centre has plentiful fast-food and satay restaurants.

Bilal (100 Jl Dato Bandar Tunggal; meals RM7) This simple eatery in the centre of town is no-frills but has filling and tasty curries; you can fill up on a plate of *pilau* (rice), dahl and chicken for around RM6.

Restoran Negeri (☎ 767 1190; 13 Jl Dato Sheikd Ahmad; meals RM7). This centrally located Muslim restaurant has a choice of filling roti and curries.

Prospect Vegetarian Restaurant (☎ 767 5760; 1B Jl Temiang; meals RM10-15) If you prefer Chinese Buddhist cuisine, this pleasant eatery, around 300m north of the Hotel Sun Lun Yik, serves tasty blood-free dishes. There are other decent Chinese restaurants in this street.

Blossom Court (☎ 762 9600 ext 3333; 1st fl, Allson Klana Resort, Jl Penghulu Cantik; meals RM25) This award-winning *(Malaysia Tatler)* Chinese restaurant serves fantastic dim sum between 8.30am and 2.30pm (RM4 per basket) and Cantonese cuisine in smart, albeit rather unexciting, surrounds. The popular RM23 buffet is worth trying.

Han Pi Yuen (☎ 766 6666; Hilton, Jl Dato AS Dawood; meals RM40) This first-rate restaurant has a fine selection of dishes from all over China in an elegant setting and with civilised service.

Yuri (☎ 762 9600 ext 3555; Lobby level, Allson Klana Resort, Jl Penghulu Cantik; meals RM40) The only Japanese restaurant in town serves genuine and superb Japanese food. It features a sushi bar, private tatami rooms and *teppanyaki* counter.

Getting There & Away

Seremban is on the main north–south rail line from KL to Singapore. KTM Komuter trains, part of KL's city rail network, have frequent departures between KL Sentral and Seremban (RM7, last train around 10pm).

Buses frequently depart to KL from the bus terminal on Jl Sungai Ujong (RM4, 1½ hours), to Melaka (RM4.70, 1½ hours), Port Dickson (RM2.65, one hour) and other peninsular destinations. The bus terminal has a **left-luggage counter** (RM1.50 per hr; 🕒 7.30am-9pm). Long-distance taxis muster upstairs for destinations including Port Dickson (RM70) and Sri Menanti (RM60).

SEREMBAN TO KUALA PILAH

East from Seremban, the road meanders through the hills to the town of Kuala Pilah, passing through the heartland of Minangkabau culture surrounding the old royal town of Sri Menanti. Along the main road are a number of **Minangkabau houses**, though the traditional thatch of buffalo-horn roofs has been replaced by more utilitarian corrugated iron. The village of Terachi, 27km from Seremban at the turn-off to Sri Menanti, has some particularly fine traditional houses, as do the villages further north including Pantai, and Sri Menanti itself.

Sri Menanti

☎ 06

Sri Menanti, 6km off the Seremban–Kuala Pilah road, is the old royal capital, first settled over 400 years ago by Minangkabau immigrants from Sumatra. This sleepy hamlet is nestled in a highland valley surrounded by jungle hills.

Just past Sri Menanti's own tiny Lake Gardens is **Istana Besar**, the impressive palace of the sultan of Negeri Sembilan (not open to the public). Originally built in the 1930s, the later addition features a blue tiled Minangkabau roof.

Just beyond Istana Besar is the marvellous **Istana Lama** (Old Palace), now a museum (admission free; 10am-6pm), remove your shoes if going upstairs. The beautiful hardwood palace, arranged over four floors, was constructed without the use of nails in 1908 as a temporary replacement for an even older palace that was razed by British soldiers during the Sungai Ujong wars. The palace is raised off the ground on 99 pillars, many of them carved, one for each of the legendary 99 *luak* (clan) warriors. Inside you can see the king and queen's bedchambers, the children's playroom, a large dining room and huge dining table as well as some kris weaponry and royal regalia. Climb to the top floor for views over the gardens.

Back towards the main road in the compound next to the mosque is the **Makam Di Raja** (Royal Cemetery), which has a distinctive Victorian/Moorish pavilion. The prominent grave of Tuanku Abdul Rahman, the first king of independent Malaysia, is immediately inside the gates.

The **Sri Menanti Resort** (☎ 497 0242; next to Istana Lama; s/d RM77/90, chalet RM108-RM126, bungalow RM360) can provide resort-style accommodation and has a restaurant.

To reach Sri Menanti from Seremban, take a bus to Kuala Pilah (RM2.20) and then a taxi (around RM20 return).

Kuala Pilah

☎ 06

Kuala Pilah, a pleasant valley town 40km east of Seremban, is one of the main townships in this strongly Minangkabau region. Attractive and not as crumbling as Seremban, Kuala Pilah has many newly painted shophouses. There are a few temples here of note including the **Kuil Sri Kanthaswamy** (Jl Melang; main prayer hall 6.30-7pm), overflowing with colour and arrayed with deities. The intriguing **Sansheng Gong** (Sansheng Temple; Jl Dato Undang Johol) has a skilfully carved boat, from the time of Qing emperor Guangxu, hanging just inside the door. The fierce-looking bearded idol in the centre is Guandi (God of War); there are marvellous carvings along the front of the temple and worn frescoes on the wall. Nearby is an elaborate Chinese-style arch dedicated to Martin Lister, the first British Resident of Negeri Sembilan.

There's no reason for you to get stranded here, but if you do, Kuala Pilah has several cheap Chinese hotels. The **Desa Inn** (☎ 481 8033; 745 Jl Dato Abdul Manap; d RM58;) has clean and comfortable rooms, all with TV. The **Hotel Hinyi** (☎ 481 8335; 227 Jl Tung Yen; d RM35;) has reasonable rooms.

From Seremban, a few companies run buses to Kuala Pilah, with departures roughly every half-hour (RM4; one hour). From Kuala Pilah it is possible to get connections east all the way to Kuantan and Kuala Terengganu, but unless you catch one of the two daily direct buses, you will first have to take a local bus to Bahau, on the highway 20km to the east.

GRAVE REMINDERS

About 23km east of Cape Rachado is the small town of Pengkalan Kempas, and just outside the town a 'Kompleks Sejarah Pengkalan Kempas' sign indicates the grave of **Sheikh Ahmad Majnun,** about 100m off the road. This local hero died in 1467 and beside his grave stand three 2m high megalithic stones known as the 'sword', 'spoon' and 'rudder'. No-one is quite sure of their purpose, but similar pairs (not trios) of monoliths have been found elsewhere. Scholars think they were originally used as grave-markers, but many monoliths evolved into village shrines, worshipped by residents who believed the stones had the power to spontaneously grow taller.

The buses that run along the coast hourly between Port Dickson and Melaka travel via Pengkalan Kempas, and the gravesite is a short distance outside town, in the direction of Lubok China and Melaka.

PORT DICKSON

☎ 06

Port Dickson is just a small port town of little interest, but it's the gateway to the stretch of beach extending 16km south to Tanjung Tuan (Cape Rachado). This beach is very popular with KL residents on weekends, and a string of hotels is spread out all the way to Tanjung Tuan.

The beaches are very popular, but nothing special, with sand varying in colour from red to grey-white. The water, like elsewhere along the Selat Melaka, is murky and very shallow for swimming. Occasional oil spills from passing tankers don't help, but even so, the views are good and Port Dickson is quite fun for a couple of days.

Originally built by the Portuguese in the 16th century, the **Tanjung Tuan lighthouse** offers fine views. On a clear day you can see Sumatra, 38km away across the Selat Melaka. The turn-off to the lighthouse is near the Km 16 marker. Head down the road for 2km and then through the forest reserve for another kilometre to the lighthouse. Nearby you'll find the small **Blue Lagoon** (Tanjung Biru), with its pretty little beach and assorted marine life.

There's not much to see in Port Dickson itself, although you can delve into the old, smoky interior of the small Taoist **Fengshan Si** (Fengshan Temple; Jl Lama) dedicated to the Taoist being Guangze Zunwang on your left as you head out on the road down to the beach. It's back to back with the vibrantly painted **Sri Maha Mariamman Temple**. At the festival of Navarathiri (September or October), the Goddess Sri Maha Mariamman is conveyed at night on a chariot procession around Port Dickson. The goddess performs a similar journey during the Anniversary Prayers procession (June or July).

Sleeping

The main attraction is the beach so head there for accommodation. The best beaches start from around the Km 8 marker. On weekends many hotels of all price ranges are fully booked (except for the hostels), but on weekdays hefty discounts drop luxury room rates practically in your lap.

Corus Paradise Resort (☎ 647 7600; www.corusparadisepd.com; Km 3.5 Jl Pantai; r RM220; ❄ 🏊) With long views over the bay to the lighthouse and up to Port Dickson, this hotel is 3.5km south of town and the best of the crop. There's a fine range of restaurants and the hotel has its own breathtaking palm tree–fringed lagoon. Rooms are comfortable and fully equipped.

Avillion Village Resort (☎ 647 6688; res@avillion.com.my; Km 5; d RM380; ❄ 🏊) This attractive and well-appointed resort has a large variety of accommodation options, including water chalets (on the sea), styled in wood, equipped with four-poster beds and open-air bathrooms. Also at hand are several good restaurants, an open-air bar, bicycle hire, a gym and a water sports centre.

Seri Malaysia (☎ 647 6070; fax 647 6028; Km 6; d Sun-Thu/ Fri & Sat RM110/130; ❄) This hotel from the nationwide chain offers good value for money, reliability and good views of the sea.

Rotary Sunshine Camp (☎ 647 3798; Km 5 Jl Pantai; dm/r RM6/20) Clean, cheap and run by friendly staff, this hostel is excellent value, despite the lack of air-con. Look for the blue painted shacks set back slightly from the road in green grass along Jl Pantai. There are shared shower and cooking facilities. On weekdays, you could well have the place to yourself.

Guoman Port Dickson Resort (☎ 662 7878; www.guomanhotels.com; Km 16 Jl Pantai, Teluk Kemang; d RM320; ❄ 🏊) Set in a wonderfully lush, green landscaped setting, the Guoman boasts a golf course, floodlit tennis courts, a magnificent pool and a breezy, open foyer. Weekday rates drop to RM180 for a deluxe room.

Also recommended:

Bayu Beach Resort (☎ 647 3703; Km 7.5; studio/apt RM140/154; ❄ 🏊) Large resort with range of apartment-style accommodation.

Regency (☎ 647 4090; Km 8; superior/deluxe RM180/250; ❄ 🏊) Minangkabau-style resort with tennis and squash courts.

Pantai Ria Hotel (☎ 662 5122; Km 12 Jl Pantai; d RM40, with air-con RM50; ❄) Simple but large rooms; seafood restaurant of same name downstairs (meals RM12)

Kong Ming (Guangming) Hotel (☎ 662 5683; Km 13 Telok Kemang; d Sun-Thu/Fri & Sat RM30/40) Cheap and right on the beach; the pricier rooms overlook the sea.

Eating

Dickson's Coffee House (☎ 647 7600; Corus Paradise Resort; meals RM25) Regular promotional menus make this a good-value restaurant. There's a wide-ranging menu including Malaysian favourites *(nasi lemak)*, Chinese dishes *(loh hon chai)* and international dishes (wild mushroom soup, and fish and chips).

Xiwang Village (☎ 662 1691; Lot 112, KM 11 Jl Pantai; meals RM8) This Chinese restaurant cooks up some good *yong tau foo* (bean curd or vegetables stuffed with fish paste) and a range of seafood dishes including sweet and sour sliced fish (RM5). If the spicy *tom* *yam* (fish slices lathered in a chilli paste) gets too spicy, reach for a chilled coconut from the fridge.

El Cactus (☎ 012-217 8555; Lot 2674, Jl Pantai; Km 3.5; meals RM25) This Mexican bar serves up food (boneless chicken fajitas RM15); there's live sports TV, music, an alfresco seating area and a relaxed atmosphere.

Getting There & Away

Port Dickson is 90km south of KL, 32km southwest of Seremban and 94km northwest of Melaka. Six buses a day go to KL (RM6.15); five a day to Seremban (RM2.65). Other destinations include Ipoh (RM17.45), Melaka (RM5) and Lumut (RM22). A taxi from Port Dickson to Melaka is around RM100. The bus and taxi stations are next to each other in the centre of town. (There is a very useful moneychanger at the bus station with much better rates than most hotels.)

From Port Dickson town, local buses (and buses to Melaka) will drop you off wherever you like along the beach.

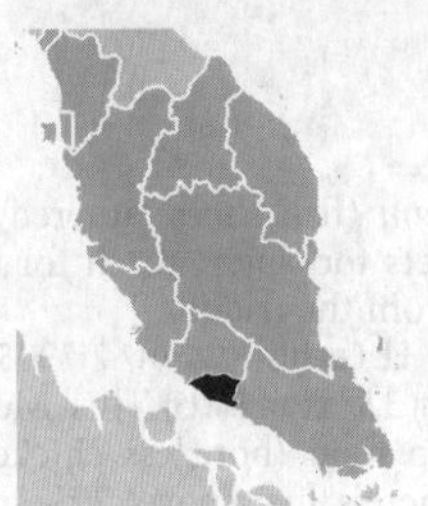

Melaka

CONTENTS

The small city-state of Melaka (Malacca) is one of the most intriguing areas on the peninsula. The highlight is the historic port city, also called Melaka, whose multicultural heritage shows up in its distinctive architecture and fantastic food. Under the Melaka sultanates, the city was a wealthy centre for trade with China, India, Siam (Thailand) and Indonesia, thanks to its strategic position on the Selat Melaka (Strait of Melaka). The Melaka sultanates were the beginning of what is today Malaysia, and some say this city is where you'll find the soul of the nation.

Modern Melaka experienced the sudden economic boom that swept Malaysia in the 1990s, starting with massive land reclamation projects, which slowed during the ensuing economic downturn. The historic waterfront retreated so far inland, however, that it endangered the traditional livelihood of the Portuguese fishing community. Despite an abundance of historical monuments, many locals argue that the city's distinctive heritage is under threat from modernisation. Nevertheless Melaka rightfully remains one of Malaysia's premier tourist destinations, with its multi-cultural heritage and a multitude of museums and other cultural attractions.

Beyond the city, there are worthwhile beach excursions to Pulau Besar and Tanjung Bidara, plus the wildlife and theme park attractions of Ayer Keroh.

HIGHLIGHTS

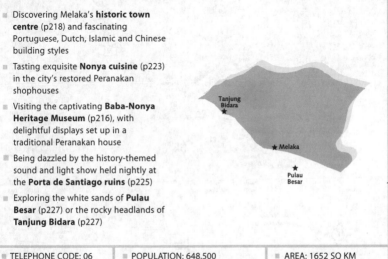

- Discovering Melaka's **historic town centre** (p218) and fascinating Portuguese, Dutch, Islamic and Chinese building styles
- Tasting exquisite **Nonya cuisine** (p223) in the city's restored Peranakan shophouses
- Visiting the captivating **Baba-Nonya Heritage Museum** (p216), with delightful displays set up in a traditional Peranakan house
- Being dazzled by the history-themed sound and light show held nightly at the **Porta de Santiago ruins** (p225)
- Exploring the white sands of **Pulau Besar** (p227) or the rocky headlands of **Tanjung Bidara** (p227)

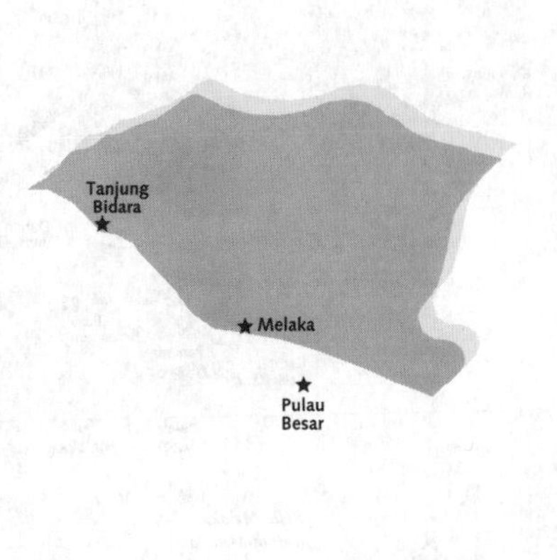

- TELEPHONE CODE: 06
- POPULATION: 648,500
- AREA: 1652 SQ KM

History

Back in the 14th century, Melaka was just another fishing village – until it attracted the attention of Parameswara, a Hindu prince from Sumatra. Parameswara had thrown off allegiance to the Majapahit empire and fled to Temasek (modern-day Singapore), where his piracy and other exploits brought on a Siamese attack in 1398, forcing him to flee again to Melaka, where he set up his new headquarters.

Under Parameswara, Melaka soon became a favoured port for waiting out monsoons and resupplying trading ships plying the strategic Selat Melaka. Halfway between China and India, and with easy access to the spice islands of Indonesia, Melaka attracted merchants from all over the East.

In 1405 Admiral Cheng Ho, the 'three-jewelled eunuch prince', arrived in Melaka bearing gifts from the Ming emperor and the promise of protection from Siamese enemies. Based on these early contacts with China, Chinese settlers followed and came to be known as the Baba and Nonya or Straits Chinese. They are the longest-settled Chinese people in Malaysia and have added many Malay customs to their own heritage. Despite internal squabbles and intrigues, by the time of Parameswara's death in 1414, Melaka was already a powerful trading state.

The cosmopolitan centre also came in contact with Islam via traders from India. The third ruler of Melaka, Maharaja Mohammed Shah (1424–44), converted to Islam, and his son, Mudzaffar Shah, took the title of sultan and made Islam the state religion.

Under the banner of Islam, Melaka became Southeast Asia's major entrepôt, attracting Muslim Indian merchants from competing Sumatran ports, and a centre for Islam, disseminating the religion throughout the Indonesian archipelago. The Melaka sultans ruled over the greatest empire in Malaysia's history, and successfully repelled Siamese attacks. The Malay language became the lingua franca of trade in the region, and Melaka produced the first major piece of Malay literature, the *Sejarah Melayu* (or *Malay Annals*), a history of the sultanate.

In 1509 the Portuguese arrived at Melaka seeking the wealth of the spice and China

PAUL BIGLAND

Baba-Nonya Heritage Museum (p216), Melaka

Christ Church (p215) and clock tower

RICHARD I'ANSON

TOM COCKREM

Cheng Hoon Teng (p216), Chinatown

CHRIS MELLOR

Young Muslim boys,
Melaka (p210)

CHRIS ROW

Malay house, **Mersing** (p240)

Sap being collected at a **rubber plantation** (p242), Johor

CHRIS ROWTHORN

MICHAEL AW

Underwater seascape, **Pulau Aur** (p244)

SIMON RIC

Johor State Tourism office (p232), Johor Bahru

trades, but after an initially friendly reception, the Melakans attacked the Portuguese fleet and took a number of prisoners.

This prompted an outright assault by the Portuguese, and in 1511 Alfonso de Albuquerque took the city, forcing the sultan to flee to Johor, where he re-established his kingdom. Under the Portuguese, the fortress of A'Famosa was constructed, and missionaries like St Francis Xavier strove to implant Catholicism. While Portuguese cannons could easily conquer Melaka, they could not force Muslim merchants from Arabia and India to continue trading there, and other ports in the area, such as Islamic Demak on Java, grew to overshadow Melaka.

The period of Portuguese strength in the East was short-lived, as Melaka suffered harrying attacks from the rulers of neighbouring Johor and Negeri Sembilan, as well as from the Islamic power of Aceh in Sumatra. Melaka declined further as Dutch influence in Indonesia grew and Batavia (modern-day Jakarta) developed as the key European port of the region. Melaka passed into Dutch hands after an eight-month siege in 1641. The Dutch ruled Melaka for only about 150 years. Melaka again became the centre for peninsular trade, but the Dutch directed more energy into their possessions in Indonesia. In Melaka they built fine public buildings and churches, which remain the most solid reminders of European presence, while Medan Portugis is still home to Portuguese Eurasians, many of whom are practising Catholics and speak Cristao, a medieval Portuguese dialect.

When the French occupied Holland in 1795, the British, allies of the Dutch, temporarily took over administration of the Dutch colonies. The British administrators, essentially traders, were opposed to the Dutch policy of trade monopoly and clearly saw the potential for intense rivalry in Malaysia between the Dutch and themselves. Accordingly, in 1807 they started to demolish A'Famosa fortress and forcibly remove Melaka's Dutch population to Penang. This would ensure that if Melaka was restored to the Dutch it would be no rival to the British Malayan centres. Fortunately Sir Thomas Stamford Raffles, the far-sighted founder of Singapore, stepped in before these destructive policies went too far, and in 1824 Melaka was permanently ceded to the British in exchange for the Sumatran port of Bencoolen (Bengkulu today).

Melaka, together with Penang and Singapore, formed the Straits settlements, the three British territories that were the centres for later expansion into the peninsula. However, under British rule Melaka was always the lesser light of the Straits settlements, and it was soon superseded by the rapidly growing commercial importance of Singapore. Apart from a brief revival of its fortunes in the early 20th century when rubber was an important crop, Melaka once again became a quiet backwater.

Climate

The temperature in Melaka ranges from 21°C to 33°C and average humidity exceeds 82%. There is rain throughout the year, with September to November the wettest months.

Getting There & Away

The North-South Highway (Lebuhraya), connecting Johor Bahru and Kuala Lumpur, is the main route through the state. Most travellers arrive and depart from Melaka overland, although there is an airport outside town. Express buses to KL and Singapore are plentiful and there are bus connections to other peninsular destinations. Trains do not stop at Melaka but at Tampin, 38km north of town. Daily boats connect with Dumai in Sumatra. For detailed information on transport to/from the city of Melaka, as well as transport options around town, see Getting There & Away (p225) and Getting Around (p226).

MELAKA

☎ 06

The city of Melaka, capital of Melaka state, is one of Malaysia's premier destinations and historical sights. Its strategic position on Selat Melaka guaranteed the city an enviable prestige and prosperity. By the 15th century the port city had become the greatest trading port in Southeast Asia, attracting waves of conquering Europeans, each adding their own cultural overlay.

Melaka's importance may have long since declined, but its distinctive history survives in its medley of Chinese, Islamic and European culture. The city's unique personality draws

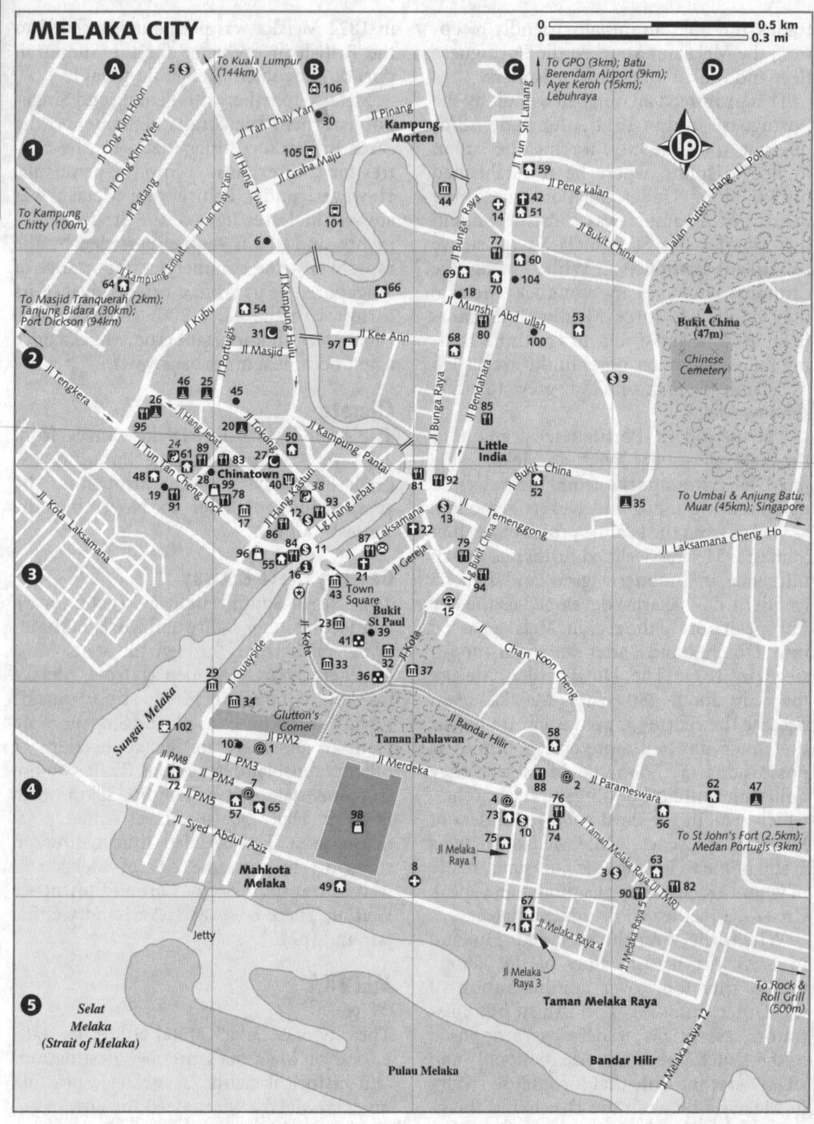

from its rare compendium of Peranakan shophouses, Portuguese and Dutch architecture, Victorian vestiges, Buddhist, Taoist and Indian temples and Islamic mosques.

When you've had your fill of Melaka's sights, food lovers can sample some of Malaysia's best cuisine here. From characteristic Peranakan dishes to Portuguese cooking, the aromas in restaurants citywide are further testament to the cultural mosaic that makes Melaka such an intriguing port.

Orientation

Melaka is a small town that's easy to navigate and compact enough to explore on foot, bicycle or *trishaw* (bicycle rickshaw).

INFORMATION
1010 Internet Cafe.....1 B4
2020 Internet Cafe.....2 C4
Bumiputra Bank.....3 D4
CEM Multimedia.....4 C4
HSBC.....5 A1
Immigration Office.....6 B1
iSURF Internet Cafe.....7 B4
Mahkota Medical Centre.....8 C4
Maybank.....9 C2
Maybank.....10 C4
MPH.....(see 98)
OCBC Bank/ATM.....11 B3
Overseas Bank.....12 B3
Public Bank.....13 C3
Southern Hospital.....14 C1
Telekom Malaysia.....15 C3
Tourist Office.....16 B3

SIGHTS & ACTIVITIES pp216-18
Baba-Nyonya Heritage Museum.....17 B3
Baoan Temple.....18 C2
Chee Mansion.....19 A3
Cheng Hoon Teng Temple.....20 B2
Christ Church.....21 B3
Church of St Francis Xavier.....22 B3
Democratic Government Museum.....23 B3
Eng Choon (Yong Chun) Association.....24 A2
Guangfu Temple.....25 A2
Guanyin Temple.....26 A2
History & Ethnography Museum.....(see 43)
Kampung Kling Mosque.....27 B2
Leong San Thong.....28 A3
Literature Museum.....(see 43)
Maritime Museum.....29 A4
Market.....30 B1
Masjid Kampung Hulu.....31 B2
Muzium Budaya (Cultural Museum).....32 B3
Muzium Rakyat (People's Museum).....33 B3
Naval Museum.....34 B4
Poh San Teng Temple.....35 D3
Porta de Santiago.....36 B3
Proclamation of Independence Memorial.....37 B3
Sanduo Temple.....38 B3
Seri Melaka.....39 B3
Sri Poyatha Venayagar Moorthi Temple.....40 B3
St Paul's Church.....41 B3
St Peter's Church.....42 C1
Stadthuys.....43 B3
Sultan's Well.....(see 35)
Villa Sentosa.....44 C1
Wah Aik shoemaker.....45 B2
Wah Teck Kiong Temple.....46 A2
Yong Chuan Tian Temple.....47 D4

SLEEPING pp221-3
Baba House.....48 A3
Century Mahkota Hotel.....49 B4
Chong Hoe Hotel.....50 B2
City Bayview Hotel.....51 C1
Eastern Heritage Guest House.....52 C3
Emperor Hotel.....53 C2
Hallmark Hotel.....54 B2
Heeren House.....55 B3
Hinley Hotel.....56 D4
Hollitel.....57 B4
Hotel Equatorial.....58 C4
Hotel Grand Continental.....59 C1
Hotel Orkid.....60 C2
Hotel Puri.....61 A3
Kancil Guest House.....62 D4
Malacca Town Holiday Lodge 1.....63 D4
Malacca Town Holiday Lodge 2.....64 A2
Mansor Hotel.....65 B4
May Chiang Hotel.....66 B2
Melaka Arasma BeliaYouth Hostel.....67 C5
Mimosa Hotel.....68 C2
Ng Fook Hotel.....69 C2
Renaissance Melaka Hotel.....70 C2
Samudra Inn.....71 C5
Seri Costa Hotel.....72 A4
Shirah's Guest House.....73 C4
Sunny's Inn.....74 C4
Travellers' Lodge.....75 C4

EATING pp223-5
Baba Cafe.....(see 48)
Bayonya.....76 C4
Bulldog Café.....77 C2
Cafe 1511.....78 B3
Capitol Satay.....79 C3
Centrepoint Food Court.....80 C2
Discovery Cafe.....81 C3
Friends Café.....82 D4
Geographér Café.....83 B2
Harper's.....84 B3
Indian Hawker Stalls.....85 C2
Jonkers Melaka Restoran.....86 B3
Long Feng.....(see 70)
Loony Planet.....87 B3
Malay Food Stalls.....88 C4
Nancy's Restoran (Old China Cafe).....89 A2
Ole Sayang.....90 D4
Restoran Peranakan.....91 A3
Selvam.....92 C3
Tart & Tart Bakery.....93 B3
UE Tea House.....94 C3
Vegan Salad & Herbs House.....95 A2

SHOPPING p225
Dr Edwin Ho.....96 B3
Ekspo Melaka.....97 B2
Mahkota Parade Shopping Complex.....98 B4
Malaqa House.....99 B3

TRANSPORT pp225-6
Avis.....100 C2
Avis.....(see 58)
Express Bus Station.....101 B1
Ferries to Dumai.....102 A4
Ferry Ticket Agents.....103 B4
Hawk.....104 C2
Local Bus Station.....105 B1
Malaysia Airlines.....(see 51)
Taxi Station.....106 B1

The interesting, older parts of Melaka are mainly on the eastern side of the river, particularly around Town Square, also known as Dutch Square, where the old Stadthuys (Town Hall) and Christ Church are solid reminders of the Dutch presence.

Rising above Town Square is Bukit St Paul (St Paul's Hill), site of the original Portuguese fort of A'Famosa. The ruins of St Paul's Church and the Porta de Santiago are the only remains of the Portuguese presence. Further north is Melaka's tiny Little India, with its night-time hawker stalls and sari shops. Chinatown to the west is lined with Chinese Peranakan shophouses and antique shops, atmospheric Buddhist temples and ancient mosques.

South of Melaka's old historical quarter are Mahkota Melaka and Taman Melaka Raya, two completely new areas built on reclaimed land.

Information

BOOKSHOPS

MPH (Ground fl, Mahkota Parade shopping complex) Good selection of English-language titles.

Popular (☎ 283 0691; 523-525 Plaza Melaka) English books on the 2nd and 3rd floors.

IMMIGRATION OFFICE

There is an **immigration office** (☎ 292 3302; 2nd fl, Wisma Persekutuan) on Jl Hang Tuah.

INTERNET ACCESS

CEM Multimedia (205 Jl Melaka Raya 1; RM3 per hr)
Geographér Café (☎ 281 6813; 83 Jl Hang Jebat; RM3 per 30 min) See also Eating (p224).
iSURF (G21, Jl PM 4, Plaza Mahkota; RM3 per hr)
1010 Internet Cafe (Jl Merdeka, opposite Glutton's Corner; RM3 per hr)
2020 Internet Cafe (56 Jl Bandar Hilir; RM3 per hr)

MEDICAL SERVICES

Hospital (☎ 282 2344)

MONEY

Moneychangers are scattered about, mainly in Chinatown and near the bus stations.

HSBC (Jl Hang Tuah) 24-hour ATMs at this bank take MasterCard, Visa, Maestro, Cirrus and Plus.

OCBC Bank (Lg Hang Jebat) This branch just over the bridge in Chinatown has a 24-hour ATM that takes Visa/Plus.

POST

A small post office can be found on Jl Laksamana off the Town Square

TELEPHONE & FAX

The **Telecom Malaysia office** (8am-5pm) is east of Bukit St Paul

TOURIST INFORMATION

Tourist Office (281 4803; www.melaka.gov.my; Jl Kota, opposite Christ Church; 8.45am-5pm, closed 12.15-2.45pm Fri) Has free (perhaps out of date) maps of Melaka.
Tourist Police (282 2222; Jl Kota)

Sights & Activities

Most sights can be visited on the Walking Tour, p218.

STADTHUYS

The massive red town hall and governor's residence, the **Stadthuys** (Town Square; 282 6526; admission RM2; 9am-6pm Sat-Thu, 9am-12.15pm & 2.45-6pm Fri), was built between 1641 and 1660 and is believed to be the oldest Dutch building in the East. Typical of Dutch colonial architecture, it features substantial solid doors and louvred windows; the port-red theme extends to the other buildings around the Town Square and the old clock tower. It also houses the **History & Ethnography Museum**. Unlike most museums in Malaysia, which give little or no explanation, here it would take a couple of hours to read your way through the detailed explanations of Melaka's past. Also within the Stadthuys is the mildly interesting **Literature Museum**, focusing on Malaysian writers. Admission to both these museums is included in the admission price to Stadthuys.

ST PAUL'S CHURCH

Originally built by a Portuguese captain in 1521 as the small Our Lady of the Hill chapel, **St Paul's Church** is a noble and sublime testament to Catholicism in East Asia and offers fine, breezy views over Melaka from the summit of Bukit St Paul upon which it sits. The church was regularly visited by St Francis Xavier and following his death in China, the saint's body was brought here and buried for nine months before being transferred to Goa in India, where it remains today. A marble statue of St Francis Xavier commemorates his interment here over 400 years ago.

In 1556 the church was enlarged to two storeys, and a tower was added to the front in 1590. The church was renamed following the Dutch takeover, but when the Dutch completed their own Christ Church at the base of the hill, it fell into disuse. Under the British it lost the tower, although a lighthouse was built at the front, and the church eventually ended up as a storehouse for gunpowder. The church has been in ruins now for more than 150 years, but the setting is beautiful, the walls are imposing and fine old tombstones stand around the interior.

MUZIUM BUDAYA

The **Muzium Budaya** (Cultural Museum; 282 7464; Jl Kota; admission RM2; 9am-5.30pm Wed-Mon) is inside a wooden replica of a Melaka sultan's palace. This building is based on descriptions from the *Malay Annals* of the original 15th-century palace, built entirely without nails. The exhibits here concentrate on traditional Melakan culture, including textiles, games, weaponry, musical instruments and even a diorama of the sultan's court. The museum also holds the Terengganu Stone with its early-14th-century Arabic and Malay inscriptions, the first evidence of Islam on the peninsula.

BABA-NONYA HERITAGE MUSEUM

This captivating **museum** (283 1273; 48-50 Jl Tun Tan Cheng Lock; adult/child RM8/4; incl tour if enough people; 10am-12.30pm & 2-4.30pm Wed-Mon), set in a traditional Peranakan townhouse in Chinatown, is arranged to look like a typical 19th-century Baba-Nonya residence. Furniture consists of Chinese hardwoods fashioned in a mixture of Chinese, Victorian and Dutch designs with mother-of-pearl inlay. There are also displays of 'Nonya ware', multicoloured ceramic designs from Jiangxi and Guangdong provinces in China, made specifically for Straits Chinese. Nonya ceramics and tilework are usually a blend of pink, yellow, dark-blue and green colours.

CHENG HOON TENG TEMPLE

Chinatown's most famous temple, the **Cheng Hoon Teng Temple** (Qing Yun Ting; Green Clouds Temple; Jl Tokong) is dedicated to the Goddess of Mercy. Dating back to 1646, it is Malaysia's oldest Chinese temple, with all building materials imported from China, along with the artisans involved in its construction. In the temple's interior (an explosion of black, gold and red), is a robed effigy of Guanyin (Goddess of Compassion) and other small shrines, as well as a small rockery at the rear decorated with small effigies of Luohan (Arhats) around an empty niche – where, one suspects, another statue of Guanyin should stand. Despite the temple's fame, it cannot compare with temples in China (its statues, as with most Chinese temples in Malaysia, are very diminutive), but it remains both a venerable and sacred site.

VILLA SENTOSA

While not an official museum, this 1920s Malay *kampung* (village) house called **Villa Sentosa** (Peaceful Villa; ☎ 282 3988; www.travel.to/villasentosa; entry by donation; 🕘 9am-1pm & 2-5pm, 2.45-5pm Fri), on the Melaka River in Kampung Morten, is open to passers-by and well worth a visit. A member of the family will show you around the house, accessed via a bridge, pointing out an interesting and varied collection of objects. These include Ming dynasty ceramics, a 100-year old copy of the *Quran* and a certificate of honour awarded by King George V to the late Tuan Haji Hashim Bin Dato Demang Haji Abdul Ghani (who lived here). Most of all, it's an opportunity to wander through a genuine *kampung* house. You will also have the chance to add to the visitor's book, copious volumes of which record congratulatory remarks from legions of visitors, some well-known. Afterwards, you can stroll around Kampung Morten, where there are a number of more traditional *kampung* houses.

ST PETER'S CHURCH

The oldest functioning Catholic church in Malaysia, **St Peter's Church** (Jl Bendahara) was built in 1710 by descendants of early Portuguese settlers. The church has stained-glass windows, the Latin words Tu es Petrus (You are the Rock) above the altar and a bell cast in Goa (India) in 1608. On Good Friday the church comes alive when the Malaccans flock here, many of them making it the occasion for a trip home from far-flung parts of the country. St Peter's was recently in the papers as Melaka folk protested the planned construction of a nearby high-rise.

BUKIT CHINA

In the middle of the 15th century the sultan of Melaka's ambassador to China returned with the Ming emperor's daughter to wed the sultan and thus seal relations between the two countries. She brought with her a vast retinue, including 500 handmaidens, and **Bukit China** (China Hill) was established as their residence. It has been a Chinese area ever since and, together with two adjoining hills, forms what is said to be the largest Chinese cemetery in the world outside China – comprised of more than 12,000 graves and covering 25 hectares. Some ornate graves date back to the Ming dynasty, but most are now in a sorry state. Chinese graveyards are often built on hillsides to maximise positive feng shui. At the foot of Bukit China, called San Bao Shan (Three Treasures Mount) in Mandarin, **Poh San Teng Temple** was built in 1795 and contains images of the Taoist entity Dabo Gong, and Guanyin. To the right of the temple is the **Sultan's Well**, a 15th-century well built by Sultan Mansor Shah for his Chinese wife, Princess Hang Li Poh. It was an important source of water for Melaka and a prime target for opposition forces wanting to take the city.

MARITIME MUSEUM & NAVAL MUSEUM

Next to the river, the **Maritime Museum** (admission RM2; 🕘 9am-6pm Wed-Mon) is housed in a huge re-creation of the *Flora de la Mar*, a Portuguese ship that sank off the coast of Melaka while trying to transport Malaysian treasures back to Europe. Closed for refurbishment at the time of writing and due to re-open by 2004, the exhibits have detailed descriptions of Melaka's history, as well as ship models, dioramas and an interesting map room featuring charts dating back to Portuguese times.

Your ticket also grants admission to the **Naval Museum** (admission RM2; 🕘 9am-6pm Wed-Mon) across the street. Salvaged remnants from the *Diana*, sunk off Melaka in 1817 while voyaging from Guangzhou (Canton) to Madras, are displayed, plus a host of discolouring photos on Malaysia's maritime past, and a guide to help you brush up on your nautical knots.

MEDAN PORTUGIS

About 3km east of the city centre on the coast is the area known as **Medan Portugis**

(Portuguese Square). The small *kampung* centred on the square is the heart of Melaka's Eurasian community, descended from marriages that took place between the colonial Portuguese and Malays 400 years ago. A French missionary first proposed the settlement to the British colonial government in the 1920s, but the square, styled after a typical Portuguese *mercado* and meant to give the settlement a cultural focus, wasn't completed until the late 1980s.

In the open square area, the Portuguese community office bulletin board displays advertisements for cultural events and news articles, some concerning the damage Melaka's land reclamation has done to local family-run fisheries.

The *kampung* is unexceptional, however, and the square often empty, except on weekends. But the sea breeze is lovely while enjoying a relaxing beer or meal at the many restaurants in and around the square (see Eating, p225). Town Bus No 17 from the local bus station will get you here; see Getting Around p226.

FORT ST JOHN

Although the British demolished most of Porta de Santiago (see Walking Tour this page), they left the small Dutch **Fort of St John** (Bukit Senjuang, off Jl Bukit Senjuang) untouched. The fort was originally a Portuguese chapel dedicated to St John the Baptist until the Dutch rebuilt it in the 18th century. It stands on a hilltop to the east of town just before the turn-off to Medan Portugis – head east along Jl Parameswara, then turn left into Jl Bukit Senjuang. Only a few walls and cannon emplacements of the fort remain, but there are fine views from the hilltop.

MASJID TRANQUERAH

Of typical Sumatran design, featuring a square, multitiered roof, the 150-year-old **Masjid Tranquerah** (Masjid Tengkera; Jl Tengkera), is 2km towards Port Dickson. In its graveyard is the tomb of Sultan Hussein of Johor, who in 1819 signed over the island of Singapore to Stamford Raffles. The sultan later retired to Melaka, where he died in 1853. Take bus No 18 from Melaka's local bus station.

BOAT TRIPS

Parameswara Tours (☎ 286 5468) offers daily riverboat tours of Melaka (RM8; 45 min; 5pm and 6pm; minimum of six people) from the quay behind the tourist office on Jl Kota. The boat travels to Kampung Morten, where Villa Sentosa is located, past old *godowns* (river warehouses). The commentary is quite droll, but some travellers complain that the river is grim and needs to be cleaned up (it is, and it does). There are also trips to Pulau Besar (RM22; 45 min; 10am; minimum of 12 people), returning at 4pm and to Pulau Upeh (RM16; 8.30am; minimum of six people), returning at 5pm.

For regularly scheduled ferries to Pulau Besar, see Around Melaka, p227.

KAMPUNG CHITTY

As well as the Baba-Nonyas, Melaka also has a small community of Chitty – Straits-born Indians, offspring of the Indian traders who intermarried with Malay women. Their area of town, known as Kampung Chitty, lies to the west of Jl Gajah Berang, about a kilometre northwest of Chinatown; look for the archway with elephant sculptures beside the Mutamariman Temple. Like Kampung Morten, it's a pretty district in which to wander and see traditional Malay-style houses. The best time to visit is during the Mariamman Festival or Pesta Datuk Charchar in May, a Hindu celebration when you might also be fortunate enough to witness a traditional Indian wedding ceremony.

Walking Tour

This walk begins at the delightful Town Square, Melaka's historic focal point. The most imposing relic of the Dutch period in Melaka is the **Stadthuys** (**1**; p216). Exiting the Stadthuys, to your right is **Christ Church (2)**. Constructed from pink bricks brought from Zeeland in Holland, the church was faced with local red laterite when constructed in 1753. Under the British this Dutch Reformed church was converted for Anglican use, and the weathercock and bell tower were added, but it still has old Dutch and Armenian tombstones laid in the floor of the church's interior. Its massive 15m-long ceiling beams were each cut from a single tree.

Walk west and cross the bridge over the Melaka River. Although Melaka has lost its prominence as a port, ancient-looking

Sumatran schooners still sail up the river and moor on its banks. Today, however, their cargo is not the varied treasures of the East, but charcoal or lumber from Indonesia. There's a good view of the river and boats from the bridge, and you can take a river boat tour (see Boat Trips, p218).

On the other shore, turn left (past Harper's restaurant) and stroll along **Jl Tun Tan Cheng Lock**. This narrow street, formerly called Heeren St, was the preferred address for wealthy Baba (Straits-born Chinese) traders who were most active during the short-lived rubber boom of the early 20th century. These typical Peranakan houses, with their intricate tiles and plasterwork, display Chinese, Dutch and British influences in a style that has been described as Chinese Palladian and Chinese Baroque. The interiors of these houses contain open courtyards that admit sun and rain – similar to Chinese temples. While walking along this street, look up at the carved lintels, cornices and other architectural flourishes.

The **Baba-Nonya Heritage Museum** (**3**; p216) is well worth exploring. Next door at No 52, the Peranakan interior of **Cafe 1511** (**4**; p224) is worth perusing. Also dotted along Jl Tun Tan Cheng Lock are several artists' studios that you can browse around. **Malaqa House** (**5**; 70 Jl Tun Tan Cheng Lock) is a gallery and antiques shop operating from a noble old building, and well worth a visit. At the end of this block sits a small, squat Taoist/Buddhist shrine, a typical reminder of how the faiths have merged in Chinese temples in Malaysia.

Further along on the right, the elegant **Hotel Puri** (**6**; p222) is well worth investigating; the Chinese characters emblazoned on the door literally mean 'Longevity Mountain, Fortuitous Sea' (the same characters are found on other buildings along this road). The impressive classical-style building set back from the street opposite is the **Chee Mansion** (**7**; 115-117 Jl Tun Tan Cheng Lock), a Chinese family shrine not open to the public.

Along from Chee Mansion is **Baba House** (**8**; see Sleeping p222), another traditional house now serving as a hotel. The **Eng Choon (Yong Chun) Association** (**9**; 122 Jl Tun Tan Cheng Lock) is an impressively well-kept Chinese temple, containing a small shrine to two Taoist deities, Tianshang Shengmu and

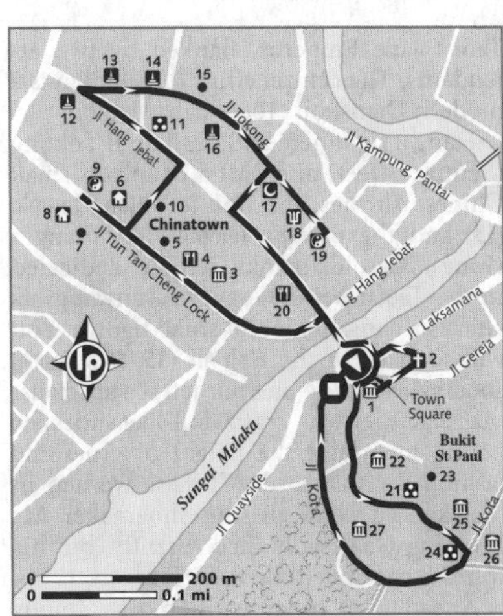

Start/Finish: Town Square/Muzium Rakyat
Distance: 2.2km
Duration: 3 hours

Zhanggong Shengjun. Admire the painted gods on the doors and the carved dragons adorning the stone pillars. Chinese characters written on the building mean 'Peace to the country and the people' – which you see elsewhere in Chinatown.

Backtrack along Jl Tun Tan Cheng Lock and walk north up the Jl Lekir (Third Cross Street). On the right-hand side is the dignified **Leong San Thong** (**10**; Dragon Hill Hall; 8 Jl Lekir) built in 1928; also arrayed along this short street are restaurants and antique shops. At the junction, turn left onto **Jl Hang Jebat**, formerly known as Jonkers St (or Junk St Melaka), famed for its interesting assortment of antique and craft shops. You can easily spend an hour or more browsing for some of the treasures of the East, but don't expect any bargains.

On Saturday and Sunday the street is for pedestrians only and is transformed into a market of stalls called the Jonker Walk; see Melaka's Endangered Heritage (p220).

As you walk west, you'll pass the all-white **Hang Kasturi's Tomb (11)** on your right and further along on your left is the small, modern and pink **Guanyin Temple** (**12**; Guanyin Tang) dedicated to the Buddhist Goddess of Compassion. Seated in the second hall is the

Taoist Jade Emperor, flanked by two attendants. The central effigy of Guanyin is a modern Qianshou (1000-arm) version.

Hang a right here and head up Jl Tokong (Temple Street) and past a couple of small Chinese shrines, the **Wah Teck Kiong Temple (13)** and the **Guangfu Temple** (**14**; Guangfu Gong), an old, smoky temple dedicated to the Taoist being Guangze Zunwang; its altar is a constellation of small figures. You will soon reach the **Wah Aik** (**15**; 56 Jl Tokong) shoemaker's shop on your left – a specialist manufacturer who crafts doll-like shoes for bound feet, once the height of gruesome fashion for well-to-do Chinese women in Melaka. The enterprising shoemaker Mr Yeo Sing Guat sadly died recently, but his son has continued the tradition.

Ahead is Chinatown's most famous Chinese temple, the **Cheng Hoon Teng Temple** (**16**; p216). Adding a splash of colour to Jl Tokong are the Chinese shops selling red and gold lanterns, paper money and funerary preparations. The street used to be famed for its goldsmiths, but most have moved to other areas.

Continue walking east to the **Kampung Kling Mosque (17)**. This hoary mosque has a multi-tiered *meru* roof (stacked form similar to that seen in Balinese Hindu architecture), which owes its inspiration to Hindu temples, and a Moorish watchtower minaret typical of early mosques in Sumatra. Further along is the **Sri Poyyatha Vinayagar Moorthi Temple (18)**, dating from 1781 and dedicated to the Hindu deity Vinayagar. Slightly further ahead is the **Sanduo Temple** (**19**; Sanduo Miao), another pretty Chinese shrine encapsulating effigies of Dabo Gong, Jinhua Niangniang and Guanyin.

Backtrack and hang a left along the exterior wall of the mosque back along Lorong Hang Lekiu (Fourth Cross St) to Jl Hang Jebat. Stroll back to Lorong Hang Jebat (First Cross St) and the bridge, noting the decorative touches along the way – mosaics, tiling, inlaid coloured stones, carvings, Western-style balustrades, balconies, shutters and ornamentations. The **Jonkers Melaka Restoran** (**20**; p224) is a noteworthy old Nonya building.

Traverse the bridge, cross the Town Square back to the Stadthuys and clamber up the steps leading to the top of Bukit St Paul, topped by the fabulous ruins of **St Paul's Church** (**21**; see Sights p216). The politically inclined can pop into the **Democratic Government Museum** (**22**; admission RM2; 9am-5.30pm Tue-Sun)

MELAKA'S ENDANGERED HERITAGE

With Nonya fast-food making an appearance along with some indiscriminate renovation of fine historic buildings, some of Melaka's citizens are gloomy. 'It is sad to see Malacca being transformed into a ludicrous theme park of fake heritage at bargain prices', complained one resident in a letter to the *New Straits Times*.

It is a familiar refrain. Residents of Jonker St in Chinatown have rounded on the organisers of the weekend Jonker Walk, accusing the market of eroding the famous street's heritage. Denizens of Jonker St blame the market for increasing pollution and noise. They also complain that traffic restrictions and the new commercial environment (soaring rents included) have forced the closure of many traditional local trades and businesses, including goldsmiths and Indian barbers.

The Wah Aik shoemaker was evicted from its premises so that the building, along with two adjacent buildings, could be torn down to build a hotel. A public outcry halted the construction of the hotel, but the buildings were demolished anyway, and the shoemaker relocated to Jl Tokong (see Walking Tour this page).

According to the Malacca Heritage Trust, between mid-2000 and December 2002, 42 buildings were demolished in Melaka's conservation area.

To outsiders, Melaka's heritage remains picturesque, but residents argue a loss of authenticity is being foisted upon them. A further complaint is that heritage buildings have been painted in garish colours in the name of conservation. The concern is that tourist development has become a higher priority than conservation.

Recently visiting Melaka, a Unesco representative (the city aims to be listed as a World Heritage Site) expressed concern at the demolition of century-old shophouses and the 'gradual degradation of the conservation area'.

en route to the church if you need to swat up on Malaysia's 20th-century history. Nearby is the **Seri Melaka** (**23**; RM2; 9am-5.30pm Tue-Sun, 9am-12.15pm & 2.45-5.30pm Fri), the former official residence of the governor and built by the Dutch in the 17th century.

There are steps from St Paul's Church down the hill to **Porta de Santiago (24)**, once the main gate – and all that remains – of the Portuguese fortress A'Famosa, originally constructed by Alfonso de Albuquerque in 1512. Stamford Raffles may have stepped in before the complete destruction of the old fortress, but it came close. Curiously, this sole surviving relic of the fort bears the Dutch East India Company's coat of arms as this was part of the fort used by the Dutch after their takeover in 1670.

To the east at the base of Bukit St Paul, is the **Muzium Budaya** (**25**; p216). Housed in a British villa dating from 1911 across the way, the **Proclamation of Independence Memorial** (**26**; admission free; 9am-6pm Sat-Thu, 9am-12pm & 3-6pm Fri) is a museum charting the history of Malaysia's progression to independence. There's too much to read and perhaps not enough to look at (although the Japanese officer's sword from occupation days is interesting). Ironically, this grand building topped by Mogul-inspired domes was once the Melaka Club, a bastion of colonialism.

Follow Jl Kota around the base of Bukit St Paul and head back to the Town Square. If you have the energy, pop into the **Muzium Rakyat** (**27**; People's Museum; admission RM2), just west of the Porta de Santiago, which was being refurbished at the time of writing. The museum has displays on Malaysian society and culture.

Festivals & Events

Melaka celebrates all the major Malaysian holidays, including Chinese New Year, Thaipusam and National Day (see the Directory chapter, p541).

The **Melaka Dragon Boat Association** (☎ 281 5649) can supply details on the Chinese dragonboat races held in June/July.

Easter (April/May) Good Friday and Easter Sunday processions are held outside at St Peter's Church.

Festa San Pedro (late June) Honouring this patron saint of the Portuguese fishing community, celebrations take place at St Peter's Church and normally include a float procession from the Porta de Santiago to Medan Portugis, with cooking, fishing, handicraft and carnival festivities.

Festa San Juan (late June) Just before the Festa San Pedro, Melaka's Eurasian community hosts this festival at the chapel on top of St John's hill.

Dragon Boat Festival (June/July) This Chinese festival, marked by a dragon boat race in the Strait of Melaka, commemorates the death by drowning of 3rd-century BC Chinese poet and statesman Qu Yuan.

Festa Santa Cruz (mid-September) This festival finishes with a candlelight procession of Melakan and Singaporean Catholics to Malim chapel.

Sleeping

BUDGET

Melaka has a wide range of accommodation, of varying quality. Many guesthouses are located in Taman Melaka Raya, the area of reclaimed land south of Jl TMR. They are virtually all on the second and third floors of rather new and characterless blocks, but offer good atmosphere and facilities: common rooms with books, TVs and notice boards; small kitchens; and a variety of rooms. Though the interior walls are often only plywood and few rooms have windows, some have skylights. Plenty of competition keeps prices down. A light breakfast may be included in the price.

Travellers' Lodge (☎ 226 5709; 214B Jl Melaka Raya 1; s/d with fan RM16/21, s/d with air-con RM33/35;) Very clean and spacious maze-like lodgings with newly decorated and tidy rooms (only pricier rooms have attached bathroom). Friendly staff, neat living room, kitchen and rooftop garden up some vertiginous steps.

Eastern Heritage Guest House (☎ 283 3026; 8 Jl Bukit China; dm/s/d RM8/18/20) Well-located, just a short walk from the town centre, this atmospheric place is housed in a superb old Melaka building dating from 1918, with Peranakan tiling and impressive carved panelling. There's a dipping pool, a downstairs common room and breakfast is included.

Malacca Town Holiday Lodge 1 (☎ 284 8830; 148B Jl TMR; s/d RM15/18) Clean and well-run establishment on the main thoroughfare of Jl TMR, opposite the Ole Sayang restaurant (see Eating p224). It may not have dorms or a decorated common room like most other hostels, but it's well-kept and is a friendly family-run place.

Malacca Town Holiday Lodge 2 (☎ 284 6905; 52 Jl Kampung Empat; s/d/tr RM16/20/27;) Despite a slightly inconvenient location, there is a variety of large rooms (all with windows);

more-expensive singles/doubles have shower and air-con. This clean and friendly place also has bike rental (RM7 per day).

Shirah's Guest House (☎ 286 1041; shirahgh@tm.ent.my; 207-209, 2nd fl, Jl Taman Melaka Raya; dm/s/tr/d RM9/15/27/18-60;) Cosy common room and informative bulletin boards, with bike hire, Internet access and kitchen facilities. Newly painted large rooms (one with four-poster bed), high ceilings, rooftop terrace and competent management.

Kancil Guesthouse (☎ 281 4044; kancil@machinta.com.sg; 177 Jl Parameswara; dm/s/d RM12/18/30;) Just west of the small Taoist Yong Chuan Tian Temple, this pleasant guesthouse offers spacious, secure lodgings (although the busy road outside has no pavement). The rooms are rather simple and the small singles are near the traffic, but there's a pleasant garden out the back. There's also bike rental (RM8 per day) and Internet access (RM4 per hour).

Hollitel (☎ 286 0607; mollykoo@yahoo.com; G-20K Jl PM 5, Plaza Mahkota; s/d RM55/70;) In the grid of blocks southwest of Jl Merdeka, this new hotel has clean rooms with electric showers (except in the cheapest singles), TV and air-con. Internet access (RM3.50 per hour) and free pick-up from the bus station are also offered.

Hinley Hotel (☎ 283 6554; 150 Jl Parameswara; s/d RM40/50;) Set back from the murderous, pavement-free road outside is this petite stand-alone orange and white hotel with just 20 rooms. Rooms come with TV, phone and shower room and make for good-value accommodation.

Also recommended:

Melaka Arasma Belia Youth Hostel (☎ 282 7915; 341A Jl Melaka Raya 3; dm RM10, with air-con RM15;) Clean place with large and quiet dorm rooms; common room with TV. There's a laundry service and a midnight curfew.

Chong Hoe Hotel (☎ 282 6102; 26 Jl Tukang Emas; s/d RM22/39;) Small, simple, fine location and good value.

Ng Fook Hotel (☎ 282 8055; 154 Jl Bunga Raya; s/d with fan RM29/37; d with air-con RM43;) More-expensive rooms have showers at this friendly place.

May Chiang Hotel (☎ 282 2101; 59 Jl Munshi Abdullah; d RM40;) Well-run, clean and friendly place with only eight rooms, all with shower, TV and air-con.

Mansor Hotel (☎ 283 7529; mansor_hotel@hotmail.com; G16-12 Jl PM 5, Plaza Mahkota; s RM25) Good discounts offered.

Sunny's Inn (☎ 227 5446; 270A-B Jl Melaka Raya 3; dm/s with fan RM9/15, d without/with air-con RM20/35;)

MID-RANGE

Many mid-range hotels are in the northern part of town but the central Chinatown area has some fabulous options.

Baba House (☎ 281 1216; thebabahouse@pd.jaring.my; 125-127 Jl Tun Tan Cheng Lock; s/d RM85/95;) In a same row of restored Peranakan shophouses, this elegant Baba building is beautifully arranged with tilework, carved panels and a cool, interior courtyard. Many rooms are windowless but come with bathroom and TV, and are clean.

Mimosa Hotel (☎ 282 1113; mimosah@tm.net.my; 108 Jl Bunga Raya; r RM100;) This recommended modern Chinatown hotel has clean, modern, fully equipped rooms, and a decent breakfast is included. The hotel also enjoys a great location in a bustling Chinese area, and offers good discounts on rates.

Century Mahkota Hotel (☎ 281 2828; Jl Merdeka; apt Sun-Thu/Fri-Sat RM178/201;) Ensconced on reclaimed waterfront south of the huge Mahkota Parade shopping complex, this lovely resort-style hotel has a range of suites and apartments, plus an ample range of facilities including two large swimming pools, a few restaurants and bars, and tennis and squash courts.

Hotel Puri (☎ 282 5588; www.hotelpuri.com; 118 Jl Tun Tan Cheng Lock; d RM110;) Chinatown has some fine buildings, and Hotel Puri is one of them. This elegant creation is a superb old renovated Peranakan manor house that once belonged to a rubber plantation owner. The elaborate lobby is decked out with beautiful old cane and inlaid furniture, and opens into a glassed-over inner courtyard. Standard rooms are very comfortable and come with all mod cons. Breakfast for two included.

Hotel Orkid (☎ 282 5555; hotelorkid@po.jaring.my; 138 Jl Bendahara; r RM99;) You'll get good value at this centrally located modern high-rise hotel. All rooms have in-house video, coffee- and tea-making facilities and minibar. There's also a health spa, restaurant and lounge with live music; breakfast is included.

Emperor Hotel (☎ 284 0777; tehmc@tm.net.my; 123 Jl Munshi Abdullah; r RM250;) Excellent promotional rates (RM98) make this smart establishment a great option. There are fine views from the upper floors, all rooms come with bath, fridge and TV with in-house video. Also at hand are a fitness centre and restaurants.

THE AUTHOR'S CHOICE *Damian Harper*

Budget

Samudra Inn (☎ 282 7441; 348B Jl Melaka Raya 3; dm/s/d RM10/18/20) It may not be located in the historic centre of Melaka, but travellers enthuse about this popular and comfy guesthouse south of Jl TMR. Clean, quiet and run by very friendly and helpful owners, the Samudra Inn offers both comfort and value.

Mid-Range

Heeren House (☎ 281 4241; fax 281 4239; 1 Jl Tun Tan Cheng Lock; d RM139;) Lodging here positions you right in the heart of Chinatown, on the waterfront and within range of some fine eateries and sights. The airy, clean and well-tended rooms in this former *godown* all overlook the river and have polished floorboards, a few pieces of antique furniture, attached bathrooms and all the mod cons. There's a popular café in the foyer (see Eating, p225) and breakfast is included in the price of the room.

Top End

Renaissance Melaka Hotel (☎ 284 8888; infomkz@po.jaring.my; Jl Bendahara; d RM400;) Plush and well managed, the high-rise five-star Renaissance offers spacious and tastefully decorated and furnished rooms, with long views over town and the port. Rooms come with in-house video and minibar, and the hotel enjoys a broad range of facilities, including squash courts, lounge and a pub (with live music regularly).

Hallmark Hotel (☎ 282 2888; fax 281 3409; 68 Jl Portugis; r RM108;) This reasonably clean and decent mid-range hotel has regular promotions and rooms come with shower room, phone and TV.

TOP END

Melaka has a couple of older high-rise hotels that are no longer up with the best, but most offer good facilities and substantial discounts.

City Bayview Hotel (☎ 283 9888; cbviewmk@tm.net.my; Jl Bendahara; r RM318;) This place is worth checking out for the awesome kitsch of the chandelier in its foyer. A high-rise hotel opposite the Southern Hospital, it has expensive rack rates but give fishing for promotional prices a go. Rooms include cable TV, minibar, and tea- and coffee-making facilities; there's a Chinese restaurant and a lounge with live music.

Seri Costa Hotel (☎ 281 6666; hotelsericosta@pd.jaring.my; Jl PM 8, Plaza Mahkota; r RM220;) This modern, clean and smart three-star hotel is southwest of Jl Merdeka. Rooms are fully equipped with satellite TV, coffee- and tea-making facilities and room safes. They come with teakwood beds and furniture, and the hotel offers good promotional rates.

Also recommended:

Hotel Equatorial (☎ 282 8333; into@mel.equatorial.com; Jl Parameswara; s/d RM380/410;) Promotional rates can dip as low as RM195.

Hotel Grand Continental (☎ 284 0088; melaka@grandhotelsinternational.com.my; 20 Jl Tun Sri Lanang; d RM200) Location in north not ideal, but breakfast is included and there are excellent promotional rates; good value.

Eating

Melaka's food reflects its history, and fantastic coffee abounds. It is the home of Portuguese Eurasian food and Chinese Nonya cuisine (done in Melaka with a salty Indonesian influence). Medan Portugis (see Restoran de Lisbon, p225) is the place to try Portuguese-influenced dishes, mostly seafood, though the fiery 'devil curry' is also worth a try. The classic Nonya dish of Melaka, laksa, is the best in Malaysia – the rich coconut base makes it tastier than the sour Penang variety.

Eats on the streets include *youtiao* (fried bread sticks; 40 sen) and *rougan* (dried meat strips; RM26 for 250gms). For drinks, look out for sugar cane juice (RM1) and soya milk (RM1). For hawker stalls, along Jl Merdeka (previously the waterfront), the permanent food stalls at Glutton's Corner serve all the usual hawker specialities.

The Mahkota Parade shopping complex down the road is mostly a centre for Western fast food, though the food court on the 1st floor has the usual Malaysian hawker favourites. Outdoor hawker venues include the daytime **Centrepoint food court** (Jl Munshi Abdullah); the night-time **Indian hawker stalls** (Jl Bendahara) in Little India, and the busy **Malay stalls** (near Jl TMR roundabout).

Restoran Peranakan (☎ 284 5001; 107 Jl Tun Tan Cheng Lock; meals RM18) Big, airy Chinatown Peranakan restaurant well worth a visit for the ambience alone. Also worth trying is the tom yam soup (RM10) and a fine piquant seafood soup (with traces of chicken). A large range of chicken and fish dishes is on the menu.

Cafe 1511 (☎ 286 0151; www.cafe1511.com; 52 Jl Tun Tan Cheng Lock; 10am-6pm Thu-Tue; meals RM8;) Next to the Baba-Nonya Heritage Museum is this Peranakan café sporting a high ceiling, original tiles along the wall and lovely carved screens, plus a mishmash of decorative objects from Southeast Asia. Served up are Nonya favourites including *nonya popiah* (spring rolls served with chilli; RM2) and *nonya otak-otak* (fish cake; RM3). Internet access is RM1.50 per 30 minutes.

Selvam (☎ 281 9223; 3 Jl Temenggong; meals RM8) This Little India eatery has a loyal band of local patrons, with its choice range of tasty and cheap curries and roti, plus a Friday afternoon vegetarian special with 10 varieties of veg (RM5).

Bayonya (☎ 292 2192; 164 Jl Taman Melaka Raya; 10am-10pm Wed-Mon; meals RM15) This authentic eatery has a great reputation for its excellent and inexpensive home-cooked Peranakan cuisine.

Long Feng (☎ 284 8888; 1st fl, Renaissance Melaka Hotel; Jl Bendahara; à la carte meals RM100) Fine Chinese dining in a classic Chinese setting, with waiting staff wearing cheongsam. There's a large selection of seafood delicacies and an 'all you can eat' dim sum buffet (11am to 2.30pm).

Geographér Café (☎ 281 6813; 83 Jl Hang Jebat; meals RM8;) The open and breezy bar with late hours in this pre-war shophouse pulls in the travellers. There's a good choice of local (*nasi lemak*, rice cooked in coconut milk served with anchovies, boiled egg, peanuts and cucumber slices; RM3.50) and Western dishes, laid-back service and live music. Internet access is RM3 per 30 minutes.

Discovery Cafe (3 Jl Bunga Raya;) A popular place of congregation for travellers, situated by the river in the centre of town, the Discovery is an excellent café/bar, and a favourite meeting place for all types. It's open late, there's Internet access at RM5 per hour, and outside seating.

Ole Sayang (☎ 283 1966; 198 Jl TMR; closed Wed; meals RM13) Famed Nonya restaurant serving a variety of Nonya dishes at decent prices and reliable standards.

Tart & Tart Bakery (☎ 282 1181; 45 Lg Hang Jebat; snacks from RM2) This simple relaxing Malay-run

THE AUTHOR'S CHOICE

Damian Harper

Harper's (☎ 282 8800; 2 & 4 Lg Hang Jebat; meals RM45) Wonderfully situated in an old Chinatown *godown* overlooking the Melaka River, Harper's is a place to dine in both history and style. This is unarguably one of Malaysia's top dining experiences – strong on character and atmosphere, with excellent value an added fillip. Take a seat, measure up the high ceiling and peruse what is an excellent menu. Harper's has hit the nail on the head with a tantalising choice of food, from Nonya specials, through a large selection of Chinese dishes, to seafood and a pronounced international selection. The creamy seafood soup is served deliciously in a hollowed-out bun, the spaghetti marinara wholesome and tasty. If you've only got one night in Melaka, book a table here.

Jonkers Melaka Restoran (☎ 283 5578; 17 Jl Hang Jebat; noon-5pm; meals RM20) Café in a craft shop and an old Nonya building, the Jonkers Melaka is highly recommended for the setting and its terrific home-made food served in a cool, central courtyard. A different Nonya specials menu (RM20) appears every week, supplemented with international dishes and vege options (vegetarian platter RM17) for those on a bloodless diet.

Capitol Satay (☎ 283 5508; 41 Lg Bukit China; meals RM8) Usually packed to the gills and one of the cheapest outfits in town, Capitol Satay not only serves up very moreish meat- and veg-kebabs (and the elusive speciality *satay celup*, a satay stick laden with raw meat and vegetables which you cook by dipping into scorching satay sauce), but a meal here is great fun and a chance for some gregarious feasting.

Chinatown snack shop does a small range of cheese tarts (RM2), cake (RM4.50), apple pies (RM2.20) and *kaya* (RM2.50) – coconut cream that you spread on bread.

Loony Planet (☎ 286 3168; 14 Jl Laksamana; meals RM10) Just north of the Town Square, the Loony Planet is ideally situated for a break at the end of the day. The cheapest beer here is Angkor (from Cambodia; not to be confused with Anchor), there's Portuguese and local food, English Premiership football (check the board for fixtures), a live band (🕒 9pm Fri & Sat), fine fried eggs and coffee.

Vegan Salad & Herbs House (☎ 282 9466; 22 Jl Kubu; 🕒 10am-4pm Fri-Wed; meals RM10) Around the corner from the Buddhist Guanyin Temple in Chinatown, this restaurant serves a range of healthy uncooked, crisp vegetables and a good-value lunch buffet (RM8).

On Friday and Saturday evenings, it's worth making the trip out to Medan Portugis and **Restoran de Lisbon** (Medan Portugis; meals RM25). At this Portuguese restaurant you can sample Malay-Portuguese dishes at outdoor tables. Try the chilli crabs (RM20) or the devil curry (RM10). You could also try **San Pedro** (4 Jl D'Aranjo), on the street immediately behind the square, with a cosy, local atmosphere for Malay-Portuguese meals.

Also recommended:

Heeren House (☎ 281 4241) The downstairs café serves an enjoyable set tea with apple crumble and ice cream (RM6), and Peranakan and Portuguese food. See also Sleeping, p223.

Nancy's Restoran (Old China Cafe) (15 Jl Hang Lekir; 🕒 Wed-Mon; meals RM8) Serves cheap Nonya set-lunches.

Baba Cafe (☎ 292 5642; 127 Jl Tun Tan Cheng Lock; meals RM15) Local Baba dishes and Western fare.

Friends Café (☎ 398 3231; 150 Jl Merdeka) Slick, trendy café with aluminium furniture.

Bulldog Cafe (☎ 292 1920; 145 Jl Bendahara; meals RM10) Nonya and Western dishes.

UE Tea House (20 Lg Bukit China; meals RM8) Simple Chinese coffee shop specialising in steamed dumplings.

Entertainment

Sound & Light Show (Son et Lumiere; adult/child RM10/2; 🕒 8.30-9.15pm) Held near the Porta de Santiago, this is Melaka's most popular form of evening entertainment. The sound system booms and the ruins are lit up to present Melaka's history from a strongly nationalistic angle. Nevertheless, it's quite good theatre (but take mosquito repellent).

Melaka's nightlife is otherwise pretty unexciting. If you're a karaoke fiend, there are innumerable bars (girly and otherwise) in the alleyways off Jl TMR.

Rock & Roll Grill (☎ 284 9652, 34 Jl Taman Melaka Raya 23; 🕒 5pm-1am Tue-Fri, 2pm-1am Sat & Sun) Though out of the way, there's a free pick-up service, pool and live music. Lots of red meat (steaks, burgers, etc) is on the menu along with rock, country, reggae and R&B.

A 'multiplex' cinema can be found in the Mahkota Parade shopping complex.

Shopping

You could easily spend a couple of hours strolling through the many antique shops along Jl Hang Jebat (Jonkers St) and Jl Tun Tan Cheng Lock in Chinatown. Here you'll find Malaysia's best range of antiques, but not all of them are old and not all are from Malaysia. Prices are high and haggling is essential. Shops are stocked with an impressive range of antique furniture, porcelain, old lamps, coins, *songket* (silk woven with gold threads), assorted bric-a-brac and crafts.

Malaqa House (☎ 281 4770; 70 Jl Tun Tan Cheng Lock) is a huge shop in an elegant building stuffed to the gills with antiques and replicas – it's not cheap, but it's full of character. **Dr Edwin Ho** (☎ 282 9663; 154 Jl Tun Tan Cheng Lock) is a local artist who sells his works for around RM350 from his studio gallery. The **Orangutan House** (59 Lg Hang Jebat) stocks work by young local artist Charles Cham, including printed T-shirts. Other galleries, souvenir stalls and more upmarket shops selling trinkets (mostly from Indonesia) can be found across from Christ Church on Jl Laksamana near the Stadthuys.

For cheap clothing and everyday goods, try **Ekspo Melaka** (Jl Kee Ann) near the river.

Getting There & Away

Melaka is 144km from Kuala Lumpur, 224km from Johor Bahru and just 94km from Port Dickson. Melaka's local bus station, express bus terminal and taxi station are all set back from Jl Hang Tuah in the Kampung Morten area.

AIR

There are currently no scheduled flights to/from Melaka, although **Malaysia Airlines** (☎ 282 9597) has an office on the 1st floor of the City Bayview Hotel.

BOAT

High-speed ferries make the trip from Melaka to Dumai in Sumatra twice daily at around 8.30am and 3pm (one way/return RM80/129, 1¾ hours;). **Madai Shipping** (☎ 284 0671) and **Fuji Express** (☎ 282 9888) have ticket offices near the wharf and close to the express bus station. Same-day tickets are on sale after 8.30am, but it's best to book the day before. Dumai is a visa-free entry port into Indonesia for citizens of most countries.

BUS

Most of the bus company ticket offices are clustered around the express bus station. Half a dozen companies have air-con buses to KL throughout the day from 6am to 7pm (RM9, 2 hours). There are so many buses to KL that you can usually just turn up and get on the next one, but it pays to book tickets for any other destination at least the day before. Phone **Transnasional** (☎ 292 2307) and **Plusliner** (☎ 281 8760) for inquiries.

To Singapore, express buses leave approximately hourly from 8am to 6pm (RM13.70, 4½ hours). On Saturday and Sunday these buses can be fully booked, so purchase your ticket well in advance or, alternatively, take one of the frequent buses to Johor Bahru, which leave roughly every hour between 8am and 8pm (RM12.50, 3 hours). Buses to Melaka can be booked at the Lavender St bus station in Singapore or from an agent operating out of the Lavender MRT station.

There are a few day and evening buses to Butterworth and Georgetown in Penang (RM30, 8 hours), Ipoh (RM20, 5 hours) and Lumut (RM26, 7 hours). To the east coast there are direct buses to Kuantan (RM17.60, 6 hours, 3 per day), Kuala Terengganu (RM29, 9 to 10 hours, 8.30pm) and Kota Bharu (RM32, 10 hours, approximately every day). Hourly buses depart for Seremban (RM4.70, 1½ hours).

From the local bus station, the No 2 bus south to Muar leaves every half-hour throughout the day (RM2, 1 hour). Regular buses also go from here north along the coast to Port Dickson (RM4.50).

To Kuala Lumpur International Airport (KLIA), take a local bus to Sepang (RM5, 1½ hours) and then another bus to the airport (RM6), between 6.30am and 8pm.

CAR

If you're driving, Melaka's one-way traffic system will probably frustrate you at every turn.

If you want to rent a vehicle, the following companies have offices in Melaka:

Avis (☎ 284 6710; Lobby, Hotel Equatorial, Jl Parameswara)

Hawk (☎ 283 7878; 126 Jl Bendahara)

TAXI

Taxis leave across the road from the local bus station, just north of the market. Whole-taxi rates include Port Dickson (RM100), Johor Bahru (RM180), Seremban (RM70), Mersing (RM200), KL (RM120) and KLIA (RM120).

TRAIN

The nearest train station is 38km north of Melaka at Tampin (☎ 411 034) on the main north–south line from KL to Singapore. Local bus No 26 from Melaka runs to the Tampin bus station, but it's a few kilometres from there to the train station, so it's more convenient to take a direct taxi from Melaka instead (RM35).

Getting Around

Melaka's airport is at Batu Berendam, 9km north of the town centre. Take bus No 65 from the local bus station, or a taxi for RM10.

Melaka is easily explored on foot, but one useful service is Town Bus No 17, which runs every 15 minutes from the local bus station, past the huge Mahkota Parade shopping complex, to Taman Melaka Raya (40 sen) and on to Medan Portugis (80 sen).

Bicycles can be hired at some guesthouses for around RM7 a day; there are also a few bike hire outfits around town.

A *trishaw* (bicycle rickshaw) is an ideal way of getting around compact and slow-moving Melaka. You'll find only a handful of these left anywhere else in Malaysia and some of the drivers are real characters, tarting up their colourful vehicles with strings of lights and jangling bells. By the hour they should cost about RM20, or RM6 for any one-way trip within the town, but you'll have to bargain.

Metered taxis should cost around RM6 for a trip anywhere around town with a 50% surcharge between 1am and 6am.

AROUND MELAKA

Ayer Keroh

☎ 06

About 15km northeast of Melaka at the Melaka turn-off on the Lebuhraya, Ayer Keroh (also spelled Air Keroh) is home to a number of contrived tourist attractions popular with Malaysian and Singaporean families on weekends. Ayer Keroh can be reached on Town Bus No 19 from the local bus station in Melaka (RM1, 30 minutes), or a taxi will cost around RM10. These attractions are deserted on weekdays and not worth much more than a passing glance.

Heading north from Melaka, the first sight is the lushly landscaped **Melaka Zoo** (adult/child RM4/2; 9am-6pm), where the small but well-fed collection includes Sumatran rhinos, Malayan sun bears and native guar oxen.

On the other side of the highway is the rather tacky **Crocodile Park** (adult/child RM5/3; 9am-6pm), where you can inspect over 200 sluggish sauries in a series of soupy tanks.

Further north along the main road is **Hutan Rekreasi Air Keroh** (Air Keroh Recreational Forest; admission free), part secondary jungle and part landscaped park with paved trails, a 250m canopy walk, picnic areas and a forestry museum. It's a pleasant place for a stroll, but it certainly ain't Taman Negara.

Just a few hundred metres on, **Taman Mini Malaysia/Asean** (adult/child RM4/2; 9am-6pm) is the so-called 'main attraction' at Ayer Keroh. This large, but surprisingly empty theme park has examples of traditional houses from all 13 Malaysian states, as well as neighbouring Asean countries. Each house contains a few handicrafts and wax dummies in traditional dress representing the region, but a lot of them look the same. Guides inside each house are usually found dozing.

About 2km further north is the **Butterfly & Reptile Sanctuary** (adult/child RM4/2; 9am-6pm), which has a landscaped enclosure with only a sampling of butterfly species. Slightly more impressive is the collection of snakes, scorpions and enormous spiders.

Pulau Besar

☎ 06

The small island of Pulau Besar, southeast of Melaka and 5km off the coast, is a popular weekend getaway. The island has a few historic graves and reminders of the Japanese occupation during WWII, but the main reason to come here is for the clean white-sand beaches. The water is a little clearer than on the mainland and the hilly island is cloaked in greenery with jungle walks.

The only place to stay on Pulau Besar is the **Pandanusa Resort** (☎ 281 8007; r Sun-Thu/Fri & Sat RM99/129, incl meals;), equipped with a pool and restaurant.

Pulau Besar is most easily reached by boat from the jetty behind the tourist office on Jl Kota in Melaka, but they are not always running (see Boat Trips p218). Boats also depart from the new jetty at Anjung Batu at 8.30am, 10am, 12pm, 2.30pm, 5pm and 6.30pm (last boat returns at 7pm). The trip takes 25 minutes and costs RM11. The jetty is several kilometres past the old pier at Umbai, both southeast of Melaka. From Umbai you'll need to charter a boat (RM80). You can reach either jetty in less than an hour by the No 2 local bus from Melaka.

Tanjung Bidara

☎ 06

About 30km northwest of Melaka on the way to Port Dickson is Tanjung Bidara, one of the better beach areas along this stretch of coast. It is well away from the main highway, requiring you to take back roads through rice paddies and farms to get to the shore. Although the water here is murky like everywhere else along the Selat Melaka, the sandy beaches are good for long, scenic walks and the greenery is reasonably prolific. The beach fills up on weekends and holidays, but otherwise you'll have it all to yourself.

The main stretch of beach is at Tanjung Bidara Beach Resort, where there is also a public beach area with food stalls. **Tanjung Bidara Beach Resort** (☎ 384 2990; fax 384 2995; r Sun-Thu/Fri & Sat RM80/120, chalets Thu-Sun/Fri & Sat RM130/200;) is quiet and relaxing with a small swimming pool and a restaurant.

Good budget accommodation is strung out several kilometres along the beach. The **Samudera Bidara Resort** (☎ 384 7587; resortsb@tm.net.my; Jl Samudera; r Sun-Thu/Fri & Sat RM60/80) in the colourful, friendly Malay village of Kampung Balik Batu has clean economy rooms. Also in Kampung Balik Batu are several simple beachside chalet guesthouses.

Bus Nos 42 and 47 from Melaka go to Masjid Tanah, from where a taxi to Tanjung Bidara Beach Resort or Kampung Balik Batu costs RM6.

Johor

CONTENTS

Connected to the dynamic city-state of Singapore by a rail and road causeway, Johor is the Malay Peninsula's southernmost and most populous state. It is also one of Malaysia's most economically significant territories, with agriculture – principally rubber, palm oil, pineapple and pepper – the traditional enterprise, alongside an increasingly vigorous manufacturing base.

Living perhaps in Singapore's shadow, the state capital Johor Bahru – Malaysia's second-largest city – has managed to forge an energetic economy. Nonetheless, most visitors see Johor Bahru and Johor as a stepping stone to or from Singapore or Pulau Tioman (Tioman Island, in Pahang state).

Johor Bahru has little to lure visitors for more than a day or two, although its nigh market and excellent museum are worthwhile. The pleasant fishing village of Mersing on the east coast of Johor sees a constant stream of wayfarers bound for the beautiful islands of the Seribuat Archipelago. Inland, trekkers seek out Endau-Rompin National Park, one of the last undisturbed stands of lowland rainforest in Peninsular Malaysia, with excellent hiking opportunities.

HIGHLIGHTS

- Exploring the lively night market and historic colonial/royal district of **Johor Bahru** (p231)
- Admiring the sultan's treasures at the **Royal Abu Bakar Museum** (p232) in Johor Bahru
- Climbing the slopes of jungle-clad **Gunung Ledang** (p239) and admiring its series of waterfalls
- Relaxing in laid-back **Mersing** (p240) en route to the islands
- Snorkelling, diving and lazing on the beautiful island beaches of the **Seribuat Archipelago** (p243)
- Discovering the pristine jungle and thundering waterfalls of **Endau-Rompin National Park** (p244)

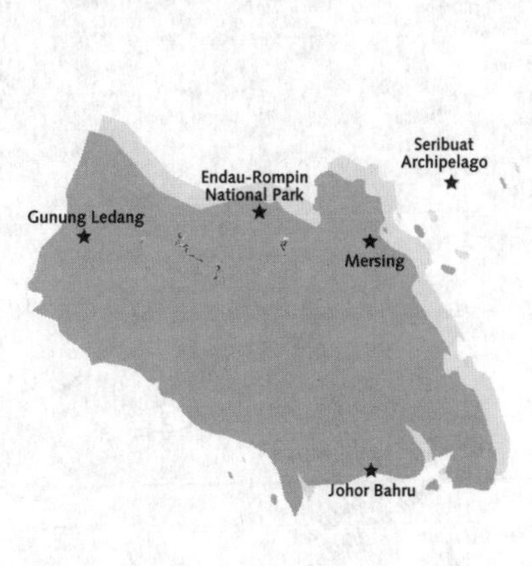

- TELEPHONE CODE: 06, 07
- POPULATION: 2.75 MILLION
- AREA: 19,984 SQ KM

History

Johor's history is really a continuation of Melaka's. When the latter fell to the Portuguese in the 16th century, Johor became the pre-eminent Malay state, and its rulers (the first of whom was the son of the last sultan of Melaka) were seen as the protectors of the western Malay states. Early on the Portuguese attacked Johor, but eventually were more or less content to let the leaders rule from their capital on Sungai (River) Johor, even though they were something of an impediment to trade in the area.

The kingdom of Aceh on the northern tip of Sumatra also had ambitions in the area. The second half of the 16th century saw a three-way struggle between the Portuguese, Johor and Aceh for control of the peninsula and the Selat Melaka (Strait of Melaka), with Acehnese attacks on Johor continuing well into the 17th century.

Johor's fortunes took a decided turn for the better with the coming of the Dutch, who allied themselves with Johor for a combined (and ultimately successful) attack against the Portuguese at Melaka in 1641. Johor was freed from virtually all the tariffs and trade restrictions imposed on other states by the Dutch, in return for cooperation in helping to defeat the Portuguese. Johor also overcame threats from the Minangkabau and by the end of the 17th century it was among the strongest Asian powers in the region.

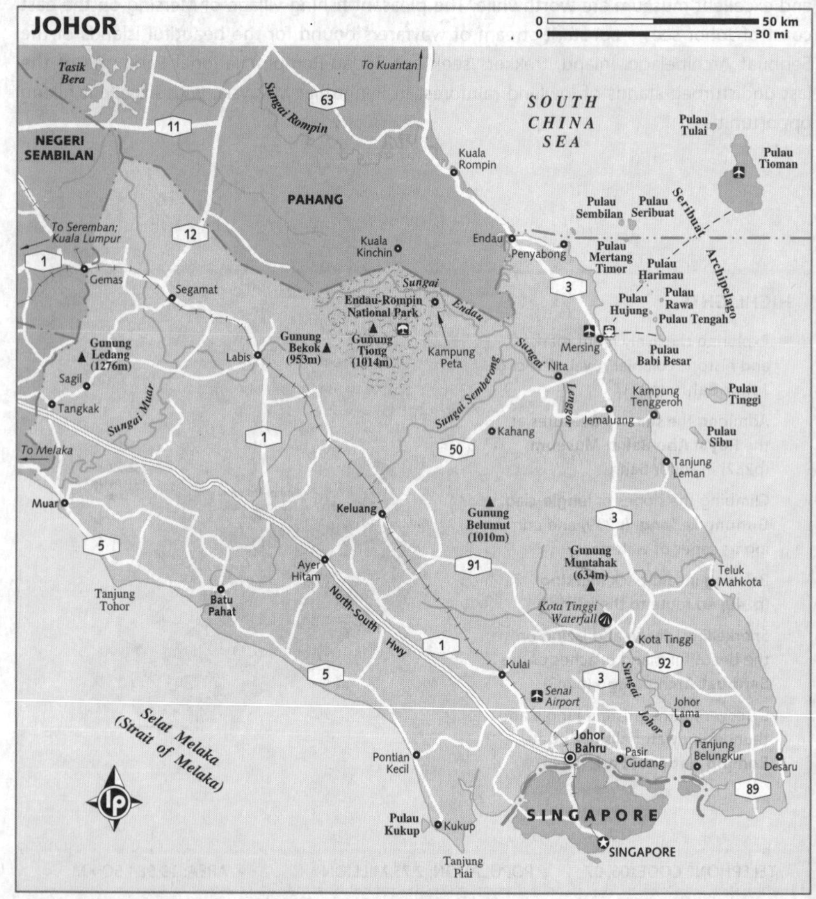

A war with the Bugis (a seafaring group of warrior-like Malay settlers from Macassar (Ujung Padang) in Celebes who rose to power in Selangor) in 1716 left Johor weakened, and further political instability followed when a Minangkabau, Raja Kecil of Siak, claimed the throne and overthrew the weak sultan in 1719. His control lasted for just two years, when the Buginese installed Sulaiman, the son of the former sultan Abdul Jalil, on the throne. His descendants ruled the state until it eventually disappeared in the early years of the 20th century. Throughout the 18th century the Bugis influence in the state increased. However, when the Dutch East India Company wrested control of Riau (in Indonesia) and Johor in 1784, the era of Bugis domination of western Malaya came to an end.

In 1819, with the court of the Johor sultan split by Malay and Bugis factions, Sir Thomas Stamford Raffles was able to bring about the cession of Singapore to the British and the pensioning-off of the sultans, while actual power went to the *temenggong* (Malay minister in charge of defence and justice). The *temenggong* continued to rule the state very ably, the most notable among them being the flamboyant Abu Bakar, who elevated himself to the position of sultan of Johor in 1886. Through his contacts with people in high places in London and Singapore, he was able to resist the British desire to bring Johor closer under its control. Abu Bakar also undertook an ambitious programme of modernisation for the state, while continuing to live the high life. Today he is fondly remembered as the Father of Johor.

Abu Bakar's successor and son, Ibrahim, was less powerful and in 1914 was forced by the British to accept a 'general adviser' who had powers similar to those exercised by the British Residents in other states. Sultan Ibrahim was still the ruler of Johor when it became part of the Federation of Malaya in 1948.

Climate

The temperature in Johor ranges from 21°C to 32°C, with an average humidity exceeding 82%. Although there is rain through the year, the wettest months are from May to December.

National Parks

Johor's prime national park, Endau-Rompin, is a remote 870-sq-km expanse of jungle in the north (see p244). For details of other parks, contact the **Johor National Parks Corporation** (☎ 07-223 7471; fax 07-223 7472; www.johorpark.com).

Getting There & Around

The North-South Hwy (Lebuhraya), connecting Johor Bahru and Kuala Lumpur, is the main transport artery to the north. Johor Bahru is also connected to Kuala Lumpur by rail and is accessed from Singapore by rail, road and boat. There are also boat services to ports in Sumatra from Johor Bahru. Airports exist at Johor Bahru and Mersing.

At Ayer Hitam on the North-South Hwy, Route 50 splits off to Mersing, which is itself connected to Johor Bahru along Route 3 in the east.

See the Getting There & Away sections in Johor Bahru (p236), Muar (p239), Kota Tinggi (p240) and Mersing (p243) for details on connections to destinations within Johor and to the rest of Peninsular Malaysia.

JOHOR BAHRU

☎ 07

Capital of the state of Johor, Johor Bahru is the southern gateway to Peninsular Malaysia. Connected to Singapore by road and rail across the 1038m-long Causeway, JB (as it is known throughout the country) inevitably suffers as a poor relation to its more glamorous neighbour. Despite its historical significance and various points of interest, few travellers pause in JB; it's just the place to get your passport stamped on the way in or out of Malaysia.

On weekends and public holidays, Singaporeans flock across the Causeway for sex, shopping and excitement, and Johor Bahru puts on a show. Central JB exudes a real border-town feel, with crowds, mostly male Singaporeans, cruising the streets. Street theatre is provided by medicine vendors dangling snakes and promising penis enlargement with their elixirs, or turbaned *bomoh* (Islamic spiritual healers) selling magical 'love oil' at astronomical prices. The *kedai gunting rambut* (barber shops) are a frequent sight, offering not haircuts, but women.

Despite its reputation as a sin centre, JB has closed its bawdier nightclubs in an effort to improve its image. A major part of the Singapore-Johor-Riau growth triangle (Sijori), JB is a burgeoning centre of investment and construction. New roads, industrial estates, shopping centres and hotels are changing the face of the city. Yet JB is still chaotic and fairly tatty. It is both a breath of fresh air and a bad smell as you arrive from squeaky-clean and sterile Singapore.

It's possible to spend an enjoyable day or two in JB; it has an excellent museum to visit and a thriving *pasar malam* (night market), where you choose from vegetables, clothes, knick-knacks and a host of local dishes. In the business centre of town you still see the footpath hawkers and other colourful stalls that are so much a part of Asia.

Orientation

The road and railway across the Causeway run straight into the middle of JB. The main area for cheap and mid-range hotels is on and around Jl Meldrum, in the centre of town. Some of JB's new shopping centres and better hotels can be found along Jl Tebrau, the main highway leading to the north and to the east coast.

West of the Causeway, Jl Ibrahim runs along JB's waterfront. Here is the city's colonial district with its parkland, colonial buildings and museum.

The Larkin bus and taxi station, where most long-distance buses operate from, is 5km northwest of the train station. Local buses operate from several bus stops around town, the most convenient being the stop in front of the post office on Jl Ibrahim. Sultan Ismail Airport is 32km northwest of the city centre, in Senai.

Note that street names in Johor Bahru often change several times in the space of a few kilometres. For example, Jl Air Molek becomes Jl Yahya Awal as it crosses Jl Gertak Merah. In similar fashion, the major Jl Ibrahim undergoes several name changes as it heads away from the Causeway.

Information

BOOKSHOPS

Popular (☎ 221 8970; Johor Bahru City Square, 108 Jl Wong Ah Fook)

Times (☎ 221 9134; Lot M4-11 & M4-12, Level 4, Johor Bahru City Square, 108 Jl Wong Ah Fook)

IMMIGRATION OFFICES

Immigration Office (☎ 224 4255; 1st fl, Block B, Wisma Persekutuan, Jl Air Molek)

INTERNET ACCESS

There are Internet cafés in most of the shopping malls around town (see Shopping, p236).

Parallel Multimedia (Lot J4-18, Level 4, Johor Bahru City Square, 108 Jl Wong Ah Fook; RM4 per hr; 🕑 10am-9.30pm)

Surflink Cafe (31-A Jl Wong Ah Fook; RM3 per hr)

MONEY

There are dozens of moneychangers in the central area and rates are competitive.

HSBC (Jl Timbalan) 24-hour ATM (Maestro, Plus, MasterCard, Visa and Cirrus)

Public Bank (Jl Wong Ah Fook) ATM (Maestro, Plus, MasterCard, Visa and Cirrus)

TELEPHONE & FAX

Telekom (Jl Abdullah Ibrahim, opposite the Puteri Pan Pacific Hotel)

TOURIST INFORMATION

Tourism Malaysia (☎ 222 3590; www.johortourism.com.my; 5th fl, Jotic Bldg, 2 Jl Air Molek; 🕑 9am-5pm Mon-Sat)

Johor State Tourism office (☎ 223 4935; 5th fl, Jotic Bldg, 2 Jl Air Molek; 🕑 9am-5pm Mon-Sat)

Sights

ROYAL ABU BAKAR MUSEUM

Set in lush, grassy grounds overlooking the Strait of Johor, the marvellous Istana Besar was once the main palace of the Johor royal family. It was built in Victorian style by Anglophile sultan Abu Bakar in 1866, and is now open to the public as the **Muzium Diraja Abu Bakar** (☎ 223 0555; Jl Ibrahim; adult/child $US7/3, payable in ringgit at a bad exchange rate; 🕑 9am-5pm Sat-Thu; ticket counter closes at 4pm).

This is undoubtedly the finest museum of its kind in Malaysia, conveying the wealth and privilege of the sultans. It contains the sultan's possessions, including furniture and hunting trophies, and is set out much as it was when in use as the palace. The superb exhibits include Chinese, Japanese, Indian and Malay carved wooden pieces and an amazing full-size crystal-glass table and chairs from France. The hunting room has some bizarre exhibits from *pukka sahib* days when wildlife was there to be shot,

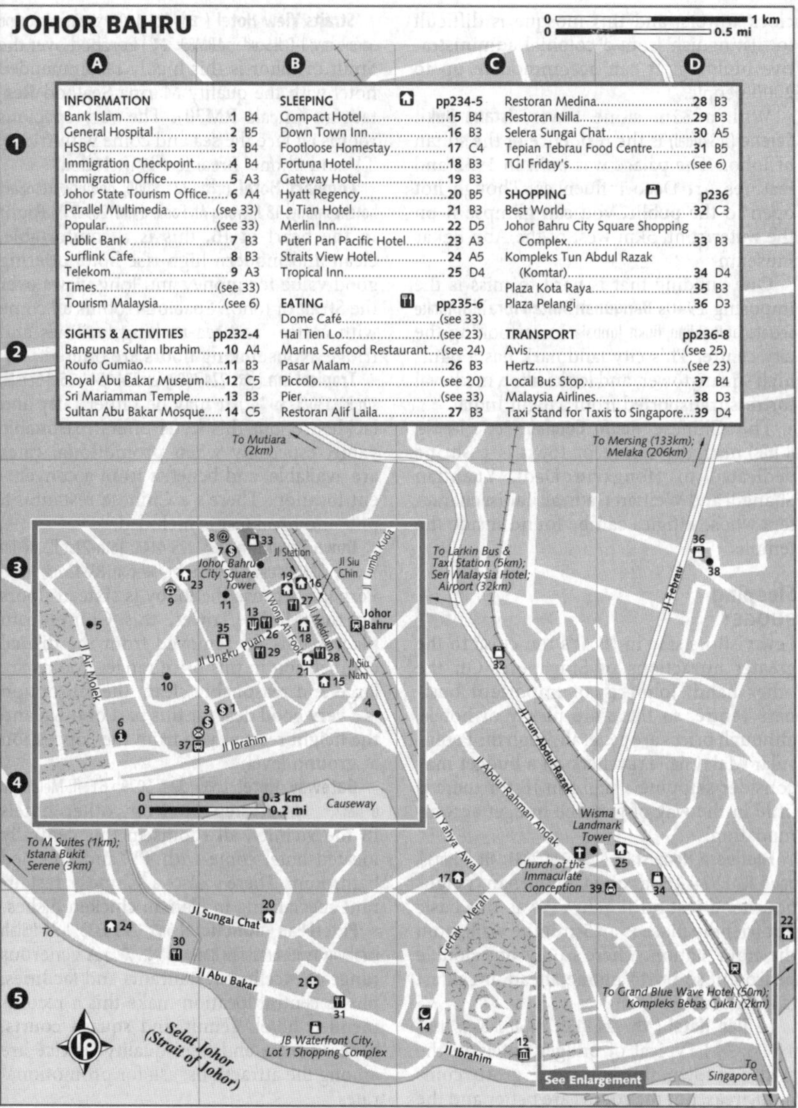

including elephant's-foot umbrella stands and antelope-leg ashtrays.

The 53-hectare palace grounds (free entry) are beautifully manicured and provide a great breathing space in this fairly cramped city. There are good views across the strait, although Singapore's industrial backside is not terribly picturesque.

OTHER SIGHTS

West of the museum is the most attractive part of Johor Bahru, the old colonial/royal district of greenery and fine buildings.

Built from 1892 to 1900, the magnificent **Sultan Abu Bakar Mosque** (Jl Ibrahim) is a mixture of architectural styles, but principally Victorian. The minarets look like British clock towers, and this mosque is difficult to distinguish from a colonial administrative building. It can accommodate up to 2000 people.

With a 32m stone tower, **Istana Bukit Serene** (Jl Skudai) is the residence of the sultan of Johor. The palace was built in 1932 and features Art Deco influences. Though not open to the public, you can glimpse it on the waterfront, 5km west of the Abu Bakar museum.

One building that is hard to miss is the imposing 1940s **Bangunan Sultan Ibrahim** (State Secretariat Building; Bukit Timbalan) overlooking the city centre. This city landmark has a 64m-high square tower, and looks like a medieval fortress transported from Mogul India.

The Chinese **Roufo Gumiao** (Roufo Temple; Jl Trus) near the centre of town is a shrine dedicated to Hongxian Dadi, Yuantian Shangdi and Weitian Dadi, all Taoist characters whose effigies can be found inside the temple.

Sleeping

BUDGET

Few visitors stay in JB; it's too close to the greater attractions of Singapore. On the other hand, Johor is an important business centre, so there are plenty of hotels, although prices are generally high for Peninsular Malaysia. Travellers on a budget may consider skipping a night in JB for there is little in the way of genuine budget accommodation.

Footloose Homestay (☎ 224 2881; 4H Jl Ismail; dm/d RM12/24) In a quiet suburban neighbourhood just off Jl Yahya Awal, this basic but friendly place is a 15-minute walk from the train station. There's only one double bedroom, so try to phone ahead; breakfast is included.

Le Tian Hotel (☎ 224 8151; 2 A-D Jl Siew Nam; d RM55; ❄) Typical of budget hotels in the centre of town, this has rather grotty common areas, but the rooms are better and the shower rooms OK.

MID-RANGE

JB's cheaper mid-range hotels cluster in the Jl Meldrum neighbourhood, just west of the train station, but the cheaper options are uniformly average. Note that all hotels in this section raise their prices on Friday, Saturday and Sunday by about 10%.

Straits View Hotel (☎ 224 1400; straitsvhjccg@po.jaring.my; 1-D Jl Scudai; d RM89; ❄) Perched over the Strait of Johor is this highly recommended hotel with the quality Marina Seafood Restaurant (meals RM30). The very spacious rooms all face the sea and come with fridge, TV and phone. Breakfast is included.

Compact Hotel (☎ 221 3000; enquiry@compacthotel.com.my; 18 Jl Wong Ah Fook; d RM126; ❄) Right in the heart of JB, this is a comfortable, clean and modern high-rise hotel offering good value for money and long views over the Strait of Johor. Spacious rooms all come with coffee- and tea-making facilities and fridge. Nonsmoking floors are offered.

Tropical Inn (☎ 224 7888; fax 224 1544; 15 Jl Gereja; s/d RM130/175; ❄) It may be rather tatty and lacklustre, but this hotel offers reasonable value, especially when promotional rates are available, and benefits from a convenient location. There's a Chinese restaurant, pub and breakfast is included.

Down Town Inn (☎ 223 4444; 16th-21st fl, Merlin Tower, Jl Meldrum; d with fan/air-con RM42/63; ❄) Perhaps because the lobby is sixteen floors up the Merlin Tower, this Chinese-run place seems far removed from the dismal competition in this price range. Rooms are large and reasonably clean, the fan option is a very good deal for this part of town and the height rescues you from the congestion at ground level.

Gateway Hotel (☎ 223 5029; 61 Jl Meldrum; d RM70; ❄) A step up from other hotels in the vicinity, all rooms in this centrally located hotel come with TV and attached bathroom. There's also a Chinese restaurant specialising in Hainan chicken dishes.

Puteri Pan Pacific Hotel (☎ 223 3333; Jl Abdullah Ibrahim; d with breakfast RM168; ❄ 🏊) A generous range of excellent restaurants and facilities, plus a central location make this a recommended hotel. Tennis and squash courts, fitness centre and high-quality service are among the attractions; ask for promotional rates.

Grand Blue Wave Hotel (☎ 221 6666; bluewavejb@po.jaring.my; 9R Jl Bukit Meldrum; d Sun-Thu/Fri & Sat RM180/190; ❄ 🏊) A range of suites and studio rooms come with fully-equipped kitchenette and dining area, free newspaper and in-room safe; good for long-term stays with coin laundry, shops and gym. Centrally located with large choice of restaurants.

SULTANS, FAST CARS & THE LAW

Like England, Malaysia has royalty and nobility – but there are nine royal families in Malaysia, not just one. Like Britain's House of Windsor, they come in for plenty of criticism – but you won't hear it, because criticising Malaysia's royalty can put you in prison on a charge of sedition. In part this relates back to Malaysia's early history as an independent state, when politicians often had royal connections, notably the first prime minister, Tunku Abdul Rahman.

Nine of the states of Malaysia are ruled by sultans, who are totally exempt from the law. They take it in turn to assume the title of *yang di-pertuan agong*, effectively the 'king' of Malaysia. Although they're not inclined towards prancing around half-naked or indulging in anguished marital separations, the Malaysian nobility does have its own colourful scandals.

The funniest in recent years has been that concerning the sultan of Kelantan and his penchant for expensive toys. Each sultan is allowed to own seven imported cars without paying import duties and taxes. This rule has customarily been treated with some flexibility – 10 is near enough to seven. Unfortunately for the sultan of Kelantan, it was finally decided that 20 was definitely more than seven, and when a brand new Lamborghini Diablo arrived in an air-freight consignment at Kuala Lumpur International Airport (KLIA) the sultan was informed he would have to pay import duties before he was allowed to take it home. 'Let me at least sit in my new toy', implored the sultan, who then proceeded to screech out of the hangar and burn rubber all the way back to the palace in Kelantan!

More serious than mere evasion of customs duty are outright cases of law breaking. In 1976 one member of the Johor royal family was actually convicted of manslaughter, then pardoned by his father, the sultan at the time. The Malaysian parliament was informed that the sultan of Johor and his son had been involved in 23 cases of assault.

Although the Malaysian government would quite like to bring the sultans to heel, their popularity in rural areas and their image as protectors of Malay culture and history make the government reluctant to meddle with the status quo. The Malaysian constitution also makes it difficult to institute changes, as it specifically states that no alteration can be made to the sultans' 'privileges, position, honours or dignities' without their agreement!

If you don't mind being outside the city centre, **Seri Malaysia Hotel** (☎ 221 1002; RM110; ❄) has clean and spacious rooms with attached bathroom. The **Fortuna Hotel** (223 3210; 29A Jl Meldrum; s RM66; ❄) is a little musty, though welcoming. The showers are small; rooms come with TV.

TOP END

Hyatt Regency (☎ 222 1234; hyatt@hrjb.com.my; Jl Sungai Chat; s/d RM430/450; ❄ 🏊) With reliable class and style from the leading chain of international business-class hotels, the fantastic Hyatt is west of the city centre, overlooking the Strait of Johor. Rooms are fully equipped, rooms for disabled travellers are available and there's a fitness centre, tennis courts and several restaurants (including the Piccolo, p236), cafés and bars.

Mutiara (☎ 332 3800; adminjb@mutiarahotels.com; Jl Dato Sulaiman; s/d RM380/410; ❄ 🏊) Travellers looking for a deluxe option can consider this former Holiday Inn, but the location 2km north of the city centre is less than desirable. All rooms come with free newspaper, satellite TV and minibar. The hotel has a recommended Chinese restaurant and live music in the Polo Lounge.

Also recommended:

Merlin Inn (☎ 276 5522; merlinjb@time.net.my; 10 Jl Bukit Meldrum; s & d RM200; ❄ 🏊) Centrally located and good value. Breakfast included.

M Suites (☎ 221 1000; m-suites@tm.net.my; 16 Jl Skudai Straits View; studio/one-bed apt/two-bed apt RM290/380/620; ❄ 🏊) Large, well-appointed and distinctly styled suites (with kitchenette) with views over Singapore. Breakfast included. Promotional rates offered.

Hotel Grand Continental (☎ 332 3999; 799 Jl Tebrau; s/d RM253/276; ❄ 🏊)

Eating

Johor Bahru is a good place for food, especially seafood. There are good hawker venues, including the nightly **pasar malam** (night market; Jl Wong Ah Fook) outside the Hindu temple. Local specialities include Johor laksa, a noodle dish relying heavily on coconut; and *mee rebus*, noodles in a thick sauce that show the Javanese influence in Johor. Also try the excellent grilled fish cooked on banana leaves, and the filling claypot rice.

Food courts can be found in shopping malls around town. Try Johor Bahru City Square and its Medena Selera food centre, where you'll also find many other Western and Asian restaurants. Also try the **Kompleks Tun Abdul Razak** (Komtar; Jl Wong Ah Fook), and there's another good food court on the upper level of the **Plaza Kota Raya** (Jl Ungku Puan) shopping centre.

Singaporeans come across the Causeway in the evenings just to eat cheap seafood. The main venues are along the waterfront to the west of the city centre. The **Tepian Tebrau** (Jl Abu Bakar) food centre is famous for its excellent seafood. One kilometre further west is **Selera Sungai Chat** (Jl Abu Bakar), another well-patronised seafood centre specialising in *ikan bakar* (grilled fish), where a meal will cost you around RM20.

Meisan (☎ 332 3800; Mutiara Hotel; 🕑 11.30am-2.30pm & 6.30-10.30pm; meals RM45-50) Meals at this fine Sichuan (Szechuan) restaurant are rather expensive, but authentically spicy and full of flavour. Set meals are available for those eager to avoid the pricier à la carte dishes.

Hai Tien Lo (☎ 223 3333; Basement level, Puteri Pan Pacific, Jl Abdullah Ibrahim; 🕑 11.30am-2.30pm & 6.30-10.30pm Mon-Fri, 7am-3pm & 6.30-10.30pm Sat & Sun; meals RM30) A smart dining environment presenting a wide range of dishes from various Chinese provinces (seafood, bean curd, claypot), with emphasis on Cantonese and Sichuan cuisine. A dim sum buffet (RM28) is served on Saturday and Sunday, there are set meals and all food is halal (pork free and specially prepared – a rarity for Chinese food).

Restoran Alif Laila (☎ 226 0445; 57 Jl Meldrum; meals RM5) With all its food on display so you can see what you are getting, this cheap and friendly outfit offers very good value for its range of roti and curries, and is popular with locals.

Restoran Medina (Cnr Jl Meldrum & Jl Siu Niam; meals RM8; 🕑 24 hr) Busy and very popular restaurant serving excellent and highly affordable *murtabak* (roti filled with mutton, chicken or vegetables), biryani and curries.

Restoran Nilla (3 Jl Ungku Puan; meals RM8) Opposite the Sri Mariamman Temple, this inexpensive eatery has filling South Indian banana-leaf set meals. Most meals are vegetarian, but fish-head curry is also featured.

Also recommended:

Marina Seafood Restaurant (☎ 224 1400; Straits View Hotel, 1-D Jl Scudai; meals RM30)

Piccolo (☎ 222 1234; Hyatt Regency, Jl Sungai Chat; meals RM35) Alfresco Italian restaurant, live music (nightly Tue-Sun).

TGI Friday's (☎ 221 3380; Unit L2-01, Bangunan Jotic; meals RM25-30; 🕑 11am-11pm) Burgers and Western dishes, plus live music and ESPN sports TV.

Dome Cafe (☎ 226 1055; J1-09, 1st floor, Johor Bahru City Square, 108 Jl Wong Ah Fook) Civilised and comfortable café.

Pier (3rd fl, Johor Bahru City Square; meals RM13) Crispy fish and chips.

Shopping

JB promotes itself as a major shopping destination. Singaporeans do come across for some shopping – petrol and groceries – but for most goods Singapore has better prices and a far better range.

Major shopping centres in central JB are **Plaza Kota Raya** (Jl Ungku Puan), the flashier **Johor Bahru City Square** (Jl Wong Ah Fook) and **Kompleks Tun Abdul Razak** (Komtar; Jl Wong Ah Fook). Other large malls to the north of the city centre include the **Plaza Pelangi** (Jl Tebrau), **Holiday Plaza** (Jl Dato Sulaiman) and **Best World** (Jl Tun Abdul Razak).

Designed specifically to cater to Singaporeans, the **Kompleks Bebas Cukai** (88 Jl Ibrahim Sultan, Stulang Laut) duty-free shopping centre is about 2km east of the Causeway (locals refer to it by its English name, Free Zone Complex). The complex also incorporates a ferry terminal that handles a lot of ferry traffic to/from Singapore and a few destinations in Indonesia (see Boat this page).

Getting There & Away

AIR

JB is well served by Malaysia Airlines and flights to other places in Malaysia are much lower than from Singapore. Regular direct flights connect JB with Kota Kinabalu, Kuala Lumpur, Kuala Terengganu, Kuantan, Kuching, Ipoh and Penang. The **Malaysia Airlines office** (☎ 334 1011; 1st fl, Menara Pelangi Bldg, Jl Kuning, Taman Pelangi) is 2.5km north of the city centre.

BOAT

Ferries leave from the Kompleks Bebas Cukai, about 2km east of the Causeway. **Sriwani Tours & Travel** (☎ 221 1677), in the complex, handles tickets to most destinations.

There are daily departures to Batu Ampar (RM50) and Tanjung Pinang (RM55), both on Sumatra in Indonesia, and two daily departures to Tanah Merah (RM38) in Singapore.

Additional boats depart from Kukup, southwest of JB, to Tanjung Balai, also in Sumatra (see Kukup p238).

BUS

Frequent buses run between Singapore's Queen St bus terminal and JB's Larkin bus station, inconveniently located 5km north of the city (a taxi to/from central JB should cost RM6). Most convenient is the Singapore–Johor Bahru Express (RM2.40/S$2.10, 6.30am-midnight, every 10 minutes). At Larkin, buy your ticket at counter No 37 at the rear facing the bus departure park. In central JB, you can buy tickets from the Merlin Tower on Jl Meldrum across the street from the train station and board the bus after clearing Malaysian immigration just before the Causeway.

The regular SBS (city bus) No 170 also runs between Larkin and Ban San terminal (RM1.70) in Singapore every 10 minutes between 6am and 11.30pm, departing from stand No 13 in Larkin. Tickets can be purchased on the bus. You can also board just before the Causeway (after clearing immigration). For either bus, disembark with your ticket and luggage for immigration clearance, as you may not board the same bus on the other side.

At Larkin bus station a large number of bus companies have regular departures for major towns in Peninsular Malaysia. Destinations include Melaka (RM12.50, 3 hours), Kuala Lumpur (RM20, 4 hours), Ipoh (RM35, 7 hours) and Butterworth (RM45, 9 hours). Most buses to Melaka come from Singapore, so it pays to book in advance. Departures to the east coast include Kota Tinggi (RM3.50, 1 hour), Mersing (RM9, 3 hours), Kuantan (RM17.90, 5 hours), Kuala Terengganu (RM28.70, 9 hours) and Kota Bharu (RM34.10, 10 hours).

There is a left luggage counter at Larkin bus station (RM2 per bag; 🕑 7am-11pm).

ON FOOT

It is possible to walk across the Causeway in both directions (about 25 minutes one way). In addition to being free of charge, this is the fastest way across when traffic clogs the roadway.

TAXI

The main long-distance taxi station (blue cabs travel outside town, red within town) is at the Larkin bus station (5km north of town), but a more useful terminal is on Jl Wong Ah Fook near the Sri Mariamman Temple. Regular taxi destinations and costs (per car) include Kota Tinggi (RM40), Kuala Lumpur (RM250), Kuantan (RM250), Melaka (RM180) and Mersing (RM150).

Registered taxis to Singapore leave from a stand near Puteri Pan Pacific Hotel. A taxi across the Causeway to the Queen St terminal should cost RM28 for the whole vehicle. From Singapore to JB the fare is S$28. Local city taxis cannot cross the Causeway.

TRAIN

Daily trains depart JB (booking office open 9am-6pm) for Kuala Lumpur and Butterworth, and these can be used to get to most places on the west coast. The line passes through Tampin (for Melaka), Seremban, Kuala Lumpur, Tapah Rd (for Cameron Highlands), Ipoh and Taiping. It is also possible to change at Gemas and board the 'jungle train' for connections to Taman Negara National Park and Kota Bharu. There are also trains to Singapore, but it's more convenient to take a bus or taxi.

Getting Around

TO/FROM THE AIRPORT

JB's Sultan Ismail Airport is 32km northwest of town at Senai, on the road to Melaka and Kuala Lumpur. Local bus No 207 runs to the airport (RM2) from the Larkin bus station, but departures are infrequent. A taxi between the airport and JB is RM25, taking 30 to 45 minutes, depending on traffic.

CAR

Car hire in JB is considerably cheaper than in Singapore, but check that the hire firm allows cars to enter Singapore.

Avis (☎ 224 4824; Tropical Inn; 15 Jl Gereja)
Hertz (☎ 223 7520; Puteri Pan Pacific Hotel, Jl Abdullah Ibrahim)
Mayflower (☎ 224 1357/227 1739; Level 2A Jl Trus, Plaza Seni)
Orix (☎ 224 1215; Grand Blue Wave Hotel, 9R Jl Bukit Meldrum)

TAXI

Taxis in JB have meters and drivers are legally required to use them. You can go almost anywhere around JB for RM5, and taxis can be hired at around RM25 per hour for sightseeing.

AROUND JOHOR BAHRU

Kukup

☎ 07

About 40km southwest of JB, on the Strait of Melaka and across from Sumatra, is the fishing village of Kukup. It's famous throughout Malaysia and Singapore for its seafood, especially prawns (shrimp), and for the open-air restaurants built on stilts over the water. Singaporeans, obsessed with the loss of their own *kampung* (village) life, flock here on weekends, mostly for the seafood. While there's no denying the quality of the seafood, some of the restaurants are geared towards tour groups; a golf course has sprung up and Kukup is a low-priority destination for many travellers.

To reach Kukup, take bus No 3 from JB to Pontian Kecil (RM5, 2½ hours), 18km north of Kukup and then take a taxi (RM10). A chartered taxi all the way to/from JB costs RM60.

Ferries run between Kukup's ferry terminal and Tanjung Balai in Indonesia. In either direction, there are up to five ferries a day (one way/return RM35/50). For more details call **PT Marina** (☎ 696 1888).

JOHOR BAHRU TO MELAKA

The main road north from JB runs to Melaka and Kuala Lumpur. It's a productive region of palm oil, rubber and pineapple plantations. Although there is little to detain the casual visitor, the coast road is fairly scenic and passes through some quaint *kampung*.

Batu Pahat

☎ 07

The riverine town of Batu Pahat has a few buildings of note, such as the town's Art Deco mosque and the Chinese Chamber of Commerce building. However, if you fancy a night in this region, it's probably better to head north to Muar.

SLEEPING & EATING

A couple of places can be found not too far from the bus station. The **Garden Hotel** (☎ 431 5999; fax 431 5759; 29 Jl Jenang; s/d RM100/110; ❄) is a reasonable mid-range hotel with a coffee garden on the ground floor, a Japanese restaurant and a health centre. The corridors are scruffy, but rooms are cleaner. The more basic **Merlin Hotel** (☎ 432 2227; 11-A Jl Sultanah; d with fan/air-con RM28/38; ❄) is a Chinese-run establishment with simple rooms. Conveniently located just by the bus station, **Restoran Zam Zam Jaya** (Jl Rugayah; meals RM5) serves up cheap roti and curry but wins no medals for service.

GETTING THERE & AWAY

Numerous buses connect with Johor Bahru (RM8), KL (RM10.20) and Melaka (RM5.90) and there are three buses a day to Singapore (RM9.80). A local bus to/from Muar costs RM3 and takes 1½ hours.

Muar

☎ 06

This riverside town, also known as Bandar Maharani, was once an important commercial centre. It is noted for its traditional Malay culture, including *ghazal* (female singers with an orchestra) music and the *kuda kepang* (horse trance) dance, originally from Java.

Muar is a typical Malaysian town with a bustling Chinatown of restaurants and hotels. Along the river you'll find the graceful colonial district, with its government offices, courthouse, customs house, school and Masjid Jamek, a Victorian fantasy of a mosque in much the same style as JB's Sultan Abu Bakar Mosque.

At the mouth of the river, just past the mosque, Tanjung Riverside Park is a pleasant place for a picnic lunch, with creeper-festooned trees and the occasional timid monitor lizard hanging about.

An Internet café is located in the Wetex Parade shopping mall in the centre of town. There is a branch of HSBC on Jl Maharani (which runs along the Muar River) with a 24-hour ATM (MasterCard, Maestro, Cirrus, Plus and Visa) near the bus station.

SLEEPING

The **Hotel Classic** (☎ 953 3888; fax 953 6333; 69 Jl Ali; s & d RM120; ❄ ▣), the smartest hotel in town, has fully equipped rooms with complimentary newspaper, coffee- and tea-making facilities and satellite TV. To find the **Rumah Persinggahan Tanjong Emas** (Muar Rest House; ☎ 952 7755; 2222 Jl Sultanah; d RM60; ❄) with its huge and good-value doubles, walk along the river past the mosque, then turn left on Jl Sultanah, and follow the signs for 'Rumah Persinggahan'. A more central mid-range option is the reasonable **Riverview Hotel** (☎ 951 3313; fax 951 8139; 29 Jl Bentayan; d RM80; ❄), while those on a budget can try the clean and affordable **Hotel Leewah** (☎ 952 1605; fax 952 2009; 44 Jl Ali; d RM36; ❄).

EATING

The clean and peaceful **Kampung Nyonya** (☎ 954 0088; 39 Jl Sayang; meals RM10; ⏰ 10.30am-3pm & 5.30-10pm) serves a range of seafood (fish, crab and squid) and Nonya favourites. Try the salty and clear *chap chai* soup (vegetable soup, RM3) and the delicious *sayur goreng* (green vegetables and garlic, RM4). For tasty buns and cakes, visit the new **Kim Hiang Bakery & Cafe** (22 Jl Yahya), run by a friendly Chinese couple. A good food court and a supermarket can be found in the **Wetex Parade shopping mall** (Jl Ali).

GETTING THERE & AWAY

There are two bus stations in Muar; the local bus station is west (downriver) of the bridge leading into town, and the long-distance bus station is east (upriver) of the bridge. Buses to/from JB (RM8.60, 2 hours) and Kuala Lumpur (RM10, 2½ hours) operate from the long-distance bus station. Buses to/from Melaka (RM3, 1 hour), Batu Pahat (RM3, 1½hours) and Gunung Ledang/Segamat (RM2.40, 1 hour) operate from the local bus station. The taxi station is just to the right of the bus station.

Ferries for Dumai (one-way/return RM80/150, 8.30am) leave from the ferry terminal at 68 Jl Maharani.

Gunung Ledang

The highest mountain in Johor, Gunung Ledang (formerly Mt Ophir; 1276m) is noted for the series of waterfalls that cascade down its jungle-clad slopes. Most visitors only climb part-way up the mountain to admire the falls, but it's possible to climb all the way to the summit on a very demanding two-day round trip (there are several camp sites along the way). This climb makes a good introduction to tropical mountaineering and is recommended for those who don't have time for longer treks in Taman Negara National Park.

Those planning to overnight can stay at the **Gunung Ledang Resort** (☎ 977 2888; fax 977 3555; BT 28, Jl Segamat, Sagil, Tangkak; tw/d RM150/200; ❄) at the base of the mountain. The resort provides a simple hiking map, but serious climbers should also try to get hold of a copy of John Briggs' *Mountains of Malaysia*, published by Longman Malaysia in 1985, which contains a detailed trail. Try to avoid the mountain on weekends, when it gets packed with local youths who come to swim in the pools at the base of the falls.

To get there, take a Segamat-bound bus No 65 (RM3, 30 minutes) from Muar and ask to be let off at Gunung Ledang (there's a large 'Gunung Ledang' sign near the bus stop). It's a 1km walk in from the main road to the start of the falls. On your return to Muar, wait at the bus stop on the opposite side of the main road.

JOHOR BAHRU TO MERSING

Kota Tinggi

☎ 07

The small town of Kota Tinggi is 42km northeast of JB on the road to Mersing. The town is of little interest, but the waterfalls at **Lumbong** (adult/child RM2.50/1.20; car park RM4; ⏰ 8am-7pm), 15km northwest of the town, are a popular weekend retreat.

The falls, at the base of 634m **Gunung Muntahak**, leap down 36m and then flow through a series of pools that are ideal for a cooling dip. The smaller pools are shallow enough for children. Unfortunately, the natural beauty of the falls has been somewhat spoiled by some artificial landscaping and the construction of the adjacent Waterfalls Resort. Those in search of a more pristine experience should try the falls at Gunung Ledang (this page).

SLEEPING & EATING

Kota Tinggi Waterfalls Resort (☎ 883 1753; fax 883 1146; chalet Sun-Thu/Fri & Sat RM130/150, d Sun-Thu/Fri & Sat RM110/130; ❄) At the falls, with the Waterfalls View Restaurant and food court; breakfast included.

Nasha Hotel (☎ 883 8000; nashahotel@hotmail.com; 40 Jl Tambatan; s/d RM48/68; ❄) This hospitable place in Kota Tinggi has reasonable rooms (with shower) and a decent Malay seafood restaurant.

Sin May Chun Hotel (☎ 883 3573; 26 Jl Tambatan; s with fan/air-con RM20/32;) More of a guesthouse, offering clean and well-kept tiled rooms (cheaper rooms have no shower).

Both Nasha and Sin May Chun are just west of the bus station.

Opposite the satisfactory **Seri Kota Hotel** (☎ 883 8111; 47 Jl Jaffar; d RM48;), the **New Mui Tou Restaurant** (☎ 883 1148; 1 & 2 Jl Jaffar; meals RM20) is a large and recommended Chinese eatery near the Johor River. The appealing menu features *tangmian* (soup noodles, RM3), fried noodles, a large choice of seafood, vegetable dishes, bean curd, duck and set lunches.

GETTING THERE & AWAY

There are regular buses, Nos 41 and 227 (RM4, 1 hour) between JB's Larkin bus station and Kota Tinggi. A local bus to/from Mersing costs RM4.90 and takes two hours. From Kota Tinggi to the waterfalls at Lumbong, take the hourly bus No 43 (RM1, one hour) or a taxi (RM12 per car). If you have your own transport, take the road heading north out of the city just east of the bridge; follow the 'Air Terjun' (Waterfalls) signs.

Desaru

☎ 07

This resort area on a 20km stretch of beach at Tanjung Penawar, 88km east of JB by road, is a popular weekend escape for Singaporeans. The attractive bend of shoreline is fringed with fine sand and set against a scenic sea view. Access to the sea is largely controlled by the resorts occupying the seafront – housing the legions of Singaporeans who journey here to swing golf clubs on Desaru's splendid course. Bicycles can be hired at several of the resorts.

SLEEPING

Accommodation at Desaru is largely resort-style, with prices rising significantly on Saturday. All resorts have restaurants serving Chinese, Japanese and international cuisine. First along the beach, the **Desaru Perdana Beach Resort** (☎ 822 2222; dpbr@tm.net.my; PO Box 29, Bandar Penawar; d Sun-Fri/Sat RM270/320;) has a large variety of rooms, loads of trips, sea sports, other recreational activities and several restaurants. About one kilometre further on, the simple **Desaru Leisure Camp** (☎ 822 2888; camping RM10, d with fan RM60) offers very spartan wooden huts along the beach.

Further ahead is the **Desaru Golden Beach Hotel** (☎ 822 1101; hotel@desaruresort.com; PO Box 50, Tanjung Penawar; d incl breakfast Sun-Fri/Sat RM180/250), and at the northern end of the beach sits the vast **Desaru Impian Resort** (☎ 838 3997/8; fax 838 3996; ste incl breakfast RM260;), with a reception block straight out of Disney.

GETTING THERE & AWAY

Buses (RM3.50, 1½ hours) and taxis (RM100 per car) run to/from Kota Tinggi. From JB, buses cost RM5 and taxis cost RM100 per car.

Daily ferries from North Changi in Singapore run to Tanjung Belungkur (return adult/child S$20/13), from where taxis can be taken to Desaru (RM40). For more details, see the Transport chapter, p561.

MERSING

☎ 07

The small fishing village of Mersing is the departure point for boats travelling between the mainland and Pulau Tioman, and the other islands of the Seribuat Archipelago. While most travellers rush through Mersing on their way to the islands, the town itself is pleasant and a relaxing stopover. The river bustles with fishing boats, kittens and cats scamper about the streets (indigenous Malaysian cats all have a kink in their tails), there are some good restaurants and you can even knock back a few beers without feeling distinctly out of place.

Orientation

From the north or south, you will enter Mersing at the town's main roundabout on Route 3. Leading off this to the east is Jl Abu Bakar, the main street down to the jetty. Jl Ismail also meets the roundabout and runs roughly parallel to Jl Abu Bakar for 150m or so. Most of the town's hotels, restaurants and banks are clustered on or near these two streets. A few hotels can also be found across the bridge to the north and down Jl Nong Yahya, to the south off Jl Ismail.

Information

INTERNET ACCESS

Cyber World! (Jl Abu Bakar; RM4 per hr; 9.30am-11.30pm)

Nasa Net Café (Jl Abu Bakar; RM3 per hr; 10.30am-10.30pm)

Cyber Café (Plaza R&R Centre; RM5 per hr)

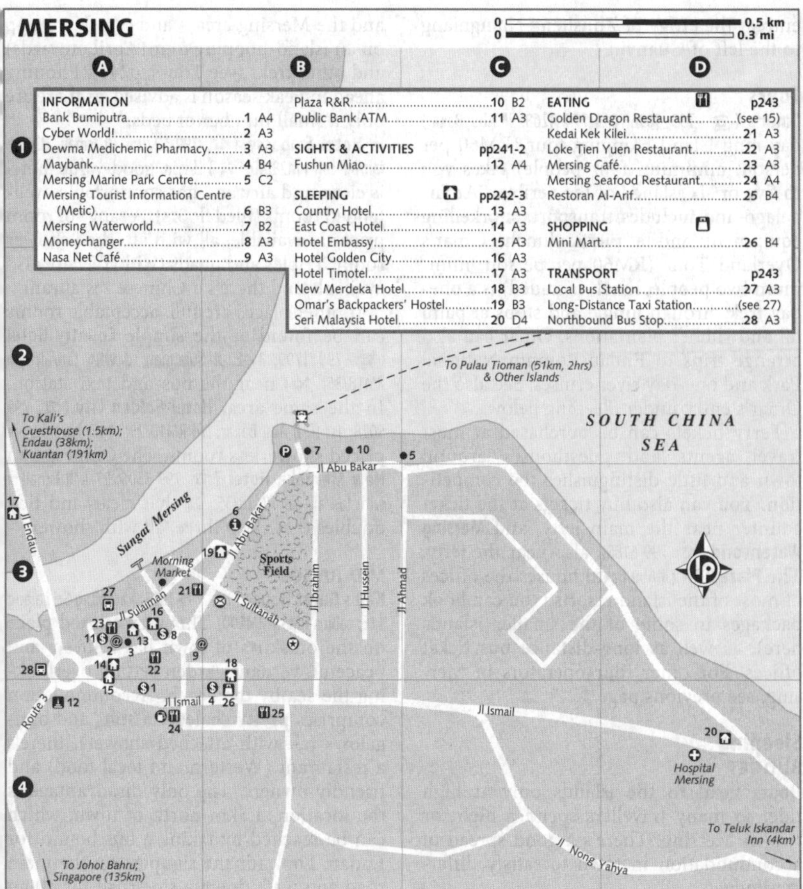

MONEY

Bank Bumiputra (Jl Ismail) and **Maybank** (Jl Ismail) can cash travellers cheques.

POST

Post Office (Jl Abu Bakar)

TOURIST INFORMATION

Mersing Tourist Information Centre (Metic; ☎ 799 5212; ⏲ 8am-1pm & 2-4.30pm Mon-Thu, 8am-noon & 2.45-4.30pm Fri, 8am-12.45pm Sat; Jl Abu Bakar)

TRAVEL AGENCIES

Agencies arranging tours and ticketing:

Giamso Safari (☎ 799 3576; 23 Jl Abu Bakar)

Island Connection Travel & Tours (☎ 799 2535; 2 Jl Jemaluang)

SS Services Agency (☎ 799 1937; No 18 Tourist Centre, R&R Plaza, Jl Abu Bakar)

Sights & Activities

There is little to see in Mersing itself. The **Fushun Miao** (Fushun Temple) is a 95-year-old Taoist and Buddhist temple. At the rear of the shrine is a splendid, gilded statue of Guanyin (Goddess of Compassion) called a Qianshou Guanyin (1000-arm Guanyin), although the effigy here sports only eight upper limbs. To her right, and below some Chinese characters announcing 'Holy Mother Tianhou', stands Tianhou (Queen of Heaven) herself, worshipped by fishing folk and those whose lives are intertwined with the sea. Women hoping for children entreat the effigy of Zhusheng Niangniang to the left of Guanyin.

Tours

Omar's (☎ 799 5096, 019-774 4268; Jl Abu Bakar) day-long Island-Hopping tour (RM60 per person, minimum four people) takes you to five or six islands of the Seribuat Archipelago and includes transport, snorkelling equipment and a picnic lunch. Omar's Overland Tour (RM60 per person, minimum two people, lunch included) is a one-day trek through jungle and stops at palm oil and rubber plantations. Omar can also arrange trips to Endau-Rompin National Park and one-day river cruises. See also the Omar's entry under Sleeping below.

Ferry tickets can be purchased at most travel agents and guesthouses around town and little distinguishes the competition. You can also buy tickets at the ticket counter near the main jetty, and **Mersing Waterworld** (☎ 799 6188), also near the jetty. The **Plaza R&R** (Jl Abu Baker) houses the offices of most of the island resorts (you can book packages to some of the smaller islands here), as well as long-distance bus ticket offices. For other tour operators in Mersing, see previous page.

Sleeping

BUDGET

Boats head to the islands only at high tide, so many travellers spend a night or two in Mersing. There's a good spread of accommodation in town to satisfy different budgets.

East Coast Hotel (☎ 799 3546, 012-762 4983; rockyanwar2002@hotmail.com; 43A Jl Abu Bakar; dm/s/d RM8/15/18; 💻) If you're looking for a friendly welcome in Mersing, this efficient and backpacker-oriented hotel gets the thumbs up. Busy, clean and well kept, there are cheap beds, informative and helpful staff and a relaxed ambience. Kitchen facilities (including a pizza oven) are at hand, along with Internet (RM4 per hour), video, a small aquarium, a rooftop sitting area and advice on local trips and treks.

Omar's Backpackers' Hostel (☎ 799 5096, 019-774 4268; Jl Abu Bakar; dm/d RM8/20) This travellers den is cheap, frugal (concrete floor) and popular. The fan doubles and four-bed dorms are clean, there's a balcony and the owners are knowledgeable about the islands and the Mersing area – and can fix you up on an island-hopping tour (April onwards) and other treks (see Tours, p241). Phoning ahead in peak season is advised, as there are only a small number of beds.

Hotel Embassy (☎ 799 5279; 2 Jl Ismail; d with fan/air-con RM28/40; ❄) This good-value hotel is clean and airy and has comfortable, well-tended rooms (tiled floors). A range of room prices is available, all with attached shower room. Triples and quads (with TV) are also available and there's a Chinese restaurant.

If other places are full, acceptable rooms can be found at the simple **Country Hotel** (☎ 799 1799; 11-E, Jl Sulaiman; d with fan/air-con RM18/35; ❄) near the bus and taxi station. In the same area, **Hotel Golden City** (☎ 799 5028; 1st fl, Jl Abu Bakar; s/d RM10/25; ❄) has low-priced showerless rooms. The Chinese-run **New Merdeka Hotel** (☎ 799 3506; 27-A Jl Ismail; r with fan/air-con RM18/35; ❄) has clean and tidy doubles that sleep three, all with shower.

MID-RANGE

Kali's Guest House (☎ 799 3613; Kampung Sri Lalang 12E; cabins RM35-RM100) This very relaxed place on the outskirts of town has a lovely and peaceful, verdant garden setting overlooking the sea by the beach. Accommodation comprises pretty chalets on stilts and bungalows (all with attached shower), there's a restaurant (Western and local food) and friendly owners. The only disadvantage is the location, 1.5km north of town, which can be reached by taking a bus bound for Endau. Look for the signpost on the main road and walk down a side road for 100m to reach the guesthouse.

Teluk Iskandar Inn (☎ 799 6037; 1456 Jl Sekakap; d RM90; ❄) Attractively located in a modern building fronted by a long lawn and perched on a hill overlooking the sea with a rocky beach, this well-groomed escape 4km south of town has large and airy two-person rooms with breakfast included. The owners can prepare Malay food by arrangement. The hotel is easy to miss, as it is not well advertised – look out for the blue Telekom phone box.

Seri Malaysia (☎ 799 1876; smmsg@serimalaysia.com.my; Lot TTB 641 Jl Ismail; d RM110; ❄ 🅿) Generally dependable, the Mersing branch of Seri Malaysia is decidedly so-so. Rooms are musty, staff indifferent, the TVs are small and there are ants in the rooms. Things may have improved by the time this goes to print, but the hotel's location remains stranded in the east of town.

Hotel Timotel (☎ 799 5888; timotel@tm.net.my; 839 Jl Endau; s/d RM115/140; ❄) Just across the bridge over the river, this is Mersing's best hotel. Offering very good value, rooms are clean and spacious. Double rooms here have showers while the twin rooms have bathtubs.

Eating

There are several places around town for a roti canai (served with dhal or curry), breakfast and coffee. Serving tasty Indian food, **Restoran Al-Arif** (44 Jl Ismail; meals RM8) is one of the best in town and very good value. Mersing, being a fishing port, is a good place for seafood, and several Chinese restaurants specialise in seafood dishes. The **Mersing Seafood Restaurant** (Jl Ismail; meals RM13) offers fine and good-value dishes, including fish slice and vegetable soup, prawns with coconut sauce and spicy Sichuan dishes such as *mapo doufu* which means pockmarked grandma dofu (the pockmarked grandma in question being the wife of a Qing dynasty restaurateur in Sichuan). Similar fare can be had at Mersing's oldest Chinese restaurant, the **Loke Tien Yuen Restaurant** (55 Jl Abu Bakar; meals RM13). For Malay and Chinese dishes, the **Golden Dragon Restaurant** (2 Jl Ismail; meals RM13) offers good-value seafood and Western breakfasts. For something approximating a Western-style breakfast, visit the **Mersing Café** (Jl Sulaiman), opposite the bus stop. Opposite the post office, the Chinese-owned **Kedai Kek Kilei** (Jl Abu Bakar; 🕒 8am-7pm) is an inexpensive coffee and cake shop that can set you up with donuts, sardine puffs, coffee and crisps.

Getting There & Away

Long-distance buses depart from the Plaza R&R, near the jetty and from the roundabout by the Restoran Malaysia. Purchase tickets at the ticket booths at Plaza R&R (or at the Restoran Malaysia). Destinations include Johor Bahru (RM7.50, one per day), Kuala Lumpur (RM19.50, six per day), Kuantan (RM10.60, four per day), Kuala Terengganu/Cherating (RM22.10, four per day), Penang (RM35, one per day) and Singapore (RM12.50, four per day).

The local bus and long-distance taxi station is on Jl Sulaiman, near the river. Taxi destinations and costs (per car) include Johor Bahru (RM80), Kota Tinggi (RM48), Kuantan (RM100), Endau (RM20) and Pekan (RM80). Local buses run to/from Johor Bahru (RM5.50) and Kota Tinggi (RM4.90).

SERIBUAT ARCHIPELAGO

☎ 07

The Seribuat Archipelago, off the east coast of Johor, contains some of Malaysia's most beautiful islands. The largest and most popular of these, Pulau Tioman, is actually in Pahang (see p250), but is usually reached from Mersing, as are the archipelago's other islands. The smaller islands of the archipelago may not have the stunning natural scenery of Tioman, but they do offer some peace and quiet, as well as some decent snorkelling and diving. In all, there are 64 islands in the archipelago.

Unfortunately, only Tioman has a regularly scheduled ferry service; the other islands are mostly the domain of private resorts. To visit these islands, it is necessary to book a package with one of the resorts, and the resort will arrange private transport to the island from Mersing. If you'd like to shop around and compare prices, most of these resorts have offices in Mersing's Plaza R&R.

Pulau Besar

☎ 07

This island, also known as Pulau Babi Besar (Big Pig Island) and one of the closest to Mersing, is 4km long and 1km wide. It has a good white-sand beach on its western side, one or two secluded beaches on its isolated eastern side and decent coral.

Most of the resorts are situated along the beach on the west of the island. **D'Coconut** (☎ 019-271 4531; chalet RM175; ❄ 🏊), one of the best resorts on the island, has a pool and restaurant. **Aseana Island Resort** (☎ 799 4152; mountain-view chalet RM138; ❄) has excellent chalets, an alfresco restaurant and a sea sports centre. South along the beach is the simply constructed **Nirwana Resort** (☎ 799 5979/5929; s/d chalets RM120/160; ❄ 🏊), with its own jetty and restaurant.

Pulau Sibu

☎ 07

The large, slender island of Pulau Sibu (6km long and 1km wide) is close to the mainland and popular with holidaymakers from

Singapore, and hence has a variety of large holiday camps. The island's terrain is not as arresting as on other islands, but there are some fine beaches and good coral.

Sibu Island Cabanas (☎ 331 7216; s/d chalet RM150/200; ❄) has a range of chalets and bungalows with en-suite bathrooms and there's a restaurant. On the east coast, the friendly **O&H Kampung Huts** (☎ 799 3124; chalet RM100) is a very popular place with island activities. The secluded and atmospheric **Rimba Resort** (☎ 010-714 7495; d with meals RM175) has its own private beach at the northern end of the island, and there is a 20% discount on room rates from Sunday to Thursday.

Pulau Rawa

☎ 07

The tiny island of Rawa, 16km from Mersing, has a fine white-sand beach, and the waters around the island are good for snorkelling.

Rawa Safaris Island Resort (☎ 799 1204; A-frames/chalets RM103/230; ❄) has a variety of accommodation, a restaurant and a wide range of facilities and activities.

Pulau Tinggi

☎ 07

Tinggi is probably the most impressive island when seen from a distance – it's an extinct volcano (tinggi means 'tall').

Accommodation is in resorts, although some locals may supply budget accommodation. **Nadia's Inn** (☎ 799 5582; d RM140) has chalets, A-frames and bungalows, a pool and a restaurant.

Pulau Pemanggil & Pulau Aur

☎ 07

Far from the mainland, these two islands are popular with divers and have crystal-clear water and excellent coral.

Aur Samudera Resort on Pulau Aur sells group diving packages in conjunction with **Dive Atlantis** (☎ 02-295 0377) in Singapore. Once on the island, chalets for up to three people cost RM60, and food is available at an extra charge.

Dagang Chalets and Longhouse (Kampung Buau; dm RM10) on Pulau Pemanggil provides cheap accommodation.

Other Islands

There are several more small islands within about 20km of Mersing. These uninhabited islands include (from north to south) Harimau, Mensirip, Gual, Hujung and Tengah. The most famous of these is Pulau Tengah, which was once a Vietnamese refugee camp but is now home only to the sea turtles who come in July to lay their eggs. The island has some superb coral on its northern side. The other islands also have good coral and some isolated white-sand beaches.

There are no regularly scheduled ferries out to these islands. About the only way to visit them without spending hundreds of ringgit to charter a boat is to join Omar's Island Hopping tour (see Tours p242).

ENDAU-ROMPIN NATIONAL PARK

Straddling the Johor-Pahang border, the 870-sq-km Endau-Rompin is the second-largest park on the peninsula after Taman Negara. The park's lowland forests are among the last remaining in Peninsular Malaysia and have been identified as harbouring unique varieties of plant life. Of these, the visitor is likely to encounter enormous umbrella palms, with their characteristic fan-shaped leaves, and *Livinstona endanensis*, a species of palm with serrated circular leaves. The park is also Malaysia's last refuge of the Sumatran rhinoceros, although they roam only the park's remote areas. Tigers also live here, but are almost never spotted by visitors. For more information on endangered species, see p54.

The vast majority of travellers come on tours arranged by private operators. It is possible to visit the park on your own, provided you have your own camping gear, but this won't necessarily work out any cheaper and the isolated location can make transport to the park inconvenient to arrange.

The accessible region of the park is confined to a small area along the banks of Sungai Endau and one of its tributaries, Sungai Jasin. A trip to the park usually involves a trek along the banks of these rivers, stopping to admire two impressive waterfalls along the way. The only other easily accessible trek in the park is the four-hour return trip up to the Janing Barat plateau, near the Kuala Jasin base camp.

Officials of the **Johor National Parks Corporation** (☎ 07-223 7471; fax 07-223 7472) generally require that you hire a guide to explore the park, but you may be able to get around this if you have experience with jungle trekking

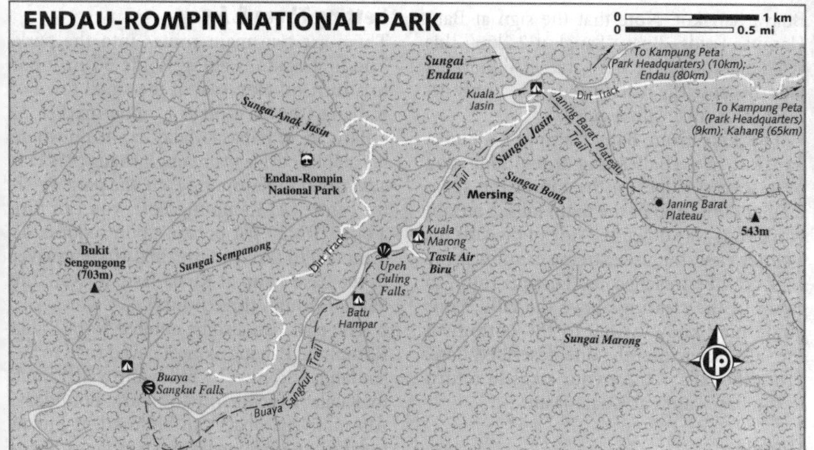

Guides can be hired for RM35 to RM40 per day at the park headquarters at Kampung Peta. A park entry permit (RM20) is also required. Also factor in further charges, including camera permit (RM10), fishing-rod permit (RM10) and further (daily) permits to travel within the park to destinations including the Buaya Sangkut and Upeh Guling waterfalls, and the Janing Barat plateau. The park entry permit charge does not apply if you enter the park from Pahang (see Getting There & Away, p246).

See 'Jungle Trekking Tips' (p537) for advice on preparing yourself for a trek.

Walks

THE JANING BARAT PLATEAU

The Janing Barat plateau is a 500m-high sandstone plateau southeast of Kuala Jasin base camp. The trail starts at the dirt track behind the camp; look for it heading into the woods opposite the path to the camp.

The trail climbs gently for the first 100m or so, then steepens into a challenging uphill slog. Soon after starting the climb, the first *Livinstona endanensis* are visible on either side of the trail. Once on the plateau, the terrain levels out and becomes marshy; keep an eye out for pitcher plants, many of which sprout from the forest floor. There is nothing to mark the high point of the trail; simply walk across the plateau for a few hundred metres and then turn around. The return to base camp from the plateau is a quick one-hour downhill hike.

WALKING THE TRAIL TO BUAYA SANGKUT FALLS

The main walk in the park follows the Sungai Jasin from Kuala Jasin base camp. Those with time for three nights in the park can usually reach the highest waterfall on the river, Buaya Sangkut; those with time for only two nights must usually turn around at Batu Hampar rocks or the falls at Upeh Guling.

After a night at Kuala Jasin base camp, the first day's hike crosses Sungai Jasin to follow the level terrain along the river bank through jungle for two hours to Kuala Marong (also known as Lembah Marong), a camp site at the confluence of Sungai Jasin and the much smaller Sungai Marong. On the far side of Sungai Marong, a narrow 300m-long track leads to Tasik Air Biru (which guides sometimes translate as `Blue Lagoon'), a fine swimming hole with translucent emerald-green water that makes a good lunch stop.

After returning to Kuala Marong, a further 10-minute hike up Sungai Jasin brings you to the impressive falls at Upeh Guling. About 8m in height, these wide falls are notable for the water-sculpted pools in the rocks just above the falls. From Upeh Guling, it's a gentle 40-minute hike to the flat rocks and camp site of Batu Hampar. Along the way you'll see some huge umbrella palms and dipterocarp trees. If you reach Batu Hampar before noon and are in excellent shape, it's possible to continue on to the Buaya Sangkut and return all the way to Kuala Jasin in one day. Otherwise, camp at Batu Hampar or at

Buaya Sangkut. Note that the sign at Batu Hampar reads 'Buaya Sangkut 2.2km'; this is a dangerous error – it's at least 4km to the falls. Because the path is quite faint, only attempt this hike with a guide.

The hike from Batu Hampar to Buaya Sangkut is a challenging three-hour slog over several ridges to the top of the spectacular 40m drop of the main falls. You can work your way down the side of the falls for a better view, but use extreme caution as the rocks can be treacherous. There is room to camp in the clearing above the falls. Your guide may know a way to the bottom of the falls other than the one described here. From the falls, retrace your steps to return to the base camp at Kuala Jasin.

Sleeping

You can camp at Kuala Jasin, Kuala Marong, Batu Hampar and above the falls at Buaya Sangkut and at Upeh Guling. Of these, Buaya Sangkut is the nicest and most remote location. A lightweight tent is the preferred option, but you can spread a ground sheet under the covered picnic platforms at Kuala Jasin and Kuala Marong – just be sure to bring some mosquito coils if you're going to sleep alfresco.

There are also simple A-frames (RM30) available in Kuala Jasin and chalets with fan (RM20) in Kampung Peta.

Getting There & Away

There are two main routes into the park. The first route is along Route 50 in Johor to a turn-off 5km east of the small town of Kahang (the turn-off is at mile marker 26 ('Batu 26' in Bahasa Malaysia), from where it's a 56km drive over rough roads (4WD is advisable) to Kampung Peta, the park's visitor centre. At Kampung Peta, you can hire a boat (RM10 per person upon request; 45 minutes) to take you the final 10km upriver to the base camp at Kuala Jasin or walk the 15km (around three hours).

The park can also be entered from Kuala Rompin in Pahang along a paved road to Selendang, and then by following a dirt track to Kuala Kinchin on the park boundary. Alternatively, boats can be hired in Endau to take you up Sungai Endau as far as Kampung Peta (RM200 one way, 7 hours).

Because of the difficulties in arranging your own transport into the park, most travellers go on a tour. Mersing is the best place to arrange this; **Omar's Backpackers' Hostel** (☎ 799 5096, 019-774 4268) can arrange tours (see Tours p242). Per-person prices for all-inclusive two-night trips are around RM400; three-night trips cost around RM500. Also in Mersing, **Giamso Safari** (☎ 799 3576; 23 Jl Abu Bakar) offers expeditions to the park (three days RM200 per person, four days RM210 per person).

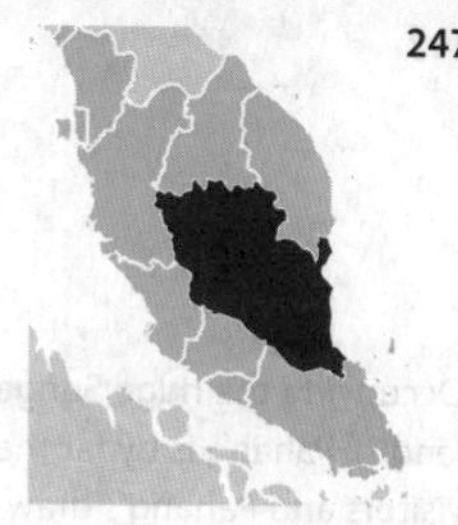

Pahang

CONTENTS

Occupying the huge Sungai Pahang Basin and bordered to the east by a coastline 209km in length, Pahang is by far the largest state in Peninsular Malaysia. The state has plenty to offer visitors and Pahang's draw-card attractions are its spectacular natural features.

The jungle-swathed island of Pulau Tioman, usually accessed via Mersing in Johor state, is fringed with coral formations and attractive beaches supporting small island communities. The national park Taman Negara lays claim to some of Peninsular Malaysia's largest tracts of virgin jungle, where ambitious trekkers can encounter its rich and primordial biodiversity. Nearby Kenong Rimba State Park may not be as popular as Taman Negara, but is more manageable. The park is often reached via the charming and easy-going town of Kuala Lipis, studded with colonial-era architecture and distinctly Chinese in flavour.

The former royal capital of Pekan deserves a visit for its museums, shophouses and stately quarters while the capital, Kuantan, sees travellers passing through en route to the beach at Teluk Chempedak outside town. Further north, many travellers are waylaid by Cherating's marvellous beach with its restaurants, bars and beach-front chalets.

HIGHLIGHTS

- Jungle trekking, snorkelling and diving on **Pulau Tioman** (p250), the island made famous in the film *South Pacific*
- Wandering around relaxed **Pekan** (p257), admiring its royal palaces, mosques and interesting museum
- Lazing, walking and promenading at **Teluk Chempedak** (p261), Kuantan's lovely resort-style beach
- Chilling out in **Cherating** (p262), a laid-back backpackers' pit stop, with a great beach, food and drinking holes
- Exploring **Taman Negara** (p267), Malaysia's first national park, one of the oldest rainforests in the world and home to endangered species and exotic plants
- Relaxing in **Kuala Lipis** (p275), a charming and hilly town in central Pahang speckled with colonial architecture
- Forest trekking on the trail of wildlife, caves and Orang Asli settlements in **Kenong Rimba State Park** (p277)

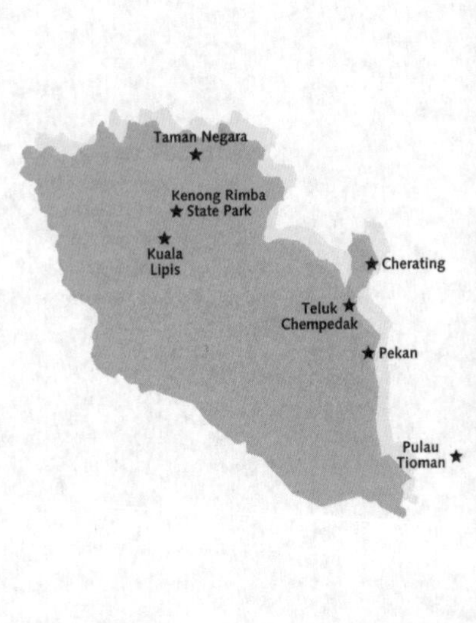

TELEPHONE CODE: 09	POPULATION: 1.26 MILLION	AREA: 35,964 SQ KM

History

Important archaeological finds dating to Neolithic times have been made along Pahang's Sungai (River) Tembeling. By the 8th century the Sumatran Srivijaya Empire held sway along the coast, until its collapse in the 14th century, after which Pahang became a Siamese dependency.

Pahang really emerged as a separate political entity only when the Melaka sultanate launched an attack against the Siamese in the middle of the 15th century and installed Muhammad, the eldest son of the Melaka sultan, as ruler.

In the 16th century the state became a pawn in the four-way struggle for ascendancy between Johor, Aceh (in what is now Indonesia), the Dutch and the Portuguese. In a period of 30 years it was sacked many times, its rich, mineral-based economy ruined, its rulers killed or abducted and much of its population murdered or enslaved. After the decline of the Acehnese empire in the mid-17th century, Pahang was ruled by Johor for 200 years.

From 1858 until 1863 Pahang suffered a protracted civil war brought about by a leadership struggle between two brothers, Wan Ahmad and Mutahir. On the death of their father, the sultan, Wan Ahmad finally won, and in 1887 he became sultan. His role from then on was reduced to a largely symbolic position as the British, who were interested in the state's commercial potential, had

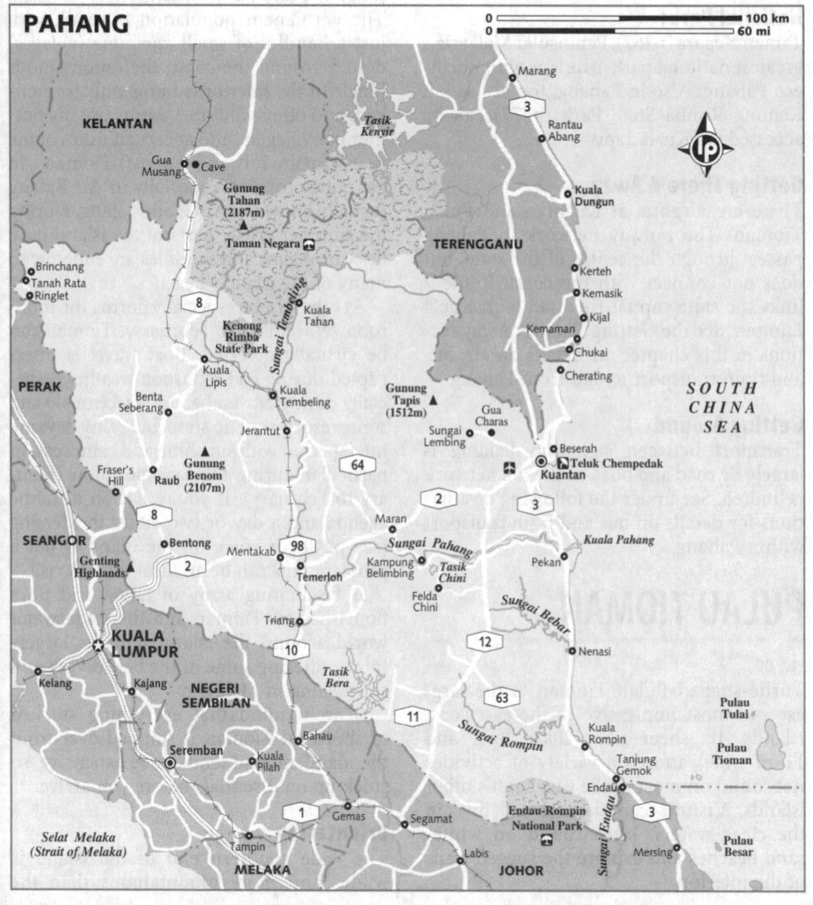

forced him to sign a treaty bringing Pahang under the control of a British Resident.

In 1896 Pahang was one of the four states that became the Federated Malay States (the others were Perak, Selangor and Negeri Sembilan). These in turn formed the Federation of Malaya in February 1948 and finally the Federation of Malaysia, as it is today, in 1963. Kuantan replaced Kuala Lipis as state capital in 1957.

Climate

The temperature in Pahang ranges from 21° to 32°C and average humidity exceeds 82%. There is rain throughout the year, but the wettest months are during the monsoon, from November to February.

National Parks

Taman Negara (p267), Peninsular Malaysia's greatest national park, overlaps with northern Pahang. Also in Pahang, the 120 sq km Kenong Rimba State Park (p277) can be accessed via Kuala Lipis.

Getting There & Away

There are airports at Kuantan and Pulau Tioman. The railway network in Pahang passes through the centre of the state, but does not connect with the coast. Route 2 links the state capital Kuantan with Kuala Lumpur. See the Getting There & Away sections in this chapter for details on air, bus and train transport to and from Pahang.

Getting Around

Transport between sights in Pahang is largely by road and boat, as the rail network is limited. See under the following destinations for details on bus and train transport within Pahang.

PULAU TIOMAN

☎ 09

Turtle-shaped Pulau Tioman is the largest and most impressive of the east coast islands. Its sheer size (20km long and 11km wide) affords a variety of activities not found on most of the east coast's other islands. Visitors can snorkel and dive in the clear waters, laze around on white-sand beaches and explore the rugged trails of the interior.

Back in the late 1950s Hollywood got wind of Tioman and famously made it the setting for the mythical Bali Hai in the film *South Pacific*. Later, in the 1970s, *Time* magazine proclaimed it one of the world's 10 most beautiful islands. The crowds have been pouring in ever since for a taste of paradise. An airport materialised, sandwiched between vertiginous mountains and the sea, a casino turned up, express boat services to the mainland multiplied and roads are now planned to convey tourists speedily from one end of the island to the other. Pulau Tioman has also become a duty-free zone, although this has yet to make the beer in the bars any cheaper.

It comes as no surprise, then, that Tioman today is geared almost entirely to tourism. The permanent population is small, with just a handful of small *kampung* (villages) dotted around the coast; the mountainous jungle of the interior is home only to monkeys and other wildlife. Visitors usually outnumber villagers, and at certain times of the year (usually July and August) Tioman can get quite crowded, especially in Air Batang (usually known as ABC) and Salang. During the summer crush, parts of the island have litter problems and sandflies are endemic to many of the island's beaches.

At other times, especially during the monsoon (November to February), Tioman can be virtually deserted. Boat travel is interrupted during bad monsoon weather (especially during November and December) and some resorts shut up shop, but rainy days are interspersed with sunshine and calm seas, in particular during the low monsoon (January to February). If you're not on a frantic agenda and a day or two either in Mersing (see p240) or stuck on the island is not a problem, this can be an ideal time to visit.

A fascinating array of fauna and flora flourishes on Tioman and the underwater world around the island remains largely intact, offering some of the best diving and snorkelling in Malaysia.

Bear in mind that everything stocked in shops on Tioman is shipped over from the mainland and tends to be expensive, so stock up on essentials before you arrive.

Orientation

The wide southern end of the island is wilder and more mountainous than the

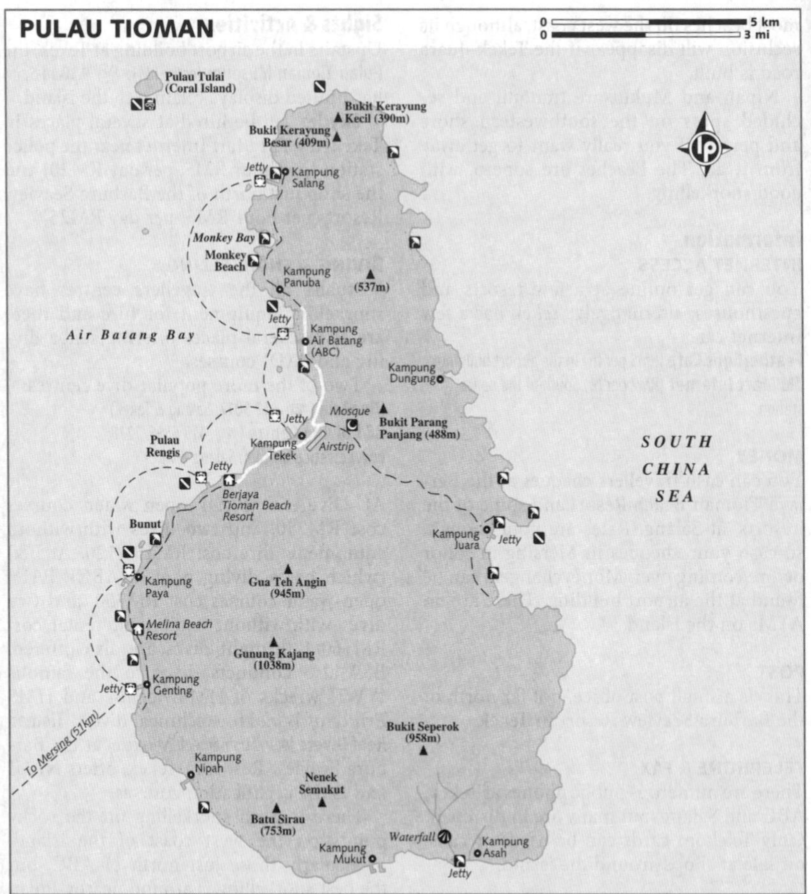

narrow northern end. At the time of writing, only one short stretch of road exists on the western side of the island, running from Berjaya Tioman Beach Resort to the northern end of Tekek. The authorities have approved the construction of roads through the jungle from Tekek to Juara, south to Kampung Mukut and north to Salang, which will speed up transport but will further commercialise the island. Until the roads are built, transport around the island is by creaky fishing boats or on foot, via rugged mountain trails.

Tekek is the island's largest village, and its administrative centre. The airport is here, as well as some well-stocked shops, but the beach isn't great. An easy walk to the north of Tekek, just over the headland, is Air Batang, commonly known as ABC. This popular beach has a string of chalet operations connected by a concrete path and is one of the two main travellers centres. The other is the small bay at Salang, 3km to the north. With its beautiful beach, good restaurants, nightlife and relative accessibility, Salang is probably the best location on Tioman. It's popular with divers – two of Tioman's better dive centres are also here (see p252). The beach is about 700m long, and the jetty is towards the southern end. Several guesthouses can arrange expensive speedboat services to ABC and around the island.

Juara, the only place to stay on the east coast, is less developed and quieter than most beaches on the west coast, although its seclusion will disappear if the Tekek–Juara road is built.

Nipah and Mukut are tranquil and secluded spots on the southwestern shore and perfect if you really want to get away from it all. The beaches are superb, with good snorkelling.

Information

INTERNET ACCESS

You can get online at a few resorts and guesthouses; alternatively, Tekek has a few Internet cafés.

Featherlight Cafe (RM5 per hr) In the airport building.
TM Mart Internet (RM7 per hr) South of the police station.

MONEY

You can cash travellers cheques at the Berjaya Tioman Beach Resort and some of the 'resorts' at Salang. Rates are poor though, so cash your cheques in Mersing in Johor before coming over. Moneychangers can be found at the airport building. There are no ATMs on the island.

POST

There's a small post office, not far north of the Barbura Seaview Resort in Tekek.

TELEPHONE & FAX

There are numerous public phones at Tekek, ABC and Salang, but many are in disrepair. Only Telekom cards can be used for calls, on sale at shops around the island.

WILDLIFE ON TIOMAN

Tioman is of great interest to biologists because its relative isolation has resulted in flora and fauna that is markedly different from mainland species. Huge swathes of jungle remain unexplored. You have a good chance of seeing monitor lizards, long-tailed macaques and sea eagles and you may even spot some of the island's reclusive mouse deer.

The waters around Tioman shelter technicolour schools of exotic fish and a surprising number of turtles. At Nipah, Juara and Pulau Tulai (Coral Island) you have a good chance of seeing turtles come ashore to lay their eggs from early July to September.

Sights & Activities

Upstairs in the airport building at Tekek, the **Pulau Tioman Museum** (entry RM1; 9.30am-5pm) has limited displays relating to the island.

Bicycles can be hired at several places in Tekek; try TM Mart Internet near the police station (per hour RM5, per day RM20) and the shop just north of the Barbura Seaview Resort (per hour RM5, per day RM25).

DIVING & SNORKELLING

Virtually all the travellers centres have snorkelling equipment for hire and there are also several places offering scuba diving and PADI courses.

Two of the more popular dive centres:

DiveAsia (☎ 419 5017; Salang & Tekek)
B&J Diving Centre (☎ 419 5555/1218; www.divetioman.com; Salang & ABC)

At DiveAsia, PADI open-water courses cost RM750, and two dives with/without equipment hire cost RM150/120. At B&J (which has a diving pool in ABC), PADI open-water courses cost RM750, and two dives with/without equipment rental cost RM160/130; night dives are also offered. B&J also conducts dives to the famous WWII wrecks of HMS *Repulse* and HMS *Prince of Wales* for technical divers. **Tioman Reef Divers** (www.tiomanreefdivers.com) at the Barbura Seaview Resort in Tekek, offers NAUI and PADI certification courses.

There is good snorkelling off the rocky points on the west coast of the island, particularly those just north of ABC, but the best snorkelling is around nearby Pulau Tulai, better known as Coral Island. Most chalet operators can arrange day trips to the island for about RM45, including equipment rental. On the east coast, the best snorkelling is around the rocks at the northern end of Juara's beach, where reef sharks sometimes make an appearance. The sea however, can be very rough during the high monsoon season (November to December).

For information about other dive sites and advice for safe and responsible diving see p534. Consult www.projectaware.com for more information on how best to protect the aquatic environment while diving.

CROSS-ISLAND WALK

This fantastic walk (around 7km) crosses the island's waist from Tekek to Juara.

While not too strenuous, parts of the walk are steep and hiking in tropical heat can be taxing. Carry plenty of water.

The walk starts about 1km north of the jetty in Tekek, just past the convenience store. Follow the concrete path, passing the mosque on your left, and then veer right onto the boulder path, leaving the concrete road as it enters a modern compound on your left. The boulder steps continue intermittently for most of the way to the top. However, crossing streams, dissolving into mud, and obscured by roots and stones, the trail can be difficult to discern, so follow the power lines overhead. Near the top of the hill, you pass a small waterfall. The jungle is awesome, with vast trees, creepers, monkeys, squirrels, butterflies, spiders and much more. About an hour beyond the waterfall, the trail levels off before becoming a concrete path that drops steeply into Juara.

The walk takes from 1½ to three hours. A sporadic ferry service leaves Juara for Salang, ABC and Tekek (RM20) at 3pm (no service during the monsoon season). To walk back to Tekek, it's not hard to find a motorcyclist willing to take you to the end of the concrete path from Juara for around RM10 (saving you the punishing uphill slog). If returning on foot, don't enter the jungle after around 4.30pm, as you can get lost in the dark. (It may be bright on the beach, but it is much darker in the jungle.) During the monsoon season, the path can be very slippery, so wear shoes with a good grip. The planned Tekek to Juara road, if completed, will replace this walk as the primary overland route between the two villages.

OTHER WALKS

You can walk along much of the west coast, but the trails are often difficult to follow; again, take water.

From Tekek you can walk south to Berjaya Tioman Beach Resort in about 30 minutes, either by the road or by rock-hopping around the headland at low tide. From there you can walk through the golf course. Just before the telecommunications tower there is a trail to the beautiful, deserted beach of Bunut. From the end of the beach, the sometimes faint trail continues over the headland to a couple of rickety bridges across the mangroves just before Paya. From Paya you can walk south to Genting – the trail is easy to follow and there are houses along the way where you can ask directions.

Further south, at secluded Mukut (reached by boat from Genting), a popular trek leads to the waterfalls near Asah.

Heading north from Tekek, you cross the small headland to ABC, and from Bamboo Hill Chalets, at the northern end of the bay, it's a 10-minute climb over the next headland to Panuba Bay. From there it's another 40 minutes through the rainforest to a deserted yellow-sand beach known as Monkey Beach. The trail continues from the other end of the beach across the next headland to the white-sand beach at Monkey Bay. At the end of this beach the trail starts the long, steep climb over the headland to Salang. The trail is not well marked here and should not be attempted during the monsoon season. (With fewer visitors, the trail becomes overgrown and it is easy to get lost.) The walk from ABC to Salang takes about three hours and is a fairly strenuous undertaking.

Boat transport to the beaches can be arranged at most of the guesthouses in ABC or Salang, if you don't want to walk back.

Sleeping & Eating

Most accommodation options are on the west coast of the island, with pricier places clustered to the south and budget places to the north, primarily in ABC and Salang. Juara, a quiet beach community on the east coast, has a few cheap places to stay for those who want to get away from it all, although the planned new road (when built) will rob the settlement of its isolation.

From June to August, when the island swarms with visitors, accommodation becomes tight. Either side of these months it's a buyer's market. During the monsoon the island is almost deserted. You can generally find accommodation from January to February, although many places shut up for the whole monsoon season (November to February).

Accommodation is mostly in small, cramped wooden chalets and longhouse rooms. For RM20 you'll get a small chalet with a double bed and bathroom. Once you start paying over RM25 you should also get a mosquito net and fan. If you want air-con, you'll pay at least RM50 per night, but these rooms are usually much nicer than fan-only rooms. Most operations have a few larger cabins for those with children. Wherever you stay, it's worth bargaining, especially for longer visits.

The only international-class hotel on the island is **Berjaya Tioman Beach Resort** (☎ 419 1000; www.berjaya.com.my; d RM260;) a sprawling place south of Tekek. With 400 rooms, it offers discounts of up to 25% from November to February. Most rooms are chalet-style with air-con, and the hotel has an impressive range of facilities – a beautiful 18-hole golf course, tennis courts, horse riding, jet-skis, scuba diving and four restaurants. The resort can be heavily booked, particularly in the school holidays.

TEKEK

Accommodation options are not as appealing as in other parts of the island and Tekek has little character. But flights arrive and depart from here, and community facilities (including a post office and a police station) are more developed.

Barbura Seaview Resort (☎ 419 1346; fax 419 1139; longhouse RM55/chalet RM132-165;) This large resort-style complex, 900m south of the jetty at the end of the beach, is equipped with a gift shop and a spacious Chinese restaurant facing the beach. There's clean accommodation, with the pricier chalets enjoying a sea view, as well as cheaper longhouse rooms without air-con. Snorkelling, boating, fishing, diving and ferry ticketing can all be arranged here.

Swiss Cottage Resort (☎ 419 1843; chalet with fan/d with sea view/large bungalow RM58/78/98) Just beyond the Barbura Seaview Resort, this place has decent, clean and spacious rooms and benefits from a good stretch of beach. Double rooms are connected to the main building while most bungalows are semi-detached. Most chalets face the sea and have a balcony. All rooms have fans.

Monte Chalet (☎ 419 1648; chalet RM60-120;) Closer to the jetty is this pleasant, well-tended place on a fine stretch of beach and all chalets (some on the beach) come with hot water. Next door, **Tekek Inn** (☎ 419 1579; chalet with fan/air-con RM60/70;) has beach-front fan and air-con chalets (with shower), and a beach bar.

The **Barbura Seaview Chinese Restaurant** (meals RM25), in the resort of the same name, offers decent food and views. Popular **Liza** (meals RM20) serves up Malay and Western food just south of the police station and Tekek Inn.

ABC (AIR BATANG)

When you're choosing somewhere to stay, bear in mind that the northern end of the beach here is somewhat rocky and poor for swimming, while the southern end, near Nazri's Place, has the best white-sand beach.

Bamboo Hill Chalets (☎ 419 1339; chalets RM70-120; open Mar-Oct;) Perched on rocks overlooking the sea at the northern end of the beach, these six well-kept chalets are in a stupendous location surrounded by vegetation and alongside a waterfall and pool. They are almost always full, so call ahead. There's no air-con, but the location benefits from cooling sea breezes. Visa and MasterCard accepted. Internet use costs RM2.50 per hour.

South Pacific (☎ 419 1176; chalet with fan RM15-30) Just north of the jetty, this basic place offers laundry, boat service, shows films in the evening, has a restaurant and a small library of second-hand books. The pricier chalets are by the sea and all come with shower and mosquito net.

Johan's Resort (☎ 419 1359; dm with fan/chalets RM12/25, chalets with air-con RM65-80;) Attractive and well laid out with chalets on the beach and up the hill, this operation beyond the South Pacific has a restaurant where you can tuck into snapper and stingray.

Nazri's Place (☎ 419 1329; d RM25;) South of the jetty and the last accommodation option before the headland, this friendly place is popular with travellers and sits by a lovely stretch of beach. At the time of writing there was limited accommodation available, as the A-frame chalets burned down. The owner is currently building stone, fire-proof chalets that will cost around RM100 to RM120 per night. There is also a restaurant and Internet access (RM5 for 15 minutes).

Nazri's II (☎ 419 1375; s/tw RM25/60, chalets with air-con RM100;) Also known as Nazri's Beach Cabanas, this roomy outfit is one of the best options and provides large and clean bungalows with sea views towards the northern end of ABC. Also here is the Hijau Restaurant, with a fine vantage point over the sea.

ABC Bungalows (☎ 419 1154; chalet with fan/air-con RM20/120, hut with bathroom RM30; ❄) Almost at the northern terminus of ABC, the beach here is good and there's a variety of chalets spread over pleasant, well-tended grounds. It's friendly and popular with travellers and a decent restaurant is out the front. The large, pricier chalets come with hot water.

Mawar Beach Chalets (☎ 419 1153; chalet RM25) Just south of the jetty. A well-tended place with a restaurant, it offers clean chalets, all with fan, shower room and mosquito net.

Tioman House (☎ 419 1196; chalet with fan RM20) Clean, comfortable chalets (all with shower) and a restaurant with sea view (local and Western fare). North of Johan's Resort.

KAMPUNG PANUBA

Over the headland from ABC, the peaceful **Panuba Inn Resort** (☎ 013-772 0454; chalet with fan/air-con RM35/58-88) has a pier and restaurant and 30 chalets built on a hill overlooking the bay.

SALANG

Khalid's Place (☎ 419 5317; salangpusaka@yahoo.com; chalet with fan/air-con RM45/100; ❄) South of the jetty and set back from the beach with a nice garden, this is a popular option. There are 42 chalets, and all those with a fan also come with a shower. The air-con chalets come with carpet and fridge and there's a restaurant.

Zaid's Place (☎ 419 5020; chalet with fan/air-con RM60/150, sea views RM80/200; ❄ 💻) Also south of the jetty, this popular outfit has an attractive garden, a restaurant and a small library (Internet use costs RM10 per hour).

Pak Long Island Chalet (☎ 419 5000; enquiry@paklongislandchalet.com.my; chalet with fan RM45, deluxe chalet/quad with air-con RM130/180; ❄) South of the jetty and over the bridge, this friendly and extensive place has a restaurant and Internet access (RM5 for 30 minutes) and is a nice setting for families.

Salang Indah Resort (☎ 419 5015; fax 419 5024; d with fan/chalet RM25/35, family chalet with air con RM150; ❄ 💻) Sprawling north of the jetty, this resort is the biggest of the bunch, with a large restaurant facing the sea, bar, shop and a wide variety of accommodation. Internet access costs RM8 per hour.

Salang Beach Resort (☎ 419 5015; d with fan/air-con RM80/110; ❄) Has wooden chalets with verandas, the more expensive of which face the sea. The resort has a sea-view restaurant and can arrange barbecues.

Salang Beach Resort Chinese Restaurant (meals RM18) Just past the resort of the same name. Attractively situated at the northern end of the beach, this resort has a large range of Chinese seafood dishes.

A few bars and cafés inject some life into the community; both Sunset Boulevard and the Four S Cafe are north of the jetty.

JUARA

Juara is the only place to stay on the east coast of the island. The beach is excellent and this is a place for serious relaxation, since there is little to do except swim and laze away the day under the coconut trees. This, however, will all change if the Tekek to Juara road is built. (See p250.)

Paradise Point (small chalet with fan RM20) Pleasantly located about 150m north of the jetty with simple chalets.

River View Place (☎ 419 3168; chalet with fan RM20) Further north, and renovating at the time of writing, this place has simple A-frame chalets (with mosquito net) and can offer cheap, long-stay options.

Juara Mutiara Resort (☎ 419 3159; chalet with fan/air-con RM25/60; ❄) South of the jetty, with largish, characterless chalets on and off the beach and there's a sizeable restaurant.

Rainbow Chalets (☎ 419 3140; fan d without/with shower RM25/30) Further south, these are pleasant clean A-frames on the beach.

Towards the southern end of the beach, **Bushman** (d with fan RM30-40) has simple A-frames, traditional Malay massage and a bar.

The beach south of the jetty is bisected by a headland. On the far side of the headland, **Mizani's Place** (☎ 419 3157; chalet with fan & shower RM25) enjoys great seclusion and the beach is fantastic. At the far end of the beach, **Juara Bay Resort** (☎ 414 5349; chalet RM30) has serviceable chalets.

Just north of the jetty, the **Ali Putra Mini Cafe** (meals RM5) serves soups, chips, fish dishes and roti canai; prices and dishes are similar at the Beach Cafe next door.

KAMPUNG PAYA

A few kilometres south of the Berjaya Tioman Beach Resort, the beach at Kampung Paya largely attracts travellers on package holidays. The ferry from Mersing stops here, but with costs higher than elsewhere, this is a poor choice for independent travellers.

The **Sri Paya Holiday** (☎ 011-765 774; chalet RM80) in the middle of the village by the jetty has 15 cheap and simple chalets, though not much else. The **Paya Resort** (☎ 07-799 1432 in Mersing; open Feb-Oct; small/large chalet RM180/200;) has clean and serviceable chalets, a restaurant and organises diving.

GENTING

Few travellers stop at Genting, and with good reason: the beach is poor and accommodation options are average.

NIPAH

Apart from a couple of longhouse blocks that are open only during the holiday periods, there's only one place to stay at this secluded spot on the southwest coast. **Nipah Beach Resort** (chalet RM30-80) has chalets on the beach, all with shower.

MUKUT

On the southern tip of Tioman, Mukut is another secluded and tranquil spot with a lovely beach. **Mukut Coral Resort** (☎ 07-799 2535/2612; r with fan RM25, chalet with air-con & TV RM88;) has traditional village-style chalets (all with air-con and hot water) set in a marvellous location. The resort has a sea-view restaurant serving Chinese and Western food.

Getting There & Away

AIR

Berjaya Air (☎ 419 1303), with offices at Berjaya Tioman Beach Resort and at the airstrip, has two daily flights to/from KL (RM246) and Singapore (RM192).

BOAT

Mersing in Johor is the main access port for Tioman. Several companies run boat services to the island. Departure times vary with the tide, with the first ferry leaving mid-morning and the last mid-afternoon. From Mersing, ferries (one way RM25, 2 to 3 hours) leave from the main jetty and stop at Genting, Paya, Berjaya Tioman Beach Resort, Tekek, ABC and Salang, in that order, picking up from those jetties in the reverse order on the return trip. Purchase tickets from one of the many tour operators around Mersing or in the R&R Plaza (you can also buy tickets at the jetty just before departure if there are spare seats). Regardless of which ferry company you use on the outbound trip, you can take any company's ferry on the return (tickets are transferable). For the return trip from Tioman, ask at the place you're staying for the next day's sailing times. There is a car park at the jetty in Mersing where you can leave your vehicle (RM7 per day).

Several speedboat companies also operate from the same jetty in Mersing for Tioman (one-way RM30, 90 minutes), departing several times a day. Buy tickets from agents in Mersing or as you board in Tioman. Boat departures during the monsoon season (November to February) can be erratic (and dangerous), although sailings become more regular during the low monsoon months (January to February).

Ferries also depart for Tioman from the **Tanjung Gemok ferry terminal** (☎ 413 1997; adult/child one way RM25/20), 35km north of Mersing. This route is useful if coming from the north and is faster, taking only an hour and a half to the Berjaya Tioman Beach Resort. The first ferry departs Tanjung Gemok at 10am and the last at 2pm. Boats return from the Berjaya Tioman Beach Resort at noon and 4.30pm.

Ferry to Singapore

A daily high-speed ferry service (one way/return S$106/174; 4½ hours) runs between Singapore and Pulau Tioman, departing Singapore's Tanah Merah Ferry Terminal daily at 8.30am, returning from Berjaya Tioman Beach Resort jetty at 2.30 pm. Bookings can be made at the desk in the lobby of **Berjaya Tioman Beach Resort** (☎ 419 1000), and in Singapore at **Penguin** (☎ 6542 7105; 02-20 World Trade Centre). Sailings stop during the monsoon season.

Getting Around

Getting around the island is, for the moment, problematic. When operating (the service has become increasingly irregular and it stops altogether during the monsoon season), the sea bus leaves Tekek for Juara at around 5pm, stopping at ABC and Salang en route (1½ hours; RM20). In the reverse direction, it departs Juara at 3pm, making the same stops. Since the construction of roads linking Tekek with Juara, Salang and Mukut has been approved, the ferry's days could be numbered.

For other journeys around the island, travellers are at the mercy of extortionate independent taxi-boat operators. A boat from Salang to ABC, for example, will cost about RM20. For Nipah and Mukut, at the southern end of Tioman, first take the sea bus to Genting, and then bargain for a taxi-boat (around RM30 and RM40 respectively). Most chalets can arrange boat charter, but it is expensive (RM300 to RM400 per day).

If you have the time, it's also possible to explore the island on foot. Bike rental is available in Tekek. (See p252).

THE COAST

ENDAU

There's little of interest in Endau, but you can hire boats to make trips up the remote Sungai Endau to Endau-Rompin National Park (see p244). There aren't any good places to stay in Endau but **Hotel Seri Malaysia** (☎ 09-413 2723; fax 09-413 2732; smrom@serimalaysia.com.my; d RM110; ❄), just across Sungai Endau in **Tanjung Gemok**, has clean air-con rooms with shower including breakfast. The hotel is 300m east of Tanjung Gemok bus station.

PEKAN

☎ 09

The relaxed former royal capital of Pahang state sports some old shophouses by the river, attractive traditional *kampung* houses, white-marble mosques and the overblown **Istana Abu Bakar**, situated next to the royal polo field (Prince Charles reputedly played here).

The state **Museum Sultan Abu Bakar** (RM1; 🕑 9.30am-5pm Tue-Sun, 9.30am-12.15pm & 2.45-5pm Fri) is housed in a wonderful building constructed by the British for the local Resident and is fronted by a Sabre jet fighter. Exhibits are largely dedicated to the lives of the Pahang royal family, such as the sultan's car and his polo achievements, but there are also weapons, pottery (including Chinese porcelain and Arab ceramics unearthed on Pulau Tioman) and exhibits on wildlife in Pahang.

Across the street is an interesting display of traditional Malaysian watercraft in **Galeri Pengangkutan Air** (🕑 9.30am-5pm Tue-Sun, 9.30am-12.15pm & 2.45-5.10pm Fri).

To the right of the Museum Sultan Abu Bakar along the river is the blue-domed **Masjid Abdullah**, dating from the 1920s and alongside it, the active **Masjid Abu Bakar**, crowned with gold domes.

Walk to the end of the road (Jl Sultan Ahmad), turn the corner and head along Jl Istana Abu Bakar away from the river, through the memorial archway fashioned like huge tusks, passing the **Chief's Resthouse** on your left. Keep walking, past the blue **Istana Mangga Tunggal** on your right and turn left after 700m towards the royal quarter, marked by the Regent of Pahang's palace, **Istana Permai**, and further on, the sultan's palace, the puffed-up **Istana Abu Bakar**. Looking like an airport terminal (no admittance), it's surrounded by lush greenery with the verdant polo field of the Royal Pahang Polo Club alongside. North of the polo field (towards the river) are some attractively coloured, traditional houses on stilts. This is a very well-tended area at odds with the rest of Pekan and well worth a stroll. North of the main shopping district and the *padang*, the **Istana Leban Tunggal** is an appealing palace of wooden construction.

Sungai Pahang, crossed at this town by a lengthy bridge, is the longest river in Malaysia and was the last east-coast river to be bridged.

Information

The **Cyber Cafe** (2nd fl, 23A Jl Engku Muda Mansor, RM3 per hr), on the road behind the Deyza Hotel, offers slow Internet connections.

Sleeping & Eating

Most accommodation in Pekan is just about tolerable and most travellers visit as a day trip from Kuantan.

Pekan Rest House (☎ 421 1240; Jl Sultan Abu Bakar; d RM30) With giant rooms, and only 15 minutes walk west of the bus station, this is the best in town.

Deyza Hotel (☎ 422 3690; 102a Jl Tengku Arif Bendahara; d with fan/air-con RM18/28; ❄) Very simple indeed. It's in the shopping area about 10 minutes west of the bus station.

Pekan Hotel Restaurant (☎ 422 1378; Jl Tengku Arif Benahara; meals RM10) A popular and cheap Chinese restaurant on the ground floor next to the Pekan Hotel (accommodation not recommended).

Restoran Islamiza (43 Jl Sultan Ahmad; meals RM8) West of the Museum Sultan Abu Bakar, this place serves simple and good-value roti and curry. On the same road, a few Chinese restaurants are open late (if you want to buy a beer). There's a large Chinese supermarket on the road behind (south of) the Deyza Hotel.

Getting There & Away

The bus station is in the centre of town and bus No 31 runs regularly to/from Kuantan (RM3). In Kuantan, these buses operate from the local bus station. Local buses also run between Pekan and Kuala Rompin (RM2.50).

The taxi station is across the road on the bank of the river. A taxi to/from Kuantan costs RM25 per car.

KUANTAN

☎ 09

About midway up the east coast from Singapore to Kota Bharu, Kuantan is the capital of the state of Pahang, and the start of the east-coast beach strip that extends all the way to Kota Bharu.

Kuantan is a well organised, bustling city and a major stopover point when you are travelling north, south or across the peninsula. There's little of interest in Kuantan itself, but it's one of the more pleasant east-coast cities and there are a few places of interest nearby.

Information

IMMIGRATION OFFICES

The **Immigration office** (☎ 514 2155; Wisma Persekutuan) is on Jl Gambut.

INTERNET ACCESS

CH Net Cafe (G013, Ground fl, Block A, Kuantan Centre Point, Jl Haji Abdul Rahman; RM2.50 per hr)

Extreme Interactive (S35, 2nd fl, Kuantan Pde; RM3 per hr)

Network 21 Cafe (Berjaya Megamall; RM4 per hr)

MONEY

Most banks are on Jl Haji Abdul Aziz (the continuation of Jl Mahkota).

Hamid Bros Books (Jl Mahkota) A licensed moneychanger; also has some English-language books available for purchase.

HSBC (cnr Jl Bank & Jl Mahkota) 24 hour Visa, MasterCard, Plus and Cirrus ATM.

POST

The post office is on Jl Haji Abdul Aziz (the continuation of Jl Mahkota), near the soaring Masjid Negeri.

TOURIST INFORMATION

The **tourist information centre** (☎ 516 1007; Jl Mahkota; 9am-4.40pm Sun-Fri, 9am-12.45pm Sat) has helpful staff and a range of useful leaflets.

Sights & Activities

Kuantan's star attraction is **Masjid Negeri** (State Mosque), the east coast's most impressive mosque, which presides regally over the *padang* (city square). It's worth taking a stroll here at night, when the mosque is illuminated and takes on the appearance of a fantasy castle.

In the daytime, take a stroll along the riverbank and watch the activity on the wide **Sungai Kuantan**. From the jetty near the local bus station you can get a ferry across the river (about 90 sen) to the small fishing village of **Kampung Tanjung Lumpur**.

The Kuantan area produces some good handicrafts, and there is a batik factory a few kilometres from the town centre, on the road to the airport. On Jl Besar, near the Hotel Classic, several shops sells local trinkets and craftwork.

Kuantan's major attraction is the beach, **Teluk Chempedak**, outside town (see p261).

Sleeping

BUDGET

Hotel Meian (☎ 552 0949; 2nd fl, 78 & 80 Jl Teluk Sisek; d with fan/air-con RM15/25;) This well-managed Chinese guesthouse has good-value double rooms and clean shower/toilet/washing area. The air-condiioned doubles come with TV.

Oriental Evergreen (☎ 513 0168; fax 513 0368; 157 Jl Haji Abdul Rahman; d RM33;) With a forbidding exterior, this five-storey hotel is in need of hefty refurbishment, but its staff are pleasant and it offers reasonable value. Credit cards (MasterCard/Visa) are accepted. Rooms are OK, with TV, phone and shower.

Hotel Sunrise (☎ 552 0949; No 6, 1st, 2nd & 3rd fl, Jl Beserah; s with fan RM15, d with fan/air-con RM18/25;) Across the wasteland from the Citiview Hotel, this is a very cheap and simple Chinese outfit.

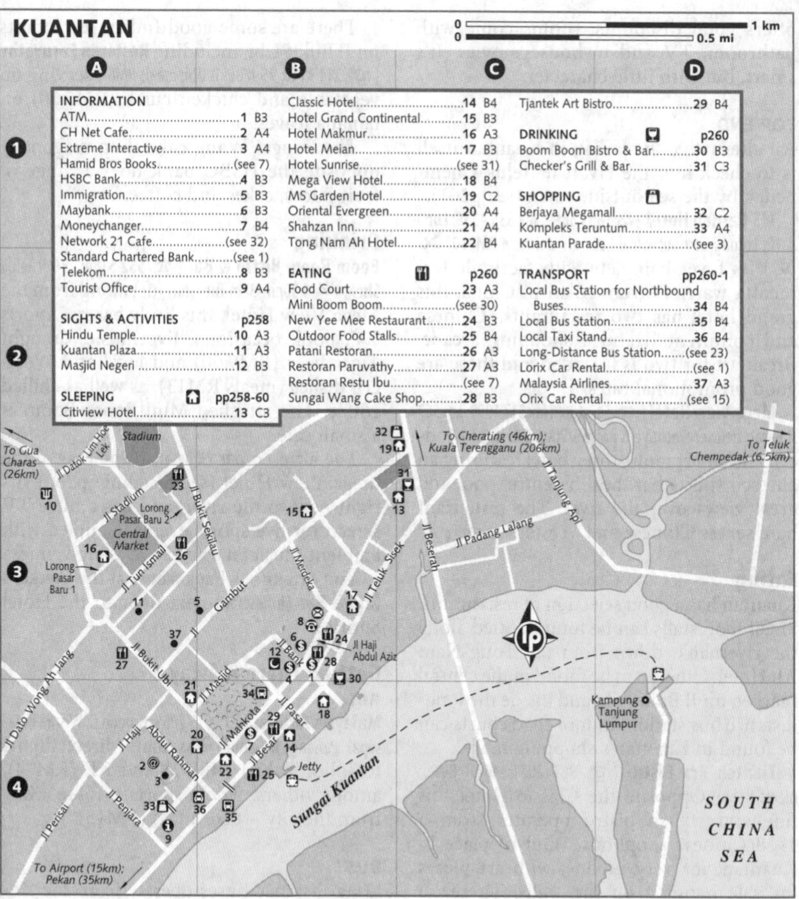

Hotel Makmur (☎ 514 1363; 1st & 2nd fl, B-14 & 16, Lorong Pasar Baru 1; d without/with bathroom RM22/35; ❄) This hotel has fairly spacious rooms (all with air-conditioning) and is close to the long-distance bus station.

MID-RANGE

Classic Hotel (☎ 516 4599; chotel@tm.net.my; 7 Jl Besar; d RM65; ❄) This very decent two-star hotel has spacious, clean rooms (some with river views) with showers and benefits from a central location. There's a restaurant and a simple breakfast is included in the price.

Hotel Grand Continental (☎ 515 8888; kuantan@grandcontinental.com.my; Jl Gambut; deluxe d RM115; ❄ 🏊) Perhaps lacklustre, this hotel still offers value for money and the ground floor restaurant has good-value set meals. Breakfast for two is included and there are good promotional rates. Rooms come with coffee- and tea-making facilities, a fridge and in-house movies. Long-stay apartments with one, two or three rooms are also available (from RM180 per day).

Citiview Hotel (☎ 555 3888; www.hotelmalaysia.com/pahang/citiviewhotel/; Jl Haji Abdul Azia; d RM120; ❄) This relatively modern high-rise hotel has friendly service and spacious rooms with bathroom, minibar, in-house movie and coffee- and tea-making facilities. Breakfast is included. Rooms for disabled guests are available.

Shahzan Inn (☎ 513 6688; fax 513 5588; 240 Jl Bukit Ubi; d RM180; ❄) This modern high-rise hotel offers good discounts; rooms come with bathroom, TV and in-house movies. It's smart, but with little character.

TOP END

An alternative to staying in Kuantan itself is to check into the Hyatt in Teluk Chempedak by the sea outside town (see p261).

MS Garden Hotel (☎ 555 5899; fax 555 4558; Lot 5 & 10, Lorong Gambut, off Jl Beserah; deluxe d RM250;) Its foyer complete with facsimile terracotta warriors from Xi'an in China, this grand hotel has two restaurants (Chinese and continental) and a shopping arcade. Breakfast for two is included and there are good promotional rates.

Mega View Hotel (☎ 517 1888; fax 517 1999; Lot 567 Jl Besar; deluxe/executive d RM150/200;) Modern and smart multistorey hotel featuring an alfresco sports bar, health centre, pool and great views over the river. The restaurant here serves Chinese and Western fare.

Eating

Kuantan has a good selection of restaurants. Small food stalls can be found dotted along the riverbank, down from the Tong Nam Ah Hotel. Others can be found in the central market, on Jl Bukit Ubi and inside the long-distance bus station. Indoor food courts can be found in Kuantan's shopping malls.

Tjantek Art Bistro (☎ 967 2021; 46 Jl Besar; meals RM20) Opposite the Classic Hotel this fine and stylish bistro operates from a 1928 Chinese shophouse. Out of place in Kuantan, it's very urbane, with art pieces for sale hanging on the walls. There's a range of pastas, cooling salads, sizzling steaks, noodles and deserts. The pasta tuna *cili padi* is a dry, hot and spicy pasta, and the fish and chips are spot-on.

Restoran Restu Ibu (☎ 935 1799; 29 Jl Mahkota; meals RM6) Recommended by locals, this clean, pleasant, good-value eatery dishes up tasty favourites such as roti *sardin* (sardine) and mee soup. There's also a buffet.

New Yee Mee Restaurant (Jl Haji Abdul Aziz; meals RM15) Chinese restaurant serving Chinese favourites and some interesting *tieban* (hotplate) dishes. This is also a good spot to enjoy an evening beer or two.

Patani Restoran (☎ 515 7800; 79 Jl Tun Ismail; meals RM8) Popular, bustling Malay restaurant (fan-cooled); among tasty dishes are nasi goreng (RM3.50) and *tom yum* soup (RM4).

There are some good Indian restaurants on Jl Bukit Ubi, including **Restoran Paruvathy** (☎ 514 3140; 75 Jl Bukit Ubi; meals RM8), serving up vegetable and chicken curry (RM5.50) on banana leaves.

The Sungai Wang cake shop diagonally opposite the HSBC bank does a range of fruit juices, cakes and coffee.

Drinking

Boom Boom Bistro & Bar (☎ 552 5184; 236 Jl Teluk Sisek; 6.30pm-3am Tue-Sun) Just along from the Mega View Hotel, this lively bar has sports TV, pool, occasional live music, draught Tiger beer (RM9.50) and local and Western dishes (meals RM13), as well as chilled coffee. The attached Mini Boom Boom is a small café.

The alfresco **bar** (Jl Besar) at the rear of the Mega View Hotel (see Sleeping, p260) sits right next to the river, and has a huge TV screen for live sports events. Coupled with ambient music, it's a very relaxing venue.

You can knock back a beer at the **Checker's Grill & Bar** (Jl Beserah) next door to the Hotel Sunrise.

Getting There & Away

AIR

Malaysia Airlines (☎ 515 7055; Ground fl, Wisma Bolasepak Pahang, Jl Gamut) has daily direct flights to Johor Bahru (RM93) and KL (RM74), among others. The airport is 15km away from the city – take a taxi (RM15).

BUS

Long-distance buses operate from the station on Jl Stadium. The ticket offices and information counter, as well as a food court, are on the 2nd floor of the building. Many companies operate the same routes, so it's simply a question of choosing your departure time.

There are services to/from the following cities (times listed here indicate departure from Kuantan): KL (RM14.20, 5 hours, frequent departures), Mersing (RM10.35, 3½ hours), Johor Bahru (RM17.90, 5 hours, frequent departures), Singapore (RM19.60, 6 hours, 5 daily), Kuala Terengganu (RM11.50, 4 hours, twice daily), Kota Bharu (RM20.50, 7 hours, frequent), Jerantut (RM10.50, 3½ hours, 3 daily), Melaka (RM16.05, 6 hours, twice daily) and Penang (RM35, 11 hours, 1 per day).

The local bus station for northbound buses is on Jl Mahkota. There are services to and from Cherating (No 27; RM2.50), Teluk Chempedak (No 39; RM1), Marang (RM7) and Sungai Lembing (No 48; RM3).

CAR

Several car rental companies have offices in Kuantan.

Hawk (☎ 516 3670; Jl Teluk Sisek)
Mayflower (☎ 538 3490; fax 539 7691; Lot 1, Terminal Bldg, Sultan Ahmad Shah Airport, Kuantan)
Orix (☎ 515 7488; Ground fl, Hotel Grand Continental, Jl Gambut)

TAXI

The long-distance taxi stand is in front of the long-distance bus station on Jl Stadium. Destinations and costs (per car) include Pekan (RM30), Mersing (RM120), Johor Bahru (RM250), Cherating (RM40), Kuala Terengganu (RM120), Jerantut (RM120) and KL (RM140).

TELUK CHEMPEDAK

☎ 09

Teluk Chempedak, Kuantan's main beach, is a lovely stretch of sand and surf around 6km east of Kuantan. It's a popular promenade and meeting place in the evening and approaches the feeling of a European seaside resort. There are several **walking tracks** in the park area on the rocky promontory at the northern end of the beach. All in all, it makes a pleasant day trip out of Kuantan, but if you're headed to the islands or to Cherating, there's little reason to stop for the night.

Taking up most of the beach front is the **Hyatt Regency Kuantan** (☎ 566 1234; hyatt_kuantan@hrktn.com.my; r RM445;). The Hyatt is spacious, breezy and effortless luxury with all the amenities you would expect (including two pools, three tennis courts, squash courts and a water sports centre). Rooms are sumptuous and a whole list of activities is arranged, including cruises along the Kuantan River (featuring a boardwalk through a mangrove jungle) and walks along the cliffs to Methodist Bay.

The only other hotel near the beach is the inadequate **Hillview Hotel** (☎ 567 0600; 41-43 Teluk Chempedak; d with air-con RM65;) in the block opposite, but at this price, stay in Kuantan.

For a bite to eat, there are several restaurants and food stalls just back from the beach. **Restoran Pattaya** (meals from RM20; 4.30pm-midnight Mon-Fri, 11.30am-12.30am Sat-Sun) is a pleasant open-air restaurant where you can feast on tiger prawns, lobster (seasonal prices), claypot rice and abalone. Fine Sichuan and Cantonese cuisine is served at the **Yue Yuen Restaurant** (7-10.30pm Tue-Sun; meals RM50) in the Hyatt Regency. The **Xing Foo** (meals RM18) restaurant in the block opposite the Hyatt does satisfactory Chinese seafood and there's more of the same at the **Steamboat Chinese Restaurant** (meals RM18). Also in this block are several bars: **Cheers Bar, Urban Beach** and **Lips TC Pub** (a sports bar featuring karaoke). A branch of McDonalds can be found on the beach.

Bus No 39 from Kuantan takes you to Teluk Chempedak. You can catch it at the local bus station, or from the more convenient stop for northbound buses on Jl Mahkota near the mosque. A taxi out to Teluk costs RM5.

GUA CHARAS

☎ 09

Twenty-six kilometres north of Kuantan at Panching, the limestone karst containing **Gua Charas** (Charas Caves; also spelt Charah; RM1) towers high above the surrounding palm plantations. The caves owe their fame to a Thai Buddhist monk who came to meditate here about 50 years ago. There's a monk in residence at the foot of the karst (where there is a small shrine and a gold four-faced statue of Avalokiteshvara), and the caretaker's wife can tell you about the caves.

It's a steep climb up a stairway to the caves' entrance – be careful. The **Sleeping Buddha Cave** (Wofo Dong) is off to the right – a colossal cave decorated with occasional, small altars to Guanyin, Puxian and other Bodhisattvas and Buddhist idols. The cavern seems to go on forever. At the back of the cave, the sleeping Buddha is a rather modest cement effort. Outside, the views are great and there is another cave further up, although this is disappointing and the climb slippery.

Take a Sungai Lembing-bound bus (No 48, RM 1.80, 1 hour) from the local bus station in Kuantan and get off at the small village of Panching, just past the sign reading 'Gua Charas 4km'. From the bus stop in town it's a hot 4km walk each way, but you may be able to get someone in Panching to give you a lift on the back of a motorcycle for around RM2. A taxi from Kuantan to the caves costs RM25.

TASIK CHINI

☎ 09

Tasik (Lake) Chini is actually a series of 12 lakes linked by vegetation-clogged channels. Around their shores live the Jakun people, an Orang Asli tribe of Melayu Asli origin, who believe the lake is home to a serpent known as Naga Seri Gumum, sometimes translated in tourist literature as 'Loch Ness Monster'. The best time to visit the lakes is from June to September when the lotus are in bloom.

It's not that easy to reach Tasik Chini – you have to make an effort to get off the beaten track – though once there, you can rent canoes and paddle around the lakes.

There's a low-key resort at the lakes, but you'll get a better feel for the area by staying at the nearby Orang Asli village of **Kampung Gumum**, from which you can make jungle treks and take boat trips. Boats cross the lake between the *kampung* and the resort on demand (RM5) but you can walk from one to the other in around 30 minutes.

Sleeping & Eating

Lake Chini Resort (☎ 477 8000; tasikchini@hotmail.com; camp/dm/d RM18/15/80-100; 💻) On the southern shore of the main lake, this place offers acceptable lodgings and the restaurant serves simple meals (dishes RM4 to 10). The resort can arrange boat trips (RM50), canoeing, night treks (RM15), fishing (RM30 per hour), an overnight climb up Mt Chini (RM70, including food) and other activities.

Across the lake at Kampung Gumum, **Rajan Jones Guest House** (r RM18), about 10 minutes' walk up the main road into the *kampung*, is good value. Rajan speaks English very well, is knowledgeable about the Orang Asli and can arrange a spectrum of activities (jungle trekking, night hikes, waterfall trips and canoeing). Longhouse accommodation is very basic (fan plus mosquito net) but breakfast and dinner is included. Open 24 hours.

Getting There & Away

The best way to reach Tasik Chini is to take a bus to Felda Chini, south of the lake, from Kuantan (RM5, 2 hours, 6 daily from 8am to 5.30pm) or Pekan (RM3.60, 4 daily from 11am to 5.45pm). From Felda Chini, hire a private car or motorbike (someone will usually offer their services) to the resort or to Kampung Gumum (RM5, 12km). To get back to Felda Chini, transport can be arranged at the resort or Kampung Gumum.

A taxi from Kuantan directly to the resort or Kampung Gumum is around RM60. You can also visit the lake as part of a group tour from Cherating for around RM60 per person (ask at the Travelpost travel agency in Cherating).

Alternatively, catch a bus from Kuantan or Temerloh to Maran (RM7.50 or RM5.50, respectively), then take a taxi for the 12km ride to Kampung Belimbing; there are no buses, and traffic on the road is unreliable for hitching. From Belimbing you must first pay RM10 for a boat across Sungai Pahang and then switch to another boat for the trip to Tasik Chini. The cost is RM60 per boat for a two-hour trip, including a tour of the lakes and a visit to an Orang Asli village.

CHERATING

☎ 09

Along with Pulau Tioman and the Perhentian Islands, Cherating is one of the most popular stops on the east coast. A travellers' *kampung*, complete with budget shacks by the sea, a handful of bars, some good restaurants and a decent beach, make Cherating a laid-back destination worth exploring. Some people visiting Cherating settle down and stay for weeks. While the beach can't compare with the white-sand beaches of the Perhentians, the mellow atmosphere of the town keeps people around.

Cherating is also a good base from which to explore the surrounding area. Most of the guesthouses and the two travel agencies on the main road can arrange tours to Gua Charas, Tasik Chini (RM60) and two-hour river cruises on Sungai Cherating (RM15).

Information

There are no banks in Cherating. Travelpost and Badgerlines will change travellers cheques and cash, but the rates are poor. On the main road:

Badgerlines Information Centre (☎ 581 9552; 🕑 9.30am-12.30pm, 2.30-4pm & 8-10pm) Offers book rental, Internet access (RM6 per hour), international phone

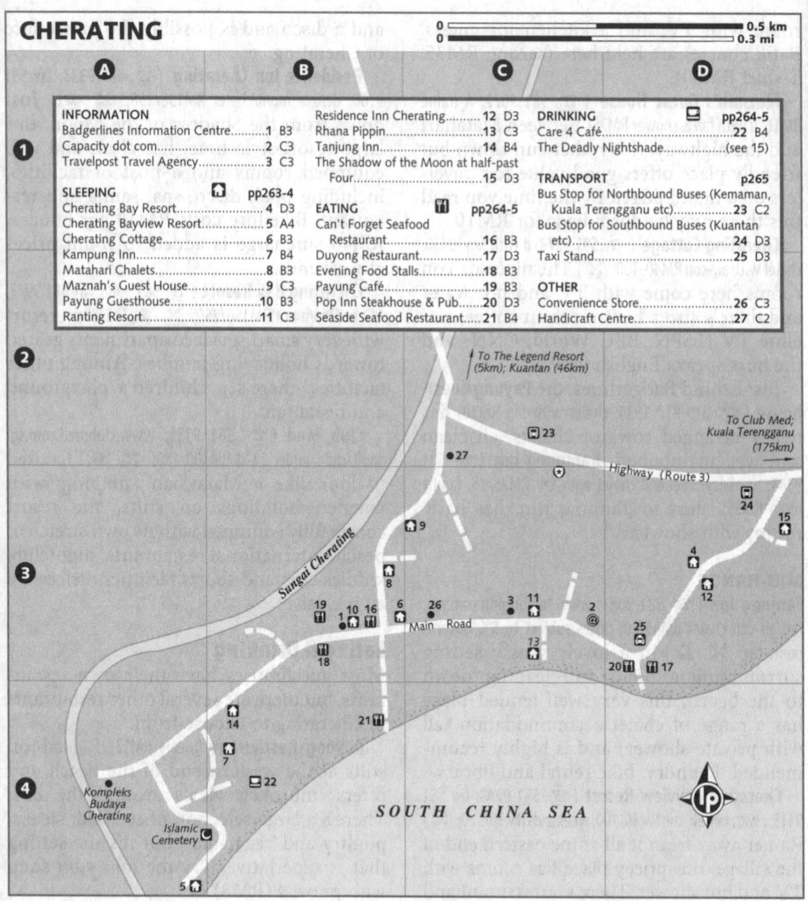

calls, a mini postal service, boat bookings, and a host of activities including sea fishing (RM85 per person), river fishing (RM45 per person) and river cruises (RM15 per person).

Capacity dot com (☎ 581 9330; Main Road) Offers phone Internet access (RM6 per hour) as well as a phone and fax service.

Travelpost Travel Agency (☎ 581 9825; 🕑 9am-11pm), also on the main road, has book rental, Internet access (RM6 per hour), international phone calls, tourist information, bike and vehicle hire, ticketing and arranges night treks, tours to watch turtles (May to August) and more.

Sleeping

BUDGET

Accommodation ranges from basic A-frame huts, each with a double mattress and light (but no fan), to more comfortable 'chalets' with fan and shower. Most places have their own restaurants.

Shadow of the Moon at Half-Past Four (☎ 581 9186; d/tr with fan RM35/55) The chalets in this quiet and secluded spot are arrayed up a hill. All rooms come with ceiling fan and shower and there is free breakfast for long stays. This is also the home of the Deadly Nightshade bar (see p264). A single bed in a shared chalet is RM16.

Matahari Chalets (☎ 581 9835; small/large chalet with fan RM20/25) On the road between the beach front and the highway, the chalets have shared showers but are clean and equipped with a fridge, windows, mosquito nets and spacious verandas. There is a very relaxed atmosphere, a common room with TV, and a kitchen for guests. Batik courses are held here (sarong RM35, T-shirt RM30).

Maznah's Guest House (☎ 581 9072; A-frame RM16, d with fan & shower RM25) Between Matahari and the highway, this rather run-down but friendly place offers good value for travellers on a tight budget. By the time you read this there may be dorm beds for RM10.

Cherating Cottage (☎ 581 9273; d with fan RM30, chalet with air-con RM40-100; ❄) The nicer air-con rooms here come with TV and hot water and there's also a bistro, decent coffee, satellite TV (ESPN, BBC World, CNN) and the boss speaks English very well.

Just behind Badgerlines, the **Payung Guesthouse** (☎ 019-917 1934; chalet with fan RM30) has neatly arranged rows of chalets, all clean and well maintained. **Kampung Inn** (☎ 581 9344; weekday/weekend chalet with fan RM25/35, family room RM65), next to Tanjung Inn, has basic rooms with shower.

MID-RANGE

Tanjung Inn (☎ 581 9081; www.tanjunginn.com.my; fan/air-con chalet RM45/90; prices subject to 5% government tax; ❄ 💻) In a lovely grassy setting surrounding a pond and leading down to the beach, this very well-tended place has a range of chalet accommodation (all with private shower) and is highly recommended. Laundry, bike rental and library.

Cherating Bayview Resort (☎ 581 9248; fax 581 9415; r with fan/air-con RM80/100, weekends RM90/120; ❄) Rather away from it all at the eastern end of the village, this pricey place has rooms with TV and hot shower. There's a restaurant and chalets are virtually on the beach.

Ranting Resort (☎ 581 9068; fan/air-con chalet RM40/60; ❄) Towards the eastern end of the main road, this is a good mid-range choice with a decent restaurant.

Rhana Pippin (fan/air-con chalet RM50/100; ❄) Has a bar (see p265) and chalets right on the beach, and can arrange windsurfing (RM25 per hour) and surfing (RM15 per hour).

TOP END

Legend Resort (☎ 581 9818; legendc@po.jaring.my; Lot 1290 Mukim Sungai Karang; d/ste RM350/750; ❄ 🏊) This luxury resort on the road to Kuantan outside Cherating has spacious rooms, a disco, two restaurants, two swimming pools, a nice stretch of beach, squash and tennis courts, a convenience store, snooker and a disco and is possibly the future face of Cherating.

Residence Inn Cherating (☎ 581 9333; fax 581 9160; deluxe room/chalet RM138/158; ❄ 🏊) Just down from the Shadow of the Moon, this large resort-style hotel has clean and well equipped rooms and a host of facilities, including pool, disco, spa, sauna and restaurant. Bike hire costs RM10 per hour. A RM40 surcharge is added to room prices at weekends.

Cherating Bay Resort (☎ 581 9988; fax 581 9977; 1/2 bedroom apt RM150/250; ❄ 🏊) Large resort with very smart serviced apartments geared towards holidaying families. Among other facilities, there's a children's playground and restaurant.

Club Med (☎ 581 9133; www.clubmed.com.sg; adult/child under 11 d RM300/180; ❄ 🏊) Crafted to look like a Malaysian *kampung* with wooden buildings on stilts, the resort comes fully equipped with its own stretch of beach, international restaurants, nightclub, kiddies club and sports facilities. Prices are all inclusive.

Eating & Drinking

Most guesthouses have their own restaurants, but there are several other restaurants in Cherating to choose from.

Duyong Restaurant (meals RM13) Raised on stilts at the western end of the beach and offers unbroken views around the bay. There's a large selection of seafood, steaks, poultry and vegetables, but it's the setting that is superlative. Try the *tom yum* soup with prawns (RM8).

Other seafood restaurants include the **Seaside Seafood Restaurant** (meals RM10), right on the beach, serving good Malay and Chinese dishes and the **Can't Forget Seafood Restaurant** (meals RM15; 🕒 11am-3pm & 6-11.30pm) which also does claypot and bean curd dishes.

Payung Café (meals RM20; 🕒 11am-11pm Mon-Sat) is a pleasant eatery with a riverside setting, specialising in pasta and pizza and late breakfasts. Great breakfasts can also be had at **Cherating Cottage** (see this page) with proper coffee and real milk.

For strictly Malay fare at rock-bottom prices, try the evening food stalls along the main road.

Deadly Nightshade, set in the woods at the Shadow of the Moon at Half-Past Four, features a lounge area, cobbled-together wooden furniture, a library and Western cooking. It may be slightly deranged, but it's very popular and undeniably appealing.

Pop Inn Steakhouse & Pub (meals RM25) has satellite TV, live music and serves up a selection of steaks, chicken and lamb. The bar at the **Rhana Pippin** (opposite the Ranting Resort), with its happy hour from 3pm to 12am (buy one get one free), starts to get crowded around midnight, and peaks at around 2am. Above the beach behind the Kampung Inn, the **Care 4 Cafe** (4.30pm-midnight) has live music on Wednesday and is an excellent place for a beer.

Getting There & Away

Cherating is most easily reached from Kuantan. From the station for northbound buses on Jl Mahkota, catch a bus marked 'Kemaman' and ask to be dropped at Cherating (look for a sign by the road that reads 'Pantai Cherating'). Buses leave every 30 minutes (RM1.80, 1 hour). When coming from the north, any bus heading for Kuantan will drop you on the main road. A taxi from Kuantan should cost about RM40. Call the **Cherating Taxi Service** (☎ 581 9355).

From Cherating to Kuantan, wave down a Kuantan-bound bus from the bus stop on the highway (Route No 3).

The two travel agencies on the main road (see pp 262–3) can arrange long-distance bus tickets and taxis (convenient for those heading north to places like Kuala Terengganu or Kota Bharu).

CENTRAL PAHANG

JERANTUT

☎ 09

The small town of Jerantut is the gateway to Taman Negara. Most visitors to the park spend at least one night here, but the town has no real attractions.

Information

There are several banks in town where you can change cash and travellers cheques (be sure to change money before heading into Taman Negara). The **Hotel Sri Emas** (☎ 266 4499; tamannegara@hotmail.com; Jl Besar) is open 24 hours, and offers Internet access, loads of travel information, ticketing, and arranges tours to Taman Negara.

Other Internet access options:

AZM Internet Café (just east of the train station; RM4 per hr)

Internet Cafe (floor below Hotel Chet Fatt, Jl Diwangsa; RM4 per hr)

Sleeping

Jerantut has plenty of hotels, but the popular places can get very busy during Taman Negara's peak period (usually April to August).

Hotel Sri Emas (☎ 266 4499; tamannegara@hotmail.com; Jl Besar; dm RM7, fan/air-con d RM15/38;) Backpacker central for those headed to Taman Negara, this place can make full arrangements for your trip to the national park. The hotel arranges minibus transport to the park or to the jetty at Kuala Tembeling as well as accommodation at Taman Negara. The hotel has free pick-up from the railway station, videos, a restaurant and there's a park briefing nightly at 8.30pm (free). Rooms are average, but cheap.

Jerantut Rest House (☎ 266 6200; dm with fan/air-con RM8/10, d RM40;) Run by the same outfit as the Hotel Sri Emas, the air-con dorms at this popular place come with shower and TV and the doubles are spacious with attached bathrooms. To get here, take Jl Besar (the main road) south past the mosque, take the left under the flyover and it's about 100m ahead.

Sakura Castle Inn (☎ 266 9663/4; 1st & 2nd fl, Jl Bomba; d/f RM40/70;) This very clean and smart mid-range hotel is near the bus station and about 500m east of the train station. Chinese-run and very new, the rooms here all come with air-con and TV.

Chong Heng Hotel (☎ 266 3693; Jl Besar; dm/d with fan RM8/15) This small, good-value hotel has a helpful and informative owner and comes with travellers' recommendations.

Eating

The food stalls between the market and train station are very good, offering Thai dishes and seafood as well as the usual Malay favourites. Cheap *kedai kopi* (coffee shops) can be found along Jl Besar and in the buildings opposite the bus station.

Jerantut Curry House (26 Jl Besar; meals RM5) A good place offering cheap and filling roti. A roti, dhal curry and soft drink will cost around RM4.

Nasi Ayamui (meals RM6) Head for this place, just east of the train station and close to

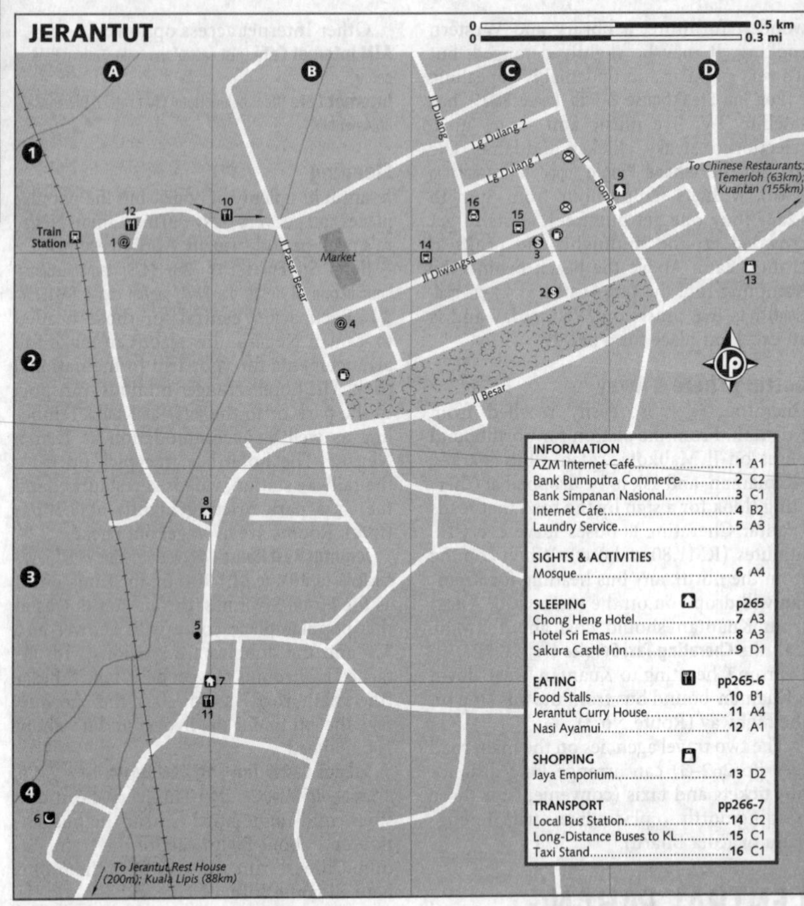

AZM Internet Café, for tasty Chinese-style chicken rice.

Food stalls can be found alongside the road just to the east of Nasi Ayamui. To stock up on food and drink for Taman Negara, visit one of the Chinese shops on Jl Besar.

Getting There & Away

BUS

Long-distance buses leave from the ticket offices near the taxi stand; local buses depart from the station across the street.

There are buses to/from KL's Pekeliling bus station (RM10.85, 3½ hours, last bus around 4pm) via Temerloh. If you miss the bus to KL, buses go every hour to Temerloh (RM4, 1 hour), from where there are more connections to KL and other destinations. There are also three daily buses to/from Kuantan (RM10.50, 3½ hours).

The buses coming through from KL continue to Kuala Lipis; otherwise, take a bus to Benta Seberang (RM3.30, hourly from 7am to 6pm) and then another to Kuala Lipis.

Kuala Tembeling (for Taman Negara)

Buses to Kuala Tembeling (RM1.20, 45 minutes), for the boat to Taman Negara, leave at 8.15am, 11.15am, 1.45pm and 5.15 pm. Be warned that bus schedules are unreliable and are not designed to arrive in time for boat departures to the park. From the jetty, buses to Jerantut come by at around 12.30pm and 4pm, but again, don't count on it.

The best bet is to take a taxi from Jerantut to Kuala Tembeling (RM16), so you don't have to worry about missing the boat.

The Hotel Sri Emas arranges minibuses to Kuala Tembeling for RM4 per person, and can arrange transport to Kuala Tahan. Most visitors prefer to take the scenic river trip to the park from Tembeling, but if you're pressed for time, you can go one way by boat and one way by minibus. Alternatively, you can drive to the park (see pp274–5).

Beware of touts at the train and bus stations who tell you that there are no boats running from Tembeling to the park; they're only trying to get you to take their very expensive alternatives.

TAXI

Per car, taxis cost RM16 to Kuala Tembeling, RM30 to Temerloh, RM140 to Cherating, RM120 to KL and RM100 to Kuantan.

TRAIN

Jerantut is on the Tumpat–Gemas railway line (also known as the jungle railway), with a daily express train to Singapore (RM19 economy) and KL (RM15 economy). A daily local train departs for Gemas (RM6.50), from where you can catch another train to Singapore (RM13 economy).

There are also two express trains (RM17) and a local train (RM12.60) to Wakaf Baharu (the nearest station to Kota Bharu on the Tumpat line). All northbound trains go via Kuala Lipis and Gua Musang.

For an up-to-date timetable and list of fares, consult **KTM** (Keretapi Tanah Melayu; ☎ 03-2267 1200, 2273 1430; www.ktmb.com.my).

TAMAN NEGARA

Peninsular Malaysia's greatest national park covers 4343 sq km and sprawls across the states of Pahang, Kelantan and Terengganu. The part of the park most visited is in Pahang.

Taman Negara is billed, perhaps wrongly, as a wildlife park. Certainly this magnificent wilderness area is a haven for endangered species such as elephants, tigers, leopards and rhinos, but numbers are low and sightings of anything more exotic than snakes, lizards, monkeys, small deer, and perhaps tapir, are rare. The birdlife is prolific, however, and chances are you'll see more insects – many at extremely close quarters – than you've ever seen in your life.

Taman Negara is not wide open savanna as in African game parks, and the jungle is so dense that you could pass within metres of an animal and never know it. Chances of spotting wildlife are greatest if you do an extended trek away from the heavily trafficked park headquarters, but sightings are never guaranteed.

For this reason, many travellers come away disappointed, but the greatest reward of a visit to Taman Negara is simply the chance to get out into one of the most pristine primary rainforests still standing. The jungle here is claimed to be the oldest in the world, having existed largely as it is for the past 130 million years. None of the ice ages affected this part of the world, and it has also been free of volcanic activity and other geological upheavals.

More than any other destination in Malaysia, the more you put into a visit to Taman Negara, the more you'll get out of it. Consider an overnight trek or at least a long boat trip up one of the park's rivers. If you aren't comfortable doing these things on your own, don't hesitate to join one of the tours that can be arranged at guesthouses and restaurants in Kampung Kuala Tahan. If you do plan on making some longer treks, you should consider bringing food and the proper equipment with you from outside the park, even from outside the country, as very little is available in Malaysia.

The 60km boat trip from Kuala Tembeling to Kuala Tahan (park headquarters) takes two to three hours, depending on the level of the river. You'll reach the park boundary near Kuala Atok, 35km from Kuala Tembeling. Along the river you'll see several Orang Asli *kampung*, local fishing people and domestic animals such as water buffalo. You might also see monkeys, otters, kingfishers and hornbills from the boat. It's a beautiful journey.

The best time to visit the park is in the dry season between February and September. Although the park is open during the rainy season, when it doesn't always rain, the number of visitors drops dramatically at this time. The peak tourist season is from April to August.

Orientation & Information

The park headquarters and the privately run Mutiara Taman Negara (National Park Resort) are at Kuala Tahan. There's an information counter at the resort's reception area capable of dealing with most queries regarding the park. The **Wildlife Department** (8am-10pm Sat-Thu, 8am-12.15pm & 3-10pm Fri) is near the reception area, where you must register before heading off into the park, or to other park accommodation outside the resort. The Wildlife Department issues copies of the *Tourism Area in Taman Negara* map; it's fine for casual rambling but inadequate for serious exploration. Unfortunately, outside the National Survey Department in KL, you won't find anything better. See Planning, p270, for recommendations about useful books.

Facilities at Kuala Tahan include chalets, a hostel, camping ground, restaurant, cafeteria, and a shop selling a range of tinned foods, toiletries, batteries and snacks – all at inflated prices (stock up in Jerantut before heading to the park, or try the shops in the village). Camping, hiking and fishing gear can be hired from the camping ground office past the shop and at the jetty on the Kuala Tahan side.

A free video presentation is held in the **Interpretive Centre** (8.45pm daily) in the resort. Other activities include jungle trekking (RM35, 9.30am), a night jungle walk (RM30, 8.45pm), cave exploration

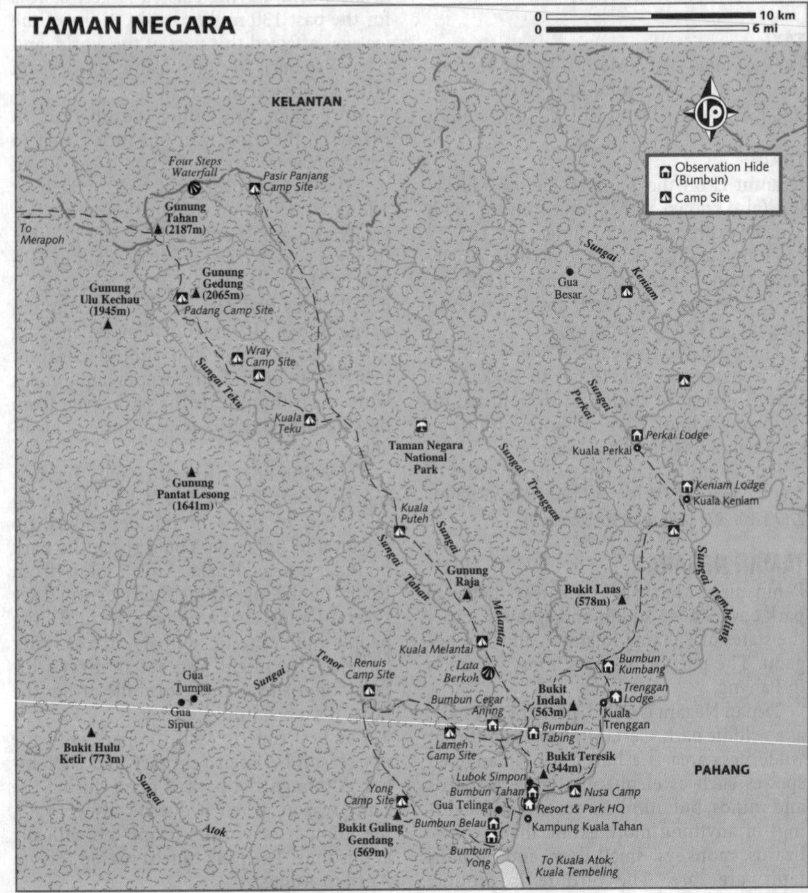

THE FUTURE OF TAMAN NEGARA

First established as a preservation area in 1937, Taman Negara is Malaysia's oldest and most prestigious national park. However, the largest protected area of primary rainforest on the peninsula is coming under increasing scrutiny. Promoted internationally as a wildlife haven and *the* place to experience the jungle in Malaysia, many doubt that the park can withstand the onslaught.

Since the park accommodation was privatised in 1991 and the facilities upgraded, visitor numbers have more than doubled to over 40,000 per year. The effects are very noticeable. Where large animals once roamed right up to park headquarters, sightings are now rare and the effective animal habitat area of the park has decreased. Trails around park headquarters are up to 4m wide and suffer from erosion due to the number of walkers.

The boom in visitors is not all bad news though, as the resort also provides necessary local employment, and the increased wealth from tourism, along with stiff government penalties, has helped eliminate poaching by villagers.

Poachers, attracted by the illicit trade in rare species and the high price of ivory and tiger bones, enter the park from the north. Poaching is largely blamed on Thais, but policing is difficult and few poachers are caught. The Orang Asli who live within the park are allowed to hunt and continue their traditional nomadic lifestyle, but their impact is relatively low.

Lack of government funding and understaffing means that the more remote parts of the park are largely beyond the control of the Wildlife Department. Taman Negara is home to perhaps 600 elephants and a high percentage of Malaysia's estimated 300 tigers, which are increasingly being pushed towards the Kelantan and Terengganu borders. However, these numbers are little more than guesswork as there have been no systematic studies of wildlife populations in the park in recent years.

Problems not only exist within the park but also outside it. Once animals would roam beyond the park boundaries into neighbouring districts, but increasing settlement along the park boundaries is eliminating this buffer zone, driving the animals further into the interior.

With all the increased traffic putting strains on the park, there has been much talk of how to best preserve Taman Negara and cater to increasing visitor interest.

Solutions to the park's problems are hard to find, and even harder to implement. Though probably put forward to highlight the problems facing the Wildlife Department and spur the government to allocate more resources, one suggestion at a recent conference was to completely privatise the park. Restricting access, by introducing quotas or raising prices, also seems unpalatable as Taman Negara is one of Malaysia's major tourist attractions. Not only does it provide foreign income but it is an important educational resource for Malaysians, increasingly aware of the ecology and natural beauty of their own wilderness areas.

(RM45, 10am and 3pm), river rafting (RM65, 10am), rapids-shooting on Sungai Tembeling (RM40, 10am), a picnic trip to Lata Berkoh rapids (RM60, 9.30am and 2.30pm) and visits to an Orang Asli settlement (RM35, 5pm).

Cheaper accommodation is available in the village of Kuala Tahan, directly across Sungai Tembeling from park headquarters, where there are also some cheaper shops and restaurants moored on the river. Just hail a boat at any one of the floating cafes to take you across the river (50 sen).

The only other places with organised accommodation (other than the hides – see p270) are Nusa Camp, about 15 minutes by boat up Sungai Tembeling from the park headquarters, and lodges at Kuala Trenggan, Kuala Keniam and Kuala Perkai, which can be booked at the Wildlife Department. At the time of writing, only the lodge at Kuala Perkai was operating (see p274).

Permits & Guides

Entrance to the park is RM1, a camera permit is RM5 and a fishing licence costs RM10. You get these at the office at the Kuala Tembeling jetty or at the Wildlife Department at the park.

Guides cost RM120 per day, whether hired at the resort or through the Wildlife Department office (one guide can lead up to 12 people), plus a RM50 fee for each night spent out on the trail. A guide is necessary for the Tenor Trail (see Longer Treks, p272) and is compulsory if you intend to climb Gunung Tahan – recommended only for experienced trekkers.

Planning

Although everyday clothes are quite suitable around Kuala Tahan, be well prepared if heading further afield. Lightweight cotton clothing is ideal. Loose-fitting, long trousers are better than shorts, protecting legs against scratches and insect bites. Whatever you wear, you'll soon be drenched in sweat and covered in mud. Take a water bottle, even on short walks, and on longer walks take water purifying tablets to sterilise stream water.

Good boots are essential; lightweight, canvas jungle boots that lace up high to keep out leeches can be hired from the camping ground office. Sleeping bags, tents, cooking gear and torches (flashlights) can also be hired here or at the Kuala Tahan jetty for trekking or for staying overnight in a hide.

River travel in the early morning hours can be surprisingly cold – bring a light jacket or a fleece. Mosquitoes can be annoying, but you can buy repellent at the park shop.

Leeches can be a nuisance after heavy rain. Mosquito repellent, tobacco, salt, toothpaste and soap can all be used to deter them, with varying degrees of success. A liberal coating of insect spray over shoes and socks works best. Leech-proof socks are also an option. See the boxed text That Clinging Feeling (p579) for more insights.

Taman Negara: Malaysia's Premier National Park by David Bowden (available in the bigger bookshops of KL or online) is an excellent book on the park, with detailed route maps and valuable background information. Another book to try is John Briggs' *Parks of Malaysia*.

See the Jungle Trekking Tips boxed text (p537) for more information on preparing yourself for trekking.

Hides & Salt Licks

Taman Negara has several readily accessible *bumbun* (hides), many close to Kuala Tahan and Kuala Trenggan. All hides are built overlooking salt licks and grassy clearings, which attract feeding nocturnal animals. There's a chance of spotting tapir, wild boar or deer, but sightings of elephant and other large game are extremely rare. Your chances of seeing wildlife will increase if you head for the hides furthest away from park headquarters.

If you're staying overnight (try to book at the Wildlife Department the day before), you need to take food and a sleeping bag. Hides cost RM5 per person per night, sleeping six to eight people and are very rustic with pit toilets. Tabing and Kumbang, easily accessible from Kuala Tahan, are the most popular hides.

Even if you don't see any wildlife, the fantastic sounds of the jungle are well worth it. The `symphony' is best at dusk and dawn.

Take a powerful torch to see any animals that wander into the salt-lick area and try to arrange shifts through the night to look out for nocturnal activity.

Rats can be a problem at some of the hides, searching for food during the night, so hang food high out of reach.

BUMBUN TAHAN

Less than five minutes' walk from the reception building, this artificial salt lick is a clearing planted with pasture grass with a nearby waterhole. This close to the resort, there's little chance of seeing any animals apart from monkeys.

BUMBUN BELAU & BUMBUN YONG

These hides on Sungai Yong sleep eight people and have water nearby. It takes about 1½ hours to walk to Bumbun Belau from the park headquarters, and you can visit Gua Telinga along the way (see Short Walks from Kuala Tahan, p271). From Belau it's less than half an hour to Bumbun Yong. Both can also be reached by the riverboat service (RM40 per 4-person boat, see Getting Around, p275).

BUMBUN TABING

The hide at this natural salt lick, about an hour's walk from Kuala Tahan, is equipped with a toilet, *tempat mandi* (bathing area) and bunks for eight people. Nearby, there's a river with fairly clean water (though it should be boiled before drinking). A four-person boat to Tabing costs RM40.

BUMBUN KUMBANG

You can either walk to Bumbun Kumbang (about five hours from Kuala Tahan) or take the riverboat service up Sungai Tembeling to Kuala Trenggan. First take a boat from Kuala Tahan (RM90 per four-person boat, 35 minutes), followed by a 45-minute walk to the hide. Animals most commonly seen here are tapir, rats, monkeys, gibbons and the occasional elephant. There are bunks for six people here.

BUMBUN CEGAR ANJING

Once an airstrip, this is now an artificial salt lick, established to attract wild cattle and deer. A clear river runs past the hide a few metres away. The hide is 1½ hours' walk from Kuala Tahan, but after rain may only be accessible by boat (RM40 per 4-person boat). There are bunks for eight people here.

Mountains & Walks

The major activity at Taman Negara is walking through the magnificent jungle. There's a wide variety of walking and trekking possibilities – from an hour's stroll to nine arduous days up and down 2187m-high Gunung Tahan.

The trails around the park headquarters are convenient but heavily trafficked. Relatively few visitors venture far beyond the headquarters, and longer walks are much less trammelled. A long day walk will take you away from the madding crowd, but getting well away from it all requires a few days trekking and/or expensive trips upriver by boat.

SHORT WALKS FROM KUALA TAHAN

Easy-to-follow trails around park headquarters are signposted and marked with approximate walking times. If you're interested in birdlife, try to set out before 8am.

Heading out past the chalets and cafeteria, the Bukit Indah (Indah Hill) trail leads along Sungai Tembeling to the **Canopy Walkway** (child/adult RM3/5; 🕑 11am-2.45pm Sat-Thu, 9am-noon Fri). Suspended 25m above the ground between massive trees, it allows closer inspection of the higher reaches of the forest.

From behind the Canopy Walkway a trail leads to **Bukit Teresik**, from the top of which are fine views across the forest. The trail is steep and slippery in parts but quite easily negotiated and takes about an hour up and back. You can descend back along this trail to the resort or, near the Canopy Walkway, take the branch trail that leads across to **Lubok Simpon**, a swimming area on Sungai Tahan. From here it is an easy stroll back to park headquarters. The entire loop can easily be done in three hours.

Past the Canopy Walkway, a branch of the main trail leads to **Bukit Indah**, another steep but rewarding hill-climb, offering fine views across the forest and the rapids in Sungai Tembeling.

The well-marked main trail along the bank of Sungai Tembeling leads 9km to **Kuala Trenggan**. This is a popular trail for those heading to the Bumbun Kumbang hide (see p270). Set out early and allow five hours. Though generally flat, it traverses a few small hills before reaching Sungai Trenggan and Trenggan Lodge. From the lodge, boats go back to Nusa Camp and Kuala Tahan, or it's a further 2km walk to Bumbun Kumbang. An alternative, longer trail leads inland, back across Sungai Trenggan from Bumbun Kumbang to the camp site at Lubok Lesong on Sungai Tahan, and then back to park headquarters (six hours). This trail is flat most of the way and crosses many small streams. Check with park headquarters for river levels – Sungai Trenggan can be forded only when levels are low.

Night jungle walks (see p268) allow you to see the jungle from a different perspective and there's also the possibility of glimpsing nocturnal animals.

Gua Telinga

It takes about 1½ hours to walk to this cave southwest of park headquarters, after first crossing Sungai Tahan by *sampan* (small boat). A stream runs through the cave and a rope guides you for the strenuous half-hour walk – and crawl – through the cave (bring a torch). Afterwards, you either return to the main path through the cave, or take the path around the rocky outcrop at its far end. Once back at the main path, it's 15 minutes' walk to the Bumbun Belau hide, where you can spend the night or from where you can walk back to Kuala Tahan.

Lata Berkoh

Heading north through the camping ground at Kuala Tahan, the trail leads all the way to Gunung Tahan, but you can do an easy day walk to Lata Berkoh, the cascading rapids on Sungai Tahan. The trail passes Lubok Simpon swimming hole and Bumbun Tabing, 1¼ hours from Kuala

Tahan. About 15 minutes further is the turn-off to Lata Berkoh. There is one river crossing before you reach the falls, which can be treacherous if the water is high; don't attempt it in high water – hail one of the boatmen waiting on the opposite side to ferry you across. You may be able to hitch a ride back on one of the boats that stop just below the falls, but don't count on it.

Around Nusa Camp

There are a couple of interesting short walks around Nusa Camp, outside the park. **Abai Falls** is only an hour's walk along a clear trail, and it's a great spot for a swim. **Gunung Warisan** is a small treeless peak a couple of hours' walk from the camp. It's an excellent walk in the very early morning, but it gets hot in the afternoon, as there is no shade.

LONGER TREKS

Rentis Tenor

From Kuala Tahan, the Tenor Trail (Rentis Tenor) takes three days. It's quite popular, but the trail is not always clear and a guide is needed. The first day involves getting a boat across Sungai Tahan at park headquarters, and then taking the trail beyond Gua Telinga to Yong camp site (about seven hours). The second day is a six-hour walk to the Renuis camp site. On the third day you have to cross Sungai Tahan (up to waist-deep) to get back to Kuala Tahan. It's about a six-hour walk, or you can stop for another night at the Lameh camp site, about halfway.

Kuala Keniam

Another popular walk is the trail from Kuala Trenggan to Kuala Keniam. It's normally done by chartering a boat to Kuala Keniam and then walking back to Kuala Trenggan (six hours). The trail is quite taxing and hilly in parts, and passes a series of limestone caves. This walk can be combined with one of the Kuala Tahan–Kuala Trenggan trails to form a two-day trip, staying overnight in the Trenggan Lodge or at Bumbun Kumbang (see p270). It is also possible to walk from Kuala Keniam to the lodge at Kuala Perkai, an easy two-hour walk.

Gunung Tahan

Really adventurous travellers climb Gunung Tahan (2187m), the highest peak in Peninsular Malaysia, 55km from park headquarters. It takes nine days at a steady pace, although it can be done in seven. A guide is compulsory (RM500 for seven days plus RM50 for each day thereafter) and either bring your own equipment or rent it; with no shelters along the way, you have to be fully equipped. For camping near the summit of Tahan you'll need a lightweight sleeping bag, blanket or tracksuit to sleep in. Try to organise this trek in advance, so you don't have to hang around park headquarters for a couple of days.

Fishing

Anglers will find the park a real paradise. Fish found in the park rivers include the superb fighting fish known in India as the *mahseer*, but here as the *kelasa*.

Popular fishing rivers include Sungai Tahan, Sungai Keniam (above Kuala Trenggan) and the remote Sungai Sepia. The best fishing months are February, March, July and August. A fishing permit costs RM10, and hiring a rod costs RM5 per day.

Boat Trips

The easiest and least expensive way to get around the park by river is the riverbus service, with scheduled departures to Nusa Camp, Bumbun Belau, Bumbun Yong, Kuala Trenggan and Kuala Keniam (see Getting Around on p275).

Boat charter can be very expensive unless you organise a group. Book a boat at park headquarters at least the day before and the staff may be able to combine individuals. Also ask at the riverside restaurants, which may be cheaper.

Boat trips to Lata Berkoh rapids, Kuala Trenggan and Kuala Keniam are all popular and can be combined with short or long walks. The following prices are for boats seating four/12 people.

Kuala Keniam RM180/220
Kuala Trenggan RM90/120
Lata Berkoh RM120 (4-seater)
Kuala Perkai RM280 (4-seater)

Tours

Many guesthouses and restaurants in Kampung Kuala Tahan organise guided tours through the park and individual guides can be found at the floating restaurants by the jetty in Kampung Kuala Tahan.

Sleeping

KUALA TAHAN

All accommodation at park headquarters is operated by the privately run **Mutiara Taman Negara** (☎ 266 3500; fax 266 1500; dm/guesthouse/chalet/bungalow RM50/185/230/800;). Bookings can also be made through its KL office (☎ 03-2145 5585; saltn@mutiarhotels.com; Lot G 01A, Ground fl, Kompleks Antarabangsa, Jl Sultan Ismail, Kuala Lumpur 50250).

The resort's hostel consists of fairly clean eight-person dorms (bunk beds, fan, separate toilets and showers). Breakfast is included in the dorm price, but at these rates you'd do much better across the river in the village.

The guesthouse rooms at the resort are grubby and dated and have no TV or phone (but come with bathroom and air-con). The pricier wooden chalets are better, with air-con, a choice of either two single beds or a double bed, and a bathroom (no TV or phone). Bungalows have two bedrooms, and bathroom and kitchen, as well as air-con and satellite TV.

Camping at park headquarters is possible (RM3) and tents can be hired although they may all be rented out during busy periods.

KAMPUNG KUALA TAHAN

The village of Kuala Tahan, directly across the river from park headquarters, is a cheaper alternative to the resort. Although it's rather scruffy, it's perfectly acceptable.

Crossing the river is easy; sampans go on demand throughout the day and evening (50 sen).

Tembeling River Hostel & Chalets (☎ 266 6766; rosnahtrv@hotmail.com; dm RM10, d/f chalet RM40/50;) First on the right as you climb the steps and offering good views over the river, dorm beds here are four to a room with fan and mosquito net; all chalets come with fan, mosquito net and shower. There's also a restaurant and Internet access (9.30am to midnight).

Teresek View Motel (☎ 266 9177; del_tvm@yahoo.com; dm/s/d RM10/20/40, d/tr with air-con RM100/120;) On the corner east of Agoh Chalets, this is one of the better places to stay with a large range of sleeping options. The RM40 A-frames come with shower, are clean and quite attractive, and the dorm is large. There's also a useful mini-mart for basics, with some of the lowest prices in the village. Internet access costs RM2 for 15 minutes.

> **TOUR WARNING**
>
> We've received a number of letters and emails, especially from women, complaining about UBAT Adventure Tours. We suggest you check the details of its tours very carefully. Other operators mentioned in this book have been checked personally by the authors and should be reliable. However, you should always check terms and conditions carefully.

Rainforest Resort (☎ 266 7888; fax 267 2352; standard/deluxe d RM150/180;) Newly built, this is the smartest and most comfortable place in the village. At the end of the road several hundred metres south of the Teresek View Motel, the very clean double rooms all come with air-con and spacious shower rooms. A restaurant was still under construction at the time of writing.

Durian Chalet (☎ 266 8940; chalet with fan RM25) Popular with travellers for its quiet setting away from the action, the Durian has decent, albeit simple, chalets (with shower) containing two single beds, and is in the process of building new deluxe twin (RM60) and double chalets. There's a restaurant with a simple Malay menu and the owner's son is a guide who can advise on trips around Taman Negara. To get there, take the paved road uphill from the restaurants, turn left before Teresek View Motel, walk past the police station and the mosque, keep going for several minutes and you'll see it on the right.

Other places in the village include **Liana Hostel** (☎ 266 9322; dm RM10) with a barracks-like but clean hostel. It's first on the left as you climb the steps and is opposite the Tembeling River Hostel & Chalets.

Ekoton Chalets (☎ 266 9897; tamannegara@-hotmail.com; dm with fan/air-con RM13/20, air-con d/chalet RM70/90;), 50m to the right from the top of the steps, has river views from its front chalets (but no restaurant).

In the middle of the village, **Agoh Chalets** (☎ 266 9570; dm/chalet with air-con RM20/40;) is basic with small chalets with fan and bathroom.

Tahan Guesthouse (☎ 266 7752; dm/d RM19/65) is a simple place next to the mosque along the way from the Teresek View Motel, before Durian Chalet.

NUSA CAMP

Quieter and away from park headquarters, **Nusa Camp** (☎ 266 3043, 266 2369; dm/A-frame RM15/55, cottage/house RM100/110) is 15 minutes up Sungai Tembeling from Kuala Tahan. Much more of a 'jungle camp' than anything at park headquarters, it has a range of accommodation for most budgets. The clean, spacious double cottages with fan and bathroom are probably the best value. The restaurant serves good but unexciting food.

Bookings can be made in **Jerantut** (☎ 266 2369; spkg@tm.net.my; 16 Jl Diwangsa), the **Kuala Tembeling jetty** (☎ 266 3043) or in **KL** (☎ 03-2070 5401; spkgkl@tm.net.my; Studio 2B, Arcadia Green, 1 Jl Sultan Ismail). It runs its own boat from Kuala Tembeling, and a riverbus service between Nusa Camp and Kuala Tahan (see Getting Around, p275).

KUALA TRENGGAN

About 35 minutes upstream from Kuala Tahan at Kuala Trenggan, **Trenggan Lodge** (☎ 266 3500; fax 266 1500; d RM100; run by Mutiara Taman Negara Resort) is a good spot to escape from the crowds. At the time of writing the lodge was being repaired after being destroyed by a rampaging elephant.

KUALA PERKAI & KUALA KENIAM

About an hour upstream from Kuala Trenggan, the lodge at Kuala Keniam was undergoing repairs. The same applies to the Wildlife Department's lodge at Kuala Perkai, a further two hours' walk past Kuala Keniam. Check with the resort to see if these are operational when you arrive in the park.

Eating

Seri Mutiara Restaurant (Mutiara Taman Negara; meals RM20) The smartest restaurant in Taman Negara is of course at the resort, with a menu consisting of local dishes (RM15 a dish) and Western fare (pizza RM19.50). Meals here are considerably more expensive if you order wine (RM60 per bottle), but beer is also available (RM15 per bottle).

Floating barge restaurants line the rocky beach opposite park headquarters, all selling basic noodle and rice meals for as little as RM3. Some of these restaurants will prepare a dinner of fresh river fish if you order early in the day (note that all of them can arrange the same activities as the resort, usually for about 10% less than the resort charges).

Getting There & Away

The main way to get to Taman Negara is to take a bus or train to Jerantut, a bus or taxi from Jerantut to Kuala Tembeling and then a boat from Kuala Tembeling to park headquarters at Kuala Tahan. You can also drive all the way to Kampung Kuala Tahan, just across the river from the resort and park headquarters. But to do so is to miss the river trip, which is a big part of the Taman Negara experience (see p267).

BOAT

The main entry point into the park is by riverboat from Kuala Tembeling, 18km north of Jerantut. At least three boats per day leave from the jetty, 500m west of the turn-off to the small village of Kuala Tembeling. Note that the boat service is irregular during the November–February rainy season.

Regular boats (RM19 one way, 2 to 3 hours) depart daily at 9am and 2pm (2.30pm on Friday) and speedboats (RM30, 1 hour) at 1 pm. Boats are run by the resort and Nusa Camp, whose boats also stop at park headquarters before continuing to Nusa Camp, so you can take either service regardless of where you stay. At Tembeling, the resort's office is up the steps above the jetty, and Nusa Camp's is near the parking area.

On the return journey, regular boats leave Kuala Tahan at 9am and 2pm (2.30pm on Friday) and speedboats leave at 10am; there is no discount for return tickets.

BUS & TAXI

For details on buses and taxis from Jerantut to Kuala Tembeling, see p266. From KL, a direct minibus (RM25) to the Kuala Tembeling jetty leaves daily at 8am (returning to KL at 1.30pm) from the Hotel Istana in the Golden Triangle. The ticket office (☎ 03-2145 5585; fax 2145 5430) is across the street in Kompleks Antarabangsa. **NKS** (☎ 03-2072 0336; www.taman-negara.com) runs tours to Taman Negara and has a daily shuttle bus from Hotel Malaya in Petaling St in Chinatown (RM30). The Pudu Hostel (p88) also runs daily shuttle buses to Kuala Tembeling. Wherever you stay, ask whether your guesthouse can arrange tours or buses to Taman Negara.

CAR

A road goes all the way from Jerantut to Kampung Kuala Tahan. As you reach Kampung Kuala Tahan, the road deteriorates but is traversable in an ordinary car.

WALKING

You can walk into or out of the park via Merapoh, at the Pahang–Kelantan border. The trail from Merapoh joins the Gunung Tahan trail, adding another two days to the Gunung Tahan trek (see p272). Guides are compulsory and can be hired in Kuala Lipis to take you in. Contact the **Kuala Lipis tourist information centre** (☎ 312 3277). However, it is easier to arrange a guide at the park for the walk out (see p269). It is also possible to enter or exit the park by walking over the mountains on the Pahang–Terengganu border and navigating the upper reaches of Sungai Tembeling by riverboat. Contact **Ping Anchorage** (☎ 09-626 2020; www.pinganchorage.com.my) in Kuala Terengganu for details and guides.

Getting Around

The resort has daily boats that go upriver to Kuala Trenggan at 10am and 2.30pm for RM12 per person. In the reverse direction, boats leave Kuala Trenggan at 11.15am and 3.15pm. These services are intended for resort guests only.

Nusa Camp also runs boats upriver to Kuala Trenggan and downriver to Bumbun Belau and Bumbun Yong (RM40 per four-person boat).

Keep in mind that these regularly scheduled riverboat services run pretty much on time during the peak season, but may be dropped entirely during the rainy season. It's best to ask at Nusa Camp or the resort for up-to-the-minute information.

In addition to these boat trips, you can arrange private boat trips at the Wildlife Department, at the resort or at the restaurants in Kampung Kuala Tahan (the latter are usually 10% cheaper).

KUALA LIPIS

☎ 09

At the confluence of the Lipis and Jelai rivers, Kuala Lipis is a small, picturesque town with a strong colonial past. The centre of town, with fine rows of shophouses down the main street, is the busy Chinese commercial district. Further south on the hilly outskirts, Kuala Lipis is dotted with reminders of the glory days when it was Pahang's most important town.

A gold-mining centre long before the British arrived in 1887, the town's heyday began in 1898 when it became the capital of Pahang. Grand colonial buildings date from this period, and trade increased when the railway came through in 1924.

In 1957 the capital shifted to Kuantan, and Kuala Lipis went into decline. It is a sleepy and pleasant town, but the gold miners are back and recent construction and the presence of a shopping mall suggest a revival of fortunes.

Besides being an important sight in itself, Kuala Lipis is the major launching pad for visits to the nearby Kenong Rimba State Park (see p277).

Information

The Public Bank and post office are both on Jl Besar, east of the train station. The **tourist office** (☎ 312 3277; 🕑 9am-5pm Mon-Fri, 9am-1pm Sat), inside the train station, is a private travel agency that sells its own trips to Kenong Rimba, but you can get a map of the town and have basic queries answered.

Internet access:

Internet Station (RM3 per hr) At the bus station.

Appu's Guesthouse (63 Jl Besar; RM6 per hr)

Sights & Activities

Kuala Lipis has some marvellous colonial-era architecture. The imposing **District Offices** are on a hill 1km south of the centre of town. The offices overlook the exclusive **Clifford School**, a grand public building that began life as the Anglo-Chinese School in 1913 and was later renamed after Sir Hugh Clifford, the second British Resident of Pahang.

The road next to the school leads up the hill to the **Pahang Club**, a sprawling wooden bungalow with wide, open verandas. With its planters chairs and hunting trophies, it clings to its colonial club traditions in the face of decay.

Accessed by a winding road or steep, overgrown steps, the gracious hilltop **Government Rest House** is a large, two-storey red building, once home to the British Resident. It serves as a hotel (see Sleeping , next page) and the foyer houses a small museum chronicling the town's history. On display are weapons and brass items (including a betel box, used for serving betel leaves and nuts) and some traditional Malay games, drums and ceramics.

The Chinese **Tianhou Temple** on Jl Jelai east of the Jelai Hotel is dedicated to the Queen of Heaven, protector of seafarers. With a carving of a ship inside the main door, on the main altar is Tianhou herself and Guanyin stands to her left. A great time to visit is during Chinese New Year, when huge incense sticks are lit in front of the temple.

A very pleasant **walk** starts on the road to the east of the Lipis Centrepoint Complex, opposite the Xin Hoi Gei restaurant. It runs south and then west alongside a lush valley, past a deserted golf club and divides at a sign listing housing numbers. These numbers indicate old colonial houses – many now abandoned and being slowly reclaimed by jungle – that can be glimpsed through the foliage on the way up.

If you're in town on Friday evening, be sure to visit the excellent **night market** held in the parking lot next to the bus station.

Sleeping

There are several hotels on Jl Besar (the main street) and Jl Jelai (the street by the river), a short walk from the bus and train stations.

Hotel Jelai (☎ 312 1192; 1st floor, 44 Jl Jelai; d with fan/air-con RM18/45; ❄) With rooms at the front affording great views over the Jelai river, this hotel is run by a helpful and informative Chinese concierge who can issue you with a rough map of Kuala Lipis and suggest walks in town. The hotel is clean and there is a variety of rooms, all good value. The air-con doubles come with hot shower and TV (with HBO movies).

Appu's Guesthouse (☎ 312 3142; jungleappu@hotmail.com; 63 Jl Besar; dm RM7, d with fan/air-con RM15/30, air-con quad RM50; ❄ 💻) Rooms here may be simple (shared toilet/shower), but this guesthouse is cheap and popular with travellers for its tours to Kenong Rimba State Park. Come out of the train station, turn left along Jl Besar and it's on the right. Free maps of the town are available and Internet access is RM6 an hour.

Government Rest House (☎ 312 2784; fax 312 2788; d RM40; ❄) The setting here is fantastic (see Sights & Activities above) although the hotel suffers from under-investment and somnolent staff. The huge air-con doubles come with TV and massive shower rooms.

Centrepoint Hotel & Apartments (☎ 312 2688; fax 312 2699; Level 5, Lipis Centrepoint; d/tw/ste RM75/82/165; ❄) Despite the forbidding stairs at ground level, this mid-range hotel is well worth the money. Fine air-con rooms (with large shower rooms) come with TV (HBO movies) plus a phone and coffee- and tea-making facilities. Breakfast is included. The executive suites are simply vast and there's an excellent restaurant here (see Eating below). Apartments are also available.

Eating

Kuala Lipis has some good Chinese restaurants, reflecting the area's largely Chinese population.

Xin Hoi Gei (Sin Hoi Kee; ☎ 312 5072; Jl Lipis; opposite the Centrepoint Hotel; meals RM18) Specialising in river and sea fish, this lively and bustling Chinese seafood restaurant, with its large alfresco seating area, seems like the social centre of Kuala Lipis.

Centrepoint Cafe (☎ 312 2688; Centrepoint Hotel, Level 5, Lipis Centrepoint; meals RM15-20) This is a great restaurant for both local and continental dishes and gets you away from the hawker stalls at ground level. Try the spring roll (RM4.50), the tasty *tom yum* soup with assorted seafood (RM5.50), and even the fish and chips (RM10).

Drinking

At the other end of Jl Jelai from the Tianhou Temple, **Flash Jacks Bar 55** (☎ 961 0307; 55 Jl Jelai) is an enterprising little Chinese-run bar, and a great place for a beer, a game of darts and a chinwag with the locals.

Getting There & Away

Six buses per day run between Kuala Lipis and KL's Pekeliling bus station (RM9.50, 4 hours) and two buses run daily to Kuantan (RM16.70). There are also buses to Temerloh (RM9.80), Raub (RM3.30) and Gua Musang (RM7), from where you can catch onward buses to Kota Bharu.

There is a daily express train to Singapore (RM21) and an express to KL (RM18, economy). Any train bound for Singapore, KL or Gemas will stop at Jerantut, the closest station for travellers on their way to Taman Negara.

Express trains run to Tumpat (RM16) and a slow but interesting local ('jungle') train connects with Wakaf Baharu, the closest station to Kota Bharu (RM16).

Taxis leave from the bus station for KL (RM130), Jerantut (RM40), Gua Musang

(RM60), Temerloh (RM100), Kota Bharu (RM200) and Kuantan (RM150).

KENONG RIMBA STATE PARK

☎ 09

This 120 sq km forest park is a sprawling area of lowland forest rising to the limestone foothills bordering Taman Negara. The park can be explored on good three- or four-day jungle treks organised from Kuala Lipis. The loop trail through the park provides an excellent opportunity to experience the jungle at close hand, and at affordable prices. For information on preparing for the jungle, see the Jungle Trekking Tips boxed text on p537.

Despite fanciful local claims that the park is a haven for elephants, tigers and rhinos escaping from over-touristed Taman Negara, sightings of big mammals are rare. Monkeys, wild pigs, squirrels, civets and possibly nocturnal tapir are all you should expect to see.

A permit from the Forestry Department is not required, contrary to what you may be told in Kuala Lipis, but you must be accompanied by a registered guide (see Tours, this page).

Walking the Trail

Access to Kenong Rimba is from a jetty on Sungai Pahang called Jeti Tanjung Kiara (see Getting There & Away on p278). From the jetty it's a 30-minute walk to the park entrance along the road through Kampung Dusun, which is just a scattering of a few houses and one small shop. Further on from the shop, past the house with the `souvenirs' sign, a side trail to the right leads to three **caves** – Gua Batu Tangga, Gua Batu Tangkup and Gua Batu Telahup. A number of confusing trails go through the swampy forest here. The guided trips include an exploration of the caves. The main trail eventually rejoins the road right at the entrance to the park, where there is a gate and a footbridge over a stream.

Thirty minutes away, the trail brings you to **Gunung Kesong**, a large limestone outcrop where there is a Forestry Department hut. Gunung Kesong contains a number of caves, the most impressive being **Gua Hijau** (Bat Cave), on a side trail around to the right (east) across two bridges. Hundreds of small bats hang from its ceiling.

The trail leads north from Gunung Kesong through lowland forest to the waterfall of **Lata Kenong** (Seven Steps). It is a three- to four-hour walk following Sungai Kenong, and crosses small streams. About an hour before the falls is the first of two log bridges across the river that require something of a balancing act to negotiate, or you can straddle your way across. The trail then crosses the foothills to the huts at the Kenong camp site just before the falls, a series of cascades.

From Lata Kenong, the trail continues up and down more hills with other river crossings to **Gunung Putih**. Though no mountain climbing is involved, this is the most strenuous part of the trek, taking about five hours and passing through some impressive forest. Gunung Putih is another rocky, cave-ridden outcrop, climbable via a side trail.

The main trail continues past Gunung Putih through the foothills, back to the lowland forest. Another side trail leads to a nearby **Orang Asli village**, home of the Batek people. The main trail leads back to Gunung Kesong, about four hours all up from Gunung Putih.

There are other side trips to make in the park, including a visit to the Lata Babi waterfall, and to Gua Batu Tinggi, across the river from Kampung Dusun.

Tours

Guides are compulsory for entry to the park and can be arranged in Kuala Lipis. Appu of **Appu's Guesthouse** (see p276) offers cheap tours – RM50 per person per day plus RM160 (minimum three people) for the boat to and from Jeti Tanjung Kiara and a RM2 per-person per-night camping fee.

Another popular operator is **Pan Holiday Travel & Tours** (☎ 312 5032; pantour@tm.net.my) in the Stesen building opposite the Kuala Lipis train station. Packages cost from RM135 per person (minimum two people). The **tourist office** (☎ 312 3598) in the Kuala Lipis train station also runs trips.

Tours include food, guide and all expenses in the park, but they are no-frills jungle experiences – you camp in the park, with all equipment and meals provided. Trips go when enough people are interested, usually every two or three days, or you can ring ahead to make a booking.

Getting There & Away

Access to Kenong Rimba is from Kuala Lipis on southbound local trains to Batu Sembilan (Mile 9), a 30-minute trip departing daily at 7.48am and 2.10pm. From Batu Sembilan, hire a boat (RM20 per person) to Jeti Tanjung Kiara, just across the river from Kampung Kuala Kenong. Alternatively, on Saturday at noon there's a direct boat from Kuala Lipis to Jeti Tanjung Kiara (RM5 per person; 1½ hours) which returns from Jeti Tanjung Kiara at around 7am on Saturday mornings. For directions from Jeti Tanjung Kiara into the park, see Walking the Trail on p277.

TEMERLOH

☎ 09

Temerloh is an old town on the banks of the enormous Sungai Pahang. It has a hint of colonial style and a colourful Sunday market. New industrial estates on the outskirts point to the future, and Temerloh is pressing to supersede Kuantan as the state capital. As the main city of central Pahang, it is a transport hub – the only real reason to visit.

The train station is 12km away at **Mentakab**, a thriving satellite of Temerloh that has a bustling nightly market.

Sleeping & Eating

Temerloh has several good hotels.

Rumah Rehat Temerloh (Temerloh Rest House; ☎ 296 3218; fax 296 3431; Jl Datok Hamzah; r RM59.50; ❄) Has 10 large and well-appointed rooms with air-con, hot water and TV.

Seri Malaysia Hotel (☎ 296 5776; fax 296 5711; Lot PT 370/6/92, Jl Hamzah; d RM110; ❄) Next door to the Rumah Rehat Temerloh, this place has decent rooms with TV, coffee- and tea-making facilities and a restaurant.

Green Park Hotel (☎ 296 3055; fax 296 2517; 373 Jl Serendit; d RM68; ❄) Of similar quality to the Seri Malaysia.

Hotel Isis (☎ 296 3136; 12 Jl Tengku Bakar; d with fan/air-con RM20/28; ❄) This is a reasonable budget option.

Getting There & Away

Temerloh's bus station is central. Buses go to all parts of the peninsula, including Kota Bharu (RM24.50), Melaka (RM9) and Penang (RM30). Regular buses depart to Jerantut (RM4), KL's Pekeliling bus station (RM6.50) and Kuantan (RM6).

Taxis at the bus station go to Mentakab (RM6), Jerantut (RM24), Kuantan (RM48) and KL (RM60).

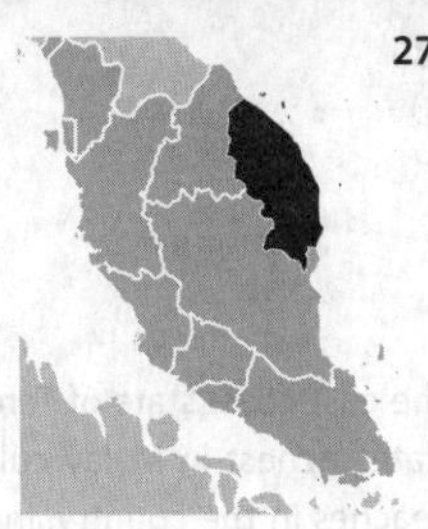

Terengganu

CONTENTS

The east-coast state of Terengganu is, along with Kelantan to its north and west, one of the states richest in Malay culture. It is also one of the most beautiful, with some of the best beaches in the country, including those of Pulau Perhentian (the Perhentian Islands), Pulau Redang and Pulau Kapas. All of these islands offer great opportunities for diving and snorkelling. On the mainland, Terengganu boasts fine beaches along most of its coastline. Inland is the vast Tasik Kenyir (Lake Kenyir), surrounded by lush rainforest.

Until the completion of the roads to Kuala Lumpur (KL) and the west coast, this part of Malaysia was fairly isolated from the rest of the country and didn't receive many Indian and Chinese migrants. Consequently, cultural influences came more from the north. Traditional activities such as kite flying, top spinning, weaving of *songket* (fabric with gold threads) and batik printing are all alive and well here.

Terengganu has always been a conservative Muslim state. Like Kelantan, it is governed by the conservative Islamic Party of Malaysia (PAS). One of the party's first acts was to remove a statue of a turtle from the city of Kuala Terengganu, to honour the injunction imposed by the Quran against the worship of idols, while other radical policies, though much discussed, have not been put into practice.

HIGHLIGHTS

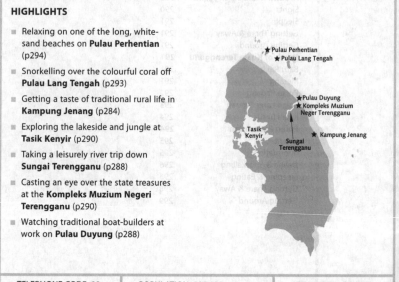

- Relaxing on one of the long, white-sand beaches on **Pulau Perhentian** (p294)
- Snorkelling over the colourful coral off **Pulau Lang Tengah** (p293)
- Getting a taste of traditional rural life in **Kampung Jenang** (p284)
- Exploring the lakeside and jungle at **Tasik Kenyir** (p290)
- Taking a leisurely river trip down **Sungai Terengganu** (p288)
- Casting an eye over the state treasures at the **Kompleks Muzium Negeri Terengganu** (p290)
- Watching traditional boat-builders at work on **Pulau Duyung** (p288)

TELEPHONE CODE: 09	POPULATION: 898,825	AREA: 12,995 SQ KM

History

When the Melaka sultanate was established in the 14th century, Terengganu was already paying tribute to the Siamese, though a 1303 inscription at Kuala Berang establishes that an Islamic state existed here at that time. Before long Terengganu became a vassal of Melaka, but managed to retain a large degree of independence during the emergence of Riau (in Indonesia) and Johor as partners in the region, and was trading with Siam (now Thailand) and China.

Terengganu was formally established as a state in 1724. The first sultan was Tun Zainal Abidin, a younger brother of one of the former sultans of Johor. The close association with Johor was to continue for some years, and in fact, in the mid-18th century Sultan Mansur spent 15 years in Johor trying to rally support. After failing there, Mansur turned his attention to Kelantan and, after some fighting and shrewd manoeuvring, had his son installed as the ruler of Kelantan. The main legacy of Mansur's reign was that Terengganu became a vassal of the Siamese.

Terengganu was controlled by the Siamese for the duration of the 19th century. However, the Terengganu sultan Baginda Omar, a man renowned for his intelligence and energy, managed to keep the Siamese at arm's length and the state flourished under his rule.

In 1909 an Anglo-Siamese treaty saw power pass to the British. It was an unpopular move locally, and in 1928 a peasant uprising erupted. It was quickly put down and the British went about consolidating their power in the state until the Japanese arrived in WWII.

During the Japanese occupation, control of the state was passed back to Thailand, but this was short-lived and Terengganu became a member of the Federation of Malaya in 1948.

Climate

Terengganu has a tropical climate, with daily temperatures ranging between 21° and 32°C. There is intermittent rain throughout the year, with heavier and more prolonged rainfall during the east-coast monsoon (November to February). Humidity levels hover around 90%.

National Parks

Taman Negara (p267), most of which is within Pahang, includes a small section of western Terengganu, stretching from the Pahang border up towards Tasik Kenyir. **Tasik Kenyir** (p290), the largest man-made lake in Southeast Asia, is surrounded by virgin rainforest. Protected **marine parks** include the islands of Pulau Perhentian, Pulau Redang and Pulau Lang Tengah.

Getting There & Away

Kuala Terengganu is the state's main transport hub, with bus links to most other major towns in Malaysia, and to Singapore. The East Coast Hwy runs the length of Terengganu, heading north towards Kelantan and the Thai border and south towards Johor Bahru. Kuala Terengganu has an airport, with regular flights to/from KL, while Pulau Redang also has an air link to KL. See Getting There & Away in Kuala Terengganu (p289) and Pulau Redang (p293).

Getting Around

There are regular bus services linking the coastal towns of Terengganu with Kuala Terengganu, the state capital, while travelling into the interior is only practical if you have your own transport. Ferries leave from Kuala Besut for Pulau Perhentian, from Merang for Pulau Redang and Pulau Lang Tengah, and from Marang for Pulau Kapas.

SOUTH OF KUALA TERENGGANU

Kemaman & Cukai

☎ 09

About 25km north of Cherating, Cukai and Kemaman are the first towns of any size north of Kuantan, and also the first towns you reach in Terengganu state when travelling up the coast. The two towns have merged into one long developed strip, with little of interest to hold passing travellers.

SLEEPING & EATING

River Garden Hotel (☎ 859 6337; K-114 Jl Sulaiman; s & d from RM71.40; ❄) If you need to stay, a reasonable mid-range option in the centre of town.

Hotel Tiara (☎ 859 1802, K-353 Jl Kg Tengah; s & d from RM45; ❄) Has basic rooms. It's down the street that is roughly opposite the bus station (turn at the 'Masjid Jamek' sign).

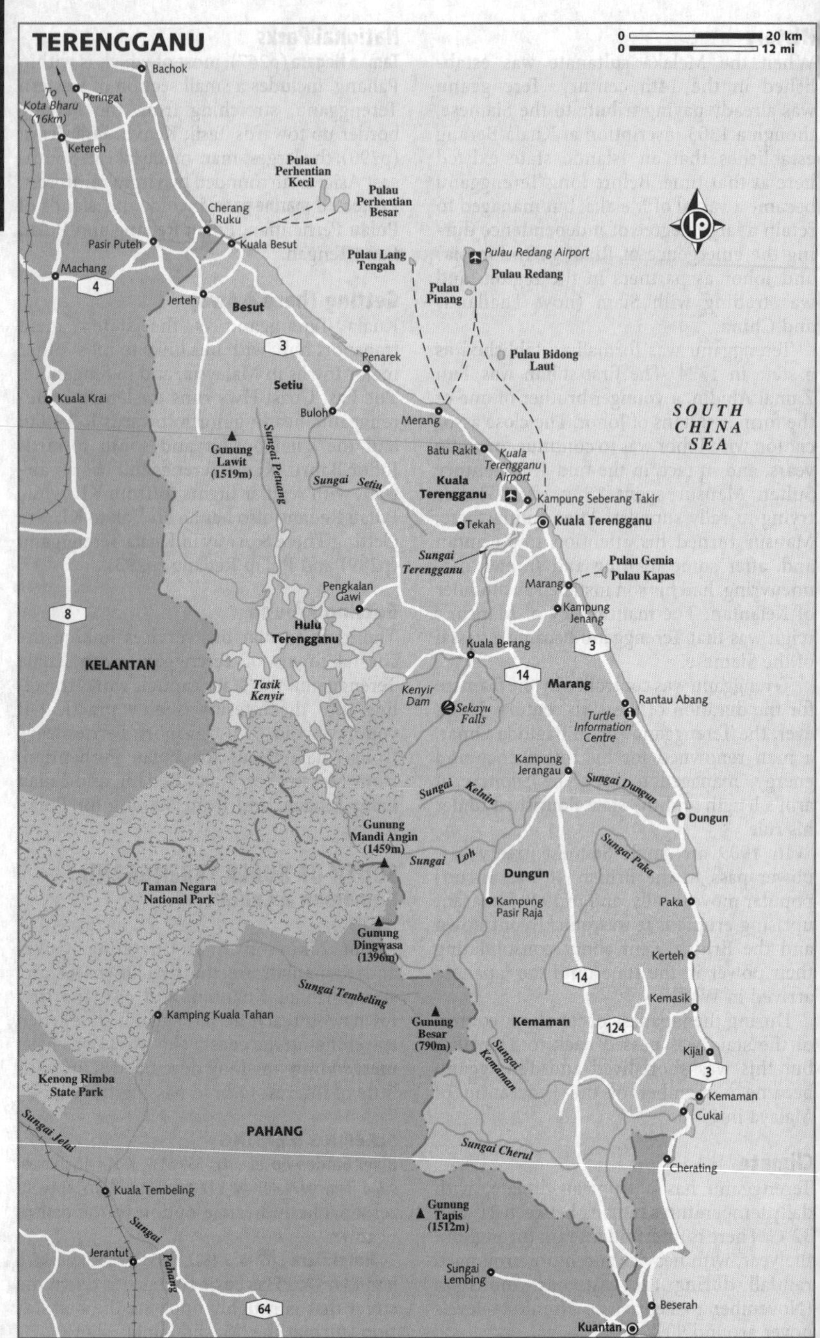
TERENGGANU
0 20 km
0 12 mi
Bachok
To Kota Bharu (16km)
Peringat
Ketereh
Pulau Perhentian Kecil
Pulau Perhentian Besar
Cherang Ruku
Kuala Besut
Pasir Puteh
Machang
4
Pulau Lang Tengah
Pulau Redang Airport
Pulau Redang
Pulau Pinang
Jerteh
Besut
3
Penarek
Setiu
Pulau Bidong Laut
Buloh
Merang
Kuala Krai
Gunung Lawit (1519m)
Sungai Petuang
Batu Rakit
Kuala Terengganu Airport
SOUTH CHINA SEA
Sungai Setiu
Kuala Terengganu
Kampung Seberang Takir
Tekah
Kuala Terengganu
Sungai Terengganu
Pulau Gemia
Pulau Kapas
Marang
Pengkalan Gawi
Kampung Jenang
8
Hulu Terengganu
Kuala Berang
3
KELANTAN
14
Marang
Tasik Kenyir
Kenyir Dam
Sekayu Falls
Rantau Abang
Turtle Information Centre
Kampung Jerangau
Sungai Kelnin
Sungai Dungun
Dungun
Gunung Mandi Angin (1459m)
Sungai Paka
Sungai Loh
Dungun
Taman Negara National Park
Kampung Pasir Raja
Paka
Gunung Dingwasa (1396m)
Kerteh
14
Sungai Tembeling
Kemasik
Kamping Kuala Tahan
Gunung Besar (790m)
Kemaman
124
Sungai Kemaman
Kijal
3
Kenong Rimba State Park
Kemaman
Cukai
Sungai Jelai
PAHANG
Sungai Cherul
Cherating
Kuala Tembeling
Gunung Tapis (1512m)
Sungai Pahang
Jerantut
Sungai Lembing
64
Beserah
Kuantan

There are several Chinese restaurants along Jl Sulaiman, including **Sin Bing Kee Restoran** (☎ 859 3097; meals RM5), which serves Western dishes as well as local specialities such as stuffed crab.

GETTING THERE & AWAY

Buses to/from Cherating and to/from Kuantan both cost RM5. Express buses cost RM7.50 to/from Marang and RM8.70 to/from Kuala Terengganu. Taxis (per car) cost RM15 to/from Cherating, RM30 to/from Kuantan, RM30 to/from Dungun and RM60 to/from Kuala Terengganu.

Kemasik

☎ 09

Kemasik's palm-fringed beach has some of the clearest water on the east coast. The nearest accommodation is at the gargantuan five-star **Awana Resort** (☎ 864 1188; www.awana.com.my; d/ste from RM245/430; ❄ 💻 🏊) on the beach around 1km south, towards Kijal. Among other things it has a golf course, tennis courts and spa, as well as a wide range of organised activities. Discounts are often available. Without your own transportation, the best way to visit the beach is to take a local bus running between Kemaman/Cukai and Dungun. If you're driving, turn off Route 3 at the 'Pantai Kemasik' sign.

Paka

☎ 09

The beach here is almost as good as the one at Kemasik, but the view is somewhat marred by the refinery a few kilometres down the coast. The village here is a little run-down but quite picturesque.

The modern **Residence Resort** (☎ 827 3366; s & d from RM160; ❄ 💻 🏊) on the beach just north of the village offers a high standard of accommodation, including luxurious beachfront suites (RM230). It also has organised activities for children. The best way to visit Paka is to take a local bus running between Kerteh and Dungun. If you're driving, turn off at the 'Pantai Paka' sign.

Dungun

☎ 09

Dungun, together with the port of Kuala Dungun, forms the largest town on the coast between Kemaman/Cukai and Kuala Terengganu. The main reason to come here is to catch a bus or taxi out again; the main bus station is here. There are plenty of hotels if you need to spend the night; most are in the old town, a few kilometres off Route 3.

Hotel Kasanya (☎ 848 1704; 225 Jl Tambun; s/d from RM21/42; ❄) This is a reasonable option, around five minutes' walk from the bus station; cross the sports field and take a left on the main road.

On the coast around 8km east of the centre of Dungun lies the luxurious **Tanjong Jara Resort** (☎ 845 1100; www.tanjongjararesort.com; Batu 8, Jl Dungun; s & d from RM805; ❄ 💻), which is one of Malaysia's most exclusive hotels. Set on a beautiful stretch of beach, the resort has an array of spacious and tastefully furnished traditional chalets, some with private verandas and sunken outdoor baths, and surrounded by landscaped gardens. There's also an excellent restaurant and a spa offering a variety of treatments.

There are buses to/from Kuala Terengganu (RM5) and Kemaman/Cukai (RM4). Kuala Terengganu–bound buses will drop you at Rantau Abang (RM1.70); the same bus heading in the opposite direction will stop at Dungan.

Rantau Abang

☎ 09

Rantau Abang once attracted large numbers of tourists who came to see the giant leatherback turtles coming ashore to lay their eggs. Now that the turtles have all but disappeared (see the boxed text Turtles Under Threat, p55), tourist numbers have dropped off, and the village has a faintly desolate air.

However, the beach is still lovely and is perfect for long, solitary walks. Swimmers should beware of the often savage undertow.

TURTLE INFORMATION CENTRE

Run by the Department of Fisheries, the **Turtle Information Centre** (☎ 845 8169; 🕐 8am-1pm & 2-4.15pm, closed Fri & 1st & 3rd Sat of the month) is close to the town's accommodation. It has a few information boards and staff will run a 10-minute film (in English) on request. At the time of writing, a new and much bigger information centre was being built nearby, possibly housing live leatherbacks in a custom-made pool, but no date had been set for its opening.

August is peak egg-laying season for the leatherbacks, but they've also been known to come ashore in June and July. With so few turtles appearing, however, you'd have to stay for all of August to be sure of a sighting, although you may well encounter the more common green turtle. For now, it's better to think of Rantau Abang just as a quiet beach resort.

SLEEPING & EATING

Awang's (☎ 844 3500; awangs_resort@hotmail.com; s & d from RM60; ❄) Right on the beach, just south of the Turtle Information Centre, this has a range of accommodation, including basic fan rooms from RM10. Ask to see a few rooms as they vary in quality.

Dahimah's Guest House (☎ 845 2843; dahimahs guesthouse@hotmail.com; s & d RM15-60; ❄) About 1km south towards Dungun, this has a wide choice, including larger family rooms with TV and fridge from RM100. Some of the best rooms are over the lagoon that separates the hotel from the beach. It's a pretty spot and makes a quiet getaway for beach lovers.

Apart from the restaurants in the various hotels, there are a few food stalls next to the Turtle Information Centre.

GETTING THERE & AWAY

Dungun–Kuala Terengganu buses run in both directions every hour from 7am to 6pm and there's a bus stop near the Turtle Information Centre. To/from Dungun costs RM1.70; to/from Kuala Terengganu costs RM4. A taxi to/from Kuala Terengganu costs RM40.

Marang

☎ 09

Marang, a fishing village on the mouth of Sungai (River) Marang, was once a favourite stopover for travellers making their way along the east coast. Unfortunately, much of the town's traditional charm has fallen victim to an ill-planned modernisation programme, and the once-picturesque waterfront area is now dominated by characterless concrete structures.

While there are a few good beaches north and south of town, the main reason to come here is to catch a ferry to Pulau Kapas (see p286), which is just 6km offshore.

SIGHTS & ACTIVITIES

If you'd like to get a glimpse of what Marang used to be like, you can travel up Sungai Marang to **Kampung Jenang** to observe traditional rural activities like *atap* (roof thatching) weaving, coconut sugar-making and the gathering of coconuts by trained monkeys. It's possible to visit the village as an easy day trip from Marang or Kuala Terengganu (see Tours in Kuala Terengganu, p288).

If you are in town on Sunday, be sure to check out the excellent **market**, which starts at 3pm near the town's jetties.

SLEEPING & EATING

Hotel Seri Malaysia (☎ 618 2889; www.serimalaysia.com.my; 3964 Jl Kg Paya; s & d from RM80; ❄) The best place in town is this bright modern chain hotel on the coast north of the centre, offering very good value.

Island View Resort (☎ 618 2006; Jl Kg Paya; s & d RM25-40; ❄) There's a clutch of ageing chalets to choose from, and several large cages full of chirpy birds, so oversleeping won't be a problem.

Marang Guesthouse (☎ 618 1976; fax 618 4386; 1367 Jl Kg Paya; s & d RM25-85; ❄) There's a range of mostly rather drab accommodation set on a hill overlooking the town. The more expensive air-con rooms are nicer, but at that price you may as well stay at the Seri Malaysia.

Anguillia Beach House Resort (☎ 618 1322; a_beach@tm.net.my; s & d from RM50; ❄) Across the bridge to the southeast is this quiet, pleasant place with a range of chalets under the palm trees on a sheltered stretch of beach, which is good for swimming. There are also larger chalets housing up to six people and there's a lovely garden restaurant.

All of the places listed have their own restaurant, but you can also find some **food stalls** (Jl Kg Paya) near the jetties.

GETTING THERE & AWAY

There are regular local buses to/from Kuala Terengganu (RM1.50) and Dungun/Rantau Abang (RM4/3). For long-distance buses, there's a **ticket office** (☎ 618 2799; Jl Tanjung Sulong Musa), near the town's main intersection. There are three buses daily to/from KL (RM25.10), two to/from Johor Bahru (RM28.70) and five to/from Kuantan/Cherating (RM11.60).

VERONICA GARBUTT

Catamaran heading for the beaches of **Pahang** (p247)

SIMON BRACKEN

Sunset, **Pulau Tioman** (p250)

Reef, off **Pulau Tioman** (p252)

MICHAEL AW

CHRISTER FREDRIKSSON

Damsel-fly, **Taman Negara** (p267)

JEAN-BERNARD CA

Traditional dance (p305) performance, Kelantan

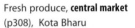

Fresh produce, **central market** (p308), Kota Bharu

RICHARD I'ANSON

CHRIS MELLOR

Spinning-top competition (p305), Kota Bharu

RICHARD I

Marang (p284), Terengganu

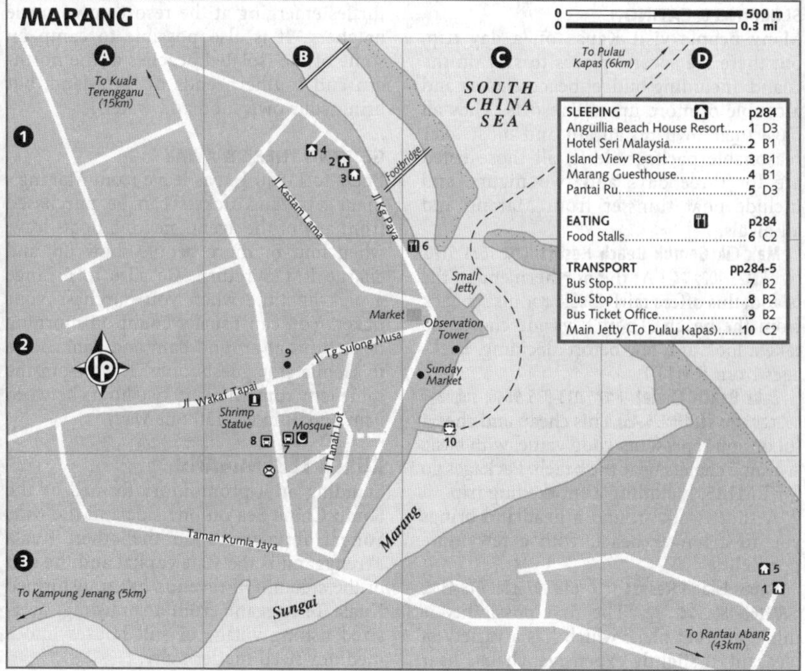

There are four bus-stops on the main road. Southbound express buses usually stop in front of the mosque and northbound services will pick you up just north of the post office. This is not a hard and fast rule, however, and it's best to ask the owner of your guesthouse or someone at the ticket office first.

Pulau Kapas

☎ 09

Six kilometres offshore from Marang is the beautiful small island of Kapas, which has clear water and beaches of powdery white sand. You'll find all the accommodation clustered together on two small beaches on the west coast, but you can walk around the headlands to quieter beaches. There is also a rough track running across the middle of the island to the rocky eastern shore, which is good for sightseeing but dangerous for swimming. Just off the north coast of Kapas is tiny Pulau Gemia; it is not usually possible to visit, though, unless you're staying at the island's exclusive Gem Island Resort (p286).

Pulau Kapas is best avoided during holidays and on long weekends, when it is overrun with day-trippers. Outside of these times, the island is likely to be very quiet. It shuts down during the east coast's monsoon season (November to March).

DIVING & SNORKELLING

Kapas is billed as a snorkelling paradise, though coral is scarce on the most accessible beaches facing the coast. Some of the best snorkelling is found around the northern end of the island and around Pulau Gemia. North of Gemia, a sunken WWII Japanese landing craft, now carpeted in coral, is a popular dive site.

All of the resorts listed can arrange snorkelling and diving trips. The **Aqua Sport Diving Centre** (☎ 019-379 6808), attached to Kapas Island Resort (p286), has scuba gear and a boat, and charges RM90/165 for one/two dives, including equipment.

Any of the budget accommodation places in town can organise snorkelling, and the cost is around RM30 for the day, including the return boat ride to Kapas.

SLEEPING & EATING

Many people visit Kapas on a day trip, but there are several places to stay on the island, including budget beach chalets and a couple of more upscale resorts. They all have their own restaurant and most offer reasonable package deals; all those listed are for three days and two nights, and include boat transfer from Marang and all meals.

Mak Cik Gemuk Beach Resort (☎ 624 5120; s & d RM25-100;) At the northern end of the island, this offers fairly basic rooms set back from the beach. There's a wide choice, so take a look at a few before deciding. Packages from RM110.

Zaki Beach Chalet (☎ 013-935 9840; zubirzr@hotmail.com; s & d RM25-45) This cheap and cheerful option represents good value, with basic A-frame chalets near the beach. Packages go for RM185, including a snorkelling trip.

A short walk around a headland brings you to a longer beach with a few more possibilities.

Kapas Island Resort (☎ 618 1976; fax 618 4386; d RM100-180;) The first possibility is this upmarket place which has a variety of pleasant, if slightly expensive, chalets near the beach, with fan or air-con, and a good restaurant. Packages from RM299.

Duta Puri Island Resort (☎ 624 6090; s & d RM50-180;) is an attractive, Indonesian-style resort offering a broad range of accommodation, from simple fan rooms to comfortable chalets in pleasantly landscaped grounds just off the beach. Packages from RM245.

On the southernmost tip of the bay is **Lighthouse** (☎ 019-215 3558; dm/s & d RM12/35), the cheapest and most atmospheric budget spot on Kapas, with all rooms in one elevated longhouse under the trees. It's rustic, but very sociable, and is popular with diving groups.

Those in search of something more exclusive can try **Gem Island Resort** (☎ 669 5910; enquiry@gemresorts.com; d from RM207;), with its airy wooden chalets, perched on tiny Pulau Gemia, 800m north of Pulau Kapas. Discounts and all-inclusive packages are available; contact **Ping Anchorage** (☎ 626 2020) in Kuala Terengganu for details. It's a peaceful spot with a couple of small private beaches, and between May and October, guests can watch baby green turtles emerging at the resort's own turtle hatchery. It is also possible to camp on some of the isolated beaches at the northern and southern ends of the island, but bring your own food and water.

GETTING THERE & AWAY

Boats to Pulau Kapas leave from Marang's main jetty and tickets can be purchased from any of the agents nearby. Boats leave when four or more people show up, and charge RM25 return. Be sure to arrange a pick-up time when you purchase your ticket. You can usually count on morning departures at around 8am and 9am. Boats to Gemia (for guests only) leave from the same jetty roughly every two hours between 9am and 3pm (RM30 one way).

KUALA TERENGGANU

Standing on a promontory formed by the South China Sea on one side and the wide Sungai Terengganu on the other, Kuala Terengganu is the state capital and the seat of the sultan. Oil revenue has transformed Kuala Terengganu from a sprawling, oversized fishing village of stilt houses into a medium-sized modern city.

At first glance Kuala Terengganu appears much like any other Malaysian city, but it remains a stronghold of Malay culture, with colourful markets and craft workshops, where you can buy hand-made batik, *songket* and basketware, while just across the river on Pulau Duyung, traditional fishing and boat-building methods are kept alive by the thriving *kampung* (village) community. The city's also a good place to sample authentic Malay cuisine, as well as some excellent Chinese seafood. Keep in mind that it remains a fairly conservative place and has a strong Islamic ethos – there's not much in the way of nightlife.

Kuala Terengganu is also convenient as a staging post to nearby attractions such as Tasik Kenyir, Pulau Kapas and Pulau Redang.

Information

Jl Sultan Ismail is the commercial hub of the town and home to most of the banks, which are open 9.30am to 3.30pm, except Friday. They are also closed on alternate Saturdays, and close at 11.30am on the first and third Thursday of the month.

Immigration Office (☎ 622 1424; Wisma Persekutuan, Jl Sultan Ismail)
Golden Wood Internet (☎ 625 2039; 59 Jl Tok Lam; RM3 per hr)
Mr Dobi Laundry (☎ 622 1671; Jl Masjid Abidin)
State Tourist Office (☎ 622 1553; Jl Sultan Zainal Abidin; 🕘 9am-5pm, closed Friday) Has a wide range of brochures on Terengganu.
Tourism Malaysia Office (☎ 622 1433; Menara Yayasen Islam Terengganu, Jl Sultan Omar; 🕘 9am-5pm, closed Friday) General information on Malaysia, a little out of the way.

Sights

Kuala Terengganu's **Chinatown** (Jl Kg Cina and around) is quite compact. It consists of the usual array of hole-in-the-wall Chinese shops and restaurants, as well as a small Chinese temple and some narrow alleys leading to the waterfront. This is a good spot to sit outdoors and enjoy an evening drink and some excellent food (see Eating p289).

The **central market** (Jl Sultan Zainal Abidin) is a lively, colourful spot, with all kinds of food on display. When they say the fish is fresh, they really mean it – the fishing boats dock right outside. Upstairs, there's a good collection of batik and *songket*.

Across the road from the market and next door to the state tourist office, look for the steep flight of steps leading up to **Bukit Puteri** (Princess Hill; admission RM1; 🕘 9am-5pm, closed Fri), a 200m hill with good views of the city. On

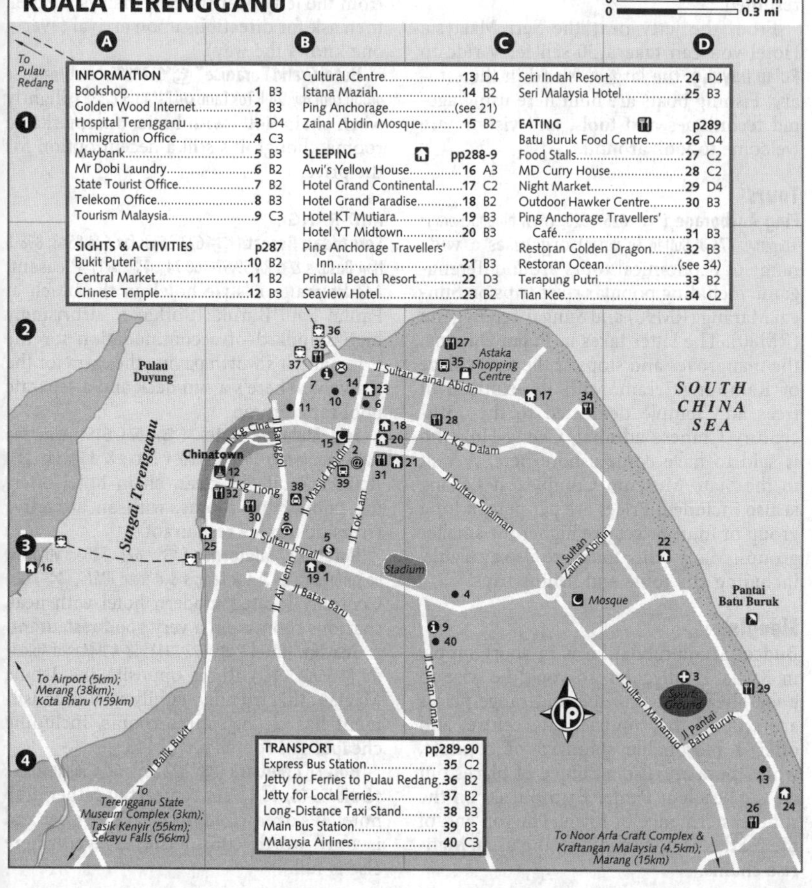

top are the scant remains of a 19th-century fort (the legacy of inter-sultanate warfare), some cannons and a bell.

Continuing past the market, you come to **Istana Maziah** (Jl Masjid Abidin), the sultan's palace, on your right. The palace is closed to the public, except for some ceremonial occasions. Nearby is the gleaming **Zainal Abidin Mosque** (Jl Masjid Abidin).

On the ocean side of town, **Pantai Batu Buruk** is the city beach and a popular place to stroll in the evening when the food stalls open. It is a pleasant stretch of sand, but swimming can be dangerous here. Across the road is the **Cultural Centre**, although at the time of writing, the cultural shows had been discontinued indefinitely; check with the state tourist office to see if they have resumed.

From the jetty near the Seri Malaysia Hotel you can take a 50-sen ferry ride to **Pulau Duyung**, the largest island in the estuary. Fishing boats are built here using age-old techniques and tools, and visitors are welcome to look around.

Tours

Ping Anchorage (☎ 626 2020; www.pinganchorage.com.my; 77A Jl Sultan Sulaiman) organises a wide range of economical tours around Terengganu, including popular river trips on Sungai Marang (RM90) and Sungai Terengganu (RM80). The latter takes in Pulau Duyung, the mangroves and stops at the tiny village of Kampung Jeram, with its exotic fruit trees and temple dedicated to the 15th-century Chinese admiral, Cheng-Ho, who is said to have come ashore here. A visit to the State Museum Complex at Losong is also included. Prices are per person for a group of four; prices are higher for smaller groups. Many other tours are also available, including city tours and fishing trips.

Sleeping

Budget accommodation is in short supply in Kuala Terengganu, so you'd be wise to book ahead. Most of the mid-range places are around the compact city centre, and offer a reasonable standard of comfort, while there are also a couple of places out on the beach at Pantai Batu Buruk, on the southeastern edge of town. The top end of the market is dominated by the usual high-rise chains.

BUDGET

Ping Anchorage Travellers' Inn (☎ 626 2020; www.pinganchorage.com.my; 77A Jl Sultan Sulaiman; dm/d from RM8/15) The number-one travellers place. It has a rooftop terrace and a café downstairs. The rooms are pristine and staff are friendly and helpful. The attached travel agency organises tours to all the east-coast islands, Sekayu Falls and Tasik Kenyir.

Awi's Yellow House (☎ 624 5046; dm/d RM6/15) Unique guesthouse built on stilts over Sungai Terengganu, on Pulau Duyung, a 10-minute ferry ride across the river. It may be a little rustic for some, and you'll need a mosquito net, but it's a friendly and relaxed place. The island is linked to the mainland by the Sultan Mahmud bridge, or you could also jump on one of the infrequent ferries from the jetty near the Seri Malaysia Hotel, then ask for directions upon arrival (everyone knows the way).

Hotel Grand Paradise (☎ 622 8888; hotel@paradisegroup.com.my; 28 Jl Tok Lam; s/d RM40/50; ❄) Slightly worn chain hotel with basic, unremarkable rooms, though it's still a decent option for the price.

MID-RANGE

Seri Indah Resort (☎ 622 2633; fax 624 8548; 898 Jl Haji Busu; s & d RM59.57-100.74; ❄ 🏊) Pleasant, Mediterranean-style hotel on the beach at Pantai Batu Buruk. It offers a surprisingly high standard of accommodation for the price, and it's worth paying the extra for the sea view. There's a sun deck and a separate pool for children.

Seri Malaysia Hotel (☎ 623 6454; www.serimalaysia.com.my; 1640 Jl Balik Bukit; s & d RM85; ❄) Reliable, squeaky-clean chain hotel offering good-value rooms, with an attractive riverside terrace restaurant.

Hotel YT Midtown (☎ 623 5288; ythotel@po.jarring.my; 23 Jl Tok Lam; s & d from RM75; ❄ 💻) Centrally located modern hotel with neat, spacious rooms and a very good restaurant.

Seaview Hotel (☎ 622 1911; 18-A Jl Masjid Abidin; s/d RM55/65; ❄) Right opposite the Istana Maziah, this friendly, family-run establishment has clean, simple rooms, including cheaper fan rooms for RM45.

Hotel KT Mutiara (☎ 622 2655; 67 Jl Sultan Ismail; s & d RM55-85; ❄) Very central but rather drab hotel. It's overpriced for what's on offer and is only worth considering if everywhere else is full.

TOP END

Hotel Grand Continental (☎ 625 1888; 4023 Jl Sultan Zainal Abidin; d/ste from RM138/400;) Modern high-rise in the centre of town with large, comfortable rooms, great service and all the amenities you'd expect.

Primula Beach Resort (☎ 622 2100; Jl Persinggahan; d/ste from RM145/322;) Luxury beachfront option with big, comfortably furnished rooms and elegant public areas, as well as a very good restaurant.

Eating

Kuala Terengganu is a good place to explore the wonders of Malay cuisine. Local specialities include *nasi dagang* (rice served on a banana leaf with curry, usually eaten for breakfast), and *kerepok* (a concoction of deep-fried fish paste and sago, usually moulded into rolls or crackers). You can sample these at the food centres listed. Beer is available in most Chinese restaurants.

QUICK EATS

One of the best food centres is Batu Buruk Food Centre, in a pleasant outdoor location near the beach; don't leave without trying the famous *ais-krim goreng* (fried ice-cream). There's a night market along the beachfront nearby every Friday evening; it's a great place to sample delicious snacks, including *kerepok*, satay and a huge array of sweets. Also worth trying is Chinatown's outdoor **hawker centre** (off Jl Kg Cina), which is divided into Chinese and Malay sections and serves up cheap and tasty meals.

RESTAURANTS

Restoran Golden Dragon (☎ 622 3034; 198 Jl Kg Cina; dishes from RM4) This excellent, and regularly crowded, restaurant serves a wide array of Chinese food; the fish is particularly good; beer is also available.

Ping Anchorage Travellers Café (☎ 626 2020; 77A Jl Sultan Salaiman; dishes from RM5) Bright, modern café under the same management as the neighbouring travel agency and guesthouse, serving an excellent Western-style breakfast and lunch menu. It's also a nice place to relax with a coffee or a cold beer and meet up with fellow travellers.

MD Curry House (☎ 013-902 6331; Jl Kg Dalam; dishes from RM4) Popular travellers hang-out offering tasty, traditional banana-leaf curries and other Indian specialities.

Restoran Ocean (☎ 623 9156; 2079 Jl Sultan Zainal Abidin; dishes from RM6) A very good Chinese restaurant specialising in seafood. It's a big place, with big, family-sized tables, though it seldom gets too crowded. It's also a good place to enjoy a few beers.

Terapung Putri (☎ 631 8946; Jl Sultan Zainal Abidin; dishes from RM3) Busy Malay restaurant perched on stilts, *kampung*-style, on the seafront next to the jetty. The usual fried rice dishes are available, as well as local items such as *kerepok*.

Tian Kee (☎ 622 4375; 136 Jl Sultan Zainal Abidin; dishes from RM5) Halal Chinese restaurant, serving very good seafood. Buttered prawns and bean curd are the specialities of the house.

Shopping

Kuala Terengganu is a good place to buy wicker goods, batik and *songket*. The **Noor Arfa Craft Complex** (9am-5pm) is a handicraft centre on the Chendering industrial estate, about 4.5km south of town, not far from the 'Floating Mosque', selling a wide variety of batik, *songket*, basketware and glass. The **Kraftangan Malaysia** (8am-4.15pm, closed Fri) outlet nearby sells a similar range of goods. Minibus No 13 from Kuala Terengganu will drop you outside (70 sen). Another good place to buy handicrafts is upstairs at the **central market** (Jl Sultan Zainal Abidin). Prices at the market average RM80 to RM250 for a 1-sq-m piece of *songket* and RM20 to RM100 for locally made wicker baskets. Bargaining is possible here – and necessary to get fair prices. Also try the **Batik Gallery** (Ping Anchorage travel agency; Jl Sultan Sulaiman), which has a wide variety of innovative batik designs.

Getting There & Away

AIR

Malaysia Airlines (☎ 622 1415; 13 Jl Sultan Omar) has direct flights daily to/from KL (RM158). **Air Asia** (☎ 631 3122; Menara Yayasan Islam, Jl Sultan Omar) has two flights daily to KL (from around RM62).

BUS

The main bus station on Jl Masjid Abidin serves as a terminus for all local buses. Some long-distance buses depart from here as well, but most use the express bus station in the north of town (ask at your lodgings or when buying your ticket if you're unsure of which station to go to).

At the local bus station, there are services to/from Marang (RM1.50), Rantau Abang (RM4), Dungun (RM5) and Merang (RM2).

From the express bus station, there are regular services running to and from the following places: Kuantan (RM11.50), Johor Bahru (RM28.70, business class RM39.10), Singapore (RM30.20, business class RM42.10), Melaka (RM29), KL (RM25.10, business class RM35.10), Ipoh (RM37), Kuala Besut (RM7) and Kota Bharu (RM9.10).

TAXI

The main taxi stand is near the bus station. Regular taxi destinations include Marang (RM12), Kota Bharu (RM60), Kuala Besut (RM48), Rantau Abang (RM28), Merang (RM20) and Tasik Kenyir (RM45).

Getting Around

A taxi to the airport costs RM20. Local buses leave from the main bus station in the town centre. Taxis around town cost a minimum of RM5, but there are not many about; try at the long-distance taxi stand.

Kuala Terengganu was once the trishaw (bicycle rickshaw) capital of Malaysia, and although numbers have dropped, they are still a popular form of inner-city transport. Cost is roughly RM3 per kilometre.

AROUND KUALA TERENGGANU

Sights

KOMPLEKS MUZIUM NEGERI TERENGGANU

A few kilometres southwest of town in Losong is the excellent **Kompleks Muzium Negeri Terengganu** (Terengganu State Museum Complex; ☎ 622 1444; adult/child RM5/2; ⏲ 9am-5pm, closed Friday). The museum, which claims to be the largest in Southeast Asia, consists of several buildings spread over attractive, landscaped grounds on the banks of the wide Sungai Terengganu. In the main building, a vast concrete reproduction of a traditional Malay house, are displays of textiles, crafts, Islamic artefacts and a gallery devoted to the state's petroleum industry. In the grounds, you'll find a collection of traditional Malay boats, as well as several wooden east-coast houses, while a small maritime gallery houses displays on ship-building and fishing. However, the real highlight of the museum is Istana Tengku Long, a wooden palace that dates from 1888 and contains displays of royal artefacts. Take minibus No 10, marked 'Muzium/Losong', from the main bus station (70 sen). A taxi from Kuala Terengganu will cost RM7.

MASJID TENGKU TENGAH ZAHARAH

The so-called 'Floating Mosque' is located 4.5km southeast of Kuala Terengganu, set in a large park. The huge, gleaming white building combines modern and traditional Moorish-style designs, and projects over the water, giving the illusion, some claim, that the whole thing is floating. Note that non-Muslims may not enter the mosque. Bus No 13 from Kuala Terengganu will drop you outside (70 sen).

SEKAYU FALLS

These waterfalls, 56km southwest of Kuala Terengganu, are part of a large park popular with locals on Friday and public holidays. The falls extend quite a way up a mountainside; the main falls are 15 minutes in from the entrance. A further 20 minutes' walk brings you to the more attractive upper falls. Swimming is possible at both of the falls. There's also an orchard with a huge variety of seasonal tropical fruit.

To get there, catch a bus from Kuala Terengganu to Kuala Berang (RM3) and switch to a taxi (RM15 each way). You can ask the taxi to wait for you (free for up to one hour, RM12 per hour thereafter) or take your chances on finding another for the ride back. **Ping Anchorage** (☎ 626 2020) in Kuala Terengganu does day trips to the falls for RM60 per person including lunch.

TASIK KENYIR

Tasik (Lake) Kenyir, formed by the construction of Kenyir Dam in 1985, covers over 260,000 hectares and contains 340 islands. The lake has been developed as an 'ecotourist' destination and there are now some 13 resorts dotted around the shore.

Waterfalls and **caves** are high on the list of Kenyir's attractions. These are reached by boat, either as day trips from the lake's main access point, Pengkalan Gawi, or from the resorts themselves. Perhaps more interesting are trips up the rivers that empty into the lake. Among these, a journey up **Sungai Petuang**, at the extreme northern end of the lake, is a real highlight of a visit to Kenyir. When the water is high, it's possible o travel several kilometres up the river into beautiful virgin jungle.

Fishing is a popular activity and the lake s surprisingly rich in species, including *oman* (snake head), *buang* (catfish), *kelah* (a kind of carp) and *kalui* (giant gourami).

Because the lake is a reservoir, the water level varies considerably, peaking at the end of the rainy season in March or April and gradually descending until the start of the next rainy season in November. When the water is high, the lake takes on an eerie atmosphere, with the tops of drowned trees poking through the surface; when the water is low, the lake is reduced to a series of canals through partially denuded jungle hills. Needless to say, the lake is at its most beautiful when the water is high, in late spring and early summer.

Sleeping

Most of the accommodation in the area is in resort chalets or floating longhouse structures built over the lake. There are no budget options. The resorts generally offer packages including meals and boat transport from the lake's main access point, Pengkalan Gawi.

Tasik Kenyir Golf Resort (☎ 666 8888; resort@lakekenyir.com; s & d from RM220;) One of the more upmarket options, with spacious, well-equipped timber chalets on the lake's edge. All-inclusive deals start at RM420 and large suites are available (RM370-880). There's a 9-hole golf course and tennis courts.

Musang Kenyir Resort (☎ 623 1888; chalet RM140;) One of the better resorts on the lake, this has a combination of floating-longhouse rooms and land-based chalets.

Kenyir Remis Rakit (☎ 681 2125; chalet RM210;) is a decent choice, with comfortable rooms and attractive views of the lake.

Another option is to explore by houseboat, which allows you to reach remote regions of the lake. The only drawback is that you generally need a large group to make a trip on a houseboat economical (it may be possible to latch onto a big group leaving from Kuala Terengganu).

It's best to organise a trip to Kenyir at a travel agency in Kuala Terengganu. **Ping Anchorage** (☎ 626 2020) offers two-night/three-day deals at Musang Kenyir Resort for RM280, or at Kenyir Remis Rakit for RM340. It can also arrange two-night/three-day houseboat tours for RM210 per person (this is the price for a 10-person tour; smaller groups cost more).

Getting There & Away

Tasik Kenyir is 15km west of Kuala Berang and 55km from Kuala Terengganu. The main access point is the jetty at Pengkalan Gawi, on the northern shore of the lake. To get there, take a taxi from Kuala Terengganu (RM60 per car each way). There are no buses to the lake from Kuala Terengganu.

Getting Around

Travel around the lake is expensive as it is necessary to hire a boat from Pengkalan Gawi (if you're staying at a resort, it will provide all transport). Boat hire costs around RM100 per hour and an all-day fishing trip costs RM400. Rather than trying to organise things on your own, try joining a day tour from Kuala Terengganu; these cost around RM80 per day for four-person groups.

NORTH OF KUALA TERENGGANU

North of Kuala Terengganu the main road (Route 3) leaves the coast and runs inland to Kota Bharu, 165km north, via Jerteh. The quiet coastal back road from Kuala Terengganu to Kuala Besut runs along a beautiful stretch of coast and is popular with cycling travellers.

Batu Rakit

☎ 09

The small fishing village of Batu Rakit lies 27km north of Kuala Terengganu. It's a quiet place with a very pleasant beach, with views of Pulau Redang on a clear day.

The best place to stay is the reasonably priced **Gem Beach Resort** (☎ 669 5910; 2135 Mukim Batu Rakit; s & d from RM98;), which occupies a stunning stretch of sand, with vast landscaped gardens. There's a range of organised activities and excursions available, and a few good restaurants.

Merang

☎ 09

Gateway to Pulau Redang, the sleepy little fishing village of Merang (not to be confused with Marang) is one of the few remaining villages of its kind where development hasn't gone ahead in leaps and bounds. There's little of interest in the village, but the beach is pleasant if you have to spend some time waiting for ferry connections to Redang.

SLEEPING

Kembara Resort (☎ 653 1770; kembararesort@hotmail.com; dm/d from RM10/30;) About 500m south of the village (follow the signs from the main road), this is the best place to stay. There are also air-con chalets for RM60, and a common kitchen is available for those who bring their own food.

In the centre of the village, **Merang Inn** (☎ 653 1435; chalet RM40;) and the neighbouring **Stingray Beach Chalet** (☎ 653 2018; chalet RM50/60;) both provide a decent standard of accommodation; Stingray has slightly better chalets on the beach, while both have their own restaurants.

Aryani Resort (☎ 653 2111; aryani@tm.net.my; Jl Rhu Tapai; s & d from RM560;) One of Malaysia's most exclusive hotels lies on a secluded stretch of coast 4km north of Merang. The detached chalets show a mix of Malay and Javanese design, and are spread out in tranquil, landscaped grounds just off the beach. All come with their own private garden and sunken outdoor bath. Spacious suites are also available, including the sumptuous Redang Suite (RM1055), a traditionally furnished 150-year-old Malay house on stilts. The restaurants serve Western and Malay cuisine, while the spa, housed in a century-old timber building, offers a wide range of indulgent body treatments and massages.

GETTING THERE & AWAY

There are daily buses from the main bus station in Kuala Terengganu to Merang (RM2). Taxis from Kuala Terengganu cost RM20 per car. Coming from the north is more difficult and it is easiest to go south as far as Kuala Terengganu and then backtrack. Otherwise, taxis from Kota Bharu cost RM48 per car.

Pulau Redang

☎ 09

One of the largest and most beautiful of the east-coast islands, Redang has, inevitably, been targeted by big developers, and there are few options for the independent traveller; nearly all visitors come on all-inclusive package deals.

Redang is one of nine islands that form a protected marine park, and it offers excellent diving and snorkelling. Silt and rubble from resort construction is said to have caused some coral damage, and there are ongoing problems with building waste, carelessly dumped on the beach. However, concerted efforts are being made to prevent further damage – even snorkelling is restricted to certain areas.

Of most interest to travellers are the beautiful bays on the eastern side of the island, including Teluk Dalam, Teluk Kalong and Pasir Panjang. The huge Berjaya Beach Resort and the airport are on the north shore and the island's main village is in the interior. There's also a small camp site near the park headquarters on nearby Pulau Pinang.

Note that Pulau Redang basically shuts down from 1 November to 1 March; the best time to visit is from mid-March to late September.

SLEEPING

Accommodation on Pulau Redang is best organised as a package in Kuala Terengganu; **Ping Anchorage** (☎ 626 2020) sells packages for all the resorts listed at competitive prices.

Note that package prices are per person, based on two sharing.

Most of the small resorts are built on a beautiful stretch of white-sand beach known as Pasir Panjang, on the east coast of the island.

Coral Redang Island Resort (☎ 623 6200; www.coralredang.com.my; s & d RM305;) At the northern end of the beach, this full-blown resort has overpriced but pleasant chalets, with meals included. There's a dive centre attached. Three-day/two-night packages start at RM535, and diving packages at RM745, which includes four dives.

Redang Pelangi Resort (☎ 624 2158; www.redangpelangi.com; s & d RM320;) This is a more casual resort-style affair that offers two- and four-bed chalets. There's a full range of kids' activities on hand.

Redang Bay Resort (☎ 620 3200; www.redangbay.com.my; s & d from RM390;) At the southern end of the beach is this rather characterless place with concrete block-style accommodation as well as chalets. The karaoke lounge is open till all hours, so it's not exactly a quiet island haven.

In the bay directly south of Pasir Panjang you will find several more places to stay strung out along an excellent white-sand beach. The cheapest is **Redang Lagoon Chalet** (☎ 666 5018; s & d RM299; ❄), which has basic wooden chalet accommodation.

Further along the beach is the vast new **Laguna Redang Island Resort** (☎ 037-805 4380; s & d from RM548; ❄), still under construction at the time of writing, but partly open in 2003; the whole place isn't due to open until 2005, so until then, noise and mess are likely to be problems. The 212-room complex has a range of luxurious accommodation and a number of restaurants.

On the headland, the **Redang Reef Resort** (☎ 622 6181; s & d from RM320; ❄) is a friendly place popular with student groups. The two-storey wooden chalets are basic but comfortable, and some have great views over the bay.

Heading south, on the secluded Teluk Kalong, is **Redang Kalong Resort** (☎ 624 3537; www.redangkalong.com; s & d from RM260; ❄), a quiet modern place set among the palm trees in a private little bay. Diving packages start at RM360 and include two dives.

On the north shore is Redang's most luxurious resort, the **Berjaya Beach Resort** (☎ 697 3988; www.berjayaresorts.com.my; s & d from RM700; ❄ 💻 🏊). It's a quiet place with a wide choice of sumptuous wooden chalets in delightful, landscaped gardens, and an excellent private beach. Special rates are available for stays of seven nights or more.

GETTING THERE & AWAY

Most visitors to Redang purchase packages that include boat transfer to the island. If you choose to go independently, you must hitch a ride on one of the resorts' boats (RM40). These run from the string of jetties along the river in Merang; the harbour has silted up and is no longer used.

Berjaya Beach Resort ferries leave Kuala Terengganu daily at 10.30am and 3pm and cost RM80 return. In the opposite direction, boats leave Redang for Kuala Terengganu daily at 8am and 1pm (8am and noon on Friday). Note that priority is given to guests of Berjaya Beach Resort and if its boat is full you will have to try to squeeze onto one of the other resorts' boats. Alternatively, you can charter your own speedboat in Merang for RM350.

If you go over on the Berjaya Beach Resort ferry, you'll be dropped at the island's main jetty. In order to get to the beaches of the east coast you will have to hire a taxi-boat for RM50 to RM60 (note that these can't dock in rough weather).

Redang also has a new airport, near the Berjaya Beach Resort; **Berjaya Air** (☎ 03-7846 8228) has three flights a week to/from KL (Subang Airport) for RM249.

It's also possible to visit Redang on a dive trip from Pulau Perhentian (see Flora Bay Divers, p296).

Pulau Lang Tengah

☎ 09

The small, idyllic island of Lang Tengah lies roughly halfway between Pulau Redang and Pulau Perhentian, and with only three resorts to choose from, it's a much quieter, less developed place than its better-known neighbours. It's a hidden gem, with soft white-sand beaches, clean turquoise waters and reputedly some of the best snorkelling in Malaysia just offshore. Like Redang, the resorts offer all-inclusive packages, as well as diving courses.

SLEEPING

The island's three resorts are spaced out on the west coast, and offer a variety of package deals (those listed are for three days and two nights, and prices are per person); discounts are sometimes available, while Ping Anchorage (p288) in Kuala Terengganu can arrange reasonably priced packages.

Square Point Resort (☎ 623 5333; www.malaysiaislandresort.com; package from RM380; ❄) This collection of modern and very pleasant chalets just off the beach also has a restaurant and dive centre. Student packages (for those with ID) start at RM220. Diving packages, which include four boat dives plus two nights full board cost RM565. Just offshore, the pristine and extensive House Reef is one of the island's best snorkelling spots; as well as the colourful coral, turtles and nurse sharks are common sights.

Redang Lang Island Resort (☎ 623 9911; package from RM380; ❄) Offers basic but neat wooden chalets just a few steps from the beach.

Blue Coral Island Resort (☎ 626 2020; www.malaysianislandresort.com; s & d from RM185; ❄ 🏊) This is the most luxurious of the island's three options, and the only one to offer nightly rates.

It has a range of comfortable chalets overlooking a beautiful stretch of unspoilt beach, and a good restaurant. Three-day/two-night diving packages which include four boat dives are also available from RM850.

GETTING THERE & AWAY

Ferries to Lang Tengah leave from the jetty in Merang at 10am and noon, and return from the island at 8.30am and 2pm. If you're travelling independently, the one-way fare for adults/children is RM40/20.

Kuala Besut

☎ 09

Kuala Besut, on the coast south of Kota Bharu, is a sleepy fishing village of little note in itself; a visit here is usually just a preliminary to a trip to Pulau Perhentian.

ORIENTATION & INFORMATION

Taxis and local buses run to and from the taxi stand in the centre of town, very near the seafront. Around the square formed by the taxi stand you will find a few simple shops and restaurants. Near the jetty, **Perhentian Pelangi Travel & Tours** (☎ 697 4353; www.perhentianpelangi.com.my) is a reliable travel agency that can arrange transport to and accommodation on the Perhentians. If you've got your own transport, there's a car park (RM5 per day) near the taxi stand.

SLEEPING & EATING

Kuala Besut's few hotels are basic, functional affairs.

Bubu Inn (☎ 697 8888; fax 697 5080; Jl Pantai; s/d from RM30/40; ❄) Near the jetty, this is the best option in town, with large simple rooms; air-con rooms go for RM60.

Nan Hotel (☎ 697 4892; Jl Haji Mohammad; s & d with fan/air-con RM40/55; ❄) Just down the road from the jetty, not far from the bus station; all rooms here can accommodate three people.

Yaudin Guesthouse (☎ 691 9611; Jl Pantai; s & d RM20-40; ❄) This is the cheapest place in town, with a few drab rooms over the travel agency of the same name.

There are several *kedai kopi* (coffee shops) around town, as well as a few shops where you can buy basic provisions.

GETTING THERE & AWAY

Kuala Besut is best reached from Kota Bharu to the north. By bus from Kota Bharu you can go via Jerteh (RM3.50) or via Pasir Puteh (RM2.50). From Jerteh to Kuala Besut it costs RM1 by bus and RM8 by taxi. From Pasir Puteh it's RM1 by bus and RM10 by taxi. However, since a taxi to/from Kota Bharu costs only RM28 per car, most people opt to go the whole way by taxi. From the south, you can go to/from Kuala Terengganu by bus (RM5.70) or taxi (RM50 per car).

PULAU PERHENTIAN

☎ 09

A short boat trip from Kuala Besut will take you to the beautiful islands of Pulau Perhentian Besar and Pulau Perhentian Kecil, just 20km off the coast. These are arguably the most beautiful islands in Malaysia, with crystal-clear aquamarine water and white-sand beaches.

While both islands have their strong points, Kecil, with its abundance of cheap chalets and lively bars and restaurants, tends to attract the younger backpacker crowd, while Besar offers higher standards of accommodation and a quieter, more relaxed ambience. The undecided can cross the strait from island to island for around RM10 (about 10 minutes).

The more expensive resorts on Besar have excellent restaurants, with seafood and barbeques being particularly good; all are open to non-guests. Over on Kecil, there are a few decent cafés serving up noodle and rice dishes, as well as various Western meals. Almost all chalet operations have their own restaurant. Alcohol is available in a few bars and hotel restaurants on both islands, though it's not openly displayed and you will have to ask for it. Prices are, naturally, higher than on the mainland

Activities on the islands include snorkelling and diving, jungle walks and just hanging around on the beach waiting for the coconuts to drop.

Note that many places, on both islands, charge 'high-season' prices, usually from late May to September, and sometimes on weekends year-round. Prices quoted here are high season. These islands basically shut down during the monsoon (usually from mid-November to early March) although some hotels remain open for hardier tourists.

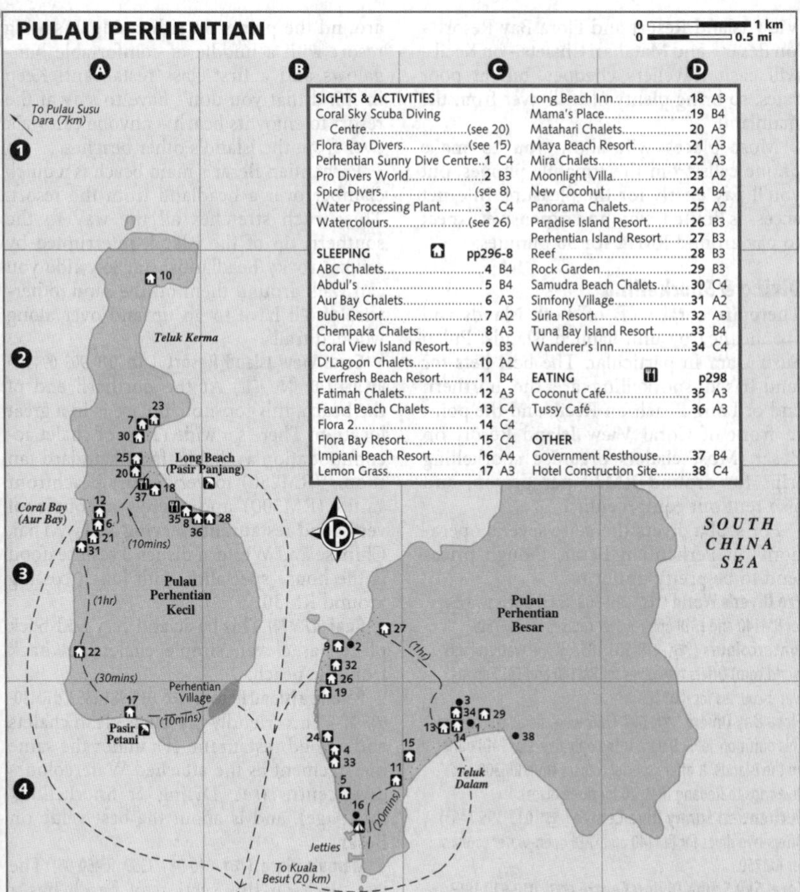

Orientation

A narrow strait separates Perhentian Besar, the big island, from Perhentian Kecil, the small island.

On Perhentian Kecil, the most popular spot is Long Beach (Pasir Panjang), an excellent white sandy beach with a string of economical bungalow operations, cafés and a few (expensive) shops. Perhentian Kecil is also the administrative centre and has a fair-sized village with a few *kedai kopi* and shops. Across the narrow waist of the island, Coral Bay is another popular spot with a decent stretch of beach and the best sunsets on the islands. The island also has several isolated bays with private beaches for those in search of solitude.

Over on Besar, most of the accommodation is clustered on the western side of the island along a series of beaches divided by rocky headlands. For those looking to get away from it all, a walk through the jungle, or a 10-minute boat ride, leads to the isolated bay of Teluk Dalam, which has a wide, palm-fringed beach. At the time of writing, however, a huge new luxury resort was under construction at the far end of the bay, which, when completed (possibly mid-2004), will no doubt change the character of this currently sedate stretch of sand.

Information

It's difficult to change money on the Perhentians. Perhentian Island Resort, Coral

View Island Resort and Flora Bay Resort – on Besar – and Matahari Chalets – on Kecil – will cash travellers cheques, but at poor rates, so bring plenty of cash over from the mainland.

Most places will allow you to make phone calls from their mobile phones, but you'll pay dearly for the pleasure. Internet access is limited, slow and expensive; expect to pay around RM12 for 30 minutes.

Diving & Snorkelling

There are coral reefs off both islands and around nearby uninhabited islands, Pulau Susu Dara in particular. The best bets for land-based snorkelling are the northern end of Long Beach on Kecil, and the point in front of Coral View Island Resort on Besar. Most chalets organise snorkelling trips for around RM30 per person, and also rent out equipment.

For scuba divers there are several operations on Perhentian Besar, though prices tend to be pretty uniform.

Pro Diver's World (☎ 010-903 0943) Offers two dives for RM140 and PADI open-water courses for RM750.

Watercolours (☎ 019-981 1852; www.watercoloursworld.com) Offers two dives for RM140 and PADI open-water courses for RM750.

Flora Bay Divers (☎ 697 7266; www.florabaydivers.com) This outfit on Teluk Dalam is the only five-star PADI outlet on the islands. It offers special courses from RM200 and dive trips to Redang (RM220 for three dives).

Perhentian Sunny Dive Centre (☎ 019-395 1463) Offers two dives for RM140 and PADI open-water courses for RM750.

Coral Sky Scuba Diving Centre (☎ 010-910 1963; www.coralskydiver.com) On Kecil, two dives cost RM120 and PADI open-water courses go for RM650.

Spice Divers (☎ 019-985 7329; www.spicedivers.com) Offers two dives for RM140.

Sleeping & Eating

PULAU PERHENTIAN BESAR

There are three main beaches on Perhentian Besar: the northern beach on the western side, which is dominated by Perhentian Island Resort; the main beach on the western side of the island; and Teluk Dalam, on the island's southeast coast.

Perhentian Island Resort (☎ 697 4900; www.perhentianresort.com; d RM250-350) Perhentian Besar's most luxurious option, this overlooks perhaps the best beach on the islands – a beautiful half-moon bay with good coral around the points on either side. It's a big resort with a huddle of comfortable bungalows and a first-class restaurant. Keep in mind that you don't have to stay at the resort to enjoy its beach – anyone can walk over from the island's other beaches.

Perhentian Besar's main beach is a quick clamber over a headland from the resort. This beach stretches all the way to the southern tip of the island, interrupted by several rocky headlands – at low tide you can walk around them on the sand, otherwise you'll have to go up and over along wooded trails.

Coral View Island Resort (☎ 010-903 0943; d RM100-210) At the northern end of the beach, this top-notch place is in a great location. There's a wide range of chalet accommodation available, from standard fan rooms (RM280) to very smart beachfront suites (RM500) and there's a couple of very good restaurants serving Malay, Thai, Chinese and Western dishes. Fresh seafood is the house speciality, with lunch costing around RM30.

Reef (d RM70) This basic and very laid-back place has eleven simple chalets set back from the beach.

Paradise Island Resort (☎ 019-981 1852; d RM30-60) This friendly place has clean chalets and a good restaurant. It's under the same management as the attached Watercolours dive centre (see Diving & Snorkelling, this page), and is about the best value on Besar.

Mama's Place (☎ 010-981 3359; RM60-95) The last place on this section of beach has a choice of reasonably comfortable chalets with or without bathrooms.

On the other side of the headland there's another stretch of beach with some quite varied accommodation.

New Cocohut (☎ 697 7988; d RM30-80) This has a good choice of rooms including pleasant beachside chalets and a two-storey longhouse, which has some great views from the upstairs balcony.

ABC Chalets (☎ 697 7568; d RM20-50) Scruffy rooms are in a tatty and not very enticing longhouse.

Tuna Bay Island Resort (☎ 697 7779; www.tunabay.com.my; d RM128-250) Immaculate chalets perch on a lovely stretch of beach, with others facing the jungle behind. Family rooms, sleeping up to four adults, are

PERHENTIAN ACCOMMODATION WARNING

In recent years, the Perhentians have exploded in popularity. In peak season, which is usually from late May to September, it can be difficult to find a place to stay on some of the island's most popular beaches, Long Beach on Kecil in particular.

The peak-season scenario goes something like this: boat after boat pulls up on Long Beach to disgorge another group of hopeful travellers. Staggering under heavy packs in the hot sun, the new arrivals make their way desperately up and down the beach in search of a vacant room, only to find that even the most wretched accommodation is full. In frustration, they either camp out on the beach and wait for a room to open up, or make the 10-minute journey across the island to Coral Bay to repeat the process all over again.

The real tragedy here is that, while these folks go through hell to secure some pretty grim rooms, there are usually plenty of openings over on Besar or at some of Kecil's lovely isolated bays. So resist the temptation to join the lemmings!

available from RM258. There's also a very good restaurant, with barbeque dinners costing around RM25.

Clambering over the next headland brings you to a quiet beach where you'll find the popular **Abdul's** (☎ 010-983 7303; d RM50-60). Options include chalets with fan and bathroom and family rooms for RM80. Just beyond is the Government Resthouse, reserved for Malaysian government officials.

It is possible to **camp** on the beach south of the Government Resthouse, although this area is far from quiet on long weekends.

An easily missed track leads from behind the second jetty over the hill to Teluk Dalam, a secluded bay with a long stretch of shallow beach.

Everfresh Beach Resort (☎ 697 7620; d RM30-80) This shabby collection of ramshackle A-frames and bungalows is serviced by indifferent staff.

Flora Bay Resort (☎ 697 7266; www.florabayresort.com; d RM50-150; ❄ 💻) This big place has a variety of chalet accommodation, set back from the beach. Prices rise by 20% on Saturday and Sunday. **Flora 2**, an extension of Flora Bay is a little further along the beach, with a smaller range of identical chalets.

Fauna Beach Chalets (☎ 697 7607; d RM40-50) This basic place also offers family chalets for RM65.

Wanderer's Inn (☎ 012-290 9300; oyaandena@hotmail.com; d RM20-25) One of the most interesting places on Teluk Dalam, this intimate and very laid-back place is run by the amiable Oya and Ena. There are only six basic huts, with shared bathroom, as well as tent sites for RM10 and a rustic little restaurant under the trees.

Samudra Beach Chalets (☎ 697 7608; d RM35-50) This pleasant, friendly place has simple beachfront bungalows and a decent restaurant. Right next door, however, is the site of a brand new luxury resort, still under construction at the time of writing, but due for completion by summer 2004, so this will no longer be the quiet and isolated place it used to be.

A trail leads from Fauna Beach Chalets around a water-processing plant over the middle of the island to Perhentian Island Resort.

PULAU PERHENTIAN KECIL

Accommodation on Perhentian Kecil tends to be more basic and prices generally lower, starting at around RM30 for a chalet with two beds, a mosquito net and a well or common shower. Recently, though, there have been a number of more upmarket developments, a trend that seems set to continue.

With a great strip of white sand out the front, Long Beach is the most popular place on the island. Unfortunately, it's becoming overdeveloped and can be quite noisy.

Rock Garden (d RM20-30) On the rocks at the southern end of the beach, this has an interesting location and some of the cheapest chalets around, though at this price you don't even get a fan. The best ones are high up on the rocks with a good view of the sea.

Lemon Grass (d RM25) This new place has a range of basic fanless huts. It's a bit scruffy, and some may find scrambling over the rocks and undergrowth awkward.

Chempaka Chalets (☎ 010-985 7329; d RM20-60) Run by the ever-cheerful Musky, there's a range of good chalets in a pleasant, laid-back setting. The spontaneous parties and beach barbeques make this a lively, sociable place.

Long Beach Inn (☎ 019-981 8999; d RM100-120; ❄) This more upmarket option has comfortable modern chalets with bathrooms.

Matahari Chalets (☎ 019-956 8726; d RM30-75) In the middle of the beach, set back among the trees, this is one of the better choices, with a good range of accommodation, from simple chalets with shared bathroom to spacious bungalows. The restaurant is quite good too.

Panorama Chalets (☎ 010-934 0123; d RM30-80; 💻) A range of chalets offering varying levels of comfort, including family chalets for four people (RM100).

Simfony Village (☎ 019-947 9421; d RM15-35) Basic A-frames have shared bathroom and nicer chalets, which aren't bad for the price have a bathroom attached.

Bubu Resort (☎ 697 8888; www.buburesort.com.my; d from RM200; ❄) At the northern end of the beach, this is the newest, and sole upscale option here. This modern three-storey hotel has light, spacious rooms, most with balconies. There's a good restaurant and seafood is barbequed on the beach regularly (RM20-30). Dorm rooms and a dive centre are planned (due to open late 2004).

Moonlight Villa (☎ 019-961 7898; d RM20-50) This popular spot right at the end of the bay is a bit shabby; the cheaper, fanless A-frame huts have certainly seen better days.

A jungle trail over the narrow waist of the island leads from Long Beach to Coral Bay (sometimes known as Aur Bay) on the western side of the island. The beach is quite pleasant and gets good sunsets but, like Long Beach, its popularity has caught up with it and it's a little crowded and noisy.

Suria Resort (☎ 697 7990; www.suriaresorts.com; s & d RM120-250; ❄) At the southern edge of the beach, Suria has spotless modern chalets in a great location, though the price is a little high.

Maya Beach Resort (☎ 019-937 9136; s & d RM40-50) With a few of the nicest A-frames on the beach, this place is often booked up.

Aur Bay Chalets (☎ 010-985 8584; d RM40-60) Fairly basic rooms set back from the sea, with a small restaurant attached. Back on the beach, **Fatimah Chalets** (☎ 019-963 0391; dm/d from RM10/30) has a few simple chalets and eight-bed dorms, as well as a nice little café.

There are a number of small bays around the island, each with one set of chalets, and often only accessible by boat. **D' Lagoon Chalets** (☎ 019-985 7089; s & d RM25-50) is on Teluk Kerma, a small bay on the northeastern side of the island. This is one of the better places on Kecil, with good coral and a tranquil, isolated location. There are longhouse rooms and chalets, as well as a more unusual tree-house for all those budding Tarzans and Janes (RM20). Tracks lead to a couple of very remote beaches in the northwestern corner of the island.

On the southwest coast, **Mira Chalets** (☎ 010-964 0582; s & d RM30-50) is an adventurous choice on a small secluded beach, with the jungle right behind. There are just eight rickety chalets set amid banana and coconut trees, in a location Robinson Crusoe would have been proud to call home. The friendly owner cooks up traditional Malay meals in the driftwood-bedecked restaurant. Walking tracks lead through the rainforest to Pasir Petani (30 minutes, about 1.5km) and north to Coral Bay (one hour, about 3km).

On the south coast is the lovely isolated beach of Pasir Petani, where you'll find the upmarket **Impiani Beach Resort** (☎/fax 697 7346; s & d RM140-180). It's a peaceful setting, and the pricier chalets facing the beach have great views out over the open sea.

There are a few basic places to eat spread out along Long Beach, including **Tussy Café** (next to Matahari Chalets), which serves Western-style breakfast (RM5) and Malaysian dishes from around RM9. Further on, **Coconut Café** serves a barbeque set dinner for RM10.

Getting There & Away

Both speedboats (RM60 return, 30 minutes) and slow boats (RM40 return, 1½ hours) run several times a day between Kuala Besut and the Perhentians, from 8.30am to 5.30pm, although you can expect delays or cancellations if the weather is bad, or if there aren't enough passengers. The boats will drop you off at any of the beaches. In the other direction, speedboats depart from the islands daily at around 8am, noon and 4pm; slow boats hourly from 8am to noon. It's a good idea to let the owner of your guesthouse know a day before you leave so they can arrange a pick-up. Tickets are sold by several travel agents around Kuala

Besut, the best of which is Perhentian Pelangi Travel & Tours (p294).

Note that you can board a speedboat in either direction with a slow-boat ticket if you pay the RM10 fare difference.

Note that the waves on Long Beach can be hazardous – when the waves are high get dropped off or picked up on the other side of the island at Coral Bay. Also, guesthouse operators on Kecil now charge RM2 for ferry pick-ups and drop-offs.

Getting Around

While there are some trails around the island, the easiest way to go from beach to beach or island to island is by boat. Most resort and chalet owners can arrange for a boat and driver. From island to island, the trip costs RM10 per boat, and a jaunt from one beach to another on the same island usually costs about RM8. You can charter a boat for a half-day tour round the islands for RM50.

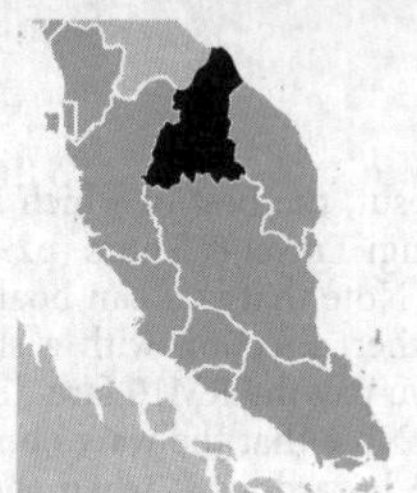

Kelantan

CONTENTS

Kelantan, the 'Land of Lightning', is Malaysia at its most Malayan. It's a largely rural state, and a prime centre for Malay culture, crafts and religion – a place to watch batik being made, see kite-flying contests, marvel at the skills of *songket* weavers and explore traditional *kampung* life in the jungled interior.

As the state shares a border with Thailand, and, indeed, was once under Thai rule, it's not surprising to find a strong Thai influence here in the local cuisine, architecture, and, of course, among the local population. Kelantan is, however, the poorest state in Peninsular Malaysia, and the economy still relies heavily on rice production, which is based mainly in the fertile river plain of Sungai Kelantan, which flows due north, reaching the sea just north of Kota Bharu. Fishing, rubber production and tobacco growing are other important commercial activities. With the Islamic Party in government, Kelantan is also Malaysia's most conservative state.

The capital, Kota Bharu, is a good place to sample the local culture and cuisine, and also makes a good base from which to explore the surrounding countryside, but the true Malay spirit is found in the villages of Kelantan.

HIGHLIGHTS

- Sampling local culinary delicacies at the lively night market, shopping for handicrafts and exploring the many museums and palaces in **Kota Bharu** (p303)
- Watching displays of traditional top-spinning, kite-making and martial arts at the **Gelanggang Seni** (p305) in Kota Bharu
- Traversing the mountainous, jungle-clad interior of Peninsular Malaysia on the **jungle railway** (p311)
- Visiting the elaborate Thai Buddhist temples in the picturesque **Tumpat district** (p310) near the Thai border

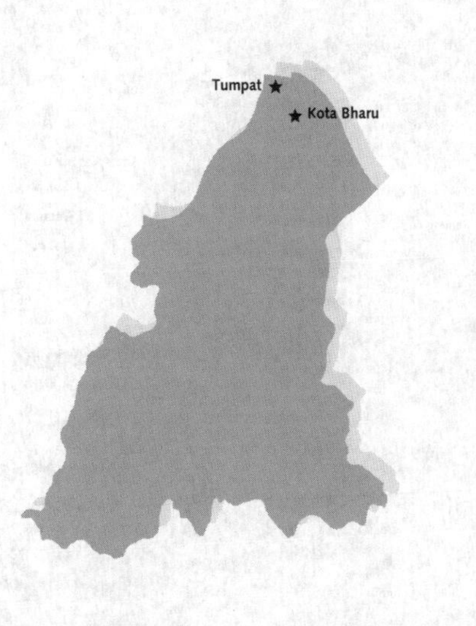

- TELEPHONE CODE: 09
- POPULATION: 1.31 MILLION
- AREA: 15,024 SQ KM

History

Archaeological finds at Gua Musang and Gua Cha have turned up evidence of human settlements dating back to prehistoric times.

In the early Middle Ages, Kelantan was influenced by the Indianised Funan kingdom on the Mekong River, whose farming methods it adopted, while there were strong links with both Siam and the Khmer Empire.

After being a vassal of first the Sumatran Srivijaya Empire, and then the Siamese, Kelantan came under the sway of the new Melaka sultanate in the 15th century. With the demise of that sultanate in the 17th century, Kelantan was ruled by Johor and then, the following century, by Terengganu.

By the 1820s Kelantan was the most populous and one of the most prosperous states on the Malay Peninsula. As was the case in Terengganu, it managed to escape the ravages of the disputes that plagued the west-coast states, and so experienced largely unimpeded development. Also like Terengganu, Kelantan had strong ties with Siam (now Thailand) throughout the 19th century, before control was passed to the British following the signing of an Anglo-Siamese treaty in 1909. Kelantan was the first place in Malaya to be invaded by Japanese troops in WWII. During the Japanese occupation, control of the state was passed to Thailand, but in 1948 Kelantan became a member of the Federation of Malaya.

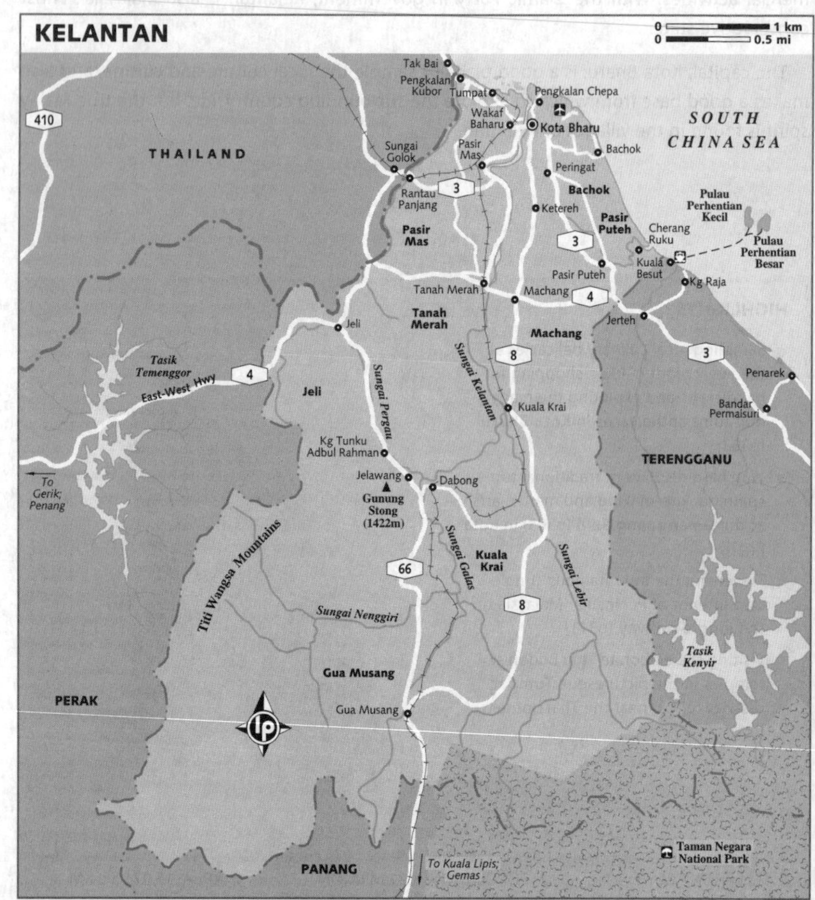

Since 1990 Kelantan has been governed by the Islamic Party of Malaysia (PAS), which has tried for years without success to impose *syariah*, or Islamic law, on its citizens; single-sex queues in supermarkets and separate public benches for men and women in Kota Bharu are largely ignored by most people.

Climate

Kelantan has a tropical climate, with temperatures between 21° and 32°C. There is intermittent rain throughout the year, and heavier, more prolonged rainfall during the east-coast monsoon season (November to January). Temperatures in Kota Bharu are often higher than in the surrounding countryside, and cooler temperatures are recorded on the coast. Humidity levels are highest in the jungled interior of the state, rarely dipping below 90%.

Getting There & Away

Kota Bharu is the transport hub of Kelantan, and can be reached by bus from most major towns in Peninsular Malaysia. The nearest train station is at Wakaf Baharu, around 5km southwest of Kota Bharu, with services to Kuala Lumpur and Singapore. There is also an airport 9km northeast of the city, offering daily flights to KL (see p308 for details). The main border crossing from Thailand is at Rantau Panjang, from where hourly buses run to Kota Bharu (see p309).

Getting Around

The so-called jungle railway runs from Tumpat, close to the Thai border, southwards through Dabong and Gua Musang to Gemas, where it meets the lines to KL and Singapore. The state-run bus company SKMK runs all regional buses and city buses in Kota Bharu, and also operates many long-distance routes.

KOTA BHARU

In the northeastern corner of the peninsula, Kota Bharu is the termination of the east-coast road, and a gateway to Thailand. At first glance, Kota Bharu, with its bustling modern centre and traffic-clogged streets, seems much like any other Malaysian city, but this is a city rich in Malay culture, with royal palaces, colourful markets and several museums to linger over; and it's also a good base for exploring the surrounding region. Many travellers plan an overnight stop here en route to or from Thailand or Pulau Perhentian (Perhentian Islands).

Orientation

The centre of town is a busy area northeast of the clock tower, bounded by Jl Pintu Pong, Jl Kebun Sultan/Jl Mahmud, Jl Hospital and Jl Temenggong.

Information

The **immigration office** (☎ 748 2126; Wisma Persekutuan) is on Jl Bayam. For Internet access try **Internet & Cyber Café** (☎ 743 1555; 176 Jl Parit Dalam; RM2.50 per hr).

Banks are open from 10am to 3pm Saturday to Wednesday, 9.30 to 11.30am Thursday, and are closed on Friday. If you need to change money after banking hours, the **Maybank moneychanger**, near the central market, is usually open to 7pm.

The **tourist information centre** (☎ 748 5534; Jl Sultan Ibrahim; 🕓 Mon-Thu 8am-1pm & 2-4.30pm, Fri 8am-12.15pm & 2.45-4.30pm, Sat 8am-12.50pm) has tour information as well as details on activities such as cookery workshops (see p306).

Sights

PADANG MERDEKA

Padang Merdeka (Independence Square) is a strip of grass that was established as a memorial following WWI. It is best-known as the place where the British exhibited the body of Tok Janggut (Father Beard), a respected elder who was killed at Pasir Puteh in 1915 after leading a 2000-strong uprising against British colonial land taxes.

MUSEUMS

The real attraction of the Padang Merdeka area is the cluster of museums close by.

Bank Kerapu (WWII Memorial Museum; Jl Sultan; RM2; 🕓 Sat-Thu 8.30am-4.45pm) is basically a collection of photographs chronicling the Japanese occupation and the 1948 Emergency, and there are also some rusty guns on display. Upstairs, there's a small gallery devoted to the history of prewar Kelantan, while there's also a garden with a reconstruction of a WWII British pillbox. The fine old wooden **Muzium Islam** (Islamic Museum; ☎ 744 0102; Jl Sultan; admission free; 🕓 Sat-Thu 8.30am-4.45pm) was once known as Serambi

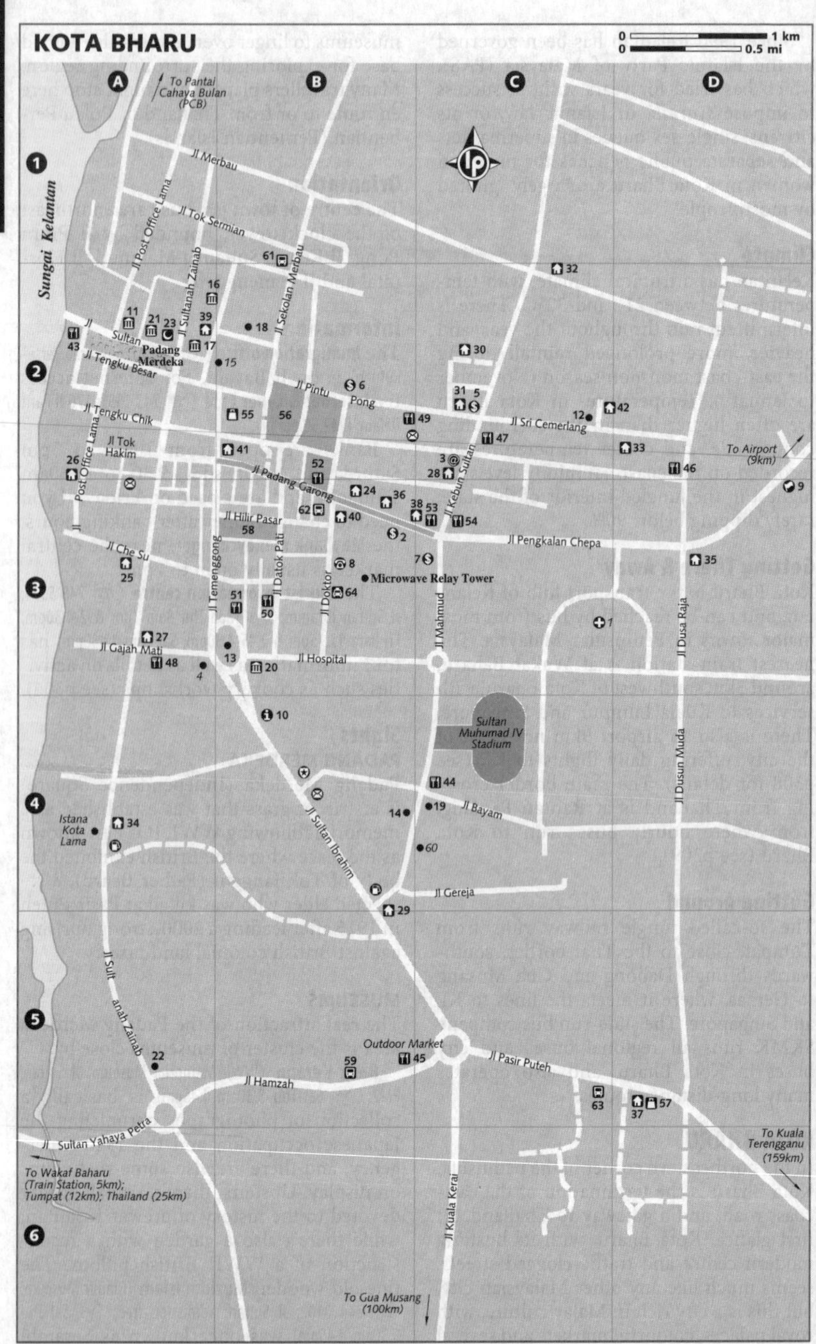
KOTA BHARU
0 1 km
0 0.5 mi
A
B
C
D
1
2
3
4
5
6
To Pantai Cahaya Bulan (PCB)
Sungai Kelantan
Jl Merbau
Jl Tok Sermian
Jl Post Office Lama
Jl Sultanah Zainab
Jl Sekolan Merbau
Jl Sultan
Padang Merdeka
Jl Tengku Besar
Jl Pintu Pong
Jl Tengku Chik
Jl Sri Cemerlang
Jl Tok Hakim
Jl Padang Garong
Jl Kebun Sultan
To Airport (9km)
Jl Hilir Pasar
Jl Pengkalan Chepa
Jl Che Su
Jl Temenggong
Jl Datok Pati
Jl Doktor
Microwave Relay Tower
Jl Mahmud
Jl Dusa Raja
Jl Gajah Mati
Jl Hospital
Sultan Muhumad IV Stadium
Jl Dusun Muda
Jl Bayam
Istana Kota Lama
Jl Sultan Ibrahim
Jl Gereja
Jl Sultanah Zainab
Outdoor Market
Jl Pasir Puteh
Jl Hamzah
Jl Sultan Yahaya Petra
To Kuala Terengganu (159km)
To Wakaf Baharu (Train Station, 5km); Tumpat (12km); Thailand (25km)
Jl Kuala Kerai
To Gua Musang (100km)

INFORMATION		
General Hospital	1	C3
Hongkong Bank	2	B3
Internet & Cyber Café	3	C2
Malaysia Airlines	4	A3
Mayban Finance	5	C2
Maybank Moneychanger	6	B2
Maybank	7	C3
Telekom	8	B3
Thai Consulate	9	D3
Tourist Information Centre	10	B4
SIGHTS & ACTIVITIES	**pp303-6**	
Bank Kerapu (WWII Memorial Museum)	11	A2
Bird-Singing Venue	12	C2
Clock Tower	13	B3
Gelanggang Seni (Cultural Centre)	14	B4
Istana Balai Besar	15	B2
Istana Batu (Royal Museum)	16	A2
Istana Jahar (Royal Customs Museum)	17	A2
Kampung Kraftagan (Handicraft Village)	18	B2
Kompleks Sultan Perdana	19	C4
Muzim Negeri Kelantan	20	B3
Muzium Islam	21	A2
Silversmith	22	A5
State Mosque	23	A2
SLEEPING	**pp306-7**	
ARM Hostel	24	B3
Crystal Lodge	25	A3
Diamond Puteri Hotel	26	A2
Dynasty Inn	27	A3
Hotel Anda	28	C2
Hotel Perdana	(see 60)	
Hotel Sentosa	29	B4
Ideal Travellers' House	30	C2
Juita Inn	31	C2
KB Garden Hostel	32	C2
Mandarin Hostel	33	D2
Menora Guest House	34	A4
New Pacific Hotel	35	D3
RV Inn Guest House	36	B3
Renaissance Hotel	37	D5
Sabrina Court	38	C3
Safar Inn	39	A2
Suria Hotel	40	B3
Temenggong Hotel	41	B2
Zeck Traveller's Inn	42	C2
EATING	**pp307-8**	
Food Stalls	43	A2
Food Court	44	C4
Food Stalls	45	B5
Four Seasons Restaurant	46	D2
Medan Selera Kebun Sultan Food Court	47	C2
Meena Curry House	48	A3
Muhibah Vegetarian Restaurant	49	B2
Muhibah Vegitarian Restaurant	50	B3
Natural Vegetarian Food	51	B3
Night Market	52	B2
Restoran Golden City	53	C3
Sri Devi Restaurant	54	C3
DRINKING		
Fame Kopitiam N' Café	(see 53)	
SHOPPING	**p308**	
Bazaar Buluh Kubu	55	B2
Central Market	56	B2
Kota Seri Mutiara Mall	57	D5
Old Central Market	58	B3
TRANSPORT	**pp308-9**	
(Jalan Hamzah) External Bus Station	59	B5
Avis	60	C4
Buses to PCB	61	B1
Central Bus Station	62	B3
Langgar Long Distance Bus Station	63	C5
Taxi Stand	64	B3
Taxi Stand	(see 62)	

Mekah (Veranda to Mecca) – a reference to its days as Kelantan's first school of Islamic instruction. Nowadays it houses a small collection of photographs and artefacts relating to the history of Islam in the state.

Istana Jahar (Royal Ceremonies Museum; ☎ 744 4666; Jl Hilir Kota; admission RM3; ⏲ Sat-Thu 8.30am-4.45pm) is a beautiful old wooden structure dating back to 1887. It houses some intriguing displays illustrating various royal rituals and ceremonies, including marriage, birth and circumcision. Inside, take note of the wrought-iron staircases that lead upstairs to a glorious wooden veranda. Outside, you'll find the **Weapons Gallery** with a small collection of spears and kris (daggers).

The sky-blue building of the **Istana Batu** (Royal Museum; ☎ 748 7737; Jl Hilir Kota; admission RM2; ⏲ Sat-Thu 8.30am-4.45pm) was constructed in 1939 and served as the palace of the crown prince until it was donated to the state. The elegantly furnished rooms give a surprisingly intimate insight into royal life, with family photos and personal belongings scattered among the fine china and glassware; you can even cast an eye over the late sultan's collection of hats.

Kampung Kraftangan (Handicraft Village; admission RM2) is a touristy affair in a pedestrian square opposite the Istana Batu, featuring a one-room museum with displays of woodcarving, batik-making and other local crafts. The complex also includes a number of souvenir shops and a restaurant.

Nearby, surrounded by walls and closed to the public, is the **Istana Balai Besar** (Palace of the Large Audience Hall). Built in 1840 as the principal royal residence, it is now used only for formal state functions.

Muzim Negeri Kelantan (State Museum; ☎ 748 2266; Jl Hospital; admission RM2; ⏲ 8.30am-4.45pm Sun-Thu) is next to the tourist information centre. It brings together an eclectic array of artefacts illustrating the history and culture of Kelantan, including traditional instruments, kites and shadow puppets, as well as an impressive collection of Chinese porcelain and furniture. There are also regular temporary exhibitions.

GELANGGANG SENI

The **Gelanggang Seni** (Cultural Centre; ☎ 744 3124; Jl Mahmud) is the place to go to see top-spinning, *seni silat* (martial arts), kite-making and other traditional activities. Free afternoon and evening sessions are held on Monday, Wednesday and Saturday from 1 March to 30 October, except during Ramadan. Check with the tourist information centre (p303) for more details, as times vary.

Activities

Roselan, the ebullient director of the tourist information centre, runs popular **Malay cookery workshops** at his home; prices vary according to the number of participants and the ingredients used. Contact the tourist information centre for details.

The **Kompleks Sultan Perdana** (Sports Complex; ☎ 743 4928; Jl Bayam; ⏰ 10am-1am) has a bowling alley (RM4.50 per game) as well as a gym and squash courts.

Tours

Some of the guesthouses, such as **Zeck Traveller's Inn** (☎ 743 1613), arrange tours around Kota Bharu and the surrounding areas. The tourist information centre (p303) keeps a list of reputable tour operators, and its director, Roselan, leads cultural tours. Popular excursions include four-hour cultural tours of Kota Bharu (RM40) and two-night/three-day trips to the Jelawang area (RM220).

Festivals & Events

Each year around August, Kota Bharu has a **bird-singing contest**, when you can see Malay songbirds perform. Every Friday morning there's also a bird-singing contest out near Zeck Traveller's Inn. Here the locals hang their decorative bird cages up on long poles, then sit back and listen. It happens to a lesser extent on other days of the week as well.

The spectacular **kite festival** is usually held in August, and the **drum festival** and the **top-spinning contest** in September. The **Sultan's Birthday** celebration involves a week of cultural events. The dates vary, so check with the tourist information centre or get hold of Tourism Malaysia's *Calendar of Events* brochure.

Sleeping

Kota Bharu has long been a popular stopover on the backpacker trail, and there's plenty of cheap hostel accommodation scattered around town, as well as a few family-run hotels. Mid-range options tend to be geared towards business travellers more than tourists, and are often pretty bland and impersonal affairs, although prices are very reasonable. The luxury end of the market, meanwhile, is dominated by a handful of gigantic high-rises on the fringes of the city centre.

BUDGET

Zeck Traveller's Inn (☎ 743 1613; www.zeck-traveller.com; 7088-G Jl Sri Cemerlang; dm/s/d from RM7/12/15; 💻) Popular hostel in a quiet location offering small but clean rooms. The friendly, informative owner can arrange tours and provides a free 24-hour pick-up service. It's around 10 minutes' walk from the centre of town.

Ideal Travellers' House (☎ 744 2246; idealtrahouse@hotmail.com; 3954-F Jl Kebun Sultan; dm/d from RM7/12) Another favourite with backpackers, located down an alley off Jl Pintu Pong, with a pleasant garden. Rooms with private bathroom start at RM30.

Menora Guest House (☎ 748 1669; Jl Sultanah Zainab; dm/d from RM6/26; ❄) Sociable place offering a variety of accommodation, including air-con rooms with shower for RM38. There's also an attractive breakfast bar and roof garden. Bike rental costs RM5 per day.

RV Inn Guest House (☎ 019-946 3620; 2981-B Jl Padang Garong; dm/s/d from RM8/10/18; ❄) Small, friendly hostel right in the centre of town. Rooms with air-con start at RM25.

ARM Hostel (☎ 743 2344; 2981-G Jl Padang Garong; dm/d from RM10/25; ❄) Comfortable, centrally located hostel right beside the RV Inn. Offers air-con doubles with bathroom for RM35.

KB Garden Hostel (☎ 748 5696; 754 Jl Dusun Raja; s/d RM30/40; ❄) Not a hostel at all, but a pleasant family-run hotel in a quiet side street, with basic but neat rooms.

MID-RANGE

Sabrina Court (☎ 744 7944; sabrinacourt@hotmail.com; 171-181 Jl Padang Garong; s & d with fan/air-con from RM29/39; ❄ 💻) Excellent value city centre hotel, with basic but perfectly comfortable rooms. On-site facilities include a Thai restaurant, snooker room and travel agency.

Crystal Lodge (☎ 747 0888; www.crystal-lodge.com.my; 123 Jl Che Su; s/d from RM69/99; ❄) Smart modern hotel in a quiet part of town, with clean, bright rooms. There are free in-house movies and daily newspapers, and the attractive rooftop restaurant has a great view over the river. Discounts often available.

Safar Inn (☎ 747 8000; fax 747 9000; Jl Hilir Kota; s/d from RM78/98; ❄) Well-placed option with cosy, spotless rooms, set amid the clutch of museums near the Padang. It also has a good Thai restaurant.

Suria Hotel (☎ 743 2255; suria.kb@tm.net.my; Jl Padang Garong; s & d from RM75;) Modern, if somewhat characterless, hotel in a good central spot, with bright and airy rooms; those overlooking the street may be subject to noise.

Temenggong Hotel (☎ 748 3844; fax 744 1481; Jl Tok Hakim; s & d from RM75;) Sister hotel of the Suria, offering a similar standard in a slightly quieter location. It has a good restaurant serving Malay and Thai food.

Juita Inn (☎ 744 6888; hotel@tm.net.my; Jl Pintu Pong; s/d from RM95/110;) Priced higher than most in this range, though the rooms are smartly furnished and the restaurant offers live entertainment.

Dynasty Inn (☎ 747 3000; dynasty@tm.net.my; 2865-D Jl Sultanah Zainab; s & d from RM100;) Modern high-rise near the better-value Crystal Lodge. Rooms with a view of the river are overpriced at RM150. There's a restaurant and a craft shop downstairs.

Hotel Sentosa (☎ 744 3200; 3180-A Jl Sultan Ibrahim; s/d from RM60/70;) A fairly basic place, but it offers a reasonable standard of comfort for the price and is handy for the bus stations at the southern edge of town.

Mandarin Hostel (☎ 748 2317; 7083-A Jl Sri Cemerlang; s & d RM60;) Despite the name, it's not a hostel, but a simple little hotel down a side street in a very quiet part of town. Rooms are unspectacular, but clean and comfortable.

Hotel Anda (☎ 747 7600; hotelanda@hotmail.com; 2529-A Jl Kebun Sultan; s & d RM45;) A no-frills option offering clean, if rather spartan rooms with private bathrooms, but no hot water.

TOP-END

Diamond Puteri Hotel (☎ 743 9988; dphkb@tm.net.my; 9 Jl Post Office Lama; d/ste from RM170/320;) Close to the river, this huge, international-class hotel offers high standards of comfort at a reasonable price, with a sauna and gymnasium, as well as a couple of excellent restaurants.

Renaissance Hotel (☎ 746 2233; www.renaissancehotels.com; Jl Pasir Puteh; d/ste RM250/375;) Gigantic chain hotel on the southern fringe of town, offering all the comforts and facilities you would expect, including a fitness centre. It's in the same block as the Kota Seri Mutiara shopping mall.

New Pacific Hotel (☎ 735 1111; www.newpacifichotel.com.my; 26 Jl Pengkalan Chepa; s/d/suites from RM158/188/350;) Another monolithic chain hotel, similar in style to the Renaissance, though not quite up to the same standard. No charge for children under 12.

Hotel Perdana (☎ 748 5000; perdana3@tm.net.my; Jl Mahmud; d/suites from RM220/550;) Slightly dated grey concrete box just south of the city centre. There's a gym, sauna and tennis court, but it's overpriced for what's on offer and there are usually big discounts available.

Eating

Kota Bharu offers a rich choice of Malay, Thai, Indian and Chinese cuisine, scattered all around the city centre, ranging from simple hawker snacks to upscale restaurant fare. No visit is complete, though, without sampling the exotic delights of the town's famed night market (see Quick Eats below).

As Kota Bharu is a conservative Muslim city, alcohol is not widely available, but there are several Chinese restaurants around town that serve beer.

QUICK EATS

The best and cheapest Malay food in town is found at the night market opposite the central bus station. The stalls are set up in the evening and there's a wide variety regional specialities on offer, including *ayam percik* (marinated chicken on bamboo skewers) and *nasi kerabu* (rice with coconut, fish and spices). Unusual options include blue rice, squid-on-a-stick and banana *murtabak*. Bear in mind, though, that the whole thing closes down for evening prayers between 7 and 7.45 pm, and Muslims and non-Muslims alike are forced to vacate the premises.

At the time of writing, the market site had been earmarked for commercial development, so you may need to ask around for its new location.

More food stalls can be found next to the river opposite the Padang Merdeka, by the Jl Hamzah bus station and on Jl Mahmud, near the Hotel Perdana.

RESTAURANTS

Four Seasons Restaurant (☎ 743 6666; 5670 Jl Dusan Raja; set meals from RM48) A little pricey by local standards, but there's an excellent range of

Chinese dishes on offer, with steamboat (RM58 for two people) being the speciality of the house.

Sri Devi Restaurant (☎ 746 2980; 4213-F Jl Kebun Sultan; dishes from RM4) As popular with locals as it is with tourists, this is a great place for an authentic banana leaf curry and a mango lassi.

Seasons Restaurant (☎ 743 9988; Jl Post Office Lama; dishes from RM20) The Diamond Puteri Hotel's main restaurant, serving 1st-class Thai and Chinese food in elegant surroundings.

Natural Vegetarian Food (☎ 746 1902; 2848 Jl Ismail; dishes from RM3.50) Serves exactly what it says on the sign; you can help yourself to as much as you like from the all-vegetarian buffet, and wash it down with a glass of wheatgrass juice.

Meena Curry House (☎ 743 0173; 3377 Jl Gajah Mati; dishes from RM4) Another basic but good-value Indian restaurant, serving a wide range of curries, roti and soft drinks.

Medan Selera Kebun Sultan Food Court (☎ 746 1632; Jl Kebun Sultan; dishes from RM3) Big, bright and clean food court with a variety of mostly Chinese fare, though there are also a few Thai and Indian options. Beer is also available.

Muhibah Vegetarian Restaurant (☎ 748 3808; Jl Datok Pati; dishes from RM4) A good-value vegetarian option which serves up an array of Malay and Chinese food as well as fruit juices, while there's also a small bakery. There's another branch on Jl Pintu Pong.

Restoran Golden City (Jl Padang Garong; dishes from RM4). Basic Chinese eatery in the centre of town, serving stir-fries and seafood. It's also good for light snacks and a cold beer on a hot day.

Shopping

Kota Bharu is a centre for Malay crafts. Batik, *songket*, silverware, woodcarving and kite-making factories and shops are dotted around town.

One of the best places to see handicrafts is on the road north to Pantai Cahaya Bulan (PCB). There are a number of workshops, representing most crafts, stretched out along the road all the way to the beach. Unfortunately, it's hard to visit these without your own transport; an alternative is to join an organised tour (see p306).

The markets are a good place to buy handicrafts, if you bargain hard. Figure on RM5 to RM100 for decorative kites and RM30 to RM200 for real flying kites, RM7 to RM50 for batik pieces and from RM60 to RM100 per sq metre of silk batik.

The **central market** (Pasar Besar Siti Khadijah; 🕑 8am-6pm) here is one of the most colourful and active in Malaysia. It's in a modern building with traders selling fresh produce on the ground floor; and spices, brassware, batik and other goods on the floors above. Near the market is **Bazaar Buluh Kubu** (closed Friday), a good place to buy handicrafts.

The **old central market** (closed Friday) consists of a block of food stalls on the ground floor, and a selection of batik, *songket* and clothing upstairs.

Getting There & Away

AIR

The **Malaysia Airlines office** (☎ 744 7000) is opposite the clock tower on Jl Gajah Mati. There are direct flights to/from Kuala Lumpur (RM158). **Air Asia** (☎ 746 1671) has flights to KL from RM81.

BUS

The state-run SKMK bus company operates city and regional buses from the **central bus station** (off Jl Padang Garong), and long-distance buses from **Langgar bus station** (☎ 748 3807) in the south of the city. All other long-distance bus companies run from the Jl Hamzah external bus station. On arrival in Kota Bharu some buses will drop you at the central bus station, but they don't depart from there.

SKMK has ticket offices at all the bus stations. While long-distance departures are from the Langgar bus station, a few evening long-distance buses also go from the central bus station. Ask which station your bus departs from when you buy your ticket, and book as far ahead as possible, especially for the Butterworth and Penang buses.

SKMK has regular buses from the central bus station to Kuala Terengganu (RM9, 3 hours), Kuantan (RM20.50, 7 hours) and Gua Musang (RM10, 3 hours). Other SKMK buses leave from Langgar bus station. Buses to Johor Bahru (RM34, 10 hours), Singapore (RM40, 12 hours) and KL (RM30, 9 hours) leave at 8pm (also 9pm to KL). 'Business class' buses (with fewer seats) are available for these routes as well, and cost roughly 30% more. The bus to Butterworth and Penang (RM19.40, 8 hours) leaves at 9pm. Other destinations include Alor Setar, Lumut, Dungun, Mersing and Melaka.

The other companies cover many of the same routes. Buy your tickets at the Jl Hamzah external bus station; or at the Bazaar Buluh Kubu, where some of the companies have agents.

Most regional buses leave from the central bus station. Destinations include Wakaf Baharu (Nos 19 and 27, 70 sen), Rantau Panjang (No 29, RM2.70), Tumpat (No 19, RM1.30), Bachok (Nos 2B, 23 and 29, RM1.70), Pasir Puteh (No 3, RM2.50), Jerteh (No 3, RM3.50) and Kuala Krai (No 5, RM4). Note that some of these may be identified by destination rather than number.

Thailand

The Thailand border is at Rantau Panjang (Sungai Golok on the Thai side), reached by bus from Kota Bharu. Bus No 29 departs on the hour from the central bus station (RM2.80, 1½ hours). From Rantau Panjang walk across the border; it's about a kilometre to the station (a trishaw costs RM5). Share-taxis from Kota Bharu to Rantau Panjang cost RM16 per car and take 45 minutes.

From Sungai Golok there is a train to Surat Thani at 6.30am, to Bangkok at 11.55am and an express train to Bangkok at 2.40pm. All stop at Hat Yai and Surat Thani.

An alternative route into Thailand is via Pengkalan Kubor, on the coast. It's more time-consuming and very few travellers go this way (see p311).

CAR

Car hire companies:

Avis (☎ 748 4457; Hotel Perdana)

Budget (☎ 773 7312; Sultan Ismail Petra Airport)

TAXI

The taxi stand is on the southern side of the central bus station, and there is an overflow stand during the day at the night market site. Although private cars will also offer their services, it's best to take an official taxi as these are cheaper and safer.

Taxi destinations and costs per car include Butterworth (RM180), KL (RM200), Kuala Terengganu (RM60) and Kuantan (RM120).

Those who plan to catch an early morning train should arrange for the taxi to Wakaf Baharu the night before they plan to leave, as it's extremely difficult to find a taxi on the street in the early morning.

TRAIN

The nearest station to Kota Bharu is **Wakaf Baharu** (☎ 719 6986). There is a daily express train all the way to KL at 3.50pm. It stops at Kuala Lipis, Jerantut and Gemas before arriving in KL at 4.50am the following day. There is also a daily express to Singapore at 8.24pm making the same stops en route before arriving at 9.40am the following day.

A local train leaves daily at 5.47am and stops at almost every station before arriving at Gemas at 7.25pm. There are also two local trains daily that only go as far as Gua Musang, one at 4am and one at 1.22pm. From there, you can catch an ongoing express train that evening to KL or Singapore, or wait until the following morning and continue south on a local train.

Note that the national railway company (KTM) schedule changes every six months, so it's a good idea to double-check departure times with the train station at Wakaf Baharu. KTM has a ticket office (counter 5) at Kota Bharu's Jl Hamzah bus station. See p569 for train timetables and fare details.

Getting Around

The airport is 9km from town. You can take bus No 9 from the old central market; a taxi costs RM15.

Most city buses leave from the middle of the old central market, on the Jl Hilir Pasar side; or from opposite the Bazaar Buluh Kubu.

Trishaws are still a common sight on the city streets. A short journey of up to 1km costs RM3.

AROUND KOTA BHARU

Masjid Kampung Laut

Reputed to be the oldest mosque in Peninsular Malaysia, **Masjid Kampung Laut** was built about 300 years ago by Javanese Muslims as thanks for a narrow escape from pirates. Built entirely of wood, without the use of nails, the mosque contains some impressive woodcarvings.

It originally stood at Kampung Laut, just across the river from Kota Bharu, but each year the monsoon floods caused considerable damage to the mosque, and in 1968 it was moved to a safer location. It now stands about 10km inland at Kampung Nilam Puri, a local centre for religious study. Note that entry is forbidden to non-Muslims.

To get there, take bus Nos 5 or 44 (RM1.50) from Kota Bharu's central bus station and get off at Nilam Puri. Try to go in the morning, when the mosque is least crowded.

Beaches

PANTAI CAHAYA BULAN (PCB)

PCB is a Malay abbreviation that sounds far more appealing translated into English: the Beach of Passionate Love. At least that's what it was once called. Pantai Cinta Berahi is now known as **Pantai Cahaya Bulan** (Moonlight Beach), in keeping with Islamic sensitivities. Fortunately, the same initials apply and everyone refers to it as PCB.

PCB is 10km north of Kota Bharu, only 30 minutes by bus. It's a shabby place, though, and the litter-strewn beach isn't overly enticing. **PCB Resort** (☎ 774 2020; chalets from RM79; ❄) is a basic beach-front option, if you do wish to stay, while there's a string of food stalls along the beach.

To get there, take bus No 10 (90 sen) from behind the Handicraft Village in Kota Bharu. A taxi costs RM15.

THE EAST COAST HOUSE

For centuries, the east coast of Malaysia was strongly influenced by both Thai and Cambodian culture, and the most obvious legacy of this exchange can be seen in the distinctive architecture of the east coast states of Kelantan and Terengganu. Traditional east coast village houses have steep roofs, often with terracotta tiles, and curved gable ends, just like those found in Thailand. There are two kinds of village house, the so-called 'bachelor house' *(rumah bujang)* which has six posts holding up the roof, and the larger 'veranda house' *(rumah serambi)*, with twelve posts. The posts raise the houses more than 2m above the ground, and they are often linked together and attached to the main village house, the *rumah ibu*. The interiors of the houses are divided up by bamboo screens, while the carved wooden panels of the outside walls are fitted with finely cut fretwork windows. The entrance is reached by means of wooden steps, at the bottom of which there is usually a large urn of water and a ladle, for visitors to wash their feet.

PANTAI IRAMA

Pantai Irama (Beach of Melody) at Bachok has landscaped gardens along the foreshore and is popular with day-trippers. It's one of the best beaches around Kota Bharu for swimming, but otherwise it's nothing special. **Motel Irama Bachok** (☎ 778 8462; s & d from RM75; ❄) offers reasonable value accommodation.

From the central bus station in Kota Bharu, bus Nos 23 and 39 (RM1.70) run out to the beach.

OTHER BEACHES

Thirteen kilometres from Kota Bharu and 3km beyond the airport, **Pantai Dasar Sabak** is a beach with a history. On 7 December 1941, the Pacific theatre of WWII commenced on this beach when Japanese troops stormed ashore, a full hour and a half before the sun rose over Pearl Harbor.

Pantai Dalam Rhu, sometimes known as Pantai Bisikan Bayu (Beach of Whispering Breeze) is near the fishing village of Semerak, not too far from the Terengganu state border. **Pantai Seri Tujuh** is a pleasant stretch of beach on a long spit of land, with a quiet bay behind. It's not far from the Thailand border and there are a few traditional villages close by.

Tumpat District

Tumpat district is a major agricultural area bordering Thailand, and the Thai influence is very noticeable. Small villages are scattered among the picturesque rice fields, and there are several interesting Thai Buddhist temples, such as Wat Phothivihan. Pengkalan Kubor is an exit point for Thailand, while Tumpat town is the terminus of the railway line, although it has no hotels.

TEMPLES

Claimed to be one of the largest Buddhist temples in Southeast Asia, **Wat Phothivihan** boasts a 40m-long reclining Buddha statue, erected in 1973. The statue itself is unremarkable, but the novelty of finding a wat in strongly Muslim Kelantan is enough to add some interest. There is a resthouse for use by sincere devotees, for a donation.

To get to Wat Phothivihan, take bus Nos 19 or 27 from Kota Bharu to Chabang Empat. Get off at the crossroads and turn left (southwest). Walk 3.5km along this

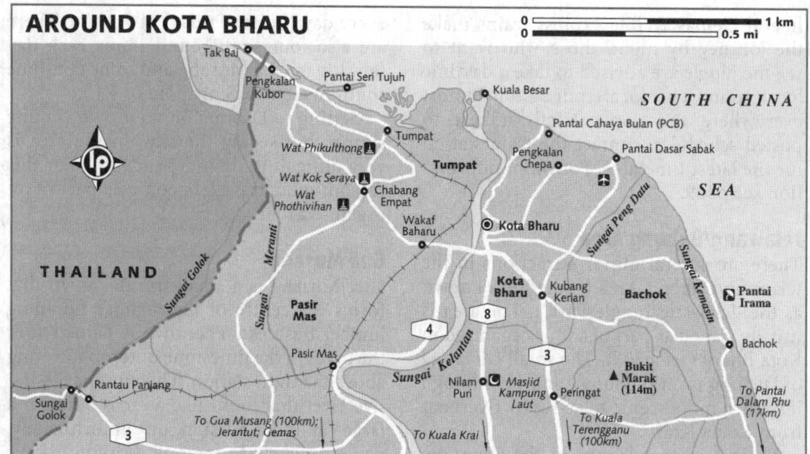

road, through interesting villages and paddies, until you reach Kampung Jambu and the reclining Buddha (about one hour). A taxi to the wat from Chabang Empat, if you can find one, costs RM4.

Thai-influenced temples dot the region, and **Wesak Day** (a celebration of Buddha's life, which is usually held in April or May) is a particularly good time to visit these temples.

At Chabang Empat, if you take the turn to the right (north) at the light in front of the police station, you will come to **Wat Kok Seraya** after about 1km. This wat houses a modest standing Buddha. Continuing north about 4km towards Tumpat, you will come to **Wat Phikulthong**, housing an impressive gold, standing Buddha. You can get to both wats on bus No 19; continue past Chabang Empat and ask the driver to let you off.

PENGKALAN KUBOR

Right on the Thai border, Pengkalan Kubor is the immigration checkpoint for this little-used back route into Thailand. During the day a large car ferry (RM1 for pedestrians) crosses the river over to busy Tak Bai in Thailand. From Kota Bharu, take bus No 27 or 43 (RM1.80) from the central bus station.

Waterfalls

There are a number of waterfalls in the Pasir Puteh area. **Jeram Pasu** is the most popular; to reach it you have to follow an 8km path from Kampung Padang Pak Amat, about 35km south of Kota Bharu en route to Pasir Puteh. Bus No 3 (RM2.90) from Kota Bharu's central bus station will take you as far as Padang Pak Amat. Other falls in this area include **Jeram Tapeh**, **Cherang Tuli** and **Jeram Lenang**.

EAST-WEST HIGHWAY

The East-West Hwy (Lebuhraya) starts near Kota Bharu and runs roughly parallel to the Thai border, eventually meeting Route 76 at the town of Gerik. It's something of an engineering masterpiece, and the views from the highway are often superb, including the vast expanse of Tasik Temenggor, a reservoir similar in appearance to Terengganu's Tasik Kenyir. The best way to travel this route, without your own car, is to take any bus between Kota Bharu and Gerik (or between Tanah Merah and Gerik). From Kota Bharu, buses to Ipoh, Alor Setar and Butterworth/Penang use this route.

JUNGLE RAILWAY

Known as the 'jungle railway' or the 'east coast railway', this line traverses Peninsular Malaysia's mountainous, jungle-clad interior. The line is an engineering marvel and the views are often superb – it's well worth the trip if you have the time.

Commencing in Tumpat, near Kota Bharu, the line runs through Kuala Krai, Gua Musang, Kuala Lipis and Jerantut (the access point for Taman Negara), and eventually meets the Singapore–KL railway line at Gemas. While express trains make the journey by night, those who want to see the jungle are advised to take a daytime local train. The local trains stop almost everywhere and don't strictly adhere to posted schedules; contact the train station for the latest timetable. For more information see p309.

Jelawang/Dabong Area

There are several minor attractions in the Jelawang/Dabong Area (sometimes known as the 'Jelawang Jungle Park'). The area is usually visited as part of a tour organised in Kota Bharu (see p306). The small *kampung* of Dabong is on the jungle railway, though it's much more scenic to arrive by riverboat from Kuala Krai.

There are several caves in the limestone outcrops a few kilometres southeast of town. Of these, the most impressive is **Stepping Stone Cave**, a narrow 30m corridor through a limestone wall that leads to a hidden grotto and then on to **Kris Cave**, named for a stalactite that resembles a kris. These two caves should not be attempted by those with claustrophobia. **Gua Ikan** (Fish Cave) is the most accessible of the caves and is consequently covered with graffiti by local youths. You may be able to find a local guide in Dabong to take you out to the caves (there is no public transport), but it's better to visit them as part of a tour from Kota Bharu.

From Dabong, you can cross Sungai Galas for 70 sen and take a minivan (RM2) out to the **falls** on 1422m-high Gunung Stong. The main falls are a 20-minute climb past the forgettable Perdana Satong Resort. A further 45 minutes of climbing brings you to the top of the falls and a camp site. From here you can make longer excursions to the summit of **Gunung Stong** and the upper falls.

Rumah Rehat Dabong (☎ 744 0725; s & d from RM20; ❄) is the only place to stay; ask at the district office opposite the resthouse. There's the usual collection of food stalls near Dabong station.

There are four trains to Dabong every day from Wakaf Baharu, a journey of between two and four hours. Alternatively, take the first morning train as far as Kuala Krai, and hop on a boat to Dabong for a more scenic three-hour jungle cruise. Boats depart 10am daily except Friday (RM5). In the opposite direction, the boat leaves Dabong every day (except Friday) at 7.30am. There are also four southbound trains each day (all stop in Gua Musang and some continue south to Gemas, Singapore or KL).

Getting to Dabong on your own is quite simple, but seeing the sites in the area is very difficult to do independently. For this reason, most travellers come as part of an organised tour (see p306).

Gua Musang

Gua Musang is a small frontier town that forms the centre of the region's booming lumber business. The town is named after the caves in the limestone outcrop towering above the train station. The *musang* is a native civet that looks like a cross between a large cat and a possum, but unfortunately, you're unlikely to see one as hunters have killed off most of these cave dwellers.

It is possible to explore the caves, but it is a very steep, hazardous climb to the entrance, which is above the *kampung* next to the railway line, 150m from the train station (walk south along the train tracks). Don't attempt the climb in wet conditions and be sure to take a torch (flashlight). A guide is recommended and local children will usually offer their services for RM5 to RM10.

Once you complete the dangerous climb to the caves, you'll have to shimmy through a narrow opening and do some scrambling to reach the main chamber, which extends some 150m before opening onto the opposite side of the mountain. There are no views, but the chamber is impressive and a good guide can point out rocks that resemble various animals.

There are several hotels on the main road that leads away from the train station. The best of these is **Evergreen Hotel** (☎ 912 2273; s/d from RM40/50; ❄) on the left just before the bend in the road. Farther down this road, around the bend on the right, **Hotel Usaha** (☎ 912 4003; s & d from RM50; ❄) is another reasonable option.

Bus No 57 to/from Kota Bharu costs RM10. Bus No 52 to/from Kuala Lipis costs RM7. Gua Musang is also on the jungle railway. Northbound local trains depart at 7.25am and 12.30pm; northbound expresses depart at 6.20am and 6.59 and 9.49pm; southbound locals depart at 5.20 and 11.50am; and southbound expresses depart at 2.30 and 4.42am and 11.34pm.

Sarawak

CONTENTS

The name 'Borneo' has long meant magic to travellers, and if you skip Sarawak you'll miss something special. The state has superb national parks, one of the most pleasant cities in Asia and a diverse, thriving tribal culture whose hospitality to strangers is unmatched. Independent travel is easy in Sarawak and the local tourist information service is excellent.

Sarawak isn't a lost paradise, however. Towns and surrounding areas are modernised and like most natural-resource economies, the state's timber and water supplies have suffered from environmental degradation. But the heart of Sarawak is still the rainforest, whose major arteries are mighty rivers snaking to the South China Sea. These rivers and their tributaries are the lifeline for the tribal longhouses, and despite the mass-transit express boats churning along huge rivers such as the Batang Rejang, traditional-style longboats (now motorised) remain the essential means of getting around upriver. Further inland and accessible by air, the Kelabit Highlands are another feature of Sarawak not to be missed. Then there's the state's system of national parks, that offers just about everything from wildlife, rainforest, beaches and rivers to vast caverns at Gunung Mulu and Niah.

Sarawak's indigenous peoples have a strong sense of identity and have made their mark in government, education and the media, keeping their heads up in the melange of cultures that make up modern Malaysia. A unique history has given Sarawak a character all its own, both part of Malaysia, yet distinct. Go there and explore. You won't regret it.

HIGHLIGHTS

- Getting to know **Kuching** (p320), an elegant city dotted with historic buildings, fine museums and great dining and drinking venues
- Trekking in clear mountain air and enjoying wonderful longhouse hospitality in the **Kelabit Highlands** (p380)
- Hiking the trails and beaches of **Bako National Park** (p334) – one of the state's finest parks, with lots of wildlife
- Climbing limestone pinnacles and hiking the Headhunters' Trail in **Gunung Mulu National Park** (p375)
- Searching out the world's largest flower – rafflesia – in **Gunung Gading National Park** (p343)
- Following the mighty **Batang Rejang** (p345) to isolated longhouse communities
- Exploring the beaches and estuary of Sarawak's pristine **Similajau National Park** (p358)

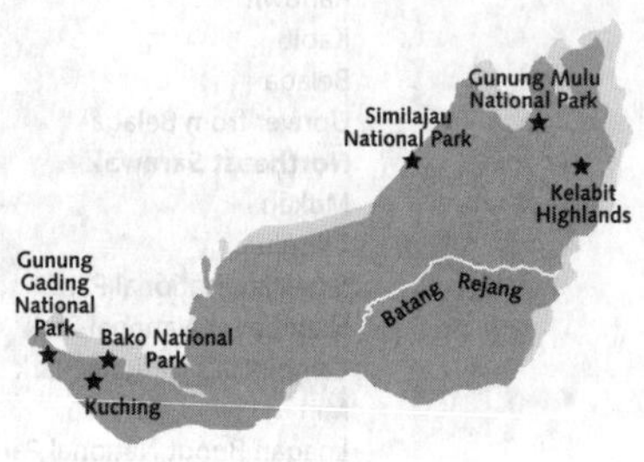

- TEL CODES: 82, 83, 84, 85, 86
- POPULATION: 2.01 MILLION
- AREA: 124,449 SQ KM

History

From the 15th until the early 19th century Sarawak was under the loose control of the sultanate of Brunei. It was only with the arrival of Sir James Brooke, the first of the three 'white raja', that it became a separate political region.

James Brooke, invalided from the British East India Company after being wounded in Burma, set off on a journey of discovery armed with a sizeable inheritance and a well-armed ship. He arrived in Sarawak in 1839 only to find the local viceroy, Prince Makota, under siege by rebellious Bidayuh and Malays of the Sungai (River) Sarawak. Brooke's fortuitous arrival put him in the perfect position to ingratiate himself with the local leaders. He put down the rebellion, and by way of reward the sultan of Brunei installed him as raja of Sarawak on 18 September 1842.

When James Brooke died in 1868 he was succeeded by his nephew, Charles Brooke. Through a policy of divide-and-rule among the local tribes, and the sometimes ruthless punishment of those who challenged his authority, Brooke extended his control and the borders of his kingdom during his long reign, which lasted until his death in 1917.

The third and last white raja was Charles Vyner Brooke, second son of Charles Brooke.

Sarawak's period as the personal kingdom of the Brooke family ended with the arrival of the Japanese in WWII. When the Japanese forces capitulated in August 1945, Sarawak was placed under Australian military administration until April 1946, when Charles Vyner Brooke, who had fled to Sydney during the war, made it known that he wanted to cede Sarawak to the British. The Bill of Cession was debated in the State Council (Council Negeri) and was finally passed in May 1946. On 1 July Sarawak officially became a British crown colony, thus putting Britain in the curious position of acquiring a new colonial possession at a time when it was shedding others.

Cession was followed by a brief but bloody anticessionist movement supported chiefly by Anthony Brooke – Charles Vyner Brooke's nephew and heir apparent to the white-raja title – and about 300 government officers who had resigned in protest at being excluded from the political process. The conflict climaxed in late 1949 when the governor of Sarawak, Duncan Stewart, was murdered by a Malay student. By 1951 the movement had lost its momentum and Anthony Brooke urged its supporters to give it up.

Along with Sabah (then North Borneo) and Brunei, Sarawak remained under British control when Malaya gained its independence in 1957. In 1962 the British proposed inclusion of the Borneo territories into the Federation of Malaya. At the last minute Brunei pulled out, as it (that is, Shell Oil) didn't want to see the revenue from its vast oil reserves channelled to the peninsula. At the same time, Malaya also had to convince the United Nations that Filipino claims to North Borneo were unfounded, as were Indonesia's claims that the formation of Malaysia was a British neocolonialist plot. The agreement was finally hammered out in July 1963, and in September of the same year the Federation of Malaysia was born.

This was also when the Indonesian Konfrontasi (Confrontation) with Malaysia erupted. The Konfrontasi was proclaimed by the Indonesian president of the time, Achmed Soekarno, and aimed to violently destabilise the fledgling state. Indonesian paramilitary raids and regular-army attacks across Kalimantan's border with Sarawak and Sabah continued until 1966. At its height 50,000 British, Australian and New Zealand forces were deployed in the border area, where some horrific confrontations occurred.

Internally, Sarawak also faced conflict during the early 1960s. The state had a large population of impoverished Chinese peasant farmers and labourers, and it was these people who found appeal in the North Kalimantan Communist Party, which supported guerrilla activity. Communist aspirations in Borneo were killed off, however, after the collapse of the Indonesian Communist Party in 1965, after which time Indonesians and Malaysians combined forces to drive communists out of their bases in Sarawak.

Today, Sarawak is doing better than its neighbour, Sabah. Kuching has weathered the Asian financial flu of the late 1990s, a situation that has given state leaders some pause in their grandiose development plans.

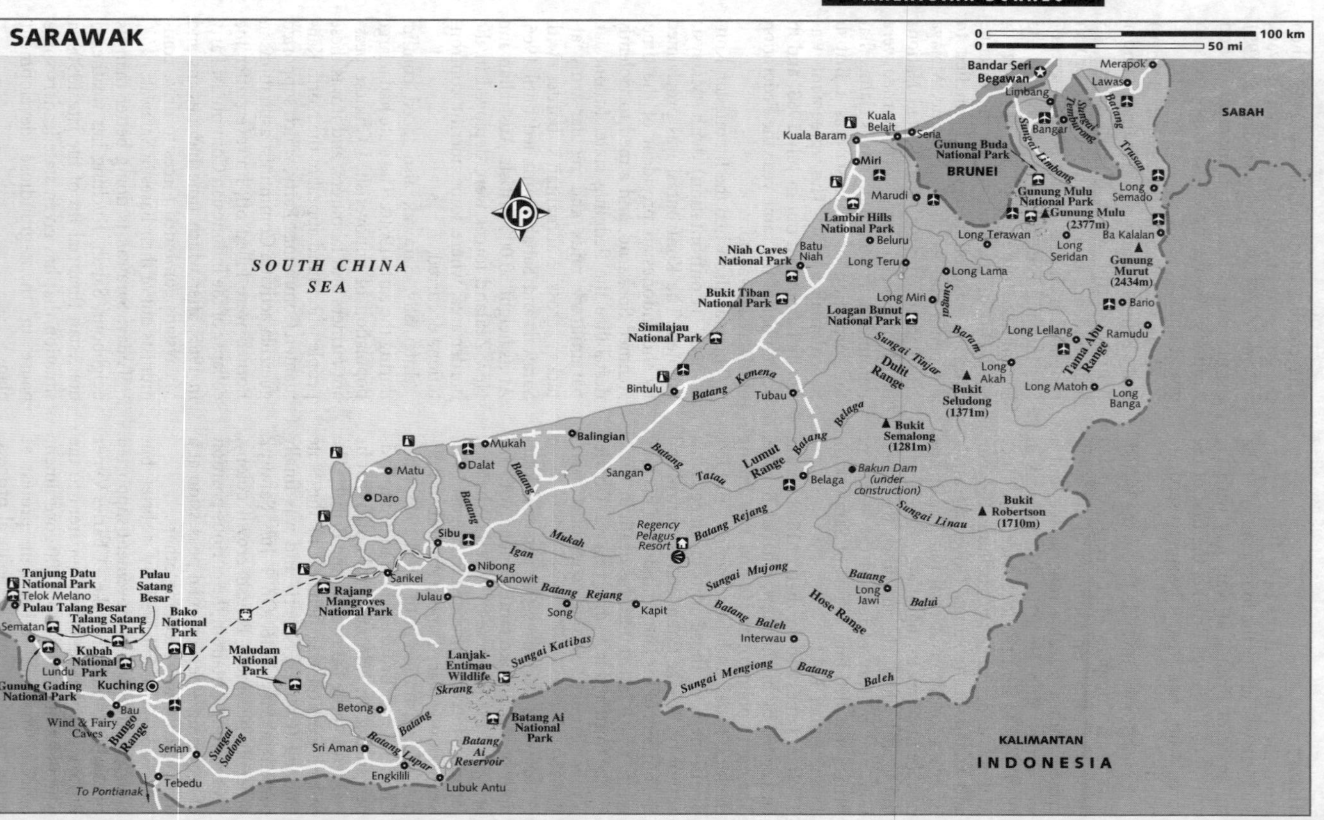
SARAWAK
0 100 km
0 50 mi
SABAH
BRUNEI
KALIMANTAN
INDONESIA
SOUTH CHINA SEA
Bandar Seri Begawan
Merapok
Lawas
Limbang
Bangar
Sungai Temburong
Batang Trusan
Sungai Limbang
Kuala Belait
Seria
Kuala Baram
Gunung Buda National Park
Miri
Marudi
Gunung Mulu National Park
Gunung Mulu (2377m)
Long Semado
Lambir Hills National Park
Beluru
Long Terawan
Long Seridan
Ba Kalalan
Gunung Murut (2434m)
Niah Caves National Park
Batu Niah
Long Teru
Long Lama
Bukit Tiban National Park
Long Miri
Sungai Baram
Bario
Loagan Bunut National Park
Similajau National Park
Long Lellang
Ramudu
Sungai Tinjar
Dulit Range
Tama Abu Range
Long Akah
Bukit Seludong (1371m)
Long Matoh
Long Banga
Bintulu
Batang Kemena
Tubau
Batang Belaga
Bukit Semalong (1281m)
Balingian
Mukah
Dalat
Matu
Daro
Batang Mukah
Sangan
Batang Tatau
Lumut Range
Belaga
Bakun Dam (under construction)
Sungai Linau
Bukit Robertson (1710m)
Regency Pelagus Resort
Batang Rejang
Sibu
Batang Igan
Nibong
Kanowit
Sarikei
Julau
Batang Rejang
Song
Kapit
Sungai Mujong
Batang Balui
Long Jawi
Hose Range
Batang Baleh
Interwau
Sungai Mengiong
Batang Baleh
Tanjung Datu National Park
Telok Melano
Pulau Talang Besar
Pulau Satang Besar
Talang Satang National Park
Bako National Park
Sematan
Kubah National Park
Lundu
Rajang Mangroves National Park
Maludam National Park
Lanjak-Entimau Wildlife
Sungai Katibas
Skrang
Gunung Gading National Park
Kuching
Bau
Wind & Fairy Caves
Bungo Range
Serian
Sungai Sadong
Betong
Batang Lupar
Sri Aman
Engkilili
Batang Ai National Park
Batang Ai Reservoir
Lubuk Antu
Tebedu
To Pontianak

DAVID ANDREW

Rafflesia (p343) in bloom, Gunung Gading National Park, Sarawak

Boatman, **Sungai Sarawak** (p323), Kuching

MARK DAFFEY

JANE SWEENEY

Kuching mosque (p325)

MARK DAFFEY

Detail of domed ceiling in the **Kuching mosque** (p325)

MARK

Traditional **longhouse** (p340), Sarawak

JANE SWEENEY

Woman of the **Penan people** (p374)

DAVID ANDREW

Sunday Market (p326) stalls, Kuching

Man of the **Iban tribe** (p345)

LOU

Climate

Sarawak has a hot and humid climate, with temperatures generally between 27° and 32°C. The heaviest rainfall occurs with the northeast monsoon from November to February, though it rains throughout the year and averages about 350mm to 450mm annually. It's cooler up in the hills, especially in the Kelabit Highlands.

Visas & Permits

Even though Sarawak is part of Malaysia, it has its own immigration controls. You will have to clear immigration every time you cross a border – travelling to or from the peninsula, Sabah, Brunei and, of course, Indonesia.

The **Indonesian Consulate** (☎ 241734; 111 Jl Tun Haji Openg; 🕑 8.30am-noon & 2-4pm Mon-Fri) in Kuching is south of the city centre. Most nationalities do not require visas to enter Indonesia by air at Pontianak, or by land at Entikong, where two-month entry permits are issued. A visa is required if entering Indonesia through a nonrecognised crossing. Two-month Indonesian visas cost RM160 and require three photographs. Visas take a day to process.

The separate controls are designed to protect indigenous people from being swamped by migrants from the peninsula and elsewhere. A major new reason for the controls is smuggling – the state government has begun to aggressively protect selected species of plants and animals from poachers.

On arrival, travellers of most nationalities will be granted a one-month stay. Since you could easily spend a month exploring Sarawak, you may have to extend your visa. Extensions can be granted at the immigration offices in Kuching (p321) and in Miri (p365).

If you plan to visit any of the longhouses above Kapit on the Rejang or Baleh Rivers, you will need a permit, which can be easily obtained in Kapit free of charge. Permits are also required from the district office in Miri or Marudi for travel to the Sungai Baram beyond Marudi.

National Parks

The Malaysian jungles contain some of the world's oldest undisturbed areas of rainforest. It's estimated they've existed for about 100 million years, since they remained largely unaffected by the far-reaching climatic changes brought on elsewhere by the Ice Ages.

Fortunately, quite large areas of some of the best and most spectacular of these rainforests have been made into national parks, in which all commercial activities are banned.

The parks closest to Kuching are probably the best value overall: Bako for beaches and wildlife, Kubah for unspoiled nature and Gunung Gading for a chance viewing of the rarely blooming rafflesia flower. Always take along your passport for registering at the park.

The most recently created parks, Bukit Tiban, Gunung Buda, Maludan and Rajang are not yet open to visitors.

Bako National Park (27 sq km) Trails and beaches to explore, about two hours north of Kuching.

Batang Ai National Park (240 sq km) This park is habitat for wild orang-utans deep in Iban country, some 250km east of Kuching.

Bukit Tiban National Park (80 sq km) A recovered logged area reforested and given park status in 2000, 50km northeast of Bintulu.

Gunung Buda (62 sq km) This park juts up on the northeast side of Gunung Mulu National Park and contains similar karst formations and caves to those found at Mulu.

Gunung Gading National Park (54 sq km) On Sarawak's extreme western tip near Sematan, a major attraction here is the rafflesia flower.

Gunung Mulu National Park (529 sq km) Sarawak's largest national park, located east of Marudi near the Brunei border.

Kubah National Park (22 sq km) Hiking trails in a pristine rainforest and clear rivers to swim in, 20km west of Kuching.

Lambir Hills National Park (69 sq km) Famous for its diverse plant species, this park is 32km south of Miri.

Loagan Bunut National Park (10.7 sq km) Includes Sarawak's largest freshwater lake, in the Miri hinterland.

Maludam National Park (431 sq km) A large sanctuary about 70km northeast of Sri Aman, protected to provide habitat for the red banded langur monkey and other primates.

Niah Caves National Park (32 sq km) Massive caves and source of the raw ingredient for bird's nest soup; about halfway between Bintulu and Miri.

Rajang Mangroves National Park (94 sq km) Provides a mangrove habitat for a variety of species, on the coast west of Sarikei in the Batang Rejang estuary.

Similajau National Park (75 sq km) A coastal park with hiking trails, beaches and rivers – known for saltwater crocodiles – northeast of Bintulu.

Talang Satang National Park (194 sq km) A large marine park to protect sea turtles, including the islands of Talang-Talang Besar, Talang-Talang Kecil and Satang Besar, off the coast between Sanbutong and Semantan.
Tanjung Datu National Park (13 sq km) Sarawak's smallest national park, with beautiful beaches, clear rivers and coral reefs, near Gunung Gading National Park.

Currently, Batang Ai, Loagan Bunut and Tanjung Datu do not have accommodation or facilities for visitors, though it's possible to visit them through travel agencies. A permit is required to visit Talang Satang, available at Kuching's **visitors' information centre** (☎ 082-410944).

PARK FEES & ACCOMMODATION

National park fees and accommodation rates were revised in July 2002. Entry passes of RM10 for adults and RM5 for children are issued at park entrances. The penalty for visiting national parks without a permit is a fine of RM1000 *and* six months in prison so always check in at the park headquarters.

Accommodation charges for national parks have been standardised across Sarawak. Most of the incidental charges are small and go towards upkeep of the park, but they can add up. There's a 10% non-refundable reservation charge for accommodation bookings, or the full amount if the total is less than RM10. In other words, if you book a room in a chalet for one night at RM120, you'll end up spending RM132. It's recommended that you book accommodation in advance either through a tourist information centre or a **National Parks & Wildlife office** (Kuching ☎/fax 082-248088; Miri ☎ 085-434184; fax 085-434179). Sarawak's **Forest Department** (www.forestry.sarawak.gov.my) has an excellent website with a section on national parks.

Accommodation

Top-end accommodation and restaurants in Sarawak add a total of 15% government tax onto their basic charges; the total you pay is the 'net' price. Published rates are mostly '++', meaning the 5% and 10% taxes have to be added. Many hotels routinely quote net rates, however, and promotions often include the tax as well. In this chapter we've given the (net) rate you'd actually pay at the time of writing.

Getting There & Away

There are regular flights to Kuching from KL, Johor Bahru and Singapore, as well as flights into other centres such as Miri and Sibu. For details, see Getting There & Away sections throughout this chapter, especially the entry under Kuching.

Getting Around

AIR

Malaysia Airlines has a comprehensive network of domestic flights, including its rural air service, which consists of 18-seater Twin Otter aircraft. The Malaysian government subsidises domestic flights, which can be a real bargain. This is just as well, because flying is sometimes the only practical means of reaching a remote area. If you plan to visit places such as Bario and Long Lellang in the highlands, chances are you'll be going by plane.

Places in Sarawak served by Malaysia Airlines flights are Ba Kelalan, Bario, Belaga, Bintulu, Kuching, Lawas, Limbang, Long Banga, Long Lellang, Long Seridan, Marudi, Miri, Mukah, Mulu and Sibu.

Twin Otter flights into the interior are subject to the vagaries of the weather. In the dry season (April to September) weather is usually not a problem, but in the wet season it can rain continuously for a few days. Make sure you have time to allow for delays.

During school holidays (mid-May to mid-June and late October to early December) it is virtually impossible to get a seat on *any* Twin Otter flight into the interior at short notice. You could turn up at the airport in the hope of a cancellation.

Flights to Mulu and Bario suffer from overbooking year-round. Vision Air, operating for a little over a year, offered an alternative for the Mulu and Bario routes, but it changed management in 2003 and is now run by Hornbill Skyways. Check at the tourist information centres for an update on fares and routes or phone the **Hornbill Skyways office** (☎ 082-455737) in Kuching.

BOAT

Transport by boat has long been the traditional way of getting around in Sarawak, though this has diminished in recent years as roads improved. War parties and traders used to rely on brute strength to get them up and down Sarawak's rivers; these days

TREKKING IN SARAWAK

Sarawak offers a range of jungle-trekking options for the fit and adventurous, as well as more-gentle ambles for those who don't aspire to superhuman status. Hiking through rainforest in hot, humid and sometimes wet conditions can be exhausting, and you'll probably have leeches for company. It may not suit everybody. The rewards are valuable though – you'll see superb rainforest and alpine plateaus in the Kelabit Highlands, stone forests and jagged peaks in Gunung (Mt) Mulu National Park. As well, there is the opportunity to visit fascinating longhouses.

Many of the treks mentioned in this chapter require a guide. A good guide should be able to gauge your abilities and have the confidence to push you a little, rather than taking the easiest way as a matter of course. In fact many people find that they get stronger the longer they stay in the jungle, and if you've done a night walk in the rainforest (this is highly recommended!), trails that previously seemed treacherous will be that much easier. When crossing those slippery log bridges, try taking off your shoes and doing it in socks – you'll get a much better grip (bare feet are as slippery as shoes).

The following information will help with planning.

When to Go

Although the wettest months in Sarawak are from November to January, the timing of monsoon seasons has been less consistent in recent years. Sarawak has high rainfall year-round and you should be prepared for heavy rain on one or more days of your stay. Flights in and out of Gunung Mulu and Bario will be cancelled if the weather is poor, so be prepared to be stranded for a couple of days on the return trip.

What to Bring

There are no special equipment requirements to enjoy walking in the region, but it can get cold at night and rain for days on end – take a waterproof jacket. Good running shoes are preferable to stiff, heavy walking boots, and a pair of thongs (flip-flops) is useful for going in and out of longhouses. Wear light cotton clothing and carry a light pullover and trousers for the evenings. If camping or staying in a longhouse, you will need a sleeping bag.

Leeches will accompany you on many walks – see the boxed text That Clinging Feeling on p579.

If you're sleeping in the jungle, a camping poncho is a definite asset. This is a lightweight sheet of tough material that is large enough for you to cocoon yourself in at night yet still breathe. It's perfect for keeping the creepy-crawlies (especially leeches) out. A good poncho costs about RM50 and should be available at camping supply shops in Miri and Kuching.

Most of your load's weight will be water. Remember to drink a lot to replace the fluids lost by sweating. It's also generally safe to drink water from streams (upstream from the longhouse, of course); ask your guide for advice. A good torch (flashlight) is a must at night; insect repellent and sunscreen will also be useful. For other tips on getting prepared, see the Jungle Trekking Tips boxed text (p537).

Responsible Trekking

Remember the golden rule of rubbish: if you carried it in, you should carry it out. Don't overlook those easily forgotten or inconvenient items, such as silver paper, plastic wrapping, water bottles, sanitary napkins and so forth. Never bury your rubbish – it may be out of sight, but it won't be out of reach of animals.

Where there's a toilet, please use it. Where there isn't one, bury your waste. Dig a small hole 15cm deep and at least 100m from any watercourse. Consider carrying a lightweight trowel for this purpose. Cover the waste with soil and a rock. Use toilet paper sparingly and bury it as well. If the area is inhabited, ask locals if they have any concerns about your chosen toilet site.

The indigenous Penan people are allowed to hunt in Gunung Mulu; otherwise, hunting is illegal for everyone in national parks and reserves.

MALAYSIAN BORNEO

travel on larger rivers, such as the Rejang and Baram, is accomplished in fast passenger launches known by the generic term *ekspres* (express). These long, narrow boats carry around 100 people, and look a bit like ex-Soviet jumbo jets with the wings removed. Powered by turbo-charged V12 diesel engines (up to 1000 horsepower), they can travel up to 60km/h, scattering motorised canoes in their wake.

The air-conditioning on express boats can be extreme, so take something warm. You can ride outside on the roof, but watch out for sunburn. Video movies of varying bad taste are usually a feature of the trip.

Where and when the express boats can't go, river travel is still mainly by longboat, though these are now motorised. Longboats are a great way to get around, but note that they aren't called 'wideboats' – watch your balance getting in and out, especially with heavy gear.

Hiring a longboat is often your only option for reaching many spots. Be prepared to pay a fair bit for the experience, as fuel isn't cheap in remote areas (that is, most of Sarawak). Getting a group together to share costs can be worth the time and effort.

CAR & BUS

Travel by road in Sarawak is generally good, and the trunk road from Kuching to the Brunei border is surfaced all the way. Travellers arriving from elsewhere in Malaysia will be pleasantly surprised by the relative sanity of Sarawakian drivers.

There are plenty of buses per day travelling between Sibu, Bintulu and Miri – an estimated 70 companies operate on these routes. Sibu to Bintulu takes 3½ hours, Bintulu to Niah Caves takes two hours, Niah Caves to Miri is two hours and Miri to Kuala Baram (on the Brunei border) is one hour. For locals, the road between Kuching and Sibu (seven hours) has all but replaced express boats as the preferred route between the two cities. There are also buses heading west from Kuching to Bau, Lundu and Sematan, and north to Bako Bazaar (for Bako National Park). The tourist information centres in Kuching, Miri and Sibu have current information on bus schedules and fares.

Hitchhiking is possible in Sarawak, although traffic can be light. In this chapter we've indicated where hitching is feasible. However, hitching is never entirely safe and travellers who decide to hitch should understand that they are taking a small but potentially serious risk. People who do choose to hitch will be safer if they travel in pairs and let someone know where they're planning to go.

WEST SARAWAK

Kuching

☎ 082

Kuching means 'cat' in Malay, and Sarawak's capital lives by its name. The spotless city combines feline grace and charm with a certain capriciousness – Kuching is sure to toy with your expectations. Many travellers consider Kuching one of the most refined, attractive cities in Southeast Asia.

Whatever your impressions, Kuching is unique, a city unlike any other you'll see in Borneo. Residents clearly love their home and are fairly fond of each other too – a long custom of intermarriage, among other reasons, has encouraged an admirable level of racial and religious tolerance. Once the city's got its claws into you it's easy to spend more time here than planned – don't forget to get out and explore the rest of Sarawak.

Kuching is the best base from which to start exploring the state, and there's plenty to keep you busy for at least several days. Nearby are longhouses, caves and a number of excellent national parks, including Bako (especially good for seeing proboscis monkeys) and Gunung Gading (known for the rafflesia, the world's largest flower).

Built principally on the south bank of the Sungai Sarawak, Kuching was known as Sarawak in the 19th century. Before James Brooke settled here, the capital had been variously at Lidah Tanah and Santubong. Kuching was given its name in 1872 by Charles Brooke.

Although Kuching is quite a large city, the centre is compact and feels isolated from the suburbs by the river. Its landscaped parks and gardens make it as green a city as you'll find in Southeast Asia. Unlike some of the other large towns in Malaysian Borneo, Kuching's historic buildings escaped damage during WWII, and many have been tastefully renovated. The south bank of the river has been paved and landscaped and a peaceful promenade links the main attractions.

ORIENTATION

The main sights – and most of the city – are on the south bank of the Sungai Sarawak. Almost all attractions are within easy walking distance of each other. The western end is overlooked by the green-and-white Kuching Mosque, and is home to markets, local bus stations and museums. All hotels, places to eat, banks, airline offices and the main post office are between the mosque and the Great Cat of Kuching, 2km east. The waterfront is a quiet thoroughfare between the eastern and western parts of town.

Looking north across the river from the open-air market is the *istana* (palace); nearby, Fort Margherita is on a low hill and visible from most points along the waterfront; the Ministerial Complex is the drab multistorey building in the background.

Public buses or taxis are only really needed to reach the Cat Museum and Timber Museum in Petra Jaya (north of the river), the airport (about 12km away), the long-distance bus station (5km) and the wharf for the boat to Sibu (6km).

Maps

Periplus produces *Sarawak & Kuching* as part of its Malaysia Regional Maps series. It also has maps of Kuching, Bintulu, Miri, Sibu, Kapit and Gunung Mulu National Park that are usually available in bookshops in Kuching. The tourist information centre also has a good map of Sarawak, which includes a detailed map of Kuching.

For good, if outdated, topographic maps, try the **Lands & Survey Department** (Jabatan Ukar & Pemetaan; ☎ 420763), on the 7th floor of the state government offices, near the end of Jl Simpang Tiga, 3km south of town. Large-scale maps (1:750 000) of Sarawak cost RM5 per sheet; to obtain the more detailed 1:50,000 maps of various parts of the state you need security clearance from the police headquarters in the centre of town.

INFORMATION

Airline Offices

Air Asia (☎ 283222; www.airasia.com; Ground fl, Wisma Ho Ho Lim, 291 Jl Abell)

Dragon Air (☎ 233322; 1st fl, Wisma Bukit Mata Kuching, Jl Tunku Abdul Rahman)

Malaysia Airlines (☎ 244144; 215 Jl Song Thian Cheok; 🕓 8am-5pm Mon-Fri, 8am-1pm Sat) Can get very crowded; you're better off dealing with a travel agent.

Royal Brunei Airlines (☎ 243344; Jl Song Thian Cheok)

Singapore Airlines (☎ 240266; Ang Chang Bldg, Jl Tunku Abdul Rahman)

Bookshops

Mohamed Yahia & Sons (☎ 416928; Holiday Inn shopping arcade & Sarawak Plaza) Has the best range of books on Borneo and Malaysia.

Belle's Bookshop (☎ 423866; 2nd fl, Sarawak Plaza) Good range of titles and maps.

Immigration Offices

The **immigration office** (☎ 245661) for visa extensions is on the 2nd floor of the state government offices on Jl Simpang Tiga, about 3km south of the city centre, towards the airport.

To get there, catch a CLL (blue-and-white) bus No 6, 11, 14A or 14B from near the Kuching Mosque; the fare is RM1.

Internet Access

Cyber City (☎ 243549; Taman Sri Sarawak; RM6 per hr; 🕓 9am-midnight) A clean, friendly place with printing and scanning services, it's in a small alley off Jl Borneo opposite the Hilton.

Waterfront Cyber Café (RM4 per hr; 🕓 10am-midnight Mon-Fri, 9am-midnight Sat & Sun) In the old Sarawak Steamship Company building.

Laundry

For quick and efficient service, try the **City Laundry & Dry Cleaning** (☎ 462906; C51, Level 1, Taman Sri Sarawak Mall) just off Jl Borneo down one of the alleys. A 2kg load costs around RM14.

Medical Services

Sarawak General Hospital (☎ 257555; Jl Ong Kee Hui) Suitable for major emergencies only, not minor ailments.

Timberland Medical Centre (☎ 234991; Mile 3, Jl Rock) A private hospital with highly qualified staff.

Chan Clinic (☎ 240307; 98 Main Bazaar) Across from the Chinese History Museum on the waterfront, a good place for cuts and scrapes, and travel ailments.

Money

There's an exchange counter and a Maybank ATM at the airport. Banks will change travellers cheques but can be very slow. Banking hours are Monday to Friday from 9.30am to 3.30pm and Saturday from 9.30am to 11.30am. The Hongkong Bank (HSBC) and Standard & Chartered Bank have 24-hour ATMs. You're probably better off changing cash at moneychangers and some change

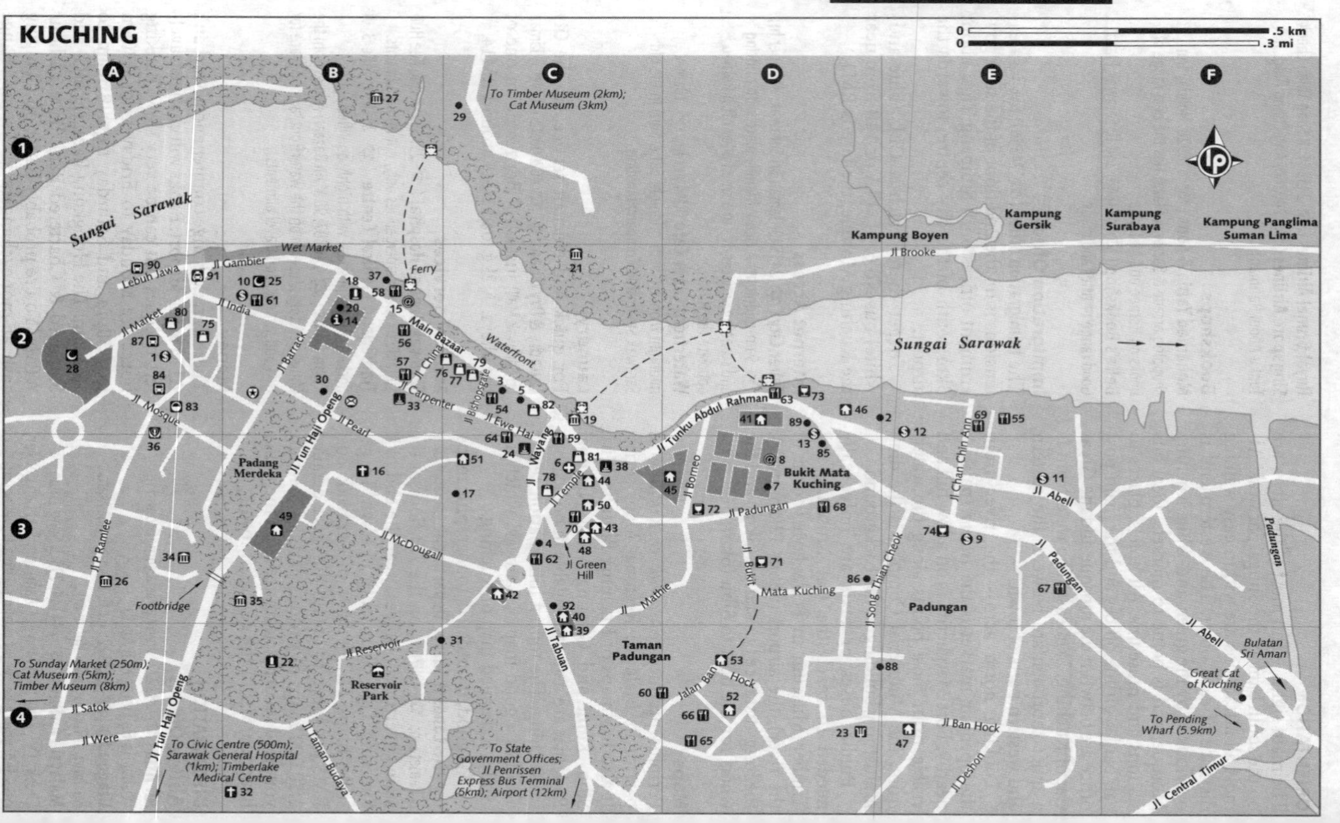
KUCHING
0 .5 km
0 .3 mi
To Timber Museum (2km); Cat Museum (3km)
Kampung Boyen
Kampung Gersik
Kampung Surabaya
Kampung Panglima Suman Lima
Sungai Sarawak
Sungai Sarawak
Jl Brooke
Wet Market
Ferry
Waterfront
Main Bazaar
Jl Gambier
Lebuh Jawa
Jl India
Jl Market
Jl Mosque
Jl Carpenter
Jl China
Jl Bishopsgate
Jl Ewe Hai
Jl Wayang
Jl Temple
Jl Barrack
Jl Pearl
Jl Tun Haji Openg
Padang Merdeka
Jl McDougall
Jl Reservoir
Reservoir Park
Jl Taman Budaya
Jl P Ramlee
Footbridge
Jl Satok
Jl Were
To Sunday Market (250m); Cat Museum (5km); Timber Museum (8km)
To Civic Centre (500m); Sarawak General Hospital (1km); Timberlake Medical Centre
To State Government Offices; Jl Penrissen Express Bus Terminal (5km); Airport (12km)
Jl Tabuan
Jl Green Hill
Jl Tunku Abdul Rahman
Jl Borneo
Jl Padungan
Bukit Mata Kuching
Jl Bukit Mata Kuching
Jl Mathie
Jalan Ban Hock
Taman Padungan
Jl Song Thian Cheok
Jl Chan Chin Ann
Jl Abell
Padungan
Padungan
Jl Ban Hock
Jl Deshon
Jl Central Timur
Great Cat of Kuching
Bulatan Sri Aman
To Pending Wharf (5.9km)

INFORMATION
Bank of Commerce ... 1 A2
Belle's Bookshop ... 2 D2
Borneo Adventure ... 3 C2
Borneo Exploration ... 4 C3
Borneo Inbound Tours & Travel ... (see 6)
Borneo Interland Travel ... 5 C2
Chan Clinic ... 6 C3
City Laundry & Dry Cleaning ... 7 D3
Cyber City ... 8 D3
Everrise Moneychanger ... 9 E3
Majid & Sons ... 10 B2
Maybank ... 11 E3
Mohamed Yahia & Sons ... (see 46)
Pacific Bank ... 12 E2
Standard Chartered Bank ... 13 D2
Visitors' Information Centre ... 14 B2
Waterfront Cyber Café ... 15 B2

SIGHTS & ACTIVITIES pp323-6
Anglican Cathedral ... 16 B3
Bishop's House ... 17 C3
Brooke Memorial ... 18 B2
Chinese History Museum ... 19 C2
Court House ... 20 B2
Fort Margherita ... 21 C2
Heroes' Monument ... 22 B4
Hindu Temple ... 23 D4
Hong San Temple ... 24 C3
Indian Mosque ... 25 B2
Islamic Museum ... 26 A3
Istana ... 27 B1
Kuching Mosque ... 28 A2
Orchid Garden ... 29 C1
Pavilion ... 30 B2
Red Crescent Building ... 31 B4
Roman Catholic Cathedral ... 32 B4
Sang Ti Miao Temple ... 33 B2
Sarawak Museum (New Wing) ... 34 A3
Sarawak Museum (Old Wing) ... 35 B3
Sikh Temple ... 36 A2
Square Tower ... 37 B2
Tua Pek Kong Temple ... 38 C3

SLEEPING pp327-8
B&B Inn ... 39 C4
Borneo Hotel ... 40 C3
Crowne Plaza Riverside Kuching ... 41 D2
Fata Hotel ... 42 C3
Goodwood Inn ... 43 C3
Harbour View Hotel ... 44 C3
Hilton Hotel ... 45 D3
Holiday Inn Kuching ... 46 D2
Hotel Grand Continental ... 47 E4
Mandarin Hotel ... 48 C3
Merdeka Palace Hotel ... 49 B3
River View Inn ... 50 C3
St Thomas Diocesan Rest House ... 51 C3
Supreme Hotel ... 52 D4
Telang Usan Hotel ... 53 D4

EATING pp328-9
Aunty Mary Kitchen ... 54 C2
Benson's Seafood Centre ... 55 E2
Biryani Café ... 56 B2
Chinese Food Centre ... 57 B2
D'Alife Restoran Sejahtera ... 58 B2
Denis' Place ... 59 C3
Hornbill's Corner Café ... 60 C4
Jubilee ... 61 B2
Junk ... 62 C3
Khatulistiwa Café ... 63 D2
Life Café ... 64 C3
Mukah Seafood Centre ... 65 D4
See Good Food Centre ... 66 D4
Tom's ... 67 E3
Top Spot Food Court ... 68 D3
Zhun San Yen Vegetarian Food Centre ... 69 E2
Zhun San Yen Vegetarian Food Centre ... 70 C3

DRINKING p330
Cottage ... 71 D3
De Tavern ... 72 D3
Riverbank Suites ... 73 D2
Royalist ... (see 72)
Soho ... 74 E3
Tribes Music Restaurant & Pub ... (see 46)

ENTERTAINMENT
Disco ... (see 63)

SHOPPING pp330-1
Atelier Gallery ... (see 81)
Electra House ... 75 A2
Galerie M ... 76 C2
Kelvin Gallery ... 77 C2
Medan Pelita Mall ... 78 C3
Nelsons Antiques & Jewellery ... 79 C2
Open Air Market ... 80 A2
Riverside Shopping Complex ... (see 41)
Sarakraf ... (see 2)
Sarawak Batik Art Shop ... 81 C3
Sarawak House ... 82 C2
Sarawak Plaza ... (see 2)
Siong Sports Trading ... (see 2)

TRANSPORT pp333-4
Borneo Highway Express ... 83 A2
CLL Buses ... 84 A2
Dragon Air ... 85 D3
Malaysia Airlines ... 86 D3
PB Ekspres ... (see 83)
Petra Jaya Bus Station ... 87 A2
Royal Brunei Airlines ... 88 D4
Singapore Airlines ... 89 D2
STC Buses ... 90 A2
Taxi Stand ... 91 A2
Teck Hun Motor ... 92 C3

travellers cheques. They also have more convenient hours than the banks and are open evenings and Sunday.

Majid & Sons (☎ 422402; 45 Jl India) Licensed moneychanger that doesn't charge a commission but only exchanges cash.

Everrise Moneychanger (☎ 233200; 199 Jl Padungan) Only exchanges cash.

Mohamed Yahia & Sons (☎ 416928; Lower Ground fl, 3 Sarawak Plaza) Changes travellers cheques at a slightly lower rate than cash.

Post

The main post office is in the centre of town on Jl Tun Haji Openg. It's open Monday to Friday from 8am to 4pm, Saturday from 8am to 6.30pm and on Sunday from 9am to 4pm; it gets very crowded on weekends.

Tourist Information

Kuching has excellent tourist information services. The **visitors' information centre** (☎ 410944/42; www.sarawaktourism.com; Sarawak Tourism Complex, Jl Tun Abang Haji Openg ; 🕑 8am-6pm Mon-Fri, 9am-3pm Sun & public holidays) is in the old courthouse. It's open from 9am to 4pm on Saturday, except for the 1st and 3rd Saturday of each month, when it's open till 3pm. The centre's staff are knowledgeable about local culture and can tell you when special events are scheduled and just about everything you need to know about travelling in Sarawak. They can supply lots of brochures, transport schedules and other information. The National Parks & Wildlife desk is in the same office and arranges accommodation at national parks. It's closed the first and third Saturday of each month.

The free *Official Kuching Guide* is an excellent publication produced locally by Travelcom Asia. It has a wealth of information on Kuching and nearby sights and is usually available in the arrivals hall at the airport, at tourist offices and at some hotel desks, but you may have to ask for it. To view it on the Internet go to www.borneotravel.com.

SIGHTS

Waterfront

The south bank of the Sungai Sarawak between the Khatulistiwa Café and the markets at the western end has been tastefully developed with a paved walkway, lawns and flowerbeds, a children's playground, cafés and food stalls. It's a quiet, pleasant place to walk or sit and watch the *tambang* (river ferries) with their lanterns glide past. In the evening its full of couples and families strolling by or eating snacks.

A *tambang* is a traditional double-oared boat, and these days motorised versions ferry passengers back and forth across the river all day until late. The river crossing costs 30 sen. Leave the exact change on the prow as you disembark. To hire a *tambang* for a river cruise, the charge is RM25 to RM30 for up to an hour – agree on the fare before you take the ride.

Sarawak Museum

Considered to be one of the best in Southeast Asia, the **museum** (☎ 244232; Jl Tun Haji Openg; admission free; ⏲ 9am-6pm) consists of two main sections, connected by a footbridge over Jl Tun Haji Openg. Both are well worth visiting.

Built in the style of a Normandy townhouse, the old wing was opened in 1891. The newer, air-conditioned wing features displays on the culture and lifestyle of Sarawak's many tribal peoples.

In the old wing you'll find stuffed and mounted animals (that look like they've been there since 1891), displays on longhouse life, with artefacts including skull trophies and photographs of tribal people from the early 20th century. There's a good collection of musical instruments. One of the best items is a reconstructed longhouse that's large enough to climb up on and explore. Arts on display include ceramics, brassware, Chinese jars and furniture, and a replica cave and description of harvesting birds' nests for soup. The museum presents slide shows and videos daily on a range of topics. There's also a souvenir and gift shop, which has a good range of postcards. The museum is closed on public holidays.

On the museum grounds past the old wing are pleasant gardens, pavilions and the **Heroes' Monument**, dedicated to fallen heroes of past military conflicts.

Islamic Museum

Islam has less hold on Sarawak than on the rest of Malaysia, but the excellent **Muzium Islam Sarawak** (☎ 244232; Jl P Ramlee; admission free; ⏲ 9am-6pm Sat-Thu) is one of Kuching's surprises. Housed in a beautifully restored building are seven galleries exhibiting aspects of the Malay Islamic heritage. Among the various exhibits are ceramics, costumes and jewellery, weaponry, science and technology displays, and Islamic art.

Istana

This shingle-roofed, white palace, set amid rolling lawns on the north bank of the river, was built by Charles Brooke in 1870. Early in the Japanese occupation prisoners were detained in the basement. It's now the governor of Sarawak's residence and not open to the public.

Fort Margherita

Built by Charles Brooke in 1879 and named after his wife, the Rani Margaret, Fort Margherita guarded the approach to Kuching against pirates. Sitting on a knoll opposite the waterfront, this little white fort, complete with battlements, offers fine views along the river. The fort now houses the **Police Museum** (Muzium Polis; ☎ 440811 ext 225; admission free; ⏲ 10am-6pm Tue-Sun), which has some interesting exhibits on the history of policing and unlawful activity in Sarawak. A short walk west of the fort through the police barracks and towards the western jetty is the **orchid garden** (☎ 444789; admission free), with over 100 orchid species on display.

To get to the fort, take a *tambang* from the promenade across the river.

Chinese History Museum

This small **museum** (☎ 231520; Main Bazaar; admission free; ⏲ 9am-6pm Sat-Thu) is lodged in one of the few original waterfront buildings to survive the redevelopment of Kuching. It began as the Chinese courthouse in 1912. Inside, historical notes and photos document the Chinese migration to Sarawak and the formation of trading associations. Examples of traditional furniture, musical instruments and costumes are also on display.

Cat Museum

Kuching's kitsch one-of-a-kind **Cat Museum** (☎ 446688; Bukit Siol, Jl Semariang; admission free; ⏲ 9am-5pm Tue-Sun) pays homage to the origins of the city's name. It's all pretty light-hearted, with plenty of trivia, photos, children's art and movie posters featuring cats. While many visitors find it as fascinating as a fur-ball, real cat-lovers (you know who you are) will adore it!

The Cat Museum is in the UFO-shaped DBKU building, north of the river. It's too far to walk, so take Petra Jaya bus No 2B; the fare is 60 sen.

Timber Museum

Some may see this **museum** (☎ 443477; Wisma Sumber Alam; admission free; 🕑 8.30am-4pm Mon-Fri, 8.30am-12.30pm Sat) as the timber industry's answer to all the criticism about logging. To learn about logging processes and the types of timber found in Sarawak, however, this is definitely the place to go. The presentations aren't exactly captivating, but there are numerous examples of various wood species in both finished and unfinished states.

The Timber Museum is across the river in Wisma Sumber Alam, Petra Jaya, about 12km by bus from downtown Kuching. Take the Kuching Matang Transport (yellow-and-orange striped) bus No 8 from near the market; the fare is 90 sen.

Courthouse & Brooke Memorial

The courthouse opened in 1874 and was the third to be built on this site. State magistrate councils were held in the courthouse until 1973, when the government complex on Jl Tun Haji Openg opened. The clock tower at the front was added in 1883, and there's a small granite memorial to Charles Brooke facing the river. At the time of writing, the block was being redeveloped as a new tourist information, cultural and retail centre.

Temples, Mosques & Churches

Kuching's Chinese temples are modest affairs, though there are a few colourful examples around town. Historically, the most significant is the **Tua Pek Kong Temple** (Jl Tunku Abdul Rahman). The temple is dedicated to the patron saint of overseas Chinese. Officially, it's dated to 1876, but written sources mention it as long ago as 1846, which would make it the oldest building in Kuching.

Other colourful, religious buildings include a **Hindu temple** (Jl Ban Hock) where visitors are welcome to wander inside the temple compound, but take your shoes off before stepping on the tiles. There's a **Sikh temple** (off Jl Mosque), and an **Indian mosque** (Jl India) dating back to the 1850s down a passageway between Nos 37 and 39 on Jl India.

Completed in 1968, the **Kuching Mosque** looks impressive, particularly from across the river, but is otherwise uninteresting. There's no admission for non-Muslims from Thursday 3pm to Friday 3pm, Saturday from 4pm to 6pm and Sunday from 2pm to 5pm.

Kuching's **Roman Catholic cathedral** (Jl Tun Haji Openg) is 500m south of the Sarawak Museum.

Civic Centre

About 1km south of the city centre, along Jl Tun Haji Openg, a white tower looking like an upside-down, half-furled umbrella on stilts dominates the skyline. This is Kuching's **Civic Centre** (admission RM2) and on a clear day it offers a panoramic view.

To get to the Civic Centre, walk down Jl Tun Haji Openg and turn left at Jl Budaya; most buses going past the main post office go there.

Reservoir Park

A peaceful oasis not many travellers get down to, this small, landscaped park south of the centre is a pleasant place for a picnic, stroll or a jog. After a few days of museums and handicraft shops, parents with young children will be grateful it exists.

To get to the park, follow the road just past the Fata Hotel (there's a small sign for the park) and take the second lane to your left (it's just past the Red Crescent building) to the car park.

Kuching Architecture

There are many historic *godowns* (river warehouses), Chinese shophouses and other buildings of note in the blocks around the waterfront and markets. Many have been beautifully restored or are in the process of being restored.

The small **Square Tower**, on the waterfront opposite the *istana*, was built in 1879 as a prison. The **main post office** (Jl Tun Haji Openg) itself is a grandiose structure fronted by Corinthian columns.

Near the Anglican cathedral, the **bishop's house** is the oldest dwelling in the state built in 1849 for the first Anglican bishop of Borneo. You can wander around the cathedral grounds but the bishop's house is not open to the public.

Cat Statues

The large white, blue-eyed pussycat perched at the eastern end of Jl Padungan is known

MALAYSIAN BORNEO

as the **Great Cat of Kuching**. Other kitsch cat statues are opposite the Holiday Inn Kuching and on the waterfront. Another statue, at the roundabout at the east end of Jl Pandungan (at one time symbolising the centre of the city), features four cats on the bottom and four rafflesia near the top. (In case you didn't read the introduction to this section, the word *kuching* means 'cat' in Malay.)

Sunday Market

Kuching's best market – and it is also one of the best in Sarawak – is the **Sunday-morning market** along Jl Satok. It's sometimes very busy and can be well worth the walk. The market actually begins late on Saturday afternoon, when villagers bring in their produce and livestock and start trading. They sleep at their stalls and resume trading at around 5am on Sunday.

The air is heady with the smell of fresh coriander, ginger and herbs, stacked among piles of bananas, mangoes, custard apples and obscure jungle fruits. Fresh fish and other seafood take up one section, while elsewhere wild boars and goats are butchered to hang with turtles and other free-range meat. (See the Turtles Under Threat boxed text, p54, and resolve not to let turtle pass your lips.). Other stalls sell beautiful orchids, live fish hanging in plastic bags of water, birds in cages, pets – you name it, it's for sale. There are also plastic toys, clothes and other odds and ends. Food stalls set up near the pedestrian overpass.

To reach the Sunday market from the museum, walk south along Jl Tun Haji Openg and turn right at Jl Satok; the market is on your left about 500m along.

Jalan Carpenter

This narrow street, lined with old Chinese shops, is signposted as Jl Ewe Hai at its eastern end. Jl Carpenter exists on two levels; the street has busy little shops and coffee shops, and above, the families who run them live cheek-by-jowl behind white-washed walls and painted shutters.

The original wooden and thatched shop-houses that occupied Jl Carpenter were all destroyed in a great fire in 1884. The buildings were replaced by more sturdy and less flammable brick terraces. It's picturesque and interesting to wander along and photograph, particularly on Sunday morning when things are quieter.

Riverside Kampung

Across the river from the waterfront are four *kampung* (villages) where you'll see traditional Malay houses and mosques stretching away to the east. It's a world away from the commerce and tourism of central Kuching. Take a *tambang* across the river and wander around.

TOURS

There's an incredible array of travel agencies and tour operators in town, and most of the hotels listed in Sleeping offer tours or have links with an operator. Some can cater for special interests, such as photography, natural history and textiles or crafts.

Most tours are priced for a minimum of at least two people (and often five or six); if you're on your own, expect to pay from RM500 to RM1200 for a few days upriver. Trips are often cancelled because of insufficient numbers, particularly with the cheaper tour operators – refunds should be immediate if a trip is cancelled.

If you're looking for a group to join, you can leave a contact number with tour operators; the tourist information centre in Kuching can also help.

Besides day trips in and around Kuching town, many travel agents offer longer trips to national parks or to longhouses along the Skrang, Lemanak and Rejang rivers. If you're interested in the Rejang and its tributaries, you may find better deals from Sibu or Kapit operators.

Half-day city tours are around RM40; day trips to longhouses at Annah Rais are around RM80 per person; and expect to pay at least RM400 each for a two-day (one-night) longhouse trip for a minimum of two people on the Lemanak. Longer trips to more remote longhouses around Batang Ai will cost more, but you're guaranteed a less touristy experience.

The MV *Equatorial* cruises up and down the Sungai Sarawak in the afternoon and evening if there is sufficient demand. A two-hour cruise costs RM35. Departures are at 3.15pm and 5.30pm from the Kuching waterfront. Smaller boats also do harbour cruises for a similar price.

Following are a few of the well-established operators:

Borneo Adventure (☎ 245175; www.borneoadventure.com; 55 Main Bazaar) Award-winning company which sets the standard for the travel experience that benefits and involves Sarawak's indigenous people. The informed staff also offer speciality tours.

Borneo Interland Travel (☎ 413595; www.bit.aus.to; 1st fl, 63 Main Bazaar) Offers a wide variety of tours near Kuching and throughout Sarawak at reasonable prices.

Borneo Exploration (☎ 252137; http://borneoexplorer.tripod.com; 76 Jl Wayang) Has packages similar to Borneo Interland at competitive prices.

Borneo Inbound Tours & Travel (☎ 233354; inboundtravel@po.jaring.my; 1st fl, 98 Main Bazaar) Arranges homestay trips to Telok Melano on the Sarawak coast, as well as various tours throughout Sarawak.

FESTIVALS & EVENTS

There's always a lot going on in Kuching; for the most current schedule of activities, contact the visitors' information centre.

Rainforest World Music Festival (www.rainforestmusic-borneo.com) Held annually either in July or August for three days at the Cultural Village (p337), another great reason to visit Kuching. Features musicians from around the world as well as highlighting indigenous music from Borneo.

Sarawak Regatta Lively event held on the river in September. Participants compete in mock war canoe races. Races are also held between speedboats and jet-skis. Makes for a big party on the waterfront.

SLEEPING

Kuching has a good selection of accommodation in the upper mid-range and top-end categories. Most of the hotels mentioned here are conveniently located within walking distance of the city centre and sights.

Budget

B&B Inn (☎ 237366; 30 Jl Tabuan; s/d RM24/32; ❄ 💻) Kuching's only backpacker hostel is close to all attractions, clean and friendly, has left-luggage facilities and a kitchen, and can help with travel information and longhouse tours. A bed in a six-bed dorm costs RM16. Cheaper singles and doubles are fan cooled.

St Thomas Diocesan Rest House (☎ 414027; Jl McDougall; s/d RM30/40) Popular with travellers on a budget, this place is at the back of the Anglican cathedral. It's sometimes full of folks on church business, but if not, you're welcome to stay – just ask for the friendly caretaker, Puli Kanto. Rooms with fan and shared bathroom are also available for RM18 to RM25. It's quiet and comfortable but guard your belongings carefully.

Fata Hotel (☎ 248111; fatahotel@hotmail.com; Jl McDougall; s/d RM45/55, s/d in new wing RM58/63; ❄) Located in a quieter area, the rooms here are clean, though a bit on the small side. Rooms at the back of the building are quieter still and look out over lovely parkland.

Mandarin Hotel (☎ 418269; 6 Jl Green Hill; s/d RM45/55; ❄) An older-style hotel with small clean rooms; many travellers have been satisfied staying here and it's good value. The friendly staff can arrange tours. There's no restaurant and it lacks an elevator, which may deter travellers with lots of luggage.

Also recommended:

River View Inn (☎ 412551; fax 256302; 22 Jl Green Hill; s/d RM45/55; ❄) A larger hotel with basic but airy rooms and slightly grungy hallways.

Goodwood Inn (☎ 244862; fax 235690; 17 Jl Green Hill; s/d RM40/55; ❄) Probably the last choice of the bunch; it also lacks an elevator.

Mid-Range

Kuching has dozens of mid-range hotels that compete keenly for business, so most are reasonably priced. Discounts are usually available. Except for the lodging houses, these places all have IDD (international direct dial) phones, and payment by credit card is accepted. Some of the good upper mid-range places provide reasonably priced alternatives to the top-end hotels.

Telang Usan Hotel (☎ 415588; www.telangusan.com; Jl Ban Hock; s/d RM90/140; ❄ 💻) Top of the list in the upper mid-range hotels, this popular place is Sarawak's first to be owned and managed by Orang Ulu (Upriver People). The colourful Kenyah décor characterised by swirling lines and shapes is just one of the touches that make it stand out. Promotional rates range from RM60 to RM90 for singles and doubles.

Harbour View Hotel (☎ 274666; www.harbourview.com.my; Jl Temple; s/d RM98/128; ❄) Close to the main bazaar shopping, sights and some of the best eating establishments, this newer hotel has top-end comfort for a mid-range price. The large bright rooms and views along the Sungai Sarawak and across to Fort Margherita make it one of the best places to stay in Kuching.

Borneo Hotel (☎ 244122; fax 254848; 30 Jl Tabuan; s/d RM75/85;) Kuching's longest-running hotel has, unfortunately, deteriorated in recent years. While some rooms are fine (notably those on the 1st floor), others are dark and cramped. But it's still a good place to stay in a pinch.

Supreme Hotel (☎ 255155; fax 252522; Jl Ban Hock; s/d RM70/90;) This is a decent hotel with a good restaurant and clean, good-sized rooms but lacks atmosphere.

Hotel Grand Continental (☎ 230399; www.grandhotelsinternational.com; Jl Ban Hock; r RM150) This large, rather nondescript hotel is nevertheless a reasonable option that's close enough to walk to/from the city centre. Rooms range from somewhat musty to quite cosy; discount rates start at RM130, including breakfast.

On Jl Green Hill there's a cluster of older 'lodging houses' that mostly cater to long-term residents. There's little difference between them – they're all acceptable, if a bit stark.

Top End

Hilton Hotel (☎ 248200; www.hilton.com; Jl Tunku Abdul Rahman; r RM335;) Not quite on the river, but just across the street, the Hilton has the finest rooms in its class and the full complement of services, plus the best handicrafts shop in town (see Galeri M, p330). Substantial discounts are often available but it's a popular hotel and bookings are advised.

Crowne Plaza Riverside Kuching (☎ 247078; www.crowneplaza.com; Jl Tunku Abdul Rahman; s/d RM380/450;) The service here is good and the rooms have good views. Discounts can bring down the rates considerably. The Riverside complex also houses a Parkson-led shopping centre.

Merdeka Palace Hotel (☎ 258000; www.merdekapalace.com; Jl Tun Haji Openg s/d RM335/440;) This large, majestic place is next to the *padang* (town square). It's tastefully fitted out, if a little gloomy and dark inside, and has a business centre and gymnasium. There's an excellent coffee shop, cigar bar, pub and good restaurant. Discounts of 40% to 45% are often available.

Holiday Inn Kuching (☎ 240277; www.holidayinn.com; Jl Tunku Abdul Rahman; s/d RM300/360;) It's worth staying here just for the location, though the service is ordinary and rooms are pretty average for the price. The lobby has some nice decorative pieces however, and there's a good range of services, such as a restaurant and the Tribes Music Restaurant & Pub (see p330).

EATING

Kuching has the best selection of food in Borneo, and the choice ranges from hawker-stall fare through good seafood to first-class Italian. Places serving standard rice and noodle dishes, beef, roti or *murtabak* (roti filled with pieces of mutton, chicken or vegetables) are everywhere. Seafood prices vary according to demand and availability – check prices before ordering. For good and even excellent Western fare look into the upmarket hotels, where prices are reasonable by Western standards.

Breakfast

This is indeed the most important meal of the day in Kuching, where breakfast is almost an art form. It seems nearly everyone converges on their favourite hang-out in the morning to savour a bowl of cheap Chinese porridge or laksa. Plenty of places also serve Western-style breakfasts. Any *kedai kopi* (coffee shop) can cook an egg and toast upon request to go with your coffee or tea, for about RM7.

Malay & Chinese

D'Alife Restoran Sejahtera (☎ 412487; Main Bazaar; dishes RM15-25) Nestled in the old Sarawak Steamship Company building on the waterfront, the tastefully decorated D'Alife features mud crab cooked in a feisty black pepper sauce. While mud crab may not sound appetizing, it's delicious if you have patience to pick out the meat from the shell. A number of other Malay dishes are also served and there's indoor (air-conditioned) and outdoor seating.

Khatulistiwa Café (☎ 248896; Jl Tunku Abdul Rahman; dishes RM8-20) This difficult-to-pronounce gathering place is in a thatched, round structure resembling Beijing's Temple of Heaven (it's actually modelled on a Bidayuh skull house) on the waterfront, next to the Riverside Suites. Kalu, as it's known to regulars, is a 24-hour open-air restaurant serving good Malay, Chinese and Western food. It's a pleasant place for breakfast or dinner, catching the breeze and watching the lantern lights of the *tambang* drift by. It's often busiest around 2am when the clubbers surface for some carbohydrates and fresh air.

Aunty Mary Kitchen (4 Jl Bishops Gate; dishes RM2.50-4; 7am-2.30pm) A few steps off Main Bazaar Aunty Mary serves a wicked 'special laksa', along with Malay and curry dishes. Try the lemon wheatgrass juice for a different taste. There's a good collection of B&W pictures of Kuching from days gone by on the walls.

Hornbill's Corner Café (☎ 252670; 85 Jl Ban Hock; adult/child RM16/8; 5.30pm-12.30am) A popular steamboat restaurant where you select your own seafood and meats, then cook them at the table, this is a lively place with good draught beer and is great for a group of people. Only take what you're going to eat, though – as elsewhere in Sarawak, you'll be charged for leftovers.

Jubilee (☎ 445626; 49 Jl India; dishes RM1.50-4) This is a small friendly café, perfect for having a light *roti canai* or *murtabak* while shopping on colourful Jl India. It also serves inexpensive Malay curries.

Biryani Café (☎ 413327; 16 Main Bazaar; dishes RM2.50-6) A good place to rest after shopping on the Main Bazaar, the Biryani has a nice variety of Indian curries and delicious *roti canai*.

Quick Eats

The so-called open-air market (it's covered) on Jl Market near the taxi stand is one of the largest and most popular food centres. One section mostly serves halal food and the other section has mostly Chinese.

The **Top Spot Food Court** (Jl Padungan) is a popular food-stall centre. It's clean and salubrious and specialises in fresh seafood.

The **Chinese Food Centre** (Jl Carpenter) is an excellent spot for breakfast or an afternoon feast of fish balls, prawn soup or satay (40 sen per stick).

Seafood

Kuching restaurants offer a good variety of seafood. Local specialities include steamed pomfret fish and *sambal* prawns.

See Good Food Centre (☎ 251397; 53 Jl Ban Hock; dishes RM5-25) At this Chinese seafood restaurant you can try local Sarawak specialities such as lobster in pepper sauce, *midin* (crispy jungle fern) or *ambol* (finger clam). The latter looks like a fleshy worm; it's delicious steamed with ginger and lemongrass, but is also known locally as *monyet punya* – literally 'monkey's got one'.

Mukah Seafood Centre (☎ 417486; 47 Jl Ban Hock; dishes RM7-26) Besides good seafood, specialities from Mukah are featured such as *umei* (Melanau raw fish in lime and onions) and Wuxi pork rib (an excellent Melanau/Chinese combination).

Benson's Seafood Centre (☎ 255262; Jl Abell; dishes RM10-20) Not only does Benson's have some of the best seafood in town, outside tables near the river offer views of paddlers, boats and the Malay *kampung* houses across the river.

Vegetarian

Life Café (☎ 411754; 108 Jl Ewe Hai; dishes RM4-12; 11am-11pm Mon-Sat) Adjacent to the Hong San Temple, this classy, tastefully decorated tea shop serves delicious Chinese vegetable dumplings and rice dishes. For the adventurous, try the crocodile-herb soup for RM12. There's also an excellent range of Chinese teas and some of the best coffee in Kuching.

Zhun San Yen Vegetarian Food Centre (☎ 230 068; 165 Jl Chan Chin Ann; RM1.10 per 100g) There's lots to choose from here at this vegetarian buffet. A second Zhun San Yen is located at 48 Jl Green Hill.

Western

Junk (☎ 259450; 80 Jl Wayang; dishes RM20-30; 6.30pm-12.30am Wed-Mon) Lamb shanks with smashed (really) potatoes is one of the favourites at this Italian restaurant. The meals are excellent and the rustic décor of this older Chinese building is worth the price of the meal alone, even if the food weren't so good. If you're looking for a quiet, intimate place for fine dining, this is it.

Denis' Place (☎ 238818; 80 Main Bazaar; dishes RM7-17) Many travellers homesick for a real Western-style restaurant rave about this café. The iced mocha coffee is worth having before a meal and for dessert again after. There's also a great range of salads.

Tom's (☎ 247672; 82 Jl Padungan; dishes RM12-20; 11.30am-11pm Tue-Sun) Tasteful décor complements the delicious meals in this Western-style restaurant serving pasta and steak dishes. For dessert, try the pastries and cakes.

DRINKING

Sarawakian hospitality is best appreciated over a drink (or several), and locals are only too happy to oblige. It's worth getting out in the evening at least once – you are much more likely to meet people in a bar than you are at a hawker stall or a restaurant.

Outside the top-end hotel bars, prices are very reasonable, with beer at around RM8 to RM10 for a bottle.

Kuching has the liveliest and most varied nightlife in Borneo. Aside from the ubiquitous karaoke lounges, there are lots of bars and nightclubs to choose from.

It's usually busy somewhere in town every night; as with elsewhere in Borneo, things don't get started until quite late – a bar may be deserted at 11pm and pumping at 1am. Established bars are packed on weekends with everyone from logging barons to transvestites. There's usually a convivial atmosphere, so be prepared for a late night.

De Tavern (☎ 419723; Taman Sri Sarawak Mall) This Kayan-run establishment has seen better days, but first-time visitors are still treated to a free tipple of *tuak*, the potent Iban rice wine.

Royalist (☎ 429479; Taman Sri Sarawak Mall) Above De Tavern it's named after James Brooke's sloop, honoured for first bringing beer to Sarawak. As at De Tavern, simply front up to the long central bar – the rest will take care of itself.

Cottage (☎ 412679; 16 Jl Bukit Mata) A nicely decorated pub with slightly subdued music during the day, Cottage serves local and pub meals. On Wednesday, Friday and Saturday local, Indonesian or Filipino live music is featured. If you like pub hopping, the corner of Jl Padungan down to the first half of Jl Bukit Mata is lined with pubs.

Soho (☎ 2247069; 64 Jl Padungan) Located away from the action-packed pub areas, one of Kuching's newest pubs is quickly becoming a favourite of Kuching's hip crowd. Jazz and Latin music plays in a relaxed atmosphere with pleasant staff.

Hornbill's Corner Café (☎ 252670; 85 Jl Ban Hock) This great open-air pub/restaurant gets packed on Saturday nights with football-mad Sarawakians watching telecasts on the TV. For details on its restaurant see p328.

Tribes Music Restaurant & Pub (☎ 424708; Holiday Inn, Jl Tunku Abdul Rahman) Terrific live music really gets this place going later into the night. There's a good restaurant with an international menu if you need some sustenance before the dancing starts. It's closed on Sunday.

Other major hotels, as well as the Riverbank Suites (across from the Crowne Plaza), have one or two pubs, karaoke lounges or live bands that go well into the wee hours.

The *Official Kuching Guide* lists most of the bars in town or get adventurous and discover your own favourite place.

SHOPPING

Kuching is the handicraft centre of Borneo. There are dozens of shops scattered around the city selling arts and crafts. Don't expect many bargains, but don't be afraid to negotiate either – there's plenty to choose from, and the quality varies as much as the price. Spend some time browsing to familiarise yourself with prices and range before committing yourself to a purchase – see the Crafty Shopping boxed text opposite.

The best area to start browsing is along Main Bazaar, where every second shop seems to be a gallery-style craft centre. Some are piled with all manner of bric-a-brac, others are presented like studios – most make for fascinating browsing and generally the shopkeepers aren't pushy.

Galeri M (☎ 411362; 26 Main Bazaar) This exquisite place is known for its fair dealings with local artists and craftspeople. It has an outstanding range of quality new and antique pieces, from beads and baskets to textiles and spears, as well as art by contemporary painters and silver jewellery. There's also a branch store in the lobby of the Hilton.

Atelier Gallery (☎ 243492; 104 Main Bazaar) At the eastern end of Main Bazaar, this shop has larger pieces, blending the traditional with a contemporary look. Aficionados of interior design will love browsing here; even if you aren't in a position to ship things back home, it's worth taking a look for inspiration on decorating ideas.

Sarakraf (☎ 258771; Ground fl, Sarawak Plaza) Set up by the Sarawak Economic Development Corporation (SEDC) to foster small-scale rural development and the handicraft industry, products here are smaller and make good souvenirs and gifts. Sarakraf supports local producers who receive equitable remuneration for their work. There's also a shop at the airport.

CRAFTY SHOPPING

If you're looking for authentic tribal artefacts in Malaysian Borneo, it's just as well to save your money for Kuching. Sabah's selection is poor and much of the stock in Sarawak towns started out in Kuching.

You can, of course, go directly to the source. Women in well-touristed longhouses often set up craft markets for visitors, and buying a basket or weaving is a good alternative to 'paying' for your visit with a T-shirt or similar gift. Further afield, ask around for items of interest – trekking guides should be able to help. However, there's not necessarily a lot out there: The Kuching art market has already absorbed a great number of trib al artefacts from longhouses as far away as the Rejang.

The most visible crafts tradition is maintained by the Iban, whose intricate paintings and carvings decorate everything from tourist leaflets to buildings. Genuine pieces may be very old, venerated or functional, and will command hundreds, if not thousands, of ringgit. The Iban are also famous for *pua kumba,* a masterful weaving style incorporating traditional motifs. Another popular craft worth a long look is beadwork. Beads originating from as far away as Venice have been traded by many Borneo tribes for centuries.

As with art markets everywhere, the onus is on the buyer to be aware. The bulk of what's on offer is churned out for tourists, and although a piece may actually come from a longhouse, it will probably have no traditional significance. Many of the more garish and polished pieces are actually mass produced outside Sarawak and even beyond Borneo.

Artificially 'aged' items are also commonplace, and many galleries have a back room where the 'real items' are kept. Sometimes these are authentic pieces, but often they aren't. Items are often composites as well: Old handles and clasps may be fixed to a medicine chest made last Wednesday in Pontianak. One way to tell the difference is by the speed the price falls. If the price quickly drops dramatically, you're almost certainly dealing with a purely tourist-trade item.

Restrictions

Most outlets can organise the necessary fumigation of wooden artefacts, as well as shipping. Some antiquities – cannons and jars in particular – are difficult to export. You'll need permission from the Sarawak Museum, and you should have this *before* you purchase the item.

The hornbill is a totally protected bird, so even though hornbill parts are sometimes sold under the counter, if you're caught trying to take them out of the state you're in a whole lot of trouble. Forget about bear and leopard teeth, too – sale of any parts of these animals is prohibited. Deer are protected but not restricted, so it is possible to apply for a licence to export deer horn.

Some countries restrict the importation of weapons as souvenirs. For example, Australian customs officials seem worried about the safety of suburban stray cats if blowpipes get in (they may have a point). The legendary *parang,* once the head-hunting tool of choice, is another trinket you may have trouble explaining to the postal worker or baggage inspector back home.

Sarawak Batik Art Shop (☎ 243739; 1 Jl Temple) Pang Ling is a noted batik artist who draws his inspiration from many years of upriver visits to longhouses. He set up this store in 1976 and he's still going strong at the age of 80. The prices are very reasonable and besides batik paintings, he also sells batik sarongs and clothes.

Among the many other shops on Main Bazaar are **Nelsons Antiques & Jewellery** (☎ 248077; 14 Main Bazaar), which sells a large range of items at reasonable prices, and **Kelvin Gallery** (☎ 252259; 32 Main Bazaar), featuring some striking Kayan carvings and beautiful ikat (fabric patterned by tie-dying the yarn before weaving) fabrics. Likewise, **Sarawak House** (☎ 252531; 67 Main Bazaar) has a good range of superb pieces.

Keep a look out for *Borneo: A Photographic Journey* by photographer Dennis Lau. The accompanying text is informative without trying to compete with the beautiful photos. Look for it in some of the shops mentioned here and also in the hotel arcades.

If you need to pick up supplies before heading out on a trek, try **Siong Sports Trading** (☎ 413609; Sarawak Plaza). It also sells gas cylinders for outdoor stoves.

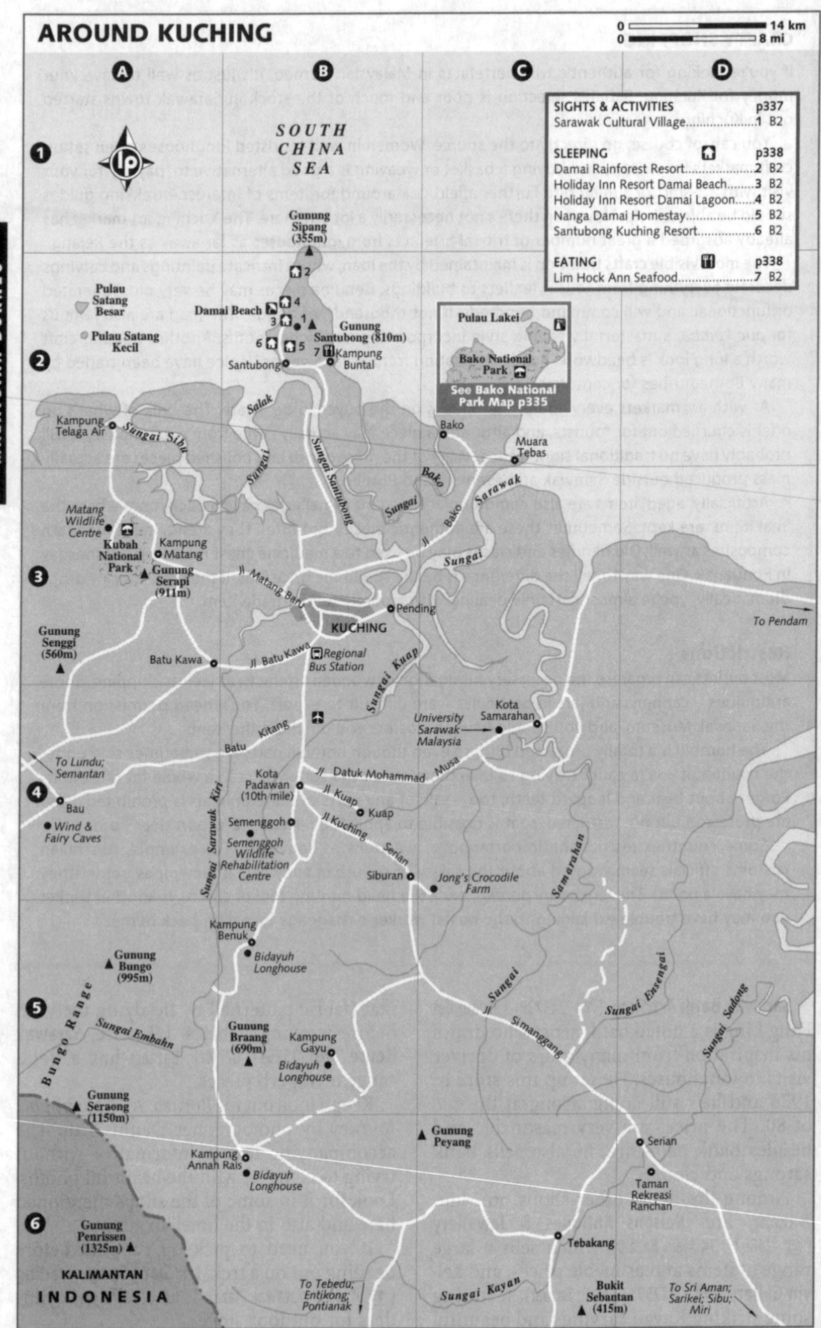

AROUND KUCHING
0 14 km
0 8 mi
SIGHTS & ACTIVITIES p337
Sarawak Cultural Village....1 B2
SLEEPING p338
Damai Rainforest Resort....2 B2
Holiday Inn Resort Damai Beach....3 B2
Holiday Inn Resort Damai Lagoon....4 B2
Nanga Damai Homestay....5 B2
Santubong Kuching Resort....6 B2
EATING p338
Lim Hock Ann Seafood....7 B2
SOUTH CHINA SEA
Gunung Sipang (355m)
Pulau Satang Besar
Pulau Satang Kecil
Damai Beach
Gunung Santubong (810m)
Santubong
Kampung Buntal
Pulau Lakei
Bako National Park
See Bako National Park Map p335
Kampung Telaga Air
Sungai Sibu
Salak
Sungai
Sungai Santubong
Bako
Muara Tebas
Sungai Bako
Sarawak
Jl Bako
Sungai
Matang Wildlife Centre
Kubah National Park
Kampung Matang
Gunung Serapi (911m)
Jl Matang Baru
Pending
KUCHING
To Pendam
Gunung Senggi (560m)
Batu Kawa
Jl Batu Kawa
Regional Bus Station
Sungai Kuap
Kota Samarahan
University Sarawak Malaysia
Batu Kitang
To Lundu; Semantan
Jl Datuk Mohammad Musa
Kota Padawan (10th mile)
Jl Kuap
Kuap
Bau
Wind & Fairy Caves
Semenggoh
Semenggoh Wildlife Rehabilitation Centre
Jl Kuching Serian
Sungai Sarawak Kiri
Siburan
Jong's Crocodile Farm
Samarahan
Kampung Benuk
Bidayuh Longhouse
Gunung Bungo (995m)
Bungo Range
Sungai Embahn
Sungai
Jl Simanggang
Sungai Ensengai
Sungai Sadong
Gunung Braang (690m)
Kampung Gayu
Bidayuh Longhouse
Gunung Seraong (1150m)
Gunung Peyang
Serian
Kampung Annah Rais
Bidayuh Longhouse
Taman Rekreasi Ranchan
Gunung Penrissen (1325m)
Tebakang
KALIMANTAN
INDONESIA
To Tebedu; Entikong; Pontianak
Sungai Kayan
Bukit Sebantan (415m)
To Sri Aman; Sarikei; Sibu; Miri

GETTING THERE & AWAY

Air

The regular Malaysia Airlines fare between KL and Kuching (1¾ hours) is RM262. There are early-morning flights for RM187. Malaysia Airlines has at least eight flights daily between KL international airport and Kuching, and two flights daily to KL's Subang airport. Air Asia has 10 flights a day to KL and some amazing offers. Past promotions have included fares as low as RM100 for the KL–Kuching route.

Malaysia Airlines has at least four flights per day to Johor Bahru (RM169) and two flights daily to Singapore (RM286).

Although Malaysia Airlines has an extensive provincial network, none of the flights to the interior operates from Kuching – they exit Sibu and Miri. From Kuching there are flights to Sibu (RM72, 10 daily), Bintulu (RM117, 6 daily), Miri (RM164, 5 daily), Kota Kinabalu (RM228, 7 daily) and Labuan (RM199, 1 daily). There's also a daily Twin Otter service to Mukah (RM76).

Malaysia Airlines operates five flights per week between Kuching and Pontianak, in Kalimantan. The fare is RM276, plus RM20 departure tax. Pontianak is a visa-free entry point to Indonesia, and travellers of most nationalities do not require a visa – but check with the Indonesian consulate first (see p317).

Malaysia Airlines flies between Kuching and Perth (Australia) once a week; the airline also flies twice a week between Kuching and Manila (Philippines). There's talk of adding a direct Kuching to London, UK route. Dragon Air flies three times a week to Hong Kong.

Boat

Bahagia (☎ 484824; 19 Jl Ban Hock) and **Sejahtera Pertama** (☎ 256736; 15 Jl Market) each run a daily boat to Sibu (four hours). Economy/1st-class tickets for the Bahagia service cost RM39/45 departing at 8.30am while Sejahtera is RM40/45 leaving at 12.45pm.

Boats depart from the Bintawa Express wharf in the suburb of Pending, about 6km east of the city centre. To get there, catch CLL bus No 17 or 19 (80 sen) from in front of the main post office, or Regas bus No 1C (90 sen) from the bus stop next to Riverbank Suite. The trip takes about 20 minutes. Taxis cost RM15

Check at the visitors' information centre for the latest on booking and for schedule changes, and get to the dock an hour before sailing to be on the safe side. Bahagia departs Sibu for Kuching at 11am and Sejahtera at 7.15am.

Bus

Long-distance buses leave from the regional express bus terminal on Jl Penrissen at Mile 3, about 5km southeast of the city centre. Several companies run buses to Sri Aman, Sarikei, Sibu, Bintulu and Miri. There's also a regular service to Pontianak in Kalimantan.

Around 18 city buses pass by the express bus terminal between 6am and 6pm, and a few buses operate until 9.30pm. Buses to the terminal stop in front of the main post office (50 sen); allow at least 20 minutes for the trip.

Except on weekends and public holidays, there's usually no need to book – just arrive, buy a ticket and hop on. Most of the long-distance bus companies have ticket offices at or near the Petra Jaya bus station. Check the daily papers for times and fares, or ask at the tourist office to see if there are changes to the schedules. Long-distance buses are modern, with air-conditioning and (loud) movies.

The main long-distance companies are:

Biaramas Ekspres (☎ 452139; Jl Khoo Hun Yeang) Biaramas has a 24-hour office at the express terminal.

Borneo Highway Express (☎ 619689; Jl P Ramlee)

Borneo Interland (☎ 413595; 63 Main Bazaar) Also sells tickets for Borneo Express.

PB Ekspres (☎ 461277, 327075; Jl P Ramlee) Some buses change over at Sarikei, phone for latest timetables.

Lanang Road Bus Company (☎ 462887) Head office is in Sibu.

SJS (☎ 455155)

Suria (☎ 575478) Head office in Miri.

Overnight buses to Sibu are a popular option. Nine buses daily leave between Kuching and Sibu (RM40, 7 hours) from 6.30am until around 11pm.

Buses go to Bintulu (RM60, 11 hours), with nine daily between 6.30am and 10pm. If you're crazy about bus rides, you can take an express bus all the way to Miri (RM80, 16 hours) with six departures daily from 6.30am to 9.30pm. The Lanang Road Bus Company has two daily departures to

MALAYSIAN BORNEO

Mukah (RM53.30, 12 hours) at 8am and 9.30pm. Most of these buses stop at Sarikei (RM28) but check at the station or phone to make sure.

Several companies have a daily service to Pontianak (around 9 hours) in Kalimantan. Biaramas Ekspres (RM34.50) has departures from Kuching at 7am, 8am, 10.30am and 12.30pm; it currently does the return trip at 8am (30,000Rp). PB Ekspres has two departures daily at 7am (RM45) and 10am (RM60). SJS does the trip in greater comfort for RM70 and includes meals.

Buses cross at the Tebeduen–Entikong border. It's a visa-free entry point into Indonesia for citizens of most nationalities, but check with the Indonesian consulate in Kuching before leaving. It's a slow haul from Serian to Tebedu on the Sarawak side, but there's a good highway from Entikong to Pontianak.

GETTING AROUND

To/From the Airport

The green-and-cream STC bus No 12A does a loop that takes in the airport (RM1, 45 minutes). It runs approximately every 50 minutes between 6.30am and 7.15pm – ask whether it's headed back to town before you board. The bus from the airport leaves from 7.15am to 7pm. The blue-and-white CLL bus No 8A (90 sen) does a direct run between the airport and city. Look for it about 100m to the right of the terminal as you exit. Airport taxis run on a coupon system and cost RM17.50 for a trip to the city centre. The coupon booth is to the right as you leave the terminal. Taxis from the city centre to the airport are between RM15 and RM20.

Boat

Small boats and express boats ply the Sungai Sarawak, connecting the small villages around Kuching. For river crossings see p323 and for river tours, see p326.

Bus

Most points of interest around the city and nearby towns are serviced by a good local bus network. At first the system may seem chaotic because there's no central terminal, but the five local companies congregate near the market at the western end of the waterfront. Bus stops are located at the western end of the Main Bazaar, in front of the post office or on the other side of the food stalls in front of Electra House shopping mall.

The *Kuching City Map*, available free at the visitors' information centre, has the latest information on local buses, times and fares. The *Official Kuching Guide* also has excellent bus information.

Kuching operates a free sightseeing bus (dressed up to look like a tram) that does a loop around the city starting from the Khatulistiwa Café (see p328) and stopping at various places where passengers can hop on or off. The visitors' information centre has a map of the route.

Car & Motorcycle

Car rental costs in Sarawak start at around RM130 per day; the Kuching visitors' information centre and upmarket hotels can also help arrange car hire. At around RM1 per litre, petrol is cheap by Western standards. **Mayflower Car Hire** (☎ 575233) has a counter at the airport and **Teck Hun Motor** (☎ 417068; 31 Jl Tabuan) rents motorcycles for RM25 per day with a RM100 deposit.

Taxi

Kuching's taxis were expected to be installed with meters by the end of 2003. Most short trips around town should cost between RM6 and RM10. Taxis can be found waiting at the market, at the express-bus station and outside major hotels. There's usually no problem flagging one down on main streets, even late at night. You can call **taxis** (☎ 343343) at any time.

Bako National Park

Bako is Sarawak's oldest national park, protecting 27 sq km of an unspoilt promontory between the mouths of the Sarawak and Bako rivers. It's a beautiful spot, where mangroves fringe the coasts and the rocky headlands are indented with clean beaches. The park features seven of the state's main vegetation types. These include rainforest and *kerangas*, a distinctive plant community that grows on the sandstone plateau, which forms the geological backbone of the national park. Botanically, Bako is a fascinating place where you can easily see four species of pitcher plant within an hour's walk of park headquarters.

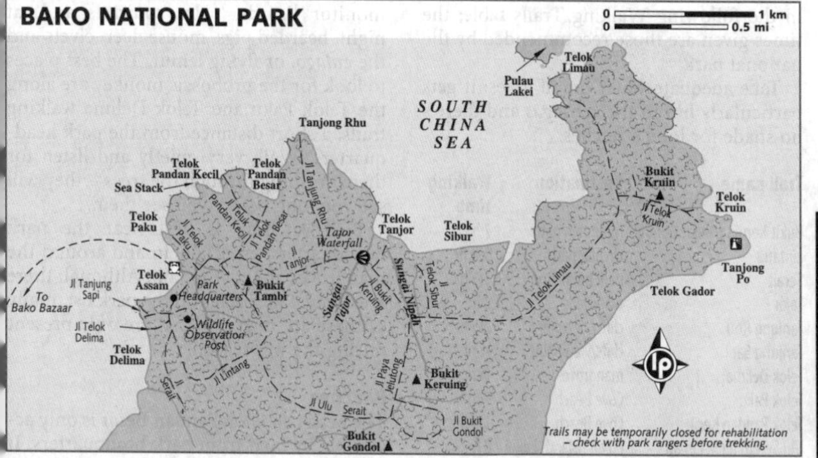

Bako is most famous for its wildlife and it's the best place in Sarawak to see the rare proboscis monkey. Macaque monkeys are common, and they're fun to watch as they forage along the beach in the evening.

For day trips you can just show up at the park headquarters, but for longer stays book your accommodation in advance. Phone bookings are accepted, but must be confirmed and paid for at least three days before your intended arrival. If you get caught short of time on a day trip, it's possible to stay overnight at the park, if a bed is available (unlikely on weekends).

Register for the park upon arrival at the boat dock in Bako Bazaar (adult/child RM10/5). Bako National Park is well worth a visit, but being only 37km north of Kuching it's also popular with day-trippers.

From Bako Bazaar it's a 30-minute boat ride to **park headquarters** (☎ 011-225049; Telok Assam) where you'll find accommodation, a cafeteria and the park office. The office is about 100m along the shore from the boat dock. Staff will show you to your quarters and can answer any questions about trails. There's a large trail map hanging outside the office; ask for a free copy. Storage lockers are available for RM5 per day.

There's a good information centre here, with photos and displays on various aspects of the park's ecology. An entertaining video on the proboscis monkey is shown at regular times and on request – ask at the office.

Permits and accommodation can be organised at the visitors' information centre in Kuching (see p323).

SIGHTS & ACTIVITIES

Walking

Bako has more than 30km of well-marked trails, ranging from short walks around park headquarters to strenuous day walks to the end of the peninsula. Guides are available (RM20 per hour), but it's easy to find your way around because all trails are colour-coded with paint on trees or rocks next to the path. You don't have to go far to see wildlife, and there are walks to suit all levels of fitness and motivation. Plan your route before starting out on longer walks, and aim to be back at Telok Assam before dark, at about 6.45pm. Some trails may be closed for maintenance after the wet season – check at the park office before setting out.

If you have only one day in Bako, try to get here early and attempt the **Jalan Lintang**. It traverses a range of vegetation and climbs the sandstone escarpment up to the *kerangas* (an Iban word for this type of landscape of dry, sandy, porous soil) where you'll find many pitcher plants.

The longest trail is **Jalan Telok Limau**, a 10km walk that's impossible to do as a return trip in one day. You will need to carry camping equipment or else be collected by boat. Arrange a pick-up with the park warden, but expect to be charged about RM100. The park's main trails are listed in the following Walking Trails table; the times given are those recommended by the national park.

Take adequate water on all hikes; it gets particularly hot in the *kerangas* and there's no shade for long stretches.

Trail name	Destination	Walking time
Bukit Keruing/Bukit Gondol	mountain path	7 hr
Lintang	circular path	3-4 hr
Serait	park boundary	1½ hr
Tajor	waterfalls	2 hr
Tanjung Rhu	cliffs/viewpoint	2½ hr
Tanjung Sapi	cliffs/viewpoint	½ hr
Telok Delima	mangroves	¾ hr
Telok Paku	Cove Beach	¾ hr
Telok Pandan Kecil	Cove Beach	1½ hr
Ulu Serait/Telok Limau	Pulau (Island) Lakei	8 hr

Wildlife

Walking trails pass through peat swamp, rainforest and, on the low sandstone plateau behind Telok Assam, *kerangas*. The latter is a fascinating ecosystem where pitcher plants are common, especially near the intersection of the Jalan Lintang and Jalan Ulu Serait trails. This *kerangas* is the spitting image of some parts of the Australian east coast, although it is botanically very different.

Common animals include the long-tailed macaque and silver leaf monkey, large monitor lizards, palm squirrels and, at night, bearded pigs, mouse deer, civets and the *culago*, or flying lemur. The best places to look for the proboscis monkey are along the Telok Paku and Telok Delima walking trails, a short distance from the park headquarters. Walk very quietly and listen for them crashing through the trees – they will see you long before you see them.

Bird-watching is best near the park headquarters, especially in and around the mangroves at Telok Assam. Although there are about 150 species on the park list, many of these are migrants that are only present during the wet season.

WARNING: MISCHIEVOUS MACAQUES

The long-tailed macaques that hang about park headquarters are great to watch but they are cunning and mischievous, an attitude fostered by tourists who persist in offering them food. Do not leave valuables, food or drink unattended, especially on the beaches, at the canteen or on verandas. Lock all doors and close all bags – they (both macaques and some tourists) are quick opportunists and will make running leaps at anything they think they can carry off, including drink bottles, food, laundry, sunglasses and hats. It's wise to leave the monkeys in peace – the males can be aggressive and put up some impressive threatening displays. If you get bailed up, yell for the park staff. Monkeys are not a problem after dark.

Beaches

The beach at Telok Pandan Besar is only accessible by boat from park headquarters. If you're thinking of hitching a boat ride to or from a beach, it's probably only cost effective for a group. Boats to beaches near park headquarters will cost around RM25 (one way or return), but to beaches further away it is quite expensive (eg, RM80 to Telok Sibur). Pulau Lakei, on the park's northeastern tip, is accessible by boat (RM120).

SLEEPING & EATING

There is plenty of accommodation at Bako National Park, including two- and three-room chalets, as well as hostels and a muddy campground. You can book accommodation through the visitors' information centre (☎ 082-410944) in Kuching.

The **hostel** (dm/r RM15/40) has four beds with shared kitchen and bathroom. Fan-cooled **chalets** (r RM75-100), with various sized rooms, are also available. Bookings are essential for the chalets and advisable for the hostel rooms, though you should be able to get a bed if you arrive on a weekday.

Camping costs RM5 per site, but the campground is a swamp for much of the year. There's a shower block and lockers can be hired for RM5 per day. Bring your own utensils, sheets and sleeping bags. The monkeys are a particular nuisance near the campground and will steal anything that is not firmly secured.

The cafeteria at park headquarters is open from 8am to 9pm. It sells cheap noodle and rice meals. The adjoining shop sells a good variety of reasonably priced tinned and dried food, chocolate, biscuits, film and toiletries, although fresh bread and vegetables are not always available.

GETTING THERE & AWAY

To get to Bako from Kuching, first take a bus to Bako Bazaar in Kampung Bako, then charter a boat to the park. Petra Jaya bus No 6 leaves from near the market in Kuching every 40 minutes (approximately) from 6.40am to 4pm (one way/return RM2.50/4 – valid for a week, 45 minutes). The last bus back to Kuching leaves Kampung Bako at 5pm.

A boat from Bako Bazaar to the park headquarters costs RM40 each way for up to 10 people. The chances are that someone on the bus will be looking to share a boat, especially on a weekend; tourists sometimes wait at the boat dock for the same reason.

Take note of the boat's number, and be sincere when you agree to a pick-up time – boat drivers have been burned by tourists who renege on a deal and return on another boat. As a result, they're often reluctant to return later the same day (tides and rough seas can also be a factor). If you do want to share a different boat back, tell park headquarters your boat number – staff are happy to call and cancel your original boat.

It's a pleasant 30-minute boat trip past coastal scenery and fishing boats. From November to February the sea is often rough, and at times it may not be possible for boats to approach or leave Telok Assam. Take a waterproof jacket to protect against spray in the open boats.

Santubong & Damai

☎ 082

The Santubong Peninsula is an exclusive tourist area 32km north of Kuching near the mouth of the Sungai Santubong. It's a picturesque place with jungle trekking on nearby Gunung Santubong and good seafood at two small fishing villages, Santubong and Buntal. The peninsula has the nearest beach to Kuching, other than those in Bako National Park, and is very popular with local people on weekends. You can see primitive rock carvings at Sungai Jaong, about 1.5km upriver from the coast, and the peninsula also has the Sarawak Cultural Village – a photogenic ethnic theme park and site of the annual Rainforest World Music Festival.

SIGHTS & ACTIVITIES

Sarawak Cultural Village

Surrounding an artificial lake at the foot of Gunung Santubong, the **Sarawak Cultural Village** (☎ 846411; www.sarawakculturalvillage.com; adult/child RM45/22.50; 🕓 9am-5.30pm) is an excellent living museum. It has examples of traditional dwellings built by different peoples of Sarawak – in this case Orang Ulu, Bidayuh, Iban and Melanau – as well as Malay and Chinese houses.

There are six buildings in all, plus a shelter of the type the nomadic Penan periodically live in. The dwellings are inhabited by tribespeople who demonstrate local arts and crafts, including basketry and weaving, blowpipe shooting, top-spinning and sago processing. Even travellers who have ventured to the Borneo interior are generally impressed by this unique opportunity to see the original styles of the now-modernised longhouses. Each longhouse usually has some musicians and dancers. It's all quite touristy, of course, but tastefully done and sincere in intent. Many of the participants speak English well and can offer a wealth of information about Sarawak. Don't miss the effusive Cecelia at the Chinese farmhouse exhibit; her stories of growing up on a pepper farm are worth the price of admission alone.

All the tribespeople are paid to take part in the daily activities, and they sell their products. Great pains are taken to make the village authentic – just to prove the point, the nomadic Penan occasionally go AWOL.

The village has a restaurant and souvenir shop and each visit is capped by a cultural show at 11.30am and 4.30pm. Hotels and travel agencies in Kuching have packages that include admission, lunch and transport ranging from RM60 to RM90. If you're planning to get married in Sarawak, this is good place to do it. You can choose to tie the knot according to Iban, Bidayuh, Orang Ulu or Malay ceremonies.

There's no public transport to the village, but a shuttle bus leaves the Holiday Inn Kuching at 9am and 12.30pm, returning at 1.45pm and 5.30pm (RM10 each way).

Jungle Walks

The Santubong Peninsula offers good jungle trekking within easy reach of Kuching, and the more adventurous can attempt the ascent of **Gunung Santubong** (810m).

MALAYSIAN BORNEO

An easy to moderate circular walk (2km, one to two hours) starts near the Holiday Inn Resort and ends near the cultural village, passing a pretty **waterfall** on the way. There's a café at the beginning where you can pick up a map, but the trail is marked with splashes of paint so you shouldn't get lost.

Rock Carvings

Although they're a little difficult to find, the Sanbutong **rock carvings** on Sungai Jaong are worth visiting if you have an interest in archaeology. There's said to be nearly 40 of these artefacts, mostly carvings on boulders, including a distinct human figure on one, though it's unlikely you'll be able to find that many without spending quite a bit of time looking around. An accurate dating of the site hasn't been made yet, but it's thought to be at least a thousand years old or more. Chinese ceramic pieces identified from the Tang dynasty and evidence of iron-making have all been found here at one of Sarawak's most important archaeological sites.

The petroglyphs are at the end of a gravel road south off the main road going into Sanbutong, about 2km after the turn-off for Kampung Buntal. There's a bus stop by the gravel road, but you may have to ask some local people to help point you in the right direction.

SLEEPING & EATING

Accommodation in Santubong and Damai is mainly resort-style.

Nanga Damai Homestay (☎ 016-8871017; nangadami@hotmail.com; Jl Sultan Tengah, Santubong; r RM80-110;) Panoramic views of jungle and sea may entice you to stay more than the minimum two days required by this family-run homestay. Breakfast is included, and lunch and dinner can be arranged.

Holiday Inn Resort Damai Lagoon (☎ 846991; www.holidayinn-sarawak.com; Teluk Penyuk, Santubong; r RM280-380;) Serene Puteri Lagoon, a lovely pool with waterfalls, nice sand beach and spacious bright rooms make this resort hard to turn down. It's five minutes' walk from the Sarawak Cultural Village, and near the stunning Damai Golf & Country Club. Guest services include tour information and shuttle service to and from Kuching as well as excellent restaurants and relaxing pubs. Discounts as low as RM180 make this an attractive proposition.

Also recommended:

Holiday Inn Resort Damai Beach (☎ 846999; www.holidayinn.com; Teluk Bandung, Santubong; r RM300-380;) Take your pick of rooms near the beach, pool or hillside suites with spectacular views. It's also close to Sarawak Cultural Village and has the same services and facilities as Damai Lagoon.

Santubong Kuching Resort (☎ 846888; fax 846666; Jl Pantai Damai Santubong; r RM138-380;) Has a wide range of services and activities such as tennis, basketball, water sports, golf and mountain biking. The beach is a five minute walk and discounts are usually available.

Damai Rainforest Resort (☎ 846487; fax 846486; Pantai Dami, Santubong; r RM120-234;) Offers decent discounts of RM80-160 on its 'eco-friendly concept' accommodation. Types of dwellings include six-person longhouse rooms, two-person treehouse rooms, six-person log cabins and camping.

There are seafood restaurants at Santubong and Buntal. **Lim Hock Ann Seafood**, in Kampung Buntal, has a wooden deck on stilts overlooking the South China Sea; it's a perfect place to sink a few beers and watch the moon rise over Bako Peninsula. The food is fresh but prices are subject to seasonal variation.

GETTING THERE & AWAY

To reach Buntal and Santubong, take Petra Jaya bus No 2B from near Kuching's open-air market (RM2.90). The last return bus leaves for Kuching at 7pm; if you want to stay for a meal the only option is to take a taxi back to Kuching (45 minutes).

There's no bus to the resorts, but there are frequent shuttle buses from the Holiday Inn in Kuching to both Holiday Inn Damai resorts (RM10 one way).

A taxi to the resorts costs RM25 to RM30; if you want to be picked up after dinner expect to pay RM60 for the return trip. Taxis can also be hired from the resorts out to Buntal and Santubong.

Kubah National Park

Just 20km west of Kuching, Kubah National Park is the nearest national park to the city and is an easy and rewarding day trip. Its 22 sq km protect a range of forested sandstone hills that rise dramatically from the surrounding plain to a height of 450m. There are waterfalls, rainforest walking trails and lookouts. Kubah's beautiful rainforest is home to a wide variety of palms and orchids, but wildlife watchers note that there is less chance of encountering animals here than in Bako National Park.

Walking trails include the paved entrance road, which runs right up to the summit of Kubah's highest peak, **Gunung Serapi**; it's a two- to three-hour walk and the peak is often shrouded in mist but there are lookouts along the way. You can probably grab a lift up then walk down. Most of the other trails run off the entrance road. The **Ulu Rayu Trail** links Kubah with the Matang Wildlife Centre, 5km from the turn-off, and takes about three hours to walk. The **Waterfall Trail** takes about 45 minutes from the turn-off and ends at a natural swimming pool.

Entrance to the park costs RM10, and trail maps are available at the **park office** (☎ 011-225003).

Kubah park headquarters offers hostel, resthouse and double-storey chalet accommodation. In the comfortable, clean **hostel** (dm/r RM15/40) rooms are fan-cooled and have shared bathrooms. There's no restaurant, but a kitchen is supplied with all facilities, including a fridge and utensils.

Air-con **chalets** (RM150) with all facilities sleep eight people. Fan-cooled **resthouses** (RM120) sleep 12. Kubah is entirely self-catering; if you have transport you can get supplies in the local *kampung* or even dine back in Kuching; otherwise you'll have to bring all your food.

Book accommodation at the Kuching visitors' information centre (see p323).

Matang Transport Co bus No 11 leaves Kuching for Kubah roughly every 50 minutes between 7am and 4.30pm (RM1.65, 30 minutes). The bus will drop you at Sungai Cina, from where it's a 300m uphill walk to the park entrance.

A taxi from town will cost at least RM60 return; arrange with the driver a time to be picked up. Another option is to drive, but the park is not well signposted. Follow the signs to Matang then turn left at the crossroads 200m past the Red Bridge; the park entrance is about 3.5km further on.

Matang Wildlife Centre

Adjacent to Kubah National Park, the **Matang Wildlife Centre** (☎ 011-225012; admission RM10) was set up as a rehabilitation centre for endangered species released from captivity.

The centre is popular with locals who come to swim in the nearby river on weekends. There's accommodation, a cafeteria and a very good information centre here. There are twice-daily feeding programs for orang-utans, hornbills, sambar deer and crocodiles, as well as rainforest walking trails – including the **Sungai Rayu Trail**, which links up with Kubah National Park (three to four hours).

Matang has a **hostel** with rooms that sleep four (RM40 per bed); a **chalet** that sleeps eight (RM150) and a **campground** (RM5 per site). Book accommodation at Kuching's visitors' information centre (see p323).

The only practical options for getting to Matang Wildlife Centre from Kuching are by taxi (about RM35 one way) or with a tour.

You can take a bus part of the way to the Kubah National Park turn-off, but it's a further 12km to Matang. Try waving down a local minibus, or you can also try hitching.

Semenggoh Wildlife Rehabilitation Centre

Semenggoh (sometimes spelled Semenggok) is Sarawak's equivalent to the orang-utan sanctuary at Sepilok in Sabah, though without the notoriety as a tourist attraction.

The **centre** (☎ 082-442180; adult/child RM3/1.50; 🕑 8am-12.45pm & 2-4.15pm) attempts to rehabilitate orang-utans, monkeys, honey bears and other unfortunate creatures that have been orphaned or illegally caged. You're not guaranteed to see wild orang-utans, because they're set free and only return when they're hungry (usually outside the forest's fruiting season).

The semi-wild orang-utans are fed at 8.30am to 9am and again at 3pm to 3.15pm, so it's best to time your visit to coincide with one of these sessions.

A (free) permit is required to visit the centre and can be arranged at the visitors' information centre in Kuching. There's no accommodation or cafeteria at Semenggoh.

Semenggoh is 32km south of Kuching. To get there, take STC bus No 6, 6A, 6B or 6C from Kuching (RM2, 40 minutes). There are eight buses running daily between 7am and 2pm. Tell the driver you wish to get off at the Forest Department Nursery, then follow a boardwalk through the forest to the centre (about 30 minutes). The last bus back to Kuching passes Semenggoh at 4pm.

Bidayuh Longhouses

The most interesting and unspoilt longhouses in Sarawak are those furthest from large settlements, particularly along the upper reaches of the Rejang, Baleh, Belaga, Balui and Baram rivers. If you're not planning on going that far, or if you would like a preview, the Bidayuh longhouses are the closest to Kuching. All have been on the tour operators' circuit for years and the communities are accustomed to tourists.

Kampung Benuk is a 35km bus ride south of Kuching, followed by a short walk. **Kampung Annah Rais**, further south, is one of the best-known 'tourist' longhouses. It's an impressive structure, with more than 100 doors; it has preserved its traditional look, apart from metal roofs and satellite dishes. The villagers also keep the tour operators informed of any special festivities taking place in the village. **Kampung Gayu** is another village visited by tour groups, and there are many others in this area.

To get to the longhouses from Kuching, take the STC bus No 9A which goes to Annah Rais between 9am and noon (RM6, 1 hour). For Kampung Benuk take STC bus No 6 (RM2) and ask the driver to let you off. Travel agencies also have set tours for about RM75.

LONGHOUSE VISITS

Many of the tribes living upstream on Sarawak's rivers reside in longhouses – gigantic wooden structures on stilts, where the entire population lives under one roof, with separate rooms leading on to one long communal veranda.

Tourism has had a big impact on the way longhouses operate, and many communities based along rivers which are easily accessible from cities have often seen their legendary hospitality turned into a business. Traditionally, the longhouse has always been open to passing travellers and traders. But with many tour companies simply depositing customers on longhouse verandas, this legendary hospitality is changing. At worst – mainly along the Skrang southeast of Kuching – you may be handed a welcoming glass of *tuak* (rice wine) with one hand while the other hand is held out for 10 ringgit.

Some of the more conscientious tour operators have made provisions for a limited number of guests with certain longhouses, and cultural shows, craft markets and other activities are laid on. In these cases, the longhouse communities have accepted tourism, but on their own terms; other communities have chosen to stay out of the tourism economy altogether.

You can of course head upriver on your own, but you'll still need to find someone to take you to a longhouse. Without an introduction local people are not going to invite you into their homes. An invitation is essential, and turning up unannounced is not just bad manners; in some circumstances it can be a minor catastrophe, particularly if there has been a recent death or if certain rituals are under way.

When you arrive at a longhouse, you may be surprised to find that it's quite modernised, with satellite TV, electric lighting, corrugated iron and other upgrades – the Iban are, after all, living in the 21st century. For a taste of the past, fine examples of traditional longhouses are on display at the Sarawak Cultural Village.

A longhouse is a way of life, not just a building. It embodies a communal lifestyle, and you may find the place all but deserted when you visit, as the younger people are often off working the fields, hunting or out on other business. Travellers often find the elders don't speak English and given the cultural differences there is little to talk about anyway – a frustration for everyone, especially the host. To avoid this, ask who will be around before you go, then try to organise some shared activities that will give you and your hosts some common ground. For example, a jungle walk or a river trip to a longhouse can be a real education if you've got a good guide. Many travellers have had unforgettable experiences participating in longhouse life by sharing in the cooking, helping out in the fields or gathering fruit and herbs.

If you're taking a tour, ask what you're in for – plenty of operators offer pretty minimal itineraries. Also be clear on the lodging arrangements if you're staying overnight. Often you'll stay at purpose-built guesthouses nearby rather than in the longhouse itself; some travellers prefer this, as there's more privacy and the facilities (eg, toilet and shower) may be cleaner and more modern.

Gunung Penrissen

Gunung Penrissen is a 1325m-high mountain just over the border in Kalimantan, Indonesia. More experienced, well-equipped climbers can climb the mountain, but it's a strenuous two- to three-day trek.

There are no regular treks up the mountain, although an adventure tour company in Kuching may be able to put together a package for you – the new resort near the mountain may also have something. It's cheaper for a group to attempt the climb because, apart from transport costs, guides need to be hired in Kampung Annah Rais or in nearby Kampung Padawan.

The **Borneo Highlands Resort** (Hornbill Golf & Jungle Club; ☎ 238266; www.hornbillgolf.com; r RM513), apparently Southeast Asia's largest hill resort, is a massive development – consisting of a golf course, hotel, chalets, gardens and whole new support town – sitting on Gunung Penrissen Plateau, an hour's drive from Kuching. Considerable discounts are usually available through travel agencies.

Jong's Crocodile Farm

Visiting **Jong's** (☎ 863570; Kuching ☎ 082-242790; adult/child RM8/4; 9am-5pm) is relatively inoffensive if you bypass the concrete holding tanks of overcrowded crocodile apartments.

Gifts are another area where misunderstandings can occur. Many tour companies will get you to buy T-shirts, coffee mugs or sweets for the kids (tooth decay is rampant in many communities). A gift is more than an object of exchange, however, and longhouse communities do not traditionally require gifts from guests; some communities need schoolbooks, others need fishing line and hooks. Your tour company or guide should be able to tell you what to bring. If visiting independently, it's polite to bring a small gift for the family of the person who invites you. Some enterprising travellers have found that buying a pig (about RM450) at a market and loading it onto an upriver-bound longboat got them invitations to stay for as long as they wished! If gifts aren't your thing (some people find handing out treats demeaning to locals), you're already contributing to the longhouse economy by taking a local longboat and buying a handicraft.

There's no getting around it: A longhouse visit is going to cost money. Tours are not cheap and if you go on your own you'll still need to pay for transport – a boat plus driver and/or Land Cruiser and driver, and maybe a guide fee along the way. But if you want a unique, once-in-a-lifetime experience, make room in your budget for a trip; the Kelabit Highlands and the Belaga area on the Batang Rejang are two good places to combine jungle and river trips with a longhouse visit.

Longhouse Etiquette

Most importantly, never enter a longhouse without permission; always wait to be invited in. If there is a *pemali* (ritual prohibition) in force (usually after a death or some misfortune), which is indicated by a bunch of branches tied to the rail at the bottom of the ladder or by a white flag near the entrance, you won't be invited in.

On arrival at the longhouse, your guide will take you to see the *tuai rumah* (chief). You'll then usually be offered a place to stay for the night and be invited to join them for a meal. Always remove your shoes. Chances are you'll be given a welcome drink of *tuak*; drink it, or at least some of it. Accept food and drinks with both hands rather than with just one.

Meals are usually taken with the *tuai rumah*; they are eaten while seated on the floor, and using both hands. Don't point your feet at anyone when sitting on the mat, and don't spit or blow your nose during a meal. The food may be very simple but eat some of it, or at the very least touch the food and then touch your mouth. Food is plentiful and vegetarians are well catered for, but note that the Iban in particular honour their guests by serving meat for special occasions. You can always take along some food of your own to throw into the communal pot.

When washing or bathing in the river, men are expected to wear at least underpants, and women should stay covered with a sarong. Nudity is definitely not on.

In the evenings there'll probably be a lot of *tuak* drinking, and you may well be expected to sing and dance. Join in and don't be afraid to make an idiot of yourself – the locals will love it! *Tuak* may taste mild but it is pretty potent stuff, and you can expect an impressive hangover the next day. The accepted way to drink it is from the glass in a single shot.

Just before the entry into the zoo are gruesome photos of a famous man-eater and its final victim, as well as a story of locals trapping a man-eater and donating it to the farm. But when crocodiles aren't eating they don't do much, and the other animals, including monkeys, hornbills and beautiful leopard cats, are probably more interesting. Along the walkway there are impressive specimens, cute baby crocs, bear and deer in fenced-off areas. While seeing birds and animals in fences or cages is never pleasant, it's unlikely you'll see many of these species in the wild without spending years in the forest or being extremely lucky. Feeding times are 11am and 3pm but to be safe call the farm or its Kuching office.

The crocodile farm is 29km southeast of Kuching, at Siburan. From Kuching, STC bus No 3, 3A, 9A or 9B (from in front of the post office) will drop you at the turn-off on the highway (RM2.70, 45 minutes), from where it's a 15-minute walk. Minibuses (RM3), also from the post office in Kuching, are faster than the bus.

Wind Cave & Fairy Cave

Two very different cave systems exist in a range of steep limestone hills a few kilometres south of Bau, an old gold-mining town, southwest of Kuching. Both of them can make an interesting day trip from Kuching. Take a picnic lunch, drinks and a good torch (flashlight) for exploring the caves (torches can also be hired at the entrance to each cave).

About 3km southwest of Bau, the **Wind Cave** is a network of underground streams on the banks of the Batang Kayan. It's easy to walk through the caves on elevated boardwalks (though it isn't lit), or else you can walk around the jungle-clad perimeter of the park. You can walk right through the caves to the river, where there are barbecues, food stalls and changing facilities. The river is usually quite shallow and safe to swim in; it's a popular spot with locals on weekends.

About 5km further south, **Fairy Cave** is an extraordinary elevated cave. A massive concrete walkway leads up to the entrance, 30m above the ground in the side of a cliff. After a steep, slippery climb, you enter a grotto formed by the collapse of the cave roof. For generations this area has been used as a shrine by Chinese, who offer incense and other goods to various anthropomorphic cave formations. It's quite large and you could easily spend an hour exploring it.

From Kuching take STC bus No 2 to Bau (RM3.30, 1 hour). Air-conditioned buses leave every 40 minutes between 6am and 6pm.

To get to the caves, take a bus from Bau bazaar and ask the driver to let you off at the turn-off, from where it is about 700m to Wind Cave and 1.3km to Fairy Cave. The 3km walk to Wind Cave from Bau takes about an hour; Fairy Cave is much further (8km) and you may have to hitch.

Lundu

☎ 082

This quiet little town sits between the forested bulk of Gunung Gading National Park and the Sungai Kayan. To most travellers it's simply the transport node for the national park, but there are far worse places to get stranded. Lundu was established by Datuk Sulaiman and his followers, who arrived from Kuching and settled the area. Some time later, they were attacked by 2100 pirates arriving in 70 vessels. The story goes that Datuk Sulaiman killed 2070 of them before he was beheaded, after which the pirates fled, leaving Lundu in peace.

Lundu has a fish market along the riverfront and a hawker centre at the western end of town. The town centre is a square bounded by old *godown* (warehouses), and brightly painted houses line the quiet country lanes. Check out the garish **rafflesia monument** near the bus station.

The road north out of town leads to the beaches at **Pandan** (10km) and **Siar** (8.5km). They're OK, but often littered with debris. STC bus No 2B (RM1.50, every hour from the bus station) goes by the beaches.

SLEEPING & EATING

Cheng Hak Boarding House (☎ 735018; fax 735091; 51 Lundu Bazaar; r RM35; ❄) This budget place has simple rooms with shared bathrooms. A few rooms with fans are RM25. The office is at the Goh Joo Hok shop, a few doors down from the Lundu Gading Hotel.

Lundu Gading Hotel (☎ 735199; 174 Lundu Bazaar; r RM58; ❄) For a little more comfort, this central establishment has fairly decent rooms. Rooms without attached bath are RM48.

MALAYSIAN BORNEO

There are Chinese *kedai kopi* around the square and the hawker centre cranks up in the evening. **Happy Seafood**, situated between the town square and Lundu Gading Hotel, serves a variety of Malay and Chinese fare.

GETTING THERE & AWAY

STC bus No EP07 leaves from Kuching and Lundu at 8am, 11am, 2pm and 4pm. The trip takes two hours and costs RM8.70.

Gunung Gading National Park

The chief attraction at **Gunung Gading** (☎ 735714; adult/child RM10/5; 🕑 8am-12.30pm & 2-5pm;) is the **rafflesia**, and it's one of the best places in Borneo to see this rarity. The rafflesia blooms year-round but at unpredictable times and places. Check whether any are in bloom before heading to the park by ringing the park headquarters or the Kuching visitors' information centre (☎ 082-410944). Because they only bloom for a few days, get to Gunung Gading as soon as you can if one is in bloom. With conservation a concern, a plankwalk was built close to where rafflesia are usually found. If a plant is deeper in the forest a park ranger may be able to guide you. It's best to follow the park ranger's instructions to protect young buds. Guiding fees are RM20 per hour (per group). November to January are the peak blooming months.

This is a pleasant and often deserted national park with well-marked **walking trails**. A large colour-coded map outside the park office indicates the walking trails and times. Trails to the two viewpoints take about one hour and 1½ hours respectively. Trekking to the tops of **Gunung Gading** (906m, three to four hours one way) and **Gunung Perigi** (five hours one way) requires a bit more effort. These treks are more enjoyable if you camp at the summit.

There's a **natural swimming pool** a few minutes from the office that's popular with locals. The information centre at the park has good photos and displays on rafflesia, wildlife and the local culture.

Park headquarters has good accommodation but no shop or canteen, so you'll have to bring your own supplies or stroll the 2km to Lundu for an evening meal.

The **hostel** (dm/r RM15/40) has fan-cooled rooms with pillows and blankets. There's a shared bathroom and fully equipped kitchen with a fridge and gas stove. Three-bedroom **chalets** (RM150) with cooking facilities and air-conditioning sleep up to six people. Park headquarters prefers bookings to be made through the visitors' information centre in Kuching (☎ 082-410944). Weekdays are less busy. Camping is also available for RM5.

To get to Gunung Gading. first take a bus from Kuching to Lundu (see Lundu's Getting There & Away section this page). From Lundu, take a Pandan bus No 17C (50 sen, hourly) and ask to be dropped off at the park; the entrance is 2km north of Lundu on the road to Pantai Pandan. If you miss a bus, it's probably just as quick to walk from Lundu as the park entrance is only 500m from where the bus drops you.

Sematan

☎ 082

Sematan is a small coastal village near the western border of Sarawak. Brightly coloured fishing boats can be viewed from an attractive promenade lining the waterfront. The northern end of the promenade leads to a park commemorating the early Malay fishermen of the area. The **beach** is clean, deserted and lined with coconut palms, but the water is very shallow. (According to Susi, from the Sematan Hotel, it's possible to walk all the way to Indonesia on the beach, though we don't recommend it.)

Semantan is a popular area with Kuching residents, many of whom have beach bungalows here and its importance may grow when visitor facilities at Tanjung Datu National Park are improved. At the moment, it's quite undeveloped and offers some good opportunities to experience local life off the beaten track.

SLEEPING & EATING

Sematan Hotel (☎ 711162; 162 Sematan Bazaar; r RM50; ❄) This friendly place is on the left-hand side of the road just before entering Sematan. If you end up here without a permit to Tanjung Datu the congenial people running the hotel can help out. They also arrange boats to Telok Melano and Talang Satang National Park (Sarawak's turtle islands); see p344.

One of the best reasons to visit Sematan is to participate in the **Telok Melano Homestay** program. The Malay village of Telok Melano is about 45 minutes away from Sematan along Sarawak's southernmost coast and offers pristine beaches and clear blue water against the backdrop of Gunung Melano. Homestay accommodation with one of the Malay villagers can be arranged in Kuching through the **Fisheries Development Authority** (☎ 082-245481) or Borneo Inbound Tours & Travel (see p327). The price with Borneo Inbound is RM280 for two days or RM360 for three days, which includes all transport from Kuching.

Sematan has a couple of Chinese *kedai kopi* facing the waterfront, and covered food stalls near the wharf.

GETTING THERE & AWAY

To get to Sematan from Kuching, first take a bus to Lundu (see p343), then catch STC bus No 17 to Sematan (RM2.80) which leaves Lundu every two hours or so between 6am and 4.30pm.

Getting to Telok Melano on your own can be a bit more complicated. Speedboats can be hired for about RM250 for the journey both ways or you might be better off getting a ride on one of the fishing boats, though you may have to wait a while. Try asking at the Sematan Hotel and on the wharf. Expect to pay about RM20 (one way) for the trip.

Tanjung Datu National Park

This is the smallest of Sarawak's national parks, located in the far west of the state, abutting the border with Kalimantan. Its 13 sq km protect rainforest, unpolluted rivers and near-pristine beaches.

There are currently no facilities for visitors. Access is only possible by boat from Sematan; ask around in the *kampung*, but negotiate a price before you set out. If you visit Gunung Gading on the way, someone at the park office may be able to organise a boat for you, otherwise try the district office in Sematan. Borneo Inbound Tours & Travel also arranges trips (see Tours in the Kuching section, p327).

Talang Satang National Park

The first marine park in Sarawak was established for the purpose of marine turtle conservation. Two islands, Pulau Satang Besar and Pulang Satang Kecil, form the Satang section (9894 hectares), part of which is open for visitors. Permits are required (see p318) and you'll be under the supervision of park staff. The Talang-Talang section (9520 hectares) is also made up of two islands, Pulau Talang-Talang Besar and Pulau Talang-Talang Kecil, which are off limits to visitors due to their small size, and to the sensitivity of the marine turtles. Local villagers and fishermen have retained their access rights and practices in conjunction with developing Pulau Satang Besar into a tourist destination. For information on getting to the park see Sematan Hotel on p343. The district office in Sematan and Borneo Inbound Tours & Travel (see Tours in the Kuching section, p327) may also be able to help.

Serian

☎ 082

Serian is a very small Bidayuh town 65km southeast of Kuching. Tour groups often stop here to pick up gifts on the way to longhouses along nearby rivers such as the Lemanak. Serian boasts a bustling **market**, where people from nearby longhouses come to sell jungle fruits and herbs, snake meat, sago worms and other unusual produce.

STC express bus Nos 3 and 3A run between Kuching and Serian (RM6.60, 1 hour) every hour between 6.30am and 5.30pm. The bus station is in the centre of Serian, near the market.

If you are going to Sri Aman, you could try hitching to Taman Rekreasi Ranchan (a popular park just off the road to Sri Aman); on weekends there's lots of traffic. The other option is to take a taxi.

Sri Aman

☎ 083

Originally known as Simanganggg, Sri Aman is a quiet town on the muddy Batang Lupar, halfway between Kuching and Sarikei. Sri Aman's main claim to fame is a tidal bore that periodically sweeps up the river, scattering all craft in its path; it nearly took the life of Somerset Maugham, an event he recorded in a short story called the *Yellow Streak*. Raja Brooke's **Fort Alice**, a little downstream, was built in 1864 and is a prominent landmark.

The Skrang, Lemanak and Ai rivers flow into the Lupar, and many of the tours organised from Kuching bring groups to the longhouses along these tributaries. See the 'Longhouse Visits' boxed text on p340.

There isn't a lot of river traffic at Sri Aman itself, and most boats to the Lemanak and Ai rivers leave from Engkilili, or outside town where the highway crosses the Batang Lupar.

Batang Ai National Park

Batang Ai covers 240 sq km and protects the catchment of the Batang Ai reservoir, formed by a hydroelectric scheme 250km east of Kuching. The park's rainforest features wildlife such as orang-utans, gibbons and hornbills. There's no visitors centre here and no accommodation in the park itself. Access is possible by chartering a boat from Batang Ai, but it's difficult and expensive. Until facilities are developed, the park is best visited as part of a longhouse tour. Some travel agencies in Kuching can arrange nearby longhouse accommodation and treks into the park (see Tours, p326).

Hilton Batang Ai Longhouse Resort (☎ 083-584338; www.sarawakmice.com.my/hiltonbatangai; r RM250;) Excellent service and high standards in cultural and nature excursions make this a well worthwhile accommodation option. All rooms have air-conditioning and the room price includes breakfast. Quality longhouse tours and jungle treks can also be arranged from this place. A transfer from Kuching (RM95) takes four to five hours, followed by a short boat ride to the resort. Discounts are often available, check with travel agencies or the office at the Kuching Hilton Hotel (p328).

BATANG REJANG

The mighty Batang Rejang is the main artery of trade with the interior for all of central and southern Sarawak. Scattered along its banks, and those of its tributaries, particularly in the upper reaches, are longhouses of the Iban and other tribes. Staying at a longhouse is one of the highlights of a trip to Sarawak. However, as with everything in Borneo, you have to pick your spot and know what to look for.

For example, if you only go as far as Kapit, the Rejang will appear to be little more than a wide, muddy conveyor belt for the insatiable logging industry. The Rejang and its tributaries – the Baleh, Belaga and Balui rivers – have been carrying topsoil and old-growth forest wasted by logging for years, and it's not a pretty sight.

Then there's the bungled Bakun Dam project, about an hour upriver from Belaga. After many delays – mainly due to mismanagement, financial problems and the sheer audacity of the project's original scale – the dam is finally near completion. The government is less paranoid about travel in the area than it once was, no doubt because there's little left about which to protest. The area south of the dam has already been emptied of an estimated 11,000 tribal people to make room for the reservoir; communities have been resettled to the north.

The best time for a trip up the Rejang is in late May and early June. This is the time of Gawai Dayak, the Harvest Festival, when there is plenty of movement on the

IBAN WORDS & PHRASES

As with other local peoples in Sarawak, the Iban use Malay for some common phrases and words:

Good morning	*Salamat pagi*
Good afternoon	*Salamat tengah-hari*
Good night	*Salamat malam*
Goodbye	*Salamat tinggal*
Thank you	*Terima kasih*

Iban words and phrases include:

How are you?	*Gerai nuan?*
Pleased to meet you	*Rindu amat betemu enggau nuan*
See you again	*Arap ke betemu baru*
What's your name?	*Sapa nama nuan?*
Where do we bathe/wash?	*Dini endor kitai mandi?*
Can I take a photograph of you?	*Tau aku ngambi gambar nuan?*
I'm sorry	*Aku minta ampun*
Where?	*Dini?*
What?	*Nama?*
I	*aku*
you	*nuan*
today	*saharitu*
tomorrow	*pegilah*
day	*hari*
night	*malam*
good	*manah*
not good	*jai also enda manah*
eat	*makai*
drink	*ngirup*
go	*bejalai*

rivers and the longhouses welcome visitors. There are also plenty of celebrations, which usually involve the consumption of copious quantities of *arak* (local liquor) and *tuak*.

Along the river, the only hotel accommodation available is in Song, Kanowit, Kapit and Belaga.

Rejang Longhouses

There are longhouses all the way along the Rejang. Most visitors head for Kapit and Belaga, but there are plenty of longhouses around Kanowit and Song. Those further upriver will not necessarily be more traditional; most are made from modern building materials. In fact, many communities are moving towards individual houses, which fare much better in the event of a fire (fire can destroy a longhouse in as little as 30 minutes).

If you don't have a lot of time, it's better to take a tour. Most travellers head for Kapit, a small administrative town upriver. Kapit is the last big settlement on the river, and it's where the longhouse people come for supplies. Further upriver, Belaga is smaller and more laid-back; it's a regular meeting place for friends and relatives from far-flung communities. In either town, the best strategy for finding someone to take you to a longhouse is to make yourself known around town – sit in the cafés and get talking to people.

Apart from a trip to the Pelagus Resort, travel beyond Kapit requires a permit (see Permits under Kapit, p350). The permit is merely a formality, and you'll probably never be asked for it.

Sibu

☎ 084

Sibu and Kuching are the Yin and Yang of urban Borneo. A rough, river town, Sibu was once known as New Foochow. It was so-named after Chinese migrants who came from Foochow (Fujian) province in the early years of the 20th century. The Melanau, then Malays and Iban were the first inhabitants.

Sibu is the gateway to the Batang Rejang and is the centre for trade between the coast and the vast upriver hinterland. The Brookes were happy to let Sibu's capitalists manage the extraction of upriver wealth. Situated 60km upstream from the sea, it's here that the interior's raw materials – logs, gravel, minerals and agricultural produce – are brought for transhipment and export. The wide, muddy river hosts a motley procession of fishing and cargo boats, tugs, barges laden with timber, express boats and speedboats skipping over their wash.

ORIENTATION

Sibu lies on the north bank of the Rejang near its confluence with Batang Igan. A graceful seven-storey Chinese pagoda marks the western edge of the waterfront and a small clock tower marks the eastern; between the two, an enormous, concrete market-building dominates the view over Jl Channel.

The wharf for express boats to Kuching is at the new River Express terminal on the western end of the Rejang Esplanade. Also on the waterfront is the local bus station; the long-distance bus terminal is at Sungai Antu, 3km west of town. The airport is 20km east of the town centre.

INFORMATION

Airline Offices

Air Asia (☎ 082-283222; www.airasia.com) Check them out if you're flying to/from KL; fares can be considerably cheaper.

Malaysia Airlines (☎ 321055; 61 Jl Tuanku Osman; 🕑 8am-5pm Mon-Fri, 8am-12.30pm Sat) A few minutes' walk north of the city centre.

Internet access

Sibu has a number of Internet cafés. The **Terazone IT Centre** (☎ 364600; Level 5, Wisma Sanyan, 1 Jl Sukan) charges RM4 per hour and stays open until about 10pm.

Money

The **Standard Chartered Bank** (Jl Tukang Besi), opposite the visitors' information centre, changes travellers cheques and has an ATM. Be prepared to wait for the cheques to go through. South of the visitors' centre, moneychanger **Yewon SDN BHD** (☎ 330577; 8 Jl Tukang Besi) is more convenient, but only changes cash.

Post

The **main post office** (☎ 332312; Jl Kampung Nyabor) is open Monday to Saturday from 8am to 5pm.

Tourist Information

The **visitors' information centre** (☎ 341280; www.sarawaktourism.com; 16 Jl Tukang Besi; 🕑 8am-4.30pm Mon-Fri, 8am-12.45pm Sat) has friendly and informative staff who can help with infor-

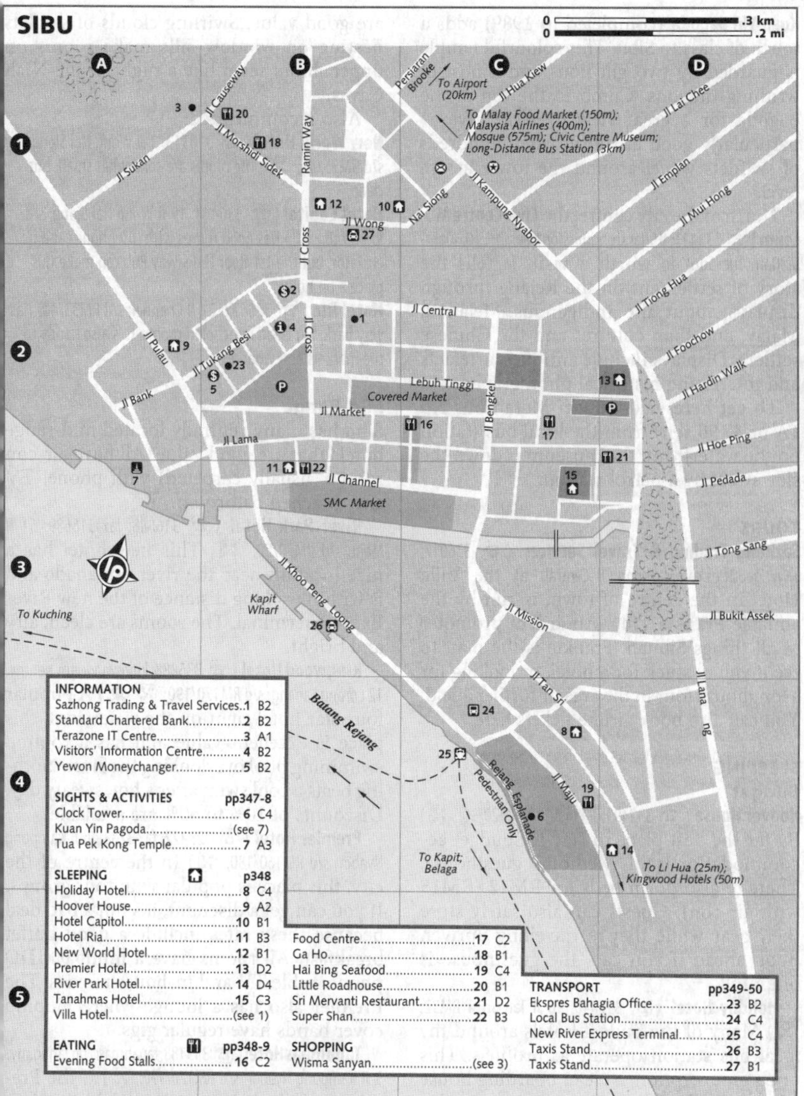

mation about upriver trips out of Song, Kapit and Belaga. Arriving in small towns alone, you'll probably have to wait until you meet someone who can help you out, so if you're short on time, it may be better to arrange things here or in Kapit. The centre has plenty of information, including brochures and maps with bus schedules to the airport, long-distance bus station, sights, and travel to other destinations in Sarawak. The tourist centre is closed every first and third Saturday of the month.

SIGHTS

The 100-year-old **Tua Pek Kong Temple** is beside the Kuching wharf, and its seven-tiered

Kuan Yin pagoda (completed in 1989) adds a touch of class to Sibu. This colourful temple is guarded by two gilt lions and a host of writhing dragons. Climb to the top of the pagoda for a great view over the river – particularly good at sunset when hundreds of swiftlets wheel around the tower at eye level.

North of the city centre, the **Civic Centre Museum** (☎ 333411; Jl Suarah; admission free; 🕑 10.30am-5.30pm Tue-Sun) is worth a visit. It tells the story of settlement on the Rejang through displays about the indigenous Melanau, Malay, and Iban cultures and the Chinese settlers. Displays include antiques, artefacts and interesting historical photographs.

To get here, take Sungei Merah bus No 1A or 4 (90 sen) from the local bus station on the waterfront; the museum is down the side street by a petrol station.

TOURS

Sazhong Trading & Travel Services (☎ 336017; www.geocities.com/sazhong; Jl Central) at the Villa Hotel in the centre of town, is run by the amiable Frankie Ting. An ardent promoter of all things Sibuan, Frankie is the man to see if you're stuck for a hotel, or looking for a longhouse tour in the area or further afield. You can also book airline tickets here.

SLEEPING

Budget

Hoover House (☎ 332491; Jl Pulau; s/d RM20/30; ❄) By far the best place to stay for budget accommodation is this Methodist guesthouse. There're also dorm beds for RM12 (RM15 with air-con). Guests can also safely store their gear while they're travelling upriver. Book ahead if you can; the guesthouse is often full.

Holiday Hotel (☎ 317440; 16 Jl Tan Sri; r RM32; ❄) Many of the budget hotels around the local bus station operate as brothels. This one's an exception, a clean boarding house where simple fan-cooled rooms are also available for RM15 and RM26.

Villa Hotel (☎ 337833; 2 Jl Central; s/d RM30/32) A fairly ordinary hotel with basic, but clean fan-cooled rooms. What makes it a good place to stay is its location next to Sazhong Travel and its proximity to the visitors' centre.

Li Hua Hotel (☎ 324000; fax 326272; 1 Lorong Lanang; s/d RM45/60; ❄) Close to the bus station, the Li Hua has decent rooms that are good value. Swirling clouds of swiflets nesting on window sills make rooms on upper floors seem like a night in the Niah Caves.

Also recommended:

New World Hotel (☎ 310313; 1 Jl Wong Nai Siong; s/d RM35/45; ❄) The rooms are somewhat small, but clean.

Hotel Capitol (☎ 336444; 19 Jl Wong Nai Siong; s/d RM42/48; ❄) Has good rooms with IDD phones and elevator, but the 1st-floor Hideaway Pub can make this place a bit noisy.

Hotel Ria (☎ 326622; 21 Jl Channel; s/d RM33/40) Has very basic but clean fan-cooled rooms. It's also handy to the markets and wharves.

Mid-Range

Sibu has many centrally located mid-range hotels that are good value. All have air-con rooms (usually carpeted) with phone, TV and attached bathroom.

River Park Hotel (☎ 316688; fax 316689; 51 Jl Maju; s/d RM70/80; ❄) This new hotel has a nice location near the river esplanade and is within walking distance of the new River Express terminal. The rooms are clean, airy and bright.

Kingwood Hotel (☎ 335888; kingwood@tm.net.my; 12 Lorong Lanang; s/d RM170/190; ❄ 🏊) A popular four-star hotel right on the waterfront, this place is excellent value and has a rooftop swimming pool overlooking the river. Nothing beats a cool swim after a hot, sweaty day. Discounts of 10% to 40% are available.

Premier Hotel (☎ 323222; fax 323399; Jl Kampung Nyabor; s/d RM160/180; ❄) In the centre of the city, this place is popular with tour groups. If you can get a discount, it's not a bad deal because these rates include a good buffet breakfast. All rooms have a minibar, IDD phone, cable TV and in-house movies. The Premier also has a lounge where Filipino cover bands have regular gigs.

Tanahmas Hotel (☎ 333188; tanahmas@po.jaring.my; 5 Jl Kampung Nyabor; s/d RM170/190; ❄) If the Premier is full, this hotel is a viable option. Discounts are sometimes available.

EATING

Some of the best food in Sibu is found at the various hawker centres and food stalls.

In the late afternoon, a host of food stalls set up near the massive, concrete SMC Market, selling delicious snacks such as *pau* (steamed dumplings), barbecued chicken wings and all manner of sweets. This is a fun way to sample local fare and the food is usually very fresh. There's a good nightly **Malay food market** at the northern end of town. To get there, follow Jl Kampung Nyabor through the roundabout past the intersection with Ramin Way – you can't miss the neon palm trees.

The Chinese *kedai kopi* along the waterfront are open for breakfast well before dawn – great if you're taking an early boat. There's also a small supermarket where you can get snacks, drinks and a paper for the trip upriver.

Hai Bing Seafood (Hai Bing Coffee Shop; 31 Jl Maju; dishes RM8-15) The Hai Bing serves excellent local dishes in both its indoor and outdoor sections. If you order seafood it will be more expensive.

Sri Meranti Restaurant (☎ 337996; 58 TKT 1 Jl Kampong Nyabor; dishes RM5-15) This pleasant, friendly restaurant serves Thai, Indonesian and Malay fare.

Little Roadhouse (☎ 319384; Jl Causeway; dishes RM4-10) This tasteful, terraced café/pub serves good burgers and pasta; beers are RM5. Just the place to land in after an arduous upriver trip. It's closed on Monday.

Ga Ho (Jl Morshidi Sidek; dishes RM2-5) A good place for snacks, the Ga Ho serves decent roti and *nasi* (rice) dishes. The best part of this place is the delicious fresh fruit juice (RM2.50), this is not so easily found in Sibu.

For self-catering and munchies for the boat, head up to the **Super Shan** (Jl Channel) supermarket near the Hotel Ria.

GETTING THERE & AWAY

Air

Malaysia Airlines flights to Sibu include KL (RM320, 1 or 2 daily), Kuching (RM72, at least 10 daily), Kota Kinabalu (RM180, 3 daily), Miri (RM112, 4 daily), Bintulu (RM64, 3 daily) and Mukah (RM45, 6 per week).

Air Asia has two flights daily between KL and Sibu and fares can be considerably cheaper.

Boat

Passenger express boats travel between Sibu and Kuching, and up the Rejang to Kanowit, Song and Kapit. Express boats leave from the new River Express terminal at the western end of the Rejang Esplanade and near the local bus terminal. Departures to Kuching (4½ hours) by **Bahagia** (☎ 319928; 20A Jl Tukang Besi) leave Sibu at 11am and tickets cost RM40/45 for economy/1st class. **Sejahtera Pertama** (☎ 321424; 20 Jl Kampong Datu) has boats leaving for Kuching at 7.15am daily. Tickets for economy/1st class are RM39/40. The express boat companies also have booths inside the terminal.

Riding the roof of the express boats is a good way to see towns and longhouse villages along the Batang Rejang. Moments rushing through the Pelagus Rapids (at times the drivers will ask passengers to go inside for the rapids) is also exciting. If you do ride on the roof, make sure you have sun protection.

Getting to Kapit is the first leg of the journey up the Batang Rejang. Boats cover the 130km or so from Sibu to Kapit (three hours) and economy/1st-class tickets are RM15/20. The boats leave between 1 and 1½ hours apart from 5.45am to 2.45pm. Just go down to the terminal and ask which boat is next to leave. People are very helpful and the boats usually have a 'clock' showing the next departure time. The Husqvarna Express boats (of chainsaw fame) make fewer stops if you are in a hurry.

All boats to Kapit pass Kanowit and Song, and may stop at smaller settlements and logging camps en route. There are also a few scheduled services to Song between around 7.30am and 1pm (RM10, 2 hours). Some services also call at Kanowit (RM6, about 1 hour). If you want to get off at Kanowit, tell the driver or ticket seller before you board.

Boats from Sibu go beyond Kapit only during the rainy season – if there's enough water they go all the way to Belaga. If there's insufficient water, you'll have to switch to a speedboat in Kapit. Getting to Belaga from Sibu, you should expect an overnight stay in Kapit, as the first express boat from Sibu doesn't always connect with the last regular service to Belaga.

Bus

Sibu is accessed by bus from all major and most smaller cities and towns in Sarawak. The main bus lines have ticket stalls at the long-distance bus station, northwest of town at Sungai Antu, as well as around the local bus station on the waterfront. Schedules

MALAYSIAN BORNEO

change often – check with the ticket agents (some are actually small shops) by the local bus station for the most recent schedule. The visitors' information centre has a city map with a detailed schedule of local and long-distance buses on the reverse side. There should be no problem getting a seat if you arrive 15 minutes before departure, but book ahead for weekends and school holidays.

Kuching Express buses leave for Kuching (RM40, 8 hours) 15 times daily from 6.30am to 11.30pm.

Miri Buses leave roughly every hour (RM40, 7½ hours) from 6am until 10pm.

Bintulu Similar to the Miri bus (RM20, 3½ hours)

Mukah Lanang Road buses make the trip (RM15.30, 3½ hours) at 6.30am, 8am, 11.30am, 12.30pm and 2.30pm daily.

Sarikei Buses run regularly to Sarikei (RM6, 1½ hours) between 6am and 4pm.

Many buses arriving at the long-distance bus station continue to the new River Express terminal in Sibu. Ask before you disembark, saving a taxi or transfer to a local bus.

GETTING AROUND

Sibu's airport is 20km east of town. Bus No 3A leaves from the blue bus shelter about 250m around to the left of the airport terminal as you exit. It runs to/from town every 1½ hours from 6.30am to 6pm (RM2.5, about 30 minutes). You could also try flagging down any rural bus that passes by. The taxi fare into town is RM20.

The local bus station is on the waterfront. To get to the long-distance bus station, take Lanang Road bus No 7 (90 sen) from the local bus station. It leaves every 20 minutes between 6am and 9pm. A taxi costs RM8.

If you arrive in Sibu by boat, the main hotels and restaurants are only a few minutes' walk from the wharves.

Kanowit

☎ 084

This small riverside settlement is the last stop on the Rejang that's connected to the coast by road – it's boat only from here on upstream. A few intrepid travellers use Kanowit as a jumping-off point for longhouse stays along the Sungai Kanowit. This can work wonderfully, but not without an invitation (see the Longhouse Visits boxed text on p340).

A white-raja fortification, **Fort Emma** sits to the right of the wharf, but it's not open to the public. There's also a colourful **clock tower** decorated in Iban 'tree-of-life' style, and a brightly painted **Chinese temple**.

Several buses leave Sibu daily for Kanowit, from 6am to around 4.30pm (RM6, 1 hour); there are five or six buses back to Sibu, leaving Kanowit between 6am and 5pm.

If travelling by boat, check at the Sibu wharf for an express boat that will drop you at Kanowit (RM6, 1 hour). Some have a scheduled stop at Kanowit, but they are few and far between.

Kapit

☎ 084

Kapit is another Rejang river town dating to the days of the white raja – historic Fort Sylvia still stands on the riverbank. The startling new District Office Council, greeting passengers off the express boats, is testament to the continuing importance of Kapit's administrative role in the area. The town is also where upriver people come to buy, sell and exchange goods, and to sample the diversions of urban life. The riverbank at Kapit is steep, but compared to many river landings is quite attractive with manicured grass, trees and plants spread between paths leading to docking areas for the many different longboats that ply the river. Kapit is a small place and everything is within an easy stroll. There's nothing much to do here, but the town offers some good accommodation.

INFORMATION

Internet Access

There's a glut of Internet cafés in Kapit. Rates are generally RM3 per hour. A couple of the quieter ones are **Goodtime Cyber Centre** (☎ 746303; 354 Jl Yong Moh Chai) and **Hyper Link Cyber Station** (17 Jl Tan Sit).

Money

The **Public Bank** (Jl Wharf) changes travellers cheques and currencies. The Maybank has an ATM near Hotel Meligai.

Moneychanger **Steven Ling** (☎ 796488; Jl Penghulu Geridang) near the Ark Hill Inn changes cash and travellers cheques.

Permits

Permits are required for foreign visitors to travel further upriver past the Pelagus

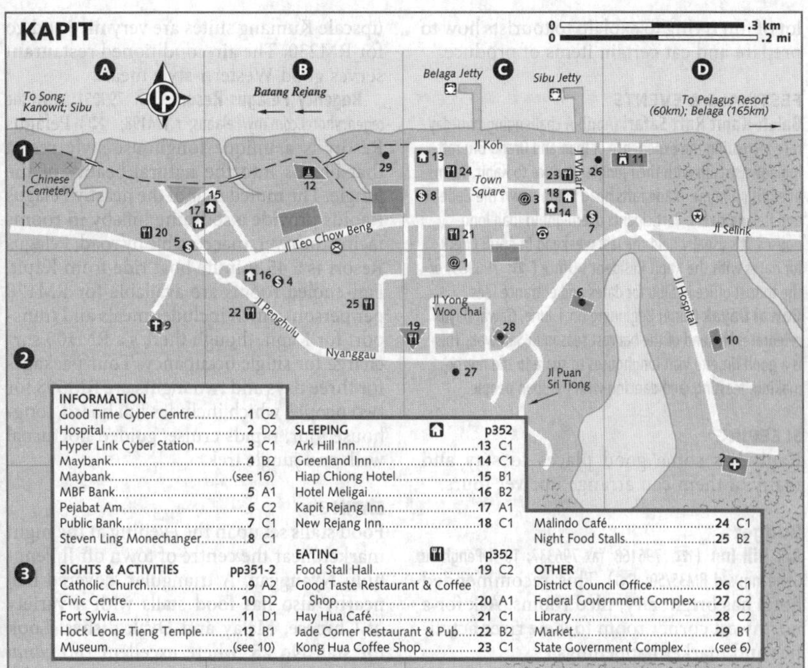

Resort to Belaga or anywhere up the Baleh River system. These are obtained from the **Pejabat Am** (Resident's Office; ☎ 796484; fax 796932; 1st fl, State Government Complex, Jl Penghulu Nyanggau). The form asks for your cholera vaccination expiry date, but this is not checked. The procedure takes about 10 minutes and the permit, which is free, is valid for one week.

SIGHTS

With its whitewashed walls, **Fort Sylvia** (☎ 799171; Jl Kubu; admission free; 🕑 10am-12pm & 2-5pm Tue-Sun) is one of the more impressive-looking raja fortifications. Formerly known as Fort Kapit, it was built in 1880 to keep peace and gain control of the upper Rejang by the Brooke administration. In 1925 the fort was renamed to honour Ranee Sylvia, wife of the third raja Charles Vyner Brooke. Built from *belian* (ironwood) timbers, Fort Sylvia lasted through the years and after independence was a base for the district office and courthouse. In 1997 it was declared a historical building. The Tun Jugah Foundation is managing the fort as a museum and resource training centre for artisans, weavers and artists in the Kapit District. At the top of the stairs to the 1st floor is a brilliant mural of a hornbill surrounded by depictions of early Iban life.

One of the most attractive features of Kapit is its **waterfront**, continually packed during the day with ferries, barges and people coming and going. It's fascinating to watch the activity on the water and to see people shouldering heavy loads of every description up from the wharf, especially when it's six slabs of beer perched precariously on a shoulder.

The lavish civic centre houses the **Kapit Museum** (Jl Hospital; admission free; 9am-12.45pm & 2-4.15pm Mon-Sat). It has a couple of cultural displays and there's a relief map showing all the longhouses in the area.

Some evenings you'll hear a frantic thrumming on big drums coming from the bright yellow-and-red **Hock Leong Tieng temple**.

Kapit has a colourful daily market, the **Pasar Teresang** (Wet Market), with an interesting mixture of people and goods near the centre of town. The friendly vendors have a lot of fun trying to explain to tourists how to prepare and eat certain items of produce.

FESTIVALS & EVENTS

Baleh-Kapit Raft Safari (April) A challenging two-day race recreating the experience of Iban and Orang Ulu rafting downstream with their jungle produce to Kapit. Teams of eight on home-made rafts head 50km down the Balleh and Rejang rivers. Participants overnight in Iban longhouses. It's usually held the last weekend in April. Check for dates with the Kapit Resident's Office (☎ 796963) or the tourist office in Sibu for dates and entrance fees.

Gawai Dayak (June) Beginning on 1 June, Gawai Dayak celebrates the end of the harvest season in Sarawak. This is a good time to visit longhouses to share in the merry-making, feasting, and dancing with the Iban people.

SLEEPING

Kapit has some good places to stay and many of them can arrange upriver tours.

Budget

Ark Hill Inn (☎ 796168; fax 796337; 10 Jl Penghulu Geridang; s/d RM35/50; ❄) This recommended hotel has bright airy, tiled rooms. Ask for a northwest corner room to view river activities and market happenings.

New Rejang Inn (☎ 796600; fax 799600; 104 Jl Teo Chow Beng; s/d RM45/50; ❄) Probably the best-value hotel in town, this hotel has comfortable rooms with phone and fridge, if you can manage the stairs. Staff will also provide free transport to and from the wharf upon request and have good information about guides and tours.

Kapit Rejang Inn (☎ 796709; fax 799600; 28 Jl Temenggong Jugah; r RM34; ❄) The management here is helpful and welcomes travellers. Cheaper fan-cooled rooms are RM18 and RM26.

Hiap Chiong Hotel (☎ 796314; 33 Jl Temenggong Jugah; s/d RM34/38; ❄) No elevator, but if you don't mind climbing the stairs there are views of the river from the 3rd and 4th floors.

Mid-Range

Greenland Inn (☎ 796388; fax 796708; Lot 463-464, Jl Teo Chow Beng; s/d RM80/90; ❄) Has immaculate but somewhat small rooms.

Hotel Meligai (☎ 798103; aswee@tm.net.my; Lot 33, Jl Teo Chow Beng; s/d RM65/75; ❄) Kapit's luxury hotel has a grand entrance and uniformed staff, though the rather ordinary rooms don't quite live up to these embellishments. If you want some pampering, however, the upscale Kumang suites are very nice and go for RM230. The air-conditioned restaurant serves good Western-style meals.

Regency Pelagus Resort (☎ 799051; www.theregencyhotel.com.my/Pelagus; r RM198; ❄) Pelagus Resort is a unique longhouse-style resort that blends into the natural beauty of the jungle. The muted roar of the nearby Pelagus Rapids provide a soothing lullaby in rooms facing the river. Inaccessible by road, Pelagus Resort is a 45-minute boat ride from Kapit. Fan-cooled rooms are available for RM178 per person, which includes meals and transport for Kapit, though there's a RM100 surcharge for single occupancy. Tour packages for three days and two nights are RM598 for two people, which includes full board, longhouse tour, rapids cruise, guided nocturnal walk and jungle trek.

EATING

Food stalls set up in the evening at the night market, near the centre of town off Jl Penghulu Nyanggau. A triangular, covered hall nearby also has food stalls with a variety of Chinese, Malay and Dyak dishes. Look for stall No 25, where excellent *roti canai* is served, made with a secret, so we're told, local recipe.

Kapit has a few good Chinese *kedai kopi* on Jl Wharf and facing the town square.

Malindo Café (☎ 798070; 40 Jl Court; dishes RM2.50-4) Located near the town square, this place has good Malay and halal food, and noodle combinations.

Kong Hua Coffee Shop (☎ 796459; 1B Jl Wharf; dishes RM3-8) The best place for breakfast, have your toast and eggs with coffee before a trip to Belaga on the express boat. Tony, the owner, is willing to answer questions on just about everything you ever wanted to know about Kapit.

Good Taste Restaurant & Coffee Shop (☎ 798658; Jl Teo Chow Beng; dishes RM6-12) Although usually crowded it's worth the wait. Three people can slake their thirst and fill their bellies to bursting for RM77.

Jade Corner Restaurant & Pub (☎ 798113; Jl Penghulu Nyanggau; dishes RM8-15) Above the café of the same name, this place is reputed to be Kapit's best Chinese restaurant. It must be true if the full tables in the evening are an indicator. Another place with good Chinese food is the **Hau Hua Café** (☎ 798636; 27 Jl Teo Chow Beng; dishes RM3-10).

GETTING THERE & AWAY

Express boats leave from Kapit to Sibu between 6.30am and 2.30pm. Times are posted on the wharf. Boats from Sibu begin at 5.45am and the last one is at 2.30pm. The trip takes 2½ to three hours and tickets are RM15/20 economy/1st class.

Boats depart for Belaga (RM25, 4½ hours) at 9am. When the river is low, express boats can't get past the Pelagus Rapids, about 45 minutes upstream, and smaller speedboats are used instead. The fare for these boats starts at RM50. If you want to do a day trip to Pelagus check around the wharf or arrange a boat through your hotel because the boats to Belaga don't stop there.

Belaga

☎ 084

Belaga is a small but pleasant bazaar town and administrative centre on the upper reaches of the Rejang where it divides into the Belaga and Balui rivers. Its close, friendly population makes it an excellent base from which to explore the interior of Sarawak; there are many Kayan and Kenyah **longhouses** along the rivers. If you speak with a local on the way upriver, you may end up being invited to stay at their longhouse – it's polite to bring a small gift for the family of the person who invited you. Otherwise, chances are you'll find someone in Belaga with a suggestion of a longhouse to visit or an offer to guide you. If you have the time, it's worth developing some real contacts.

A few part-time operators offer jungle treks at reasonable rates, about RM150 for three days/two nights; longer treks are also available. The nearest longhouse to Belaga is a 45-minute walk, and a pretty **waterfall** is a short boat ride away.

Boats will drop you at the bottom of a steep set of concrete steps leading up to the small town centre; the hotels and café are all here, across from the small park.

INFORMATION

The **Malaysia Airlines** office (☎ 461240; www.malaysiaairlines.com.my; 3 Belaga Bazaar; 9am-5pm) is on the main street. It's open daily and has several terminals for Internet access (RM6 per hour). For information on tours and longhouse stays check their website.

The informative and congenial **John Belarik** (☎ 013-633 1527; www.geocities.com/freeland_blg/) is a registered guide in Belaga. As well, another freelance guide is **Hamdani Louis** (☎ 013-836 5850). Daniel's Corner (see below) also has information on guides and tours out of Belaga. Guides can arrange transport and cultural events if you contact them beforehand.

SLEEPING & EATING

Belaga's accommodation is basic and inexpensive, catering for local people dropping into town for extended stays.

Belaga Hotel (☎ 461244; 14 Belaga Bazaar; s/d RM30/35; ❄) The rooms here are a little small, but the friendly proprietor makes up for this shortcoming. Fan-cooled rooms are also available for RM20. There's a good coffee shop downstairs.

Daniel's Corner (☎ 461997, 013-848 6351; udiontheroad@yahoo.com; 34 Jl Bato Luhat) Besides feeding you with local pancakes when his cook shows up, Daniel the jovial Orang Ulu entrepreneur can link you up with homestays, longhouse stays, guides for treks, fishing and hunting. Email before your trip and you can join in wood gathering, harvesting and land clearing activities. Daniel's Corner is two streets back from Main Bazaar, off the street leading from the Belaga wharf and past the post office and clinic.

Also recommended:

Bee Lian Inn (☎ 461439; 11 Belaga Bazaar; s/d RM35/40; ❄) Has decent rooms with warm-water showers.

Hock Chiang Inn (☎ 461258; 1 Belaga Bazaar; s/d RM35/40; ❄) Conveniently close to the wharves, it also has a nice café.

Lai Bin Ong Café (☎ 461309; Jl Bato Luhat; dishes RM2.50-8) This is the place to try out some wild boar and meet local Kayan and Kenyah people. Some boar, local vegetables and rice with beer for two is a good deal at RM21.

GETTING THERE & AWAY

Air

There are two weekly flights between Belaga and Bintulu (RM40, 1 hour). Belaga's tiny airstrip is 20 minutes downriver by longboat (RM8), followed by a short jungle walk after clambering up a set of precarious riverbank steps! Check in at the Malaysia Airlines office (see Information this page) the day before your flight to arrange transport to the airport. The airline clerk will arrange a boat at the Belaga dock about two hours before the flight. They'll get you to the quaint hut that functions as the airport terminal, where you and your gear are carefully weighed like boxers before a title bout.

Flights are sometimes cancelled due to inclement weather but new logging roads mean it's possible to go overland. There are four 4WD pick-ups going to Bintulu (RM50, 4½ hours) or you can also arrange to go to Batu Niah. Arrange things the night before (at the latest) through the Malaysia Airlines office, your hotel, your guide if trekking, or Daniel from Daniel's Corner. The 4WD pick-ups wait in front of the Welcome Inn in Bintulu for customers to make the return trip.

Boat

See the Kapit section (p353) for details of boat departures from Kapit to Belaga (RM25, 4½ hours). Returning to Kapit, express boats leave Belaga early (between 6am and 6.30am) to hook up with the boats from Kapit to Sibu. The fare is the same but the trip downstream can be faster. A boat schedule may be posted outside the Hock Chiang Inn.

Boats go upriver from Belaga as far as the Bakun Dam area near Rumah Apan (RM10, about 1 hour), from where you can explore the resettled river country north of the Rejang. It's possible to do a loop back to Bintulu this way.

Upriver from Belaga

With the Bakun Dam expected to be completed in 2005 or 2006, the forest beyond Belaga has changed forever. The forest around the dam site was long ago clear-cut for quick profit, and a massive reservoir will soon inundate all that remains. Longhouses along the lower Sungai Balui have been emptied of their communities, and families resettled in the Sungai Asap area north of the Rejang.

When the Asian financial crisis of 1997–98 began to bite, the Bakun Dam, like other grandiose development schemes, was scaled down. It is, however, still a massive project that has uprooted an estimated 11,000 people from their small river communities. They were given financial compensation for the loss of ancestral homelands, but it was often less than the amount of a house in

NIGHTLIFE, ORANG ULU STYLE

If you don't fancy the idea of having your face smeared with greasy soot and being dumped unceremoniously in the river, then perhaps you should steer well clear of the Kayan and Kenyah tribes. But if you do give them a wide berth, be warned that you'll miss out on one of the best travel experiences in Borneo.

The two tribes are numbered among the Orang Ulu (a general term, literally meaning 'upriver people', which covers a host of different inland tribes). The Kayan and Kenyah tribes are the people you're most likely to meet when travelling on the upper Rejang or upper Baram rivers.

Both tribes are originally from central Kalimantan (Indonesia), and have been moving downriver into Sarawak for centuries, fighting fierce territorial wars with the Iban that ended as recently as 1923. They have different languages but similar cultures, based on settled dry rice-farming. Sarawak's most artistic peoples, the Kayan and Kenyah build imposing longhouses, with exquisite woodcarvings and 'tree of life' paintings, and like all Sarawakians, they take hospitality very seriously.

If you visit a longhouse around Belaga or the upper Baram, you won't encounter a boisterous Iban-style welcome, but appearances can be deceptive. The Kayan and Kenyah are more reserved and refined than the Iban, but if you spend a day or two with them they will start to let their hair down. At sunset, huge glasses of *borak* (sour, very potent rice wine) are handed out and downed to a chorus of *'duiiiii ...'*, the local drinking song. Cigarettes made from fierce local tobacco are passed around. *Sape* players weave complex and haunting melodies on their mandolin-like instruments, and long-eared, tattooed women sing songs of praise to the guests, all the while chewing on betel nut.

You may be treated to warrior dances from the men and fan dances from the young women, and even a display of traditional wrestling. And if you're lucky, the festivities will last to sun-up, when the soot-smearing and dunking take place. It's the traditional Orang Ulu sense-of-humour test, given only to true friends. After such a memorable night you probably need a bath anyway.

Asap. Furthermore, the situation in Asap is not good; endemic unemployment and a poor transport infrastructure have left people in a sorry state. Some 100 families refused to move to Asap and have settled upriver from the Bakun site, though the government claims they are squatting on government land.

It remains unclear what purpose the dam serves – Sarawak doesn't need the electrical power and plans to move in aluminium smelters and other industries to utilise the excess energy worries environmentalists.

With a permit from Kapit, you can travel to near the dam – boat drivers will refuse to take you further than you're permitted to travel. The nearest longhouses to Belaga – such as Uma Aging and Uma Kahei – are mostly Kayan, but Uma Neh is a Kejaman longhouse and Long Semiang is a Lahanan longhouse within a 30-minute boat ride of Belaga.

Boats will not turn up unannounced, so you'll need an invitation to a longhouse from someone in town. A paved road to Bakun was recently completed linking it to the Bintulu–Miri highway.

NORTHEAST SARAWAK

Mukah

☎ 084

This small town on the coast north of Sibu is seldom visited by travellers, but it's a delightful spot to relax for a day or two, especially after the rigours of travel up the Rejang.

Most of the local people are Melanau, and the area's major attraction is the **Kaul Festival**, currently held on the second Sunday in April. *Pesta Kaul*, as it is called locally, is a lively beach celebration that includes enchanting enactments of the Melanau's rituals, and games to honour the spirits of the sea.

Kampung Tellian is a pleasant water village just beyond the centre of town; here you'll find **Lamin Dana** (☎ 871543; adult/child RM3/1; ⏰ 9am-5pm), a Melanau cultural centre and guesthouse built from traditional materials on the grounds of a Melanau highhouse. The folks who run this museum also live in it – the house features exhibits including heirlooms and handicrafts. Among things offered are traditional massage (two sessions are recommended) by the village midwife (RM30, 1 hour), river tours that visit a sago farm and old-style sago bakehouse, and Melanau delicacies such as *umai* (raw fish marinated in lime and onions), smoked fish and sago shoots (RM10). Cultural shows can also be arranged. Keep in mind that during Chinese New Year, the fourth week of December and the Kaul Festival, plane bookings and accommodation are usually full.

To reach Lamin Dana from Mukah, take a Tellian bus (50 sen) and tell the conductor where you want to go. Lamin Dana can also arrange longboat transport (RM3 per person) to or from the water village – an enjoyable way to reach the town centre. A taxi will cost RM5. Walking takes about 45 minutes. There are good photo opportunities from the bridge about 10 minutes outside Mukah.

SLEEPING & EATING

Lamin Dana (☎ 871543; www.lamindana.com; Kampung Tellian Tengah; r RM50) The rooms here are simply furnished and the toilets and showers are clean. A Melanau-style breakfast is included in the price. There are also four-person rooms for RM100 (discounts are available for stays of three nights or longer). The house has only nine rooms, so booking is a good idea, especially if you want to take part in activities, giving the staff time to arrange boats, dancers, or massage experts.

King Ing Hotel (☎ 871403; fax 871800; 182 Jl Boyan; s/d RM50/55) This new hotel has bright rooms and is close to the food court on the riverbank. The bus stop is a five-minute walk away. Nice corner rooms overlooking the river and temple are RM75.

Nelayan Melanau Café (☎ 019-817 7277; Block 1-3 New Town; dishes RM3-15) Malay and Chinese meals are served in this very clean café. To get to the New Town walk southeast from the old chimney (near the Chinese temple) to Jl Boulevard. At the end of the path turn west of the circle, which has a clock tower in the centre.

Located right on the river, the **food court** (Jl Pasar; dishes RM2-6) is a great place to have lunch or sip a beer and observe life in a small fishing village.

GETTING THERE & AWAY

Mukah's airstrip is just outside town; a Malaysia Airlines van will drop you at your

MALAYSIAN BORNEO

lodging for RM5. Malaysia Airlines Twin Otters fly between Mukah and the following centres: Bintulu (RM44, weekly), Kuching (RM76, daily), Miri (RM55, daily) and Sibu (RM30, six per week).

The **Lanang Road Bus Company** (☎ 332696) runs buses between Mukah and Sibu six times daily, starting at 6.30am in Mukah and 6am in Sibu. The last bus from Sibu to Mukah is at 4pm and from Mukah to Sibu at 4.30pm. The trip takes 3½ hours and tickets are RM13.80 (RM15.30 with air-con).

Buses leave Mukah for Bintulu (RM20, 4 hours) at 7am and 1pm daily and from Bintulu to Mukah at 8am and 1pm.

Bintulu

☎ 086

At the mouth of the Batang Kemena, Bintulu is a commercial centre servicing offshore oil and gas installations and upriver logging. Bintulu came under James Brooke's sway in 1861, and a simple **memorial** near the town centre commemorates Sarawak's first Council Negeri (State Council), formed in 1867. There's a colourful **Chinese temple** near the waterfront and a bathing beach north of town, but Bintulu is really only a transit stop for most travellers.

Travellers heading north to Niah Caves and Miri, and south to Sibu, the Rejang and Kuching, may need to use Bintulu's bus station as a staging post. If you're going to nearby Similajau National Park, you might also end up overnighting in Bintulu.

Similajau National Park (see p358), a 45-minute drive northeast of Bintulu, has a scenic estuary and some nice beaches. If you are self-catering at Niah Caves, Bintulu is a good place to stock up with provisions, Although Niah has a good cafeteria.

ORIENTATION & INFORMATION

Bintulu lies along the east bank of the Batang Kemena, within walking distance of the river mouth. All the places to stay and eat, banks and other services are situated between the old airport, which bisects the town, and the riverbank. The waterfront just north of the shopping area along Jl Masjid has several clean, bustling markets. The long-distance bus station is 5km north of town at Medan Jaya; take a local bus or taxi between here and the town centre.

Malaysia Airlines (☎ 331554; 🕑 8.30am-4.30pm Mon-Fri, 8.30am-12.30pm, Sat) is on Jl Masjid. The **Hong Leong Bank**, opposite the local bus station, is a good place to change cash or travellers cheques. For Internet access try **Star Internet** (☎ 312209; Jl Law Gek Soon; RM3 per hr) on the 1st floor of the building beside the **HSBC** bank.

SLEEPING

Budget

Bintulu's budget lodging is nothing to write home about and you're better off staying in mid-range hotels.

Dragon Inn (☎ 315150; 1 New Commercial Centre; s/d RM25/35) Of the budget possibilities, this hotel is probably the best one. The rooms are bright and clean but it can get noisy at night.

Sea View Inn (☎ 339228; fax 339226; 254 Taman Sri Dagang; s/d RM40/45; ❄) This one has the best location, it's on the waterfront and is basic but good value. Make sure to ask for a window facing the river.

Queen's Inn (☎ 338922; fax 330889; 238 Taman Sri Dagang; s/d RM40/45; ❄) It's always refreshing to find a hotel in the tropics that rejects carpets in favour of tiles. The rooms here are clean and the location is central.

My House Inn (☎ 336399; 161 Jl Masjid; s/d RM35/40; ❄) Among a cluster of hotels at this end, the inn is quieter than its neighbours, which are sandwiched between karaoke bars and discos, and has reasonable rooms.

Also recommended:

Fata Inn (☎ 332998; 113 Jl Masjid; s/d RM42/48; ❄) Very good value and it's clean and friendly.

Welcome Inn (☎ 315266; fax 315266; 186 Taman Sri Dagang; s/d RM30/40; ❄) Has small rooms but it's clean.

Mid-Range

Most of the hotels in Bintulu are in this category; they're fairly new and have TV, IDD phone and attached bathrooms.

Riverfront Inn (☎ 333111; fax 339577; 256 Taman Sri Dagang; s/d RM63/90; ❄) A very pleasant hotel, popular with expatriate oil workers and business people. If you're lucky enough to get a room overlooking the river, the view of boats travelling up and down is very much worth the extra cost at RM97 per room.

Regency Plaza Hotel (☎ 335111; hotel@plazabintulu.com.my; 116 Jl Abang Galau; s/d RM120/140, ❄ 🏊) This large hotel has all the personality of

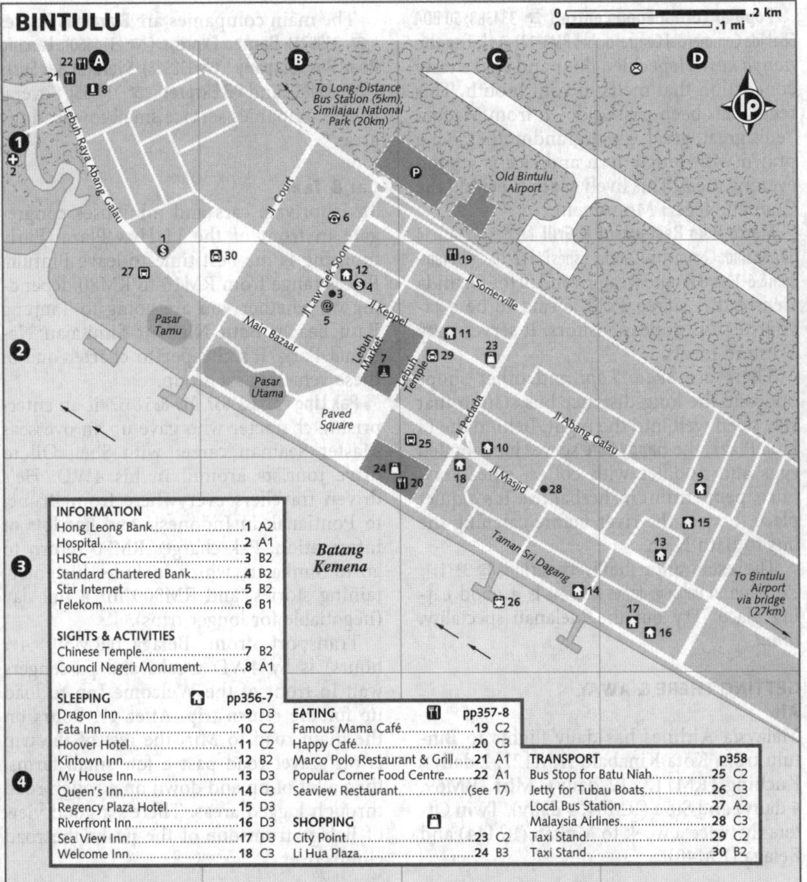

a suburban shopping mall, but the rooms are good value if you get a discount (quite likely) at RM90 for a double. There's also a rooftop swimming pool, which makes it an attractive place to stay.

Also recommended:

Kintown Inn (☎ 333666; 93 Jl Keppel; s/d RM75/80) These are clean, quiet and good value.

Hoover Hotel (☎ 337166; fax 337597; 92 Jl Keppel; s/d RM78/86;) The rooms are a bit stuffy but otherwise OK and the staff are friendly.

EATING

The top floor of the **pasar utama** (new market) is the place to go for hawker food. It has dozens of food stalls, and you can sit and look out over the river. The stalls at the **pasar tamu** (night market), near the local bus station, are good for takeaway satay, grilled chicken and fish.

There are literally dozens of Chinese *kedai kopi* along Jl Masjid, all offering very similar fare.

Seaview Restaurant (☎ 334929; 254 Taman Sri Dagang; dishes RM3-8) is a *kedai kopi* with standard Chinese food, but it you're tired of noodles for breakfast, they have nice toasted sandwiches and coffee.

Famous Mama Café (☎ 336541; 10 Jl Somerville; dishes RM2-4) A good place for quick and tasty halal Indian food. If you see a middle-aged woman with a red headscarf, ask her if she's the restaurant's namesake and you'll get a big smile in return.

Popular Corner Food Centre (☎ 334388; 50 BDA Shahida Commercial Centre; dishes RM3-12) Ask for the *nonya kavih* (speckled flour and egg) a tasty concoction that melts in your mouth. This recipe has been passed down from Madam Yeo's great, great, great grandmother. King prawn with jungle fern and rice is a good evening meal. This lively place is behind the Council Negeri Monument.

Marco Polo Restaurant & Grill (☎ 334214; 114 BDA Shahida Commercial Centre; dishes RM12-30; 🕑 11am-2pm & 6-11pm) At the western end of the Shahida Centre the Marco Polo is said to be a favourite of European visitors. It serves tasty Western meals.

There are *kedai kopi* and other shops opposite the long-distance bus station that stay open well into the night. Behind the Li Hua Plaza, the **Happy Café** serves hard-boiled eggs and noodles with coffee, wheatgrass juice, peppermint or herbal tea. It's a quiet place to view the river before catching the bus to Batu Niah.

The restaurant at the **Riverfront Inn** (☎ 333111; 256 Taman Sri Dagang; dishes RM5-24) is a good eating place. Try out the Melanau speciality, *umai*.

GETTING THERE & AWAY

Air

Malaysia Airlines has daily flights to Bintulu from Kota Kinabalu (RM127, 2 daily), Kuching (RM117, 12 daily), Miri (RM69, 4 daily) and Sibu (RM64, 4 daily). Twin Otters fly twice a week to Mukah (RM44) and Belaga (RM40).

Bus

It's easy to travel to Bintulu by bus as there are daily services from major cities leaving anywhere from every half-hour to two hours apart. Routes include Kuching (RM60, 9 daily), Miri (RM20, 15 daily) and Sibu (RM17, 18 daily). Take a local bus from the station near the covered markets, departing hourly from 7.15am to 9.15pm (50 sen). A taxi to the bus station costs RM10.

Various bus companies occupy the ticket booths at the long-distance bus station and display departure times and fares. Usually you can just buy a ticket and get on the next bus. Note that the posted bus services aren't always running, so it's best to ask ahead of time.

The main companies are **Biaramas Ekspres** (☎ 339821), **Borneo Express** (☎ 314460); **Lanang Road Bus Company** (☎ 338518), **Syarikat Bas Suria** (☎ 335489), and **PB Ekspres** (☎ 314355). Several other companies service small towns in the area.

Car & Taxi

Taxis, private cars and minibuses congregate in front of the Li Hua Plaza. Early morning is the best time to leave Bintulu. Prices range from RM15 to RM80 depending on whether you are going to Tanjung Batu beach, Batu Niah or Similajau National Park. It's cheaper to charter one of these vehicles as a group.

Pak Ling (☎ 335857, 019-885 8657) is an enterprising character who gave up an overseas Master Seaman career with Shell Oil to drive tourists around in his 4WD. He's driven travellers everywhere from Brunei to Pontianak in Indonesia and has lots of information. Pak charges RM70 return to go to Similajau, which includes his entertaining stories, and RM300 for a full day (negotiable for longer trips).

Transport from Belaga (RM50, 4½ hours) is by 4WD trucks and passengers wait in front of the Welcome Inn to load up for the return trip. After 1½ hours on the main road to Miri the rest of the trip is on gravel road past a few small farms, then a lot of up and down on a rough road through logged areas. There's a good view of Belaga from one of the peaks the road climbs over.

GETTING AROUND

Bintulu's airport is 27km west of the city centre. A taxi there will cost RM25.

Taxis congregate at the Chinese temple and at the big taxi stand near the markets. Most taxi fares around town are RM5. The trip to the long-distance bus station costs RM10, and the fare to Similajau is RM35.

Similajau National Park

☎ 086

A 45-minute drive northeast of Bintulu, this park's deserted, sandy beaches are among the best in Sarawak. Similajau does not have the variety of Bako National Park but it's perfect if you want a quiet, relaxing place during the week. It's easy to spend a day or two walking in the coastal rainforest or lazing on the beach. Permits for the park can be obtained on arrival; if the gatehouse is abandoned just sign your name and go on in. The gatekeeper will have gone fishing to break the boredom; they'll find you later to give you the permit and collect fees. Access to the park is by car or taxi only.

Similajau occupies a narrow coastal strip 30km long but only a few kilometres wide. Because Similajau is flanked by logged forest it's a haven for wildlife. A recent survey recorded 230 bird species, making it one of the most diversely inhabited areas in Sarawak. The forest is also home to 24 species of mammals; there are a few shy macaques around the park headquarters.

The park occupies the south bank of the mouth of the Sungai Likau, though most of it lies north of the river, and is accessed by a suspension bridge. The river crossing is a bit Tarzanesque – saltwater crocodiles occasionally lurk around the mouth of the river, especially in the early morning and evening. Swimming in the river is not recommended as crocodiles killed three locals in 2002. A warning sign is posted.

You might be able to arrange a boat up the mangrove-lined Sungai Likau for RM50 per hour (one hour should be enough). If you go in the early morning, you'll see a range of birds, including hornbills, and maybe mammals or even crocodiles.

There are pavilions along the casuarina-lined beach as well as decent accommodation and an information centre at the **park headquarters** (☎ 391284; fax 391251; admission RM10; ⌚ 8am-noon & 2-5pm). Accommodation for the park can be booked through the park headquarters or the **National Parks & Wildlife Office** in Miri (☎ 085-434184; fax 434179).

WALKS

Similajau has a limited trail network, the backbone of which is a long trail (9.8km from park headquarters) to Golden Beach. It's a long, hot trek so take lots of water.

Trails are well marked and a guide isn't necessary. After crossing the river from headquarters, head left off the boardwalk towards the headland. It's about half an hour's walk to a pavilion from where you can enjoy the view back along the coast towards Bintulu.

Further along the coast, the main trail leads to **Turtle Beach** (7km) and **Golden Beach** (9.8km), two beautiful, deserted spots where turtles come ashore to lay their eggs. Other trails forge into the low hills behind the coast to **Selunsur Rapids** (6.9km). To get to **Kolam Sebubong** you'll have to organise a boat at park headquarters (about RM75 – based on a rate of RM15 per person for a minimum of five people for one hour). The trip takes 30 minutes and Kolam Sebubong is a 15-minute walk from the boat drop-off. If you take the boat, you could also be dropped off at one of the other beaches along the way and walk back.

SLEEPING & EATING

Similajau can be visited as a day trip from Bintulu, but to tackle the trails, you'll need to stay overnight. Accommodation is comfortable, at least in the newest building, called Hostel 3. The **hostels** (dm RM10 with fan) each have four rooms. The air-conditioned **chalets** (RM60) have two rooms, each sleeping four people. There's also a **campground** (RM5 per person).

The park's **cafeteria** (⌚ 9.30am-6pm) has decent food and some sundry items for sale. There are no cooking facilities.

GETTING THERE & AWAY

Access to Similajau is off the road that leads to Bintulu's fairly impressive port. The first 2km is on a road under construction that will eventually be part of a new coastal highway linking Bintulu and Miri. From the marked turn-off, there's a 10km road through logged areas. There's no public transport; a taxi or private car will cost RM35 each way and you'll have to arrange a time to be picked up. Boat operators might do a trip from Bintulu, but it's expensive – this would only be economical for a group.

Niah Caves National Park

☎ 085

This small national park (32 sq km) near the coast between Miri and Bintulu protects one of Sarawak's most famous attractions, the Niah Caves. Niah Caves National Park is about 115km south of Miri and its centrepiece is the Great Cave, one of the largest caves in the world. The park is dominated by a 394m-high limestone massif, Gunung Subis, that is usually visible from quite a distance.

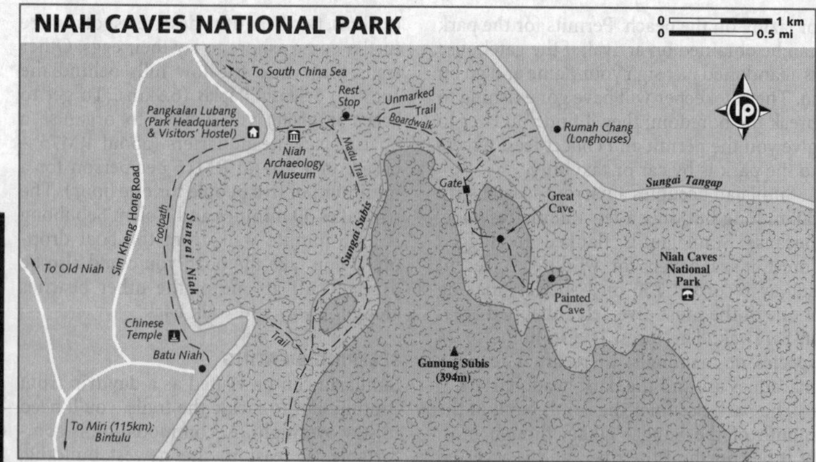

In 1958, archaeologists discovered evidence of human occupation of the caves area dating back some 40,000 years. Rock paintings were found in what has become known as the Painted Cave, and the discovery of several small canoe-like coffins (death ships) indicate that this site was once used as a burial ground. A reconstruction of the cave and some of the artefacts found here can be seen in the Sarawak Museum in Kuching.

The Niah Caves are home to a whole lot of bats and are also an important nesting site for swiftlets, which supply the vital ingredient for the famous bird's nest soup. Traditionally, the Penan have been custodians and collectors of the nests, while the Iban have had the rights to the caves' other commodity, bat guano. During the harvesting season nest collectors live in the caves, and the tools of their trade can be seen inside: massive bamboo poles lashed together and wedged against the cave roof above.

The bus from Bintulu or Miri will drop you in the centre of **Batu Niah** town. It's a 3km walk along the river to the park headquarters (follow the path past the red Chinese temple); you can also go by taxi, by longboat (if one is available) or someone in town may offer to drive you for a small fee. The road to the headquarters is behind the town centre to the left of where the bus stops, and the boat dock is directly to the right. Batu Niah has some decent food and lodging – see Sleeping & Eating p361.

Internet access is available at **Y2K Computer and Cyber Café** (☎ 736093; RM4 per hr), two blocks north of the Tung Poh Restaurant.

PERMITS, FEES & BOOKINGS

A permit is needed to visit Niah Caves; it is issued without fuss at **park headquarters** (☎ 737450; adult/child RM10/5; 8am-5pm). Upon arrival you must register at the park office and pay the entrance fee.

Bookings are advisable for accommodation at the park chalets. You can book accommodation at the visitors' information centres in Miri or Kuching, but make sure you get a receipt to present if requested at the park office at Niah. If you're staying at the hostel you can usually turn up without a booking, especially during the week. If it's busy and there's no accommodation, the worst you'll have to do is head the 3km back to Batu Niah, where there are three hotels.

SIGHTS

Niah Archaeology Museum

The **Niah Archaeology Museum** (admission free; 9am-6pm Tue-Sat) is a lovely Malay-style building with interesting displays on the geology, archaeology and ecology of the caves. It's in the park, just across the river from the park headquarters.

Niah Caves

To get to the caves from park headquarters first take a boat across the Sungai Niah; the jetty is down the path between the office building and the cafeteria. During the day the ferry costs 50 sen; from 5.30pm until the last crossing at 7.30pm it costs RM1.

Once across the river, follow the 3km-long raised boardwalk to the caves (note that it can get very slippery when it's raining). The boards are loose in places and make a lot of noise, but if you stop for a while you'll hear lots of birds and may also see macaques. As well as the hundreds of beautiful butterflies, wildlife includes squirrels, flying lizards and a striking emerald-green lizard that sometimes sits on the boardwalk.

Shortly after the rest stop, about 500m along, you'll pass an unmarked boardwalk branching off to the left – keep going straight. Approaching the caves, the trail skirts jagged limestone outcrops that appear like ancient ramparts festooned with giant vines and creepers. Just before the cave entrance the boardwalk forks; head to the right for the caves – the left fork goes to the village of Rumah Chang, where there are a couple of longhouses. Villagers usually sit at the junction selling cold beer and soft drinks. The trail goes under a large overhang with stout stalactites, called the **Trader Cave**. As the name implies, this is where early bird's nest and guano collectors carried on their business. The trail then rounds a corner to enter the vast **Great Cave**.

The impressive Great Cave measures 250m across at the mouth and 60m at its greatest height. Since you approach the cave from an angle, its enormity probably won't strike you straight away. It's usually only after descending the steep stairs into the bowels of the cavern for a half-hour or so that visitors pause to look back at where they've come.

At one time, some 470,000 bats and four million swiftlets called Niah home. There are no current figures today, but the walls of the caves are no longer thick with bats and there are fewer birds' nests to harvest. Several species of swiftlet nest on the cave walls; the most common by far is the glossy swiftlet, whose nest contains vegetation and is not harvested. For obvious reasons, the species whose nests are edible are far less abundant and can only be seen in the remotest corners of the cavern. Several species of bat also roost in the cave, but they're not in dense colonies and must be picked out in the gloom among the birds' nests – take a powerful torch (flashlight).

The best time to see the cave wildlife is at dusk, during the 'changeover', when the swiftlets return to their nests for the night and the bats come hurtling out for the night's feeding. You'll have to hurry back to the river, though, as the last ferry crossing is at 7.30pm.

Inside the cave, the boardwalk continues down to the right, but you'll need a torch to explore any distance. The stairs and handrails leading down into **Gunung Subis** are usually covered with dirt or guano, and can get very slippery in places. Allow a good hour to explore the Great Cave; the trail branches around a massive central pillar but both branches finish at the same point and it's impossible to get lost if you stick to the boardwalk. There's no need to hire a guide, although you can hire torches (RM5) from the first house beyond the visitors centre.

After following the pathway all the way through the Great Cave, a short forest pathway emerges beyond the larger cavern's opening and leads to the **Painted Cave**. To protect the death ships (empty now) and paintings, this area is fenced off. A set of small travel binoculars are useful to make out figures in and around the death ships. The paintings, done with a red hematite, are along a narrow 30m-strip at the back of the cave.

Outside the main entrance to the Great Cave, trails through the jungle will take you to the summit of Gunung Subis. The park headquarters provides a trail map.

SLEEPING & EATING

In the Park

Accommodation in the park is next to the Sungai Niah about 3km from Batu Niah. The **hostel** (dm/r RM15/42) has comfortable four-bed dorms with fan. **Chalets** (r RM105, with air-con RM158) have four beds. Bedding is provided, as well as utensils if you want to cook. **Camping** (RM5) is also possible. The park has a canteen with quite a good range of noodle and rice meals, and provisions are on sale here. In the dry season the rainwater tanks may dry out, so the water is drawn from the river and must be boiled before drinking.

Rumah Chang Niah Homestay Program (☎ 434181; stb@po.jaring.my) Staying in Rumah Chang, you'll be rubbing shoulders with bird's nest collectors from the Niah Caves.

It's a good base to visit the caves (15-minute walk), as well as exploring the park's other features. Visits to pepper gardens, jungle treks, and fishing trips are also available from the villagers. Reservations can be made through Niah park headquarters or Miri visitors' information centre.

Batu Niah

If you arrive outside the park office hours, or don't want to stay at the park, there are three hotels in Batu Niah.

Niah Cave Hotel (☎ 737726; s/d RM22/30; ❄) This friendly place has nice wood floors and the rooms are simple and clean, with shared bathrooms. It's back from the town square along the river. The bar downstairs sometimes serves food, but there are plenty of other eateries around the small town.

Park View Hotel (☎ 737021; fax 737023; 117 New Commercial Centre; s/d RM38/45; ❄) This place has decent rooms with tile floors and also offers economy rooms for RM25. You may not get much sleep though, as there's a late-night disco next door.

Niah Cave Inn (☎ 737333; fax 737332; 621 Batu Niah Bazzar; s/d RM52/58; ❄) This is the big hotel on the corner as you arrive in Batu Niah. It's the best hotel (and the best pun) in town, with TV, fridge and IDD phones.

Seng Kee Seafood Restaurant (☎ 737472; 622 Batu Niah Bazzar; dishes RM4-10) Right next door to the Niah Cave Inn, this place serves excellent Chinese food and has plenty of vegetarian options, as well as seafood of course.

Tung Poh Restaurant (☎ 737349; 599 Batu Niah Bazzar; dishes RM8-15) Across the road from the Niah Cave Inn, the Tung Poh is a good place for breakfast and opens at 8am, one hour earlier than the Seng Kee.

GETTING THERE & AWAY

Access to Batu Niah, the town nearest the caves, is by road only. Batu Niah is 13km west of the highway between Miri and Bintulu; the turn-off is 102km south of Miri. Express buses make a brief stop at the junction, which has a small market and a few shops, but if you take one of these buses you'll have to make your own way to Batu Niah.

There are ordinary long-distance bus services to Batu Niah from both Miri and Bintulu; check departure times with the visitors' information centres in Miri or Bintulu.

From Miri, **Syarikat Bas Suria** (☎ 085-434317) has five buses to Batu Niah (RM10, 1¾ hours) leaving between 6.30am and 4pm from the Miri bus station.

From Bintulu, **Syarikat Bas Suria** (☎ 086-335489) has six coaches a day leaving between 6am and 3.30pm from the Bintulu bus station or from Li Hua Plaza (RM11.50, 2 hours). Minibuses, share-taxis and private cars also make the trip, especially in the morning (see Getting There & Away for Bintulu, p358).

Leaving Batu Niah, the last bus is at 3.30pm, so if you're visiting the caves as a day trip, arrive early. If you do miss the last bus, private cars will offer lifts from Batu Niah to the highway turn-off (you shouldn't pay more than RM15) so you can catch an express bus back to Miri or Bintulu. Express buses stop at the junction, and the fare may be a bit higher than normal (eg RM10 to Miri instead of the regular RM8.50).

Returning to Bintulu, ordinary buses leave Batu Niah from the open area in the centre of town (6am to 3.30pm). There's no ticket agency – pay as you board. Buses back to Miri leave between 6.30am and 3pm.

GETTING AROUND

Transport to the park headquarters from Batu Niah is usually by taxi or boat. The boat trip costs RM10, plus RM2 per person for more than five people. Taxis also cost RM10. Boats do most of their business in the morning; in the afternoon it's usually quicker to get a taxi, a few of which are always waiting next to the bus stand. The boat trip is a short but exhilarating journey past jungle-clad limestone cliffs.

Lambir Hills National Park

☎ 085

A regional attraction and a popular weekend retreat for Miri residents, Lambir Hills National Park has pleasant rainforest walking trails, a picturesque natural swimming pool and riverside picnic shelters. At its closest point, the park is only 20km from Miri and city residents come by the car load to do the 15-minute walk to the pretty waterfalls, one of which cascades into a good swimming hole.

Lambir Hills makes an easy and enjoyable day trip from Miri, though you can always stay longer. While it doesn't have the spectacular scenery of Niah Caves and

Gunung Mulu National Parks or the diversity of Bako National Park, Lambir Hills is excellent for short jungle walks.

The national park covers 69 sq km and protects a range of low sandstone hills that reach a height of 465m at Bukit Lambir. Much of the forest was logged before the park was declared, but the secondary forest is beautiful in its own right and has a good range of wildlife.

Officially, the trails are open from 8am to 4pm Monday to Friday, and from 8am to 5pm on weekends and public holidays, but if you are seriously interested in wildlife-watching you will have to get an earlier start. Wildlife here includes gibbons, tarsiers, pangolins and barking deer, though you are unlikely to see any of these close to the park headquarters. Lambir Hills is also home to many species of birds.

Located next to the highway, the **park headquarters** (☎ 491030; adult/child RM10/5 ⌚ 8am-5pm) is 32km from Miri. Here you'll find the park office and information centre, a canteen and accommodation. Permits and accommodation bookings can be arranged at the visitors' information centre in Miri (see p365).

WALKS

Walking times given here are those posted at park headquarters; halve them if you are fit. The most popular walk is to **Latak Waterfall** – an easy 15-minute stroll from headquarters. The trail passes two minor falls before reaching the main waterfall, where there are picnic shelters, a changing shed and a large, clear pool, ideal for swimming. This walk is much quieter on weekdays.

From Latak Waterfall the main trail heads off to **Bukit Pantu** (about 1½ hours), the nearest peak to the headquarters, and Bukit Lambir. Just above the falls, at the start of the trail, is a 40m-high tree tower. The view of the forest canopy is magnificent, though the tower sways a bit in the breeze.

The main trail goes all the way to **Bukit Lambir** (3½ hours), from where there are fine views. Off the main trail there are many worthwhile waterfall detours: Nibong (about two hours); Pantu (just over one hour); Pancur (2½ hours), Dinding (about 2½ hours), and Tengkorong (2 hours). The trail is steep and slippery in places, but the walks are not overly strenuous. Bukit Pantu is a straightforward climb, but the stretch to Bukit Lambir can be tiring. From the headquarters, the Inoue Trail (45 minutes) is a short-cut that links up to the Pantu Trail.

It is possible to arrive at the park in the morning, walk to Bukit Lambir and back, then be on your way to Miri or Niah Caves National Park, but this doesn't leave much time to appreciate the forest or its wildlife. Register your name at the booth at the start of the trail before you head off.

SLEEPING & EATING

Accommodation at the park is comfortable, but it's only a few hundred metres from the main highway so you won't feel like you're in the middle of the jungle. Book at the visitors' information centre in Miri (see p365) in advance, particularly on weekends, though you are unlikely to be turned away if you don't have a reservation.

The three-bed **resthouses** (r RM50, with air-con RM100) have shared bathrooms.

There are no cooking facilities at the park, but a **canteen** sells rice and noodle dishes, drinks and basic provisions. Opening hours depend on demand, but are generally from 8am to about 7pm.

GETTING THERE & AWAY

Lambir Hills National Park is on the main highway and is easily accessible by bus from Miri. Take any Batu Niah bus for RM2.40 (see Getting There & Away in the Niah Caves National Park section p362), or any nonexpress bus going to Bintulu. Returning to Miri, buses from Batu Niah pass Lambir Hills and cost RM6.

From the park you must stand out the front and hail a bus; park staff can tell you when they pass. Heading south, the last buses to Batu Niah and Bintulu pass at around 3 pm. Heading north to Miri, the last buses leave at around 4.30 pm. Taxis cost about RM40.

Miri

☎ 085

Miri, Sarawak's most northerly city, evolved from a small and humble fishing town to a major commercial centre in a relatively short time with the discovery of oil in 1910. Besides the petroleum industry, timber, palm oil, pepper, rubber, and coconut oil have all played a part in the economy. The city is also an important service centre for

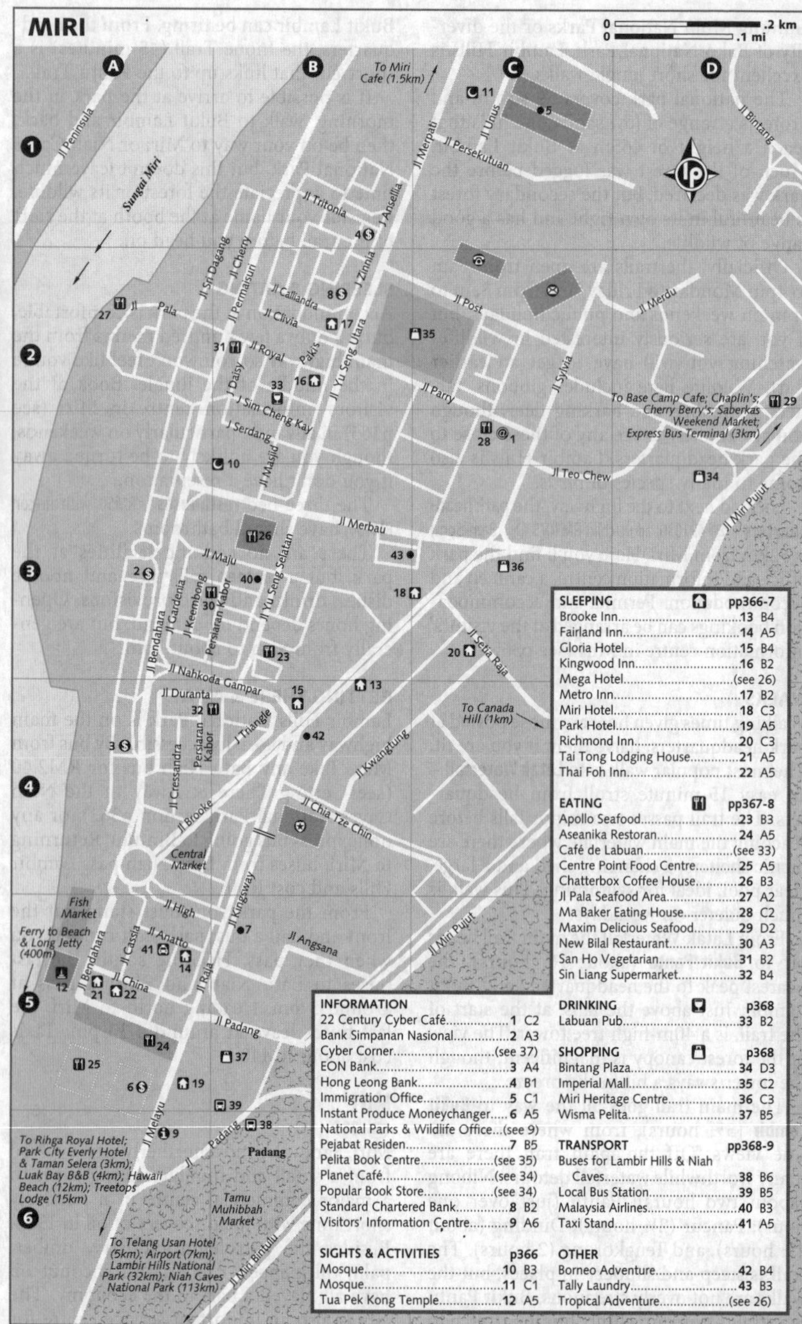
MIRI
0 .2 km
0 .1 mi
A
B
C
D
1
2
3
4
5
6
To Miri Cafe (1.5km)
Jl Peninsula
Sungai Miri
Jl Merpati
Jl Unus
Jl Persekutuan
Jl Bintang
Jl Tritonia
Jl Ansellia
Jl Sri Dagang
Jl Cherry
Jl Permaisuri
Jl Zinnia
Jl Calliandra
Jl Clivia
Jl Pala
Jl Royal
Pakis
Jl Yu Seng Utara
Jl Post
Jl Merdu
Jl Daisy
Jl Sim Cheng Kay
Jl Parry
Jl Sylvia
Jl Serdang
Jl Masjid
To Base Camp Cafe; Chaplin's; Cherry Berry's; Saberkas Weekend Market; Express Bus Terminal (3km)
Jl Teo Chew
Jl Miri Pujut
Jl Merbau
Jl Maju
Jl Yu Seng Selatan
Jl Bendahara
Jl Gardenia
Jl Keembong
Persiaran Kabor
Jl Setia Raja
Jl Nahkoda Gampar
Jl Duranta
Jl Triangle
To Canada Hill (1km)
Jl Kwangtung
Jl Cressandra
Persiaran Kabor
Jl Brooke
Jl Chia Tze Chin
Central Market
Fish Market
Jl High
Jl Kingsway
Ferry to Beach & Long Jetty (400m)
Jl Cassia
Jl Anatto
Jl Angsana
Jl Miri Pujut
Jl Bendahara
Jl China
Jl Raja
Jl Padang
Jl Melayu
Jl Padang
Padang
To Rihga Royal Hotel; Park City Everly Hotel & Taman Selera (3km); Luak Bay B&B (4km); Hawaii Beach (12km); Treetops Lodge (15km)
Tamu Muhibbah Market
To Telang Usan Hotel (5km); Airport (7km); Lambir Hills National Park (32km); Niah Caves National Park (113km)
Jl Miri Bintulu
INFORMATION
22 Century Cyber Café....1 C2
Bank Simpanan Nasional....2 A3
Cyber Corner....(see 37)
EON Bank....3 A4
Hong Leong Bank....4 B1
Immigration Office....5 C1
Instant Produce Moneychanger....6 A5
National Parks & Wildlife Office....(see 9)
Pejabat Residen....7 B5
Pelita Book Centre....(see 35)
Planet Café....(see 34)
Popular Book Store....(see 34)
Standard Chartered Bank....8 B2
Visitors' Information Centre....9 A6
SIGHTS & ACTIVITIES p366
Mosque....10 B3
Mosque....11 C1
Tua Pek Kong Temple....12 A5
SLEEPING pp366-7
Brooke Inn....13 B4
Fairland Inn....14 A5
Gloria Hotel....15 B4
Kingwood Inn....16 B2
Mega Hotel....(see 26)
Metro Inn....17 B2
Miri Hotel....18 C3
Park Hotel....19 A5
Richmond Inn....20 C3
Tai Tong Lodging House....21 A5
Thai Foh Inn....22 A5
EATING pp367-8
Apollo Seafood....23 B3
Aseanika Restoran....24 A5
Café de Labuan....(see 33)
Centre Point Food Centre....25 A5
Chatterbox Coffee House....26 B3
Jl Pala Seafood Area....27 A2
Ma Baker Eating House....28 C2
Maxim Delicious Seafood....29 D2
New Bilal Restaurant....30 A3
San Ho Vegetarian....31 B2
Sin Liang Supermarket....32 B4
DRINKING p368
Labuan Pub....33 B2
SHOPPING p368
Bintang Plaza....34 D3
Imperial Mall....35 C2
Miri Heritage Centre....36 C3
Wisma Pelita....37 B5
TRANSPORT pp368-9
Buses for Lambir Hills & Niah Caves....38 B6
Local Bus Station....39 B5
Malaysia Airlines....40 B3
Taxi Stand....41 A5
OTHER
Borneo Adventure....42 B4
Tally Laundry....43 B3
Tropical Adventure....(see 26)

the river towns in northern Sarawak. With a declining timber industry due in part to a growing worldwide awareness of endangered forests, Miri is entering another phase and is focusing on developing tourism services. The city has created theme gardens, an artificial lake garden, the largest open-air amphitheatre in Malaysia and is building an esplanade along the river.

While still mainly a stopover en route to longhouse visits, trekking or exploring caves, there's actually a little of everything for the visitor in and around Miri. There are parks and beaches outside town and an abundance of shops, good restaurants, several nightlife areas and friendly people. All of this makes Miri an enjoyable place to spend that extra day to acclimatise before heading off on an excursion or to unwind when you've finished.

ORIENTATION

Miri lies on a narrow plain between the east bank of the Sungai Miri and low hills that were once covered in oil wells – the source of the city's wealth. Most places to stay and eat are within walking distance of each other, but you'll need a bus or taxi to get to the long-distance bus station or airport. A few blocks north of the town centre are a couple of modern shopping malls, the main post office and the immigration office.

The local bus station and the stop for Lambir Hills and Niah Caves are close to the visitors' information centre.

INFORMATION

Airline Offices

Air Asia (www.airasia.com)

Malaysia Airlines (☎ 417315; Lot 239, Beautiful Jade Centre) Behind the Mega Hotel.

Bookshops

Pelita Book Centre (☎ 414116, Level 3, Imperial Mall) Has a small range of Borneo-related books and some maps. Look for the sign outside saying Kwan's bookstore.

Popular Book Store (☎ 439052; 2nd fl, Bintang Plaza) A large place with a good general selection.

Internet Access

Cyber Corner (1st fl, Wisma Pelita; RM5 per hr) Near the local bus station.

Planet Café (☎ 412260; 1st fl, Bintang Plaza; RM4 per hr)

22 Century Cyber Café (☎ 428922; Jl Parry; RM4 per hr) Above Ma Bakers.

Immigration Offices

The **Immigration Department** (☎ 442105; Wisma Persekutuan; Jl Persekutuan) is in a complex of government buildings in the northwest section of Miri.

Laundry

Tally Laundry Services (☎ 430322; Jl Merbau; 8am-6pm) has next-day laundry service.

Money

The **Standard Chartered Bank** (Jl Calliandra) changes travellers cheques, but it charges a hefty RM20 per transaction and 15 sen per cheque. Other major banks are clustered near the Imperial Mall. Moneychangers are common. **Instant Produce** (☎ 413233; 7 Jl Raja; 🕓 7.15am-9pm), near the visitors' information centre, changes cash.

Permits

In this area the only travel permits you'll need are for visiting longhouses upriver from Marudi or if you plan to go on a trek that goes past the Indonesian border in the Kelabit Highlands.

Present your passport at the **Pejabat Residen** (☎ 433202; fax 432876; Jl Kingsway; 🕓 8am-12.30pm & 2-5pm Mon-Fri, 8am-1pm Sat). Fill in a form with details of your intended visit (keep it simple), including your expected length of stay – there's currently no time limit. Your passport will be photocopied, then the Resident will sign the permit, which is free of charge.

Post

The post office is about 10 minutes' walk north of the city centre along Jl Sylvia.

Tourist Information

The **visitors' information centre** (☎ 434181; stb@po.jaring.my; Lot 452, Jl Melayu; 🕓 8am-6pm Mon-Fri, 8am-4pm Sat) is at the southern end of the town centre. The helpful staff can provide city maps, transport schedules and information on accommodation and tours.

National Parks & Wildlife (☎ 434184; fax 434179) is housed in the visitors' information centre. You can arrange permits and accommodation for Gunung Mulu, Niah Caves, Lambir Hills and Similajau National Parks here.

The visitors' centre was expecting to have a Miri guide available by late 2003. The centre is closed on the first and third Saturday of every month.

SIGHTS & ACTIVITIES

The atmospheric old part of town begins around the southern end of Jl Brooke; this is the area most worth exploring. The markets here are lively, especially in the morning, and there's plenty of commerce along the covered walkways in the Chinese shophouse blocks. The **central market** offers discounts on items such as cigarettes and alcohol; **Tamu Muhibbah** is a newer market complex where local Dayaks come to Miri to sell their vegetables. The wide courtyard of **Tua Pek Kong temple** near the fish market is a good spot to watch the river traffic float by. The recently built **Taoist Temple**, the biggest in Southeast Asia, features intricate façades brought over from China.

Canada Hill, on the low ridge behind the town centre, is Malaysia's first oil well, a wooden structure dating from 1910, from where you can get good views across Miri to the South China Sea.

If you land in Miri on a weekend, don't miss the **Saberkas Weekend Market** that takes place about 3km northeast of Bintang Plaza. It's one of the most colourful and friendly markets in Sarawak and vendors are more than happy to answer questions about the various products displayed.

About 3km south of town, Miri has a passable beach at **Taman Selera**. Further south, **Hawaii Beach** is a clean, palm-lined beach about 15 minutes outside town by bus. To get there, take Bakam bus No 13 (RM1.50); it runs between 6.30am and 6.30pm from the local bus station.

Diving

Aside from the islands of Talang-Talang near Kuching, Miri is about the only area in Sarawak where it's possible to dive. A short boat trip away are several small shoals (45 minutes) and a reef (2 hours). A Japanese WWII wreck, the *Atago-maru*, lies off the long jetty south of town. Outside the rainy season, visibility is good at the reef (up to 20m), though there's less to see here than at Sabah's better dive spots. Seridan Mulu (see Tours below) can organise trips, equipment and training.

TOURS

Miri has plenty of travel agencies that can book flights and confirm tickets. Numerous tour operators organise trips to Gunung Mulu and Niah Caves National Parks, as well as to other places – the visitors' information centre has plenty of brochures. Visiting the caves in Mulu is easy and cheaper as an independent traveller, but if you want to trek to the Pinnacles or along the Headhunters' Trail, you should compare tour company prices.

A full-day tour to Niah Caves costs about RM80 to RM100. Published prices for Mulu trekking vary depending on the accommodation and food arrangements. You don't have to stay at the resort but you'll have to negotiate another price with the tour company. Some established tour operators:

Borneo Adventure (☎ 438741; www.borneoadventure.com; 2nd fl, Lot 171A, Jl Brooke) A long-established and reliable operator with imaginative itineraries and commitment to responsible tourism.

Seridan Mulu (☎ 414300; www.seridanmulu.com; Lobby Arcade, Rihgah Royal Hotel) This outfit, 4km south of town, does trips to Mulu as well as scuba diving off Miri.

Tropical Adventure (☎ 419337; hthee@pc.jaring.my; Ground fl, Mega Hotel) Arranges trips throughout Sarawak and Sabah, including adventure caving tours to Mulu, hiking the Headhunters' Trail and trekking in the Kelabit Highlands.

SLEEPING

Budget

Miri has some budget accommodation but the mid-range hotels offer much better value for money.

Thai Foh Inn (☎ 418395; www.thaifoh.8k.com; 19 Jl China; s/d RM25/38; ❄) The air-conditioned rooms here are good value, and there's an in-house laundry service. Singles/doubles with fans are RM20/25 and dorms have three beds (RM15 per bed per night) with attached bathroom.

Fairland Inn (☎ 413898; Jl Anatto; s/d RM30/32; ❄) A quiet place that has small, clean rooms with attached bathrooms, the Fairland has a good location within walking distance of the local bus station, visitors' information centre and most of the restaurants.

Tai Tong Lodging House (☎ 411498; 26 Jl China; r RM40; ❄) This basic place recently has been cleaned up, though women travellers might still prefer a room to a dorm bed. Singles/doubles with fan are RM25/30 and a dorm bed in the lobby is RM10.

Brooke Inn (☎ 412881; brookeinn@hotmail.com; 14 Jl Brooke; s/d RM40/45; ❄) Travellers have recommended this hotel for its clean and basic accommodation; it's very good value.

Metro Inn (☎ 411663; fax 424663; 592 Jl Merpati; s/d RM55/58; ❄) Located up in the northern part of Miri, this place has bright, airy rooms.

Treetops Lodge (☎ 482449; mrmiri@tm.net.my; Lot 210, Siwa Jaya; dm RM20,) About half an hour outside Miri, Mike and Ester have a beautiful place on spacious grounds close to the ocean, and can also arrange tours. Air-conditioned rooms are available for RM50 and include breakfast. There's a gorgeous deck to lounge on and enjoy the sea breezes. Accommodation here can also be booked through www.borneo-holidays.com.

Mid-Range

As is the case elsewhere in Sarawak, there's plenty of choice in mid-range hotels. All have attached bathrooms, air-con and carpet, and most provide a TV and IDD phone.

Luak Bay B&B (☎ 424327; www.kelabit.net; 13 Jl Pantai; r RM60; ❄) David and Pauline have a serene place three minutes from the beach where you can watch the sunset from the jetty before returning for a barbeque and beer. David is an avid ambassador for Miri and its environs. To get there, take bus No 11 for Tanjong from Miri's local bus station.

Park Hotel (☎ 414555; fax 410003; Jl Raja; s/d RM58/78; ❄) A large hotel with a great location right by the visitors' information centre and the bus station. Decent-sized rooms make it a comfortable and convenient place to stay.

Miri Hotel (☎ 421212; fax 412002; 47 Brooke Rd; s/d RM60/75; ❄) The rooms here are clean and spacious, and breakfast at the small restaurant downstairs is included.

Also recommended:

Telang Usan Hotel (☎ 411433; tusan@po.jaring.my; s/d RM58/70; ❄) Large, friendly place run by an Orang Ulu family, on the road to the airport.

Richmond Inn (☎ 413289; fax 413297; 243 Jl Setia Raja; s/d RM50/65; ❄) Larger rooms make this hotel good value.

Kingwood Inn (☎ 415888; fax 415009; 826 Jl Yu Seng Utara; s/d RM45/70; ❄) A quiet place with clean, spacious rooms; breakfast included.

Gloria Hotel (☎ 416699; fax 418866; 27 Jl Brooke; s/d RM78/92; ❄) Has large, clean rooms in an older attractive building.

Top End

Mega Hotel (☎ 432432; www.megahotel.net; 907 Jl Merbau; s/d RM280/320; ❄) This upmarket hotel dominates Miri's skyline and is right in the centre of town. The service is excellent and there are two good restaurants. It's popular with tour groups and people doing business in Miri. Discounts are often available.

Rihga Royal Hotel (☎ 421121; www.rihgamiri.com; Jl Temenggong Datuk Oyong Lawal; s/d RM270/304; ❄) Miri's only five-star hotel is on the beach about 4km south of the town centre. There's a gym, business centre, restaurants, coffee shops and a beautiful swimming pool. Rooms with discounts (RM148) are great value.

Park City Everly Hotel (☎ 418888; fax 419999; r RM200;) The former Holiday Inn has been spruced up and is under new management. Close to the Rihga and also on the beach, the Everly has beautiful ocean views and 50% discounts were available at the time of writing.

EATING

There are plenty of good places to eat in Miri, especially in the blocks between Jl Brooke and the waterfront, with something to suit every budget.

Ma Baker Eating House (☎ 417307; Jl Parry; dishes RM2-6) This small bakery serves lunches, fresh fruit juices as well as baked goods. It's a pleasant place to cool off from Miri's heat during the day.

New Bilal Restaurant (☎ 418440; 250 Jl Persiaran Kabor; dishes RM4-10) For delicious Indian food, this unpretentious eating place is one of the better Indian restaurants you'll find. It serves all kinds of *roti canai* and the RM12 set meal of tandoori, saffron rice and raita is irresistible. You can even go there for breakfast at 6.30am. Another place serving excellent roti, as well as Indonesian food is **Aseanika Restoran** (☎ 424491; Jl Oleander; dishes RM4-8).

Apollo Seafood (☎ 420813; 4 Jl Yu Seng Selatan; dishes RM15-25) Miri seems to have a seafood restaurant on every second block, but this one is among the best. It also serves superb Chinese food and steamboat. Prices are reasonable, but it can get packed in the evening.

Maxim Delicious Seafood (☎ 413329; 1063 Jl Miri-Pujuit; RM15-40 per selection) A short walk north of the Bintang Plaza, Maxims is a well-known stop for seafood in Miri. Fresh fish in banana leaves is a speciality, which, depending on the type of fish, can cost up to RM80.

MALAYSIAN BORNEO

Another place for great seafood is a collection of restaurants with a common seating area right on the riverbank on **Jl Pala**, just north of the main Miri waterfront area. There are fabulous sunsets here between 5.30pm and 6.30pm, so bring your camera. Sit down and someone will come and take your order. Expect to pay RM25 and up for seafood dishes. Other food is also served.

Chatterbox Coffee House (☎ 432432; Mega Hotel; dishes RM10-30) This air-conditioned oasis serves delicious Malay and Western-style meals, on the ground floor of the Mega Hotel. It's also good for breakfast (opening at 6.30am) and the buffet dinner for RM30 is wonderful.

Miri Cafe (☎ 425122; Lot 2120-2121, Taman Yakin Commercial Centre, Jl Bulan Sabit; dishes RM10-20) About 1.5km north of the city centre, this friendly open-air bar and restaurant serves a wide range of delicious Western-style meals as well as Chinese and Malay food.

Café de Labuan (☎ 417353; Jl Sim Cheng Kay; dishes RM4-12) This covered bar and food-stall zone is fine for lunch or a cheap evening meal and a beer. Malay and Western-style meals are served.

San Ho Vegetarian (☎ 420688; Jl Royal; dishes RM6-10) Tucked down a quiet street, the San Ho serves up all kinds of Chinese-style tofu dishes masquerading as chicken, beef and seafood.

If you've just got off the bus and are famished, try the **Centre Point Food Centre** (dishes RM2-6), west of the visitors' information centre, has reasonably priced fast-food places dispersed around a very clean new mini shopping block.

For self-catering, the **Sin Liang Supermarket** (☎ 413762; Jl Duranta; 🕑 8.30am-9pm) is centrally located and a good place to stock up for trips to the interior.

DRINKING

Chaplin's (☎ 430339; Jl Miri Pujut, Pelita Commercial Centre) They don't make pubs like this any more – it's a classic expat bar and a very friendly spot for a beer.

Labuan Pub (☎ 417353; Jl Sim Cheng Kay) One of Miri's oldest pubs and still popular with some crowds. It can get rowdy at times. Follow the sounds or people to a few other pubs within a couple of blocks from Labuan.

Clippers is an English-style pub out at the Park City Everly Hotel where techno music is played; it attracts many Miri locals on the weekends. **Rigs**, next door at the Rihga Royal, is a trendy spot in a luxurious setting. Also at the Rihga, **Flags Bar** has a happy hour between 5pm and 9pm, when drinks are two for the price of one.

A few other notable pubs and lounges around the Pelita Commercial Centre include the **Other Office**, **Talking Point** and **Cherry Berry's**, which has live bands.

SHOPPING

Miri Heritage Centre (☎ 410280; Jl Merbau) Owned by the Miri municipal council, the centre was set up for various ethnic groups including Iban, Orang Ulu, Malay, and Chinese to sell their handicrafts such as beaded work, baskets, musical instruments, jewellery and curios. Cultural dances are sometimes performed, which you may be coerced to join in. Aweh and some of the other Kelabit, Kayan and Bidayuh vendors enjoy challenging customers to blow-pipe competitions. You have to get a bull's-eye to beat them.

GETTING THERE & AWAY

Air

Miri is well served by Malaysia Airlines. For flights in and out of Bario and Mulu, book as far in advance as possible. If flights are full to Bario or Mulu, try your luck at the airport. Check with the visitors' information centre for alternative flights to Mulu offered by Hawksbill Airways.

Malaysia Airlines has Twin Otter services to Bario (RM70; daily and an extra flight Monday and Sunday); Lawas (RM59, at least 3 daily); Limbang (RM45, at least 2 daily); Long Banga (RM67, 2 weekly); Long Lellang (RM66, 2 weekly); Long Seridan (RM57, 2 weekly); Marudi (RM29, 2 to 5 flights daily); Mukah (RM55, daily); and Mulu (RM69, 3 daily).

Larger aircraft fly direct to Bintulu (RM69, 4 daily), Sibu (RM112, 4 daily), Kuching (RM164, at least 7 daily), Labuan (RM66, daily) and Kota Kinabalu (RM104, 5 daily).

Malaysia Airlines has numerous daily flights from Kuala Lumpur to Miri (RM422), three of them nonstop. Air Asia has four flights a day to Miri from KL, which can be up to 50% cheaper than the Malaysia Airlines price.

Bus

For the latest bus information, check the English-language newspapers or ask the Miri visitors' information centre. The long-distance bus station is about 4km north of the centre along Jl Miri Pujut. If you're in a hurry to get to Batu Niah (RM15 to RM40) taxis, minivans and private cars are waiting for customers across the road from the local bus station by the visitors' information centre.

Buses to Kuala Baram and the crossing to Brunei depart from the local bus station at the southern end of the town centre.

Major bus companies serving Miri include **Syarikat Bas Suria** (☎ 430416), **PB Ekspres** (☎ 435816), **Biaramas Ekspres** (☎ 434319), **Lanang Road Bus Company** (☎ 433116), **Borneo Amalgamated Transport Company** (☎ 430420) and **Belait Transport Company** (☎ 419129).

Bintulu Express bus services go daily to Bintulu (RM20, about 4½ hours), roughly every hour between 6am and 8.30pm.

Batu Niah Syarikat Bas Suria has buses (RM10, 2 hours) leaving hourly from around 6.30am to 4pm from the bus shelter on Jl Padang (over the road from the local bus station).

Lambir Hills Syarikat Bas Suria buses go to Lambir Hills (RM3, 45 minutes).

Marudi The Belait Transport Company has buses to Kuala Baram every half-hour between 5.30am and 9.30pm (RM2.50, 1 hour). From Kuala Baram, express boats to Marudi (RM18, 3 hours) leave from about 7am to 3pm.

Kuching It's a long haul that can be done direct (RM70-80, 15 to 16 hours). The major companies each have a couple of buses daily from Miri with frequent departures throughout the day. The last one is at 10pm.

Mukah Syarikat Bas Suria has a bus from Miri to Mukah/Dalat (RM50, 12 hours) at 7.30am; it returns from Mukah at 8.30am.

Sibu Among other bus companies, Syarikat Bas Suria travels to Sibu (RM38, 8 hours) six times daily between 7am and 9pm and on Sunday at 5.30pm.

If you're headed to Brunei, it's a convoluted bus journey from Miri to Bandar Seri Begawan, Brunei's capital. The Belait Transport Company plies the route between Miri and Kuala Belait, the first leg of the trip, and has its office at the local bus station. Five services daily run to Kuala Belait between 7am and 3.30pm (RM12.20, 2½ hours).

There's a river crossing at Kuala Baram, where vehicles often have to queue for the ferry; passengers can wait by the edge of the river, leaving their bags on the bus. The Malaysian immigration checkpoint is just across the river. After clearing immigration you reboard the bus for the two-minute ride to the Brunei immigration checkpoint. Here you must take all your belongings with you through passport control and customs.

A Brunei bus will then take you to the Sungai Belait for another ferry crossing. The queues here are often horrendous and can last for hours; the driver and passengers leave the bus on one side, cross on the ferry (free), then board a bus on the other side of the river for Kuala Belait.

At Kuala Belait bus station you can change to a connecting bus to Seria. Start your journey early unless you want to spend the night in Kuala Belait. If you need to change money, there's a branch of the HSBC (Hongkong Bank) opposite the Kuala Belait bus station.

From Seria, you must take another bus to Bandar Seri Begawan. See the Brunei chapter for details.

GETTING AROUND

The Miri visitors' information centre has a handy schedule of local buses, printed on the back of the town map.

For the long-distance bus station, bus No 33 (70 sen) leaves regularly from the local bus station next to the visitors' information centre. Bus Nos 28 and 30 run frequently between the local bus station and the airport from 6am to 7pm (RM1.20, 20 minutes). Heading into town, the airport bus stop is to the left of the terminal as you exit.

Taxis from the airport run on a coupon system; a cab to a central hotel costs RM14. Other destinations are by negotiation – a taxi from the city centre to the long-distance bus station should be RM10. A taxi between Miri and Kuala Baram costs RM20.

Loagan Bunut National Park

☎ 085

This little-visited park in the Miri hinterland covers 10.7 sq km and protects the largest natural freshwater lake in Sarawak – although at 650 hectares it's not exactly huge. The surrounding forest hosts breeding colonies of **water birds** such as darters, herons and egrets. Local Berawans practise a unique form of fishing that has enabled them to keep the lake stocked with fish even during times of drought, which happens annually when the lake dries up completely for about two weeks.

For keen wildlife-watchers, or those trying to get off the tourist trail, Loagan Bunut is an interesting trip. Access is difficult and there are no visitor facilities in the park, but there's a nearby **hostel** (dm with fan RM15) with cooking facilities and fresh water (bring your own supplies).

Most travellers visit the park as a day trip with a tour. To visit independently, you're better off in a group since expensive river travel is involved. From the local bus station in Miri, take a bus to Tinjar or Lapok (RM8.50, 2½ hours). From there charter a car or Land Cruiser to Logan Pengkalan, and from there a boat to the park. Contact the **National Parks & Wildlife office** (☎ 434184) in Miri for the most current transport to the park. As with Sarawak's other national parks, entry is RM10 and a permit is required.

Marudi

☎ 085

Marudi is situated upriver from Miri. Its main attraction is yet another of the Brooke outposts, **Fort Hose** (admission free; 🕒 10am-6pm Tue-Sun) built in 1898 and named after Charles Hose, who became administrator of the district in 1891. The site became the Baram District Museum in 1997 and features some historical photographs and other items and is worth visiting if you get to Marudi. It's on a low hill at the eastern end of town.

Marudi sits on the north bank of the Batang Baram, and the main street, Jl Cinema, is aligned roughly east–west. It's a small town and most places to stay and eat are within a block or two of the main street. A square runs from Jl Cinema down to the river and all boats moor at the adjacent jetty.

Although the forest between Marudi and Kuala Baram on the South China Sea has long since been demolished, travel beyond Marudi to upriver longhouses is still quite pleasant and rewarding – at least once you get to Long Lama. Locals in Marudi can help arrange a visit – the longhouses are welcoming if you're expected. The **district office** (☎ 085-755 211) can help arrange permits.

There is a road network around Marudi and you can visit longhouses at Long Selaban and Long Moh. You can travel much further afield, though you'll have to arrange a lift locally. A road connecting Marudi to Miri may be finished by the time of this book's publication.

SLEEPING & EATING

Marudi has a lot of inexpensive hotels but it's doubtful anyone would spend much time here unless they're en route to Gunung Mulu National Park. The best place to stay is the **Grand Hotel** (☎ 755711; fax 755293; Marudi Bazzar; s/d RM45/68; ❄), two blocks north of Jl Cinema. Spacious air-conditioned rooms have TV and video.

There are plenty of *kedai kopi* around the square and along the main street at the western end of town. The Grand Hotel also has a good restaurant.

GETTING THERE & AWAY

Air

The Malaysia Airlines agent is **Tan Yong Sing** (☎ 755480), next to the Grand Hotel. Twin Otter flights go to Bario (RM55, 4 daily); Long Banga (RM59, weekly); Long Lellang (RM46, weekly); Long Seridan (RM42, weekly); and Miri (RM29, 2 to 5 daily).

Flights are often full – especially to Bario – and it's advisable to book ahead but you can always turn up in the hope of a cancellation. The airport is a 10-minute walk (1km) from the centre of town.

Boat

The express boats between Marudi and Kuala Baram operate roughly every hour between 7am and 3pm (RM18, 3 hours). The schedule may change when the road to Miri is finished.

Heading upriver from Marudi, express boats to Long Terawan (depending on the water level) leave when there's enough passengers (RM20, 4 hours), usually at around 11am. Speedboats are RM32. If you're heading into Gunung Mulu National Park from Long Terawan, you'll need to hire a boat. See Getting There & Away in the Gunung Mulu section, p376.

Batang Baram

The Batang Baram is northeast Sarawak's main artery. From Marudi this massive river runs deep into the interior through Kayan and Kenyah territory, and via its Dapur tributary continues right up into the Kelabit Highlands around Bario. Its upper reaches are home to the Penan, the seminomadic hunter-gatherers who have become symbolic of a disappearing way of life for the indigenous Dayak tribespeople of Sarawak. The Baram region is one of the major remaining areas of primary forest in Borneo, and one of the most heavily logged. The northeast has long been the centre of dispute between the government, logging companies and local tribes.

Logging roads in the Baram catchment have been blockaded many times in the past, and activists, including tribespeople, have been arrested. These days barricades are less common than briefs brought to the courts; in fact, the main problem for travellers – and locals – is the illegal logging operators, who are not always happy to see strangers. You may be turned back from certain routes, especially where fresh logging roads are being cut.

A permit is required to travel upriver from Marudi. They're available at the Pejabat Residen in Miri (see p365). If you want to experience a remote longhouse, exploring this region can be worthwhile. Travel agents in Miri can arrange tours along the Baram. However, be warned: much of the forest has been devastated and it's not a pleasant sight.

Going independently is not particularly easy or cheap. Express boats travel from Marudi as far as Long Lama, and from there it's possible to go by regular boat to Long Miri. From Long Miri travel is by smaller longboat, which must be chartered (at least RM150 per day, plus fuel). It's a full day's travel by boat to Long Akah, and then a day or more to Long Matoh.

The alternative is by road, which involves expensive 4WD hire. From the main highway south of Miri it is possible to go by a good logging road to Long Miri and all the way to Long Akah. This road is being pushed further into the jungle towards Long Lellang and beyond.

Gunung Mulu National Park

☎ 085

Gunung Mulu is the most heavily promoted of Sarawak's national parks and one of the most popular destinations in the state. The park is an unspoilt wilderness offering caving, trekking and wildlife-viewing. It can be enjoyed simply for its beauty or as a challenge that even experienced outdoors enthusiasts will relish.

At 529 sq km, Gunung Mulu is also Sarawak's largest national park. Among its remarkable features is the fact that two mountain ranges, one of sandstone and one of limestone, abut within its boundaries. The sandstone peak of Gunung Mulu is 2377m, and the limestone Gunung Api reaches 1750m. In between are more rugged mountains, deep gorges with clear rivers, and a unique mosaic of habitats supporting fascinating and diverse wildlife. Beneath the ground is a network of underground passages, stretching some 51km. A few years ago cave explorers here discovered the largest chamber in the world, the Sarawak Chamber, reputed to be the size of 16 football fields.

Keen cavers will get their money's worth at Mulu, but many travellers will want more reasons for making the trip to the park. Mulu's most famous attractions are the Pinnacles – a forest of razor-sharp limestone peaks towering 45m above the rainforest – and the so-called Headhunters' Trail, which follows an old tribal war path (see the 'Trekking in Gunung Mulu' National Park boxed text, p374).

Access to the park is either a long trip by boat from Marudi or a 40-minute flight. Expect to wait several days to a week to be confirmed on one flight. You can probably get to Mulu easily enough on standby, but getting back this way might mean a few extra days at the park.

Transport hassles are one reason many travellers resort to tours, even though Mulu is easily explored without a prearranged package. The other reason is cost. Trekking on your own can be expensive; guide fees and boat hire can seem unreasonably high because the rates are based on groups. Once you get to the park, though, it's also possible to get together with people and hire freelance guides.

PERMITS, FEES & BOOKINGS

When you get to the park office, a park permit will be issued and you'll be allocated a room or bed. Here you must also pay the RM10 park entry fee.

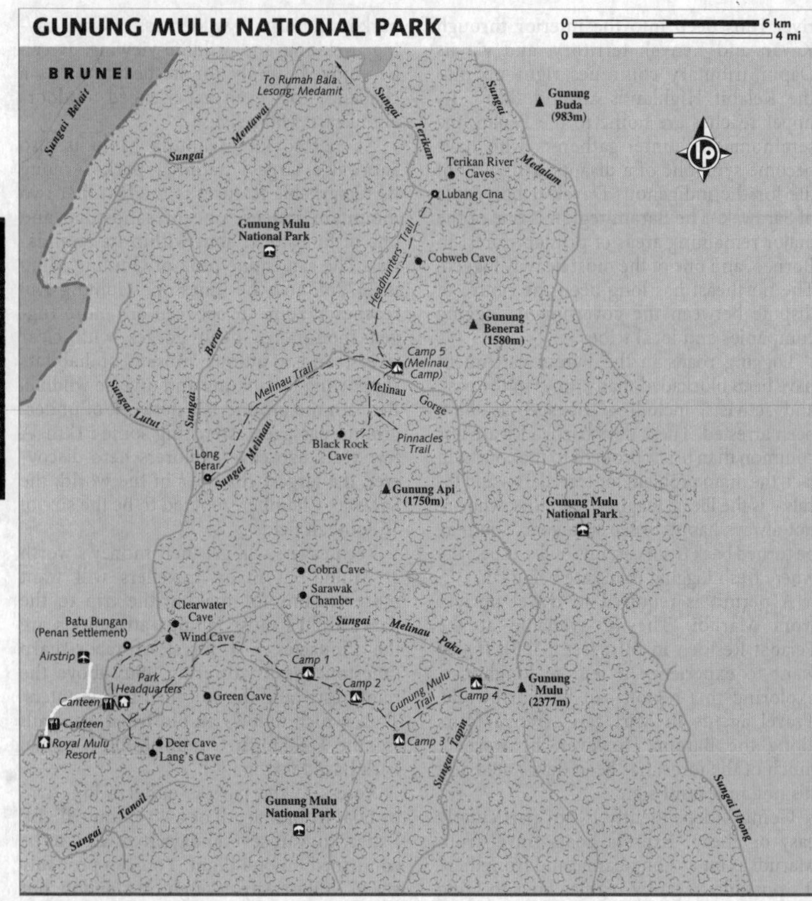

Accommodation bookings can be made at the visitors' information centre in Miri (see p365). You can simply turn up at the park office and book, but it's a popular spot and you run the risk of finding all the accommodation booked out. There's accommodation outside the park but it may also be full, though someone would probably put you up in their house in a pinch.

SIGHTS & ACTIVITIES

Show Caves

The Deer, Lang, Clearwater and Wind Caves are all known as the Show Caves, and are easily accessible to visitors. Other caves are closed to the public because they are inaccessible or considered dangerous, while others contain fragile formations that park authorities want to protect from further deterioration.

Due to the availability of power for lighting, the Clearwater and Wind Caves are officially open only in the morning and the Deer and Lang Caves only in the afternoon. Power failures are not uncommon, but natural light to some extent illuminates much of the Clearwater and Wind Caves in particular.

A park fee of RM20 gives access to the Deer and Lang Caves or to the Clearwater and Wind Caves.

Deer Cave & Lang's Cave

Deer Cave and adjoining Lang's Cave are the closest caves to the park headquarters, an easy 3km walk along a boardwalk. At 2160m long and 220m deep, they have the world's largest cave passage. Both are very safe, with walkways and wooden steps.

Lang's Cave is lit each afternoon until 4pm, though a strong torch is still useful for the darker areas. There are pretty **stalagmites** and **stalactites** and some other strange formations. Water cascades from openings in the roof after heavy rain. You enter the cave on one side of the mountain and exit from the other; it takes about 30 minutes to walk the entire length.

Deer Cave is a gaping cavern in the mountainside, huge beyond comprehension. It doesn't have the attractive formations of Lang's Cave and there's the added stink of ammonia from the piles of guano on the floor. Look up and you'll see the cause – some two million **free-tailed bats** clinging to a roof so distant that they appear as a seething black mass. The bats emerge from the cave entrance between 5pm and 7pm each night in a vast chittering stream that can last for half an hour. They can be seen from quite a distance, and a 'bat observatory' station has been built; there are also picnic tables from where you can get a great view. The swarm is a sight not to be missed and is one of the wildlife highlights of Mulu.

Clearwater Cave & Wind Cave

Wind Cave is part of the Clearwater Cave system and the starting point for some of the longest tunnels. It opens out in a cliff above the Sungai Melinau and has a boardwalk and stair system that does a loop around some impressive caverns and beautiful limestone formations.

It's not marked on park maps, but to get to the Wind Cave you first have to pass through the small **Moon Milk Cave**, which is at the top of a steep set of stone steps. A good torch and caution are essential: Roots snake around your feet, rock formations hang at head height and parts of the boardwalk are rotten.

The Clearwater Cave is 51km long (the longest cave passage in Southeast Asia) and 355m deep. It takes its name from an underground river that spills through a natural grate to form a crystal-clear **swimming pool** near the cave entrance. A bridge over the river is reached by the path on the left of the cave entrance. The path on the right passes some of the cave's finer features. Access is via steep concrete steps up a hillside then along a walkway, which can be slippery in places.

There's a pleasant but slippery trail from the park headquarters to the Wind and Clearwater Caves that takes about an hour to walk, and which follows the Sungai Melinau for part of the way. The walk from the Wind Cave to Clearwater Cave takes about 15 minutes.

Adventure Caving

There are plenty of other caves in the park, and new caves are regularly discovered. It's estimated that the number already explored represents only about 40% of the total number of caves in Gunung Mulu National Park.

It's possible to explore the nooks and crannies of the Show Caves away from the pedestrian boardwalks, and a few other caves are open to experienced cavers. The park offers guides for adventure caving, though it doesn't supply equipment, and needs at least a day's notice. The price ranges from RM200 to RM300 for groups of up to five people, depending on the cave. Tour companies also offer caving expeditions that allow you to crawl, climb and swim your way through the many passages of the caves.

Other Activities

Non-guests can hire **kayaks** and **mountain bikes** (RM25 for the first hour) from the Royal Mulu (see p376). There are some good biking trails near the resort, and **rock climbing** (RM36 per hour) on the premises.

Wildlife

Gunung Mulu National Park features eight types of forest, including peat swamp, tall dipterocarp and, at the summits of the higher peaks, stunted moss forest. Thousands of species of plants have been recorded here, and each new scientific expedition finds new species. Among the finds are over 170 species of orchid and 10 species of pitcher plant.

A staggering 275 species of birds have been recorded at Mulu, as well as 75 species of mammals, 74 of frogs, 281 species of butterflies and – while we're counting – 458 species of ants. Mulu is part of traditional Penan hunting grounds and the tribe is still allowed

MALAYSIAN BORNEO

TREKKING IN GUNUNG MULU NATIONAL PARK

Gunung Mulu National Park offers excellent jungle trekking for the fit and determined. There are three main treks in Mulu – the Gunung Mulu Trail, the Pinnacles Trail and the Headhunters' Trail. An attempt at any of them will involve some expense and it's best to go with a group to reduce guide and transport costs. Ask around when you get to park headquarters to see if anyone's interested in sharing costs.

You should not attempt any of the following trails without a guide – and you won't be permitted to anyway. Expect rain, leeches, slippery and treacherous conditions, and a very hot workout – carry lots of water. Your guide should let you go at your own pace. Many who attempt the Pinnacles or Gunung Mulu don't make it to the top. Guides can be arranged at the park headquarters.

The Pinnacles

The Pinnacles is an incredible stone forest towering 45m, halfway up the side of Gunung Api.

The trek to the Pinnacles starts with a two- or three-hour boat trip (depending on the level of the river) from park headquarters to Long Berar. From here it is a tough 8km trek to Camp 5 by the Sungai Melinau. Camp 5 is hostel-style accommodation with running water, cold showers, a cooking area, 'American' toilet and covered sleeping quarters. Sleep overnight at this picturesque spot before climbing Gunung Api.

You'll have to climb virtually the whole distance to see the Pinnacles – there's no easy way out. The three- to four-hour ascent is very steep and slippery in parts. It's best to start early in the morning, when it's a lot cooler and you're more likely to see wildlife. The ultimate destination is a small viewing point looking out over the Pinnacles. It is possible to camp here, but the Pinnacles trip is usually done in one day and most trekkers return to Camp 5. If you start at sunrise it's possible to return to park headquarters the same day.

Guides' fees are RM400 per group for a three-day/two-night trek; each extra day costs RM20 plus a RM10 allowance per night. The rate for boat hire to Long Berar from park headquarters is RM350 return for one to four people, or RM85 per person for five or more. One way costs RM200 per boat for up to four people, or RM45 per person for five or more.

Gunung Mulu Trail

The climb to the summit is normally done as a four-day trek and is the highlight of many a traveller's visit to Mulu. You must carry enough food for the entire trip, as well as your own cooking utensils and a sleeping bag (it gets quite cold at night). It's not unusual for it to rain every day, so

to hunt in the park. Don't worry about encountering the business end of a blowpipe on your travels – tourism has made larger birds and mammals scarce near trails.

Around the park headquarters you'll see a few common species of birds, such as bulbuls and sunbirds, but look out for the white-fronted falconet – the world's smallest bird of prey and only slightly larger than a sparrow. The walks to the Show Caves can be very good for spotting birds, particularly in the early morning. At the caves themselves you'll see plenty of swiftlets nesting on the cave walls, as well as a selection of birds of prey that pick off the bats as they come pouring out in the evenings. Along the rivers you can see the stork-billed kingfisher, with its massive red bill, and the amazing black-and-red broadbill – a clownish-looking bird with a fat blue bill.

With the exception of bats, most of Mulu's mammals are shy and difficult to see, although you'll probably encounter squirrels along the trails. Look out for the pygmy squirrel along the boardwalks, and the striking Prevost's squirrel in the trees.

If it's not raining you'll see an incredible variety of butterflies along the trails. When it's raining you can expect lots of leeches (but not many different species) to appear as if from nowhere. See That Clinging Feeling boxed text in the Health chapter, p579.

Batu Bungan Penan Settlement

The Gunung Mulu region is mainly home to the Berawan people, but the government you could find yourself wallowing in mud all the way. Good walking shoes are a must. The guide fees are RM1000 per group.

There are several camps (basic wooden huts) along the trail; Camps 1, 3 and 4 are the ones usually used for overnight stops. The most common schedule involves an easy first day (about three or four hours' walking) and overnight at Camp 1 beside a beautiful river. On day two you're faced with a long (four or five hours), hard and extremely steep climb to Camp 4. If it hasn't rained, there won't be any water at Camp 4, so carry some up from Camp 3.

On day three leave your pack at Camp 4 and climb to the summit of Gunung Mulu. You can either sleep at Camp 3 another night and return to park headquarters on day four, or descend the mountain in one day. The latter is quite tough on the legs, but you can cool down in the river along the way.

Headhunters' Trail

The Headhunters' Trail is a backdoor route from Gunung Mulu to Limbang and can be done in either direction, though most organised trips start in the national park. This trail is named after the Kayan war parties that used to make their way up the Sungai Melinau from the Baram area to the Melinau Gorge, then drag their canoes overland to the Sungai Terikan to raid the peoples of the Limbang region. A 3m-wide road lined with poles was used to move the canoes, and a canal was dug around Batu Rikan.

To do the Headhunters' Trail independently you should gather a group together to share costs, and ask around for a guide at park headquarters. The usual procedure is to take a boat to Long Berar (RM250), walk to Camp 5 (about four hours) and overnight there (RM10 per person) on the first day. Day two involves an 11km walk to the Sungai Terikan (four or five hours), where you can spend the night at the rangers' station (Mentawai) or proceed to Rumah Bala Lesong, an Iban longhouse another three or four hours away. After overnighting in the longhouse, it's a boat trip farther downriver to Medamit, from where it is possible to travel by minibus to Limbang.

The boat from the Sungai Terikan to Medamit should cost about RM350 to RM400; the guide's fee will come to about RM400 (per group); a suitable payment for food and lodging at the longhouse will be about RM20 per person; and the minibus from Medamit to Limbang costs RM5. Extra costs include food for the stay at Camp 5, gifts for the longhouse and a tip for your guide if you feel it is warranted.

You could do the Pinnacles trek, return to Camp 5 then set off on the Headhunters' Trail the following day. This trip is equally possible in the opposite direction – take a bus to Medamit, where a boat can be arranged to the longhouse or the ranger's station at Mentawai.

has settled a Penan group on the banks of the Sungai Melinau as part of its campaign to change the nomadic lifestyle of these people, since logging and development have increasingly threatened their traditional way of living.

There are actually two Penan settlements at Mulu: Long Iman is well south of the park headquarters along the Sungai Tutoh and is not open to tourists without an invitation; Batu Bungan is a stark reminder of the consequences of 'modernisation' for people who never asked for its blessings in the first place.

In fact, Batu Bungan has never been blessed. Its sorry patchwork housing can be seen through the trees across the river as you walk to the Clearwater Cave. Boats carrying tour groups drop by the small market where people set up on the riverbank at around 9am. There's some fine **rattan weaving** on sale (the plain, dark-coloured bracelets are worn by the Penan in the jungle; the more colourful, patterned bracelets are for tourist trade), but the rest of the village is private housing.

The Penan are highly regarded by Borneo tribes as 'the true people of the forest'. They are a shy people, even when dealing with other tribes, so if you visit the market, folks will be more at ease if you speak softly, move slowly and avoid large, sudden gestures. Hardly any English is spoken here, but there will probably be a tour guide around in the mornings to help with translations.

A large primary school serving the two Penan settlements has been built nearby, and you'll probably hear the children before you see them. The settlement can also be reached by a path leading towards the river from the airport – take a left on the boardwalk and then the first right to reach the river.

TOURS

The park office handles all bookings and fees for guides, and can also arrange transport. On arrival, some boat operators will offer to arrange a cave tour for you on the spot. Avoid them if you are looking for a group to join – transport and a guide can be arranged at any time at the park office.

The cost for trekking guides depends on the distance covered and the number of people trekking – the park office has a schedule of fees. For example, for a group of five trekking to the Pinnacles over three days and two nights a guide will cost RM400; and to the summit of Gunung Mulu RM1000. There's an additional fee of RM10 per night at Camps 3, 4 and 5. Bigger groups bring down the cost for each individual, but if a group is too large you'll see less wildlife along the way.

Boat costs are relatively high, for example, RM85 per boat (up to four people) for Clearwater Cave and RM350 return to Long Berar for the Pinnacles trek. If you want to visit all the caves and do a lot of trekking, an organised tour starts to look cost effective. Most travel agents charge around RM1000 for four days and three nights at the park. This includes a visit to all the caves, a trek, all transfers and mid-range accommodation. Packages that include accommodation at Royal Mulu Resort will cost a little more.

SLEEPING & EATING

Given Mulu's popularity and the preference for tour groups, it can sometimes be difficult to book a place to stay, but private accommodation is available outside the park. Note that there are no cooking facilities at the park, though you can boil water and make toast at the hostel.

The standard of accommodation at the park won't win any awards. There's a roomy 18-bed **hostel** (dm RM15) and a 15-bed **cabin** (r RM50). There are also air-conditioned three-bed rooms in the **longhouse** (r RM100) and three-bed **chalets** (RM150).

There are two places to eat near the park headquarters; a canteen with a pool table (inside the park just along from the hostel) and a canteen across the river from the park headquarters (at the end of the suspension bridge). The one across the river is a good place to buy basic noodle and rice dishes, as well as soft drinks. It's also a good spot for an evening beer. Each is open from 8am to around 9pm (though the canteen inside the park often closes earlier); cheap and simple meals, soft drinks, beer and bottled water are available at both. The latter has a deck over the river and is a pleasant place for a meal.

Royal Mulu Resort (☎ 790100; www.rihgamulu.com; r RM290; ❄ 🅿) This luxury hotel complex, about 3km from the park entrance, is tastefully built around limestone bluffs overlooking the river. Rooms are nicely appointed and the garden is full of flowers, butterflies and birds. The food at the resort's coffee shop/restaurant is good but expensive and it's not worth a special trip from the park unless you're dying for fish and chips.

The Royal Mulu ownership itself is embroiled in a dispute with Berawan tribespeople, who originally sanctioned the use of the land for Mulu National Park, not for a luxury resort funded by foreign and government investment. Plans by the hotel to occupy more land for a golf course have only added fuel to the fire.

GETTING THERE & AWAY

The only practical way in and out of this popular park is currently via Miri, and the vast majority of travellers make the trip by air. Book as far in advance as possible. If you arrive at Mulu overland and plan to leave by air, make a booking as soon as you arrive.

Air

Malaysia Airlines has Twin Otter flights between Mulu and Miri (RM69, 3 daily), though cancellations due to weather are not uncommon. Hawksbill Airways also has flights into Mulu, ask at the visitors' information centre in Miri (see p365).

Bus & Boat

For a more adventurous trip, it's possible to get to Mulu by a combination of bus and boat. From Miri take a local bus to Kuala

Baram (RM2.50, 1 hour). Buses leave regularly, but if you want to get to the park in one day, take the 6am bus; alternatively, stay in Marudi overnight.

From Kuala Baram there are express boats to Marudi (RM18, 3 hours) leaving between 7am and 3pm. Launches go from Marudi to Long Terawan when there are enough passengers (RM20). If the water is high enough they go all the way through; if not, change boats at Long Apoh.

Travel from Long Terawan to the national park is by charter boat. Ask around in Marudi before you set off to try and pre-arrange this, or if you arrive early enough in Long Terawan you can probably find someone there. The boat will cost at least RM150. The journey takes around two hours.

It's easier to arrange a Long Terawan boat from Mulu (ask at park headquarters or at the canteens) and it's easier to fly into Mulu than back out, so it makes sense to do the river trip on the way out of the park. You need to be up at 4am to get the boat to Long Terawan in time to connect with the express boat to Marudi. The Mulu–Miri run will take eight to 10 hours. If you're up for the time and effort, the river route to Mulu is a unique experience and a great alternative to flying.

GETTING AROUND

The park headquarters is a 3km walk from the airport along the road to Royal Mulu Resort; the park turn-off is on the left, about 10 minutes' walk from the airport. Minivans run between the airport and headquarters, but there's no regular service. You can catch a lift with one of the resort vans (about RM2).

Bario

☎ 085

Bario is a small settlement in a beautiful valley 1500m up in the Kelabit Highlands, close to the Indonesian border. A trip to the Kelabit Highlands is a highlight of any visit to Borneo.

Sleepy Bario played a pivotal role in Borneo's modern history. It was to here that Major Tom Harrisson and a British commando unit parachuted during WWII to organise resistance against the Japanese occupation. During the Konfrontasi with

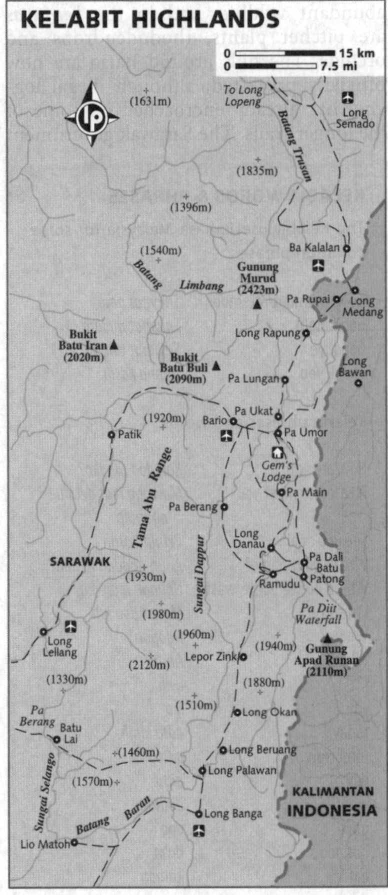

Indonesia in the early 1960s, the area was again the scene of aerial strafing and nasty guerilla fighting. Some people near the Indonesian border relocated to the Bario area during this time and stayed.

Bario's appeal lies in the hospitality of the Kelabit people, the clear mountain air and the splendid isolation (access is by air only). The valley northeast of Bario past Pa Ukat offers stunning views. The region features Kenyah and Kelabit longhouses, great highland treks to suit all levels of fitness and motivation and vistas of highland farming. Bario rice is renowned Asia-wide and considered by some Japanese as the best in the world. The nearby hills are covered in largely untouched forest with abundant wildlife, and in the *kerangas* are pitcher plants, rhododendrons and orchids. The hills around Bario are now officially protected, although illegal logging has already encroached on some of the longer trails. The Sarawak government has tentative plans for the Kelabit Highlands to become a major tourist destination in the next three to five years. There's mixed feelings on the subject among the locals; many feel they haven't been asked for enough input.

Travellers should bring enough cash for accommodation, food and guides; small denominations, such as RM10, RM5 and RM1, will be useful – and take extra in case you are stranded. There are no credit-card facilities in the Kelabit Highlands. Bario and Ba Kelalan have shops where you can stock up on basic supplies.

KELABIT WORDS & PHRASES

The Kelabit use Bahasa Malaysia for some common phrases:

Good morning/afternoon	*Salamat pagi*
Good night	*Salamat malam*
Goodbye	*Salamat tingga*
Thank you	*Terima kasih*

Kelabit phrases and words:

How are you?	*Kan doo tah iko?*
Pleased to meet you	*Mawang niat petulu nganuih*
See you again	*Petulu baruh*
What's your name?	*Anun ngadan nuidih?*
Where do we bathe/wash?	*Ngapah inan diu?*
I'm sorry	*Mutuh doo iuh*
Where?	*Ngapah?*
What?	*Anun?*
I	*u-ih*
you	*iko*
today	*adto kinih*
tomorrow	*adto riak*
day	*adto*
night	*dadtan*
good	*doo*
not good	*da'at*
eat	*kuman*
drink	*mirup*
go	*ame*
go for a walk	*ame nalan-nalan*
sleep	*rudap*
lodge	*rumah tumpang*
longhouse	*rumah kadang*
jungle	*pulung*
leech	*lamatak*
wild boar	*baka*
bucking deer	*tela'o*

Kelabit forms of address:

grandmother/grandfather	*tapu*
older man	*tamah*
older woman	*sinah*
chief	*tua kampung*

ORIENTATION & INFORMATION

Bario is not actually a town in the usual sense; rather, it's a lush valley settlement dotted with longhouses, wet-rice fields, a church or two and a couple of rough dirt roads. There's a long row of tiny shops selling a few necessities (expensive, as they have to be flown in), which might be considered the centre of town. This is also where you'll find the Malaysia Airlines desk and the police office. The immigration office is near the junction of the airport road and the rutted road to the shophouses (turn left from the airport) and Gem's Lodge (turn right).

The airport is about a 30-minute walk south of the blue-roofed shophouses. To reach the centre of town from the airport, head up the road (bear right at first), then take a left at the junction where Labang's Longhouse sits. You probably won't have to walk anyway – everyone here is welcoming and you are bound to be offered a lift.

There's a public telephone near the middle of the shophouses. Internet service is available at the nearby **Telecentre** (11am-4pm; RM4 per hr).

Guide fees are generally RM50 per day for one-day treks or tours, and RM65 per day for overnight treks; add RM50 per day if a porter is required to carry gear and cook. Some guides may have raised their rates to RM80 by the time this book is published. Guides are generally arranged by the lodges, or you're bound to meet one yourself. Tour operators from Miri also do package trips to Bario. To plan your trip and get more information about the Kelabit Highlands, check out the website www.kelabit.net.

SLEEPING & EATING

Gem's Lodge (☎ 019-815 5779; gems_lodge@yahoo.com; dm RM15-25) If you're looking for tranquility away from the beaten path, this simple and comfortable lodge, situated in the trees on a riverbank, is the place to stay. Just 6km southeast of Bario near the longhouse village of Pa Umor, Jaman and his wife make your stay a memorable one with delicious Kelabit-style meals made with produce from the garden, as well as a few jungle delicacies. Going out with Jaman, one of Bario's best and informative guides, is a real treat. Accommodation with meals ranges from RM50 to RM75 and separate chalets are in the works. To reserve from Miri call **Gerawat Gala** (☎ 019-855 3546).

De Plateau Lodge (www.kelabit.net; dm RM15, with meals RM50) Douglas (Munney) and Millie Bala are the gracious hosts here, 2km east of Bario, and staying in this lovely home (designed by Munney), surrounded by beautiful gardens, is a joy. Great meals are served up, made with local produce and Bario's world renowned rice. An early morning coffee outside or an evening beer inside with Munney is equally pleasurable. He loves talking about the Bario area and will arrange trips according to his customers' abilities and wishes.

Labang's Longhouse (☎ 016-8952102; ncbario@yahoo.com; dm/r RM20/40) Labang's Longhouse, 1km east of Bario, has 17 rooms (two beds per room) and more under way. The longhouse-style lodge is good for large groups, especially educational, cultural or nature tours. Meals are optional, at RM45. Having spent many years in his work and own interest campaigning for nature conservation in Malaysian Borneo, David, the owner, is very knowledgeable about environmental issues.

Also recommended:

JK View Lodge (rose_sabot@hotmail.com; dm RM15, with meals RM50) Rose's place is 0.5km west of Bario, near the shophouses, and close to longhouses where she can arrange rooms to stay for intimate views of longhouse living. Rose also arranges guided treks and tours.

Bario Asal Longhouse Stay (www.kelabit.net; dm RM15, with meals RM50) Peter Matu guides and provides accommodation out of his family longhouse 2km west of Bario.

GETTING THERE & AWAY

The only way into Bario (other than by walking) is by air. Booking one to two weeks in advance is advisable.

Malaysia Airlines Twin Otters fly daily from Miri (RM70) and twice daily on Sunday and Monday. Flights are in the morning and return to Miri the same day. Flights from Bario currently have to be booked at the Malaysia Airlines office in Bario or at the airport. Book as early as possible to coincide with your trekking plans. Flights are dependent on the weather and cancellations are not uncommon, so make sure your schedule isn't too tight. Many flights are overbooked so show up at the airport (Miri or Bario), even if you have no reservation, in the hope of getting a stand-by flight. For the Harvest Festival in June, flights will be full.

Hornbill Skyways was taking over Vision Air at the time of writing and will fly into Bario. Check with the visitors' information centres in Miri (p365) or Kuching (p323).

Limbang

☎ 085

This small, prosperous town on the Batang Limbang is sandwiched between the two parts of Brunei. There's not much to do here except have a few beers in the evening by the river. Then again, if you've just come from Brunei or the Headhunters' Trail, this may be all you need.

ORIENTATION & INFORMATION

The main part of Limbang sits along the east bank of the Sungai Limbang, which loops across a forested plain before emptying into Brunei Bay. A range of low hills further east marks the border with Brunei's Temburong district.

The older part of town is only a couple of hundred metres square and is bordered on the riverbank by a two-storey, blue-roofed market. The massive peach-and-green complex looming over the wharf area is the Purnama Hotel and its attendant shopping mall, the Limbang Plaza. Beyond this, and downstream about 200m from the old town, are concrete blocks of shophouses with cafés, karaoke bars and snooker halls; here you'll find accommodation and some good riverside eateries. On the opposite bank of the river stretches a pleasant stilt village punctuated by the domes of mosques.

Boats to Brunei and Labuan leave from the wharf below the blue-roofed new market, and taxis park just outside. Boats to Lawas tie up at the jetty a few hundred

BARIO & THE KELABIT HIGHLANDS

Bario is ringed by forested hills, and a network of basic roads and tracks offer some great trekking options. There are plenty of possibilities for easy walks to nearby longhouses, longer hikes into Kalimantan and tough treks to the spectacular peaks guarding the Kelabit Highlands.

Day Walks

Of the longhouses close to Bario, you can walk southeast to **Pa Umor** (about one hour) and nearby **Pa Ukat**. The trail then continues to Pa Lungan. There's a Kelabit burial ground close to the centre of town on the way to **Pa Ramapuh**, a village in Bario about a 1½ hour-walk away. There is a **waterfall** about 7km beyond Pa Ramapuh.

Another day walk is to **Pa Berang**, a Penan settlement approximately 15km from Bario where it's possible to continue on the loop back to Bario (see the Bario Loop on the following page). Keep an eye out for the *dolmen* (stone burial markers) dotted throughout the highlands; new ones are sometimes found when a trail is blazed through the forest.

Gem's Lodge and De Plateau Lodge (see p379) organise a wide variety of tailor-made shorter walks and longer treks. A day trip to the **salt lick** *(main tudtuh)* an hour's walk from Gem's Lodge is fascinating. You'll learn the local method of salt processing, done in giant vats over a roaring fire; though ask at the lodge if there's any work going on, as this method is beginning to die out.

Treks

Longer, more strenuous walks can take you through superb rainforest and on to alpine plateaus, staying overnight at longhouses en route; or across the Indonesian border and back. For certain sectors you are strongly advised to hire a guide – trails are sometimes indistinct, terrain can be rugged, and it may be wet and slippery. Visitors occasionally get lost up here and you should seek local information before setting out.

The guestbooks in the lodges and longhouses are full of good information. Note that longhouses in the area normally charge for an overnight stay – RM20 is the usual charge, and meals are extra.

Gem's Lodge and De Plateau Lodge offer a five-day **wildlife-spotting** trip, which involves trekking to undisturbed jungle patches and *leeks* (watering holes) tracking wildlife (here's your chance to add a few bird and animal calls to your repertoire) and staying in jungle camps and a longhouse

metres downstream. Buses leave from a stand a couple of blocks east of the river, behind the old part of town. The airport is about 4km south of town.

There are several moneychangers across the road from the Brunei–Labuan wharf, and there's a Maybank near the Muhibbah Inn.

SIGHTS

A **tamu** (weekly market) is held on Friday in the car park in front of the new market. Villagers come in from the surrounding district, who are mainly Bisayah and speak the Brunei Malay dialect, which is still strong here.

The small but excellent **Limbang Regional Museum** (Muzium Wilayah; admission free; 9am-6pm Tue-Sun) is upstairs in another of Charles Brooke's forts, built in 1897. It's definitely worth the five-minute walk along the river. The collection is well presented and features exhibits of archaeology, culture and crafts of the region. To get here, follow the riverbank upstream (south) past the police station; there's a well-carved replica of the totemic Pagul pole at Batang Pirak (near Medamit) out the front.

Down the road from the museum and up a steep drive is a pretty **park** with an artificial lake backed by forest. It's a pleasant place to pass some time if you're waiting for a flight.

SLEEPING & EATING

Some of the cheap-looking places on and around the main street opposite the wharf are decidedly sleazy. The decent places are mostly mid-range, air-conditioned hotels, some of which accept credit cards.

Muhibbah Inn (☎ 212488; fax 212153; 30-31 Jl Bank s/d RM40/55;) Right in the centre of town, this older hotel looks a little worse for wear, along the way. Wild boars and bucking deer, as well as the endangered black monkey *(wawa)* and hornbill are among the wildlife you might see.

Because of encroaching logging in Sarawak, much of the wildlife has moved south, and the Kalimantan loop from Pa Umor can offer the best chance to see birds and animals. Long Bawan is the main border town and one of two entry points to Kalimantan in the area.

Pa Umor–Lembudud–Long Bawan–Pa Umor

This is a three-day trip; Lembudud is the first settlement across the Indonesian border south of Pa Umor.

Pa Umor–Tang Paya–Long Bawan–Jungle Camp–Pa Umor

This is either a four- or five-day trip; the longer hike involves staying in a jungle camp an extra night and walking via Long Medang.

Bario Loop

This five-day trek goes through some varied country (Pa Berang, Ramadu and Pa Dali), staying in longhouses, and ending up back in Bario. It's a good idea to add on a day or two for exploring the area around Pa Dali. Pa Main is an alternative stop at the beginning or end of the loop, depending which direction you go. Long Danau, another stop on the loop, can be reached in one day, but it's about an eight-hour hike.

Bario–Ba Kalalan

Another possibility is to walk to Ba Kalalan, a day's walk beyond Pa Lungan, and then fly to Lawas (RM46, 5 weekly). Walks in this area are difficult – you'll need to have your own food and shelter and be prepared for some hard slogging. It's a good idea to hire a local guide. A border permit is also required from the immigration office in Bario, as the route takes you into Kalimantan via Pa Rupai. De Plateau Lodge or Gem's Lodge can help arrange this.

Bario–Long Lellang

It's also possible to walk to Long Lellang and catch one of the flights to Marudi (RM46, once weekly) or Miri (RM66, twice weekly) though you'll have to time your arrival. The trip to Long Lellang is a four- to six-day trek. Guides are recommended.

but has decent and clean rooms if you can find them through the maze of corridors.

National Inn (☎ 212922; fax 212282; 69 Jl Buangsiol; s/d RM50/53; ❄) This is a good hotel with clean rooms and views of the river.

Purnama Hotel (☎ 216700; fax 216711; r RM150; ❄) A four-star hotel with friendly staff, the Purnama has large, adequate rooms. They're good value when discounted (RM80).

There are food stalls on the 1st floor of the waterfront market and at the bus station. Basic Malaysian food, roti and *murtabak* is served in the halal cafés in the same building as the Muhibbah Inn.

Maggie Café (☎ 212278; Jl Buangsiol; dishes RM8-20) Near the National Inn, this is a good spot for dinner. It serves excellent grilled fish and cold beer at tables overlooking the river.

Kuali Cafeteria (Purnama Hotel; ☎ 216700; dishes RM10-25) There's a range of Western-style dishes here if you're craving a sirloin steak at the end of the Headhunters' Trail. It also has a good breakfast buffet.

GETTING THERE & AWAY

Air

Malaysia Airlines has Twin Otter flights to Miri (RM45, 3 daily), Lawas (RM25, 4 weekly) and KK (RM60, 3 weekly). The airport is 4km south of the town centre. A taxi to the airport costs RM5 per person if there's a full load; it's hard to get a taxi to take you on your own for less than RM10.

Boat

Speedboats make mostly morning runs between Limbang and Bandar Seri Begawan (RM20 or B$10, about 30 minutes). The boats go when they have a full load of 12 passengers, so you may have a bit of a wait after 9am or so. The last boat in each direction leaves at around 4.30pm.

An express boat goes to Lawas every morning at 7.30am (RM20, 30 minutes). The express boat to Labuan in Sabah leaves at 7.30am and 8am (RM22, 2 hours). From Labuan to Limbang the boat leaves at 12.30pm and 2.30pm. Buy your ticket at the wharf.

Bus

It's possible to travel by road between the two halves of Brunei via Limbang. For connections to Bandar Seri Begawan, Brunei's capital, there's a scheduled bus from Limbang to Kuala Lurah on the Brunei border (12 buses daily between 5.30am and 5.30pm).

There's no bus service to the nearby eastern Brunei border, but taxis regularly make the trip for about RM20, and all the way to Bangar by negotiation. Make sure you call at the Brunei immigration checkpoint on the road into Bangar; it's open daily from 6am to 10pm. From Bangar it's possible to go overland to Lawas and on to Sabah, but it involves an expensive taxi ride (see Lawas Car & Taxi on this page).

Regular buses to other parts of the Limbang district leave from the bus station at the northeastern corner of the old town. There are services to Pandaruan, Buagsiol, Batu Danau, Kubong, Ukong and Tedungan. If you're planning to follow the Headhunters' Trail into Gunung Mulu National Park, the bus for Medamit leaves roughly every hour between 5.30am and 4.30pm and costs RM5.

Lawas

☎ 085

Lawas is a busy little town on the banks of the Batang Lawas. Like Limbang, it's a transit point where you may find yourself en route to/from Miri, Brunei or Sabah. Logging is a big industry in this part of Sarawak and a logging road runs from Lawas to Long Semado. It's impossible to get lost here; the bus station is in the middle of town and places to stay and eat are in the surrounding shophouses. There are several budget to mid-range hotels in town; rooms are basic but OK and cost around RM35 to RM50. A couple of top-end options are located near the airport, about 2km from town.

GETTING THERE & AWAY

Air

The Malaysia Airlines agent is **Ngan Travel Services** (☎ 285570; Lot 455, 2 Jl Liaw Siew Ann). Twin Otters fly to Kota Kinabalu (RM47, 2 weekly), Miri (RM59, at least 3 daily), Limbang (RM25, 5 weekly) and Ba Kalalan (RM46, 5 weekly).

Boat

All boats leave from the riverside wharf east of the town centre.

An express boat to Limbang (RM20, 30 minutes) leaves between 8am and 9am – check the current schedule at the wharf. If you're heading to Brunei, the only boat leaves at 7am daily (RM25); it returns at 1.30pm. Boats to Labuan (RM22, 2 hours) leave at 9am daily, but this schedule changes often.

Bus

There are daily buses to KK (RM20, 4 hours) and the towns en route, leaving Lawas at 7am.

If you miss the express service to KK, there's a direct minibus to Beaufort (RM15).

Car & Taxi

If you happen to miss the boat to Brunei, you could travel by taxi to Bangar, in Temburong, and from there then take a boat to Bandar Seri Begawan. You'll first need to clear Malaysian immigration at Lawas wharf, then get the taxi to take you to the Brunei immigration office (a few kilometres past Bangar) before bringing you back to the Bangar wharf. All up, this should take about 40 minutes and the taxi should cost RM100. Boats for Bandar Seri Begawan leave regularly from Bangar until about 4.30pm (B$7).

It's possible to reach Ba Kalalan in the Kelabit Highlands overland from Lawas or vice-versa by 4WD Land Cruiser. With eight people squeezed in, the price is RM40 per person, or RM400 to hire the vehicle. The trip takes five to six hours.

Sabah

CONTENTS

Sabah

Travellers venturing from Sarawak into Sabah will discover another side of Malaysian Borneo. Sabah is something of a frontier state, and a sense of history in the towns and landscape is hard to find. Sabah's past masters have included Sulu sultans and foreign invaders hungry for the state's natural resources; the present masters are plantation owners, real estate barons and those with the power to grant logging concessions in irreplaceable rainforests.

Even the Malaysian government's hold on parts of the territory is tenuous: Sabah's proximity to Indonesia and the Philippines ensures both nations claim areas of the state as their own. Sabah, Indonesia and the southern Philippines have many cultural similarities – not least of which is a strong Islamic tradition. Filipino migrants eke out a living here along with Indonesians, many of whom come to work in the vast palm – oil plantations covering the southeast. Sabah's own people – the Kadazan, Dusun, Murut, Bajau, Bugis and Rungus are among the main groups – seem to take all this in their stride.

The state is known abroad mainly for its incredible natural features. There are gorgeous beaches to lie on and coral reefs to explore, birds, animals, trees and plants to seek out and a huge mountain to climb, Mt Kinabalu (4095m), one of the highest yet most accessible mountains in Southeast Asia.

HIGHLIGHTS

- Climbing **Mt Kinabalu** (p414), an immense granite peak with unbeatable summit-view sunrises
- Drifting on the tributaries of **Sungai Kinabatangan** (p432) for some of the best wildlife-viewing in Southeast Asia
- Diving in the pristine waters surrounding **Pulau Sipadan** (p438) and other coral reef islands off Sabah's coast
- Experiencing the thrill of trekking in the primary rainforest of the **Danum Valley** (p434)
- Getting an intimate glimpse of orang-utans at the **Sepilok Orang-Utan Rehabilitation Centre** (p429)
- Exploring the islands and beaches of **Tunku Abdul Rahman National Park** (p398)
- Wandering the streets and markets of **Kota Kinabalu** (p388), Sabah's lively capital
- Witnessing the regeneration of the endangered green turtles at **Turtle Islands National Park** (p431)

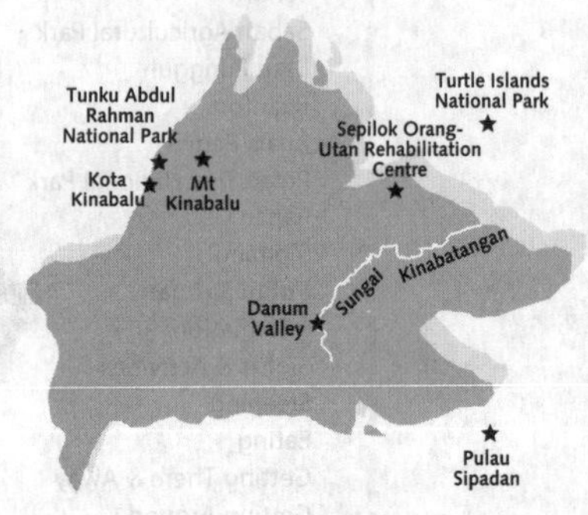

■ TEL CODES: 087, 088, 089 ■ POPULATION: 1.7 MILLION ■ AREA: 73,619 SQ KM

History

Before Malaysia's independence Sabah was known as North Borneo and administered by the British North Borneo Company. After WWII both Sabah and Sarawak were handed over to the British government, and both decided to merge with the peninsular states to form the new nation of Malaysia in 1963.

But Sabah's natural wealth attracted other prospectors and its existence as a state was disputed by two powerful neighbours – Indonesia and the Philippines. There are close cultural ties between the people of Sabah and the Filipinos of the nearby Sulu Archipelago and Mindanao. Several small islands to the north of Sabah are disputed by the Philippines, and a busy smuggling trade operates from Sabah into Mindanao. Mindanao's Muslim rebels often retreat down towards Sabah when pursued by government forces, and pirates based in the Sulu Sea continue to raid parts of Sabah's coast.

After independence, Sabah was governed for a time by Tun Mustapha, who ran the state almost as a private fiefdom and was often at odds with the central government in Kuala Lumpur (KL). In 1967 he even threatened secession. He disappeared from the political scene in 1975. In 1985 the Kadazan-controlled Sabah United Party (Parti Bersatu Sabah; PBS) came into power and joined the National Front Alliance.

However, tensions with the federal government were rife. In 1990 the PBS pulled out of the alliance with the National Front just days before general elections. The PBS claimed that the federal government was not equitably returning the wealth that the state generated and, in 1993, it banned the export of logs from Sabah, largely to reinforce this point. The federal government used its powers to overturn the state decision. Though there's always talk of handing back more of the profits that Sabah's natural resources deliver to KL, to date nothing has changed – the crumbs KL leaves on the table for each state amounts to only 5% of the pie.

Partly as a result of its bad relations with the federal government, Sabah is currently the poorest of Malaysia's states. Although it's rich in natural resources, one-third of the population lives below the poverty line. Part of the problem is a bizarre rotation system that forces a change of political administration in Sabah every two years. This serves the federal government well, since politicians aren't in power long enough to implement anything autonomous; in fact, they aren't around long enough to do much of anything – beyond perhaps setting themselves up for a comfortable life after office.

Climate

Like the rest of Malaysia, Sabah's climate is hot and humid. Expect temperatures in the high twenties and low thirties throughout the lowlands. The state's rainfall averages about 300cm annually and though it can rain anytime during the year, the heaviest rainfall generally occurs between November and April. At higher elevations, the temperature is refreshingly cool and downright cold at night. Mt Kinabalu has its own climate and temperatures can drop to freezing above 3500m.

Visas & Permits

Sabah is semi-autonomous, and like Sarawak it has its own immigration controls. On arrival most nationalities are likely to be given a visa for two months' stay and it is rare to be asked to show money or onward tickets. Most visitors arrive at the state capital, Kota Kinabalu (KK), but it is possible to travel into Sabah overland from Sarawak via Brunei (see p529); by boat from Kalimantan (Indonesia) to Tawau (see p442), or from the Philippines city of Zamboanga to Sandakan (see p429).

Visas can be renewed at immigration offices at or near most points of arrival, even at small places like Merapok near Beaufort. If you miss them it's not a problem – just report to another immigration office, even if it's several days later, and explain your situation to the officials.

Apart from entry to national parks and other reserves, permits are required to visit Pulau Sipadan (Sipadan Island), the Danum Valley Conservation Area and the Maliau Basin. With the exception of the Maliau Basin, you can obtain these permits at each destination upon arrival.

National Parks & Reserves

Sabah's national parks and their inhabitants are among the main reasons tourists visit the

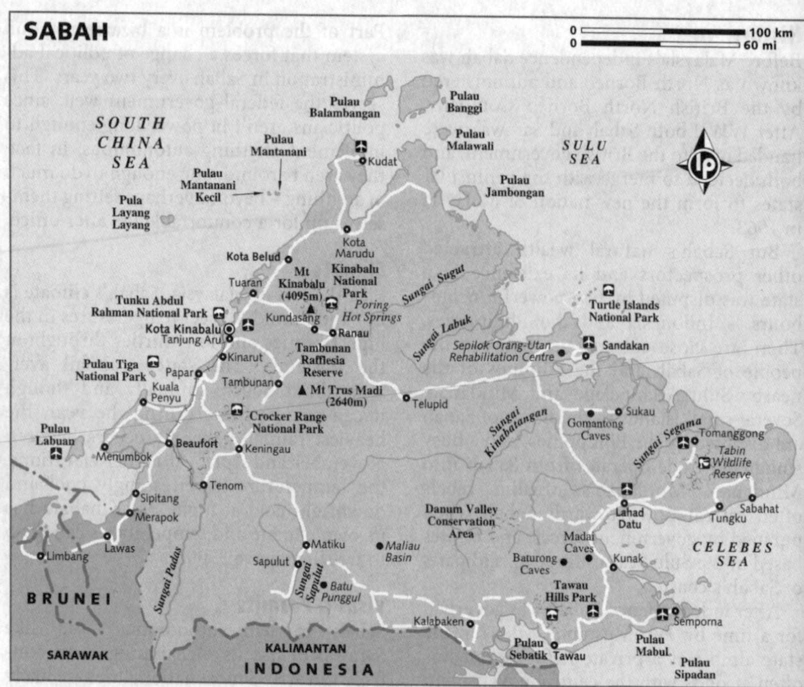

state; they feature beautiful scenery and an astonishing variety of plant and animal life. Accommodation and facilities can vary in quality, from excellent (such as Manukan) to marginal (such as the Laban Rata Resthouse on Mt Kinabalu). Budget accommodation is available in or near the major reserves and, depending on the area and weather, camping is also possible. The parks are generally well maintained and accessible.

Sabah's major parks are:

Crocker Range National Park Preserving a huge swathe (139 sq km) of forested escarpment overlooking the coast, this park has no facilities.

Kinabalu National Park Easily accessible from KK, this is the state's largest and most popular national park (754 sq km). It offers straightforward climbing at Mt Kinabalu, along with beautiful forest walks at the park's headquarters and at Mesilau. It also includes Poring Hot Springs.

Pulau Tiga National Park This park (15 sq km) comprises three islands 50km southwest of KK: one was formed by volcanic mud eruptions, one is famous for breeding sea snakes and the third has been virtually washed away by wave action. The islands take some effort to reach independently, but both resort and park accommodation is available.

Tawau Hills Park Near Tawau in the state's southeast, this park (29 sq km) has forested volcanic hills, waterfalls and hot springs. There's basic accommodation and facilities and it's a popular weekend getaway for Tawau residents.

Tunku Abdul Rahman (TAR) National Park A group of five islands (49 sq km), one quite large, a few kilometres west of the capital. Features of TAR National Park include beaches, snorkelling and hiking. There's good accommodation on two of the islands and it's possible to camp on Pulau Gaya, Sapi and Mamutik, though a camping permit is required from the Sabah Parks office in KK (see next page).

Turtle Islands National Park This national park (17 sq km) comprises three tiny islands 40km north of Sandakan that protect the nesting ground of green and hawksbill sea turtles. There's accommodation on one of the islands.

Two cave systems – **Gomantong** and **Madai** – are administered by the Wildlife Department and can be visited; reserves run by the Sabah Foundation include the **Danum Valley Conservation Area** and the **Maliau Basin**. The **Tabin Wildlife Reserve** is managed by both the Forestry & Wildlife Department though visitor facilities are run by a private company. The **Sepilok Orang-Utan Rehabilitation Centre** is a nongovernmental reserve.

BOOKINGS

Accommodation in Kinabalu National Park (including the lodges at Laban Rata, Poring Hot Springs and Mesilau) and on Manukan Island in Tunku Abdul Rahman National Park is privately run. Bookings are handled by **Kinabalu Nature Resorts** (☎ 088-243629; www.kinabalunatureresorts.com; Lot G15, Ground fl, Wisma Sabah; 🕑 8.30am-4.30pm Mon-Sat, 8.30am-12.30pm Sun). You can book your guide and accommodation for Mt Kinabalu here, but it's also possible to book online or by phone; it's not necessary to make a special trip to KK just to make a booking.

Sabah Parks (☎ 088-211881; sipadan@po.jaring.my; Lot 1-3, Ground fl, Block K, Compleks Sinsuran; 🕑 8am-1pm & 2-4.30pm Mon-Thu, 8am-11.30am & 2-4.30pm Fri, 8am-12.50pm Sun) handles reservations for park accommodation at Pulau Tiga National Park and camping permits for Tunku Abdul Rahman National Park.

Bookings and permits for the Danum Valley Conservation Area and Maliau Basin can be arranged through **Innoprise Jungle Lodge** (☎ 243245; cijl@ po.jaring.my; 3rd fl, Block D, Kompleks Sadong Jaya).

Getting There & Away

There are regular flights to Kota Kinabalu from KL, Singapore and Johor Bahru (see p396). You can also fly into Pulau Labuan, Sandakan and Tawau from KL; see Getting There & Away for the respective sections later in this chapter.

Getting Around

Independent travel in Sabah is limited compared to neighbouring Sarawak. Many travellers will have to rely on tour outfits at some point, whether it's for diving, watching turtles lay eggs or roaming along Sungai (River) Kinabatangan. At the same time, the state's highlights are concentrated in a few spots and some (like Mt Kinabalu) are easy to reach on your own.

Sabah has a good road system and most major roads are sealed, including the highway from KK to Sandakan and Tawau. If you're planning to rent a car, it's a good idea to ask tourist information centres which roads are paved, depending on your destination. Probably the worst stretch is between Ranau and Keningau, where minivans sometimes have to turn back because the perilous cliffside gravel road is impassable after heavy rain.

Subsidence and washouts frequently put stretches of highway under repair and can slow down a trip considerably – the route between Ranau and Sandakan can be unreliable

MALAYSIAN BORNEO

COSTS

Depending on where you're coming from in the region, Sabah may seem an expensive place to travel around. It's still possible, however, to find a whole range of acceptable budget and mid-range accommodation options, particularly in KK, Sepilok, Mt Kinabalu and the national parks. Here, you can generally expect to pay anywhere from RM20 up for a place to sleep. B&Bs are popular economical alternatives but are often located outside city centres (and don't necessarily include breakfast!). Keep in mind that cheaper places to stay might also be brothels. At the other end of the spectrum, on many of the islands (such as Sipadan or the Turtle Islands) accommodation choices are more limited and usually only available as part of a tour package.

An interesting alternative is to investigate the growing number of homestays offered in Sabah's smaller towns and rural areas. The **Sabah Tourism Board** (www.sabah-homestay.com) publishes a booklet on available homestays, along with contact numbers, but it's possible to book everything online. Some travel agencies can also arrange homestays. Prices vary depending on what is offered in terms of activities, but the bare minimum includes accommodation in a family's home plus food. Taking part in a homestay programme means being completely respectful of the beliefs and customs of the local people. Read the list of 'dos and don'ts' posted on the website (www.sabah-homestay.com/advise.asp) to see if it's right for you.

Top-end accommodation and restaurants in Sabah add a total of 15% government tax onto their basic charges; the total you pay is the 'net' price. Published rates are mostly '++', meaning that 5% and 10% taxes have to be added. Many hotels routinely quote net rates, however, and promotions often include the tax as well. In this chapter we've given net prices. In federally administered Labuan, the total tax is 10%.

in wet weather. The route from Tawau to Keningau is unsealed for most of the way, though it's possible to get through on 4WD Land Cruisers crammed with passengers.

Express buses, minibuses and minivans run between KK and most major centres, including Mt Kinabalu. The big state-of-the-art express buses are all air-conditioned; the smaller, often older, minibuses may or may not be. Minivans are small, eight-seater vans (usually white), which are often stuffed with as many passengers and gear as the laws of physics permit. Express buses are relatively punctual and usually cost only a few ringgit more than minivans. Minivans only leave when full but, once under way, they are quick and efficient. They don't have air-conditioning and can get crowded; on the other hand, if you want to share an experience with the locals and don't mind a toddler or two on your lap, minivans are a good option.

There are frequent departures of buses and minivans from most centres until around noon; afternoon departures can be scarce. See individual destination entries for more information.

Hitchhiking is possible in Sabah, though traffic is usually light. In this chapter we've indicated where hitching is feasible. However, hitching is never entirely safe and people who decide to hitch should understand that they are taking a small but potentially serious risk. People who choose to hitch will be safer if they travel in pairs and let someone know where they are planning to go.

Sabah's only railway runs between KK and Tenom via Papar and Beaufort (see p397).

KOTA KINABALU

☎ 088

Sabah's capital, Kota Kinabalu, sits on the edge of the South China Sea overlooking a cluster of coral-fringed islands. With the towering Crocker Range as a backdrop and the cloud-shrouded peaks of mighty Mt Kinabalu in the far distance, the modern suburbs of KK – as everyone calls it – sprawl aimlessly for many kilometres along the coast and inland.

KK is not without appeal, but it's a functional place built mainly for state functionaries and their business partners. Part of the reason for KK's undistinguished character goes back to WWII when Jesselton, as it was then known, was razed by the retreating British in order to prevent the Japanese using it as a base for operations. Just three years later Jesselton was again flattened, this time by Allied bombing as the Japanese were pushed out of Borneo. The city was rebuilt from scratch and renamed Kota Kinabalu in 1963. Since then, reclamation projects have created the land that today holds a good chunk of the city centre.

While Sandakan to the southeast is also a good base from which to explore Sabah, KK is definitely worth spending a couple of days in. It's a good place to get information and organise your itinerary, pick up supplies, take a break on an offshore island and sample a wide variety of restaurants.

Orientation

The international airport at Tanjung Aru is 7km south of the city centre, which is bounded on the north by the upmarket bayside suburb of Likas. Downtown KK is a dense, concrete grid of buildings nestled between the waterfront and a range of low, forested hills to the east. It's compact and walkable – most of the restaurants, accommodation, tourist offices, tour operators, the main post office and transport centres are located here, though at first the lack of distinguishing landmarks may make it seem a bit confusing to find your way around.

KK's main shopping complexes line the main road, which changes name four times in a relatively short distance. On the western side of Jl Tun Razak there are two sprawling, grid-like blocks of dilapidated two- and three-storey shophouses: Kompleks Segama and Kompleks Sinsuran. Between Jl Haji Saman and the waterfront is Wisma Merdeka and at the opposite end, on the way to the airport, are the huge Centre Point and Api-Api centres. Asia City, which also has some good restaurants, is opposite the Api-Api Centre. Between town and the airport the massive reclamation project, Sutera Harbour, is a luxury resort development.

KK has two areas downtown where buses congregate (see p396). Taxis are common in the city centre. Ferries leave for the islands of TAR National Park, as well as for Pulau Labuan, from the waterfront at the northern end of town.

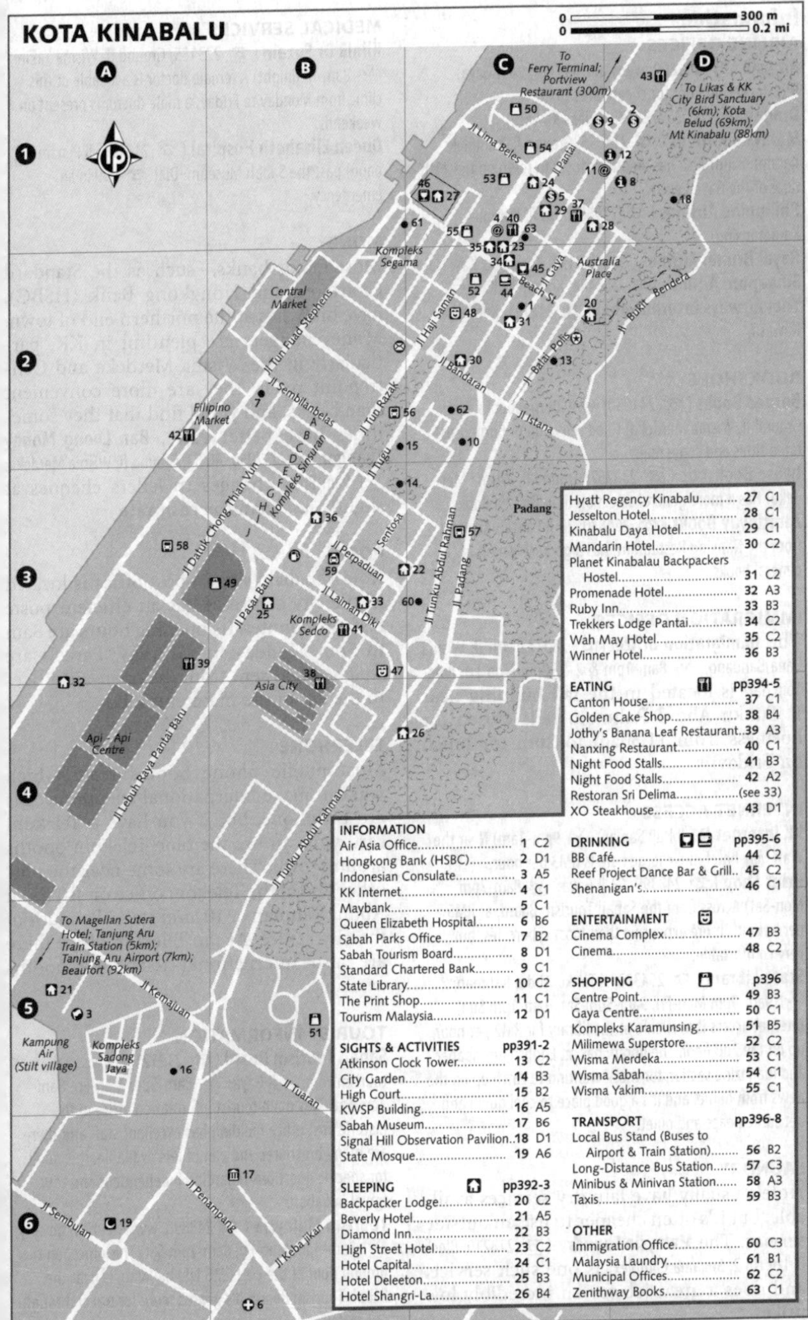
KOTA KINABALU
0 300 m
0 0.2 mi
To Ferry Terminal; Portview Restaurant (300m)
To Likas & KK City Bird Sanctuary (6km); Kota Belud (69km); Mt Kinabalu (88km)
Jl Lima Beles
Jl Pantai
Jl Gaya
Beach St
Australia Place
Jl Bukit Bendera
Kompleks Segama
Central Market
Jl Tun Fuad Stephens
Jl Haji Saman
Jl Bandaran
Jl Balai Polis
Jl Istana
Jl Sembilanbelas
Filipino Market
Kompleks Sinsuran
Jl Tun Razak
Jl Tugu
Padang
Jl Datuk Chong Thian Vun
Jl Sentosa
Jl Perpaduan
Jl Tunku Abdul Rahman
Jl Padang
Jl Pasar Baru
Jl Laiman Diki
Kompleks Sedco
Asia City
Api - Api Centre
Jl Lebuh Raya Pantai Baru
To Magellan Sutera Hotel; Tanjung Aru Train Station (5km); Tanjung Aru Airport (7km); Beaufort (92km)
Jl Kemajuan
Kampung Air (Stilt village)
Kompleks Sadong Jaya
Jl Tuaran
Jl Penampang
Jl Sembulan
Jl Keba Jikan
MALAYSIAN BORNEO
INFORMATION
Air Asia Office 1 C2
Hongkong Bank (HSBC) 2 D1
Indonesian Consulate 3 A5
KK Internet 4 C1
Maybank 5 C1
Queen Elizabeth Hospital 6 B6
Sabah Parks Office 7 B2
Sabah Tourism Board 8 D1
Standard Chartered Bank 9 C1
State Library 10 C2
The Print Shop 11 C1
Tourism Malaysia 12 D1
SIGHTS & ACTIVITIES pp391-2
Atkinson Clock Tower 13 C2
City Garden 14 B3
High Court 15 B2
KWSP Building 16 A5
Sabah Museum 17 B6
Signal Hill Observation Pavilion 18 D1
State Mosque 19 A6
SLEEPING pp392-3
Backpacker Lodge 20 C2
Beverly Hotel 21 A5
Diamond Inn 22 B3
High Street Hotel 23 C2
Hotel Capital 24 C1
Hotel Deleeton 25 B3
Hotel Shangri-La 26 B4
Hyatt Regency Kinabalu 27 C1
Jesselton Hotel 28 C1
Kinabalu Daya Hotel 29 C1
Mandarin Hotel 30 C2
Planet Kinabalau Backpackers Hostel 31 C2
Promenade Hotel 32 A3
Ruby Inn 33 B3
Trekkers Lodge Pantai 34 C2
Wah May Hotel 35 C2
Winner Hotel 36 B3
EATING pp394-5
Canton House 37 C1
Golden Cake Shop 38 B4
Jothy's Banana Leaf Restaurant 39 A3
Nanxing Restaurant 40 C1
Night Food Stalls 41 B3
Night Food Stalls 42 A2
Restoran Sri Delima (see 33)
XO Steakhouse 43 D1
DRINKING pp395-6
BB Café 44 C2
Reef Project Dance Bar & Grill 45 C2
Shenanigan's 46 C1
ENTERTAINMENT
Cinema Complex 47 B3
Cinema 48 C2
SHOPPING p396
Centre Point 49 B3
Gaya Centre 50 C1
Kompleks Karamunsing 51 B5
Milimewa Superstore 52 C2
Wisma Merdeka 53 C1
Wisma Sabah 54 C1
Wisma Yakim 55 C1
TRANSPORT pp396-8
Local Bus Stand (Buses to Airport & Train Station) 56 B2
Long-Distance Bus Station 57 C3
Minibus & Minivan Station 58 A3
Taxis 59 B3
OTHER
Immigration Office 60 C3
Malaysia Laundry 61 B1
Municipal Offices 62 C2
Zenithway Books 63 C1

Information

AIRLINE OFFICES

Air Asia (☎ 284669; www.airasia.com; 94 Jl Gaya) Worth checking out for cheap fares to KL.

Dragonair (☎ 254733; Kompleks Kawasa)

Malaysia Airlines (☎ 213555; Ground fl, Kompleks Karamunsing) Also has an office closer to town on the 11th floor of the Gaya Centre.

Philippine Airlines (☎ 239600; 3rd fl, Kompleks Karamunsing)

Royal Brunei Airlines (☎ 242193; Kompleks Kawasa)

Singapore Airlines (☎ 255444; Kompleks Kawasa)

Thai Airways International (☎ 242193; Kompleks Kawasa)

BOOKSHOPS

Borneo Books (☎ 241050; www.borneobooks.com; Ground fl, Wisma Merdeka) Good selection of Borneo-related titles and some maps.

Iwase Bookshop (☎ 233757; Ground fl, Wisma Merdeka) Has a more general selection than Borneo Books.

Zenithway Books (☎ 264830; 29 Jl Pantai) Across from the Nanxing Restaurant; has a good selection of general books.

IMMIGRATION OFFICES

The **immigration office** (☎ 280772; 4th fl, Wisma Dana Bandang; 🕓 8am-1pm & 2-4.30pm Mon-Fri, 8am-1pm Sat) is located in the tall building near Jl Tunku Abdul Rahman. It is closed for business from 11.30am to 2pm for lunch on Friday.

INTERNET ACCESS

KK Internet (31 Jl Haji Saman; 🕓 9pm-1am) Near the Wah May hotel, the charge here is RM3 per hour.

Print Shop (☎ 248399; 63 Jl Gaya; 🕓 8am-7pm Mon-Sat) Across from the Sabah Tourism Board, at RM5 per hour it's more expensive than most cybercafés, but very comfortable.

State Library (☎ 254333; Jl Tunku Abdul Rahman; 🕓 9am-9pm Mon-Fri, 9am-5pm Sat, 9am-1pm Sun) Internet access is available at the library for RM2 per hour, up on the 2nd floor. The library has an English newspaper and magazine section for those wanting to catch up on the news from home, and it's a good place to cool down and get some peace and quiet.

LAUNDRY

Hotels usually have laundry services available, but it's often cheaper to use an outside service. The **Malaysia Laundry** (☎ 218210; Block D, Lot No 2, Segama Complex) is one such service, and does a great job for an incredibly low price.

MEDICAL SERVICES

Klinik Dr Suzain (☎ 223185; Ground fl, Wisma Yakim; 🕓 8am-midnight) A female doctor is available at this clinic from Monday to Friday; a male doctor is present on weekends.

Queen Elizabeth Hospital (☎ 218166; Jl Penampang) past the Sabah Museum. Dial ☎ 999 in an emergency.

MONEY

Most major banks, such as the Standard Chartered and Hongkong Bank (HSBC), have branches at the northern end of town. Moneychangers are plentiful in KK, particularly in the Wisma Merdeka and Centrepoint malls; they are more convenient than banks, and you'll find that they sometimes have better rates. **Ban Loong Money Changer** (☎ 237950; AG 52, Ground fl, Wisma Merdeka; 🕓 9am-8pm) changes travellers cheques at slightly less than the cash rate.

POST

Kota Kinabalu's main post office is located in the city centre; it has an efficient poste restante counter. Its opening hours are 8am to 5pm Monday to Saturday. Parcels are weighed and sent from the open-air offices to the left of the main entrance.

TELEPHONE

Most public phone booths from which you can make international telephone calls are Uniphone, but if you have a Telekom card you can use the blue Telekom booths around town. There are some near the post office and at the Telekom office on Jl Tunku Abdul Rahman, a 10-minute walk south of the city centre. At the Telekom office there are also international telephone booths available.

TOURIST INFORMATION

Sabah Tourism Board (☎ 212121; www.sabahtourism.com; 51 Jl Gaya; 🕓 8am-5pm Mon-Fri, 8am-2pm Sat) This main tourist information office in the historic post office building has excellent staff and there are many brochures and pamphlets available. It is good for specific questions regarding independent and tour travel in Sabah.

Tourism Malaysia (☎ 248698; www.tourism.gov.my; 🕓 8am-5pm Mon-Fri, 8am-2pm Sat) This office, on the ground floor of the EON CMG Life building, is near the Sabah Tourism Board. It's geared more for travel throughout Malaysia.

Dangers & Annoyances

When the usual precautions are taken, KK is a reasonably safe city. Late at night, streets and alleys near the waterfront, such as in Kompleks Sinsuran, are probably best avoided if you are alone. Women travellers are wise to be cautious about walking around on their own after dark, though it's probably safer than many Western cities.

Sights & Activities

SABAH MUSEUM & SCIENCE CENTRE

The **Sabah Museum** (☎ 253199; E-M-jmuzium@tm.net.my; Jl Muzium; admission RM5; ⏲ 9am-5pm Sat-Thu) is a modern four-storey structure inspired by the longhouses of the Rungus and Murut tribes. It's a little south of the city centre, on a hill on the corner of Jl Tunku Abdul Rahman and Jl Penampang. The museum and gardens are definitely worth a visit. There are good collections of tribal and historical artefacts, including ceramics; nicely presented exhibits of flora and fauna, with a display of Sabah's spectacular butterflies and other insects; and the 'time tunnel', an absorbing walk that traces the history of KK with artefacts, old photos, costumes and weaponry. The top floor is devoted to Muslim culture and history.

The adjoining **science centre** has an informative exhibition on the petroleum industry, from drilling to refining and processing. The **art gallery** was undergoing renovations at the time of writing, but features shows by local artists.

To get there, catch a bus (50 sen) along Jl Tunku Abdul Rahman and get off just before the mosque.

STATE MOSQUE

This is a fine example of contemporary Islamic architecture, set some distance from the heat and noise of central KK. It's south of the city centre past the Kampung Air stilt village, not far from the Sabah Museum; you'll see it on your way to or from the airport.

The majesty of this mosque has been upstaged by the glittering newer mosque at Likas Bay; nonetheless, the state mosque is impressive from a distance, and can accommodate 5000 male worshippers and has a balcony where there's room for 500 women to pray. Non-Muslim visitors are allowed inside, but must remove their shoes before entering and dress appropriately.

To reach the mosque, take a bus along Jl Tunku Abdul Rahman.

ATKINSON CLOCK TOWER

This relic of the colonial era has the dubious distinction of being one of the only structures to survive the Allied bombing of Jesselton in 1945. It's a square, 15.7m-high wooden clock tower that was completed in 1905 and named after the first district officer of the town, FG Atkinson, who died of malaria aged 28.

The clock tower stands on a low hill near the main police station on Jl Balai Polis, close to the city centre.

KOTA KINABALU CITY BIRD SANCTUARY

Opened in 2000, this **sanctuary** (☎ 246955; likaswetlands@hotmail.com; Jl Bukit Bendera Upper; adult/child RM10/5; ⏲ 8am-6pm Tue-Sun) covers 24 hectares of mangrove swamp in the KK suburb of Likas northeast of the city centre. It's not exactly *teeming* with bird and other animal life, but there are some rare treats, like the majestic purple herons visible from a blind in the northwest section of the reserve. Run by the local Likas Wetlands Society in association with WWF, the sanctuary reception has a small library and you can rent binoculars for RM5. Bird books are available on loan. It's best to visit early in the morning or late afternoon from September to April.

NORTH BORNEO RAILWAY

A luxurious ride is offered by the **North Borneo Railway** (☎ 263933; www.northborneorailway.com.my), a tourist attraction set up by the Sutera Harbour group. It features a refurbished wood-burning Vulcan steam train going as far as Papar on Wednesday and Saturday, departing KK at 10am and returning at 2.30pm. The RM160 fare includes lunch.

OTHER ATTRACTIONS

KK has its own stilt village, **Kampung Air**, just south of the city centre off the main drag, Jl Lebuh Raya Pantai Baru. Once an extensive settlement stretching south along the shore, all that remains is a small collection of rickety dwellings cut off from the sea by the land reclamation that's occurred over the years.

You can wander up to the observation pavilion on **Signal Hill**, at the eastern edge of the city centre, to escape the traffic and to get another take on the squatters' stilt village at Pulau Gaya. The view is best as the sun sets over the islands. To get there, take the path behind the Backpacker Lodge to the steps leading up to Jl Bukit Bendera. From the top, it's also possible to hike down to the bird sanctuary on the other side.

There's a lively **fish & meat market** on the waterfront adjacent to the Filipino market (see p396) with numerous vendors selling mouth-watering snacks and seafood. It's a good place to watch the sun go down while munching on a tasty *murtabak*.

Tours

KK has a huge number of tour operators, enough to suit every taste and budget. It's not absolutely necessary to go through a travel agency to visit Sabah's major sights, but a good tour operator can make life easier if you're short on time. If you run into problems with a tour agency, take your complaint to the Sabah Tourism Board (see p390).

Some of the more established companies include:

Borneo Adventure (☎ 238731; www.borneoadventure.com; 5th fl, 509-512 Gaya Centre) Award-winning company with very professional staff, imaginative itineraries and a genuine interest in local people and the environment. Definitely worth checking out.

Borneo Divers (☎ 222226; www.borneodivers.info; 9th fl, Menara Jubili, 53 Jl Gaya) Longest-established Borneo dive outfit; can arrange courses and dives just about anywhere and has a dive shop (☎ 222227; Ground fl, Wisma Sabah). It's possible to get discounted rates as a walk-in.

Borneo Eco Tours (☎ 234009; www.borneoecotours.com; 2nd fl, Shop Lot 12A, Lorong Bernam 3, Taman Soon Kiong) This is a place with a good reputation, arranging tours throughout Malaysian Borneo, including travel to the Kinabatangan area with exclusive accommodation at the tranquil Sukau Rainforest Lodge. The KK office is near the Sabah Golf & Country Club southeast of the city centre.

Borneo Sea Adventures (☎ 230000; www.bornsea.com; 1st fl, 8A Karamunsing Warehouse) Runs dive tours and has the only resort on the beautiful Mantanani Islands, home to dugongs, off Kota Belud. Also has accommodation on Sipadan.

Borneo Wildlife Adventure (☎ 213668; www.borneo-wildlife.com; 1st fl, Lot F, GPO). Arranges a variety of tours throughout Sabah, including day trips outside KK; good for the mid-range budget.

Intra Travel Service (☎ 261 558; www.intra-travel.com.my; Level 1, No 5 Airport Terminal 2, Jl Old Airport) Specializes in trips to the Tabin Wildlife Reserve.

Wildlife Expeditions (☎ 259701; www.wildlife-expeditions.com; 1st fl, Wisma Sabah) Similar programmes as Borneo Eco Tours, with accommodation at the Sukau River Lodge on the Kinabatangan. Specializing in wildlife and rainforest trips. Also has an office in the Tanjung Aru Resort in KK (☎ 246000) and in Sandakan (see p427).

Sleeping

There's no shortage of accommodation in KK. Mid-range bargains are plentiful, offering air-conditioned comfort, TV, IDD phones, private bathroom and (if you're lucky) a small fridge. Top-end choices are more limited, but feature supreme luxury at nearby resort hotels.

BUDGET

KK has the best range of backpackers' hostels in Sabah which are excellent places to gather travel information and meet other travellers, even if you choose to stay somewhere else.

Planet Kinabalu Backpackers Hostel (☎ 319168; planetkinabalu@hotmail.com; 98-100 Jl Gaya; dm RM18) A clean, well-managed and friendly place in the heart of KK, the price includes a good breakfast. Certainly the best budget option in central KK.

Backpacker Lodge (☎ 261495; www.welcome.to/backpackerkk; Lot 25, Lorong Dewan, Australia Pl; dm/r RM18/40) Although the location is convenient, the facilities here are a bit crowded, with more than a dozen beds in each segregated dormitory, but it's clean and quite popular with budget travellers. Breakfast is included.

Trekkers Lodge Pantai (☎ 213888; www.trekkerslodge.com; 3rd fl, 46 Jl Pantai; dm/r RM17/37, with air-con RM20/43; ❄ 💻) Although it's been a long-standing hang-out for budget travellers, this place has seen better days and is quite noisy because of the nearby bars and clubs. It may be your only option, however, if the other places are full.

MID-RANGE

Most of KK's hotels fall into this price range (RM60 to RM200) and the competition makes it possible to find some good bargains.

Kinabalu Daya Hotel (☎ 240000; www.kkdayahotel.com; Lot 3 & 4, Block 9, Jl Pantai; s/d RM78/88; ❄) This large hotel gets rave reviews from travellers. Rooms have wooden floors and some have good views. The price includes breakfast. Cheaper rooms without windows are also available.

Mandarin Hotel (☎ 225222; jw3333@hotmail.com; 138 Jl Gaya; s/d RM50/70;) Large rooms, marble floors and location make this hotel one of the best bargains in town, especially with the frequently available discounts. More expensive rooms are larger and worth the extra money.

Ruby Inn (☎ 213222; Lot 17, Block 36, Jl Laiman Diki) and **Diamond Inn** (☎ 261222; Lot 7, Block 37, Jl Haji Yaacob), both near the Sedco Complex, are run by the same company and have similar facilities.

Hotel Capital (☎ 231999; fax 237222; 23 Jl Haji Saman; r RM85;) Although not quite as nice as the Kinabalu Daya, the rooms here are still good value and the location can't be beat. There's an attractive Italian restaurant on the ground floor.

Hotel Deleeton (☎ 252222; fax 267999; Lot 45-46, Block E, Asia City; s/d RM130/180;) This accommodating business-style hotel, across from the Centre Point, is just outside the more bustling neighbourhood to the north. It's possible to get a room for up to 50% off the published room rates. The staff are friendly and professional. Deluxe rooms for an additional RM10 are more spacious and comfortable than the standard rooms.

Hotel Shangri-La (☎ 212800; kkshang@po.jaring.my; 75 Bandaran Berjaya; r RM185;) Not quite as conveniently located as the Hyatt, but certainly cheaper, this 10-storey hotel offers comfortable rooms and is popular with local businesspeople. Despite the name, this hotel is not part of the Shangri-La hotel chain and not to be confused with the Shangri-La Tanjung Aru.

Other recommendations:

Winner Hotel (☎ 243222; fax 217345; 9-10 Jl Pasar Baru; s/d RM55/65;) Just north of the Hotel Deleeton, this place is a little cramped but friendly.

Wah May Hotel (☎ 266118; wahmayhtl@pd.jaring.my; 36 Jl Haji Saman; s/d RM60/70;) Has smaller rooms but is well run and a good lower mid-range option.

High Street Inn (☎ 218111; fax 219111; 38 Jl Pantai; s/d RM60/70;) Rooms are similar to the Wah May, but there's no elevator. A 15% government tax is added to the room rate.

TOP END

KK doesn't lack for some top-notch four- and five-star hotels. Promotional discounts allow for some worthwhile bargains in this category if you're looking for a little luxury.

Promenade Hotel (☎ 265555; www.promenade.com.my; 4 Lorong Api-Api 3, Api-Api Centre; r RM270;) This large four-star hotel is north of Centre Point in the upscale Api-Api Centre. Readers have recommended it for its good value, and discounts up to 50% make it a solid bargain. Rooms with views of the South China Sea are a little extra.

Jesselton Hotel (☎ 223333; www.jesseltonhotel.com; 69 Jl Gaya; r RM280;) The oldest of KK's many hotels, it was built in the '50s, but renovated in the '90s as a luxury boutique hotel. It's tastefully decorated in mock-colonial wood and marble and has 31 rooms, including one gorgeous suite with a rock pool and alcove. There's also a very good restaurant, coffee shop, business centre and a red London taxi-cab to shuttle you to the airport. Discounts of up to 40% are available.

Hyatt Regency Kinabalu (☎ 221234; www.kinabalu.regency.hyatt.com; Jl Datuk Salleh Sulong; r RM310;) The Hyatt has a perfect location opposite the waterfront, though it lacks the class and charm of the Jesselton. Facilities include a swimming pool, restaurants, business centre, childcare, medical services and popular pub. Discounts are often available, especially on rooms without a sea view.

Shangri-La Tanjung Aru Resort (☎ 225800; www.shangri-la.com; Tanjung Aru; r RM370;) If you have no reason to stay in the city centre, it's worth considering this beautiful five-star resort on the beach at Tanjung Aru near the airport. The hotel is the flagship of upmarket travel in Sabah and hosts plenty of dignitaries. It has an impressive array of facilities, including a medical clinic and childcare, tasteful rooms and a relaxing setting.

Magellan Sutera (☎ 312222; www.suteraharbour.com; 2 Jl Sutera; r RM565;) Another five-star option is at the sprawling Sutera Harbour Resort & Spa south of the city centre. The Magellan is one of two hotels on this reclamation site, which features a golf course, luxury condos and numerous bars and restaurants.

Other recommendations include:

Pacific Sutera (☎ 318888; 2 Jl Sutera; r RM400;) Alternative wing of the Magellan Sutera, has rooms at slightly lower rates.

Beverly Hotel (☎ 258998; www.infosabah.com.my/karamunsing; Jl Kemajuan; r RM280;) Smart, business-style hotel with 200 rooms close to the airport.

Eating

For variety and quality, KK ranks up there with Kuching as the best restaurant city in Malaysian Borneo. Besides the ubiquitous Chinese *kedai kopi* (coffee shops) and Malaysian halal restaurants scattered everywhere, other choices include fine seafood, Chinese, Japanese and Western restaurants in the city centre and hotels. The abundance of small supermarkets and shops also makes self-catering a good option, especially if you have a room with a fridge.

CHINESE

Nanxing Restaurant (☎ 215284; 34 Jl Pantai; dishes RM5-10; 🕑 5.45am-9pm) Numerous *kedai kopi* line Jl Pantai and its adjoining streets but this is one of the most popular. It's packed for breakfast, serving up Cantonese-style dim sum, noodles and delicious thin pancakes topped with a fried egg. Just point at what you want to order.

Canton House (☎ 267399; 70 Jl Gaya; dishes RM 6-15) This air-conditioned restaurant is a little more upscale than the average *kedai kopi*, and serves up tasty dim sum, noodles and other Cantonese-style dishes.

Port View Seafood Restaurant (☎ 538178; 16-17 Jl Haji Saman; dishes RM20-30) A large Chinese establishment specializing in seafood, it serves lunch and dinner. The buffet on Sunday is a bargain at RM22 per person.

MALAY

Restoran Sri Delima (☎ 213361; Block 36, 17 Jl Laiman Diki; dishes RM10-15) A clean, simple restaurant adjoining the Ruby Inn that serves Malay and Baba Nonya-style dishes. It claims its *assam ikan* (fish steamed with tamarind juice) is the best in KK.

Tivoli Restaurant (☎ 212800; Hotel Shangri-La; dishes RM10-20) Air-conditioned restaurants in the upmarket hotels serve more expensive (but good) Malay fare as well as Western favourites. This restaurant in the Hotel Shangri-La has a good evening Malay buffet.

Halal restaurants serving Malay dishes are common in the streets around Jl Gaya and Jl Pantai, and Segama Plaza.

QUICK EATS

The best night market in town is at the square at Kompleks Sedco where the speciality is seafood though other dishes are also available. The proprietors can get a bit pushy urging you to choose their place. Make sure you find out the price of each item because the seafood in particular can get expensive. The Sabah green vegetables and satay are particularly good here. For great snacks and inexpensive seafood, try out the food stalls on the waterfront side of the Filipino Market that set up at around 5pm and are open until midnight.

KK's shopping malls are good for quick meals. During the day, the **Wisma Merdeka food court** (☎ 213686; 6th fl, Wisma Merdeka) is the place to go for simple meals. There are nice views over to the islands.

Season Cake House (☎ 242750; Ground fl, Wisma Merdeka) is a good place for picking up snacks for self-catering. They also make delicious waffles. Take the Wisma Merdeka main entrance on Jl Haji Saman, turn right and follow your nose.

There's a whole variety of delicious pastry desserts available at the **Golden Cake Shop** (☎ 263370; Block A, Ground fl, Asia City). Try the mouth-watering custard tarts.

VEGETARIAN

Jothy's Banana Leaf Restaurant (☎ 261595; Block 1, Lot 9 Api-Api Centre; RM8-15) If you're looking for some good vegetarian (getting tired of chicken?) Jothy's is the ideal place. Fine curries and roti are served on banana leaves in quiet, air-conditioned comfort. Another place for vegetarian food is the Wisma Merdeka food court (see above).

WESTERN

Little Italy (☎ 232231; 23 Jl Haji Saman; dishes RM15-25) A bright and breezy place on the ground floor of the Capital Hotel, what this place lacks in terms of Italian ambience it makes up for in the no-nonsense delivery of pasta, pizza and other tasty items. There's also outdoor seating where you can watch the hectic traffic of KK.

XO Steakhouse (☎ 237077; 54 Jl Gaya; dishes RM20-30) Outside of the luxury hotels, this is probably the best place to find a good steak in downtown KK. The meat is flown in from Australia and the USA. Seafood dishes are also served and the three-course set lunch is good value at RM25.

Gardenia (☎ 223333; dishes RM30-50) This elegant restaurant in the Jesselton Hotel has some of the best Western food in town. The diverse menu includes good beef cuts and fresh fish. The hotel's **Wishbone Café & Restaurant** serves less formal dishes, like fish and chips and burgers. Try the durian ice cream for dessert.

Coffee Bean Wisma Merdeka (☎ 232333; Ground fl, Wisma Merdeka; dishes RM6-15; 7.30am-9pm Tue-Sun) This Western-style coffee shop is right on the corner of Jl Tun Razak and Jl Tun Fuad Stephen and is a veritable refuge if you're looking to cool off with a good cup of iced coffee. They also serve snacks and Western breakfasts.

Drinking

Much of KK's nightlife is limited to hotel bars and discos, though a new outdoor venue in the centre of town is set to change all that. Known as **Beach Street**, it's an attractive area surrounded by eating places and cafés during the day and bars that fill up at night. Live music or dancing performances often take place in the evening and it's a popular place for young people to congregate. It's certainly lively, with all the various bars' sound systems competing for dominance of the air waves. Like other nightlife in KK, things keep going until 4am.

Reef Project Dance Bar & Grill (☎ 233013; 48 Jl Pantai) This multilevel establishment overlooks Beach Street and the exterior balconies are a choice place to perch yourself and see what's going on down below. Inside, there's a bar and dance floor. Live bands play every night except Mondays and usually don't start until 9pm. Meals and snacks are also served.

BB Café (☎ 233882; 1 Jl Jati) Diagonally across from the Reef Project on Beach Street, this open-air drinking place feels more like a tropical pub than a café. It's a relaxing space furnished with lovely wooden chairs and decor. The enthusiastic staff are friendly and it's a good place for a late afternoon cold beer, or better yet, three cold beers for RM10 during happy hour.

Shenanigan's (☎ 221234; Ground fl, Hyatt Regency Hotel) Modelled on an Irish pub, this has long been a popular establishment in KK. Live bands perform most nights from 9pm and the place gets packed on weekends. Entry is free and drinks are reasonably priced during happy hour (beer is RM7.50 till 9.30pm); the dress code – no singlets or flip flops (thongs) – is usually enforced.

Hunter's Bar (☎ 240000; 1st fl, Kinabalu Daya Hotel) If you've never experienced karaoke in Asia before, this is as good a place as any to try it out. If you don't want to sing, there's darts and billiards. Meals and snacks are available during the day as well as the evening.

MALAYSIAN BORNEO

AND THE BANDS PLAY ON

Wander into a hotel bar in Sabah or Sarawak and chances are a microphone will occupy centre stage. The odds are about even that the mike will be firmly gripped by a besotted businessman croaking his favourite karaoke tune, or by a smooth Filipina songstress (or two or three) dressed in go-go boots and backed by an organ-grinder with a bad perm.

Welcome to the world of live entertainment, Borneo-style. Because of its proximity to the southern Philippines, most of the live bands making the rounds of bigger hotels and nightclubs are from Mindanao. These are often family affairs, someone's cousin filling in on guitar while the elder brother makes a visit back home.

The quality of the music is as variable as the line-up – while most singers have Mariah Carey and Britney Spears down pat, attempts at a Santana guitar solo may be hit-and-miss. Still, as cover bands go, they can be very entertaining, and often note-perfect. The Piccolo Band, most of whom are from the Philippine island of Palawan, bring the house down with an uncanny version of George Michael doing Queen. And you'd swear Matchbox 20 had turned up for a gig until you saw the six-piece Indonesian band on stage.

The same goes for the increasing number of bands from KL on the scene. The talent is sometimes stretched thin, but there are some outstanding musicians that play a wide range of music, from country and western to hip-hop. One of the best bar bands around is the Headliners – big Bob and the band know what you want, and can deliver on everything from classic Bread to Pink Floyd and the Beastie Boys. There isn't a cooler bass player in Borneo, and the lead female vocalist may be tiny but she hardly needs a microphone to out-sing Whitney Houston.

Other recommendations:

Blue Note (☎ 225800; Shangri-La Tanjung Aru Resort; 🕑 5pm-1am Wed-Sun) A new venue at the Tanjung Aru, offering DJ tunes, a dance floor and lots of space.

KK's (☎ 318888; Pacific Sutera, Sutera Harbour Resort & Spa) Live bands from the Philippines perform every night.

Shopping

Although a major centre, KK isn't a great place for handicrafts compared to Kuching in Sarawak. Wisma Merdeka has a few outlets for souvenirs on its ground floor but the mother of all souvenir markets is at the Filipino Market on the waterfront, opposite the west side of the Sinsuran Complex. Here you can buy everything from the most tacky of souvenirs to worthwhile items like pearls and woven baskets. Many of the products come from the Philippines, but there are some crafts from Sabah as well.

A night market fills Jl Sentosa and adjoining streets selling cheap clothes, watches and sunglasses but it's not terribly interesting. A more lively market occurs each Sunday morning along Jl Gaya.

Getting There & Away

AIR

KK is the hub of the Malaysia Airlines network in Sabah and there are regular flights to Bintulu (RM127, 1 or 2 daily), Kuching (RM228, up to 7 daily), Pulau Labuan (RM52, up to 7 daily), Lahad Datu (RM106, at least 3 daily), Miri (RM104, at least 5 daily), Sandakan (RM83, usually 7 daily), Sibu (RM180, usually 3 daily,) and Tawau (RM96, usually 9 daily).

The cheapest way of getting from Peninsular Malaysia to KK on MAS is by purchasing a seven-day advance-purchase ticket from Johor Bahru (RM295, daily flights) or economy night flight (RM260); the regular fare is RM347. There are also economy night flights from KL for RM306, advance-purchase fares for RM372 or the regular fare of RM437. Air Asia has five flights a day between KL and KK for nearly half the price of MAS's regular fare, depending on the promotions being offered.

The KK–Singapore fare is RM584, so it's cheaper to take the flights to/from Johor Bahru and cross the Causeway on the Malaysia Airlines bus, which takes you right into Singapore.

Malaysia Airlines has at least one flight daily to Bandar Seri Begawan (BSB) in Brunei (RM103) and to Hong Kong and Kaoshiung in Taiwan. The airline also flies to Taipei and Manila three times a week, Cebu City twice a week, Tokyo twice a week and Seoul once a week.

BOAT

Passenger boats (☎ 236834) leave daily for Pulau Labuan (RM28/33 for economy/1st class, about 2½ hours) from the ferry terminal north of the city centre. From Labuan there are connecting services to Brunei. The boats are long and narrow and completely enclosed. Bring earplugs if you don't want to be assaulted by the soundtrack of the (usually) violent movies played en route. The ride is generally smooth as long as the sea is not too rough.

Two boats leave at 8am, 10am, 1.30pm and one boat leaves at 3pm. Boats from Labuan to KK leave at 8.30am, 10.45am, 1pm and 3pm. Boarding time is 15 minutes before departure, and because Labuan is a federal territory you will need to take your passport with you.

For boats to KK's offshore islands, see p400.

BUS

There is no main bus station in KK; long-distance air-con express buses and long-distance minibuses and minivans depart from two depots around the city centre. Note that transport may leave for some destinations from both depots, and the asking price may not be quite the same.

Air-con express buses are the best way to reach Mt Kinabalu and the east coast towns. Buses leave from the area southeast of the municipal offices on Jl Tunku Abdul Rahman; long-distance buses leave from about 6.30am. Some minibuses and minivans also operate from here.

You'll be greeted by touts upon reaching the bus lot, asking about where you're going; don't be offended – most are helpful and will guide you to the right bus. A myriad of companies service the main routes. Many (but not all) have wooden shacks where you can check current schedules and make advance bookings. It's probably better to book ahead on weekends for Sandakan, but generally you can just turn up before the scheduled departure time and hop on. In any case, the bus may wait for an hour or so for more passengers. Schedules for express buses on the longer routes should be checked in advance. Main destinations and fares from here are as follows:

Beaufort Minibuses do the run at 7am and 1.30pm (RM8, 2hr).

Keningau Buses leave at 7am, 10am, 1pm and 4pm (RM15, 2½hr).

Kota Belud Departures until 5pm but most are in the morning (RM7, 1½hr).

Kudat Buses leave every hour between 8am and 5pm (RM15, 3hr).

Lahad Datu There's an express bus at 7.30am (RM35, 8hr).

Lawas (Sarawak) Buses leave at 7.30am and1.30pm and pass through Papar, Beaufort and Sipitang (RM20, 4hr).

Mt Kinabalu Buses (RM15, 3hr) leave for the national park around 7.30am daily – check the schedule in advance, and book on weekends. You could also take any bus going to Ranau or Sandakan and ask to be dropped off at the entrance road, 100m from park headquarters. Minivans do the trip for RM10.

Ranau (for Poring Hot Springs) There are morning departures (RM15, 3½hr) from around 8.30am. All Ranau buses and minivans pass the entrance to Mt Kinabalu National Park (RM10); ask to be dropped off.

Sandakan Services depart at 6.30am, 7am, 2pm and 8pm; it's advisable to book ahead on weekends (RM30, 6hr).

Semporna An express bus leaves at 7.30am (RM50, 10hr).

Tawau Express buses leave at 7.30 daily (RM50, 10hr).

Tenom Express buses leave at 8am, noon and 4pm (RM20, 3½hr).

The large vacant lot behind Centre Point is a busy minibus and minivan depot. Most transport from here is local, but there are plenty of departures for centres around KK, such as Penampang, Papar and Tuaran, and further north to Kota Belud and Kudat.

Minivans have rough schedules, but leave when they're full. You'll be pressured by touts to take a certain van, but don't commit yourself until you see how many people are on board. It's always a bit of a gamble. If you get to the bus stand and there isn't a minivan with even one passenger going your way, hang back for a few minutes; chances are there's one that's nearly full doing a lap of the town trying to fill the last couple of seats.

Departures are frequent in the early morning; there are often far fewer later in the day. The general rule is to travel early, and the further you travel the earlier you should leave.

Some examples of services from KK are as follows:

Beaufort Regular departures until about 5pm (RM10, 2 hours).

Kampung Likas (Likas Bay) Frequent departures between 6.30am and 5pm (RM1).

Keningau Regular departures until about 5pm (RM13, 2½ hours).

Kudat Departures until about 5pm (RM15, 3 to 4 hours).

Papar Buses leave until 5pm (RM3, 1 hour).

Ranau Mainly early-morning departures, but may leave as late as 6pm; all buses and vans pass Kinabalu National Park (RM10 or RM15, 3½ hours).

Tambunan Departures to about 5pm (RM10, about 1½ hours).

Tuaran Buses leave throughout the day (RM2, 40 minutes).

TAXI

There are share-taxis to many minivan destinations. They also leave when full, but the fares are much higher than the minivans. Their big advantage is that they are much quicker and more comfortable.

A couple of share-taxis do a daily run between KK and Ranau (RM15 per person or RM60 for the whole taxi), and can get you to/from the turn-off to park headquarters at Mt Kinabalu (also RM15).

TRAIN

Tanjung Aru train station (☎ 254611) is 5km south of the city centre, close to the airport. Sabah's only railway runs between Tanjung Aru, Papar, Beaufort and Tenom. The four-hour journey to Tenom from KK is very cheap (RM7.50) but the most scenic section begins after Beaufort (see p407).

Getting Around

TO/FROM THE AIRPORT

KK's modern international airport is at Tanjung Aru, 7km southwest of the city centre. Minivans run to the airport till 10pm from behind Centre Point; the fare is RM2.

Buses marked `Putatan' from the local bus station also pass the airport turn-off. Departures are irregular, but there is usually at least one an hour during the day; the fare is RM1. This bus stops opposite the access road, from where it's a 10-minute walk to the terminal. Heading into town, there's a bus stop to the right as you leave the airport, 10 minutes' walk from the terminal.

The airport is new and modern, with a post office, hotel and car-rental booking kiosks (often unattended), a Telekom office, moneychanger and ATM, a good bookshop and fast-food outlets.

The 15-minute taxi ride to the airport normally costs RM13 or RM14, but you may be charged more late at night. Leaving the terminal, there's a taxi desk on the ground floor where you can buy a fixed-price coupon for RM20 into town.

BUS

Local buses leave from the stand between the municipal offices and Jl Tun Razak. The only time you'll probably need one is to get to the airport (RM1) or to Tanjung Aru train station (50 sen). Minivans that pass the airport also pass the train station. If you don't feel like walking to Kompleks Karamunsing south of the city centre, jump on a bus going along Jl Tunku Abdul Rahman (50 sen).

CAR

There are a couple of car-rental booths near the taxi stand at the airport, though they are often unstaffed. The bigger hotels and the Tourism Malaysia office can also help arrange car rental. While more expensive than the bus, there are many advantages to renting a car; it's a lot easier to get around because public transport to remote areas is often limited. The average rate for a Proton Iswara is RM180 per day, while a Toyota Land Cruiser costs around RM480 per day. **Adaras Rent A Car** (☎ 222137; adarasrac@hotmail.com) has some good deals and can also arrange drop-offs in major towns, something many other companies won't do.

TAXI

KK's taxis are plentiful and by the time you read this they should all have meters installed. There are several hubs in the city centre where taxis congregate – try outside the Kinabalu Daya Hotel or near the Millimewah Superstore. Most trips around town cost about RM5 and renting a taxi by the hour will cost about RM35.

AROUND KOTA KINABALU

Tunku Abdul Rahman National Park

Five lovely islands a short distance west of KK – Pulau Manukan, Gaya, Sapi, Mamutik and Sulug – and the reefs in between make up TAR National Park, which covers a total area of just over 49 sq km. Only a short boat ride from the city centre, they have some nice beaches and the water in the outer areas is usually clear.

Unfortunately, much of the coral around the islands has been destroyed by dynamite fishing, and experienced divers and snorkellers are likely to be disappointed. There are still plenty of colourful fish, however, and if you've had few opportunities for tropical snorkelling, the park offers easy and affordable access. It's possible to hire snorkelling gear on Manukan and Sapi, or try hiring beforehand at your hotel.

Gaya and Manukan have accommodation and it's possible to **camp** on Gaya, Sapi and Mamutik for RM5 per person, if you bring your own tent or, alternatively, use park tents that cost RM30/40 for four-person and six-person tents, respectively. You need to get a permit from the Sabah Parks office (see p387). Only Pulau Gaya and Manukan actually have restaurants. Snacks and drinks are sold on Sapi but for camping on Sapi or Mamutik bring your own water.

It's easy enough to get to any of the islands to enjoy a day's snorkelling, hiking, lazing on a beach – or all three.

There's a park entrance fee of RM10 per person, which is valid for all the islands.

PULAU MANUKAN

Manukan is the most popular destination for KK residents and has well-developed facilities. It is the second-largest island in the group and its 20 hectares are largely covered in dense vegetation. There's a good beach with coral reefs off the southern and eastern shores, and a walking trail around the perimeter. There's quite a good range of tropical fish and many can be seen simply by looking down from the jetty.

Other wildlife includes the Tabon scrubfowl, a primitive bird that lays its eggs in piles of rotting vegetation. The birds are shy, but can be seen by walking quietly along the island's jogging path early or late in the day.

Kinabalu Nature Resorts manages **Manukan Island Resort** (☎ 243629; www.kinabalunatureresorts.com; chalets RM230; ❄ 🏊) on Manukan, which has chalets, a restaurant, swimming pool and tennis courts. The chalets sleep up to four and are fully furnished with a desalinated shower, and kitchen/dining facilities.

In the gardens around the chalets you may see sunbirds and fruit pigeons.

Equipment for hire includes mask, fins and snorkel (RM15), surf mats (RM5) and rubber tubes (RM5); a security deposit is payable. There's also a shop selling postcards, T-shirts, sun hats, ice creams and souvenirs.

The **Coral Garden Seafood Restaurant** (7am-9pm) on Manukan serves a wide range of Western and Malay dishes, and good seafood, though price depends on availability.

Boats out to the islands are arranged inside the waiting room at the KK ferry terminal and the service runs from 7.30am to 5.30pm. Travellers are discouraged from hiring boats on their own. It's best to go early and you may have to wait until there's enough people to fill up the boat. Manukan is the most popular destination and costs RM14 return. You can usually get to the other islands for RM20, if you can't find anyone to share a boat.

The Gayan Eco Resort has its own ferry service to Gaya starting at 8am until 11pm (RM10 return, 1½ to 2 hours).

A ferry terminal fee of RM1 is added to all tickets.

PULAU GAYA

With an area of about 15 sq km and rising in places to an elevation of 300m, Pulau Gaya is by far the largest island in the park. It's also the closest to KK and is virtually covered in undisturbed tropical forest. There are about 20km of marked hiking trails and a good stretch of white sand – Police Beach – at Bulijong Bay. The trails can be rather overgrown, and the shallow water at Police Beach washes a fair bit of garbage ashore. If you're lucky, you may see monkeys, pangolins or even a bearded pig.

Worth checking out is the **Marine Ecology Research Centre** (MERC; ☎ 301131; www.gayana-ecoresort.com/merc; Gayana Eco Resort; adult/child RM9/7; 9am-9pm) where research is conducted and seminars given to raise public awareness about coral-reef destruction. On Monday and Thursday the aquariums are cleaned and the centre doesn't open until 6pm.

There's a large **stilt village** in front of Pulau Gaya – it's clearly visible from the KK waterfront. It is mainly inhabited by Filipino refugees, who you'll see hopping into speedboats to be ferried back home. The village is generally considered a no-go area, and it wouldn't be wise to hop in a boat and go exploring through the maze of rickety plankwalks – someone may be poor and desperate enough to relieve you of your valuables.

A study in contrast to the stilt village is the **Gayana Eco Resort** (☎ 301131; www.gayana-ecoresort.com; s/d RM156/202), a luxury development similar to the Dragon Inn at Semporna (see p438), where thatched bungalows sit on stilts over the water. There's a restaurant and water-sports centre as well as the Marine Ecology Research Centre (see this page). The standard of service has slipped in the last couple of years, but it's worth checking out for the research centre. The resort has a **KK sales office** (☎ 245158) on the ground floor of Wisma Sabah.

The two restaurants at the Gayana Eco Resort are the **Island Seafood Restaurant** and the **Waterfront Bistro.** A buffet lunch for RM30 every Sunday includes the return boat trip out to the resort.

PULAU SAPI

Pulau Sapi (Cow Island) lies just off the southwestern tip of Pulau Gaya and has some of the best snorkelling in the park. With an area of only 0.1 sq km, the island has good beaches and a nature trail. Macaques live in the forest and sometimes go down to the beach to look for crabs – they also come looking for foolish tourists handing out food and can be quite aggressive; mind your bags and other gear if macaques are about.

There's no accommodation on Sapi, unless you plan to camp, but there are shelters, changing rooms, toilets and barbecue pits. Snorkelling equipment can also be hired (RM15 for a snorkel and mask).

PULAU MAMUTIK

This is the smallest island in the park and is less visited than its neighbours. There are good beaches right around the island and some good coral reefs, particularly on the eastern side.

PULAU SULUG

This island has an area of 8.1 hectares and is the least visited of the group, probably because it's the furthest away from KK. It has only one beach, on the eastern shore, but the snorkelling is quite good and it makes for a quiet day trip.

Beaches

There are a few shallow paddling beaches near the highway south of KK. The nearest is at the plush Shangri-La Tanjung Aru Resort (see p393), but other accommodation is available along the coast between the airport and Papar. The beaches won't win any awards, but you could pleasantly laze away a day or two before catching a plane.

SLEEPING

Seaside Travellers Inn (☎ 750555; www.infosabah.com.my/seaside; Km 20 Jl Papar, Kinarut; bungalows RM77/88;) This small, family-run resort is 20km south of KK on the way to Papar and is a reasonable mid-range alternative to the more lavish establishments. A dorm bed in a fan-cooled room with shared bathroom costs RM25 and economy rooms with air-con or fan range from RM30 to RM66. All prices include a continental breakfast.

Casuarina Hotel (☎ 221000; www.casuarinahotel.com; Lorong Ikan Lais, Jl Mat Salleh, Tanjung Aru; r RM130;) Named for the casuarina tree, found in abundance on Sabah's beaches, this hotel is a comfortable place to stay near the beach at Tanjung Aru and close to the airport. It's very good value if you want to be close to the beach, with discounts available of up to 50%.

GETTING THERE & AWAY

To get to the beaches south of KK, take a Papar minivan (RM3) from behind Centre Point. For the Seaside Travellers Inn, get off near the Km 20 marker; the inn is a short walk past the school.

Pulau Layang Layang

Some 300km northwest of KK, Layang Layang is a tiny island surrounded by a coral atoll. It's an exclusive dive location and part of the famous (among divers, at least) Borneo Banks.

Layang Layang has a growing reputation among divers as a good alternative to the wasted coral found in many other spots around Sabah. Another part of the appeal is the chance to splash around in a geopolitical hot spot, as Layang Layang is one of the disputed Spratlys, a collection of about 600 islands, reefs and atolls strategically located in the South China Sea. With the prospect of undersea oil reserves and rich fishing, parts of the Spratlys are claimed by China, Vietnam, Taiwan, the Philippines, Malaysia and Brunei. China and Vietnam have already clashed over Chinese occupation of several islands, and Malaysia has a small naval base on Layang Layang.

Layang Layang covers less than 1 sq km, but is surrounded by an atoll more than 7km long and 2km wide. The diving is excellent, particularly down the wall, where pelagic species such as tuna and barracuda are encountered, and reef sharks and hammerheads are seen regularly. Soft corals are a feature and manta rays are visible in shallower water. The island is also a breeding ground for sea birds such as boobies and terns.

Layang Layang can only be visited as part of an expensive tour. There is only one resort on the island, **Layang Layang Island Resort** (☎ 03-2162 2877; www.layanglayang.com) run by a company based in KL. Access to the resort and dive areas is only possible between February and October. For outfits offering dive charters and live-aboard trips to the area see p392.

SOUTH OF KOTA KINABALU

The Crocker Range is the backbone of western Sabah, rising from near Tenom in the south and peaking in the north at massive Mt Kinabalu and its outlier, Mt Trus Madi. Nearly 1500m below the range is the fertile coastal plain, where KK and other large settlements sit. Logging has taken a devastating toll on most of Sabah, but the Crocker still has some good stands of intact forest, and much of it is now preserved as the Crocker Range National Park. Unfortunately, the park has no facilities, trails or accommodation.

A highway climbs steeply from KK over Gunung Alab to Tambunan then veers south to the central valley towns of Keningau and Tenom. From here you can travel by road to Batu Punggul.

Heading south from KK, another road follows a coastal plain past Papar before reaching Beaufort, Sipitang and the Sarawak border. A popular and scenic way of closing the loop is to take the railway from Beaufort to Tenom (see p405), and then back to KK via Keningau and Tambunan.

Tambunan Rafflesia Reserve

Near the top of the range next to the highway is the Tambunan Rafflesia Reserve, devoted to the world's largest flower. The rafflesia is a parasitic plant that grows hidden within the stems of jungle vines until it bursts into bloom. The large bulbous flowers can be up to 1m in diameter. The 12 or so species of rafflesia are found only in Borneo and Sumatra; several species are unique to Sabah, but their blooming is unpredictable.

The **Rafflesia Information Centre** (☎ 087-774691; admission free; 🕓 8am-4.30pm), on the highway 59km from KK, has interesting displays and information on the rafflesia. From the centre, trails lead into the forest where the rafflesias can be found. Whether you will find one in bloom is very much a matter of luck, though the staff at the centre can tell you of the latest sightings. The flowers may be close to the information centre or involve a walk deep into the forest. In theory, guides are available to take you to the flowers at fixed times, but staff are actually rarely available. If the centre is closed, you can still walk down the trail. For information on whether there are flowers blooming, give the centre a call first.

Even if there are no rafflesias, there are pleasant walks at the reserve. There is also a good walk to **Sensuron Waterfall**, just off the highway about 4km from the information centre towards KK. It's a 45-minute walk down to the falls from the highway, and near the starting point on the other side of the road is a lookout point and picnic tables.

SLEEPING & EATING

While there is no accommodation at the reserve, there are options nearby.

Gunung Emas Highlands Resort (☎ 088-215499; fax 238158; Km 55, Jl KK-Tambunan; s/d RM60/80) This ramshackle place is perched on the side of the mountain 7km back towards KK from the Rafflesia Information Centre. The views are superb and the climate is refreshing but very damp. The term 'resort' is a little grandiose; the buildings are quite run-down and there's a very depressing little zoo. The restaurant at the 'resort', however, serves good Chinese dishes and you can also sample a taste of wild boar and venison. On weekends it can get crowded with day-trippers from KK.

Gunung Alab Resort (☎/fax 08-302279, Mile 33, Jl Penampang; r without/with shower RM35/45) This is a smaller and newer hotel further on towards Tambunan with a **halal restaurant** and more superb views over the Crocker Range.

GETTING THERE & AWAY

Take a Tambunan or Keningau minivan from KK to the reserve or the resort for RM10. From Tambunan the cost is RM5, but you may be charged for the whole trip to KK. The journey takes 30 minutes. Minivans pass by fairly frequently until dusk.

Tambunan

☎ 087

Tambunan, a small agricultural service town set in a bucolic valley about 81km from KK, is the first settlement across the Crocker Range. The region was the last stronghold of Mat Salleh, who became a folk hero for rebelling against the British late in the 19th century. He eventually negotiated a truce with the British, which so outraged his own people that he was forced to flee to the Tambunan plain where he was eventually besieged and killed. His gravestone is in a cemetery just off the main road, 750m out of town towards Ranau.

There's little of interest in the small town but the surrounding hills and farm fields make this a tranquil spot to stay for a couple of days. A good time to visit is in May, when activities associated with the **Pesta Kaamatan** (Harvest Festival) take place. If you have your own 4WD, or are well equipped for trekking, there are some interesting side trips. **Mawar Waterfall** is a pretty waterfall in the Crocker Range, though getting to it is an expedition. From Tambunan head towards Ranau; 7.5km past the turn-off to KK there is a small shop and a very difficult-to-see sign to 'Air Terjun Mawar'. Turn left and keep going past rural areas and new settlements, high up into the mountains. It is beautiful countryside, though the road is long and tortuous and fords a small river. Alternatively you can make the trek up Mt Trus Madi (next page).

SLEEPING & EATING

Tambunan Village Resort Centre (☎ 774076; info@tvrc.net; Kampung Keranaan, Tambunan; r without/with shower RM100/120; a) Many travellers have recommend this delightful place on the riverside, where you can stay in a bamboo longhouse for RM60 or in private rooms and individual chalets. It's also possible to camp for RM10. The centre arranges trips to surrounding areas including Mt Trus Madi (see next page). If you want to experience local life for a couple of days, Tambunan is a good place to try out

Sabah's **homestay programme** (☎ 018-665 5836; tambunanvillage@sabah-homestay.com). Check out the Sabah homestay website at www.sabah-homestay.com for more details.

GETTING THERE & AWAY

Regular minivans ply the roads between Tambunan and KK (RM10, 1½ hours), Ranau (RM10, 2 hours), Keningau (RM5, 1 hour) and Tenom (RM10, 2 hours).

Mt Trus Madi

On the opposite side of the highway from Tambunan's shopping area, a road leads to Sabah's second-highest peak, 2642m-high **Mt Trus Madi**. Though Trus Madi is surrounded by logging concessions, the upper slopes and peak are wild and jungle-clad and classified as forest reserve.

There are a couple of muddy trails to the summit that are treacherous in parts – just the thing for those who find Mt Kinabalu a bit pedestrian. Independent trekkers must be well equipped and take all food and water up the mountain.

Before setting off you are strongly advised to hire a guide, or at least get maps and assistance from the **Forestry Department** (Jabatan Perhutanan; ☎ 774691) at the district office in Tambunan.

Also in Tambunan, the **Tambunan Village Resort Centre** (☎ 774076; info@tvrc.net; Kampung Keranaan) can arrange a trek to Mt Trus Madi for about RM500 per day per group, which includes the rental of a 4WD vehicle, provisions, and guide hire.

Unless you are very fast or get ferried up by 4WD, expect it to take three days altogether. There are camping spots halfway up the mountain and on the summit.

To get to the mountain from Tambunan, take the road towards Kaingaran. Past Kampung Batu Lapan take the road to the southeast which leads to a network of logging roads. With good maps or a guide, it is possible to go by 4WD up to about 1500m, from where it is a five- to seven-hour climb to the top of Trus Madi. From Tambunan it's a 28km walk along the pleasant valley road then up through logging roads to the peak.

Keningau

☎ 087

Keningau is a sprawling timber and agricultural town. Arriving here is a bit of a shock after the rustic splendour of Tambunan and Tenom and there's not much reason to stay here except to arrange ongoing transport. Attracted by the prospect of well-paid employment, people have flocked here from neighbouring districts, as well as from Indonesia and the Philippines, and the town's population has more than doubled since the 1960s. There is a large *tamu* (weekly market) every Thursday. Though the town is deep in the heart of Murut country, it's most unlikely you'll see anyone dressed in traditional tribal wear.

SLEEPING & EATING

Keningau has plenty of hotels. The cheaper places are very seedy, but Keningau has been feeling hard times for a while and top-end accommodation can be a bargain.

Hotel Juta (☎ 337888; www.sabah.com.my/juta; s/d RM230/270; ❄) has comfortable rooms and incredible discounts – room prices can be as much as 50% off. This multistorey white building is a short walk from where the minivans gather in the parking lot on the edge of the highway.

There's a number of small restaurants in the streets off the market near the Chinese temple.

GETTING THERE & AWAY

An express bus from Tenom (RM12) passes through three times daily at about 8am, 1pm and 5pm.

Minivans and share-taxis (the main form of transport here) congregate in a large parking area off the main highway, leaving for KK (RM10, 2½ hours), Ranau (RM15, 3 hours) and Tenom (RM5, 30 minutes). The last minivan to Ranau leaves at noon, so don't be late arriving in Keningau. The road to Ranau is a hairpin gravel road which follows a deep river-chasm much of the way. After heavy rain the bank is often washed away in places and vehicles may have to turn back. If you make it to Ranau from here, you can go on to either Sandakan or Kinabalu National Park.

Other transport gathers in complete chaos near the Chinese temple, about 200m southwest of the highway parking lot. From here, minivans and Land Cruisers make the journey deep into the centre of Sabah to Sapulut. From Sapulut, travellers go by chartered boat to Batu Punggul then back to Sapulut and on through to Tawau (see p405). The roads are rough and it's not a comfortable journey.

A logging road also runs down the rugged and spectacular Crocker Range from Keningau towards the coast, then links up with the Papar–Beaufort road. It's only recommended for 4WD vehicles, and logging trucks always have right of way.

Tenom

☎ 087

Nestled in a lovely, cool, cloud-shrouded valley, Tenom is the home of the friendly Murut people, most of whom are farmers. Soya beans, maize and vegetables are grown in this fertile area, and there are several cocoa plantations. The area is also populated by Dusun, Indians and Chinese. Tenom is the end of the railway line from Tanjung Aru in KK.

Despite the peaceful setting, there's nothing to do in the town. **The Sabah Agricultural Park** makes an interesting diversion (see p404).

About 10 minutes out of town on the road towards Beaufort is a recently built replica of a Murut longhouse, which houses the fledgling **Murut Cultural Centre**. The centre was built to record something of the area's local traditions, as longhouses as far away as Tomani have either been burnt or abandoned in the last few years.

Tenom is a compact little place and it's very easy to find your way around. Minivans park near the *padang* (town square) and cruise up and down the main street, while taxis wait near the Hotel Sri Perdana.

SLEEPING

Hotel Sri Perdana (☎ 734001; fax 734009; Lot 77, Jl Tun Mustapha; s/d RM30/45; ❄) A clean and friendly place with the added advantage of tile floors, this hotel is good value and quite popular. It's only three minutes' walk from the train station.

Orchid Hotel (☎ 737600; excelng@tm.net.my; Block K, Jln Tun Mustapha; s/d RM42/48; ❄) Centrally located on the main road running through town, the Orchid has nice bright rooms, also with tile floors.

Hotel Perkasa Tenom (☎ 735811; perkasa-tm@hotmail.com; r RM65; ❄) Perched high on the hill above Tenom, the Perkasa is a quiet place to stay and is surrounded by low forest with walking trails. At the right time of year it's possible to see rafflesia flowers near a stream about 15 minutes' walk away from the hotel parking lot. It has all the services of an upper mid-range hotel, including a bar and restaurant. The 1km road up to the hotel is very steep and a bit long to walk up. A taxi there will cost RM5.

EATING

There are plenty of *kedai kopi* in town selling basic Chinese food. Food stalls set up in the evening in the car park down the main road from the *padang* and are open until about midnight.

Restaurant Happy Café (88 Jl Datuk Yassin; dishes RM3-5) Run by a very friendly Indian family, the *murtabak* and *nasi ayam* (rice with chicken) have more of a zingy taste than usual. They also serve Indian dishes.

Chi Hin Restaurant (☎ 736133; dishes RM5-10) Tucked away behind one of the shopping block alleys, there's good Chinese food here.

For other Indian food, roti and *murtabak*, try the restaurant attached to the **Hotel Sri Perdana**; it's friendly and is open from 7.30am to 9.30pm. The **Sapong Restaurant** in the Hotel Perkasa serves moderately priced Chinese, Malay and Western food.

GETTING THERE & AWAY

Bus

Lots of minivans park around the *padang* and near the Hotel Sri Perdana; when they're ready to go, they cruise up and down the street drumming up business. Most are going to Keningau (RM5, 1 hour), but some go to KK (RM20, 3 to 4 hours). There are also regular services to Tambunan (RM10, 2 hours). An **express bus** (☎ 264315) to KK (RM20, 3½ hours) leaves daily from the train station at 7am, noon and 4pm.

Taxi

Taxis congregate opposite the petrol station near the Hotel Sri Perdana. Share-taxis also make the run to Keningau (RM5), Ranau (RM20) and KK (RM25). Early morning is the best time to catch one.

Train

Although the railway line goes as far as Melalap, further up the valley, Tenom is the railhead as far as passenger trains are

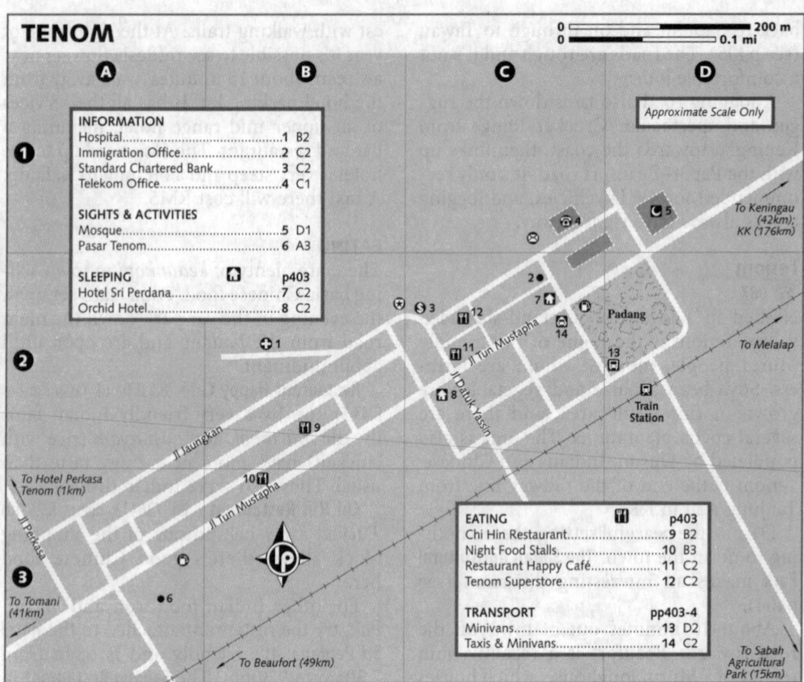

concerned. A fire destroyed the train station in early 2003, but the train is still in service. Taking the 2½-hour trip to Beaufort (RM2.65) and then a bus to onward destinations is worth considering. The trip is a bit of a novelty and there's good scenery along the way (the road follows Sungai Padas). Bring lots to eat and drink, as there can be delays, especially if there's been heavy rain.

Sabah Agricultural Park

Located in Lagud Seberang, about 15km southeast of Tenom, this research and tourist facility is one of the best reasons to visit the Tenom area. If you're the least bit interested in tropical horticulture, it can't be missed. **Sabah Agricultural Park** (Taman Pertianian Sabah; ☎ 737952; www.sabah.net.my/agripark; adult/child RM25/10; 9am-5.30pm Tue-Sun) is run by the Department of Agriculture and altogether covers about 1500 acres (610 hectares). The visitors centre is an expansion of the former Orchid Centre, established over a period of years by a British man, Anthony Lamb, who spent many years in Borneo.

There's a lot to do, in terms of getting to know plants. Seeing everything in detail could take about two or three days, and it's possible to stay overnight. Highlights include the largest collection of orchid species in Southeast Asia, walking trails in the forested hills surrounding the park, a bee centre and the **Living Crop Museum**, which explains how various plants are used and cultivated. You can rent bicycles to get around for RM3 per hour (plus RM1 for each additional hour) or take a guided tour on the tractor-trailer that takes visitors to all the different gardens and sights. The Tenom area is known for its **coffee** and it's on sale here at the centre's shop. The instant coffee (powdered grounds that come in what looks like a large teabag) is a pleasant surprise, though some heavy-duty coffee drinkers might find it less robust than they're used to.

The park has a **hostel** (dm RM25), a restaurant, shop and information centre. It's also possible to camp for RM10 per person.

To get there take a minivan from Tenom heading to Lagud Seberang (RM3). Services run every hour or so throughout the morning, but dry up in the late afternoon. Tell the driver you're going to Taman Pertianian. The park entrance is about 1km off the main road. Taxis do the return trip from Tenom for RM25, though you'll have to negotiate how long you want the driver to wait.

Batu Punggul

Not far from the Kalimantan border, Batu Punggul is a jungle-topped limestone outcrop towering nearly 200m above Sungai Sapulut. This is deep in Murut country and Batu Punggul was one of several sites sacred to these people. It can be difficult and expensive to get here, but this is a beautiful part of Sabah that few tourists visit, and it offers a chance to rub shoulders with the Murut. The trip involves a long ride over rough logging roads via Keningau to the village of **Sapulut**, from where it is about three to five hours (depending on the water level) by motorised longboat along the jungle-lined Sungai Sapulut.

The only place to stay is the **Batu Punggul Lodge**. Accommodation is on floor mats and must be pre-arranged by the **Rural Development Corporation** (☎ 088-440158 in KK); contact Sansi Mansir. The resort centres on a traditionally styled Murut longhouse, and offers jungle walks, canoeing and visits to nearby caves. It's a popular place with youth groups and can get crowded during school holidays, but mostly it's nearly empty. Tours are arranged by **Borneo Eco** (☎ 088-234009, fax 233688; cbetsb1@po.jaring.my) in KK (see p392).

It's possible to do a trip independently, but hiring a boat for the river transport is expensive (about RM200 to RM250 per group). Minivans and Land Cruisers leave from Keningau (RM20, 3 hours) for Sapulut. You can also get to Sapulut from Tawau in East Sabah. It's a long journey over rough roads by Land Cruiser (RM20, 8 hours).

Beaufort

☎ 087

Beaufort is a quiet provincial town on Sungai Padas, about 90km south of KK. Its blue-painted, two-storey wooden shophouses have a certain dilapidated charm, and the people make you feel welcome, but the main reason to come here is to catch the train.

There's a branch of the HSBC on Jl Masjid that will change travellers cheques.

White-water rafting is popular through the Padas Gorge south of Beaufort, and is at its best between April and July, when the water level of Sungai Padas creates Grade 2 to 3 conditions. Rafting day trips organised out of KK cost RM150 to RM200 per person, and normally require 24 hours advance notice to arrange. For tour companies, see p392.

SLEEPING & EATING

If you miss your connections, you'll have to spend a night in Beaufort. The **Beaufort Hotel** (☎ 211911; Jl Pasar Awam; s/d RM42/56; ❄), near the mosque, has simple but clean rooms. The **Mandarin Inn** (☎ 212800; s/d RM35/42; ❄), across the river, has similar facilities, but is further from the train and bus station.

Restoran Rasa Sayang (☎ 016-840 7636; Jl Pasar Awam; dishes RM9-18) This is a friendly place for lunch or dinner with decent roti dishes and an excellent rice dish with chicken and vegetables.

Restoran Kim Wah (☎ 211911; Jl Pasar Awam; dishes RM5-10) You can find good Chinese food here and there's a separate air-conditioned section around the corner. The restaurant is underneath the Beaufort Hotel.

Beaufort Baker (☎ 223262, 211262; Lot 5, Jl Chung) For a good selection of cakes, buns and other pastries, look no further than this bakery just across the river on the south side of the road. A second branch is near the market. If you're just passing through Beaufort, you'll have time to duck in and grab something when the bus stops.

Kedai Teck Loong (☎ 016-841 4812; Lot 31, Beaufort Jayah) A couple of blocks south of the bakery, this is a great place to try out a wide range of very refreshing fresh fruit juices for RM2 each.

GETTING THERE & AWAY

Bus

Buses and minivans gather along Jl Pasar Awam in the town centre, and behind the Beaufort Hotel. A couple of express buses leave morning and afternoon for KK (RM14, 1½ hours). The KK to Lawas express bus passes through Beaufort at around 3pm; the fare from Beaufort to Lawas is RM15. Express buses to Sipitang (from KK) pass through until 1.30pm. Minibuses to Kuala Penyu (RM6) leave in the morning.

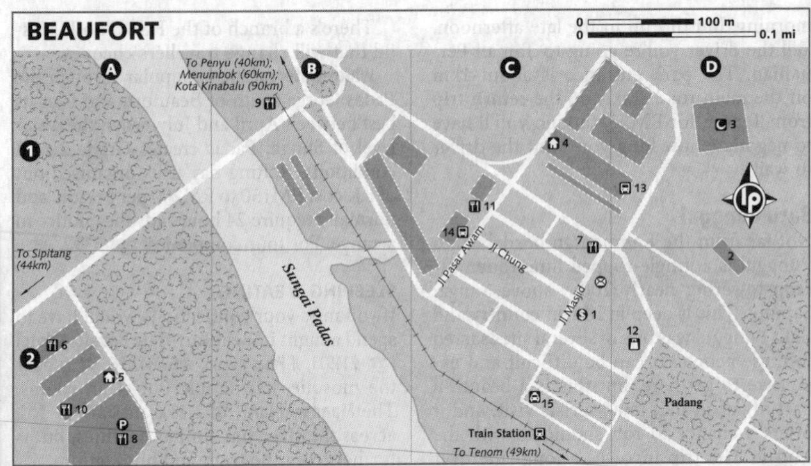

INFORMATION
Hongkong Bank (HSBC)....1 C2

SIGHTS & ACTIVITIES
Council Office....2 D2
Mosque....3 D1

SLEEPING p405
Beaufort Hotel....4 C1
Mandarin Inn....5 A2

EATING p405
Beaufort Baker....6 A2
Beaufort Baker....7 C1
Food Stalls....8 A2
Food Stalls....9 B1
Kedai Teck Loong....10 A2
Restoran Rasa Sayang....11 C1

SHOPPING
Food and Clothing Market....12 D2

TRANSPORT pp405-6
Minibus & Minivan Stands....13 D1
Minibus & Minivan Stands....14 C1
Taxis....15 C2

Minivans that are nearly full cruise around town honking hopefully at pedestrians. There are frequent departures for Papar (RM6) and KK (RM7, 2 hours), and less-frequent departures for Sipitang (RM6, 1½ hours), Lawas (RM15), Kuala Penyu (until around 2.30pm, RM5) and Membakut (RM6). The road to Kuala Penyu is a disaster, so start out early to make sure you get back on the same day – there's nowhere to stay there. To Menumbok (for Labuan) there are plenty of minivans until early afternoon (RM6, 1 hour).

Train

It is possible to take the Sabah State Railway from KK to Beaufort, but it's a slow trip (RM5.60, 2½ hours) and a bus or minivan is quicker. For schedules and bookings, contact the stations at **Beaufort** (☎ 211518), **Tenom** (☎ 087-735514) and **Tanjung Aru** (☎ 088-254611).

The stretch of track between Beaufort and Tenom (RM2.65, 2½ hours) following Sungai Padas is more scenic, and worth doing if you have the time. There's no air-conditioning on the train and major delays can be expected when there are problems with the track due to heavy rain. Make sure you bring something to eat and drink because it could be a long journey.

Kuala Penyu

Kuala Penyu is at the northern end of a flat, swampy peninsula dotted with water buffalo. If you want to get to Pulau Tiga National Park, this is the place to come. The town is unremarkable, but there are some good **beaches** nearby. The best is around the headland from the estuary, 8km out of town; there are picnic tables and toilets but no other facilities.

Readers have recommended a quiet lodge about 13km outside of town in the village of Tempurong. The **Tempurong Seaside Lodge** (☎ 088-773066; info@borneoauthenticadventure.com; r RM110) sits on a small hill with views of the South China Sea and is a beautiful place to unwind for a couple of days. The room price includes breakfast, lunch and dinner. The facilities are clean, but basic, with fan-cooled rooms and mosquito nets. There's access to a white sandy beach close by. The only problem is getting out to the lodge. Your best bet is to phone or email the lodge (ask for Yanti) and see about getting picked up in KK or Kuala Penyu. Even if you have your own transport, it's a good idea to contact them for directions because it's not easy to find.

The lodge also runs tours of nearby **Sungai Klias**, which is habitat for proboscis monkeys, various birds and crocodiles. The cruise costs RM60 per person and includes dinner and refreshments.

GETTING THERE & AWAY

From KK minivans leave from behind Centre Point (RM10, 2 hours). From Beaufort minivans to Kuala Penyu (RM5) leave throughout the morning until around 2.30pm, minibuses (RM6) leave in the morning only. From the turn-off on the Menumbok road, it's a long, dusty road that ends at a river on the other side of the town – a car ferry shuttles across to Kuala Penyu between 6am and 6pm. A minivan from Kuala Penyu to Menumbok costs RM5.

Pulau Tiga National Park

The name Pulau Tiga means simply 'Three Islands', but only two of the original three remain in this 15-sq-km park north of Kuala Penyu. Pulau Tiga is the largest island; about 1km to the northeast lies tiny Pulau Kalampunian Damit; and in between are the remains of the third island, now only a sandbar eroded by wave action. In 2001 it was the location for the reality TV show 'Survivor' and is often referred to now as **Survivor Island**. While its association with the TV show has attracted tourists (and possibly repelled some), it's still a quiet and relaxing place to visit, blessed with fine sandy beaches and good snorkelling throughout the year.

The islands themselves are recent creations, formed in 1897 by the eruption of mud volcanoes. The main island, **Pulau Tiga,** has since been covered by dense vegetation. Continuous volcanic activity has taken place over the last hundred years, and still continues in the form of bubbling mud and escaping methane gas visible from the highest point of the island.

Pulau Kalampunian Damit is little more than a large rock covered in dense vegetation but is famous for the sea snakes that come ashore in their hundreds to mate. On any one day up to 150 snakes can be present, curled up under boulders, among roots and in tree hollows. It's a fascinating phenomenon made enigmatic by the fact that the snakes are never seen on nearby Pulau Tiga. Not surprisingly, the local name for this islet is Pulau Ular – **Snake Island**. If you make a trip out to this island by hiring a boat, beware of the snakes – they are extremely poisonous.

SLEEPING & EATING

The island has one resort and there's also basic accommodation available through the Sabah Parks office.

Pulau Tiga Resort (☎ 885650; sdc@sipadandivers.com) If you're looking for a little luxury and a relaxing escape from everything try out this comfortable resort. Packages from KK are available for various durations. For example, a two-day package is about RM300 and includes meals, transport from KK and the park entrance fee, as well as a visit to Snake Island (discounts may be available). Other activities like diving and boating incur additional costs. The resort also offers survivor-wannabes the chance to recreate their own experience in the jungle.

More rustic lodgings on the island are run by **Sabah Parks** (☎ 88-211881 in KK; dm/d cabins RM30/120). Camping spots cost RM5 per person. Facilities here are basic and there's no restaurant, though a cooking area is provided for preparing your own food.

GETTING THERE & AWAY

To get to Pulau Tiga, take a minibus from KK to Kuala Penyu, then ask around for a boat – it should cost around RM120 for the return trip. If you're just visiting for the day, arrange a time for the boat's return, but don't leave it too late or you may miss out on a minivan from Kuala Penyu. The Pulau Tiga Resort arranges its own transport from KK.

Papar

This is a cosy little coastal Kadazan town 38km south of KK. Local produce includes coconut wine and there's a *tamu* (weekly market) on Sunday. There's a beach out of town where you can swim, and you can take a boat ride along Sungai Papar.

Minivans leave throughout the day from KK (RM3, 1 hour). Express buses also pass by and can drop you in the town.

On Wednesday and Saturday, Sutera Harbour operates the **North Borneo Railway** (☎ 088-263933; www.northborneorailway.com.my) featuring a renovated British Vulcan steam engine that does the run from Tanjung Aru train station in KK to Papar and back. The train leaves KK at 10am and returns from Papar at 2.30pm (RM160 including lunch, 3 hours).

You can also hop on a Beaufort-bound diesel train with the locals, get off at Papar (RM2.40, 1 hour) and return to KK later. **Tanjung Aru train station** (☎ 088-254611) in KK will have the latest schedule.

Sipitang

Sipitang is 44km south of Beaufort, 144km from KK and the closest town in Sabah to the Sarawak border. Located on a wide, shallow bay, Sipitang is pleasant enough, though the only reason to stop here is to organise bus connections. If you are heading to Lawas for a boat to Brunei or Limbang, you should spend the night in Lawas or you'll miss the early-morning departures.

The Sarawak border is 18km south and buses stop at **Merapok**, where passports and visas are checked at both Sabah and Sarawak immigration offices. The offices are open every day from 6am until 10pm.

Sipitang has a number of *kedai kopi* and food stalls on the main street, and some reasonable, easy-to-find hotels if you have to stay the night.

Minivans ply between Beaufort and Sipitang (RM6, 1½ hours) throughout the day. Buses go to Merapok in Sarawak for RM3. From Beaufort there are buses and trains to KK and Tenom (see p405).

PULAU LABUAN

☎ 087

Labuan is an island about 8km off the coast of Sabah at the mouth of Brunei Bay. It's had its historical moments, especially during WWII, but is pretty quiet these days. Many travellers pass through Labuan en route to Brunei, but it's a pleasant place, with a spotlessly clean, compact town and a relaxed lifestyle.

Just to confuse regional politics, Labuan is a federal territory governed directly from KL. Before the Asian financial crisis a few years ago, the government poured money into the island and pushed it as a major offshore banking haven. Labuan hasn't quite taken off as envisioned, but still offers incentives to investors, more recently one to try and attract foreign senior citizens to make it their place for retirement. The sultan of Brunei ceded Labuan to the British in 1846 and, apart from three years under Japanese occupation, it remained British for 115 years. Labuan's modern anonymity belies the fact that it played a major role in the Borneo arena during WWII. The Japanese landed here and the Allies counter-invaded; the Japanese forces in North Borneo surrendered here at the end of the war; and the Japanese officers responsible for the 'death marches' from Sandakan (see p426) were tried by an Australian War Crimes Court on Labuan. There's a war cemetery and peace park to mark these horrific events, and many remaining WWII veterans and their families make annual pilgrimages to see the memorials.

Labuan also was once a coal-mining centre and now has major petroleum gas installations. In 2003, newspaper reports mentioned plans for building a bridge to mainland Borneo, which might change the economic outlook for Labuan, but would also destroy some of its uniqueness as an island.

Bandar Labuan is the main town and the transit point for ferries. The population is a mix of Muslim Malays, a large contingent of Indians and Chinese, plus a sprinkling of Bugis and Bajau people.

Information

INTERNET ACCESS

There's a good choice of terminals at **Family Fun Internet** (1st fl, Financial Park; RM2 per hr; 9.30am-9.30pm), in the midst of an amusement arcade; thankfully it's closed off in a separate section from the arcade and gamers.

Aquarius Internet Café (☎ 411860; Jl Tun Mustapha; RM3 per hr; 9am-midnight) is a small cybercafé on the ground floor of the Millimewah Superstore; it can get a bit noisy with gamers.

LAUNDRY

A small hole-in-the-wall laundry service, the **Super Wash Laundry** (☎ 411305; Unit 0255 Jl Tun Mustapha) is near the local bus station.

MONEY

There are numerous banks around town, including the HSBC bank near the town

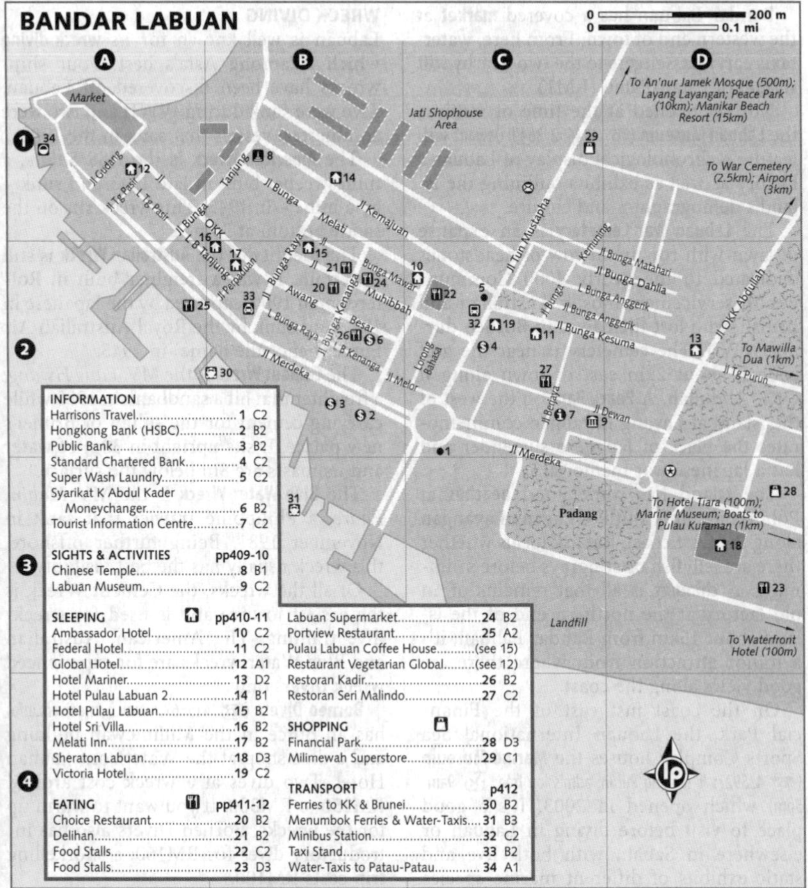

centre and a Maybank in the Financial Park shopping complex. Moneychangers around town will change cash and travellers cheques at good rates.

Syarikat K Abdul Kader (☎ 412545; 168 Jl OKK Awang Besar; ⏰ 8am-6.30pm) changes cash and travellers cheques.

TOURIST INFORMATION

Labuan has a helpful **Tourism Information Centre** (☎ 417862; www.labuantourism.com.my; ⏰ 9am-5pm) on the corner of Jl Dewan and Jl Berjaya.

TRAVEL AGENCIES

Harrisons Travel (☎ 412557; htshipkk@tm.net.my; 1 Jl Merdeka) is a handy and reputable travel agency on the southeast side of the roundabout at the intersection of Jl Merdeka and Jl Tun Mustapha.

Sights & Activities

If you're arriving by boat, you can't miss the looming steel-and-glass shopping fortress, **Financial Park**; the town's No 1 'attraction', and the place where duty-free spending is meant to happen; but prices are generally no cheaper than elsewhere. Financial Park is open from 10am to 10pm daily, but most of its shops are closed by 8pm on weekdays.

North of the city centre, on Jl Mustapha is the **An'nur Jamek Mosque**. This is one distinctive house of worship – futuristic is too mild a word. The mosque is a 15-minute walk up Jl Tun Mustapha from the centre of town.

Bandar Labuan has a covered **market** at the western end of town. From here, water-taxis carry passengers to the two nearby **stilt villages** of Patau-Patau (RM1).

Not yet opened at the time of writing, the **Labuan Museum** (☎ 414462; 364 Jl Dewan) will feature a chronological display of Labuan's history as well as exhibits outlining the island's demographics and culture.

The **Labuan War Cemetery** is an expanse of lawn with row upon row of headstones dedicated to the nearly 4000 Commonwealth servicemen, mostly Australian and British, who lost their lives in Borneo during WWII. The cemetery is near the golf course, about 2km east of town along Jl OKK Abdullah. A **Peace Park** on the west of the island at Layang Layangan commemorates the place of Japanese surrender and has a Japanese war memorial.

The island has some good **beaches** at Pohon Batu and south of Layang Layangan along the west coast, but ask locals whether there are jellyfish or stingrays before swimming. A **chimney** is all that remains of an old factory at the northern end of the island about 15km from Bandar Labuan; it's a minor attraction from where there are good views along the coast.

On the coast just east of the Financial Park, the Labuan International Sea Sports Complex houses the **Marine Museum** (☎ 425927; Jl Tanjung Purun; admission free; 🕑 9am-5pm) which opened in 2003. It's a good place to visit before diving in Labuan or elsewhere in Sabah, with both live and static exhibits of different marine species and ecosystems.

NEARBY ISLANDS

Pulau Kuraman, Pulau Rusukan Kecil and Pulau Rusukan Besar are uninhabited islands lying southwest of Labuan that are now protected as the **Labuan marine park**. The beaches are pristine, but dynamite fishing has destroyed much of the coral.

Pulau Papan is another island, 5km southeast of Bandar Labuan, which has been developed as a tourist attraction – it makes for a pleasant day trip. Basic accommodation is available at the **Kuraman Resort** (☎ 016-849 0931; cabins from RM40 per night).

Boats to Pulau Kuraman leave from the jetty at the Labuan International Sea Sports Complex (see p412).

WRECK DIVING

Labuan is well known for its **wreck diving** which is among Asia's best. Four shipwrecks have been discovered off Labuan. Two were sunk during WWII and two were commercial vessels that sank in the 1980s.

The **American Wreck** is the USS *Salute*, a minesweeper built in late 1943 and sunk – by a mine – in 1945. This wreck sits on the sandy bottom at 33m.

The identity of the **Australian Wreck** is still uncertain. It was a freighter built in Rotterdam in 1900, captured by the Japanese in 1942 and sunk by the Royal Australian Air Force (hence the name) in 1945.

The **Cement Wreck** is the MV *Tung Hwang*, a freighter that hit a sandbank in 1980 while carrying cement for the sultan of Brunei's new palace. It sits upright in 30m of water and its masts are 8m below the surface.

The **Blue Water Wreck** is the MV *Mabini Padre*, a Philippine trawler that sank in November 1981. Being further offshore, this wreck usually has the best visibility.

Of all the wrecks, the Cement Wreck is the easiest to dive and is used for wreck-dive training. The American, Australian and Blue Water wrecks are for experienced wreck divers only.

Borneo Divers (☎ 415867; www.bornedivers.info) has an office in the Millimewah building and a dive shop at the Waterfront Labuan Hotel. Two dives at a wreck cost around RM250 to RM300. If you want to warm up for the wrecks, Borneo Divers also has introductory dives for RM160; a snorkelling trip costs RM100.

Sleeping

BUDGET

Budget accommodation in Bandar Labuan is limited. There's much better value to be found at mid-range and top-end hotels, especially if you scam a discount when business is slow.

Melati Inn (☎ 416307; Unit 0061 Jl Perpaduan; r RM48; ❄) This place is a little run-down, but is clean and was undergoing some renovation at the time of writing. It has large rooms that sleep four people, with shared bathroom.

Hotel Sri Villa (☎ 413605; Jl OKK Awang Besar; s/d RM35/40 ❄) Around the corner from the Melati, this is another low-rent option. The rooms here are basic and the toilets are shared.

MID-RANGE

Labuan has a variety of mid-range hotels, ranging in quality and price. Most are within walking distance of the ferry terminal.

Hotel Mariner (☎ 418822; mhlabuan@tm.net.my; Unit 0468 Jl Tanjung Purun; s/d RM82/136; ❄) A large, brightly lit hotel with a grand lobby, this popular hotel has good rooms, though the singles are a bit small.

Global Hotel (☎ 425201; www.skynary.com/global/hotel; Unit 0017 Jl OKK Awang Besar; s/d RM69/99; ❄) Rooms here are a little small, but they're clean and the staff downstairs is friendly. A traditional-style Malay breakfast is included in the attached Global Vegetarian Restaurant.

Ambassador Hotel (☎ 423233; fax 428233; Unit 0142 Jl Bunga Mawar; s/d RM60/80; ❄) Located behind the Labuan Supermarket, this is a smaller, new hotel with plain but clean and comfortable rooms.

Manikar Beach Resort (☎ 418700; manikar@tm.net.my; Jl Batu Manikar; r RM110-130; ❄ 🏊) At the northern tip of the island, this medium-sized resort is one of the best places to stay in Labuan if you're looking for a little luxury at bargain prices. Discounts of 50% are often available. The rooms are very large, with slate floors, and the bathrooms are spacious. It's right on the beach, with a nice swimming pool, restaurant and quiet surroundings. It's on the local bus route.

Other recommendations:

Victoria Hotel (☎ 412411; fax 412550; Unit 0360 Jl Tun Mustapha; s/d RM58/88) Right on Jl Tun Mustapha; has comfortable rooms.

Federal Hotel (☎ 411711; fax 411337; Jl Bunga Kesuma; s/d RM50/75; ❄) Large and clean rooms and offers substantial discounts.

Hotel Pulau Labuan (☎ 416288; fax 416255; 27-28 Jl Muhibbah; s/d RM78/102; ❄) A busy hotel with decent rooms, but a little noisy.

Hotel Pulau Labuan 2 (☎ 422388; fax 421422; 9-12 Jl Kemajuan; s/d RM82/118; ❄) Another version of the same hotel, both places have good restaurants serving Western and Asian food.

TOP END

Labuan's best hotels are east of the town centre.

Waterfront Labuan Hotel (☎ 418111; leslbn@tm.net.my; 1 Jl Wawasan; s/d RM178/200; ❄ 🏊) A large, luxurious and beautiful hotel with a small marina attached, the rooms here are extremely good value with discounts. Rooms with views of the sea are a little more. There's a comfortable coffee shop open 24 hours, and some nice bars and eating places outside.

Sheraton Labuan (☎ 422000; www.sheraton.com; 462 Jl Merdeka; s/d RM185/220; ❄ 🏊) This has everything you would expect from a Sheraton hotel, five-star rooms, good restaurants, a pub with live bands (and a reasonable happy hour till 9.30pm) and wall safes in the rooms. It's in the Labuan Financial Centre.

Hotel Tiara (☎ 414300; www.tiaralabuan.com; Jl Tanjung Batu; s/d RM180/308; ❄ 🏊) The Asian financial crisis hasn't been kind to this luxury hotel, but it's nicely positioned near a quiet beach a little out of town, towards the Labuan War Cemetery.

Eating

Bandar Labuan has plenty of cafés and restaurants. In duty-free Labuan alcohol is cheap and a big bottle of beer can cost as little as RM3.

You'll find food stalls on Jl Muhibbah between the Labuan Supermarket and the cinema. There are also excellent and affordable **food stalls** next to the park between the Sheraton Labuan and the Waterfront Financial Hotel; they're open all day but evenings are when it's all happening – there's plenty of variety to choose from.

Restoran Seri Malindo (☎ 416072; Jl Dewan; dishes RM5-15) A large, breezy open-air restaurant near the museum, this place opens early (6.30am) and has decent breakfast for RM10. Meals are served throughout the day until 11.30pm. It also offers delicious fruit drinks and banana splits (RM4.50) – good to cool down with in the afternoon.

Choice Restaurant (☎ 418086; Unit 0104 Jl OKK Awang Besar; dishes RM5-15) This air-conditioned and clean Indian restaurant serves tasty chicken tandoori and other delicious items, like roti canai and *puri*. It's hard to know where to begin on the huge potato *masala dosa* that arrives at the table like a work of art.

Restoran Kadir (Jl OKK Awang Besar; dishes RM3-5) This Indian restaurant is a little more basic, but also has delicious food. The staff is friendly and serves food from breakfast to dinner.

Portview Restaurant (☎ 422999; Jl Merdeka; dishes RM20-30) A Chinese-style seafood place like its branch in KK, the setting is a little nicer here, overlooking the harbour.

Restaurant Vegetarian Global (☎ 426206; Jl OKK Awang Besar; 🕑 7.30am-3pm; dishes RM5-10) A spotlessly clean eating establishment beside the Global Hotel that serves an eclectic menu of Malay-style vegetarian food. Try the coconut-flavoured rice wrapped up in a banana leaf and the vegetarian *sambal*.

Pulau Labuan Coffee House (☎ 416288; 28 Jl Muhibbah; dishes RM10-25) This air-conditioned Western-style coffee shop in the Pulau Labuan Hotel serves Western meals like hamburgers and milkshakes as well as Chinese and Malay dishes. It's open for breakfast, lunch and dinner.

Delihan (☎ 408787; Jl Bunga Mawar; 🕑 8am-4.30pm; dishes RM3-8) Small bakery with excellent pastries and good sandwich buns.

Getting There & Away

AIR

Malaysia Airlines has a desk at the airport, and Labuan is well served by the Malaysia Airlines domestic network. There are regular flights to KK (RM52, 6 daily), KL (RM437, 2 nonstop daily), Kuching (RM199, daily) and Miri (RM66, twice daily). Air Asia also has flights to KK twice a day, often much cheaper than Malaysia Airlines.

BOAT

Passenger boats are plentiful and some morning boats can fill up quickly; tickets can be bought in advance or just before departure at the small kiosk at the ferry terminal building. You pay a 50 sen departure tax at the gate before boarding.

Speedy passenger ferries (☎ 412262) connect Labuan to KK (RM28/33 economy/1st class, 1½ hours). Buy tickets at the dock. Boats leave for KK at 8.30am, 10.45am, 1pm and 3pm, but check the schedules beforehand. Boats leave from KK at 8am, 10am, 1.30pm and 3pm for the trip to Labuan.

Car ferries (☎ 417333) go to Menumbok (RM5, 2 hours) from the dock next to the customs wharf at 10am, 1pm and 6pm. From Menumbok they leave at 8am, 4pm and 8pm. Speedboats (RM10) do the journey in about 30 minutes and leave roughly every hour between 8am and 4pm.

Express boats to Limbang (RM22, 2 hours) leave at 12.30pm and 2.30pm; from Limbang departures are at 7.30am and 8am. Boats to Lawas (RM22, 2 hours) leave at 12.30pm daily except Tuesday and Thursday.

Numerous express boats go to Muara port in Brunei daily (RM24/30 economy/1st class, 1 hour). From Brunei the cost is B$15/18 for economy/1st class. Normal departure times from Labuan are between 8.30am and 4.30pm; departures from Brunei begin at 7.30am and end at 4.40pm. The schedule changes, however, and extra services may be available on weekends and public holidays. There's usually no problem buying your tickets at the dock, except on public holidays.

Getting Around

TO/FROM THE AIRPORT

The airport is serviced by bus Nos 4 and 6 (RM2); a taxi should cost around RM8 from town.

BOAT

Boats to Pulau Kuraman (RM28 per person, min 10 people) leave from the jetty at the Labuan International Sea Sports Complex. You can also hire boats from here or from the water-taxi dock opposite the stilt village to explore the nearby marine park. Chartering boats for the day costs around RM350 to RM500 per group of six people.

BUS

Labuan has a good minibus network. Buses leave regularly from the parking lot off Jl Mustapha. Their numbers are clearly painted on the front, and fares range from 50 sen for a short trip to RM2 for a trip to the top of the island.

Other destinations and fares around Labuan are as follows:

No 1 War Cemetery (RM1).
No 2 Mosque and Patau-Patau (RM1.20).
No 3 Bebuloh (RM1.50).
No 4 Mosque, Peace Park and Layang Layangan (RM1.20).
No 6 Mosque and chimney (RM1.50).

TAXI

Taxis are plentiful. The standard fare for a journey of up to a few kilometres is RM5.

NORTH OF KOTA KINABALU

The road north from the capital leads to small coastal towns and stilt villages, then over low hills to the small market town of Kota Belud. The route to Kota Belud is well travelled and almost *de rigueur* on the itineraries of tour groups – although many

MALAYSIAN BORNEO

travellers may find the crowded Sunday market at Kota Belud a bit disappointing.

Beyond Kota Belud the highway traverses fertile plains planted with rice, coconut palm, oil palm and bananas. A scenic peninsula with some nice beaches leads into the country of the Rungus people and on to the isolated town of Kudat.

Kudat doesn't see many tourists, which is another reason for visiting. Ownership of the islands to the north and east is disputed by the Philippines and out of bounds to most foreigners.

Tuaran

☎ 088

Tuaran, 33km from KK, is a bustling little town with tree-lined streets and a distinctive nine-storey **Chinese pagoda**.

There's a turn-off 2km before Tuaran that leads to two luxury resorts and **Mengkabong Water Village**, a Bajau stilt village built over an estuary. It was once a very picturesque spot, though it's not very special now, in terms of scenery, and is hardly the 'Venice of the East' claimed in tourist brochures.

There's a much more attractive stilt village at **Penimbawan**. To get there, take a minivan to Serusup (RM2); these leave a block back from the main street in Tuaran – look for the cluster of minivans. You then charter a motorboat at the Serusup jetty for RM40. The trip up the river takes about 15 minutes, and the boat will wait while you wander the plankwalks of the village. The villagers are friendly, but you're better off going with someone who speaks Malay, because it can feel a bit intrusive just wandering around.

SLEEPING & EATING

Sulaman Lake Resort (☎ 791500; fax 792500; Jl Kampung Serusup; r RM60-70) If you want to spend more time around the estuary at Serusup there's a new lodge built on stilts on the water by the Serusup jetty. The rooms are basic, but it's quiet on weekdays and the lodge can arrange boat tours and fishing.

There are a couple of luxury resorts on the road to Mengkabong Water Village; both are set on nice beaches:

Sabandar Bay Resort (☎ 088-787722, fax 787575; KK sales office; off Jl Pantai Dalit; r RM260-480) A four-star luxury hotel with rooms and semidetached and detached chalets. Discounts are usually available.

Shangri-La's Rasa Ria Resort (☎ 792888; rrr@po.jaring.my; Panti Dalit; r RM325-850) This is a large development adjoining the Dalit Bay Golf & Country Club; rooms are the last word in luxury and there are a couple of good restaurants. Special packages are offered on the Internet and through travel agencies.

GETTING THERE & AWAY

Minivans go regularly between KK and Tuaran (RM2, 30 minutes). Minivans from Tuaran to Tamparuli are RM1; to Mengkabong they are less frequent and cost 60 sen. Regular minivans go from Tuaran to Kota Belud (RM5, 30 minutes).

Kota Belud

☎ 088

Every Sunday a huge *tamu* takes place on the outskirts of this small, sleepy town. This market is a congested, colourful and dusty melee of vendors, hagglers and innumerable goods piled under one roof and spilling out into the car park – everything your average family could want is here, from polyester pants and plastic toys to fresh fish and fruit.

A *tamu* is not simply a market where villagers gather to sell their farm produce and to buy manufactured goods from traders; it's also a social occasion where news and stories are exchanged. Farmers haggle all morning over the price of a buffalo calf and the Bajau sell their horses, although tourists now outnumber cattle and the horsemen have mostly moved to a quieter spot away from the car park.

Visitors looking for tribal handicrafts and traditional clothing are likely to be disappointed, but the market is fun and you can enjoy a very good breakfast here after looking around.

SLEEPING & EATING

Most people visit Kota Belud as a day trip from KK, since you can make it from KK in plenty of time for the market. One reason to overnight here is the stunning view of Mt Kinabalu at first light.

SIU Motel (☎ 976617, 019-862 4123; Km 1, Jl Kuala Abai (Uskan Port Rd); s/d RM25/86 ❄) Readers have recommended this place, just outside Kota Belud 1km northwest of the roundabout turn-off to Kudat. It's run by a friendly family who can help arrange trips to Kuala Abai fishing village, the beach and to the

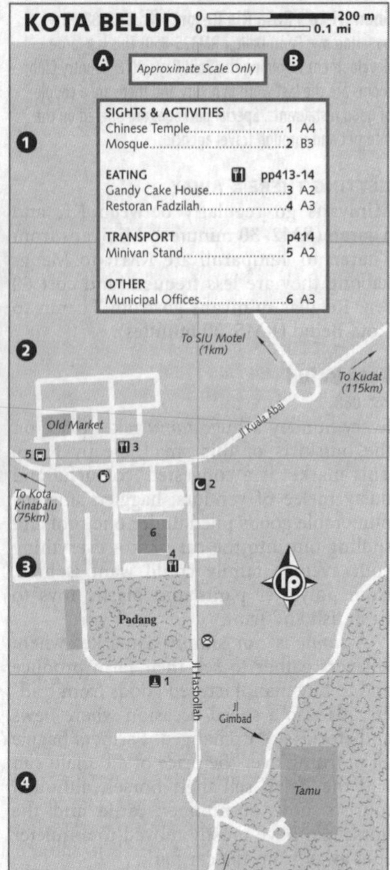

Sunday *tamu*. The rooms are plain but clean and the price includes breakfast. Discounts are sometimes available.

Kota Belud is not a gastronome's delight, but plenty of tasty snacks can be picked up at the Sunday market. There are a few Chinese and halal **coffee shops** in the northern part of town around Pasar Besar – these are close to transport, so they're handy if you're not on a tour.

Restoran Fadzilah (☎ 975330; dishes RM4-7) In the centre of town, opposite the municipal offices, this seems to be one of the few places open later in the evening.

There are a couple of small eating places near the SIU Motel. For cakes and pastries as well as nice sandwich buns for bus snacks, try the **Gandy Cake House** (☎ 013-854 2129) east of the minivan stop.

GETTING THERE & AWAY

The main area for minivans and share-taxis is at the bus station in front of Pasar Besar, the old market. Most of these serve the Kota Belud–KK route, (RM5, 2 hours) departing between 7am and 5pm. They leave when they're full. A freeway covers most of the route from KK to Kota Belud. On Sunday, *tamu* day, the number of minivans and taxis has to be seen to be believed. On other days it's much quieter.

Minivans go north to Kudat (RM10, 2 hours) between 7am and 5pm; the trip is quite pleasant.

To get to Kinabalu National Park, take any minibus going to KK and get off at Tamparuli, about halfway there (RM5, 30 minutes). There are several minivans from Tamparuli to Ranau every day until about 2pm. All of them pass the park entrance – tell the driver to drop you off there. The ride to the park is RM5 (about an hour on a good sealed road). To go all the way to Ranau costs RM8.

Kinabalu National Park

☎ 088

Towering above the coastal plain and what's left of the lush tropical forests of northern Borneo, Mt Kinabalu is the biggest tourist attraction in Sabah and the centrepiece of the vast 754-sq-km Kinabalu National Park. At 4095m, it is the highest mountain between the mighty Himalayas and New Guinea. And it's still growing: researchers have found it increases in height by about 5mm a year. It is 50km inland, but on a clear day you can see the Philippines from the summit; clear days are rare, however, as the mountain is usually socked-in with cloud by mid-morning.

Mt Kinabalu is one of the easiest mountains in the world to climb, and thousands of people of all ages and fitness levels scale the summit every year. All you need is some stamina, determination and weatherproof clothing – it can get very cold and wet up there.

Even if you decide not to do the climb, the park itself is a beautiful spot, and many visitors come just to escape the heat and humidity of the coast. There are walking trails in the rainforest at the base of the mountain, the climate is agreeably cool – even cold at night – and the accommodation both inside and outside the park is good.

HISTORY

The first recorded ascent of the mountain was made in 1851 by Sir Hugh Low, the British colonial secretary on Pulau Labuan. Kinabalu's highest peak is named after him, as is the mile-deep 'gully' on the other side of the mountain.

In those days the difficulty of climbing Mt Kinabalu lay not in the ascent, but in getting through the jungle to the mountain's base – and finding willing local porters. The tribesmen who accompanied Low believed the spirits of their dead inhabited the mountain. Low was therefore obliged to protect the party, and a guide carried a large basket of quartz crystals and teeth, as was the custom. In time, the spirit-appeasement ceremonies performed by the guides upon reaching the summit became more elaborate, so that by the 1920s they had come to include loud prayers, gunshots, and the sacrifice of seven eggs and seven white chickens.

These days there's a sealed road all the way from KK to the foot of the mountain, but Low's Gully – the abyss on the other side of the summit – didn't give up its secrets as easily as Low's Peak. One of the groups in the first expedition in 1994 to abseil into the gully got stuck and could not be rescued for three weeks. It was only as recently as February 1998 that a joint British-Malaysian expedition explored the bottom, returning with several newly discovered species of plants and insects.

GEOLOGY

From its immense size you might think Mt Kinabalu is the ancient core of Borneo, but the mountain was actually formed relatively recently. Its origins go back a mere nine million years, to when a mass of igneous rock was pushed up from the depths below. This upward movement is still continuing.

In geological terms Mt Kinabalu is still very young. Little erosion has occurred on the exposed granite rock faces around the summit, though the effects of glaciers that used to cover much of the mountain can be detected by striations on the rock. The glaciers have disappeared, but at times ice forms in the rock pools near the summit.

ORIENTATION & INFORMATION

Kinabalu park headquarters is 88km from KK and set in gardens with a magnificent view of the mountain. At 1588m the climate is agreeably cool; the average temperature ranges from 20°C in the day to 13°C at night.

Accommodation at park headquarters can be tight and even tighter on the mountain. Reservations are made through **Kinabalu Nature Resorts** (☎ 088-243629; www.kinabalunatureresorts.com) in KK (see p387). In theory only advance reservations are accepted but if you just show up at the park, you might get lucky and find space but don't count on it. During public holidays and in particular, Chinese New Year, it's almost impossible to get a place.

On arrival, once you've paid your entry fee at the park gate (adult/child under 18

FLORA & FAUNA OF MT KINABALU

Mt Kinabalu is a botanical paradise, with over half the species growing above 900m unique to the area. Among the more spectacular flowers are **orchids, rhododendrons**, and the insectivorous **Nepenthes (pitcher plants)**. Around park headquarters, there's **dipterocarp forest** (rainforest); creepers, ferns and orchids festoon the canopy, while fungi grow on the forest floor. Between 900m and 1800m, there are **oaks**, **laurels** and **chestnuts**, while higher up there's dense, **rhododendron** forest. On the windswept slopes above Laban Rata, vegetation is stunted, with **sayat-sayat** a common shrub. The mountain's uppermost slopes are bare of plant life.

More mammal species are seen in the lowland rainforest around Poring Hot Springs than at higher altitudes around park headquarters. **Deer** and **monkeys** are not common anymore; but there are squirrels, including the handsome **Prevost's squirrel** and **mountain ground squirrel. Tree shrews** can sometimes be seen raiding rubbish bins. Common birds are **Bornean treepies**, **fantails**, **bulbuls**, **sunbirds** and **laughing thrushes**, while birds seen only at higher altitudes are the **Kinabalu friendly warbler**, the **mountain black-eye** and the **mountain blackbird**. Other wildlife includes colourful **butterflies** and the huge green **moon moth**.

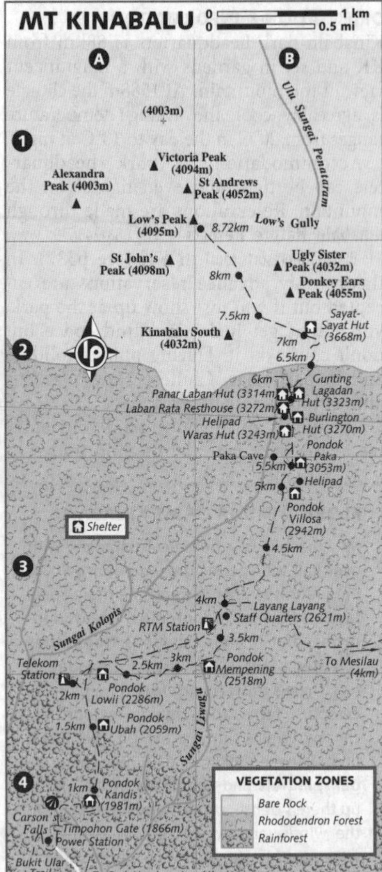

RM15/10) you check in at the park office. If you're staying overnight, present your reservation slip from KK and you'll be allocated your bed or room. Valuables can be deposited in safety boxes at the office and excess baggage can be stored here (RM1 per item) until you return from the mountain.

The security is not great up at Laban Rata and travellers have reported thefts of personal items.

All the hostels and resthouses are within walking distance of the park office. In the visitors centre down the road past the hostels is the Liwagu Restaurant and an **exhibit centre**; a slide show (RM2) presented here (weekdays at 2pm and weekends at 7.30pm) gives an excellent introduction to the mountain. The **Kinabalu Conservation Centre** (admission RM3; 9am-3pm) is also worth visiting; it has good displays on the natural and cultural history of the area.

Next to the park office is a **souvenir shop** selling film, ice creams and souvenirs. If you don't have a raincoat, you can buy one here for RM15. There's also a reasonable range of books on the park and other places in Sabah, and a 30-minute film processing service. The shop is open from 7am to 7pm.

PERMITS & GUIDES

A climbing permit and insurance (RM3.50) are compulsory for any ascent of Mt Kinabalu. The permit fee for foreigners is RM100 for adults and RM40 for anyone under 18. Pay this at park headquarters before you climb.

A guide is only compulsory if you intend to venture beyond Laban Rata, ie to the summit. Guide fees are RM60 per trip for one to three persons, RM65 per day for four to six people, and RM70 per trip for seven to eight climbers (the maximum per guide).

A guide is assigned to you on the morning you begin your hike. If you ask, the park staff will try to attach individual travellers to a group so that guide fees can be shared. Couples can expect to be given their own guide.

The guides and porters are usually Kadazan from local villages, and not employees of the national park. Some of these professional guides are amazing: one is 55 years old and has climbed Mt Kinabalu more than 700 times in his 16 years as a guide! On the other hand, some travellers have complained that their guides are useless. A good guide should be able to point out pitcher plants and other interesting sights. You can ask for a knowledgeable guide, but usually it's the luck of the draw.

Porters can also be hired. The fee is RM70/80/90 per trip for a maximum load of 10kg up to the Panar Laban huts, Sayat-Sayat and the summit, respectively.

EQUIPMENT

As long as it's not raining you can walk as far as Laban Rata in normal hiking gear. Dress in layers so you can take off and put on clothes as necessary. It's only at the summit that you'll need warm clothes – you can rent jackets at Laban Rata but you should also bring a woollen hat, gloves and long pants. A raincoat or rain poncho is also recommended. Wear strong, comfortable shoes with good grip.

A torch (flashlight) is required if you're getting up before dawn – these can be hired for RM5 at Laban Rata. Bring snacks for the climb and food if you intend to do your own cooking. Water bottles can be filled along the trail. Don't be fooled by the clouds – the sun is fierce at that altitude and to avoid sunburn sun block is necessary.

WALKS

It's well worth spending a day exploring the marked trails around park headquarters; if you have time, it may be better to do it before you climb the mountain as you may not feel like it afterwards. All the trails and lookouts are shown on the Kinabalu Park Headquarters & Trails map (p419).

All the trails link up with others at some stage, so you can spend the whole day, or indeed days, walking at a leisurely pace through the beautiful forest. Some interesting plants, plenty of birds and, if you're lucky, the occasional mammal can be seen along the **Liwagu Trail**, which follows the river of the same name. When it rains, watch out for slippery paths and armies of leeches.

At 11am each day a **guided walk** (RM3) starts from the park office and lasts for one to two hours. The knowledgeable guide points out flowers, plants, birds and insects along the way. If you set out from KK early, it's possible to arrive at the park in time for the guided walk.

Many of the plants found on the mountain are cultivated in the **Mountain Garden** behind the visitors centre; it's open at 9am, noon and 3pm, and is also well worth a look (entry RM5).

THE CLIMB

Climbing Mt Kinabalu is normally a two-day exercise. Most people climb as far as Laban Rata or the nearby huts on the first day, then climb to the summit at dawn and return to park headquarters on the next day. The park headquarters recommends that you be under way by 10am to make Laban Rata in good time, but this is probably conservative – leaving by 11am should be fine if you're reasonably fit, though most people set off between 8am and 9am.

Dawn on the summit is often an all-too-brief glimpse across Borneo at 6am before the clouds roll in along the mountainous spine stretching towards the morning light. Sometimes the summit is socked-in already, at other times the sun shines through till 10am or later. You won't know until you get there, but that's part of the adventure.

Either way, it is wise to stay overnight at the park headquarters at least the night before the climb. This will allow you to make an early start and to acclimatise a bit – Mt Kinabalu is high enough for altitude sickness to occur.

The climb is uphill 99% of the way; it is unrelenting, steep in places and there are seemingly endless steps – actually there are 2500 – as far as Laban Rata. Then it gets a whole lot tougher. The trail becomes even steeper as you approach the summit then disappears altogether on vast, near-vertical fields of slippery granite. Every step can be a struggle as you gasp for breath in the thin air.

The secret to climbing Mt Kinabalu is stamina. Take it slowly – very slowly if you are tired and out of breath. Many people start off briskly then have to take frequent and increasingly longer rest breaks, while the old hands just keep trudging along. Take it easy and walk at a comfortable pace.

Signboards showing your progress are spaced along the trail and there's a marker every 500m. There are rest shelters *(pondok)* at regular intervals, with clean, squat-style toilets and tanks of cool, fresh drinking water. The walking times that follow are conservative estimates published by the Sabah Parks office.

You can also access the trail to Laban Rata from the Mesilau Nature Resort (see p421).

Park Headquarters–Power Station

The trail officially starts at the Timpohon Gate (1866m), from where it's an 8.72km walk to the summit. Unfortunately it's nearly an hour's uphill walk from park headquarters to the gate – or power station, as it's commonly called. A bus shuttles back and forth from the park office area to the power station between 7am and about 5pm; it takes only 15 minutes and will considerably shorten your day's walking. An earlier start can be negotiated with the park office. The cost for a group of five people is RM2.50 per person.

It is not much fun walking along the road, though the Liwagu Trail to the power station is a scenic alternative for those who can afford to add an extra three hours or so to the climb.

Power Station–Layang Layang

After a short, deceptive descent, the trail leads up steep stairs through magnificent tall forest. There's a small waterfall **Carson's Falls** beside the track shortly after the start, and the forest can be alive with birds and squirrels in the morning. Five pondok are spaced at intervals of 15 to 35 minutes and it's about three hours to Layang Layang (2621m), where there are staff quarters. At Pondok Kandis (1981m) the tall forest gives way to dense, stunted rhododendron forest. Near Pondok Lowii (2286m) the trail follows an open ridge giving great views over the valleys and up to the peaks.

Layang Layang–Pondok Paka

It's about 1¾ hours on to Pondok Paka (3053m), the seventh shelter on the trail and 5.5km from the start. The trail passes through increasingly stunted rhododendron forest, leaving walkers more exposed to the elements. Occasional flat sections come as a relief after the endless steps. This stretch is good for pitcher plants, although you probably won't see any growing by the side of the track – look among the dense vegetation.

A half-hour detour can be made to **Paka Cave** – a rock overhang with a bamboo platform where the early explorers spent the night before tackling the summit. It is not that interesting and can be left for the descent, when the lungs are less taxed.

Pondok Paka–Laban Rata

Laban Rata (3272m) marks the treeline and is the night's resting spot for most people attempting the summit. This leg takes about 45 minutes to walk. The main resthouse has heating, hot water, comfortable beds and a restaurant with fine views. Three other accommodation units have basic cooking facilities, bathroom but no heater, though there were plans to install heaters by the end of 2003.

Laban Rata–Sayat-Sayat

The one-hour climb to Sayat-Sayat hut (3668m) involves crossing the sheer Panar Laban rock face. Vegetation is no more than waist high, except where overhangs provide some respite from the wind. It is one of the toughest parts of the climb and doesn't get any easier in the dark and cold at 4am, when the early risers from Laban Rata are urged onwards to see the dawn.

Thick ropes are used to haul yourself up the granite sheets; it's hard work, hauling and juggling a torch, but in a way it's good to be using arm muscles instead of legs! Narrow wooden steps and hand rails help in places, but often you'll use the smooth, gnarled branches of bushes for support as you gasp for breath.

Sayat-Sayat–Summit

The steepest and hardest part of the climb is also the last. Past Sayat-Sayat, more desolate rock faces and hoisting await the string of climbers stretched out in the dark, trying to keep warm while holding ropes and torches. In the daylight, thick veins of quartz seem like painted lines on the rock face.

The summit looks deceptively close and, though it's just over 1km, the last burst can take up to two hours from Sayat-Sayat. Many people are reduced to crawling on hands and knees up the last few boulders to the small area that is the top of Borneo. Climbers crowd together, perched over the mysterious abyss of Low's Gully, and huddle against the cold, priming their cameras for a shot of the sunrise and nearby peaks. And it can get very crowded up there; don't be surprised to be sharing your experience with a hundred or more people. When the sun has risen and the photos are taken, there's a quick exodus down the mountain to Laban Rata, while the late risers, perhaps the wisest of all, make their way to the less crowded summit.

The climb down to the power station takes about five hours – don't underestimate the descent, and leave plenty of time to get back before nightfall. Allow another hour to walk from the power station to your accommodation. While easier than the climb up, it can be a lot more damaging on under-used muscles. Aim to leave the summit by about noon and to be well underway by 1pm. The weather can close in very quickly and, although you probably won't get lost, the granite is slippery even when it's dry – and it can get very wet at the top.

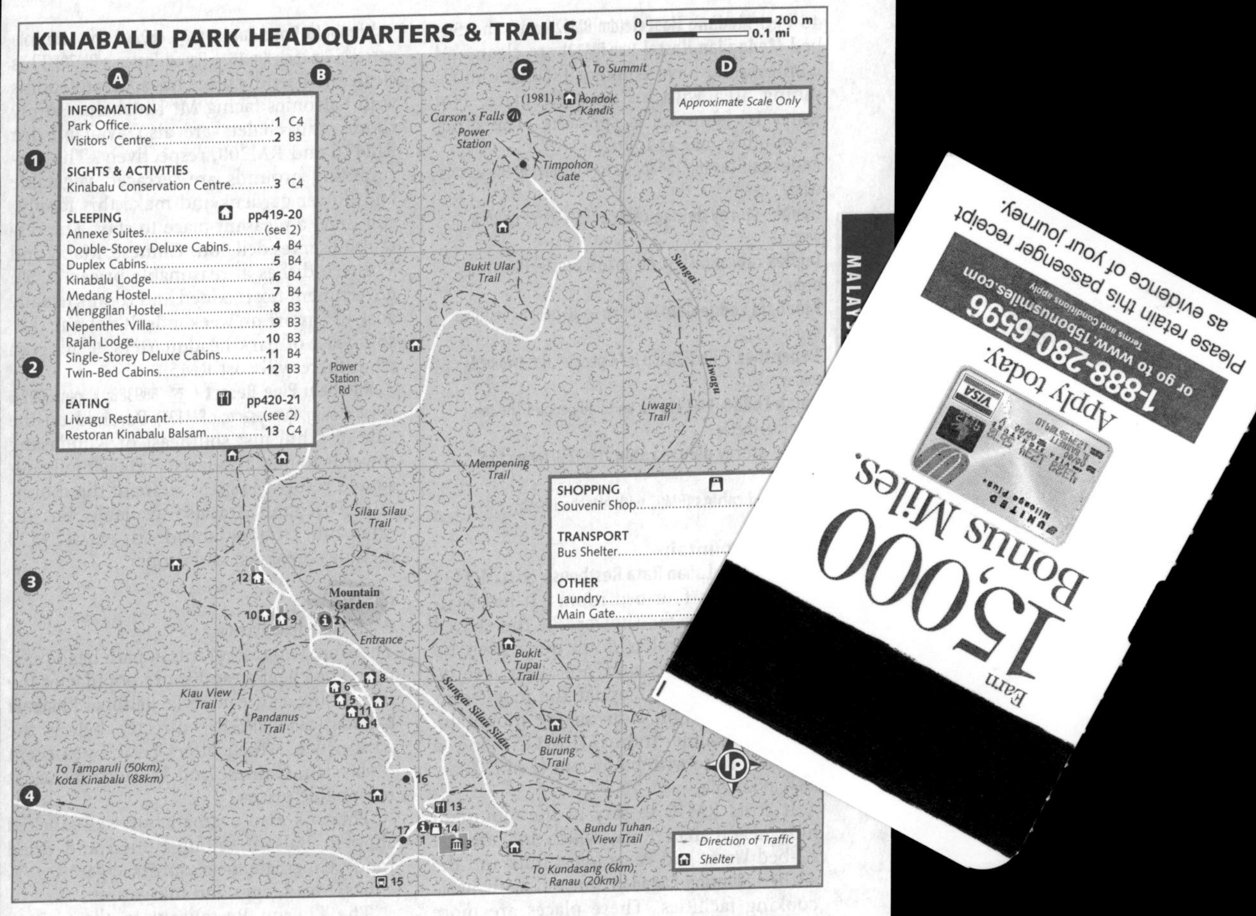

A 1st-class certificate can be purchased for RM10 by those who complete the climb; 2nd-class certificates are issued for making it to Laban Rata – no mean feat in itself. They can be collected at the park office.

SLEEPING

Overnight accommodation is available around park headquarters, on the Ranau road between the park turn-off and Kundasang, at Mesilau, at Poring Hot Springs and at Laban Rata on the mountain.

Accommodation in the park, including mountain huts, is booked through **Kinabalu Nature Resorts** (☎ 088-243629; www.kinabalunatureresorts.com); see p387. Book as far in advance as possible (at least several days to a week) and note that on weekends, school holidays and public holidays all the accommodation may be taken. Prices can double during major holidays like Chinese New Year.

Reservations can be made by email, fax or phone, but they will not be confirmed until fully paid for. Deposits are theoretically required for accommodation in the park (eg, RM20 for a dorm bed and RM100 for an annexe suite), payable when you check in at park headquarters. In fact you may not be asked to leave a deposit, but bring some extra cash for the purpose.

Park Headquarters

There's a variety of good accommodation at park headquarters to suit all budgets. The

46-bed **Medang Hostel** (dm RM12) and the 54-bed **Menggilan Hostel** (dm RM12) are clean and comfortable, have cooking facilities and a dining area with an open fireplace. Hot water for showers is sporadic. The other possibilities are as follows:

Annexe suites (RM184 for up to 4 people) In the visitors centre.
Double-storey deluxe cabins (RM288 for up to 7 people)
Duplex cabins (RM230 for up to 6 people) Have two bedrooms.
Kinabalu Lodge (RM414 for up to 10 people) Has five bedrooms.
Nepenthes Villa (RM288 for 4 people) Has two bedrooms.
Rajah Lodge (RM1150 for up to 10 people) The most luxurious choice.
Single-storey deluxe cabins (RM230 for up to 5 people)
Twin-bed cabins (RM92 with attached bath)

On the Mountain

The 54-bed **Laban Rata Resthouse** costs RM34 per person in four-bed rooms. It has heating and hot-water showers in the shared bathroom; the toilets don't quite keep up with the demand and are quite grotty. Nevertheless, this is by far the most comfortable overnight stop on the mountain. Limited double rooms (RM115) and a four-bed suite with bathroom (RM230) are also available.

It costs RM17 to stay in the mountain huts near Laban Rata, which include the 12-bed **Waras** and **Panar Laban** huts and the 44-bed **Gunting Lagadan** hut, all with basic cooking facilities. These places are more spartan and aren't heated, but a sleeping bag is provided and they're close to the restaurant.

Outside the Park

It's preferable to stay in the park, mainly because the lodging is reasonable value and it's convenient. Keep your entry receipt if you plan to make trips outside the park.

There are numerous places to stay outside the park, however, on the road between the park headquarters and Kundasang. Some have great mountain views, though most look out over the cultivated valley south of the park. The two mentioned here are very comfortable and both have good views of the mountain.

Kinabalu Rose Cabin (☎ 889233; www.kinabalurosecabin.8m.com; Km 18, Jl Ranau-Tuaran; r RM70) This clean and friendly place has spacious rooms with balconies facing Mt Kinabalu. Family rooms and chalets are also available for RM126 and RM200, respectively. The surrounding grounds are terraced vegetable and flower gardens and make this family-run hotel a pleasant place to stay. The restaurant serves delicious Chinese, Malay and Western dishes at reasonable prices. A 5% government tax is added and rooms usually cost 40% more on weekends. It's about 1km southeast of park headquarters; a minivan from there will cost RM5.

Kinabalu Pine Resort (☎ 889388; k_pine2002@yahoo.com.sg; Kundasang; r RM125) Perched on the side of a hill just southeast of Kundasang towards Ranau, this large and tastefully designed resort has great views of the mountain. Discounts are also available, but it's often full, so book ahead. An extra RM20 includes breakfast and dinner.

EATING

Park Headquarters

There are two restaurants at park headquarters. The cheaper and more popular of the two is the canteen-style **Restoran Kinabalu Balsam** (dishes RM5-10), directly below the park office, which offers basic but decent Malaysian, Chinese and Western dishes at reasonable prices.

There is also a small but well-stocked shop in Balsam selling tinned and dried foods, chocolate, beer, spirits, cigarettes, T-shirts, bread, eggs and margarine.

The Liwagu Restaurant in the visitors centre is more expensive than the Balsam, but there's a huge range of dishes, including noodles, rice and seafood standards. An 'American breakfast' is pretty ordinary here for RM12; the cheaper breakfast at the Balsam canteen is better value.

Both restaurants are open every day at 6am, closing at 10pm on weekdays and 11pm on weekends and public holidays.

On the Mountain

At Laban Rata, on the mountain, there's a **restaurant** selling hot noodle dishes and rice meals for about RM8 to RM15; the restaurant is open for regular meals, and also from 2am to 3am so you can grab some breakfast before the summit climb.

There's also a shop selling film, cold drinks, headache tablets and other basic medicines, chocolates and walking sticks (useful for the descent).

GETTING THERE & AWAY

Kota Kinabalu Air-con express buses (RM15, 3 hours) leave for the national park around 7.30am daily. Check the schedule and book on weekends. Buses going to Ranau or Sandakan will drop you off at the entrance road, 100m from the park headquarters. Minivans do the trip for RM10. Buses and minibuses pass the turn-off between 8am and noon heading towards KK. You can wave them down.

Kota Belud & Tamparuli Tamparuli is where the road up the coast to Kudat branches for Kota Belud and Ranau. From Kota Belud to Kinabalu National Park, first go to Tamparuli and take a minivan (RM10, 2 hours) heading to Ranau.

Poring Hot Springs Minivans leave park headquarters for Poring (RM15, 45 minutes) three times a day until 4pm. You can hire a minivan for RM60, or go to Ranau and catch a minivan from there.

Ranau & Sandakan Air-con express buses to Sandakan (RM20, 4 hours) pass the park headquarters twice in the morning and once in the afternoon. Minivans (RM5) heading to Ranau are more frequent but usually dry up by 5pm.

Mesilau Nature Resort

The trip to Mt Kinabalu can also be approached from the Mesilau Nature Resort, and in fact this is preferable because it's much less crowded than the park headquarters. The 5.5km trail from Mesilau meets up with the main trail to Laban Rata at Layang Layang. Arrange your trip with **Kinabalu Nature Resorts** (☎ 088-243629; www.kinabalunatureresorts.com) and your guide will meet you at Mesilau. It takes a little longer (four hours) but the advantages are less people and more sightings of pitcher plants. The guide fee for Mesilau is RM70.

Even if you don't plan to climb Mt Kinabalu it's worth spending a day or two at the resort. It has superb accommodation, nature trails and three knowledgeable guides, Anson, Suikaibeen and Rosebeyani, who know a lot about the area. There's also an **exhibit centre** (admission free; 🕓 8am-4pm).

Nearby is the **Mount Kinabalu Golf Club** (☎ 088-888255; mkgc@tm.net.my) an 18-hole 80-acre course. At an elevation of just under 2000m, it's the highest golf club in Southeast Asia. Playing on this golf course adds yards to your drive because of the thin air.

The turn-off for Mesilau on the highway in Kundasang is also the site of the **Kundasang War Memorial** (admission free; 🕓 8.30am-5pm Mon-Sat, 9am-4pm Sun). An embankment built up with a stone wall contains a memorial plaque for the POWs who died here after their forced march from Sandakan during WWII (see p426). The garden laid out on two levels of the embankment is exquisite, with a host of beautiful tropical flowers like bougainvillea and heliotrope. It's a fitting testament to the men who lost their lives here and a peaceful oasis literally a stone's throw off the highway and Kundasang's ramshackle vegetable market.

SLEEPING & EATING

Mesilau's accommodation is also run by **Kinabalu Nature Resorts** (☎ 088-243629; www.kinabalunatureresorts.com) and is made up of small chalets tucked away in shaded areas of the forest. The **Bishop's Head Resthouse** has dormitory beds for RM30 per person, which includes breakfast. The **Crocker Range Lodges** and **Witti Range Lodge** are three-bedroom units priced from RM320 to RM350. The remaining buildings are chalets with kitchens that sleep four (RM350) to six people (RM400).

The **Kedamaian Restaurant** (dishes RM10-20; 🕓 7.30pm-9pm) serves Malay, Chinese and Western meals, and the **Malaxi Café** serves breakfast, drinks and snacks.

GETTING THERE & AWAY

Mesilau is 20km from park headquarters and there's no public transport going there. The road to the resort turns north off the main highway at Kundasang. It's 10km to the resort from this intersection. A taxi or minivan to Mesilau costs RM65 from Kinabalu park headquarters.

Ranau

☎ 088

Ranau is a curious collection of concrete shophouse blocks set in a lovely green valley on the route between KK and Sandakan. There's a busy *tamu* on Saturday at the bridge a few hundred metres south of town, but few travellers stay overnight since the main attraction is Poring Hot Springs about 19km to the north. Ranau is primarily a place to get a bus connection to/from Poring or Mt Kinabalu.

Ranau is only a few hundred metres square. Express buses park at the top end of town near the square. In the blocks of shophouses across the road there are cafés and hotels, and minibuses line up along the main street to the west of the bus stand. There's an ATM at the **Bank Simpanan Nasional** and an Internet café called the **Internet Station** (RM2 per hour), visible by its large red sign, by the Millimewah Superstore.

SLEEPING & EATING

If you get stuck in Ranau between buses, there are a couple of hotels in town. The **Rafflesia Inn** (☎ 879359; Block N, Sedco Shophouse; s/d RM30/50; ❄), west of the main street, has small, adequate rooms. Rooms with hot showers are RM5 extra.

Ranau has plenty of **coffee shops**; most are Chinese but simple Malay meals are also available.

GETTING THERE & AWAY

Morning bus and minivan services operate regularly from Ranau. Minivans to Tambunan (RM10, 2 hours) and Keningau (RM15, 3 hours) traverse a hazardous mountain road (see p402). Express buses leave Ranau for KK (RM15, 3½ hours) from 7am to about 1.30pm. Minivans (RM10 or RM15) and share-taxis (RM15) leave Ranau daily until about 3pm. The morning runs are more frequent.

All bus services to KK pass the entrance to Mt Kinabalu National Park (RM5). If you get stuck, you can charter a minivan to park headquarters for RM50.

All buses to Sandakan pass the Sepilok Orang-Utan Rehabilitation Centre; ask to be dropped off. Air-conditioned express buses are the best way to travel, and these leave Ranau for Sandakan between 7.30am and noon (RM25, 4 hours). Minivans go throughout the day but can take a while to fill up, especially in the afternoon.

On weekends it's easy and cheap to get to the hot springs from Ranau. Drivers cruise around the blocks, shouting 'Poring, Poring!'. The price is RM5 per person and the transport leaves when it's full. On weekdays it isn't quite so easy, especially if you arrive in Ranau during the afternoon – you may have to charter a minivan or taxi for RM25.

Poring Hot Springs

Developed by the Japanese during WWII, the **Poring Hot Springs** (admission adult/child under 18 RM15/6) have become a popular weekend retreat for locals. The complex is actually part of the Kinabalu National Park, but the park headquarters is 43km away via Ranau.

Steaming, sulphurous water is channelled into pools and tubs in which visitors can relax their tired muscles after the trek to the summit of Mt Kinabalu. The pools are in a pretty garden setting with hibiscus and other flowers attracting hordes of butterflies. Poring is also famous among bird-watchers, and a good variety of birds can be seen around the gardens and along walking trails.

SIGHTS & ACTIVITIES

Baths

The **outdoor tubs** (admission free; 🕓 7.30am-6.30pm) are of varying sizes and can easily fit a couple of people. They have hot- and cold-water taps to regulate the temperature. The water from the springs is extremely hot.

Western women may not feel comfortable in the public baths just wearing swimsuits and may want to wear shorts and a T-shirt over their suits.

Private spa cabins (standard/deluxe RM15/20 per hr) are also available. A standard cabin has a tub and shower, while the deluxe versions have a lounge area, spa, shower and toilet and can accommodate up to eight people.

After a hot bath you can take a cooling dip in the rock pool.

Gardens

Although the springs are the main attraction, also part of the Poring complex are a **Tropical Garden** (adult/child RM3/1.50; 🕓 9am-4pm), a **Butterfly Farm** (adult/child RM4/2; 🕓 9am-4pm Tue-Sun) and an **Orchid Garden** (adult/child RM10/5; 🕓 9am-4pm) You may see two rescued orang-utans who frequent the area in the Tropical Garden.

Canopy Walkway

The unusual **Canopy Walkway** (adult/child RM5/2.50; 🕓 9am-4pm) consists of a series of walkways suspended from trees up to 40m above the jungle floor and offers a unique view of the surrounding forest. The springy walkways are not for the faint-hearted, but they're quite safe and great fun. Get there early if you want to see birds or other wildlife.

Walks

There are several kilometres of forest trails around the springs. The **Kipungit Waterfalls** are only about 15 minutes' walk away; there's a beautiful spot in a cool glade where you can swim at the base of the falls.

Over the stream the trail gets steeper, and after another 15 minutes you reach what are known as the **Bat Caves**, which are just a jumble of huge boulders between which bats and swiftlets roost. There's not much to see but the surrounding forest is very pretty. A trip to the **Langanan Waterfall** is 1¾ hours away on the same trail via Kipungit and the bat caves. This walk is legendary among bird-watchers as a haunt of the rarely seen blue-banded pitta. Let the parks office at the entrance to Poring know if you plan to walk to Langanan.

SLEEPING & EATING

It's a good idea to book your accommodation at Poring in advance at the Kinabalu Nature Resorts office (☎ 088-243629; www.kinabalunatureresorts.com) in KK (see p387). It's possible to just show up, but Poring is a popular place, especially on weekends.

The older **Kelicap Hostel** has 24 beds and the **Serindit Hostel** is a newer, 44-bed dorm. Both have clean, spacious kitchens with gas cookers and cost RM12 per bed. Blankets and pillows are provided free of charge.

Cabins with cooking facilities, and chalets with air-con and all facilities are also available. The four-bed **Tempua Cabin** is RM92; **Enngang Cabin** and **Rajawali Chalet** each sleep six people and cost RM115 and RM288, respectively. A **camp spot** is also available for RM6 per tent. Tents can be hired through the park office at the springs for RM3. The mosquitoes at Poring can be vicious, so take coils and insect repellent.

The **Kalibambang Restaurant** (🕑 7am-9pm) serves Chinese, Malay and Western food and overlooks the rock pool and the river. There are also inexpensive eating places right opposite the park entrance. If you're self-catering, you can buy food for cooking here as well, though it's cheaper if you bring your own from KK.

GETTING THERE & AWAY

Poring is 19km north of Ranau along a sealed road and can be reached by minivan, taxi or hitching. Access is generally from Ranau (see p422), but minivans run from the park headquarters at Mt Kinabalu to Poring three times a day (RM15).

Leaving Poring can be tricky. Minivans depart for Ranau from outside the park office at the springs at around 6.30am, and then at roughly 10am and 2pm, depending on demand (RM5). On weekends there are nearly always share-taxis parked near the office; the fare is by negotiation but with a full load it should only cost RM5 per person.

Kudat

☎ 088

Kudat is a quiet port town in the very north of Sabah, 190km from KK. Kudat has a noticeable Filipino influence, as much of the trade here is with the Philippines, and the surrounding countryside is the home of the friendly Rungus people, tribal cousins of the Kadazan.

There are some good beaches west of town and it's possible to visit Rungus longhouses near the highway, but you'll need a car or taxi to reach them.

SLEEPING & EATING

Hotel Sunrise (☎ 611517; Jl Ibrahm Arshao; s/d RM 25/60; ❄) A friendly place in the old part of town near the minivan station, it's the best value if you're on a budget.

Hotel Kinabalu (☎ 613888; 1234 Jl Melor; s/d RM42/70; ❄) This is one of several similar hotels on Jl Melor in the new section of town. It has decent air-conditioned rooms, though not much character.

The **Upper Deck Hotel** (☎ 622272; fax 622300; Jl Lintas; s/d RM80/160; ❄) An aptly named hotel on top of the Millimewah Superstore, this place has good views of the harbour. It opened in August 2002 and the rooms are big, very bright and clean.

Kudat Golf & Marina Resort (☎ 611211; www.kudatgolfmarinaresort.com; off Jl Urus Setia; s/d RM99/115; ❄ 🏊) This is a new top-end hotel in a serene setting opposite a well laid out, almost deserted golf course – perfect for fans of the game. For non-golfers it's still worth staying for the sea views alone. There's a 1st-class restaurant serving Western, Chinese and Malay meals.

For inexpensive Malay and Chinese dishes try the **Restoran Ainey** (☎ 019-899 5607; Jl Melor; dishes RM2-4; 🕑 24 hr) near the Hotel Kinabalu. Various combinations of roti are served as well. Opposite the Chinese temple just off Jl Lintas, the **Restoran Saijana** is a welcoming halal place that serves tasty Malay dishes.

GETTING THERE & AWAY

There are Malaysia Airlines Twin Otter flights from Kudat to KK (RM50, 3 weekly) and Sandakan (RM54, 6 weekly).

Several minivans a day make the three- to four-hour trip from KK for RM15. The two-hour journey from Kota Belud costs RM10.

There is an express boat leaving from the old part of town for nearby Pulau Panggi (RM10); there are no tourist facilities on the island, however, and foreigners don't seem to be encouraged to visit.

Around Kudat

BEACHES

You'll find some of the best beaches in Sabah around Kudat, where the water is shallow and safe for paddling. **Bak Bak**, about 11km from Kudat, is the town beach. It has clear water, picnic and toilet facilities and food stalls on weekends, though the beach itself is only a narrow strip of sand against a retaining wall. The fishing villages further north of Bak Bak have some even better white-sand beaches, but there is no accommodation and they are difficult to get to. The northern end of the peninsula is said to have the best sunsets in Sabah, and there are plans to develop this area for tourism.

LONGHOUSE TOURS

Many Rungus people build their own houses in preference to living in the highly flammable traditional longhouses, but there are still some interesting longhouses around Kudat. The best known of these is **Matunggung**, on the highway south of Kudat. It's a traditional thatched-roof longhouse with enclosed bamboo-slatted sides. Inside, each family's living quarters, called *valai*, is composed of sleeping, dining and living areas, and an attic. Matunggung is well frequented by tour groups, but there are other longhouses found further inland from the highway.

The **Rungus Longhouse Homestay Programme** (☎ 621971; fax 621971) lets visitors experience the culture of northern Sabah's indigenous people. Performances such as *mongigol* (dance and music), *mangatip-atip* (bamboo show) and *monguruali* (nose flute) can be arranged with advance notice. The soothing massage-like effect of walking on the bamboo floors is excellent therapy for the feet if you've recently climbed Mt Kinabalu. The two-day, one-night packages include dinner and breakfast as well the cultural events. For people who want privacy there are a few bamboo huts with concrete foundations and toilets. A one-hour hike up the highest hill around Kudat allows for good views of Mt Kinabalu.

Tour operators in KK (see p392) can arrange a homestay including transport. If you're planning to go on your own, phone ahead and catch a bus to the turn-off (it's well marked but ask the driver) where you'll be picked up.

For day trips the entrance fee is RM45 for one or two adults. Staying overnight is RM120/140 for one/two people, which includes breakfast and dinner and the entrance fee.

The traditional dress for Rungus women is a black sarong and colourful, beaded necklaces. On festive occasions, heavy brass bracelets are worn as well. The Rungus tribes produce some elaborate beadwork and you can sometimes buy their handicrafts at the Sunday *tamu* held at **Sikuati**, 23km south of Kudat. Sikuati is on the highway, 1km from the coast, where there is a good beach. Teluk Sikuati has a long, sweeping white-sand beach, though the water can be choppy and it is not as clear as that around Bak Bak.

GETTING THERE & AWAY

Bak Bak is difficult to get to from Kudat without your own transport – count on at least RM20 for a taxi there and back; arrange a time for pick-up. Sikuati and Matunggung are both on the highway and minibuses can drop you off.

EAST SABAH

After enjoying Sabah's main tourist attraction, Mt Kinabalu, many travellers head for the Sepilok Orang-Utan Rehabilitation Centre near Sandakan. Sepilok's orang-utans are a major draw, but this part of Sabah offers plenty more, especially if it's wildlife you're after.

One or two sights are pretty well the exclusive preserve of tour groups – but an enthusiast's route could take in Sepilok, a half-day at the Gomantong Caves, a trip to the fabulous Sungai Kinabatangan and some world-class diving or snorkelling at the islands off Semporna. And if your budget allows it, you could indulge in a few days at the magnificent Danum Valley for an upmarket rainforest experience, or even explore the Lost World of the Maliau Basin.

Sandakan

☎ 089

Sandakan is a busy commercial centre at the entrance to a beautiful, island-studded bay. Most activity centres on the docks and wharves that sprawl along the waterfront. Barges, ferries and motorboats of every description buzz around, unloading fish and other produce, and taking away rattan, timber, rubber, copra, palm oil and even birds' nests. West of town, passenger ferries shuttle back and forth to Zamboanga in the Philippines. In the bay, container vessels ride at anchor awaiting their turn to unload.

Compared to Sabah's relatively anonymous state capital, Sandakan has character and even a certain downmarket charm. The real attractions lie outside town, but there's excellent seafood to enjoy and beautiful views from the hills at sunset.

Further afield there's the Gomantong Caves and superb wildlife-watching along Sungai Kinabatangan. Forty kilometres offshore is Turtle Islands National Park, one of the world's few turtle sanctuaries.

HISTORY

At the height of the timber boom Sandakan was said to have the world's greatest concentration of millionaires. It was perhaps an extravagant claim, but the area has always been renowned for luxury goods such as pearls, sea cucumbers and birds' nests, and so attracted trade from the nearby Philippines and as far away as China.

In the 18th century Sandakan came under the suzerainty of the sultan of Sulu, who ruled the southern islands of what is now the Philippines. British traders came to the region in the 19th century, but the first foreign settlement was mainly by Germans who settled on Pulau Timbang, in Teluk Sandakan, in the 1870s.

In 1878 Baron von Overbeck, an Austrian, acquired a lease from the sultan of Sulu for much of eastern Sabah, and this

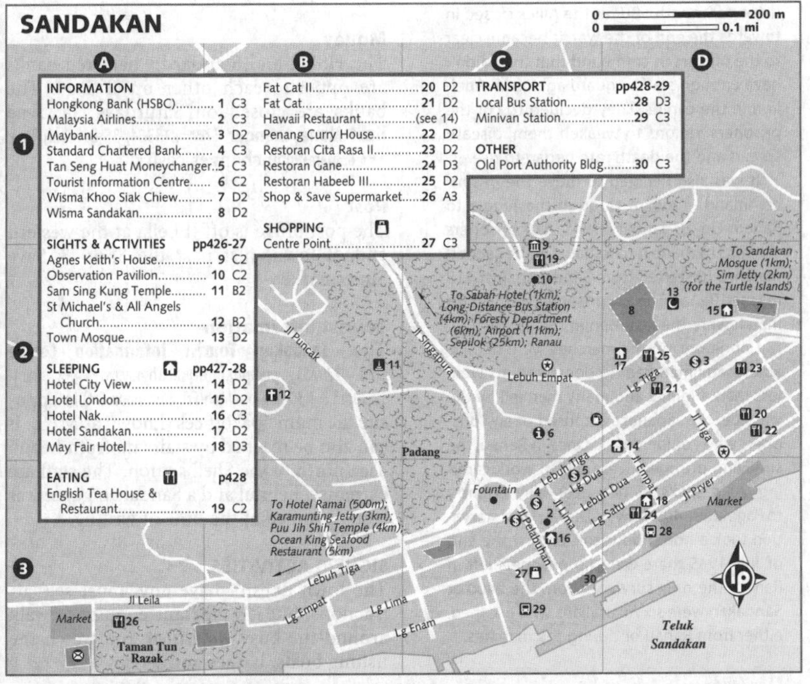

was later sold to Alfred Dent, a Hong Kong-based publisher. Sandakan was established by the British Resident William Pryer, and it boomed. In 1884 Sandakan became the capital of British North Borneo, and it remained the capital until the Japanese invasion; subsequent Allied bombing in 1945 virtually destroyed the town. In 1946 the capital was moved to Jesselton, now called Kota Kinabalu.

ORIENTATION

The centre of Sandakan consists of only a few blocks squashed between the waterfront and a steep escarpment from where you can look out over the bay. In the centre you'll find most of the hotels and restaurants, banks, the Malaysia Airlines office, and the local and long-distance bus stations. The main road west along the bay, Jl Leila, passes the commercial centres of Bandar Ramai-Ramai and Bandar Leila, where there are more hotels and places to eat.

The local bus station is right by the markets along the waterfront. Local buses and minivans also leave from the open area just past the old Port Authority building. Express buses to KK and other destinations leave from the long-distance bus station, 4km north of the town centre.

THE SANDAKAN DEATH MARCHES

Sandakan was the site of a Japanese prisoner-of-war camp during WWII, and in September 1944 there were 1800 Australian and 600 British troops interned here. What is probably not widely known is that more Australians died here than during the building of the infamous Burma Railway.

Early in the war, food and conditions were bearable (the death rate was around three per month). But as the Allies closed in towards the end of the war, it became clear to the officers in command that they didn't have enough staff to guard against a rebellion in the camps. They decided to cut the prisoners' rations to weaken them; disease spread and the death rate began to rise.

It was also decided to move the prisoners inland – 250km through the jungle to Ranau. On 28 January 1945, 470 prisoners set off; 313 made it to Ranau. On the second march, 570 started from Sandakan; just 118 reached Ranau. The 537 prisoners on the third march were the last men in the camp.

Conditions on the marches were deplorable: many men had no boots, rations were less than minimal and many men fell by the wayside; the Japanese disposed of any prisoners who couldn't walk. Once in Ranau, the surviving prisoners were put to work carrying 20kg sacks of rice over hilly country to Paginatan, 40km away. Disease and starvation took a horrendous toll, and by the end of July 1945 there were no prisoners left in Ranau. The only survivors from the 2400 at Sandakan were six Australians who escaped, either from Ranau or during the marches.

INFORMATION

Airline Offices

The **Malaysia Airlines office** (☎ 273966; 8.30am-5pm Mon-Fri, 8.30am-noon Sat) is at Wisma Sabah, opposite the Hotel Nak.

Internet Access

Cyberjazz (1st fl Centre Point; until 9.30pm) Charges RM4 per hour.

Sandakan Cybercafé (3rd fl, Wisma Sandakan; until 9pm) Charges RM4 per hour.

Money

The HSBC and Standard Chartered banks are opposite each other on Jl Tiga. The banks are closed on Saturdays. **Tan Seng Huat Moneychanger** (☎ 213364; 35-B Lebuh Tiga; 8.30am-9pm) changes cash.

Post

The post office is off Jl Leila at the western end of town, just past the Shop & Save Supermarket.

Tourist Information

The **Sandakan Tourist Information Centre** (☎ 229751; pempt.j.mps@sabah.gov.my; 8am-12.30pm & 1.30-4.30pm Mon-Fri, 8am-noon Sat) is opposite the municipal offices (known as MPS). It can also be reached by stairs up from Lebuh Tiga north of the Shell station. The staff are extremely helpful and a Sandakan guide was being planned at the time of writing.

SIGHT & ACTIVITIES

The town doesn't have any 'must see' attractions, but it's pleasant enough to walk around the busy **waterfront** and watch the fishing boats, barges and ferries.

The **market** is always a hive of activity, though it can get a bit fetid in the heat of the day. Locals will warn you about pickpockets; it's a good idea to avoid the market area after 9pm, especially if you're alone.

The **Puu Jih Shih Temple**, 4km west of the town centre, is a large Buddhist temple perched on a steep hill overlooking Teluk Sandakan. Take a bus to Tanah Merah and ask for the temple. Closer to the centre of town, the **Sam Sing Kung Temple** dates from 1887 and fronts the *padang*. Another building of note is **St Michael's & All Angels Church**, built in the 19th century and one of the few stone buildings in Malaysian Borneo.

For a fine view over the town and bay, head up the hill towards the Renaissance Sandakan Hotel and turn right at Jl Istana near the roundabout. An **observation pavilion** a few hundred metres along offers panoramic views. Just behind is **Agnes Keith's House**, an old two-storey wooden villa; at the time of writing the house was being renovated as a museum. Keith was an American who came to Sandakan in the 1930s with her husband, who was the Conservator of Forests. She wrote about her experiences in three books, the most famous being *Land Below the Wind*. She was imprisoned by the Japanese during WWII – just one of her many adventures in Sabah.

Sandakan Memorial Park

The **Sandakan Memorial Park** (admission free; ⏲ 9am-5pm) is in a quiet, wooded park just past the government buildings at Batu 8 (Km 12) on the road to Ranau. Despite its tranquil appearance, this was the site of the Japanese POW camp and the starting point for the infamous 'death marches' to Ranau (see facing page). Large, rusting machines under the trees have plaques telling how many men died during their construction and how prisoners tried to sabotage them. There's a very good exhibit with surviving prisoners' accounts and photographs, in a chapel-like building at the centre of the park. It's a moving experience to visit this place.

To get there, take any Batu 8 or higher bus and get off at the Esso petrol station about 1km on the right past the government buildings at the airport roundabout. Walk along Jl Rimba for about 10 minutes; the park is on the right across from the Taman Sri Rimba housing estate. A taxi will cost about RM10.

TOURS

It's easy to visit the Sepilok Orang-Utan Rehabilitation Centre independently. The Gomantong Caves and Sungai Kinabatangan are more difficult to reach with public transport, but it is possible. To see wildlife, however, you'll need a guide and the easiest way to arrange this is by going on a tour.

Sandakan has plenty of tour operators offering trips to these places and further afield. Hotels in Sandakan and Sepilok can also arrange tours, as can tour operators in KK (see p392).

Crystal Quest (☎ 212711; cquest@tm.net.my; Jl Buli Sim Sim) Exclusive agent running trips to Turtle Islands (see p431).

Jungle Sanctuary (☎ 019-873 4289; www.junglesanctuary.cjb.net; based in Traveller's Rest Hostel, 2nd fl, Lot 2 Block E, Bandar Ramai Ramai, Jl Leila) Has guided jungle walks and night boating forays from its jungle camp on Sungai Kinabatangan (see p432). Recommended by many travellers; budget rates but the accommodation is spartan.

SI Tours (☎ 213502; www.sitours.com.my; 1st fl, Wisma Khoo Siak Chiew) Can arrange trips to Pulau Seligan and organise Sukau lodging for the Kinabatangan.

Uncle Tan's (☎ 531917; fax 531639; tansulim@tm.net.my; Block B, Sedco Complex, Mile 16, Jl Labuk) Has a jungle camp on Sungai Kinabatangan and provides guided tours in the jungle (see p432).

Wildlife Expeditions (☎ 219616; www.wildlife-expeditions.com; Room 901-904, 9th fl, Wisma Khoo Siak Chiew) Runs tours to the Kinabatangan and operates the Sukau River Lodge there. It also has an office in KK.

SLEEPING

Budget & Mid-Range

If you're only visiting Sandakan en route to the Orang-Utan Rehabilitation Centre, it's better to stay at Sepilok, since the centre is about 25km from Sandakan. Besides, there is hardly any budget lodging in Sandakan, and the few really cheap places are usually establishments of ill-repute or serve as housing for immigrants.

May Fair Hotel (☎ 219855; 24 Jl Pryer; s/d RM36/45; ❄) This spotlessly clean 1st-floor walk-up is close to the bustling fish market and is one of the best cheaper mid-range places to stay in Sandakan. The rooms are bright and spacious. There's a DVD player in each one and the proprietor has a generous repertoire of (mostly action) movies. Another convenience is the in-house laundry service.

Hotel London (☎ 216371; 10 Lebuh Empat; s/d RM40/50; ❄) This is a basic but clean and well-run place with an elaborate rooftop garden. The staff can help with local information and maps.

Hotel City View (☎ 271122; fax 273115; 23 Lebuh Tiga; s/d RM60/90 ❄) Rooms are well appointed but the street noise (and other guests) can be a bit loud. There's a decent restaurant downstairs that serves Western breakfasts.

Hotel Nak (☎ 272988; fax 272879; Jl Pelabuhan; s/d RM60/80; ❄) What was once Sandakan's best hotel is looking a little worse for wear these days and prices have dropped. It's still liveable though; ask for a room facing the harbour.

Hotel Ramai (☎ 273222; fax 271884; Jl Leila; s/d RM65/95 ❄) This newer hotel has spacious rooms and suites. While it's quite far from the city centre (about 1km west of the post office), it's conveniently close to the wharves for boats to the Philippines.

If you're catching an early bus and want accommodation near the station outside town, the **Seagull B&B** (☎ 218328; fax 210328; 1st fl, Mile 2.5, Jl Utara; dm RM20; ❄) is a handy place, located right beside the bus terminal. It also arranges tours to Turtle Islands National Park.

Top End

Hotel Sandakan (☎ 221122; tengis@tm.net.my; Lebuh Empat; s/d RM173/219; ❄) This two-star hotel, next to Wisma Sandakan, has a restaurant, lounge and business centre. Discounts of up to 20% may be available.

Sabah Hotel (☎ 246149; shsdksm@tm.net.my; Km 1, Jl Utara; s/d RM320/340; ❄ 🅿) The only international-standard hotel in town, and a favourite of the Sepilok tour groups, this is a comfortable, luxurious place set in quiet gardens with a swimming pool, sporting facilities, lounge and restaurants.

EATING

Sandakan has many cheap **Chinese restaurants** and *kedai kopi*, particularly near the waterfront, serving standard rice or noodle dishes.

For no-frills food, some of it fine Filipino fare, try one of the stalls in the waterfront **market** next to the local bus station. A couple of ringgit will get you a decent meal but choose carefully, as hygiene might not be 1st class. The food-court-style restaurants on the 1st floor of **Centre Point** are a bit more expensive, but the quality is generally reliable. There's more market food at the **night market** that sets up outside the post office each evening.

Penang Curry House (☎ 226675; Lorong Satu; dishes RM5-10) There's excellent curry rice dishes and other Indian food here, especially the delicious *masala dosa*.

Restoran Gane (☎ 221549; Jl Pryer; dishes RM4-8) An unpretentious place near the market, there's good Malay food here and an air-conditioned section upstairs. Try the excellent *murtabak*. A couple of similar places are close by, including one of the many branches of **Restoran Habeeb**.

For light snacks and meals the **Restoran Cita Rasa II** (☎ 224588; Lebuh Tiga; RM5-10) is a good place to cool off. It also has freshly squeezed vegetable and fruit juices for RM2 to RM3.50. **Fat Cat II** is a Malay fast-food-style restaurant opposite the other **Fat Cat** on Lebuh Tiga.

English Tea House & Restaurant (☎ 222544; 2002 Jl Istana; dishes RM15-25) Tropical elegance permeates this exquisite colonial-house restaurant on the grounds of the historic Agnes Keith House. Enjoy the beautiful decor inside or sit in rattan chairs on the lawn overlooking Sandakan Bay. Try the delicious cornish pastry (RM17.50) and the creamy custard cheesecake (RM8.50). This restaurant is a special treat.

For less refined Western food, the **Hawaii Restaurant** in the City View Hotel has decent Western food and good breakfast combinations at reasonable prices.

Ocean King Seafood Restaurant (☎ 618111; Batu 2.5, Jl Batu Sapi; dishes RM10-25) About 5km west along the coast from Sandakan's city centre, you'll find this large restaurant perched on stilts jutting out from the shore. It's perfect for watching sunsets while munching on prawns fried in garlic butter. Seafood dishes are more expensive.

GETTING THERE & AWAY

Air

Sandakan is well served by the Malaysia Airlines domestic network, and there are direct flights to KK (RM83, 7 daily) and Tawau (RM74, 2 daily). There are also Twin Otter flights to Kudat (RM54, 4 weekly), KK (RM69, 3 weekly) Tawau (RM61, twice weekly) and Tomanggong (RM42, twice weekly), near the Tabin Wildlife Reserve.

Air Asia has a direct flight from KL to Sandakan twice daily.

MALAYSIAN BORNEO

CHRISTER FREDRIKSSON

Kinabalu National Park (p414), Sabah

MICHAEL AW

Nudibranch, **Pulau Sipadan** (p438)

MARK DAFFEY

Stilt village, **Semporna** (p437)

Rhinoceros hornbill (p432), Sungai Kinabatangan

CHRISTER FREDRIKSSON

TOM CC

Musician (p424), Sabah

Orang-utan orphan, **Sepilok Orang-Utan Rehabilitation Centre** (p429)

MARK DAFFEY

MICHAEL AW

Baby turtles in the hatchery at Pulau Selingan, **Turtle Islands National Park** (p431)

MARK

Mosque, **Semporna** (p437)

Boat

A couple of companies run passenger ferries between Sandakan and Zamboanga (18 hours) in the Philippines; it is a popular route with overseas Filipinos returning to visit their families. The most reliable outfit is **Timarine** (☎ 212063). They have boats leaving twice a week in the evening and fares are RM130 (RM150 with air-con) and RM170 for a cabin. Tickets can be bought in advance from the Karamunting jetty, about 4km west of town, where you also clear immigration when boarding. To get to the jetty, take a Pasir Putih bus (90 sen).

Bus

The long-distance bus station is inconveniently located in a large parking lot at Batu 2½, 4km north of town. Air-con express buses to KK, Semporna and Tawau wait here. Most buses, and all minivans, leave in the morning. To get to the bus station, catch a local bus from the stand at the waterfront. A taxi from the station to town is RM5.

Bus companies have booths at the station, but it's hardly worth coming all the way out here to find out when the next day's buses run. **Tung Ma Express** (☎ 210054) is one of the larger companies; **SIDA Ekspress** (☎ 019-833 9746) is another. The tourist office can also help with schedules.

Most express buses to KK (RM30, 6 hours) leave between 7am and 1.30pm. The same buses pass the turn-off to Kinabalu National Park headquarters (RM25).

Buses depart daily for Lahad Datu (RM15, 2½ hours) and Tawau (RM30, 5½ hours) every half-hour between 6.30am and 5pm.

There's also a bus to Semporna (RM30, 5½ hours) at 8am. If you miss the bus to Semporna, you can take one to Lahad Datu from where there are more-frequent minivans to Semporna.

Minibuses to Ranau cost RM25 and the journey takes about four hours. Minivans depart frequently throughout the morning for Lahad Datu, some going on to Tawau. There are also minibuses for Sukau (RM15), but these leave from the local bus station in town.

GETTING AROUND

To/From the Airport

The airport is about 11km from the town centre. The Batu 7 Airport bus (70 sen) runs by the airport but stops on the main road about 500m from the terminal. Airport-bound buses leave from behind Centre Point in town. A coupon taxi from the airport to the town centre costs RM17.50; going the other way, you can get a cab for RM15.

Taxi

Taxis are plentiful. They cluster near the markets and main hotels and are easy to hail along main roads. Trips around the town centre should cost RM5 and a trip out to Sepilok is RM25.

Sepilok Orang-Utan Rehabilitation Centre

☎ 089

One of only four orang-utan sanctuaries in the world, Sepilok is about 25km north of Sandakan. The centre was established in 1964; it now covers 40 sq km and has become one of Sabah's top tourist attractions.

The centre has doubtless suffered from its own success – so many camera-clicking tourists are turned loose on the viewing platforms that the atmosphere can seem more like a circus than a sanctuary. More seriously, constant contact with humans has exposed the orang-utans to diseases, which can make rehabilitation to the wild all but impossible.

Orang-utans are the only species of great ape found outside Africa. A mature male is an impressive, not to mention hairy, creature with an armspan of 2.25m, and can weigh up to 144kg. It was once said that an orang-utan could swing from tree to tree from one side of Borneo to the other without touching the ground. Sadly this is no longer the case, and hunting and habitat destruction continue to take their toll.

Orphaned and injured orang-utans are brought to Sepilok to be rehabilitated to return to forest life, and so far the centre has handled about 100, although only about 20 still return regularly to be fed. It's unlikely you'll see anywhere near this number at feeding time – three or four is more likely. Females that have returned to the wild often come back to the feeding platforms when they're pregnant and stay near the centre until they've given birth, after which they go back to the forest.

The orang-utans are fed fruit, such as bananas, twice daily from a platform in the forest, about 10 minutes' walk from the centre. This feeding is just to supplement what they can find for themselves in the jungle – if trees are fruiting, few apes will turn up.

Young orang-utans in particular are endlessly appealing, with ginger fur and intelligent eyes. Macaques may also join the feeding and photo frenzy – it's quite dim under the forest canopy and if you're taking photographs, you'll need ASA 400 film.

INFORMATION

The feeding schedule is usually at 10am and 3pm but it can change, and the morning and afternoon programmes are posted at the **visitor reception centre** (☎ 531180; soutan@po.jaring.my; admission RM30; ⌚ 9am-12.30pm & 2-4.30pm) where there's a souvenir shop and a cafeteria.

The **Nature Education Centre** has some interesting displays about the wildlife in the reserve. Make sure you look at the exhibit on the main factor threatening orang-utans today. A 25-minute video, *Orphans of Borneo*, is shown at the park office at 8.40am, 10.40am and 3.30pm. The whole centre closes at 11.30am on Fridays.

There are lockers for your valuables – orang-utans have been known to relieve tourists of hats, sunglasses, cameras and even clothing.

WALKS

Walking trails lead further into the forest, but they are only open at specified times and you have to register at the visitor reception centre to use them. Trails range in length from 250m to 2km, and different trails are open during the year. There's a 5km trail through a mangrove forest to Sandakan Bay, where it's possible to get a boat back to Sandakan though you need to arrange this with the **Forestry Department** (☎ 213135 ext 32; Jl Labuk) in Sandakan, or a travel agency.

Note that you wander through the forest at your own risk. Although orang-utans are not usually aggressive, on no account should you provoke or pester any wild animal. If you are carrying any food, the macaques will scent it and try to relieve you of it – don't argue with them because they'll probably win.

Make sure you wear hiking boots and take water; expect to find leeches and plenty of mosquitoes.

SLEEPING & EATING

Sepilok has some very good accommodation, scattered along Jl Sepilok (the 2.5km-long road off the main highway to the rehabilitation centre) and also nearby on the main highway. All these places can arrange tours to Sungai Kinabatangan and Turtle Islands.

Sepilok Resthouse (☎ 534900; imejbs@tm.net.my; dm RM18, r with fan/air-con RM45/65; ❄) This comfortable place is only a five-minute walk from the centre, and is very popular with travellers. It's clean, breezy and there's a nice yard to relax in. Breakfast is included.

Sepilok Jungle Resort (☎ 533031; www.borneo-online.com.my/sjungleresort/; dm RM18, r with fan/air-con RM40/65; ❄) Set on a garden with amazing sculpted concrete buildings and ornaments, this place is about 100m east off Jl Sepilok. There's a shuttle service to Sandakan.

Sepilok B&B (☎ 532288; nbp@tm.net.my; dm RM20, r with fan/air-con RM45/60; ❄ 💻) This is another place occupying a large acreage with fruit trees and gardens about 250m off Jl Sepilok (don't be fooled by the sign on the road that says '100m'), about 1km short of the rehabilitation centre entrance. It's not quite as nice as the Sepilok Resthouse, but all room rates include breakfast and free tea and coffee. Camping is also possible (RM5/10 with/without your own tent) and Internet access costs RM1 for eight minutes.

Labuk B&B (☎ 533190; labukbb@tm.net.my; Mile 15, Jl Labuk; r RM20 per person) A couple of kilometres from Sepilok on the main highway towards KK, Robert Chong and his wife Annie run this small place housed in a renovated Malay-style house. There's room for 14 people, and a delicious American-style breakfast is included. Dinner is also available. Labuk often acts as an informal host to visiting wildlife researchers and you'll probably find yourself in stimulating company here. It's a great place to pick up information about Sabah. Buses passing the Sepilok turn-off can drop you back at Labuk B&B (Batu 15 bus and higher). Just ask the driver and remind him as you get closer; the fare is 40 sen, or RM1.50 from the centre of town.

The rehabilitation centre **cafeteria** (⌚ 7am-4pm) serves breakfast, sandwiches, noodle and rice dishes, and drinks. At busy times it may run out of all but the basics. There's a small **supermarket** about 1.5km back towards the highway, not far from the Sepilok B&B turn-off.

GETTING THERE & AWAY

To get directly to the rehabilitation centre from Sandakan, look for the blue bus marked 'Sepilok Batu 14' from the local bus stand next to the market on the waterfront (RM2, 30 minutes). Minivans also make the trip every hour or so.

Regular buses, also marked 'Batu 14' or higher, can drop you at the turn-off to Jl Sepilok, 1.5km from the orang-utan centre.

Returning from Sepilok, the last bus leaves the centre for Sandakan at 4.30pm.

Most of the B&Bs and guesthouses can organise transport to/from the bus station and the airport for a nominal fee.

Turtle Islands National Park

Also known as the Pulau Penyu National Park, this park comprises three small islands – Pulau Selingan, Pulau Bakungan Kecil and Pulau Gulisan – that lie 40km north of Sandakan, within swimming distance of nearby islands of the Philippines.

Though their numbers have fallen off, two species of marine turtles – the green and hawksbill – come ashore here to lay their eggs at certain times of the year. Since their laying seasons are virtually complementary, it's possible to see either species at almost any time of year.

Sea turtles are harmless vegetarians that spend most of their lives at sea. They are strong, graceful swimmers that grow to a great age and size. The green turtle commonly lays on Pulau Selingan and Pulau Bakungan Kecil between July and October; and the smaller hawksbill turtle lays its eggs on Pulau Gulisan from February to April. The eggs are collected by permanent staff based on Pulau Selingan and transferred to fenced hatcheries, where they are safe from illegal collection by fishermen who eat or sell them.

For more information on sea turtles (and how you can make sure you do them no harm), see p55.

Besides accommodation prices listed below, an RM10 conservation fee is also charged.

SLEEPING & EATING

All visits to the Turtle Islands must be arranged through a travel agency or directly through **Crystal Quest** (☎ 089-212711; cquest@tm.net.my; Jl Buli Sim Sim, Sandakan).

Accommodation is in chalets on Pulau Selingan, ranging in price from RM130 per person (no bathroom) to RM165 and up, with bathroom. All rooms have air-con and the price includes at least two meals.

Try to book ahead because facilities are limited and tour companies often take bulk bookings.

GETTING THERE & AWAY

Transport to the islands is from the wharf on Jl Buli Sim Sim east of Sandakan's centre. The trip to the islands takes about two hours. Tickets with Crystal Quest cost RM100/50 for adults/children (a child is under 10 years of age). You may be able to get a better deal arranging your transport through another tour company.

Gomantong Caves

These limestone caves are Sabah's most famous source of the swiftlets' nests used for bird's-nest soup. The caves are 5km south off the road to Sukau, 20km from the main highway. They're difficult, but not impossible, for independent travellers to reach without their own transport.

The most accessible of the caves is a 10-minute walk along the trail near the **information centre** (☎ 230189; www.sabah.gov.my/jhl; adult/child RM30/15; ⌚ 8am-noon & 2-4.30pm). A boardwalk leading off to the right doubles back to the entrance road – it's a pleasant walk but it won't get you to the caves. Continue past the living quarters of the nest collectors to get to the main cave, **Simud Hitam** (Black Cave). You can venture in, though it involves wading through ankle-deep guano alive with insects. In the nesting season, you can watch the nests being collected from the cave roof, as they are at Niah Caves in Sarawak, by men climbing long, precarious-looking bamboo poles.

The left-hand trail from the office leads to the top of the mountain. After a few metres the trail forks again. To the right, a 15-minute walk brings you to a top entrance to the cave, while the left-hand trail continues for 30 minutes and leads high up the mountain to **Simud Putih** (White Cave). This cave contains the more-valuable white nests. Both trails are steep and involve some sweaty rock climbing.

The area around the caves is covered in forest and dense vegetation. There's plenty of wildlife, especially birds, and the walks are worthwhile, but the caves are difficult to reach. The great caves of Gunung Mulu and Niah national parks in Sarawak are more spectacular and easier to visit, and the Madai Caves (see p436) near Lahad Datu are quite interesting and more accessible.

From Sandakan, minivans go directly to Sukau (RM15) – ask to be dropped at the turn-off for the caves. You can also take a minivan for Lahad Datu, get out at the Sukau turn-off and take another minivan to Sukau (RM10) which can drop you at the turn-off for the caves. You may have to walk 5km down the road to the ticket office unless there's a vehicle going down at the same time. Bring your passport because the guard at the gatepost at the start of the road may ask to see it.

An easier way to see the caves is to take a tour; most operators include it as part of a package to Sungai Kinabatangan (see p427 for a list of tour operators).

Sungai Kinabatangan

Sungai Kinabatangan is Sabah's longest river and measures 560km from its headwaters in the southwest of the state to the point where it empties into the Sulu Sea, east of Sandakan. Logging and clearing for plantations have devastated the upper reaches of the river, but by a strange irony the riverine forest near the coast is so hemmed in by oil-palm plantations that an astonishing variety of wildlife is common and easy to see.

This is one of the best places in Borneo – indeed, in all of Southeast Asia – to observe wildlife, and the Kinabatangan is a high-

BANKING ON THE KINABATANGAN

One of Borneo's treasures, the lower Sungai Kinabatangan floodplain is home to an astonishing variety and richness of plant and wildlife. Like many wetland environments however, its survival is tenuous. The area is seriously threatened by Sabah's economic reliance on plantations and logging. Larger animals, like the Asian elephant and Sumatran rhino, as well as proboscis monkeys and orang-utans, are being squeezed out of their habitat for the sake of palm oil, and the river is slowly choking on silt from upriver logging. Hunting parties from the logging camps and plantations have been known to cruise the river, and soon after the bodies of bullet-riddled proboscis monkeys end up along the banks. Fortunately, in the last few years, some action has been taken to try and save this precious environmental resource from further destruction.

In 1999 some 27,000 hectares in the lower Kinabatangan were declared a protected area, and the World Wide Fund for Nature (WWF) has been actively working on its Partners for Wetlands project in the area for 10 years. In 2001 the organisation succeeded in upgrading lower Kinabantangan to bird sanctuary status. The next step is to have the area declared a wildlife sanctuary. The WWF conservation project has been trying to convince logging companies and plantation owners to establish corridors for animals to pass through, an essential factor to sustain wildlife populations. It seems the foreign banks funding these plantations would like to see a few environmentally friendly gestures before renewing loans, so the landowners are inclined to oblige.

Despite some successes and the clout given to the project by the government, the WWF has been criticised for its strategy of forming links with big business. Also, some feel that the WWF brief is quite limited, where upriver communities are, so far, simply slated to fit in to the new tourism economy generated by conservation and more upmarket lodges. The organisation is trying to involve the local community more, however, and recently opened a modest site office in Sukau. It has also been active in supporting tourist homestay initiatives in the village of Batu Puteh on the river.

There's also the sad reality, however, that unless the upriver logging stops, the Kinabatangan has a short future, regardless of what happens in the floodplain downstream – the damage from silting and deforestation is simply too great. Nonetheless, in Sabah money does all the talking (and listening), and the WWF 'partnership' with big business recognises that the loggers and palm-oil barons are not going away any time soon. At least the Wetlands project is a start, and a chance for the unique Kinabatangan's survival, where virtually none existed a few years ago.

You can contact **Partners for Wetlands** (☎ 089-225101; fax 225103; wetlandp@tm.net.my) in Sandakan or visit its website at www.borneo-online.com.my/wwf or write to WWF Malaysia, Partners for Wetlands Project, WDT 49, PPJU, 90309 Sandakan, Sabah.

light of any nature-lover's trip to Sabah. The river is interesting at any time of year. Most bird activity happens in the wet season (October to March), but conditions are uncomfortable – and mammals can be seen at any time of year. However, during the dry season, the river's oxbow lakes may not have water in them.

A narrow corridor of rainforest clings to the northern riverbank from the Sandakan–Lahad Datu road downstream to the mangrove-fringed estuary. Sightings of the unique proboscis monkeys are common among the mangroves in the late afternoon; two macaque species – long-tailed and pig-tailed – are common; and orang-utans are also seen, particularly downstream.

There's a chance of seeing marbled cats in the forest, and flat-headed cats are seen regularly at night along the Menungal (a tributary of the Kinabatangan); other mammals include elephant (very shy), deer and giant squirrel.

Bird lovers will find the **bird-watching** incredible: all eight of Borneo's hornbill species are seen regularly; two species of the gorgeous pittas are reasonably common; as well as Storm's stork and the bizarre Oriental darter, or snake-bird.

The success rate of animal-spotting largely depends on the local knowledge of your guide and luck – don't be afraid to ask hard questions about the specifics of your trip before you sign up. Elephants and other larger animals come and go – herds often break up to get through the palm plantations encroaching in many areas.

SLEEPING & EATING

Independent travel to the Kinabatangan is virtually impossible, and good guides are a must off the beaten track, but if wildlife is your passion, make room in your budget to visit this incredible place. Backpackers and budget travellers are catered for in jungle camps, and there's a cluster of more expensive lodges near the riverside village of Sukau.

Jungle Camps

Both the **Jungle Sanctuary** (☎ 019-873 4289; www.junglesanctuary.cjb.net; based in Traveller's Rest Hostel, 2nd fl, Lot 2, Block E, Bandar Ramai Ramai, Jl Leila, Sandakan) and **Uncle Tan's Wildlife Camp** (☎ 089-31917; fax 531639, tansulim@tm.net.my; Block B, Sedco Complex, Mile 16, Jl Labuk, Sandakan) have places to stay in the jungle. There are many opportunities to view wildlife, either on river trips or on guided walks. Their prices are similar, about RM150 to RM200 for a two-night, three-day stay in the forest, which includes meals and transport. The accommodation here is very basic, however, and it's a good idea to bring lots of mosquito repellent. The grounds at Uncle Tan's in particular can get very muddy in the rain.

Lodges

Sukau is the main village on the lower Kinabatangan, reached by gravel road, 42km off the main highway between Lahad Datu and Sandakan. Lodges operated by tour companies near Sukau offer wildlife experiences and more, in luxurious comfort. There's not much difference between them – all have comfortable, mosquito-proof rooms with fan and bathroom, fully catered meals and bar, and trained guides. The Sukau Rainforest Lodge, run by Borneo Eco Tours, is the most isolated, being on the other side of the river from the others.

On a twin-share basis, expect to pay RM250 to RM300 per night at a lodge, including transfers. Most tours include Gomantong Caves as part of the package, but you can opt out of this if you wish. See Tours in the Sandakan (p427) and KK (p392) sections for companies that use the lodges.

Other Accommodation

Another option if you have time is to stay in Sukau and hire a local guide for a day trip on the river and its tributaries. A three-hour trip on the river is about RM60. The **Tomanggong B&B** (☎ 230275; r RM20) is a pleasant place by the river, with small cabins and attached baths. It's about 1km east of the village, past the Muslim cemetery. Local-style meals are served and breakfast is included.

GETTING THERE & AWAY

Minivans go to Sukau from Sandakan (RM15, 2 hours), or you can take a minivan to Lahad Datu and get out at the Sukau turn-off. Expect to wait awhile for a minivan from here to Sukau (RM10, 1 to 1½ hours). If you're on a tour, transport will be arranged.

SABAH HOMESTAY PROGRAMME

After visiting Sukau, another option in the Kinabatangan region is the Sabah Homestay Programme at Batu Puteh, on Sungai Kinabatangan. Batu Puteh is accessible from the main highway about 15km south of the Sukau turn-off on the way to Lahad Datu. The **Miso Walai Homestay Association** (☎/fax 089-562601; 019-863 1520; www.misowalai.com.my) was established with the participation of local villagers, the Tourism Ministry, the Forestry Department and the Worldwide Fund for Nature (WWF) to encourage local tourism development at community level. There's a variety of activities that travellers can take part in, including community service in the villages, while living with a village family. It's designed for short visits (up to four days) and can be arranged by travel agencies in Sepilok and Sandakan or you can contact the association yourself. Visitors must expect very basic facilities and above all have a respectful attitude towards local customs and beliefs. This means dressing appropriately and following the rules, regardless of your own political and cultural assumptions and the fact that you'll be paying for this privilege. The website has a comprehensive list of 'dos and don'ts' which is good to read if you're thinking of taking part in this homestay, or any other homestay, in Sabah.

If you're heading further south from Sukau, ask to be dropped at the highway, from where you can catch a minivan to Lahad Datu or possibly a bus to Semporna – it'll save you repeating the long drive from Sandakan.

Lahad Datu

☎ 089

Lahad Datu is a bustling boomtown bordering a lovely bay. This area of eastern Sabah around the Celebes Sea is known for its pirates, who are equipped with the essentials of modern piracy – machine guns and speedboats. Pirate raids on ships and coastal villages are not uncommon and it's not recommended to hire boats for exploring around here.

There's no real reason to stop in Lahad Datu, except to arrange ongoing transport or to visit the Danum Valley or Tabin Wildlife Reserve. The **Danum Valley Field Centre office** (☎ 881092; danum@care2.com; Block 3, Fajar Centre) and **Borneo Nature Tours** (☎ 880207; www.brl.com.my; 1st fl, Block 1, Lot 6, Fajar Centre) are in the upper part of town. Both run trips to the Danum Valley Conservation Area (this page).

If you plan to visit the Tabin Wildlife Reserve independently (see p436) it's best to contact the **Wildlife Department office** (Pejabat Hidupan Liar; ☎ 884416), just in case a permit is necessary. It's four blocks south of the Danum Valley Field Centre office.

Don't be surprised if cars frequently slow down and honk as you walk by. These are private taxis that shuttle people between the upper and lower parts of town (where the bus station is) for RM3.

SLEEPING & EATING

Lahad Datu has plenty of hotels and restaurants, both in the upper and lower parts of town. Try the comfortable **Executive Hotel** (☎ 881333; fax 881777; Jl Teratai; s/d RM80/165; ❄) in the main part of town on the waterfront, just west of the city centre.

GETTING THERE & AWAY

Lahad Datu has an airport, with at least three daily flights to KK (RM106).

Express buses, minibuses and minivans leave from a vacant lot near the waterfront in the lower part of town. There are frequent minivan departures for Sandakan (RM15, 2½ hours), Semporna (RM12, 2½ hours) and Tawau (RM12, 2½ hours). Air-con minibuses to Sandakan are RM12. A bus to Tomanggong (RM7, 2 hours) leaves at noon.

There are plenty of departures to all places until around 3pm; buses and vans to Semporna and Tawau pass the Kunak turn-off for Madai Caves; the fare is RM7. The road north to Sandakan and south to Semporna and Tawau is a relentless monotony of palm plantations – if you go all the way to Tawau, you'll be seeing the tidy rows of squat palm trees in your sleep.

Danum Valley Conservation Area

Danum Valley is part of a vast logging concession owned by the Sabah Foundation, which set aside the conservation area to preserve 43 sq km of pristine wilderness on Sungai Segama, about 81km west of Lahad Datu. For some years research into rainforest ecology was carried out at a field studies centre, and the area has been well patronised by foreign politicians and Hollywood starlets.

In 2000, a massive new pulp-wood plantation project planned for the Kalabakan area southwest of the Danum Valley caused outrage among conservation groups around the world; it would, in effect, eliminate an important wildlife corridor between the Danum Valley and the Maliau Basin. Preliminary wildlife surveys in the area discovered more wildlife (including orang-utans) than expected but it remains under threat from logging and other development.

Despite the logging, the conservation area still manages to support an incredible diversity of wildlife. At present, botanical riches include 200 tree species per hectare; 275 bird species (many endemic to Borneo); and 110 species of mammals, including great rarities such as the Sumatran rhino and the beautiful clouded leopard.

Recent changes now make the valley more accessible to independent travellers. It's now possible to stay at the Danum Valley Field Centre as well as the Borneo Rainforest Lodge. Either way, the Danum Valley is one of the highlights of Sabah.

Entry to the area is RM30 per person.

SIGHTS & ACTIVITIES

Jungle Walks

A number of trails have been cleared around the Borneo Rainforest Lodge (BRL), although you won't be allowed on most without a guide, either arranged by the field centre or the lodge. If you have a particular interest, insist on a specialist – some travellers have complained that their guides didn't seem to know much.

There's a short nature trail near the lodge that points out interesting facts about the surrounding forest, but you'll probably be so overwhelmed by the colours and sounds that you'll just want to absorb it as you walk along.

Longer trails follow Sungai Segama, but one of the best climbs is up a bluff where there's an ancient hardwood coffin and the remains of bodies buried in a cliff face. On the return it's possible to swim at refreshing waterholes.

Guided night walks are organised most nights, with the chance of seeing snakes, frogs and mammals such as flying squirrels and bearded pigs.

Comfortable, durable footwear is a must. Leeches are common when it's wet. See the boxed text 'That Clinging Feeling' (p579) for leech insights.

Canopy Walk

One of the attractions of the BRL is a walkway suspended 25m above the rainforest floor. It's an ideal spot to look for bird life and saves you craning your neck to look into the treetops.

Night Drives

This may be one of the best ways to see some of the valley's mammals, though sensitive souls might empathise with the 'caught-in-the-headlights' surprise experienced by the animals. On the other hand, this may be as close as you'll get to an African safari in Southeast Asia. Expect to see one or two species of giant flying squirrels, sambar deer, civets, porcupines and possibly even leopard cats; lucky sightings could include elephants, slow loris and clouded leopards.

Night drives leave the BRL most evenings; the best trips are the extended night drives, which depart at about 8.30pm and return at 1 or 2am. The cost is about RM50 per person. Things you'll be glad you brought include a light waterproof jacket, camera with flash, binoculars and powerful torch.

Bird-Watching

Although there is a high diversity of bird species, rainforest bird sightings can oscillate between spectacular and spare; you have to put in the hours. The best vantage points are along the access road to the BRL – see if you can get a lift up to the entrance in the late afternoon, and then walk the 4km back to the lodge. There's more to hear than see, but hornbills are relatively common and argus pheasants are often heard.

Field Studies Centre

The field centre was set up by the Sabah Foundation, the Royal Society and a number of private companies to provide facilities for research and education in the rainforest. Many of the sponsors are involved in logging and one of the main areas of study is forest regeneration. It's possible to stay at the field centre (see below).

SLEEPING & EATING

Danum Valley Field Centre (☎ 881092; danum@care2.com; dm RM46, r RM80) Accommodation here is comfortable, if not luxurious. You can also camp for RM20 per person, and there's a chalet for RM105 per person. Bookings are made at the **Danum Valley Field Centre office** (Block 3, Fajar Centre, Lahad Datu) or through **Peter Chong** (☎ 088-326318; ces@icsbrbj.po.my in KK). You're wise to book ahead rather than just showing up in Lahad Datu. March can get especially busy.

Borneo Rainforest Lodge (☎ 880207; www.borneorainforestlodge.com; chalets s/d RM690/900 with full board) This is a 1st-class resort with vast, comfortable rooms, good dining and a bar. The price includes three meals a day and activities such as day and night walks, the canopy walk and a night drive. Extended night drives cost extra. In Lahad Datu you can book at **Borneo Nature Tours** (☎ 880207; www.brl.com.my; 1st fl, Block 1, Lot 6, Fajar Centre) or in KK you can book with one of the many tour companies (see p392).

GETTING THERE & AWAY

The Danum Valley is 81km by road from Lahad Datu. Transport provided by the Field Studies Centre leaves at 3.30pm (Monday, Wednesday and Friday) and costs RM60. It may be more if there are too few people. If you have your own car, a vehicle permit costs RM5.

Guests of the Borneo Rainforest Lodge can be met at the Lahad Datu airport and shuttled out to Danum Valley for RM150/100 for one/two people.

Tabin Wildlife Reserve

The **Tabin Wildlife Reserve** (☎ 821060; www.tabinwildlife.com) was created in 1984 to help preserve some of Sabah's disappearing wildlife. Straddled by palm-oil plantations 48km east of Lahad Datu, it covers a huge area (1205 sq km) of mostly lowland dipterocarp forest, with some mangrove forests in the reserve's northern reaches. Tabin falls under the auspices of the Forestry & Wildlife Department though visitor facilities, which only opened in 2002, are run by a private company. While not completely made up of primary forest, like the Danum Valley it's still a rich area for wildlife viewing; there's a good chance you'll see Asian elephants, grey-leaf monkeys and an abundance of bird life. It's also home to the endangered Sumatran rhino, though it's unlikely you'll get a glimpse of this rarely seen animal. There's also a mud volcano, similar to those found on Pulau Tiga.

It's possible to visit Tabin on your own, though, like many places in Sabah it's easier to go with a tour. **Intra Travel Service** (☎ 088-261558; www.intra-travel.com.my) in KK (see p392) runs a variety of tours to Tabin, involving varying degrees of comfort depending on your budget. Tours start at RM400. Facilities at the reserve include a restaurant and accommodation in fan-cooled chalets linked together by timber walkways or in tents on wooden platforms. A visitor information centre was also scheduled to open in mid-2003.

If you plan on visiting Tabin on your own it's best to contact the **Wildlife Department office** (Hidupan Liar; ☎ 089-884416) in Lahad Datu. It's four blocks south of the Danum Valley Field Centre office. Permits may not be necessary, but it's best to check first.

Intra Travel Service can arrange transport from Lahad Datu to Tabin, which is included in the tour price. For independent travellers, a bus leaves Lahad Datu at noon daily for Tomanggong, passing the reserve entrance on the way (RM7, 1 hour). Tomanggong is served by flights from Sandakan (RM42, twice weekly), though you'll still have to get to or from the park entrance by bus or car.

Madai Caves

Like the better-known Gomantong Caves to the north, these limestone caves are famed for their birds' nests. At the entrance to the cave system is a sprawling *kampung* (village) of empty wooden shanties. When the swiftlets start nesting these become the temporary dwellings of the nest collectors. So highly prized are these little cups of bird saliva that the collectors risk life and limb by climbing to the roof of the caves on precarious bamboo poles to gather the nests. The most valuable – and rarest – nests are the white ones, which can fetch RM2000 or more for a kilogram.

There have been environmental concerns because harvesting the nests before the swiftlet young are mature has decimated the population of swiftlets in the region. There's been an attempt to manage the harvesting in Malaysia, as well as innovations like creating environments for 'farming' the nests, but illegal harvesting is also a threat to swiftlet populations

Seeing the caves requires a bit of planning if you intend to do the right thing. The caves shelter ancestral tombs, and you must have permission from the local villagers to enter; an experienced local guide is needed to go any distance inside. When you arrive, the villagers will arrange things for you. The entrance fee is RM30.

The caves are near the Lahad Datu–Tawau Hwy. The turn-off (signposted 'Gua Madai') is 69km from Lahad Datu, and then it's 3km to the caves.

All buses between Lahad Datu and Semporna or Tawau pass the turn-off to the caves; you should be able to get a minivan to take you all the way to the caves, but you may have to walk back out to the highway. Buses run to the caves from the small town of Kunak for RM2, but you could be in for a long wait. Traffic on the road to the caves is light.

Semporna

☎ 089

Semporna is just about the end of the road in southeastern Sabah. This mainly Bajau town really comes alive at the end of March when a colourful regatta takes place, but normally it's quiet. The town is on a pretty bay sprouting sprawling stilt villages (one of which burned down in March 2003), and there are islands with good beaches not far offshore. Its proximity to Indonesia and the Philippines ensures a hefty police presence, especially since the Abu Sayyaff kidnapping incident on Pulau Sipadan in 2000 (see p439); the patrol boats are also there to deter dynamite fishing, which has done considerable damage to many of the reefs around the popular dive destinations lying off Semporna.

Semporna is usually only visited as a base for diving and snorkelling day trips or live-aboards to Pulau Mabul or Pulau Sipadan, the famous dive island 36km southeast of the town. The best dive seasons are between April and July/August – especially between April and June – and during November and December. Be warned: apart from the legitimate dive operators – who will produce a licence and dive-master certification if asked – there are a lot of cheapo operators out there (the names change as soon as they get a bad rep) who are happy to take your money and leave you high and dry on an isolated island. A deal that sounds too good to be true almost certainly is – which is not to say the pricey big companies are always good value (just a whole lot safer).

The Dragon Inn and Semporna Tourism Centre is a large development of thatched huts on stilts over the harbour. It consists of a hotel, restaurant, souvenir shop and a pathetic aquarium at the end of the pier. The complex is connected to the shore by a causeway; along this road, just past the entrance to the Dragon Inn, are dive shops and further along, the Seafest Hotel.

Minivans will drop you in the centre of town; to reach the causeway from there, walk east past the small children's park and playing field, and follow the road around to the left. On the shore between the town centre and the causeway is a fish market and outdoor food stalls.

Sukaria Cyber (☎ 782019; 29 Bandar Baru), in the next block over from Lee's Resthouse, has Internet access for RM2.50 per hour.

DIVING

For details of dive outfits based in KK that run trips in the area see p392. Many of these also have their own resorts.

Sipadan Water Village Resort (☎ 752996; www.sipadan-village.com.my; bookings 1st fl Wisma MAA, Bandar Sabindo, Tawau) Has a resort on Pulau Mabul.

Pulau Sipadan Resort & Tours (☎ 761899; www.sipadan-resort.com) This company can arrange lodging on Kapalai and Lankayan. Its head office is in Tawau (see p440), but it also has an office in Semporna, at the far end of the causeway.

North Borneo Dive & Sea Sports (☎ 769950; www.fortunecity.com/marina/paradise/132) This is another good operator with offices in both Tawau and Semporna. Its Semporna office (☎ 781788) is at the Dragon Inn pier complex.

Borneo Jungle River Island Tours (Uncle Chang's; ☎ 019-803 0988; unclechang99@hotmail.com) Located at the entrance to the Dragon Inn complex, this multi-purpose travel agency can do just about anything. Snorkelling day trips to Pulau Sibuan cost RM150 per small group.

Prices can vary for dive packages, depending on the choice of accommodation and whether you include all transport arrangements to Semporna. Booking ahead with a tour agency beforehand isn't necessarily cheaper, though it will guarantee you a place. If you just show up in Semporna, it's possible to book a package to Sipadan for two days and one night for RM500 per person, which includes dive equipment. A package booked from KK or abroad, including transport from Tawau, can be three times that.

If you don't plan to dive and have no interest visiting Pulau Sipadan, some operators offer a small discount for snorkellers.

SLEEPING & EATING

Dragon Inn (☎ 781088; fax 781099; r RM82.50; ❄) This is a huge place, built on stilts over the water and is quite attractive really, except when the tide brings in garbage. Dormitory beds in the roomy air-conditioned longhouse costs RM15, with attached toilets and *mandi* (Southeast Asian washbasin). Beds are also available in less roomy four-bed dorms for RM20. Discounts make this place very good value.

The menu at the inn's breezy **Pearl City Restaurant** (dishes RM10-20) includes Chinese, Malay and some Western dishes. Seafood costs a little more, depending on what you order. It does a decent breakfast from 6.30am and is open late if you want to sip a beer while the world floats by.

Seafest Hotel (☎ 782333; seafest.tm.net.my; rooms RM108; ❄) A new six-storey tourist hotel built at the end of the causeway, this place is comfortable but not as much of a novelty as the Dragon Inn. Rooms on the top floor are slightly more expensive.

Lee's Resthouse & Café (☎ 784491; joejack@tm.net.my; s/d RM50/60; ❄) If you want accommodation near the bus stand, this small, clean hotel is a good option. Breakfast is included in the refreshingly cool air-conditioned restaurant.

There are bakeries and cafés in town, a short walk from the causeway.

GETTING THERE & AWAY

Coming into Semporna, buses and minivans drop passengers around the Shell petrol station in the town centre. Minivans leave for Tawau (RM5, 1½ hours), Lahad Datu (2½ hours, RM12) and Sandakan (RM25).

Pulau Sipadan

This small island 36km off the southeast coast of Sabah attracts experienced and novice divers from all over Asia and further afield. Sipadan is the tip of a limestone pinnacle that rises 600m from the seabed. Within 25m of the eastern side of the island you can float over a near-vertical 'wall' and gaze into the inky depths. It's rather awe-inspiring; myriads of colourful tropical fish swim in the warm water near the surface, but deep down huge gropers and wrasse nose about, and the water gets so dark you don't know what may be lurking there.

The best way to find out is to scuba dive down the wall. The sea is teeming with marine life and the island is billed as one of the world's great diving destinations.

Sipadan is fringed by a beautiful white-sand beach, but it takes only half an hour to walk around the island and the real fun is under the water. To get the most out of a visit it's best to do a dive package. If you don't dive (yet), you can take a course here.

DIVING

Dives are held from early morning until after dark by all operators, and qualified personnel accompany each trip. All visitors are briefed on local conditions when they arrive, and equipment can be hired on the island or is included in the price of a package.

Diving off the wall can be exhilarating and frightening. The deeper water offshore is home to schools of barracuda and tuna, occasional whale sharks and friendly hammerheads, which sometimes investigate a dive team. Sea turtles are common, and experienced divers can explore an undersea cavern in which turtles periodically lose their way and perish.

The best snorkelling is near the jetty, where you can float over the drop-off and watch a good variety of common wrasse, parrotfish, batfish and others. In the shallow water around the island you won't have to go far to see turtles and you can also snorkel around the dive boats in deeper water. The current over the reef can be quite strong.

Borneo Divers has installed a hyperbaric (decompression) chamber on the island. Make sure your travel insurance covers diving accidents, because the decompression chamber costs US$1000 an hour. Besides, a chamber is not a magic cure for the bends – casualties may need urgent evacuation to Sandakan – so it's worth taking diving-safety instructions to heart.

SLEEPING & EATING

Sipadan has suffered considerably from uncontrolled resort construction and waste from the large number of tourists staying on the island. The number of visitors is now strictly limited to 80 to 100 people per night and permits are required to keep track of numbers. Plans also call for the six remaining dive operators with resorts on Sipadan to form a consortium to provide accommodation – a development that may squeeze out a few of the smaller players. The companies currently operating dive resorts on Sipadan have huts on the causeway by the Dragon Inn – see p392 for a list of dive contacts.

The small number of people allowed on the fragile island, plus the fact that permits need to be arranged, makes booking at least 24 hours in advance necessary. If you don't have time to wait, book early to ensure you get a place.

Accommodation is in comfortable, rather than luxurious, fan-cooled chalets with bathrooms and desalinated showers (some of which have been known to flood the bedroom floor). All meals are included in the packages and the food is generally but not always good; alcoholic drinks are extra.

GETTING THERE & AWAY

The 45-minute boat ride from Semporna is usually included in the dive package. Getting to Sipadan under your own steam is expensive. Hiring a fishing boat for a day trip from Semporna costs around RM250, but a group could share the fee. Dive centres ask about RM400 for their speedboats.

> **SAFETY IN SIPADAN**
>
> In April 2000 the island made world headlines when gunmen from the Filipino Muslim separatist terrorist group Abu Sayyaff landed on the island, overpowered the lone policeman and made off to the Philippines with 20 hostages, including a number of foreign tourists. The island was closed off for a couple of days, but soon got back to business as normal; security on the island and in nearby waters has noticeably increased and visitors can expect more protection than they previously had in these troubled waters. Both geography and ubiquitous traffic between the islands make enforcing security a daunting task, however. The Sipadan hostages were eventually released after nearly five tense months in captivity, but at least one other kidnapping (of Malaysians) has since occurred on the surrounding islands.

Tawau

☎ 089

A mini-boomtown way down south near the Indonesian border, Tawau (pronounced like 'bow-wow') is a centre for the shipping of timber, rubber, Manila hemp, cocoa, copra, tobacco and palm oil. Though Tawau is known as a Bugis city, a massive stilt village east of town houses many of the Filipino and Indonesian immigrants you'll encounter eking out a living on the waterfront. Travellers, especially women, may feel much more comfortable in pairs after dark.

The nearby Tawau Hills Park (see p442) has hot springs and waterfalls and facilities for staying overnight, though it's a little difficult to get to without your own transport.

For most travellers Tawau is a transit point for dive-trip packages to Sipadan or Mabul, and the embarkation point for Tarakan in Kalimantan; but it has its charms nevertheless, especially the fishing boat activity around the fish market.

Tawau is a visa-free port for travel to/from Tarakan and Nunakan in Kalimantan, Indonesia.

INFORMATION

Airline Offices

The **Malaysia Airlines** office (☎ 765522; 8.30am-5pm Mon-Fri, 8am-1pm Sat) is in Wisma SASCO on the eastern edge of the town centre.

Internet Access

Cyberland (☎ 768805; 9am-1am) Upstairs off Jl Musantara near the waterfront. Charges RM3 per hour.

City Internet Zone (☎ 760016; 9am-midnight) Very comfortable place in the eastern part of town on Jl Perbandaran. Rates are RM2 per hour (Monday to Thursday) and RM3 per hour (Friday to Sunday).

MALAYSIAN BORNEO

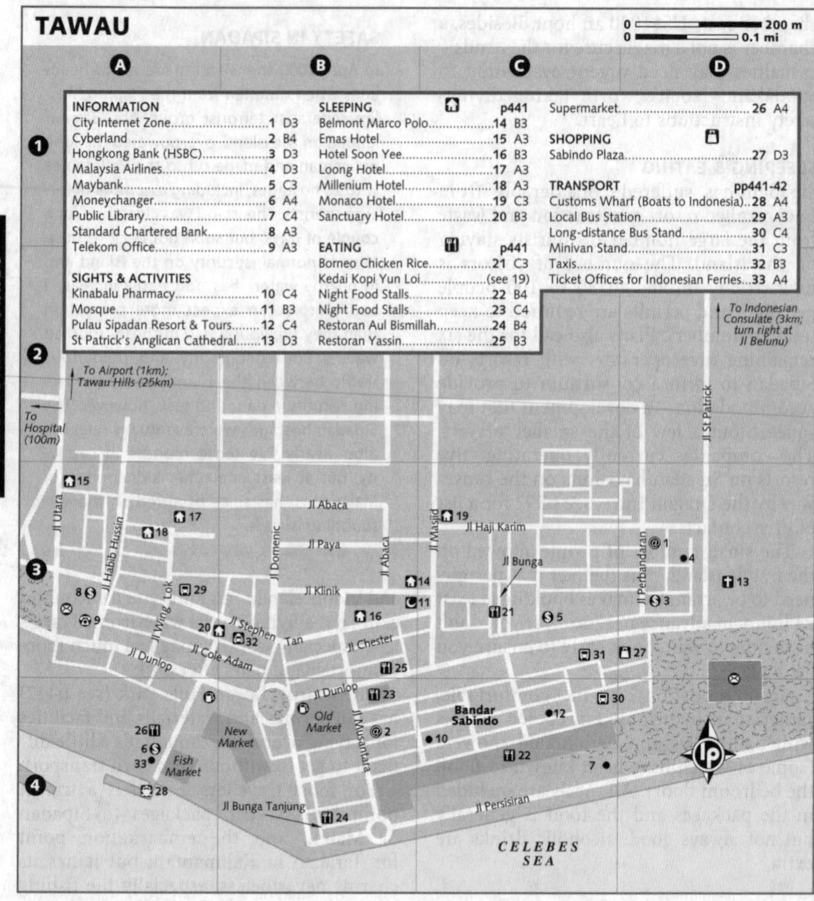

Money

There's a **Maybank** (Jl Dunlop) at the eastern end of town. **PH Pengurup Wang Moneychanger** (☎ 776389; Kompleks Kojasa) is opposite the fish market and only changes cash.

Tourist Information

There's no tourist office, although the reception desk at the Belmont Marco Polo Hotel may be able to help with inquiries.

DIVING

There is so-so diving off **Roach Reef**, halfway between Tawau and Pulau Sipadan. The reef is mainly used for PADI training, though it's best to do training in KK, since transport costs are lower. If you are based in Semporna, you'll have to transfer to Roach Reef via Tawau.

Bookings for Pulau Sipadan, Mabul and other islands off Semporna can be made at the following dive outfits in Tawau:

North Borneo Dive & Sea Sports (☎ 769950; www.fortunecity.com/marina/paradise/132; Ground fl, Grace Inn, Jl Haji Karim) Offers dive courses as well as trips to Sipadan, Roach Reef and other islands, including some across the border in Indonesia.

Pulau Sipadan Resort & Tours (☎ 765200; www.sipadan-resort.com) Does trips to islands around Semporna, including Sipadan. Also does trips to Pulau Lankayan.

Sipadan Water Village Resort (☎ 752996; www.sipadan-village.com.my) Runs the luxurious resort on Pulau Mabul, off Semporna.

Recent government agreements have opened the door for dive trips from Sabah to unexploited areas nearby in Indonesia, such as **Pulau Sangalaki**, about 150km southeast of Tarakan; there are 11 dive sites around the island, which is noted for its varied and abundant sightings of larger fish and marine species. Other dive spots include Pulau Kakaban and Pulau Maratua.

SLEEPING

Budget

The so-called budget hotels in Tawau are poor value for money. The best of the bunch is the **Hotel Soon Yee** (☎ 772447; 1362 Jl Stephen Tan; s/d RM30/34; ❄) This is generally a well-run place, though rooms may be a bit musty. There are a few simple fan-cooled rooms for RM18.

Mid-Range

By far the bulk of Tawau's hotels are mid-range and there are lots of decent choices.

Loong Hotel (☎ 765308; fax 750236; 3868 Jl Abaca; s/d RM45/70; ❄) This well-run and clean hotel has fairly large rooms, though the double rooms are better value. Its location on the relatively quiet Jl Abaca makes it a good mid-range choice.

Millenium Hotel (☎ 771155; fax 755511; 561 Jl Bakau; s/d RM65/75; ❄) Similar to the Loong Hotel but slightly higher in quality, this friendly place has airy, bright rooms and is located on a quiet street.

Monaco Hotel (☎ 776655; fax 756655; Jl Masjid; r RM70; ❄) The rooms here are good value, even without a RM20 discount. The staff are accommodating and it's in a quiet spot away from the main thoroughfare.

Sanctuary Hotel (☎ 751155; fax 751555; 4263 Jl Chester; s/d RM55/70; ❄) Another good mid-range option with clean and spacious rooms though not as quiet as some of the hotels already mentioned. It compensates by being close to the wharves and fish market. The taxi stand is right outside the door.

Top End

Belmont Marco Polo (☎ 777988; bmph@tm.net.my; Jl Klinik; s/d RM165/178; ❄) Definitely the best place to stay in Tawau. The rooms are roomy and comfortable. There's a business centre, coffee shop and an elegant Chinese restaurant. The front desk can arrange airport transfer for RM28 and car hire.

Emas Hotel (☎ 762000; fax 763569; Jl Utara; s/d R130/145; ❄) This business-style hotel isn't as nice as the Belmont, but certainly a step up from the mid-range offerings. The rooms are a little small; larger executive suites are available for RM210. An airport pick-up and drop-off shuttle service is RM15.

EATING

There's plenty of choice in Tawau. Hawkers' stalls are plentiful and seem to spring up wherever there's a vacant lot. Tawau is also renowned in Sabah for its seafood, not least because it is comparatively cheap. The evening food stalls that set up in the large parking area off Jl Dunlop are very good, with all kinds of Indonesian and Malay favourites and some of the best seafood in town. There's a lively atmosphere and it's popular with locals.

Kedai Kopi Yun Loi (☎ 765798; Jl Masjid; dishes RM5-10) For delicious noodles, dumplings and fruit juices, try this bustling Chinese *kedai kopi*. It's a good place to have Chinese-style breakfast if you can find a place to sit down. The Loong Hotel also has a decent Chinese coffee shop.

Restoran Aul Bismillah (☎ 764675; Jl Bunga Tan Jung; dishes RM4-10) An unpretentious outdoor restaurant that's good for catching the ocean breeze, this is a nice spot to have a break or eat dinner and watch the sunset. Malay halal dishes are the main items available.

Borneo Chicken Rice (☎ 773989; 250 Jl Masjid; RM10-20; 🕑 9.30am-9.30pm Sat-Thu) A popular place for family outings on Sunday, this buffet-style restaurant has a wide range of Malay dishes to choose from as well as tasty desserts and delicious juices, floats and milkshakes. In the evening, it turns the tables into *steamboats* (hotpot) at RM18 per person.

A good standby for *murtabak* and curries is the **Restoran Yassin** (☎ 754701; 52 Jl Dunlop; dishes RM3-6).

If you're craving Western food, the **Belmont Marco Polo** has a Sunday brunch from 11am to 2pm (RM16.80 per person) and a BBQ buffet every Friday from 6.30pm to 9.30pm (RM27.50 per person).

GETTING THERE & AWAY

Air

Malaysia Airlines has flights to KK (RM96, 8 daily) and Sandakan (RM74, 2 daily). Twin Otters also fly twice-weekly to Sandakan

(RM61) and Tarakan in Kalimantan, Indonesia (RM89, 40 minutes).

Air Asia has two daily direct flights to Tawau from KL.

Boat

Boats for Indonesia leave from the customs wharf next to the fish market. Purchase tickets at either of the shipping booths near the customs wharf opposite the fish market. There are daily departures to Pulau Nunukan and a sign displays the next sailing times. To get to Tarakan you first have to take a boat to Pulau Nunukan (RM25, 1 hour). Tarakan is another three hours from Nunukan by boat (RM70).

Although this route is ostensibly visa-free, don't take any chances. Check with the Indonesian consulate in Tawau (see p540) or plan on getting a visa beforehand as some travellers have run into problems when they got to Nunukan. Ringgit can be exchanged for rupiah at the moneychanger near the ticket booths.

Bus

Express buses for KK and Sandakan depart from the vacant lot in front of the public library at the eastern end of the town centre. Minibuses and minivans for other destinations depart from the block next to Sabindo Plaza, off Jl Dunlop.

Express buses to KK (RM50, 10 hours) and Sandakan (RM28, 5 hours) leave daily between 7am and 8pm; there are frequent departures till 9.30am. Book ahead if travelling on the weekend – ticket booths line the street where the buses park. **Tung Ma Express** (☎ 748455) is one of the companies doing the route.

There are frequent minivans to Semporna (RM5, 1½ hours) and Kunak (RM5), Lahad Datu (RM12, 2½ hours) and Sandakan (RM25, 5½hours). These leave from around 8am.

Land Cruisers leave for the long journey over rough roads to Keningau (RM30, 11 hours) from in front of the public library (starting at 8am). This is also an alternative route to Sapulut (RM20, 8 hours) if you are planning to visit Batu Punggul (see p405).

GETTING AROUND

Tawau has a new airport 25km from town on the main highway to Sandakan. At the time of writing there was no bus to the airport; check with your hotel. A taxi will cost RM35. The Belmont (RM28) and Emas (RM15) hotels have shuttle services which you may be able to take.

Tawau Hills Park

Hemmed in by agriculture and human habitation this small reserve has forested hills rising dramatically from the surrounding plain. The park was declared in 1979 to protect the water catchment for settlements in the area, but not before most of the accessible rainforest had been logged. Much of the remaining forest clings to steep-sided ridges that rise to 1310m Gunung Magdalena. Admission to the park costs RM10.

On a clear day the park's peaks make a fine sight. A trail leads to **hot springs** and a waterfall three hours' walk north of the park headquarters, and there's a 30-minute walk to 530m **Bombalai Hill** to the south.

There's accommodation at **Tawau Hills Park headquarters** (Taman Bukit Tawau; ☎ 753564; dm RM20, chalet RM200). Rates are lower on weekdays.

Tawau Hills is about 25km northwest of Tawau. A taxi there will cost about RM30. It's very popular with local residents and can get crowded on weekends.

Singapore

RICHARD I'ANSON

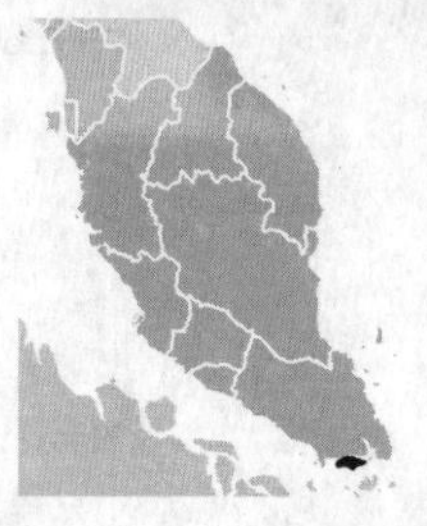

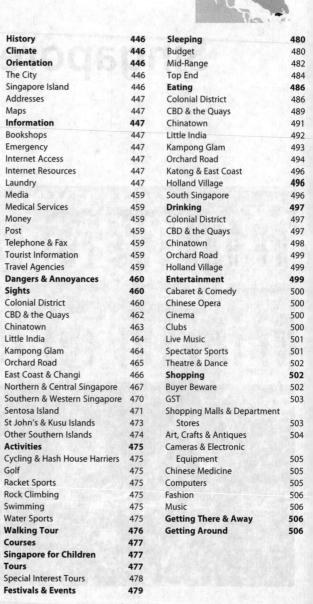

Singapore

CONTENTS

Ditch the image of Singapore as boringly sterile – to our minds it's one of the more enjoyable of the region's cities. As you zoom from marvellous Changi International Airport, one of the world's top travel hubs, along the lushly tree-shaded expressway or on the zippy Mass Rapid Transit (MRT) train line you'll soon realise why it's also known as a garden city and is famous for its smooth efficiency. Greenery is everywhere, as are shops – Orchard Road being the irresistible magnet of this island's consumerist economy.

Singapore's mouthwatering food scene is its biggest draw card, though. A night at a bustling hawker centre will not only introduce you to a fantastic range of Asian dishes but will also be light on your pocket. If you want to indulge, then Singapore also delivers, with some of the most innovative, stylish restaurants in the region and a range of top-class hotels culminating in Raffles, a timeless symbol of colonial luxury.

It's not all about shopping and eating. Singapore offers a good range of outdoor activities including walking, mountain biking and water sports. The striking architecture of the Esplanade – Theatres on the Bay is the latest, most high-profile example of Singapore's desire to pitch itself as the epitome of a modern metropolis and an arts hub for the region. Thankfully, elements of Singapore's colourful, rakish past still survive, as do the cultures of China, India and Malay Muslims, all combining for a unique Southeast Asian experience.

HIGHLIGHTS

- Discovering the region's art and culture in the fascinating **Asian Civilisations Museum** (p460)
- Sneaking up on lions and tigers on the night safari, and checking out monkeys and elephants at the **Singapore Zoological Gardens** (p467)
- Admiring the orchids and other tropical finery in the serene **Botanic Gardens** (p465)
- Visiting **Little India** (p464) on Sunday evening when it's as colourful as a Bollywood musical
- Taking tea, attending Chinese opera and visiting the Chinatown Heritage Centre – the full **Chinatown** experience (p463)
- Getting your tired shopper's limbs massaged by a reflexologist on **Orchard Road** (p465)
- Tucking into **hawker stall delights** (p487) at the utterly authentic Tiong Bahru Cooked Food Centre, or Chomp Chomp in Serangoon Gardens
- Taking in a cultural performance at the modern architectural landmark **Esplanade – Theatres on the Bay** (p460)
- Swimming with the sharks at **Underwater World** (p472) on Sentosa Island
- Slinging back cocktails at the regal **Raffles Hotel** (p460)

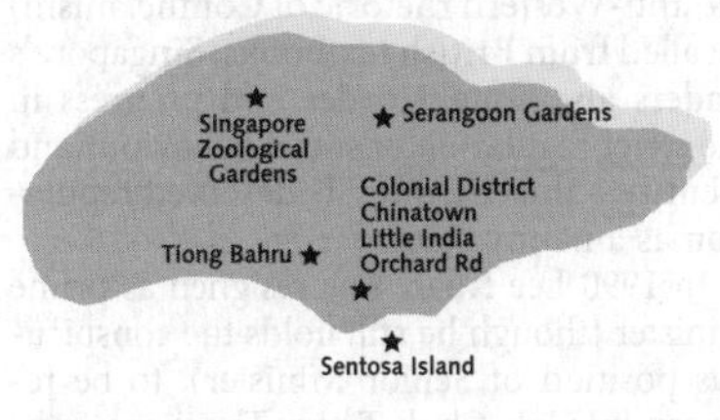

NO LOCAL TELEPHONE CODE	POPULATION: 4.13 MILLION	AREA: 6823 SQ KM

HISTORY

Singapore got its big break on the world stage when Sir Thomas Stamford Raffles arrived in 1819 to make the island into a bastion of the British Empire. It prospered in its role as a trade hub for Southeast Asia, attracting large scale immigration of Chinese workers, some of whom intermarried with local Malay women to form the Peranakan people and culture (p43).

The glory days of Empire came to an abrupt end on 15 February 1942 when the Japanese invaded Singapore. For the rest of WWII the Japanese ran the island with much brutality, infamously encapsulated for many foreigners in the internment of prisoners of war at Changi Prison (it should also be noted though that thousands of locals, particularly Chinese, suffered too). Although the British were welcomed back to the island after the war, it was clear that the Empire's days in the region were numbered.

The socialist People's Action Party (PAP) was founded in 1954 with Lee Kuan Yew, a third-generation Straits-born Chinese, Cambridge-educated lawyer, as its secretary general. The shrewdly political Lee led the PAP to victory in elections held in 1959, becoming the first Singaporean prime minister – a post he held in his iron grip for over 30 years. Although Singapore's situation looked grim when it was kicked out of the nascent federation of Malaysia in 1965, Lee set to work making the most of one-party rule, pushing through an ambitious industrialisation programme for the island which had no natural resources beyond its labour force.

Housing and urban renovation, in particular, have been keys to PAP's success – by the mid-1990s, the city-state had the world's highest rate of home ownership. Living out 'social engineering dreams' (as couched in the anti-Western rhetoric of Confucianism) recalled from British textbooks, Singapore's leaders also sought order and progress in the strict regulation of social behaviour and identity – thus earning its deserved reputation as a nanny state.

In 1990 Lee Kuan Yew resigned as prime minister (though he still holds the conspicuous position of Senior Minister), to be replaced by Goh Chok Tong. There are signs that the government is loosening up in its paternalistic role, but as the 2001 election showed – when the PAP won before even one vote was cast because of the lack of opposition candidates – it's not ready to let Singaporeans grow up fully yet. Goh announced in 2002 that he would be stepping down before the next election in 2007, to make way for a new generation of leaders. His anointed successor, Lee Hsien Loong, Deputy Prime Minister and Minister for Defence as well as being Lee Kuan Yew's son, is expected to take over the top job well before this election.

CLIMATE

Practically on the equator, Singapore is constantly hot (the temperature never drops below 20°C) and humid, and gets fairly steady year-round rainfall. The wettest months are November to January, the driest May to July.

ORIENTATION

Singapore is a city, an island and a country. While there are built-up, high-density areas all around the island, the main city area is in the south.

The City

The Singapore River is at the heart of the city. Just south of the river mouth is the central business district (CBD), centred on Raffles Place, and along the river banks are the popular renovated districts of Boat Quay, Clarke Quay and Robertson Quay. To the southwest Chinatown adjoins the CBD.

North of the river is the colonial district, which has many reminders of British rule, as well as a number of top-end hotels and shopping centres. Further north are Little India, centred on Serangoon Rd, and Kampong Glam, the Muslim centre of the city.

From the colonial district, Bras Basah Rd heads northwest to become Orchard Rd, Singapore's premier shopping centre, with dozens of luxury hotels, shopping malls, restaurants and bars. Orchard Rd becomes Tanglin Rd at its far western end, leading into Napier Rd and on to the Botanic Gardens.

Singapore Island

To the west of the island, the predominantly industrial area of Jurong contains a number of tourist attractions. Heading south you'll find the recreational island of Sentosa.

Eastern Singapore has some interesting suburbs (Geylang, Katong), a major beach park and Changi International Airport. The northeastern parts are home to some huge housing developments. The central north of the island has much of Singapore's undeveloped land, most of the remaining forest and Singapore's zoo.

Addresses

Unlike many cities in Asia, Singapore is well laid out, with signposted streets and logically numbered buildings. As many of the shops, businesses and residences are in high-rise buildings, addresses are often preceded by the number of the floor and then the shop or apartment number. Addresses do not quote the district or suburb. For example, 05-01 The Heeren, 260 Orchard Rd, is outlet No 01 on the 5th floor of The Heeren building.

Maps

Various maps, many in Japanese as well as English, are available free at tourist offices, the airport on arrival, and at some accommodation and shopping centres. *The Official Map of Singapore*, free from the Singapore Tourism Board (STB) and hotels everywhere, is very good and very easy to follow. Of the commercial maps, Nelles and Periplus maps are good. The *Singapore Street Directory* is essential if you plan to drive. Check out Lonely Planet's *Singapore City Map*, a full-colour, laminated fold-out map with a full index of streets and sights.

INFORMATION

Bookshops

Borders (Map pp456-7; ☎ 6235 7146; 01-00 Wheelock Place)
Kinokuniya (Map pp456-7; ☎ 6737 5021; 03-10/15 Ngee Ann City, 391 Orchard Rd)
Select Books (Map pp456-7; ☎ 6732 1515; www.selectbooks.com.sg; 03-15 Tanglin Shopping Centre,19 Tanglin Rd) Specialises in Southeast Asian titles. Check their website; it has a wealth of information on local writers and books.
Sunny Books (Map pp456-7; ☎ 6733 1583; 03-58/59 Far East Plaza, 14 Scotts Rd; 🕒 10am-8pm Mon-Sat, 11am-6pm alternate Sun) For second-hand books.

Emergency

Fire/Ambulance (☎ 995)
Police (☎ 999)

Internet Access

There are numerous outlets where you can access the Net in Singapore (from around S$5 per hour), and many places to stay (even budget places) have Internet access. Try the following places:

Book Café (Map pp452-3; 01-02 Seng Kee Bldg, 20 Martin Rd; 🕒 8.30am-10.30pm Sun-Thu, 8.30am-1.30pm Fri & Sat)
Chills Café (Map pp452-3; 01-07 Stamford House, 39 Stamford Rd; 🕒 9am-midnight)
E-Games (Map pp456-7; 03-08 Cathay Cineleisure Orchard, 8 Grange Rd; 🕒 10am-midnight)
Mega Cybernet (Map pp452-3; 04-16 Pearl Centre, 100 Eu Tong Sen St; 🕒 11am-11.30pm)
Pacific Coffee Company (Map pp452-3; -26 City Link Mall; 🕒 8am-10.30pm Mon-Fri, 9am-midnight Sat-Sun)
Selegie Cyber (Map p458; 185 Selegie Rd; 🕒 10am-midnight)
Wheelpower Rent-a-Bike (Map p458; ☎ 1800-238 2388; 91 Bencoolen St; 🕒 9.30am-7pm)

There's also an Internet café in the transit lounge of Terminal 2 at Changi International Airport.

Internet Resources

Asia One (www.asia1.com.sg) The website of the company that owns Singapore's newspapers, with links to the *Straits Times*, the *New Paper* and the *Business Times*
Changi Airport (www.changi.airport.com.sg) A detailed guide to Singapore's world-leading airport
Happening.com (www.happening.com.sg) An offbeat, online listings magazine with articles, reviews and regularly updated 'what's on' information
Singapore Government (www.gov.sg) This website has all the official info you could wish for on the island state
Singapore Tourism (www.visitsingapore.com) Singapore Tourism's site, with plenty of links to things to see and do
Unorthodox Singapore (www.geocities.com/TheTropics/7222/) Local guy Robin has created this interesting, quirky look at the island with plenty of useful info and links

Laundry

Singapore has plenty of laundries – there's one in the basement of **Tanglin Mall** (Map pp456-7; 163 Tanglin Rd; 🕒 10am-9pm) – although you will generally have to wait a couple of days for your laundry to come back to you washed and pressed. Laundries are listed in the buying guide of the *Yellow Pages*. Expect to pay around S$3 to have a small item such as a skirt, blouse or slacks/trousers washed, and S$5 for dresses.

(Continued on page 459)

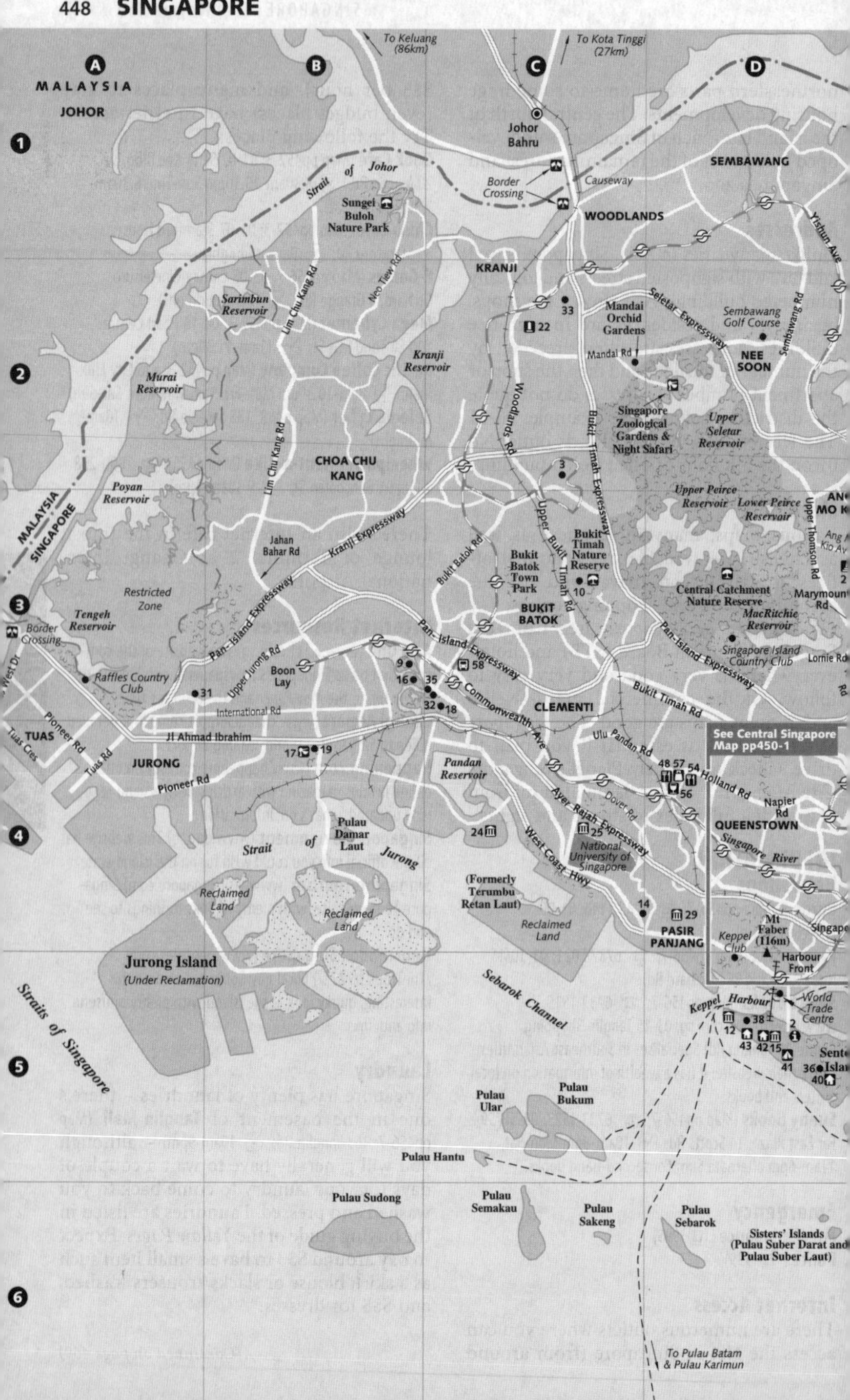

MALAYSIA
JOHOR
To Keluang (86km)
To Kota Tinggi (27km)
Johor Bahru
Strait of Johor
Border Crossing
Causeway
SEMBAWANG
WOODLANDS
Sungei Buloh Nature Park
KRANJI
Sarimbun Reservoir
Lim Chu Kang Rd
Neo Tiew Rd
Mandai Orchid Gardens
Seletar Expressway
Sembawang Golf Course
Sembawang Rd
Yishun Ave
Mandai Rd
NEE SOON
Kranji Reservoir
Murai Reservoir
Woodlands Rd
Bukit Timah Expressway
Singapore Zoological Gardens & Night Safari
Upper Seletar Reservoir
CHOA CHU KANG
Poyan Reservoir
Upper Peirce Reservoir
Lower Peirce Reservoir
Upper Thomson Rd
MALAYSIA
SINGAPORE
Kranji Expressway
Jahan Bahar Rd
Bukit Batok Rd
Bukit Batok Town Park
Upper Bukit Timah Rd
Bukit Timah Nature Reserve
Restricted Zone
Pan-Island Expressway
Tengeh Reservoir
Central Catchment Nature Reserve
MacRitchie Reservoir
Marymount Rd
BUKIT BATOK
Singapore Island Country Club
Lornie Rd
Border Crossing
Raffles Country Club
Upper Jurong Rd
Boon Lay
Commonwealth Ave
CLEMENTI
Bukit Timah Rd
International Rd
TUAS
Pioneer Rd
Tuas Cres
Tuas Rd
Jl Ahmad Ibrahim
JURONG
Pioneer Rd
Pandan Reservoir
Ulu Pandan Rd
Holland Rd
See Central Singapore Map pp450-1
Napier Rd
QUEENSTOWN
Dover Rd
Ayer Rajah Expressway
West Coast Hwy
Pulau Damar Laut
Strait of Jurong
National University of Singapore
Singapore River
(Formerly Terumbu Retan Laut)
Reclaimed Land
Reclaimed Land
Reclaimed Land
PASIR PANJANG
Mt Faber (116m)
Keppel Club
Harbour Front
Jurong Island (Under Reclamation)
Sebarok Channel
Keppel Harbour
World Trade Centre
Straits of Singapore
Pulau Ular
Pulau Bukum
Pulau Hantu
Pulau Sudong
Pulau Semakau
Pulau Sakeng
Pulau Sebarok
Sisters' Islands (Pulau Suber Darat and Pulau Suber Laut)
To Pulau Batam & Pulau Karimun

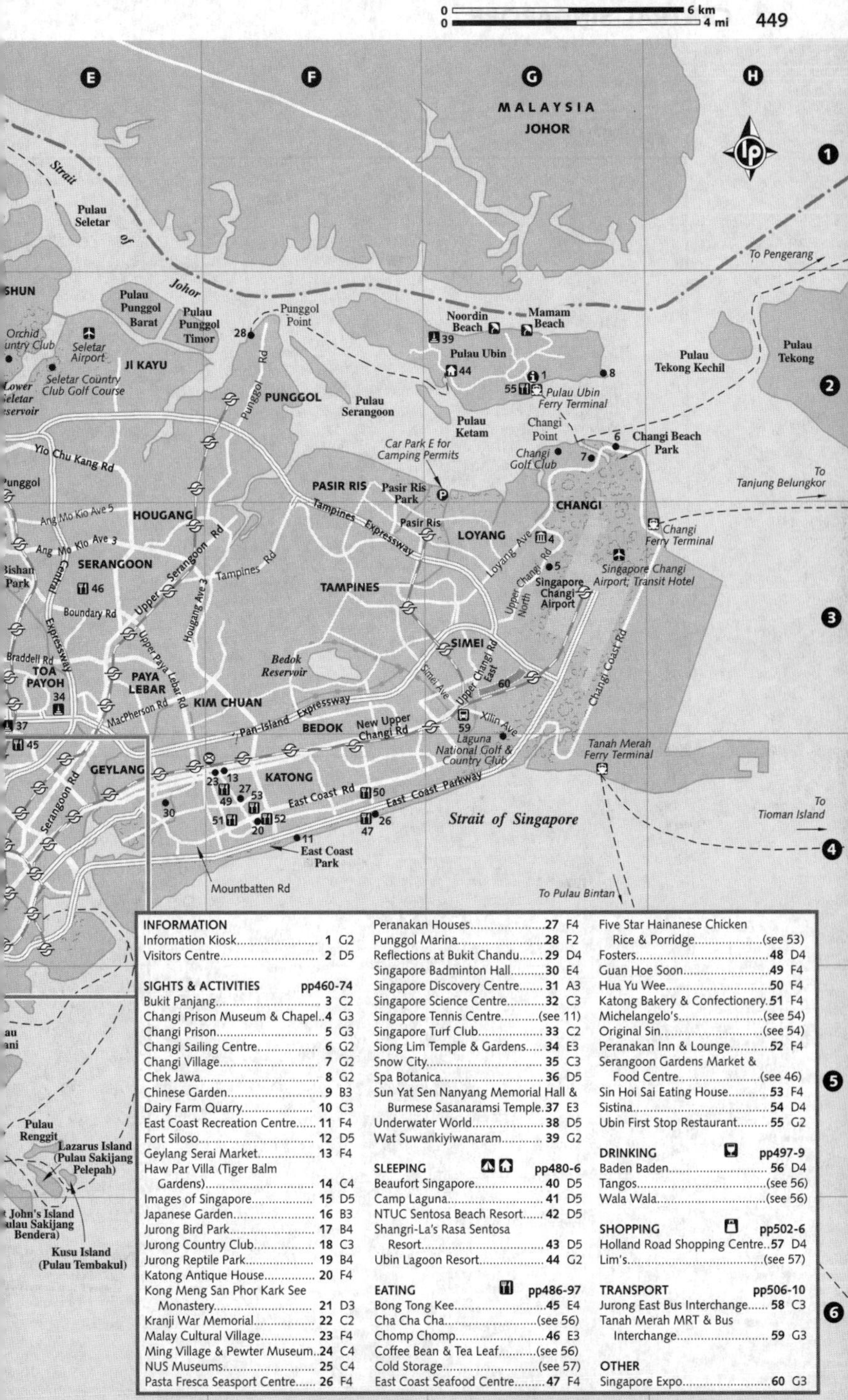
0 6 km
0 4 mi
E
F
G
H
MALAYSIA
JOHOR
Strait of Johor
Pulau Seletar
Pulau Punggol Barat
Pulau Punggol Timor
Punggol Point
Noordin Beach
Mamam Beach
Pulau Ubin
Pulau Ubin Ferry Terminal
Pulau Tekong Kechil
Pulau Tekong
To Pengerang
Orchid Country Club
Seletar Airport
JI KAYU
Seletar Country Club Golf Course
Lower Seletar Reservoir
PUNGGOL
Punggol Rd
Pulau Serangoon
Pulau Ketam
Changi Point
Changi Beach Park
Car Park E for Camping Permits
Changi Golf Club
Yio Chu Kang Rd
PASIR RIS
Pasir Ris Park
Pasir Ris
Tampines Expressway
CHANGI
To Tanjung Belungkor
Changi Ferry Terminal
HOUGANG
Ang Mo Kio Ave 5
Ang Mo Kio Ave 3
SERANGOON
Upper Serangoon Rd
Tampines Rd
LOYANG
Loyang Ave
Upper Changi Rd North
Singapore Changi Airport; Transit Hotel
Singapore Changi Airport
Bishan Park
Central Expressway
Boundary Rd
Hougang Ave 3
TAMPINES
Upper Paya Lebar Rd
SIMEI
Simei Ave
Upper Changi Rd East
Changi Coast Rd
Braddell Rd
TOA PAYOH
PAYA LEBAR
Bedok Reservoir
MacPherson Rd
KIM CHUAN
Pan-Island Expressway
BEDOK
New Upper Changi Rd
Xilin Ave
Laguna National Golf & Country Club
Tanah Merah Ferry Terminal
GEYLANG
KATONG
Serangoon Rd
East Coast Rd
East Coast Parkway
Strait of Singapore
To Tioman Island
East Coast Park
Mountbatten Rd
To Pulau Bintan
Pulau Renggit
Lazarus Island (Pulau Sakijang Pelepah)
St John's Island (Pulau Sakijang Bendera)
Kusu Island (Pulau Tembakul)
INFORMATION
Information Kiosk 1 G2
Visitors Centre 2 D5
SIGHTS & ACTIVITIES pp460-74
Bukit Panjang 3 C2
Changi Prison Museum & Chapel 4 G3
Changi Prison 5 G3
Changi Sailing Centre 6 G2
Changi Village 7 G2
Chek Jawa 8 G2
Chinese Garden 9 B3
Dairy Farm Quarry 10 C3
East Coast Recreation Centre 11 F4
Fort Siloso 12 D5
Geylang Serai Market 13 F4
Haw Par Villa (Tiger Balm Gardens) 14 C4
Images of Singapore 15 D5
Japanese Garden 16 B3
Jurong Bird Park 17 B4
Jurong Country Club 18 C3
Jurong Reptile Park 19 B4
Katong Antique House 20 F4
Kong Meng San Phor Kark See Monastery 21 D3
Kranji War Memorial 22 C2
Malay Cultural Village 23 F4
Ming Village & Pewter Museum 24 C4
NUS Museums 25 C4
Pasta Fresca Seasport Centre 26 F4
Peranakan Houses 27 F4
Punggol Marina 28 F2
Reflections at Bukit Chandu 29 D4
Singapore Badminton Hall 30 E4
Singapore Discovery Centre 31 A3
Singapore Science Centre 32 C3
Singapore Tennis Centre (see 11)
Singapore Turf Club 33 C2
Siong Lim Temple & Gardens 34 E3
Snow City 35 C3
Spa Botanica 36 D5
Sun Yat Sen Nanyang Memorial Hall & Burmese Sasanaramsi Temple 37 E3
Underwater World 38 D5
Wat Suwankiyiwanaram 39 G2
SLEEPING pp480-6
Beaufort Singapore 40 D5
Camp Laguna 41 D5
NTUC Sentosa Beach Resort 42 D5
Shangri-La's Rasa Sentosa Resort 43 D5
Ubin Lagoon Resort 44 G2
EATING pp486-97
Bong Tong Kee 45 E4
Cha Cha Cha (see 56)
Chomp Chomp 46 E3
Coffee Bean & Tea Leaf (see 56)
Cold Storage (see 57)
East Coast Seafood Centre 47 F4
Five Star Hainanese Chicken Rice & Porridge (see 53)
Fosters 48 D4
Guan Hoe Soon 49 F4
Hua Yu Wee 50 F4
Katong Bakery & Confectionery 51 F4
Michelangelo's (see 54)
Original Sin (see 54)
Peranakan Inn & Lounge 52 F4
Serangoon Gardens Market & Food Centre (see 46)
Sin Hoi Sai Eating House 53 F4
Sistina 54 D4
Ubin First Stop Restaurant 55 G2
DRINKING pp497-9
Baden Baden 56 D4
Tangos (see 56)
Wala Wala (see 56)
SHOPPING pp502-6
Holland Road Shopping Centre 57 D4
Lim's (see 57)
TRANSPORT pp506-10
Jurong East Bus Interchange 58 C3
Tanah Merah MRT & Bus Interchange 59 G3
OTHER
Singapore Expo 60 G3

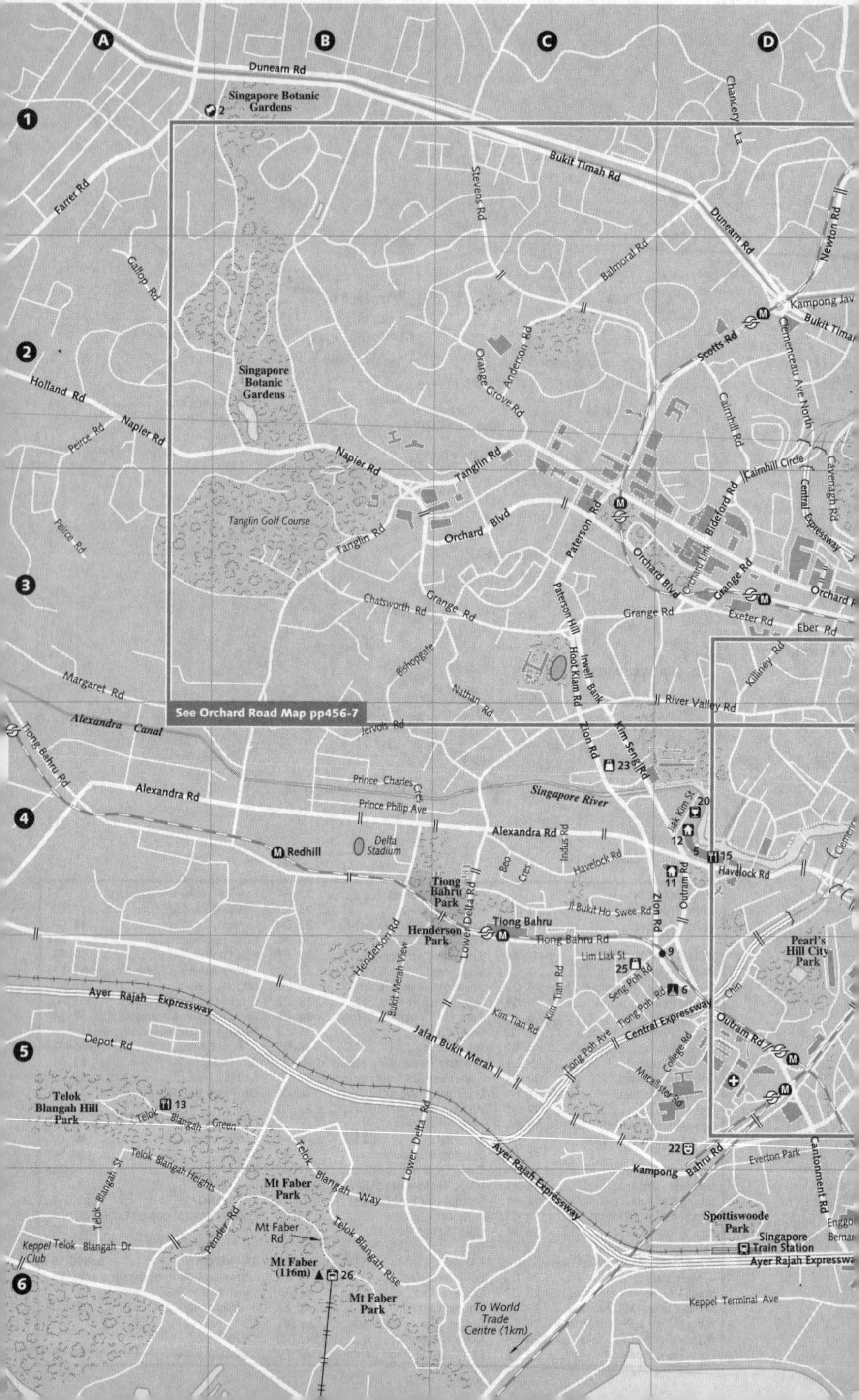

A
B
C
D
1
2
3
4
5
6

Dunearn Rd
Singapore Botanic Gardens
2
Farrer Rd
Bukit Timah Rd
Stevens Rd
Chancery La
Dunearn Rd
Newton Rd
Gallop Rd
Balmoral Rd
Kampong Java
Bukit Timah
Scotts Rd
Clemenceau Ave North
Anderson Rd
Orange Grove Rd
Singapore Botanic Gardens
Holland Rd
Napier Rd
Peirce Rd
Cairnhill Rd
Cairnhill Circle
Cavenagh Rd
Central Expressway
Napier Rd
Tanglin Rd
Bideford Rd
Tanglin Golf Course
Orchard Blvd
Paterson Rd
Peirce Rd
Tanglin Rd
Orchard Link
Orchard Blvd
Grange Rd
Orchard Rd
Chatsworth Rd
Grange Rd
Paterson Hill
Grange Rd
Exeter Rd
Eber Rd
Hoot Kiam Rd
Iwell Bank
Bishopgate
Killiney Rd
Margaret Rd
Nathan Rd
River Valley Rd

See Orchard Road Map pp456-7

Alexandra Canal
Jervois Rd
Tiong Bahru Rd
Zion Rd
Kim Seng Rd
23
Prince Charles Cres
Alexandra Rd
Singapore River
Prince Philip Ave
Jiak Kim St
20
12
Alexandra Rd
Indus Rd
Redhill
Delta Stadium
5
15
Havelock Rd
Beo Cres
Havelock Rd
11
Outram Rd
Tiong Bahru Park
Lower Delta Rd
Bukit Ho Swee Rd
Zion Rd
Henderson Rd
Henderson Park
Tiong Bahru
Tiong Bahru Rd
Pearl's Hill City Park
Lim Liak St
9
25
Seng Poh Rd
Tiong Poh Rd
6
Bukit Merah View
Kim Tian Rd
Ayer Rajah Expressway
Kim Tian Rd
Central Expressway
Chin
Outram Rd
Depot Rd
Jalan Bukit Merah
Tiong Poh Ave
College Rd
Macalister Rd
Telok Blangah Hill Park
13
Telok Blangah Green
Lower Delta Rd
22
Telok Blangah Heights
Telok Blangah Way
Ayer Rajah Expressway
Kampong Bahru Rd
Everton Park
Cantonment Rd
Telok Blangah St
Mt Faber Park
Spottiswoode Park
Mt Faber Rd
Telok Blangah Rise
Enggor
Bernam
Keppel Club
Telok Blangah Dr
Pender Rd
Singapore Train Station
Ayer Rajah Expressway
Mt Faber (116m)
26
Mt Faber Park
To World Trade Centre (1km)
Keppel Terminal Ave

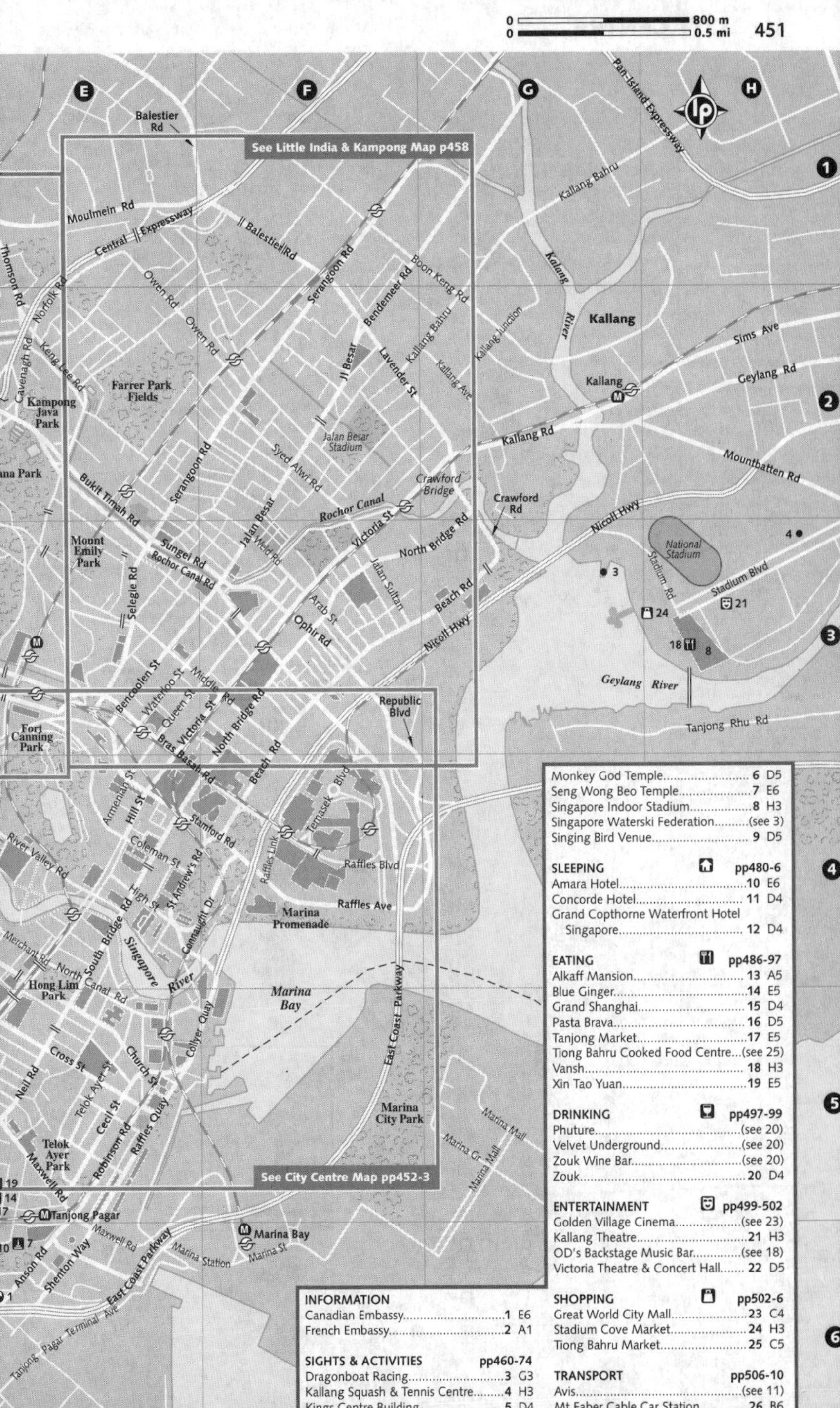
0 800 m
0 0.5 mi
E
F
G
H
1
2
3
4
5
6
See Little India & Kampong Map p458
See City Centre Map pp452-3
Balestier Rd
Moulmein Rd
Central Expressway
Balestier Rd
Thomson Rd
Norfolk Rd
Owen Rd
Serangoon Rd
Bendemeer Rd
Boon Keng Rd
Kallang Bahru
Pan-Island Expressway
Kallang Junction
Kallang River
Kallang
Sims Ave
Geylang Rd
Cavenagh Rd
Keng Lee Rd
Kampong Java Park
Farrer Park Fields
Jl Besar
Lavender St
Kallang Ave
Jalan Besar Stadium
Kallang Rd
Mountbatten Rd
Syed Alwi Rd
Crawford Bridge
Crawford Rd
Rochor Canal
Victoria St
North Bridge Rd
Nicoll Hwy
National Stadium
Stadium Rd
Stadium Blvd
Bukit Timah Rd
Jalan Besar
Weld Rd
Jalan Sultan
Beach Rd
Mount Emily Park
Sungei Rd
Rochor Canal Rd
Selegie Rd
Arab St
Ophir Rd
Geylang River
Bencoolen St
Waterloo St
Middle Rd
Queen St
Republic Blvd
Tanjong Rhu Rd
Fort Canning Park
Bras Basah Rd
Temasek Blvd
Armenian St
Hill St
Stamford Rd
River Valley Rd
Coleman St
St Andrew's Rd
Raffles Link
Raffles Blvd
Raffles Ave
High St
Connaught Dr
Marina Promenade
Merchant Rd
North Canal Rd
South Bridge Rd
Singapore River
Hong Lim Park
Marina Bay
East Coast Parkway
Collyer Quay
Cross St
Church St
Neil Rd
Telok Ayer St
Cecil St
Robinson Rd
Raffles Quay
Marina City Park
Marina Mall
Marina Cr
Telok Ayer Park
Maxwell Rd
Tanjong Pagar
Maxwell Rd
Marina Bay
Marina St
Marina Station
Anson Rd
Shenton Way
East Coast Parkway
Tanjong Pagar Terminal Ave
INFORMATION
Canadian Embassy....1 E6
French Embassy....2 A1
SIGHTS & ACTIVITIES pp460-74
Dragonboat Racing....3 G3
Kallang Squash & Tennis Centre....4 H3
Kings Centre Building....5 D4
Monkey God Temple....6 D5
Seng Wong Beo Temple....7 E6
Singapore Indoor Stadium....8 H3
Singapore Waterski Federation....(see 3)
Singing Bird Venue....9 D5
SLEEPING pp480-6
Amara Hotel....10 E6
Concorde Hotel....11 D4
Grand Copthorne Waterfront Hotel Singapore....12 D4
EATING pp486-97
Alkaff Mansion....13 A5
Blue Ginger....14 E5
Grand Shanghai....15 D4
Pasta Brava....16 D5
Tanjong Market....17 E5
Tiong Bahru Cooked Food Centre...(see 25)
Vansh....18 H3
Xin Tao Yuan....19 E5
DRINKING pp497-99
Phuture....(see 20)
Velvet Underground....(see 20)
Zouk Wine Bar....(see 20)
Zouk....20 D4
ENTERTAINMENT pp499-502
Golden Village Cinema....(see 23)
Kallang Theatre....21 H3
OD's Backstage Music Bar....(see 18)
Victoria Theatre & Concert Hall....22 D5
SHOPPING pp502-6
Great World City Mall....23 C4
Stadium Cove Market....24 H3
Tiong Bahru Market....25 C5
TRANSPORT pp506-10
Avis....(see 11)
Mt Faber Cable Car Station....26 B6

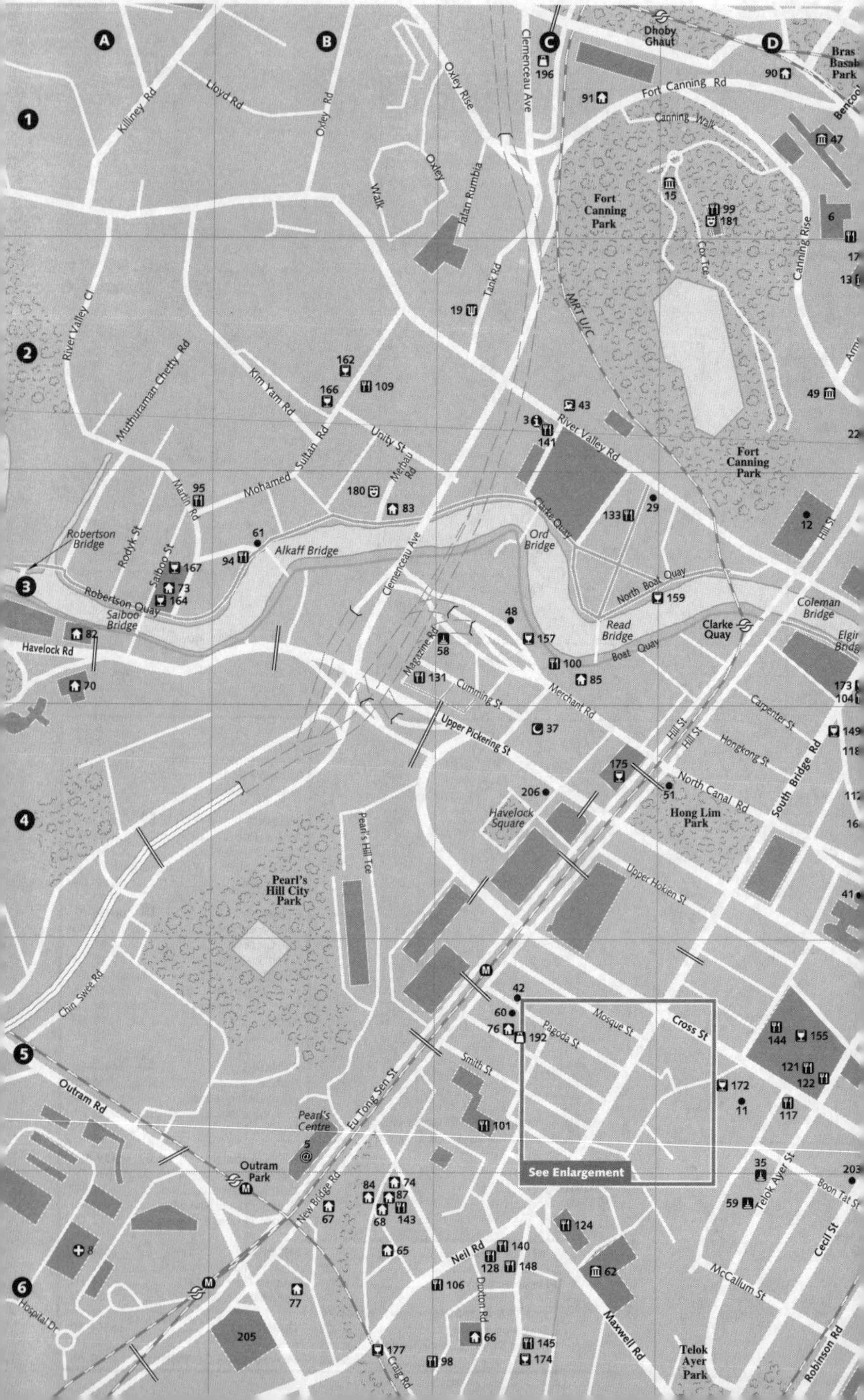

A B C D

1 2 3 4 5 6

Dhoby Ghaut

Bras Basah Park

Bencoolen

Clemenceau Ave

Oxley Rise

Oxley Rd

Lloyd Rd

Killiney Rd

Fort Canning Rd

Canning Walk

Oxley Walk

Jalan Rumbia

Tank Rd

Fort Canning Park

Cox Tce

Canning Rise

MRT U/C

River Valley Cl

Muthuraman Chetty Rd

Kim Yam Rd

Unity St

Merbau Rd

Mohamed Sultan Rd

River Valley Rd

Martin Rd

Rodyk St

Saiboo St

Robertson Bridge

Robertson Quay

Saiboo Bridge

Alkaff Bridge

Havelock Rd

Clarke Quay

Ord Bridge

North Boat Quay

Read Bridge

Boat Quay

Coleman Bridge

Elgin Bridge

Hill St

Magazine Rd

Cumming St

Merchant Rd

Upper Pickering St

Carpenter St

Hongkong St

North Canal Rd

South Bridge Rd

Hong Lim Park

Havelock Square

Pearl's Hill Tce

Pearl's Hill City Park

Upper Hokien St

Chin Swee Rd

Mosque St

Pagoda St

Cross St

Smith St

Eu Tong Sen St

Outram Rd

Pearl's Centre

Outram Park

New Bridge Rd

Neil Rd

Duxton Rd

Maxwell Rd

Telok Ayer St

Boon Tat St

Cecil St

McCallum St

Telok Ayer Park

Robinson Rd

Hospital Dr

Craig Rd

See Enlargement

90 91 196 47 15 99 181 6 17 13 19 162 166 109 49 43 3 141 22 95 180 83 29 133 12 61 94 167 73 164 82 70 159 48 157 58 100 85 131 173 104 37 149 118 175 51 206 112 16 41 42 60 76 192 144 155 121 122 172 11 117 101 5 35 203 59 84 74 87 67 68 143 124 65 140 128 148 62 8 106 77 205 66 177 98 145 174

0
800 m
0
0.5 mi
MRT Marina Line (2005)
Marina Line (2005)
Waterloo St
Queen St
Victoria St
Bras Basah Rd
North Bridge Rd
Middle Rd
Liang Seah St
Purvis St
Seah St
Beach Rd
Rochor Rd
Republic Ave
Republic Blvd
Nicoll Hwy
Temasek Blvd
Temasek Ave
Stamford Rd
War Memorial Park
City Hall
City Link Mall (Underground)
Raffles Link
Raffles Blvd
Coleman St
Hill St
East Coast Parkway
Colombo Ct
High St
St Andrew's Rd
The Padang
Connaught Dr
Esplanade Park
Raffles Ave
Marina Promenade
Esplanade Bridge
Anderson Bridge
Cavenagh Bridge
Singapore River
Marina Bay
Raffles Place
Collyer Quay
Raffles Quay
East Lagoon Link
Mosque St
Cross St
Pagoda St
Temple St
South Bridge Rd
Smith St
Sago St
Ann
Siang Rd
Marina City Park
E
F
G
H
1
2
3
4
5
6

INFORMATION

Chills Cafe....1 E2
Eu Yan Sang....2 G6
Liang Court Tourist Service Centre....3 C2
Malaysian Embassy....4 E2
Mega Cybernet....5 B5
National Library....6 D1
National Parks Board....7 G1
Pacific Coffee Company....(see 97)
Singapore General Hospital....8 A6
Site of New National Library....9 F1
STB Suntec City....(see 189)
STB....(see 187)

SIGHTS & ACTIVITIES pp460-74

Amrita Spa....(see 80)
Armenian Church....10 D2
Art Seasons....11 D5
Art-2 Gallery....12 D3
Asian Civilisations Museum....13 D2
Asian Civilisations Museum....14 E4
At-Sunrice Cooking Academy....(see 181)
Battle Box....15 D1
Bird Sculpture....16 E4
Campers' Corner....17 E2
Cathedral of the Good Shepherd....18 E1
Central Fire Station....(see 22)
Chettiar Hindu Temple....19 C2
Chinatown Heritage Centre....20 F5
City Hall....21 E3
Civil Defence Heritage Gallery....22 D2
Civilian War Memorial....23 F2
Esplanade Jetty....24 F3
First Generation Sculpture....25 E4
Fountain of Wealth....26 G2
Gajah Gallery....(see 12)
Homage to Newton Sculpture....27 E4
Jamae Mosque....28 G5
Keeper Collection....29 C3
Kenko Wellness Boutique....30 G6
Kucinta Sculpture....31 E4
Lim Bo Seng Memorial....32 F3
Maghain Aboth Synagogue....33 E1
Merlion Statue & Merlion Park....34 F4
Nagore Durgha Shrine....35 D6
Old Parliament House....36 E3
Omar Kampong Melaka Mosque....37 C4
Parliament House....38 E3
Progress & Advancement Sculpture....39 E4
Raffles Hotel Museum....(see 193)
Raffles Landing....40 E4
Reclining Figure Sculpture....41 D4
Red Peach Gallery....42 C5
River Valley Swimming Complex....43 C2
Shing's Antique Gallery....44 G5
Singapore Art Museum....45 E1
Singapore Cricket Club....46 E3
Singapore History Museum (closed until 2006)....47 D1
Singapore History Museum....48 C3
Singapore Philatelic Museum....49 D2
Singapore Recreation Club....50 F2
Soobin Art Gallery....(see 12)
Speakers' Corner....51 D4
Sri Mariamman Temple....52 G6
St Andrew's Cathedral....53 E2
St Joseph's Catholic Church....54 E1
Struggle for Survival Sculpture....55 E5
Suntec City Fountain Terrace....(see 103)
Supreme Court....56 E3
Tan Kim Seng Fountain....57 F3
Tan Si Chong Su Temple....58 C3
Thian Hock Keng Temple....59 D6
Thow's Gallery....60 C5
Tyler Print Institute....61 B3
URA Gallery....62 C6
Wak Hai Cheng Bio Temple....63 E5
Yong Gallery....64 G6

SLEEPING pp480-6

Backpacker Cozy Corner Hotel....65 B6
Berjaya Hotel Singapore....66 C6
Chinatown Homestay....67 B6
Chinatown Hotel....68 B6
Conrad Centennial Singapore....69 G2
Copthorne King's Hotel....70 A3
Damenlou Hotel....71 G6
Fullerton Hotel....72 F4
Gallery Hotel....73 A3
Hotel 1929....74 B6
Hotel Inter-Continental Singapore....75 F1
Inn on Temple Street....76 C5
Majestic Hotel....77 B6
Pan Pacific Singapore....78 G2
Raffles Hotel....79 F2
Raffles, The Plaza....80 F2
Ritz-Carlton, Millenia Singapore....81 H3
River View Hotel....82 A3
Robertson Quay Hotel....83 B3
Royal Peacock Hotel....84 B6
Swissôtel Merchant Court Singapore....85 C3
Swissôtel The Stamford Singapore....86 F2
Tropical Hotel....87 B6
Victoria Hotel....88 E1
Waterloo Hostel....89 E1
YMCA International House....90 D1
YWCA Fort Canning Lodge....91 C1

EATING pp486-97

Ah Teng's Bakery....92 F2
Akashi....(see 97)
Belachan....93 F6
Bon Gout....94 B3
Book Café....95 A3
Bras Basah Food Court....96 F1
Bread Talk....97 F2
Broth....98 B6
Café at-sunrice....99 D1
Café Iguana....100 C3
Chinatown Complex Food Centre....101 C5
Christa & Naomi Café (CAN)....102 F1
Coffee Bean & Tea Leaf....103 G1
Coffee Bean & Tea Leaf....104 D3
Colours by the Bay....105 F3
Coriander Leaf....(see 73)
Crystal Jade Kitchen....(see 103)
Da Paolo E Judie....106 C6
Da Paolo....107 G6
Damenlou Swee Kee....(see 71)
Duo....108 G6
Empire Café....(see 92)
En Japanese Dining Bar....109 B2
Equinox....(see 86)
Fat Frog Café....110 D1
Garlic Restaurant....(see 105)
Hai Tien Lo....(see 78)
Haru....111 F4
House of Sundanese Food....112 D4
Ichiban Boshi....(see 105)
Imperial Herbal Restaurant....113 F1
Inagiku....(see 129)
Indochine Alfresco....114 E1
Indochine....115 G6
Indochine....116 E4
Keyaki....(see 78)
Killiney Kopitiam....117 D5

SINGAPORE IN...

Two Days

Start with a refreshing dawn stroll in the **Singapore Botanic Gardens** (p465), followed by breakfast at **Halia** (p494) or **Café Les Amis** (p494). If you don't fancy hitting the shops of nearby Orchard Rd so soon, head over to **Chinatown** (p463) to explore the many temples and the shophouse-lined streets, or browse the antique and art emporiums. Revive yourself with a lunch of Singaporean hawker food at the **Maxwell Rd Food Centre** (p487) or learn to take your tea the Chinese way at **Yixing Yuan Teahouse** (p493).

For an air-conditioned injection of culture take in some of the museums of the colonial district, in particular the **Singapore Art Museum** (p461) or the **Asian Civilisations Museum** (p460). It's now 6pm, so time for a sundowner at **Raffles** (p460) followed by a meal and a sparkling view at either **Equinox** on the 70th floor of the Swissôtel The Stamford Singapore, or **Indochine** (p489) overlooking Boat Quay.

On day two, shop for colourful souvenirs in **Little India** and stop off for a curry at **Banana Leaf Apolo** (p492) or a *dosa* at **Komala Vilas** (p493) before heading over to Kampong Glam to experience a more Islamic side of Singapore.

At night check out the restaurants and bars along **Club St** (p498), or head over to **Mohamed Sultan Road** (p498), the liveliest strip of watering holes in Singapore.

Kinara 118 D4
L'Angelus 119 G6
Lau Pa Sat 120 E6
Lei Garden (see 187)
Lingzhi Vegetarian 121 D5
Maison de Fontaine (see 187)
Mama Africa 122 D5
Marché Movenpick 123 G2
Marché Movenpick (see 189)
Maxwell Rd Food Centre 124 C6
Moomba 125 E4
My Humble House (see 105)
Nan Tai Eating House 126 E1
Nectar 127 G6
Nooch (see 97)
Qun Zhong Eating House 128 C6
Raffles City Food Court 129 F2
Rang Mahal (see 78)
Saffron Bistro 130 E4
Saint Pierre 131 B3
Sakana 132 G1
Sanur (see 103)
Satay Club 133 C3
Seah Street Deli 134 F1
Senso 135 G6
Si Chuan Dou Restaurant 136 E4
Smith St Hawker Stalls 137 F6
Soup Restaurant 138 F6
Soup Restaurant (see 103)
Spizza for Friends 139 G6
Tea Chapter 140 C6
Teaspa (see 129)
Tung Lok 141 C2
Victoria Street Food Centre 142 F1
Vietlang (see 187)
Xin Min Vegetarian Food Court 143 B6
Ya Kun Kaya Toast & Coffee 144 D5
Ya Kun Kaya Toast & Coffee 145 C6
Yet Con 146 F1
Yhingthai Palace 147 F1
Yixing Yuan Teahouse 148 C6

DRINKING pp497-9

Actors' Bar 149 D4
Aphrodisiac Bar 150 G6
Backstage Bar 151 F5
Bar & Billiard Room 152 F2
Bar Sá Vanh (see 115)
Barrio Chino 153 G6
Beaujolais Wine Bar 154 G6
Boom Boom Room 155 D5
bq bar 156 E4
Brewerkz 157 C3
Centro 158 F4
Crazy Elephant 159 C3
Davis Café 160 F6
Embargo (see 158)
Father Flanagans 161 E2
Front Page 162 B2
Gazebo Bar (see 195)
Harry's 163 E4
Insomnia (see 161)
Introbar (see 86)
Liberté (see 161)
Liquid Room 164 A3
Live Jazz @ The Green Room (see 188)
Long Bar (see 195)
Lot, Stock & Barrel 165 F1
Madam Wong's 166 B2
Metz 167 A3
Molly Malone's 168 D4
New Asia Bar & Grill (see 86)
Next Page (see 162)
Paulaner Brauhaus 169 G2
Penny Black 170 E4
Post (see 72)
Red Lantern Beer Garden 171 E5
Shidong 172 D5
Sound Bar (see 164)
South Bridge Jazz 173 D3
Taboo 174 C6
Tong Heritage Bar 175 C4
Union 176 G6
Water Bar 177 B6

ENTERTAINMENT pp499-502

Action Theatre (see 114)
Black Box (see 181)
CalendarOne TicketCharge 178 D2
CalendarOne TicketCharge (see 186)
China Jump (see 161)
Chinese Theatre Circle 179 F6
City Space (see 86)
DBS Drama Centre 180 B3
Drama Centre (see 181)
Fort Canning Centre 181 D1
Guinness Theatre (see 178)
Jubilee Hall (see 193)
Marina Square Complex Cinemas 182 G3
Shaw Towers Cinemas 183 G1
SISTIC 184 E3
Somerset's (see 129)
Substation (see 178)
Suntec City Cinemas (see 185)

SHOPPING pp502-6

British India (see 194)
Carrefour 185 H2
Challenger Superstore 186 E3
CHIJMES 187 E2
Esplanade Mall 188 F3
Funan – The IT Mall (see 186)
Harvey Norman 189 G2
HMV 190 F2
Island & Archipelago (see 187)
Lajeunesse Asian Art 191 G6
Lim's 192 C5
MPH (see 190)
MPH (see 194)
Pagoda House 193 F1
Peter Hoe Evolution (see 187)
Plum Blossoms (see 12)
Plum Blossoms (see 193)
Project Shop Blood Brothers 194 F2
Raffles Hotel Arcade 195 F1
Robinsons (see 194)
Singapore Shopping Centre 196 C1
SISTIC (see 189)
Suntec City Mall 197 G2
Thieves' Market 198 G5
Thossb (see 193)
Tower Records (see 189)
Woods & Woods 199 G6

TRANSPORT pp506-10

Air New Zealand 200 E5
Budget Rent a Car 201 E5
Cathay Pacific Airways (see 200)
Malaysian Airlines (see 196)
Singapore Motor Launch Owners' Association 202 F5
Thai Airways International 203 D6
Thrifty (see 75)

OTHER

Nanyang Academy of Fine Arts 204 F1
Police Cantonment Complex 205 B6
Raffles City Convention Centre (see 194)
Small Claims Tribunal 206 C4

Four Days

To take in Singapore in four days, start off by following the two-day itinerary outlined earlier.

Kick off the third day by venturing out to **Sentosa Island** (p471). Sentosa (which means peace and tranquility) offers plenty to see and do for both adults and children: a great aquarium, beaches, museums, and outdoor activities like bicycling and golf. If it's good weather, take the cable car there or back as the ride offers spectacular views and is one of the best things about visiting the island. In the evening there's a laser light and musical fountain show which is well worth staying on for.

Day four could see you head out to **Pulau Ubin** (p467) for a breather from the fast pace and urban lifestyle of mainland Singapore. Catch bus No 2 in the city and head for the terminal at Changi Village – during the journey you'll have plenty of time to see life as it's lived by millions of Singaporeans in their Housing Development Board (HDB) flats. From Changi Village board the ferry for Pulau Ubin where bikes can be hired for a pedal around this leafy, rural island.

On the way there or back pay your respects at the WWII pilgrimage site, the **Changi Prison Museum & Chapel** (p467). The Changi chapel at the site was built by Allied POWs captured by invading Japanese forces.

Finish off with a slap-up seafood meal at the **East Coast Seafood Centre** (p496), the prime waterfront location ideal for winding down and getting your fingers all messy on a firm Singaporean favourite, delicious Singapore chilli crab.

INFORMATION

Australian High Commission 1 B4
Borders 2 E4
British Council 3 C4
British High Commission 4 C4
Chinese Embassy 5 C4
Comcentre 6 F6
E-Games (see 74)
German Embassy 7 E4
Gleneagles Hospital 8 C4
Indian High Commission 9 D6
Indonesian Embassy 10 C5
Internet 11 E4
Japanese Embassy 12 C3
Kinokuniya (see 80)
Mt Elizabeth Hospital 13 F4
New Zealand Embassy 14 F5
Royal Thai Embassy 15 E4
Select Books (see 82)
Singapore Airlines 16 F5
Singapore Tourism Board (STB) 17 C5
STA Travel 18 G5
Sunny Books (see 79)
Tanglin Clinic (see 82)
US Embassy 19 C4

SIGHTS & ACTIVITIES pp460-74

Istana 20 H4
Kenko (see 82)
Midpoint Orchard 21 G5
National Orchid Garden 22 A3
National Youth Centre Skate Park 23 F5
Ngee Ann Foot Reflexology (see 21)
Peranakan Place 24 G5
Youth Park 25 F5

SLEEPING pp480-6

Elizabeth Singapore 26 F4
Four Seasons Hotel 27 D4
Goodwood Park Hotel 28 F3
Grand Hyatt Singapore 29 E4
Hilton International 30 D4
Le Meridien Singapore 31 G5
Lloyd's Inn 32 G6
Metro-Y Apartments (see 42)
New Sandy's Place 33 F2
Orchard Hotel 34 D4
Regalis Court 35 G6
Regent Singapore 36 C4
RELC International Hotel 37 D3
Sheraton Towers Singapore 38 F3
Singapore Marriott 39 E4
Sloane Court Hotel 40 E2
Traders Hotel Singapore 41 C4
YMCA Metropolitan 42 D2

EATING pp486-97

Akashi (see 44)
Blood Café 43 F5
Bombay Woodlands Restaurant 44 D4
Boon Tong Kee 45 E6
Bread Talk 46 G5
Bread Talk 47 E4
Café Les Amis 48 B3
Coffee Bean & Tea Leaf 49 E4
DKNY Cafe 50 D4
Don (see 63)
Great Treat (see 31)
Halia 51 A3
House of Peranakan Cuisine 52 E4
Imperium 53 F5
Killiney Kopitiam 54 G6
Lingzhi Vegetarian 55 E4
Marché Movenpick 56 F5
Marmalade Pantry (see 50)
Mezza9 (see 29)
Newton Food Centre 57 G3
Nooch 58 E4
Nooch (see 43)
Picnic at Scotts 59 E4
Samy's Curry Restaurant 60 A4
Shashlik 61 D4
Supernature 62 D5
Supernature (see 58)
Takashimaya Food Village (see 53)
Tanglin Mall Food Junction 63 C4
Tanglin Market Place (see 81)
Teaspa (see 43)
Ubar 64 E4

DRINKING pp497-99

Alley Bar 65 G5
Brix (see 29)
Dubliners 66 G5
Ice Cold Beer 67 G5
Martini Bar (see 29)
Mitre Hotel 68 G6
Muddy Murphy's 69 D4
No 5 70 G5
Que Pasa 71 G5
Vincent's 72 E4

ENTERTAINMENT pp499-502

Anywhere 73 D4
Bar None (see 39)
CalendarOne TicketCharge (see 76)
Cineleisure Orchard 74 F5
Cinema (see 75)
Cinema (see 77)
Milieu (see 65)
Punchline Comedy Club (see 39)
SISTIC (see 78)

SHOPPING pp502-6

Akemi Gallery (see 82)
Apple Centre (see 2)
Best Denki (see 80)
Boon's Pottery (see 81)
British India 75 H5
British India (see 81)
British India (see 80)
Forum – Shopping Mall 76 D4
HaKaren Art Gallery (see 82)
Hilton Shopping Gallery (see 30)
Isetan 77 E4
Isetan 78 E4
Kwan Hua Art Gallery (see 82)
Level One Far East Plaza 79 E4
M)phosis (see 80)
Project Shop Blood Brothers (see 16)
Project Shop Blood Brothers (see 78)
Sembawang Music Centre (see 74)
Song+Kelly21 (see 76)
Takashimaya 79 E4
Tanglin Mall 81 C4
Tanglin Shopping Centre 82 D4
Toys 'R' Us (see 76)
Woods & Woods 83 E4

TRANSPORT pp506-10

British Airways 84 F4
Garuda Indonesia 85 H1
Hertz 86 E4
KLM-Royal Dutch Airlines (see 80)
Lufthansa (see 16)
Qantas (see 84)

OTHER

Alliance Française 87 F2
American Club 88 E3
Gymboree Play & Music (see 81)

0 500 m
0 0.3 mi
E
F
G
H
1
2
3
4
5
6
Novena
Moulmein Rd
Barker Rd
Gilstead Rd
Buckley Rd
Gentle Rd
Dunearn Rd
Rochel Canal
Bukit Timah Rd
Chancery La
Khiang Guan Ave
Thomson Rd
Keng Chin Rd
85
United Square
Eew Boon Rd
Newton Rd
Evelyn Rd
Surrey Rd
Balmoral Cres
40
Lincoln Rd
Wee Nam Rd
Norfolk Rd
Balmoral Rd
Sarkies Rd
87
33
Goodwood Hill
Keng Lee Rd
Kampong Java Rd
Newton Circus
Newton
57
Stevens Rd
Cavenagh Rd
Kampong Java Park
Hooper Rd
Monk's Hill Tce
Goodwood Hill
38
Draycott Park
Scotts Rd
Anthony Rd
Winstedt Rd
Clemenceau Ave North
Monk's Hill Rd
Draycott Dr
Draycott Rd
Peck Hay Rd
Cairnhill Rd
28
Claymore Hill
88
86
Cairnhill Circle
Cairnhill Rise
Istana Park
20
Claymore Rd
52
Palais Renaissance
Pacific Plaza
Far East Plaza
79
Mount Elizabeth Rd
26
64
83
Claymore Hill
29
15
Far East Shopping Centre
Shaw Centre
47
59
Scotts Shopping Centre
Cairnhill Circle
Emerald Hill Rd
Cavenagh Rd
11
77
13
55
Liat Towers
2
39
Tangs
Nutmeg Rd
84
Saunders Rd
Central
58
Wheelock Place
72
Lucky Plaza
Bideford Rd
Cairnhill Rd
Orchard
78
49
The Paragon
43
16
Wisma Atria Shopping Centre
Hullet Rd
Cuppage Tce
Expressway
Sophia Rd
Edinburgh Rd
Paterson Rd
Orchard Turn
Ngee Ann City
80
14
67
71
70
Centrepoint
Orchard Blvd
53
The Heeren
56
Cuppage Plaza
74
21
65
18
24
Orchard Plaza Shopping Centre
Orchard Link
Grange Rd
46
Plaza Singapura
Oldham La
Handy Rd
23
25
Somerset Rd
31
75
Paterson Rd
Somerset
Orchard Rd
Penang Rd
Devonshire Rd
Grange Rd
Exeter Rd
66
Eber Rd
Devonshire Rd
6
54
See City Centre Map pp452-3
Dhoby Ghaut
Leonie Hill
Leonie Hill Rd
Killiney Rd
Irwell Bank
Hoot Kiam Rd
St Thomas Walk
35
Oxley Rise
Clemenceau Ave
Penang La
68
Lloyd Rd
32
Oxley Rd
Fort Canning Rd
Cox Tce
Oxley Walk
Jl Rumbia
Fort Canning Park
River Valley Rd
5

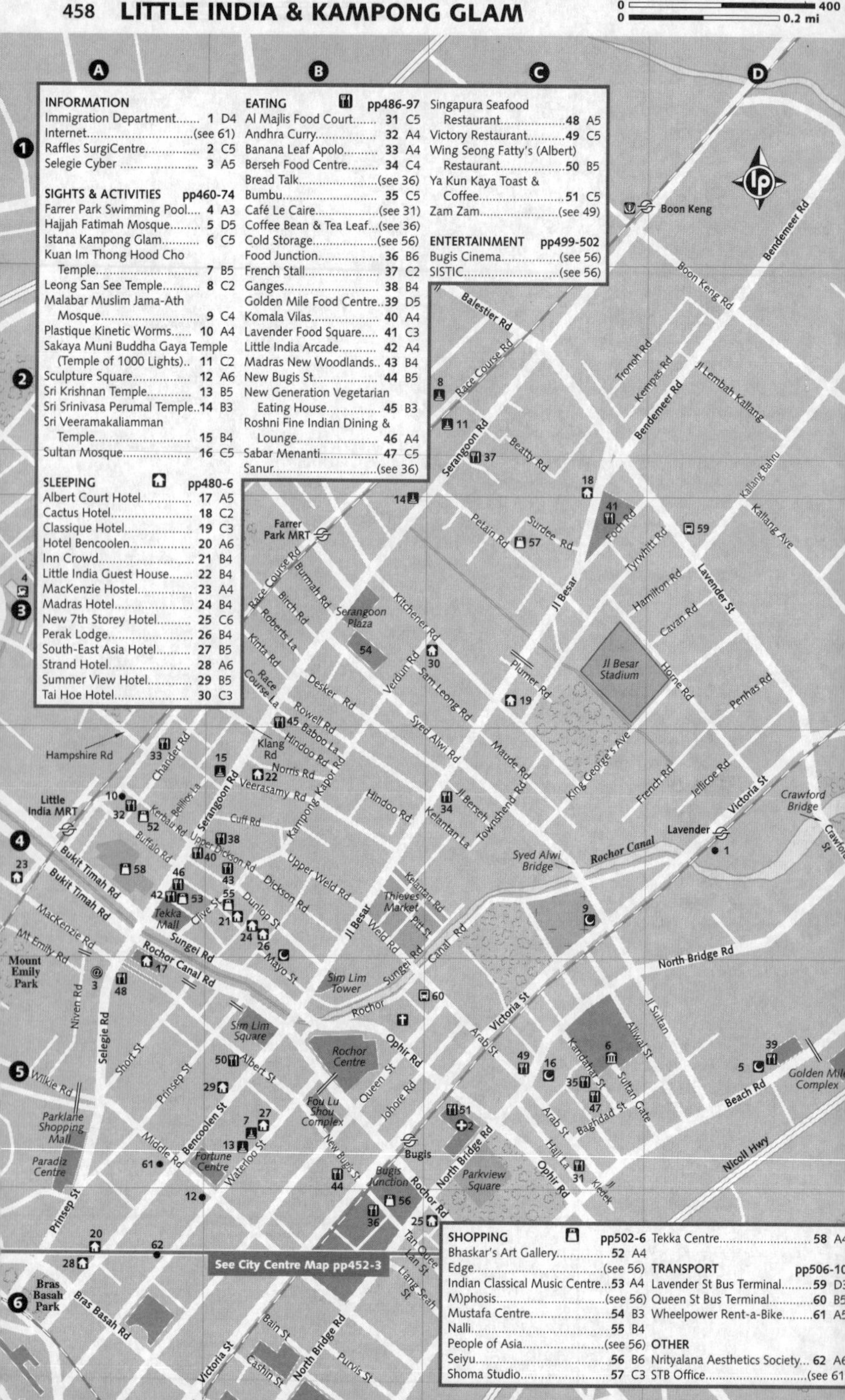
0 400 m
0 0.2 mi
A
B
C
D
1
2
3
4
5
6
INFORMATION
Immigration Department 1 D4
Internet (see 61)
Raffles SurgiCentre 2 C5
Selegie Cyber 3 A5
SIGHTS & ACTIVITIES pp460-74
Farrer Park Swimming Pool 4 A3
Hajjah Fatimah Mosque 5 D5
Istana Kampong Glam 6 C5
Kuan Im Thong Hood Cho Temple 7 B5
Leong San See Temple 8 C2
Malabar Muslim Jama-Ath Mosque 9 C4
Plastique Kinetic Worms 10 A4
Sakaya Muni Buddha Gaya Temple (Temple of 1000 Lights) 11 C2
Sculpture Square 12 A6
Sri Krishnan Temple 13 B5
Sri Srinivasa Perumal Temple 14 B3
Sri Veeramakaliamman Temple 15 B4
Sultan Mosque 16 C5
SLEEPING pp480-6
Albert Court Hotel 17 A5
Cactus Hotel 18 C2
Classique Hotel 19 C3
Hotel Bencoolen 20 A6
Inn Crowd 21 B4
Little India Guest House 22 B4
MacKenzie Hostel 23 A4
Madras Hotel 24 B4
New 7th Storey Hotel 25 C6
Perak Lodge 26 B4
South-East Asia Hotel 27 B5
Strand Hotel 28 A6
Summer View Hotel 29 B5
Tai Hoe Hotel 30 C3
EATING pp486-97
Al Majlis Food Court 31 C5
Andhra Curry 32 A4
Banana Leaf Apolo 33 A4
Berseh Food Centre 34 C4
Bread Talk (see 36)
Bumbu 35 C5
Café Le Caire (see 31)
Coffee Bean & Tea Leaf (see 36)
Cold Storage (see 56)
Food Junction 36 B6
French Stall 37 C2
Ganges 38 B4
Golden Mile Food Centre 39 D5
Komala Vilas 40 A4
Lavender Food Square 41 C3
Little India Arcade 42 A4
Madras New Woodlands 43 B4
New Bugis St 44 B5
New Generation Vegetarian Eating House 45 B3
Roshni Fine Indian Dining & Lounge 46 A4
Sabar Menanti 47 C5
Sanur (see 36)
Singapura Seafood Restaurant 48 A5
Victory Restaurant 49 C5
Wing Seong Fatty's (Albert) Restaurant 50 B5
Ya Kun Kaya Toast & Coffee 51 C5
Zam Zam (see 49)
ENTERTAINMENT pp499-502
Bugis Cinema (see 56)
SISTIC (see 56)
SHOPPING pp502-6
Bhaskar's Art Gallery 52 A4
Edge (see 56)
Indian Classical Music Centre 53 A4
M)phosis (see 56)
Mustafa Centre 54 B3
Nalli 55 B4
People of Asia (see 56)
Seiyu 56 B6
Shoma Studio 57 C3
Tekka Centre 58 A4
TRANSPORT pp506-10
Lavender St Bus Terminal 59 D3
Queen St Bus Terminal 60 B5
Wheelpower Rent-a-Bike 61 A5
OTHER
Nrityalana Aesthetics Society 62 A6
STB Office (see 61)
Boon Keng
Bendemeer Rd
Boon Keng Rd
Balestier Rd
Race Course Rd
Tronoh Rd
Kempas Rd
Jl Lembah Kallang
Serangoon Rd
Beatty Rd
Kallang Bahru
Kallang Ave
Farrer Park MRT
Petain Rd
Surdee Rd
Foch Rd
Tyrwhitt Rd
Jl Besar
Hamilton Rd
Lavender St
Cavan Rd
Serangoon Plaza
Kitchener Rd
Jl Besar Stadium
Horne Rd
Plumer Rd
Penhas Rd
Sam Leong Rd
Verdun Rd
Desker Rd
Rowell Rd
Baboo La
Hindoo Rd
Syed Alwi Rd
Maude Rd
King George's Ave
Hampshire Rd
Chander Rd
Klang Rd
Norris Rd
Veerasamy Rd
Kampong Kapor Rd
French Rd
Jellicoe Rd
Victoria St
Crawford Bridge
Little India MRT
Kerbau Rd
Cuff Rd
Jl Berseh
Townshend Rd
Kelantan La
Lavender
Upper Dickson Rd
Buffalo Rd
Bukit Timah Rd
Syed Alwi Bridge
Rochor Canal
Upper Weld Rd
Dickson Rd
Thieves Market
Kelantan Rd
Pitt St
Tekka Mall
Clive St
Dunlop St
Weld Rd
MacKenzie Rd
Mt Emily Rd
Sungei Rd
Rochor Canal Rd
Mayo St
Canal Rd
North Bridge Rd
Mount Emily Park
Niven Rd
Selegie Rd
Sim Lim Tower
Rochor
Jl Sultan
Sim Lim Square
Rochor Centre
Ophir Rd
Arab St
Aliwal St
Wilkie Rd
Short St
Prinsep St
Albert St
Queen St
Kandahar St
Sultan Gate
Golden Mile Complex
Beach Rd
Parklane Shopping Mall
Bencoolen St
Fou Lu Shou Complex
Johore Rd
Baghdad St
Middle Rd
Waterloo St
New Bugis St
Bugis
Haji La
Nicoll Hwy
Paradiz Centre
Fortune Centre
Bugis Junction
Parkview Square
Jl Kledek
See City Centre Map pp452-3
Tan Quee Lan St
Liang Seah St
Bras Basah Park
Bras Basah Rd
Bain St
Victoria St
Cashin St
Purvis St

(Continued from page 447)

Media

English dailies in Singapore include the *Straits Times* (which includes the *Sunday Times*), the *Business Times*, the afternoon tabloid *New Paper*, and *Today*, a free paper available at the MRT stations and offering an opposition point of view. *Eight Days* is a weekly television and entertainment magazine.

Where Singapore, *I-S Magazine* and *Juice* are all free from tourist offices, most major hotels and several restaurants, cafés and bars. They also have listings information and are worth a look.

Medical Services

Gleneagles Hospital (Map pp456-7; ☎ 6473 7222; www.gleneagles.com.sg; 6A Napier Rd)
International Medical Clinic (www.imc-healthcare.com) Tanglin Clinic (Map pp456-7; ☎ 6733 4440; tanglin@imc-healthcare.com; 04-20 Tanglin Shopping Centre, 19 Tanglin Rd) Jelita Clinic (Map pp448-9; ☎ 6465 4440; jelita@imc-healthcare.com; 02-08 Jelita Cold Storage Shopping Centre, 293 Holland Rd)
Mt Elizabeth Hospital (Map pp456-7; ☎ 6737 2666; www.mountelizabeth.com.sg; 3 Mount Elizabeth)
Raffles SurgiCentre (Map pp456-7; ☎ 6334 3337; www.raffleshospital.com; 585 North Bridge Rd) Open 24 hours.
Singapore General Hospital Accident & Emergency Department (Map pp452-3; ☎ 6321 4311; Block 1, Outram Rd) Open 24 hours.

Money

Banks can be found all over the city. Exchange rates tend to vary from bank to bank and some even have a service charge on each exchange transaction – this is usually S$2 to S$3, but can be more, so ask first. Most banks are open from 9.30am to 3pm on weekdays (to 11.30am Saturday).

Moneychangers do not charge fees, so you will often get a better overall exchange rate for cash and travellers cheques with them than at the banks. You'll find moneychangers in just about every shopping centre in Singapore. Most shops accept foreign cash and travellers cheques at a slightly lower rate than you'd get from a moneychanger.

ATMs are also liberally scattered across Singapore – there's usually at least one in all shopping malls and MRT stations.

Post

Postal delivery in Singapore is very efficient. All post offices are open 8am to 6pm Monday to Friday, 8am to 2pm Saturday. Call ☎ 1605 to find the nearest branch or check www.singpost.com.sg.

Letters addressed to 'Poste Restante' are held at the **Eunos Post Office** (☎ 6741 8857; 10 Eunos Rd), next to the Paya Lebar MRT.

Handy central branches include **Comcentre** (Map pp456-7; 31 Exeter Rd) and **Ngee Ann City** (Map pp456-7; 04-15 Takashimaya, 391 Orchard Rd), and Terminals 1 and 2 at Changi airport also have branches open 8am to 9pm.

Telephone & Fax

You can make local and international calls from public phone booths. International calls can be made from booths at the **Comcentre** (Map pp456-7; 31 Exeter Rd) 24 hours a day and at selected post offices. Most phone booths take phonecards, and some take credit cards, although there are still booths around that take coins. For inquiries see www.singtel.com.

Local phone cards are widely available from 7-Eleven stores, post offices, Telecom centres, stationers and bookshops, and come in denominations of S$2, S$5, S$10, S$20 and S$50.

Useful numbers:
Directory information (☎ 100)
Flight information (☎ 1-800-542 4422)
STB 24-hour Touristline (☎ 1-800-736 2000)

Tourist Information

The STB head office is on Orchard Spring Lane, but the office at Suntec City is open daily and provides a wide range of services, including tour bookings and event ticketing.
CHIJMES (Map pp452-3; ☎ 6338 2529; 2nd fl, CHIJMES, 30 Victoria Rd; 🕒 10am-6pm Mon-Sat)
Liang Court (Map pp452-3; ☎ 6336 2888; Level 1, Liang Court Shopping Centre, 177 River Valley Rd; 🕒 10.30am-9.30pm)
Suntec City (Map pp452-3; ☎ 1-800-332 5066; 01-35/37/39/41 Suntec City, 3 Temasek Blvd; 🕒 8am-6.30pm Mon-Sat, 9am-6.30pm Sun)
Tourism Court (Map pp456-7; ☎ 1-800-736 2000; 1 Orchard Spring Lane; 🕒 8.30am-5pm Mon-Fri, 8.30am-1pm Sat)

Travel Agencies

There are many travel agencies in Singapore, including international operators such as

STA Travel. The *Yellow Pages* phone directory has listings.

Harharah Travel (Map p458; ☎ 6337 2633; harharah@singnet.com.sg; 171A Bencoolen St)

STA Travel (Map pp456-7; ☎ 6737 7188; www.statravel.com.sg; 33A Cuppage Rd, Cuppage Terrace)

DANGERS & ANNOYANCES

Singapore is a very safe country with low crime rates. Pickpockets are not unknown, but in general, crime is not a problem – unsurprising, given the harsh penalties meted out to offenders. The importation of drugs carries the death penalty, which is regularly carried out. Quite simply, drugs in Singapore should be avoided at all costs.

The nanny state takes a tough line on antisocial issues. Smoking in all public places earns a S$500 fine. You can smoke at food stalls and on the street (as long as you dispose of your butt in a bin, of course). Jaywalk, by crossing the road within 50m of a designated crossing, and it could cost you S$50. Get caught littering and you could be looking at a fine of up to S$1000; not surprisingly, Singapore is amazingly clean.

SINGAPORE

SIGHTS

Colonial District

The mark of Sir Stamford Raffles remains indelibly stamped on central Singapore. His early city plans moved the business district south of the river and made the north bank the administrative area. This north bank area is known today as the colonial district and it's where you'll find most of the imposing monuments of British rule (see Walking Tour, p476). Thanks to land reclamation it's also where you'll find a host of mega shopping malls and the dazzlingly contemporary Esplanade – Theatres on the Bay.

ASIAN CIVILISATIONS MUSEUM — Map pp450-1

The jewel in the National Heritage Board's bevy of museums, the **Asian Civilisations Museum** is now split across two locations, both worth visiting. The new **Empress Place wing** (☎ 6332 7789; 1 Empress Place; adult/child S$3/1.50; ⏰ noon-6pm Mon, 9am-6pm Tue-Thu, Sat & Sun, 9am-9pm Fri) occupies a grand building (1865) named in honour of Queen Victoria. Ten thematic galleries explore different aspects of Asian culture – from the Islamic world to the glories of China. There are also regular touring and programmed exhibitions. A visit here is a fine way to get a handle on Singapore's historic development and see how it relates to the region.

The **Armenian St branch** (☎ 6332 3015; 39 Armenian St; adult/child S$3/1.50; ⏰ noon-6pm Mon, 9am-6pm Tue-Thu, Sat & Sun, 9am-9pm Fri) is housed in the beautifully restored Tao Nan School, dating from 1910. The permanent displays here include excellent ones on Peranakan culture, Chinese ceramics and Buddhist artefacts. A ticket for both branches is adult/child S$5/2.50.

ESPLANADE – THEATRES ON THE BAY

Love it or hate it, Singapore's S$600 million **Esplanade – Theatres on the Bay** (Map pp452-3; ☎ 6828 8222; www.esplanade.com; 1 Esplanade Dr) has fast become the posterboy of contemporary Singapore, a shining example of the artsy, creative side of the island state.

Dubbed 'the durians' by local wags, the theatre complex's twin glass domes, covered in 7,139 variously angled aluminium shades, do not take their design reference from the tropical fruit, but from the natural geometries of nature and traditional Asian reed weavings. Most likely you'll come here to see a cultural performance at one of its several auditoria, to eat at one of the many restaurants that are in the rest of the complex, or to hang out around the outside of the building where free performances are frequently held.

RAFFLES HOTEL — Map pp452-3

A block north of the Padang, **Raffles Hotel** (1 Beach Rd) is a Singapore institution. It's hard to believe, viewing the regal edifice that stands today, that Raffles Hotel started life as a 10-room bungalow. It was opened in December 1887 by the Sarkies brothers, immigrants from Armenia and proprietors of two other grand colonial hotels, the Strand in Yangon (Rangoon) and the Eastern & Oriental in Penang.

The hotel's heyday began with the opening of the main building in 1899, the same one that guests stay in today. Raffles soon became a byword for oriental luxury. By the 1970s, however, Raffles had become a shabby relic and seemed destined for demolition. Fortunately the government designated the building a national monument in

GLENN BEANLAND

Opera performers, **Chinese Theatre Circle** (p500)

GLENN BEANLAND

Interactive displays,
Singapore Science Centre (p470)

View over **Sentosa Island** (p471)

TOM COCKREM

DOMINIC ARIZONA BONUCCELLI

Trishaw (p510) driver, Little India

GLENN BEA

Shop fronts, **Little India** (p464)

GLENN BEANLAND

Singapore Sling, Raffles' **Long Bar** (p497)

LIZ THOMPSON

Worshipper in a Hindu temple, **Little India** (p464)

Raffles Hotel (p460)

GLENN BEA

1987 and, in 1991, it was reopened after an expensive restoration project that has seen the hotel all but swallowed up by a fancy shopping and dining arcade.

For nonresidents the hotel lobby is open to the public (dress standards apply, so no shorts or sandals please!) and high tea is served in the Tiffin Room. Drinks can be taken at any of its bars – the Bar & Billiard Room has the best ambience.

Hidden away on the 3rd floor of the Raffles Hotel Arcade, the **Raffles Hotel Museum** (admission free; 10am-7pm) is worth hunting out. Here you'll find a fascinating collection of memorabilia, including photographs and posters from bygone eras and a fine city map showing how Noel Coward could once sip his gin sling and stare out at the muddy sea from the hotel veranda.

SINGAPORE ART MUSEUM

Two blocks west of Raffles Hotel is the fine **Singapore Art Museum** (Map pp452-3; ☎ 6332 3222; 71 Bras Basah Rd; adult/child S$3/1.50; noon-6pm Mon, 9am-6pm Tue-Thu, Sat & Sun, 9am-9pm Fri), based in St Joseph's Institution, a former Catholic boys' school. The gallery's collection focuses on Singaporean and regional artists, with exhibitions ranging from classical Chinese calligraphy to contemporary works that examine issues of Asian identity and the modern Singaporean experience. Look out for works by prominent local artists Liu Kang and Ng Eng Teng. Many interesting temporary exhibitions from overseas are also mounted here.

FORT CANNING HILL Map pp452-3

Once known as Bukit Larangan or Forbidden Hill, **Fort Canning Hill** is home to a shrine to Sultan Iskander Shah, the last ruler of the ancient kingdom of Singapura. Archaeological digs in the park have also uncovered Javanese artefacts from the 14th-century Majapahit Empire.

When Stamford Raffles arrived, the only reminder of the sultan's long-gone kingdom was an earthen wall that stretched from the sea to the top of Fort Canning Hill. Raffles built his modest *atap*-roofed residence atop the hill in 1822, and it later became Government House until the military replaced it with Fort Canning in 1860, named in honour of Viscount Canning, first Viceroy of India.

> **FREE MUSEUM ADMISSION**
>
> The **National Heritage Board** (☎ 6837 9940; www.nhb.gov.sg) administers the following museums in the city's colonial district: Asian Civilisations Museum; Singapore Art Museum; Singapore History Museum (closed for renovation until 2006 but with a satellite exhibition over by Clarke Quay); and Singapore Philatelic Museum. All except the Philatelic Museum have free admission on Friday from 6pm to 9pm. Check the website for details of free guided tours of each museum.

Little is left of the hill's historic buildings; a couple of Gothic gateways lead into the pleasant park where gravestones from the old Christian cemetery are embedded in the brick walls. There's also a spice garden here, on the site of Raffles' original botanic garden; guided tours can be arranged through the **at-sunrice cooking academy** (p477) based in the monumental **Fort Canning Centre**, the former barracks building dating from 1926.

Also on Fort Canning Hill is the **Battle Box** (☎ 6333 0510; 51 Canning Rise; adult/child S$8/5; 10am-6pm Tue-Sun), Singapore's largest underground military operations complex during WWII. This warren of 26 rooms and tunnels now houses a fascinating hi-tech exhibition on the fall of Singapore in 1942. In one room you can gaze through binocular-like lenses to view holographic figures tapping out Morse messages; the Japanese codes are still etched on the walls.

The park hosts several outdoor events each year including WOMAD and Ballet under the Stars.

SINGAPORE PHILATELIC MUSEUM

Devoted to stamps and unlikely to thrill all, the **Singapore Philatelic Museum** (Map pp452-3; ☎ 6337 3888; www.spm.org.sg; 23B Coleman St; adult/child S$2/1; 9am-6pm Tue-Sun) has its moments. Housed in the attractive former Methodist Book Room Building dating from around 1895, the museum holds a well-presented collection of rare and not-so-rare stamps from both Singapore and around the world; some of the artwork and design is impressive. Kids will enjoy designing stamps and other interactive displays.

CHURCHES **Map pp452-3**

Singapore's oldest church is the charming **Armenian Church** (☎ 6334 0141; 60 Hill St). Designed by eminent colonial architect George Coleman, this neoclassical style church dates from 1836 and is dedicated to St Gregory the Illuminator. In its grounds lie the graves of several Sarkies (but not the brothers of Raffles Hotel fame) and Agnes Joaquim, discoverer of the island's first hybrid orchid, now the national flower.

Coleman also designed the original **St Andrew's Cathedral** (☎ 6337 6104; 11 St Andrew's Rd) in 1837 but this was demolished after lightning damage and rebuilt between 1856 and 1862. The oldest Catholic church (consecrated in 1846) is the **Cathedral of the Good Shepherd** (☎ 6337 2036; 4 Queen St). Another attractive central church is **St Joseph's Church** (☎ 6338 3167; 143 Victoria St) built in Gothic style and dating from 1912.

KUAN IM THONG HOOD CHO TEMPLE **Map p458**

Bugis (see 'The Reinvention of Bugis St' boxed text opposite) may have lost a lot of its atmosphere over the decades, but one part of the area that is always lively is the precinct in front of the colourful **Kuan Im Thong Hood Cho Temple** (178 Waterloo St). Dedicated to Kuan Yin (Guan Yin), one of the most popular Chinese deities, the temple attracts a daily crowd of devotees seeking divine intervention in their lives. Flower sellers can always be found outside the temple and it's particularly busy on the eve of Chinese New Year when it stays open all night.

Next door is the recently renovated and even more polychromatic **Sri Krishnan Temple** (Waterloo St), which also attracts worshippers from the Kuan Yin Temple, who show a great deal of religious pragmatism by also burning joss sticks and offering prayers at this Hindu temple.

Central Business District & the Quays **Map pp452-3**

South of the river is the central business district (CBD), the financial pulse of Singapore. Once the city's vibrant heart, **Raffles Place** is now a rare patch of grass above the MRT station surrounded by the gleaming towers of commerce. There are some interesting sculptures here and along the nearby Singapore River (see Walking Tour, p476). You'll also find at the river mouth into the harbour the **Merlion statues**, the weird half-fish, half-lion icon designed in the 1960s by the tourism board as the island's mascot.

Amid all the modern architecture are a few preserved relics of olden days. **Clifford Pier** is the place to hire a boat or catch a harbour cruise (p478) while the **Fullerton Building**, once the general post office, now houses one of Singapore's swankiest hotels (p485). Further south along the waterfront you'll find **Lau Pa Sat** (19 Raffles Quay), a hawker centre that occupies the old Telok Ayer Market building, a fine piece of cast-iron Victoriana.

Splitting the colonial district from the CBD is the Singapore River, the site of the first British arrivals and for over a century the main artery of trade. Riverside walkways make it possible to stroll along the water, or you could take a bumboat (motorised *sampan*) tour between the quays (see p478). **Boat Quay** was the location of the city's leading *towkays* (Chinese business chiefs) and remained busy right up until the 1960s. In the mid-1980s the long-dilapidated area was declared a conservation zone by the government and its revival into one of the island's top entertainment districts began.

Clarke Quay, named after Singapore's second colonial governor, Sir Andrew Clarke, was developed like Boat Quay into a dining and shopping precinct in the early 1990s. A fleamarket is held here on Sundays.

While its main building on Stamford Road is being renovated the **Singapore History Museum** (☎ 6332 3659; 03-09/17, Riverside Point, 30 Merchant Rd; admission S$2; 🕓 noon-6pm Mon, 9am-6pm Tue-Thu, Sat & Sun, 9am-9pm Fri) has a small exhibition here about the Singapore River.

Nearby, the **Chettiar Hindu Temple** (☎ 6737 9393; 15 Tank Rd; 🕓 8am-noon, 5.30-8.30pm) was completed in 1984 and replaces a much earlier temple built by Indian chettiars, or moneylenders. This Shaivite temple, dedicated to the six-headed Lord Subramaniam and properly known as the Sri Thandayuthapani Temple, is at its most active during the festival of Thaipusam, when the procession ends here.

Robertson Quay was used for storage of goods. Now some of the old godowns (warehouses) have been tarted up into flash places to party, such as the mega-club Zouk (p500). You'll also find several good hotels and restaurants clustered around here.

The **Tyler Print Institute** (☎ 6336 3663; www.stpi.com.sg; 41 Robertson Quay; admission free; 🕑 1-5pm Sun & Mon, 9.30am-6pm Tue-Sat) established by the American printmaker Kenneth E Tyler features an interesting gallery with new exhibitions every few months on various aspects of printmaking, as well as a paper mill and educational facility.

Chinatown

Map pp452-3

Roughly bounded by the Singapore River to the north, New Bridge Rd to the west, Maxwell and Kreta Ayer Rds to the south and Cecil St to the east, **Chinatown** is packed with temples and provides a glimpse of the ways of the Chinese immigrants that shaped and built modern Singapore. The area has changed incredibly since the early 1990s, and although it's become sanitised and gentrified it's still a fascinating place to wander around and to eat, shop and party.

THIAN HOCK KENG TEMPLE

Its name translates as **Temple of Heavenly Bliss** (☎ 6423 4626; 158 Telok Ayer St) – entirely apt given the gorgeous decoration of this, the oldest and most important Hokkien temple in Singapore. Built between 1839 and 1842 on the site of a joss house the temple was magnificently restored in 2000. It houses a shrine to Ma-Chu-Po, the Goddess of the Sea, from whom sailors asked for protection.

As you wander through the courtyards of the temple, look for the rooftop dragons, the intricately decorated beams, the gold-leafed panels and, best of all, the beautifully painted doors. During the restoration a calligraphic panel dating from 1907 and from the Emperor of China, Guang Xu of the Qing Dynasty, was discovered above the central altar.

SRI MARIAMMAN TEMPLE

Right in the heart of Chinatown, the **Sri Mariamman temple** (☎ 6223 4064; 244 South Bridge Rd; 🕑 7.30-11.30am & 5.30-8.30pm) is Singapore's oldest, originally built in 1823, then rebuilt in 1843. The colourful *gopuram* (tower) crowded with deities, soldiers and floral decoration over the entrance gate clearly identifies this as a South Indian Dravidian-style temple.

At the end of October each year the temple is the scene for the Thimithi festival, during which devotees walk barefoot over burning coals – supposedly feeling no pain, although spectators report that quite a few hot-foot it over the final few steps!

CHINATOWN HERITAGE CENTRE

A reflection of the often frenetic atmosphere of Chinatown itself, the **Chinatown Heritage Centre** (☎ 6325 2878; www.chinatownheritage.com.sg; 48 Pagoda St; adult/child S$8/4; 🕑 10am-7pm) is a new museum crammed to the rafters with interactive, imaginative displays on the history of the area. Three restored shophouses have been combined to make the three-storey centre which partly recreates the cramped living quarters that many Chinese once had to endure. The oral and video histories of local people are truly fascinating. There's a lot to take in here in one go, so keep your ticket stub if you fancy a break, and the attendants will let you return the same day.

THE REINVENTION OF BUGIS ST

Until the 1980s, Bugis and Malay Sts, a few blocks northeast of Raffles Hotel, were infamous as Singapore's raucous sexual playground, a haunt of prostitutes, transvestites and transsexuals. Bugis St was never, officially, more than another food stall centre but, in practice, it was the place to be until the early hours of the morning, to join the crowds and watch the goings on. It was proof that Singapore had a life. Eventually, it had to go – and did so during the building of Bugis MRT and Bugis Junction shopping mall.

The reinvented Bugis St, partly swallowed up inside the mall, is complete with new terrace lookalikes and a glass-covered roof allowing patrons to browse and dine in air-conditioned comfort. The open-air market section of the street, west across Victoria St, has more flavour of the old Bugis; here the food stalls and bars stay open late and there are some colourful souvenir stalls to poke around. It's hardly what it used to be like but the really sharp sighted might catch a fleeting transvestite – like a ghost of the past – heading off to Little India's Desker Rd for a night's business.

URA GALLERY
To see how Singapore's urban environment has changed over recent decades and how it will change further in the future, pop into the **URA Gallery** (☎ 6321 8321; www.ura.gov.sg; 45 Maxwell Rd; admission free; 🕑 9am-4.30pm Mon-Fri, 9am-12.30pm Sat). This showcase of the Urban Redevelopment Authority (URA) includes video shows, interactive exhibits and a huge scale model of the island state with its own six-minute sound and light show.

WAK HAI CHENG BIO TEMPLE
On the CBD edge of Chinatown, the Taoist **Wak Hai Cheng Bio Temple** (cnr Phillip & Church Sts) is also known as the Yueh Hai Ching Temple, which translates as Calm Sea Temple. Dating from 1826, it's an atmospheric place, with giant incense coils smoking over its empty courtyard, and a whole village of tiny plaster figures populating its roof.

Little India

Map p458

Focused around Serangoon Rd, Little India is another great area to peruse, taking in the various flavours and culture of the local Indian community.

SRI VEERAMAKALIAMMAN TEMPLE
One of the most colourful and bustling Shaivite temples in Little India, the **Sri Veeramakaliamman Temple** (☎ 6293 4634; 141 Serangoon Rd; 🕑 8am-12.30pm & 4-8.30pm) is dedicated to Kali. Kali, bloodthirsty consort of Shiva, has always been popular in Bengal, the birthplace of the labourers who built this temple in 1881. Images of Kali within the temple show her garlanded with skulls and ripping out the guts of her victims, and in less violent poses with her sons Ganesh and Murugan.

SRI SRINIVASA PERUMAL TEMPLE
Dedicated to Vishnu, the **Sri Srinivasa Perumal Temple** (☎ 6298 5771; 397 Serangoon Rd; 🕑 6.30am-noon, 6-9pm) dates from 1855 but the 20-metre tall *gopuram* (tower) is a relatively recent addition, built in 1966. Inside the temple you will find statues of Perumal, or Vishnu, and his consorts Lakshmi and Andal, as well as his bird-mount, Garuda.

This temple is the starting point for devotees who make the walk to the Chettiar Hindu Temple during the Thaipusam festival.

SAKAYA MUNI BUDDHA GAYA TEMPLE
In 1927 a Thai monk founded the **Sakaya Muni Buddha Gaya Temple** (☎ 6294 0714; 366 Race Course Rd; 🕑 8am-4.45pm), popularly known as the Temple of 1000 Lights. This Buddhist temple is dominated by a brightly painted 15m-high, 300-tonne Buddha who sits alongside an eclectic range of deities including Guan-Yin, the Chinese goddess of mercy, and Brahma and Ganesh (both Hindu deities). You can walk round the back of the giant Buddha and go inside it through a low door. Here you will see a smaller image of the reclining Buddha, Maitreya. Around the base of the statues, models tell the story of the Buddha's life, and, of course, there are the electric lights that give the temple its name.

LEONG SAN SEE TEMPLE
Across the road from the Temple of 1000 Lights is the less gaudy Taoist **Leong San See Temple** (☎ 6298 9371; 371 Race Course Rd; 🕑 6am-6pm), dating from 1917 and dedicated to Kuan Yin, Goddess of Mercy. The name translates as Dragon Mountain Temple and it's beautifully decorated with timber beams carved with chimeras, dragons, flowers and human figures.

Kampong Glam

Map p458

This quarter, roughly bounded by Victoria St, Jl Sultan and Beach Rd, all immediately northeast of Bugis MRT, is the Muslim centre of the city. Its name derives from the Malay for village *(kampong)* and *gelam*, a type of tree that once grew here. Although it certainly has a distinct atmosphere, and a clutch of interesting shops, it is not as lively as Chinatown or Little India.

SULTAN MOSQUE
The golden domed focal point of Kampong Glam is **Sultan Mosque** (☎ 6293 4405; 3 Muscat St; 🕑 to visitors 5am-8.30pm), Singapore's biggest mosque. It was originally built in 1825 with the aid of a grant from Raffles and the East India Company, as a result of Raffles' treaty with the sultan of Johor. A hundred years later, the original mosque was replaced by the present magnificent building.

ISTANA KAMPONG GLAM
The Kampong Glam area is the historic seat of the Malay royalty, resident here before

the arrival of Raffles, and the **Istana Kampong Glam** (Sultan Gate Rd, between Baghdad St & North Bridge Rd) was the palace built for the last sultan of Singapore, Ali Iskander Shah, between 1836 and 1843. An agreement allowed the palace to belong to the sultan's family as long as they continued to live there. Even though this was repealed in 1897, the family stayed on for over another century, the palace gradually sliding into ruin.

In 1999 the family moved out and ever since the walled compound, which also includes the Gedong Kuning (Yellow Villa) of the sultan's treasurer, the *bendahara*, and Pondok Java, a small community house, has been under renovation with the aim of opening it as a Malay heritage park. At the time of research the repairs were still underway.

OTHER MOSQUES

The architecturally interesting **Hajjah Fatimah Mosque** (☎ 6297 2774; 4001 Beach Rd) was built in 1846 and is, unusually, named after a Malaccan-born Malay woman named Hajjah Fatimah. Its most distinctive feature is a European-style minaret that leans about six degrees off-centre.

The blue-tiled **Malabar Muslim Jama-Ath Mosque** (☎ 6294 3862; 471 Victoria St) is one of the most distinctive in Singapore, but it didn't always look this way; the tiles were added after the mosque, the only one on the island dedicated to Malabar Muslims from the southern Indian state of Kerala, was opened in 1963.

Orchard Road

Map pp456-7

The trees that shade the ever present crowds along Singapore's wall-to-wall consumerist nirvana hint at the area's 19th century incarnation as an orchard lined with nutmeg and pepper plantations; dotted between the malls, hotels and designer boutiques you'll stumble across the odd architectural relic from this time. When you've had your fill of the shops, the serene Botanic Gardens are a short stroll from the west end of the road.

ISTANA

Home of Singapore's president, the Istana (palace) was built in 1867–69 as Government House, a neoclassical monument to British rule. Public works were never a high priority in laissez-faire colonial Singapore, but the need to impress the visiting Duke of Edinburgh convinced the island's Legislative Council to approve the building's huge budget. The actual construction was done by Indian convicts transported from Bencoolen on Sumatra.

The **Istana** (☎ 6737 5522; www.gov.sg/istana/openhouse.html) is set about 750m back from Orchard Rd in beautifully maintained grounds including a nine-hole golf course and terraced garden. Most of the time the closest you are likely to get to it are the well-guarded gates on Orchard Road, but the Istana is open to the public on selected public holidays such as New Year's Day – call or check the website for details. If you are lucky enough to be in Singapore on one of these occasions, take your passport and join the queues to get in.

EMERALD HILL

Take some time out to wander up from pedestrianised Peranakan Place to **Emerald Hill Road**, where some fine terrace houses remain; the quiet atmosphere feels a million miles from bustling Orchard Rd. Check out Nos 39–45, built in 1903 with an unusually wide frontage and grand Chinese-style entrance gate, and the Art Deco-style Nos 121–129 dating from 1925.

SINGAPORE BOTANIC GARDENS

An ideal spot to recover from your jet lag, have a picnic or just lie around reading or daydreaming, is the **Botanic Gardens** (☎ 6471 7361; www.nparks.gov.sg; 1 Cluny Rd; admission free; 🕑 5am-midnight).

Established around 1860 and covering 52 hectares, the gardens originally acted as a test ground for potential cash crops – such as rubber – and botanical research. Today they still host a herbarium housing more than 600,000 botanical specimens and a library whose archival materials date back to the 16th century.

Visitors can enjoy manicured garden beds or explore a four-hectare patch of 'original Singaporean jungle', a sample of the kind of forest that once covered the entire island. Don't miss the extraordinary **National Orchid Garden** (adult/child S$2/1; 🕑 8.30am-7pm) one of the world's largest orchid displays featuring over 60,000 of these delicate looking but incredibly hardy plants, including the *Vanda Miss Joaquim*.

This hybrid orchid, Singapore's national flower, was discovered in 1893 by Agnes Joaquim, in her garden.

Future developments include a prehistoric garden charting the development of plants from the time when there were no land plants, and a 'cool house' – the opposite of a hothouse – which will house Southeast Asian plants from milder climes and high elevations. The gardens contain several decent restaurants and host free open-air music concerts on Sunday evenings for most of the year – call the garden or check with the Singapore Tourism Board (STB) for details.

Bus Nos 7, 77, 123 and 174 all run to the Gardens from the Orchard MRT exit on Orchard Blvd.

East Coast & Changi

Map pp448-9

Heading east of the city centre, the most interesting places to visit are Geylang and Katong, both largely Malay districts rarely frequented by foreign visitors. Further east is the WWII pilgrimage site of the Changi Prison Museum and Chapel; and sleepy Changi Village, the jumping off point for the rural retreat of Pulau Ubin.

GEYLANG

Geylang Serai is a Malay residential area, but you are not going to see traditional *atap* (thatched-roof) houses or any sarong-clad cottage industry workers. The area is Singaporean high-rise, though there are some older shophouses around, especially in the *lorong* (alleys) that run off Geylang Rd and which house one of Singapore's most active red-light districts.

Geylang Serai is easily reached by taking the MRT to Paya Lebar station, from where it's a short walk down Tanjong Katong Rd to Geylang Rd, the area's busy main shopping street. While in the area you could check out the **Malay Cultural Village** (☎ 6748 4700; 39 Geylang Rd; adult/child S$5/3; ⏰ 10am-10pm). This complex of traditional Malay-style houses was built as a showpiece of native culture, though it hasn't really taken off and is very quiet; it's largely free to walk around, the admission fee being for the small museum housing Malay cultural artefacts such as costumes and furniture, and the Kampung Days display which recreates an idealised Malay village.

For more atmosphere duck into the nearby **Geylang Serai Market**, hidden behind some older-style housing blocks on Geylang Rd; its entrance is through a small lane that leads to a crowded, traditional Asian market, much more interesting than most of Singapore's new concrete box markets.

KATONG

From the Geylang Serai Market you can head down Joo Chiat Rd to East Coast Rd and explore the Katong district. Along and just off **Joo Chiat Road** are some of the finest **Peranakan terrace houses** in Singapore, decorated with plaster stucco dragons, birds, crabs and brilliantly glazed tiles. *Pintu pagar* (saloon doors) at the front of the houses are another typical feature, which allow breezes in while retaining privacy.

Joo Chiat Rd runs into traffic-plagued **East Coast Road**, noted for its restaurants, many serving top class Nonya cuisine. Combining Peranakan food and culture is the **Katong Antique House** (☎ 6345 1220; 208 East Coast Rd; ⏰ 11am-6pm) where owner Peter Wee will show you round his large collection of antiques including beautifully beaded slippers, wedding costumes and traditional ceramics and furniture. Call in advance if you'd like tea (S$10) or a meal (from S$23) here including Peranakan delicacies. Heading west back to the city, East Coast Rd changes its name to **Mountbatten Road** – around here you'll see a number of grand bungalows dating from the early 20th century.

From East Coast Rd, bus Nos 12 and 32 head into the city along North Bridge Rd in the colonial district, while bus No 14 goes down Stamford Rd and then Orchard Rd.

EAST COAST PARK

This pleasant waterside stretch of park, running for 10km along East Coast Parkway, is where Singaporeans come to swim, windsurf, lie on the sand, rent a bike or inline skates, and eat. The beach, born of reclaimed land and made of sand from Indonesia, wouldn't win any awards as a tropical paradise, but it is one of Singapore's more popular, and the park has decent facilities, including some great seafood restaurants.

The **East Coast Recreation Centre** midway along the park, has bowling, squash, crazy golf, fun rides, and a selection of restaurants and food stalls. You can hire bicycles (from around S$5 an hour), rollerblades (S$8 per hour) and canoes. Bus No 401 runs between Kallang and Bedok MRT stations via Mountbatten Rd and stops along the service road in the park.

CHANGI PRISON MUSEUM & CHAPEL

The quietly moving **Changi Prison Museum** (☎ 6214 2451; www.changimuseum.com; 1000 Upper Changi Rd North; admission free; guided tour S$6; 🕒 9.30am-4.30pm) commemorates the Allied POWs who were captured, imprisoned and suffered horrific treatment at the hands of the invading Japanese forces during WWII. It was shifted from the original Changi Prison site in 2000 when Singapore Prisons reclaimed the land to expand its operations.

The museum's centrepiece is a replica of the original Changi chapel built by inmates as a focus for worship and presumably as a sign of solidarity and strength. Tucked into the walls beside the altar with its cross made of ammunition casings, are little mementos and hand-written notes left by visitors. Services are held on Sundays (9.30am and 5.30pm), but the shadeless courtyard heats up like an oven.

The exhibition section poignantly tells the story of Changi and wartime suffering in Singapore through photographs, artefacts and survivors' testimonials. You can also view full-sized replicas of the famous **Changi Murals** painted by POW Stanley Warren in the old POW hospital. The originals are now off limits in what is now Block 151 of the nearby Changi Army Camp.

Bus No 2 from Victoria St or Tanah Merah MRT will take you past the entrance (ask the driver to alert you to the nearest stop). The bus terminates at Changi Village.

CHANGI VILLAGE

On the far northeast coast of Singapore, **Changi Village** is an escape from the hubbub of central Singapore. The buildings are modern but there's still a village atmosphere with the lively hawker centre next to the bus terminus being a focal point. Changi's beach (where thousands of Singaporean civilians were executed during WWII), lapped by the polluted waters of the Johor Straits, is hardly a tropical paradise, but there's a good stretch of sand. It's popular on weekends but almost deserted during the week. Bus No 2 from Victoria St or Tanah Merah MRT runs here.

PULAU UBIN

Changi Village's ferry jetty, a minute's walk from the bus terminus, is where bumboats leave for **Pulau Ubin** (S$2, 6am-10pm). There's no timetable; boats depart when a quota of 12 people is reached, which usually doesn't take too long.

Rural Pulau Ubin with its quiet beaches and *kampung* atmosphere is as unlike modern Singapore as you will find. It's also a natural haven for many species of bird that inhabit the mangroves and forest areas. Public pressure has halted government policy of developing Ubin, the most notable victory being scored over **Chek Jawa**, a flood plain teeming with marine life at the eastern tip of the 8km long island. Still with less than 100 people now living here, development plans are unlikely to be deferred indefinitely – visit sooner rather than later.

There's an **information kiosk** (☎ 6542 4108; 🕒 8am-4.30pm) a minute's walk from the jetty where the bumboats dock; call them to inquire about guided tours out to Chek Jawa. Pick up here a free leaflet with a map of the island showing the main walking and cycling trails. The best way to explore the island is by bicycle, which can be hired from around S$6 per day from numerous stalls next to the jetty.

Heading out to the west of Ubin you'll pass several of the abandoned quarries where granite was once mined; note that swimming in the quarry lakes is strictly forbidden. You'll also find **Wat Suwankiyiwanaram**, a Thai Buddhist temple with robed monk statues inside.

There are several inexpensive, informal eateries near the jetty, the best of which is **Ubin First Stop Restaurant** (☎ 6543 2489; 🕒 11am-8pm Thu-Tue) where a seafood meal will set you back around S$30.

Northern & Central Singapore

Map pp448-9

SINGAPORE ZOOLOGICAL GARDENS

In the far north of the island, the world-class **Singapore Zoological Gardens** (☎ 6269 3411; www.zoo.com.sg; 80 Mandai Lake Rd; adult/child S$12/5; 🕒 8.30am-6pm) has 3600 animals, representing 410 species including endangered white rhinos, Bengal white tigers and even polar bears. Wherever possible, moats replace bars and the zoo is spread out over 28 hectares of lush greenery beside the Upper Selator Reservoir.

As zoos go (and in spite of the animal shows – some of which come close to circus-style antics) this is one of the best. New and innovative exhibits include the S$2.4m 'Hamadryas Baboons – The Great Rift Valley of Ethiopia' enclosure, housing a 50-strong troupe of these rare primates, which attempts to convey an entire ecosystem. You can also get up close to an otter, reticulated python and one of the zoo's famous orang-utans at the 'wild breakfast or tea' (breakfast adult/child S$15.45/11.33; tea S$13/10.30) at 9am and 4pm.

You can get around the zoo on foot or by tram (adult/child S$2.50/1.50).

NIGHT SAFARI

Next door but completely separate from the zoo, and equally worth visiting, is the **Night Safari** (☎ 7269 3412; www.nightsafari.com.sg; adult/child S$15.45/10.30; 🕑 7.30pm-midnight). This 40-hectare forested park allows you to view 120 different species of animal, including tigers, lions and leopards. In the darkness the moats and other barriers seem to melt away, and inside the enclosed Mangrove Walk bats flap around your head – a truly electric experience!

You are asked to *not* use a flash on your camera since they disturb the animals and annoy fellow visitors.

As well as exploring the park on foot, it's worth taking the Night Safari tram tour (adult/child S$5/2) lasting about 45 minutes with a live commentary. Expect queues since it's very popular.

You can save some money with a combined zoo and Night Safari ticket (adult/child S$23/13) – but specify when you buy this whether you want to view both parks on the same or different days. Both parks have plenty of food outlets and the zoos boast award-winningly clean and creatively designed toilets!

To get here, take the MRT to Ang Mo Kio station, and then catch bus No 138 from the same side of the road as the MRT. When returning from the night safari you should catch a bus at around 10.45pm to ensure you make the last train leaving Ang Mo Kio at 11.28pm. A taxi to/from the city centre costs around S$15; there is a taxi stand at the zoo entrance.

BUKIT TIMAH NATURE RESERVE

Nature walks and jungle treks can be enjoyed at the 164-hectare **Bukit Timah Nature Reserve** (www.nparks.gov.sg), the only large area of primary forest left in Singapore. It's a haven for wildlife and boasts the highest point on the island, 163.63m Bukit Timah – don't expect much of a view though; it's blocked by dense vegetation.

The most popular and easiest walk in the park is along a paved road to the top of Bukit Timah. Even during the week it attracts a number of walkers, but few venture off the pavement to explore the side trails which are more interesting; try the North View, South View or Fern Valley paths, where it is hard to believe that you are in Singapore. These involve some scrambling over rocks and tree roots and can be quite testing in parts.

Pick up a map of the park's trails from the **information desk** (☎ 1800- 468 5736; 🕑 8.30am-6pm) above which is a small natural history exhibition area. There's a shop here selling drinks, snacks, nature guidebooks and mosquito repellent (it's a good idea to apply some).

Bukit Timah has two challenging **mountain bike trails**, 6km in all, running around the edge of the nature reserve between Chestnut Ave and Rifle Range Rd. The trails cut though jungle and abandoned quarry sites and are hilly in parts. There's also a bike trail running through the neighbouring Central Catchment Nature Reserve to the MacRitchie Reservoir, 5.8km east.

Several buses run close to the park, including Nos 65 and 170 from Newton MRT, No 75 from the CBD and Chinatown, and No 171 from the YMCA on Orchard Rd. Get off at the Bukit Timah Shopping Centre; the park's entrance is about 1km north along Hindhede Drive.

KONG MENG SAN PHOR KARK SEE MONASTERY

A fascinating few hours can be had exploring **Kong Meng San Phor Kark See Monastery** (☎ 6453 4046; kmspks.org; 88 Bright Hill Dr; 🕑 7am-6pm), Singapore's largest. Founded in 1921, the monastery's main function is as a crematorium – on any day you'll be able to watch

SINGAPORE

cremations and if you contact the monastery in advance it's also possible to get a tour of the facilities including the large columbarium (repositories for cremation urns). Also worth seeing here are several monumental halls of worship, the highlight being the **Pagoda of 10,000 Buddhas**, with its golden cone-shaped stupa lined on the inside with 9999 Buddha images – the 10,000th Buddha is the giant one inside the pagoda.

Bus No 410 with the white plate (not the green plate) runs here from Bishan MRT station.

MACRITCHIE RESERVOIR

Part of the 2000 hectares of the **Central Catchment Nature Reserve**, Singapore's largest nature reserve the **MacRitchie Reservoir** park has a great trail running along the reservoir and into the jungle to a tree-top walkway. To complete the reasonably well signposted 12km trail takes around three hours and you're guaranteed to see plenty of long-tailed macaques along the way. For more details see the national parks board website www.nparks.gov.sg.

SUNGEI BULOH WETLAND RESERVE

One of Singapore's least visited but potentially most interesting parks is **Sungei Buloh Wetland Reserve**, an 87-hectare wetland nature reserve (☎ 6794 1401; www.sbwr.org.sg; 301 Neo Tiew Cres; adult/child S$1/50c; 🕑 7.30am-7pm Mon-Fri, 7am-7pm Sat & Sun), in the far northwest of the island, overlooking the Straits of Johor. It's home to 140 species of bird, most of which are migratory. From the visitors centre, with its well-presented displays, trails lead around ponds and mangrove swamps to hides for observing the birds. The best time for viewing birds is before 10am, but you can enjoy the walks and solitude here anytime.

Audiovisual shows on the park's flora and fauna are held at 9am and 11am, and 1pm, 3pm and 5pm (hourly between 9am and 5pm on Sunday). Allow yourself three hours to do the park justice.

To reach the park take the MRT to Kranji and then the No 925 TIBS bus.

MANDAI ORCHID GARDENS

Singapore has a major business in cultivating orchids, and the **Mandai Orchid Gardens** (☎ 6269 1036; Mandai Lake Rd; adult/child S$2/50c; 🕑 8.30am-5.30pm), near the zoo, is one of the best places to see them – four solid hectares of orchids. You can arrange to have a giftbox of fresh orchids flown to just about anywhere in the world. To get here see the transport details for the zoo.

SIONG LIM TEMPLE

Nestled in a corner of the Toa Payoh HDB housing estate, **Siong Lim Temple** (☎ 6259 6924; 184E Jl Toa Payoh; 🕑 7am-5pm) is also known as Lian Shan Shuang Lin Monastery (and literally translated as Twin Groves of the Lotus Mountain). The original buildings were built in 1912, the main hall being wonderfully atmospheric, a towering space stained by decades of incense smoke and perpetually buzzing with visitors. The adjoining complex of newer temples is also beautifully decorated and surrounded by neatly clipped bonsai. Sadly the ambience is ruined by traffic thundering by on the expressway.

You can walk to the temple – it's about 1km east of Toa Payoh MRT station – or take one of several buses (including No 238) for three stops from Toa Payoh bus interchange.

KRANJI WAR MEMORIAL

Near the Causeway off Woodlands Rd, the **Kranji War Memorial** (☎ 6269 6158; 9 Woodlands Rd; admission free; 🕑 24hr) includes the graves of thousands of Allied troops who died in the region during WWII. The walls are inscribed with the names of 24,346 men and women. Registers, stored inside unlocked weatherproof stands, are available for inspection. The memorial can be reached by bus No 170 from Rochor Rd.

SUN YAT SEN NANYANG MEMORIAL HALL

Built in the 1880s, the **Sun Yat Sen Nanyang Memorial Hall** (☎ 6256 7377; 12 Tai Gin Rd; admission S$2; 🕑 9am-5pm Tue-Sun), was once the residence of Sun Yat Sen, a Chinese revolutionary Republican leader. This national **monument** is a fine example of a colonial Victorian villa and houses a museum with items pertaining to Sun Yat Sen's life and work. Bus No 145 from Toa Payoh bus interchange stops on Balestier Rd near the villa and temple.

HOLLAND VILLAGE

This popular expat enclave, a short bus ride from the Botanic Gardens, is best known for its fashionable restaurants and cafés, concentrated on Lorong Mambong, just back from the main road. The **Holland Shopping Centre** is a good place to root around for souvenirs.

The nearest MRT station is Buona Vista, about a 15-minute walk along Buona Vista Rd from Holland Village. Or take bus No 7, 105 or 106 from Penang Rd/Orchard Blvd.

Southern & Western Singapore

Map pp448-9

MT FABER PARK & THE CABLE CAR

Off Kampong Bahru Road, the 116m-high Mt Faber forms the centrepoint of the pleasant Mt Faber Park. The hillside slopes offer fine views over the harbour and the city, and on the hike up here you'll catch glimpses of colonial-era black-and-white bungalows and the strikingly stripy **Danish Seaman's Mission** built in 1909.

If you don't want to walk up, the **cable car** (☎ 6270 8855; www.cablecar.com.sg; adult/child S$8.50/3.90; ⏰ 8.30am-9pm) connects the summit with the World Trade Centre (WTC; next to Harbour Front MRT station) and Sentosa Island. Every Saturday from 6.30pm to 8.30pm it's also possible to dine in the cable car; the four course meal (you have a choice of entrée, either steak or salmon) plus a glass of wine and tea or coffee is served *à deux* at each of the stations as the cable car glides from Mt Faber to Sentosa and back. It's S$120 per couple and bookings are essential.

HAW PAR VILLA

'What I have in mind will be unique, like nothing anybody has seen,' said Aw Boon Haw, one of the brothers behind the Tiger-Balm miracle ointment fortune, who stumped up over S$1 million in the 1930s to build this tacky, unbelievably kitsch **Chinese mythology theme park** (☎ 6872 2780; 262 Pasir Panjang Rd; admission free; ⏰ 9am-7pm). The Aw's glamorous villa is long gone and the park is really running to seed these days, but it's still worth swinging by to gawp at the infamous '10 courts of hell'. This cave-like enclosure inside the body of a giant dragon, holds a series of graphic, bloody tableaus depicting the hideous tortures awaiting a multitude of sinners.

Bus No 200 from Buona Vista MRT runs here as well as bus Nos 10, 30 or 188 from Harbour Front MRT.

NUS MUSEUMS

On the campus of the National University of Singapore (NUS), this trio of small but exquisite **art museums** (☎ 6874 4616; www.nus.edu.sg/museums/; 50 Kent Ridge Cres; admission free; ⏰ 9am-5pm Mon-Sat) each hold fine collections. On the ground floor is the **Lee Kong Chian Art Museum** with works spanning 7000 years of Chinese culture, from ancient ceramics to modern paintings done in traditional style.

The concourse level houses the **South & Southeast Asian Gallery** with a mixture of art from across the region, including textiles and sculptures. On the top level is the **Ng Eng Teng Gallery** which displays the paintings, drawings and sculptures of Ng Eng Teng (1934–2001) one of Singapore's foremost artists specialising in imaginative, sometimes surreal depictions of the body.

JURONG BIRD PARK

Over 8000 birds representing around 600 species can be seen at the beautifully landscaped 20-hectare **Jurong Bird Park** (☎ 6265 0022; www.birdpark.com.sg; 2 Jurong Hill; adult/child S$12.25/5.10; ⏰ 8am-6pm) that's fun to visit even if you're only mildly interested in our feathered friends. Highlights include the walk-through Waterfall Aviary (with its 30m-high custom-made waterfall); the Penguin Parade, which simulates a slice of Antarctica; and a lake teeming with pink flamingos. A monorail (adult/child S$3.05/2.05) will transport you around it all.

As with the zoo (which is run by the same management) there are bird shows at various times during the day, kicking off with the 'breakfast with the birds' show (adult/child S$13.35/11.10; 8am to 10.30am) and including the birds of prey show at 10am.

To get here take bus No 194 or 251 from Boon Lay MRT.

While here you might want to check out the less impressive **Jurong Reptile Park** (☎ 6261 8866; 241 Jl Ahmad Ibrahim; adult/child S$8/7.50; ⏰ 9am-6pm), across the car park from the bird park. Crocodiles are the star attraction here, although there's also a scaly collection of other reptiles and amphibians, including giant tortoises and arapaima fish.

SINGAPORE SCIENCE CENTRE & SNOW CITY

For kids, but not bad entertainment for adults too, is the fun **Singapore Science Centre**

(☎ 6425 2500; www.sci-ctr.edu.sg; 15 Science Centre Rd; adult/child S$6/3; 🕑 10am-6pm Tue-Sun). All aspects of science come alive through a range of high- and low-tech hands-on displays. Outside is the free **Kinetic Garden**, an interactive scientific sculpture garden.

Next door is the **Omni-Theatre** (adult/child S$10/5; 🕑 10am-8pm), which features special huge screen movies, and the **Virtual Voyages** (adult/child S$6/4) simulation theatre, which has shows every 15 to 20 minutes between 10am and 8.30pm.

Also nearby is **Snow City** (☎ 6560 1511; www.snowcity.com.sg; 21 Jurong Town Hall Rd; admission S$8 Tue-Fri, S$12 Sat, Sun & public holidays; 🕑 9am-8.30pm Tue-Sun), a hangar-size deep freeze with a small ski slope and area for chucking snow balls or building snowmen. Obviously a huge novelty if you live in the tropics, visitors from colder climes will find it at best mildly amusing. Entrance includes a warm jacket and boots.

Jurong East is the nearest MRT station. To reach the centre take the left-hand exit and walk through the shopping centre and across Jurong Town Hall Rd (Jurong East's main road). A taxi from Orchard Rd will take around 20 minutes and cost around S$15.

REFLECTIONS AT BUKIT CHANDU

Atop Bukit Chandu (Opium Hill), this new WWII **interpretive centre** (☎ 6375 2510; www.s1942.org.sg; 31K Pepys Rd; admission S$2; 🕑 9am-5pm Tue-Sun) is based in an old renovated villa. Its focus is the brave stand made by the 1st and 2nd Battalions of the Malay Regiment defending the hill in the Battle of Pasir Panjang when the Japanese invaded in 1942. High-tech displays, using films from the period and audio effects to transport you to the scene of the battle, are all quite evocative. The nearest bus stops (for Nos. 10, 30, 51 and 143) are on Pasir Panjang Rd, from where it's a steep hike up the hill – you may want to take a taxi.

CHINESE & JAPANESE GARDENS

Not especially worth going out of your way for, these spacious gardens (☎ 6261 3632; 1 Chinese Garden Rd; admission free; 🕑 6am-10pm Mon-Fri, 6am-11pm Sat & Sun) each occupying 13.5 hectares in the vicinity of Jurong Lake, are nonetheless quite pleasant.

The Chinese Garden is actually an island. It contains a number of Chinese-style pavilions and a seven-storey pagoda providing a great view. The main attraction is the extensive *penjing* (Chinese bonsai) display. The less-interesting Japanese Garden – which is almost an island – has large grassed areas and a few buildings.

The Gardens are easily accessed from Chinese Garden MRT station.

MING VILLAGE & PEWTER MUSEUM

Reproduction Ming and Qing dynasty pottery is made in this **workshop** (☎ 6265 7711; 32 Pandan Rd; admission free; 🕑 9am-5.30pm) where you can watch the craftspeople at work. The complete production process is done on the premises and guided tours are available.

Ming Village is owned by Royal Selangor Pewter, so there's also a small pewter museum here with some interesting pieces. The pewter is made in Malaysia, but the polishing and hand-beaten designs are demonstrated at the village. The showroom sells an extensive selection of pewter as well as porcelain.

The company runs a free shuttle service from Orchard Hotel, Mandarin Hotel, Raffles Hotel and Pan Pacific Hotels daily from 9.20am; inquire with the hotel concierges.

Sentosa Island

Map pp448-9

Five hundred metres off the south coast of Singapore is **Sentosa Island** (☎ 1800-736 8672; www.sentosa.com.sg; basic admission adult/child S$2; 🕑 7am-midnight), the city's favourite resort getaway. Like its beaches of imported sand, Sentosa is almost entirely a synthetic attraction, but it is a good place for children and adults won't be disappointed either by the decent museums, a fine aquarium, and outdoor activities including bicycling and golf. There's easily enough to do to fill a day and night and if that isn't enough you could stop over.

Most of the attractions cost extra and the charges can really add up if you want to see them all. If that's your plan, it's a good idea to invest in one of the ticket packages, starting at adult/child S$19.90/13.90 – check the website for details. There's also quite a bit that's free on the island, including the buses, monorail and the entertaining nightly musical fountain and laser show.

Over 30 years old now, Sentosa (meaning peace and tranquillity in Malay) is in the midst of a makeover. Some old attractions are being revamped, and new ones added. All-night rave parties on the beaches have also become popular – check the local press for details. By 2005 a new monorail should link the island directly with Harbour Front MRT station, replacing the old round-island monorail.

UNDERWATER WORLD

This spectacular **aquarium** (☎ 6275 0030; www.underwaterworld.com.sg; adult/child S$17/11; ⌚ 9am-9pm) is deservedly one of Sentosa's most popular attractions. Its star attraction is the travellator, an acrylic tunnel with a moving walkway that takes spectators through the main tanks. There is nothing quite like the sight of 60kg giant groupers, brown stingrays or sharks swimming overhead. You can watch divers feeding the fish, and even get in the tank yourself on the 90-minute *Dive with the Sharks* experience (from S$70 per person, bookings required; call the aquarium or email ayu@uws.hawpar.com). After 7pm, when the lights are turned off and torches handed out to visitors, the aquarium takes on a whole new atmosphere.

Your entry ticket also includes admission to the specially constructed **Dolphin Lagoon** (⌚ 10.30am-5.30pm) at Palawan Beach. Here you can see the Indo-Pacific humpbacked dolphins, commonly known as pink dolphins, perform in shows at 1.30pm, 3.30pm and 5.30pm with an extra 11am session on the weekends. It's possible to get in the water to feed the dolphins, too.

FORT SILOSO

This surprisingly entertaining attraction is a slice of history, dating from the time when the island was called Pulau Blakang Mati (Malay for 'island behind which lies death'). **Fort Siloso** (adult/child S$5/3; ⌚ 9am-6.30pm) was built in the 1880s as a military base with a series of gun emplacements linked by underground tunnels. But when it came to the test with the Japanese invasion in WWII, the guns were all pointing in the wrong direction. The fort was later used by the Japanese as a POW camp.

The path around the fort leads to the gun emplacements, tunnels and buildings, with jolly waxwork re-creations and voice-overs about life in a colonial barracks. There's also a small obstacle course to try your army skills out on.

From 1989 until 1993, Fort Siloso housed Sentosa's most unusual 'attraction', political prisoner Chia Thye Poh. Arrested in 1966 for allegedly being a Communist, Chia served 23 years in jail before being banished to complete his sentence among the holiday delights of Sentosa.

IMAGES OF SINGAPORE

This diverting historical and cultural **museum** (adult/child S$8/5; ⌚ 9am-9pm) starts with Singapore as a Malay sultanate and takes you through its establishment as a busy port and trading centre, its trials during WWII and the subsequent Japanese surrender. Scenes are recreated using lifelike wax dummies, film footage and dramatic light and sound effects. The Festivals of Singapore section is particularly colourful and the new Stories of the Sea exhibition offers an interactive 'all-sensory' journey through Singapore's maritime heritage.

BEACHES & RECREATIONAL FACILITIES

Along Sentosa's southern coast are three **beaches**: Siloso at the western end, Palawan in the middle and Tanjong Beach at the eastern end. As a beach paradise, Sentosa has a long way to go to match the islands of Malaysia or Indonesia, but the imported sand and planted coconut palms do lend it a tropical ambience even if the muddy Singapore Straits make uninviting swimming. Aquabikes, canoes, kayaks and sailboards are available for hire.

Sentosa has a 5.7km **bicycle track** that loops the island and takes in most of the attractions. Bicycles (S$4 to S$10 per hour) can be hired at bicycle stations at Siloso and Palawan Beaches or at the ferry terminal.

The **Sentosa Riding Centre** (☎ 6273 7492) offers everything from five-minute pony rides (adult/child S$8/6) to two-hour rides for qualified riders (S$70).

There are two 18-hole golf courses at the **Sentosa Golf Club** (☎ 6275 0022). On a mini-scale **Sijori Wondergolf** (adults/child S$8-10/4-7; ⌚ 9am-9pm) offers 54 putting greens in three fun courses, two of international tournament standard.

OTHER ATTRACTIONS

The free **Musical Fountain** (⌚ 5 & 5.30pm) and, in particular, the **Magical Sentosa shows** (⌚ 7.40pm, 8.40pm Mon-Fri, extra 9.30pm show Sat, Sun and public holidays) combining the musical fountain with a spectacular S$4 million sound, light and laser extravaganza, are well worth hanging around for.

More than 50 species of butterfly flutter around you inside the conservatory of the **Butterfly Park & Insect Kingdom** (adult/child S$8/5; 9am-6pm). In the Insect Kingdom museum there are thousands of mounted butterflies, rhino beetles, Hercules beetles (the world's largest) and scorpions, among other, thankfully dead, creepy crawlies – kids will be entranced.

Among the trashier of Sentosa's attractions are the **Merlion** (adult/child S$3/2; 9am-9.30pm), the 37-metre hybrid lion-mermaid statues towering over the island; it does offer a good view but you can see the same from the cable car. Equally naff is **VolcanoLand** (adult/child S$12/6; 10am-7pm) dominated by a concrete volcano, which you can see 'erupting' every half hour with a bang and a puff of smoke. **Cinemania** (adult/child S$12.50/8; 11am-7.30pm) offers two different 3-D virtual-reality–style thrill rides per admission.

As well as the florid ferry terminal, Fountain Gardens and Flower Terrace, there's a **Nature Walk**, livened up – in typical Sentosa fashion – with plaster dragons and fossils. Long-tailed macaques are common, but hide your food from these aggressive monkeys.

There's no shortage of places to eat on the island, although none are particularly outstanding. The hawker centre and the **SEA Village** restaurant next to the bus terminal are both good value. **Bora Bora Beach Bar** at Palawan beach also does OK food and has a pleasant location.

GETTING THERE & AWAY

All the following transport costs include island admission of S$2.

The easiest way of getting to Sentosa is to take the MRT to Harbour Front station and then either walk across the causeway or hop on the service bus. Alternatively you can take the Sentosa bus from Tiong Bahru MRT station directly to the island. Sentosa bus fares are S$3.

Ferries (S$4.30) run every 20 to 30 minutes to/from the WTC between 9.30am and 10pm on weekdays, and from 8.30am to 10pm weekends and public holidays.

The cable car from either the top of Mt Faber or from the Cable Car Towers adjacent to the WTC itself costs S$10.50. It operates every 20 minutes between 8.30am and 9pm. The cable-car ride, with its spectacular views, is one of the best parts of a visit to Sentosa; if the weather is fine, take it at least one-way.

GETTING AROUND

All the transport on the island is covered in the admission price. The monorail, operating on a continuous loop between 9am and 10pm, has seven stops, including the ferry terminal. A beach 'train' (it's actually a kind of bus) (9am to 7pm) runs continuously between Siloso, Palawan and Tanjong beaches. The Fort train (9am to 7pm) travels the short distance between Underwater World and Fort Siloso. There are also four different colour-coded buses running set routes around the island: The *Sentosa Island Guide*, a free pamphlet available at the WTC, the ferry terminal and the Visitor Arrival Centre, has maps and details on times. You can also cycle – see p507 for details.

St John's & Kusu Islands

The Sentosa Development Corporation is also in charge of two other tiny islands that are popular with locals as city escapes: St John's (Pulau Sakijang Bendera) and Kusu (Pulau Tembakul). On weekends they can both become rather crowded but during the week you'll find them fairly quiet, and good places for a peaceful swim – though the water can be a bit on the polluted side, hardly surprising given all the ships that pass through. Both islands have changing rooms, toilet facilities, grassy picnic spots and swimming areas.

St John's Island is much the bigger of the two. It was once a quarantine station for immigrants, drug rehabilitation centre and prison. There's not much to do here other than walk along its rather uninspiring concrete pathways and relax in its shady picnic areas. Bring your own picnic, as the culinary offerings are limited. It's possible to stay overnight in colonial-style bungalows, or camp; contact the **Sentosa Development Corporation** (☎ 6275 0388) for details.

Kusu Island is more interesting, famous for both its Taoist temple and Malay *kramat*

SINGAPORE

(shrine), where people come to pray for health, wealth and fertility. Tua Pek Kong temple and turtle sanctuary is next to the ferry jetty, the yellow-painted shrine atop a small wooded hill, reached by a steep flight of steps – both can be visited in less than an hour, leaving you the rest of the day to laze around on the quiet beaches. Again bring your own food and water.

The liveliest time to visit Kusu is during the annual pilgrimage of Taoists in the ninth lunar month (around October), when there are constant daily ferries from Clifford Pier; try to avoid weekends in this period, though, as the island is literally swamped with visitors.

GETTING THERE & AWAY

The ferry from the WTC (☎ 6321 2802; round trip adult/child S$9/6) runs to both islands at 10am and 1.30pm Monday to Saturday – more frequently on Sunday and public holidays – stopping first at Kusu and then St John's. The only way to see both islands without hanging around for hours is on Sunday when you can hop off the ferry at Kusu, then get on again when the next one passes through to St John's.

During the annual Kusu pilgrimage, ferries leave every 30 minutes from Clifford Pier (round trip S$10 Monday to Saturday, S$11.50 Sunday). Also most harbour tours pass St John's Island and stop at Kusu for 20 minutes or so (see p473).

Other Southern Islands

Many of the islands on Singapore's southern shore have refineries that provide much of Singapore's export income. Among the ones that are relatively unspoilt are the **Sisters' Islands** – Pulau Subar Darat and Pulau Subar Laut. The sea is much better for swimming and snorkelling here and the nearby coral reefs make it a good spot for divers, too (you'll need to bring your own equipment). Bring your own food and water too since there are no amenities on the islands.

To reach these islands you must rent a bumboat, with operator, from Clifford Pier at Marina Bay. Expect to pay around S$100 per hour per boat, which takes from six to 12 people. You can approach individual boat owners or contact the **Singapore Motor Launch Owners' Association** (Map pp450-1; ☎ 6532 5652) at Clifford Pier.

SINGAPORE

MASSAGE & SPA SELECTION

Reflexology is an integral part of Chinese medical culture, and foot and/or shoulder massages have long been available across Singapore – walk in off the street and relax for 30 or 40 minutes of gentle (and sometimes not so gentle) pummelling and prodding. Try **Ngee Ann Foot Reflexology** (Map pp456-7; ☎ 6235 5538; 4th fl, Midpoint Orchard, 220 Orchard Rd; ⌚ 10am-8pm) run by visually impaired masseurs. A 40-minute foot massage costs S$22, a full body massage S$40 for a hour.

Kenko (www.kenkofootreflexology.com) is the McDonald's of reflexology with outlets all over the city. The most upmarket of their operations are the **'wellness boutique'** (Map pp452-3; ☎ 6223 0303, 211 South Bridge Rd) in Chinatown, and the spas at the **Esplanade Mall** (pp452-3; ☎ 6363 0303) and **DFS Galleria Scottswalk** (Map pp456-7; ☎ 6565 0303; 25 Scotts Rd). Thirty-minute foot massages start at S$30.90.

If you're looking for something more luxurious in the way of bodily pampering, then hasten over to Sentosa where the super-sybaritic (and expensive) **Spa Botanica** (Map pp448-9; ☎ 6820 6788; www.spabotanica.com) has recently opened as the island state's first indoor and outdoor spa. The signature treatment here is the galaxy steam bath (S$100), a 45-minute wallow in medicinal chakra muds in a specially designed steam room. There's also a mud pool outside as well as landscaped grounds and pools.

Amrita Spa (Map pp452-3; ☎ 6336 4477; www.amritaspas.com; Level 6, Raffles The Plaza, 2 Stamford Rd) boasts of being Asia's most extensive spa with 35 treatment rooms, a fitness centre, a variety of plunge and bubble pools and a long menu of spa treatments; their day spa escape package with back massage and express facial is S$150. There are branches at Swissôtel Merchant Court and Raffles Hotel.

The spas at Amara Singapore Hotel, Fullerton Hotel, Grand Hyatt Hotel and Goodwood Park Hotel (see Sleeping on p485) are also open to the public.

ACTIVITIES

A great resource for finding out about all manner of sports and activities in Singapore – from archery to martial arts – is the website www.singaporesports.com.sg.

Cycling & Hash House Harriers

Bikes can be hired for a leisurely pedal along the foreshore of the east coast, around Sentosa or on Pulau Ubin. For a more energetic workout take to the mountain bike trails around Bukit Timah Nature Reserve. See p507 for bike-hire details.

Two Wheel Action (☎ 6463 2143) organises Sunday rides in collaboration with the Singapore chapter of the Hash House Harriers (full details are on www.singaporesports.com.sg). You bring your own bike and meet at a pre-arranged point for a casual ride. Cost is S$10 per session.

Golf

Singapore has plenty of golf courses; most are members only so they charge visitors a premium and usually don't allow you to play on weekends. A game of golf costs around S$90 on weekdays, and from S$100 to S$220 on weekends. Club hire is expensive. The following courses have 18 holes:

Jurong Country Club (Map pp448-9; ☎ 6560 5655; 9 Science Centre Rd)

Laguna National Golf & Country Club (Map pp448-9; ☎ 6541 0289; 11 Laguna Golf Green)

Raffles Country Club (Map pp448-9; ☎ 6861 7655; 450 Jl Ahmad Ibrahim)

Sentosa Golf Club (Map pp448-9; ☎ 6275 0022; Sentosa Island)

Racket Sports

Tennis and squash courts can be hired at **Kallang Squash & Tennis Centre** (Map pp450-1; ☎ 6440 6839; Stadium Rd). A game at **Singapore Tennis Centre** (Map pp448-9; ☎ 6442 5966; 1020 East Coast Parkway; 🕑 7am-11pm) starts from S$10.50 per hour.

You can also whack shuttlecocks around at **Singapore Badminton Hall** (Map pp448-9; ☎ 6345 7554; 102 Guillemard Rd; 🕑 7am-10pm). Bookings are essential with court fees starting at S$3.50 off-peak.

Rock Climbing

Dairy Farm Quarry (Map pp448-9) near Bukit Timah, with some 20 routes, is the only legal place to climb in Singapore. Most routes are bolted and can be done with a 50m rope; you'll need to bring your own gear. To find out about joining up with climbers who come here regularly on weekends, contact an outdoor equipment shop such as **Campers' Corner** (Map pp452-3; ☎ 6337 4743; 01-13 Capitol Bldg, 11 Stamford Rd; 🕑 11am-8pm Mon-Sat, noon-7pm Sun).

> **DRAGONBOAT RACING**
>
> A popular weekend workout with expats and locals alike is a furious paddle in a dragonboat – it's a great way to sweat off your Friday night hangover! Groups meet at Water Sports Centre, Stadium Lane, a short walk from the Indoor Stadium at Kallang (Map pp450-1). The British team (www.britishdragonboat.com) meets every Saturday between 3.30pm and 4pm. You don't need to be British, or even an expat, to join in – bring S$10, a change of clothes and some water to drink on the boat. Refreshments are provided afterwards. Fun competitions are held occasionally between the different dragonboat teams.

Swimming

Given the polluted waters, none of Singapore's beaches are particularly great for swimming, although there are safe swimming areas at East Coast Park, Sentosa or the other islands.

A better option, if you're not staying at a hotel with its own pool, are the excellent public pools at **Farrer Park** (Map p458; ☎ 6299 1002; 2 Rutland Ave) and **River Valley Swimming Complex** (Map pp452-3; ☎ 6337 6275; 1 River Valley Rd) at the foot of Fort Canning Park. Both are open 8am to 9.30pm and admission is adult/child S$1/0.50 or S$1.30/0.60 on weekends.

Water Sports

The **Pasta Fresca Seasport Centre** (Map pp448-9; ☎ 6449 5118; sailing@singaporesport.com.sg; 1212 East Coast Parkway) is the place to go for windsurfing and sailing. Sailboards cost S$30 for two hours' hire; lessons are also available. The centre also rents laser-class boats for S$30 per hour and organises sailing courses.

Sailboards and aquabikes are also available for hire on Sentosa.

The **Changi Sailing Centre** (Map pp448-9; ☎ 6545 2876; www.csc.org.sg; 32 Netheravon Rd) rents out j-24s (24-foot keel boats) on one-day charters for

S$180 a day, including petrol. You will need to show a sailing proficiency certificate.

At the **Singapore Waterski Federation** (Map pp450-1; ☎ 6440 9763; Water Sports Centre, 10 Stadium Lane, Kallang) you can arrange water-skiing and wakeboarding (like a snowboard) lessons and equipment (from S$90 per hour on weekdays and S$120 on weekends, including boat, driver and equipment; bookings are required).

WALKING TOUR

From Raffles Place cut through the **Clifford Centre (1)** and across the Change Alley arcade bridge on the second level to the historical **Clifford Pier (2)**. Walk north up the promenade and admire the **Fullerton Hotel (3**; p485), once the city's post office, from One Fullerton, the modern office and dining complex fronting the bay. Here you'll also find the **Merlion statues** (**4**; p462) and across the bay the spiky domes of **Esplanade – Theatres on the Bay** (**5**; p460).

Start/Finish: Raffles Place MRT
Distance: 2.5km
Duration: 2hrs

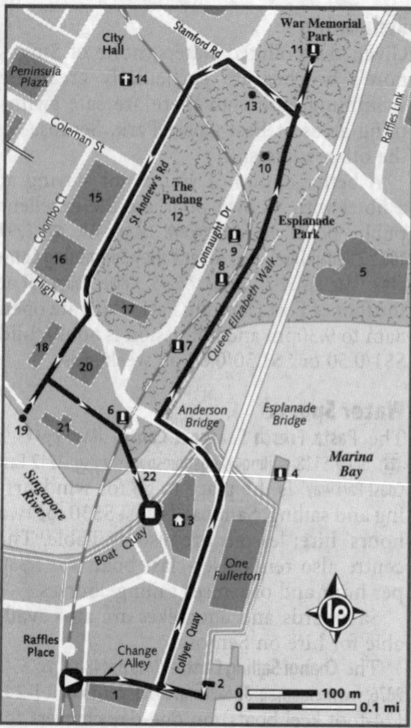

If the footway under the Esplanade Bridge is still closed, walk up and over the bridge and cross the adjacent Anderson Bridge. The **Dalhousie Obelisk (6)**, dedicated to free trade, is to your left. Turn right along the pedestrian Queen Elizabeth Walk, passing the **Lim Bo Seng Memorial (7)**, built in honour of a WWII hero, followed by the **Indian National Army Monument (8)**. Continue to the British war memorial, the **Cenotaph (9)**, and along to the Victorian-style **Tan Kim Seng Fountain (10)**. Across Stamford Rd is the **Civilian War Memorial (11)**, locally known as the chopsticks – you'll easily see why.

On the south side of Stamford Rd is the green expanse of the **Padang (12)**, the colonial cricket pitch where the game is still played. At the north end you'll pass the ugly modern **Singapore Recreation Club (13)**. Turn left onto St Andrew's Rd, pausing by **St Andrew's Cathedral** (**14**; p462) off Coleman St. Continue walking south – on one side will be the Padang, on the other the handsome colonial duo of **City Hall (15)**, built in 1929, and the **Supreme Court (16)**. Built in 1939, the court was the last classical building to be erected in Singapore, replacing the Grand Hotel de L'Europe, which once outshone Raffles as Singapore's premier hotel. A new supreme court designed by Sir Norman Foster is being built behind the current building.

As St Andrew's Rd swings left past the **Singapore Cricket Club (17)** you'll reach **Old Parliament House (18)**, built in 1827, Singapore's oldest government building and now an arts centre. Cut through Old Parliament Lane to **Raffles Landing (19)**, where you'll find the quintessential Raffles statue, arms folded, looking resolute against the incongruous backdrop of the CBD's skyscrapers. There's a smaller but identical statue of the man in front of the nearby **Victoria Theatre & Concert Hall (20)** built in 1826.

If you have time, explore the new branch of the **Asian Civilisations Museum** (**21**; p460) at Empress Place. Otherwise take the cute, pedestrian **Cavenagh Bridge (22)**, built in 1869, over to the Boat Quay side of the river, noting several modern sculptures clustered along the bank (see the boxed text next page). Nip into the Fullerton for refreshments, or head down to Boat Quay when you're done.

COURSES

The best cookery courses are offered by **at-sunrice** (Map pp452-3; ☎ 6336 3307; www.at-sunrice.com) in the Fort Canning Centre in Fort Canning Park. Their half-day courses (S$75) include a guided tour of the park's spice garden and then move into the fully-equipped teaching kitchens for a hands-on experience of making local dishes such as laksa, chilli crab and chicken rice. The tutors are excellent and you'll get to enjoy your efforts at the end in a meal on the centre's terrace. There are also kids' classes during school holidays.

Raffles Culinary Academy (Map pp452-3; ☎ 6412 1256, fax 6339 7013; rca@raffles.com) on the second level of the Raffles Hotel Arcade, offers a wide variety of day-long cookery classes (Tue-Sat; from S$55) for groups of up to 20 people. Very few are hands on, but you will get lunch or dinner at the end of them.

The Asian fusion restaurant **Coriander Leaf** (Map pp452-3; ☎ 6732 3354; www.corianderleaf.com; 02-01 The Gallery Hotel, 76 Robertson Quay) also occasionally runs cookery courses, although their demonstration kitchen is small and doesn't allow the hands-on experience either.

SINGAPORE FOR CHILDREN

Singaporean society is very family orientated, making travelling with children here a breeze. Eating out as a family is commonplace and hotels are well geared to providing family rooms, extra beds and cots. A great website to check for information and to entertain the kids is www.sg/kids/index.htm.

There are plenty of places to let your kids run around safely and burn off all that excess energy not already soaked up by the humidity. Try the **Botanic Gardens** (p465) or the kinetic park in front of the **Singapore Science Centre** (p470). There's also the **National Youth Centre Skate Park and Youth Park** (Map pp456-7) near Somerset MRT off Orchard Rd, set up for skateboarders and one of the rare places you'll see government-sanctioned graffiti in Singapore. Bikes can be hired in the **city** (p507) or on **Pulau Ubin** (p467).

For lessons on the local wildlife you certainly won't go wrong at the **Zoo** (p467) and **Night Safari** (p468), **Jurong Bird Park** (p470) and **Underwater World** on **Sentosa** (p472) where there's also a dolphin show. For other types of instruction sign up for a kid's cooking course at **at-sunrice** (this page) or the arts classes at **Sculpture Square** (Map p458; ☎ 6333 1055; www.sculpturesq.com.sg; 155 Middle Rd).

Of course there's also **Sentosa** (p471) for beaches, the cable car and a host of other diversions. Also guaranteed to bring joy to a child and to game adults is splashing through the leaping, dancing **fountain** at Parco Bugis Junction (p504).

For the very young, check out **Gymboree Play & Music** (Map pp456-7; ☎ 6735 5290; 03-17/18 Tanglin Mall, 163 Tanglin Rd) a playgroup with classes daily for kids from birth up to four years old. A trial class is S$30.90.

THE SCULPTURE TRAIL

Start at Raffles Place and tick off the following sculptures:

1. Aw Tee Hong's boat-shaped *Struggle for Survival* at the south end of Raffles Place.
2. The Singapore streetscape *Progress & Advancement* by Yang Ying-Feng at the north end of Raffles Place.
3. Henry Moore's *Reclining Figure* in front of the OCBC centre on Chulia St.
4. The surreal *Homage to Newton* by Salvador Dali in the atrium of the UOB Plaza on Chulia St.
5. Fernando Botero's giant, fat *Bird*, on the river in front of UOB Plaza.
6. The river diving boys of *First Generation* by Chong Fat Cheong, on the right side of Cavenagh Bridge.
7. The family of tiny *kucinta* cats on the left side of Cavenagh Bridge.

TOURS

A wide variety of tours can be booked at the travel agents or the desks of the big hotels. Itineraries included trips to the zoo, the night safari and the Jurong Bird Park, all of which can easily be visited independently.

CHILD-MINDING FACILITIES

The **YMCA Metropolitan** (Map pp456-7; ☎ 6731 0763; www.mymca.org.sg; 60 Stevens Rd) runs a crèche open to anyone with children on weekdays from 9am to noon (S$15). For all other times, the best option is to ask your hotel to arrange babysitting for you.

SINGAPORE

More original tours include *Painted Faces*, in which you get a behind-the-scenes look at Chinese opera; *In Harmony with Feng Shui*; and *Flavours of New Asia*, which takes you around Singapore's main ethnic areas. The STB offices have full details and brochures, and can also make bookings.

Special Interest Tours

Singapore-born **Geraldene Lowe-Ismail** (☎/fax 6737 5250; geraldenestours@hotmail.com) has been leading walking tours of Singapore for nigh on 40 years. A mine of information, her wide variety of tours give you a unique insight into Singapore's history and culture. Geraldene charges S$80 an hour – you may be able to join a group to reduce costs. She will also tailor tours to suit your particular interests. In addition to English, she conducts tours in Italian.

Another guide recommended for walking tours is **Diana Chua** (☎ 9489 1999; dime@pacific.net.sg). She also charges S$80 an hour and offers similar tours to Geraldene.

Subaraj Rajathurrai (☎/fax 6787 7048; serin@swiftech.com.sg) specialises in bird-watching and nature tours. His enthusiastic and knowledgeable guidance is highly regarded.

RIVER CRUISES

One of the best ways to get a feel for central Singapore and its history is to take a river cruise. Bumboat cruises depart from several places along the Singapore River including Clarke Quay, Raffles Landing and Boat Quay, as well as Merlion Park and the Esplanade Jetty on Marina Bay; and generally run between 8.30am and 10.30pm.

Singapore Explorer (☎ 6339 6833; www.singaporeexplorer.com.sg) offer trips in a glass-top boat (adult/child S$15/6) or a traditional bumboat (adult/child S$12/6). **Singapore River Cruises** (☎ 6336 6111; www.rivercruise.com.sg) offer bumboat tours of 30 minutes (adult/child S$12/5) or 45 minutes (adult/child S$15/8). At night red Chinese lanterns hang from the boats' canopies and the whole experience becomes quite romantic.

HARBOUR CRUISES

A host of operators have harbour cruises departing from **Clifford Pier**, just east of Raffles Place. Companies offer *towkang* (Chinese junk) cruises as well as a number of lunch and dinner cruises. Most of them do the rounds of the harbour, which involves a lot of time passing oil refineries, then a look at Sentosa and the southern islands of St John's, Lazarus and Kusu. The short stop at Kusu is worthwhile and you will get some good views of the city and harbour.

Fairwind (☎ 6533 3432) offers 2½-hour tours aboard a Chinese junk (adult/child S$20.60/10.30), which leave at 10.15am and 3pm. Their sunset cruise (S$15/10) departs at 4pm and lasts one hour while their dinner cruise (S$36/18) leaves at 6pm and goes for 2½ hours.

WaterTours (☎ 6533 9811; www.watertours.com.sg) operates tours on the *Cheng Ho*, a gaudy

OFFBEAT SINGAPORE

- Relax to the sound of **singing birds** housed in ornate cages and displayed by the owners on the corner of Tiong Bahru and Seng Poh Rds (Map pp450-1). Sunday morning from around 7am till 11am is the best time to visit
- Walk clockwise three times around the **Fountain of Wealth** at Suntec City, the world's largest fountain – locals say it will bring you good luck
- Have your fortune read by a parrot on the corner of Dunlop St and Serangoon Rd in **Little India** (Map p458), then maybe get a traditional henna tattoo
- Look out for the mobile **ice-cream sandwich** sellers along Orchard Rd, among the last real food hawkers in Singapore. If you're feeling adventurous go for the durian-flavoured ice cream layered between pink and green dyed bread slices.
- Observe Buddhist cremation rites at the **Kong Meng San Phor Kark See Monastery** (p468), Singapore's largest temple complex
- Discover what hellish punishment awaits you for being an ungrateful child at the gloriously tacky **Haw Par Villa** (p470)

replica of a Ming dynasty junk. They leave at 10.30am (adult/child S$23/11) and 3pm, and last 2½ hours. They also offer a high-tea cruise at 3pm (S$29/14) and a dinner cruise at 6.30pm (S$49/25).

Combining a harbour cruise with a city centre bus tour is the **DUCKtour** (☎ 6333 3825; adult/child S$33/17). Starting from Suntec City mall, an amphibious truck drives around the colonial centre before dipping into the harbour for a quick splutter around; the accompanying commentary is dire.

It is also possible to charter boats – the STB can put you in touch with charter-boat operators.

FESTIVALS & EVENTS

With so many cultures and religions, there are an amazing number of celebrations in Singapore. Although some have fixed dates, the Hindus, Muslims and Chinese follow a lunar calendar that varies annually. In particular, the Muslim festivals change constantly, moving back 11 days each year – for details of these and other festivals held across the region see the Directory chapter (p541). The STB puts out an annual *Festivals & Events* brochure.

JANUARY–FEBRUARY

Ponggal This four-day harvest festival is celebrated by south Indians, especially at the Sri Mariamman Temple (Map pp452-3) on South Bridge Rd, where rice, vegetables, sugar cane and spices are offered to the gods for thanksgiving.

Chingay Singapore's biggest street parade occurs on the 22nd day after the Chinese New Year. It's a multicultural event, held along Orchard Rd, with flag bearers balancing 6m- to 12m-long bamboo flag poles, and lion dancers, floats and other cultural performers.

MARCH–APRIL

Qing Ming Festival On 'All Souls' Day', Chinese traditionally visit the tombs of their ancestors to clean and repair them and make offerings. Singapore's largest temple complex, Kong Meng San Phor Kark See Monastery (Map pp448-9) in the centre of the island is the place to be.

Good Friday A candlelit procession bearing the figure of the crucified Christ takes place at St Joseph's Catholic Church at Victoria St (Map pp452-3).

Singapore Food Festival Celebrating the national passion, this month-long festival (www.singaporefoodfestival.com) from the end of March to the end of April has special offerings at everything from hawker centres to top-end restaurants. The festival includes the two-week **World Gourmet Summit** (www.worldgourmetsummit.com), a gathering of top international chefs and gourmet events.

TAKE ART! This is a month-long season of arts events, featuring both local and international performers, including the **Singapore International Comedy Festival** and **Singapore International Film Festival** (www.filmfest.org.sg).

MAY–JUNE

Birthday of the Third Prince The child-god is honoured with processions, and devotees go into a trance and spear themselves with spikes and swords during this Chinese festival. Celebrations, if you can call them that, are held at various temples and on Queen St (Map p458), near Bencoolen St.

Dragon Boat Festival Commemorating the death of a Chinese saint who drowned himself as a protest against government corruption, this festival is celebrated with boat races at East Coast Park. Rice dumplings are traditionally made and eaten during this festival.

Great Singapore Sale Orchard Rd is decked with banners and merchants are encouraged by the government to drop prices in an effort to boost Singapore's image as a shopping destination. It is held for one month from the end of May to the beginning of July.

Singapore Arts Festival (www.singaporeartsfest.com) Organised by the National Arts Council, this is Singapore's premier arts festival with a world-class programme of art, dance, drama and music.

JULY–AUGUST

Singapore National Day On 9 August a series of military and civilian processions and an evening firework display celebrate Singapore's independence in 1965. Held on alternate years at the Padang (Map pp452-3) and National Stadium (Map pp450-1).

SEPTEMBER–OCTOBER

Festival of the Hungry Ghosts The souls of the dead are released for this one day of feasting and entertainment on earth. Chinese operas and other events are laid on for them (head to Chinatown) and food is put out – the ghosts eat the food's spirit but leave the substance for mortal celebrants.

Birthday of the Monkey God The birthday of T'se Tien Tai Seng Yeh is celebrated twice a year at the Monkey God Temple (Map pp450-1) on Seng Poh Rd near the Tiong Bahru Market. Mediums pierce their cheeks and tongues with skewers and go into a trance, during which they write special charms in blood.

Mooncake Festival Celebrated on the full moon of the eighth lunar month and also known as the Lantern Festival, the overthrow of the Mongol warlords in ancient China is celebrated by eating mooncakes and lighting colourful paper lanterns. Mooncakes are made with bean paste, lotus seeds and sometimes a duck egg.

Navarathri In the Tamil month of Purattasi, the Hindu festival of 'Nine Nights' is dedicated to the wives of Shiva, Vishnu and Brahma. Young girls are dressed as the goddess Kali; this is a good opportunity to see traditional Indian dancing and singing. The Chettiar (Map pp452-3), Sri Mariamman (Map pp452-3) and Sri Srinivasa Perumal (Map p458) temples are centres of activity.
For Art's Sake! The third of Singapore's banner arts events encompasses a wide range of events, from the **WOMAD** festival of world music held in Fort Canning Park to **ARTSingapore**, a fair of contemporary Southeast Asian Art.

OCTOBER–NOVEMBER

Pilgrimage to Kusu Island Tua Pek Kong, the god of prosperity, is honoured by Taoists in Singapore who make a pilgrimage to the shrine on Kusu.
Thimithi (Fire-Walking Ceremony) Hindu devotees prove their faith by walking across glowing coals at the Sri Mariamman Temple (Map pp452-3).

DECEMBER

Christmas Orchard Road celebrates Christmas with shop-front displays and the Christmas light-up (which actually are in place from November), another of the illuminations that Singapore is so fond of.

SLEEPING

Singapore might be one of the most expensive cities in Southeast Asia in which to bed down, but top hotels are constantly offering promotional deals, sometimes slashing up to half off their official rates (and chucking in breakfast for good measure). It pays to call around before you book.

It really doesn't matter where you stay – the island's zippy public transport system puts everywhere within a few minutes of everywhere else. For atmosphere we'd recommend Chinatown or Little India, both of which harbour most of the budget accommodation, and characterful small hotels in shophouse conversions.

Orchard Rd and its environs is crammed with identikit upmarket hotels, as is the area around Marina Bay, where you'll find the Esplanade complex and Suntec City Mall. There are also several good options dotted close by the redeveloped quays of the Singapore River. If you favour having the beach close at hand, Sentosa's the go (but note that rates and occupancy levels over the weekends at all the recreational island's properties are higher).

For details of the hotel price categories and taxes see p531.

Budget

Rooms in the cheapest places are cubicle-like, cramped, often windowless and facilities are invariably shared. Most places offer both air-con and fan rooms, with fan rooms being cheaper. Note that both YMCA International House and YWCA Fort Canning Lodge (listed under Mid-Range) also have dorm beds.

GAY & LESBIAN SINGAPORE

Singapore has an increasingly active and visible local gay and lesbian scene.

Backstage Bar (Map pp452-3; ☎ 6227 1712; 13A Trengganu St; ⌚ 7pm-2am Sun-Thu, 7pm-3am Fri & Sat) is hands down one of the best bars in Singapore. It's very friendly and relaxed with a roomy balcony on which to hang out if the cosy interior gets too packed. Most people drop by here first before heading on to the clubs later. The entrance is up the stairs on Temple St.

Its lesbian-friendly sibling is **The Actors' Bar** (Map pp452-3; ☎ 6533 2436; 13/15 South Bridge Rd; ⌚ 5pm-2am Mon-Thu, 5pm-3am Fri & Sat), a classy two-storey bar over the 7-Eleven shop. There are different theme nights, with pool (S$2) being a popular pastime.

Taboo (Map pp452-3; ☎ 6225 4172; 01-04, 21 Tanjong Pagar Rd; ⌚ 9pm-2am Mon-Sat) is the dance club-de-jour, a pumping spot where the patrons are not afraid to rip off their shirts and strut on the podiums and bar tops (Singaporean rules be damned!). Similarly fun behaviour pervades their sister establishment the **Water Bar** (Map pp452-3; ☎ 6221 5739; 38/39 Craig Rd; ⌚ 9pm-2am Mon-Sat) in a dazzlingly whitewashed shophouse, hung with luxurious velvet drapes.

Vincent's (Map pp456-7; ☎ 6736 1360; 6th fl, Lucky Plaza, 304 Orchard Rd) is a small bar that's been going forever and attracts a regular, older crowd.

Also check out the fabulous drag cabaret at **Boom Boom Room** (p500) and the Sunday night dance parties at **Centro** (p501). For more details of where to go and what to do check out the websites listed on p544.

AIRPORT HOTEL DESK & THE TRANSIT HOTEL

If you arrive in Singapore without a hotel booking, don't despair. The efficient Singapore Hotel Association has four desks at Changi airport: Terminal 1's east wing desk is open from 10am to 11.30pm, while in the west wing it's open 24 hours; the desk in the north wing of Terminal 2 is open from 7am to 11pm, and open 24 hours in the south wing.

There are dozens of hotels on its lists, ranging from S$37 a night right up to Raffles Hotel at S$650-plus. There's no charge for the service, and promotional/discounted rates, when available, are passed on to you. You can also book the hotels over the Internet on the Association's website: www.stayinsingapore.com.sg.

Also, if you're only in Singapore for a very short time or have a long wait between connecting flights, there's the **Ambassador Transit Hotel** (Terminal 1: ☎ 6542 5538; t1@airport-hotel.com.sg; Terminal 2: ☎ 6542 8122; t2@airport-hotel.com.sg; s S$40 & 57, d S$63.50). The rates quoted are for the first six hour stay; none of the rooms have windows and the cheaper singles use shared bathroom. The Terminal 1 branch has a sauna, gym and outdoor pool. If you just want to nip in for a shower, that will cost you S$5.15.

COLONIAL DISTRICT

New 7th Storey Hotel (Map p458; ☎ 6337 0251; 229 Rochor Rd; dm/d S$17/52, d with bathroom S$75;) Well run and reliable, the New 7th Storey Hotel sits in splendid isolation on a patch of cleared land near Bugis MRT. Its four-bed dorms are all air-conditioned, its other rooms clean and spacious. Pluses include delightful garden patios on which to sunbathe and bike rental from S$2.50 per hour.

Waterloo Hostel (Map pp452-3; ☎ 6336 6555; www.waterloohostel.com.sg; 55 Waterloo St, 4th fl, Catholic Centre Building; dm/s/d S$23/53/58, s/d with bathroom S$68/69;) This spick-and-span, Catholic-run operation is one of Singapore's best hostels. Its dorm sleeps eight and there's a variety of other spacious rooms all with breakfast included in the prices.

Also worth considering is the simple, clean **Victoria Hotel** (Map pp452-3; ☎ 6338 2381; fax 6334 4853; 87 Victoria St; d/tr S$50/60, d/tr with bathroom S$60/75;).

CHINATOWN

Chinatown Homestay (Map pp452-3; ☎ 9758 3200; teoannie@singnet.com.sg; 5th fl, 325D New Bridge Rd; dm/s/d S$25/40/45;) This guesthouse has decent-sized, clean rooms, a fully equipped kitchen, and some rooms come with bathrooms. At the time of writing, the place was scheduled to move to another location. Call Annie for new details.

Backpacker Cozy Corner Hotel (Map pp452-3; ☎ 6225 4812, fax 6225 4813; 5 Teck Lim Rd; d S$45-65;) There's neither anything particularly backpackerish nor cosy about this hotel, but the rooms are freshly-painted and clean.

Tropical Hotel (Map pp452-3; ☎ 6225 6696, fax 6225 6626; 22 Teck Lim Rd; s/d from S$60/80;) This gay-friendly hotel is in a shophouse conversion, but lacks style inside. Some singles are without windows and the larger rooms at the front with balconies go for S$100, but they're open to bargaining for longer stays.

LITTLE INDIA Map p458

MacKenzie Hostel (☎ 6837 2887, fax 6334 3277; 114A Mackenzie Rd; dm/s/d S$10/20/35;) In a quiet area southwest of Little India is this clean, well-run hostel – and for company, there's Singapore's president in the Istana! The cheapest rooms are tiny and windowless, but the others are fine and there's a pleasant open patio, laundry facilities and a kitchen.

Little India Guest House (☎ 6294 2866, fax 6298 4866; 3 Veerasamy Rd; s/d/f S$35/40/50, with air-con S$40/45/60;) The rooms are stripped to bare essentials at this guesthouse in the heart of Little India – doubles have a bunk-bed with a double bed on the base and single on top. All share common bathrooms which are very clean.

Cactus Hotel (☎ 6391 3913; cactus98@singnet.com.sg; 407 Jl Besar; d S$50;) This simple hotel, handy for Lavender Food Square and the buses to Malaysia, offers reasonable rooms with attached bathrooms. Once upon a time guests Tony and Maureen Wheeler wrote the first edition of *South-East Asia on a Shoestring* in this building. Rates are slightly more expensive on Friday and Saturday.

THE AUTHOR'S CHOICE *Simon Richmond*

Inn Crowd (Map p458; ☎ 6296 9169; www.the-inncrowd.com; 35 Campbell Lane; dm/dS$18/48;) If only all hostels were as welcoming as this brightly painted and well-equipped one. The air-con dorm sleeps 16 in bunk beds, the common bathrooms are spotless and its modern kitchen has a washing machine. Rates include breakfast, use of a locker and free Internet access in its comfy ground-floor lounge/Internet café. The one double room is quite cosy and has a TV and video.

Hotel 1929 (Map pp452-3; ☎ 6347 1929; www.hotel1929.com; 50 Keong Saik Rd; s/d S$101.20/207) This dazzling new place is one of the most successful conversions of shophouses into a boutique hotel. The rooms are on the small side (even the suites are far from large) but all immaculately decorated in contemporary style with nice touches such as flat-screen, wall-mounted TVs and broadband Internet connections. There's also a cute outdoor Jacuzzi and the very decent Restaurant Ember.

Raffles Hotel (Map pp452-3; ☎ 6337 1886; raffles@raffles.com; 1 Beach Rd; st from S$650;) Raffles' reputation precedes it, but would you want to spend upwards of S$650 a night for putting up here? We think you would, despite the snootiness that means guests are expected to keep up appearances – no shorts or sandals for men here. There are 103 suites, all with timber floors, lofty ceilings, chintzy colonial furnishings, marble-clad bathrooms and lovely touches such as red pompom slippers, sun parasols made from paper and fresh roses.

Classique Hotel (☎ 6392 3838, fax 6392 2828; 240 Jl Besar; d S$55;) More stylish and spacious than most in this price bracket, the Classique is worth considering even though it's on one of Little India's less than charming main roads.

ORCHARD ROAD

New Sandy's Place (Map pp456-7; ☎ 6734 1431; sandygiam@hotmail.com; 3C Sarkies Rd; s/d S$18/55;) In a residential home (so there's no sign) this guesthouse is a 200m walk from Newton MRT, next to the Alliance Française. It's a simple friendly place with a scrappy garden where the pet poodle scampers. The rooms range from a broom-cupboard single on the 1st floor to a spacious double room, with a fan and attached bath, on the 3rd floor (overlooking a playing field). Breakfast is included.

SENTOSA

NTUC Sentosa Beach Resort (Map pp448-9; ☎ 6275 1034; www.ntucclub.com; 30 Imbiah Walk; kampung huts from S$24, rooms from S$98;) Sentosa's budget accommodation option has 15 small air-con wooden huts sleeping up to three people and using shared bathrooms. Use of the BBQ pit is S$5 extra. Scoring one over the weekend can be near impossible unless you book months ahead, but during the week shouldn't be too much of a problem. The resort, owned by the National Trade Union Congress, also has smart and good value hotel rooms.

Mid-Range

COLONIAL DISTRICT

Strand Hotel (Map p458; ☎ 6338 1866; fax 6338 1330; 25 Bencoolen St; d S$95;) What a pleasant surprise – the room furnishings here eschew boring conformity in favour of jazzy fabrics. If you're really up for it, ask for the 'special rooms', with their funkier decor and glass-walled bathrooms (popular with honeymooners apparently!). The café-bar on the ground floor is also pleasingly decked out in contemporary colours.

City Bayview Hotel (☎ 6337 2882; bayintl@pacific.net.sg; 30 Bencoolen St; s/d S$188.10/199.50;) The City Bayview is nothing grand but has reasonably good rooms. The self-serve laundry is on the roof, beside the pool, so you can cool off while your smalls are in the wash.

Hotel Bencoolen (Map p458; ☎ 6336 0822; www.hotelbencoolen.com; 47 Bencoolen St; s/d S$93/103;) A good value choice, the rooms at the Bencoolen are reasonably sized with big beds and the full range of facilities. The outdoor spa pool is just big enough for a soak.

Also recommended are **Summer View Hotel** (Map p458; ☎ 6338 1122; summerviewhtl@pacific.net.sg; 173 Bencoolen St; d S$154;) and **South-East Asia Hotel** (Map p458; ☎ 6338 2394; www.seahotel.com.sg; 190 Waterloo St; d S$77;).

THE QUAYS **Map pp452-3**

Robertson Quay Hotel (☎ 6735 3333; www.robertsonquayhotel.com.sg; 15 Merbau Rd; s/d S$138/172.50;) This modern, distinctive round building has a round swimming pool on the roof. Its contemporary-styled rooms are good value especially if the promotional rates of S$92/103 are on offer.

River View Hotel (☎ 6732 9922; www.riverview.com.sg; 382 Havelock Rd; s/d from S$161/184;) This is a great value option considering its riverside location close by trendy Robertson Quay. Its rooms are comfortable and a good size and there's a free shuttle service to the city centre and Chinatown. Its speaking elevator will greet you in three languages!

Copthorne King's Hotel Singapore (☎ 6733 0011; www.copthornekings.com.sg; 403 Havelock Rd; d from S$155.25;) The older river-facing rooms at this hotel have delightful balconies hung with flowers and there are lots of facilities including a gym, pool and self-service laundry.

CHINATOWN Map pp452-3

Damenlou Hotel (☎ 6221 1900; fax 6225 8500; 12 Ann Siang Rd; d from S$80;) Handily placed for trendy Club St, Damenlou Hotel has bags of character and a good restaurant with a section on the roof offering a spectacular view of Chinatown – a great place to come for a drink at sundown. It's worth paying a bit more for its larger rooms.

Royal Peacock Hotel (☎ 6223 3522; www.royalpeacockhotel.com; 55 Keong Saik Rd; s/d S$140/155;) The rooms don't quite match the plushness and contemporary chic of the lobby but it's certainly one of the fanciest shophouse conversions along this stretch. If you want a room with a window then you'll be paying extra.

Chinatown Hotel (☎ 6225 5166; www.chinatownhotel.com; 12-16 Teck Lim Rd; s/d S$88/99;) The doors automatically swing open as you enter the Chinatown Hotel. It's a pleasant place that's slightly better appointed than similar establishments.

The Inn on Temple Street (☎ 6221 5333; www.theinn.com.sg; 36 Temple St; rooms S$88;) Occupying five restored shophouses in the heart of Chinatown, the Inn's rooms have nice wooden furniture and fixtures but they're a little cramped and some singles are windowless. Attached is a cute café.

Majestic Hotel (☎ 6222 3377; www.majestic-singapore.com; 31-37 Bukit Pasoh Rd; s/d S$60/69;) In a restored shophouse, the Majestic has been around for decades. The rooms (some with balconies) are fine, if a little worn. The rates include breakfast and it's run by friendly people.

LITTLE INDIA Map p458

Perak Lodge (☎ 6299 7733; www.peraklodge.net; 12 Perak Rd; d from S$80) This tastefully decorated guesthouse in a renovated Peranakan-style building is a deservedly popular place. The staff are very helpful and there's a quiet communal area where you serve yourself breakfast (which is included in the rates). The cheaper rooms don't have windows but they're all nicely furnished and come with access to some cable TV channels. If you're planning to be in Singapore for a while they offer attractive rates for longer stays.

Madras Hotel (☎ 6392 7889; www.madrassingapore.com; 28-32 Madras St; s/d S$60/70;) The plainly decorated but clean Madras Hotel is a great place to stay. Ask for a room with a balcony at the front of this attractive art-deco–style building. The rates include breakfast.

Tai Hoe Hotel (☎ 6293 9122; www.taihoehotel.com; 163 Kitchener Rd; d S$68;) This modern hotel offers tidy and good-value rooms. The rooms overlooking Kitchener Rd have a lovely leafy aspect.

CAMPING

The best place for camping is Sentosa Island (p471). **Camp Laguna** (Map pp448-9; ☎ 6270 7888; accommodation@sentosa.com.sg; 4/6/8-person tents S$12.50/15.60/20.80) is beside Palawan beach. Camp beds cost an extra S$1 each. It caters primarily for groups, but with space for 300, individuals are welcome too.

The **National Parks Board** (Map pp452-3; ☎ 6391 4488; www.nparks.gov.sg; 18-01/08 Gateway West, 150 Beach Rd) administers several free camp sites around the island, including East Coast Park and Pasir Ris Park. You need a permit to camp but these can usually be obtained on the spot. For East Coast Park go to Carpark C3 near McDonald's. The permits are free but there's a small fee to use the barbeque pits or shower facilities.

St John's Island has camping facilities; contact the **Sentosa Development Corporation** (☎ 6275 0388) for details.

On **Pulau Ubin** (p467) you can camp at Noordin Beach and nearby Mamam Beach on Ubin's north coast. The sites are free, but very basic and there's no drinking water, so bring your own.

SINGAPORE

Albert Court Hotel (☎ 6339 3939; www.albertcourt.com.sg; 180 Albert St; d from S$185;) At the southern edge of Little India is this smart hotel in a shophouse redevelopment that now shoots up eight storeys. All rooms have the usual mod-cons, and include a choice of fan or air-con. Their promotional rates go as low as S$99.

ORCHARD ROAD **Map pp456-7**

Regalis Court (☎ 6734 7117; 64 Lloyd Rd; d from S$166.75;) Savour Peranakan style in this hotel based in a charming colonial era building with polished teak floors. Standard rooms don't have windows, but are quite spacious and rates include breakfast.

Sloane Court Hotel (☎ 6235 3311; sloane@singnet.com.sg; 17 Balmoral Rd; s/d S$83.20/93.60;) This mock-Tudor-style hotel in a garden setting is a pleasant place to escape the consumerist onslaught of nearby Orchard Rd. Rooms are reasonably sized and have character. Sometimes the rates include breakfast.

Lloyd's Inn (☎ 6737 7309; www.lloydinn.com; 2 Lloyd Rd; d from S$70;). A short walk south from Orchard Road in a quiet street surrounded by old villas is this popular hotel. The rooms are spread out, motel style, around the reception building. It's slightly dated but is tidy and good value (deluxe rooms are larger and with fridge). Bookings are advisable.

RELC International Hotel (☎ 6885 7888; relcih@singnet.com.sg; 30 Orange Grove Rd; d S$133.85;) Plain, but good value is this hotel which has large, well-appointed rooms, each with a balcony. RELC stands for Regional English Language Centre, and the bottom floors are devoted to conference rooms and teaching facilities. A free shuttle runs downtown to Orchard Road every hour during the day.

Top End

COLONIAL DISTRICT **Map pp452-3**

Hotel Inter-Continental Singapore (☎ 6338 7600; singapore@intercontinenti.com; 80 Middle Rd; d from S$440;) Built into the Parco Bugis Junction mall, this hotel is decorated in a very appealing Peranakan/colonial style. Ask for one of their shophouse-style rooms or suites which have wooden floors, oriental rugs and hand-painted lampshades. The comfy lobby lounge is a fine alternative to Raffles if just for a quiet, classy drink.

Swissôtel The Stamford Singapore (☎ 6338 8585; www.swissotel.com; 2 Stamford Rd; d from S$360;) The tallest hotel tower in Southeast Asia contains 1200 smartly decorated rooms with obviously great views, the best being from the 29 suites occupying what the management like to call their 'hotel within a hotel' *Stamford Crest*. On hand is the excellent Amrita Spa and trendy Equinox dining/drinking complex.

Ritz-Carlton, Millenia Singapore (☎ 6337 8888; www.ritzcarlton.com; 7 Raffles Ave; s/d from S$465/515;) The entrance to this classy number

THE Ys

Singapore has three YMCAs, which take all visitors. They provide good mid-range accommodation and, though not the bargain they used to be, are still very popular. Advance booking of at least three weeks with one night's deposit is usually essential. The following prices include all taxes and breakfast. Non-YMCA members must pay a small charge for temporary membership.

YMCA International House (Map pp456-7; ☎ 6336 6000; www.mymca.org.sg; 1 Orchard Rd; dm/s/d/f S$28.33/111.03/128.03/147.29;) has a handy location at the colonial district end of Orchard Rd. The place has good facilities, including a fitness centre, rooftop swimming pool, squash and badminton courts and a billiard room. There's also a restaurant, which offers a cheap set meal. Although most rooms have recently been upgraded, they're still pretty average.

YWCA Fort Canning Lodge (Map pp452-3; ☎ 6338 4222; reservations@ywcafclodge.org.sg; 6 Fort Canning Rd; d/s/tw from S$50.85/$135.60/158.20;) has a similar list of facilities and a good location. The five bed dorms have air-con, TV and attached bathrooms, the standard rooms are quite stylish with wooden floors.

The cheapest rooms at the **YMCA Metropolitan** (Map pp456-7; ☎ 6737 7755; www.mymca.org.sg; 60 Stevens Rd; d from S$74.50;) have no windows, but are spacious and well-appointed. It's a good 1km walk, though, north of Orchard Rd; a shuttle bus runs from the YMCA to Orchard Rd Monday to Friday. The place also offer apartments, known as the Metro-Y, for long-term visitors.

has a striking entrance dominated by a Frank Stella sculpture. The rooms have harbour views to die for, including from the bathrooms, which have a strong claim to being the sexiest in Singapore.

Pan Pacific Singapore (☎ 6336 8111; panpac@pacific.net.sg; 7 Raffles Blvd, Marina Square; d from S$420;) The Pan Pac takes the prize for most dramatic atrium – soaring up 35 storeys, this is Asia's highest internal space. The rooms are decorated in a contemporary style (the business rooms even have ergonomic Aeron desk chairs); those with a balcony and a view are a bit pricier.

Conrad Centennial Singapore (☎ 6334 8888, fax 6333 9166; 2 Temasek Blvd; s/d from S$260/310;) The feel is stylish and contemporary at the Conrad, with rooms tastefully decorated in light browns. There's a decent sized pool and butler service on the executive floor. A sweet touch is that all guests get a complimentary teddy bear.

CBD & THE QUAYS **Map pp452-3**

Fullerton Singapore (☎ 6733 8388; www.fullertonhotel.com; 1 Fullerton Sq; d from S$470;) The Fullerton is elegance to a tee. Occupying the magnificent colonnaded Fullerton Building (named after Robert Fullerton, the first Governor of the Straits Settlements) the former home of the GPO and the exclusive Singapore Club was renovated at a cost of S$400 million and reopened in 2001 to general acclaim. The heritage principles involved in the restoration mean some of the Armani-beige rooms overlook the inner atrium. Spend a bit extra to gain access to the hotel's private Straits Club and upgrade to rooms with river or marina views.

Gallery Hotel Singapore (☎ 6849 8686; general@galleryhotel.com.sg; 76 Robertson Quay; d from S$295;) This strikingly designed riverside building is about as trendy as they come, from its primary colour fixtures and fittings to its gorgeous lap pool and the ultra-hip restaurants and bars within the complex. The rates include breakfast.

Swissôtel Merchant Court Singapore (☎ 6337 2288; www.swissotel-merchantcourt.com; 20 Merchant Rd; s/d from S$285/315;) The riverside Merchant Court is a classy number with a pleasant design throughout and a great location. Their executive club rooms (S$345/375) come with all the usual business class extras.

Grand Copthorne Waterfront Hotel Singapore (☎ 6733 0880; grandcopthorne@copthorne.com.sg; 392 Havelock Rd; s/d from S$300/330;) Of the several hotels clustered at the far west end of the river this is the fanciest by far. It's the best of the Copthorne's group of hotels, with light-filled comfortable rooms.

CHINATOWN

Berjaya Hotel Singapore (Map pp452-3; ☎ 6227 7678; berjayaresorts.com; 83 Duxton Rd; d/ste from S$210/290;) All rooms are plushly furnished at this top-class shophouse conversion hotel. The suites have an attractive mezzanine bedroom reached by spiral staircase, or you can opt for one of the two suites opening onto landscaped gardens.

Amara Singapore (Map pp450-1; ☎ 6879 2555; www.amarahotels.com; 165 Tanjong Pagar Rd; d from S$320;) Following its sleek contemporary makeover the Amara is a fine choice. Tasteful black-and-white photos of Singapore hang in the rooms, and facilities include a pool, spa and tennis court as well as several good restaurants.

ORCHARD ROAD **Map pp456-7**

Goodwood Park Hotel (☎ 6737 7411; www.goodwoodparkhotel.com.sg; 22 Scotts Rd; s/d from S$385/425;) Designed to resemble a Rhine castle and dating from 1900, the Goodwood Park has a venerable history. This lends the place an old-fashioned feel but bags of class, from its two swimming pools to the hotel's pet cat roaming the lobby. Nice touches in the rooms include arty black-and-white photos of Singapore, Persian rugs and neatly hidden TVs and minibars. If you have S$3000 to spare, treat yourself to a night in the opulent Brunei Suite.

Regent Singapore (☎ 6733 8888; www.regenthotels.com; 1 Cuscaden Rd; d from S$350;) At this classy hotel all the colourfully decorated, spacious rooms are ranged around an airy central atrium. There are acres of marble and gorgeous furnishings in the lobby, which is a top place for afternoon tea.

Four Seasons Hotel Singapore (☎ 6734 1110; www.fourseasons.com/singapore; 190 Orchard Blvd; s/d from S$435/475;) In a quiet, tree-lined street just off bustling Orchard Road, the Four Seasons has a beautiful lobby matched by its elegant antique style rooms. Among its many facilities are air-conditioned tennis courts.

Sheraton Towers Singapore (☎ 6737 6888; www.sheraton.com/towerssingapore; 39 Scotts Rd; d from S$460;) The Sheraton oozes opulence. The rooms are decorated in mossy greens with beautiful pictures of flowers, the service is efficient and pleasant. Their grand lobby is a lovely place for tea.

Traders Hotel Singapore (☎ 6738 2222; reservations@traders.com.sg; 1A Cuscaden Rd; s/d from S$275/305;) The good value Traders has stylish, plush rooms. An attractive water-wall runs the length of its spacious lobby (flowing at peak times only). If you pay the full tariff, extras thrown in include complimentary airport transfers, laundry service, breakfast and local calls.

Elizabeth Singapore (☎ 6738 1188; www.theelizabeth.com; 24 Mount Elizabeth Rd; d from S$220;) In a quiet spot a short walk north of Orchard Road, the Elizabeth has an exclusive, clubby feel. The rooms are thoroughly pleasant with William Morris–style print bedspreads and there's a soothing leafy aspect to the lobby.

SENTOSA — Map pp448-9

Beaufort Singapore (☎ 6275 0331, fax 6275 0331; www.beaufort.com.sg; 2 Bukit Manis Rd; d from S$380;) This low-rise, elegantly designed five-star resort has a cliff-top setting. Contemporary furnishings in the rooms, a new al-fresco restaurant and Singapore's only garden spa (see Spa Botanica, p474) make this a splendid choice. The promotional rate takes it as low as S$178 during the week.

Shangri-La's Rasa Sentosa Resort (☎ 6275 0100; reservations@shangri-la.com.sg; 101 Silosa Rd; d from S$290;) Singapore's only beachfront resort, so you'll want to pay a bit more for the sea-facing rooms all of which have spacious balconies. The resort has a fresh, clean feel and is well set up for families. Their rates include breakfast.

PULAU UBIN

Ubin Lagoon Resort (Map pp448-9; ☎ 6542 9590; www.clubendeavour.com.sg; chalets weekdays/weekends from S$150/190, duplexes S$210/250;) At Sungei Puaka, this is an upmarket outdoor activities-style resort. Modern chalets sleep up to three, the duplexes up to six, and the rates include breakfast and return ferry trips from Pongol Marina on Singapore. For details on how to get to Pulau Ubin, see p467.

EATING

Singapore is far and away the food capital of Asia. The variety is enormous and the prices reasonable (as long as you don't indulge in wine, which is expensive). The local enthusiasm for food is reflected in the huge number of restaurants, cafés and hawker centres that are invariably busy night and day, and in the constant newspaper and magazine coverage about the best and the latest places – good publications to check include *Where Singapore*, *I-S Magazine* and the glossy monthly magazine *Wine & Dine*. A great website is www.makansutra.com from the TV food show Makansutra; they also publish an extensive guidebook to all the best budget eating options.

Most restaurants open from around 11.30am to 2.30pm for lunch and 6pm to 10.30pm for dinner; some places are shut at lunch on the weekends and all day Sunday so it's always best to call ahead to check. Food courts are generally open from 10.30am through to 10pm; at these most dishes range from S$2 to S$6.

Colonial District

AMERICAN

Seah Street Deli (Map pp452-3; ☎ 6337 1886; 01-22 Raffles Hotel Arcade, 1 Beach Rd; mains S$10-15; 11am-10pm Sun-Thu, 11am-11pm Fri & Sat) Swing back to 1950s New York at this authentically styled deli serving bagels, pastrami sandwiches, pumpkin pie, pretzels and salads.

CAFÉS

Christa & Naomi Café (CAN) (Map pp452-3; ☎ 6337 3732; 01-12/14, 1 Liang Seah St; 3pm-1am) Perpetually packed with lounging, mobile-phone connected youths, CAN is a delightful snub to Singaporean order, decked out in mismatched furniture, quirky whatnots and old movie posters. Grab a coffee, a beer, a snack or one of their trademark strawberry soda icecream floaters.

Fat Frog Café (Map pp452-3; ☎ 6338 6201; 45 Armenian St; 11.30am-11pm Sun-Thu, 11.30am-1am Fri & Sat) This pleasantly offbeat café is an alternative place to hang out and often has live music at the weekends (see Entertainment p501).

Pacific Coffee Company (Map pp452-3; ☎ 6821 0098; B1-26 City Link Mall; 8am-10.30pm Mon-Fri, 9am-midnight Sat-Sun) This Hong Kong coffee chain brings its free Internet, comfy sofas

MAGNIFICENT SEVEN HAWKER CENTRES

Hawker centres, also known as food centres, are a Singaporean institution you should not miss. Among our favourites:

Chomp Chomp (Map pp448-9; Serangoon Gardens)
Golden Mile Food Centre (Map p458; 505 Beach Rd)
Lau Pa Sat (Map pp452-3; 18 Raffles Quay)
Lavender Food Square (Map p458; Jl Besar)
Maxwell Rd Food Centre (Map pp452-3; cnr South Bridge & Maxwell Rds)
Newton Food Centre (Map pp456-7; Scotts Rd)
Tiong Bahru Cooked Food Centre (Map pp450-1; cnr Seng Poh & Lim Liam Sts)

and fine range of drinks to Singapore in this branch next to the MPH bookstore in the underground City Link mall.

CHINESE

Crystal Jade Kitchen (Map pp452-3; ☎ 6338 3511; B1-013/014 Suntec City, 3 Temasek Blvd; mains S$10-20; 🕑 11am-10.30pm) This busy Cantonese place is one of the reliable Crystal Jade group of restaurants with outlets across the city. There's an extensive à la carte menu and several set menus.

Imperial Herbal Restaurant (Map pp452-3; ☎ 6337 0491; 3rd fl, Metropole Hotel, 41 Seah St; mains from S$20) Here a Chinese physician will check you over, then prescribe something on the menu to rebalance your Yin and Yang. Some of the concoctions will sound more appetising than others – double boiled crocodile soup with cordyceps (dried worms), anyone? Worth going with a group since individual dishes can be pricey.

Lei Garden (Map pp452-3; ☎ 6339 3822; 01-24 CHIJMES, 30 Victoria St; mains from S$20) This stylish and popular place is a good place to try double-boiled soups, for which it is particularly noted, and dim sum. There are also branches on Orchard Rd (Map pp456-7; No 321, Orchard Shopping Centre and No 150 Orchard Plaza).

My Humble House (Map pp452-3; ☎ 6423 1881; 02-27/29 Esplanade Mall; mains S$15-20; 🕑 11.30am-3pm, 6.30-10.30pm) With decor that's Alice in Wonderland meets Phillipe Starck this place is anything but humble. The food is equally hip Chinese dishes with poetic names such as 'Memories of Waikiki' (fried prawns with macadamia nuts and wasabi mayonnaise). Service is below par but it's worth enduring for the ambience.

Soup Restaurant (Map pp452-3; ☎ 6333 9388; 39 Seah St) Soup celebrates dishes enjoyed by Samsui women, tough Chinese gals famous for working on building sites and for their distinctive red headscarves. Sample one of the MSG-free, double-boiled herbal soups (all under S$12) and the luscious Samsui ginger chicken (S$13 or S$24). The setting is traditional shophouse style. Among several other outlets are ones in **Chinatown** (Map pp452-3; ☎ 6222 9923; 25 Smith St) **Suntec City** (Map pp452-3; ☎ 6333 9886; B1-059 Suntec City) and DFS Galleria Scottswalk (Map pp456-7; ☎ 6333 8033; 25 Scotts Rd).

Yet Con (Map pp452-3; ☎ 3637 6819; 25 Purvis St; mains under S$10; 🕑 11am-8pm) For honest, authentic Hainanese chicken rice this simple place is hard to beat.

Also recommended is **Hai Tien Lo** (Map pp452-3; ☎ 6434 8338; 37th fl, The Pan Pacific Singapore, 7 Raffles Blvd; mains from S$20), noted for its fine food and views.

FRENCH

Maison de Fontaine (Map pp452-3; ☎ 6336 0286; 01-29A, CHIJMES, 30 Victoria Rd; mains S$15-25) The country-style decor is a bit cheesy but lends a welcome informal note compared with some other stuffy French temples of gastronomy. The menu includes traditional dishes such as burgundy escargots (S$12), pan-fried foie gras (S$28), steak tartare (S$18) and rack of lamb Provençale (S$28).

INDIAN

Rang Mahal (map pp452-3; ☎ 6333 1788; 3rd fl, The Pan Pacific Singapore, 7 Raffles Blvd; mains S$15-25) An ultra-contemporary setting and fine North Indian cuisine, including excellent tandoori dishes and freshly made naans. Watch the chefs at work in the open kitchen.

Annalakshmi (Map pp452-3; ☎ 6339 9993; 02-10 Excelsior Hotel & Shopping Centre, 5 Coleman St) This is a vegetarian restaurant where you 'eat as you like, give as you feel'. It's run by volunteers and the profits help support various Indian arts foundations and charitable causes.

INDONESIAN

Sanur (Map pp456-7; ☎ 6333 9339; 02-48, Parco Bugis Junction, 200 Victoria St; mains S$15-25) This long-time favourite for Indonesian dishes like *sambal udang* (prawns in chilli sauce), *gado gado* (vegetables, bean curd and prawn crackers, served with a spicy peanut sauce) and Javan oxtail soup, has other branches including **Suntec City** (Map pp452-3; ☎ 6338 2777; B1-010) and **Ngee Ann City** (Map pp456-7; ☎ 6734 3434; 04-16).

INTERNATIONAL

Colours by the Bay (Map pp452-3; ☎ 6835 7988; 01-13A/G Esplanade Mall, 8 Raffles Ave; mains S$10-20; 11.30am-11pm) Colours by the Bay comprises seven different restaurants covering most major cuisines, where you can sit at one and order from any of the others. We were impressed with the Garlic Restaurant which has the pungent bulb in many of its dishes, including ice cream!

Equinox (Map pp452-3; ☎ 6431 5669; Level 70, Swissôtel The Stamford Singapore, 2 Stamford Rd; noon-2.30pm, 7-11pm) Equinox offers stunning views, dramatic Oriental-style decor and very good, inventive food that is either east or west, but not both together. It's not to be missed. The funky New Asia Bar & Grill (see p497), upstairs, offers a range of nibbles, including seafood, and is slightly kinder to the budget.

JAPANESE

Ichiban Boshi (Map pp452-3; ☎ 6423 1151; 02-14 Esplanade Mall; mains S$10-15; 11.30am-11pm Sun & Mon, 11.30am-1am Tue-Thu, 11.30am-2am Fri & Sat) Good conveyor belt sushi (S$1.50-3.80) and other Japanese delicacies are offered here at very reasonable prices. It's a classier and tastier operation than others of its ilk in Singapore.

Sakana (Map pp452-3; ☎ 6336 0266; 01-03/04 Liang Seah St; mains S$10-20; noon-2.30pm, 6-10pm Mon-Sat) Sakana is one of those great little informal places that you find so rarely outside Japan. The set lunch (S$9.90) is fab, but come for dinner to sample the full range of their tasty, well presented dishes and sake.

A couple of upmarket places are **Inagiku** (Map pp452-3; ☎ 6431 6156; Level 3, Raffles The Plaza Singapore, 2 Stamford Rd; mains from S$20), known for its tempura and sashimi; and **Keyaki** (Map pp452-3; ☎ 6434 8335; 4th fl, The Pan Pacific Singapore, 7 Raffles Blvd; mains from S$20), where you can enjoy a bento-box lunch looking out on a landscaped garden that could be in the midst of Kyoto.

PERANAKAN

Empire Café (Map pp452-3; ☎ 6337 1886; Level One, Raffles Hotel Arcade, 1 Beach Rd; mains S$9-15; 11am-11pm) On the corner of Bras Basah and North Bridge Rd and next to the totally yummy **Ah Teng's Bakery** (7.30am-2am), the Empire Café offers Singaporean favourites in a classy setting. Their chicken rice and *congee* are excellent.

THE AUTHOR'S CHOICE

Simon Richmond

Café at-sunrice (Map pp452-3; ☎ 6336 3307; Fort Canning Centre; mains S$4-6; 11am-9pm) This self-serve café not only has a lovely quiet spot in the leafy surrounds of Fort Canning Park, but also serves great value Asian meals. It's about the only place in Singapore to sample the wonderful Burmese dishes *mohingar* (a laksa-style noodle soup) and young tea leaf and nut salad. Their chicken on lemongrass skewers is utterly delicious.

Vansh (Map pp450-1; ☎ 6345 4466, 01-04 Singapore Indoor Stadium, 2 Stadium Walk; mains S$20-30; noon-2.30pm, 6-11pm). Among Singapore's many Indian restaurants Vansh – one of the gaggle of restaurants nestling at the base of the riverside Indoor Stadium – stands out for its tasty modern Indian cuisine and strikingly contemporary interior design. As with its sibling restaurant Rang Mahal in the Pan Pacific you can watch the chefs at work, yanking naans in and out of the tandoor. Wash down scrumptious chicken *tikka masala* with their refreshing rose petal sherbet.

Chomp Chomp (Map pp448-9; welcome.to/chomp-chomp; 6pm-1am) Although they've been challenged by newly located and good Serangoon Gardens Market & Food Centre across the way, the old hands at Chomp Chomp still justly attract the crowds. Here 36 hawker stalls churn out dishes such as *satay been hoon* (peanut sauce flavoured noodles) and carrot cake. Wander the smoky aisles to see what else takes your fancy. Since it's out of the way in the north of the island you're likely to be the only tourist in sight.

SINGAPORE

QUICK EATS

The third floor of **Raffles City** (Map pp456-7; 252 North Bridge Rd) and the basements of **Funan Centre** (Map pp452-3; 109 North Bridge Rd) and **Seiyu** department store at Bugis (Map p458; 200 Victoria St), have busy, modern food courts. Seiyu's Food Junction offers a decent selection of Japanese food, including *takoyaki* (deep-fried octopus and batter balls), plus Thai, bubbling claypot concoctions, chicken rice and more.

Victoria Food Centre (Map pp452-3; 143 Victoria St; 24hr) with a distinctive small shrine outside, is a great place for a late night feed or beer. **Bras Basah Food Court** (Map pp452-3; 232 Victoria St; 7am-9pm) offering Malay and Indian tandoori food as well as Chinese favourites – the *bak chor mee* (noodles with pork, meat balls and fried scallops) from Parklane Noodle House at stall 01-79/06 is popular. At **Nan Tai Eating House** (Map pp452-3; Blk 262 Waterloo St) the *rojak* (a fruit and vegetable salad tossed in peanut and prawn paste sauce) from Sajis Indian Food at stall 01-29 is justly famous.

New Bugis St (Map p458) beside the market stalls has Malay, Indonesian, Thai and Chinese food and does a brisk evening trade. **Suntec City Fountain Terrace** is where you can watch the largest fountain in the world do its stuff, after trawling through a fine selection of food stalls, including Shanghainese, Thai, Malay, Indian and Korean.

SELF-CATERING

The supermarket **Cold Storage** (www.coldstorage.com.sg) has several branches across the city, including ones in the basement of **Seiyu Department Store** (Map p458) and at 293 Holland Rd in **Holland Village** (Map pp448-9). If you can not find what you want here, try the French hypermarket **Carrefour** (Map pp452-3; Suntec City Mall).

THAI

Yhingthai Palace (Map pp452-3; 6337 1161; 01-04, 36 Purvis St; mains S$10-15) This long-running favourite serves all the classic Thai dishes and does them well. Their branch further down at 01-01, 36 Purvis St is halal so the dishes are free of pork or lard.

VIETNAMESE

Indochine Alfresco (Map pp452-3; 6333 5003; 42 Waterloo St; mains S$15-25) Among the three outlets this is the Indochine we prefer, set in a tranquil colonial-style building (which also houses Action Theatre). The food is from all over Indochina and uniformly delicious.

Indochine Waterfront (Map pp452-3; 6339 1720; 1 Empress Place) There's lots to recommend here too, but we've not been too impressed with the service. The original wine-bar and restaurant in this mini-chain is in Chinatown (6323 0503, 49 Club St) and is also worth checking out.

Vietlang (Map pp452-3; 6337 3379; 01-26/27 CHIJMES, 30 Victoria St; mains S$10-20; 11.30am-10.30pm Sun-Thu, 11.30am-11.30pm Fri & Sat) One of the newer additions to CHIJMES's bamboozling range of restaurants, Vietlang offers excellent-value Vietnamese food in a Hanoi-chic setting.

CBD & the Quays

ASIAN FUSION

Coriander Leaf (Map pp452-3; 6732 3354; www.corianderleaf.com; 02-01 The Gallery Hotel Singapore, 76 Robertson Quay; mains S$15-25) At this contemporary Asian-chic restaurant a selection of starters (may we recommend the *mezze* plate and the soft-shell crab tempura?) will do you fine. Their desserts are stellar. The restaurant also has a small deli and cooking studio for courses.

AUSTRALIAN

The Moomba (Map pp452-3; 6438 0141; 52 Circular Rd; mains from S$20) Aboriginal painting-style murals decorate the walls at The Moomba and complement the excellent modern Australian cuisine and wine list. Dine on barbecued kangaroo loin and char-grilled Australian beef.

CAFÉS

Book Café (Map pp452-3; 6887 5430; 01-02 Seng Kee Bldg, 20 Martin Rd; mains S$10-15; 8.30am-10.30pm Sun-Thu, 8.30am-1.30pm Fri & Sat;) This is a convivial place with a reasonable selection of old books, magazines and foreign newspapers to browse while you slump on a sofa enjoying breakfast or a coffee. There's free Internet access for customers, and literary events are occasionally held here too – check www.qlrs.com for details.

CHINESE

Tung Lok (Map pp452-3; 6336 6022; 04-07/09 Liang Court Shopping Centre, 177 River Valley Rd; mains over S$20) The original Tung Lok (the first of what is now one of Singapore's biggest restaurant groups) is renowned for its shark's fin dishes, although braised abalone is also popular and they do a large range of dim sum (from S$2.50 a dish).

Grand Shanghai (Map pp450-1; ☎ 6836 6866; Level 1 King's Centre, 390 Havelock Rd; mains S$15-25) The concept – retro chic surroundings, traditional dishes with a contemporary twist – here is a winner, and the minced chicken stuffed pastry pockets are to die for.

Si Chuan Dou Hua Restaurant (Map pp452-3; ☎ 6535 6006; 60-01 UOB Plaza 1, 80 Raffles Place; mains S$15-20) Perched 60 floors above the Singapore River this classy restaurant specialises in Sichuan, Cantonese and Hunan dishes – the dim sum and Peking duck are worth sampling. For added interest, traditional Chinese tea is usually served by a silk pyjama-clad gent who mixes dance and gymnastics as he pours your cuppa.

FRENCH

Saint Pierre (Map pp452-3; ☎ 6438 0887; 01-01 Central Mall, 3 Magazine Rd; mains over S$30) St Pierre serves very modern French (with a hint of Japan) cuisine, in a stylishly minimalist setting. Try their three- or five-course set lunch (S$26.50/50) to see why some hail this the best French restaurant in town.

INDIAN

Kinara (Map pp452-3; ☎ 6533 0412; 57 Boat Quay; mains S$10-20) This Chinese shophouse has been renovated into a *haveli* (a traditional, ornately decorated Indian residence). You can look over the river while feasting on moderately priced Punjabi food.

Saffron Bistro (Map pp452-3; ☎ 6536 5025; 50 Circular Rd; mains S$10-15) Saffron Bistro offers a modern take on classic Indian dishes, their chefs using less oil for a healthier product. The set lunches (from S$9.90) and dinner (S$24.90) are good value.

INDONESIAN

House of Sundanese Food (Map pp452-3; ☎ 6534 3775; 55-55A Boat Quay; mains S$15-25) Sample the spicy cuisine of West Java, such as crisp fried prawns with *sambal* (sauce of fried chilli, onions and prawn paste), *cumi cumi bakar* (charcoal-grilled squid) or *ikan sunda* (fried dancing fish). There are other outlets at **Suntec City** (Map pp452-3; ☎ 6334 1012; Suntec City Mall, B1-063) and **Katong** (Map pp448-9; ☎ 6345 5020; 218 East Coast Rd).

JAPANESE

Bon Gout (Map pp452-3; ☎ 6732 5234; 01-01 The Quayside, 60 Robertson Quay; mains S$5-10; ⏲ noon-10pm) Selling new and used Japanese books & CDs, this laid-back place whips up comforting Japanese meals of the less fancy variety – think noodles, rice bowls and mild curries.

En Japanese Dining Bar (Map pp452-3; ☎ 6735 2212; 207 River Valley Rd; mains S$15-25) En is one of the best places to dine on the Mohamed Sultan strip, with its outdoor tables and a keenly priced menu of Japanese favourites supplemented by more exotic Okinawan dishes using pork, bitter gourd and fish.

Haru (Map pp452-3; ☎ 6536 3080; 01-07 One Fullerton; 1 Fullerton Rd; mains S$15-25) This classy eatery does good lunchtime set menus and is a nice spot in the evening for bayside views. The food is authentic and they also have a sake bar.

BRUNCH, TIFFIN & HIGH TEA

Singaporeans have a mania for elaborate buffet brunches, toff-style high teas and tiffin (the traditional midday light meal of colonials). The five-star hotels all do a good job in laying out Eastern and Western savouries, cakes, puddings, fruits and even champagne for the hungry hordes. Prices range from S$45-80 per head, young kids sometimes eat for less (or even free) and child-minding facilities may be available.

For the latest deals it's best to check the local papers and magazines. To be assured of a seat book several days ahead. Try **Mezza9** at the Grand Hyatt (Map pp456-7; ☎ 6416 7189), renowned for its free-flow champagne Sunday brunch; the charming waterfall room at **Sheraton Towers** (Map pp456-7; ☎ 6737 6888); Raffles' colonial style **Bar & Billiard Room** (pp452-3) or pukka **Tiffin Room** (Map pp452-3; ☎ 6331 1612); **One-Ninety** at the Four Seasons Hotel Singapore (Map pp456-7; ☎ 6831 7250); the **Regent** (Map pp456-7; ☎ 6733 8888); or the **Fullerton Singapore** (Map pp452-3; ☎ 6733 8388) at either the main restaurant Town with its riverside location or in the cool of the atrium lobby – the cakes here are divine.

MEXICAN

Café Iguana (Map pp452-3; ☎ 6438 2311; 02-07 Riverside Point, 30 Merchant Rd; mains S$15-20; ⏲ 6pm-1am Mon-Fri, noon-1am Sat & Sun) Singapore doesn't have many good Mexican restaurants, but if you're hanging out for fajitas or nachos then this bright and breezy place will hit the spot. It has a pleasant riverside location and they do brunch on the weekend from noon to 4pm.

QUICK EATS

Lau Pa Sat (Map pp452-3;18 Raffles Quay) means 'old market' in Hokkien, which is appropriate since this fine food court occupies a handsome iron lacework structure shipped out from Glasgow in 1894 and once used as a market. A few souvenir stalls hug its perimeter, but the main emphasis is on eating. Additional hawker stalls, many specialising in satay, set up in the evening on **Boon Tat St** (Map pp452-3; 7pm-3am Mon-Fri, 3pm-3am Sat & Sun), where you can dine alfresco – the chilli crab here is excellent.

More of the Indonesian-style kebabs are available at the **Satay Club** (Map pp452-3; Clarke Quay; ⏲ 5pm-3am). There are several mobile stalls from which to choose. You pay 40¢ per satay stick – they're generally served in a bunch of 10.

Chinatown

AFRICAN

Mama Africa (Map pp452-3; ☎ 6532 9339; 01-01 Far East Square, 88 Telok Ayer St; mains S$15-25) If all you've been craving since hitting Singapore is *bobotie* (mince pie) and *boerewors* (sausages), then this faux-African joint is for you. The atmosphere is suitably upbeat.

CHINESE

Damenlou Swee Kee (Map pp452-3; ☎ 6221 1900; 12 Ann Siang Rd; mains S$10-15) The Swee Kee is a long-running family restaurant, famed for its *ka shou* fish-head noodles; dine in the Peranakan-style ground floor room, or phone ahead and get them to set up a table on the roof for a postcard view across Chinatown.

Qun Zhong Eating House (Map pp452-3; ☎ 6221 3060; all dishes under S$10; 21 Neil Rd; ⏲ 11.30am-3pm, 5.30-9.30pm Thu-Tue) Join the queue outside this cosy eatery for the yummy handmade seafood, pork and vegetable dumplings or the interesting Chinese-style pizza. The red bean paste pancake makes for a great dessert.

Xin Min Vegetarian Food Court (Map pp452-3; ☎ 6324 2481; 29 Kreta Ayer Rd; mains S$5-10) Just a few doors down from the Chinese Buddhist Association this is an inexpensive vegetarian option. Dine on bean curd, noodles, rice and vegetables in a traditional shophouse.

Xin Tao Yuan (Map pp452-3; ☎ 6323 6367; 63 Tanjong Pagar Rd; mains S$5-10) Watch fresh Taiwanese-style noodles being made in the restaurant window, then try them cold with sesame paste and cucumber – if you don't want the shredded pork which goes in this dish, tell them. Their dumplings are good, too.

FRENCH

Club St brims over with French and French-inspired restaurants.

L'Angelus (Map pp452-3; ☎ 6225 6897; 85 Club St; mains around S$30) has a Provençale flavour both to its decor and food.

Nectar (Map pp452-3; ☎ 6323 4544; 87 Club St; mains S$25-35) serves dishes occasionally as dramatic as its alabaster, gold and gauze interior.

Duo (Map pp452-3; ☎ 6224 4428; 38 Club St; mains from S$30) is elegant and intimate – they prefer to serve couples.

INTERNATIONAL

Broth (Map pp452-3; ☎ 6323 3353; 21 Duxton Hill; mains S$15-25) Based in a smartly converted shophouse, Broth's short menu zips from the daily soup (S$6.90) to rare tuna *tataki*, pies and veal saltimbocca (S$22.90). The friendly staff and modern-meets-colonial interior give this place a welcoming, informal feel.

ITALIAN

Pasta Brava (Map pp450-1; ☎ 6227 7550; 11 Craig Rd; mains S$15-25) Fabulous Italian food, particularly the homemade pasta, is served here. Every table comes with a white paper sheet over the table cloth, and a basket of chalks – doodle away and, if they like your artwork, it will get pinned on the wall.

Spizza for Friends (Map pp452-3; ☎ 6224 2525; 29 Club St; pizzas S$14-17) One of the best places in Singapore for authentic thin-crust pizzas – hence its popularity.

Da Paolo (Map pp452-3; ☎ 6224 7081; 80 Club St; mains S$15-30) is one of an expanding chain of chi-chi Italian eateries. Their famous dish is squid ink pasta, also available at the sleek, minimalist **Da Paolo E Judie** (Map pp452-3; ☎ 6225 8306; 81 Neil Rd; mains S$15-25) which specialises in fish.

PERANAKAN

Blue Ginger (Map pp450-1; ☎ 6222 3928; 97 Tanjong Pagar Rd; mains S$15-25) Blue Ginger is justly renowned for the quality of its Peranakan cooking. The colonial atmosphere of this old shophouse is enlivened by the striking contemporary paintings of local artist Martin Loh.

Belachan (Map pp452-3; ☎ 6221 9810; 10 Smith St; mains S$15-25) Free of the kitsch decorations present in some other Peranakan restaurants, Belachan is worth visiting for its prawn and papaya soup or Grandma's *itek manis*, duck simmered in ginger and black bean sauce. It's closed Mondays.

QUICK EATS Map pp452-3

As you'd expect, the large, eternally busy **Chinatown Complex** (cnr Sago & Trengganu Sts) has some great Chinese food stalls on the 2nd floor. The choice is vast. Some of the vendors from here and other renowned hawker stalls and restaurants across the city have set up along **Smith St** where you can sit on the street under red lanterns bobbing in the breeze – it's very touristy, but fun and popular with locals too.

One of Singapore's best food courts is **Maxwell Road Food Centre** (cnr South Bridge & Maxwell Rds) in an open-sided shed-like structure. It's an interesting place to spend some time watching the hawkers at work. Don't miss the *ham chin pang* (long pieces of deep-fried dough) or the fine chicken rice at **Tian Tian** (stall 10) or the dim sum at stall 79/80.

Around 1.5km along Outram Rd, northwest of Outram Park MRT is the truly excellent and authentic **Tiong Bahru Cooked Food Centre** (cnr Seng Poh & Lim Liam Sts). Come here for the *char kway teow* (fried flat noodles; stall 11A), oyster omelette (stall 19C), the *chwee kueh* (steamed radish cakes; stall 15E) or the Koh Brothers' famed pig's organ soup.

SELF-CATERING

In the **Chinatown Complex** (Map pp452-3; cnr Sago & Trengganu Sts) you'll find one of Singapore's best wet markets (so named for the water on the floor). The seafood, meat, fruit and vegetables sold here are very fresh; dig around and you'll find all kinds of exotic produce.

THAI

Thanying (Map pp450-1; ☎ 6222 4688; 2nd fl, Amara Hotel, 165 Tanjong Pagar Rd; mains S$15-25) Thanying has long been considered one of Singapore's best Thai restaurants – known for its grilled chicken, roast duck red curry and other royal Thai dishes.

Little India Map p458

CHINESE

New Generation Vegetarian Eating House (☎ 6398 0878; 5 Hindoo Rd; mains S$5-10; 🕒 8am-9pm Tue, Wed, Fri-Sun, 8am-6pm Mon & Thu) This simple café serves tasty, cheap Chinese vegetarian dishes; try the mock duck or pineapple rice.

Singapura Seafood Restaurant (☎ 6336 3255; Block 9, Selegie House, 01-31 Selegie Rd; mains S$15-25) Foochow-style food from southern China is not that common in Singapore, but this unpretentious family-run place has made its reputation based on it. Try their excellent cold crab, fragrant crispy duck, honey pork ribs and prawn rolls.

Wing Seong Fatty's (Albert) Restaurant (☎ 6338 1087; 01-31 Burlington Square, 175 Bencoolen St; mains from S$5) The Cantonese menu is extensive at this long-running expat hangout. Most dishes come in a choice of small, medium and large sizes (small will be fine for most appetites).

FRENCH

The French Stall (☎ 6299 3544; 544 Serangoon Rd; mains S$10-20; 🕒 3-6pm drinks & dessert only, 6-10pm Tue-Sun) It's cash only at this charming Gallic hawker stall owned and run by a two-star Michelin chef from Brittany. Enjoy scrumptious set French meals (from S$11.80) and wine at a bargain S$6.80 per glass, amid a Euro-savvy crowd.

INDIAN

Andhra Curry (☎ 6293 3935; 41 Kerbau Rd; mains S$8-10; 🕒 11.30am-10.30pm) Andhra Curry specialises in the fiery flavours characteristic of the central Indian state of Andhra Pradesh. Try Andhra Hyderabadi biryani or the traditional vegetarian wedding dish *kalyana bhojara*.

Banana Leaf Apolo (☎ 6293 8682; bananaleafapolo.com; 54-58 Race Course Rd; meals from S$6; 🕒 10am-10pm) Come here to dine off the eponymous leaf in a modern, air-con setting. Their speciality is fish-head curry (S$18 small, S$22 medium, S$26 large) but they also do cheap thalis; there's a plusher branch at 66-68 Race Course Rd too, serving north Indian cuisine and open slightly later (11am to 11pm).

TOM COCKREM

Katong Antique House (p466)

Expo MRT station (p49)

SIMON RICHMOND

DOMINIC ARIZONA BONUCCELLI

Neon glow from the bars and cafés that line **Singapore River** (p446)

Chinese **movie** (p500) poster, Orchard Rd

GLENN BEANLAND

ALAIN

Motorcyclist, **Chingay parade** (p479)

CHRISTINE OSBORNE

Fortune teller, **Chinatown** (p463)

Flamingos, **Singapore Zoological Gardens** (p467)

GLENN BEA

Esplanade – Theatres on the Bay (p460), Colonial District

GLENN BEANLAND

THE ART OF TEA APPRECIATION

Taking time out in a teahouse is a pleasant way to relax, and to learn about the many kinds of tea available and how to appreciate them. The best place to start is **Yixing Yuan Teahouse** (Map pp452-3; ☎ 6224 6961; 30/32 Tanjong Pagar Rd; 🕑 11am-11pm), where former banker Vincent Low explains all you need to know about sampling different types of tea. The demonstration with tastings lasts around an hour (S$15). If you choose to sample a few snacks it's S$20, or if you go for the dim sum lunch S$25 – bookings are necessary.

Once you know your green tea from your oolong, nip around the corner to **Tea Chapter** (Map pp452-3; ☎ 6226 1175; www.tea-chapter.com.sg; 9-11 Neil Rd; 🕑 10am-11pm), where Queen Elizabeth and Prince Philip dropped by for a cuppa in 1989. There are several different areas in which to sit, but choose carefully – the more private incur a higher surcharge. If you don't know the drill, the waiter will give you a brief demonstration of how to make tea. Then sit back and enjoy a leisurely afternoon of sipping and chatting.

Teaspa (Map pp456-7; ☎ 6336 4113; 03-12 Raffles City, 252 North Bridge Rd; 🕑 noon-9.30pm) is a trendy contemporary café/restaurant/tea gallery, offering a staggering 86 types of tea and herbal and fruit infusions – you can even get ones blended to suit your horoscope. There another branch at the Paragon on Orchard Rd.

Komala Vilas (☎ 6293 6990; 76-78 Serangoon Rd; 🕑 7am-10.30pm; mains S$5-10) Don't miss out on Komala Villas terrific, inexpensive vegetarian food. Their *dosa* (paper-thin pancakes made from lentil flour) are great and the vegetable biryani is particularly tasty. At 82 Serangoon Rd the restaurant has an outlet selling a tempting range of Indian sweets.

Madras New Woodlands (☎ 6297 1594; 12-14 Upper Dickson Rd; mains S$5-10; 🕑 7.30am-11.30pm) This place is looking smarter after a recent revamp, but nothing's changed with their filling thalis on banana leaves, which are delicious. The service is gracious and the portions immense.

Two places that serve good value buffets are **The Ganges** (☎ 6294 3547; 3A-9A Upper Dickson Rd; lunch/dinner S$9.50/11.50) and **Roshni Fine Indian Dining & Lounge** (☎ 6292 4808; 48 Serangoon Rd; lunch/dinner S$13/17) where on Wednesday to Saturday nights you can kick your heels to live bhangra music from 10pm.

QUICK EATS

Pick from a good range of Indian-Muslim food stalls at the **Tekka Centre** (cnr Serangoon & Buffalo Rds). Across the road, the smaller **Little India Arcade** (Serangoon Rd) has several stalls that sell vegetarian, Muslim, Keralan and Sri Lankan food. It is very busy on Sunday evenings when Indian, Pakistani and Sri Lankan workers gather to socialise on their day off. If you aren't up to a full meal, come for a cold drink, spicy Indian tea and a snack such as *idli* (steamed rice cakes) or *vadai* (a fried, spicy lentil patty, served with savoury lentil sauce or yogurt).

Lavender Food Square (Jl Besar; 🕑 24hr) is a great place to dine on interesting dishes such as frogs' legs and turtle soup. The dim sum here is good too.

Berseh Food Centre (Jl Besar) Closer to the heart of Little India, this is also a lively and authentic place to drop by for a feed.

Kampong Glam

Zam Zam (Map p458; ☎ 6298 7011; 699 North Bridge Rd; 🕑 7am-11pm) and **Victory Restaurant** next door, is where you can watch the skilful *murtabak* (*roti prata* filled with mutton, chicken or vegetables) makers at work. Both restaurants have been turning out good, inexpensive food in this part of town since the early 1900s.

Bumbu (Map p458; ☎ 6392 8628, 44 Kandahar St; mains S$10-15) This place serves delicious Thai and Indonesian dishes in a charming shophouse setting. Further down the street, terrific Malay fare is on the menu at the simple **Sabar Menanti** (Map p458; ☎ 6293 0284; 50/52 Kandahar St; meals under S$10; 🕑 8am-8pm Mon-Sat, 8am-5pm Sun).

Malay food can also be had from the small **Al Majlis Food Court** (Map p458; 39 Arab St) where you'll also find the relaxing **Café Le Caire** (Map p458; ☎ 6292 0979; 🕑 10am-2am) serving some Middle Eastern dishes and offering hookah pipes (S$8) with 12 flavours of tobacco including cappuccino and rose scented.

QUICK EATS

The excellent **Golden Mile Food Centre** (Map p458; 505 Beach Rd) is one of the best spots in Singapore to sample soup *tulang* (stalls 13 and 15 in the basement – open from 4pm till late). Soup *tulang* (S$4) consists of meaty bones stewed in a rich, spicy, blood-red tomato gravy. Gnaw off the flesh; suck out the marrow (a straw comes in handy) and sop up the tomato sauce with bread. It's very messy and filling. If you have any room left, head to **Zhao An Granny Grass Jelly** (stall 01-58) and try a glass of this dark, refreshing substance (grass jelly) sweetened with syrup. Or go to stall **Ah Balling Peanut Soup** (stall 01-75) serving chewy rice balls filled with peanut, sesame, red bean or yam paste in a peanut- or ginger-infused soup.

In the Golden Mile Complex across the road, you'll find many Thai food stalls (as well as a giant Thai supermarket); try **Diandin Leluk** (Map p458; 01/67-69; mains under S$10; 11am-11pm) known for its tasty *tom yum* soup and beef noodles.

SELF-CATERING

The **Tekka Centre** (Map p458; cnr Serangoon and Sungei Rds) is another of Singapore's best wet markets selling all you need to put together your own Indian banquet.

SINGAPORE

Orchard Road

ASIAN

Nooch (Map pp456-7; 6235 0880; 02-16 Wheelock Place, 501 Orchard Rd; mains S$10-15) Slurp and scoff both Thai- and Japanese-style noodle and rice dishes at this stylish, casual restaurant. A new branch is set to open in the **City Link mall** (Map pp452-3; 6341 9288) and the **Paragon** (Map pp456-7; 6732 3313, Orchard Rd).

Halia (Map pp456-7; 6476 6711; Singapore Botanic Gardens, 1 Cluny Rd; mains S$10-20; 8am-10am Sat & Sun, 11am-5.30pm, 6.30-10.30pm) Halia's outdoor deck surrounded by the verdant fronds of the Botanic Gardens is a lovely place for a buffet breakfast (S$15) or lunch; their laksa is a hearty meal in a bowl. Dine by candlelight in the evening when the tourist crowds have gone.

CAFÉS

Marmalade Pantry (Map p456-7; 6734 2700; B1-08 Palais Rennaissance, 390 Orchard Rd; 11.30am-9pm) The delicious cakes alone are worth a visit to this quietly sophisticated place where the food is contemporary international, with something for everyone. Bookings for their good Sunday brunch (10.30am-4pm) are essential.

Blood Café (Map pp456-7; 6735 6765, 02-20/21 The Paragon, 290 Orchard Rd; 10am-8.30pm) This cool café tucked away at the back of the trendy Project Shop Blood Bros boutique serves great food and drinks and has tons of style mags to flick through.

DKNY Café (Map pp456-7; 6734 0811; 01-03 Palais Rennaissance, 390 Orchard Rd; 11am-7pm Mon-Sat, 11.30am-5.30pm Sun) This is another café inside a fashion store – but don't feel like a shop dummy; they serve some interesting sandwiches and cakes – enough to send supermodels scurrying.

Café Les Amis (Map pp456-7; Singapore Botanic Gardens, Cluny Rd entry; 7.30am-10.30pm) Nothing fancy but locals flock here for a quiet breakfast (Western or Asian), drinks, sandwiches and light meals at around S$10 a pop; it's just beside the main Cluny Rd entrance to the gardens.

Ubar (Map pp456-7; 6238 6648; 01-04 Pacific Plaza, 9 Scotts Rd; 10am-11pm Sun-Thu, 10am-midnight Fri & Sat) Get healthy with the various freshly squeezed and whizzed juice combinations at Ubar. Take a table, fill in the order slip, pay at the counter and wait for your juice to arrive.

CHINESE

Boon Tong Kee (Map pp456-7; 6736 3213; 425 River Valley Rd; mains S$5-15; 10am-midnight) As well as their superlative chicken rice, we can recommend the marinated raw fish (S$5 to S$13) and prawns in soya bean paste (S$12). Dine alfresco at their original store near **Toa Payoh** (6256 0138; 399 Balestier Rd), handy if you are visiting Sun Yat-Sen Nanyang Memorial Hall.

Imperium (Map pp456-7; 6733 9833; Ngee Ann City, 391 Orchard Rd; mains S$10-20) Tucked away on the 7th floor of Ngee Ann City, like the long lost set from a 1940s Hollywood musical, Imperium is a great place for a dim sum pig out.

Jiang Nan Chun (Map pp456-7; 6831 7220; Four Seasons Hotel, 190 Orchard Blvd; mains from S$20) Discreet and artistically furnished, Jiang Nan Chun is the place to bring someone you want to impress. Their modern Chinese dishes flit all around the country for inspiration.

Lingzhi Vegetarian (Map pp456-7; ☎ 6734 3788; 05-01 Liat Towers, 541 Orchard Rd; mains S$12-20) This place offers traditional and imaginative modern Chinese vegetarian dishes. At the entrance is a takeaway outlet selling vegetarian dumplings, cakes and spring rolls. There's also a branch in Far East Square in Chinatown.

INDIAN

Bombay Woodlands Restaurant (Map pp456-7; ☎ 6235 2712; B1-01/02 Tanglin Shopping Centre, 19 Tanglin Rd; mains S$5-7; 9.30am-10pm) This all-vegetarian joint offers a great set price buffet lunch as well as thalis for S$14. It's patronised by the Indian traders so can be relied on.

Samy's Curry Restaurant (Map pp456-7; ☎ 6472 2080; Civil Service Club, Blk 25 Dempsey Rd; mains S$10) The legendary Samy's is *the* place for banana leaf feasts. They do a mean fish-head curry and other traditional north and south Indian food, all served in the pricelessly unpretentious surroundings close by the Botanic Gardens. Arrive early if you want to get a table on the veranda.

INTERNATIONAL

Marché Movenpick (Map pp456-7; ☎ 6737 6996; basement, The Heeren, 260 Orchard Rd; mains S$10-20; 11am-11pm) This kind of European-style hawkers centre is best known for its *rosti*, sausages and crêpes. Frazzled parents will appreciate the kid's playground. They also have a branch at Suntec City (Map pp452-3; ☎ 6336 3113).

Mezza9 (Map pp456-7; ☎ 6416 7189; Grand Hyatt Singapore, 10-12 Scotts Rd; Mains around S$20; noon-11pm) On the mezzanine floor of the Hyatt's expansive lobby, this flashy number wows with six display kitchens offering everything from sushi to elaborate desserts; sit where you like and order from any one of them. High tea is served 3pm to 5pm and their champagne Sunday brunch is popular.

JAPANESE

Akashi (Map pp456-7; ☎ 6732 4483; B1-9-11 Tanglin Shopping Centre, 19 Tanglin Rd; mains S$10-20) This is one of the best value Japanese restaurants around. Its photo menu shows you what to expect from each of the set meal deals. There's a sushi bar where the more adventurous and knowledgeable can indulge their fishy passions. There's a branch in the City Link mall (Map pp452-3; ☎ 6238 7767).

Don (Map pp456-7; ☎ 6738 3188; 01-16 Tanglin Mall, 163 Tanglin Rd; mains S$10-15; 11.30am-10pm) Another fine pick for fuss-free Japanese – teppanyaki and noodles are the speciality at this bright, modern place.

QUICK EATS

The basements of many shopping malls and department stores have good, inexpensive food courts, most open from 10.30am-9.30pm; try **Lucky Plaza** (Map pp456-7; 304 Orchard Rd), which offers the usual variety of noodle, chicken rice and claypot outlets, as well as drinks and desserts.

Beneath Le Meridien Hotel is a fine new Thai-themed food centre **Great Treat** (Map pp456-7; 100 Orchard Rd; open 10.30am-10pm). Fourteen out of the 17 outlets are devoted to different types of Thai food, and there's a branch of the famous Bangkok seafood stall Rut & Lek.

Picnic at Scotts (Map pp456-7; Scotts Shopping Centre, 6 Scotts Rd), is glossier than most and has a variety of Asian cuisines, including Thai and Japanese, which you'll also find in plentiful supply at **Takashimaya Food Village** (Map pp456-7; Takashimaya, Ngee Ann City, 391 Orchard Rd). Another modern place with a good range is **Tanglin Mall Food Junction** (Map pp456-7; Tanglin Mall, 163 Tanglin Rd).

Newton Food Centre (Map pp456-7; Scotts Rd; 24hr) is near Newton MRT and best visited late in the evening when the atmosphere is liveliest. It's a long-time favourite with tourists (even though it's a bit more expensive than other hawker centres and some of the stall holders have a horrible habit of overcharging the more gullible). Sample *popiah* (rice paper rolls) and satay at stall 68, and noodles at either stall 64 or 79.

RUSSIAN

Shashlik (Map pp456-7; ☎ 6734 3090; 06-19 Far East Shopping Centre, 545 Orchard Rd; mains around S$25) The food is not really Russian but they do decent borscht and very tender beef, chicken or pork shashlik. The retro ambience (the place hasn't been changed for decades) is priceless, as are the old waiters pushing around trolleys and expertly setting flame to bombe Alaskas.

SELF-CATERING

Tanglin Market Place (Map pp456-7; Tanglin Mall, 163 Tanglin Rd) is a good place to shop for groceries. In the same mall you'll find all kinds of organic, chemical-free products, including fresh fruit and vegetables, at **Brown Rice Paradise** (Map pp456-7; 03-15/16 Tanglin Mall, 163 Tanglin Rd), or nearby at **Supernature** (Map pp456-7; ☎ 6735 4338; 01-21 Park House, 21 Orchard Blvd).

Bread Talk (www.breadtalk.com.sg) is a highly popular bakery chain, serving a very tempting range of buns, cakes and other local sweet and savoury nibbles. It has several outlets along or near Orchard Rd; you'll also find them in the City Link Mall (Map pp456-7) and Parco Bugis Junction (Map p458).

VEGETARIAN

Supernature (Map pp456-7; ☎ 6737 1768; 03-04 Wheelock Place; mains S$10-15; 🕓 10am-7pm Mon, Tue, Thu & Fri, 10am-8pm Wed & Sat, 11am-6pm Sun) Feeling rough after a night on the tiles? Then drop in for a super detox juice (S$7.50) and a healthy organic-produce sandwich or a soy burger. Vegans and those avoiding wheat products are catered for too.

Katong & East Coast

CAFÉS

Katong Bakery & Confectionary (Map pp448-9; 187 East Coast Rd; 75 East Coast Rd; 🕓 11.30am-8pm) This pre-WWII cake and coffee shop serves up cream rolls, dark honey cakes and fluffy sponges to customers sitting at marble-topped tables and on rickety wooden chairs. If they aren't already heritage listed, we'd like to nominate the whole shop including the recipes and the sweet, grey-haired proprietor as national treasures.

CHINESE

Sin Hoi Sai Eating House (Map pp448-9; 187 East Coast Rd; mains S$5-10; 🕓 5pm-3am) This simple place serving good, cheap Cantonese dishes is always packed. Next door at No 191 **Five Star Hainanese Chicken Rice & Porridge** (Map pp448-9; 🕓 11am-2am) dishes up chicken rice for a bargain S$3.

PERANAKAN

Guan Hoe Soon (Map pp448-9; ☎ 6344 2761; 214 Joo Chiat Rd; mains under S$20; 🕓 11am-2.30pm, 6-9.30pm Wed-Mon) They have been turning out fine Nonya cuisine here for around 50 years, and it's where Lee Kuan Yew gets his takeaways from. This is the place to try *ayam buah keluak*, a chicken and ground-nut curry.

Peranakan Inn & Lounge (Map pp448-9; 187 East Coast Rd; ☎ 6440 6195; 210 East Coast Rd; mains S$10-20; 🕓 11am-3pm & 6-10.30pm) Delicious smells waft from the air-conditioned interior of this restaurant, run by the same people as those behind the equally good **House of Peranakan Cuisine** (Map pp456-7; ☎ 6733 4411, Meritus Negara Hotel) just off Orchard Rd.

SEAFOOD

Hua Yu Wee (Map pp448-9; ☎ 6241 1709; 462 Upper East Coast Rd; mains S$10-20; 🕓 5-11.30pm) In an old villa at the far east end of the trendy Siglap area, this local institution gets packed at weekends. Sit out the back and let the shuffling aunties bring you seafood (great chilli crab and crispy baby squid) and steamboat dishes.

East Coast Seafood Centre (Map pp448-9; East Coast Parkway; 🕓 5pm-midnight) The breezy waterside location makes this a prime spot to enjoy some of the best seafood in Singapore. There are eight operations to choose from although lunch is served from noon at the **Gold Coast Seafood** restaurant only.

Holland Village Map pp448-9

You'll find most of Holland V's dining options clustered around buzzy Lorong Mambong, or along quieter Jl Merah Saga on the Chip Bee Gardens side of this smart residential area favoured by expats.

Along Lorong Mambong several of the bars do decent food, such as Baden Baden (see p499) for German fare, or you could go for Mexican at **Cha Cha Cha** (☎ 6462 1650; 32 Lorong Mambong; mains S$10-20).

Fosters (☎ 6466 8939, 277 Holland Ave; 🕓 11am-11pm Sun-Thu, 11am-1am Fri & Sat) Subtitled 'an English rose café', Fosters is a pleasant spot for a bite with a rustic outdoor terrace and comfy interior. They are famous for their scones and cream afternoon teas.

Sistina (☎ 6476 7782; 01-58, 44 Jl Merah Saga; mains S$15-20) churns out consistently good pizzas, calzone and *stromboli* (a rolled pizza). **Michelangelo's** (☎ 6475 9069, 01-60, 44 Jl Merah Saga; mains over S$20) offers a good selection of pastas (the penne vodka in a creamy orange sauce is the signature dish) and salads. **Original Sin** (☎ 6475 5605; 01-62, 43 Jl Merah Saga; mains S$20-30) does upmarket Mediterranean-style vegetarian dishes.

South Singapore

INDONESIAN

Alkaff Mansion (Map pp450-1; ☎ 6415 4888; 10 Telok Blangah Green, Telok Blangah Hill; mains from S$30; 🕓 noon-2.30pm, 7-10.30pm) The reason for visiting here is

SINGAPORE

mostly to take in the hilltop ambience of the historic 1920s mansion. They're also known for their dinnertime rijstaffel (rice table, usually consisting of at least 10 dishes; S$70) served by women wearing traditional Malay dress. Western food is also available.

DRINKING

Despite relatively high prices for alcohol, Singapore's bar scene is incredibly lively – you're bound to find somewhere to suit your mood. Hit the bars early to take advantage of their happy hours, which typically stretch from around 5pm to 8pm or even 9pm. At these times you'll typically get two of most drinks for the price of one. On Wednesday nights some bars offer cheaper if not free drinks to women.

The main places to party include Mohamed Sultan Rd, CHIJMES in the colonial centre, Boat Quay, Chinatown, Emerald Hill just off Orchard Rd and Holland Village. Unless otherwise stated you can expect most bars to be open from 5pm until at least midnight Sunday to Thursday, and through to 2am on Friday and Saturday.

Colonial District Map pp452-3

There's a good selection of bars at **CHIJMES** (30 Victoria St), a lively place to drop by of an evening with charming outdoor areas in which to relax. **Liberté** (☎ 6338 8481) is one of the newest and choicest watering holes. Nearby, **Insomnia** (☎ 6334 4693) hosts foot-tapping live bands and is very popular at weekends. The unmistakably Irish pub **Father Flanagans** (☎ 6333 1418) is also good for jolly partying; ours will be a Guinness, thanks!

Lot, Stock & Barrel (☎ 6338 5340; 29 Seah St; 🕒 11.30am-3pm Mon-Fri, 5pm-1am Sun-Thu, 5pm-2am Fri, 6pm-2am Sun) If you're looking for a regular bar, this fits the bill nicely with its pool table, darts, cable TV sports channels and decent range of beers.

Introbar (☎ 6431 6156; Swissôtel The Stamford, 2 Stamford Rd). Just off the hotel's lobby, this is a handy and loungy place to meet (although the service can be a bit sloppy) before you zip up 70 floors to take in the panoramic views from trendy New Asia Bar & Grill for which there is a S$25 cover charge (including one drink) on Friday and Saturday nights after 10pm.

Paulaner Brauhaus (☎ 6883 2572; 01-01 Times Square@Millenia Walk, 9 Raffles Blvd; 🕒 11.30am-1am Sun-Thu, 11.30am-2am Fri & Sat) We recommend the Munich Lager and Munich Dark brewed on the premises of this three-storey German microbrewery bar and restaurant. There's live music in the evenings.

We know it's a cliché, but a visit to Singapore is practically incomplete without a drink at Raffles Hotel (p460). Of the several options our favourite is the Bar & Billiard Room, underneath which a tiger was shot in 1904. It has live jazz nightly and a nice veranda on which to sip your drink. The Gazebo Bar in the courtyard of the attached Raffles Hotel Arcade is also a top spot for a tipple with live music in the evening. The plantation style Long Bar, on the Arcade's second level, is where you can chuck peanut shells on the floor without copping a fine. If you must, order a Singapore Sling (S$16 or S$25 with a souvenir glass) – in our opinion, it's a sickly sweet, pre-mixed monstrosity.

> **CHAIN CAFÉS**
>
> Starbucks' domination of the caffeine scene continues apace in Singapore, with numerous outlets across the city centre, but it's not alone – nor necessarily the best place for a coffee.
>
> Hot on the heels of the Seattle-based behemoth – and other imported chains such as Gloria Jeans and Deli France – is the **Coffee Bean & Tea Leaf** (www.coffeebean.com) with over 30 branches (including 82 Boat Quay; 01-79 Parco Bugis Junction; 10 Lorong Mambong, Holland Village; two outlets in Suntec City; and 03-40 Wisma Atria, Orchard Rd). They do gourmet sandwiches, salads and pastas as well as a wide range of brews.
>
> Trading on the nostalgia factor are **Ya Kun Kaya Toast & Coffee** (branches at Far East Square, 18 China St, and 21 Tanjong Pagar Rd, both in Chinatown and 585 North Bridge Rd) and **Killiney Kopitiam** (67 Killiney Rd; 36 Purvis St; and 21 Amoy St). Visit either for a traditional breakfast of strong coffee *(kopi)* and *kaya* (coconut jam) on toast.

CBD & the Quays

Embargo (Map pp452-3; ☎ 6220 2288; One Fullerton, 1 Fullerton Rd) Trendy Embargo, womblike inside, is the spot for pre-party drinks if you're heading to the club Centro above, or if you just want to gaze out on the bay at night.

Post (Map pp452-3; ☎ 6733 8388; The Fullerton Singapore, 1 Fullerton Sq) The Fullerton's swish bar boasts some impressive cocktails (not all of which they know how to make) and a *long* list of vodkas. One for the style mavens.

For a taste of old Singapore, head to the seedy, bayside **Red Lantern Beer Garden** (50 Collyer Quay) where bands often play, cheap meals are served and you can get a reasonably priced beer.

BOAT QUAY **Map pp452-3**

Visit during the day or early in the evening if you want a quiet drink here – it can get rowdy later on. There are so many bars, most with outdoor tables, that you can just wander along until one takes your fancy.

Harry's Bar (☎ 6538 3029; 28 Boat Quay; 11am-1am Sun-Thu, 11am-2am Fri & Sat) One-time hangout of Barings Bank breaker Nick Leeson, Harry's is still a city slickers' favourite, with the suits flocking here for happy hour until 8pm. Later it turns into a good jazz venue (9.30pm-12.30am Tue-Sat). The upstairs bar is quieter and a comfortable place for Sunday brunch (S$30 or S$50 with free flow champagne, Bloody Marys or margaritas).

Penny Black (☎ 6538 2300; No 26/27 Boat Quay) Homesick Brits will find comfort at this traditionally English pub; ditto the Irish at **Molly Malone's** (☎ 6536 2029; 42 Circular Rd), just off the main strip. Both serve hearty food appropriate to their mock surroundings.

bq bar (☎ 6536 9722; 39 Boat Quay; 11.30am-midnight) Comfy sofas and a stylish vibe make bq bar the most laid-back option. It also does tapas-style finger food after 5pm.

CLARKE QUAY **Map pp452-3**

Brewerkz (☎ 6438 7438; 01-05 Riverside Point Centre, 30 Merchant Rd; noon-midnight Sun-Thu, noon-1am Fri & Sat) Across the river from Clarke Quay, this microbrewery and restaurant offers no fewer than five beers brewed on site, including the popular India Pale Ale; a seven set sampler (S$12.50) is a good way to discover which is your favourite.

Crazy Elephant (see p501) has plenty of room on the pavement outside for chatting if the live music isn't to your taste.

ROBERTSON QUAY & MOHAMED SULTAN ROAD

Note that most of the bars along Mohamed Sultan will have a cover charge of around S$10 on Friday and Saturday nights after 9pm, which will include one drink.

Next Page (Map pp452-3; ☎ 6238 7826; 17/18 Mohamed Sultan Rd) On a strip where places regularly change names and concepts, this bar and the adjoining Front Page have remained consistently popular places with locals and visitors alike. The Next Page has ye-olde-Shanghai decor (think lots of red lanterns), the Front Page a more modern vibe and an outdoor area.

Metz (Map pp452-3; ☎ 6887 2490; Gallery Hotel, 76 Robertson Quay) Metz has a very appealing Bali-esque outdoor area for chilling, while indoors an acoustic band and DJ provide the dance music in a minimalist chic setting.

Sound Bar (Map pp452-3; ☎ 6333 8117; Gallery Hotel, 76 Robertson Quay) The prelude to trendy club Liquid Room (p501) has a twinkling alfresco riverside frontage and a dreamy interior with glowing fish tanks. Groovy baby!

Zouk Wine Bar (Map pp450-1; ☎ 6738 2088; 17 Jiak Kim St) This bar, with African mask as a design feature, is the place to hang and check out the scene while waiting for the action to get going at the attached mega-club.

Chinatown **Map pp452-3**

The main focus of action is Club St where there are oodles of restaurants and bars housed in attractive restored shophouses (note most are closed Sunday). Starting at the foot of the hill at No 7 you'll find **Shidong** (☎ 6220 6587) where the contemporary Asian decor is undermined by middle-of-the-road background music.

Bar Sá Vanh (☎ 6323 0503), at No 49A, is an atmospheric place, tastefully decked out with Laotian and Vietnamese art, a koi pond and six-metre long opium bed. Next door, **Aphrodisiac Bar** (☎ 6325 8616) sports classical Greek statues and contemporary chrome and leather furniture – all very Hugh Heffner!

The bar at **Union** (☎ 6327 4990), at No 81, with its squishy retro sofas and bags of room, is a good spot from which to survey the goings on of the street. From here you can keep an eye on the salsa stylings of **Barrio Chino** (☎ 6324 3245) at No 60.

Beaujolais Wine Bar (☎ 6224 2227; 1 Ann Siang Hill) This *très* cute bar is a good spot for the vino and has cheese and wine nights occasionally (S$30).

Tong Heritage Bar (☎ 6532 6006; 50 Eu Tong Sen St; 6pm-1am Mon-Wed, 6pm-3am Thu-Sat) This bar housed in a historic former medical institute is worth visiting to enjoy the atmospheric architecture and traditional Chinese courtyard alone. The main entrance is on New Market Rd.

Davis Café (☎ 6220 9390; 28 Smith St) Pitched at the backpacker crowd, this café-bar with a prime view on to the hawker stalls is a relaxed, unstuffy place for a drink.

The Far East Square complex hosts several drinking options. **Carnegies** (☎ 6534 0850; 44/45 Pekin St) is a rock-and-roll theme bar and unabashed expat hangout. **Mama Africa** (88 Telok Ayer St) is part-restaurant, part-bar. The Disneyland-Africa decor is supplemented by foot-tapping African music. There is also the more laid-back **Bisous Bar** (☎ 6226 5505; 25 Church St) with outdoor tables and an Asian colonial bar ambience inside.

Also see the boxed text Gay & Lesbian Singapore (p480); many of the best bars are in the Chinatown area and are welcoming to friendly drinkers of all sexual persuasions.

Orchard Road Map pp456-7

Brix (☎ 6738 1234; basement Grand Hyatt Singapore, 10 Scotts Rd) This popular place is divided into distinct sections each with their own atmosphere; the music bar is the spot for dancing. The decor is plush and the crowd is in their 20s and 30s. Also worth checking out for a sophisticated tipple is the Hyatt's Martini Bar, part of the Mezza9 restaurant (p495).

The Dubliners (☎ 6735 2220; 165 Penang Rd) A cut above the rest of the Irish crowd, The Dubliners gains kudos not only for its location in a smartly decorated, historic former colonial plantation mansion, but also for the quality of its food – the Sunday roast here is said to be worth dragging across town for.

Muddy Murphy's (☎ 6735 0400; Orchard Hotel Shopping Arcade, 442 Orchard Rd) No prizes for guessing that this is an Irish Bar. The quieter top bar is narrow and smoky and only opens in the evening.

Emerald Hill Rd has a collection of bars in the renovated terraces just up from Orchard Rd. At No 2 is one of the best, **Alley Bar** (☎ 6235 9810), occupying part of the former premises of the Peranakan Showcase Museum. Not much imagination went into naming **No 5** (☎ 6732 0818), which is at No 5; it's popular with tourists and its chilli vodka has a mean reputation. With a tad more class at No 7 is **Que Pasa** (☎ 6235 6626), an authentic wine and tapas bar. Then it's back to a rowdy old time at No 9, **Ice Cold Beer** (☎ 6735 9929), which offers an enormous range of chilled brews from around the world, all downed to a rock soundtrack.

Mitre Hotel (☎ 6737 3811; 145 Killiney Rd) Decrepit beyond belief this bar in a ramshackle black-and-white bungalow is the ultimate antidote to sanitised Singapore. Drop by for a beer and to experience a side of Singapore that's all but vanished.

Holland Village Map pp448-9

The bar and restaurant strip Lorong Mambong is where the expat community gathers to eat, drink and socialise. All within a coaster's throw of each other are **Wala Wala** (☎ 6462 4288; No 31) a fun American-style place that's generally packed most nights, with seating on two floors, as well as alfresco dining; **Tangos** (☎ 6463 7364; No 35) a sleek, minimalist place with beer, wine and a good selection of pasta; and **Baden Baden** (☎ 6468 5585; No 42) which has Carlsberg and Erdinger on tap plus a reasonable range of German bottled beers, along with the schnitzel and sausages.

ENTERTAINMENT

There's no excuse for an early night in Singapore – the lion city offers plenty of entertainment options. Singapore's theatre scene is diverse and creative; the cinemas show the latest movies (with pretty cheap ticket prices compared to other countries); and there's a good range of clubs to dance the night away at.

The live music scene is less healthy, limited to a few venues with only a small roster of bands and performers – the magazine *Big O* will give you the low down on what's happening. Still, there's excellent classical music, jazz is popular and you've the chance to get to grips with Chinese opera, not to mention fun cabaret and comedy shows.

To find out what's on check out the *Straits Times* newspaper and *Eight Days*, Singapore's weekly television and entertainment magazine. *Where Singapore*, *I-S Magazine* and *Juice*, all free, also have listings information.

Tickets for most events can be bought either through **SISTIC** (☎ 6348 5555, www.sistic.com.sg) or **CalendarONE TicketCharge** (☎ 6296 2929, www.ticketcharge.com.sg). It's best to call or check their websites first since both have exclusive deals with certain venues. Both agencies have outlets where you can buy tickets on site: SISTIC's include Bugis Junction, Takashimaya and Wisma Atria on Orchard Rd, Suntec City, and the Victoria Concert Hall box office; TicketCharge's include The Substation, Tanglin Shopping Centre and the Funan Centre.

Cabaret & Comedy

Boom Boom Room (Map pp452-3; ☎ 6435 0030; Far East Square, 130-132 Amoy St; Thu-Sat S$15/25 including one drink; 🕑 8.30pm-2am Thu-Sat) The fabulous drag divas here (including the quick-witted local TV star Kumar) perform glitzy song, dance and comedy reviews worthy of Las Vegas. The shows, which change regularly to remain topical, kick off at 11pm and 12.30am on Thursday, 11pm and 1.30am on Friday and Saturday. If you want a seat, make a booking or come early.

Singapore has two regular comedy clubs, both of which charge around S$50 a ticket for top acts from the UK, US and Australia. **1nitestand Comedy Club** (www.1nitestand.com; tickets from CalendarOne TicketCharge) has a regular gig at **Milieu** (Map pp456-7; 6738 1000; Peranakan Place, 180 Orchard Rd) while **The Punchline Comedy Club** (Map pp456-7; ☎ 6831 4656; Bar None, Marriott Hotel; tickets from SISTIC) usually has shows on the last Tuesday and Wednesday of the month.

Chinese Opera

A low-key introduction to Chinese opera can be had at one of the teahouse evenings organised by the nonprofit opera company, the **Chinese Theatre Circle** (Map pp452-3; ☎ 6323 4862; www.ctcopera.com.sg; 5 Smith St; tickets through SISTIC). Every Friday and Saturday evening at 8pm there is a brief talk (in English) on Chinese opera, followed by a short excerpt from a Cantonese opera classic, performed by professional actors in full costume. Delicious lychee tea and little tea cakes are included in the price of S$15. The whole thing lasts around 45 minutes and you are able to take photos. Bookings are recommended.

Cinema

Movie-going is hugely popular in Singapore – and at around S$8.50 per ticket one of the best value forms of entertainment. Multiplex cinemas are common and you can find city centre ones at Parco Bugis Junction (Map p458), Shaw Towers on Beach Rd (Map pp452-3), Suntec (Map pp452-3), Marina Square Complex (Map pp452-3), Cineleisure Orchard, Plaza Singapura and Shaw House all on or near Orchard Road (Map pp456-7), among other places.

If you really want pampering, head to the **Golden Village multiplex** (Map pp450-1; ☎ 6735 8484; www.gv.com.sg; 1 Kim Seng Promenade) on the 3rd floor of the Great World City Mall; S$25 admits you to the 'gold class' cinema with lush carpets, reclining seats, foot rests, and food and drink service. There's also a giant IMAX screen, Singapore's first, at this complex.

The roster of movies will comprise mainly Hollywood blockbusters, Chinese, Korean and Japanese crowd-pleasers, plus a few art house hits from around the world. The **Singapore International Film Festival** (www.filmfest.org.sg) held each April further widens the choice. Take along something warm to wear; Singaporean cinemas are notoriously chilly places. Also be prepared for plenty of mobile phones to go off (and conversations to be engaged in!) during the movie.

Clubs

All clubs have cover charges of around S$15 to S$25, but this will almost always include at least one drink; women sometimes pay less. Venues frequently change names and concepts so check the local press before venturing out. Also look out for outdoor rave parties, usually held on Sentosa. For those wanting to hang with the happening crowd, at the time of research there were really only three venues to care about: Zouk, Centro and The Liquid Room.

Zouk (Map pp450-1; ☎ 6738 2988; www.zoukclub.com; 17 Jiak Kim St) The enduring legend of the Singapore clubbing scene, Zouk still pulls them in and attracts top-name DJs from around the world. It's actually three clubs in one, plus a wine bar, and we'd recommend going the whole hog and paying the entrance to them all (S$35 including two drinks). The **main event** (S$25; 🕑 7pm-3am, Wed, Fri & Sat), is an Ibiza-inspired party space on several levels throbbing to techno and happy house beats. For the same cover charge you'll gain access to the spacey **Phuture**, too, where you can catch the more experimental DJs and music. Plush and decorated with original modern art is **Velvet Underground** (S$35; 🕑 9pm-3am Tue-Sat), which caters to a slightly older, dance-loving crowd.

Centro (Map pp452-3; ☎ 6220 2288; www.centro360.com; One Fullerton, 1 Fullerton Rd; S$15-25; ⏰ Tue-Sun 9pm-3am) Hot on Zouk's heels is this dreamy, roomy venue, with a knock-them-dead view across the bay to the Esplanade, that really gets going on Friday, Saturday and Sunday nights.

Liquid Room (Map pp452-3; ☎ 6333 8117; www.liquidroom.com.sg; Gallery Hotel, 76 Robertson Quay) Don't let size put you off at this tiny venue – it is Singapore's most progressive dance space, hosting some of the island's best DJ's. They occasionally organise parties on Sentosa – see the website for details. Also there's no cover charge.

Bar None (Map pp456-7; ☎ 6831 4656; www.barnoneasia.com; basement, Marriott Hotel, 320 Orchard Rd) Bar None is one of the more popular spots along Orchard Road. There's live music and the DJs play more mainstream music, from R&B and pop classics to salsa and rock. It's also home to the monthly performances by the Punchline Comedy Club (p500).

Milieu (Map pp456-7; ☎ 6738 1000; Peranakan Place, 180 Orchard Rd) One of the most stylish clubs in the Orchard Road area is also the place where you can catch the monthly 1nite-stand comedy club nights (see p500).

China Jump (Map pp452-3; ☎ 6338 9388; Fountain Court, CHIJMES, 30 Victoria St) This club gets very lively at the weekends. There's free entry for women on Wednesdays and local drag star Kumar (see Boom Boom Room, p500) does a show here on Tuesday.

Madam Wong's (Map pp452-3; ☎ 6834 0107; 28/29 Mohamed Sultan Rd; ⏰ 9am-3am) This perennially popular club has Chinese theme decor and features poppy dance music for a boozy crowd.

Live Music

CLASSICAL

The 1800-seater state-of-the-art concert hall at the **Esplanade – Theatres on the Bay** (Map pp452-3; ☎ 6828 8222; www.esplanade.com; 1 Esplanade Dr) is now home to the respected Singapore Symphony Orchestra (SSO), who used to play at the **Victoria Concert Hall** (Map pp452-3; ☎ 6338 4401) across the Padang. Keep an eye out for concerts at either venue and also check out the SSO's free concerts in the Botanic Gardens. The SSO play most Friday and Saturday nights throughout the year (except for June). Also worth catching are the **Singapore Chinese Orchestra** (☎ 6557 4034; www.sco.com.sg), Southeast Asia's only such professional group, playing Indian and Malay music as well as Chinese orchestral pieces.

BANDS

Fat Frog Café (Map pp452-3; ☎ 6338 6201; The Substation, 45 Armenian St) This is one of the best places to catch local indie bands such as Force Vomit, The Oddfellows and Urban Karma. Shows tend to be on the weekends in the evenings in the outdoor courtyard.

Crazy Elephant (Map pp452-3; ☎ 6337 1990; www.crazyelephant.com; 01-07 Clarke Quay, 3E River Valley Rd) There's a lively atmosphere at Crazy Elephant which has some decent rock bands and a Sunday night blues jam.

OD's Backstage Music Bar (Map pp450-1; ☎ 6346 5303; Stadium Waterfront, Singapore Indoor Stadium, Kallang; ⏰ 6am-3am Tue-Sat) At this sophisticated place with a cool, waterside setting, jazz, blues and R&B artists play.

Anywhere (Map pp456-7; ☎ 6734 8233; 04-08/09 Tanglin Shopping Centre, 19 Tanglin Rd) A house band belts out all your favourite cover versions.

JAZZ

Somerset's (Map pp452-3; ☎ 6431 5331; Level 3 Raffles the Plaza; 2 Stamford Rd) A pleasant place to while away an evening, Somerset's lays claim to being Singapore's top jazz venue in terms of comfortable ambience and its ability to attract top international acts.

City Space (Map pp452-3; ☎ 6837 3322; 70th fl, Swissôtel The Stamford Singapore) Equally classy, with a knockout view to boot.

South Bridge Jazz (Map pp452-3; ☎ 6327 4671; www.southbridgejazz.com.sg; 82B Boat Quay) This convivial, small jazz venue is upstairs overlooking Boat Quay. The sets kick off around 9.15pm, and sometimes there's a cover charge of S$15 if someone famous is playing.

Live Jazz @ The Green Room (Map pp452-3; ☎ 6334 1032; 01-05/07 Esplanade Mall) Like its sister venue Harry's Bar over on Boat Quay, this new place offers good live jazz along with a mixture of Eastern and Western food.

Spectator Sports

Most large-scale sporting and entertainment events – from pop concerts and soccer games to celebrity wrestling – take place at **Singapore Indoor Stadium** (Map pp450-1; ☎ 6344 2660, www.singaporeindoorstadium.com; 2 Stadium Walk). Also check www.singaporesports.com.sg for details of sporting events across the island.

Monthly races are held at the **Singapore Turf Club** (Map pp448-9; ☎ 6879 1000; www.turfclub.com.sg; 1 Turf Club Ave). There is a four-level grandstand which seats up to 35,000. Admission is S$5 (S$10 for air-con). For S$20 (bring your passport) tourists can access the air-con gold card room. A dress code applies here: men must wear a collar – shorts and jeans are out, and men and women must wear closed shoes (no sandals).

Theatre & Dance

Among the local companies to watch are **Action Theatre** (Map pp452-3; www.action.org.sg; ☎ 6837 0842; 42 Waterloo St), which performs plays with contemporary themes; **Theatreworks** (www.theatreworks.org.sg), one of the more experimental and interesting companies; and **Wild Rice** (☎ 6223 9081; www.wildrice.com.sg) whose productions broach issues of sexuality and other such risqué areas for Singapore. The **Singapore Repertory Theatre** (www.srt.com.sg), based at the DBS Drama Centre but also performing at other venues, offers up repertory standards such as works by Shakespeare, Tennessee Williams and Arthur Miller, plus some modern Singaporean plays.

Nrityalaya Aesthetics Society (Map p458; ☎ 6336 6537; www.nas.org.sg; 01-01 Stamford Arts Centre, 155 Waterloo St) is Singapore's only full-time Indian dance and music troop. They hold an annual drama festival.

Singapore Dance Theatre (www.singaporedance theatre.com) is the top dance company, performing traditional ballets alongside contemporary works. Their *Ballet Under the Stars* season at Fort Canning Park is a lovely event to attend – bring a picnic.

Apart from the Esplanade (p460), other venues include:

Black Box (Map pp452-3; ☎ 6338 4077; Fort Canning Centre)

DBS Drama Centre (Map pp452-3; ☎ 6733 8166; 20 Merbau Rd)

Drama Centre (Map pp452-3; ☎ 6336 0005; Canning Rise)

Jubilee Hall (Map pp452-3; ☎ 6331 1732; 3rd fl, Raffles Hotel Arcade; 328 North Bridge Rd)

Kallang Theatre (Map pp450-1; ☎ 6345 8488; Stadium Rd)

Guinness Theatre at the Substation (Map pp452-3; ☎ 6337 7800; www.substation.org; 45 Armenian St; box office 4-8.30pm Mon-Fri)

Victoria Theatre (Map pp450-1; ☎ 345 8488; Empress Place)

SHOPPING

Indifference is not an option. Singapore's plethora of shops will either seduce you instantly into maxing out your credit cards and emptying your wallet, or send you screaming back to your hotel room.

Prices are usually fixed except at markets and in some shops in touristy areas. If you do have to haggle, stay good humoured and don't get petty – this causes everyone to lose face. Also don't start bargaining if you have no real interest in buying.

Singapore is not an early bird's shopping destination. Most shops are open from 10am or 11am through until 9pm and 10pm.

The Singapore Tourism Board promotes the **Great Singapore Sale** (www.greatsingaporesale .com.sg), held every year from the end of May to the beginning of July. Many stores offer discounts at this time but, again, it pays to shop around. For details on this and other shopping possibilities see the *Singapore Shopping Guide* free from STB offices. Also check out the free monthly magazine *Where Singapore* which has the latest on the shopping scene.

Buyer Beware

Singapore has stringent consumer laws and promotes itself as a safe place to shop; however, you should still be wary when buying. This is particularly true in smaller shops where a salesperson may match your low price but short-change you by not giving you an international guarantee or the usual accessories. Guarantees are an important consideration if you're buying electronic gear, watches, cameras etc. Make sure it's international and that it is filled out correctly, with the shop's name and the serial number of the item written down.

Make sure you get exactly what you want before you leave the shop. For example, check for the right voltage and cycle when you buy electrical goods. Singapore, Australia, New Zealand, Hong Kong and the UK use 220V to 240V at 50 cycles, while the USA, Canada and Japan use 110V to 120V at 60 cycles. Most shops will also attach the correct plug for your country. Also note that there are two main types of TV systems: PAL in Australia and Europe, and NTSC in the USA and Japan – video equipment must be compatible with your system. If you're buying a DVD player you'll also want to check that it plays the discs available in your home country.

When buying antiques, ask for a certificate of antiquity, which is required in many countries to avoid paying customs duty.

Singapore enforces international copyright laws, so being palmed off with pirated goods is not really a problem. If you do run into trouble, take your purchases back to the shop. If you fail to get satisfaction, contact the **Small Claims Tribunal** (Map pp452-3; ☎ 6241 3575; www.smallclaims.gov.sg/SCT-General_Info.html; 2 Havelock Rd) or any of the Singapore Visitors Centres.

GST

Almost all goods and services incur a 5% Goods and Services Tax (GST). A tax refund on goods worth S$300 or more can be applied for through shops participating in the GST Tourist Refund Scheme. These shops will display a 'tax-free shopping' logo.

Shopping Malls & Department Stores

ORCHARD ROAD Map pp456-7

Orchard Road has a mind-boggling array of department stores and shops selling whatever you want. The prices aren't necessarily the best, but the range is superb and this is certainly the spot for high-quality, brand-name items. The following is an overview of the main malls and is by no means exhaustive.

The Heeren (☎ 6733 4725; www.heeren.com.sg; 260 Orchard Rd) is teen heaven, housing CD emporium HMV and two levels of tiny, market-like cutting edge fashion shops.

The enormous **Ngee Ann City** (☎ 6733 0337; 391 Orchard Rd) pretty much has it all: glitzy department store **Takashimaya** (☎ 6738 1111); the giant Kinokuniya bookstore; scores of fashion shops including Louis Vuitton, Chanel, Burberry and the latest Spanish-import hit Zara; a post office, Internet café, library and oodles of places to eat.

The Paragon (☎ 6738 5535; 290 Orchard Rd) is a stylish mall, currently being expanded. Here you'll find Singapore Airlines' main office, Marks & Spencers, and trendy fashion shops such as Diesel, Salvatore Ferragamo and street-wear favourite Project Shop Blood Brothers.

Much more downmarket is **Lucky Plaza** (☎ 6235 3294; 304 Orchard Rd), a bustling place that's good for cheap clothes, bags and shoes, and electronic goods; make sure you bargain hard and shake off the touts and pesky tailors. Next door is the long-running department store **Tangs** (☎ 6737 5500; 320 Orchard Rd).

Wisma Atria (435 Orchard Rd) has **Isetan** department store (☎ 6733 7777) and lots of boutiques such as Topshop and People of Asia. There's another branch of **Isetan** (☎ 6733 1111; 350 Orchard Rd) across from **Wheelock Place** (501 Orchard Rd) where you'll find Borders bookstore.

DFS Galleria Scottswalk (☎ 6229 8100; www.dfsgalleria.com; 25 Scotts Rd) is a swanky new four-storey duty free shopping centre with all the perfumes, luxury goods and souvenir items you could wish for.

Far East Plaza (☎ 6734 2325; 14 Scotts Rd) has carved out a niche as a funkier, bargain place to shop, somewhere to buy second-hand books and get a tattoo. The new Level One Far East Plaza, packed with some 80-odd different fashion shops, pitches itself at the more adventurous dresser.

Hilton Shopping Gallery (581 Orchard Rd) is where Calvin Klein, Donna Karan, Giorgio Armani, Gucci and Paul Smith all gather as if in a designers' convention. If you can't find your favourite label there, it's likely to be across the road at **Palais Renaissance** (390 Orchard Rd), home to DKNY, Gianni Versace and Prada.

Forum The Shopping Mall (☎ 6732 2479; 583 Orchard Rd) is dominated by Toys'R'Us, with other children's speciality shops such as Baby Guess and Oshkosh in the same centre.

Continuing on to Tanglin Rd you'll find **Tanglin Shopping Centre** (☎ 6732 8751, 19 Tanglin Rd) with Singapore's best selection of Asian arts and antiques outlets.

Tanglin Mall (163 Tanglin Rd) has a fine range of ethnic homewares and gift shops as well as the largest branch of fashion chain British India, good shops and facilities for kids and a great supermarket in the basement.

COLONIAL DISTRICT Map pp452-3

Raffles City (☎ 6338 7766; 252 North Bridge Rd) with its soaring atrium and wide range of shops, including a branch of Robinsons department store and some interesting gift shops, is a focus for spenders, eaters and browsers. It's linked to the enormous **Suntec City Mall** (☎ 6821 3668; 3 Temasek Blvd) by the underground **City Link Mall** (accessed from the City Hall MRT station).

SINGAPORE

From Suntec City an underpass will lead you to **Millenia Walk** (☎ 6333 5761; 9 Raffles Blvd) where you'll find homeware shops. There's also an underground link to the new **Esplanade Mall** (8 Raffles Ave), mainly a dining destination, but also with a few interesting shops – Potter's Cove selling handmade pottery, The Tatami Shop for Japanese-style home furnishings, and the Esplanade Shop for stylish souvenirs.

Attached to the Hotel is the stylish **Raffles Hotel Arcade** (328 North Bridge Rd) which, as expected, is firmly upmarket, with designer clothes, galleries (including one selling fossils) plus the excellent Raffles Hotel gift shop and Thossb gourmet food shop.

BUGIS & LITTLE INDIA **Map p458**

Parco Bugis Junction (200 Victoria St) comprises the large **Seiyu** department store (☎ 6223 2222; 230 Victoria St), the Hotel Inter-Continental and shophouse recreations covered by an atrium. Its **Edge** (3rd fl) subsection is another good spot for checking out local fashions.

Sim Lim Square (☎ 6332 5839; 1 Rochor Canal Rd), is known as the place to buy computers and electronic goods. **Sim Lim Tower** (☎ 6295 4361; 10 Jl Besar) is a big electronic centre with everything from capacitors to audio and video gear. These two centres are popular with tourists so expect to bargain.

The bustling **Mustafa Centre** (☎ 6298 2967; 145 Syed Alwi Rd) in Little India has electrical and everyday goods at honest prices.

CHINATOWN **Map pp452-3**

There are Chinese instruments, laquerwork and jade among other things at the **People's Park Complex** (1 Park Rd). On the next corner **People's Park Centre** (110 Upper Cross St) is also a good place to browse with plenty of electronics, clothing and department stores.

Chinatown Point (133 New Bridge Rd) has a section with lots of handicraft shops. **The Pearl's Centre** (100 Eu Tong Sen St) is known for its Chinese medicine shops, as well as its cinema showing racy Chinese flicks.

Art, Crafts & Antiques

If you're after anything of note artistically, it pays to know your original piece from your cheap copy. While there are many dedicated art galleries and antique shops in Singapore, there's a fair degree of overlap between them and craft shops. Obviously for Chinese crafts and antiques the best place to head is Chinatown, for Indian crafts Little India. Kampong Glam's Arab St is known for Southeast Asian crafts, such as caneware, batik and leather goods. Note many galleries are closed on Mondays.

COLONIAL DISTRICT **Map pp452-3**

The **CHIJMES** complex (30 Victoria St) is a good place to browse for crafts. Here you'll find **Island & Archipelago** (☎ 6883 0221; 01-06A) with items from across the region including beaded boxes from India and Indonesian puppets; and **Peter Hoe Evolution** (☎ 6339 6880; 01-05) which does a nice line in modern batik clothing as well as the usual craft items.

Pagoda House (☎ 6883 0501; 02-34 Raffles Hotel Arcade; 328 North Bridge Rd) sells antiques and gifts, while their branches at 143/145 Tanglin Rd and 44 Pagoda St in Chinatown specialise in chic, contemporary Chinese furniture as well as Buddhas, architectural artefacts and the like.

FLEA MARKETS

Looking for a real bargain or just something quirky as a souvenir? Then try the following flea and craft markets.

Clarke Quay (Map pp452-3; ☎ 6337 3292; 3 River Valley Rd; 🕒 10am-6pm Sun) is not as busy as it once was, but is worth a look for old clothes and knickknacks. **Far East Square** (Map pp452-3; ☎ 6532 7868; 76 Telok Ayer St; 🕒 noon-10pm Sat & Sun) doesn't have that many vendors but is worth a look at the same time as checking out the old folk hawking retro watches, medals, semi-precious stones and the like beside the car park on Mohammed Ali Lane at the end of Club St. More of a crafts and street fashion market, **Stadium Cove** (Map pp450-1; ☎ 6344 2660; 2 Stadium Walk; 🕒 4-11pm Sat, 11am-11pm Sun) is a pleasant spot to head on the weekend; there's a free shuttle bus from Raffles City here every hour after 3.30pm until 10.30pm. The sprawling **Thieves Market** (Map pp452-3; 🕒 11am-6pm Sun), held around Pasar Lane, is where anyone and everyone comes to offload their old wares.

You find several good art galleries in the brightly coloured, colonial **MITA Building** (140 Hill St), including **Art-2 Gallery** (☎ 01 6338-8713), the well respected **Plum Blossoms** (☎ 6339 9768), **Gajah Gallery** (☎ 6737 4202) and **Soobin Art Gallery** (☎ 6392 9366), representing the best of China's vibrant avant-garde scene.

CHINATOWN Map pp452-3

The classy **Lajeunesse Asian Art** (☎ 6224 7975; 94 Club St) has art, artefacts and furniture from throughout Southeast Asia. Similarly upmarket is the **Red Peach Gallery** (☎ 6222 2215, 68 Pagoda St) with lots of decorative homewares.

Shing's Antique Gallery (☎ 6224 4332, 24A-26 Pagoda St) is one of the better options along this tourist strip; they stock beautiful wooden screens and antique window grills.

Both **Thow's Gallery** (☎ 6223 8600; 63 Temple St) and **Yong Gallery** (☎ 6226 1718; 260 South Bridge Rd) specialise in Chinese antiques, old jade, calligraphy, wood carvings etc.

Art Seasons (☎ 6221 1800; The Box, 5 Gemmill Lane), just off Club St, specialises in contemporary art sourced from China, Myanmar, Korea and Japan.

LITTLE INDIA Map p458

Shoma Studio (☎ 6296 2285; 34 Petain Rd; 11am-6pm Thu-Sun or by appointment), a striking modern gallery in a renovated shophouse, has floors of beautiful art, craft and furniture from all over Southeast Asia.

For art, it's worth dropping by **Bhaskar's Art Gallery** (☎ 6396 4523; 19 Kerbau Rd) which promotes Indian artists from Singapore, India and Malaysia, although the works can be hit-and-miss.

Plastique Kinetic Worms (☎ 6292 7783; 61 Kerbau Rd) is Singapore's only artist-run, non-profit gallery promoting the works of young and contemporary visual artists.

ORCHARD ROAD Map pp456-7

Tanglin Shopping Centre (☎ 6732 8751; 19 Tanglin Rd) is the best one-stop place to hunt for antiques, crafts and art in Singapore. Within the building **HaKaren Art Gallery** (☎ 6733 3382), **Kwan Hua Art Gallery** (☎ 6733 8368) and **Akemi Gallery** (☎ 6735 6315) are all good places to start your treasure hunt, but be prepared to bargain.

Boon's Pottery (☎ 6836 3978, 01-30 Tanglin Mall, 163 Tanglin Rd) has many striking pieces by local potters.

HOLLAND VILLAGE

The **Holland Road Shopping Centre** (Map pp448-9; 211 Holland Ave) has dozens of shops selling everything from cloisonné ware to Korean chests. Try **Lim's** (☎ 6467 1300) a great place to rummage for all kinds of Asian gifts and homewares. They also have a smaller branch in **Chinatown** (Map pp452-3; at 46 Smith St).

Cameras & Electronic Equipment

Cameras, TVs, CDs, VCRs, VCDs, DVDs – you name it, all the latest high-tech audiovisual equipment is available all over Singapore, much of it at very competitive prices. It will certainly pay to do a little research into makes and models before you arrive. Make sure your guarantees are worldwide, your receipts are properly dated and stamped and your goods are compatible with electricity supplies and systems in your country of origin (see Buyer Beware, p502).

Lucky Plaza (Map pp456-7), Sim Lim Square, Sim Lim Tower and the Mustafa Centre (see Shopping Malls & Department Stores, p503) are all good places to start looking, but you'll have to be prepared to bargain.

If bargaining isn't your bag, decent discount prices can be had for all kinds of electronic goods at **Best Denki** (Map pp456-7; ☎ 6835 2855; 05-01/05 Ngee Ann City, 391 Orchard Rd) and **Harvey Norman** (Map pp452-3; ☎ 6332 3461; 02-001 Suntec City Mall).

Chinese Medicine

The venerable **Eu Yan Sang** (Map pp452-3; ☎ 6223 6333; 269A South Bridge Rd) has been revamped into looking like a modern chemist – until you get a load of the traditional remedies on the shelves. A consultation with the resident herbalist is S$8, and most stock comes with English instructions.

Computers

Funan – The IT Mall (Map pp452-3; ☎ 6337 4235; 109 North Bridge Rd) is the main computer centre, with dozens of computer shops on the top floors as well as a large **Challenger Superstore** (☎ 6336 8327).

The top floors of Sim Lim Square (Map p458) are good for cheap computers and peripherals.

Macintosh equipment can be bought at the **Apple Centre** (Map pp456-7; ☎ 6238 9378; 02-07/08 Wheelock Place; 501 Orchard Rd).

Fashion

For clubbing fashions the best places to scope are The Heeren, Far East Plaza and Parco Bugis Junction (see Shopping Malls & Department Stores, p503), all of which have sections packed with fun boutiques and stalls.

M)phosis (Map pp456-7; ☎ 6737 6539; B1-09/10 Ngee Ann City, 391 Orchard Rd) carries the wispy, slinky designs of Singaporean Colin Koh; there's also a branch at Parco Bugis Junction, where you'll find one of the outlets of flash streetware shop **POA People of Asia** (Map p458; ☎ 6333 4582; 02-10 Parco Bugis Junction, 200 Victoria St).

It's hard to resist the hip male and female clobber and accessories of **Project Shop Blood Brothers** (Map pp456-7; ☎ 6735 0071; 02-20/21 Paragon; 290 Orchard Rd). Find them also in Ngee Ann City and Wisma Atria (Map pp456-7) and Raffles City (Map pp452-3).

A couple of upmarket local designers to browse are **Song+Kelly21** (Map pp456-7; ☎ 6735 3387; 01-38 Forum Galleria; 583 Orchard Rd) and **Woods & Woods** (Map pp456-7; ☎ 6887 5054; 02-16 Pacific Plaza, 9 Scotts Rd) which also has a branch at 56 Club St, Chinatown (Map pp452-3).

You can buy saris and sari material, as well as Punjabi suits, at numerous shops along Serangoon Rd in Little India as well as at **Nalli** (Map p458; ☎ 6334 0341; 27 Campbell Lane) where a deluxe gold-threaded silk sari can cost anything from S$200 to S$1000.

Music

Arguably the most extensive selection of CDs can be found at **HMV** (Map pp456-7; ☎ 6733 1822; 01-11 The Heeren, 260 Orchard Rd), where there are separate floors dedicated to Western pop, Asian pop, and classical and jazz. There's a smaller branch in the City Link Mall (Map pp452-3).

Both **Tower Records** (Map pp452-3; ☎ 6338 5755; Suntec City Mall, 3 Temasek Blvd) and **Borders** (Map pp456-7; ☎ 6235 9113; 01-00 Wheelock Place, 501 Orchard Rd) have good selections. If you want to save a bit of money, then check out the discount pop selection at **Sembawang Music Centre** (Map pp456-7; ☎ 6738 7727; 03-01 Orchard Cineleisure, 8 Grange Rd).

As well as Indian music CDs, the **Indian Classical Music Centre** (Map p458; ☎ 6291 0187; 01-29 Hastings Block, Little India Arcade, 48 Serangoon Rd) also sells sitars, tabla, bells – everything you need to create your own Bollywood soundtrack.

GETTING THERE & AWAY

Air

Singapore is a major Southeast Asian travel hub and a good place to buy air tickets. Practically all international air traffic goes through Changi International Airport – for full details of this, airlines flying in and out of the country and prices see the Transport chapter (p555).

Boat

Singapore has a number of ferry connections to Malaysia and the Indonesian islands of the Riau Archipelago. The main departure point for ferries is the **World Trade Centre** (WTC; Map pp448-9), next to Harbour Front MRT station. **Tanah Merah ferry terminal** (Map pp448-9) south of Changi airport has ferries to the Indonesian island of Bintan and Tioman Island in Malaysia; Changi ferry terminal and the pier at Changi Village, both north of Changi airport, have ferries to Malaysia. For details see the Transport chapter (p561).

Bus

Buses run frequently from Singapore to many destinations in Malaysia and some in Thailand from the Queen St bus terminal, Lavender St bus terminal and the Golden Mile Complex (all on Map p458). For details of the services see the Transport chapter (p559).

Taxi

There are shared taxis to many places in Malaysia from Singapore's Queen St bus terminal (Map pp458); but it will be cheaper to take a bus to Johor Bahru and take a taxi from there to your ultimate destination.

Train

Singapore's railway station (Map pp448-9) is the southern termination point for the **Malaysian railway system** (KTM; www.ktmb.com.my). For details of services to and from Malaysia see the Transport chapter (p559).

GETTING AROUND

Singapore is undoubtedly the easiest city in Asia to get around. With a typical mixture of far-sighted social planning and authoritarianism, the government has built, and continues to extend, its Mass Rapid Transit (MRT) rail system and improve its already excellent roads.

Traffic is kept to a minimum as the government controls private cars by a restrictive licensing system and prohibitive import duties that make owning an auto primarily a preserve for the rich. Cars entering the central business district (CBD) have to buy special licenses.

For information about public transport online check out www.sbstransit.com.sg.

To/From the Airport

CHANGI AIRPORT

The airport, about 20km from the city centre, is now served by the MRT. From Changi to City Hall is a bargain S$1.35 and takes 26 minutes with trains departing roughly every seven minutes.

The most convenient bus is the airport shuttle service (adult/child S$7/5) – six-seater maxicabs that will take you to your hotel or anywhere in the CBD. The shuttle operates daily from the arrivals halls of both terminals from 6am to midnight, departing every 15 minutes. Bookings can be made at the airport shuttle counters at the arrivals halls in both terminals, and you pay the driver.

Public bus No 36 leaves the airport for the city approximately every 10 minutes between 6am and midnight. You should have the right change (S$1.50) when you board. It takes around 20 minutes to reach the city centre, passing through the colonial district on to Orchard Blvd (which runs parallel to Orchard Rd). When heading to the airport catch this bus on Orchard or Bras Basah Rds.

Taxis from the airport are subject to a supplementary charge on top of the metered fare (S$3 to S$5 depending on the time), which is around S$12 to most places in the city centre. This supplementary charge only applies to taxis from the airport, not from the city.

There's also a limousine taxi service (S$35) available between 6am and 2am to any destination in Singapore. You can choose between a Mercedes and a London cab.

SELETAR AIRPORT

You may come to this small airport to catch the daily Pelangi Airways flights to Tioman Island in Malaysia. Seletar is in the north of the island, and the easiest way to get there is to take a taxi for around S$11; otherwise bus No 103 will take you from outside the National Library to the gates of the Seletar Air Force base, from where you change to a local base bus to the airport terminal. Also from the base gates, bus No 59 will take you to the nearest MRT station (Yio Chu Kang).

Boat & Ferry

You can charter a bumboat to take a tour up the Singapore River or to go to the islands around Singapore. **Singapore River Cruises** (☎ 6336 6111) and **Singapore Explorer** (☎ 6339 6833) both charge S$3/5 from Boat Quay to Clarke Quay/Robertson Quay, with sailings at least every hour roughly between 9am and 10.30pm.

There are regular ferry services from the WTC to Sentosa and the other southern islands, and from Changi Village to Pulau Ubin. You can also take river cruises, or boat cruises around the harbour – see Tours (p478).

Bicycle

If you can cope with the heat and sometimes fast-moving traffic, getting around Singapore by bicycle isn't too bad an idea. Cycling up to Changi Village and then taking the bike over to Pulau Ubin is a very popular activity among expat cyclophiles and there's a great mountain bike track circling the base of the Bukit Timah Nature Reserve (p468).

In the city centre bicycles can be hired from **Wheelpower Rent-a-Bike** (Map p458; ☎ 1800-238 2388, 01-09 Sunshine Plaza, 91 Bencoolen St; 24-hour hire S$28; 🕑 9.30am-7pm); and **Treknology Bikes 3** (Map pp456-7; ☎ 6732 7119; 01-02 Tanglin Pl, Tanglin Rd; 24-hour hire S$35; 🕑 11am-7.30pm Mon-Sat, 11.30am-3.30pm Sun). Bikes can also be rented cheaply at several places along East Coast Parkway, on Sentosa Island and Pulau Ubin.

Bus

Singapore's extensive bus service should be the envy of the world. You rarely have to wait more than a few minutes for a bus and they will take you almost anywhere you want to go. There are even TV programmes aired on many buses, providing in-ride entertainment.

Bus fares start from 60c (70c for air-con buses) for roughly the first 3.2km rising to a maximum of S$1.20 (S$1.50 air-con). There are also a few flat-rate buses. When you board the bus drop the exact money into the fare box, as no change is given.

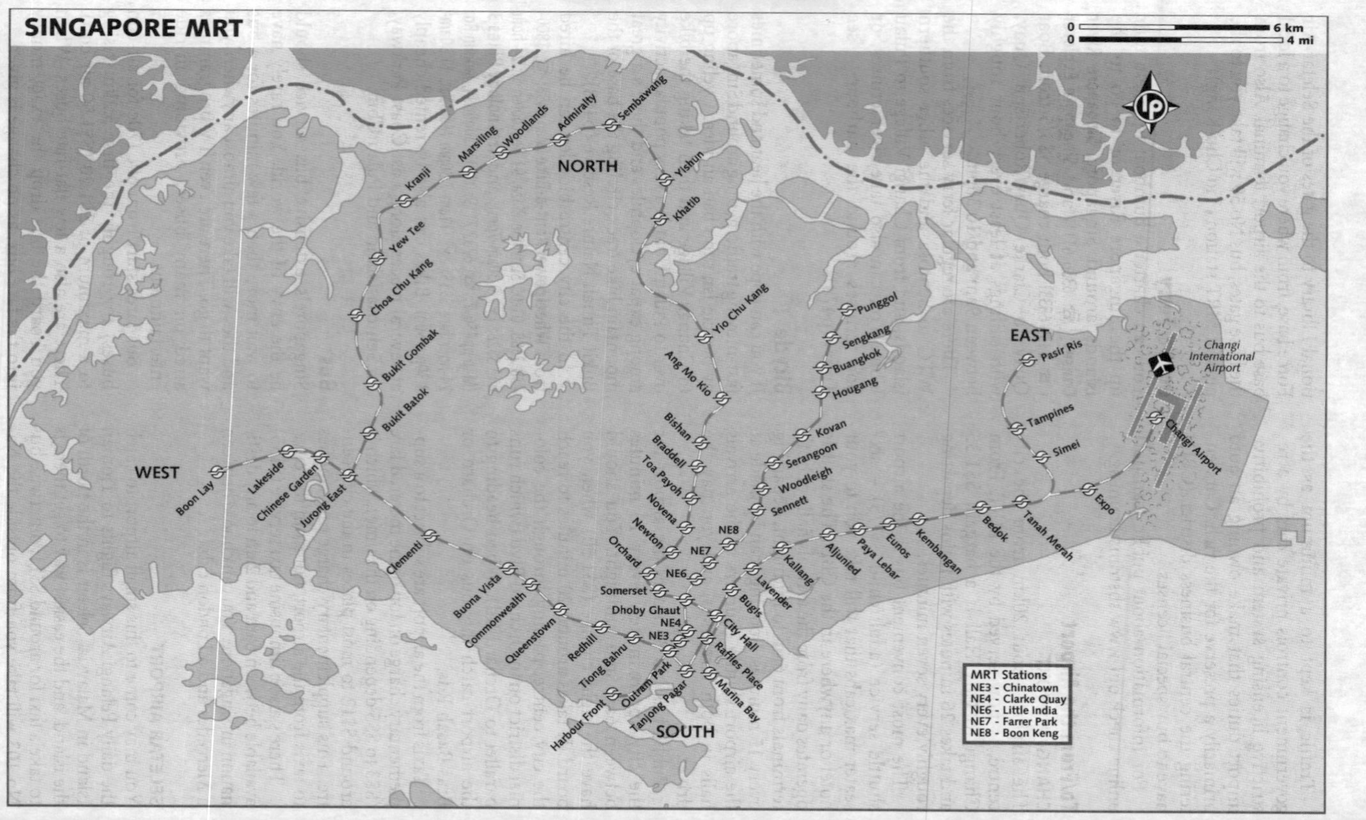
SINGAPORE MRT
0 6 km
0 4 mi
NORTH
SOUTH
EAST
WEST
Changi International Airport
Boon Lay
Lakeside
Chinese Garden
Jurong East
Bukit Batok
Bukit Gombak
Choa Chu Kang
Yew Tee
Kranji
Marsiling
Woodlands
Admiralty
Sembawang
Yishun
Khatib
Yio Chu Kang
Ang Mo Kio
Bishan
Braddell
Toa Payoh
Novena
Newton
Orchard
Somerset
Dhoby Ghaut
NE3
NE4
NE6
NE7
NE8
Clementi
Buona Vista
Commonwealth
Queenstown
Redhill
Tiong Bahru
Outram Park
Tanjong Pagar
Harbour Front
Raffles Place
Marina Bay
City Hall
Bugis
Lavender
Kallang
Aljunied
Paya Lebar
Eunos
Kembangan
Bedok
Tanah Merah
Expo
Changi Airport
Simei
Tampines
Pasir Ris
Punggol
Sengkang
Buangkok
Hougang
Kovan
Serangoon
Woodleigh
Sennett
MRT Stations
NE3 - Chinatown
NE4 - Clarke Quay
NE6 - Little India
NE7 - Farrer Park
NE8 - Boon Keng

Ez-link cards (see p510) can be used on all buses. You'll need to flash it in front of the card reader on boarding the bus and once again on leaving – if you forget to do this, you'll be charged the maximum fare for the bus journey, rather than for the section you travelled, the next time you use your card.

TOURIST BUSES

The **SIA Hop-On**, run by Singapore Airlines, passes Orchard Rd, Bugis Junction, Suntec City, the Colonial District, Clarke Quay, Boat Quay, Chinatown and the Botanic Gardens. It operates daily (every 30 minutes) between 8.30am and 7pm and runs on a continual loop. It's free if you are on a Singapore Stopover Holiday (show your SSH identification card); S$3 for passengers on either Singapore Airlines or Silk Air (show your ticket or boarding card). Other passengers pay S$6 (S$4 children) for an all-day pass. Tickets can be bought either from the bus driver or from hotels and Singapore Airlines offices.

The **Singapore Explorer** (☎ 6339 6833) is a red bus made up to look like an old-fashioned tram. Its route takes in the Botanic Gardens, the Orchard Rd area, the Colonial District, the CBD, Chinatown and the World Trade Centre (WTC) with the trolley stopping at all the major hotels and points of interest. An all-day ticket (adult/child S$14.90/9.90) includes a riverboat tour along the Singapore River, and can be bought from the bus driver or hotels.

Car

Singaporeans drive on the left-hand side of the road and it is compulsory to wear seat belts. Unlike in most Asian countries, traffic is orderly, but the profusion of one-way streets and streets that change names (sometimes several times) can make driving difficult for the uninitiated. The *Singapore Street Directory* is essential for negotiating the city.

RENTAL

If you want a car for local driving only, many of the smaller rental operators quote rates that are slightly cheaper than the major companies. Rental rates are more expensive than in Malaysia – if you intend driving from Singapore to Malaysia and spending time there, it will be better to rent your car in Johor Bahru.

Rates start from around S$170 a day, while collision damage waiver will cost about S$20 per day for a small car such as a Toyota Ford Laser or Mitsubishi Lancer. Special deals may be available, especially for longer-term rental. There are hire booths at Changi airport and in the city. Contact details for the major companies are:

Avis (Map pp450-1; ☎ 6737 1668; 01-01 Concorde Hotel, 317 Outram Rd)

Budget Rent a Car (Map pp452-3; ☎ 6532 4442; 26-01A Clifford Centre, 24 Raffles Place)

Hertz Rent-a-Car (Map pp456-7; ☎ 1800-734 4646; 15 Scotts Rd)

Thrifty (Map pp452-3; ☎ 6338 7900; 80 Middle Rd)

RESTRICTED ZONE & CAR PARKING

Between 7.30am and 6.30pm weekdays, and from 10.15am to 2pm Saturdays, the area encompassing the CBD, Chinatown and Orchard Rd is a restricted zone. Cars may enter as long as they pay a surcharge. Vehicles are automatically tracked by sensors on overhanging gantries that prompt drivers to insert a cashcard into their in-vehicle unit, which then extracts the appropriate toll. The same system is also in operation on certain major highways. Rental cars are subject to the same rules.

Anyone who doesn't pay the entry toll is automatically photographed by cameras on the gantries and a fine will soon arrive at the car owner's address.

Parking in many places in Singapore is operated by a coupon system. You can buy a booklet of coupons at parking kiosks and post offices. You must display a coupon in your car window with holes punched out to indicate the time, day and date your car was parked.

Mass Rapid Transit (MRT)

The ultramodern Mass Rapid Transit (MRT) subway system is the easiest, quickest and most comfortable way to get around Singapore. The system operates from 6am to midnight, with trains at peak times running every three minutes, and off-peak every six minutes.

Most of the MRT's 85km of track runs underground in the inner-city area, emerging overground out towards the suburban housing estates. The system connects with

TRISHAWS

Trishaws had their peak just after WWII when motorised transport was practically nonexistent and trishaw riders could make a very healthy income. Today there are only around 300 trishaws left in Singapore, and they are mainly used by tourists. At Bugis trishaws congregate in large numbers in the pedestrian mall at the junction of Waterloo and Albert Sts (Map p458), but you'll also come across them in other tourist haunts such as Chinatown and around Raffles.

Always agree on the fare beforehand: we were quoted S$60 for half an hour, but with a bit of haggling you could probably get this down to S$40. Trishaw tours of Chinatown and Little India are run from a number of the larger hotels.

the Light Rapid Transit (LRT) trains at Choa Chu Kang MRT station; LRT systems are also under construction at Punggol and Sengkang.

A new 20km North East MRT Line running from the World Trade Centre (Harbour Front MRT) in the south to Punggol in the north opened in 2003 intersecting with the existing lines at Dhoby Ghaut and Outram MRT stations. Construction is also underway on a central loop line that will link the city centre with Suntec City and the Singapore Indoor Stadium area in Kallang.

FARES & FARECARDS

Single-trip tickets cost from 80c to S$1.80, but you'll save money and find it more convenient to buy a S$15 Ez-link card from any MRT station. This electronic card, which includes S$10 of value (you'll get back the S$5 deposit and any remaining value on the card when you return it), can be used on all public buses and can easily be topped up using the ticket machines in MRT stations. Fares using an Ez-link card range from 60c to S$1.65. Apart from cutting out all that fiddling with change in ticket machines, the card needn't even be removed from your wallet when you tap it on the ticket gate sensor when entering and leaving an MRT station.

A tourist day-ticket (S$10), giving you 12 rides on buses and trains and valid for one day's travel, can be bought from MRT stations and bus interchanges.

Taxi

There are close on 19,000 taxis in Singapore and most of the time you should have no problem getting one. The three major cab companies are **City Cab** (☎ 6552 2222), **Comfort** (☎ 6552 1111) and **TIBS** (☎ 6555 8888).

Fares start from S$2.10 (TIBS off peak) and S$2.40 for the other companies for the first kilometre, then 10c for each additional 220m. There are various surcharges to note:

- S$3.20 or 50% on top of the meter fare from midnight to 6am.
- S$5 5pm to midnight Friday to Sunday, S$3 all other times for journeys from the airport, but not to.
- S$3-S$3.20 for current (less than an hour before needed) telephone bookings depending on which taxi company you use. For advance bookings you'll pay S$5-S$5.20.
- S$2 on all trips from the CBD between 4.30pm and 7pm on weekdays and from 11.30am to 2pm Saturdays. You may also have to pay a surcharge (see p509) if you take the taxi into the CBD during restricted hours.
- Payment by credit card incurs an extra 10% on the fare.

You can flag down a taxi any time. Also look for the special taxi stands (they have signs) where you can queue for the next available taxi. Ordering a taxi by phone is a computerised process that's extremely efficient. After telling the operator your name and location, you'll be transferred to an automatic message that gives you the number (ie numberplate) of your designated cab. All you do then is wait and watch for the cab with this numberplate.

Brunei

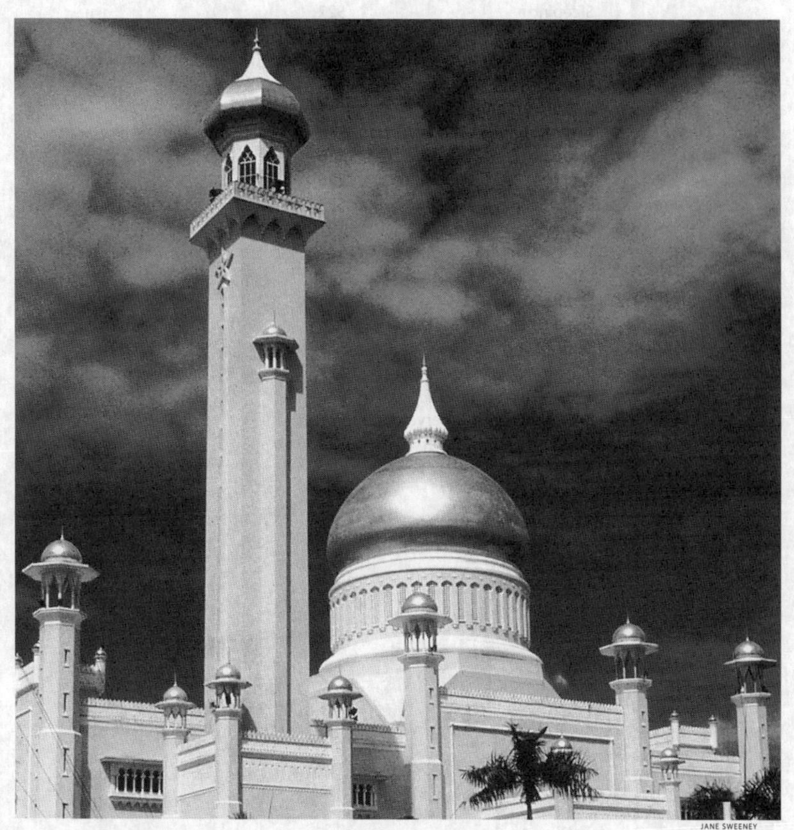

JANE SWEENEY

Brunei

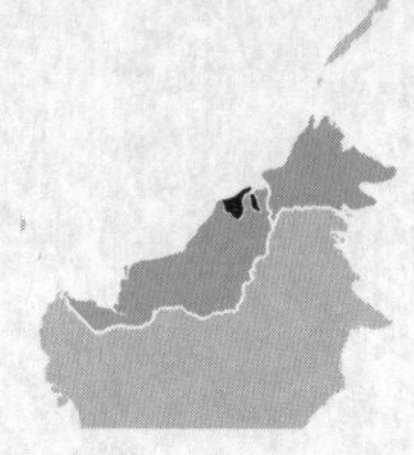

CONTENTS

Brunei is one of the smallest countries in the world – and one of the wealthiest. It's a tiny Islamic sultanate, wedged between the northeastern corner of Sarawak and the South China Sea. A curious reminder of the British colonial legacy, and the power of companies (in this case Shell Oil) to shape countries, it's all that remains of an empire that controlled all of Borneo in the 16th century.

The country's full name is Negara Brunei Darussalam, which is usually translated as 'Brunei – the Abode of Peace'. With alcohol virtually unobtainable, no nightlife or active political culture, it certainly is peaceful.

Presiding over it all is His Majesty Sultan Haji Hassanal Bolkiah Mu'izzaddin Waddaulah, the 29th of his line and better known as the Sultan of Brunei. Brunei's economy is almost wholly fuelled by oil, which comes mainly from offshore wells at Seria and Muara. As long as the oil lasts (2020 is tagged as the watershed year by conservative estimates), Brunei's upriver forests are safe from the fate of those of neighbouring Sabah and Sarawak – clean, clear rivers still flow through towns like Tutong and the beautiful Temburong district in the country's east.

Brunei and its natural attractions are only now being actively promoted as a tourist destination. With its stunning mosques, forests and welcoming people, who combine an international outlook with respect for both Malay and Islamic traditions, Brunei is a unique place to visit, a fascinating anomaly of monarchical rule preserved in modern times.

HIGHLIGHTS

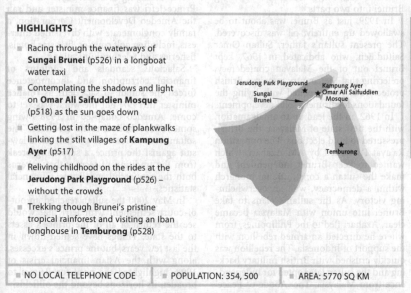

- Racing through the waterways of **Sungai Brunei** (p526) in a longboat water taxi
- Contemplating the shadows and light on **Omar Ali Saifuddien Mosque** (p518) as the sun goes down
- Getting lost in the maze of plankwalks linking the stilt villages of **Kampung Ayer** (p517)
- Reliving childhood on the rides at the **Jerudong Park Playground** (p526) – without the crowds
- Trekking though Brunei's pristine tropical rainforest and visiting an Iban longhouse in **Temburong** (p528)

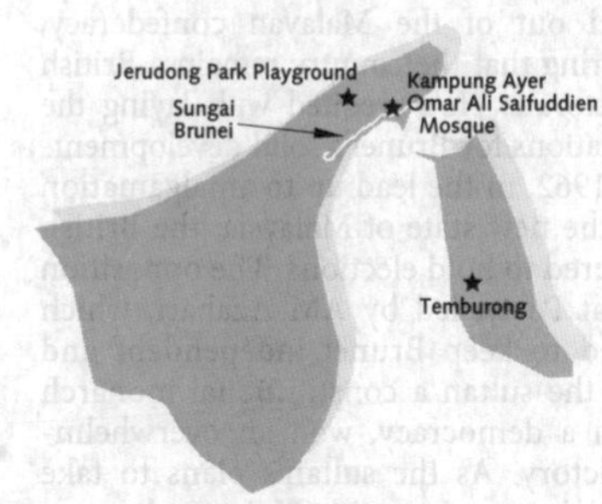

NO LOCAL TELEPHONE CODE	POPULATION: 354, 500	AREA: 5770 SQ KM

History

The earliest recorded references to Brunei's presence relate to China's trading connections with 'Puni' in the 6th century, during the Tang dynasty. Prior to the region's embrace of Islam, Brunei was within the boundaries of the Sumatran Srivijaya Empire, then the Majapahit Empire of Java. By the 15th and 16th centuries, Brunei Darussalam had become a considerable power itself in the region, with its rule extending throughout Borneo and into the Philippines.

The Spanish and Portuguese were the first European visitors, arriving in the 16th century. The Spanish made a bid to take over, but were soon ousted.

In the early 19th century, the arrival of the British in the guise of James Brooke, the first white raja of Sarawak, spelt the end of Brunei's power. A series of 'treaties' was forced onto the sultan as Brooke consolidated his hold over Kuching. He aimed to develop commercial relationships and suppress piracy, a favourite Bruneian and Dayak occupation (piracy was a common excuse for justifying European land grabs). Brunei became a British protectorate in 1888 and was gradually whittled away until, with a final dash of absurdity, Limbang was ceded to Sarawak in 1890, thus dividing Brunei into two parts.

In 1929, just as Brunei was about to be swallowed up entirely, oil was discovered. The present sultan's father, Sultan Omar Saifuddien, who abdicated in 1967, kept Brunei out of the Malayan confederacy, preferring that the country remain a British protectorate. He's credited with laying the foundations for Brunei's solid development.

In 1962, in the lead up to amalgamation with the new state of Malaysia, the British pressured to hold elections. The opposition Ra'ayat Party, led by AM Azahari, which wanted to keep Brunei independent and make the sultan a constitutional monarch within a democracy, won an overwhelming victory. As the sultan's plans to take Brunei into union with Malaysia became clear, Azahari fled to the Philippines, from where he directed an armed rebellion with the support of Indonesia. The rebellion was quickly crushed with British military backing and the sultan later opted for independence from Malaysia. The 'Abode of Peace' has been under emergency laws ever since, though you'll see little evidence of this.

Early in 1984 the popular young sultan and *yang di-pertuan* ('he who is lord'), Hassanal Bolkiah, somewhat reluctantly led his tightly ruled country into complete independence from Britain. The then 37-year-old leader rather enjoyed the British umbrella and the country still has close ties to Britain.

Since independence, Brunei has veered towards Islamic fundamentalism; Melayu Islam Beraja (MIB) is the name given to the national ideology. It stresses Malay culture, Islam and monarchy, and is promulgated through the ministries of education, religious affairs and information. In 1991 the sale of alcohol was banned and stricter dress codes were introduced; in 1992 the study of MIB became compulsory in schools.

Despite the emergency laws still in place and little evidence of a gathering tide of democratic reform, things are changing. In recent years the government has recognised a relatively small but growing unemployment problem, and disaffected youths have been blamed for isolated incidents of crime.

Symbolic of the country's economic and familial underbelly are the misadventures of the sultan's younger brother, Prince Jefri. While indulging in a flamboyant lifestyle, Prince Jefri was finance minister and ran the Amedeo Development Corporation, a family conglomerate with diversified interests, including golf courses, five-star hotels, fisheries and telecommunications.

Salacious scandals and rumours of financial corruption and incompetence forced the sultan to sack Jefri as finance minister in 1997, but the worst was yet to come. Amedeo collapsed in 1998 owing some US$16 billion to its creditors. The sultan went so far as to publicly file a lawsuit against the prince, a surprising break from the tradition of secrecy that governs both the monarchy and Brunei's financial statistics.

In May 2000 the sultan reached an out-of-court settlement with Jefri that would see the return of all of the prince's assets to the state. Things have settled down in the last few years, but the prince's excesses, along with the Asian financial crisis of 1998, highlighted the need for Brunei to broaden its horizons beyond the oilfields.

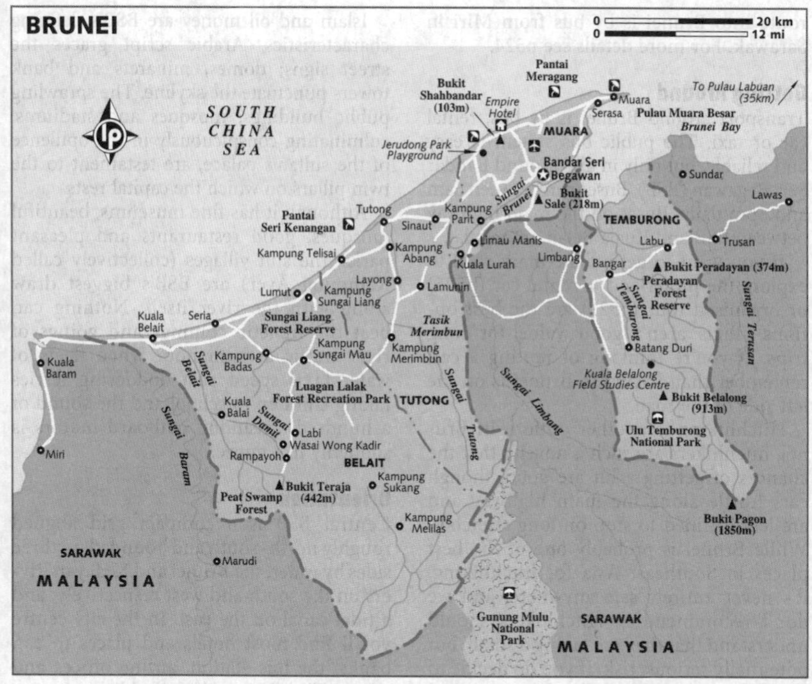

In the meantime, due to its wealth, Brunei's citizens enjoy a standard of living and benefits unheard of in most countries. There are pensions for all, free medical care, free schooling, free sport and leisure centres, cheap loans, subsidies for many purchases (including cars), short working weeks, no taxes and the highest minimum wages in the region. Keeping things that way is the major challenge facing Brunei right now.

Climate

Being a slice of Borneo, Brunei is subject to the huge island's prevailing climatic conditions. It's out of the typhoon belt and experiences high average temperatures, humidity and rainfall. Temperatures consistently fall between 24° and 31°C, with an average humidity of 79%. Average annual rainfall is about 3295mm. Although Brunei doesn't really have marked wet and dry seasons, the wettest months are from September to January, during the northeast monsoon, and the driest period is February to April.

National Parks & Reserves

Brunei has one major national park and several forest reserves that have sections designated as forest recreation parks.

Luagan Lalak Forest Recreation Park A small wetland (270 hectares) that's part of the Labi Forest Reserve, 25km inland south of Seria.

Merimbun Heritage Park Centred on Brunei's largest lake (120 hectares), this park, 27km inland south of Tutong, has trails and nature observation posts.

Peradayan Forest Recreation Park A section (10.7 sq km) of the Peradayan Forest Reserve in Brunei's Temburong district; treks through the jungle lead to the summits of Bukit Patoi (310m) and Bukit Peradayan (410m).

Ulu Temburong National Park An untouched expanse of forest (500 sq km), with trails and a canopy walk, accessible by boat only.

Getting There & Away

The Brunei International Airport is about 8km from BSB. Airlines flying into Brunei include Royal Brunei Airlines, Malaysia Airlines, Singapore Airlines and Thai Airways International. Regular boats go between Brunei, Sarawak and Sabah in Malaysian Borneo. The main overland route into Brunei is by bus from Miri in Sarawak. For more details see p524.

Getting Around

Transport around Brunei is by bus, rental car or taxi. The public bus system is easy and reliable, but only in and around Bandar Seri Begawan (BSB). Buses run between 6am and 6pm daily. Buses on the main highway between BSB and Kuala Belait are regular.

If you want to get off the main road to explore the hinterland, a rental car (p525) or organised tour (p521) are the best options. Taxis aren't good value for long trips. If you're thinking of renting a car, remember that driving in Brunei is on the left side of the road.

Hitchhiking is another option. In Brunei, hitchhikers are such a novelty that the chances of getting a lift are good, though cars hurtle along the main highway and are less inclined to stop on long stretches. While Brunei is probably one of the best places in Southeast Asia for hitchhiking, it's never entirely safe anywhere, and we don't recommend it. Hitchhikers should understand that they are taking a small, but potentially serious, risk. If you do decide to hitchhike, it is safer to travel in pairs and wise to let someone know where you are planning to go.

Regular boats connect Bangar in the Temburong district with BSB. Temburong has a limited road network and taxis are the only way to get around independently.

BANDAR SERI BEGAWAN

Images of Brunei's capital and largest town, Bandar Seri Begawan, conjure up a kind of Southeast Asian version of Arabian splendour, with gorgeous palaces and curvaceous mosques. BSB, as it's more prosaically known, isn't quite so fantastical, but there's definitely an air of banal exoticism to the place – banal in the sense of a calm, clean, compact town of some 75,000 people, with uncrowded streets and orderly traffic, a high standard of living and no visible poverty. Its exoticism is evident in the glorious curves of the Omar Ali Saifuddien Mosque that literally glows in the dark, and the waterborne lifestyle of residents who live amid the tangle of plankwalks and pilings that make up Kampung Ayer's stilt villages.

Islam and oil money are BSB's defining characteristics. Arabic script graces the street signs; domes, minarets and bank towers punctuate the skyline. The sprawling public buildings, mosques and stadiums, culminating conspicuously in the opulence of the sultan's palace, are testament to the twin pillars on which the capital rests.

Although it has fine museums, beautiful mosques, good restaurants and pleasant parks, the stilt villages (collectively called Kampung Ayer) are BSB's biggest draw along with the river itself. Nothing can beat the frenetic comings and goings of river traffic at rush hour when fleets of water taxis speed past doddering ferries taking children to school and the sound of a hundred screaming outboard motors is suddenly like music.

Orientation

Central BSB is a compact grid aligned roughly north–south and bounded on three sides by water: the Brunei and Kedayan Rivers on the south and west respectively, and a tidal canal on the east. In the city centre you'll find most hotels and places to eat, banks, the bus station, airline offices and shops. The Omar Ali Saifuddien Mosque on the western edge of the city centre dominates the landscape. Most sights are within walking distance, or a short bus ride, of the city centre.

Between Omar Ali Saifuddien Mosque and the riverfront are two massive Malay-style buildings, which form an ultra chic shopping mall – the Yayasan Sultan Haji Hassanal Bolkiah Complex. Usually written as the YSHHB Complex and simply called Yayasan, the mall leads to Jl MacArthur, across which are waterfront cafés and the customs wharf for boats to Sabah and Sarawak.

Stilt villages sprawl along the opposite bank of Sungai Brunei, and along both banks of the Sungai Kedayan to the northwest. Long, rickety-looking plankwalks connect the stilt villages to the shore.

Information

BOOKSHOPS

Paul & Elizabeth Book Services (☎ 222 0958; Lot 2.14-2.19 YSHHB Complex; 🕑 10am-10pm) Largest range of books and magazines. It sometimes has maps in stock.

Wordzone Bookshop (☎ 223 2764; Basement, YSHHB Complex; 🕑 9.30am-10pm) Has a small range of periodicals and newspapers. It also carries the useful *Road Map & Street Index of Brunei*, published by Shell.

CULTURAL CENTRES

British Council (☎ 223 7742; Lot 2.01, 2nd fl, YSHHB Complex; 🕑 8am-12.15pm & 1.45-4.30pm Mon-Thu, 8am-12.30pm Fri & Sat) It's in the same office as the British Embassy.

Alliance Française (☎ 234 3245; Simpang 465, Ting Sing Garden, Kampung Sungai Tilong, Jl Muara) Outside town on the way to the airport.

INTERNET ACCESS

LA Ling Cybercafe (☎ 223 2800; 2nd fl, YSHHB Complex; B$3 per hr; 🕑 9.30am-9.30pm Mon-Sat, 10am-6pm Sun) A comfortable and quiet place for checking your email.

Cyberstar Café (☎ 224 0666; B$1 per hr; 🕑 9am-10pm) Opposite the Apek Utama Hotel.

MEDICAL SERVICES

Jerudong Park Hospital (☎ 261 1433; fax 2612461; Royal Brunei Polo Club, Jerudong Park)

Ripas Hospital (☎ 224 2424; fax 224 2690; Jl Tutong, Bandar Seri Begawan)

MONEY

All banks in BSB charge to cash travellers cheques, with some exceptions. The Hongkong Bank (HSBC) doesn't charge for American Express travellers cheques it has issued but charges B$15 for all others (including American Express issued elsewhere). The Standard Chartered Bank usually offers slightly better rates but charges B$15 commission per transaction up to US$200! It charges B$5 for Thomas Cook travellers cheques issued by Standard Chartered.

A handy moneychanger by the bus station is **Perniagaan & Perusahaan Liyana** (☎ 222 1961; Ground fl, Britannia House, 1 Jl Cotor; 🕑 8am-5.30pm Mon-Sat, 8am-3pm Sun). ATMs are common in the city centre and there's one in the departure hall at the airport. There's also a moneychanger at the airport.

POST

The main post office is on the corner of Jl Sultan and Jl Elizabeth Dua.

TOURIST INFORMATION

The **Tourist Information Centre** (☎ 884 9110; wildlifeadventure@hotmail.com; Ground fl, Post Office Bldg, cnr Jl Sultan & Jl Elizabeth Dua; 🕑 8am-noon & 2pm-4.30pm Mon-Thu & Sat, 8am-noon Fri) is run under the auspices of ZQ Tours and you can book a variety of nature tours here. These range in price from B$50 per person for a three-hour tour to B$135 for a day trip to Ulu Temburong National Park. The staff are helpful and there are brochures and maps available. They can also supply the *Explore Brunei* guide, published by the government, which contains useful information for visitors, including the bus routes. The centre is within walking distance of Jl MacArthur, beside the post office.

For more information on Brunei visit the official website at www.tourismbrunei.com.

Sights

KAMPUNG AYER

Kampung Ayer is made up of 28 water villages (housing up to 30,000 people) built on either side of Sungai Brunei – exploring it is probably one of the most interesting experiences you'll have in Brunei. A maze of wooden plankwalks connects brightly painted shacks to shops, villages to schools, clinics to workshops. It's fascinating to wander at random – even if you do end up in someone's kitchen! BSB's people are at their least reserved and most friendly in their close-knit riverside homes – you can expect to be mobbed along the plankwalks by children and heartily heralded from verandas. A traditional way of life continues in these mostly prefab dwellings with modern plumbing, electricity and colour TVs.

There are many ways to get to Kampung Ayer, all of them interesting. Either get dropped off at one of the stilt villages by water taxi, or find a plankwalk heading out from the shore. There's one on the south-east side of the YSHHB Complex. Among the houses in Kampung Ayer are all sorts of shops and businesses. You might stumble across a handicraft shop selling silverwork, brass, woven cloth and baskets. If not, ask a boat operator to take you to one.

Water taxis from BSB cost about B$1, but if you're coming from further up or down the river the cost is about B$2. Water taxis shuttle people back and forth between early morning and late evening, and congregate like schools of fish at the area next to the customs wharf. They also stop at various piers along the riverside and villages. Wave frantically and they'll come by and pick you up.

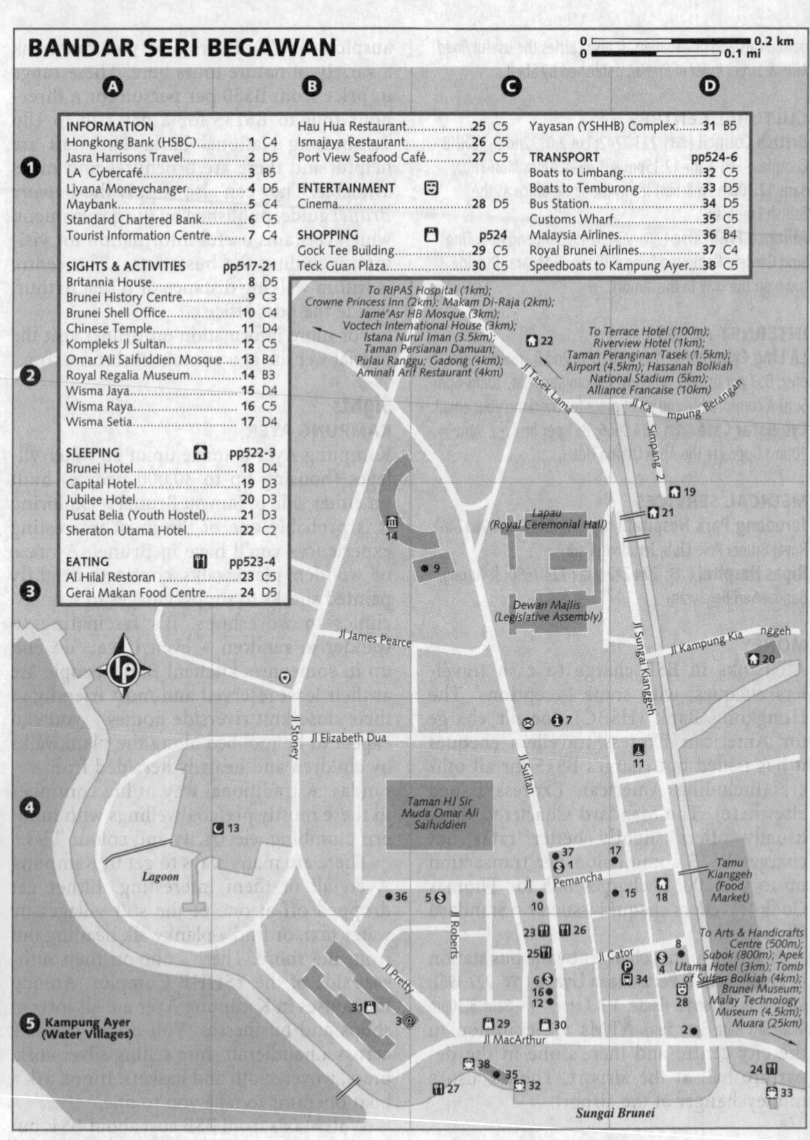

A **boat trip** right around Kampung Ayer in the early morning or evening is highly recommended and, when combined with a stopover at Taman Persiaran Damuan (p521) near the sultan's palace, should take about an hour. Chartering a water taxi should cost B$20 per hour, though bargaining is expected.

OMAR ALI SAIFUDDIEN MOSQUE

Named after the 28th sultan of Brunei, the golden-domed **Omar Ali Saifuddien Mosque** (☎ 222 2623; admission free; 8am-noon, 1-3pm, 4.30-5pm Sat-Wed, 4.30-5pm Fri, closed to non-Muslims Thu) is open to non-Muslims outside prayer times. The compound is open between 8am and 8.30pm. Remember to dress appropriately and to remove your shoes before entering the mosque (not the compound). Muslim travellers can enter the mosque to pray at any time.

This grand mosque was built in 1958 and stands next to Sungai Kedayan in its own artificial lagoon. It's one of the tallest buildings in BSB and one of the most impressive structures in Southeast Asia, especially when lit up at night, or silhouetted as the sun sinks over the stilt village next door. Listen for the call to prayer that echoes throughout the city centre, starting before dawn or at dusk.

The interior is simple but tasteful, though it's no match for the stunning exterior. The floor and walls are made from the finest Italian marble, the stained-glass windows were crafted in England and the luxurious carpets were flown in from Saudi Arabia and Belgium. A Venetian mosaic of 3.5 million pieces decorates the inside of the main dome, and pools and quadrants surrounding the building throw beautiful reflections. The ceremonial stone boat sitting in the lagoon is a replica of a 16th-century *mahligai* (royal) barge.

You may be able to take the elevator to the top of the 44m minaret or walk up the winding staircase (look for one of the mosque personnel to ask permission). The view over the city and Kampung Ayer is excellent.

BRUNEI MUSEUM

Situated 6.5km east of the centre of BSB, the excellent **Brunei Museum** (☎ 222 6495; Kota Batu; admission free; 9.30am-5pm Sat-Thu, 9-11.30am & 2.30pm-5pm Fri) overlooks Sungai Brunei. It contains one of the finest galleries in the world, and combined with a visit to the Malay Technology Museum (next page), it's definitely worth the short trip from town.

The Brunei Museum has displays of artefacts representing the cultural heritage of Brunei, including musical instruments, baskets and brassware, and a large collection of Chinese ceramics dating from AD 1000. A natural history section features exhibits of mounted mammals, birds and insects. There are also interesting exhibits on shipwrecks and their cargoes.

These exhibits are fine, but they give little hint of what awaits in the breathtaking **Islamic gallery**. Here you'll find an astonishing, brilliantly arranged collection of beautiful ceramics, jewellery, silverwork and weaponry from across the Islamic world. The illuminated Quran alone are worth the trip out to the museum, but the jade sword handles inlaid with gems and the begging bowls intricately carved from coconut husks are also to be admired.

The exhibit on the oil industry may be less alluring, but offers worthwhile insights into the source of Brunei's modern wealth. There are interesting models of different oil rigs and the extraction process.

Purple bus Nos 11 and 39 pass the museum (B$1). Otherwise, it's a bit of a walk from town, but you may be able to catch a lift. After visiting the museum, you can walk down the steep bank to the Malay Technology Museum.

THE REAL 'VENICE OF THE EAST'

Kampung Ayer is the place that spawned all those 'Venice of the East' clichés common throughout the region – except in this case it was, and in many ways still is, an apt description. At least Antonio Pigafetta – who was on one of Magellan's voyages – thought so. He coined the phrase in honour of the vast collection of wooden stilt villages he encountered at Kota Batu (just east of modern central BSB) in 1521.

Except for the *istana* (palace) and a few royal houses, the capital of the sultan's then extensive empire was built entirely on poles and plankwalks over Sungai Brunei. By the 18th century, the *kampung* (villages) had become known abroad for their artisan guilds – a certain kampung was famed for its brasswork, another for weaving. Today the kampung are serviced by schools and clinics, shops, mosques and a waterborne fire brigade. Although buildings are increasingly of concrete rather than wood, fires are not uncommon, and the average dwelling takes all of seven minutes to burn to the waterline. Watch for the little ferries shuttling schoolchildren back and forth. Instead of in a schoolyard, the kids hang out on the wharf. Not surprisingly, anyone growing up in Kampung Ayer learns to swim before they can walk. Considering the miles of narrow plankwalks to be traversed, maybe it's a good thing Brunei prohibits the use of alcohol.

MALAY TECHNOLOGY MUSEUM

Built on the edge of the river below the Brunei Museum, the **Malay Technology Museum** (☎ 224 4545; admission free; 9.30am-5pm Sat-Thu, 9-11.30am & 2.30-5pm Fri) has three galleries devoted to traditional lifestyles and artisans and shouldn't be missed.

Gallery 1 features water villages and includes reconstructions of how *kampung* architecture has evolved over the last 150 years or so. Gallery 2 has exhibits of handicrafts and fishing techniques practised by the people of the water villages. These include some fine examples of silversmithing, brass casting and weaving. Gallery 3 shows the tools and techniques used by the indigenous tribes of the interior for food gathering, agriculture and hunting. Brunei's first gunboat is on display in front of the museum.

ROYAL REGALIA MUSEUM

Right in the heart of BSB, the **Royal Regalia Museum** (☎ 223 8358; Jl Sultan; admission free; 8.30am-5pm Sat-Thu, 9-11.30am & 2.30-5pm Fri) lies between Jl Sultan and Jl Stoney, a short walk north of the waterfront. Gutted by fire early in 1998, the building has been carefully reconstructed; the contents fortunately survived the blaze. The museum is devoted to the sultan of Brunei and, unsurprisingly, consists mainly of photographs of His Majesty and other members of the royal family, along with artefacts of the monarchy. Among these are his report from Sandhurst Royal Military Academy, and coronation hardware such as the throne, crowns, ceremonial sceptres, kris (traditional swords) and costumes.

Visitors must remove their shoes before entering.

BRUNEI HISTORY CENTRE

Adjacent to the Royal Regalia Museum, the **Brunei History Centre** (☎ 223 8368; Jl Sultan; admission free; 7.45am-12.15pm & 1.30-4.30pm Mon-Thu & Sat) is devoted to researching Brunei's history and recording the sultan's family history. There's a small museum at the entrance that details the lineage of the sultan. It also has replicas of all the royal tombs and shows their locations around BSB.

ARTS & HANDICRAFTS CENTRE

Built to help develop local craftwork, the grandiose **Arts & Handicrafts Centre** (☎ 224 0676; Jl Kota Batu; admission free; 7.45am-12.15pm & 1.30-4.30pm Mon-Thu & Sat) is on the waterfront towards the Brunei Museum, visible from town and within easy walking distance. While the concept of such a centre is a marvellous idea, if you're interested in traditional crafts it's a little disappointing; only new silverwork and weaving produced by the students are available and some items are very expensive. A traditional umbrella costs about B$20, model water taxis start at B$200, a kris and scabbard will set you back about B$500, and silverwork starts at B$10, going up to thousands of Brunei dollars for intricate pieces. It's more interesting to visit the workshops, though there's not always a lot of activity.

TAMAN PERANGINAN TASEK

This park, a short distance from town, is a pleasant retreat from the city. It has picnic areas and peaceful walks to a small waterfall and reservoir. If you're lucky, you may get a glimpse of proboscis monkeys in the early morning or late afternoon. Walk north along Jl Tasek Lama past the Terrace Hotel and after two sets of traffic lights, turn right. From the entrance gates by the parking lot, it's about 1km to the falls – continue past the flowerbeds and picnic tables, then follow the stream to the falls. They're best in the wet season, when the water is deeper. You can swim here but women should remember that the usual rules of modesty apply; T-shirts and shorts are OK. Another road by the gate leads to a 15-minute uphill walk to a view over the reservoir.

The Sheraton Utama Hotel hands out a map for joggers that shows the park walks.

JAME'ASR HASSANAL BOLKIAH MOSQUE

Another stunning example of Islamic architecture is the **Jame'Asr Hassanal Bolkiah Mosque** (☎ 223 8741; Jl Hassan Bolkiah; admission free), the largest mosque in Brunei. It was built at great expense for the 25th anniversary of the sultan's reign in 1992 and is a fabulous sight. Situated in Kampung Kiarong, a few kilometres from the city centre, it's known locally as the Kiarong Mosque. Opening times are similar to those of the Omar Ali Saifuddien Mosque. Take bus No 1 or 22 to get there.

ISTANA NURUL IMAN

The sultan's palace, or **Istana Nurul Iman** (☎ 222 9988; Jl Tutong), is an impressive sight,

BRUNEI

especially when lit up at night. It's larger than the Vatican Palace and no expense was spared in its construction; it cost US$350 million and, among other features, has 1788 rooms, 200 toilets and a banquet hall with seating for 4000. Unfortunately, the istana is open to the public only during Hari Raya Aidilfitri, the end of the fasting month of Ramadan, when the sultan is often willing to meet his people.

The istana is about 3.5km out of town on the Tutong road, and the grounds look on to Sungai Brunei. You could spend a leisurely hour walking there, or charter a water taxi (p517) to **Taman Persiaran Damuan**, a large landscaped park along the riverbank nearby, which also has some of the best views of the palace.

OTHER SIGHTS

About halfway between downtown BSB and the istana is the **Makam Di-Raja** (Royal Mausoleum), overlooking the river. This is the burial place of the last four sultans; other members of the royal family are buried in the grounds. It's a short walk from the Crowne Princess Inn.

On the other side of town on the way to the Brunei Museum is the **Tomb of Sultan Bolkiah**, the fifth sultan of Brunei, who lived from 1473 to 1521, during a period when Brunei was the dominant power in the region. The small tomb and garden are in the historic setting of Kota Batu and the view across the river is nice; otherwise, it's a very minor attraction.

There's a brightly painted **Chinese temple** on the corner of Jl Elizabeth Dua and Jl Sungai Kianggeh. You'll probably pass by it at some point. It's a busy place on Saturday evenings, and Chinese opera is sometimes staged here.

For good views of Kampung Ayer and the approach to BSB take a walk or taxi up **Bukit Subok** (Subok Hill). After passing the handicraft centre on Jl Kota Batu heading away from the city, turn left and follow the road up the hill. The Foreign Affairs ministry is also on Bukit Subok.

In the middle of the river across from the Istana Nurul Iman, **Pulau Ranggu** is home to a large colony of proboscis monkeys – Brunei is one of the strongholds of these amazing primates. Macaques also inhabit the island. If you take a water taxi along the river around sunset you may glimpse a monkey; the bargaining price will probably start at B$30 but you should be able to hire a boat for B$20. For a good trip in the late afternoon, plan a water taxi reconnaissance of the island to look for monkeys then get dropped off at Taman Persiaran Damuan (this page) for views of the illuminated istana. Take a water taxi back or get a bus or taxi on Jl Tutong.

Activities

The **Hassanal Bolkiah National Stadium** (☎ 238 0700; Jl Berakas; 🕑 8am-noon & 1.30-4.30pm) is of Olympic proportions and includes a track-and-field complex, tennis centre, squash courts and swimming pool. It's open to the public and prices to use it are reasonable. The pool is often nearly deserted. The stadium is 5km north of the city; to get there, take purple bus No 1 or 34.

Brunei has three golf courses close to BSB. Green fees range from B$120 to B$150 on weekdays.

Mentiri Golf Club (☎ 279 1021; Jl Pengkalan Si Babaunear) International standard golf course northeast of BSB on the shore near the mouth of Sungai Brunei.

Empire Golf & Country Club (☎ 241 7815; www.empire.com.bn) Waterfront golf course designed by Jack Nicklaus, in the grounds of the luxurious Empire Hotel.

Royal Brunei Recreation Club (☎ 234 3724; Lebuhraya Sultan Haji Hassanal Bolkiah) Driving range near the airport north of BSB city centre.

Some tour operators run **dive trips** to a few spots in the area, including the wrecks off Pulau Labuan, but you're probably better off dealing with Labuan operators or saving your money for the islands off Semporna in Sabah.

Tours

In the city centre there's a host of travel agencies where you can book flights and local tours. Prices for tours depend on the number of paying customers, and are cheaper if there are two or more people. Half-day tours of BSB start at around B$50 per person, and a range of trips into the countryside cost from B$50 to B$100 per day (more for overnight trips). Operators are as follow:

Eco Tours & Travel (☎ 222 3420; ecotvl@hotmail.com; Ground fl, Britannia House, Jl Cator) Offers tours to the sights in and around BSB, as well as trips to Ulu Temburong.

Freme Travel Service (☎ 223 4280; fremeinb@brunet.bn; Unit 403B Wisma Jaya, Jl Pemancha) Offers a variety of tours, including city and Kampung Ayer, and trips to Ulu Temburong and Pulau Selirong.

Jasra Harrisons (☎ 224 3911; jasratvl@brunet.bn; cnr Jl MacArthur & Jl Sungai Kianggeh) A good general travel agency, and the sales agent for British Airways and Qantas; it also organises trips to Ulu Temburong.

Sunshine Borneo Tours & Travel (☎ 244 1791; www.exploreborneo.com; No 2, Simpang 146, Jl Kiarong) Runs tours of the city, and farther afield in Brunei and the rest of Borneo.

ZQ Tours (☎ 266 1941; zq_tours@hotmail.com; Tourist Information Centre, Ground fl, Post Office Bldg) Currently runs Brunei's Tourist Information Centre and specialises in outdoor and wildlife tours around Brunei.

Festivals & Events

Brunei has many of the same holidays as Malaysia, based on the Islamic calendar but including holidays on Chinese New Year, Christmas Day and New Year's Day. The most important are:

National Day (23 February) Parade and procession in downtown BSB to celebrate Brunei's independence.

Sultan's Birthday (15 July) A lively event marked by fireworks, parades and various processions in downtown BSB and around Brunei.

Hari Raya Aidilfitri (Variable timing, based on Islamic calendar) Probably the best time to visit Brunei, when feasting and celebration mark the end of Ramadan and the sultan's palace is open to receive visitors.

Sleeping

BUDGET

Budget prices in Brunei are more like the mid-range options in the rest of Malaysia. Even if it seems expensive, however, the accommodation listed here certainly offers mid-range comfort.

Apek Utama Hotel (☎ 222 0808; fax 222 6166; Simpang 229, Kampung Pintu Malim, Jl Kota Batu; r B$30;) The friendly and helpful people who run the Apek are a mini tourist information centre in themselves. Bright clean rooms with bathrooms, and a TV lounge make this a great place to stay. It's about 3km east from town along Sungai Brunei on the way to the museum. Purple bus No 39 goes right by. Once you're settled, the best way to get back and forth to town is by water taxi. Opposite the hotel are Cyberstar Café (see Internet Access, p517) and a comfortable restaurant serving Western breakfasts.

Pusat Belia (Youth Hostel; ☎ 222 2900; 8765515; Jl Sungai Kianggeh; per bed B$10;) This hostel is part of a youth centre, a short walk from the city centre. It's the cheapest you'll find in BSB with comfortable rooms and shared bathrooms. The hostel is often empty but can sometimes fill up with sports groups. It may be hard to find someone at reception, but persevere. The hostel does not accept guests after 9pm. Office hours are from 7.45am to noon from Monday to Saturday; the desk should also be attended from 2.30pm to 9pm on Friday and Sunday. Entry to the wonderfully inviting swimming pool is B$1; there is also a café with a very limited menu.

Voctech International House (Seameo Voctech; ☎ 244 7992; www.voctech.org.bn; Jl Pasar Baharu Gadong; s/d B$40/50;) Although it's 4km from downtown, the facilities here are first rate. This educational centre runs conferences and hosts overseas groups, but welcomes travellers as well. It's within walking distance of the Gadong shopping area northwest of the city centre and is accessible from downtown by bus No 22. The staff are friendly and helpful. Each room has a TV and fridge, and there's Internet access downstairs between 9am and 5pm (B$2.50 per hour). The cafeteria serves good food at very reasonable prices (around B$3.50 to B$5 per dish). It's best to phone first to make sure there's a room available.

MID-RANGE

If you are on a tight budget, the jump in price from budget to mid-range accommodation will be a shock. If it's any consolation, all rooms have air-con, TV, hot water and IDD phones.

Capital Hotel (☎ 222 3561; No 7 Simpang 2, Kampung Berangan; s/d B$58/68;) The Capital has somewhat faded rooms but at fairly acceptable prices. The restaurant downstairs serves reasonably priced meals and Western breakfasts.

Terrace Hotel (☎ 224 3554; www.terracebrunei.com; Jl Tasek Lama; s/d B$66/90;) The Terrace Hotel has comfortable, basic rooms. Its restaurant is good, but the best part of staying here is the outdoor swimming pool for cooling off.

Jubilee Hotel (☎ 222 8070; jubilee@brunet.bn; Jl Kampung Kianggeh; s/d B$70/125;) Rooms here have spacious bathrooms and breakfast is included. A small supermarket, restaurants and travel facilities are on site.

Grand City Hotel (☎ 245 2188; grandcity@brunet.bn; 1-12 Kampung Pengkalan Gadong; r B$88;) If you're flying into Brunei and need a short rest, this hotel near the airport has six-hour 'transit' rooms available for B$44. Discounts for regular rooms bring the price down to B$60.

Crowne Princess Inn (☎ 224 1128; teph@brunet.bn; Km 2.5, Jl Tutong; r B$110;) This compact, comfortable hotel is about halfway between downtown and the Istana Nurul Iman across Edinburgh Bridge. It's good value, with discount rates of B$70 routinely offered.

TOP END

BSB has a good selection of top-end hotels, although the mid-range accommodation is perfectly adequate. For the extra money you can take advantage of added luxuries such as golf courses, sports centres and theatres.

Empire Hotel & Country Club (☎ 241 8888; www.empire.com.bn; Muara-Tutong Hwy, Kampung Jerudong; s/d B$450/605;) If you're looking for something special in a world-class luxury hotel, think about staying here. One of Prince Jefri's projects, the Empire is estimated to have cost US$1.1 billion to build. Some of the contractors haven't been paid yet due to the prince's financial misdemeanours; unpaid or not, they certainly did a brilliant job in putting things together, right down to the beautiful inlaid marble and wooden mouldings. The place is practically empty and discounts can be as much as 50%. Everything is here: a golf course, a beach, a cinema, a bowling alley and a dinner theatre. If you don't feel up to the luxury, at least enjoy some afternoon tea in the magnificent lobby with its 80m-high atrium.

Brunei Hotel (☎ 224 2372; www.quanix.com/business/bruhotel; 95 Jl Pemancha; s/d B$160/180;) Smack in the middle of downtown BSB, this hotel has a convenient location and is good value when discounts are available.

Sheraton Utama Hotel (☎ 224 4272; fax 222 1579; Jl Tasek Lama; s/d B$240/270;) Has the luxury you would expect from the chain and is within walking distance of the city centre. Convenient and comfortable.

Riverview Hotel (☎ 223 8238; rivview@brunet.bn; Km 1, Jl Gadong; s/d B$165/185;) The river in view here is Sungai Kedayan. This hotel is pleasant and luxurious and offers discounts. It is north of town on the way to the airport.

THE EMPIRE STRIKES BACK

The Empire Hotel was just one among many of Prince Jefri's projects that got him into trouble with the sultan. The list of his acquisitions makes Imelda Marcos seem like a penny-pinching grandmother. Under the auspices of the Amedeo Development Corporation, Prince Jefri bought five luxurious hotels overseas, including the Beverly Hills Hotel in Los Angeles. But that's nothing compared to some of Jefri's possessions audited in the wake of the sultan's lawsuit against the prince in 2000. It's one thing to covet Asprey's, the jeweller for the British royal family, but what about the gold-plated toilet brushes included among his household items? Wasn't he satisfied with the usual accoutrements of wealth, like his 2000 cars, private jets and lavish residences around the world?

It's difficult to reconcile the relatively devout and quietly conservative Brunei with a man who names his 50m yacht *Tits* and its two accompanying speedboats *Nipple I* and *Nipple II*. But then again, maybe Prince Jefri is a symbol of Brunei's alter ego, an adolescent nation struggling to get out and party. The problem is what to do with the morning after.

Centrepoint (☎ 243 0430; www.arhbrunei.com; Abdul Razak Complex, Gadong; s/d B$150/185;) This luxurious hotel is located in the rather uninspiring Gadong shopping neighbourhood, far from the riverfront. There's an impressive range of marble-clad facilities, including an expensive a Chinese restaurant, a business centre, a sports centre and private dining rooms.

Eating

Most of the hotels and the youth centre have their own restaurants and there are places in town to suit every budget. For outdoor eating hawker-style, the **Gerai Makan** (food centre; Jl MacArthur) on the riverfront just over the canal from the customs wharf, has some delicious choices. Good food can also be found at the local food market, **Tamu Kianggeh** (cnr Jl Sungai Kianggeh & Jl Pemancha), across the canal. It's not very extensive but has plenty of local colour and is a popular spot for lunch. Water taxis hurtle up and down the canal transporting passengers to and fro, while patrons munch on satay, barbecued fish, chicken wings and *kueh melayu* (sweet pancakes filled with peanuts, raisins and sugar).

If the heat's getting to you and you're in the northeast of the city centre, try the clean, air-conditioned **food courts** (2nd fl, Wisma Setia Bldg, Jl Pemancha). West of the city centre is the **Padian Food Court** (1st fl, YSHHB Complex). For good coffee and Western-style breakfasts and lunches try **Delifrance** (☎ 223 1209; dishes B$4-8; ⏲ 8.30am-10pm).

Also in the YSHHB Complex, the **Hua Ho Supermarket** (☎ 223 1120; ⏲ 10am-10pm) is good for self-catering.

For quick, inexpensive Malay and Indian meals, try the crowded **Ismajaya Restaurant** (☎ 2220229; Jl Sultan; dishes B$1-4). The *roti canai*, for only B$1, is delicious. Across the road is the comparably priced **Al Hilal Restoran** (☎ 2223690; Jl Sultan; dishes B$2-4), serving similar types of meals. Both places open early for breakfast.

Hau Hua (☎ 222 5396; 48 Jl Sultan; dishes B$5-10; ⏲ 7am-9pm) This comfortable, air-conditioned Chinese café-restaurant has delicious Chinese meals. It's one of the very few in downtown BSB that serves pork. Western breakfasts and a variety of delicious fresh juices, including wheatgrass health drinks, are on the menu.

Port View Seafood Café (☎ 223 1467; Jl MacArthur; dishes B$4-8) The best part about this place, besides the food, is its outside eating area on the river, a strategic place to enjoy the sunset. At night the water taxis look like huge fireflies zipping through the darkness. The menu includes simple Western, Chinese and Malay dishes, as well as mouth-watering desserts. Upstairs, the menu is a little more expensive and features Thai, Chinese and Japanese food.

Aminah Arif (☎ 245 6447; 7 Jl Gadong; dishes B$8-13) If you're interested in trying a traditional and rather peculiar Bruneian dish, this restaurant specialises in *ambuyat*, sago that's served in a gluey mass eaten with chopsticks. Set meals are B$16 and B$26 per couple, served in an unpretentious, clean air-conditioned space. Little English is spoken here, but the menus have photographs. The Aminah is located in Gadong, too far to walk from downtown, but fairly easy to get to by bus. Take bus No 1, get off at the Centrepoint Hotel in Gadong, then walk about a block northwest. The restaurant is just behind the Mercedes Benz dealership.

Fratini's (☎ 223 2892; Ground fl, YSHHB Complex; dishes B$15-20) This upmarket restaurant has a relaxing ambience and features an imaginative selection of pizzas and pasta dishes. A good place for lunch or dinner if you're hankering for a Western-style atmosphere and flavours.

BSB's top-end hotels have lots of restaurant choices. For a special treat, try the afternoon tea (B$15 per person) at the luxurious Empire Hotel (see previous page).

Shopping

Most of the quality shopping is in the air-conditioned plazas. The gigantic YSHHB Complex has a dazzling selection of ritzy shops selling watches, sunglasses, Iranian chandeliers and other essentials. It also houses franchises like the Body Shop.

The other big shopping centre is at Gadong, about 4.5km from the city centre. There's no reason to make a special trip here, but there are plenty of supermarkets and department stores, a couple of decent bookshops, and a number of restaurants all collected together in the massive air-conditioned Centrepoint shopping centre.

There are numerous photo-processing, camera and film shops in the shopping malls in the city centre and at Gadong, though if you have any special film requirements you should fulfil them before you come to Brunei. There's no advantage in buying duty-free in Brunei, since you will get far more for your money in Malaysia.

Getting There & Away

AIR

Airline tickets to Malaysia and Singapore from BSB are at a fixed rate, but other international fares are cheaper if bought through travel agents rather than the airlines. Royal Brunei Airlines often has promotional fares out of BSB as well.

For airline offices or general sales agents in BSB see p517.

BOAT

Apart from flying, the most convenient way to travel between Brunei and Sabah or Sarawak is by boat. Boats to Lawas

BRUNEI

JANE SWEENEY

Jame'Asr Hassanal Bolkiah Mosque (p520), Bandar Seri Begawan

Omar Ali Saifuddien Mosque (p518)

LIZ BARRY

LIZ BARRY

Water taxis heading for the floating village of **Kampung Ayer** (p517)

LIZ BARRY

Flat-bottomed boats, **Temburong** (p528)

Night market, **Gadong** (p524)

Children, **Kampung Ayer** (p517)

LIZ BARRY

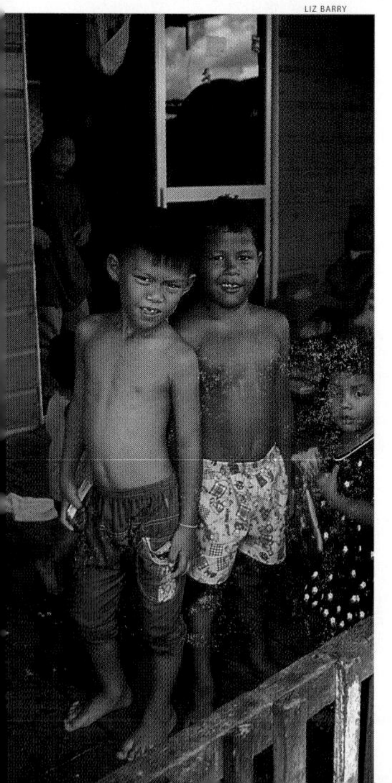

GRAHAM TWEEN

Istana Nurul Iman (p520), Bandar Seri Begawan

JANE S

Buildings on stilts, **Kampung Ayer** (p519)

(Sarawak) and Pulau Labuan (for connections to Sabah) leave from the **ferry terminal** (☎ 277 3071) at Muara, 25km northeast of BSB. Numerous express boats go between Muara port and Pulau Labuan (B$15 economy, B$18 1st class; 1 hour) between 7.30am and 4.40pm. Departures from Labuan (economy RM24, 1st class RM30) are between 8.30am and 4.30pm. Extra services may be added at weekends and on public holidays. A daily boat leaves for Lawas in Sarawak (B$10, 2 hours) at 11.30am. Boats leave from Lawas (RM25) for Muara at 7am daily. An express bus between town and the terminal costs B$2. The website www.bruneibay.net has a useful ferry schedule link for the most up-to-date information.

Boats to Limbang (B$10, 30 minutes) leave between 6am and 6pm from the customs wharf at the end of Jl Roberts in BSB and depart when full, which means you could be waiting a while.

For the Temburong district, speedboats go between BSB and Bangar throughout the day (B$6, 45 minutes). The first departure is around 7am and the last at 5pm; boats leave (when full) from the jetty near the Gerai Makan (food centre). From Bangar, it's a short taxi ride (about B$15) to the Sarawak border and on to Limbang. A taxi from Bangar to Lawas, 20km from Brunei's eastern border with Sarawak costs around B$80.

BUS

Brunei's main highway links BSB with the town of Kuala Baram in Sarawak via Seria and Kuala Belait. Overland from BSB to Miri (Sarawak) or vice versa involves changing buses at least four times. Public buses also go to the Sarawak border southwest of BSB at Kuala Lurah, where you can continue on to Limbang in Sarawak.

The BSB bus station is on Jl Cator, beneath the multistorey car park. For Miri, take a bus to Seria (B$6, 2 hours) and at the Seria bus station, buy a combined ticket for the three buses you'll need to get to Miri. This comes to B$11.20 and includes your ticket to Kuala Belait (B$1, 20 minutes), from Kuala Belait to the border (B$5.50) and from the border to Miri (the fare is RM4.70, but you're charged B$4.70). You change buses in Kuala Belait, cross the river, and switch again at Kuala Baram for the border. Immigration and customs formalities are taken care of on both sides of the Brunei–Sarawak border.

The journey to Miri takes about four hours. Buses leave BSB for Seria about every half-hour between 7.30am and 5pm. It's best to get an early start to reach Miri by the early afternoon. From Seria, buses to Kuala Belait (B$1) leave roughly every half-hour up to 3pm. Buses from Kuala Belait to the border leave at 7.30, 9.30 and 11am, and at 1.30 and 3.30pm, though this isn't quite written in stone. The fare is B$10.20 for the 2½-hour trip to Miri. Before you board, ask at the bus station in Seria if the bus will make the Miri connections.

Public bus No 44 goes to the Sarawak border at Kuala Lurah.

CAR

It's possible to travel by road to Lawas in Sarawak from Bangar in the Temburong district of Brunei but you'll have to hire a taxi.

Hiring a car is the only feasible way to explore the hinterland of Brunei, though you could comfortably see most sights in two days. Prices range from B$80 to B$120 for a sedan; rates for luxury cars like Mercedes or Volvos and 4WD SUVs are much higher. Mileage and insurance are included, though surcharges may apply if the car is taken into Sarawak. Most rental agencies will bring the car to your hotel and arrange to pick it up when you've finished with it. Petrol is cheap and the main roads are in good condition, but many of the back roads require 4WD. An international driver's permit is required for driving in Brunei.

Ask at your hotel about renting a car and they can probably help you out. A reasonable and recommended company is **Azizah Car Rentals** (☎ 222 9388).

Getting Around

TO/FROM THE AIRPORT

Purple bus Nos 11, 23, 24, 36, 38 and 57 will get you to/from the airport, about 8km northwest of the city, for B$1. Leaving the terminal, keep to the right and walk south for about 300m to the bus stops.

Some major hotels have courtesy phones at the arrivals hall that you can use to request a free pick-up. Taxis go between the airport and town for about B$20, but cost more after 9pm.

BUS

The government bus network covers most sights in and around the city, and the international ferry terminal at Muara. Routes for local buses are displayed at the bus station, beneath the multistorey car park on Jl Cator, and numbers are displayed on each bus. The *Explore Brunei* book and map brochure available from the Tourist Information Centre also includes a good bus routes map. Apart from the Muara express service (B$2), all fares are B$1. Most buses run every 15 to 20 minutes, and the system operates daily between 6.30am and 6pm. Useful routes:

Airport Bus Nos 11, 23, 24, 36, 38 and 57
Apek Utama Hotel, Brunei Museum & Malay Technology Museum Bus No 39
Gadong Shopping Precinct and Centrepoint Bus No 1
Voctech International House Bus No 22
Hassanal Bolkiah National Stadium & Immigration Department Bus Nos 1 and 34
Jame'Asr Hassanal Bolkiah Mosque Bus Nos 1 and 22
Jerudong Park Playground Bus Nos 55 and 57
Muara Bus Nos 37, 38 and 39

Express buses travel between BSB and the Muara ferry terminal every half-hour between 6.50am and 4.50pm; the trip takes 40 minutes and the fare is B$2.

TAXI

Taxis are metered at B$3 for the first 1km and B$1 for each additional kilometre. The rates go up from B$3 to B$4.50 after 9pm. A charge of B$1 is added for each piece of luggage and there's an added B$5 for trips to and from the airport. Lots of taxis congregate at the bus station, but you may have trouble flagging one down farther afield. Booking a **taxi** (☎ 222 2214) also incurs a charge of B$3.

WATER TAXI

Water taxis are longboats with powerful outboard motors that hurtle up and down Sungai Brunei, transporting passengers to/from Kampung Ayer's stilt villages. Getting in and out of them can sometimes be a bit of a balancing act, but they're lots of fun and only mildly life-threatening. Wave them down near the customs wharf or the Tamu Kianggeh food market or in front of the YSHHB Complex. Fares for short trips are between B$1 and B$2. To charter a boat for a tour of Kampung Ayer and the river shouldn't cost more than B$20 per hour.

AROUND BANDAR SERI BEGAWAN

None of Brunei's sights is more than a few hours from the capital, but a car is essential to reach most of them. There are some beaches and forest reserves that make pleasant day trips, and with some extra effort and expense you can take some river trips and visit a longhouse, a traditional-style communal tribal dwelling. For trekking and wildlife-viewing in pristine rainforest, head for Temburong, though to get into the national park and the Kuala Belalong Rainforest Field Studies Centre, you'll need to take a tour or get special permission from the Forestry Department (p530).

Jerudong Park Playground

The sultan presented the sprawling **Jerudong Park Playground** (☎ 261 1894; Jerudong; adult/child B$15/5; 🕑 5pm-midnight Wed-Fri & Sun) to his adoring subjects to mark his 48th birthday in 1994. The park is near the coast north of BSB and claims to be the biggest amusement park in the world (although the Disney Corporation may dispute this). It's certainly huge – even if the whole of Kampung Ayer turned up on a Sunday (unlikely), the place would probably still seem deserted. Chances are you'll have the place to yourself and it's a dreamworld for kids (and some adults). Sleeveless blouses or shirts are not allowed and proper footwear is required to board the rides. On Saturdays it's open until 2am and there are food and drink stalls in the parking lot.

It's easy to get to the playground – just take purple bus No 55 or 57 from the bus station – but the last bus leaves at 5.30pm and getting back to town can be a problem. Major hotels have shuttle services with prearranged pick-up times for about B$20 per person. A taxi back to BSB will cost about B$30 to B$35.

Beaches

Muara is a small container port at the top of the peninsula north of BSB. Two kilometres from town, **Pantai Muara** (Muara Beach) is a popular weekend retreat. The white sand is clean, but like many beaches in Borneo, it's littered with driftwood and other flotsam that comes in with the tide. It's quiet during the week and has food stalls, picnic tables and a children's playground.

Other beaches around Muara include **Pantai Serasa**, a thin bit of beach on an equally thin spit of land jutting out into the sea. The Royal Brunei Yacht Club is here, as well as a water sports centre and lots of food stalls on the weekend. About 4km west of Muara along the Muara–Tutong highway, **Pantai Meragang** is another beach that's pleasant and not quite as crowded as the others on weekends, though its local English name of Crocodile Beach may dissuade swimmers. There's a couple of food stalls and it's a good place for a picnic, but difficult to get to without your own transport.

Take bus No 37, 38 or 39 from BSB to Muara town (B$2); purple bus No 33 will take you from there to Pantai Muara or Pantai Serasa; the fare is B$1.

Pulau Selirong

This small island (25 sq km) off Brunei Bay, about one hour by boat from Muara, is on the itinerary of some tour companies for day trips. Tours leave early in the morning for the best opportunities to see wildlife (see p521 for details). The island is a good example of mangrove ecology and there's 2km of wooden walkways and an observation tower. A guide is necessary and caution is advised because of venomous snakes.

Tutong

Tutong is the main town in Tutong district and is about halfway between Seria and BSB. Buses to Seria pass by on the main highway, but if you want to see the attractions around Tutong the most feasible way is to rent a car.

PANTAI SERI KENANGAN

This popular beach (often simply referred to as Pantai Tutong) has picnic tables, and a simple restaurant and food hawkers on the weekend. It's on a spit of land with the ocean on one side and the pleasant vista of Sungai Tutong on the other. The white-sand, casuarina-lined beach is probably the best in Brunei. The royal family has a surprisingly modest **istana** at Pantai Seri Kenangan, which is a couple of kilometres off the highway just outside Tutong town. The turnoff to the beach is near the Tamu Tutong, where a **market** is held daily in the morning. The road to the beach continues for another 5km to Kuala Tutong; the beach at the end of the road is quiet and ideal for camping.

Tasik Merimbun

Tasik Merimbun, also known as Merimbun Heritage Park, is 27km inland from Tutong, and, at 7800 hectares, contains Brunei's largest lake. It's a pretty, tranquil spot surrounded by forest where you might see monkeys and birds. Wooden walkways lead around the shore to picnic pavilions and this picturesque, swampy lake has an island in the middle. There's a restaurant overlooking the lake near the car park.

The Tourist Information Centre in BSB (p517) has day trips to Merimbun for B$78 per person. The only way to get there on your own is by car and the road is a little rough in places.

Labi

East of Seria, a road branches inland to Labi. About halfway to Labi is the **Luagan Lalak Forest Reserve**, where there's a wetland that becomes a lake after it rains. A weathered wooden boardwalk traverses the area, crossing a brilliant green field of lush swamp grasses. About 10km further south, on the road to Kampung Labi, there are several modern, relatively small **Iban longhouses** open to visitors, including Rumah Panjang Mendaram Besar and Rumah Panjang Teraja. Off the road near here a trail through the forest leads to the **Wasai Wong Kadir**, a waterfall and crystal-clear pool. The trek takes around 45 minutes and is quite steep, but the pool is an apt reward.

There are more trekking possibilities south of Kampung Labi. A trail leads to **Rampayoh Waterfall**, about a 10km walk from the end of the sealed road south of Kampung Rampayoh. Further along the road, past Rumah Panjang Teraja, there's Sungai Teraja and a trail to another waterfall and **Bukit Teraja**, the highest hill in the area, with good views across Brunei and Sarawak. The main trail to the summit is signposted and starts about 6km beyond Rampayoh. The walk through primary forest takes about two hours to the top. Travel agencies do day trips to Bukit Teraja and charge between B$80 and B$100 per person. To get there on your own you'll need to rent a car.

For a more extensive trip to visit Dusun and Penan villages at Kampung Sukang and Kampung Melilas deep in the interior jungle along Sungai Belait you have to go by boat. The best place to hire a boat (expect to pay around B$300 per day) is at Kampung Sungai Mau, on the Labi road where it meets Sungai Belait before Luagan Lalak.

Seria

Seria is a transit stop on the road to Sarawak, a sprawling company town on the coast between Tutong and Kuala Belait. In fact, it's hard to tell where Seria ends and Kuala Belait begins. This is where Shell Brunei has its major installations and is home to the Gurkha troops that protect them and hundreds of houses where company staff live.

The coastal plain between here and Kuala Belait is the main centre for oil production in Brunei, and at a beach just outside of town the **Billionth Barrel Monument** commemorates the billionth barrel of oil produced at the Seria field. From the beach, oil rigs are visible jutting up on the horizon.

There are a few modern blocks of shops and a market, but the nearest accommodation is in Kuala Belait. If you're travelling by bus to Miri, you must change at Seria.

About 10 antiquated buses a day bounce along the road from BSB (B$6, 2 hours), with frequent departures on the half-hour between 7.30am and 5pm.

If you're going to Sarawak, you can buy your tickets all the way through to Miri from the bus station in Seria (see p525 for details).

Kuala Belait

The last town before Malaysia, Kuala Belait is the main town in Belait district and the place to get buses to Miri. 'KB' (not to be confused with Kuala Baram on the Sarawak side of the border) has colonial shophouses in the town centre and a reasonable beach, though most travellers just pass through on their way to or from Sarawak. The HSBC bank has an ATM, diagonally opposite the bus station on Jl McKerron.

You can hire a boat by the market for trips south up the river to **Kuala Balai**, a small river village that was once the largest settlement in the district. It's now almost deserted because the residents have left to find work in the oil industry on the coast. The 45-minute trip (one way) passes by lush jungle at the river's edge. Price is by negotiation, but expect to pay about B$150 each way.

EATING & SLEEPING

Government Rest House (☎ 333 4288; Jl Carey; r B$50; ❄) It's best to phone here before arriving. The rooms are comfortable and this place is right on the beach, a 10-minute walk along Jl McKerron from the bus station, then 200m to the right on Jl Carey.

Hotel Sentosa (☎ 333 4341; fax 333 1129; 92 Jl McKerron; s/d B$95/105; ❄) This hotel in town is near the bus station and is convenient if you miss your connections. The rooms are ordinary, but comfortable.

Seaview Hotel (☎ 333 2651; fax 334 2770; Jl Maulana; s/d B$95/115; ❄) About 4km out of town along the beach road towards Seria, this is probably the best place to stay if you're planning to do trips around Kuala Belait. Breakfast is included and there's a well-stocked supermarket frequented by expats. The hotel can also arrange car rental.

Kuala Belait has plenty of *kedai kopi* (coffee shops) within striking distance of the bus station.

GETTING THERE & AWAY

See p525 for details of buses to Kuala Belait and on to Miri.

From Kuala Belait it's a five-minute bus ride (20-minute walk) to Sungai Belait, where a car ferry plies back and forth to the other side. Once across the river it's a short ride to the Brunei immigration checkpoint. After going through Brunei customs a Malaysian bus takes passengers to the Malaysian immigration checkpoint. From here it's a short ride to the queue at Sungai Baram, which usually takes 15 to 30 minutes to cross.

TEMBURONG

Covered by lush tropical rainforest, Temburong district is the eastern slice of Brunei, surrounded by Sarawak and cut off from the sultanate when Raja Brooke grabbed what is now the Limbang district. Temburong has little industry or development and much of it is unspoilt forest, which the government has recently began promoting as an adventure tourism destination.

Bangar is the main town, a backwater reached by boat from BSB and the base for trips into the Temburong district. The boat trip itself is great, roaring down Sungai Brunei and into the open sea, then weaving through the maze of dense mangroves fringing Brunei Bay into the mouth of Sungai

Temburong. Sitting on the roof of the boat is like going on a minor ride at Jerudong Park, but make sure you use plenty of sunscreen.

Bangar can be visited as a day trip from BSB if you catch an early boat. The Peradayan Forest Reserve is a good outing for a jungle walk, or you can visit the Iban longhouse at Batang Duri. For a longer and richer jungle experience, Ulu Temburong National Park and the Kuala Belalong Rainforest Field Studies Centre in the Batu Apoi Forest Reserve receive visitors, but you must obtain a permit for the reserve from the **Forestry Department** (BSB ☎ 238 1687; Bangar ☎ 522 1839) or go in with a tour (p521). Brunei also has an **Outward Bound centre** (www.kkbs.gov.bn/program.htm) on Sungai Temburong offering outdoor adventure programs.

It's not necessary to take a tour to visit the Peradayan Reserve: you can pick up a permit at the entrance.

From Bangar it's possible to travel overland to Sarawak, either west to Limbang or east to Lawas.

Bangar

Bangar is a sleepy, pleasant little town on the banks of Sungai Temburong. It's the district centre and has a row of shops, a mosque and government offices, and a couple of coffee shops, which also have information about arranging transport.

The immigration office is a few kilometres west of Bangar on the way to Limbang; it's open from 6am to 10pm daily.

SLEEPING & EATING

Bangar Resthouse (☎ 522 1239; Jl Batang Duri; dm/s/d B$10/25/30; chalets B$80; ❄) Dormitory-style rooms here have six beds and a shared bathroom. The resthouse is opposite the covered market and food stalls. Head west up the main road from the boat wharf about 300m and turn left at the Jl Batang Duri turn-off.

Youth Hostel (☎ 522 1694; dm B$10-15; ❄) This hostel was being renovated at the time of writing and air-conditioning was being installed. Heading west from the boat wharf it's a 300m walk up the main road, which continues on to the western border with Sarawak. Walk past the row of shops and look for the hostel on your right, on the north side of the street.

A local Iban named Labar who runs **Labar Bin Hussin Traditional Crafts** (☎ 522 2258, 885 5980; 5 Kedat Rakya) can arrange for people to stay at longhouses and learn about forest traditions of the Iban and other tribes. He may also have a four-bedroom house available for accommodation by the time you read this. Expect to pay around B$5 to B$10 to stay at a longhouse and more for a complete program which includes a translator/guide. Labar's shop is off the main road leading from the boat wharf, in front of the new mini-mart at the end of the row of shops.

Bangar Restoran (☎ 522 1341; dishes B$2.50-7) Look for this *kedai kopi* up the road from the boat wharf past the shops. It's a good spot to sit with a coffee or a cold drink and get all the information you need about what to do around Bangar. If no one here can answer your questions they'll certainly find someone who can.

GETTING THERE & AWAY

Boat

From BSB, speedboats leave when they're full from the wharf near the food centre (B$6, 45 minutes). If you're coming back to BSB, buy a return ticket for B$12. Boats leave BSB and Bangar approximately every 30 minutes between 7am and 5pm.

Hitching

Hitchhiking is possible, though you may be in for a wait, especially on the way back from Batang Duri. The road to the Peradayan Forest Reserve – and Lawas – is across the bridge from Bangar wharf on the east side of the river.

Taxi

Temburong has two main roads; both are sealed but traffic is light. One leads south to Batang Duri and the other runs between the east and west borders with Sarawak.

Taxis are the only form of transport in the district and they congregate near the wharf. They don't have meters and prices must be negotiated.

Taxis go to Limbang in Sarawak for about B$15. There's no border post, so make sure you stop at the immigration office in Bangar before leaving Brunei. Report to immigration in Limbang.

It's possible, but expensive, to cross the eastern border to Lawas in Sarawak. A taxi to Lawas costs about B$80, including a trip to the immigration office near Bangar. In

Lawas, clear immigration at the jetty where the Brunei ferries tie up. From Lawas you can proceed on to Sabah.

Batang Duri

Batang Duri is an Iban longhouse on Sungai Temburong, 17km south of Bangar. Boats to the Kuala Belalong Rainforest Field Studies Centre leave from the village jetty. If you visit the longhouse, introduce yourself first, preferably to the *penghulu* (chief). Take your shoes off when you enter and don't wander up and down the veranda; this is like walking unannounced into someone's living room. Batang Duri can be visited as a day trip or as part of a tour, but overnight stays must be pre-arranged. Check with Labar at Labar Bin Hussin Traditional Crafts for more information about where to stay (p529) for information about where to stay. A taxi to Batang Duri from Bangar costs B$15 each way.

Batu Apoi Forest Reserve

This reserve protects a large area of primary rainforest that covers most of southern Temburong, and includes **Ulu Temburong National Park**. A permit is required to visit the reserve. Travellers usually take a tour, though you could try phoning the **Forestry Department** (BSB ☎ 238 1687; Bangar ☎ 522 1839) to inquire about individual permits. As travel within the park requires hiring a boat, it may be easier to go on a tour.

Tour companies in BSB (p517) can arrange accommodation at the Field Studies Centre. With a minimum of two people, prices start at B$198 per person for a two-day trip, which includes staying overnight at a Murut village on the way up the Sungai Temburong and a day trip to the national park.

KUALA BELALONG RAINFOREST FIELD STUDIES CENTRE

This scientific research centre is in Ulu Temburong National Park, and was developed by Brunei Shell and the Universiti Brunei Darussalam to provide facilities for research into tropical rainforest. It's primarily for scientists and is visited by school groups, though interested overseas visitors can stay at the centre, usually arranged through a tour.

The forest is rich in flora and fauna, and the jungle can be explored along walking trails. The main trail is a rugged two-day walk to Bukit Belalong, and there's a canopy walkway that's among the longest in the world.

Access to the centre is by longboat from Batang Duri and costs about B$150.

Peradayan Forest Reserve

This forest reserve is about 15km from Bangar along the road to Labu. It protects the forested peaks of Bukit Patoi and Bukit Peradayan. Walking trails lead to the summits and this is the most accessible rainforest for visitors to Brunei. You'll have to start early to maximise chances of seeing the mainly nocturnal mammals, but the park also contains many bird species, including hornbills.

The most popular walk is to **Bukit Patoi**, and starts at the entrance to the park. The trail is steep in parts but is well marked, with rest huts along the way. The plank walkway was badly in need of repair in 2003, so watch out for broken areas. It's about a 20-minute walk to Batu Berdinding, a sandstone outcrop, and then another hour to the summit. From the summit there are fine views to the east across the South China Sea and the Lawas area of Sarawak. Most walkers descend back along the trail, but it's possible to continue over the other side of the summit and around to **Bukit Peradayan**. This trail is harder and indistinct in parts, though trees are marked to show the way. The trail eventually rejoins the road, 12km from Bangar near the Labu Km 5 marker. Allow at least three hours for the walk from Bukit Patoi to Bukit Peradayan and back to the road.

There are picnic tables and a toilet block at the start of the trail, but bring water and food for the walk. The return taxi trip from Bangar should cost around B$30. The driver will wait for you to do the summit walk, or if you want to spend more time in the reserve, arrange for a pick-up.

Directory

CONTENTS

ACCOMMODATION

The region's accommodation possibilities range from rock-bottom budget to luxurious international-standard hotels. Most hotels quote similar prices for single and double rooms, so it is a lot cheaper to travel with another person. Singapore and, particularly, Brunei have less selection at the budget end of the market.

It's worth knowing that outside the peak holiday seasons (around major festivals such as Chinese New Year in January/February) big discounts are frequently available at the region's hotels – it's always worth asking about special offers.

Throughout this book we have divided accommodation into budget, mid-range and top-end categories; the corresponding price ranges are detailed below.

MALAYSIA

In Malaysia, budget places are those under RM60 per room; at such hotels and guesthouses don't expect much in the way of comfort, although most will offer a choice of rooms with or without air-conditioning and with or without attached bathrooms.

In mid-range (RM60 to RM200) you'll get more for your money with the better places offering pleasant extras such as swimming pools, nicely designed rooms, and facilities such as restaurants and business centres. All top-end establishments (RM200 and above) will have such facilities, and much more as a matter of course.

A 5% government tax applies to all hotel rooms. On top of this there's a 10% service charge in all top-end places. You are not expected to tip in addition to this.

Top-end places sometimes quote prices exclusive of tax and service charge – these charges are represented as ++ (called plus-plus), for example RM120++ for a double. Net means that tax and any service charges are included – these are the prices quoted in most budget (and some mid-range) places. Tax and service charges are also applied to food, drinks and services in the more expensive hotels and restaurants. We quote net prices for all budget and mid-range places.

SINGAPORE

In Singapore, budget-hotel prices are under S$60 a night per room, mid-range is S$60 to S$200 and top end is over S$200. The charging system is similar to Malaysia's, except it's +++, which covers 10% service charge, 5% Goods and Services Tax (GST) and 1% government tax; again a net price means all taxes are included – we quote net prices for all budget and mid-range places.

BRUNEI

In Brunei budget places are under B$60, mid-range is B$60 to B$150; and top end is over B$150. Most prices are quoted net, with only some of the top-end places adding 10% for government tax.

PRACTICALITIES

Electricity

- You'll need the UK-type three-square-pin plug to connect to the region's reliable electricity supply (220–240V, 50 cycles).

Newspapers

- Read Malaysia's English-language newspapers including the *New Straits Times*, the *Star* and the *Malay Mail*.
- In Malaysian Borneo there are dailies such as the *Borneo Post* and the *Sarawak Tribune*.
- In Singapore try the *Straits Times*, the afternoon tabloid *New Paper* and *Today*, a free paper available at the Mass Rapid Transit (MRT) stations.
- The *Borneo Bulletin* is Brunei's English-language daily.

Radio

- Listen to Radio Malaysia's three main radio stations: HITZ FM (92.9 FM; top 40), MIX FM (94.5 FM; adult contemporary) and Light & Easy FM (105.7 FM; easy listening). Note that the frequencies given are for the KL area, and may differ in other parts of Malaysia. These stations are not available in Malaysian Borneo.
- Singapore offers a wide range of radio stations, including five English-language ones: Gold 90.5FM, Symphony 92.4FM, NewsRadio 93.8FM, Class 95FM and Perfect 10 98.7FM. Private stations include Passion 99.5FM, which is an arts and world music station, and Safra Radio's English-language Power 98FM, a 24-hour station aimed at the 18- to 35-year-old market.
- In Brunei, English radio broadcasts can be heard on the FM bands Pilihan Network and Pelangi Network. London's Capital Radio and Capital Gold can also be picked up on the FM band.

Television

- Switch on the box to watch Malaysia's two government television channels, TV1 and TV2, and two commercial stations, TV3 and NTV7.
- Singapore has seven free-to-air channels: Channel 5 (English); Channel 8 (Mandarin); Suria (Malay-language programmes); Central (the arts channel in English, plus a section of children's programming and Indian-language broadcasts); Channel News Asia, a news and information channel; Channel i, a general entertainment channel broadcasting mainly movies and news; and Channel U, the Mandarin-language channel.
- In Brunei, RTB can be received on Channel 5.

Videos

- Buy or watch videos in the PAL system.

Weights & Measures

- Use the metric system for weights and measures.

Camping

Many of Malaysia's national parks have official camping grounds and will permit camping in nondesignated sites once you are deep in the jungle. There are also many lonely stretches of beach, particularly on the east coast of the peninsula, which are ideal for camping. Likewise, it is possible to camp on uninhabited bays on many of Malaysia's islands. If you do decide to camp in Malaysia, a two-season tent with mosquito netting is ideal. A summer-weight sleeping bag is OK, but the best choice is a lightweight bag-liner, since even the nights are warm.

In Singapore, the **National Parks Board** (☎ 6391 4488; www.nparks.gov.sg; 18-01/08 Gateway West, 150 Beach Rd) administers several free camp sites around the island, including at East Coast Park and Pasir Ris Park. The best place for camping is on Sentosa Island. See the Camping boxed text (p483) in the Singapore chapter.

Hostels & Guesthouses

At beach centres and in the major tourist cities of Malaysia there's a variety of cheap accommodation that can be grouped together under the terms hostels and guesthouses. These may be huts on the beach, private homes or rented houses divided by partition walls into a number of rooms. Dormitory accommodation is usually available. Rooms are spartan, but this is the cheapest accommodation around and often the nicest, with a real family atmosphere. These places often cater only to foreign travellers and offer their customers lots of little extras, such as free tea and coffee, bicycles and transport, to outdo the competition. A dorm bed will cost RM6 to RM10, and rooms will cost from RM12, up to RM60 for a hotel-style room with air-con.

Hotels

Standard rooms at top-end hotels are often called 'superior' in the local parlance. Most hotels have slightly more expensive 'deluxe' or 'club' rooms, which tend to be larger, have a better view, and include extras such as breakfast or free Internet access. Many also have suites.

At the low end of the price scale are the traditional Chinese hotels. They are generally fairly spartan – bare floors and just a bed, a couple of chairs and a table, a wardrobe and a sink. The showers and toilets (which will sometimes be Asian squat-style) may be down the corridor. A point to note: couples can sometimes economise by asking for a single, since in Chinese-hotel language 'single' means one double bed, and 'double' means two beds. Don't think of this as being tight; in Chinese hotels you can pack as many into one room as you wish.

The main catch with these hotels is that they can sometimes be terribly noisy. They're often on main streets, and Chinese hotels on the bottom rung of the ladder have a serious design flaw – the walls rarely reach the ceiling. The top is simply meshed or barred in. This is great for ventilation but terrible for acoustics. Every noise carries throughout the hotel, and guests all

GRAND HOTELS & LUXURY RESORTS

Fancy a spot of pampering? Then you've come to the right place – choose from grand colonial-era hotels, glitzy beach resorts and jungle or mountain hideaways.

Live it up in grand colonial style at Singapore's **Raffles Hotel** (p460), Penang's the **E&O** (p168) and KL's **Carcosa Seri Negara** (p91). For luxurious getaways, kick back at the **Pangkor Laut Resort** (p143) on Pulau Pangkor, the **Datai** (p194) on Langkawi, the **Aryani Resort** (p292) in a secluded corner of Terengganu, or the **Beaufort** (p486) on Singapore's Sentosa Island. Over in Sabah, the **Borneo Rainforest Lodge** (p436) combines comfort with the eco-tourism experience, while Brunei's glittering **Empire Hotel** (p523) is fit for a sultan.

wake to a terrible dawn chorus of hawking, coughing and spitting.

Longhouses in Malaysian Borneo

Longhouses are the traditional dwellings of the indigenous peoples of Borneo. These communal dwellings may contain up to 100 individual family 'apartments' under one long roof. The most important area of a longhouse is the common veranda, which serves as a social area. These days there are two main types of longhouse: tourist longhouses and authentic longhouses. While a visit to a tourist longhouse is arranged easily enough, it is unlikely to be of much interest. A visit to an authentic, living longhouse can be a magical experience, but it is easier said than done – one does not merely show up on the veranda with a carton of cigarettes and expect to be welcomed inside. Indeed, there is a very specific etiquette to visiting a longhouse. For details, see the Longhouse Visits boxed text (p340) in the Sarawak chapter.

Resthouses

Some of the old British-developed resthouses in Malaysia are still operating. These were set up during the colonial era to provide accommodation for travelling officials, and later provided excellent shelter for all types of travellers. Many of the resthouses are still government-owned but are now privately operated. Some have been turned into mid-range resorts, but many retain old colonial decor. The average price for a room in a resthouse is RM70, and this usually includes air-con and attached bathroom.

ACTIVITIES

Malaysia and the region offer a great range of activities, from craft classes to caving. The following is a brief list of some of the more popular activities.

Bird-Watching

Malaysia's tropical jungles and islands are home to a tremendous variety of bird species. On the peninsula, Taman Negara (p267), Kenong Rimba State Park (p277) and Endau-Rompin National Park (p244) all offer excellent bird-watching. In Malaysian Borneo, Mt Kinabalu (p414), Gunung Mulu (p371), Similajau National Park (p358) and Gunung Gading (p343) are similarly rich in bird species.

In Singapore, the wetlands of the Sungei Buloh Wetland Reserve (p469) shouldn't be missed by twitchers. See the Environment chapter (p53) for information on the region's bird species.

Cycling

Malaysia is one of the best places in Southeast Asia for bike touring. Perhaps the most popular route is the one up the east coast of Peninsular Malaysia, with its relatively quiet roads. However, if you're fit and energetic, you may prefer the hillier regions of the peninsula's interior or Malaysian Borneo.

Caving

Malaysia's limestone hills are riddled with caves *(gua)* to lure spelunkers. Some of these are easily accessible and can be visited without any special equipment or preparation while others are strictly the terrain of the experienced caver. There are caves on the peninsula – Gua Charas (p261), Gua Musang (p312) and in Taman Negara (p271), among others – and dotted around Malaysian Borneo, including one of the world's premier caving destinations, Gunung Mulu National Park (p372).

Diving & Snorkelling

With its tropical location and wealth of islands, it's not surprising that Malaysia has some great snorkelling and diving. The main centres include Pulau Perhentian (p296), Pulau Redang (p292), Pulau Tioman (p252), the Seribuat Archipelago (p243) and Pulau Sipadan (p438). While neither as cheap as Thailand nor as spectacular as Indonesia, reasonable prices, good variety and easy access make diving in Malaysia a good choice for both first-timers and old hands. Dives can be arranged in Singapore and Brunei, too, but you'll find prices cheaper in Malaysia.

Located in a series of marine parks established in the 1970s and 1980s, most of Malaysia's dive sites are now protected from the destructive activities of the past, such as dynamite fishing, collection of rare species and pollution from motorboat engines, that wreaked havoc on coral reefs. Reefs are regenerating and the diving industry is booming. There's an RM5 entry fee to dive in any of Malaysia's marine parks, but there's often no-one around to collect the money.

Island-based boat dives are the most common, but a few areas, like Sabah's Pulau Sipadan (Sipadan Island), have some great sites right off the beach. Also increasing is the number of live-aboards that take divers to previously inaccessible spots. Most sites are over fairly shallow reefs, but there are also a couple of islands with deep drop-offs and even a few wreck dives in Malaysian Borneo.

The standards of diving facilities in Malaysia are generally quite high and equipment rental is widely available. Most places offer instruction leading to Professional Association of Diving Instructors (PADI) certification (which will then allow you to dive), and this certification is almost universally recognised. While it is possible simply to show up and dive at some of the larger dive centres like Pulau Tioman, it is usually a good idea to make arrangements in advance, if only to avoid waiting a day or two before starting.

Most dive centres charge around RM180 to RM250 for two dives, including equipment rental. PADI open-water courses average around RM800. Many resorts and dive operators also offer all-inclusive dive packages, which vary widely in price.

The northeast monsoon brings strong winds and rain to the east coast of Peninsular Malaysia from early November

RESPONSIBLE DIVING

Please consider the following tips when diving or snorkelling, and help preserve the ecology and beauty of the reefs:

- Do not use anchors on the reef, and take care not to ground boats on coral. Encourage dive operators and regulatory bodies to establish permanent moorings at popular dive sites.
- Avoid touching living marine organisms with your body, or dragging equipment across the reef. Polyps can be damaged by even the gentlest contact. Never stand on coral, even if it looks solid and robust. If you must hold onto the reef, touch only exposed rock or dead coral.
- Be conscious of your fins. Even without contact the surge from heavy fin strokes near the reef can damage delicate organisms. When treading water in shallow reef areas, take care not to kick up clouds of sand. Settling sand can easily smother the delicate organisms of the reef.
- Practise and maintain proper buoyancy control. Major damage can be done by divers descending too fast and colliding with the reef. Make sure you are correctly weighted and that your weight belt is positioned so that you stay horizontal. If you have not dived for a while, have a practice dive in a pool before taking to the reef. Be aware that buoyancy can change over the period of an extended trip: initially you may breathe harder and need more weight; a few days later you may breathe more easily and need less weight.
- Take great care in underwater caves. Spend as little time in them as possible as your air bubbles may be caught within the roof and thereby leave previously submerged organisms high and dry. Taking turns to inspect the interior of a small cave will lessen the chances of damaging contact.
- Resist the temptation to collect or buy coral or shells. Apart from the ecological damage, taking home marine souvenirs depletes the beauty of a site and spoils the enjoyment of others. The same goes for marine archaeological sites (mainly shipwrecks). Respect their integrity; some sites are even protected from looting by law.
- Ensure that you take home all your rubbish and any litter you may find. Plastics in particular are a serious threat to marine life. Turtles can mistake plastic for jellyfish and eat it.
- Resist the temptation to feed fish. You may disturb their normal eating habits, encourage aggressive behaviour or feed them food that is detrimental to their health.
- Minimise your disturbance of marine animals. In particular, do not ride on the backs of turtles as this causes them great anxiety.

to late February, during which time most dive centres simply shut down. Visibility improves after the monsoon, peaking in August and September. On the west coast conditions are reversed and the best diving is from September to March.

In Malaysian Borneo the monsoons are less pronounced and rain falls more evenly throughout the year. However, the same general seasons apply, with the best diving on the east coast from May to October and on the west from October to March.

Jungle Trekking

Despite the pressures of logging, Malaysia is still home to some of the world's most impressive stands of virgin tropical jungle. Almost all of Malaysia's national parks offer excellent jungle-trekking, including Taman Negara (p271) on the peninsula and Gunung Mulu National Park (p374) in Malaysian Borneo. There are treks to suit all levels of ability, from 20-minute jaunts to 10-day expeditions.

Singapore doesn't offer anything on the same scale as Malaysia, but there are some good day-walks in the Bukit Timah Nature Reserve (p468) and the Central Catchment Reserve around MacRitchie Reservoir (p469).

Brunei has treks in the Peradayan Forest Reserve (p530).

Mountain Climbing

Mt Kinabalu (p414) is an obvious choice for those interested in mountain climbing. However, this is not the only mountain worth climbing in Malaysia. Gunung Mulu (p374), in Sarawak's Gunung Mulu National Park, is a challenging four-day climb. On the peninsula, there are several good climbs in Taman Negara, including Gunung Tahan (p272) which stands at 2187m. There are also a few lesser peaks scattered around that make pleasant day-outings. Keen mountain climbers should try to pick up a copy of *Mountains of Malaysia – A Practical Guide and Manual* by John Briggs.

Water-Sports

In Singapore water-skiing and wakeboarding (water-skiing on a single surfboard-like ski) can be arranged at the Singapore Water Ski Federation, while windsurfing equipment is available at East Coast Park and on Sentosa Island. See Water Sports (p475) in the Singapore chapter.

BUSINESS HOURS

Malaysia

Government offices are usually open from 8am to 4.15pm Monday to Friday. Most close for lunch from 12.45pm to 2pm, and on Friday the lunch break is from 12.15pm to 2.45pm for Friday prayers at the mosque. The offices are open from 8am to 12.45pm on Saturday.

Bank hours are generally 10am to 3pm on weekdays and 9.30am to 11.30am on Saturday.

Shop hours are variable, although a good rule of thumb for small shops is that they're open from 9am to 6pm from Monday to Saturday. Major department stores, shopping malls, Chinese emporiums and some large stores are open from around 10am until 9pm or 10pm, seven days a week.

Most of Malaysia follows this working week: Monday to Friday, with Saturday a half-day. But in the more Islamic-minded states of Kedah, Perlis, Kelantan and Terengganu, government offices, banks and many shops are closed on Friday and on Saturday afternoon. These states have declared Friday the holiday, and their working week is from Saturday to Thursday, which is a half-day. However, federal government offices follow the same hours as the rest of the country.

Singapore

Government offices are usually open from Monday to Friday, and on Saturday morning. Hours vary, starting at around 7.30am to 9.30am and closing between 4pm and 6pm. On Saturday, closing time is between 11.30am and 1pm.

Shop hours are similar to those in Malaysia. Most small shops in Chinatown and Arab St close on Sunday, though Sunday is the busiest shopping day in Little India. Banks are open from 9.30am to 3pm weekdays (to 11.30am on Saturday).

Brunei

Government offices are open from 7.45am to 12.15pm and 1.30pm to 4.30pm (closed on Friday and Sunday); private-business offices are generally open from 8am to 5pm Monday to Friday and from 8am to noon on Saturday. Banks are open from 9am to 3pm weekdays and from 9am to 11am on Saturday. Most shops in the central area of Bandar Seri Begawan open daily around 9am and are closed by 6pm. Shopping malls generally open an hour or so later and close between 9.30pm and 10pm (some may close earlier on Sunday). In major shopping precincts, such as Jl Tutong and in Gadong, shops stay open until 9pm or 9.30pm. Hours may be shorter during the fasting month of Ramadan.

CHILDREN

Practicalities

Travelling with children in Malaysia, Singapore and Brunei can be a lot of fun as long as you come with the right attitudes and the usual parental patience. *Travel with Children* by Cathy Lanigan and others contains useful advice on how to cope with kids on the road and what to bring along to make things go more smoothly, with special attention paid to travelling in developing countries.

There are discounts for children for most attractions and for most transport in Malaysia, Singapore and Brunei. Many beach resorts have special family chalets. Chinese hotels are also a good bargain as they charge by the room rather than the number of people. Cots, however, are not widely available

JUNGLE TREKKING TIPS

Jungle trekking can be one of the true highlights of a trip to Malaysia. To the uninitiated, however, it can be something of a shock – like marching all day in a sauna with a heavy pack strapped to your back. The following guidelines will help to make the experience as painless as possible. See the boxed text That Clinging Feeling in the Health chapter, p579, for information on how to deal with leeches.

- On overnight trips, bring two sets of clothing: one for hiking and one to put on at the end of the day (keep your night kit in a plastic bag so that it stays dry). Within minutes of starting out, your hiking kit will be drenched and it will stay that way throughout your trip. If you'll be travelling through dense vegetation, wear long trousers and a long-sleeved shirt. Otherwise, shorts and a T-shirt will suffice. Whatever you wear, make sure that it's loose fitting.
- Drink plenty of water. If you're going long distances, you'll have to bring a water filter or a water purification agent like iodine (most people opt for the latter to keep carrying weight down).
- Get in shape long before coming to Malaysia and start slowly – try a day hike before setting out on a longer trek.
- Take a guide if you're setting off on a longer and/or lesser-travelled trek.
- Bring talcum powder to cope with the chafing caused by wet undergarments. Wearing loose underwear (or better yet, no underwear at all) will also help prevent chafing.
- If you wear glasses, be sure to treat them with an anti-fog solution (ask at the shop where you buy your glasses). Otherwise, you may find yourself blinded by steamed-up glasses soon after setting out.

in cheap accommodation. Public transport is comfortable and relatively well organised, although pushing a stroller around isn't likely to be easy given there are often no footpaths and kerbs are high.

Baby formula, baby food and nappies (diapers) are widely available across the region. However, it makes sense to stock up on these items before heading to remote destinations or islands.

For the most part, parents needn't be overly concerned, though it pays to lay down a few ground rules – such as regular hand-washing – to head off potential problems. All the usual health precautions apply (see the Health chapter, p580); children should especially be warned not to play with animals, as rabies occurs in Malaysia.

If you're travelling with children, a useful website for general information and ideas is www.travelwithyourkids.com.

Sights & Activities

Some beach destinations suitable for families with younger children include Pulau Perhentian (p294), Pulau Kapas (p285) and Tunku Abdul Rahman National Park (p398). Those with older children might enjoy some of the jungle parks of the country, including Taman Negara (p267) and, over in Sarawak, the Bako (p334) and Gunung Mulu (p371) national parks. You might also want to consider the Sepilok Orang-Utan Rehabilitation Centre (p429) in Sabah.

Singapore is a very child-friendly place (the government actively encourages couples to have children) so you'll have no problem entertaining the kids at attractions such as the zoo (p467) and bird park (p470) or on Sentosa Island (p472). A day biking around Pulau Ubin (p467) or along the East Coast Park (p466) is also recommended.

Brunei's top kids' attraction is the Jerudong Park Playground (p526), a largely free funfair – a present from the sultan to his people.

CLIMATE

Malaysia, Singapore and Brunei have a typically tropical climate – it's hot and humid year-round. The temperature rarely drops below 20°C, even at night, and usually climbs to 30°C or more during the day. The tropics can take some adjusting to.

Take it easy when you first arrive and try to avoid running around in the heat of the midday sun.

Rain tends to arrive in brief torrential downpours and is soon replaced by more of that ever-present sunshine. At certain times of the year it may rain every day, but it rarely rains all day. Although the region is monsoonal, it's only the east coast of Peninsular Malaysia that has a real rainy season – elsewhere it's just a time of year when the average rainfall is heavier than at other times of the year.

Throughout the region the humidity tends to hover around the 90% mark, but on the peninsula you can always escape from heat and humidity by retreating to the delightfully cool hill stations.

For tips on the best times to visit, see When to Go (p13) in the Getting Started chapter.

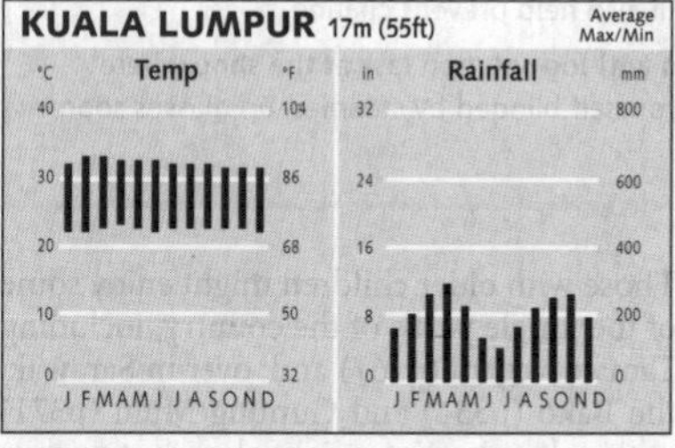

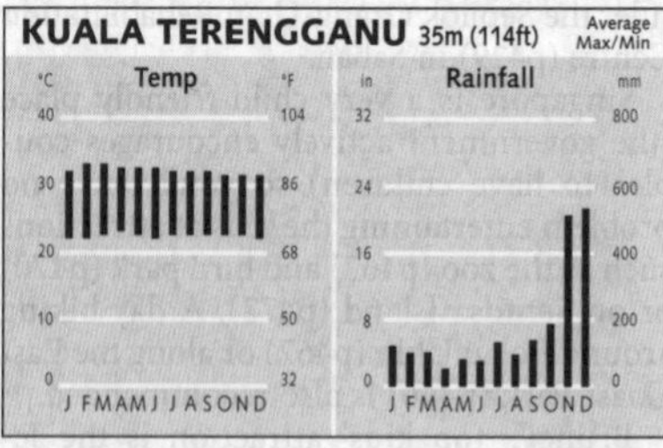

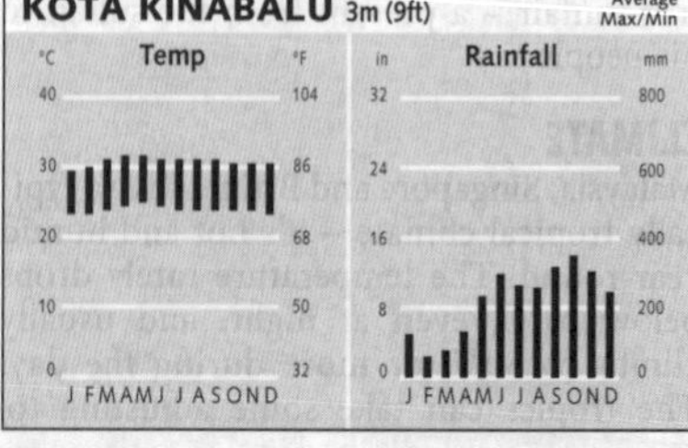

CUSTOMS

Malaysia

The following can be brought into Malaysia duty free: 1L of alcohol, 225g of tobacco (200 cigarettes or 50 cigars) and souvenirs and gifts not exceeding RM200 (RM500 when coming from Labuan or Langkawi). Cameras, portable radios, perfume, cosmetics and watches do not incur duty.

The list of prohibited items: counterfeit currency, weapons (including imitations), fireworks, drugs and 'obscene and prejudicial articles' (pornography, for example, and items that may be considered inflammatory, or disruptive to Malaysia's ethnic harmony).

Visitors can carry only RM1000 in and out of Malaysia; there is no limit on foreign currency. When you enter Malaysia, you must fill out a Currency Declaration Form on which you are required to declare both the amount of ringgit notes, if the figure exceeds RM1000, and any amount of foreign currency you are carrying. Keep this form in your passport as you must produce it when leaving Malaysia.

Drug trafficking carries the death penalty.

Singapore

Visitors to Singapore are allowed to bring in 1L of wine, beer or spirits duty-free. Electronic goods, cosmetics, watches, cameras, jewellery (but not imitation jewellery), footwear, toys, arts and crafts are not dutiable; the usual duty-free concession for personal effects, such as clothes, applies. Singapore does not allow duty-free concessions for cigarettes and tobacco.

Duty-free concessions are not available if you are arriving from Malaysia or if you leave Singapore for less than 48 hours (so you cannot stock up on duty-free goods on a day trip to Batam in Indonesia).

Illicit drugs, firecrackers, play currency and coins, obscene or seditious material, gun-shaped cigarette lighters, endangered species and their by-products, pirated recordings and publications, and retail quantities of chewing gum are prohibited. If you bring in prescription drugs, you should have a doctor's letter or a prescription confirming that they are necessary. There is no restriction on the importation of currency.

Drug trafficking carries the death penalty.

Brunei

Duty-free allowances for persons over 17 years of age are 200 cigarettes or 250g of tobacco, 60ml of perfume and 250ml of eau de toilette. Non-Muslims may import two bottles of liquor (about 2L) and 12 cans of beer, which must be declared upon arrival.

The importation of drugs carries the death penalty.

DANGERS & ANNOYANCES

Operators mentioned in this book have been personally checked by the authors and should be reliable. However, you should always check terms and conditions carefully.

Animal Hazards

The chances of being savaged by a tiger or other wild cat in the Malaysian jungle are pretty close to impossible. You should certainly keep an eye out for snakes though (see the Health chapter for details on how to deal with snake bites, p580). Rabies occurs in Malaysia, so any bite from an animal should be treated very seriously.

Scams

When in Kuala Lumpur (KL) beware of scams. Many of these involve card games or the purchase of large amounts of gold jewellery. Still others involve people who claim to have a relative studying abroad; these always start with the scammer asking you where you come from – the best answer is none at all.

Theft & Violence

None of the countries covered in this book are theft or violence-prone – compared with Indonesia or Thailand they are extremely safe. Nevertheless, it pays to keep a close eye on your belongings, especially your travel documents (passport, travellers cheques etc), which should be kept with you at all times. We've had reports of bag snatchings by thieves on motorbikes – particularly in (KL); carry your bags on the side facing away from the road and be aware that such attacks can happen.

Credit card fraud is a growing problem in Malaysia. Use your cards only at established businesses and guard your credit card numbers closely.

A small, sturdy padlock is well worth carrying, especially if you are going to be staying at any of the cheap chalets found on Malaysia's beaches, where flimsy padlocks are the norm.

While Malaysia is generally safe for travellers of both sexes, physical attacks have been known to occur, particularly after hours and in the poorer, run-down areas of cities. It's a good idea to avoid all street demonstrations in Malaysia – public gatherings of over three people need police permission and there have been ugly clashes in the past.

> **TRAVEL ADVISORIES**
>
> The SARS health crisis and terrorist attacks in the region have put Malaysia and Singapore on several countries' watch lists. For latest travel advisories check the following websites:
>
> **Australia** (www.dfat.gov/travel/)
> **Canada** (www.voyage.gc.ca)
> **New Zealand** (www.mft.govt.nz)
> **UK** (www.fco.gov.uk/travel)
> **US** (travel.state.gov/travel_warnings.html)

DISABLED TRAVELLERS

For the mobility impaired, Malaysia can be a nightmare. In most cities and towns there are often no footpaths, kerbs are very high, construction sites are everywhere, and crossings are few and far between. On the upside, the modern urban rail lines in KL are at least reasonably accessible, and both Malaysia Airlines and KTM (the national rail service) offer 50% discounts on travel for disabled travellers.

Similarly, if you're confined to a wheelchair, travelling around Singapore will be a chore. Check out *Access Singapore*, a useful guidebook for the disabled produced by the Singapore Council of Social Services. It is available from Singapore Tourism Board (STB) offices, or contact the **National Council of Social Services** (☎ 6336 1544; www.ncss.org.sg).

Three travel-information sources for the mobility-impaired:

Global Access Disability Travel Network (www.geocities.com/Paris/1502/)
Holiday Care Service (☎ 01293-774535, fax 784647; Imperial Buildings, Victoria Rd, Horley, Surrey, RH6 7PZ, England)
Mobility USA (☎ 1-541 343 1284; PO Box 1076, Eugene, OR 97440, USA)

DISCOUNT CARDS

A Hostelling International (HI) card is of limited use in Malaysia, as only KL, Melaka and Port Dickson have HI hostels, though the card can also be used to waive the small initial membership fee at some YMCAs and YWCAs. Bring it if you have one.

An international student identity card (ISIC) is worth bringing. Many student discounts, such as for train travel, are available only for Malaysian students, but some places do offer discounts for international students.

In Singapore, visitors over 55 are eligible for discounts at many attractions and for tours, upon presentation of a passport or other form of identity with the date of birth on it.

EMBASSIES & CONSULATES

Malaysia

Malaysian Embassies & Consulates

For a full list of Malaysian embassies and consulates outside the country check out www.tourism.gov.my.

Australia (☎ 02-6273 1543; 7 Perth Ave, Yarralumla, ACT 2600)

Brunei (☎ 02-345652; 27 & 29 Simpang 396-39 Kampung Sungai Akar, Jl Kebangsaan, Bandar Seri Begawan)

Canada (☎ 613-241 5182; 60 Boteler St, Ottawa, ON K1N 8Y7)

France (☎ 01-45 53 11 85; 2, bis rue Benouville, Paris 75116)

Germany (☎ 030-885 7490; Klingelhofer Strasse 6, 10785 Berlin)

Indonesia (☎ 021-522 4947; Jl HR Rasuna Said Kav X/6, No 1-2 Kuningan, Jakarta Selatan, Jakarta)

Netherlands (☎ 070-350 6506; Rustenburgweg 2, 2517 KE, The Hague)

New Zealand (☎ 04-3852 4399; 10 Washington Ave, Brooklyn, Wellington)

Thailand (☎ 0 2679 2190; 35 South Sathorn Rd, Tungamahamek, Bangkok 10120)

UK (☎ 020-7235 8033; 45-46 Belgrave Square, London SW1X 8QT)

USA (☎ 202-328 2700; 2401 Massachusetts Ave NW, Washington DC 20008)

Embassies & Consulates in Malaysia

The following countries are among nations with diplomatic representation in Malaysia.

Australia Kuala Lumpur (☎ 03-2146 5555; www.australia.org.my; 6 Jl Yap Kwan Sweng) Kota Kinabalu (☎ 088-236569; 10th fl, Wisma Yakim Bldg, Kota Kinabalu, Sabah; 🕑 8am-1pm Mon-Fri)

Brunei (☎ 03-2161 2800; Tingkat 19, Menara Tun & Tan, Jl Tun Razak, Kuala Lumpur)

Canada (☎ 03-2718 3333; 7th fl, Plaza OSK, 172 Jl Ampang, Kuala Lumpur)

France Kuala Lumpur (☎ 03-2148 4122; 196 Jl Ampang, Kuala Lumpur) Georgetown (☎ 04-262 8816; Wisma Rajab, 82 Bishop St, Georgetown, Penang)

Germany (☎ 03-2142 9666; 3 Jl U Thant, Kuala Lumpur)

Indonesia Kuala Lumpur (☎ 03-2142 1151; 233 Jl Tun Razak) Georgetown (☎ 04-227 4686; 467 Jl Burma, Georgetown, Penang) Kota Kinabalu (☎ 088-219110; Jl Kemajuan; 🕑 8am-1pm, Mon-Fri) Tawau (☎ 089-772052; Jl Apas, Tawau, Sabah) Kuching (☎ 082-241734; 111 Jl Tun Haji Openg, Kuching, Sarawak; 🕑 8.30am-noon & 2-4pm Mon-Fri)

Ireland (☎ 03-2161 2963; Ireland House, Amp Walk, 218 Jl Ampang, Kuala Lumpur)

Netherlands (☎ 03-2168 6200; 7th fl, Amp Walk, 218 Jl Ampang, Kuala Lumpur)

New Zealand (☎ 03-2138 2533; Level 21 Menara IMC, 8 Jl Sultan Ismail, Kuala Lumpur)

Singapore (☎ 03-2161 6277; 209 Jl Tun Razak, Kuala Lumpur)

Thailand Kuala Lumpur (☎ 03-2148 8222; 206 Jl Ampang, Kuala Lumpur) Kota Bharu (☎ 09-744 0867; 4426 Jl Pengkalan Chepa, Kota Bharu, Kelantan) Georgetown (☎ 04-226 9484; 1 Jl Tunku Abdul Rahman, Georgetown, Penang)

UK (☎ 03- 2148 2122; 185 Jl Ampang, Kuala Lumpur)

USA (☎ 03-2168 5000; 376 Jl Tun Razak, Kuala Lumpur)

Singapore

Singaporean Embassies & Consulates

For a list of Singaporean missions abroad check out www.visitsingapore.com/index_main.html, where you'll also find a full list of foreign embassies and consulates in Singapore.

Australia (☎ 02-6273 3944; 17 Forster Cres, Yarralumla, ACT 2600)

Brunei (☎ 02-262741/2/3; fax 262752; 8 Simpang 74, Jl Subok, Bandar Seri Begawan)

France (☎ 01-45 00 33 61; 12 Square de l'Avenue Foch, Paris 75116)

Germany (☎ 030-226 3430; Friedrichstrasse 200, 10117 Berlin)

Indonesia (☎ 021-520 1489; fax 520 1486; Blk X/4 Kav No 2, Jl HR Rasuna Said, Kuningan, Jakarta 12950)

Malaysia (☎ 03-2161 6277; 209 Jl Tun Razak, Kuala Lumpur 50400)

New Zealand (☎ 04-470 0850; fax 479 4066; 17 Kabul St, Khandallah, PO Box 13-140, Wellington)

Thailand (☎ 0 2286 2111; fax 286 6977; 9th & 18th fl, Rajanakam Bldg, 183 South Sathorn Rd, Bangkok)

UK (☎ 020-7235 8315; 9 Wilton Cres, Belgravia, London)
US (☎ 202-537 3100; 3501 International Place, NW, Washington DC 20008)

Embassies & Consulates in Singapore

Australia (☎ 836 4100; www.australia.org.sg; 25 Napier Rd)
Canada (☎ 6325 3200; www.cic.gc.cai; IBM Towers, 80 Anson Rd)
France (☎ 6880 7800; www.france.org.sg; 101-103 Cluny Park Rd)
Germany (☎ 6737 1355; www.germanembassy-singapore.org.sg; 14-01 Far East Shopping Centre, 545 Orchard Rd)
Indonesia (☎ 6737 7422; 7 Chatsworth Rd)
Malaysia (☎ 6235 0111; fax 6733 6135; 30 Hill Street 02-01)
New Zealand (☎ 6235 9966; fax 6733 9924; www.nz-high-com.org.sg; 15-06/10 Ngee Ann City, 391A Orchard Rd)
Thailand (☎ 6737 2644; www.thaiembsingapore.org; 370 Orchard Rd)
UK (☎ 6424 4200; www.britain.org.sg; 100 Tanglin Rd)
USA (☎ 9100; www.usembassysingapore.org.sg; 27 Napier Rd)

Brunei

Bruneian Embassies & Consulates

Australia (☎ 02-6285 4500; fax 6285 4545; 10 Beale Cres, Deakin, ACT 2600)
Canada (☎ 613-234 5656; fax 234 4397; 395 Laurier Ave East, Ottawa, ON K1N 6R4)
France (☎ 01-53 64 67 60; fax 53 64 67 83; No 7, Rue de Presparg, Paris 75017)
Germany (☎ 030-206 07 600; fax 206 07 666; Kronenstrasse 55-58, 10117 Berlin)
Indonesia (☎ 021-574 1437; fax 574 1463; Suite 1194, Wisma GKBI, 28 Jl Sudirman, Jakarta 10210)
Malaysia (☎ 03-2161 2800; Tingkat 19, Menara Tun & Tan, Jl Tun Razak, Kuala Lumpur)
Singapore (☎ 065-733 9055; fax 737 5275; 325 Tanglin Rd, Singapore 247955)
Thailand (☎ 0 2204 1476; fax 204 1486; No 132, Sukhumvit Soi 25, Sukhumvit Rd, Bangkok 10110)
UK (☎ 020-7581 0521; fax 7235 9717; 19 Belgrave Square, London SW1X 8PG)
USA (☎ 202-237 1838; info@bruneiembassy.org; 3520 International Court, Washington DC 2008)

Embassies & Consulates in Brunei

Countries with diplomatic representation in Bandar Seri Begawan:

Australia (☎ 229 435; ozcombrn@brunet.bn; 4th fl, Teck Guan Plaza, Jl Sultan)
Canada (☎ 220 043; hiomcda@brnet.bn; 5th fl, Jl McArthur Bldg, No 1 Jl McArthur)
France (☎ 220 960; france@brunet.bn; 301-306, 3rd fl, Kompleks Jl Sultan, Jl Sultan)
Germany (☎ 222 574; prgerman@brunet.bn; 2nd fl, Unit 2.01, Block D, YSHHB Complex)
Indonesia (☎ 330 180; www.indonesia.org.bn; Simpang 528, Lot 4498, Jl Muara, Kampung Sungai Hanching)
Malaysia (☎ 381 095; mwbrunei@brunet.bn; Lot 27 and 29, Simpang 396-39, Jl Kebangsaan Lama, Kampung Sungai Akar)
New Zealand (☎ 331 612; 36A Seri Lambak Complex, Jl Berakas)
Singapore (☎ 262 741; www.mfa.gov.sg/brunei/; No 8, Simpang 74, Jl Subok)
UK (☎ 222 231; www.britain-brunei.org/gov; 2nd fl, Unit 2.01, Block D, YSHHB Complex)
USA (☎ 229 670; Amembbsb@brunet.bn; 3rd fl, Teck Guan Plaza, Jl Sultan)

Austria, Bangladesh, Belgium, China, Denmark, Finland, India, Iran, Korea, Myanmar (Burma), the Netherlands, Norway, Oman, Pakistan, Saudi Arabia, Sweden, Thailand and Vietnam also have diplomatic representation in Brunei.

FESTIVALS & EVENTS

With so many cultures and religions in the region, there's quite an amazing number of occasions to celebrate. Although some of them have a fixed date each year, the Hindus, Muslims and Chinese all follow a lunar calendar, so the dates for many events vary each year. Tourism Malaysia and the Singapore Tourism Boards both publish Calendar of Events pamphlets with specific dates and venues of various festivals and parades – state tourist offices have more detailed listings.

The major Islamic events each year are connected with Ramadan, the month during which Muslims do not eat or drink from sunrise to sunset. Fifteen days before the start of Ramadan, on Nisfu Night, it is believed the souls of the dead visit their homes. During Ramadan Lailatul Qadar (Night of Grandeur), Muslims celebrate the arrival of the Quran on earth, before its revelation by Mohammed. A Quran-reading competition is held in KL (and extensively televised) during Ramadan.

Hari Raya Puasa marks the end of the month-long fast, with two days of joyful celebration. This is the major holiday of the Muslim calendar and it can be difficult to find accommodation in Malaysia, particularly on the east coast. During this time everyone wears new clothes, homes are cleaned and redecorated, and everyone seems to visit everyone else.

Hari Raya Haji is the day when pilgrims mark the successful completion of the hajj (pilgrimage to Mecca). It is a two-day holiday in many of the peninsular states, and is marked by the consumption of large amounts of cakes and sweets.

The major Chinese event of the year is Chinese New Year; the major Indian celebration is Deepavali, though Thaipusam is the most spectacular, celebrated with a painful-looking spectacle in some states of the peninsula (see the Piercing Devotions boxed text (p109) in the Selangor chapter.

There are many other special events, ranging from fun runs, kite-flying and fishing competitions to the Malaysian Grand Prix – see the destination chapters for details of events specific to particular towns and cities.

January–February

Thai Pongal A Hindu harvest-festival marking the beginning of the Hindu month of Thai, considered the luckiest month of the year. Celebrated by Tamils.

Chinese New Year Dragon dances and pedestrian parades mark the start of the new year. Families hold open house, unmarried relatives (especially children) receive *ang pow* (money in red packets), businesses traditionally clear their debts and everybody wishes you *kong hee fatt choy* (a happy and prosperous New Year).

Birthday of the Jade Emperor Nine days after New Year, this Chinese festival honours Yu Huang, the supreme ruler of heaven, with offerings at temples.

Chap Goh Meh 15 days after Chinese New Year, the celebrations officially end.

Thaipusam One of the most dramatic Hindu festivals (now banned in India), in which devotees honour Lord Subramaniam with acts of amazing physical resilience- see the Piercing Devotions boxed text, p109.

March–April

Malaysian Grand Prix Held at the Sepang International Circuit in Selangor around March 20. This is Formula 1's big outing in Southeast Asia.

Singapore Food Festival Kicking off in March and lasting a month, this is one of Singapore's best festivals with mouthwatering events held all over the city.

Panguni Uttiram The marriage of Shiva to Shakti and of Lord Subramaniam to Theivani is celebrated on the full-moon day of the Tamil month of Panguni.

Birthday of the Goddess of Mercy Offerings are made to the very popular Kuan Yin at her temples across the region.

Cheng Ming On Cheng Ming, Chinese traditionally visit the tombs of their ancestors to make offerings, and to tend, clean and repair the tombs.

Sri Rama Navami A 9-day festival held by those of the Brahmin caste to honour the Hindu hero of the Ramayana, Sri Rama.

Birthday of the Monkey God The birthday of T'se Tien Tai Seng Yeh is celebrated twice a year. Mediums pierce their cheeks and tongues with skewers and go into trances during which they write special charms in blood.

April–May

Songkran Festival A traditional Thai Buddhist New Year in which Buddha images are bathed.

Chithirai Vishu The start of the Hindu New Year.

Birthday of the Queen of Heaven Ma Cho Po, the queen of heaven and goddess of the sea, is honoured at her temples.

Wesak Day Buddha's birth, enlightenment and death are celebrated with various events, including the release of caged birds to symbolise the setting free of captive souls.

June

Gawai Dayak Annual Sarawak Dayak Festival on 1 and 2 June to mark the end of the rice season, with war dances, cockfights and blowpipe events.

Festa de San Pedro Christian celebration on 29 June in honour of the patron saint of the fishing community, particularly celebrated by the Eurasian-Portuguese community of Melaka.

Birthday of the God of War Kuan Ti, who has the ability to avert war and to protect people during war, is honoured on his birthday.

Dragon Boat Festival Commemorates the death of a Chinese saint who drowned himself. In an attempt to save him, the local fishing community paddled out to sea, beating drums to scare away any fish that might attack him. To mark the anniversary, this festival is celebrated from June to August, with boat races in Penang and other places.

July–August

Birthday of Kuan Yin The goddess of mercy has another birthday!

Prophet Mohammed's Birthday Muslims pray and religious leaders recite verses from the Quran.

Sri Krishna Jayanti A 10-day Hindu festival celebrating popular events in Krishna's life is highlighted on day eight with celebrations of his birthday. The Laxmi Narayan Temple in KL is a particular focus.

August–September

Festival of the Seven Sisters Chinese girls pray to the weaving maid for good husbands.

Festival of the Hungry Ghosts The souls of the dead are released for one day of feasting and entertainment on earth. Chinese operas and other events are laid on for them and food is put out. The ghosts eat the spirit of the food, but thoughtfully leave the substance for mortal celebrants. Mainly in Penang and Singapore.
National Day (Hari Kebangsaan) Malaysia celebrates its independence on 31 August with events all over the country, but particularly in KL where there are parades and a variety of performances in the Lake Gardens.
Vinayagar Chathuri During the Tamil month of Avani (around August and September), prayers are offered to Vinayagar, another name for the popular elephant-headed god Ganesh.
Moon Cake Festival The overthrow of the Mongol warlords in ancient China is celebrated by eating moon cakes and lighting colourful paper lanterns. Moon cakes are filled with bean paste, lotus seeds and sometimes a duck egg-yolk.

September–October

Navarathri In the Tamil month of Purattasi, the Hindu festival of 'Nine Nights' is dedicated to the wives of Shiva, Vishnu and Brahma. Young girls are dressed as the goddess Kali.
Festival of the Nine Emperor Gods Nine days of Chinese operas, processions and other events honour the nine emperor gods. Fire-walking ceremonies are held on the evening of the 9th day at the Kau Ong Yah Temples in KL and Penang.
Puja Ketek Offerings are brought to Buddhist shrines, or *ketek*, in the state of Kelantan during this festival in October. Traditional dances are often performed.

October–November

Thimithi (Fire-Walking Ceremony) Hindu devotees prove their faith by walking across glowing coals at temples in Melaka and Singapore.
Kantha Shashithi Subramaniam, a great fighter against the forces of evil, is honoured during the Hindu month of Aipasi.
Deepavali Later in the month of Aipasi, Rama's victory over the demon king Ravana is celebrated with the Festival of Lights, when tiny oil-lamps are lit outside the homes of Hindu people, as it's believed that Lakshmi, the goddess of wealth, will not enter an unlit home. For business people, this is the time to start a new financial year, and for the family a pre-dawn oil bath, new clothes and lots of sweets is the order of the day.
Birthday of Kuan Yin This popular Goddess of Mercy gets to celebrate her birthday for the 3rd time in the year.
Kartikai Deepam Huge bonfires are lit to commemorate Shiva's appearance as a pillar of fire following an argument with Vishnu and Brahma. The Thandayuthapani Temple in Muar is a major site for this festival.
Guru Nanak's Birthday The birthday of Guru Nanak, founder of the Sikh religion, is celebrated on 22 November.

December

Winter Solstice Festival A Chinese festival to offer thanks for a good harvest.
Christmas Day On 25 December Christians celebrate the birth of Jesus Christ.

FOOD

While travelling around some parts of Asia is as good as a diet session, Malaysia, Singapore and Brunei are quite the opposite. The food is simply terrific, the variety unbeatable and the costs pleasantly low. Whether you're looking for Chinese food, Malay food, Indian food, Indonesian food or even a Big Mac, you'll find happiness! There's also a good range of nonalcoholic and alcoholic drinks. For a complete description, see the Food & Drink chapter (p60).

GAY & LESBIAN TRAVELLERS

Legally, gays have a bad time in this part of the world. In Malaysia, homosexuality is punishable by imprisonment and caning. Although you're perfectly free to be homosexual in Singapore, homosexual sex is illegal and you can be sentenced to between 10 years and life if you're caught having it. In Brunei, too, you can also be thrown in jail for up to 10 years and fined B$30,000 for being caught in homosexual acts.

Fortunately, outright persecution of gays and lesbians is rare. Nonetheless, while travelling in the region, gay and lesbian travellers should avoid behaviour that attracts unwanted attention. Malaysians and Singaporeans are quite conservative about displays of public affection; women, and straight Indian men, can get away with same-sex hand holding, but an overtly gay couple doing the same would attract attention. It is highly unlikely, however, that you will encounter vocal or aggressive homophobia.

In light of all this, you may be surprised to hear that there is actually a fairly active gay scene in KL and Singapore – see the destination chapters for listings of bars and clubs. The lesbian scene is less obvious but, naturally, exists for those willing to seek it out. If you want to find out more about local attitudes, as well as what's going on now, read *People Like Us – Sexual Minorities in*

Singapore, edited by Joseph Lo and Huang Gouqin, which takes an upfront look at a variety of queer issues.

A good place to start looking for information is on www.utopia-asia.com or www.fridae.com, both of which provide excellent coverage of gay and lesbian events and activities across Asia. The website **Yawning Bread** (www.geocities.com/yawning_bread/) covers Singaporean gay issues from a more serious angle. Gay men can also check out www.sgboy.com for Singaporean happenings and hangouts.

HOLIDAYS

In addition to national public holidays, each state has its own holidays, usually associated with the sultan's birthday or a Muslim celebration. Muslim holidays move forward 10 or 11 days each year. Hindu and Chinese holiday dates also vary, but fall roughly within the same months each year. Unless otherwise specified, the following holidays apply across Malaysia, Singapore and Brunei.

Public Holidays

January–February

New Year's Day 1 January (except in Johor, Kedah, Kelantan, Perlis and Terengganu)
Thaipusam Variable (in Johor, Negeri Sembilan, Perak, Penang and Selangor only)
Federal Territory Day 1 February (in KL, Labuan and Putrajaya only)
Sultan of Kedah's Birthday 7 February (in Kedah only)
Chinese New Year Variable, 2 days in late January/early February (1 day only in Kelantan and Terengganu)
Brunei's National Day 23 February (in Brunei only)

March

Hari Raya Haji (Hari Raya Aidiladha in Brunei) Variable February/March
Sultan of Selangor's Birthday 2nd Saturday of March (in Selangor only)
Anniversary of Installation of Sultan of Terengganu 21 March (in Terengganu only)
Muslim New Year (Hizrah in Brunei) Variable (no holiday in Singapore)
Sultan of Kelantan's Birthday 30 & 31 March (in Kelantan only)

April

Sultan of Johor's Birthday 8 April (in Johor only)
Good Friday Variable (in Sarawak, Sabah and Singapore only)
Melaka Historical City Day 15 April (in Melaka only)
Sultan of Perak's Birthday 19 April (in Perak only)
Sultan of Terengganu's Birthday 29 April (in Terengganu only)

May

Labour Day 1 May (in Malaysia and Singapore only)
Raja of Perlis' Birthday Variable, April/May (in Perlis only)
Wesak Day Variable (no holiday in Brunei)
Harvest Festival Variable (in Sabah and Labuan only)
Royal Brunei Armed Forces Day 31 May (in Brunei only)

June

Yang di-Pertuan Agong's (King's) Birthday 1st Saturday in June (in Malaysia only)
Dayak Festival 1 & 2 June (in Sarawak only)
Prophet's Birthday Variable (in Malaysia and Brunei only)

July

Governor of Penang's Birthday 2nd Saturday in July (in Penang only)
Sultan of Brunei's Birthday 15 July (in Brunei only)
Governor of Negeri Sembilan's Birthday 19 July (in Negeri Sembilan only)

August

Singapore's National Day 9 August (in Singapore only)
Malaysia's National Day (Hari Kebangsaan) 31 August (in Malaysia only)

September

Malaysia Day 16 September (in Sabah only)

October–November

Governor of Melaka's Birthday 2nd Saturday in October (in Melaka only)
Sultan of Pahang's Birthday 24 October (in Pahang only)
Israk Mikraj (Ascension of the Prophet) Variable (in Kedah, Negeri Sembilan and Brunei only)
Deepavali Variable (no holiday in Sarawak, Labuan and Brunei)
Awal Ramadan (Beginning of Ramadan) Variable (in Johor and Melaka only)

December

Nuzul Al-Quran Variable (in Kelantan, Pahang, Perak, Perlis, Selangor and Terengganu)
Hari Raya Puasa (Hari Raya Aidilfitri in Brunei) Variable
Christmas Day 25 December

School Holidays

Schools in Malaysia break for holidays five times a year. The actual dates vary from state to state but the breaks are generally in January (one week), March (two weeks), May (three weeks), August (one week) and October (four weeks).

In Singapore there's a week's holiday towards the end of March, three weeks in June, one week in early September, and the long break from the end of November until the beginning of January.

In Brunei the holidays fall in the last week of March, the last two weeks of June, the second week of September, and from mid-November to the beginning of January.

INSURANCE

Although Malaysia, Singapore and Brunei are generally safe countries in which to travel, it's still a good idea to take out a travel insurance policy to cover theft, loss and medical problems. There are a wide variety of policies and travel agents have recommendations. Check the small print to see if the insurance policy covers potentially dangerous sporting activities, such as diving or trekking, and make sure that it adequately covers your valuables. Healthwise, you may prefer a policy that pays doctors or hospitals directly rather than your having to pay on the spot and claim later. If you have to claim later, make sure that you keep all documentation. Check that the policy covers ambulances or an emergency flight home

A few credit cards offer limited, sometimes full, travel insurance to the holder.

For information on health insurance see the Health chapter (p571), and for car insurance see the Transport chapter (p566).

INTERNET ACCESS

Internet access is freely and cheaply available at numerous internet cafes and centres across the region, generally on fast broadband connections. Many hotels also have Internet access either in their business centres or directly in their rooms. If you plan to carry your notebook or palmtop computer with you, note all three countries use the three-pronged, square-pin plugs used in the UK; if your computer doesn't have such a plug, you'll need an adaptor.

Also, your PC-card modem may or may not work once you leave your home country – and you won't know for sure until you try. The safest option is to buy a reputable 'global' modem before you leave home, or buy a local PC-card modem if you're spending an extended time abroad. Keep in mind that the telephone socket will probably be different from the one at home, so ensure that you have at least a US RJ-11 telephone adaptor that works with your modem. You can almost always find an adaptor that will convert from RJ-11 to the local variety. For more information on travelling with a portable computer, see www.teleadapt.com.

If you intend to rely on cybercafés, you'll need to carry three pieces of information with you to enable you to access your Internet mail account: your incoming (POP or IMAP) mail server name, your account name and your password. Your Internet Service Provider (ISP) or network supervisor will be able to give you these.

For details of useful websites to kick-start your research into a trip throughout this region see Internet Resources (p16) in the Getting Started chapter. Among the Internet providers in Malaysia and Singapore:

Jaring (☎ 03-8996 1900; www.jaring.my/)
Pacific (☎ 6336 6622; www.pacific.net.sg)
SingTel (www.singtel.com.sg)
Telekom Malaysia (www.telekom.com.my)

LEGAL MATTERS

In any of your dealings with the local police forces it will pay to be deferential. You're most likely to come into contact with them either through reporting a crime (some of the big cities in Malaysia have tourist police stations for this purpose) or while driving. Minor misdemeanours may be overlooked, but don't count on it and don't offer anyone a bribe – these are not those sort of countries.

Singapore is notorious as a place where large fines are levied against all manner of antisocial behaviour, from littering and smoking in public places to urinating in lifts. If you do jaywalk or casually drop your ciggie stubs on the pavement, it's unlikely the cops will nab you, but with everyone else being so well-behaved you're going to look pretty foolish not falling in line. At the more extreme end of the scale of transgressions you will be punished.

Drug trafficking in all three countries carries a mandatory death penalty. All drug offenders are considered equal, and being a

COMING OF AGE

For the record:

- The legal age for voting in Malaysia and Singapore is 21. In Brunei nobody gets to vote.
- You can drive legally in Malaysia and Brunei at 18, and in Singapore at 16.
- Heterosexual sex is legal in Malaysia and Singapore at 16, and in Brunei at 14.
- To legally buy alcohol you need to be 21 in Malaysia and 18 in Singapore. Alcohol is banned in Brunei.

foreigner will not save you from the gallows. A number of foreigners have been executed in Malaysia, some of them for possession of amazingly small quantities of heroin. Even possession of tiny amounts can bring down a lengthy jail sentence and a beating with the *rotan* (cane). Just don't do it.

MAPS

Malaysia

The most useful overall map for Peninsular Malaysia is the 1:650,000 *West Malaysia* map produced by Nelles Verlag. It has most of the major and minor roads and shows some topographical features. Nelles also produces *Malaysia,* a decent map that shows both Peninsular Malaysia and Malaysian Borneo. Periplus produces an excellent series of Malaysian city and state maps, including *Johor*, *Kuala Lumpur*, *Melaka*, *Penang*, *Sabah* and *Sarawak*.

It may be difficult to find some of these maps outside of KL – you may even have difficulty finding them in KL. In fact, the best place to buy maps of Malaysia is in Singapore or in your home country.

It's worth picking up Tourism Malaysia's *The Map of Malaysia,* which has useful distance charts, facts about the country and inset maps of many major cities.

If you're intent on getting accurate maps of rural areas, visit the **National Survey & Mapping Department** (Ibu Pejabat Ukur & Pemetaan Malaysia; ☎ 03-2617 0800; Jl Semarak, Kuala Lumpur). You'll have to apply for permission to purchase maps here, and you may need a Malaysian national to vouch for you.

Singapore

Various maps are available free in Singapore, including *The Official Map of Singapore*, from the STB, as well as from hotels everywhere. Of the commercial maps, Nelles and Periplus maps are good. The *Singapore Street Directory* is essential if you plan to drive. Also check out Lonely Planet's *Singapore City Map*, a durable, full-colour, laminated fold-out map with a full index of streets and sights.

Brunei

Shell publishes a folding road-map of Brunei, but it's not as useful as their larger and more comprehensive *Road Map and Street Index of Brunei Darussalam.*

MONEY

See the Quick Reference page (inside the front cover) for currency exchange rates.

ATMs & Credit Cards

Credit cards are readily accepted for purchases in many establishments, with MasterCard and Visa the most widely accepted brands. Banks all over the region accept credit cards for over-the-counter cash advances, or you can make ATM withdrawals if you have your PIN. Many banks are also linked to international banking networks such as Cirrus (the most common), Maestro and Plus, allowing withdrawals from overseas savings accounts.

Maybank, Malaysia's biggest bank with branches everywhere, accepts both Visa and MasterCard. Hongkong Bank accepts Visa, and the Standard Chartered Bank accepts MasterCard. If you have any questions about whether your cards will be accepted in Malaysia, ask your home bank about its reciprocal relationships with Malaysian banks.

Credit card companies in Singapore:

American Express (☎ 6299 8133)
Diners Card (☎ 6294 4222)
JCB (☎ 6734 0096)
MasterCard & Visa (☎ 1800-345 1345)

Currency

MALAYSIA

Here you'll be spending ringgit (RM) made up of 100 sen. Coins in use are 1 sen, 5 sen, 10 sen, 20 sen and 50 sen, and RM1; notes come in RM1, RM2, RM5, RM10, RM50 and RM100.

In September 1998 Malaysia fixed the ringgit at RM3.8 to US$1 (other currency rates remain variable) and recalled foreign holdings of ringgit in an attempt to protect the economy from currency speculators. It is now technically illegal to trade the ringgit outside Malaysia; in practice, you can (usually) buy and sell ringgit in southern Thailand, Singapore and Brunei. US dollars can still be exchanged for ringgit in Malaysia.

Because of the fixed rate, it pays to make some calculations before deciding where to change your money. If you're travelling to Malaysia from Thailand, for example, work out whether changing your dollars into baht there, then changing baht into ringgit in Malaysia, will earn you more for your dollar. You could also calculate whether exchanging currency other than the US dollar for ringgit would be more profitable.

Malaysians sometimes refer to ringgit as 'dollars', the old name for the country's currency. Unless someone makes it clear that they are talking about US dollars, you can be sure they mean ringgit. Be sure to carry plenty of small bills with you when venturing outside cities – people often cannot change bills larger than RM10.

SINGAPORE

The unit of currency is the Singaporean dollar (S$), made up of 100 cents. Singapore uses 1c, 5c, 10c, 20c, 50c and S$1 coins, while notes come in denominations of S$2, S$5, S$10, S$50, S$100, S$500 and S$1000; Singapore also has a S$10,000 note – not that you'll see many.

BRUNEI

The official currency is the Brunei dollar (B$), but Singapore dollars are exchanged at an equal rate and can be used.

Brunei uses 1c, 5c, 20c and 50c coins, and B$1, B$5, B$10, B$50, B$100, B$500, B$1000 and B$10,000 notes.

Taxes & Refunds

MALAYSIA

There is no general sales tax but there is a government tax of 10%, plus a service tax of 5% at larger hotels and restaurants.

SINGAPORE

A 5% Goods and Services Tax (GST) is applied to all goods and services. Visitors purchasing goods worth S$300 or more through a shop participating in the GST Tourist Refund Scheme can apply for a GST refund. These shops display a 'tax-free shopping' logo, and when you purchase an item you must fill in a claim form and show your passport. You will receive a global-refund cheque – these are issued only for purchases of S$100 and above.

Present this cheque (or cheques), your passport and goods at the Customs GST Inspection counter in the departure hall at Changi airport, *before* you check your bags (and the goods) in. Customs then stamps your cheque(s), which you can then cash at the cash-refund counters inside the airport, or have credited to your credit-card or bank account. Refer to the STB brochure *Singapore Shopping Guide* for more details.

In addition to the GST, a 10% service charge and 1% 'cess' (government entertainment tax) is added to the bill at the more expensive hotels and restaurants, as well as at most nightspots and bars. This is the 'plus-plus-plus' that follows some quoted prices (as in S$120+++). Some of the cheaper establishments don't add taxes but absorb them into the quoted price, which is 'net', for instance S$70 net.

BRUNEI

There is no general sales tax in Brunei. Some hotels charge a 10% service charge, though this is mostly included in the price that's quoted and charged.

Travellers Cheques & Cash

Banks in the region are efficient and there are plenty of moneychangers. For changing cash or travellers cheques, banks usually charge a commission (around RM5 per transaction in Malaysia, around S$3 in Singapore and B$15 in Brunei), whereas moneychangers have no charges but their rates vary more – so know what the current rate is before using moneychangers. Compared with a bank, you'll generally get a better rate for cash at a moneychanger – it's usually quicker too. Away from the tourist centres, moneychangers' rates are often poorer and they may not change travellers cheques.

All major brands of travellers cheques are accepted across the region. Cash in major currencies is also readily exchanged, though like everywhere else in the world the US dollar has a slight edge.

Note that in Brunei, Malaysian ringgit are not accepted in hotels or shops, though Singapore dollars are. If you haven't already purchased Brunei dollars in Labuan, there are moneychangers in Muara to tide you over till you get to Bandar Seri Begawan (BSB).

PHOTOGRAPHY

Malaysia, Singapore and Brunei are delightful countries to photograph. There's a lot of natural colour and activity, and the people usually have no antipathy to being photographed. However, it is, of course, polite to ask permission before photographing people or taking pictures in mosques or temples. If you're looking for tips, *Travel Photography: A Guide to Taking Better Pictures* is written by travel photographer Richard I'Anson. The guide is designed for taking on the road and is full colour throughout.

Print film is commonly available at good prices – a 36-exposure roll averages RM10. Slide film is a little harder to come by and more expensive – a 36-exposure roll of Fuji Velvia averages RM29 and a 36-exposure roll of Sensia averages RM18. Professional slide film can be found only in the biggest cities – if you're a serious photographer, you may want to bring your own slide film, especially since most of what's available in Malaysia show signs of improper storage.

Colour film can be developed quickly and competently in Malaysia. Processing prices for a 36-exposure roll of slide film range from RM15 to RM18 (mounted), and 60 sen to 70 sen per exposure for print film. In bigger cities like KL, you'll find photo shops with a decent range of equipment at reasonable prices, but Malaysia isn't really the place to buy camera equipment (try Singapore).

In Singapore print film costs around S$5 for a 36-exposure roll. Processing costs around S$3.50 plus 30 to 40 cents per print (the price varies depending on the size and the finish). Expect to pay around S$12.50 for a roll of 36-exposure transparency film to be developed and mounted (usually same-day service as long as you drop the film off in the morning).

POST

Malaysia

Malaysia has an efficient postal system with good poste restante at the major post offices. Post offices are open daily from 8am to 5pm, and closed on Sunday and public holidays (closed on Friday and public holidays in Kedah, Kelantan and Terengganu).

Aerograms and postcards cost 50 sen to send to any destination. Letters weighing 10g or less cost 55 sen to Asia, Australia or New Zealand, 90 sen to the UK and Europe, and RM1.10 to North America.

It's easy to send parcels from any major post office, although the rates are fairly high (from around RM20 to RM35 for a 1kg parcel, depending on the destination).

Main post offices in larger cities have POS2020 stores, which sell packaging materials and stationery.

Singapore

Postal delivery in Singapore is very efficient. All post offices are open 8am to 6pm Monday to Friday, 8am to 2pm Saturday. Call ☎ 1605 to find the nearest branch or check its website at singpost.com.sg.

Letters addressed 'Poste Restante' are held at the **Eunos Post Office** (Map pp448-9; ☎ 6741 8857; 10 Eunos Rd), next to the Paya Lebar MRT. Handy central branches include **Comcentre** (Map pp456-7; 31 Exeter Rd) and **Ngee Ann City** (Map pp456-7; 04-15 Takashimaya, Ngee Ann City, 391 Orchard Rd). Terminals 1 and 2 at Changi airport also have branches open from 8am to 9pm daily.

Airmail postcards and aerograms cost 50c to anywhere in the world. Letters cost from 70c to S$1.

POSTAL CODES

There is a six-digit postal code system that should be used when addressing mail to and within Singapore. Ask for the *Postal Code Directory* at any post office or call the **Postal Code HelpLine** (☎ 1800-842 7678) to find a particular code. Alternatively, visit www.singpost.com.sg for full details.

The system is, not surprisingly, very efficient. The first two digits are the sector code, which defines a particular area in Singapore, and the last four digits are the delivery point – the house or building. In theory you could address a mail item to someone using the postal code only and it should get there.

Brunei

Post offices open from 7.45am to 4.30pm Monday to Thursday and Saturday (8am to 11am and 2pm to 4pm Friday; closed Sunday).

Letters (up to 10g) cost 75c to Australia and New Zealand, 90c to the UK, and B$1.20 to the USA and Canada. An airmail postcard to Malaysia and Singapore is 20c; to most other places in Southeast Asia it's 35c; to the Pacific, Europe, Africa and Australia it's 50c; and to the Americas it's 60c. Aerograms are 45c regardless of destination.

TELEPHONE

Malaysia

FAX

Fax facilities are available at Telekom offices in larger cities and at some main post offices. You can also send and receive faxes at travel agencies, but the rates are usually pretty steep. Large hotels also have fax machines but these are generally only for the use of guests.

INTERNATIONAL CALLS

Making international calls from Malaysia can be an exercise in frustration. In addition to the legion of broken pay phones, the traveller is beset by a bewildering number of mutually exclusive services and phonecards.

International direct dial (IDD) calls and operator-assisted calls can be made from any private phone. The access code for making international calls to most countries is ☎ 00. Call ☎ 108 for the international operator and ☎ 103 for directory inquiries.

To make an IDD call from a pay phone, you'll have to find a Telekom pay phone marked `international' (with which you can use coins or Telekom phonecards; dial the international access code, ☎ 00, and then the number). A more convenient option is to buy a Time phonecard from a newsagent and dial from a small coin-phone of the type found in most guesthouses, or from the occasional Uniphone pay phone that accepts international calls. The third option is to go to a Telekom office, where you can make IDD or operator-assisted international calls. These days, there are very few regular pay phones that allow IDD calls, apparently because of a rash of counterfeit phonecards.

For calls to a number of countries, it's possible to make Home Country Direct calls, which allow you to deal directly with an operator in your home country . These can be made from participating Uniphone pay phones for the cost of a local call (10 sen for three minutes); from private phones there is no charge.

If you're making a call to Malaysia from outside the country, dial ☎ 60, drop the 0 before the Malaysian area code, then dial the number you want. See the list in the Phone Codes section (next page) for area codes for Malaysia's major cities and destinations.

LOCAL CALLS

Making domestic telephone calls in Malaysia is usually a simple matter, provided you can find a working pay phone (at least one-third seem to be out of order). You can direct-dial long-distance between all major towns in Malaysia. Local calls cost 10 sen for three minutes.

All over the country you'll come across card-operated telephones run by Telekom Malaysia and a private communications company, Uniphone. These telephones take coins or plastic cards, but you need different cards for each company. For most calls Telekom card-phones are the most reliable and convenient, but you'll have to use Uniphone phones for 1-800 calls. In the larger cities, you'll also find Cityphone card telephones, but since these are only found in the cities it makes little sense for travellers to buy one of these cards.

Uniphone cards can be bought from 7-Eleven stores and some other shops. They come in denominations of RM3, RM5, RM10, RM30 and RM50. Telekom cards are available from Telekom offices, post offices and some shops (news vendors in particular). They come in similar denominations.

MOBILE PHONES

As long as you have arranged to have `global-roaming' facilities with your home provider, your GSM digital phone will automatically tune into one of the region's digital networks. If not, and you have your phone with you, the simplest way to go mobile is to buy a prepaid SIM card for one of the services on arrival in the country – telephone shops can advise on which is the best plan based on how long you'll be in the country.

In Malaysia, Maxis (numbers beginning with 012) and Celcom (numbers beginning with 019) both offer good coverage and service, with call rates of around 60 sen a minute.

PHONE CODES

Phone calls to Singapore are STD (long-distance) rather than international calls. Area codes for Malaysia:

Town/region	Area code
Cameron Highlands	☎ 05
Ipoh	☎ 05
Johor Bahru	☎ 07
Kota Bharu	☎ 09
Kota Kinabalu	☎ 088
Kuala Lumpur	☎ 03
Kuala Terengganu	☎ 09
Kuantan	☎ 09
Kuching	☎ 082
Labuan	☎ 087
Langkawi	☎ 04
Melaka	☎ 06
Miri	☎ 085
Penang	☎ 04
Sandakan	☎ 089
Singapore	☎ 02

Singapore

CREDIT-CARD PHONES

Singapore has credit-card phones, which means you can just swipe your Amex, Diners Club, MasterCard or Visa card through the slot. At some Singtel centres, there are also Home Country Direct phones – press a button designated to a particular country to speak to that country's operator and reverse the charges, or have the call charged to an international telephone card acceptable in your country. The Home Country Direct service is available from any phone by dialling the appropriate code listed in the front pages of the phone book.

FAX

Faxes can be sent from all post offices, Telecom centres and hotels.

INTERNATIONAL CALLS

To call Singapore from overseas, dial your country's international access number and then ☎ 65, Singapore's country code, before entering the eight-digit telephone number.

Calls to Malaysia are considered to be STD (trunk or long-distance) calls. Dial the access code ☎ 020, followed by the area code of the town in Malaysia that you wish to call (minus the leading zero) and then your party's number. Thus for a call to 346 7890 in Kuala Lumpur (area code ☎ 03) you would dial 020 3 346 7890. Call ☎ 104 for assistance with Malaysian area codes.

To call overseas from Singapore dial 001.

LOCAL CALLS

From public phones, local calls cost 10c for three minutes. There are no area codes within Singapore; telephone numbers are eight digits unless you are calling toll-free (1-800). Mobile phone numbers start with 9.

MOBILE PHONES

Mobile phone numbers in Singapore start with 9. As long as you have arranged to have `global roaming' facilities with your home provider, your GSM digital phone will automatically tune into one of Singapore's two digital networks, MI-GSM or ST-GSM. There is complete coverage across the whole island and phones will also work in the underground sections of the MRT rail network. Rates are variable, but quite reasonable in comparison with other countries in the region.

From post offices and 7-Eleven stores it's also possible to buy SIM cards for one of the three local mobile phone services (Singtel, Starhub and MI) from S$20 per card. Just slip the new SIM card into your handset, check your new Singapore phone number and you're away.

PHONECARDS

Local phonecards are widely available from 7-Eleven stores, post offices, Telecom centres, stationers and bookshops, and come in denominations of S$2, S$5, S$10, S$20 and S$50. Most phone booths take phonecards, and some take credit cards, although there are still booths around that take coins. For inquiries see www.singtel.com.

Brunei

To call Brunei from outside the country, the country code is 673; from Brunei, the international access code is 00.

Hallo Kad and JTB are the most common types of phonecard. They're available from Telecom offices and retail stores in denominations of B$10, B$20, B$50 and B$100, and can be used in public booths to make international calls. Most hotels have IDD phones, and faxes can be sent from the Telecom office or from major hotels.

TIME

Malaysia, Singapore and Brunei are all 16 hours ahead of US Pacific Standard Time (San Francisco and Los Angeles), 13 hours ahead of US Eastern Standard Time (New York), eight hours ahead of GMT/UTC (London) and two hours behind Australian Eastern Standard Time (Sydney and Melbourne). Thus, noon in the region is 8pm in Los Angeles and 11pm in New York (the previous day), 4am in London, and 2pm in Sydney and Melbourne. See the World Map (pp582-3) for international time zones.

TOILETS

Toilets in these parts are not nearly as horrifying as those in other Southeast Asian countries. You will find both Western-style and Asian squat-style toilets, the former rapidly replacing the latter. In places with squat-style toilets, toilet paper is not usually provided. Instead, you will find a hose which you are supposed to use as a bidet or, in cheaper places, a bucket of water and a tap. If you do not find this to your liking, make a point of taking packets of tissues or toilet paper wherever you go.

TOURIST INFORMATION

Malaysia

Malaysia's national tourist body, **Tourism Malaysia** (Map p74-5; ☎ 03-293 5188; fax 293 5884, www.tourismmalaysia.gov.my; 17th fl, Putra World Trade Centre, 45 Jl Tun Ismail, Kuala Lumpur) has an efficient network of overseas offices, which are useful for predeparture planning. Unfortunately, its domestic offices are less helpful and are often unable to give specific information about destinations and transportation. Nonetheless, they do stock some decent brochures as well as the excellent *Map of Malaysia*.

Within Malaysia there are also a number of state tourist-promotion organisations, such as the Penang Tourist Association, which often have more detailed information about specific areas.

Where there are representatives, Tourism Malaysia and state tourism offices are listed in individual destination entries.

Tourism Malaysia maintains the following offices overseas:

Australia Sydney (☎ 02-9299 4441; Level 2, 171 Clarence St, Sydney 2000) Perth (☎ 08-948 0400; MAS Bldg, 56 William St, Perth, WA 6000)
Canada (☎ 604-689 8899; 830 Burrard St, Vancouver)
France (☎ 01-42 97 41 71; 29 rue des Pyramides, Paris)
Germany (☎ 069-28 37 82; Rossmarkt 11, 60311 Frankfurt-am-Main)
Japan Tokyo (☎ 03-3501 8691; 5F Chiyoda Biru, 1-6-4 Yurakucho, Chiyoda-ku, Tokyo) Osaka (☎ 06-6444 1220; 10F Cotton Nissay Biru, 1-8-2 Utsubo-Honmachi, Nishi-ku, Osaka)
Singapore (☎ 02-6532 6321; 01-01 B/C/D, 80 Robinson Rd, Singapore)
Thailand (☎ 02-631 1994; Unit 1001 Liberty Square, 287 Silom Rd, Bangkok)
UK (☎ 020-7930 7932; 57 Trafalgar Square, London WC2N 5DU)
USA Los Angeles (☎ 213-689 9702; 818 West 7th St, Suite 804, Los Angeles, CA 90017); New York (☎ 212-754 1113; 120 East 56th St, Suite 804, New York, NY 10022)

Singapore

Before your trip, the **Singapore Tourism Board** (www.visitsingapore.com) is the best place to check for information. It includes a list of Singapore Tourism offices around the world.

In Singapore, the STB head office is on Orchard Spring Lane, but the office at Suntec City is open daily and provides a wide range of services, including tour bookings and event ticketing. For a full list of offices see the Singapore chapter, p459.

Brunei

The government has an official tourism website at www.tourismbrunei.com. There are no overseas tourist offices; just the small **Tourist Information Centre** (Map p518; ☎ 884 9110, wildlifeadventure@hotmail.com, Ground fl, Post Office Bldg) in Bandar Seri Begawan.

VISAS

Visitors must have a valid passport or internationally recognised travel document valid for at least six months beyond the date of entry into Malaysia, Singapore or Brunei.

Malaysia

Commonwealth citizens (except those from India, Bangladesh, Sri Lanka and Pakistan), and citizens of the Republic of Ireland,

Switzerland, the Netherlands, San Marino and Liechtenstein do not require a visa to visit Malaysia.

Citizens of Austria, Belgium, the Czech Republic, Denmark, Finland, France, Germany, Hungary, Iceland, Italy, Japan, Luxembourg, Norway, Slovak Republic, South Korea, Sweden, the USA and most Arab countries do not require a visa for a visit not exceeding three months.

Citizens of Greece, South Africa and many South American and African countries do not require a visa for a visit not exceeding one month. Most other nationalities are given a shorter stay-period or require a visa.

Citizens of Israel cannot enter Malaysia.

For full details of visa regulations see the website www.kln.gov.my/english/visainfo/.

Nationals of most countries are given a 30- or 60-day visa on arrival, depending on the expected length of stay. As a general rule, if you arrive by air you will be given 60 days automatically, though coming overland you may be given 30 days unless you specifically ask for a 60-day permit. It's possible to get an extension at an immigration office in Malaysia for a total stay of up to three months. This is a straightforward procedure that is easily done in major Malaysian cities (immigration offices are listed under Information in the relevant destination chapters).

Sabah and Sarawak are treated in some ways like separate countries. Your passport will be checked on arrival in each state and a new-stay permit issued. You are usually issued with a 30-day permit on arrival in Sarawak or Sabah. Travelling directly from either Sabah or Sarawak back to Peninsular Malaysia, however, there are no formalities and you do not start a new entry period, so your 30-day permit from Sabah or Sarawak remains valid. You can then extend your initial 30-day permit, though it can be difficult to get an extension in Sarawak. For more information see the Sabah (p385) and Sarawak (p317) chapters.

VISA STAMPS

We've heard of travellers having problems when they leave Malaysia, after having entered the country by train from Singapore – this is because the Malaysian immigration officials at Singapore's railway station, which is the southern termination point for Malaysia's Keretapi Tanah Melayu (KTM), do not stamp your passport. This shouldn't be a problem as long as you keep your immigration card and your train ticket to show how you entered the country. Your details will have been input into the Malaysian immigration computer and should come up when you exit. Stand your ground if anyone asks you to pay a fine.

Singapore

Citizens of British Commonwealth countries (except India) and citizens of the Republic of Ireland, Liechtenstein, Monaco, the Netherlands, San Marino, Switzerland and the USA do not require visas to visit Singapore. Citizens of Austria, Belgium, Denmark, Finland, France, Germany, Iceland, Italy, Japan, Korea, Luxembourg, Norway, Spain and Sweden do not require visas for stays of up to 90 days for social purposes.

You will be given a 30-day visitor's visa if you arrive by air and a 14-day visa if you arrive by land or sea. Apply for extensions at the **Immigration Department** (☎ 6391 6100; 10 Kallang Rd), one block southwest of Lavender Mass Rapid Transit (MRT) station.

Brunei

For visits of up to 14 days, visas are not necessary for citizens of Belgium, Canada, France, Germany, Indonesia, Japan, Luxembourg, the Netherlands, New Zealand, Norway, the Philippines, South Korea, Sweden, Switzerland, Thailand and the Republic of the Maldives. British, Malaysian and Singaporean citizens do not require a visa for visits of 30 days or less. US citizens do not need a visa for visits of up to 90 days.

People of all other nationalities must have a visa to visit Brunei. Brunei embassies overseas have been known to give incorrect advice, so you should double-check if your nationality is not listed in this section and you are told that you do not require a visa to enter the country.

Note that if you need a visa for Brunei and don't already have one, you cannot enter the country by land or sea – there are no visa-granting facilities at its Sabah and Sarawak borders. Australian citizens entering Brunei by air, however, can get visas for up to 14 days, as well as multiple-entry visas for re-entering Brunei. Multiple-entry visas can also be arranged in advance through Canberra (the cost is A$22 for a 14-day visa valid for three months). Assuming your visas are in order, entering from Sarawak or Sabah is pain free – there's no money-showing, no requirement for an onward ticket and it's unlikely your bags will even be looked at.

Transit passengers are issued a 72-hour visa at the airport and if you intend to make a short trip to Brunei, it would be worth taking advantage of this visa. Three days is enough to see most of the sights, but this visa does tie you to travelling by air.

WOMEN TRAVELLERS

In these generally safe countries, the key to women travelling with minimum hassle is to blend in with the locals, which means dressing modestly and being respectful, especially in areas of stronger Muslim religious sensibilities, such as the east coast of Peninsular Malaysia and Brunei. Trying to fathom just what is appropriate can be confusing – some female readers report covering themselves carefully despite the heat, only to find local Chinese women in Muslim states scantily clad! Still, it's better to be safe than sorry – in the past we've had reports of attacks on women ranging from minor verbal aggravation to full-on physical assault.

Hard as it is to say, the truth is that the closer you get to conservative Muslim areas, the more aggressive Malay men can be towards women who look obviously foreign. In contrast, you are unlikely to be hassled too much in the Indian-populated highland resorts or the Little Indias of major west-coast cities. You're even safer in Malaysia's many Chinatowns, where harassment of foreign women is just about unheard of.

Be proactive about your own safety. Treat overly friendly strangers, both male and female, with a good deal of caution. Many travellers have reported the existence of small peepholes in the walls and doors of cheap hotels, some of which operate as boarding houses or brothels (often identified by their advertising 'day use' rates). You could always plug the holes with tissue paper or try asking to change rooms, but if you're on a budget you may not have much of a choice in some towns. This is especially true in Sarawak, where if there's a cage around the reception desk, you can bet it's probably a brothel and/or a gambling den. When you have a choice, stay in a Chinatown, or at least in a Chinese-operated hotel. On island resorts, stick to crowded beaches, and choose a chalet close to reception and other travellers.

No matter how limited your budget, it sometimes pays to upgrade – pay for taxis after dark or in seedy areas of town, and treat yourself to a mid-range hotel if all your other options are brothels. You won't regret it.

Keep in mind that the majority of Malaysians are Muslim and modesty in dress is culturally important. In conservative Muslim areas, you can halve your hassles just by tying a bandanna over your hair (a minimal concession to the headscarf worn by most Muslim women). When visiting mosques, you must cover all limbs, and either borrow a headscarf at the mosque entrance or buy one of the cheap silk ones (RM3) available on the street. At the beach, most Malaysian women swim fully clothed in T-shirts and shorts, so don't go topless – cover up.

Tampons and pads are widely available in Malaysia, especially in the big cities, and over-the-counter medications for common gynaecological health problems (like yeast infections) are also fairly easy to find.

In Singapore, women travellers are highly unlikely to suffer any harassment; in fact, in some bars you may come to feel invisible as the expats ogle the local girls.

In Brunei, Western women on their own may get propositioned by elderly gentlemen, but it's more amusing than annoying – dress modestly and you should be able to avoid most problems.

WORK

Malaysia

Being neither extremely poor nor extremely rich, Malaysia lacks some of the work and volunteer opportunities of its Asian neighbours. However, there are possibilities for those who seek them out. At the upper end of the scale there are professional-level jobs in finance, journalism and the oil industry. Likewise, those with teaching credentials can find English-teaching jobs in Malaysia, though pickings are slim compared to Japan and Korea. At the other end of the scale, temporary jobs can be found at some guesthouses and dive centres in popular resort areas.

The Web is the best place to start your search. JobStreet.com advertises a wide variety of jobs at www.jobs.com.my. Teachers can check some of the many TEFL sites, including the TEFL Job Centre at www.jobs.edunet.com. Those looking for volunteer work should contact the major volunteer organisations in their home country.

Depending on the nature of your job, you'll need either an Expatriate Personnel Visa or Temporary Employment Visa. For details and requirements, check the Immigration Department of Malaysia's website at www.imi.gov.my.

Singapore

While Singapore does have a fairly large expatriate European community, this is more a reflection of the large representation of overseas companies than a shortage of skills in the local labour market. However, the vacancies pages of the *Straits Times* are often crammed with job notices.

In the great majority of cases, foreign workers obtain employment with multinationals based in Singapore before they come to Singapore. One of the main reasons for this is the high cost of accommodation and car ownership, which overseas companies normally cover. The overwhelming majority of positions are for domestic servants (newspapers are full of agencies advertising Filipino housemaids) and unskilled labourers.

Some foreigners arrive in Singapore and find work. Business experience and economic training are a bonus, or those with easily marketable job skills can do the rounds of companies that might be interested. It has become fashionable for some of the restaurants serving Western food to employ Westerners, and some travellers have picked up temporary work as waiters. Finally, check out **Contact Singapore** (www.contactsingapore.org.sg/home.htm), where jobs are posted.

Transport

CONTENTS

THINGS CHANGE...

The information in this chapter is particularly vulnerable to change. Check directly with the airline or a travel agent to make sure you understand how a fare (and ticket you may buy) works and be aware of the security requirements for international travel. Shop carefully. The details given in this chapter should be regarded as pointers and are not a substitute for your own careful, up-to-date research.

GETTING THERE & AWAY

ENTERING THE REGION

There are no particular difficulties for most travellers entering the region. The main requirement is a passport that's valid for travel for at least six months. To enter Malaysia, Singapore or Brunei you'll need to show an onward ticket. For Malaysia, proof of adequate funds for your stay is also required. For Brunei, many travellers will need to obtain a visa in advance. Sabah and Sarawak are treated in some ways as countries separate from Peninsular Malaysia, with additional entry procedures.

Citizens of Israel, Serbia and Montenegro cannot enter Malaysia, and Brunei may not admit nationals of Israel or North Korea. According to some sources, anyone of 'scruffy appearance' may be denied entry to Malaysia.

For more details of visa and other entry requirements, see p551.

AIR

Airports & Airlines

MALAYSIA

Kuala Lumpur (KL) is the major gateway to Malaysia, handling almost all international flights with the exception of a few regional flights from Asia, which may come via Penang, Kota Kinabalu and a few other cities (see the relevant chapters for airport details). Many airlines service Malaysia, but the country's international airline, Malaysia Airlines, is the major carrier.

The hi-tech **Kuala Lumpur International Airport** (Map pp74-5; KLIA; www.klia.com.my) is 75km south of the city centre at Sepang.

Some airlines with offices in KL (area code ☎ 03):

Aeroflot (☎ 2161 0231; www.aeroflot.com; Wisma Tong Ah, 1 Jl Perak)

Air India (☎ 2142 0166; www.airindia.com; Angkasaraya Bldg, 123 Jl Ampang)

British Airways & Qantas (☎ 2167 6188; www.britishairways.com; 8th fl, West Wing, Rohas Terkasa, 8 Jl Perak)

Cathay Pacific Airways (☎ 2078 3377/55; www.cathaypacific.com; Suite 22, Level 1, Menara IMC, 8 Jl Sultan Ismail)

China Airlines (☎ 2142 7344; www.china-airlines.com; Amoda Bldg, 22 Jl Imbi)

Garuda Indonesian Airlines (☎ 2162 2811; www.garuda-indonesia.com; Level 19, Menara Citibank, Jl Ampang)

Japan Airlines (☎ 2161 1722; www.japanair.com; Level 20, Menara Citibank, Jl Ampang)

Lufthansa (Map p82; ☎ 2161 4666; www.lufthansa.com; 3rd fl, Pernas International Bldg, Jl Sultan Ismail)

Malaysia Airlines (☎ 2161 0555; www.malaysiaair.com; 24-hr reservations ☎ 7846 3000; Bangunan MAS, Jl Sultan Ismail; ☎ 2272 4260; KL Sentral station)
Royal Brunei Airlines (Map p82; www.bruneiair.com; ☎ 2070 7166; Menara UBN, 10 Jl P Ramlee)
Singapore Airlines (☎ 2692 3122; www.singaporeair.com; Wisma SIA, 2 Jl Dang Wangi)
Thai Airways International (☎ 2031 2900; www.thaiair.com; 30 Wisma Goldhill, 67 Jl Raja Chulan)
Virgin Atlantic (☎ 2143 0322; www.virgin-atlantic.com; 2nd fl, 77 Jl Bukit Bintang)

SINGAPORE

Practically all international air traffic goes through **Changi International Airport** (Map pp448-9; ☎ 6541 2267; www.changi.airport.com.sg).

Regularly voted the world's best airport, Changi is vast, efficient and amazingly organised. Among its many facilities are foreign-exchange booths, a post office (open 24 hours), free phones for local calls, Internet access, left-luggage facilities (S$3.09 per small bag for the first day and S$4.12 per day thereafter), scores of shops, as well as restaurants, fitness centres, saunas, showers, and business and medical centres (including one that is open 24 hours in the basement of Terminal 2).

Currently Changi has two terminals (the newer Terminal 2 handles most major international flights). A third terminal is under construction. On your way through the arrivals concourse, pick up the free booklets, maps and other guides (including the airport's own magazine) available from stands.

Following are some of the major airline offices in Singapore, including that of the national carrier, Singapore Airlines.

Air New Zealand (☎ 6532 3846; www.airnewzealand.com; 24-07/08 Ocean Bldg, 10 Collyer Quay)
British Airways & Qantas (☎ 6589 7000; www.britishairways.com; 06-05 Cairnhill Place, 15 Cairnhill Rd)
Cathay Pacific Airways (☎ 6533 1333; www.cathaypacific.com; 16-01 Ocean Bldg, 10 Collyer Quay)
Garuda Indonesia (☎ 6250 5666; www.garuda-indonesia.com; 12-03 United Square, 101 Thomson Rd)
KLM-Royal Dutch Airlines (☎ 6737 7622; www.klm.com; 12-06 Ngee Ann City Tower, 391A Orchard Rd)
Lufthansa Airlines (☎ 6835 5933; www.lufthansa.com; 05-01 Palais Renaissance, 390 Orchard Rd)
Malaysia Airlines (☎ 6336 6777; www.malaysiaair.com; 02-09 Singapore Shopping Centre, 190 Clemenceau Ave)
Singapore Airlines (☎ 6223 8888; www.singaporeair.com; Level 2, Paragon Bldg, Orchard Rd)
Thai Airways International (☎ 1-800 224 9977; www.thaiair.com; The Globe, 100 Cecil St)

BRUNEI

Brunei International Airport (☎ 233 2531/3315, flight inquiries ☎ 233 1747) is about 10km out of the centre of Bandar Seri Begawan (BSB). Royal Brunei Airlines has direct flights between Bandar Seri Begawan and many destinations in Asia, and to Darwin and Perth in Australia, and to and from Abu Dhabi and Dubai. Other flights with stopovers go to Los Angeles and to Europe. Discounts are often available when you buy the ticket in the country of your departure, and promotional fares are offered out of Brunei as well. If you need a drink on long-haul flights, keep in mind that Royal Brunei does not serve alcohol.

Airlines flying into Brunei and with offices in BSB:

British Airways & Qantas (☎ 222 5871; www.britishairways.com) For ticket sales, contact Jasra Harrisons (☎ 224 3911; cnr Jl MacArthur & Jl Sungai Kianggeh)
Garuda Indonesia (☎ 223 5870; www.garuda-indonesia.com; 3rd fl, Wisma Raya Bldg, 49-50 Jl Sultan)
Malaysia Airlines (☎ 222 4141; www.malaysiaair.com ; 144 Jl Pemancha)
Royal Brunei Airlines (☎ 224 2222; www.bruneiair.com; RBA Plaza, Jl Sultan)
Singapore Airlines (☎ 224 4901; www.singaporeair.com; 1st fl, Wisma Raya Bldg, 49-50 Jl Sultan)
Thai Airways International (☎ 224 2991; www.thaiair.com; 401-403, 4th fl, Kompleks Jl Sultan, 51-55 Jl Sultan)

Tickets

When shopping for a ticket, be sure to compare the costs of flying into Malaysia versus flying into Singapore. From Singapore, you can travel overland to almost any place in Peninsular Malaysia in less than 18 hours, and Singapore also has direct flights to Malaysian Borneo and Brunei.

KL, Penang and Singapore are good places to buy tickets for onward travel from Malaysia, but if you're really in search of bargains, you'll almost always do better in Bangkok (just a train ride away).

To research and buy a ticket on the Internet, try these online booking services:

www.lonelyplanet.com Use the TripPlanner service to book multistop trips.

> **DEPARTURE TAX**
>
> **Malaysia**
>
> There's a RM45 airport tax on all flights out of KLIA (RM11 for flights out of Penang and Johor Bahru). If you buy your ticket in Malaysia, the tax is included in the price.
>
> **Singapore**
>
> The airport departure tax, or Passenger Service Charge (PSC), from Changi is $15 and will be included in the cost of your air ticket.
>
> **Brunei**
>
> There's a departure tax of B$5 when flying to Malaysia and Singapore, and B$12 to all other destinations.

www.bridgetheworld.co.uk Good for holiday bargains and speciality travel (all prices quoted in pounds only).

www.travel.com.au There is also a New Zealand version (www.travel.co.nz).

www.cheapflights.com No-frills website offering flights to a number of destinations.

www.onetravel.com Another covering a number of destinations.

From Australia

Discounted fares from Melbourne or Sydney to KL or Singapore start at A$800 return in the low season, rising to A$1100 in the high season (December to February). Flying from Brisbane is about A$100 cheaper, from Perth A$200 cheaper. Qantas' budget-flight subsidiary **Australian Airlines** (☎ 1300 799 798; www.australianairlines.com.au) flies from Cairns to Singapore and may be launching direct flights to Kota Kinabalu; check its website for details.

Malaysia Airlines, Singapore Airlines and Qantas Airways all offer good deals; also check some of the Middle-Eastern airlines that fly between Europe and Australia.

The travel sections of weekend newspapers such as the *Age* in Melbourne and the *Sydney Morning Herald* are good places to look for air-fare deals.

Local travel agencies:

Flight Centre (☎ 131 600 Australia-wide; www.flightcentre.com.au) Has dozens of offices throughout Australia.

STA Travel (☎ 03-9349 2411; www.statravel.com.au) Has offices in all major cities. Call ☎ 131 776 Australia-wide for the location of your nearest branch.

From Canada

There are no direct flights between Canada and Malaysia; the cheapest fares are going to be on an airline like **Eva Air** (☎ 04-6823576; www.evaair.com/html/global/english/gb_en_home/) via Taiwan. For flights to Malaysia, low-season return fares from Vancouver average C$1400; from Toronto they're closer to C$2200.

The fare from Vancouver to Singapore starts at one-way/return C$1170/1545. Prices are similar from Montreal.

The *Globe & Mail*, the *Toronto Star*, the *Montreal Gazette* and the *Vancouver Sun* carry travel agency ads.

Travel CUTS (☎ 1866-246 9762; www.travelcuts.com) is Canada's national student travel agency.

From Continental Europe

From Paris to KL or Singapore costs as little as €830 return.

Nouvelles Frontières (☎ 01-45 68 70 00; www.nouvelles-frontieres.fr; 87 blvd de Grenelle, 75015 Paris) sometimes has special deals on Gulf Air.

From Hong Kong

Hong Kong is not the discount-flight centre it once was. The cheapest one-way flights to Malaysia cost around HK$2013, to Singapore HK$1270, and to Brunei HK$2014. In addition to KL, it is possible to fly from Hong Kong to Penang, Pulau Langkawi and Kota Kinabalu.

The Tsim Sha Tsui area is Hong Kong's budget travel-agency centre. Most of the operators nowadays are reliable. One of the best is **Phoenix Services Agency** (☎ 2722 7378; info@phoenixtrvl.com). **Royal Brunei Airlines** (☎ 2242222; www.bruneiair.com) flies between Brunei and Hong Kong (B$686) three times a week.

From Indonesia

The short hop from Medan in Sumatra to Penang costs around US$60 to US$140 (depending on discounts). There are also weekly flights between Pontianak in Kalimantan (the Indonesian part of the island of Borneo) and Kuching in Sarawak for around US$80. Similarly, at the eastern end of Borneo there is a weekly connection between Tawau in Sabah and Tarakan in Kalimantan.

From Java, the cheapest connections are to Singapore, for as little as one-way/return US$70/US$115. A flight from Bali to

Singapore costs from US$145/197 with **Boraq Airlines** (www.bouraq.com/); which also has direct flights between Singapore and Medan and Surabaya. Internal flights are cheaper if tickets are bought in Indonesia.

The travel agencies on Jl Jaksa, Jakarta's budget accommodation area, are good places to look for international flights; **Indo Shangrila Travel** (☎ 021-625 6080) is a large ticketing agent that often has good deals.

Royal Brunei Airlines (☎ 2242222; www.bruneiair.com) flies between Brunei and Jakarta (B$471) four times a week.

From Japan

Return flights from Japan to KL cost between ¥50,000 and ¥70,000. One-way tickets are expensive, averaging around ¥50,000. It's usually around ¥10,000 cheaper to fly to/from Tokyo, rather than Osaka/Kansai International Airport.

Reliable travel agencies used to dealing with foreigners:

A'Cross Travel (☎ 03-3340 6741; www.crosstravel.com)
No 1 Travel (☎ 03-3200 8871; www.no1-travel.com)
STA Travel (www.statravel.co.jp; Tokyo ☎ 03-5485 8380; Osaka ☎ 06-262 7066)

For information on the latest discount prices, pick up a copy of *Tokyo Classified* or, if you're in the Kansai region, get hold of *Kansai Time Out*. The four English-language newspapers also run advertisements from the major travel agents.

From New Zealand

Low-season one-way/return tickets start at NZ$1000/1400 between Auckland and KL or Singapore; add around NZ$400 for high-season fares. Round-the-World (RTW) and Circle Pacific fares for travel to/from Malaysia are often a good value.

The *New Zealand Herald* has a travel section in which travel agents advertise fares.

Flight Centre (☎ 09-309 6171) Has a large office in Auckland and many branches throughout the country.
STA Travel (☎ 09-309 0458; www.statravel.co.nz) Has offices in all major towns and cities.

From Thailand

The place to buy tickets to Malaysia or Singapore in Bangkok is Khao San Rd. The agents here deal in discounted tickets; rip-offs do occur from time to time, so take care. Flights from Bangkok to KL cost from 4800B/6500B one way/return and flights from Bangkok to Penang cost from 3600B/6800B. **Royal Brunei Airlines** (☎ 2242222; www.bruneiair.com) flies between Brunei and Bangkok (B$520, 3 weekly)

From the UK

London has the best deals for flights to Malaysia and Singapore. You can take your pick from a wide range of carriers, but the cheapest are Aeroflot, Pakistan International Airlines and Air Lanka. Low-season discount tickets start from one-way/return UK£240/380. Other airlines such as Lufthansa Airlines, Virgin Atlantic and Malaysia Airlines have return fares from around UK£565, but there are seasonal fluctuations of around UK£100. Over the peak Christmas to New Year period return fares can top UK£600.

Advertisements for many travel agents appear in the travel pages of the weekend broadsheets, such as the *Independent* on Saturday and the *Sunday Times*. Look out for free magazines such as *TNT*.

Reputable agencies in London:

Bridge the World (☎ 0870-444 7474, 020-7813 3350)
Flightbookers (☎ 0870-010 7000; www.ebookers.co.uk)
STA Travel (☎ 0870-1600 599; www.statravel.co.uk)
Trailfinders (☎ 020-7938 3939; www.trailfinders.co.uk)

From the USA

It's possible to find fares from the US west coast to Malaysia for around US$900 return, with Malaysia Airlines offering some of the cheapest. Other airlines to check include Singapore Airlines, Air China and Cathay Pacific. From New York, fares start at US$1100. Some cheap fares may include a stopover in Hong Kong.

Singapore Airlines and others have direct flights but it is usually cheaper to fly via another port, such as with China Airlines via Taipei or with Cathay Pacific Airways via Hong Kong. Low season tickets start from one-way/return US$507/619 from Los Angeles, US$615/763 from New York.

If you're going to be travelling the region, look into Circle Pacific flights. There are numerous combinations of destinations you can include. Expect to pay around US$2000 to go from Los Angeles to Singapore via Tahiti, Auckland (New Zealand), Sydney and Bali, then back home via Hong Kong.

San Francisco consolidators (discount travel agents) have some of the cheapest fares, although good deals can also be found in Los Angeles, New York and other big cities. The *San Francisco Examiner*, the *New York Times*, the *Los Angeles Times* and the *Chicago Tribune* all produce weekly travel sections in which you'll find any number of travel agency ads. A good place to start is **STA Travel** (☎ 800-781 4040; www.statravel.com) which has a wide network of offices.

BORDER CROSSINGS

LAND

Malaysia

FROM BRUNEI

The main overland route into Brunei is via bus from Miri in Sarawak. See the Getting There & Away section under Bandar Seri Begawan (p525) for details. It's possible to travel overland between Limbang or Lawas in Sarawak and Bangar in the eastern part of Brunei, although a boat to Bandar Seri Begawan is the usual and far more convenient option. Overland travel between Lawas and Bangar involves hiring a taxi, so it's a little more expensive than the other routes. See the Getting There & Away sections under Bangar (p529), and Limbang (p381) and Lawas (p382) for details on these border crossings.

FROM INDONESIA

It is easy to cross the border between Malaysian Borneo and Indonesia. A daily express bus (10 hours) runs between Pontianak in Kalimantan and Kuching in Sarawak. The bus crosses at the Tebedu/Entikong border, a visa-free entry point into Indonesia. See the Kuching Getting There & Away section (p333) for details.

FROM SINGAPORE

The Causeway linking Johor Bahru (JB) with Singapore handles most traffic between the countries. Trains and buses run from all over Malaysia straight through to Singapore, or you can take a bus to JB and get a taxi or one of the frequent buses from JB to Singapore.

There is also a causeway linking Tuas, in western Singapore, with Geylang Patah in JB. This is known as the Second Link, and some bus services to Melaka and up the west coast head this way. If you have a car, tolls on the Second Link are much higher than the charge on the main Causeway.

Bus

From Singapore, both the air-con express buses (S$2.40) and the public SBS bus No 170 (S$1.10) depart for Johor Bahru every 15 minutes between 6.30am and 11pm from the **Queen St bus terminal** (Map p458; cnr Queen & Arab Sts). Bus No 170 can be boarded anywhere along the way, such as on Rochor, Rochor Canal or Bukit Timah Rds. Share taxis to many places in Malaysia also leave from the Queen St terminal.

The buses stop at the Singapore checkpoint before the Causeway – keep your ticket and hop on the next bus that comes along after you've cleared immigration. You'll go through the same process at Malaysian immigration and customs at the other end of the Causeway, 1km away. The bus continues from here (your ticket is still valid) to the Johor Bahru bus terminus on the outskirts of town, or you can walk the 100m or so to town from the Causeway.

If you are travelling beyond JB, it is easier to catch a long-distance bus straight from Singapore, but there is a greater variety of bus services from JB and the fares are cheaper.

In Singapore, long-distance buses to Melaka and the east coast of Malaysia leave from and arrive at the **Lavender St bus terminal** (Map p458; cnr Lavender St & Kallang Bahru). The terminal is a 500m walk from Lavender MRT station; otherwise take bus No 5 or 61. For destinations north of Kuala Lumpur, including to Thailand, most buses leave from the **Golden Mile Complex** (Map p458; Beach Rd); Lavender MRT station is about 500m away.

Train

From Singapore, **KTM** (Keretapi Tanah Melayu; ☎ 6222 5165; www.ktmb.com.my) runs three air-conditioned express trains daily to Malaysia (approximately six hours to KL); from KL you can take a train to Thailand.

FROM THAILAND

You can cross the border into Thailand at Padang Besar (p198) by road or rail; at Bukit Kayu Hitam (p196) or Keroh–Betong

TRANSPORT

by road in the west; or at Rantau Panjang – Sungai Golok or Pengkalan Kubor in the east (p309).

Bus & Car

On the west coast, although there are border points at Padang Besar and Keroh, most travellers cross by road at Bukit Kayu Hitam on the Lebuhraya (North-South Hwy) for Hat Yai. The easiest way to cross here is to take a bus from Georgetown (see the Penang chapter, p155) to Hat Yai for around RM30.

Buses also run from Alor Setar to the Malaysian customs post at Bukit Kayu Hitam. From here you can walk the roughly 2km to the border crossing or hop on one of the passing motrobikes which ply the route for around RM3. On the other side, buses and taxis run to Sadao and Hat Yai. Buses and trains run from Hat Yai to Phuket, Krabi, Surat Thani, Bangkok and other places.

The alternative is to cross at Padang Besar, where it is an easy walk across. The only reason to go this way by road is if you're heading to/from Langkawi. Buses run from Kuala Perlis to Padang Besar via Kangar. The train from Alor Setar all the way to Hat Yai is the easiest way to cross this border.

On the east coast the Thai border is at Rantau Panjang (Sungai Golok on the Thai side), 1½ hours by bus from Kota Bharu. From Rantau Panjang walk across the border, and it's about 1km to the station, from where trains go to Hat Yai, Surat Thani and Bangkok. Buses also take this route. See the Kota Bharu Getting There & Away section (p309) for more details.

An alternative route into Thailand is via Pengkalan Kubor on the coast. It's more time-consuming and fewer travellers go this way. See the Pengkalan Kubor (p311) section in the Kelantan chapter for more details.

Train

The rail route into Thailand is on the Butterworth–Alor Setar–Hat Yai route, which crosses into Thailand at Padang Besar. You can take the **International Express** (☎ 6222 5165; www.ktmb.com.my) from Butterworth all the way to Bangkok with connections from Singapore and KL. From Hat Yai there are frequent train and bus connections to other parts of Thailand (see the *International Express* table on this page for train fares and schedules). One train a day also goes from Alor Setar to Hat Yai (see the Alor Setar Getting There & Away section, p187, for details).

The luxurious **Eastern & Oriental Express** (☎ 6392 3500; www.orient-express.com) departs Singapore on alternate Wednesdays, Fridays and Sundays. The train, done out in antique opulence, takes 42 hours to do the 1943km journey to Bangkok. Don your linen suit, sip

INTERNATIONAL EXPRESS FARES (2ND CLASS)

	Singapore	Kuala Lumpur	Butterworth
Hat Yai	S$64.20	RM43.50	RM14.90
Bangkok	S$91.70	RM70.30	RM44.90

INTERNATIONAL EXPRESS SCHEDULE

Train No 36 (from Butterworth; daily)	
Butterworth	14:20
Alor Setar	16:17
Hat Yai	18.25*
Bangkok	11:10*

Train No 35 (from Bangkok; runs daily)	
Bangkok	14.20*
Hat Yai	06.55*
Alor Setar	11:08
Butterworth	12:55

*Thai time (one hour behind Malaysian time).

There is an express surcharge on the *International Express* of RM13.60 for air-con and RM8.10 for non-air-con, plus RM7.20 for the Thai leg of the journey. Sleeping berths in 2nd class cost an additional RM22.30 for an upper berth and RM28.50 for a lower berth. Surcharges may also apply to fares in Singapore dollars; check with KTM or visit its web site at www.ktmb.com.my.

a gin and tonic and dig deep for the fare: from S$2350 per person in a double compartment, up to S$6000 in the presidential suite. You can go as far as Kuala Lumpur or Butterworth for a lower fare.

SEA

Malaysia

FROM BRUNEI

Boats connect Brunei to Lawas and Limbang in Sarawak, and to Pulau Labuan, from where boats go to Sabah. With the exception of boats destined for Limbang, all international boats now depart from Muara, 25km northeast of Bandar Seri Begawan, where Brunei immigration formalities are also handled. Besides flying, the boat route is the most convenient; normally the South China Sea is quite smooth, but during the wet season it can get choppy. Bring anti-nausea pills if you're prone to sea-sicknessness. See the Bandar Seri Begawan Getting There & Away section (p524) for more information.

Buy your ticket at the dock the previous day if you are catching an early boat, especially on weekends and public holidays, and aim to check in 45 minutes before departure time to clear immigration. You'll need to catch the first express bus to Muara from BSB to get the first ferry.

From Muara, there are numerous express boats daily to Pulau Labuan (1 hour) between 7.30am and 4.40pm. The fare from Brunei is adult/child B$15/8. The 1st-class fare is only B$3 (or RM6) more and a lot more comfortable.

Pulau Labuan is a duty-free island between Brunei and Sabah from where you can take a ferry direct to Kota Kinabalu or Menumbok (for a bus to Kota Kinabalu); and flights to Sabah, Sarawak or West Malaysia. For more details, see the Pulau Labuan Getting There & Away section (p412) in the Sabah chapter.

Boats to Limbang in Sarawak leave from the customs wharf at the end of Jl Roberts in Bandar Seri Begawan, where there's also an immigration office. Private express boats do this run between 7am and 4pm, and depart when full. Buy your ticket at the customs wharf. The fare is B$10 and the trip takes about 30 minutes.

Limbang is an uneventful river town and is also one end of the famed Headhunters' Trail. From Limbang you can fly to Miri, Lawas or Kota Kinabalu (see p381 for more information).

One express boat daily goes from Muara to Lawas in Sarawak (B$10, 2 hours) at 11.30am. Returning to Muara, a boat leaves Lawas at 7am and costs RM25. From Lawas there are buses to Sabah and flights to Miri and Kota Kinabalu. See the Lawas Getting There & Away section (p382) for more details.

FROM INDONESIA

The three main ferry routes between Indonesia and Malaysia are Medan–Penang and Dumai–Melaka connecting Sumatra with Peninsular Malaysia, and Tarakan–Tawau linking Kalimantan with Sabah.

The popular crossing between Medan in Sumatra and Penang is handled by two companies that between them have services most days of the week. The boats actually leave from Belawan in Sumatra (the bus journey from Medan is included in the price). See the Penang, Getting There & Away (p155) for more details.

Twice-daily high-speed ferries run between Dumai in Sumatra and Melaka. See the Melaka chapter (p226) for details.

Boats also operate most days from Tarakan and Pulau Nunukan in Kalimantan to Tawau in Sabah. Tarakan is three hours from Pulau Nunukan, and it's another hour to Taway. See the Sabah chapter (p442) for details.

Boats go directly from Batu Ampar and Tanjung Pinang, both in Sumatra, to the Bebas Cukai ferry terminal in Johor Bahru (see p236 for more information). You can also take a ferry from Tanjung Balai in Sumatra to Kukup, 40km southwest of Johor Bahru (see p238 for more information).

FROM THE PHILIPPINES

Passenger ferries now run between Sandakan and Zamboanga in the Philippines. The trip takes 18 hours and costs from RM60.

FROM SINGAPORE

Singapore has a number of ferry connections to Malaysia. Cruise trips in the region are also very popular with locals.

The big cruise centre at the **World Trade Centre** (WTC), next to HarbourFront MRT station, is the main departure point for cruises and many ferries; a host of agents here handle bookings.

Changi ferry terminal (☎ 6545 3600) and the pier at Changi Village, both north of Changi airport, have ferries to Malaysia. To get to Changi ferry terminal, take bus No 2 to Changi Village and then a taxi. The ferry terminal is just off Changi Coast Rd.

The ferry from Changi ferry terminal to Tanjung Belungkor, east of Johor Bahru, is primarily a service for Singaporeans going to Desaru in Malaysia. The 11km journey takes 45 minutes and costs S$18/28 one way/return. There are usually four services daily in each direction. From the Tanjung Belungkor jetty, buses operate to Desaru and Kota Tinggi.

From Changi Village, ferries also go to Pengerang across the Johor strait in Malaysia. This is an interesting back-door route into Malaysia. There's no fixed schedule; ferries leave throughout the day when full (12 people). The cost is S$10 per person or S$60 for the whole boat. The best time to catch one is early in the morning before 8am. Clear Singapore immigration at the small post on the Changi River dock.

Between March and mid-October **Penguin** (☎ 6542 7105; 02-20 World Trade Centre) runs a high-speed catamaran service (one-way/return S$106/174; 4½ hours) to Pulau Tioman. Departures are at 8.30am from the **Tanah Merah ferry terminal** (☎ 6542 7102) south of Changi airport.

FROM THAILAND

Regular daily boats run between Satun in Thailand and Pulau Langkawi (see p196). There are customs and immigration posts here, so you can cross quite legally, although it's an unusual and rarely used entry/exit point. Make sure you get your passport stamped on entry. In the main tourist season (around Christmas) yachts run irregularly between Langkawi and Phuket in Thailand, taking in Thai islands on the way. The trip usually takes five days and costs around US$70 per person, per day.

Singapore

FROM INDONESIA

No direct ferries run between Singapore and the main ports in Indonesia, but it is possible to travel between the two countries via the islands in the nearby Riau Archipelago. Most services run via Pulau Batam and Pulau Bintan. The ferries are modern, fast and air-conditioned. From Sumatra, boats go to Batam.

Pulau Batam

From Sekupang and Batu Ampar (both on Pulau Batam), it takes half an hour and 45 minutes respectively to reach Singapore. The main ferry agents are at Batu Ampar. Between them they have dozens of departures every day to Singapore, at least every half-hour from 7.30am to 8pm. Tanjung Buton on the Sumatran mainland is a three-hour bus ride from Palembang. From Tanjung Buton you can take a boat to Sekupang.

Batu Ampar is close to the main town of Nagoya; ferry departures are roughly every hour from 7.50am to 8.15pm. Dino Shipping also has several ferries a day from Nongsa in the north of Pulau Batam to the the **Tanah Merah ferry terminal** (☎ 6542 7102) south of Changi Airport in Singapore.

Pulau Bintan

The same companies that operate ferries from Batam also have several ferries a day from Bintan to Singapore's Tanah Merah ferry terminal. From Tanjung Pinang, the main city on the island, there are several ferries a day to Singapore from around 9am with most services on the weekends. The journey takes about 1½ hours.

GETTING AROUND

AIR

Domestic Air Services

Malaysia's main domestic operator is **Malaysia Airlines** (☎ 03-2161 0555; www.malaysia-airlines.com.my). The Malaysian Air Fares map (opposite) details some of the main regional routes and the standard one-way fares in Malaysian ringgit. Malaysia Airlines has many other regional routes in Sarawak and Sabah. It operates Airbuses, Boeing 737s and Fokker F50s/F70s on its main domestic routes, plus 18-seater Twin Otters on most of the more remote Sarawak and Sabah routes.

Malaysia's other main domestic carrier is **Air Asia** (☎ 03-7651 2222 in KL; www.airasia.com) covering Alor Setar, Kota Bharu, Kota Kinabalu, Kuala Terengganu, Kuching, Labuan, Langkawi, Miri, Penang, Sandakan, Sibu and Tawau.

The tiny **Berjaya Air** (☎ 03-7847 6828; www.berjaya-air.com) has flights between Kuala Lumpur, Pulau Tioman and Pulau Pangkor in Peninsular Malaysia.

In Singapore, tickets for flights within Malaysia are only sold by **Malaysia Airlines** (Map pp452-3; ☎ 6433 0612; 02-09 Singapore Shopping Centre, 190 Clemenceau Ave), 200m southwest of Dhoby Ghaut MRT.

From Kuala Lumpur International Airport the domestic departure tax is RM45, from Penang and Johor Bharu RM11. These taxes are included in the ticket prices.

DISCOUNTS & SPECIAL FLIGHTS

A variety of worthwhile discounts (typically between 25% and 50%) are available for flights around Malaysia on Malaysian Airlines, including for families and groups of three or more – it's worth enquiring when you book tickets in Malaysia. Student discounts are available, but only for students enrolled in institutions in Malaysia. Air Asia also discounts ticket prices if you book them yourself over the Internet.

Malaysia Airlines also has special seven-day advance-purchase one-way tickets (YOX fares) and advance-purchase 30-day return tickets (YEE30 fares) for the following flights from Johor Bahru and KL:

Flight	fare (RM) YOX/YEE30
JB-Kuching	144/305
JB-Kota Kinabalu	295/624
JB-Penang	228/483
KL-Kuching	227/425
KL-Kota Kinabalu	372/689
KL-Miri	359/679
KL-Labuan	372/656
KL-Sibu	–/510
Kuching-Penang	–/544

There are also a few economy night-flights between Kuala Lumpur and Kota Kinabalu (RM306), Kuching (RM187), Alor Setar (RM112) and Penang (RM111), and between JB and KK (RM260).

MALAYSIA

If you are flying to Sarawak or Sabah, you can save quite a few ringgit by flying from Johor Bahru rather than Kuala Lumpur or Singapore. The regular economy fare is RM169 from Johor Bahru to Kuching against RM262 from KL and S$199 from Singapore. To Kota Kinabalu, the respective fares are RM347, RM437 and S$403. To persuade travellers to take advantage of these lower fares, Malaysia Airlines runs the **SPS** (☎ 250 3333) bus service directly from its office at the **Copthorne Orchid Hotel** (214 Dunearn Rd) in Singapore to the Johor Bahru airport for S$12 (2 hours).

Malaysia Airlines has lots of local flights in Malaysian Borneo, where many communities rely on air transport as the only quick

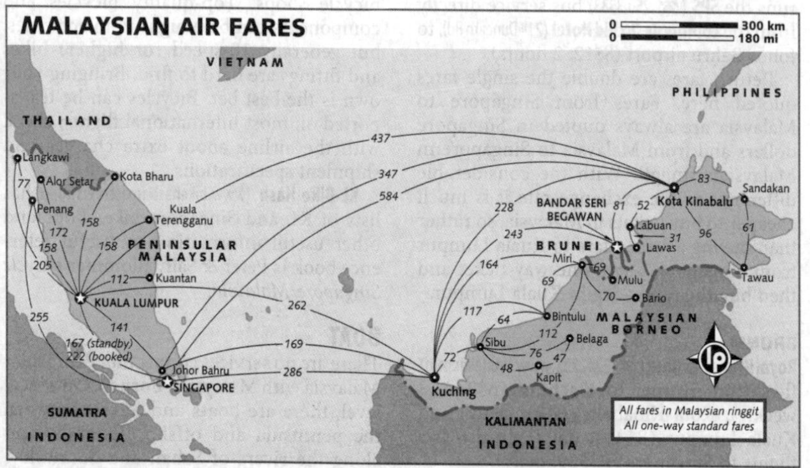

way in or out. These flights are very much reliant on the vagaries of the weather. In the wet season (October to March in Sarawak and on Sabah's northeast coast; May to November on Sabah's west coast), places like Bario in Sarawak can be isolated for days at a time, so don't venture into this area if you have a very tight schedule. These flights are completely booked during school holidays. At other times it's easier to get a seat at a few days' notice, but always book as far in advance as possible. See the Sabah (p383) and Sarawak chapters (p313) for more detail.

SINGAPORE

Malaysia Airlines and Singapore Airlines operate a shuttle service with frequent flights between Kuala Lumpur and Singapore for one-way stand-by from RM167 (S$115 from Singapore); seats are available on a first-come, first-served basis. Malaysia Airlines also connects Singapore to Langkawi (RM305, S$211) and Penang (RM255, S$176) in Peninsular Malaysia, and Kuching (RM286, S$199) and Kota Kinabalu (RM584, S$403) in Malaysian Borneo.

Silk Air (☎ 1-800-223 8888; www.silkair.com), the 'regional wing' of Singapore Airlines, has daily flights between Singapore and Pulau Langkawi (RM478, S$211).

Going to Malaysia, you can save quite a few dollars if you fly from Johor Bahru rather than Singapore. For example, to Kota Kinabalu the fares are RM347 from Johor Bahru but S$403 from Singapore. Malaysia Airlines runs the **SPS** (☎ 250 3333) bus service directly from the **Copthorne Orchid Hotel** (214 Dunearn Rd), to Johor Bahru airport (S$12, 2 hours).

Return fares are double the single fares quoted here. Fares from Singapore to Malaysia are always quoted in Singapore dollars and from Malaysia to Singapore in Malaysian ringgit. With the considerable difference in the exchange rate it is much cheaper to buy tickets in Malaysia, so rather than buying a return fare to Kuala Lumpur from Singapore, buy a one-way ticket and then buy the return leg in Kuala Lumpur.

BRUNEI

Royal Brunei Airlines (☎ 2242222; www.bruneiair.com) flies from Brunei to Kuching (B$244, 3 weekly), Kota Kinabalu (B$81, daily) and Kuala Lumpur (B$411, daily). It also has flights to Singapore (B$389, daily).

Air Passes

The Discover Malaysia pass costs US$199 for five flight coupons and can be used on any Malaysia Airlines service within a 28-day period.

For flying around the region the Asean Air Pass needs to be bought at the same time as a ticket from your home country to the region on one of the following airlines: Singapore Airlines, Malaysia Airlines, Thai, Garuda, Silk Air, Philippine Airlines, Air Vietnam, Laos Airlines and Myanmar Airlines. You can buy a minimum of three coupons (US$360) covering three flights, up to a maximum of six coupons (US$720).

If you are going to be flying a lot between countries, it will be better for you to purchase the New Asean Circle Fare. This can be used with any outward bound airline to the region and starts at US$500 for three coupons rising to US$650 for six coupons.

BICYCLE

Cycling is a cheap and healthy way of travelling, and bicycle touring from Singapore, around Malaysia, and on to Thailand is an increasingly popular activity.

The main road system is well engineered with good surfaces, but the secondary road system is limited. Road conditions are good enough for touring bikes in most places, but mountain bikes are recommended for forays off the beaten track.

Both KL and Singapore have plenty of bicycle shops. Top-quality bicycles and components can be bought in major cities, but generally 10-speed (or higher) bikes and fittings are hard to find. Bringing your own is the best bet. Bicycles can be transported on most international flights; check with the airline about extra charges and shipment specifications.

KL Bike Hash (www.bikehash.freeservers.com) has lists of KL and Singapore bike shops and other useful information. A useful reference book is Peter & Sally Blommer's *Cycle Singapore/Malaysia*.

BOAT

There are no services connecting Peninsular Malaysia with Malaysian Borneo. On a local level, there are boats and ferries between the peninsula and offshore islands, and along the rivers of Sabah and Sarawak –

check the relevant chapters for details. Note that some ferry operators are notoriously lax about observing safety rules, and local authorities are often nonexistent. If a boat looks overloaded or otherwise unsafe, *do not board it* – no one else will look out for your safety.

BUS

All the countries covered in this book have good bus systems.

In Malaysia, there are public buses on local runs, and a variety of privately operated buses on the longer trips, some of which are listed below:

Gunung Raya (www.gunungraya.com)
Plusliner (www.plusliner.com.my)
Supercoach (www.supercoach.com.my)

In larger towns there may be a number of bus stations; local/regional buses often operate from one station and long-distance buses from another; in other cases, KL for example, bus stations are differentiated by the destinations they serve.

Buses are fast, economical and comfortable and seats can be reserved. There are so many buses on major runs that you can often turn up and get a seat on the next bus. On main routes most private buses have air-con and cost only a few ringgit more than regular buses. They make travel a sweat-free activity, but you should take note of one traveller's warning: 'Malaysian air-conditioned buses are really meat lockers on wheels with just two settings: cold and suspended animation'.

Getting off the beaten track is only marginally more difficult. Small towns and *kampung* (villages) all over the country are serviced by public buses, usually non-air-conditioned rattlers. Unfortunately, they are often poorly signed and sometimes the only way for you to find your bus is to ask a local. These buses are invariably dirt cheap and are great for sampling rural life. In most towns there are no ticket offices, so buy your ticket from the conductor after you board.

CAR & MOTORCYCLE

Driving in Malaysia is a breeze compared to most Asian countries; the roads are generally of a high quality, there are plenty of new cars available and driving standards are not too hair-raising.

The Lebuhraya, or North-South Hwy, is a six-lane expressway that runs virtually the whole length of the peninsula from the Thai border in the north to Johor Bahru in the south. There are toll charges for using the expressway, and these vary according to the distance travelled. It's not all that cheap, and is the result that the normal highways remain crowded while traffic on the expressway is light. As an example, the trip from KL to Johor Bahru costs RM39.90. Many other highways are in excellent condition and many are under construction.

Driving in the big cities, especially KL, is confusing, chaotic and not much fun, but once out in the countryside driving is relatively easy and a car gives you a great deal of flexibility.

Petrol is inexpensive at around RM1.10 a litre; diesel fuel costs 75 sen per litre.

The **Automobile Association of Malaysia** (☎ 03-262 5777; fax 262 5358; 25 Jl Yap Kwan Seng, 50450 Kuala Lumpur) will let you join its organisation if you have a letter of introduction from your own automobile association.

In Singapore driving is pure cruise control as the city-state has excellent roads and signage.

Bring Your Own Vehicle

It's possible to bring your vehicle into Malaysia, but the cost and hassle of shipping it here makes it an unrealistic proposition for all but the most determined.

Driving Licence

A valid overseas licence is needed to rent a car. An International Driving Permit is usually not required by local car-hire companies but it is recommended that you bring one. Most rental companies also require that drivers are at least 23 years old.

Hire

Rent-a-car operations are well established in Malaysia. Major rental companies include Avis, Budget, Mayflower, Hertz, National and Thrifty; there are many others, though, including local operators only found in one city. Unlimited distance rates for a 1.3L Proton Saga, the cheapest and most popular car in Malaysia, are posted at around RM150/900 per day/week, including insurance and collision-damage waiver. The Proton Wira is a step up in standard and

ROAD DISTANCES FOR PENINSULAR MALAYSIA (KM)

	Alor Setar	Bukit Fraser	Butterworth	Ipoh	Johor Bahru	Klang	Kota Bharu	Kuala Lumpur	Kuala Terengganu	Kuantan	Melaka	Mersing	Pelabuan Klang	Port Dickson	Seremban	Taiping
Alor Setar	---															
Bukit Fraser	443	---														
Butterworth	93	350	---													
Ipoh	257	186	164	---												
Johor Bahru	830	467	737	573	---											
Klang	495	132	400	236	401	---										
Kota Bharu	409	406	386	391	689	507	---									
Kuala Lumpur	462	99	369	205	368	33	474	---								
Kuala Terengganu	521	453	498	503	521	488	168	455	---							
Kuantan	684	253	591	427	325	292	371	259	209	---						
Melaka	606	243	513	349	224	177	607	144	508	292	---					
Mersing	815	436	722	558	134	386	568	353	401	191	255	---				
Pelabuan (Port) Klang	503	140	410	246	409	8	515	41	496	300	185	394	---			
Port Dickson	552	189	459	295	318	115	564	90	503	291	94	321	123	---		
Seremban	526	163	433	269	304	97	538	64	471	259	80	289	105	32	---	
Taiping	183	272	90	86	659	322	369	291	481	513	435	644	332	387	355	---

a bit more expensive. The Proton is basically a Mitsubishi assembled under licence in Malaysia. Charges for a Ford Laser are around RM200/1200 per day/week.

These are the standard rates from the major car-hire companies but you can often get better deals, either through smaller local companies or when the major companies offer special deals. Rates drop substantially for longer rentals and if you shop around by phone you can get a Proton Saga for as little as RM2000 per month, including unlimited kilometres and insurance. The main advantage of dealing with a large company is that it has offices all over the country, giving better backup if something goes wrong and allowing you to pick up in one city and drop off in another (typically for a RM50 surcharge). Mayflower is one local company with offices all over and some competitive rates.

The best place to look for car hire is KL (p101), though Penang is also good (p155). In Sabah and Sarawak there is less competition and rates are higher, partly because of road conditions.

Insurance

Rental companies will provide insurance when you hire a car, but always check what the extent of your coverage will be, particularly if you're involved in an accident. You might want to take out your own insurance or pay the rental company an extra premium for an insurance excess reduction.

Road Rules

Driving in Malaysia follows much the same rules as in Britain and Australia – cars are right-hand drive, and you drive on the left side of the road. The only additional precaution you need to take is to be aware of possible road hazards: stray animals and the large number of motorcyclists. And take it easy on the *kampung* (village) back roads.

Wearing safety belts *is* compulsory, although they are fitted to the front seats only.

Although most drivers in Malaysia are relatively sane, safe and slow, there are also a fair few who specialise in overtaking on blind corners and otherwise trusting to divine intervention. Malaysian drivers also use a curious signalling system, where a flashing left indicator means 'you are safe to overtake', or 'I'm about to turn off', or 'I've forgotten to turn my indicator off', or 'look out, I'm about to do something totally unpredictable'. Giving a quick blast of the horn when you're overtaking a slower vehicle is common practice and helps alert otherwise sleepy drivers to your presence.

HITCHING

Keep in mind that hitching is never entirely safe in any country in the world, and we don't recommend it. Travellers who decide to hitch, particularly single women, should understand that they are taking a small but potentially serious risk. People who do choose to hitch will be safer if they travel in pairs and let someone know where they are planning to go.

This said, Malaysia has long had a reputation for being an excellent place for hitchhiking and it's generally still true, though with convenient bus travel most travellers don't bother.

On the west coast of Malaysia, hitching is generally quite easy but it is not possible on the main Lebuhraya expressway. On the east coast, traffic is lighter and there may be long waits between rides. Hitching in Malaysian Borneo also depends on the traffic, although it's quite possible.

You might get odd looks if you try hitching in Singapore – but someone might eventually stop for you. Why bother though when the public transport system is so good and relatively inexpensive.

LOCAL TRANSPORT

Local transport varies widely from place to place. Large cities in Malaysia have local taxis (as opposed to long-distance taxis, see this page). These taxis usually have meters but there are exceptions to this rule (usually in smaller towns like Kuantan in Pahang). For metered taxis, rates are as follows: flagfall (first 2km) is RM2; 10 sen for each 200m or 45 seconds thereafter; 20 sen for each additional passenger over two passengers; RM1 for each piece of luggage in the boot (trunk); plus 50% between midnight and 6am. Drivers are legally required to use meters if they exist – insist that they do so.

In major cities there are also buses – in KL the government buses are backed up by private operators. Where they exist, these buses are extremely cheap and convenient, provided you can figure out which one is going your way. KL also has commuter trains and Light Rail Transit (LRT); see p103, in the Kuala Lumpur chapter.

Some towns have bicycle rickshaws. While they have died out in KL and have become principally a tourist gimmick in many Malaysian cities, they are still a viable form of transport. Indeed, in places like Georgetown, with its convoluted and narrow streets, a bicycle rickshaw is probably the best way of getting around.

In the bigger cities of Malaysian Borneo, like Kuching and Kota Kinabalu, you will find taxis, buses and minibuses. Once you're out of the big cities, though, you're basically on your own and must either walk or hitch. If you're really in the bush, of course, riverboats and aeroplanes are the only alternatives to lengthy jungle treks.

Singapore has one of the best public transport systems in the region with clean buses that arrive on time, inexpensive tickets, and subway trains connecting all parts of the island

Long-Distance Taxi

Long-distance taxis make Malaysian travel, already easy and convenient even by the best Asian standards, a real breeze. In almost every town there will be a 'teksi' stand where the cars are lined up and ready to go to their various destinations.

Taxis are ideal for groups of four, and are also available on a share basis. As soon as a full complement of four passengers turns up, off you go. Between major towns you have a reasonable chance of finding other passengers to share without having to wait too long, but otherwise you will have to charter a whole taxi, which is four times the single-fare rate (in this book we generally quote the rate for a whole taxi). As Malaysia becomes increasingly wealthy, and people can afford to hire a whole taxi, the share system is becoming less reliable. Early morning is generally the best time to find people to share a taxi, but you can inquire at the taxi stand the day before to see when is the best time.

Taxi rates to specific destinations are fixed by the government and are posted at the taxi stands; usually the whole-taxi rate is

> **MALAYSIAN RAILWAY HISTORY**
>
> Malaysia's first railway line was a 13km route from Taiping to Port Weld that was laid in 1884, but it's no longer in use. By 1903 you could travel all the way from Johor Bahru to near Butterworth; the line was extended to the Thai border in 1918 and across the Causeway to Singapore in 1923. In 1931 the east-coast line was completed, effectively bringing the railway system to its present state.
>
> Keppel Railway Station in Singapore, built in 1932, is actually still part of Malaysia, as is land on which the tracks run up to the Causeway; this was part of the deal done at the time of federation.

listed. Air-con taxis cost a few more ringgit than non-air-con, and fares are generally about twice the comparable bus fares. If you want to charter a taxi to an obscure destination, or by the hour, you'll probably have to do some negotiating. As a rule of thumb, you should pay around 50 sen per kilometre.

Taxi drivers often drive at frighteningly high speeds. They don't have as many head-on collisions as you might expect, but closing your eyes at times of high stress certainly helps! You also have the option of demanding that the driver slow down, but, this is met with varying degrees of hostility. Another tactic is to look for aging taxis and taxi drivers – they must be doing something right to have made it this far!

No one would use long-distance shared taxis for getting around Singapore, but they do use them to get from Singapore to Malaysia. The place to find these taxis is the Queen St Bus Terminal, 100m north of Bugis MRT station.

TOURS

Reliable tours of both Peninsular Malaysia and Malaysian Borneo are run regularly by international operators:

Exodus (www.exodus.co.uk)
Explore Worldwide (www.explore.co.uk)
Peregrine Adventures (www.peregrine.net.au)
Intrepid Travel (www.intrepidtravel.com.au)

Such tours are often a good way to see the best of Malaysian Borneo in a short period of time and without having to worry about possibly problematic transport connections. In contrast, getting around the peninsula under your own steam should be of little hassle, making a tour less necessary. For luxurious Orient-Express-based tours check out the offerings by **Abercrombie & Kent** (www.abercrombiekent.com).

One Malaysia-based operator which offers some interesting variations on the usual tours is **My-Gap** (☎ 03-2039 4767; www.kembara; Level 26, Menara IMC, Jl Sultan Ismail, Kuala Lumpur). It runs programs which include homestays and wildlife, marine, conservation and cultural education. Costs start at US$50 a day for the homestays programs which includes transfers, lodging and all meals. Its website also has some good background information on the country, its culture and people.

For tours of Malaysian Borneo, Kuching-based **Borneo Adventures** (www.borneoadventures.com) has an excellent reputation and runs good tours.

Tours of Singapore are often tacked on to tours of Malaysia. There are several local tours available of the island, see Tours (p477) in the Singapore chapter.

TRAIN

Malaysia has a modern, comfortable and economical railway service, although there are basically only two lines. One runs from Singapore to Kuala Lumpur, and to Butterworth and on into Thailand. The other branches off from this line at Gemas and runs through Kuala Lipis up to the northeastern corner of the country near Kota Bharu in Kelantan. Often referred to as the 'jungle train', this line is properly known as the 'east-coast line'. Other lines are just minor branches off these two routes and are not used much.

In Sabah there's a small narrow-gauge railway line that can take you through the Sungai Padas gorge from Tenom to Beaufort. The trip is scenic, but can be very slow. The train crawls along, stopping at stations along the way and delays are common during heavy rains because of obstructions on the track.

Train Passes

The privatised national railway company, **Keretapi Tanah Melayu** (KTM; ☎ 03-2267 1200 or 2773 1430; www.ktmb.com.my), offers a Tourist Railpass for five days (adult/child US$35/18);

TRAIN FARES IN MALAYSIA & SINGAPORE

From Butterworth (fares in RM)

Destination	Express 1st class	2nd class	3rd class	Local 1st class	2nd class	3rd class
Padang Besa	34.00	20.00	11.00	25.50	11.10	6.30
Taiping	23.00	15.00	8.00	14.40	6.30	3.60
Ipoh	36.00	21.00	11.00	27.80	12.10	6.90
Tapah Road	44.00	24.00	13.00	36.00	15.60	8.90
Kuala Lumpur	67.00	34.00	19.00	58.50	25.40	14.40
Tampin	85.00	42.00	23.00	76.50	33.20	18.90
Johor Bahru	122.00	58.00	33.00	114.00	49.40	28.10
Singapore	127.00	60.00	34.00	118.50	51.42	9.90

From Kuala Lumpur (fares in RM)

Destination	Express 1st class	2nd class	3rd class	Local 1st class	2nd class	3rd class
Padang Besar	–	–	–	81.00	35.10	20.00
Butterworth	67.00	34.00	19.00	58.50	25.40	14.40
Taiping	53.00	28.00	16.00	45.00	19.50	11.10
Ipoh	40.00	22.00	12.00	31.50	13.70	7.80
Tapah Road	32.00	19.00	10.00	23.30	10.10	5.80
Tampin	27.00	17.00	9.00	18.80	8.20	4.70
Johor Bahru	64.00	33.00	18.00	55.50	24.10	13.70
Singapore	68.00	34.00	19.00	60.00	26.00	14.80
Jerantut	48.00	35.00	15.00	–	–	–
Kuala Lipis	56.00	36.50	18.00	–	–	–
Wakaf Baharu	78.00	45.50	28.00	–	–	–
Tumpat	80.00	46.50	29.00	–	–	–

From Singapore (fares in S$)

Destination	Express 1st class	2nd class	3rd class	Local 1st class	2nd class	3rd class
Padang Besar	–	–	–	139.50	60.50	34.40
Butterworth	127.00	60.00	34.00	118.50	51.40	29.20
Taiping	112.00	53.00	30.00	103.50	44.90	25.50
Ipoh	100.00	48.00	27.00	91.50	39.70	22.60
Tapah Road	92.00	45.00	25.00	84.00	36.40	20.70
Kuala Lumpur	68.00	34.00	19.00	60.00	26.00	14.80
Tampin	50.00	27.00	15.00	42.00	18.20	10.40
Johor Bahru	13.00	10.00	6.00	4.20	1.90	1.10
Kuala Lipis	76.00	31.00	21.00	–	29.30	16.70
Wakaf Baharu	119.00	41.00	32.00	–	48.10	27.40
Tumpat	121.00	57.00	32.00	–	48.80	27.70

Supplementary berth charges for Malaysian services are: RM70 for 1st-class lower berth; RM50 for 1st-class upper berth; RM14 for 2nd-class air-con lower berth; RM11.50 for 2nd-class air-con upper berth. Supplementary charges may also apply to ex-Singapore fares.

10 days (adult/child US$55/28); and 15 days (adult/child US$70/35). This pass entitles the holder to unlimited travel on any class of train but does not include sleeping-berth charges. Railpasses are available only to foreigners and can be purchased at KL, Johor Bahru, Butterworth, Pelabuhan Klang, Padang Besar, Wakaf Baharu and Penang train stations.

Services & Classes

Malaysia has three main types of rail services: express, limited express and local trains. Express trains are air-conditioned and generally 1st and 2nd class only, and on night trains there's a choice of berths or seats. Limited express trains may have 2nd and 3rd class only but some have 1st, 2nd and 3rd class with overnight sleepers. Local trains are usually 3rd class only, but some have 2nd class.

Express trains stop only at main stations. Limited express trains stop at a few more stations but still provide a quick service; however, these are being gradually phased out. These two options are much faster than the local trains, and in most respects are definitely the ones to take. The local services, which operate mostly on the east-coast line, are colourful experiences for short journeys. They stop everywhere, including the middle of the jungle, to let passengers and their goods on and off, but they take more than twice as long as the express trains and run to erratic schedules.

Contact KTM (see Train Passes this page) for more information on schedules and fares. Train schedules are reviewed biannually, so check before you make detailed plans.

Health

CONTENTS

Health issues and the quality of medical facilities vary depending on where and how you travel in the region. The major cities are now well developed, but travel to rural areas can expose you to a variety of health risks and inadequate medical care. Travellers tend to worry about contracting infectious diseases when in the tropics, but infections rarely cause serious illness or death in travellers. Pre-existing medical conditions, such as heart disease, and accidental injury (especially traffic accidents) account for most life-threatening situations. Becoming ill in some way, however, is relatively common. Fortunately most common illnesses can either be prevented with some common-sense behaviour or be treated easily with a well-stocked traveller's medical kit.

The following advice is a general guide only and does not replace the advice of a doctor trained in travel medicine.

BEFORE YOU GO

Pack medications in their original, clearly labelled containers. A signed and dated letter from your physician describing your medical conditions and medications, including generic names, is also a good idea. If carrying syringes or needles, be sure to have a physician's letter documenting their medical necessity. If you have a heart condition, bring a copy of your ECG taken just prior to travelling.

If you take any regular medication, bring double your needs in case of loss or theft, and carry these extra supplies separately. You may be able to buy some medications over the counter in Malaysia without a doctor's prescription, but it can be difficult to find some of the newer drugs, particularly the latest antidepressants, blood pressure medications and contraceptive pills.

INSURANCE

Even if you are fit and healthy, don't travel without health insurance – accidents do happen. Declare any existing medical conditions you have – the insurance company will check if your problem is pre-existing and will not cover you if it is undeclared. You may require extra cover for adventure activities such as rock climbing. If your health insurance doesn't cover you for medical expenses abroad, consider getting extra insurance – check subwwway on www.lonelyplanet.com for more information. If you're uninsured, emergency evacuation is expensive, bills of over US$100,000 are not uncommon.

Find out in advance if your insurance plan will make payments directly to providers or reimburse you later for overseas health expenses. (Doctors may expect payment in cash.)

RECOMMENDED VACCINATIONS

Specialised travel-medicine clinics are your best source of information; they stock all available vaccines and will be able to give specific recommendations for you and your trip. The doctors will take into account factors such as past vaccination history, the length of your trip, activities you may be undertaking and underlying medical conditions.

Most vaccines don't produce immunity until at least two weeks after they're given, so visit a doctor four to eight weeks before departure. Ask your doctor for an International Certificate of Vaccination (otherwise known as the yellow booklet), which will list all the vaccinations you've received.

Proof of vaccination against yellow fever will be required only if you have visited a country in the yellow fever zone (parts of Africa and South America) within six days prior to entering Southeast Asia. If you're coming from Africa or South America, check to see if you require proof of vaccination.

The World Health Organization recommends the following vaccinations for travellers to Malaysia, Singapore and Brunei:

Adult diphtheria and tetanus Single booster recommended if none in the previous 10 years. Side effects include a sore arm and fever.

Polio In 2002, no countries in Southeast Asia reported cases of polio. Only one booster required as an adult for lifetime protection. Inactivated polio vaccine is safe during pregnancy.

Measles, mumps and rubella Two doses of MMR required unless you have had the diseases. Occasionally can develop a rash and flu-like illness a week after receiving the vaccine. Many young adults require a booster.

Hepatitis A Provides almost 100% protection for up to a year; a booster after 12 months provides at least another 20 years' protection. Mild side effects such as headache and sore arm occur in 5% to 10% of people.

Hepatitis B Now considered routine for most travellers. Given as three shots over six months. A rapid schedule is also available, as is a combined vaccination with hepatitis A. Side effects are mild and uncommon, usually headache and sore arm. In 95% of people lifetime protection results.

Typhoid Recommended unless your trip is less than a week and only to developed cities. The vaccine offers around 70% protection, lasts for two to three years and comes as a single shot. Tablets are also available; however, the injection is usually recommended as it has fewer side effects. Sore arm and fever may occur.

Varicella If you haven't had chickenpox discuss the vaccination with your doctor.

These immunisations are recommended for longer-term travellers (more than one month) or those at special risk:

Rabies Three injections in all. A booster after one year will then provide 10 years' protection. Side effects are rare; a headache or a sore arm.

Japanese B encephalitis Three injections in all. Booster recommended after two years. Sore arm and headache are the most common side effects. Rarely, an allergic reaction comprising hives and swelling can occur up to 10 days after any of the three doses.

Meningitis Single injection. There are two types of vaccination. The quadravalent vaccine gives two to three years' protection. Meningitis group C vaccine gives around 10 years' protection. Recommended for long-term backpackers aged younger than 25.

Tuberculosis A complex issue. Adult long-term travellers are usually recommended to have a TB skin test before and after travel, rather than vaccination. Children may be recommended to have the vaccination; only one is necessary in a lifetime.

MEDICAL CHECKLIST

Recommended items for a personal medical kit:

- For diarrhoea consider an oral rehydration solution (eg Gastrolyte), diarrhoea 'stopper' (eg Loperamide) and antinausea medication (eg Prochlorperazine)
- Antibiotics for diarrhoea – Norfloxacin or Ciprofloxacin or Azithromycin for bacterial diarrhoea; Tinidazole for giardiasis or amoebic dysentery
- Laxative, eg Coloxyl
- Antispasmodic for stomach cramps, eg Buscopan
- Indigestion tablets, eg Quick-Eze, Mylanta
- Throat lozenges
- Antihistamine – there are many options, eg Cetrizine for daytime and Promethazine for night
- Decongestant, eg Pseudoephedrine
- Paracetamol
- Ibuprofen or another anti-inflammatory
- Your personal medicine if you are a migraine sufferer
- Sunscreen and hat
- Antiseptic, eg Betadine
- Antibacterial cream, eg Muciprocin
- Steroid cream for allergic/itchy rashes, eg 1% to 2% hydrocortisone
- Antifungal cream, eg Clotrimazole
- For skin infections, antibiotics such as Amoxicillin/Clavulanate or Cephalexin
- Contraceptive method
- Thrush (vaginal yeast infection) treatment, eg Clotrimazole pessaries or Diflucan tablet
- Ural, or equivalent, if prone to urinary-tract infections
- DEET-based insect repellant
- Mosquito net impregnated with a substance like permethrin
- Permethrin to impregnate clothing

- Iodine tablets (unless you are pregnant or have a thyroid problem) to purify water
- Basic first-aid items such as scissors, elastoplasts, bandages, gauze, thermometer (but not mercury), sterile needles and syringes, safety pins, tweezers

ONLINE RESOURCES

There's a wealth of travel health advice on the Internet. For further information:

Lonely Planet (www.lonelyplanet.com) A good place to start.

World Health Organization (www.who.int/ith/) Publishes a superb book called *International Travel and Health*, which is revised annually and is available online at no cost.

MD Travel Health (www.mdtravelhealth.com) Provides complete travel health recommendations for every country and is updated daily.

CDC (www.cdc.gov) Has good general information.

FURTHER READING

Lonely Planet's Healthy *Travel Asia & India* is a handy pocket size and packed with useful information including pretrip planning, emergency first aid, immunisation and disease information and what to do if you get sick on the road. *Travel with Children* from Lonely Planet includes advice on travel health for young children. Other recommended references include *Traveller's Health* by Dr Richard Dawood (Oxford University Press), and *Travelling Well* by Dr Deborah Mills, available at www.travellingwell.com.au.

HEALTH ADVISORIES

It's usually a good idea to consult your government's travel health website before departure, if one is available:

Australia www.dfat.gov.au/travel/

New Zealand www.mfat.govt.nz/travel

South Africa www.dfa.gov.za/travelling

Canada www.travelhealth.gc.ca

United Kingdom www.doh.gov.uk/traveladvice/

United States www.cdc.gov/travel/

IN TRANSIT

DEEP VEIN THROMBOSIS (DVT)

Blood clots forming in the legs during plane flights, chiefly because of prolonged immobility, is known as deep vein thrombosis (DVT). The longer the flight, the greater the risk. Though most blood clots are reabsorbed uneventfully, some may break off and travel through the blood vessels to the lungs, where they may cause life-threatening complications.

The chief symptom of DVT is swelling or pain of the foot, ankle or calf, usually but not always on just one side. When a blood clot travels to the lungs, it may cause chest pain and difficulty breathing. Travellers with any of these symptoms should immediately seek medical attention.

To prevent the development of DVT on long flights you should walk about the cabin, perform isometric compressions of the leg muscles (ie contract the leg muscles while sitting), drink plenty of fluids, and avoid alcohol and tobacco.

JET LAG & MOTION SICKNESS

Jet lag is common when crossing more than five time zones; it results in insomnia, fatigue, malaise or nausea. To avoid jet lag try drinking plenty of fluids (nonalcoholic) and eating light meals. Upon arrival, seek exposure to natural sunlight and readjust your schedule (for meals, sleep etc) as soon as possible.

Antihistamines such as dimenhydrinate (Dramamine) and meclizine (Antivert, Bonine) are usually the first choice for treating motion sickness. Their main side effect is drowsiness. A herbal alternative is ginger, which works like a charm for some people.

IN MALAYSIA, SINGAPORE & BRUNEI

AVAILABILITY & COST OF HEALTH CARE

In Malaysia, the standard of medical care in the major centres is good, and most problems can be adequately dealt with in Kuala Lumpur.

Singapore has excellent medical facilities and acts as the referral centre for most of Southeast Asia. You cannot buy medication over the counter without a doctor's prescription in Singapore.

In Brunei, general care is reasonable. There is no local medical university, so expats and foreign-trained locals run the health care system. Serious or complex cases are better managed in Singapore, but adequate primary health care and stabilisation are available.

Clinics catering specifically to travellers and expatriates are usually more expensive than local medical facilities, but they offer a superior standard of care and are aware of the best local hospitals and specialists. They can also liaise with insurance companies should you require evacuation. Recommended clinics are listed under Information in the capital city sections in this book. Your embassy and insurance company are also good contacts.

It can be difficult to find reliable medical care in rural areas.

Self-treatment may be appropriate if your problem is minor (eg traveller's diarrhoea), you are carrying the appropriate medication and you cannot attend a recommended clinic. If you think you may have a serious disease, especially malaria, don't waste time. Travel to the nearest quality facility to receive attention. It's always better to be assessed by a doctor than to rely on self-treatment.

INFECTIOUS DISEASES

Cutaneous Larva Migrans

Found in Malaysia and Brunei, and caused by the dog hookworm, the rash symptomatic of cutaneous larva migrans starts as a small lump, then slowly spreads in a linear fashion. It's intensely itchy, especially at night, but it's easily treated with medications; it should not be cut out or frozen.

Dengue Fever

This mosquito-borne disease is becomingly increasingly problematic throughout Asia, including Malaysia, Singapore and Brunei, especially in the cities. As there's no vaccine available, it can only be prevented by avoiding mosquito bites. The mosquito that carries dengue bites both day and night, so use insect avoidance measures at all times. Symptoms include high fever, severe headache and body ache (dengue was previously known as 'breakbone fever'). Some people develop a rash and experience diarrhoea. The southern islands of Thailand are particularly high risk. There's no specific treatment, just rest and paracetamol – don't take aspirin as it increases the likelihood of haemorrhaging. See a doctor to be diagnosed and monitored.

Filariasis

Occurring in Malaysia and Brunei, filariasis is a mosquito-borne disease, very common in local populations, yet very rare in travellers. Mosquito-avoidance measures are the best way to prevent this disease.

Hepatitis A

This food- and water-borne virus infects the liver, causing jaundice (yellow skin and eyes), nausea and lethargy. There's no specific treatment for hepatitis A, you just need to allow time for the liver to heal. All travellers to Malaysia, Singapore and Brunei should be vaccinated against hepatitis A.

Hepatitis B

The only sexually transmitted disease that can be prevented by vaccination, hepatitis B is spread by body fluids, including sexual contact. In some parts of Asia up to 20% of the population are carriers of hepatitis B, and usually are unaware of this. The long-term consequences can include liver cancer and cirrhosis.

Hepatitis E

Hepatitis E is transmitted through contaminated food and water, has similar symptoms to hepatitis A, but is far less common. It's a severe problem in pregnant women and can result in the death of both mother and baby. There is currently no vaccine, and prevention is by following safe eating and drinking guidelines while you're travelling in Malaysia, Singapore and Brunei.

HIV

HIV is rapidly increasing through much of Southeast Asia, including Malaysia, Singapore and Brunei, with heterosexual sex now the main method of transmission.

Influenza

Present year-round in the tropics, influenza (flu) gives you a high fever, muscle aches, a runny nose, a cough and sore throat. Flu can be very severe in people over the age of 65 or in those with underlying medical conditions such as heart disease or diabetes. Vaccination is recommended for these high-risk individuals travelling in Malaysia, Singapore and Brunei. There's no specific treatment, just rest and paracetamol.

Japanese B Encephalitis

Rare in travellers, this viral disease transmitted by mosquitoes is found in Malaysia and Brunei. Most cases of Japanese B encephalitis occur in rural areas and vaccination is recommended for travellers spending more than one month outside cities. There is no treatment, and a third of infected people will die while another third will suffer permanent brain damage.

Leptospirosis

Present in Malaysia, leptospirosis is most commonly contracted after river rafting or canyoning. Early symptoms are very similar to the flu and include headache and fever. It can vary from a very mild to a fatal disease. Diagnosis is through blood tests and it is easily treated with Doxycycline.

Malaria

For such a serious and potentially deadly disease, there is an enormous amount of misinformation concerning malaria. You must get expert advice as to whether your trip actually puts you at risk, especially if you will be travelling in Malaysia. Many areas, particularly city and resort areas, have minimal to no risk of malaria, and the risk of side effects from the tablets may outweigh the risk of getting the disease. For some rural areas, however, the risk of contracting the disease far outweighs the risk of any tablet side effects. Remember that malaria can be fatal. Before you travel, seek medical advice on the right medication and dosage for you.

Malaria is caused by a parasite transmitted through the bite of an infected mosquito. The most important symptom of malaria is fever, but general symptoms such as headache, diarrhoea, cough or chills may also occur. Diagnosis can be made only by taking a blood sample.

Two strategies should be combined to prevent malaria – mosquito avoidance and antimalarial medications. Most people who catch malaria are taking inadequate or no antimalarial medication.

Travellers are advised to prevent mosquito bites by taking these steps:

- Use a DEET-containing insect repellent on exposed skin. Wash this off at night, as long as you are sleeping under a mosquito net treated with permethrin. Natural repellents such as citronella can be effective, but must be applied more frequently than products containing DEET.
- Sleep under a mosquito net impregnated with permethrin.
- Choose accommodation with screens and fans (if not air-con).
- Impregnate clothing with permethrin in high-risk areas.
- Wear long sleeves and trousers in light colours.
- Use mosquito coils.
- Spray your room with insect repellent before going out for your evening meal.

There are a variety of antimalarial medications available:

Chloroquine & Paludrine The effectiveness of this combination is now limited in most of Southeast Asia. Common side effects include nausea (40% of people) and mouth ulcers. Generally not recommended.

Lariam (Mefloquine) Lariam has received much bad press, some of it justified, some not. This weekly tablet suits many people. Serious side effects are rare but include depression, anxiety, psychosis and having fits. Anyone with a history of depression, anxiety, other psychological disorders or epilepsy should not take Lariam. It's considered safe in the second and third trimesters of pregnancy. It's around 90% effective in most parts of Asia, but there's significant resistance in parts of northern Thailand, Laos and Cambodia. Tablets must be taken for four weeks after leaving the risk area.

Doxycycline This daily tablet is a broad-spectrum antibiotic that has the added benefit of helping to prevent a variety of tropical diseases, including leptospirosis, tick-borne diseases, typhus and meliodosis. The potential side effects include photosensitivity (a tendency to sunburn), thrush in women, indigestion, heartburn, nausea and interference with the contraceptive pill. More serious side effects include ulceration of the oesophagus – you can help prevent this by taking your tablet with a meal and a large glass of water, and never lying down within half an hour of taking it. Must be taken for four weeks after leaving the risk area.

Malarone This new drug is a combination of Atovaquone and Proguanil. Side effects are uncommon and mild, most commonly nausea and headache. It is the best tablet for scuba divers and for those on short trips to high-risk areas. It must be taken for one week after leaving the risk area.

Artesunate Artesunate derivatives are not suitable as a preventive medication. They are useful treatments under medical supervision.

A final option is to take no preventive medication but to have a supply of emergency medication should you develop the symptoms of malaria. This is less than ideal, and you'll need to get to a good medical facility within 24 hours of developing a fever. If you choose this option the most effective and safest treatment is Malarone (four tablets once daily for three days). Other options include Mefloquine and quinine but the side effects of these drugs at treatment doses make them less desirable. Fansidar is no longer recommended.

Measles

Occurring in Malaysia, this highly contagious bacterial infection is spread via coughing and sneezing. Most people born before 1966 are immune, as they had the disease in childhood. Measles starts with a high fever and rash and can be complicated by pneumonia and brain disease. There is no specific treatment.

Rabies

This fatal disease, present in Malaysia, is spread by the bite or lick of an infected animal – most commonly a dog or monkey. You should seek medical advice immediately after any animal bite and commence post-exposure treatment.

Having pre-travel vaccination means the post-bite treatment is greatly simplified. If an animal bites you, gently wash the wound with soap and water, and apply an iodine-based antiseptic. If you are not prevaccinated you will need to receive rabies immunoglobulin as soon as possible.

STDs

Among the most common sexually transmitted diseases in Southeast Asia, including Malaysia, Singapore and Brunei, are herpes, warts, syphilis, gonorrhoea and chlamydia. People carrying these diseases often have no signs of infection. Condoms will prevent gonorrhoea and chlamydia but not warts or herpes. If after a sexual encounter you develop any rash, lumps, discharge or pain when passing urine, seek immediate medical attention. If you've been sexually active during your travels, have an STD check on your return home.

Tuberculosis

While tuberculosis (TB) is rare in travellers in Malaysia and Brunei, medical and aid workers and long-term travellers who have significant contact with the local population should take precautions. Vaccination is usually given only to children under the age of five, but adults at risk are recommended to have TB testing both before and after travelling. The main symptoms are fever, cough, weight loss, night sweats and tiredness.

Typhoid

This serious bacterial infection is spread via food and water and is found in Malaysia, Singapore and Brunei. It causes a high, slowly progressive fever, a headache, and may be accompanied by a dry cough and stomach pain. It's diagnosed by blood tests and treated with antibiotics. Vaccination is recommended for travellers spending more than a week in the region, or travelling outside the major cities. Be aware that vaccination is not 100% effective so you must still be careful with what you eat and drink.

Typhus

Murine typhus is spread by the bite of a flea, whereas scrub typhus is spread via a mite. Although present in Malaysia, these diseases are rare in travellers. Symptoms include fever, muscle pains and a rash. You can prevent typhus by following general insect-avoidance measures. Doxycycline will also prevent it.

TRAVELLER'S DIARRHOEA

Traveller's diarrhoea is by far the most common problem affecting travellers – between 30%-50% of people will suffer from it within two weeks of starting their trip. In over 80% of cases, traveller's diarrhoea is caused by a bacteria (there are numerous potential culprits), and therefore responds promptly to treatment with antibiotics. Treatment with antibiotics will depend on your situation – how sick you are, how quickly you need to get better, where you are etc. Traveller's diarrhoea is defined as the passage of more than three watery bowel-actions within 24 hours, plus at least one other symptom such as fever, cramps, nausea, vomiting or feeling generally unwell. Treatment consists of staying well-hydrated; rehydration solutions like Gastrolyte are the best for this. Antibiotics such as Norfloxacin, Ciprofloxacin or Azithromycin will kill the bacteria quickly.

Loperamide is just a 'stopper' and doesn't get to the cause of the problem. It can be helpful, for example if you have to go on a long bus ride. Don't take Loperamide if you have a fever, or blood in your stools. Seek medical attention quickly if you do not respond to an appropriate antibiotic.

Amoebic Dysentery

Amoebic dysentery is very rare in travellers but is often misdiagnosed by poor quality labs in Asia. Symptoms are similar to bacterial diarrhoea, ie fever, bloody diarrhoea and generally feeling unwell. You should always seek reliable medical care if you have blood in your diarrhoea. Treatment involves two drugs – Tinidazole or Metroniadzole to kill the parasite in your gut and then a second drug to kill the cysts. If left untreated complications such as liver abscess and abscess in the gut can occur.

SARS

In March 2003 the world's attention was drawn to the outbreak of an apparently new and serious respiratory illness that became known as SARS (Severe Acute Respiratory Syndrome). At the time of writing SARS appears to have been brought under control. During the outbreak, 8500 cases were confirmed, resulting in 800 deaths. The peak of disease activity was in early May 2003. The outbreak started in the Chinese province of Guangdong, and numerous cases were reported in Hong Kong, Vietnam, Singapore and Canada. The World Health Organization soon issued a global alert to health authorities and the public. Although this helped to bring the disease under control, it also resulted in widespread panic.

The symptoms of SARS are identical to many other respiratory infections, namely high fever and cough. There's no quick test for SARS but certain blood-test and chest x-ray results offer support for the diagnosis. There's also no specific treatment available and death from respiratory failure occurs in about 10% of patients. Fortunately, it appears it's not as easy to catch SARS as was initially thought. Wearing masks has a limited effect and is not generally recommended.

Giardiasis

Giardia is a parasite that is relatively common in travellers. Symptoms include nausea, bloating, excess gas, fatigue and intermittent diarrhoea. 'Eggy' burps are often attributed solely to Giardia, but work in Nepal has shown that they are not specific to Giardia. The parasite will eventually go away if left untreated but this can take months. The treatment of choice is Tinidazole, with Metronidazole being a second line option.

ENVIRONMENTAL HAZARDS

Air Pollution

Air pollution, particularly vehicle pollution, is an increasing problem in most of Asia's major cities. If you have severe respiratory problems, speak with your doctor before travelling to any heavily polluted urban centres. Air pollution can cause minor respiratory problems such as sinusitis, dry throat and irritated eyes. If troubled by the pollution, leave the city for a few days to get some fresh air.

Diving

Divers and surfers should seek specialised advice before they travel, to ensure their medical kit contains treatment for coral cuts and tropical ear infections, as well as the standard problems. Divers should ensure their insurance covers them for decompression illness – get specialised dive insurance through an organisation such as **DAN** (Divers Alert Network; www.danseap.org). Have a dive medical before you leave your home country – there are certain medical conditions that are incompatible with diving and economic considerations may override health considerations at some dive operations in Asia.

Food

Eating in restaurants is the biggest risk factor for contracting traveller's diarrhoea. Ways to avoid it include eating only freshly cooked food and avoiding shellfish

DRINKING WATER

- Never drink tap water.
- Bottled water is generally safe – check the seal is intact at purchase.
- Avoid ice.
- Avoid fresh juices – they may have been watered down.
- Boiling water is the most efficient method of purifying it.
- The best chemical purifier is iodine. It should not be used by pregnant women or those with thyroid problems.
- Water filters should also filter out viruses. Ensure your filter has a chemical barrier such as iodine and a small pore size, ie less than 4 microns.

and food that has been sitting around in buffets. Peel all fruit, cook vegetables, and soak salads in iodine water for at least 20 minutes. Eat in busy restaurants with a high turnover of customers.

Heat

The Southeast Asian region is mostly hot and humid throughout the year. Most people take at least two weeks to adapt to the hot climate. Swelling of the feet and ankles is common, as are muscle cramps caused by excessive sweating. Prevent these by avoiding dehydration and too much activity in the heat. Take it easy when you first arrive. Don't eat salt tablets (they aggravate the gut) but drinking rehydration solution or eating salty food helps. Treat cramps by stopping activity, resting, rehydrating with double-strength rehydration solution and gently stretching.

Dehydration is the main contributor to heat exhaustion. Symptoms include feeling weak, headache, irritability, nausea or vomiting, sweaty skin, a fast, weak pulse and a slightly elevated body temperature. Treatment involves getting the victim out of the heat and/or sun, fanning them and applying cool wet cloths to the skin, laying the victim flat with their legs raised and rehydrating with water containing a quarter of a teaspoon of salt per litre. Recovery is usually rapid although it's common to feel weak for some days afterwards.

Heatstroke is a serious medical emergency. Symptoms come on suddenly and include weakness, nausea, a hot dry body with a body temperature of over 41°C, dizziness, confusion, loss of coordination, fits, and eventual collapse and loss of consciousness. Seek medical help and commence cooling by getting the sufferer out of the heat, removing their clothes, fanning them and applying cool, wet cloths or ice to their body, especially to the groin and armpits.

Prickly heat is a common skin rash in the tropics, caused by sweat being trapped under the skin. The result is an itchy rash of tiny lumps. If you develop prickly heat, treat it by moving out of the heat and into an air-conditioned area for a few hours and by having cool showers. Creams and ointments clog the skin so they should be avoided. Locally bought prickly-heat powder can be helpful.

Tropical fatigue is common in long-term expatriates based in the tropics. It's rarely due to disease but is caused by the climate, inadequate mental rest, excessive alcohol intake and the demands of daily work in a different culture.

Insect Bites & Stings

Bedbugs don't carry disease but their bites are very itchy. They live in the cracks of furniture and walls and then migrate to the bed at night to feed on you. You can treat the itch with an antihistamine. Lice inhabit various parts of your body but most commonly your head and pubic area. They can be difficult to treat and you may need numerous applications of an anti-lice shampoo such as permethrin. Transmission is via close contact with an infected person. Pubic lice are usually contracted from sexual contact.

Ticks are contracted after walking in the bush. Ticks are commonly found behind the ears, on the belly and in armpits. If you have had a tick bite and experience symptoms such as a rash at the site of the bite or elsewhere, a fever or muscle aches you should see a doctor. Doxycycline prevents tick-borne diseases.

Leeches are found in humid rainforest areas. They do not transmit any disease but their bites are often intensely itchy for weeks afterwards and can easily become infected. Apply iodine-based antiseptic to any leech bite to help prevent infection (see also the boxed text, this page).

Bee and wasp stings mainly cause problems for people who are allergic to them. Anyone with a serious bee or wasp allergy should carry an injection of adrenaline (eg an EpiPen) for emergency treatment. For others, pain is the main problem – apply ice to the sting and take painkillers.

Most jellyfish in Southeast Asian waters are not dangerous, just irritating. First aid for jellyfish stings involves pouring vinegar onto the affected area to neutralise the poison. Don't rub sand or water onto the stings. Take painkillers, and anyone who feels ill in any way after being stung should seek medical advice. Take local advice if there are dangerous jellyfish around and keep out of the water.

Parasites

Numerous parasites are common in local populations in Southeast Asia; however, most of these are rare in travellers. The two rules to follow if you wish to avoid parasitic infections are to wear shoes and to avoid eating raw food, especially fish, pork and vegetables. A number of parasites are transmitted via the skin by walking barefoot including strongyloides, hookworm and cutaneous larva migrans.

Skin Problems

Fungal rashes are common in humid climates. There are two common fungal rashes that affect travellers. The first occurs in moist areas that get less air such as the groin, armpits and between the toes. It starts as a red patch that slowly spreads and is usually itchy. Treatment involves keeping the skin dry, avoiding chafing and using an antifungal cream such as Clotrimazole or Lamisil. Tinea versicolour is also common – this fungus causes small, light-coloured patches, most commonly on the back, chest and shoulders. Consult a doctor.

Cuts and scratches become easily infected in humid climates. Take meticulous care of any cuts and scratches to prevent complications such as abscesses. Immediately wash all wounds in clean water and apply antiseptic. If you develop signs of

THAT CLINGING FEELING

On any rainforest walk, the subject of leeches invariably comes up. Actually, you may not encounter any of these slimy little vampires while walking through the Malaysian jungle, but if the trail is leafy and it's been raining, chances are you'll be preyed upon.

The local leeches are maddeningly tiny – so small, in fact, they can squeeze through tight-knit socks. They don't stay tiny for long, however, since once a leech has attached to your skin, it won't let go until it has sucked as much blood as it can hold. Only then will the bloated, sated little parasite release itself and make its way back to the forest floor. Your souvenir of the experience will be bloody, but consider it a flesh wound.

Two species are common: the brown leech and the tiger leech. The tiger leech is recognisable by its cream and black stripes, but you'll probably feel one before you see it. Unlike the brown leech, whose suction is painless, tiger leeches sting a bit. Brown leeches hang around on, or near, the forest floor, waiting to grab onto passing boots or pants. Tiger leeches lurk on the leaves of small trees and tend to attack between the waist and neck, and that can mean any orifice there and around. Keep your shirt tucked in.

Leeches are harmless, but bites can become infected. Prevention is better than the cure and opinion varies on what works best. Insect repellent on feet, shoes and socks works temporarily; loose tobacco in your shoes and socks also helps – Kelabit hunters swear by it. Better yet, invest in some leech-proof socks, which are a kind tropical gaiter that covers the foot and boot heel and fastens below the knees.

Safe and effective ways to dislodge leeches include flicking them off sideways (pulling a leech off by the tail might make it dig in harder), burning them with a cigarette (though you may burn yourself as well), or sprinkling salt on them. Tiger balm, iodine or medicated menthol oil (a common brand is the Axe Brand Universal Oil) will also get leeches off. High-pitched screaming doesn't seem to affect them much. Succumb to your fate as a reluctant blood donor and they will eventually drop off.

HEALTH

infection (increasing pain and redness) see a doctor. Divers and surfers should be particularly careful with coral cuts as they become easily infected.

Snakes

Southeast Asia is home to many species of poisonous and harmless snakes. Assume all snakes are poisonous and never try to catch one. Always wear boots and long pants if walking in an area that may have snakes. First aid in the event of a snakebite involves pressure immobilisation via an elastic bandage firmly wrapped around the affected limb, starting at the bite site and working up towards the chest. The bandage should not be so tight that the circulation is cut off; the fingers or toes should be kept free so the circulation can be checked. Immobilise the limb with a splint and carry the victim to medical attention. Don't use tourniquets or try to suck the venom out. Antivenin is available for most species.

Sunburn

Even on a cloudy day, sunburn can occur rapidly. Always use a strong sunscreen (at least factor 15), making sure to reapply it after a swim, and always wear a wide-brimmed hat and sunglasses outdoors. Avoid lying in the sun during the hottest part of the day (10am to 2pm). If you become sunburnt, stay out of the sun until you have recovered, apply cool compresses and take painkillers for the discomfort. One-percent hydrocortisone cream applied twice daily is also helpful.

TRAVELLING WITH CHILDREN

There are specific issues you should consider before travelling with your child.

All their routine vaccinations should be up to date, as many of the common childhood diseases that have been eliminated in the West are still present in parts of Southeast Asia. A travel health clinic can advise you on specific vaccines, but think seriously about rabies vaccination if you're visiting rural areas or travelling for more than a month, as children are more vulnerable to severe animal bites.

Children are more prone to getting serious forms of mosquito-borne diseases such as malaria, Japanese B encephalitis and dengue fever. In particular, malaria is very serious in children and can rapidly lead to death – you should think seriously before taking your child into a malaria-risk area. Permethrin-impregnated clothing is safe to use, and insect repellents should contain between 10% and 20% DEET.

Diarrhoea can cause rapid dehydration and you should pay particular attention to keeping your child well hydrated. The best antibiotic for children with diarrhoea is Azithromycin.

Children can get very sick very quickly so locate good medical facilities at your destination and make contact if you are worried – it's always better to get a medical opinion than to try and treat your own children.

WOMEN'S HEALTH

Pregnant women should receive specialised advice before travelling. The ideal time

TRADITIONAL & FOLK MEDICINE

Throughout Asia, traditional medical systems are widely practised. There is a big difference between these traditional healing systems and 'folk' medicine. Folk remedies should be avoided, as they often involve rather dubious procedures with potential complications. In comparison, traditional healing systems, such as traditional Chinese medicine, are well respected, and aspects of them are being increasingly utilised by Western medical practitioners.

All traditional Asian medical systems identify a vital life force, and see blockage or imbalance as causing disease. Techniques such as herbal medicines, massage and acupuncture bring this vital force back into balance or maintain balance. These therapies are best used for treating chronic disease such as chronic fatigue, arthritis, irritable bowel syndrome and some chronic skin conditions. Traditional medicines should be avoided for treating serious acute infections such as malaria.

Be aware that 'natural' doesn't always mean 'safe', and there can be drug interactions between herbal medicines and Western medicines. If you are using both systems, ensure you inform both practitioners as to what the other has prescribed.

to travel is in the second trimester (between 16 and 28 weeks), when the risk of pregnancy-related problems is at its lowest and pregnant women generally feel at their best. During the first trimester there's a risk of miscarriage and in the third trimester complications such as premature labour and high blood pressure are possible. It's wise to travel with a companion. Always carry a list of quality medical facilities available at your destination and ensure you continue your standard antenatal care at these facilities. Avoid travel in rural areas with poor transport and medical facilities. Most of all, ensure travel insurance covers all pregnancy-related possibilities, including premature labour.

Malaria is a high-risk disease in pregnancy. The World Health Organization recommends that pregnant women do not travel to areas with malaria resistant to Chloroquine. None of the more effective antimalarial drugs is completely safe in pregnancy.

Traveller's diarrhoea can quickly lead to dehydration and result in inadequate blood flow to the placenta. Many of the drugs used to treat various diarrhoea bugs are not recommended in pregnancy. Azithromycin is considered safe.

In urban areas, supplies of sanitary products are readily available. Birth-control options may be limited so bring adequate supplies of your own form of contraception. Heat, humidity and antibiotics can all contribute to thrush. Treatment is with antifungal creams and pessaries such as Clotrimazole. A practical alternative is a single tablet of Fluconazole (Diflucan). Urinary-tract infections can be precipitated by dehydration or long bus journeys without toilet stops; bring suitable antibiotics.

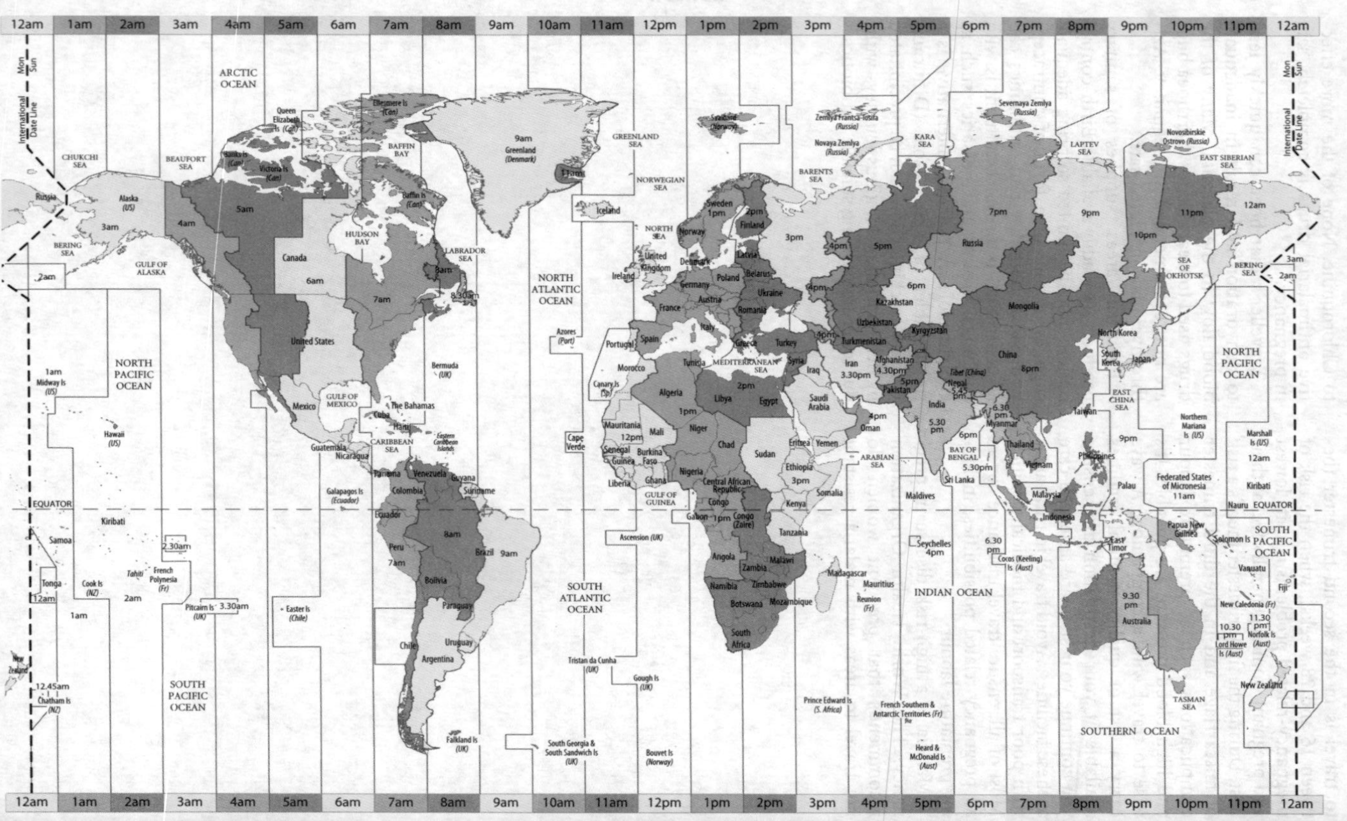

12am
1am
2am
3am
4am
5am
6am
7am
8am
9am
10am
11am
12pm
1pm
2pm
3pm
4pm
5pm
6pm
7pm
8pm
9pm
10pm
11pm
12am
International Date Line
Mon
Sun
ARCTIC OCEAN
CHUKCHI SEA
BEAUFORT SEA
BERING SEA
GULF OF ALASKA
HUDSON BAY
BAFFIN BAY
LABRADOR SEA
GREENLAND SEA
NORWEGIAN SEA
NORTH SEA
BARENTS SEA
KARA SEA
LAPTEV SEA
EAST SIBERIAN SEA
SEA OF OKHOTSK
NORTH PACIFIC OCEAN
NORTH ATLANTIC OCEAN
GULF OF MEXICO
CARIBBEAN SEA
MEDITERRANEAN SEA
ARABIAN SEA
BAY OF BENGAL
EAST CHINA SEA
GULF OF GUINEA
EQUATOR
SOUTH PACIFIC OCEAN
SOUTH ATLANTIC OCEAN
INDIAN OCEAN
TASMAN SEA
SOUTHERN OCEAN
Russia
Alaska (US)
Queen Elizabeth Is (Can)
Ellesmere Is (Can)
Banks Is (Can)
Victoria Is (Can)
Baffin Is (Can)
Greenland (Denmark)
Iceland
Canada
United States
Mexico
The Bahamas
Cuba
Haiti
Eastern Caribbean Islands
Bermuda (UK)
Guatemala
Nicaragua
Panama
Venezuela
Guyana
Suriname
Colombia
Ecuador
Peru
Brazil
Bolivia
Paraguay
Chile
Uruguay
Argentina
Falkland Is (UK)
Galapagos Is (Ecuador)
Midway Is (US)
Hawaii (US)
Kiribati
Samoa
Tonga
Cook Is (NZ)
Tahiti
French Polynesia (Fr)
Pitcairn Is (UK)
Easter Is (Chile)
New Zealand
Chatham Is (NZ)
Azores (Port)
Canary Is (Sp)
Cape Verde
Ascension (UK)
Tristan da Cunha (UK)
Gough Is (UK)
South Georgia & South Sandwich Is (UK)
Bouvet Is (Norway)
Svalbard (Norway)
Zemlya Frantsa-Iosifa (Russia)
Novaya Zemlya (Russia)
Severnaya Zemlya (Russia)
Novosibirskie Ostrovo (Russia)
Ireland
United Kingdom
Norway
Sweden
Finland
Denmark
Latvia
Belarus
Poland
Germany
Austria
Ukraine
France
Romania
Italy
Spain
Portugal
Greece
Turkey
Syria
Iraq
Iran
Morocco
Tunisia
Algeria
Libya
Egypt
Mauritania
Mali
Niger
Chad
Sudan
Senegal
Guinea
Burkina Faso
Ghana
Liberia
Nigeria
Central African Republic
Gabon
Congo
Congo (Zaire)
Eritrea
Yemen
Ethiopia
Somalia
Kenya
Tanzania
Angola
Zambia
Malawi
Namibia
Zimbabwe
Botswana
Mozambique
South Africa
Madagascar
Mauritius
Reunion (Fr)
Seychelles
Saudi Arabia
Oman
Kazakhstan
Uzbekistan
Turkmenistan
Kyrgyzstan
Afghanistan
Pakistan
India
Nepal
Tibet (China)
Sri Lanka
Maldives
Myanmar
Thailand
Vietnam
Malaysia
Indonesia
China
Mongolia
North Korea
South Korea
Japan
Taiwan
Philippines
Palau
East Timor
Papua New Guinea
Australia
Northern Mariana Is (US)
Federated States of Micronesia
Marshall Is (US)
Nauru
Solomon Is
Vanuatu
Fiji
New Caledonia (Fr)
Norfolk Is (Aust)
Lord Howe Is (Aust)
Cocos (Keeling) Is (Aust)
Prince Edward Is (S. Africa)
French Southern & Antarctic Territories (Fr)
Heard & McDonald Is (Aust)
12.45am
2.30am
3.30am
8.30am
3.30pm
4.30pm
5.30 pm
5.45 pm
5.30pm
6.30 pm
9.30 pm
10.30 pm
11.30 pm
11am

Language

CONTENTS

Bahasa Malaysia (also known simply as Malay and, officially, as *Bahasa Melayu*) and Bahasa Indonesia are virtually the same language; only a few differences in vocabulary distinguish the two. Many of these differences are in the loan words – English-based for Malay and Dutch-based for Indonesian. If you're coming from Indonesia and have developed some proficiency in the language, you may initially be confused by Malay pronunciation. Bahasa Indonesia is a second language for most Indonesians – pronunciation is learnt in schools and thus tends to remain fairly standard. Bahasa Malaysia, however, is subject to a greater degree of regional variation in pronunciation and slang – so much so that a Malaysian from Negeri Sembilan may have difficulty understanding someone from Kelantan.

In its most basic form, Malay is very simple. Verbs aren't conjugated for tense; the notion of time is indicated by the use of adverbs such as 'yesterday' or 'tomorrow'. For example, you can change any sentence into the past tense by simply adding *sudah* (already). Many nouns are pluralised by simply saying them twice – thus *buku* is 'book', *buku-buku* is 'books', *anak* is 'child', *anak-anak* is 'children'. There are no articles (a, an, the). Thus 'a good book' or 'the good book' is simply *buku baik*. There is no verb 'to be', so again it would be *buku baik* rather than 'the book is good'. Malay is also a very poetic and evocative language – 'the sun', for example, is *matahari*, or 'the eye of the day'.

Many Malay terms have found their way into the everyday English of Malaysia. You'll often see the word *bumiputra* (literally 'sons of the soil') in English-language newspapers, usually in ads for positions vacant; it's a term used to indicate that the job is open only to 'native' Malays, not Indian Malaysians or Chinese Malaysians. Similarly, you may see English-language articles about *jaga keretas*, the people who operate car-parking rackets – pay them to 'protect' your car while it's parked or you'll wish you had. Another expression is *khalwat* (literally 'close proximity') – unmarried Muslim couples definitely do not wish to find themselves suspected of *khalwat*!

For a more comprehensive guide to the language, get hold of Lonely Planet's *Malay phrasebook*. It's a handy pocket-sized introduction to the language.

PRONUNCIATION

Most letters are pronounced the same as their English counterparts, although a few vowels and consonants differ.

Vowels

a as the 'u' in 'hut'
e a neutral vowel like the 'a' in 'ago' when unstressed, eg *besar* (big); when the stress falls on **e** it's more like the 'a' in 'may', eg *meja* (table). Unfortunately, there's no single rule to determine whether **e** is stressed or unstressed.
i as in 'hit'
o as in 'note'
u as in 'flute'
ai as in 'aisle'
au a drawn out 'ow', as in 'cow'
ua each vowel is pronounced, as 'oo-a'

Consonants

c always as the 'ch' in 'chair'
g always hard, as in 'go'
ng as the 'ng' in 'singer'

SINGLISH

One of the most intriguing things the visitor to Singapore will notice is the strange patois spoken by the locals. Nominally English, it contains borrowed words from Hokkien and Malay, such as *shiok* (delicious) and *kasar* (rough). Unnecessary prepositions and pronouns are dropped, word order is flipped, phrases are clipped short, and stress and cadence are unconventional, to say the least. The result is known locally as Singlish. Singlish is frowned upon in official use, though you'll get a good idea of its pervasive pronunciation characteristics if you listen to the news bulletins on TV or the radio.

While there isn't such a thing as Singlish grammar, there are definite characteristics. First off, there's the reverse stress pattern of double-barrelled words. For example, in standard English the stress would be '*fire*-fighter' or '*theatre* company' but in Singlish it's 'fire-*fighter*' and 'theatre *company*'. Word-final consonants – particularly **l** or **k** – are often dropped and vowels are often distorted; a Chinese-speaking taxi driver might not understand 'Perak Road' since they pronounce it 'Pera Roh'. The particle *lah* is often tagged on to the end of sentences as in, 'No good, *lah*', which could mean (among other things) 'I don't think that's such a good idea'. Requests or questions will often be marked with a tag ending since direct questioning is considered rude. So a question such as 'Would you like a beer?' might be rendered as 'You want beer or not?', which might come across to speakers of Western English as being extremely rude. Verb tenses tend to be nonexistent; future, present or past actions are all indicated by time phrases, so in Singlish it's 'I go tomorrow' or 'I go yesterday'.

The following are some of the most frequently heard Singlishisms:

ah beng – unsophisticated person with no fashion sense or style; red neck
Aiyah! – 'Oh, dear!'
Alamak! – exclamation of disbelief, frustration or dismay, like 'Oh my God!'
ayam – Malay word for chicken; adjective for something inferior or weak
blur – a slow or uninformed person
buaya – womaniser, from the Malay for crocodile
Can? – 'Is that OK?'
Can! – 'Yes! That's fine.'
char bor – babe, woman
cheena – old-fashioned Chinese in dress or thinking (derogatory)
go stan – to reverse, as in 'Go stan the car' (from the naval expression 'go astern'; pronounced 'go stun')
heng – luck, good fortune (Hokkien)
hiao – vain
inggrish – English
kambing – foolish person, literally 'goat' (Malay)
kena ketuk – literally 'get knocked'; ripped off
kiasee – scared, literally 'afraid to die'; a coward
kiasu – literally 'afraid to lose'; selfish, pushy, always on the lookout for a bargain
lah – generally an ending for any phrase or sentence; can translate as 'OK', but has no real meaning; added for emphasis to just about everything
looksee – take a look
malu – embarrassed
minah – girlfriend
Or not? – general suffix for questions, as in 'Can or not?' (Can you or can't you?)
see first – wait and see what happens
shack – tired
shiok – good, great, delicious
steady lah – well done, excellent; expression of praise
Wah! – general exclamation of surprise or distress
ya ya – boastful, as in 'He always *ya ya*'

ngg as 'ng' + 'g' (as in 'anger')
j as in 'join'
r pronounced clearly and distinctly
h as the English 'h' but slightly stronger (like a sigh); at the end of a word it's almost silent
k as English 'k', except at the end of the word, when it's more like a glottal stop (ie the 'non-sound' created by the momentary closing of the throat before each syllable in the expression 'oh-oh!')
ny as in 'canyon'

Word Stress

In Malay words, most syllables carry equal emphasis, but a good rule of thumb is to put stress on the second-last syllable. The main exception is the unstressed **e** in words such as *besar* (big), pronounced 'be-SAR'.

ACCOMMODATION

I'm looking for a ... *Saya mencari ...*
guesthouse *rumah tetamu*
hotel *hotel*
youth hostel *asrama belia*
bed *katil*

Where is a cheap hotel?
Di mana ada hotel yang murah?
What is the address?
Apakah alamatnya?
Could you write the address, please?
Tolong tuliskan alamat itu?
Do you have any rooms available?
Ada bilik kosong?

I'd like a ...	*Saya hendakkan ...*
single room	*bilik untuk satu orang*
double room	*bilik untuk dua orang*
room with two beds	*bilik yang ada dua katil*
room with air-con	*bilik dengan alat hawa dingin*
room with a fan	*bilik dengan kipas*
room with a bathroom	*bilik dengan bilik mandi*

I'd like to share a dorm.
Saya nak berkongsi (bilik hostel/asrama).

MAKING A RESERVATION

(for phone or written inquiries)

To ...	*Ke ...*
From ...	*Daripada ...*
I'd like to book ...	*Saya nak tempah ...* (see the list under 'Accommodation' for bed and room options)
for the nights of ...	*untuk malam ...*
in the name of ...	*atas nama ...*
credit card	*kad kredit*
type	*jenis*
number	*nombor*
expiry date	*tempoh tamat*
Please confirm availability and price.	*Tolong sahkan tempahan dan harga.*

How much is it ...?	*Berapa harga ...?*
per night	*satu malam*
per week	*satu seminggu*
per person	*satu orang*

May I see it?
Boleh saya lihat biliknya?
Where is the bathroom?
Bilik mandi di mana?
I (don't) like this room.
Saya (tidak) suka bilik ini.
I'm/We're leaving today.
Saya/Kami nak mendaftar keluar hari ini.

CONVERSATION & ESSENTIALS

Hello.	*Helo.*
Good morning.	*Selamat pagi.*
Good day. (said around midday)	*Selamat tengah hari.*
Good afternoon.	*Selamat petang.*
Good night.	*Selamat malam.*
Goodbye. (said by person leaving)	*Selamat tinggal.*
Goodbye. (said by person staying)	*Selamat jalan.*
Yes.	*Ya.*
No.	*Tidak.*
Please.	*Tolong/Silakan.*
Thank you (very much).	*Terima kasih (banyak).*
That's fine/ You're welcome.	*Boleh/Sama-sama.*
Excuse me, ...	*Maaf, ...*
Sorry/Pardon.	*Maaf.*
I'm sorry. (forgive me)	*Minta maaf.*
How are you?	*Apa khabar?*
Fine thanks.	*Khabar baik.*
What's your name?	*Siapa nama kamu?*
My name is ...	*Nama saya ...*
Where are you from?	*Dari mana asal saudara?*
I'm from ...	*Saya dari ...*
How old are you?	*Berapa umur saudara?*
I'm (20 years old).	*Umur saya (dua puluh tahun).*
I like ...	*Saya suka ...*
I don't like ...	*Saya tidak suka ...*
Just a minute.	*Sebentar/Sekejap.*
Good/Very nice.	*Bagus.*
Good/Fine.	*Baik.*
No good.	*Tidak baik.*

DIRECTIONS

Where is ...?	*Di mana ...*
Which way?	*Ke mana?*
Go straight ahead.	*Jalan terus.*
Turn left.	*Belok kiri.*
Turn right.	*Belok kanan.*
at the corner	*di simpang*
at the traffic lights	*di tempat lampu isyarat*
at the T-junction	*di simpang tiga*
behind	*di belakang*
in front of	*di hadapan*
next to	*di samping/di sebelah*
opposite	*berhadapan dengan*
near	*dekat*
far	*jauh*
here	*di sini*
there	*di sana*

SIGNS

Masuk	Entrance
Keluar	Exit
Pertanyaan	Information
Buka	Open
Tutup	Closed
Dilarang	Prohibited
Di Larang Merokok	No Smoking
Awas	Caution
Bahaya	Danger
Ada Bilik Kosong	Rooms Available
Penuh/Tak Ada Bilik Kosong	Full/No Vacancies
Polis	Police
Balai Polis	Police Station
Tandas	Toilets
Lelaki	Men
Perempuan	Women
Panas	Hot
Sejuk	Cold
Tarik	Pull
Tolak	Push

north *utara*
south *selatan*
east *timur*
west *barat*

beach *pantai*
bridge *jambatan*
island *pulau*
mosque *masjid*
museum *muzium*
palace *istana*
ruins *runtuhan*
sea *laut*
square *dataran*

HEALTH

Where is a ... *Di mana ada ...*
chemist/pharmacy *apotik/farmasi*
dentist *doktor gigi*
doctor *doktor*
hospital *hospital*

I'm ill. *Saya sakit.*
It hurts here. *Sini sakit.*

I'm allergic to ... *Saya alergik kepada ...*
to antibiotics *antibiotik*
to aspirin *aspirin*
to penicillin *penisilin*
to bees *lebah*
to nuts *kacang*

I'm ... *Saya ...*
asthmatic *sakit lelah*
diabetic *sakit kencing manis*
epileptic *sakit gila babi*
pregnant *hamil*

antiseptic *antiseptik*
condoms *kondom*
contraceptive *kontraseptif* or *pencegah hamil*
diarrhoea *cirit-birit*
fever *demam panas*
headache *sakit kepala*
medicine *ubat*
sunblock cream *krim pelindung cahaya matahari*
pill/tablet *pil/tablet*
quinine *kina/kuinin*
sanitary napkins *tuala wanita*
sleeping pills *pil tidur*
tampons *tampon*

EMERGENCIES

Help! *Tolong!*
There's been an accident! *Ada kemalangan!*
I'm lost. *Saya sesat.*
Go away! *Pergi!*
Stop! *Berhenti!*
I've been robbed! *Saya dirompak!*

Call ...! *Panggil ...!*
a doctor *doktor*
an ambulance *ambulans*

LANGUAGE DIFFICULTIES

Do you speak English?
Bolehkah anda berbicara bahasa Inggeris?/ Adaka anda berbahasa Inggeris?
Does anyone here speak English?
Ada orang yang berbahasa Inggeris di sini?
How do you say ... in Malay?
Macam mana cakap ... dalam Bahasa Melayu?
What does ... mean?
Apa ertinya ...?
I understand.
Saya faham.
I don't understand.
Saya tidak faham.
Please write it down.
Tolong tuliskan.
Please write that word down.
Tolong tuliskan perkataan itu.
Please repeat it.
Tolong ulangi.

LANGUAGE

Can you show me (on the map)?
Tolong tunjukkan (di peta)?

NUMBERS

0	*kosong/sifar*
1	*satu*
2	*dua*
3	*tiga*
4	*empat*
5	*lima*
6	*enam*
7	*tujuh*
8	*delapan/lapan*
9	*sembilan*
10	*sepuluh*
11	*sebelas*
12	*dua belas*
13	*tiga belas*
14	*empat belas*
15	*lima belas*
16	*enam belas*
17	*tujuh belas*
18	*lapan belas*
19	*sembilan belas*
20	*dua puluh*
21	*dua puluh satu*
22	*dua puluh dua*
30	*tiga puluh*
40	*empat puluh*
50	*lima puluh*
60	*enam puluh*
70	*tujuh puluh*
80	*lapan puluh*
90	*sembilan puluh*
100	*seratus*
200	*dua ratus*
1000	*seribu*
2000	*dua ribu*

PAPERWORK

name	*nama*
nationality	*bangsa*
date of birth	*tarikh lahir*
place of birth	*tempat kelahiran tempat lahir*
sex/gender	*jantina*
passport	*pasport*
visa	*visa*

QUESTION WORDS

Who?	*Siapakah?*
What?	*Apa?*
When?	*Bilakah?*
Where?	*Di mana?*
How?	*Berapa?*
Which?	*Yang mana?*

SHOPPING & SERVICES

I'd like to buy ...	*Saya nak beli ...*
How much (is it)?	*Berapa (harganya)?*
I don't like it.	*Saya tak suka ini.*
May I look at it?	*Boleh saya lihat barang itu?*
I'm just looking.	*Saya nak tengok saja.*
It's cheap.	*Murah.*
It's too expensive.	*Mahalnya.*
Can you lower the price?	*Boleh kurang sedikit?*
No more than ...	*Tak lebih daripada ...*
That's a good price.	*Harganya dah murah.*
I'll take it.	*Saya nak beli ini.*

Do you accept ...?	*Boleh bayar dengan ...?*
credit cards	*kad kredit*
travellers cheques	*cek kembara*

more	*lebih banyak*
less	*kurang*
big	*besar*
bigger	*lebih besar*
small	*kecil*
smaller	*lebih kecil*
this	*ini*
that	*itu*

I'm looking for a/the ...	*Saya nak cari ...*
bank	*bank*
barber	*tukang cukur*
bookshop	*kedai buku*
city centre	*pusat bandar*
chemist/pharmacy	*apotik/farmasi*
... embassy	*kedutaan besar ...*
grocery	*kedai makanan*
market	*pasar*
night market	*pasar malam*
police station	*stesen polis*
post office	*pejabat pos*
public telephone	*telepon umum*
public toilet	*tandas awam*
shop	*kedai*
shopping centre	*pusat membeli-belah*
telephone centre	*pusat telefon*
tourist office	*pejabat pelancong*

I want to change ...	*Saya nak tukar wang ...*
money (cash)	*wang tunai*
travellers cheques	*cek kembara*

What time does it open/close?
Pukul berapa buka/tutup?
I want to call ...
Saya mau menelefon ...

TIME & DATES

What time is it?	*Pukul berapa?*
(It's) 7 o'clock.	*Pukul tujuh.*
When?	*Bila?*
in the morning	*pagi*
in the afternoon	*tengahari*
in the evening	*petang*
at night	*malam*
today	*hari ini*
tomorrow	*besok/esok*
yesterday	*semalam*
How long?	*Berapa lama?*
hour	*jam*
week	*minggu*
year	*tahun*

Monday	*hari Isnin*
Tuesday	*hari Selasa*
Wednesday	*hari Rabu*
Thursday	*hari Khamis*
Friday	*hari Jumaat*
Saturday	*hari Sabtu*
Sunday	*hari minggu*

January	*Januari*
February	*Februari*
March	*Mac*
April	*April*
May	*Mei*
June	*Jun*
July	*Julai*
August	*Ogos*
September	*September*
October	*Oktober*
November	*November*
December	*Disember*

TRANSPORT

Public Transport

What time does the ... leave?	*Pukul berapakah ... berangkat?*
boat	*bot*
bus	*bas*
plane	*kapal terbang*
ship	*kapal*
train	*keretapi*

I'd like a ... ticket.	*Saya nak tiket ...*
one-way	*sehala*
return	*pergi-balik*
1st class	*kelas satu*
2nd class	*kelas dua*
economy class	*kelas ekonomi*

I want to go to ...
Saya nak ke ...
How can I get to ...?
Bagaimana saya pergi ke ...?
How many kilometres?
Berapa kilometer?
The (train/bus) has been delayed.
Kereta api/bas itu telah terlambat.
The (train/bus) has been cancelled.
Kereta api/bas itu telah dibatalkan.

the first (bus)	*(bas) pertama*
the last (train)	*keretapi terakhir*
airport	*lapangan terbang*
bus station	*stesen bas*
bus stop	*perhentian bas*
platform number	*nombor platform*
rickshaw/trishaw	*beca*
ticket office	*pejabat tiket*
ticket window	*(tempat/kaunter) tikit*
timetable	*jadual*
train station	*stesen keretapi*

Private Transport

I'd like to hire a/an ...	*Saya nak menyewa ...*
car	*kereta*
4WD	*4WD*
motorbike	*motosikal*
bicycle	*basikal*

ROAD SIGNS

Beri Jalan	Give Way
Lencongan	Detour
Dilarang Masuk	No Entry
Tidak Boleh Memotong	No Overtaking
Dilarang Letak Kereta	No Parking
Masuk	Entrance
Kosongkan	Keep Clear
Jalan Tol	Toll Way
Plaza Tol	Toll Gate
Bahaya	Danger
Perlahan-Perlahan	Slow Down
Jalan Sehala	One Way
Keluar	Exit

Is this the road to ...?	*Inikah jalan ke ...?*
Where's a service station?	*Stesen minyak di mana?*
Please fill it up.	*Tolong penuhkan tangki.*
I'd like (30) litres.	*Saya nak (30) liter.*
petrol	*minyak/petrol*
diesel	*disel*

leaded petrol *petrol plumbum*
unleaded petrol *tanpa plumbum*

The English terms such as Super Leaded, Super/Premium Unleaded, Leaded, Unleaded are displayed at the pumps, depending on the oil company.

(How long) Can I park here?
(Beberapa lama) Boleh saya letak kereta di sini?
Where do I pay?
Di mana tempat membayar?
I need a mechanic.
Kami memerlukan mekanik.
The car/motorbike has broken down (at ...)
Kereta/motosikal saya telah rosak (di ...)
The car/motorbike won't start.
Kereta/motosikal saya tidak dapat dihidupkan.
I have a flat tyre.
Tayarnya kempis.
I've run out of petrol.
Minyak sudah habis.
I've had an accident.
Saya terlibat dalam kemalangan.

Also available from Lonely Planet:
Malay phrasebook

TRAVEL WITH CHILDREN

Do you have a/an ...? *Ada ...?*
I need a/an ... *Saya perlukan ...*
baby change room *bilik salin bayi*
car baby seat *tempat duduk bayi*
child-minding service *penjagaan anak*
children's menu *menu kanak-kanak*
(disposable) nappies/diapers *(pakai buang) kain lampin*
formula (milk) *(susu) rumusan bayi*
(English-speaking) babysitter *penjaga anak (yang tahu bercakap dalam Bahasa Inggeris)*
highchair *kerusi tinggi*
potty *bekas najis*
stroller *kereta tolak bayi*

Do you mind if I breastfeed here?
Adakah anda keberatan jika saya meneteki/menyusui bayi di sini?
Are children allowed?
Adakah kanak-kanak dibenarkan masuk?

LANGUAGE

Glossary

See p66 for culinary terms.

A

adat – Malay customary law
adat temenggong – Malay law with Indian modifications, governing the customs and ceremonies of the sultans
air – water
air terjun – waterfall
alor – groove; furrow; main channel of a river
ampang – dam
ang pow – red packets of money used as offerings, payment or gifts
APEC – Asia-Pacific Economic Cooperation
arak – Malay local alcohol
arrack – see *arak*
Asean – Association of Southeast Asian Nations
atap – roof thatching

B

Baba-Nonya – descendants of Chinese immigrants to the Straits Settlements (namely Melaka, Singapore and Penang) who intermarried with Malays and adopted many Malay customs; also known as Peranakan, or Straits Chinese; sometimes spelt Nyonya
Bahasa Malaysia – Malay language; also known as Bahasa Melayu;
bandar – seaport; town
Bangsawan – Malay opera
batang – stem; tree-trunk; the main branch of a river
batik – technique of imprinting cloth with dye to produce multicoloured patterns
batu – stone; rock; milepost
belukar – secondary forest
bendahara – chief minister
bendang – irrigated land
bomoh – spiritual healer
British Resident – chief British representative during the colonial era
bukit – hill
bumboat – motorised *sampan*
bumiputra – literally, sons of the soil; Malay people
bunga raya – hibiscus flower (national flower of Malaysia)

D

dadah – drugs
dato, datuk – literally, grandfather; general male nonroyal title of distinction
dipterocarp – family of trees, native to Malaysia, that have two-winged fruits
dusun – small town; orchard; fruit grove

G

genting – mountain pass
godown – river warehouse
gua – cave
gunung – mountain

H

hilir – lower reaches of a river
hutan – jungle; forest

I

imam – keeper of Islamic knowledge and leader of prayer
istana – palace

J

jalan – road

K

kain songket – traditional Malay handwoven fabric with gold threads
kampung – village; also spelt kampong
kangkar – Chinese village
karst – characteristic scenery of a limestone region, including features such as underground streams and caverns
kedai kopi – coffee shop
kerangas – distinctive vegetation zone of Borneo, usually found on sandstone, containing pitcher plants and other unusual flora
khalwat – literally, close proximity; exhibition of public affection between the sexes which is prohibited for unmarried Muslim couples
kongsi – Chinese clan organisations, also known as ritual brotherhoods, heaven-man-earth societies, triads or secret societies; meeting house for Chinese of the same clan
kopi tiam – coffee shop (Singapore)
kota – fort; city
kramat – Malay shrine
KTM – Keretapi Tanah Melayu; Malaysian Railways System
kuala – river mouth; place where a tributary joins a larger river

L

laksamana – admiral
langur – small, usually tree-dwelling monkey
laut – sea
lebuh – street
Lebuhraya – expressway or freeway; usually refers to the North–South Highway, which runs from Johor Bahru to Bukit Kayu Hitam at the Thai border
lorong – narrow street; alley

LRT – Light Rail Transit (Kuala Lumpur)
lubuk – deep pool

M
macaque – any of several small species of monkey
mandi – bathe; Southeast Asian wash basin
masjid – mosque
MCP – Malayan Communist Party
Melayu Islam Beraja – MIB; Brunei's national ideology
merdeka – independence
Merlion – half-lion, half-fish animal; symbol of Singapore
MIB – Melayu Islam Beraja; Brunei's national ideology
MRT – Mass Rapid Transit (Singapore)
muara – river mouth
muezzin – mosque official who calls the faithful to prayer

N
negara – country
negeri – state
nonya – see *Baba-Nonya*

O
orang asing – foreigner
Orang Asli – literally, Original People; Malaysian aborigines
Orang Laut – literally, Coastal People
Orang Ulu – literally, Upriver People

P
padang – grassy area; field; also the city square
pantai – beach
PAP – People's Action Party
parang – long jungle knife
PAS – Parti Islam se-Malaysia
pasar – market
pasar malam – night market
Pejabat Residen – Resident's Office
pekan – market place; town
pelabuhan – port
pencak silat – martial-arts dance form
penghulu – chief or village head
pengkalan – quay
Peranakan – literally, half-caste; refers to the *Baba-Nonya* or Straits Chinese
PIE – Pan-Island Expressway, one of Singapore's main road arteries
pua kumbu – traditional finely woven cloth
pulau – island
puteri – princess

R
raja – prince; ruler
rakyat – common people
rantau – straight coastline
rattan – stems from climbing palms used for wickerwork and canes
rimba – jungle
rotan – cane used to punish miscreants
roti– bread

S
sampan – small boat
samsu – Malay alcohol
sarung – all-purpose cloth, often sewn into a tube, and worn by women, men and children; also spelt sarong
seberang – opposite side of road; far bank of a river
selat – strait
semenanjung – peninsula
silat – see *pencak silat*
simpang – crossing; junction
songkok – traditional Malay headdress worn by males
Straits Chinese – see *Baba-Nonya*
sungai – river
syariah – Islamic system of law

T
tambang – river ferry; fare
tamu – weekly market
tanah – land
tanjung – headland
tasik – lake
teluk – bay; sometimes spelt telok
temenggong – Malay administrator
towkang – Chinese junk
tuai rumah – longhouse chief (Sarawak)
tuak – local 'firewater' alcohol (Malaysian Borneo)
tunku – prince

U
ujung – cape
UMNO – United Malays National Organisation

W
warung – small eating stalls
wayang – Chinese opera
wayang kulit – shadow-puppet theatre
wisma – office block or shopping centre

Y
yang di-pertuan agong – Malaysia's head of state, or 'king'
yang di-pertuan besar – head of state in Negeri Sembilan
yang di-pertuan muda – under-king
yang di-pertuan negeri – governor

Behind the Scenes

THIS BOOK

The 1st edition of this guide was written by Geoff Crowther and Tony and Maureen Wheeler in 1982. Mark Lightbody handled the research for the 2nd edition. The 3rd edition was the joint effort of Sue Tan and Joe Cummings. Hugh Finlay and Peter Turner updated the 4th and 5th editions. The 6th edition was researched and written by Peter Turner and Chris Rowthorn. Chris Rowthorn, David Andrew, Paul Hellander and Clem Lindenmayer teamed up on the 7th edition. The 8th edition was updated by Chris Rowthorn, Sara 'Sam' Benson, Russ Kerr and Christine Niven. This 9th edition was updated by Simon Richmond, Marie Cambon, Damian Harper and Richard Watkins. The Food & Drink chapter was based on Lonely Planet's *World Food Malaysia & Singapore* by Su-Lyn Tan and adapted for this title by Simon Richmond. Alan D'Cruz wrote the History chapter, while Trish Batchelor did Health. Additional reviews of Malaysian films were contributed by Richard Lau.

THANKS FROM THE AUTHORS

Simon Richmond Steve and Emiko, I can't thank you enough for the many times you have played gracious hosts and willing accomplices on my dining forays around Singapore. A huge thanks also to my playmate Kim, and to Arnel (and the girls) for many fun nights out. Ian, your helpful suggestions are much appreciated. At STB, Yul Chin Kok and Su Lin Oh did a great job on sorting out facts and contacts. Cheers also to Maggie Perry, Su-Lyn Tan, Jenny Tan Che Gee and Terry Ong for various insights and advice.

Marie Cambon Many thanks to staff at the tourist information centres in Sarawak and Sabah, especially Robin Chin in KK and Deckson and Angela in Kuching. Thanks to Paul for a great introduction to Kuching, and to Robert Chong, Elvina, Borneo Adventure, Julia and the folks at Rose Cabin, Esther, and Max for his wonderful tour of Brunei. Special thanks to Helen Rowley at LP for her notes and comments and to the readers who sent in useful suggestions. Thanks also to Ruth Marzetti, Stephen Macdonald and Randy Schuks for their support and encouragement. Finally, thanks Simon Richmond and Mary Neighbour for their patience.

Damian Harper Thanks to all the helpful individuals I met on my journey in Peninsular Malaysia, and special thanks to Anne Louis and her friends for some fine Chinese food in Johor Bahru. Cheers also to the youths of Pekan and to both Ron the gold miner and Mr Zheng in Kuala Lipis. A nod of thanks also to staff at Lonely Planet and a big hug for my wife and son for their marvellous support.

Richard Watkins Many thanks to Alex Lee Ping and his friendly and knowledgeable staff, who made my stay in Terengganu such an interesting and enjoyable one. Thanks also go to Madi and to Jimmy Lee in Pulau Perhentian, who went out of their way to show me the very best their beautiful islands had to offer. Thanks are also due to Roselan in Kota Bharu, a real character whose dry humour and knowledge of British TV sitcoms made me laugh. I would also like to thank Edward Oh in Pulau

THE LONELY PLANET STORY

The story begins with a classic travel adventure: Tony and Maureen Wheeler's 1972 journey across Europe and Asia to Australia. There was no useful information about the overland trail then, so Tony and Maureen published the first Lonely Planet guidebook to meet a growing need.

From a kitchen table, Lonely Planet has grown to become the largest independent travel pub-lisher in the world, with offices in Melbourne (Australia), Oakland (USA), London (UK) and Paris (France).

Today Lonely Planet guidebooks cover the globe. There is an ever-growing list of books and information in a variety of media. Some things haven't changed. The main aim is still to make it possible for adventurous travellers to get out there – to explore and better understand the world.

At Lonely Planet we believe travellers can make a positive contribution to the countries they visit – if they respect their host communities and spend their money wisely.

Pangkor, Khairul Syahar Khalid in KL and all the staff at the Tourism Malaysia office in Penang.

CREDITS

Malaysia, Singapore & Brunei 9 was commissioned and developed in Lonely Planet's Melbourne office by Mary Neighbour. Cartography for this guide was developed by Corie Waddell, and the project was managed by Chris Love.

This book was coordinated by Maryanne Netto (editorial), Jack Gavran (cartography) and David Kemp (layout). The cover was designed by Pepi Bluck. Maryanne was assisted by Simone Egger, Anastasia Safioleas, Miriam Cannell, Cathryn Game, Andrea Baster, Sally Steward, David Andrew, Gabbi Wilson, Jocelyn Harewood and Diana Saad. Quentin Frayne prepared the Language chapter and Peter Cruttenden compiled the index. Many thanks to managing editor Jane Thompson for her support and guidance throughout, and to Darren O'Connell and Jennifer Garrett for rallying to calls for help.

Jack was assisted by Bonnie Wintle, Tony Fankhauser, Mike Mammarella, Anneka Inkamp, Valentina Kremenchutskaya, Csanad Csutoros and Sarah Sloane. Assisting David Kemp were Pablo Gastar, Steven Cann, Indra Kilfoyle, Vicki Beale, Katherine Marsh, Laura Jane and Angela Robinson. A big thanks to Adriana Mammarella and Kate McDonald, who oversaw layout; to Carol Chandler and Graham Imeson from print production; Lachlan Ross and Chris Lee Ack for production support; and to Ben Handicott for editorial production assistance.

Series Publishing Manager Virginia Maxwell oversaw the redevelopment of the country guide series with help from Maria Donohoe. Virginia also steered the development of this title. The series was designed by James Hardy, with mapping development by Paul Piaia and Wayne Murphy. The series development team included Anna Bolger, Dave McClymont, Erin Corrigan, Howard Ralley, Jenny Blake, Lynne Preston, Nadine Fogale, Rachel Peart, Shahara Ahmed, Susie Ashworth and Verity Campbell.

THANKS FROM LONELY PLANET

Many thanks to the travellers who used the last edition and contacted us with helpful hints, advice and interesting anecdotes:

A Heidi Abbott, Dr Baharudin Abdullah, Lisa Abra, Sander Abruti, David Ackley, Fairuz Adzahan, Susan Aistrop, Marielle Al, Mascha Alberts, Tennille Alford, Silvia Allami, Craig Allatt, Isaac Allen, Matthew Allen, Ingrid Alten, Ian Andersen, Lene Cecilie Andersen, Ryan Anderson, Cynthia Ang, Anita Montvazski, Mardi Arkinstall, Tim Armstrong, Luke Arnold, Tom Ash, Brett Ashby, Philip Asher, Caroline & Phil Ashton, Susan & Paul Atkinson, Colin Attenborough, Azrai Azhari, Azmi Abdul Aziz **B** Rob Baarda, Allen Bageant, Chris Bain, Patricia Ball, Mark & Dianne Barber-Riley, Will Barclay, Larona Barnes, Robert Barnes, John Barnett, Calude Barrelet, Greg Barrie, Tom Barry, Melvin Bashner, Jannik Bausager, Janny Beare, Chloe Beesley, Danica Beharkova, Peter Beirinckx, Aocha Belhaddad, Freeda Bell, Emily Bellish, Bernarda Benka Pulka, Lene Berge, Lesley Berger, Joakim Bergmark, Joan Berings, Peter Beswick, Gisela Beukema, John Biale, Lee Bibring, Darin Bielby, Radjender Bindesrisingh, Neville Bingham, Gillian & David Bird, Sam Birtles, Genevieve Bisset, Valerie Black, Shannon Blackmore, William Blake, Sally Blakemore, Bill Blick, Cedar Blomberg, Helga Bloom, Paul Bloomfield, Abi Blyth, Ben Blythe, Nicole Boelens, Ruben & Hanneke Boer, Rene Bohlen, Julia Bonn, Simon Booth, Jeroen Borggreve, Marjolein Borstlap, Arnaud Bos, Teresa Boulton, Jasper Bouman, David Bowden, Suzanne Bradbrook, Jenny Brain, Christian Beccer Brandvold, Shelly Branson, James Bravant, Andrea Bremner, Siobhan Breslin, Jean-Noel Brevet, Samantha Brierley, Bert Brilleman, Dr Andreas P Briner, Mrs LP Britt, Anne & David Brock, Johnathan Brook, Marc Brookhuis, Dave Broughton, Chris Brown, Laura Brown, Rosamund Brown, Joan Browne, Lisbeth Brunthaler, Erik Bryer, Zaliha Buang, Richard Buck, Maxine Buckingham, Richard Buckley, Ivan Buholzer, Thawatchai Buparat, Frank Bures, Linda Burgin, Martin Burke, Richard Burnham, Bob Burns, Ben Buston, Alan Butterworth, Kathy Butts **C** Marilyn Cable, Claudia Caflisch, Victoria Cairns, Fergy Campbell, Kathy Canavan, Steve P Cannings, Jared Cantlon, Jennifer Carriage, Alister Carroll, Tony Carthy, Kim Cartledge, Rusty Cartmill, Silvy Carvalho, Maura Celli, Lina Chakrabarty, Joanna Champion, Georgia Chandler, Vic Chapman, Gavin Chart, Briar Charteris, WK Chee, Anna Cheetham, David Cheetham, David Chen, Gabriel Chew, Lim Huck Chin, Terrie Chin, Beth Chong, Ng Koh Chong, Vivian Chong, Tan Hui Choon, Wendy Chouinard, Charlie Chow, Lennert Christensen, Jo Chua, Tan Teck Chuan, Lee Yu Chuang, Len Clampett, David Clark, Rita Clayfield, Joanna Clough, John Cockroft, Andy Cole, Yvonne Colebatch, Dennis Collins, Jody Collins, Bea & Matthias Colyer, Ruby Cooper, Justin Corfield, Chris Courtheyn, Patrick Couzens, Nicholas Covelli, Douglas Cowan, Jehan Coyajee, Adele Crabtree, Roby Cran, Kelly Crawford, Sue Crawford, Mark Creery, Annick Criekemans, Simona Crolla, Tim & Marika Crosby, Ben Crowe, Rob Cruts, Peter Cunningham **D** Natasha Dahanayake, Anne Danaher, Edward Dang, Tim Daniels, Mireille Dauphinais, Annette Davey, Barry Davies, Paul Davies, Stephanie Davies, Oliver Davis, Jan Davison, Katie Day, Shantha D'Cruz, Georg de Boer, Wouter de Boer, Manuel Dona de Guzman, Arno De Jong, Yvonne de Jong, Dietrich De Roeck, Marco de Rosa, Jarin De Wit, Steve Deadman, Ellen Deckers, Kamiel Deinum, Kevin Denny, Alison Denton, Katharine Dickens, Annemiek Dijkstra, John Dimino, Anthony Diorio, Dan Dispain, Dan Dixon, David Dobell, Sasha Dodimead, Ineke Dohrmann, Tracy Donaldson, Hugues Donato, Frank A Doonan, David Dorn, Tim Dowdall, Sebastian Down, Michael Doyle, Remon Drenth, Dory Drijver, Manuela Druml, Shani Duggan, Klaus Dunder, Russell Dunne, Roger Dunscombe, Mike Dunthorne, Chloe & Michael Dutton, Gabriella Dvorak, Elizabeth Dwomoh, Dan Dyksztejn

E Vicky Earl, John Eaton, Steve Ebury, Mel & Kathy Eckhaus, Lisa Edwards, Rachel Edwards, Erik Klein Egelink, Irene Eiermann, Rick Eling, Troy Ellis, Annette & Andrew Emms, Steve Emms, Angie Eng, Anna Eng, Bob Ennis, Michelle Enticknap, Kurt Epper, David Escat, Clive Essame, Ralph Essers, Greg Evans, Simon Evans, Paul Eveniss **F** Guido Faes, Richard Fahrni, John Fahy, Mindi and Brian Farran, Jimmy Fauske, Raphael Favre, Geoff Fawcett, Luke Fawcus, David Fearn, Marvin Feldman, Ferdinand Fellinger, Keow Mei Fern, Pablo Strubell Fernandez, Arnout Fischer, Nicki Fishlock, Tim Fitzsimmons, Amy Fletcher, Elizabeth Fletcher, Katie Flood, Petrina Flynn, Joseph Fok, Lcien Fokker, Marco Fontana, James Forbes, Steve Fosher, Evan Foster, Kent Foster, Judith M Fothergill, Michael Francis, Beauchamp Francois, D'Haenens Frank, Mark Freshney, Lucy Friedland, Matt Friend, Richard Frost, Alexandra Fuchs, Sarah Fullinger, Michael Fung **G** Mike Galante, Rachel & Stuart Gale, Bruce Gall, Nemo Galletti, Vicki Gallichan, G L Galusha, Mike Galvin, Katherine Gantzer, Joan Gates, Barbara Geis, Chris Geisow, Gerhard Geldenhuys, András Gelencsér, Craig Gerrior, Dave Gerrish, Guido Gevels, Razman Ghazaly, Andy Gilbert, Steve Gill, Bob Gillick, Jose Francisco Giraldo, Sue Glauser, Christian Glossner, Simon Goddard, Stephanie Godfrey, Laura Goldie, Stephanie Gordon, Zsolt Gordos, Glyn & Beverley Goronwy, Rene Gouweleeuw, Puspanathan Govindasamy, Tom & Carol Greber, David Greenlee, Andy & Maiko Greenshields, Jan Grenner, Peter Grills, Ivette Groenendijk, Eelko-Jan Groenevelt, Patch Groenweleger, Catherine Gross, Andrea Gryak, Chew Chang Guan, Chantel Guidry, Bernard Guillelmon, Jane Guillelmon, Peter Gustafsson **H** Natasja Hagenaar, A Hagon, Robert Haines, Angela Hall, Jennifer Hall, Kenneth Hall, Dave Hankin, Nicholas Paul Hanlon, Paul Hannon, Susanne Hansson, Heather Hapeta, Darren Hare, Stephen Harper, Fred Harris, Harvey Harris, Paul Harris, Valerie Harris, Niek Hartmann, Oliver Harwood, Gunther Haschberger, Eric Haskell, Noel Hathorn, Karin Haugen, Juliet Haughton, Graeme Hay, Nick Hays, Janis Hearn, Janos Hee, John B Hee, Shana Hermie, Justine Herridge, Kevin Herring, Amy Hetherington, Josee Heuts, Peggy Heyder, Rowan Hibbett, Ritchie Hicks, Anselm Hi'ilawe, Victoria Hill, Michiel Hillenius, Michael Hilt, Eva Himmelberg, Lol Hind, Simon Hodge, Geoff & Carol Hodgson, Cyrill Hofer, Kirsty Hogg, Paul Holbourne, Siri Holm, Suzanne Holm, John Holmes, Joanna Holt, Steve Holt, Somneuk Homteeb, Marita Honerud, Marita & Kjersti Honerud, Duncan Hope, Gwalgen Hops, Dawn Horridge, Mark Horsfield, Anne Hosking, Edward Housley, Caroline Howe, Caroline & Greg Howe, Stella Hristova, Marjolaine Hubault, Lee Hubbard, Doris Hug, David Hughes, Laura Hughes, Rhidian Hughes, Jeannot Huijnen, Paul & Karen Hull, Elisabeth Hunel, Steve Hurst, Darci Hutchinson, Simon Hutchinson, Simon & Alex Hutchinson, Riina Hynninen **I** Mary Guat Looi Iceton, Christine Ingemorsen, Brian Irwin, Nana Ito, Faiz Izwan Izwan **J** Jessey Jacco, Beatrix Jacobs, Kenneth Jademo, Hana Jaitnerova, Haoli James, Steven James, H Jamieson, Shaun & Meriah Jamieson, Remco Jansen, Jiri Jaros, Ms Jaswinder, the Jatnell Family, Khudija Javed, David Jeffcock, Phillip & De Jeffries, Wolfgang Jenet, Neil Jenkinson, Riaz Jensen, Rachel Job, Louise T Johansen, Tina Johnson, Ian Jones, Tess Jones, Wally Jones, Antje Jos, Isabelle & YC Jost **K** Glen Kabumoto, Laura Kallenberg, Beate Kampmann, Adam Kaoullas, Terima Kasih, Peter Kaye, John Kearins, Alison Keeler, Peter Keenan, D Kelly, Marian Kelly, Patricia Kelly, Peter Kelly, Jeltsje Kemerink, Stephan Kennedy, Dianna Kennewell, Lamar Kerley, Birgit Kern, Rudy Kerremans, John Ketelhohn, David Kidd, Daniel Kiernan, Kalervo Kiianmaa, Tom Kleijwegt, Janica Kleiman, Adam Klinger, Keetie Klinkenberg, Ad Klok, Stefan Knau, Nick Knight, Martha Knox, Wong Kin Kok, Andrea & Serge Kolijn, Bartlomiej Kolodziejczyk, Edward Kommers, Bianca & Francisco Kooijman, Dr Ernst J Kopp, Sally Kowal, Christian Kowalkowski, Jochem Kramer, John Kramer, Poul E Kristensen, Sidse Kristensen, Joe Kuhn, Joep Kusters **L** Simon Lai, Sean Laing, Elaine Lam, Eric Lambert, Yvonne Lane, Steve Langford, Johanna & Bruno Langoe Ivanoff, Kris Laplace, Fredrik Larsen, Kai Larsen, Tea Larsen, Tanja & Paul Lasee, Ken Lau, Winnie Lau, Sylvie Laurenty, Thomas Laursen, Alex & Sabina Lautensach, Kevin Lavery, Varry Lavin, Anna Lawley, Mark & Emma Lawton, Damien Le Gal, Marcia Leath, Michael Ledwidge, Tania Lee, Dr Juliane Leichter, R N Lelievre, Mikelson Leong, Peter Leong, Paola Leoni, Eric Lepelaar, Xavier Lepretre, Toine Leroi, Sara LeRoy, Camma Leth, Steffen Leth, Paul Lewis, Dirk Leysen, David Lezy, Yum Shoen Liang, Pete Lidbetter, Anna Liden, Alice Lim, Charles Wei Siong Lim, Huck Lim, Charles Lim Wei Song, Anna Gil Lindell, Ian Lindner, Stefan Lindquist, Michelle & Matthew Linhardt, Harm Linssen, Jodie Linz, Julia Lippold, Alan Livingstone-Smith, Delyth Lloyd, Noel Long, Dylan Longworth, Meng Loong, Harald Loos, Christina Lorenz, Chris Louie, Marina Louter, Jerry Low, Michelle Lowings, Cecilia Lozano, Britt LP, Lau Siu Lun, Tommy Lundstrom, Brian Lynch **M** Ewen Macauley, Helen Maddock, Rian Maelzer, Uma Mahadevan-Dasgupta, Sophie Maher, Jon Maisey, Kari Makelainen, Susan Manchester, Delyan Manchev, Bram Manck, Thomas Manhart, Corrado Mantovani, Ato Mariano, Salvatore Marino, Catelijne Markenstein, Helen Marsland, Lotte Martens, Carla Martin, Conor Martin, Kali Martin, Peter Martin, Rosa Martinez-Arias, Max Mauro, Wolfgang Mayrhofer, Neil McBain, John & Megan McCallum, Kelly McCarthy, Janet McCluskey, Chris McCullough, Derek McDermott, Garry McKellar-James, John McLachlan, Simon McLaughlin, Henry McLean, An Mees, Henry Meester, Tora Mehlsen, David Meiklejohn, Leo Meyer, Jill Middleton, Fred Midtgaard, Laurent Mieville, Chris Miller, Kym Miller, Michelle Mills, Lynda Millspaugh, Yu Min, Ming Ming Teh, Claire Missing, Kim Moden, Bettina Moellring, Wolfgang Mohl, Jock Moilliet, Jock & Janice Moilliet, Eefje Mol, Camilla Moller, Harriet Molyneux, Ugo Monticone, David Moodie, Ian Moody, Paul Mooney, Tom Mooney, Annalee Moore, Frank Moore, Stu Moore, Nnenna Morah, Andrew Morritt, Caroline Moulin, Alex Moyler, John Mulhall, Olwyen Mulholland, Edan Mumford, Mary Munnik, Sonja Munnix, L Muntinga, Allan Murphy, Odile Murphy, Jim Murray, Nicky Muscat **N** Belinda Naden-Turner, Lukas Nardella, Liz Nash, George Natuman, Tytli Natunen, Carlo Navalta, Dina Nelson, Joclyn Neo, Diana Neuner, Wendy Ng, Henry Nguyen, Martin Nigg, Sonja Nightingale, Ray Nijeboer, Alex & Diane Nikolic, Terry Nixon, Oya Mat Nor, Siti Nor **O** Gary O'Brien, Shane O'Brien, Alexa Obsieger, Anne & Andy O'Carroll, Lorenzo Occhi, Eline Odegaard, Shula O'Dowd, James Oehlcke, Simon O'Kelly, Shannon O'Laughlin, Teresa Ong, Johan Oosterloo, Laszio Orban, Brendan

O'Rourke, David Osborn, Sian O'Sullivan, Daniel & Susan Otahal, Tina Ouellette, Alain Ouimet, Dafydd Owen, Hester Ozinga **P** Ben Pace, Julie Page, Kerri Lee Page, Phil Palmer, Emmanuel Parabakaran, Lewa Pardomuan, Simon Parker, JS Parkes, Colin Parsons, Adam Pasley, Alison Payne, Helen Pegden, Paul Pelczar, Lisa Pelles, Emily Pelter, Richard Pennington, James & Ann Percival, Bridget Pereira, Chris Perez, Gualberto Perez, Maria Perkins, Christine Perroud, Tim Phelps, Reni E Pihl, Hannah Pike, Kalai Pillay, Christophe Pinelli, Barry & Sarah Pitt, Andrew Plant, Tom Plocher, Niklas Plumpe, Roland Poath, Michael Pocock, Adriana Poli, Alberto Poli, Lisa & Ilias Pollard, Rob Pompey, Martijn & Danielle Poort, Tim & Gayle Pope, Adrian Portal, Alex Portnoy, Denise Potter, Laura Pountney, Lawrence Powell, Julie Power, Daniel & Catherine Price, Nick Price **Q** Naz Quadri, Jean-Pierre Quaedvlieg, Martie Quick **R** Althea Radford, Deki Radha, Jan Rae, Ole Rahbek, Kelly Rains, Steven Ramm, Claire Ramsay, Suzanne Randall, Jannet Rangel, Lisa Rapley, Jan Raposa, Michael Rausch, Luke Rees, Tim Reeve, Dietrich Rehnert, Gordon Reid, Max Reimpell, Fran Rein, Natalie Rempal, Roland Reynier, Sue Reynolds, Sydney Richardson, Garry & Carol Richens, Renee Riddle, Robert Riegel, Linze Rijswijk, Rory Riley-Gillespie, Robert & Medy Rillema, Carla Rimondi, Julia Ripol, Lucy Roberts, Toby Roberts, Kate Robins-Browne, Daniel Robinson, Sarah Robinson, Seth Roby, Aldo Rodenhaeuser, Elwin Roetman, Edi Rohrer, Esther Roling, Jasper Rothuizen, Peter Rowan, Mark Rowlatt, Andreas Rudin, Jaroslaw Rudnik, Peter Ruston **S** Karen S, Rob S, Pradipta Saha, Mary Saldanha, Claire Sampson, Per Samuelsson, Ben Sand, Jonathan Sargant, Carmen Savella, Sian Sayward, Rick Scavetta, Peter Schaaf, Jack & Joan Schafer, Axel Schechert, Bert-Jan Scheffer, Ditte Schlüntz, Remi Schmaltz, Martin Schmidt, Kara Schmieder, Joerg Schnabel, Sabine Schneider, Jeffrey Schoeman, Robert Schoenfeld, Piet Schouten, Harald Schubert, Michael Schubert, Janna Scopel, Stephen Scott, Thomas Sczepanek, Emma Searle, Susanne Seegers, Jochen Seidenspinner, Merron Selenitsch, Manjira Sen-Gosain, Yien Lein Seow, Gloria Ser, Lasse Settem, Richard Sevicke-Jones, Victor & Tram Shao, Bill & Wannee Shaw, Maj Shaw, Achim Shcuhmacher, Caroline Shelton, Norman Shepherd, Nolan Shulak, Fredrik & Line Sibbern, Ganes Sichamar, Michael Siefert, Ralf Siemieniec, Larry Siga, Caroline Simms, David Simpson, John Simpson, Peter Simpson, Lim Wei Siong, Ayesha Sitter, Viktor Sjoblom, Caroline Skitmore, Kaja & Sigbjoern Skjaerven, Gurdeep Skolnik, Margaret Slater, Sandy Slater-Jones, Ross Slotten, Matthew Smedley, Julie Smith, Kathy Smith, Reuben Smith, Suzette Smith, Peter Smits, Anne Sofie, Miquel Sola, Chee Soo Lian, Deb Southerland, Lucy Sparks, Colin Speed, Kristel Speier-Jenet, Peter Speldewinde, Kelli Speller, Petr Sperling, Ann & Frank Spowart Taylor, Doreen & Tim Spurdens, Clare Standing, Michael Stein, Tom Stein, Katerina Stenman, Jill & John Stephenson, Helen Steward, Joe Pietro Stiphout, Andy Stock, Eduard Stomp, Merryn Stoyle, Anna Streatfeild, Wolfram Strempfer, Bernhard Stummer, Jasper Stuurman, Tim Sumner, Jorge Luis Supelano, Jacqueline Ann Surin, Taka Suzuki, Martin Svenningsen, Keith Swartz, Aidan Sweeney, JFP Swift **T** Marja Talahaturuson-van-Donk, Trevor Talbot, Jan Talsma, Parry Tan, Tong-Khee Tan, Rieman Tang, Anna Tapp, Olivia Tay, Doreen Teo, Sharon Teo, Victor Teo, Martin Terry, Rebecca Terry, Ben Theaker, Barbara Theiler, Julie Thewlis, Cece Thomas, Birgid Thompson, Birgid & Keith Thompson, Nicholas Thompson, Andrea & Gareth Thomson, Janine Thorstein, Aranea Tigelaar, Neil & Lynne Tilbrook, Jennie Timar, Sally Tio, Olga & Annia Titus, Derek Tokashiki, Marianne Tomkies, Simon Tomlin, Stephen Totterman, Deborah Townsend, Lara Trafford, Jeff Tsay, Tony Tuch, Tore Tunold, Alexia & Paul Turner, Grant Turner, Liz Turner, Sarah Turner, Nic & Tamara Turner-Moore, Rachel Tyler **U** Fabio Umehara, Jen Utterson **V** Carl Vadivella Belle, Kim van Bussel, Don van Dalen, Toine van den Berk, M van den Hoek, Lesta van den Ouden, Jo-Anne van der Horst, Hilary van der Starre, Leo van der Water, Kevin van Dijck, Stefan van Eijk, Jan van Gendt, Wilbert Van Haneghem, Hiske van Haren, Wilmar van Hengel, Marcel van Leeuwen, Pien van Leeuwen, Tjomme van Norden, Ab van Peer, Martin van Rongen, Kees & Hyke van Stralen, Link Van Ummersen, Anton van Veen, Louis van Wermeskerken, Laura van Willenswaard, Josie Vendramini, Peter Vergeer, Amanda Verhaege, Nancy Vermeiren, David Verrelli, Martien & Hanneke Versteeg-van Adrichem, Carsten Vestero Jensen, Cher Vialle, Viktor Kaposi, Andrea Villa, Sabine Villmann, Nur Viratan, Berry Visscher, Elke Visser, Rene Rudolf von Rohr, Kai Vonk, Dennis Vorouxis, Reinier Vrolijk **W** Claudia Wagner, Laszlo Wagner, Camilla & Linda Waldal, Taryn Walker, Janelle Wallace, Kelvin Walls, Luke Walshe, Sally Walton, Jeff Ward, Kevin Waterfall, Val Waterfall, David Watkins, Luke & Hannah Watson, Mona Weckes, Nah Wee Kee, Chris Weeks, Shang Wei, Judith Weibrecht, Viktor Weisshaupl, David & Lynn Wellington, Ruud Welman, Sue Welsh, Jenni Westcott, Birthe

SEND US YOUR FEEDBACK

We love to hear from travellers – your comments keep us on our toes and help make our books better. Our well-travelled team reads every word on what you loved or loathed about this book. Although we cannot reply individually to postal submissions, we always guarantee that your feedback goes straight to the appropriate authors, in time for the next edition. Each person who sends us information is thanked in the next edition – and the most useful submissions are rewarded with a free book.

To send us your updates – and find out about LP events, newsletters and travel news – visit our award-winning website: **www.lonelyplanet.com**.

Note: We may edit, reproduce and incorporate your comments in Lonely Planet products such as guidebooks, websites and digital products, so let us know if you don't want your comments reproduced or your name acknowledged. For a copy of our privacy policy visit www.lonelyplanet.com/privacy.

Westerby, Marten Westerink, Rachel & Andy Westnidge, Marc Weustink, Rebeca & Anna Whitworth, Jeffrey Wicharuk, Michael Wiebe, Katy Wigmore, Leigh Wilbrey, Suzanne Wild, Kathy Wilhelm, Dave Wilkie, Robyn Wilkin, Marjan Willemsen, Ian Williams, Justin Williams, Reg Williams, Suresh Williams, Harald Willms, Craig Wilson, Paul Wilson, Venessa Wilson, Robert Winser, Kim Winter, Alison Winward, Faye Withecomb, Schelto F Witsen Elias, Werner Wohland, Michelle Woo, Ashley Wood, Charlie Woods, Julian Woon, Loh Woon Yee, Michael Wray, Eoin Wrenn, Ralp Wurzbacher **Y** Mark Yabsley, Rosalind Yang, Wade Yenowine, Eddie KC Yeo, Mike Yeomans, Teo Swee Yew Norman, Lee Yik Hun, Sui Yin Yoon, Muhammad Ali Yusof **Z** Pei Zan, H Zhongyi, Andrew Zimmerman, Oliver Zoellner, Ahmed Zulkiflie, Nicole Zweifel

ACKNOWLEDGMENTS

Many thanks to the following for the use of their content:

Mike Reed for permission to use the boxed text 'Nightlife, Orang Ulu Style', and Mountain High Maps® © 1993 Digital Wisdom, Inc.

Index

INDEX

000 Map pages
000 Location of colour photographs

INDEX

000 Map pages
000 Location of colour photographs

INDEX

T

INDEX

MAP LEGEND

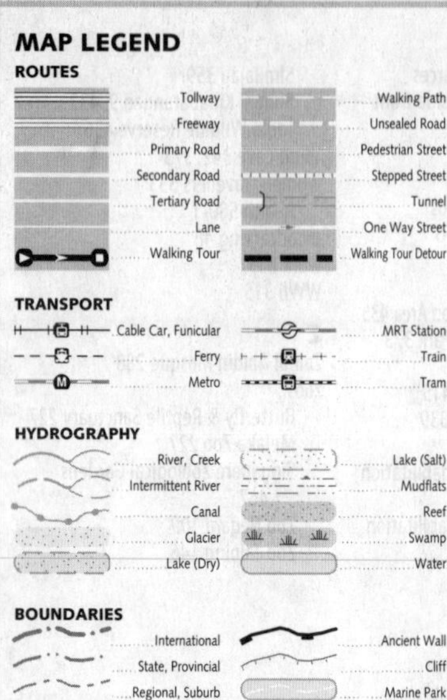

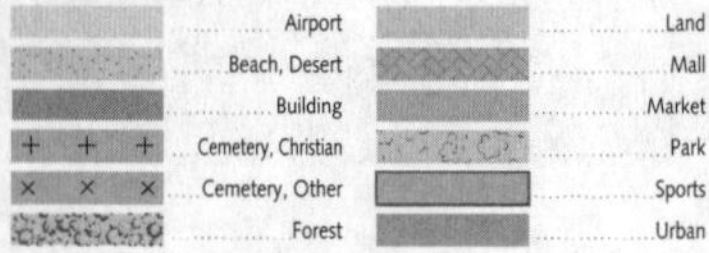

POPULATION

CAPITAL (NATIONAL) · CAPITAL (STATE)
Large City · Medium City
Small City · Town, Village

AREA FEATURES

Airport · Land
Beach, Desert · Mall
Building · Market
Cemetery, Christian · Park
Cemetery, Other · Sports
Forest · Urban

SYMBOLS

SIGHTS/ACTIVITIES
Beach
Buddhist
Castle, Fortress
Christian
Confucian
Diving, Snorkelling
Hindu
Islamic
Jain
Jewish
Monument
Museum, Gallery
Picnic Area
Point of Interest
Ruin
Shinto
Sikh
Skiing
Taoist/Chinese
Winery, Vineyard
Zoo, Bird Sanctuary

INFORMATION
Bank, ATM
Embassy/Consulate
Hospital, Medical
Information
Internet Facilities
Parking Area
Petrol Station
Police Station
Post Office, GPO
Telephone
Toilets

SLEEPING
Sleeping
Camping

EATING
Eating

DRINKING
Drinking
Café

ENTERTAINMENT
Entertainment

SHOPPING
Shopping

TRANSPORT
Airport, Airfield
Border Crossing
Bus Station
Ferry/Boat Terminal
General Transport
Taxi Rank
Trail Head

GEOGRAPHIC
Hazard
Lighthouse
Lookout
Mountain, Volcano
National Park
Oasis
Pass, Canyon
River Flow
Shelter, Hut
Spot Height
Waterfall

NOTE: Not all symbols displayed above appear in this guide.

LONELY PLANET OFFICES

Australia
Head Office
Locked Bag 1, Footscray, Victoria 3011
☎ 03 8379 8000, fax 03 8379 8111
talk2us@lonelyplanet.com.au

USA
150 Linden St, Oakland, CA 94607
☎ 510 893 8555, toll free 800 275 8555
fax 510 893 8572, info@lonelyplanet.com

UK
72–82 Rosebery Ave,
Clerkenwell, London EC1R 4RW
☎ 020 7841 9000, fax 020 7841 9001
go@lonelyplanet.co.uk

France
1 rue du Dahomey, 75011 Paris
☎ 01 55 25 33 00, fax 01 55 25 33 01
bip@lonelyplanet.fr, www.lonelyplanet.fr

Published by Lonely Planet Publications Pty Ltd
ABN 36 005 607 983

Cover photographs: Pulau Rawa, Malaysia, Gloria Maschmeyer/photolibrary.com/superstock (front); Petronas Towers, Kuala Lumpur, Malaysia, Simon Bracken/Lonely Planet Images (back). Many of the images in this guide are available for licensing from Lonely Planet Images: www.lonelyplanetimages.com.

Printed by SNP SPrint (M) Sdn Bhd, Malaysia